CONTENTS

THE NATIONWIDE FOOTBALL ANNUAL 2022–2023

Published by SportsBooks Limited, 9 St Aubyns Place, York, YO24 1EQ
First published in 1887

Copyright © Stuart Barnes and SportsBooks 2022
www.sportsbooks.ltd.uk

The 136th edition of this publication is the last one to be published by Randall Northam of SportsBooks and edited by Stuart Barnes. Both are retiring. Attempts are being made to hand over the baton, so the world's oldest football annual can have a new lease of life. As we went to press, some interest was being shown in taking over, but nothing had been confirmed.

A CIP catalogue record for this book is available from the British Library.

Editorial compilation by Stuart Barnes

ISBN-13 9781907524639

Front cover shows Manchester City celebrating their Premier League title victory. Back cover has Liverppol enjoying the second of their cup wins, the FA Cup. Photos from Alamy/PA Images.

Printed and bound in the UK by CPI Group (UK) Ltd, Croydon CRO 4YY

COMMENT

By Stuart Barnes

At some point in the new season, one of the game's most prestigious records will change hands. Barring serious injury or loss of form, Harry Kane will score his 54th international goal and take over the mantle of England's leading marksman from Wayne Rooney. It could happen in their two remaining Nations League matches against Italy and Germany in the autumn. A more likely setting would be the winter World Cup in Qatar, the perfect stage for the England captain, who took his tally last season to 50 with a dozen strikes, seven of them in successive qualifiers against Albania and San Marino. Kane has made the most of playing against minnows like that, but reaching his half-century in 73 matches still sits impressively, pro rata, in the list of the country's most prolific marksmen. With probably three or four more years remaining at the top level, he looks set to take the record far beyond the reach of anyone else for the foreseeable future. A successful Tottenham campaign under new manager Antonio Conte followed his summer flirtation with Manchester City and, at 29, he is at the peak of his powers. He remains without a trophy, restricted to two League Cup runners-up medals and one in the 2019 Champions League against Liverpool. Tottenham's last silverware was the 2008 League Cup, too long for a club of that stature. All could change in Conte's first full season in charge. The early-summer signing of Richarlison from Everton bodes well and while the Brazilian's new side might still not be equipped to contest the big prize with Manchester City and Liverpool, success in one of the cup competitions seems a real possibility.

Wayne Rooney's resignation as Derby County manager came as no surprise, despite having indicated in the immediate aftermath of relegation from the Championship that he wanted to stay on. Clearly, the prospect of spending the summer back on the treadmill putting together an entirely new squad after so many departures, was not an appealing one. Even an experienced manager, let alone one in his first full season in charge, would probably have needed a break after such a traumatic experience. There were also family issues to be considered before committing to another under-pressure campaign, this one with the expectation of an immediate return to the second tier. Rooney tackled what most regarded as an impossible job with conviction and composure, qualities which will stand him in good stead on his eventual return to the game.

As Wayne Rooney found out, relegation has nothing to do with a club's size, status or history. Oldham Athletic and Scunthorpe United also discovered that the table does not lie. Oldham, part of the Premier League's inaugural season of 1992-93, dropped into non-league football after 115 years. Scunthorpe's 72-year stay in the Football League also came to an end – for me personally a sad day for my home-town club. Neither could have any complaints. They were simply not good enough. And while supporters remain angry at the running of the two clubs, we welcome back on merit Stockport County, the most enterprising of the National League teams, and play-off winners Grimsby Town, restored to membership at the first time of asking by manager Paul Hurst. The likes of Notts County, who had a National League record crowd of nearly 13,000 against Solihull, Wrexham and Chesterfield missed out on a return, prompting renewed calls for the introduction of a third promotion place. There is also talk of the competition becoming League Three in the not-too-distant future. Such is its overall strength, the proposals carry considerable weight.

WINTER WORLD CUP COUNTDOWN

England and Wales will carry contrasting expectations into the World Cup in Qatar this winter. Despite a sobering end-of-season experience against Hungary, Gareth Southgate's side know they must live up to the standards set when reaching the semi-finals of the previous tournament in Russia and the final of last year's European Championship. Anything less is likely to have implications for some international careers and indeed for the manager's own position. Southgate took some stick following that Nations League drubbing at Molineux– an exact reversal of the 4-0 win in Budapest at the start of the campaign – which ended a worrying 11-day, four-match schedule during which England failed to score a goal from open play. It wasn't their strongest line-up, with the manager continuing to look for new blood, having used 13 players in all during 13 World Cup qualifiers, Nations League and friendly matches. Even so, a tired, disjoined performance was exposed embarrassingly by a team not good enough to qualify for Qatar. Unless one or two of the fringe players make an impact in the autumn fixtures, it looks like there will be little change from the tried and tested line-up when England kick-off against Iran on November 21. By then, Southgate will hope that Harry Maguire will have regained the defensive authority missing from so many of his performances for both club and country, that Phil Foden and/or Jack Grealish can provide much-needed some creativity and that Harry Kane will find someone to share the responsibility of scoring goals as he approaches Wayne Rooney's 53 goals for his country. If the Tottenham striker does not make it before the finals, what a stage the World Cup would be for him to make the record his own. England complete their group against Wales, who will at the tournament for the first time for 64 years after defeating Ukraine 1-0 in an emotional play-off match in Cardiff – a result Gareth Bale described as the 'greatest in the history of Welsh football.' No country will enjoy the occasion more or as determined to repeat the achievement of reaching the last 16 of Euro 2020. Robert Page developed a successful relationship with his players during his time as caretaker-manager after Ryan Giggs concentrated on contesting court proceedings. With Giggs now having resigned because of the time his case is taking, that bond will surely continue to flourish. Page faces none the pressure that faces Southgate when Wales open against the United States. If Bale's presence continues to inspire those around him, it would be no surprise to see both go through from the group.

● These will be the first finals not to be held during the summer, with most countries suspending their domestic league seasons as a result. Qatar is the smallest nation to play host and its selection has been controversial from the start over issues involving human rights and migrant workers brought in to build the stadiums. With an initial budget of £4.7bn, seven of the eight have been built from scratch, with the other extensive redeveloped. All are within an hour's drive if each other and are powered by solar-panel farms.

MATCHES

GROUP STAGE (UK times)
November 21
Group A: Senegal v Holland (10am); Qatar v Ecuador (4pm)
Group B: England v Iran (1pm); USA v Wales **(7pm)**
November 22
Group C: Argentina v Saudi Arabia (10am); Mexico v Poland (4pm)
Group D: Denmark v Tunisia (1pm); France v Australia (7pm)
November 23
Group E: Germany v Japan (1pm); Spain v Costa Rica (4pm)
Group F: Morocco v Croatia (10am); Belgium v Canada (7pm)
November 24
Group G: Switzerland v Cameroon (10am); Brazil v Serbia (7pm)
Group H: Uruguay v South Korea (1pm); Portugal v Ghana (4pm)
November 25
Group A: Qatar v Senegal (1pm)' Holland v Ecuador (4pm)
Group B: Wales v Iran (10am); England v USA (7pm)
November 26

Group C: Poland v Saudi Arabia (1pm); Argentina v Mexico (7pm)
Group D: Tunisia v Australia (10am); France v Denmark (4pm),
November 27
Group E: Japan v Costa Rica (10am); Spain v Germany (7pm)
Group F: Belgium v Morocco (1pm); Croatia v Canada (4pm)
November 28
Group G: Cameroon v Serbia (10am); Brazil v Switzerland (4pm)
Group H: South Korea v Ghana (1pm); Portugal v Uruguay (7pm)
November 29
Group A: Holland v Qatar (3pm), Ecuador v Senegal (3pm)
Group B: Wales v England (7pm); Iran v USA (7pm)
November 30
Group C: Poland v Argentina (7pm); Saudi Arabia v Mexico (7pm);
Group D: Tunisia v France (3pm); Australia v Denmark (3pm)
December 1
Group E: Japan v Spain (7pm); Costa Rica v Germany (7pm)
Group F: Croatia v Belgium (3pm); Canada v Morocco (3pm)
December 2
Group G: Cameroon v Brazil (7pm); Serbia v Switzerland (7pm)
Group H: South Korea v Portugal 3pm); Ghana v Uruguay (3pm)

LAST 16
December 3
Game 49: Winners of Group A v runners-up of Group B (3pm)
Game 50: Winners of Group C v runners-up of Group D (7pm)
December 4
Game 51: Winners of Group D v runners-up of Group C (3pm)
Game 52: Winners of Group B v runners-up of Group A (7pm)
December 5
Game 53: Winners of Group E v runners-up of Group F (3pm)
Game 54: Winners of Group G v runners-up of Group H (7pm)
December 6
Game 55: Winners of Group F v runners-up of Group E (3pm)
Game 56: Winners of Group H v runners-up of Group G (7pm)

QUARTER-FINALS
December 9
Game 57: Winners of 53 v Winners of 54 (3pm)
Game 58: Winners of 49 v. Winners of 50 3pm)
December 10
Game 59: Winners of 55 v winners of 56 (3pm)
Game 60: Winners of 51 v winners of 52 (7pm)
SEMI-FINALS
December 13
Game 61: Winners of 57 v winners of 58 (7pm)
December 14
Game 62: Winners of 59 v winners of game 60 (7pm)

THIRD PLACE PLAY-OFF
December 17
Game 63: Losers of 61 v losers of 62 (3pm)

FINAL
December 18
Game 64: Winners of 61 v winners of 62 (3pm or 7pm)

HOW THE TEAMS QUALIFIED

EUROPE

(Group winners qualified, plus winners of play-off matches)

GROUP A

	P	W	D	L	F	A	Pts
Serbia Q	8	6	2	0	18	9	20
Portugal Q	8	5	2	1	17	6	17
Republic of Ireland	8	2	3	3	11	8	9
Luxembourg	8	3	0	5	8	18	9
Azerbaijan	8	0	1	7	5	18	1

GROUP B

	P	W	D	L	F	A	Pts
Spain Q	8	6	1	1	15	5	19
Sweden	8	5	0	3	12	6	15
Greece	8	2	4	2	8	8	10-
Georgia	8	2	1	5	6	12	7
Kosovo	8	1	2	5	5	15	5

GROUP C

	P	W	D	L	F	A	Pts
Switzerland Q	8	5	3	0	15	2	18
Italy	8	4	4	0	13	2	16
Northern Ireland	8	2	3	3	6	7	9
Bulgaria	8	2	2	4	6	14	8
Lithuania	8	1	0	7	4	19	3

GROUP D

	P	W	D	L	F	A	Pts
France Q	8	5	3	0	18	3	18
Ukraine	8	2	6	0	11	8	12
Finland	8	3	2	3	10	10	11
Bosnia-Herzegovina	8	1	4	3	9	12	7
Kazakhstan	8	0	3	5	5	20	3

GROUP E

	P	W	D	L	F	A	Pts
Belgium Q	8	6	2	0	25	6	20
Wales	Q 8	4	3	1	14	9	15
Czech Republic	8	4	2	2	14	9	14
Estonia	8	1	1	6	9	21	4
Belarus	8	1	0	7	7	24	3

GROUP F

	P	W	D	L	F	A	Pts
Denmark Q	10	9	0	1	30	3	27
Scotland	10	7	2	1	17	7	23
Israel	10	5	1	4	23	21	16
Austria	10	5	1	4	19	17	16
Faroe Islands	10	1	1	8	7	23	4
Moldova	10	0	1	9	5	30	1

GROUP G

Holland Q	10	7	2	1	33	8	23
Turkey	10	6	3	1	27	16	21
Norway	10	5	3	2	15	8	18
Montenegro	10	3	3	4	14	15	12
Latvia	10	2	3	5	11	14	9
Gibraltar	10	0	0	10	4	43	0

GROUP H

Croatia Q	10	7	2	1	21	4	23
Russia	10	7	1	2	19	6	22
Slovakia	10	3	5	2	17	10	14
Slovenia	10	4	2	4	13	12	14
Cyprus	10	1	2	7	4	21	5
Malta	10	1	2	7	9	30	5

GROUP I

England Q	10	8	2	0	39	3	26
Poland Q	10	6	2	2	30	11	20
Albania	10	6	0	4	12	12	18
Hungary	10	5	2	3	19	13	17
Andorra	10	2	0	8	8	24	6
San Marino	10	0	0	10	1	46	0

GROUP J

Germany Q	10	9	0	1	36	4	27
North Macedonia	10	5	3	2	23	11	18
Romania	10	5	2	3	13	8	17
Armenia	10	3	3	4	9	20	12
Iceland	10	2	3	5	12	18	9
Liechtenstein	10	0	1	9	2	34	1

Play-offs (on aggregate): Poland 2 Sweden 0; Portugal 2 Macedonia 0; Wales 1 Ukraine 0

SOUTH AMERICA

(Top four qualified)

	P	W	D	L	F	A	GD	Pts
Brazil	17	14	3	0	40	5	35	45
Argentina	17	11	6	0	27	8	19	39
Uruguay	18	8	4	6	22	22	0	28
Ecuador	18	7	5	6	27	19	8	26
Peru	18	7	3	8	19	22	-3	24
Colombia	18	5	8	5	20	19	1	23
Chile	18	5	4	9	19	26	-7	19
Paraguay	18	3	7	8	12	26	-14	16
Bolivia	18	4	3	11	23	42	-19	15
Venezuela	18	3	1	14	14	34	-20	10

Brazil v Argentina abandoned

NORTH AMERICA

(Top four qualified)

Canada Q	14	8	4	2	23	7	16	28
Mexico Q	14	8	4	2	17	8	9	28
USA Q	14	7	4	3	21	10	11	25
Costa Rica Q	14	7	4	3	13	8	5	25
Panama	14	6	3	5	17	19	-2	21
Jamaica	14	2	5	7	12	22	-10	11
El Salvador	14	2	4	8	8	18	-10	10
Honduras	14	0	4	10	7	26	-19	4

Inter-confederation play-off: Costa Rica 1 New Zealand 0

AFRICA

(Group winners into play-offs – five winners qualified)

GROUP A

Algeria	6	4	2	0	25	4	21	14
Burkina Faso	6	3	3	0	12	4	8	12
Niger	6	2	1	3	13	17	-4	7
Djouti	6	0	0	6	4	29	-25	0

GROUP B

Tunisia Q	6	4	1	1	11	2	9	13
Eq Guinea	6	3	2	1	6	5	1	11
Zambia	6	2	1	3	8	9	-1	7
Mauritania	6	0	2	4	2	11	-9	2

GROUP C

Nigeria	6	4	1	1	9	3	6	13
Cape Verde	6	3	2	1	8	6	2	11
Liberia	6	2	0	4	5	8	-3	6
Central Africa Rep	6	1	1	4	4	9	-5	4

GROUP D

Cameroon Q	6	5	0	1	12	3	9	15
Ivory Coast	6	4	1	1	10	3	7	13
Mozambique	6	1	1	4	2	8	-6	4
Malawi	6	1	0	5	2	12	-10	3

GROUP E

Mali	6	5	1	0	11	0	11	16
Uganda	6	2	3	1	3	2	1	9
Kenya	6	1	3	2	4	9	-5	6
Rwanda	6	0	1	5	2	9	-7	1

GROUP F

Egypt	6	4	2	0	10	4	6	14
Gabon	6	2	1	3	7	8	-1	7
Libya	6	2	1	3	4	7	-3	7
Angola	6	1	2	3	6	8	-2	5

GROUP G

Ghana Q	6	4	1	1	7	3	4	13
South Africa	6	4	1	1	6	2	4	13
Ethiopia	6	1	2	3	4	7	-3	5
Zimbabwe	6	0	2	4	2	7	-5	2

GROUP H

Senegal Q	6	5	1	0	15	4	11	16
Togo	6	2	2	2	5	6	-1	8
Namibia	6	1	2	3	5	10	-5	5
Congo	6	0	3	3	5	10	-5	3

GROUP I

Morocco Q	6	6	0	0	20	1	19	18
Guinea-Bissau	6	1	3	2	5	11	-6	4
Guinea	6	0	4	2	5	11	-6	4
Sudan	6	0	3	3	5	12	-7	3

GROUP J

Congo DR	6	3	2	1	9	3	6	11
Benin	6	3	1	2	5	4	1	10
Tanzania	6	2	2	2	6	8	-2	8
Madagascar	6	1	1	4	4	9	-5	4

Play-offs (on agg): Cameroon 2 Algeria 2 (aet, Cameroon won on away goals); Morocco 5 DR Congo 2; Nigeria 1 Ghana 1 (Ghana won on away goal); Senegal 1 Egypt (aet, Senegal won 3-1 on pens); Tunisia 1 Mali 0

ASIA

(Five qualified)

GROUP A

Iran Q	10	8	1	1	15	4	11	25
South Korea Q	10	7	2	1	13	3	10	23
UAE	10	3	3	4	7	7	0	12
Iran	10	1	6	3	6	12	-6	9
Syria	10	1	3	6	9	16	-7	6
Lebanon	10	1	3	6	5	13	-8	6

GROUP B

Saudi Arabia Q	10	7	2	1	12	6	6	23
Japan Q	10	7	1	2	12	4	8	22
Australia Q	10	4	3	3	15	9	6	15
Oman	10	4	2	4	11	10	1	14
China	10	1	3	6	9	19	-10	6
Vietnam	10	1	1	8	8	19	-11	4

Group play-off: UAE 1 Australia 2. **Inter-confederation play-off**: Australia 0 Peru 0 (aet, Australia won 5-4 on pens)

OCEANIA

Group play-off
Solomon Is 0 New Zealand 5

DAY-BY-DAY DIARY 2021–22

JULY 2021

15 Former Everton and Republic of Ireland midfielder Lee Carsley is promoted from head coach of the England under-20 team to manager of the national under-21 side.

16 Reading's Madejski Stadium is renamed after club sponsor Select Car Leasing, with the ground's East Stand rebranded in honour of former chairman Sir John Madejski.

17 Wembley retains hosting rights to the 2024 Champions League Final, despite violence at the Euro 2020 Final between England and Italy. Dublin's Aviva Stadium will stage that season's Europa League Final.

18 Former Bristol Rovers manager Ben Garner takes over at Swindon.

19 Daniel Farke, manager of promoted Norwich, signs a four-year contract extension through to 2025.

20 Steve Cooper, manager of beaten Championship play-off finalists Swansea, leaves the club by mutual agreement.

21 The FA plans life bans from England matches and Wembley for those identified of having broken into the stadium at the Euro 2020 Final. Brentford break their transfer record with the £13.5m signing of Celtic defender Kristoffer Ajer. Two goals by Ellen White give GB a 2-0 victory over Chile in their opening group match at the Tokyo Olympics.

22 Tottenham's Son Heung-min and Arsenal's Emile Smith Rowe sign new five-year contract extensions.

23 Jadon Sancho becomes the second most expensive English player after Harry Maguire when signing for Manchester United from Borussia Dortmund for £73m.

24 Manchester United manager Ole Gunnar Solskjaer signs a new three-year contract. Ellen White is on the mark again as GB reach the quarter-finals with a 1-0 win over Japan.

26 John Terry, assistant to Aston Villa manager Dean Smith, leaves the club to pursue his own managerial ambitions.

27 Former England defender Ashley Cole secures his first major coaching appointment, alongside new under-21 manager Lee Carsley. GB complete their Olympic group matches with a 1-1 draw against Canada.

28 Responding to growing numbers of former players with dementia, English football introduces limits on the number of headers in training for the new season. Celtic are knocked out of the Champions League at the first qualifying hurdle, losing 3-2 on aggregate to the Danish team Midtjylland.

29 Arsenal sign Ben White from Brighton, who receive a club-record £50m for the England defender. Liverpool's Trent Alexander-Arnold signs a new contact until 2025 with Liverpool.

30 A hat-trick by Ellen White is not enough to prevent GB from losing 4-3 to Australia after extra-time at the Olympics.

31 Rangers open their defence of the title with a 3-0 victory over Livingston as the new Scottish season opens with restricted crowds.

AUGUST 2021

1 Russell Martin leaves MK Dons to become Swansea's new manager.

2 Harry Kane, pressing for a move to Manchester City, misses the start of pre-season training at Tottenham. The England captain says his absence was always planned.

3 Two Liverpool players sign new long-term contracts – Alisson until 2027 and Fabinho through to 2026. Arsenal's Granit Xhaka agrees a new four-year deal.

4 Aston Villa pay £25m for Southampton's Danny Ings and sign Bayer Leverkusen's Jamaica winger Leon Bailey for the same amount. Leicester's Wesley Fofana suffers a broken leg in a pre-season friendly against Villarreal.

5 Jack Grealish becomes the most expensive English player with a £100m move from Aston Villa to Manchester City. Grealish signs a six-year contract reported to be worth £230,000 a week.

6 Tottenham agree a £47.5m deal for Atalanta defender Cristian Romero.

7 After nearly 18 months of matches behind closed doors, supporters make a full return for the start of the EFL season. Newcomers Sutton are beaten 2-1 by Forest Green. Hartlepool, back after four years in the National League, defeat Crawley 1-0. Biggest crowd of 31,549 watch Sunderland defeat Wigan. Harry Kane returns to Tottenham and goes straight into quarantine after a holiday abroad. Leicester beat Manchester City 1-0 in the Community Shield with an 89th minute penalty by Kelechi Iheanacho.

8 Lionel Messi bids an emotional farewell to Barcelona after a 20-year career at the club. He blames La Liga's spending restrictions for his departure.

9 Scottish clubs receive permission for a return to full attendances. Swansea's Liberty Stadium is renamed Swansea.com Stadium in a sponsorship deal with a local investment company. Harrogate have their next three fixtures postponed after a Covid outbreak at the club.

10 Lionel Messi signs a two-year contract with Paris Saint-Germain on a free transfer from Barcelona. Rangers are knocked out of the Champions League qualifiers by Malmo 4-2 on aggregate.

11 Chelsea beat Villarreal on penalties in the UEFA Super Cup at Windsor Park after Kepa Arrizabalaga replaces Edouard Mendy near the end of extra-time and saves two spot-kicks.

12 Seven years after leaving Chelsea for Everton, Romelu Lukaku returns to Stamford Bridge in a club-record £97.5m move from Inter Milan. Marcelo Bielsa signs a one-year-contract to stay as Leeds manager.

13 Brentford make a dream start to their first season in the top division for 74 years with a 2-0 win over Arsenal. Virgil van Dijk extends his contract with Liverpool until 2025. Former West Ham and Ipswich youth coach Liam Manning takes charge at MK Dons.

14 Nine months after suffering a fractured skull against Arsenal, Raul Jimenez plays his first competitive match – Wolves' Premier League opener against Leicester.

15 Manchester City begin their defence of the title with a 1-0 defeat by Tottenham, who do not include Harry Kane.

17 Tammy Abraham ends a 16-year association at Chelsea with a £34m move to Jose Mourinho's Roma.

18 Parick Bamford (Leeds) and James Ward-Prowse (Southampton) sign new five-year contracts.

19 Denis Law, former Manchester United and Scotland star, reveals he has been diagnosed with dementia, saying he wants to be 'open' about the condition.

20 Harvey Barnes signs a new four-year contract with Leicester.

21 Terry McDermott, winner of three European Cups and five League titles with Liverpool, admits he is suffering from dementia.

23 A group of 60 former players call on the football authorities to set up a support fund for those with dementia and other neurodegenerative diseases. Peterborough and Cardiff are both fined £5,000 by the FA for a players' melee.

24 Premier League clubs refuse to release players for international matches next month in Covid 19 red list countries.

25 Harry Kane accepts that his hopes of a summer move from Tottenham to Manchester City are over. City manager Pep Guardiola hints that he will leave the club at the end of the 2022-23 season. Southampton score a club-record 8-0 away win over Newport in the second round of the League Cup. Liverpool's Andrew Robertson signs a new five-year contract.

26 Harry Kane marks his first start of the season with two goals in Tottenham's 3-0 win over the Portuguese side Pacos de Ferreira which earns a place in the group stage of the new Europa Conference League. Aberdeen, St Johnstone and Shamrock Rovers are beaten in other play-off matches. Celtic and Rangers reach the group stage of the Europa League.

27 Twelve years after leaving Old Trafford for Real Madrid, Cristiano Ronaldo, 36, rejoins Manchester United. The £19.8 transfer from Juventus is confirmed soon after Manchester City make it clear they will not be signing the five-time World Player of the Year.

28 Manchester City unveil statues of club legends Vincent Kompany and David Silva at the Etihad Stadium.

29 Manchester United break the English record with a 28th successive away league game without defeat – a 1-0 victory over Wolves.

30 Aston Villa allow Emiliano Martinez and Emiliano Buendia to fly to South America for Argentina's World Cup qualifiers – against the wishes of the Premier League. Kalvin Phillips is voted England's Player of the Year by supporters. Ruben Dias signs a new contract with Manchester City until 2027.

31 Transfer deadline-day deals take Nikola Vlasic from CSKA Moscow to West Ham for £26.8m, Emerson Royal from Barcelona to Tottenham for £25.8m and Daniel James from Manchester United to Leeds for £25m. Spending by Premier League clubs during the summer window totals £1.1bn.

SEPTEMBER 2021

1 Cristiano Ronaldo becomes the leading scorer in international football with headers in the 89th and 96th minutes to give Portugal a 2-1 World Cup qualifying win over the Republic of Ireland, who have John Egan on the mark for the first time. Ronaldo overtakes Iran's Ali Dael with 111 goals in 180 matches. Scotland concede twice in the opening quarter-of-an-hour and lose 2-0 to Denmark. In a friendly international, Wales share a goalless draw with Finland. Ederson signs a new five-year-contract with Manchester City.

2 England players are racially abused and Raheem Sterling is pelted with plastic cups after putting them on the way to a 4-0 qualifying victory over Hungary. Daniel Ballard and Shayne Lavery score their first international goals and Bailey Peacock-Farrell saves a penalty as Northern Ireland win 4-1 in Lithuania.

3 Gareth Southgate's players receive FA backing to walk off the pitch if there is a repeat of the abuse in Budapest.

4 The Republic of Ireland face missing out on the finals in Qatar are being held 1-1 by lowly Azerbaijan. Scotland revive their chances of qualifying by beating Moldova 1-0 with a goal by Lyndon Dykes.

5 Gareth Bale scores a hat-trick to give Wales a 3-2 victory over Belarus in a qualifier played behind closed doors in the Russian city of Kazan because of sanctions against the Belarus Government. His first two goals are penalties and the winner comes in stoppage-time. England, with a completely new starting line-up ahead of a tough qualifier in Poland, defeat Andorra 4-0. Jesse Lingard's two goals are his first for nearly three years. Chelsea's Romelu Lukaku marks his 100th cap for Belgium with his 67th international goal in a 3-0 victory over the Czech Republic. The Brazil-Argentina qualifier in Sao Paulo is abandoned five minutes after kick-off when public health officials come on the pitch and accuse four Argentine Premier League players – Aston Villa's Emiliano Martinez and Emiliano Buendia and Tottenham's Giovani Lo Celso and Cristian Romero – of breaking quarantine rules. Chelsea open their defence of the Women's Super League title with a 3-2 defeat by Arsenal.

6 Gareth Bale, Manchester City and Leeds come out strongly against a proposal from Arsene Wenger, FIFA's head of global football development, to hold the World Cup every two years. ITV announces a four-year deal to broadcast England women's matches.

7 Lyndon Dykes is again on the mark for Scotland, this time with a penalty which delivers a 1-0 win in Austria and second place in the group. An 86th minute own goal gives the Republic of Ireland a 1-1 draw against Serbia.

8 England concede in stoppage-time and surrender their 100 per cent group record with a 1-1 draw in Poland. Wales lose ground in a goalless draw against Estonia. Bailey Peacock-Farrell saves another penalty as Northern Ireland also share a 0-0 scoreline with Switzerland.

9 Chelsea are fined £25,000 by the FA for failing to control their players following the reaction to the sending-off of Reece James against Liverpool.

10 The Premier League joins Europe's top competitions in opposing FIFA's proposal for a World Cup every two years.

11 Cristiano Ronaldo marks his return to Manchester United with two goals in his first match – a 4-1 win over Newcastle.

12 England move into third place behind Belgium and Brazil in the FIFA world rankings – their highest for nine years,

13 Harvey Elliott, 18-year-old Liverpool midfielder, says the tackle by Leeds defender Pascal Struijk which left him with a dislocated ankle was a 'freak accident.'

14 The FA dismisses an appeal by Leeds against the sending-off of Pascal Struijk and confirms a three-match ban.

15 Sean Dyche, appointed in 2012 and the longest-serving Premier Leage manager, signs a new four-year contract with Burnley.

16 Chris Hughton becomes the season's first managerial casualty, sacked with Nottingham Forest bottom of the Championship.

17 England women defeat North Macedonia 8-0 in new manager Sarina Wiegman's first match – a World Cup qualifier.

19 Jimmy Greaves, England's record scorer in top-flight football with 357 goals, dies aged 81.

20 Tottenham supporters call for a lasting memorial for the club's all-time leading scorer Jimmy Greaves.

21 Former Swansea manager Steve Cooper takes charge at Nottingham Forest, the club's 14th manager in the last ten years. Two players score four goals in League Cup third round ties – Brentford's Marcus Forss against Oldham (7-0) and Burnley's Jay Rodriguez against Rochdale (4-1).

22 Derby are deducted 12 points for going into administration. The club blame the pandemic, an EFL investigation into their accounts and the collapse of a takeover bid for serious financial problems.

23 FIFA imposes a two-match stadium ban and £160,000 fine on the Hungarian FA for racial abuse directed at England players during the World Cup qualifier.

24 Peterborough's Jonson Clarke-Harris is banned for four matches and fined £5,300 by the FA for abusive historical posts on social media.

25 Australian referee Jarred Gillett becomes the first overseas official to take charge of a Premier League match – Watford against Newcastle.

27 Leicester are fined £17,000 by UEFA for scuffles between fans and Napoli supporters at the end of the Europa League game. The Italian club receive a £13,000 fine.

28 Roger Hunt, World Cup winner with England in 1966 and Liverpool's record league scorer, dies aged 83. The FA fines Stoke £10,000 and Barnsley £8,000 for a touchline fracas. Stoke coaches Dean Holden and Rory Delap, along with Barnsley's Tonda Eckert and Joe Laumann receives fines and bans.

29 Cristiano Ronaldo celebrates a record 178th appearance in the Champions League with a goal in the fifth minute of stoppage-time to give Manchester United a 2-1 group win over Villarreal. West Ham unveil a statue of Bobby Moore, Sir Geoff Hurst and Martin Peters at the London Stadium to mark the club's 1965 European Cup-Winners' Cup success. Derby are fined £5,000 by the FA for their players surrounding referee David Webb following the dismissal of Kelle Roos against Sheffield United – the club's first match after going into administration.

30 Fewer than half of the players at most Premier League clubs and just five members of the England squad have had Covid vaccines, according to reports.

OCTOBER 2021

1 Liverpool manager Jurgen Klopp criticises players who have not been vaccinated. Mike Flynn steps down after four years as Newport manager.

2 To avoid the problems during September's international break, the Government relaxes Covid regulations to allow players to travel to red-list countries for World Cup qualifiers, providing they are fully vaccinated.

3 Xisco Munoz is sacked after ten months as Watford manager with the side he led to promotion on seven points from their first seven Premier League games.

4 Claudio Ranieri returns to the Premier League after leading Leicester to the title along with spells at Chelsea and Fulham.

5 Fara Williams, England's most-capped international with 172 appearances, become the first player to be inducted into the Women's Super League Hall of Fame.

6 Manchester City's Ferran Torres scores both goals as Spain end Italy's 37-match unbeaten run to reach the final of the UEFA Nations League. Huddersfield are fined £5,000 for players' protests against Blackburn.

7 Newcastle are taken over by a Saudi Arabia-led consortium in a £305m deal which ends Mike Ashley's 14-year ownership of the club and puts manager Steve Bruce under pressure, with his side still to win a match this season. Coventry's Matt Godden is banned for two matches for diving to win a penalty against Fulham.

8 Wales recover from goalkeeper Danny Ward's own goal to keep alive their World Cup qualification hopes with a 2-2 away draw against the Czech Republic. Peterborough manager Darren Ferguson receives a one-match touchline ban and £2,000 fine for swearing at a match official after the defeat by Bristol City.

9 Ben Chilwell scores his first goal for England, who win 5-0 in Andorra in their first match to be refereed by a woman – Kateryna Monzul from the Ukraine. Scott McTominay scores in the fourth minute of stoppage-time to give Scotland a 3-2 success against Israel. Northern Ireland are left six points adrift of second place in their group after Jamal Lewis is sent off for a controversial second yellow card in a 2-0 defeat by Switzerland. Despite a first competitive victory for manager Stephen Kenny at the 13th attempt, the Republic of Ireland can no longer qualify because of results elsewhere. His side defeat Azerbaijan 3-0, with Chiedozie Ogbene on the mark for the first time.

10 France beat Spain 2-1 to win the Nations League. Carlisle manager Chris Beech is sacked after a fourth defeat in five matches.

11 Kieffer Moore scores the only goal of the match for Wales in Estonia. Germany become the first team to qualify for the World Cup finals in Qatar.

12 Lyndon Dykes scores for the fourth successive qualifier, his 86th minute goal giving Scotland a 1-0 victory over the Faroe Islands. England are held 1-1 by Hungary, whose supporters at Wembley are involved in fights with police. Northern Ireland's fate is sealed by a 2-1 defeat by Bulgaria.

13 With manager Steve Bruce's position under threat following the Newcastle takeover, Leicester's Brendan Rodgers rules himself out of the job. David Brooks, Bournemouth and Wales midfielder, announces he has been diagnosed with cancer.

14 Manchester City's Raheem Sterling says he will consider his future unless he starts more matches.

15 The EFL approves an increase from three to five substitutes in League Cup ties for the rest of the season.

16 Liverpool manager Jurgen Klopp hails Mohamed Salah as the best player in the world on current form after another impressive performance capped by a solo goal in a 5-0 win over Watford.

17 Newcastle manager Steve Bruce takes charge of his 1,000th match as a manager – a 3-2 home defeat by Tottenham which puts his position under further threat.

18 England are ordered by UEFA to play one home match behind closed doors following violent scenes at the final of Euro 2020 at Wembley. A second game is suspended for two years and the FA is fined £84,560.

19 Cardiff coach James Rowberry is appointed the new manager of Newport, the club he supported as a boy.

20 Steve Bruce is dismissed by Newcastle's new owners with a reported pay-off of £8m. Coach Graeme Jones takes temporary charge.

21 UEFA fines West Ham £50,500 for crowd trouble at the Europa League game against Rapid Vienna. Manchester United must pay £7,000 for incidents during the Champions League match against Villarreal. Nigel Adkins, manager of Charlton for seven months, is sacked with his side third from bottom in League One.

22 Zambia striker Patson Daka scores all four goals in Leicester's 4-3 Europa League win over Spartak Moscow. Southampton manager Ralph Hasenhuttl is fined £20,000 by the FA for questioning the integrity of VAR official Mike Dean after the defeat by Chelsea.

23 Mick McCarthy, manager of Cardiff for eight months, loses his job after eight successive Championship defeats and a single goal scored.

24 Manchester United manager Ole Gunnar Solskjaer comes under pressure after a 5-0 home defeat by Liverpool.

25 Bristol Rovers manager Joey Barton is reminded of his responsibilities by the FA but escapes a formal sanction for comparing his team's poor performance against Newport to the Holocaust.

26 Walter Smith, winner of 21 trophies as manager of Rangers, dies aged 73. Former Bristol City manager Keith Millen takes charge at Carlisle.

27 Manchester City, League Cup winners for the previous four seasons, are beaten on penalties by West Ham in a fourth-round tie.

28 Brentford goalkeeper David Raya is ruled out for four months with a knee ligament injury sustained against Leicester.

29 Blackpool and Preston are both fined £5,000 by the FA for a players' confrontation.

30 Tottenham supporters turn on manager Nuno Espirito Santo during a 3-0 home defeat by Manchester United.

31 Nuno Espirito Santo is sacked after four months in charge. Arsenal and Chelsea reach the delayed final of the Women's FA Cup with 3-0 wins over Brighton and Manchester City respectively.

NOVEMBER 2021

1 Barnsley sack manager Markus Schopp after a single win in his 15 Championship matches. Neil Cox is dismissed by Scunthorpe, bottom of League Two. Dave Challinor leaves Hartlepool, six weeks after signing a new three-year contract, to become National League Stockport's new manager.

2 Antonio Conte, a Premier League and FA Cup winner at Chelsea and latterly coach to Inter Milan, is appointed Tottenham's new manager. Middlesbrough's Neil Warnock takes charge of a record 1,602nd English league match – a 3-1 defeat at Luton.

3 Unai Emery, Villarreal coach and former Arsenal manager, turns down the chance to take over at Newcastle. Liverpool qualify for the knockout stage of the Champions League as group winners with two matches to spare.

4 David Moyes reaches 1,000 matches as a manager in West Ham's 2-2 draw with Genk which guarantees a place in the Europa League's knockout stage.

5 Former Tranmere and Bolton manager Keith Hill takes over at Scunthorpe.

6 Four months after signing a new four-year contract, Norwich manager Daniel Farke is sacked after his bottom-of-the-table team score their first win of the season against Brentford. Four days after his record number of matches, Neil Warnock is dismissed by Middlesbrough with his team in the bottom half of the table.

7 Dean Smith becomes the season's fifth Premier League manager to be sacked, following Aston Villa's fifth successive defeat, this one by Southampton. Former Sheffield United manager Chris Wilder replaces Neil Warnock at the Riverside.

8 Eddie Howe returns to the Premier League as Newcastle's new manager, 15 months after leaving Bournemouth.

9 A move for clubs to support a homeless charity by wearing their away strip at home on Boxing Day is blocked by the Premier League because it would breach regulations.

10 Steven Gerrard leaves Rangers after three-and-a-half years in charge to become Aston Villa's new manager.

11 The Republic of Ireland hold their World Cup qualifying group leaders Portugal to a goalless draw. Caretaker Steve Morison is appointed Cardiff manager until the end of the season. Hartlepool's Victoria Park is renamed the Suit Direct Stadium in a sponsorship deal with a menswear retailer.

12 Harry Kane overtakes Wayne Rooney as England's leading marksman in competitive matches with a hat-trick in a 5-0 win over Albania, taking his total to 39 goals. In front of a Wembley

crowd of more than 80,000, his side score five times in the first half to move to the brink of automatic qualification for the tournament in Qatar. Nathan Patterson's first international goal, together with Craig Gordon's penalty save, ensure a play-off place for Scotland after a 2-0 away victory over Moldova. Northern Ireland defeat Lithuania 1-0. Businessman David Henderson, who organised the illegal flight which crashed in the English Channel, killing Cardiff's new signing Emiliano Sala in January 2019, is jailed for 18 months.

13 Gareth Bale wins his 100th cap and Ben Davies scores his first international goal in a 5-1 win for Wales against Belarus.

14 Fulham's Aleksandar Mitrovic heads a 90th minute winner in Lisbon to earn Serbia automatic qualification and force Portugal into the play-offs. The Republic of Ireland complete their group matches with a 3-0 victory in Luxembourg. Stevenage sack manager Alex Revell after one League Two win in 14 matches. West Ham are fined £30,000 by UEFA for crowd trouble at the Europa League match against Genk.

15 England confirm an automatic place with a record-breaking 10-0 win against San Marino – their biggest in a competitive match and the highest tally of 39 goals in any major qualifying campaign. Harry Kane scores four times, twice from the penalty spot, while Tyrone Mings and Emile Smith Rowe are on the mark for the first time. John Souttar heads his first international goal on his first appearance for three years after injuries as Scotland earn a seeded place in the play-offs with a sixth successive victory – 2-0 against Denmark. Northern Ireland deny Italy an automatic place by holding the European champions to a goalless draw. Dean Smith makes a rapid return to the managerial ranks, tasked with trying to keep Norwich in the Premier League. A record National League crowd of 12,843 watch Notts County's match against Solihull.

16 Wales seal the runners-up place in their qualifying group, earning a home semi-final in the play-offs, by holding Belgium to 1-1 with a goal from Kieffer Moore. Derby are deducted another nine points, this time for historic breaches of EFL spending rules, leaving the club 18 adrift and facing the threat of relegation from the Championship. Following criticism by some clubs of the Premier League's handling of the Newcastle takeover, chairman Gary Hoffman announces his resignation.

17 Reading are deducted six points for breaching EFL spending rules. Barnsley appoint Sweden under-21 coach Poya Asbaghi as their new manager.

18 The Premier League announces an additional £25m of Covid-impact funding – £20m to clubs in Leagues One and Two and £5m to those in the National League. Exeter are ordered to replay their FA Cup first round tie against Bradford after fielding a sixth substitute against the rules in a 3-1 win.

19 Giovanni van Bronckhorst, winner of five trophies as a player with Rangers, succeeds Steven Gerrard as manager. Eddie Howe tests positive for Covid and has to miss his first match as Newcastle manager against Brentford.

20 Manchester United manager Ole Gunnar Solskjaer is sacked after a fourth Premier League defeat in five matches – 4-1 at Watford. Celtic defeat holders St Johnstone 1-0 to reach the Scottish League Cup Final.

21 Coach Michael Carrick is appointed Manchester United's caretaker manager. Hibernian defeat Rangers 3-1 with a hat-trick by Martin Boyle in the second Scottish League Cup semi-final.

22 Wigan striker Charlie Wyke suffers a cardiac arrest in training and is taken to hospital. England manager Gareth Southgate signs a new contract through to December 2024.

23 Covid vaccine passes for matches with more than 10,000 spectators are introduced in Scotland. Manchester United reach the knockout stage of the Champions League with a 2-0 away win over Villarreal. Chelsea also go through by beating Juventus 4-0. Two managers of struggling teams lose their jobs – Fleetwood's Simon Grayson after ten months in charge and Oldham's Keith Curle after eight months in the job.

24 A report which could transform English football calls an independent regulator to prevent the game 'lurching from crisis to crisis.' More help from the Premier League for other clubs via a transfer levy is another recommendation of the fan-led review, headed by former Sports

Minister Tracey Couch., Manchester City qualify for the last 16 of the Champions League as group winners by defeating Paris Saint-Germain 2-1. Liverpool, already through, win their fifth successive match – 2-0 against Porto.

25 West Ham top their Europa League group and qualify for the last 16. Rangers, runners-up in their section, reach the play-off round. Celtic, third in their group, go out. Slavisa Jokanovic, manager of Sheffield United for six months, is sacked with his side in the bottom half of the Championship. Paul Heckingbottom, caretaker after Chris Wilder's departure the previous season, returns to Bramall Lane on a four-and-a-half-year contract.

26 Manchester United appoint German coach Ralf Rangnick from Lokomotiv Moscow as interim manager until the end of the season. Former Barnsley coach Tommy Wright is banned by the FA from all football-related activity, apart from coaching, for six years for bribery offences.

27 Ellen White marks her 100th England appearance with the only goal of a Women's World Cup qualifier against Austria.

28 Paul Tisdale, former Bristol Rovers, MK Dons and Exeter manager, takes over at Stevenage.

29 Lionel Messi is voted the world's best player for the seventh time. Champions League winners Chelsea are named the top team of 2021.

30 Ray Kennedy, winner of three European Cups and five First Division titles with Liverpool and part of Arsenal's League and FA Cup Double-winning side, dies aged 70. Ellen White passes Kelly Smith as England's all-time leading scorer, taking her tally to 48 goals with a hat-trick in their record 20-0 World Cup qualifying win over Latvia.

DECEMBER 2021

1 Richie Wellens is sacked after six months as Doncaster manager with his side second from bottom. Former Hartlepool defender Graeme Lee is appointed the club's new manager.

2 Cristiano Ronaldo becomes the first player to score 800 top-level goals with two in Manchester United's 3-2 win over Arsenal. Michael Carrick, United's caretaker-manager, announces he is leaving the club after handing over to interim-manager Ralf Rangnick. Ten days after his cardiac arrest, Charlie Wyke leaves hospital after being fitted with an implantable defibrillator. The Wigan striker says he owes his life to the quick actions of manager Leam Richardson and club doctor Jonathan Tobin.

3 Ticketless hooligans on the rampage at the Euro 2020 Final at Wembley 'turned a potentially glorious national occasion into a day of national shame,' according to an independent report. The FA and Scotland Yard apologise 'for a collective failure in planning.' Bournemouth (£15,000) and Millwall (£5,000) are fined by the FA for a players' confrontation.

4 Paul Cook, manager of Ipswich for nine months, is sacked after a goalless draw against Barrow in the FA Cup and with his side seven points off a play-off place.

5 Chelsea beat Arsenal 3-0 in the delayed Women's FA Cup Final at Wembley to complete the Treble for the 2020-21 season, having retained the Super League title and won the League Cup.

6 Frankie McAvoy, manager of Preston for seven months following a spell as caretaker, is sacked with his side 18th in the table. Director of football Marcel Brands leaves Everton over 'a difference of opinion on the direction of the club.'

7 Liverpool become the first English club to win all six Champions League group matches, completing their programme by defeating AC Milan 2-1 in the San Siro with a starting line-up containing only three senior regulars. Ryan Lowe leaves Plymouth to become Preston's new manager and is replaced by his Home Park assistant Steven Schumacher. Jude Bellingham, Borussia Dortmund's England midfielder, is fined £34,000 by the German FA for questioning the appointment of referee Felix Zwayer for the Bundesliga match against Bayern Munich.

8 Manchester United finish top of their Champions League group with a 1-1 draw against Young Boys. They include six teenagers, including Charlie Savage, son of former Wales midfielder Robbie Savage, who is commentating on the match for BT Sport. Chelsea concede a stoppage-time equaliser to Zenit St Petersburg and surrender top spot in their group to Juventus. Barcelona miss out on the knockout stage for the first time in 21 years.

9 Leicester lose 3-2 to Napoli in their final Europa League group game, finish third and go out. Tottenham's final Europa Conference League group fixture against Rennes is postponed after eight players test positive for Covid. Hibernian dismiss manager Jack Ross, ahead of the Scottish League Cup Final against Celtic, after a single win in nine Premiership matches.

10 Tottenham's weekend Premier League match against Brighton is postponed. Bournemouth's Jefferson Lerma is fined £4,000 and banned for an additional two matches by the FA for improper behaviour after being sent off against Coventry.

11 Chris Armas, former United States midfielder and New York Red Bulls coach, joins Manchester Unted as Ralf Rangnick's No 2.

13 Covid vaccine passes are brought in for Premier League and EFL matches with more than 10,000 spectators. The draw for the last 16 of the Champions League has to be redone after Manchester United's ball is added to the wrong pot. Doncaster's Keepmoat Stadium becomes the Eco-Power Stadium in a sponsorship deal with the local recycling company.

14 With the Omicron variant of the virus spreading rapidly, Brentford v Manchester United is postponed. Pierre-Emerick Aubameyang is stripped of the Arsenal captaincy for disciplinary breaches. Manchester City score the season's biggest win – 7-0 against Leeds.

15 Burnley v Watford is called off. Northern Ireland manager Ian Baraclough signs a new two-year contract. Manchester City manager Pep Guardiola flies to Barcelona for Sergio Aguero's tearful announcement that a heart condition has forced him to retire at 33.

16 EFL figures show 25 per cent of players at clubs have not been vaccinated. Kieran McKenna, Manchester United's assistant first-team coach, is appointed the new Ipswich manager. Crystal Palace (£45,000) and Aston Villa (£20,000) are fined by the FA for protesting players surrounding referee Michael Salisbury. Walsall's Manny Monthe is banned for seven matches and fined £1,200 for a homophobic comment to a Forest Green Rovers player while with Tranmere.

17 Former Charlton midfielder Johnnie Jakson is named permanent manager after seven wins in ten games as caretaker. Christian Eriksen, who has not played since suffering a cardiac arrest in Denmark's Euro 2020 match against Finland, has his contract with Inter Milan terminated by mutual consent.

18 Five of the day's six Premier League matches and 19 games in the EFL are postponed because of Covid infections.

19 Two goals by Japan striker Kyogo Furuhashi give Celtic a 2-1 victory over Hibernian in the Scottish League Cup Final. Phil Foden and Jack Grealish are dropped for Manchester City's game at Newcastle for disciplinary reasons.

20 The Premier League rejects calls to postpone a round of festive fixtures. Figures show 16 per cent of players have not been vaccinated – the worst among Europe's top leagues. EFL matches also go ahead. Third and fourth round FA Cup replays are scrapped to ease a backlog of matches. Tottenham are eliminated from the Europa Conference League after UEFA rules the club must forfeit the postponed match against Rennes. Former Celtic and Scotland winger Shaun Maloney is named Hibernian's new manager. Leeds are fined £20,000 by the FA for protesting players surrounding referee Chris Kavanagh during the match against Chelsea.

21 Cardiff, Swansea, Newport and Wrexham are ordered to play home matches behind closed doors from Boxing Day onwards for an unspecified period by new Welsh Government Covid restrictions covering all Welsh sporting events. Liverpool and Manchester City are fined £4,270 by UEFA for pitch invasions during Champions League matches against Porto and Paris Saint-Germain respectively. Tottenham receive a £6,600 fine for crowd trouble at their Europa Conference League game with Vitesse Arnhem. Celtic (£32,580) and Rangers (£4,700) are fined for crowd incidents in Europa League games against Bayer Leverkusen and Sparta Prague respectively. Former Scotland defender Stephen Crainey takes charge at Fleetwood until the end of the season after a successful spell as interim manager.

22 The Scottish Premiership's three-week winter break is brought forward to lessen the impact of new Covid restrictions limiting attendances across all four divisions to 500.

23 With Covid cases continuing to rise and more postponements imminent, Liverpool captain Jordan Henderson accuses the authorities of failing to pay enough attention to the welfare of players.

24 Manchester City manager Pep Guardiola adds his voice to the dangers of a growing backlog of fixtures.

26 The traditional Boxing Day programme takes a hit, with three Premier League fixtures and 24 in the EFL called off. Defending champions Rangers take a six-point lead over Celtic into the Scottish Premiership winter break.

27 The Premier League reports a record 103 positive Covid tests for players and staff in the seven days up to and including Boxing Day.

28 Chelsea's Ben Chilwell is ruled out for the rest of the season with a knee injury requiring surgery. Ferran Torres, Manchester City's Spain striker, joins Barcelona for £46.3m.

29 Former Chelsea captain John Terry returns to Stamford Bridge in a part-time role to coach Academy players. The club posts an annual loss of £145.6m.

30 Former Coventry and Birmingham midfielder Gary McSheffrey is appointed Doncaster's new manager.

31 Chelsea manager Thomas Tuchel gives a frosty reaction to record-signing Romelu Lukaku declaring he is unhappy at the club, calling his comments an unwelcome distraction. Celtic sign three players from Japanese clubs – midfielders Yosuke Ideguchi and Reo Hatate and striker Daizen Maeda.

JANUARY 2022

1 Manchester City celebrate new year with a commanding lead at the top of the Premier League, 11 points ahead of Chelsea and 12 clear of Liverpool, after 11 successive victories. Ten fixtures across the four divisions are postponed. Chelsea women's manager Emma Hayes receives an OBE in the New Year Honours. England assistant manager Steve Holland is made an MBE.

2 Chelsea become the first of five Premier League and Championship clubs to trial safe-standing – 24 years after supporters were banned from standing in the wake of the Hillsborough disaster. The club's match against Liverpool has special areas in the Matthew Harding Stand and Shed End at Stamford Bridge.

3 Romelu Lukaku apologises to Chelsea fans for his comments and pledges to restore their trust in him.

4 Southampton are taken over by a consortium led by Serbian tycoon Dragan Solak which purchases the 80 per cent majority shareholding of Chinese businessman Gao Jisheng.

5 Rangers receive a club-record fee of £12m from Everton for Scotland full-back Nathan Patterson.

6 Arsenal are fined £20,000 by the FA for protesting players surrounding referee Stuart Atwell during the home defeat by Manchester City. Bournemouth are fined £25,000 and Queens Park Rangers £5,000 for a players' fracas. Managing director Richard Arnold is appointed the successor to Ed Woodward as Manchester United's most senior executive.

7 England defender Kieran Trippier returns to the Premier League in a £12m move to Newcastle from Spanish champions Atletico Madrid. Aston Villa manager Steven Gerrard signs his former Liverpool team-mate Philippe Coutinho on loan from Barcelona.

8 Newcastle, with Kieran Trippier making his debut, are beaten 1-0 at home by League One Cambridge in the third round of the FA Cup. Kidderminster, the lowest-ranked side left in the competition, defeat Reading 2-1.

9 Arsenal, record 14-time winners of the FA Cup, lose 1-0 to Nottingham Forest at the City Ground. Gillingham manager Steve Evans has his contract terminated 'by mutual consent' after a 4-0 home defeat by Ipswich leaves his side seven points adrift.

10 Eight men who sued Manchester City after being abused by coach Barry Bennell lose their case for damages at the High Court.

11 Two months after beating Blackburn 7-0, Fulham defeat Reading by the same scoreline, becoming the first club to win two away league games by seven goals or more in the same season since Liverpool in 1895-96.

12 Chelsea reach the League Cup Final with a 3-0 aggregate win over Tottenham.

13 Newcastle sign Chris Wood from relegation rivals Burnley for £25m. Brentford captain Pontus Jansson extends his contract until 2023.

14 With a preferred bidder for the club still to emerge, Derby are asked to provide proof to the EFL of funding to complete the season.

15 Three league matches are postponed as the effects of the Omicron variant continue to wane.

16 Rafael Benitez, manager of Everton for six-and-a-half-months, is sacked after a single Premier League win in 13 matches.

17 Chelsea's Thomas Tuchel and Emma Hayes are named FIFA Coaches of the Year for 2021. Capacity crowds return in Scotland after Covid restrictions are lifted.

18 Fulham become the first second-tier club to score six or more goals in three successive league games since Everton in 1954, following up wins over Reading (7-0) and Bristol City (6-2) by beating Birmingham 6-2.

19 Turkish businessman Acun Ilicali buys Hull from the Allam family, owners of the club for 12 years. Colchester sack manager Hayden Mullins after five successive league defeats.

20 Liverpool reach the League Cup Final with a 2-0 aggregate win over Arsenal. Bristol City manager Nigel Pearson is fined £5,000 by the FA for 'improper' comments after the defeat by Queens Park Rangers.

21 Everton owner Farhad Moshiri takes his stake in the club to 94 per cent with a £100m capital injection. Tottenham captain Hugo Lloris signs a new two-year contract. Spectators return to matches in Wales after Covid restriction are eased.

22 Scottish Cup holders St Johnstone are knocked out in the fourth round by fourth-tier village team Kelty Hearts, who win 1-0 with an extra-time goal by Kallum Higginbotham. Brentford's game against Wolves is halted for 20 minutes when a drone flying over the Community Stadium is deemed to be a safety risk.

23 Brentford manager Thomas Frank signs a new contract through to the end of the 2024-25 season. John Sheridan is named Oldham manager for the sixth time – four full-time appointments and two as caretaker.

24 Claudio Ranieri is sacked after 14 matches as Watford manager with his side in the bottom three after a single point from his final eight games.

25 Hull's new owner sacks manager Grant McCann, despite successive victories over promotion-chasing Blackburn and Bournemouth taking the club seven points clear of the drop zone.

26 Roy Hodgson replaces Claudio Ranieri and becomes Watford's 15th 'permanent' manager in ten years. It's the 74-year-old's 17th club appointment in a 46-year managerial career.

27 The Premier League calls on clubs to show proof of at least four positive Covid tests in order to have a fixture postponed. Former Rangers, Ajax and Georgia international striker Shota Arveladze is appointed Hull's new manager.

28 Brentford manager Thomas Frank is fined £8,000 by the FA for confronting referee Peter Bankes after the home defeat by Wolves.

29 Former Liverpool midfielder Cameron Brannagan makes English football history by scoring four penalties in Oxford's 7-2 win at Gillingham.

30 Frank Lampard, formerly in charge at Chelsea and Derby, is appointed Everton's new manager. Sunderland sack Lee Johnson following a 6-0 defeat at Bolton. Neil Harris, former Cardiff and Millwall manager, takes over at Gillingham.

31 Transfer deadline day brings former Inter Milan and Tottenham midfielder Christian Eriksen back to the Premier League – seven months after suffering a cardiac arrest in Denmark's Euro 2020 match against Final. Eriksen, who has not played since, signs for Brentford until the end of the season. Pierre-Emerick Aubameyang, stripped of the Arsenal captaincy, joins Barcelona. And another high-profile free-transfer takes Tottenham's Dele Alli to Everton. Spending by Premier League clubs during the winter window totals £295m, with Liverpool's £37.5m acquisition of Porto's Colombia winger Luis Diaz the biggest fee.

FEBRUARY 2022

1 Joao Cancelo signs a new contract with Manchester City through to 2027.

2 Valerien Ismael, manager of West Bromwich Albion for seven months, is sacked after one win in eight league and cup games. Nottingham Forest and Derby are both fined £10,000 by the FA for a players' melee.

3 Former Newcastle manager Steve Bruce succeeds Valerien Ismael at the Hawthorns – his 11th club appointment.

4 Middlesbrough knock Manchester United out of the FA Cup 8-7 on penalties in a round four tie at Old Trafford.

5 Sixth-tier Kidderminster are two minutes away from one of the FA Cup's biggest-ever upsets when West Ham equalise in stoppage-time and win 2-1 with a goal in the first added minute of extra-time.

6 FA Cup holders Leicester are beaten 4-1 by Nottingham Forest. Sadio Mane scores the winning spot-kick as Senegal beat his Liverpool team-mate Mohamed Salah's Egypt on penalties in the Africa Cup of Nations Final.

7 The four home nations, together with the Republic of Ireland, launch a joint bid for Euro 2028 after agreeing not to target the 2030 World Cup. Chelsea settle a High Court case brought by four former youth team players over alleged historical racial abuse.

8 West Ham's Kurt Zouma is condemned by his club, fined two weeks' wages of £250,000 and has two pet cats taken away by the RSPCA after he is filmed kicking and slapping one of them.

9 Kurt Zouma is dropped by his sportswear company and West Ham lose other sponsorship after including the defender in the midweek match against Watford. His brother Yoan is suspended by his club, National League Dagenham and Redbridge, for his part in filming the incident. Chelsea defeat Asian champions Al Hilal 1-0 with a Romelu Lukaku goal to reach the Club World Cup Final in Abu Dhabi.

10 Lee Johnson receives a four-match touchline ban and £3,000 fine from the FA for his involvement in a touchline fracas while Sunderland manager. Sunderland (£5,000) and Lincoln (£4,000) are fined for failing to control their players. Matt Taylor, manager of Walsall for nine months, is sacked after a seventh successive defeat leaves his team fourth from bottom.

11 After Roy Keane turns down a return to the club, Sunderland appoint former Preston and Norwich manager Alex Neil.

12 Chelsea become world champions by beating Palmeiras of Brazil 2-1 with a goal by Romelu Lukaku and an extra-time penalty from Kai Havertz.

13 Stephen Glass, manager of Aberdeen for 11 months, is sacked after a Scottish Cup defeat by Motherwell and with his side fourth from bottom of the Premiership.

14 Emiliano Martinez and Emiliano Buendia of Aston Villa and Tottenham's Cristian Romero and Giovani Lo Celso are banned by FIFA for two Argentina World Cup qualifiers after failing to comply with Covid rules for the abandoned match against Brazil. Barnsley are fined £12,000 and Cardiff £10,000 by the FA for a confrontation involving players and coaches.

15 Bradford, eight points adrift of a play-off place, dismiss Derek Adams, manager for eight months. Former Newport manager Mike Flynn takes the Walsall job.

16 Dundee manager James McPake is sacked with his side second from bottom of the Premiership. Mark McGhee, formerly in charge of Motherwell and Aberdeen, takes over until the end of the season, but misses the first six matches because of an outstanding touchline ban.

17 Barrow manager Mark Cooper is given an eight-match touchline ban and fined £3,000 by the FA for abusive comments, including a reference to gender, made to assistant referee Helen Edwards during the match against Exeter.

18 Reading, two points above the relegation zone, sack manager Veljko Paunovic. Jim Goodwin leaves St Mirren to become Aberdeen's new manager.

19 Eight years after his last managerial job, former England midfielder Paul Ince is appointed caretaker at Reading. Eight EFL matches are postponed in the aftermath of Storm Eunice.

20 Darren Ferguson, in his third spell as Peterborough manager, resigns with his side second from bottom.

21 Stephen Robinson leaves Morecambe after eight months as manager to take over at St Mirren. Barnsley are fined £10,000 by the FA for protesting players surrounding referee Andy Davies in the match against Luton.

22 Kenny Jackett, manager of Leyton Orient for nine months, loses his job after a run of two points and two goals scored in ten matches.

23 Carlisle part company with Keith Millen, manager for four months, after his team drop into the relegation zone. Paul Simpson is appointed until the end of the season, 15 years after leaving the club for Preston. England women defeat Germany 3-1 at Molineux to win a four-team tournament also featuring Spain and Canada.

24 The managerial merry-go-round continues. Grant McCann, ousted at Hull, returns to Peterborough for a second spell. Derek Adams goes back to Morecambe, nine months after leaving for Bradford. Mark Hughes, out of management since being sacked by Southampton in December 2018, takes over at Bradford. Rangers reach the last 16 of the Europa League with a 6-4 aggregate win over Borussia Dortmund in the play-off round. Leicester defeat Randers 7-2 over two legs to go through in the Europa Conference League. Celtic are defeated 5-1 by Norwegian champions Bodo/Glimt. ITV announces a new two-year broadcast deal, taking over EFL, League Cup and League Trophy highlights from Quest.

25 St Petersburg is stripped of the Champions League Final following Russia's invasion of Ukraine, with UEFA moving the match to Paris. Manchester United cancel their sponsorship deal with Aeroflot, Russia's national airline. Chelsea manager Thomas Tuchel admits the invasion could turn public feeling against the club, owned by Russian billionaire Roman Abramovich since 2003.

26 Roman Abramovich announces he is handing the 'stewardship and care' of Chelsea to trustees of the club's charitable foundation. His statement has no mention of the invasion. Critics say the move is purely 'symbolic' and he remains the owner. The Wembley arch is lit up in Ukraine's colours of blue and yellow ahead of the League Cup Final. Poland, Sweden and the Czech Republic boycott any World Cup qualifying matches against Russia.

27 Liverpool and Chelsea players stand in support of Ukraine below the League Cup Final. Liverpool win 11-10 on penalties after a goalless draw. England, Scotland and Wales say they will not play Russia 'for the foreseeable future.' Leeds manager Marcelo Bielsa is sacked after four successive defeats and 17 goals conceded leave his side two points off the drop zone.

28 FIFA and UEFA suspend Russian national and club teams from all competitions, including the World Cup and Europa League. The European governing body also terminates a Champions League sponsorship deal with the energy company Gazprom. American coach Jesse Marsch, formerly with RB Leipzig, replaces Marcelo Bielsa at Elland Road. Arsenal post a club-record annual loss of £107m.

MARCH 2022

1 Former Norwich manager Daniel Farke leaves the Russian Premier League club Krasnodar 'by mutual agreement' without taking charge of a match. Middlesbrough reach the FA Cup quarter-finals by beating Tottenham 1-0.

2 Roman Abramovich announces his intention to sell Chelsea after 19 years of ownership. Abramovich says he will not ask for loans to the club of £1.5bn to be repaid and that net proceeds of the sale will go to victims of the war in Ukraine, without saying to which side.

3 Everton sever links with major sponsor Alisher Usmanov, a Russia oligarch. The Premier League is reviewing its owners' and directors' test, chief executive Richard Masters tells a football business forum.

4 Everton suspend sponsorship deals with three Russian companies. Derby's administrators say there is sufficient cash for the club to complete the season.

5 Manchester City come from behind to beat Chelsea 3-1 in the women's League Cup Final.

6 Former Celtic manager Neil Lennon is appointed coach to the Cypriot club Omonia Nicosia.

7 Wesley Fofana, recovering from a broken leg sustained in a pre-season friendly, signs a two-year contract extension with Leicester

8 The Premier League, EFL and FA terminate broadcasting deals with Russia. The Premier League also donates £1m to Ukraine victims of the war. Scotland's World Cup play-off semi-final against Ukraine, scheduled for March 24 at Hampden Park, is postponed. Liverpool reach the quarter-finals of the Champions League with a 2-1 aggregate win over Inter Milan.

9 Manchester City qualify for the last eight by defeating Sporting 5-0 over the two legs. Pedro Neto signs a new five-year contract with Wolves. Republic of Ireland manager Stephen Kenny signs a contract extension through to Euro 2024. Former Doncaster and Salford manager Richie Wellens takes over at Leyton Orient.

10 Roman Abramovich is sanctioned by the Government over links with the Russian leader Vladimir Putin and accused of 'having blood on his hands.' All his UK assets, including Chelsea, are frozen, with major repercussions for the club. Transfers, sales of tickets and merchandise are banned.

11 The Government opens negotiations with Roman Abramovich's advisers over the sale of Chelsea and wants to push through a deal as quickly as possible.

12 Cristiano Ronaldo, the 59th hat-trick of his career in Manchester United's 3-2 win over Tottenham, becomes FIFA's all-time leading scorer on 807 goals for club and country

13 On an emotional afternoon at the London Stadium, Ukraine winger Andriy Yarmolenko scores for West Ham on his first appearance since the invasion of his homeland.
  Chelsea manager Thomas Tuchel, whose future has been shrouded in uncertainly, says he will remain at the club until at least the end of the season. Bournemouth manager Scott Parker is given a one-match touchline ban and £2,000 fine by the FA for abusive language during the match against Preston. The FA announces a tenfold increase in prize money to £3million for the Women's FA Cup from season 2022-23.

15 Manchester United are knocked out of the Champions League 2-1 on aggregate by Atletico Madrid. Chelsea are criticised by FA Cup opponents Middlesbrough for asking for the quarter-final tie at the Riverside to be played behind closed doors 'for matters of sporting integrity.' The request to the FA is later withdrawn. Brentford's Christian Eriksen is named in Denmark's squad for the first time since his cardiac arrest at Euro 2020.

16 Chelsea progress to the quarter-finals of the Champions League with a 4-1 victory over the two legs against Lille. Paul Tisdale, in charge of Stevenage for three-and-a-half-months, is sacked after nine matches without a win leaves his team third from bottom. He is replaced by former Gillingham manager Steve Evans. Swansea are fined £5,000 by the FA for protesting players surrounding referee Jarred Gillett in the match against Fulham.

17 Andriy Yarmolenko delivers another special goal, this one in extra-time, to send West Ham through to their first European quarter-final since 1981. It brings a 2-1 aggregate success against Sevilla and they are joined in the last eight of the Europa League by Rangers, 4-2 winners against Red Star Belgrade over the two legs. Leicester's Wesley Fofana, out all season, marks his return with the goal which secures a 3-2 victory over Rennes in the last 16 of the Europa Conference.

18 The deadline for bids to buy Chelsea from Roman Abramovich passes with an estimated 20 interested parties.

19 On the pitch, Chelsea continue their successful run, defeating Middlesbrough 2-0 to reach the semi-finals of the FA Cup.

20 Barrow's Mark Cooper, serving an eight-match touchline ban and with his side fourth from bottom, becomes League Two's latest managerial casualty. Former Southend manager Phil Brown is appointed until the end of the season.

21 Liverpool and Manchester City supporters' groups call for the clubs' FA Cup semi-final to be moved from Wembley, with no direct trains to London from either city that weekend because of engineering work.

22 Wayne Rooney and Patrick Vieira are the latest additions to the Premier League's Hall of Fame.

23 Chelsea supporters are given permission to buy tickets for away matches after amendments to the club's special licence.

24 Two spectacular Gareth Bale goals, the first a free-kick, give Wales a 2-1 victory over Austria in a World Cup play-off semi-final. European champions Italy lose to North Macedonia and fail to qualify for the tournament in Qatar. Kieran Tierney scores his first goal for Scotland, who draw 1-1 with Poland in a friendly international which raises £500,000 for the children of war-torn Ukraine.

25 Jermain Defoe, 39, brings down the curtain on a distinguished 22-year career for club and country, having made 762 appearances for six teams, scored 162 Premier League goals and won 57 England caps. The FA announces 50 free buses each for Liverpool and Manchester City supporters for the FA Cup semi-final at Wembley.

26 Harry Kane draws level with Sir Bobby Charlton on 49 goals in England's all-time list with a penalty in a 2-1 friendly win over Switzerland. Alan Browne's 86th minute goal earns the Republic of Ireland a 2-2 draw against Belgium. Christian Eriksen scores two minutes after coming off the bench in his international comeback for Denmark, who are beaten 4-2 by Holland. Kelty Hearts become League Two champions with five matches still to play in their first season of senior Scottish football.

27 Parties shortlisted to buy Chelsea are told they can make new and improved offers for the club.

28 Everton post an annual loss of £120m. AFC Wimbledon manager Mark Robinson is sacked with his side fourth from bottom after 20 games without a win. Newcastle's Isaac Hayden is fined £19,000 by the FA for criticising referee David Coote after the defeat by Chelsea.

29 Goalkeeper Wayne Hennessey wins his 100th Wales cap and Rubin Colwill scores his first international goal in the 1-1 draw with the Czech Republic. In other friendlies, England defeat the Ivory Coast 3-0, Scotland draw 2-2 against Austria after leading 2-0, Northern Ireland are beaten 1-0 by Hungary and Troy Parrott scores a 97th minute winner for the Republic of Ireland against Lithuania. Manchester United's Bruno Fernandes scores both goals to send Portugal to the World Cup with a 2-0 victory over Macedonia in their play-off final. In a repeat of the Africa Cup of Nations decider, Sadio Mane scores the winning spot-kick as Senegal qualify with victory over Liverpool team-mate Mohamed Salah's Egypt on penalties.

30 AFC Wimbledon appoint former Reading manager Mark Bowen until the end of the season. A world record crowd for a women's match of 91,553 watch Barcelona play Real Madrid in the quarter-finals of the Champions League.

31 Annual payments to agents by Premier League clubs reach a record £272.6m. Manchester City (£35m), Manchester United (£29m) and Chelsea (£28.2m) top the spending list, with Brentford (£3.5m) paying the lowest amount. Premier League clubs vote to reintroduce five substitutions from season 2022-23.

APRIL 2022

1 England are handed a favourable World Cup draw in a group with Iran, the United States and either Wales, Scotland or Ukraine. Bruno Fernandes extends his contract with Manchester United to 2026 with a new one-year deal.

3 Celtic remain on course to regain the Scottish Premiership title by beating defending champions Rangers 2-1. Rotherham defeat Sutton 4-2 in the EFL Trophy Final after equalising in the fifth minute of stoppage-time to take the match into extra-time.

4 Leicester unveil a statue of their late former owner Vichai Srivaddhanaprabha, who died in a helicopter crash outside the King Power Stadium in October 2018.

5 American businessman Chris Kirchner is named by Derby's administrators as the preferred bidder for the club.

6 Karim Benzema scores a hat-trick for Real Madrid at Stamford Bridge in a 3-1 win over Chelsea in the first leg of their Champions League quarter-final.

7 UEFA announces new financial regulations limiting clubs' spending on wages, transfers and agents' fees to 70 per cent of their revenue. League Two Crawley are taken over by an American investment group.

8 Neil Warnock, 73, announces his retirement after 42 years and 1,603 games in management with 16 clubs.

9 Crewe become the first EFL team to be relegated, dropping into League Two with four matches remaining.

10 Manchester City and Liverpool remain separated by a single point at the top of the Premier League after a 2-2 draw.

11 Atletico Madrid are ordered to close part of their stadium for the Champions League quarter-final second leg against Manchester City after Nazi salutes by supporters during the first game. Crewe manager David Artell is sacked after the club's relegation.

12 Chelsea, leading 3-0 at the Bernabeu with ten minutes of normal time remaining, are poised for one of the great overall Champions League comebacks. But Real Madrid pull a goal back and a second from Karim Benzema in extra-time gives them a 5-4 aggregate victory and a place in the semi-finals.

13 Manchester City overcome a hostile crowd and an intimidatory approach by Atletico Madrid to reach the last four with a goalless draw and a 1-0 aggregate success. Police are called in to deal with violence in the tunnel after the match. Liverpool, showing seven changes from the first leg in Lisbon, go through 6-4 on aggregate against Benfica after a 3-3 draw at Anfield.

14 West Ham are 3-0 winners in Lyon to go through to the European League semi-finals 4-1 on aggregate. They are joined by Rangers, who beat Braga 3-2 over the two legs. Leicester defeat PSV Eindhoven 2-1 on aggregate to reach the last four of the Europa Conference. Queens Park Rangers are fined £5,000 by the FA for protesting players against Fulham.

15 Sean Dyche, appointed in October 2012 and the longest serving manager in the Premier League, is sacked with Burnley third from bottom with eight games remaining. Scunthorpe are relegated after 72 years in the Football League.

16 Liverpool score three goals in the first half to defeat Manchester City 3-2 and reach the FA Cup Final. Hearts beat Hibernian 2-1 in Scotland. Manchester City overcome West Ham 4-1 in the first women's semi-final.

17 Chelsea beat Crystal Palace 2-0 to set up a repeat of the League Cup Final against Liverpool. Rangers are 2-1 winners against Celtic. Chelsea women defeat Arsenal 2-0.

18 Wayne Rooney promises to stay as manager and rebuild Derby after the club's relegation from the Championship.

19 Liverpool and Manchester United supporters come together at Anfield to show support for Cristiano Ronaldo following the death of his baby son. Fulham are promoted straight back to the Premier League.

20 Shaun Maloney is sacked after four months as Hibernian manager, with his side missing out on a top-six place and beaten by Hearts in the semi-finals of the Scottish Cup. Oliver Skipp signs a new four-year contract with Tottenham.

21 Ajax coach Erik ten Hag is appointed Manchester United's new permanent manager on a three-year contract through to June 2025.

22 Crawley suspend manager John Yems over allegations of discriminatory behaviour and language towards his players. Kilmarnock win the Scottish Championship and regain their Premiership place at the first attempt. Huddersfield (£5,500) and Luton (£5,000) are fined by the FA for a players' confrontation.

23 Oldham are relegated after 117 years in the Football League.

24 Poya Asbaghi, manager of Barnsley for five months, is sacked after his team are relegated. Southampton's Tino Livramento sustains a serious knee injury against Brighton and is expected to be out or the remainder of 2022.

25 The Government says it will establish an independent regular for football after endorsing recommendations in a fan-led review of the game.

26 Manchester City defeat Real Madrid 4-3 in an epic Champions League semi-final first leg at Anfield. Aston Villa's Jacob Ramsey signs a new five-year contract.

27 Liverpool beat Villarreal 2-0 in the second semi-final first leg. Alex Morris, David Artell's former assistant at Crewe, is appointed permanent manager. Stoke are fined £9,000 and Bristol City £7,000 by the FA for a players' melee.

28 Liverpool's Mohamed Salah is named the football writers' Footballer of the Year. Rangers are fined for the sixth time this season for crowd trouble in Europa League games – £39,000 for fireworks being lit and a late kick-off against Braga. Manchester United are fined £8,400 for objects thrown at Atletico Madrid coach Diego Simeone after the Champions League match. Liverpool must pay the same amount for a late kick-off against Benfica.

29 Ralf Rangnick, Manchester United's interim manager, is appointed head coach to the Austrian national team.

30 Norwich are relegated from the Premier League with four matches to be played. Lincoln manager Michael Appleton leaves the club at the end of his contract.

MAY 2022

1 UEFA bans Russian clubs from all European competitions in season 2022-23 The women's national team are disqualified from the European Championship finals.

2 Fulham clinch the Championship title with a third 7-0 win of the season, against Luton.

3 Liverpool overturn a 2-0 deficit in the second leg against Villarreal with three second-half goals to reach the Champions League Final 5-2 on aggregate. Bournemouth return to the Premier League after an absence of two seasons as runners-up to Fulham. Johnnie Jackson is sacked by Charlton after four-and-a-half months as permanent manager.

4 Manchester City concede three goals in five minutes at the end of their second leg against Real Madrid, lose 3-1 and go down 6-5 on aggregate in one of the most remarkable Champions League ties of all time. Watford manager Roy Hodgson confirms he will leave the club at the end of the season. Hearts goalkeeper Craig Gordon becomes the first three-time winner of the Scottish football writers' Footballer of the Year award.

5 Manager David Moyes is shown a red card for kicking the ball at a ball boy as West Ham are beaten 3-1 on aggregate by Eintracht Frankfurt in the semi-finals of the Europa League. Defender Aaron Cresswell is also sent off, after 18 minutes, in the second leg of the tie which his side lose 1-0. Rangers, trailing from their first leg, defeat RB Leipzig 3-2 on aggregate to reach the final. Hartlepool sack Graeme Lee after five months as manager.

6 Arsenal manager Mikel Arteta signs a new contract through to the end of the 2024-25 season. Crawley manager John Yems is dismissed after an investigation by the club into allegations he racially abused his own players.

7 Chelsea announce agreement for the sale of the club for £4.25bn to an American-Swiss consortium headed by Todd Boehly, co-owner of the LA Dodgers baseball team. Watford are relegated from the Premier League. Tony Mowbray, appointed in February 2017 and the Championship's longest-serving manager, leaves Blackburn at the end of his contract. Mark Warburton leaves Queens Park Rangers after three years in charge. Chelsea retain the women's Super League title.

8 Celtic's Callum McGregor and Angelos Postecoglou are named PFA Scotland's Player and Manager of the Year.

9 UEFA approves an increase from 32 to 36 teams in Champions League groups from season 2024-25

10 Watford appoint Forest Green's League Two title-winner Rob Edwards as their new manager. Former Celtic and Scotland captain Scott Brown takes charge at Fleetwood.

11 Celtic regain the Scottish Premiership title. Dundee are relegated. Kevin De Bruyne scores four goals in Manchester's 5-1 win over Wolves. Manchester United win the FA Youth Cup for a record 11th time, defeating Nottingham Forest 3-1 at Old Trafford in front of a record crowd for the competition of 67,492.

12 Former Republic of Ireland winger Mark Kennedy, assistant to Lee Bowyer at Birmingham, is appointed Lincoln's new manager.

13 Manchester City unveil a statue at the Etihad of record-scorer Sergio Aguero on the tenth anniversary of his Premier League title-winning goal.

14 Liverpool beat Chelsea on penalties after a goalless draw in the FA Cup Final – a repeat of the League Cup Final. Cowdenbeath are relegated after 117 years in the Scottish League, losing a play-off 4-0 to Lowland League champions Bonnyrigg Rose, who take their place.

15 Stockport return to the Football League after an 11-year absence as champions of the National League. Chelsea women complete the Double by beating Manchester City 3-2 after extra-time in the FA Cup at Wembley in front of a record crowd for the competition of 49,094.

16 Blackpool's Jake Daniels, 17, becomes the country's first male professional footballer to come out as gay since Justin Fashanu in 1990. Stoke caretaker Paul Ince is appointed permanent manager. Wayne Brown is confirmed in the job at Colchester. Johnnie Jackson, sacked by Charlton, takes over at AFC Wimbledon.

17 The Premier League title race goes to the final day of the season after Liverpool win at Southampton to close to within a point of Manchester City. Salford dismiss manager Gary Bowyer after failing to reach the play-offs.

18 Rangers lose 5-4 on penalties to Eintracht Frankfurt after a 1-1 draw in the Europa League Final in Seville.

19 The FA, Premier League and EFL pledge to crack down on pitch invasions after violent incidents at play-off matches at Huddersfield, Nottingham Forest, Port Vale and Mansfield and Everton's match against Crystal Palace. Premier League referees Michael Oliver and Anthony Taylor are selected to officiate at the Qatar World Cup.

20 Manchester City's Kevin De Bruyne is named the Premier League's top player for the season. Liverpool's Jurgen Klopp wins the managerial award. Lee Johnson, formerly in charge at Sunderland and Bristol City, is appointed Hibernian's new manager. Salford appoint Neil Wood, Manchester United's under-23 coach as their manager.

21 Rangers defeat Hearts 2-0 after extra-time to win the Scottish Cup. Sunderland, with more than 46,000 supporters at Wembley, defeat Wycombe 2-0 in League One's Play-off Final.

22 On a dramatic final day of the Premier League season, Manchester City overturn a 2-0 deficit against Aston Villa with three goals in five minutes to become champions for the fourth time in five years, a point ahead of Liverpool. Burnley are relegated alongside Norwich and Watford. Bromley win the FA Trophy for the first time, defeating Wrexham 1-0 in the final.

23 St Johnstone retain their Scottish Premiership place with a 6-2 aggregate win over Inverness in the Play-off Final.

24 Jurgen Klopp receives a second accolade – the League Manager's Association Manager of the Year award.

25 The Government approves the takeover of Chelsea after it passes the Premier League's owners' and directors' test.

26 Egypt midfielder Mohamed Elneny signs a new one-year contract with Arsenal.

27 Two clubs appoint new managers. Promoted Forest Green bring in Notts County's Ian Burchnall. Pete Wild, formerly in charge at Halifax, takes over at Barrow.

28 Liverpool lose the Champions League Final 1-0 to Real Madrid after kick-off at the Stade de France in Paris is delayed for 36 minutes amid chaotic, frightening scenes involving police and Liverpool supporters, who are pushed back in the crush with tear gas and pepper spray. Port Vale beat Mansfield 3-0 in the League Two Play-off Final.

29 UEFA's claim that late-arriving Liverpool fans, some with fake tickets, were responsible for the trouble is rejected by the club, who point the finger at poor management of the match by Europe's governing body and demand an apology. Nottingham Forest return to the Premier League after an absence of 23 years with a 1-0 victory over Huddersfield in the Championship Play-off Final.

30 The £4.25bn takeover of Chelsea is completed. UEFA launches an independent inquiry into the Champions League Final. Everton manager Frank Lampard is fined £30,000 by the FA for comments 'implying bias' about referee Stuart Attwell after the defeat by Liverpool. Ralph Rangnick and Manchester United agree to scrap his planned two-year consultancy role.

31 Players present and past feature in the Queen's Birthday Honours. Gareth Bale and James Milner are both awarded an MBE. Rio Ferdinand, Luther Blissett and Mike Summerbee each receive an OBE.

JUNE 2022

1 On an emotional night at Hampden Park, Scotland are beaten 3-1 by Ukraine in their World Cup qualifying play-off semi-final. A crowd of more than 87,000 at Wembley watches Argentina defeat Italy 3-0 in a match between the champions of South America and Europe. Michael Beale, Steven Gerrard's No 2 at Aston Villa, is appointed the new manager of

Queens Park Rangers. Kurt Zouma is ordered by magistrates to undertake 180 hours of community service for kicking his cat. Brother Yoan receives 140 hours.

2 Blackpool manager Neil Critchley leaves the club to replace Michael Beale at Villa Park. Northern Ireland lose 1-0 to Greece in their opening Nations League game.

3 UEFA apologises for what happened at the Champions League Final, admitting to mismanagement. Paul Hartley, manager of the Scottish League One champions Cove Rangers, takes charge at Hartlepool. Kevin Betsy, Arsenal's under-23 coach, is appointed Crawley's new manager.

4 England begin their Nations League programme with a 1-0 defeat against Hungary in Budapest, where a match expected to be played behind closed doors is watched by 30,000 children and 3,000 accompanying adults under a little-known UEFA regulation. The Republic of Ireland lose by the same scoreline in Armenia. Grimsby return to the Football League at the first attempt by defeating Solihull 2-1 in the National League Play-off Final.

5 Wales qualify for their first World Cup for 64 years by overcoming Ukraine 1-0 in the Play-off Final with a free-kick from Gareth Bale turned into his own net by former West Ham winger Andriy Yarmolenko. Northern Ireland's run without a Nations League win extends to 12 matches in a goalless draw in Cyprus.

6 James McArthur and James Tomkins sign new one-year contract extensions with Crystal Palace.

7 Harry Kane reaches a half-century of international goals with a penalty in England's 1-1 draw against Germany, overtaking Sir Bobby Charlton's tally and closing to within three of Wayne Rooney's record of 53. England's under-21 team confirm a place in European Championship finals. Ben Garner leaves Swindon to become Charlton's new manager. Gary Bowyer, sacked by Salford, takes over at relegated Dundee.

8 The Premier League suspends its broadcasting deal with Russia. Anthony Ralston and Scott McKenna scores their first international goals as Scotland defeat Armenia 2-0. Rhys Norrington-Davies opens his account with Wales, who suffer a stoppage-time 2-1 defeat by Holland. The Republic of Ireland lose 1-0 to Ukraine.

9 Liverpool's Mohamed Salah is voted the Professional Footballers' Association Player of the Year. Northern Ireland are beaten 3-2 by Kosovo.

10 Billy Bingham, who led Northern Ireland to the World Cup finals in 1982 and 1986, dies aged 90.

11 England share a goalless draw with Italy at a virtually empty Molineux, UEFA's punishment for crowd trouble at the Euro 2020 Final between the two teams. The Republic of Ireland win their first Nations League match at the 13th attempt, defeating Scotland 3-0 with Michael Obafemi scoring his first international goal. Brennan Johnson's first for Wales earns a 1-1 draw against Belgium

12 A stoppage-time goal by Jonny Evans gives Northern Ireland a 2-2 draw at home to Cyprus.

13 American businessman Chris Kirchner's bid to buy Derby, backed by manager Wayne Rooney, collapses. Manchester City pay £51.2m for Borussia Dortmund striker Erling Haaland.

14 England suffer their worst home defeat since 1928, beaten 4-0 by Hungary at Molineux and facing relegation from their Nations League group. Wales go down 3-2 to another stoppage-time goal by Holland. Scotland win 4-1 in Armenia, who have two players sent off. Nathan Collins scores his first goal for the Republic of Ireland, a brilliant solo effort, in a 1-1 draw with Ukraine in a match switched to Lodz in Poland because of the war. Dundee United manager Tam Courts leaves to take charge at the Hungarian club Honved.

15 Vincent Kompany, former Manchester City captain and Anderlecht coach, becomes Burnley's new manager. Cheltenham manager Michael Duff takes over at Barnsley. Liverpool sign Uruguay striker Darwin Nunez from Benfica for an initial £64m.

16 Blackburn appoint the former Newcastle and Denmark forward Jon Dahl Tomasson as their new manager.

17 Liverpool agree to sell Sadio Mane to Bayern Munich for £35.1m, signalling the break-up of the club's successful strike force of Mane, Mohamed Salah and Roberto Firmino. England midfielder Declan Rice is given a two-match European ban for accusing Spanish referee

Jesus Gil of 'corruption' after West Ham's Europa League defeat by Eintracht Frankfurt. Manager David Moyes receives a one-match ban for kicking the ball at a ballboy.

18 Arsenal's Eddie Nketiah signs a new five-year contract. Former Lincoln manager Michael Appleton takes over at Blackpool, his second spell at the club.

20 Ryan Giggs, who stood aside temporarily as Wales manager to contest assault allegations, resigns because of delays with the case coming to court. Scott Lindsey, Swindon's assistant manager, is promoted to replace Ben Garner. Former Hibernian and Sunderland manager Jack Ross takes over at Dundee United.

21 Todd Boehly, head of the consortium taking over Chelsea, becomes chairman in place of Bruce Buck, who steps down after 19 years. Director Marina Granokskaia also leaves the club.

22 Cardiff manager Steve Morison speaks to Gareth Bale about the possibility of a move to the club.

23 Wayne Rooney resigns as Derby manager, maintaining that 'fresh energy' is needed at the club.

24 Manchester City close in on a £45m deal for England midfielder Kalvin Phillips from Leeds.

25 Promoted Nottingham Forest sign Nigeria striker Taiwo Awoniyi from Union Berlin for a club-record £17m.

26 Local property developer David Clowes has his bid to buy Deby accepted. Referees' chief Mike Riley announces he is stepping down after 13 years in the job.

27 Gareth Bale signs a 12-month contract with Major League Soccer club Los Angeles after nine years at Real Madrid.

28 Petr Cech, technical and performance adviser, becomes the third high-profile figure to leave Chelsea. Coach Wade Elliott is appointed Cheltenham's new manager. Goalkeeper Mark Travers signs a new five-year contract with promoted Bournemouth.

29 A year after his record £97.5m move to Chelsea from Inter Milan, Romelu Lukaku returns on loan to the Italian club.

30 Tottenham pay a club-record £60m for Everton's Richarlison. Record-signing Paul Pogba and Jesse Lingard leave Manchester United at the end of their contracts.

JULY 2022

1 Mohamed Salah ends speculation about his future by signing a new three-year contract with Liverpool. Derby come out of administration on completion of the takeover by lifelong supporter David Clowes.

2 Birmingham sack manager Lee Bowyer after finishing the season fifth from bottom of the Championship.

3 John Eustace, assistant manager at Queens Park Rangers and with the Republic of Ireland, replaces Lee Bowyer.

4 Manchester City pay Leeds £45m for Kalvin Phillips and receive the same amount from Arsenal for Gabriel Jesus.

5 Duncan Ferguson, Everton's assistant manager, leaves the club to pursue his own managerial ambitions. Richarlison, Tottenham's new-signing, is given a one-match ban and £25,000 fine by the FA for throwing a flare after scoring the winner for Everton against Chelsea

6 Raheem Sterling agrees terms with Chelsea after telling Manchester City he wants to leave the club. Liverpool's Joe Gomez is given a new five-year contract.

7 Carlos Corberan resigns as manager of beaten Championship play-off finalists Huddersfield and is replaced by coach Danny Schofield. Safe standing is given the go-ahead at Premier League and Championship grounds.

8 Former FIFA president Sepp Blatter and former UEFA president Michel Platini are cleared of fraud by a Swiss court.

ENGLISH TABLES 2021–2022

PREMIER LEAGUE

		P	W	D	L	F	A	W	D	L	F	A	GD	PTS
				Home						**Away**				
1	Man City	38	15	2	2	58	15	14	4	1	41	11	73	93
2	Liverpool	38	15	4	0	49	9	13	4	2	45	17	68	92
3	Chelsea	38	9	7	3	37	22	12	4	3	39	11	43	74
4	Tottenham	38	13	1	5	38	19	9	4	6	31	21	29	71
5	Arsenal	38	13	2	4	35	17	9	1	9	26	31	13	69
6	Man Utd	38	10	5	4	32	22	6	5	8	25	35	0	58
7	West Ham	38	9	5	5	33	26	7	3	9	27	25	9	56
8	Leicester	38	10	4	5	34	23	4	6	9	28	36	3	52
9	Brighton	38	5	7	7	19	23	7	8	4	23	21	-2	51
10	Wolves	38	7	3	9	20	25	8	3	8	18	18	-5	51
11	Newcastle	38	8	6	5	26	27	5	4	10	18	35	-18	49
12	Crystal Palace	38	7	8	4	27	17	4	7	8	23	29	4	48
13	Brentford	38	7	3	9	22	21	6	4	9	26	35	-8	46
14	Aston Villa	38	6	5	8	29	29	7	1	11	23	25	-2	45
15	Southampton	38	6	7	6	23	24	3	6	10	20	43	-24	40
16	Everton	38	9	2	8	27	25	2	4	13	16	41	-23	39
17	Leeds	38	4	6	9	19	38	5	5	9	23	41	-37	38
18	Burnley	38	5	6	8	18	25	2	8	9	16	28	-19	35
19	Watford	38	2	2	15	17	46	4	3	12	17	31	-43	23
20	Norwich	38	3	3	13	12	43	2	4	13	11	41	-61	22

Manchester City, Liverpool, Chelsea, Tottenham into Champions League group stage; Arsenal, Manchester Utd into Europa League group stage; West Ham into Europa Conference play-off round

Prize money/TV revenue (approx sums; league position = amount received): 1 £164m, 2 £162m, 3 £155m, 4 £155m, 5 £154m, 6 £150m, 7 £143m, 8 £134m, 9 £131m, 10 £130m, 11 £129m, 12 £123m, 13 £122m, 14 £120m, 15 £119m, 16 £114m, 17 £112m, 18 £104m, 19 £101m, 20 £99m

Biggest win: Chelsea 7 Norwich 0, Manchester City 7 Leeds 0
Highest aggregate score: Manchester City 6 Leicester 3
Highest attendance: 73,564 Manchester Utd v Chelsea
Lowest attendance: 16,479 Brentford v Arsenal
Player of Year: Kevin De Bruyne (Manchester City)
Manager of Year: Jurgen Klopp (Liverpool)
Golden Boot: 23 Mohamed Salah (Liverpool), Son Heung-min (Tottenham)
Golden Glove: 20 clean sheets Alisson (Liverpool), Ederson (Manchester City)
Team of Year: Alisson (Liverpool), Alexander-Arnold (Liverpool), Van Dijk (Liverpool), Rudiger (Chelsea), Joao Cancelo (Manchester City), De Bruyne (Manchester City), Thiago Alcantara (Liverpool), Bernardo Silva (Manchester City), Salah (Liverpool), Ronaldo (Manchester Utd), Mane (Liverpool)
Leading league scorers: 23 Salah (Liverpool), Son Heung-min (Tottenham); 18 Ronaldo (Manchester Utd); 17 Kane (Tottenham); 16 Mane (Liverpool); 15 De Bruyne (Manchester City), Diogo Jota (Liverpool), Vardy (Leicester); 14 Zaha (Crystal Palace); 13 Sterling (Manchester City); 12 Bowen (West Ham), Maddison (Leicester), Toney (Brentford); 11 Mahrez (Liverpool), Mount (Chelsea), Pukki (Norwich), Raphina (Leeds), Saka (Arsenal), Watkins (Aston Villa)

SKY BET CHAMPIONSHIP

		P	W	D	L	F	A	W	D	L	F	A	GD	PTS
				Home						Away				
1	Fulham	46	14	4	5	56	20	13	5	5	50	23	63	90
2	Bournemouth	46	13	7	3	41	21	12	6	5	33	18	35	88
3	Huddersfield	46	13	6	4	35	23	10	7	6	29	24	17	82
4	Nottm Forest*	46	13	4	6	43	22	10	7	6	30	18	33	80
5	Sheff Utd	46	13	5	5	38	15	8	7	8	25	30	18	75
6	Luton	46	12	7	4	37	22	9	5	9	26	33	8	75
7	Middlesbrough	46	14	2	7	34	21	6	8	9	25	29	9	70
8	Blackburn	46	12	5	6	36	26	7	7	9	23	24	9	69
9	Millwall	46	13	4	6	32	16	5	9	9	21	29	8	69
10	WBA	46	12	8	3	33	16	6	5	12	19	29	7	67
11	QPR	46	10	6	7	30	25	9	3	11	30	34	1	66
12	Coventry	46	10	5	8	32	26	7	8	8	28	33	1	64
13	Preston	46	9	10	4	33	28	7	6	10	19	28	-4	64
14	Stoke	46	10	5	8	30	23	7	6	10	27	29	5	62
15	Swansea	46	9	9	6	30	27	7	5	11	28	41	-10	61
16	Blackpool	46	11	3	9	29	26	5	9	9	25	32	-4	60
17	Bristol City	46	8	8	7	33	29	7	2	14	29	48	-15	55
18	Cardiff	47	7	4	12	22	29	8	4	11	28	39	-18	53
19	Hull	47	7	4	12	22	28	7	5	11	19	26	-13	51
20	Birmingham	46	7	6	10	27	33	4	8	11	23	42	-25	47
21	Reading	47	7	5	11	33	44	6	3	14	21	43	-33	41
22	Peterborough	46	6	7	10	27	33	3	3	17	16	54	-44	37
23	Derby	46	11	7	5	30	22	3	6	14	15	31	-8	34
24	Barnsley	46	5	7	11	18	29	1	5	17	15	44	-40	30

*Also promoted. Derby 21 pts deducted, Reading 6pts deducted

Biggest win: Blackburn 0 Fulham 7, Fulham 7 Luton 0, Reading 0 Fulham 7
Highest aggregate score: Fulham 6 Birmingham 2, Fulham 6 Bristol City 2, Reading 4 Swansea 4, Sheffield Utd 6 Peterborough 2
Highest attendance: 32,211 Derby v Birmingham
Lowest attendance: 6,832 Peterborough v Swansea
Player of Year: Aleksandar Mitrovic (Fulham)
Manager of Year: Nathan Jones (Luton)
Team of Year: Nicholls (Huddersfield), Worrall (Nottm Forest), Kelly (Bournemouth), Adarabioyo (Fulham), Spence (Nottm Forest), Robinson (Fulham), Billing (Bournemouth), Yates (Nottm Forest), Wilson (Fulham), Mitrovic (Fulham), Solanke (Bournemouth)
Leading league scorers: 43 Mitrovic (Fulham); 29 Solanke (Bournemouth); 22 Brereton Diaz (Blackburn), Piroe (Swansea), Weimann (Bristol City); 18 Grant (WBA); 17 Gyokeres (Coventry); 16 Adebayo (Luton), Johnson (Nottm Forest), Riis (Preston); 14 Sharp (Sheffield Utd), Ward (Huddersfield); 13 Brown (Stoke); 12 Afobe (Millwall), Clarke-Harris (Peterborough), Cornick (Luton), Godden (Coventry), Grabban (Nottm Forest), Lewis-Potter (Hull), Martin (Bristol City)

SKY BET LEAGUE ONE

			Home				Away						
	P	W	D	L	F	A	W	D	L	F	A	GD	PTS
1 Wigan	46	13	5	5	36	22	14	6	3	46	22	38	92
2 Rotherham	46	15	3	5	43	22	12	6	5	27	11	37	90
3 MK Dons	46	13	5	5	34	21	13	6	4	44	23	34	89
4 Sheff Wed	46	16	5	2	48	18	8	8	7	30	32	28	85
P Sunderland*	46	16	3	4	49	19	8	9	6	30	34	26	84
6 Wycombe	46	14	5	4	39	26	9	9	5	36	25	24	83
7 Plymouth	46	14	4	5	32	19	9	7	7	36	29	20	80
8 Oxford	46	13	6	4	47	27	9	4	10	35	32	23	76
9 Bolton	46	12	7	4	45	26	9	3	11	29	31	17	73
10 Portsmouth	46	14	5	4	46	25	6	8	9	22	26	17	73
11 Ipswich	46	11	9	3	38	22	7	7	9	29	24	21	70
12 Accrington	46	12	6	5	41	33	5	4	14	20	47	-19	61
13 Charlton	46	10	4	9	32	28	7	4	12	23	31	-4	59
14 Cambridge	46	8	8	7	28	29	7	5	11	28	45	-18	58
15 Cheltenham	46	10	7	6	33	30	3	10	10	33	50	-14	56
16 Burton	46	10	6	7	34	26	4	5	14	17	41	-16	53
17 Lincoln	46	7	5	11	25	29	7	5	11	30	34	-8	52
18 Shrewsbury	46	9	7	7	30	25	3	7	13	17	26	-4	50
19 Morecambe	46	7	8	8	33	35	3	4	16	24	53	-31	42
20 Fleetwood	46	5	8	10	33	37	3	8	12	29	45	-20	40
21 Gillingham	46	4	8	11	13	36	4	8	11	22	33	-34	40
22 Doncaster	46	7	3	13	20	32	3	5	15	17	50	-45	38
23 AFC Wimbledon	46	2	14	7	27	34	4	5	14	22	41	-26	37
24 Crewe	46	5	5	13	22	40	2	3	18	15	43	-46	29

*Also promoted

Biggest win: Bolton 6 Sunderland 0, Ipswich 6 Doncaster 0, Sheffield Wed 6 Cambridge 0
Highest aggregate score: Wycombe 5 Cheltenham 5
Highest attendance: 38,395 Sunderland v Doncaster
Lowest attendance: 1,746 Accrington v AFC Wimbledon
Player of Year: Scott Twine (MK Dons)
Manager of Year: Leam Richardson (Wigan)
Team of Year: Cooper, (Plymouth), Whatmough (Wigan), Ihiekwe (Rotherham), Darling (MK Dons), Burns (Ipswich), McClean (Wigan), Bannan (Sheffield Wed), Barlaser (Rotherham, Twine (MK Dons), Smith (Rotherham), Stewart (Sunderland)
Leading league scorers: 26 Keane (Wigan); 24 Stewart (Sunderland); 23 May (Cheltenham), Stockton (Morecambe); 20 Taylor (Oxford), Twine (MK Dons); 19 Smith (Rotherham); 16 Gregory (Sheffield Wed), Hardie (Plymouth), Vokes (Wycombe); 15 Lang (Wigan), Smith (Cambridge); 14 Brannagan (Oxford), Ironside (Cambridge); 13 Hirst (Portsmouth), Stockley (Charlton), Udoh (Shrewsbury); 12 Afolayan (Bolton), Bonne (Ipswich), Burns (Ipswich), Eisa (MK Dons), Rudoni (AFC Wimbledon)

SKY BET LEAGUE TWO

			Home					Away						
		P	W	D	L	F	A	W	D	L	F	A	GD	PTS
1	Forest Green	46	14	4	5	34	18	9	11	3	41	26	31	84
2	Exeter	46	14	6	3	37	19	9	9	5	28	22	24	84
3	Bristol Rov	46	14	4	5	38	20	9	7	7	33	29	22	80
4	Northampton	46	13	5	5	32	15	10	6	7	28	23	22	80
5	Port Vale*	46	11	6	6	35	22	11	6	6	32	24	21	78
6	Swindon	46	9	7	7	35	25	13	4	6	42	29	23	77
7	Mansfield	46	15	4	4	40	24	7	7	9	27	28	15	77
8	Sutton	46	14	5	4	38	20	8	5	10	31	33	16	76
9	Tranmere	46	16	3	4	36	16	5	9	9	17	24	13	75
10	Salford	46	10	9	4	33	21	9	4	10	27	25	14	70
11	Newport	46	9	6	8	40	31	10	6	7	27	27	9	69
12	Crawley	46	9	6	8	28	29	8	4	11	28	37	-10	61
13	Leyton Orient	46	9	5	9	36	22	5	11	7	26	25	15	58
14	Bradford	46	6	10	7	29	29	8	6	9	24	26	-2	58
15	Colchester	46	6	9	8	25	28	8	4	11	23	32	-12	55
16	Walsall	46	10	5	8	30	29	4	7	12	17	31	-13	54
17	Hartlepool	46	9	7	7	24	26	5	5	13	20	38	-20	54
18	Rochdale	46	7	11	5	28	23	5	6	12	23	36	-8	53
19	Harrogate	46	6	7	10	32	36	8	4	11	32	39	-11	53
20	Carlisle	46	8	7	8	19	23	6	4	13	20	39	-23	53
21	Stevenage	46	9	6	8	29	30	2	8	13	16	38	-23	47
22	Barrow	46	5	9	9	25	28	5	5	13	19	29	-13	44
23	Oldham	46	5	4	14	29	42	4	7	12	17	33	-29	38
24	Scunthorpe	46	3	7	13	15	36	1	7	15	14	54	-61	26

*Also promoted

Biggest win: Bristol Rov 7 Scunthorpe 0
Highest aggregate score: Oldham 5 Forest Green 5
Highest attendance: 18,283 Bradford v Carlisle
Lowest attendance: 1,290 Salford v Crawley
Player of Year: Kane Wilson (Forest Green)
Manager of Year: Rob Edwards (Forest Green)
Team of Year: Wollacott (Swindon), Guthrie (Northampton), Clarke (Tranmere), Turnbull (Salford), Wilson (Forest Green), Cadden (Forest Green), Dieng (Exeter), Azaz (Newport), McKirdy (Swindon), Telford (Newport), Stevens (Forest Green)
Leading league scorers: 25 Telford (Newport); 23 Stevens (Forest Green); 19 Matt (Forest Green), McKirdy (Swindon); 15 Collins (Bristol Rov), Keillor-Dunn (Oldham); 14 Jay (Exeter), Sears (Colchester); 13 Diamond (Harrogate), Drinan (Leyton Orient), Norris (Stevenage), Payne (Swindon), Smith (Leyton Orient); 12 Armstrong (Harrogate), Cook (Bradford), Dieng (Exeter), Garrity (Port Vale); Miller (Walsall), Muldoon (Harrogate), Proctor (Port Vale)

PREMIER LEAGUE RESULTS 2021–2022

Home \ Away	Arsenal	Aston Villa	Brentford	Brighton	Burnley	Chelsea	Crystal Palace	Everton	Leeds	Leicester	Liverpool	Man City	Man Utd	Newcastle	Norwich	Southampton	Tottenham	Watford	West Ham	Wolves
Arsenal	—	3-1	2-1	1-2	1-0	0-2	2-2	2-1	2-1	2-0	0-2	1-2	3-1	2-0	1-0	3-0	3-1	1-0	2-0	2-1
Aston Villa	0-1	—	1-1	2-0	1-0	1-3	2-1	0-3	3-3	2-1	1-2	1-2	2-2	1-0	2-0	4-0	0-4	0-1	1-4	2-3
Brentford	2-0	1-1	—	0-1	0-3	1-1	0-0	1-0	1-2	1-2	3-3	0-1	1-3	2-0	1-2	3-0	0-0	2-1	2-0	1-2
Brighton	0-0	0-2	0-1	—	0-3	1-1	1-1	0-2	1-1	1-1	0-2	1-4	4-0	0-0	0-0	2-2	0-2	2-0	3-1	0-1
Burnley	0-1	3-1	0-0	3-0	—	0-4	3-3	1-1	1-1	1-2	0-1	0-2	1-1	1-0	0-0	2-0	1-0	0-0	1-3	0-0
Chelsea	2-0	3-0	1-3	1-1	0-4	—	3-0	1-1	3-0	1-2	2-2	0-1	1-1	2-0	7-0	2-2	2-0	2-1	3-2	2-2
Crystal Palace	3-0	2-3	3-2	1-1	3-3	1-0	—	3-1	0-0	2-2	1-3	0-0	1-0	1-1	3-0	2-2	3-0	1-1	2-2	2-0
Everton	2-1	1-0	1-0	2-3	3-1	0-1	3-1	—	0-0	1-1	1-4	0-1	1-0	1-1	2-0	1-2	0-0	2-5	0-1	0-1
Leeds	1-4	3-3	1-2	0-0	1-1	3-0	1-0	2-2	—	1-1	0-3	0-4	4-2	1-0	2-1	1-1	0-4	0-0	1-2	1-1
Leicester	0-2	2-1	1-2	1-1	2-2	3-0	2-1	2-0	1-0	—	1-0	0-1	1-0	4-0	3-1	4-1	2-3	4-2	2-2	1-0
Liverpool	2-0	1-0	3-3	2-0	0-1	2-2	1-0	1-0	6-0	2-0	—	2-2	0-0	3-0	5-0	4-0	1-1	2-0	1-0	3-1
Man City	5-0	3-2	0-0	1-1	2-0	1-0	0-0	3-0	4-0	6-3	2-2	—	4-1	5-0	3-2	0-0	2-3	5-1	2-2	1-0
Man Utd	3-1	2-2	1-3	4-0	1-1	1-1	1-0	1-0	4-2	4-1	0-5	0-2	—	1-1	1-0	2-1	3-2	4-1	1-1	0-1
Newcastle	2-0	1-0	2-0	2-1	1-0	0-3	1-0	1-0	1-1	2-1	1-3	0-4	1-1	—	1-2	2-1	2-3	1-1	1-2	1-0
Norwich	1-0	2-0	1-2	0-0	0-0	1-3	3-0	2-1	2-1	1-2	1-3	0-4	1-2	1-2	—	1-2	0-3	0-0	2-1	0-1
Southampton	3-0	4-0	3-0	2-2	2-0	3-1	2-2	3-1	1-1	4-1	0-4	1-3	2-1	1-1	1-1	—	2-1	0-1	2-3	3-1
Tottenham	3-0	2-1	0-0	2-0	1-0	0-2	3-0	0-0	2-1	3-2	1-1	3-2	0-0	5-1	3-0	2-1	—	0-1	3-1	2-0
Watford	2-3	3-2	1-2	1-2	0-0	1-2	2-2	2-1	0-3	2-5	0-5	1-3	4-1	1-1	3-0	2-3	1-0	—	1-4	0-4
West Ham	1-2	2-1	2-0	1-1	0-0	3-2	2-2	2-1	2-3	4-1	3-2	2-2	1-1	1-1	4-0	3-1	1-1	1-0	—	1-0
Wolves	0-1	2-1	0-2	0-3	1-0	0-0	1-1	2-1	2-3	1-0	0-1	1-5	1-0	1-0	2-1	3-1	0-2	4-0	1-0	—

SKY BET CHAMPIONSHIP RESULTS 2021–2022

	Barnsley	Birmingham	Blackburn	Blackpool	Bournemouth	Bristol City	Cardiff	Coventry	Derby	Fulham	Huddersfield	Hull	Luton	Middlesbrough	Millwall	Nottm Forest	Peterborough	Preston	QPR	Reading	Sheff Utd	Stoke	Swansea	WBA
Barnsley	—	1-1	0-0	0-2	0-1	2-0	0-1	1-0	2-1	1-1	1-1	0-2	0-1	3-2	0-1	1-3	0-2	1-3	1-0	1-1	2-3	1-1	0-2	0-0
Birmingham	2-1	—	1-2	1-1	0-3	3-0	0-1	0-0	2-2	6-2	0-0	0-5	0-0	1-1	3-1	2-0	2-0	0-0	2-0	1-2	1-2	0-0	2-1	1-0
Blackburn	2-1	4-0	—	1-1	2-1	0-1	0-1	2-2	1-2	2-0	3-2	1-1	0-0	1-1	3-1	1-2	5-0	1-4	2-1	1-0	3-1	0-1	1-0	1-2
Blackpool	1-0	6-1	1-1	—	1-2	3-1	1-1	1-1	1-1	3-2	1-1	0-1	1-2	2-1	1-1	1-2	5-0	1-0	2-1	4-1	0-0	0-1	1-0	0-0
Bournemouth	3-0	3-1	0-2	2-2	—	3-2	3-0	0-1	0-2	0-3	0-0	1-0	3-2	1-1	1-1	2-3	0-0	0-0	2-3	3-0	2-1	2-1	4-0	2-2
Bristol City	1-1	1-2	1-1	0-1	0-2	—	1-1	0-1	1-0	1-0	2-1	2-1	2-1	2-0	2-3	0-2	2-2	1-2	2-3	2-2	1-1	1-0	1-0	2-2
Cardiff	1-0	0-1	0-1	1-1	0-2	1-2	—	2-0	1-0	0-1	2-1	2-1	2-1	1-2	1-1	2-1	1-2	1-2	2-1	2-1	2-3	2-1	0-4	0-4
Coventry	2-0	0-0	2-2	1-1	0-1	0-1	2-0	—	2-0	1-1	1-2	2-1	2-1	0-0	1-1	2-1	4-0	0-0	2-0	2-3	4-1	1-0	1-2	1-2
Derby	2-0	2-2	1-2	1-1	0-2	1-0	1-0	2-0	—	4-1	1-2	2-1	2-0	2-1	3-1	2-1	3-0	0-0	2-0	1-1	0-1	0-1	1-0	0-0
Fulham	4-1	6-2	2-0	3-2	0-3	1-0	0-1	1-1	0-0	—	1-2	3-1	7-0	3-1	1-1	0-1	3-0	1-0	3-1	4-0	3-0	3-0	3-1	1-0
Huddersfield	2-1	0-0	3-2	1-1	0-0	2-1	2-1	1-2	1-2	1-2	—	0-2	1-3	1-2	2-2	1-1	1-2	0-1	2-3	3-0	1-1	1-1	1-1	1-0
Hull	0-2	0-5	1-1	0-1	1-0	2-1	2-1	2-1	2-1	3-1	0-1	—	1-3	1-2	2-0	2-0	3-0	0-1	2-0	2-3	0-2	0-2	0-1	0-2
Luton	2-1	0-0	0-0	1-2	3-2	2-1	2-1	2-1	2-0	7-0	1-3	1-0	—	0-0	2-1	2-0	3-0	4-0	2-3	2-1	0-0	1-0	2-1	2-0
Middlesbrough	2-1	1-1	1-1	2-1	1-1	2-0	1-2	0-0	2-1	3-1	2-1	0-1	2-1	—	0-0	3-1	2-0	3-0	3-1	1-0	2-0	3-1	3-3	2-0
Millwall	4-1	3-1	3-1	1-1	1-1	2-3	1-1	1-1	3-2	1-1	2-2	2-0	0-1	3-1	—	0-1	3-0	1-1	2-0	4-0	3-1	2-1	1-0	2-1
Nottm Forest	3-0	2-0	1-2	1-2	2-3	0-2	2-1	2-1	2-1	0-1	1-1	1-0	1-0	0-4	1-1	—	3-0	0-1	2-1	0-2	1-1	2-2	5-1	4-0
Peterborough	2-1	2-0	5-0	5-0	0-0	2-2	1-2	4-0	3-0	3-0	1-2	3-0	3-0	1-3	1-1	3-0	—	1-0	1-3	1-3	6-2	2-2	2-3	0-1
Preston	2-2	1-1	1-4	1-0	0-0	1-2	1-2	0-0	0-0	1-0	0-1	3-0	4-0	4-1	1-1	0-1	1-3	—	3-3	4-0	3-0	1-1	3-1	0-1
QPR	1-0	2-0	2-1	2-1	2-3	2-3	2-1	3-1	2-0	3-3	0-3	0-3	2-3	2-3	2-0	3-1	1-3	3-2	—	1-2	3-1	0-2	0-0	1-1
Reading	2-0	1-0	1-0	1-0	3-0	2-2	1-2	2-1	2-2	4-0	3-0	2-1	1-0	4-1	1-2	2-0	6-2	1-2	4-0	—	4-0	1-1	4-4	0-1
Sheff Utd	1-1	0-1	1-0	0-1	1-0	0-2	3-3	4-1	2-3	0-2	1-3	0-2	0-0	4-1	3-1	1-1	0-1	3-0	0-1	0-1	—	2-1	2-1	4-0
Stoke	1-1	2-2	0-1	1-1	2-1	1-0	3-0	1-0	0-1	3-0	0-2	0-2	1-0	3-1	2-1	2-2	2-2	1-1	1-0	2-3	1-0	—	3-0	0-2
Swansea	1-1	0-0	2-1	1-1	4-0	1-0	0-4	1-2	1-0	3-1	1-1	0-1	2-1	3-3	1-0	5-1	2-3	3-1	0-0	2-3	4-0	1-3	—	2-1
WBA	4-0	4-0	1-0	0-0	2-0	3-0	0-0	1-2	0-0	1-0	1-0	0-2	2-0	2-0	2-1	4-0	0-1	0-1	1-1	0-1	4-0	1-3	0-2	—

SKY BET LEAGUE ONE RESULTS 2021–2022

	Accrington	AFC Wimbledon	Bolton	Burton	Cambridge	Charlton	Cheltenham	Crewe	Doncaster	Fleetwood	Gillingham	Ipswich	Lincoln	MKDons	Morecambe	Oxford	Plymouth	Portsmouth	Rotherham	Sheff Wed	Shrewsbury	Sunderland	Wigan	Wycombe
Accrington	—	0-2	1-0	0-0	2-1	2-1	4-4	4-1	1-0	5-1	0-0	0-1	2-1	1-1	2-2	2-0	4-0	2-2	1-0	2-3	1-0	1-1	1-4	3-2
AFC Wimbledon	3-4	—	3-3	1-1	1-0	1-1	2-2	3-2	2-2	2-2	1-1	0-2	2-1	1-1	2-1	3-1	2-1	0-0	0-1	1-2	1-0	1-1	0-2	1-1
Bolton	3-1	4-0	—	0-0	2-0	2-1	1-1	3-2	3-0	4-2	1-3	2-0	3-3	3-1	1-1	2-1	1-0	1-1	0-1	1-1	2-1	6-0	0-4	2-1
Burton	4-0	1-1	3-1	—	2-2	0-1	1-1	4-1	2-0	3-2	1-0	2-0	1-2	0-1	3-0	1-3	0-0	2-1	2-0	3-1	0-2	1-0	0-0	1-0
Cambridge	2-0	1-0	2-2	3-0	—	0-2	2-2	1-0	3-1	2-2	2-0	2-0	1-5	0-2	3-2	2-1	2-0	0-0	0-1	2-2	2-0	1-2	0-0	1-4
Charlton	2-3	1-4	1-0	0-2	0-2	—	1-2	2-0	4-0	2-0	1-0	2-0	2-0	0-2	2-3	1-0	2-1	0-1	0-1	1-1	2-1	0-0	2-2	0-1
Cheltenham	1-0	3-1	1-4	1-1	1-1	1-1	—	1-2	4-0	2-0	0-1	1-1	2-2	1-1	3-1	1-0	0-2	2-2	0-2	2-2	2-1	2-1	0-0	1-3
Crewe	0-1	3-1	1-2	1-2	3-1	2-1	1-1	—	1-1	1-3	0-1	2-0	2-0	1-4	1-3	0-1	1-4	1-3	0-2	1-3	2-1	0-4	0-2	1-3
Doncaster	2-0	1-1	2-0	2-0	4-0	0-1	4-0	4-0	—	2-0	1-0	0-1	2-0	2-1	1-3	0-0	0-2	1-0	0-5	0-2	2-1	0-4	0-2	0-2
Fleetwood	1-2	1-1	0-1	0-1	1-1	1-2	3-2	3-0	0-0	—	0-1	0-1	0-0	1-1	1-2	1-2	3-3	1-3	0-5	1-3	0-3	0-3	2-3	0-2
Gillingham	0-0	0-0	1-3	1-0	1-0	3-2	0-2	3-0	0-0	0-0	—	0-4	1-1	1-4	2-1	2-7	1-0	0-1	0-2	0-0	0-3	1-2	0-2	1-1
Ipswich	2-1	2-2	0-1	1-2	0-1	4-0	0-0	2-1	6-0	2-1	1-0	—	2-0	2-3	2-2	0-0	1-1	2-3	0-0	3-1	2-0	1-1	2-3	1-0
Lincoln	0-1	0-1	2-0	3-0	1-2	2-1	3-1	2-0	0-1	3-3	0-0	0-0	—	0-4	2-0	1-2	2-1	1-0	0-1	1-0	1-0	0-1	1-1	1-0
MKDons	2-0	2-0	3-0	4-1	4-2	1-0	1-1	2-1	4-0	0-0	2-1	0-0	1-4	—	2-0	1-2	1-3	3-0	0-0	1-0	3-1	1-0	2-3	3-2
Morecambe	3-3	3-4	1-1	3-0	0-2	2-2	1-3	1-2	0-1	3-3	2-1	0-0	2-0	2-3	—	2-0	2-1	0-3	3-0	0-0	1-0	0-1	1-1	0-0
Oxford	5-1	3-0	2-3	4-1	4-2	3-1	1-0	2-0	2-1	3-1	1-1	0-1	3-1	0-5	3-1	—	1-0	3-2	0-0	3-2	1-0	1-2	2-3	1-0
Plymouth	4-0	3-0	1-0	3-0	1-2	1-1	2-0	1-0	4-0	2-4	1-0	2-1	3-2	1-2	2-0	2-2	—	2-2	4-1	1-0	1-0	5-0	3-2	0-3
Portsmouth	4-0	1-0	1-0	2-1	1-2	1-2	1-1	1-1	4-0	3-3	3-1	0-4	3-2	1-0	2-0	2-1	2-2	—	4-1	0-0	1-2	5-0	3-2	0-0
Rotherham	1-0	3-0	1-0	2-0	4-1	3-1	1-0	4-1	3-3	1-0	1-0	1-1	1-1	1-0	5-0	1-2	2-0	4-1	—	0-2	1-0	1-0	1-1	2-2
Sheff Wed	1-1	2-1	1-0	1-0	0-1	4-1	1-0	1-1	3-3	1-1	1-0	1-1	1-0	1-1	4-0	1-0	4-2	1-2	1-0	—	3-2	3-0	1-1	1-2
Shrewsbury	0-0	0-1	1-1	0-1	1-1	3-1	2-1	1-1	1-2	3-1	1-3	1-1	1-0	1-0	5-0	0-3	4-2	1-2	1-1	1-0	—	1-1	0-3	0-0
Sunderland	2-1	1-0	1-1	1-1	5-1	5-0	1-1	2-0	1-2	3-1	1-0	1-3	1-2	1-0	5-0	1-1	4-2	1-2	1-1	5-0	3-2	—	2-1	3-1
Wigan	3-0	1-0	1-1	2-0	1-2	2-1	2-1	2-1	2-0	2-0	3-2	1-1	1-2	2-1	4-1	1-1	2-0	0-3	1-0	1-2	1-1	0-3	—	1-3
Wycombe	2-1	2-2	1-0	1-4	1-4	0-1	1-3	2-1	2-0	1-0	1-1	1-0	1-0	0-1	4-3	1-0	2-0	0-0	3-1	0-0	0-0	3-3	1-3	—

SKY BET LEAGUE TWO RESULTS 2021–2022

	Barrow	Bradford	Bristol Rov	Carlisle	Colchester	Crawley	Exeter	Forest Green	Harrogate	Hartlepool	Leyton Orient	Mansfield	Newport	Northampton	Oldham	Port Vale	Rochdale	Salford	Scunthorpe	Stevenage	Sutton	Swindon	Tranmere	Walsall
Barrow	—	1-2	1-0	2-0	0-2	1-0	2-1	2-0	2-1	3-1	2-0	0-1	2-1	1-3	0-0	0-3	0-0	2-2	0-1	1-0	1-0	2-0	1-1	1-1
Bradford	1-2	—	2-1	3-0	1-2	1-2	0-0	1-1	0-2	0-2	2-3	0-2	2-1	1-3	2-1	1-2	1-2	2-1	1-1	4-1	2-2	2-1	1-1	1-1
Bristol Rov	1-0	2-1	—	1-0	1-0	1-0	2-1	3-0	1-0	2-1	1-3	0-0	1-3	2-1	1-0	2-1	4-2	1-0	7-0	4-1	0-2	1-2	2-2	1-0
Carlisle	0-0	2-0	1-0	—	0-0	1-1	1-1	0-2	3-0	0-0	1-1	0-0	1-2	0-1	0-0	1-3	2-0	0-2	2-2	0-1	0-2	0-3	0-1	0-0
Colchester	0-2	3-0	1-1	2-2	—	1-1	2-2	0-1	1-1	1-2	2-2	0-0	1-1	1-0	2-2	1-1	2-0	0-2	2-2	2-2	1-3	1-1	1-0	2-2
Crawley	1-0	1-2	2-1	2-1	3-1	—	2-1	0-0	1-3	2-3	1-0	1-2	1-1	0-1	1-0	1-4	1-0	2-1	0-0	2-1	0-1	1-1	1-0	1-0
Exeter	2-1	0-0	4-1	2-1	2-1	2-1	—	4-3	0-0	0-0	1-0	2-1	2-2	1-2	2-2	0-1	2-0	2-1	2-0	2-1	2-0	3-1	0-1	2-2
Forest Green	2-0	0-2	2-0	3-0	0-1	0-0	0-0	—	1-3	1-1	1-0	1-0	2-0	1-2	2-1	0-2	2-1	3-1	1-0	0-0	2-0	0-2	0-1	0-1
Harrogate	2-1	0-2	3-0	1-2	1-2	6-3	2-1	1-4	—	1-2	0-3	1-1	2-0	1-2	3-0	1-1	3-2	0-2	6-1	0-0	2-1	1-4	2-2	1-1
Hartlepool	3-1	0-2	2-1	0-1	0-1	1-0	1-0	1-3	3-2	—	0-3	2-2	1-1	2-1	3-0	3-1	0-2	0-2	7-0	1-1	0-3	0-3	0-0	2-0
Leyton Orient	2-0	1-0	2-0	3-0	2-1	1-2	0-1	1-1	1-1	5-0	—	0-0	0-1	2-4	4-0	3-1	3-1	0-2	3-0	2-2	4-1	4-1	0-1	2-0
Mansfield	0-1	2-3	2-1	2-1	2-0	2-0	1-1	2-2	3-2	3-2	2-0	—	2-1	0-1	0-0	2-1	0-2	2-1	3-1	5-0	2-3	3-2	4-2	2-0
Newport	2-1	1-0	1-0	2-0	1-2	0-1	2-2	3-0	4-0	2-3	2-0	1-0	—	1-2	2-1	1-4	2-0	2-1	0-0	3-0	0-2	2-3	1-0	2-2
Northampton	0-3	0-0	2-0	1-0	2-1	3-3	0-2	2-0	0-2	0-0	2-0	2-0	1-0	—	2-1	3-2	1-3	1-0	1-0	3-0	3-2	1-3	4-2	1-3
Oldham	3-1	1-1	2-1	1-2	3-3	4-1	3-2	1-1	0-1	0-0	2-0	1-2	1-2	0-2	—	0-0	1-3	0-1	1-3	5-0	0-2	1-3	0-0	0-1
Port Vale	0-0	0-0	1-3	2-1	0-1	0-1	2-0	2-0	0-1	1-0	0-1	1-0	1-0	1-0	3-2	—	2-3	1-1	6-1	3-0	3-2	1-3	0-0	2-2
Rochdale	2-2	1-0	1-1	0-3	1-3	2-1	0-3	1-1	0-0	1-1	1-1	3-0	3-0	2-2	2-0	0-0	—	1-1	0-0	1-0	3-2	2-2	1-0	0-1
Salford	0-1	1-1	2-3	0-1	1-3	2-1	1-1	1-1	1-0	2-0	2-1	0-4	0-2	0-0	0-1	0-0	2-3	—	5-1	1-0	3-2	2-1	1-0	2-0
Scunthorpe	2-2	1-0	1-0	0-1	1-2	2-1	1-2	0-3	2-2	0-1	1-1	0-1	2-2	0-0	2-0	0-0	0-0	1-1	—	1-0	3-2	1-0	0-0	1-0
Stevenage	0-1	1-4	2-3	1-3	0-2	2-1	0-0	0-4	3-0	3-0	0-0	1-2	0-0	2-2	0-1	1-2	1-1	1-1	1-1	—	1-0	2-1	2-1	0-0
Sutton	1-0	1-1	0-1	0-1	3-0	2-1	3-0	1-0	1-1	1-1	1-2	2-0	2-0	0-2	1-2	4-3	3-0	0-0	4-1	2-1	—	1-2	3-1	1-0
Swindon	2-1	1-0	1-3	4-0	3-2	3-0	1-2	2-1	1-2	3-1	1-2	4-3	2-3	5-2	1-2	1-2	2-2	0-0	3-0	2-1	2-1	—	1-1	3-0
Tranmere	2-0	1-1	1-1	2-0	2-0	2-1	0-4	0-4	1-1	1-0	1-0	3-2	1-1	0-1	2-1	1-1	2-0	2-1	4-0	0-0	2-1	3-0	—	1-0
Walsall	2-2	1-2	1-2	0-0	1-0	1-1	2-1	1-3	1-1	2-0	0-2	2-0	3-3	0-1	2-1	2-2	0-0	2-1	1-1	1-0	1-0	0-3	1-0	—

HIGHLIGHTS OF THE PREMIER LEAGUE SEASON 2021–22

AUGUST 2021

13 Brentford make a dream start to their first season in the top division for 74 years, beating an Arsenal side weakened by the absence of Pierre-Emerick Aubameyang and Alexandre Lacazette 2-0 with goals from Sergi Canos and Christian Norgaard.

14 Bruno Fernandes, with a hat-trick, and Paul Pogba, with four assists, treat a crowd of nearly 73,000 at Old Trafford to a 5-1 victory for Manchester United against Leeds as clubs throughout the Premier League welcome back spectators for the first time since March 2020. The two teams promoted with Brentford experience mixed fortunes. Cucho Hernandez scores 49 seconds after coming off the bench and fellow new-signing Emmanuel Dennis is also on the mark as Watford are 3-2 winners over Aston Villa, for whom Danny Ings converts a penalty in his first match for the club. Norwich lose 3-0 to Liverpool, who have Virgil van Dijk returning after ten months out with a knee injury and Mohamed Salah scoring on the opening day for a record fifth successive season. Academy product Trevoh Chalobah marks his debut by completing Chelsea's 3-0 victory over much-changed Crystal Palace, who have Patrick Vieira in charge for the first time after succeeding Roy Hodgson. Adam Armstrong scores on his first appearance for Southampton at Goodison Park, but Everton deliver a successful start for their new manager Rafael Benitez. A 3-1 success is launched by Richarlison, who had a busy summer playing for Brazil in the Copa America and the Olympics. Brighton come from behind to prevail 2-1 at Burnley, while Leicester are 1-0 winners over Wolves, whose new manager Bruno Lage welcomes back Raul Jimenez for his first competitive start in nine months following a fractured skull.

15 Harry Kane is deemed not match-fit to face Manchester City, the club he wanted to join. But Tottenham defeat the defending champions – and their £100m signing Jack Grealish – with a goal from Son Heung-min to give Nuno Espirito Santo a winning start as manager. West Ham twice come from behind at Newcastle and go on to a 4-2 victory, rounded off by the impressive Michail Antonio.

21 Jack Grealish opens his account for Manchester City following his move from Aston Villa in fortuitous fashion – a cross from Gabriel Jesus bouncing in off his thigh in the 5-0 win over Norwich. Grealish's former team defeat Newcastle 2-0 with a spectacular overhead kick by Danny Ings, an early contender for goal of the season. Shane Duffy, back in Brighton's defence after a loan spell at Celtic, puts them on the way to a 2-0 victory over Watford which brings the club maximum points from their opening two matches in the top-flight for the first time. Harvey Elliott, 18, makes an impressive first Premier League start as Liverpool overcome Burnley 2-0, while Leeds twice come from behind for a point against Everton.

22 Romelu Lukaku, Chelsea's £97.5m signing from Inter Milan, takes just a quarter-of-an-hour to mark his return to Stamford Bridge with a goal, paving the way for a 2-0 success at Arsenal. Harry Kane, resigned to staying at Tottenham, comes of the bench as Nuno Espirito Santo makes a winning return to Molineux 1-0.

28 Arsenal lose a third successive league match at the start of a season for the first time since 1954–55. They are crushed 5-0 by Manchester City – Ferran Torres scoring twice – and have Granit Xhaka sent off at 2-0 for a two-footed lunge on Joao Cancelo. Chelsea's Reece James is also shown a straight red card, for handling, but his side hold on to a 1-1 scoreline during the second 45 minutes at Liverpool. Crystal Palace twice come from behind for a point at West Ham, with Chelsea loanee Conor Gallagher scoring both their goals. Newcastle and Southampton also share a 2-2 scoreline after a dramatic period of stoppage-time in which Allan Saint-Maximin puts Newcastle ahead and James Ward-Prowse levels from the penalty spot.

29 Manchester United stretch their unbeaten away run to an English League record 28 matches, beating Wolves 1-0 with a disputed goal by Mason Greenwood which is allowed to stand following Paul Pogba's strong challenge on Ruben Neves in the build-up. After the third programme of matches, Tottenham are the only team with a 100 per cent record after defeating Watford 1-0 – with pointless Arsenal bottom.

SEPTEMBER 2021

11 Twelve years after leaving Old Trafford, Cristiano Ronaldo returns to the Premier League with two goals in Manchester United's 4-1 victory over Newcastle, whose consolation is Javier Manquillo's first for the club. Odsonne Edouard, Crystal Palace's signing from Celtic, comes off the bench for a record-breaking Premier League debut – a goal after 28 seconds. He adds a second in stoppage-time to complete a 3-0 win over Tottenham, who have Japhet Tanganga sent off for two yellow cards in the space of three minutes with the match goalless. Patrick Vieira collects his first three points and so does the new Wolves manager Bruno Lage, whose side defeat Watford 2-0 at Vicarage Road with Leipzig loanee Hwang Hee-chan scoring on his debut. Romelu Lukaku nets twice as Chelsea overcome Aston Villa 3-0, while Arsenal are up and running by beating Norwich 1-0. West Ham have Michail Antonio dismissed for a second yellow in a goalless draw at Southampton.

12 Liverpool's 3-0 victory at Leeds is clouded when 18-year-old midfielder Harvey Elliott sustains a dislocated ankle in a mistimed tackle by Pascal Struijk, who receives a straight red card.

13 Everton come from behind to score three times in six minutes to defeat Burnley 3-1.

18 Sadio Mane savours a special goal in Liverpool's 3-0 success against Crystal Palace, reaching 100 in all competitions for the club and becoming the first Premier League player to score in nine successive appearances against a specific team. A red-letter day, too, for Matty Cash and new-signing Leon Bailey, who are on the mark for Aston Villa for the first time as Everton are on the receiving end of a goal blitz, conceding three in nine minutes to go down 3-0. VAR intervenes at the Etihad and Turf Moor. Jon Moss shows a red card to Manchester City's Kyle Walker for his challenge on Adam Armstrong, awards Southampton a penalty, then changes his mind on both decisions after consulting the pitch-side monitor and the game finishes goalless. Anthony Taylor also has second thoughts after giving Burnley a penalty when Matej Vydra tumbles over goalkeeper Aaron Ramsdale. Arsenal win that game 1-0. Brentford hold on to a 2-0 lead away to Wolves after losing Shandon Baptiste to a second yellow card, while Ismaila Sarr nets twice in Watford's 3-1 victory at Norwich.

19 David Moyes gambles by bringing on Mark Noble to take a stoppage-time penalty against Manchester United. West Ham's club captain has his spot-kick saved by David de Gea and United hold on to a 2-1 advantage established in the 89th minute by Jesse Lingard against the side he served so well on loan the previous season. Tottenham and Chelsea fans unite in tribute to Jimmy Greaves before a match of contrasting fortunes for two of the clubs he served. Chelsea substitute N'Golo Kante sparks an impressive second-half performance by his team, rewarded by a 3-0 away win. Brighton maintain an impressive start to the season by beating Leicester 2-1.

25 Mohamed Salah scores his 100th Premier League goal in Liverpool's 3-3 draw at Brentford, who twice come behind to maintain their bright start to the season. Pep Guardiola becomes Manchester City's most successful manager with his 221st victory – 1-0 against Chelsea at Stamford Bridge with a goal by Gabriel Jesus. Leicester's Jamie Vardy has a match to remember – an own goal followed by two at the right end in a 2-2 draw against Burnley, for whom Maxwel Cornet delivers an eye-catching volley on his first league start, then limps off with a hamstring injury. A stoppage-time penalty miss by the normally reliable Bruno Fernandes costs Manchester United a first defeat, inflicted by an 88th minute Kortney Hause header for Aston Villa at Old Trafford. Australian referee Jarred Gillett, the Premier League's first overseas official, shows seven yellow cards in Watford's 1-1 draw against Newcastle.

26 Raul Jimenez completes his recovery from a career-threatening fractured skull with a superb solo goal to give Wolves a 1-0 win at Southampton. Arsenal take their much-improved form to a new level with three goals in the first 34 minutes to defeat Tottenham 3-1.

2 Watford's 1-0 defeat at Elland Road spells the end for manager Xisco Munoz, sacked after ten months in the job with his side 14th in the table. Leeds win for the first time, while Norwich record their first point in a goalless draw at Burnley, whose manager Sean Dyche takes charge of his 400th game for the club. James Ward-Prowse puts Southampton level from the penalty spot at Stamford Bridge, then has a yellow card for lunging at Jorginho upgraded to red after Martin Atkinson views the pitchside monitor. Chelsea score twice in the final six minutes of normal time for a 3-1 victory. Wolves account for Newcastle 2-1 courtesy of two goals by Hwang Hee-chan.

3 Mohamed Salah scores a goal rated one of the finest of the Premier League era by Alan Shearer as Liverpool and Manchester City draw an enthralling match 2-2. Salah evades three defenders before scoring from an acute angle, but his side twice concede the lead and are lucky not to lose James Milner for a second bookable offence ignored by Paul Tierney. Crystal Palace, retrieve a 2-0 deficit for a point against Leicester thanks to two substitutes - Michael Olise scoring his first goal for the club and Jeffrey Schlupp equalising 48 seconds after coming on. Yoane Wissa also makes his mark off the bench, earning Brentford a 2-1 success at West Ham with the last kick of the match.

16 Jurgen Klopp hails Mohamed Salah as the world's best player on current form after another majestic performance in a 5-0 away win over Watford. Salah even outshines Roberto Firmino's hat-trick with another brilliant solo goal, alongside a crossfield pass delivered with the outside of the boot to set up Sadio Mane's 100th in the Premier League. They make it a sobering return to English football for new Watford manager Claudio Ranieri. The Italian's former title-winning side, Leicester, end Manchester United's record 29-match unbeaten away run with a 4-2 success in which Patson Daka becomes the first Zambian player to score in the Premier League. Chelsea loanee Armando Broja becomes the first Albanian to do so, earning Southampton their first three points of the season – 1-0 against Leeds. Wolves, trailing 2-0 at Villa Park, rally in the final ten minutes of normal time to draw level, then complete a superb comeback with a deflected free-kick by Ruben Neves five minutes into stoppage-time. Ben Chilwell is on the mark for the third successive match for club and country and Chelsea hang on to defeat Brentford thanks to a world-class display by goalkeeper Edouard Mendy.

17 A new era at Newcastle following the club's £305m Saudi Arabia-backed takeover starts on a high note with Callum Wilson's second-minute goal. But a 3-2 defeat by Tottenham at St James' Park in Steve Bruce's 1,000th match as a manager, puts a damper on the big day as Harry Kane scores his first league goal of the season and Jonjo Shelvey is sent off for a second yellow card. Bruce is dismissed three days later.

18 Patrick Vieira is seconds away from a successful first return to Arsenal as a manager when Alexandre Lacazette equalises for the home side and Crystal Palace have to be satisfied with a 2-2 scoreline.

22 Thomas Partey scores his first goal for Arsenal in a 3-1 defeat of Aston Villa, whose consolation from Jacob Ramsey is his first for the club.

23 Hat-tricks by Joshua King and Mason Mount highlight a high-scoring day. King, given a free-transfer by Everton after 11 blank appearances the previous season, sparks Watford to a 5-2 victory over his former club at Goodison Park, with four of their goals coming in the final 12 minutes. Mount, without a goal in his previous 25 appearances for club and country, takes pride of place in Chelsea's 7-0 drubbing of Norwich, who have Ben Gibson sent off for a second yellow card at 5-0. Phil Foden nets twice in Manchester City's 4-1 success at Brighton, while Maxwel Cornet's brace earns Burnley a 2-2 draw away to Southampton, who have Tino Livramento on the scoresheet for the first time. Graeme Jones, appointed Newcastle caretaker-manager after the dismissal of Steve Bruce, starts with a point at Crystal Palace thanks to Callum Wilson's spectacular overhead volley.

24 Mohamed Salah delivers the weekend's third hat-trick as Liverpool crush Manchester United 5-0 at Old Trafford. Salah becomes the club's first player to score in ten successive matches in all competitions. United concede four goals in the first-half, lose substitute Paul Pogba to a straight red card for lunging at Naby Keita and have six other players booked. Mathias Jorgensen's first goal for Brentford is not enough to prevent a 2-1 home defeat by Leicester.

30 What a difference a week makes. Cristiano Ronaldo's superb volley puts Manchester United on the way to a 3-0 success at Tottenham, eases the pressure on Ole Gunnar Solskjaer and deflects all the attention towards the home side's manager Nuno Espirito Santo. He comes under fire from supporters and is sacked two days later. For once, United put Manchester City in the shade, with Pep Guardiola's team beaten 2-0 at home by Crystal Palace, for whom Wilfried Zaha becomes the club's first player to score 50 top-flight goals. Zaha is also brought down by Aymeric Laporte, who is shown a straight red card for a professional foul. Liverpool also falter, held 2-2 at Anfield after leading 2-0 against Brighton, who have Enock Mwepu on the mark for the first time in the Premier Legue. Chelsea take advantage to go three points clear of Liverpool and five ahead of City. They win 3-0 at Newcastle, Reece James scoring twice with carbon-copy angled drives. Improving Arsenal also impress away from home, defeating Leicester 2-0 with the help of one of the saves of the season by Aaron Ramsdale from James Maddison's free-kick. Burnley beat Brentford 3-1 for their first victory of the season.

31 Buoyant West Ham retain fourth place with a 4-1 victory away to Aston Villa, who have Ezri Konsa sent off at 2-1 when Chris Kavanagh upgrades yellow to red after consulting the pitchside monitor. Andrew Omobamidele, 19-year-old Norwich defender, heads his first senior goal, but it's not enough to prevent a 2-1 home defeat by Leeds.

NOVEMBER 2021

1 Max Kilman puts Wolves on the way to a 2-1 victory over Everton with his first goal for the club.

5 Aston Villa suffer a fifth successive defeat, 1-0 at Southampton, and manager Dean Smith is sacked two days later after three years in charge.

6 Daniel Farke, manager of Norwich for four-and-a-half-years, is dismissed immediately after their first win of the season – 2-1 at Brentford with loanee Mathias Normann scoring his first goal for the club. Ole Gunnar Solskjaer comes under fire again after Manchester United are outplayed by Manchester City at Old Trafford and have goalkeeper David de Gea to thank for restricting the scoreline to 2-0. Eddie Howe watches from the stand as Newcastle earn a point at Brighton and are denied the chance of a winner when Callum Wilson, clean through, is brought down by goalkeeper Robert Sanchez, who is shown a straight red card. Another 1-1 scoreline brings Burnley a battling point at Chelsea.

7 Kurt Zouma heads his first goal for the club as West Ham are 3-2 winners over Liverpool, whose club-record-equalling unbeaten run in all competitions ends on 25 matches. Watford's Ben Foster marks his 500th career appearance by saving Pierre-Emerick Aubameyang's penalty at the Emirates. But his side have Kucka sent off for a second yellow card and Claudio Ranieri accuses Arsenal of a lack of respect for not returning possession after an injury stoppage moments before Emile Smith Rowe's controversial winning goal. Antonio Conte's first match as the new Tottenham manager is a goalless draw at Everton.

20 Despair for Ole Gunnar Solskjaer, delight for Steven Gerrard and Dean Smith on a dramatic day. Solskjaer is sacked after Manchester United suffer a fourth defeat in five Premier League matches – 4-1 at Watford despite David de Gea saving Ismaila Sarr's twice-taken penalty – and have Harry Maguire sent off for a second yellow card. Gerrard celebrates a 2-0 victory over Brighton in his first match in charge of Aston Villa after goals from Ollie Watkins and Tyrone Mings in the final ten minutes of normal time. The man Gerrard replaced, Dean Smith, marks a rapid return to management at Norwich with a 2-1 win over Southampton, Grant Hanley scoring the decisive goal on his 30th birthday. Eddie Howe has to watch his first match as Newcastle manager on a live stream after testing positive for Covid. His new side draw 3-3 with Brentford – a scoreline repeated at Turf Moor, where Marc Guehi scores his first goal for Crystal Palace, alongside a brace for Christian Benteke, against Burnley. Two more managers make the headlines, with Jurgen Klopp and Mikel Arteta shown yellow cards for an angry touchline exchange during Liverpool's 4-0 success against Arsenal. – the follow-up to Sadio Mane's challenge on Takehiro Tomiyasu. Leicester's Brendan Rodgers also has his say after a 3-0 home defeat by Chelsea, criticising supporters for booing their team at the end of each half.

21 Sergio Reguilon's first goal for Tottenham delivers Antonio Conte's first victory – 2-1 against Leeds, who have Daniel James on the mark for the first time. Raheem Sterling launches Manchester City 3-0 defeat of Everton on his 300th Premier League appearance.

27 Liverpool take their goals tally to 39 in 13 matches by beating Southampton 4-0, Diogo Jota scoring twice. Eddie Howe's first appearance on the touchline for Newcastle ends in a 2-0 defeat at Arsenal, completed by Gabriel Martinelli's second touch of the ball after coming off the bench. Aston Villa continue a successful start under Steven Gerrard – 2-1 winners away to Crystal Palace.

28 With Michael Carrick in temporary charge and Cristiano Ronaldo dropped, Manchester United earn a 1-1 draw at Chelsea, courtesy of Jadon Sancho's first Premier League goal. Fernandinho's first for three years completes Manchester City's 2-1 victory over West Ham. It leaves his side in second place on 29 points, one behind Chelsea and ahead of Liverpool (28) and West Ham (23). Jamie Vardy's brace highlight's Leicester's 4-2 success against Watford, while Ivan Toney's penalty for Brentford accounts for Everton. In the bottom three, Burnley and Norwich have nine points and Newcastle six.

30 Ten-man Newcastle hold out for a 1-1 draw against Norwich after having Ciaran Clark shown a straight red card for pulling back Teemu Pukki in the ninth minute.

DECEMBER 2021

1 Everton manager Rafael Benitez comes under pressure after a 4-1 home defeat by Liverpool, for whom Mohamed Salah scores twice. Bernardo Silva delivers a contender for goal of the season in Manchester City's 2-1 success at Villa Park which makes Pep Guardiola the quickest Premier League manager to reach 150 wins. With Villa supporter Prince William looking on, Bernardo rounds off a swift counter-attack with a stunning volley on the run. Another spectacular goal comes from Brighton's Neal Maupay, whose 89th minute overhead kick earns a 1-1 draw at West Ham. Chelsea are 2-1 winners at Watford in a match halted for 30 minutes after a supporter suffers a cardiac arrest.

2 On a dramatic night at Old Trafford, Cristiano Ronaldo becomes the first player to reach 800 top-level goals. He nets twice in Manchester United's 3-2 win over Arsenal, for whom Emile Smith Rowe's goal into an unguarded net with goalkeeper David de Gea down injured is allowed to stand. The night ends with Michael Carrick, United's caretaker-manager, announcing he is leaving the club ahead of Ralf Rangnick's appointment until the end of the season.

4 Substitute Arthur Masuaku's first Premier League goal, an 87th minute intended cross which drifts in at the near post, gives West Ham a 3-2 victory over Chelsea. Two more matches produce late efforts. Neal Maupay follows up his midweek point-saver against West Ham to earn Brighton a point at Southampton in the eighth minute of stoppage-time. Divock Origi comes off the bench to give Liverpool the verdict in the 94th minute at Wolves. Bernardo Silva, the league's best player on current form according to his manager Pep Guardiola, nets twice as Manchester City go top for the first time with a 3-1 win at Watford. Newcastle collect their first three points at the 15th attempt with the only goal of the game from Callum Wilson against Burnley.

5 Ralf Rangnick's first match in charge of Manchester United is a 1-0 defeat of Crystal Palace, earned by Fred's eye-catching 20-yard drive. Patrick Bamford's first game back for Leeds after two-and-a-half-months out with an ankle injury ends on a high with his 95th minute equaliser for 2-2 against Brentford. Centre-back Ezri Konsa also has an afternoon to savour with both goals for Aston Villa, who come from behind to beat Leicester.

6 Demarai Gray strikes from 25 yards in stoppage-time to give Everton their first victory in nine matches – 2-1 against Arsenal.

10 Pontus Jansson's first goal for the club and Bryan Mbeumo's 95th minute penalty enable Brentford to come from behind and beat Watford.

11 Penalties dominate the day's programme, alongside the season's most foolish sending-off. Jorginho is on the spot twice for Chelsea, his second coming in stoppage-time for 3-2 against Leeds. Joe Gelhardt scores his first Leeds goal with his first touch after coming off the bench, while Manchester City's Raheem Sterling nets his 100th in the Premier League against Wolves, who have Raul Jimenez booked on the stroke of half-time for a foul, then dismissed for standing in the way of the resulting free-kick. Sterling's spot kick for 1-0 is disputed and so is the one converted by Liverpool's Mohamed Salah for the same scoreline against Aston Villa. For good measure, Cristiano Ronaldo makes no mistake with his penalty for the only goal of Manchester United's visit to Norwich.

12 Chelsea loanee Conor Gallagher continues his outstanding form for Crystal Palace with two goals in a 3-1 win over Everton, who have Salomon Rondon on the mark for his first time. Youri Tielemans also nets twice for Leicester – his first goal a penalty – as Newcastle are beaten 4-0 at the King Power.

14 Leeds suffer their worst-ever Premier League defeat, crushed 7-0 by Manchester City with Kevin De Bruyne netting twice and five other players on the scoresheet.

15 Alexandre Lacazette, captaining Arsenal after Pierre-Emerick Aubameyang is stripped of the position for disciplinary breaches, has a penalty saved by Lukasz Fabianski. But his side go fourth with a 2-0 victory over West Ham, who have Vladimir Coufal sent off at 1-0 for a second yellow card. Jordan Ayew scores his first goal in 43 Premier League games to earn Crystal Palace a 2-2 draw with Southampton.

16 Jarrad Branthwaite, 19-year-old Everton defender, scores his first goal for the club to secure a 1-1 draw away to Chelsea. Liverpool come from behind to overcome Newcastle 3-1, Trent Alexander-Arnold making sure with a 25-yard drive.

18 With the Omicron strain of Covid spreading rapidly, five of the day's six scheduled matches are postponed – Aston Villa against Burnley just two hours before kick-off. The one to survive is at Elland Road, where a depleted Leeds side go down 4-1 to Arsenal, who have Gabriel Martinelli on the mark twice.

19 England captain Harry Kane and Scotland skipper Andy Robertson are at the centre of controversy in a full-blooded 2-2 draw between Tottenham and Liverpool. Kane escapes with a yellow card from Paul Tierney for diving in, studs-up on Robertson. Later, after consulting the pitchside monitor, Tierney upgrades yellow to red for the Liverpool player's foul on Emerson Royal. Slow-motion replays underline the threat to serious injury posed by both challenges. Manchester City set a top-flight record of 34 victories in a calendar year by beating Newcastle 4-0 at St James' Park. Chelsea drop more points in a goalless draw against Wolves.

26 Manchester City take their goals tally to 17 in three matches by defeating Leicester 6-3 – the season's highest aggregate scoreline. They lead 4-0 in 25 minutes, are pegged back to 4-3, then move clear again, with Raheem Sterling's second of the match making sure. His first is a penalty and there are two successful spot-kicks for Chelsea's Jorginho in a 3-1 victory at Villa Park. Bukayo Saka also nets twice, highlighting Arsenal's 5-0 success at Norwich. There are much needed wins for Brighton and Southampton. Graham Potter's side achieve their first in 12 matches – 2-0 against Brentford. Southampton, twice lose the lead at West Ham, but have the final say for the first time in seven fixtures thanks to Jan Bednarek's header. Crystal Palace have Wilfried Zaha sent off for a second yellow card in their 3-0 defeat at Tottenham.

27 Newcastle's improved performance in a 1-1 draw against Manchester United is overshadowed by a calf injury sustained by leading scorer Callum Wilson, who is ruled out for much of the season.

28 Mohamed Salah has a penalty saved by Kasper Schmeichel and Liverpool lose 1-0 at Leicester to a goal by substitute Ademola Lookman. West Ham find their touch again with a 4-1 victory at Watford, rounded off by a first goal for the club from Nikola Vlasic. Southampton hold on at 1-1 against Tottenham following Mohammed Salisu's second yellow card six minutes before half-time. But Norwich's revival under Dean Smith looks a distant memory after a fifth successive defeat without a goal scored – 3-0 at Crystal Palace.

29 Manchester City go into the new year with a commanding lead as Phil Foden marks his return to the side after being dropped for a breach of club discipline with the only goal at Brentford for a tenth successive victory. His side have 50 points from 20 matches, eight more than Chelsea and nine ahead of Liverpool, who have a game in hand. Chelsea drop more points at home to Brighton, who equalise in stoppage-time through Danny Welbeck.

30 Manchester United give the watching Sir Alex Ferguson an 80th birthday present with a 3-1 win over Burnley, who remain in the bottom three on 11 points, the same as Newcastle and one more than Norwich. Sean Dyche's side have three games in hand on their relegation rivals because of Covid postponements.

JANUARY 2022

1 Pep Guardiola admits Manchester City are fortunate to bank another three points at the Emirates. Arsenal, with Mikel Arteta isolating at home, dispute Riyad Mahrez's equaliser from the penalty spot. And despite losing Gabriel to a second yellow card in the space of 78 seconds, they are set for a deserved point until Rodri's 93rd minute decider. Tottenham also strike late – a 96th minute header from Davinson Sanchez for the only goal at Watford. Two from Manuel Lanzini, his first a penalty, point West Ham to a 3-2 success at Crystal Palace.

2 Record-signing Romelu Lukaku is dropped after declaring he is unhappy at Stamford Bridge and supporters are also down in the dumps when Liverpool lead 2-0 in 26 minutes. Chelsea recover for a point, but both teams fall further behind Manchester City. Brentford go one better after trailing Aston Villa, with Mads Roerslev's first goal for the club in the 83rd minute delivering a 2-1 success. Anthony Gordon opens his Everton account with a brace at home to Brighton. But Dominic Calvert-Lewin misses a penalty on his return from four months out with injury and two from Alex Mac Allister spark Brighton's 3-2 victory. Jack Harrison nets his first in the league since making his loan move from Manchester City permanent as Leeds defeat Burnley 3-1.

3 Wolves win at Old Trafford for the first time since 1980, Joao Moutinho's 82nd minute goal inflicting Manchester United interim manager Ralf Rangnick's first defeat.

11 Southampton treat new owner Dragan Solak to their biggest win of the season – 4-1 against Brentford.

12 West Ham go back up to fourth by beating Norwich 2-0 with two goals from Jarrod Bowen.

15 Kevin De Bruyne's sweet strike enables Manchester City to tighten their grip on top spot with a 12th successive victory - 1-0 over Chelsea, whose title bid is effectively ended 13 points adrift. At the bottom Adam Idah scores his first Premier League goal in Norwich's 2-1 win over struggling Everton, whose manager Rafael Benitez is sacked the following day. Joao Pedro's 88th minute goal earns Watford a point at Newcastle, while on-loan Philippe Coutinho makes an immediate impact for Aston Villa after Steven Gerrard introduces his former team-mate from the bench against Manchester United. Four years on from a £142m move from Liverpool to Barcelona, Coutinho delivers an assist and a goal to cancel out a brace from Bruno Fernandes for a 2-2 scoreline.

16 A red-letter day for Leeds delivers a 3-2 success at West Ham. Jack Harrison scores his first hat-trick and his club make Premier League history by bringing the total of debut-making teenagers in a single season to eight. Liverpool, with Mohammed Salah and Sadio Mane at the Africa Cup of Nations, defeat Brentford 3-0 to climb above Chelsea.

19 Tottenham are heading for a 2-1 defeat at Leicester until substitute Steven Bergwijn scores twice in the space of 80 seconds in stoppage-time. Manchester United close to within a point of fourth place with a 3-1 victory at Brentford.

21 Two goals by United States international Josh Sargent, his first in the Premier League, point Norwich to a 3-0 win at Watford which takes them out of the bottom three for the first time. Watford, beaten for the seventh time in eight matches, drop into the relegation zone for the first time and have Emmanuel Dennis shown a second yellow card at 2-0. Manager Claudio Ranieri is sacked three days later.

22 Manchester City's unbeaten run comes to an end in a 1-1 draw at Southampton, for whom Kyle Walker-Peters scores his first Premier League goal. Marcus Rashford's winner seconds from the end enables Manchester United to replace opponents West Ham in fourth place. Jonjo Shelvey's free-kick provides Newcastle with only their second win of the season, at Leeds. And Aston Villa provide a third 1-0 scoreline, courtesy of Emiliano Buendia's strike at Everton, who have Duncan Ferguson back as caretaker-manager. Two Villa players celebrating the goal, Matty Cash and Lucas Digne, are struck by a bottle thrown from the crowd. Wolves overcome Brentford 2-1 in the day's most eventful game, which referee Peter Bankes halts for 20 minutes for safety reasons when a drone flies over the Community Stadium. There are two concussion substitutions, while Wolves defender Toti Gomes has a red card downgraded to yellow by Bankes and VAR, then Brentford manager Thomas Frank is shown yellow and red after the final whistle for continuing to argue with the referee.

23 Liverpool, for once, steal a march on Manchester City by beating Crystal Palace 3-1 at Selhurst Park. They go into the winter break nine points adrift of the leaders, with a game in hand. Chelsea are a point further back after defeating Tottenham for the fourth time – a league double after this 2-0 success and the two-leg League Cup semi-final. Burnley hold Arsenal to a goalless draw at the Emirates, but remain bottom, with matches in hand, on 12 points. Watford have 14 and Newcastle 15.

FEBRUARY 2022

5 Roy Hodgson, back in management with Watford at the age of 74, begins the job of trying to save the club from relegation with a goalless draw away to fellow-strugglers Burnley.

8 Kieran Trippier's free-kick, his first goal for the club, completes a 3-1 victory over Everton which lifts Newcastle out of the bottom three. A 100th career league goal for Jay Rodriguez earns Burnley a 1-1 draw against Manchester United. West Ham's 1-0 win over Watford is soured by both sets of supporters jeering Kurt Zouma over a video of him kicking and slapping one of his pet cats.

9 Ralph Hasenhuttl hails a 3-2 win at Tottenham as the finest of his tenure as manager of Southampton, who twice come from behind and clinch victory with a header from Che Adams in the 82nd minute. Another cracking match ends 3-3 at Villa Park, where Philippe Coutinho scores one and provides assists for two from Jacob Ramsey. Daniel James is on the mark twice for Leeds, while Villa's Ezri Konsa is dismissed late on for a second yellow card. Teemu Pukki scores after 38 seconds for Norwich against Crystal Palace, who reply through Wilfried Zaha, then miss the chance of all three points when Zaha slips while taking a penalty which goes wide. No such problem for Riyad Mahrez, who converts his fourth spot-kick in successive Premier League and FA Cup appearances as Manchester City defeat Brentford 2-0.

10 Diogo Jota scores both goals as Liverpool keep alive their chances of catching Manchester City by beating Leicester 2-0. Arsenal hold on to a 1-0 lead away to Wolves in the final 26 minutes after losing Gabriel Martinelli to two bookable offences six seconds apart.

12 Raheem Sterling completes the perfect hat-trick – right-foot, header, left-foot – in Manchester City's 4-0 success at Norwich after Angus Gunn pushes out his penalty. Seamus Coleman's first goal for three years launches Everton's 3-0 victory over Leeds, their first in the league under new manager Frank Lampard. Watford remain deep in trouble after a sixth successive home defeat – 2-0 against Brighton.

13 Newcastle's revival continues with another Kieran Trippier free-kick against Aston Villa, but is clouded when the England defender sustains a broken bone in his left foot. Liverpool are also 1-0 winners, at Burnley, courtesy of Fabinho's fifth goal in seven matches. Leander Dendoncker scores his first league goal of the season in Wolves' 2-0 success at Tottenham, while Craig Dawson's stoppage-time equaliser earns West Ham a 2-2 draw at Leicester. A troubled time for team-mate Kurt Zouma continues when he is withdrawn from the team after leaving the warm-up complaining of dizziness.

15 Cristiano Ronaldo ends a run of six goalless matches with a brilliant individual effort in Manchester United's 2-0 victory over Brighton, who have Lewis Dunk sent off after a VAR check for bringing down Anthony Elanga.

19 Manchester City's dominance is interrupted by Harry Kane, the player the club tried four times to buy during the summer. Kane's 95th minute goal, his second of the match, delivers a 3-2 success for Tottenham at the Etihad to cut City's lead and boost his own side's chances of a top-four place. Dejan Kulusevski is also on the mark with his first for the club and another new signing makes an impact as Liverpool take advantage by coming from behind to defeat Norwich 3-1. Luis Diaz nets their third after Mohamed Salah take his tally to 150 from a 70-yard pass by goalkeeper Alisson. A third newcomer, Wout Weghorst, puts Burnley on the way to a 3-0 win at Brighton, while Watford's Emmanuel Dennis delivers Roy Hodgson's first three points with the only goal at Villa Park.

20 Manchester United players are pelted with objects from the crowd in a stormy match of nine bookings at Elland Road, where they establish a two-goal lead, are pegged back by Leeds, then reassert supremacy for a 4-2 victory.

23 Sadio Mane scores twice and Mohamed Salah converts two penalties as Liverpool crush struggling Leeds 6-0. Two by Wilfried Zaha in the final five minutes of normal time complete a 4-1 success for Crystal Palace at Watford, while captain Ben Mee breathes new life into Burnley's bid to beat the drop with the only goal against Tottenham.

26 On the day clubs, players and supporters unite in support of Ukraine following the invasion by Russia, Christian Eriksen completes one of the game's great personal comebacks. Eight months after his cardiac arrest, the midfielder makes his debut as a substitute for Brentford in a 2-0 home defeat by Newcastle. Eriksen comes on for Mathias Jensen, the player sent on to replace him in Denmark's opening Euro 2020 match against Finland. Brentford have Josh Dasilva shown a straight red card, confirmed by VAR, after 11 minutes for a high challenge on Matt Targett. There is another moving moment at Goodison Park, where Everton's Vitaliy Mykolenko embraces fellow Ukrainian Oleksandr Zinchenko of Manchester City during the warm-up. Both remain on the bench during City's 1-0 victory in which they are fortunate to escape a red card for Rodri handling in his own penalty box. Referees' chief Mike Riley apologies for the error by match official Paul Tierney and video assistant referee Chris Kavanagh. Matt Doherty scores his first goal for Tottenham in a 4-0 away win over Leeds, whose fourth successive defeat, with 17 goals conceded, is followed by the dismissal of manager Marcelo Bielsa. City (66) lead Liverpool by six points, from an extra game played, with Chelsea on 50. Norwich (17), Watford (19) and Burnley (21) fill the bottom three places.

MARCH 2022

1 Jamie Vardy, out for two months with a hamstring injury, returns with Leicester's second goal in a 2-0 win over Burnley.

5 Newcastle, revitalised under Eddie Howe, make it eight games unbeaten by defeating Brighton 2-1 with two goals in the opening 14 minutes from Ryan Fraser and Fabian Schar. Brentford, without a win in eight, also ease the pressure thanks to Ivan Toney, whose hat-trick in a 3-1 success at Norwich includes two penalties. But Burnley remain in big trouble after a 4-0 home defeat by Chelsea, who have Kai Havertz on the mark twice. Anxious times, too, for Leeds, who lose to the only goal of the game at Leicester – a fifth successive defeat with American Jesse Marsch having replaced Marcelo Bielsa. Philippe Coutinho inspires Aston Villa to their biggest win of the season, 4-0 against Southampton, while Liverpool defend Sadio Mane's goal in the face of a strong challenge from West Ham.

6 Kevin De Bruyne and Riyad Mahrez share the goals as the leaders dominate the Manchester derby, City seeing off United 4-1. Arsenal climb to fourth with a 3-2 win at Watford and with three fixtures in hand look well placed for a return to Champions League football.

7 Harry Kane scores twice as Tottenham are 5-0 winners against Everton, who are left a single point off the drop zone.

10 On a day of turmoil at Stamford Bridge after owner Roman Abramovich is sanctioned by the Government over his links to Russian president Vladimir Putin, Chelsea consolidate third place by beating Norwich 3-1 at Carrow Road. Newcastle stretch their unbeaten run with a 2-1 win at Southampton, Chris Wood and Bruno Guimaraes scoring their first goals for the club to virtually seal Premier League survival. Calum Chambers nets his first for Aston Villa,

3-0, victors away to struggling Leeds, while Watford's problems also mount in a 4-0 drubbing at Wolves.

12 Cristiano Ronaldo becomes FIFA's all-time leading scorer on 807 goals for club and country with a hat-trick in Manchester United's 3-2 success against Tottenham. Brentford look safe after defeating Burnley 2-0, thanks to two goals by Ivan Toney, one a penalty, in the final five minutes of normal time. Liverpool win for the eighth successive match – 2-0 at Brighton.

13 In one of the season's most powerful images, a tearful Andriy Yarmolenko sinks to his knees and points to the sky after scoring West Ham's first goal in the 2-1 defeat of Aston Villa – the Ukraine winger's first appearance since his homeland's invasion by Russia. A different kind of emotion, following the sanctioning of owner Roman Abramovich, accompanies Chelsea's 1-0 victory over Newcastle, who lose for the first time in ten league matches. Leeds end a run of six straight defeats with substitute Joe Gelhardt's 94th minute goal against Norwich. Watford also boost their chances of staying up in another 2-1 scoreline, Cuco Hernandez netting a brace at Southampton. But Everton lose for the eighth time in nine matches – Conor Coady heading Wolves' winner at Goodison Park – and have Jonjoe Kenny dismissed for two yellow cards. Two more goals for Brentford's Ivan Toney, one a penalty, account for Burnley 2-0.

14 Manchester City come under pressure from Liverpool after being held to a goalless draw by Crystal Palace.

16 Liverpool close to within a point of the leaders by defeating Arsenal 2-0 at the Emirates with goals from Diogo Jota and Roberto Firmino. Cristian Romero scores his first for the club in Tottenham's 2-0 victory away to Brighton, who are pointless for the sixth successive match.

17 Everton have Allan sent off when Craig Pawson upgrades the midfielder's yellow card for taking out Newcastle's Allan Saint-Maximum after reviewing the incident on the pitchside monitor. But his side earn a much-needed victory with Alex Iwobi's goal in the ninth of 14 minutes of stoppage-time, caused by a protester attaching himself to one of the goalposts. Leeds retrieve a two-goal deficit at Molineux following a second yellow card for Wolves striker Raul Jimenez and complete the comeback with Luke Ayling's 91st minute winner. Ahead of the international break, Manchester City have 70 points, Liverpool 69 and Chelsea 59. Norwich (17), Burnley (21) and Watford (22) remain in the bottom three.

APRIL 2022

2 Brentford deliver one of the season's finest performances to dispel any lingering doubts about staying up. They come from behind to crush Chelsea 4-1 at Stamford Bridge, with Christian Eriksen scoring his first goal for the club and Vitaly Janelt on the mark twice. Liverpool go top for a few hours after a 2-0 lunchtime victory over Watford, their tenth in succession. Manchester City regain pole position by winning at Burnley by the same margin, Ilkay Gundogan's goal making him the highest scoring German player in the Premier League with 34. Brighton and Norwich end runs of six successive defeats in a goalless draw, the home side wasting the chance of all three points when Neal Maupay fires a penalty into the crowd.

3 Emerson Royal scores his first goal for Tottenham, who trail Newcastle, then turn on the style for a 5-1 success to go fourth. Everton have a player sent off for the third successive match – Michael Keane for a second yellow card – in a 2-1 defeat at West Ham.

4 Patrick Vieira denies Arsenal an immediate return to a Champions League place, engineering a 3-0 victory for Crystal Palace against his old club.

6 Nathan Collins scores his first goal for Burnley in a 3-2 win over relegation rivals Everton, whose two goals are both Richarlison penalties.

9 Son Heung-min's hat-trick puts Tottenham in the driving seat for fourth place. They win 4-0 at Villa Park, while Arsenal are beaten again – 2-1 at home to Brighton, for whom Leandro Trossard and Enock Mwepu secure their first three points for two months. After successive defeats by Brentford and, in the Champions League by Real Madrid, Chelsea give Southampton a 6-0 drubbing at St Mary's, with two goals each for Timo Werner, who also hits the woodwork three times, and Mason Mount. Leeds are also convincing winners away from home, 3-0 at Watford, while Anthony Gordon eases the pressure on Everton with the only goal against Manchester United.

10 Honours even at the Etihad as Manchester City twice lead through Kevin De Bruyne and Gabriel Jesus and Liverpool reply each time with goals from Diogo Jota and Sadio Mane. Brentford's fourth win in five matches, 2-0 against West Ham, completes an impressive move clear of the bottom three while effectively ending their opponents' chances of a top-four place. Pierre Lees-Melou scores his first goal for Norwich, who overcome Burnley 2-0, while Kiernan Dewsbury-Hall gets his first in the Premier League for Leicester, who beat Crystal Palace 2-1.

16 Cristiano Ronaldo's second hat-trick in a month revives Manchester United's chances of fourth place. They defeat Norwich 3-2, while Arsenal go down for the fourth time in five matches, 1-0 at Southampton, and Tottenham are beaten at home by Brighton by the same scoreline. Pontus Jansson's header in the fifth minute of stoppage time gives Brentford a fifth victory in six – 2-1 at Watford.

17 Maxwel Cornet misses a penalty in Mike Jackson's first match as Burnley's interim manager following the dismissal of Sean Dyche – a 1-1 draw at West Ham.

19 Mohamed Salah scores twice as Liverpool outplay Manchester United 4-0 to go top.

20 Manchester City regain the leadership with three goals in the second half to defeat Brighton 3-0. Arsenal return to winning ways 4-2 away to Chelsea with Eddie Nketiah on the mark twice.

21 Connor Roberts scores his first goal for Burnley, who beat Southampton 2-0 to keep alive their chances of staying up.

23 Gabriel Jesus takes pride of place with four goals, one a penalty, as Manchester City overcome Watford 5-1. Nuno Tavares scores his first for Arsenal in the 3-1 defeat of Manchester United, for whom Cristiano Ronaldo reaches 100 Premier League goals on his return to the side after the death of his new-born son and Bruno Fernandes misses a penalty at 2-1. Tottenham lose ground in the race for fourth place in a goalless draw at Brentford, while two Joelinton goals lift Newcastle, 3-0 winners at Norwich, into the top half.

24 Liverpool continue to go toe-to-toe with Manchester City, substitute Divock Origi's sixth goal in nine Merseyside derbies completing a 2-0 victory over Everton. Frank Lampard's side drop into the bottom three, overtaken by Burnley, who beat Wolves 1-0. A brace by James Ward-Prowse, one a free-kick, enable Southampton to retrieve a two-goal deficit for a point at Brighton. Lukasz Fabianski saves Jorginho's penalty and West Ham are set for a point at Stamford Bridge until Craig Dawson is shown a straight red card for denying Romelu Lukaku a scoring chance after 86 minutes and Chelsea break the deadlock four minutes later through Christian Pulisic.

30 Norwich are relegated for the sixth time in the Premier League era, this time after a 2-0 defeat at Villa Park with four games still to play. Burnley, written off three weeks ago, win a third successive match. They come from behind to defeat Watford 2-1 away with goals in the final ten minutes, Jack Cork scoring for the first time for three years. Watford become the first team in English top-flight history to lose 11 successive home games. Brighton surpass their previous best Premier League points tally of 41 when beating Wolves 3-0 at Molineux, set on the way by Alexis Mac Allister's penalty after his first one nine minutes earlier strikes a post. The top two remain separated by a single point. Manchester City are 4-0 winners at Leeds, who lose Stuart Dallas with a broken leg, and Liverpool defeat Newcastle 1-0 at St James' Park. City have 83, Liverpool 82, Chelsea 66. Norwich go down on 21, Watford have 22, Everton 32 and Leeds and Burnley both on 34.

MAY 2022

1 England goalkeeper Jordan Pickford caps a man-of-the-match performance with one of the saves of the season from Cesar Azpilicueta as Everton beat Chelsea 1-0. Rob Holding's first goal for the club puts Arsenal on the way to a 2-1 win at West Ham. Tottenham beat Leicester 3-1 with two from Son Heung-min.

2 Raphael Varane's first goal for Manchester United completes a 3-0 victory over Brentford.

7 On the day Watford's relegation is confirmed and the sale of Chelsea is agreed, the title race takes a new twist. Liverpool are held 1-1 by a resolute Tottenham at Anfield, offering

Manchester City to chance assume pole position. Watford make an immediate return to the Championship after losing 1-0 to Crystal Palace and having Hassane Kamara dismissed for a second yellow card. Meanwhile, Burnley's survival bid stalls after three successive wins, beaten 3-1 at home by Aston Villa. Hours after an American-Swiss consortium agrees a £4.25bn deal to take over at Stamford Bridge, its leader Todd Boehly sees two Romelu Lukaku goals set up a likely victory over Wolves, until Conor Coady's 97th minute equaliser for 2-2. Two Brighton players, Marc Cucurella and Moises Caicedo, score for the first time for the club in a 4-0 win over Manchester United. Former Celtic defender Kristoffer Ajer also nets his first for Brentford, who defeat Southampton 3-0.

8   Manchester City take full advantage with a 5-0 win over Newcastle, launched and completed by Raheem Sterling goals. Eddie Nketiah is also on the mark twice for Arsenal, who punish Leeds 2-1 for ill-discipline which heightens their relegation worries. Goalkeeper Illan Meslier gifts Nketiah his first goal, while captain Luke Ayling misses their final three games following his dismissal for a two-footed lunge at Gabriel Martinelli. Another fine performance by Jordan Pickford highlights another priceless victory for Everton – 2-1 at Leicester, with Ukraine international Vitaly Mykolenko's spectacular volley delivering his first goal for the club.

10   Liverpool win 2-1 at Villa Park after falling behind to a Douglas Luiz goal after three minutes.

11   Kevin De Bruyne scores four goals – his first three in the opening 24 minutes – as Manchester City cruise past Wolves 5-1 at Molineux. Leeds have another player shown a straight red card – Daniel James for a reckless challenge on Mateo Kovacic in a 3-0 home defeat by Chelsea. Everton move two points clear of the relegation zone, with a game in hand, in a goalless draw at Watford.

12   Two Harry Kane goals, the first a penalty, direct Tottenham to within a point of fourth-place Arsenal with a 3-0 victory over their rivals, who have Rob Holding sent off for a second yellow card.

15   Riyad Mahrez misses the chance to virtually seal the title for Manchester City at the London Stadium. Mahrez has a penalty saved by Lukasz Fabianski seven minutes from time after his side retrieve West Ham's 2-0 lead established by two from Jarrod Bowen. Everton also pay a price at the other end of the table. They twice lead Brentford, but have Jarrad Branthwaite sent off for a professional foul on Ivan Toney, Salomon Rondon dismissed for lunging at Rico Henry and lose 3-2. Pascal Struijk's stoppage-time equaliser against Brighton revives Leeds' chances of staying up, but Burnley lose to Harry Kane's penalty at Tottenham, who overtake Arsenal in fourth place. Rob Edwards, Watford's incoming manager, watches their record 15th home defeat – 5-1 to Leicester, for whom Jamie Vardy and Harvey Barnes share four of the goals.

16   Arsenal's chances of fourth place hang by a thread after a 2-0 defeat at Newcastle.

17   Liverpool stretch the title race to the final day of the season, by overcoming Southampton 2-1 at St Mary's with a team showing nine changes from their FA Cup win over Chelsea.

19   Dominic Calvert-Lewin's diving header in the 85th minute completes Everton's recovery from two goals down against Crystal Palace and a 3-2 win keeps Frank Lampard's side up. Burnley move above Leeds on goal difference with a 1-1 draw at Villa Park.

22   Manchester City are crowned champions for the fourth time in five seasons after an extraordinary comeback in the final round of matches. Trailing Aston Villa 2-0 at the Etihad, they score three goals in five minutes, two of them by substitute Ilkay Gundogan and one from Rodri, to stay one point ahead of Liverpool. Jurgen Klopp sends congratulations after his side come from behind to defeat Wolves 3-1 – a result which ends their chances of an unprecedented four trophies. Burnley lose at home to two Callum Wilson goals for Newcastle and are relegated. Leeds stay up with a 2-1 win at Brentford, clinched by Jack Harrison in the fourth minute of stoppage-time. Tottenham's 5-0 victory at Norwich confirms fourth place and a return to the Champions League at Arsenal's expense. Son Heung-min's two goals takes him to 23 for the season and a share of the Golden Boot with Liverpool's Mohamed Salah. Arsenal, 5-1 winners over Everton, and Manchester United, beaten 1-0 by Crystal Palace in front of new manager Erik ten Hag, go forward to the Europa League. West Ham miss the chance to overtake United in a 3-1 defeat at Brighton and will play in the Europa Conference.

HOW MANCHESTER CITY WON ANOTHER TITLE

AUGUST 2021

14 Tottenham 1 (Son Heung-min 55) Manchester City 0. Att: 58,262
21 Manchester City 5 (Krul 7 og, Grealish 22, Laporte 64, Sterling 71, Mahrez 84) Norwich 0. Att: 51,437
28 Manchester City 5 (Gundogan 7, Ferran Torres 12, 84, Gabriel Jesus 43, Rodri 53) Arsenal 0. Att: 52,276

SEPTEMBER 2021

11 Leicester 0 Manchester City 1 (Bernardo Silva 62). Att: 32,087
18 Manchester City 0 Southampton 0. Att: 52,698
25 Chelsea 0 Manchester City 1 (Gabriel Jesus 53). Att: 40,036

OCTOBER 2021

3 Liverpool 2 (Mane 59, Salah 76) Manchester City 2 (Foden 69, De Bruyne 81). Att: 53,102
16 Manchester City 2 (Bernardo Silva 12, De Bruyne 70) Burnley 0. Att: 52,711
23 Brighton 1 (Mac Allister 81 pen) Manchester City 4 (Gundogan 13, Foden 28, 31, Mahrez 90). Att: 31,215
30 Manchester City 0 Crystal Palace 2 (Zaha 6, Gallagher 88). Att: 53,014

NOVEMBER 2021

6 Manchester Utd 0 Manchester City 2 (Bailly 7 og, Bernardo Silva 43). Att: 73,086
21 Manchester City 3 (Sterling 44, Rodri 55, Bernardo Silva 86) Everton 0. Att: 52,571
28 Manchester City 2 (Gundogan 33, Fernandinho 90) West Ham 1 (Lanzini 90+4). Att: 53,245

DECEMBER 2021

1 Aston Villa 1 (Watkins 47) Manchester City 2 (Ruben Dias 27, Bernardo Silva 32). Att: 41,400
4 Watford 1 (Hernandez 74) Manchester City 3 (Sterling 4, Bernardo Silva 31, 63). Att: 20,673
11 Manchester City 1 (Sterling 66 pen) Wolves 0. Att: 52,613
14 Manchester City 7 (Foden 8, Grealish 13, De Bruyne 32, 62, Mahrez 49, Stones 74, Ake 78) Leeds 0. Att: 52,401
19 Newcastle 0 Manchester City 4 (Ruben Dias 5, Joao Cancelo 27, Mahrez 63, Sterling 86). Att: 52,127
26 Manchester City 6 (De Bruyne 5, Mahrez 14 pen, Gundogan 21, Sterling 25 pen, 87, Laporte 69) Leicester 3 (Maddison 55, Lookman 59, Iheanacho 66). Att: 53,226
29 Brentford 0 Manchester City 1 (Foden 16). Att: 17,009

JANUARY 2022

1 Arsenal 1 (Saka 31) Manchester City 2 (Mahrez 57 pen, Rodri 90+3). Att: 59,757
15 Manchester City 1 (De Bruyne 70) Chelsea 0. Att: 53,319
22 Southampton 1 (Walker-Peters 7) Manchester City 1 (Laporte 65). Att: 31,178

FEBRUARY 2022

9 Manchester City 2 (Mahrez 40 pen, De Bruyne 69) Brentford 0. Att: 51,658
12 Norwich 0 Manchester City 4 (Sterling 31, 70, 90, Foden 48). Att: 27,010
19 Manchester City 3 (Gundogan 33, Mahrez 90+2 pen) Tottenham 3 (Kulusevski 4, Kane 50, 90+5). Att: 53,201
26 Everton 0 Manchester City 1 (Foden 82). Att: 39,028

MARCH 2022

6 Manchester City 4 (De Bruyne 5, 28, Mahrez 68, 90) Manchester Utd 1 (Sancho 22). Att: 53,165

14 Crystal Palace 0 Manchester City 0. Att: 25, 309

APRIL 2022

2 Burnley 0 Manchester City 2 (De Bruyne 5, Gundogan 25). Att: 21,200

10 Manchester City 2 (De Bruyne 5, Gabriel Jesus 37) Liverpool 2 (Diogo Jota 13, Mane 46). Att: 53,197

20 Manchester City 3 (Mahrez 53, Foden 65, Bernardo Silva 82) Brighton 0. Att: 52,226

23 Manchester City 5 (Gabriel Jesus 4, 23, 49 pen, 53, Rodri 34) Watford 1 (Kamara 28). Att: 53,013

30 Leeds 0 Manchester City 4 (Rodri 13, Ake 54 Gabriel Jesus 78, Fernandinho 90+3). Att: 35,771

MAY 2022

8 Manchester. City 5 (Sterling 19, 90+3, Laporte 38, Rodri 61, Foden 90) Newcastle 0. Att: 53,336

11 Wolves 1 (Dendoncker 11) Manchester City 5 (De Bruyne 7, 16, 24, 60, Sterling 84). Att: 31,500

18 West Ham 2 (Bowen 24, 45) Manchester City 2 (Grealish 47, Coufal og 69). Att: 59,972

22 Manchester City 3 (Gundogan 76, 81, Rodri 78) Aston Villa 2 (Cash 37, Coutinho 69). Att: 53,395 – Manchester City clinched title

... AND HOW LIVERPOOL JUST MISSED OUT

AUGUST 2021

14 Norwich 0 Liverpool 3 (Diogo Jota 26, Firmino 65, Salah 74). Att: 27,023

21 Liverpool 2 (Diogo Jota 18, Mane 69) Burnley 0. Att: 52,591

28 Liverpool 1 (Salah 45 pen) Chelsea 0. Att: 53,100

SEPTEMBER 2021

12 Leeds 0 Liverpool 3 (Salah 20, Fabinho 50, Mane 90+2). Att: 36,507

18 Liverpool 3 (Mane 43, Salah 78, Keita 89) Crystal Palace 0. Att: 52,985

25 Brentford 3 (Pinnock 27, Janelt 63, Wissa 82) Liverpool 3 (Diogo Jota 31, Salah 54, Jones 67). Att: 16,876

OCTOBER 2021

3 Liverpool 2 (Mane 59, Salah 76) Manchester City 2 (Foden 69, De Bruyne 81). Att: 53,102

16 Watford 0 Liverpool 5 (Mane 8, Firmino 37, 52, 90+1, Salah 54). Att: 21,085

24 Manchester Utd 0 Liverpool 5 (Keita 5, Diogo Jota 13, Salah 38, 45, 50). Att: 73,088

30 Liverpool 2 (Henderson 4, Mane 24) Brighton 2 (Mwepu 41, Trossard 65). Att: 53,197

NOVEMBER 2021

7 West Ham 3 (Alisson 4 og, Fornals 67, Zouma 74) Liverpool 2 (Alexander-Arnold 41, Origi 83). Att: 59,909

20 Liverpool 4 (Mane 39, Diogo Jota 52, Salah 73, Minamino 77) Arsenal 0. Att: 53,092

27 Liverpool 4 (Diogo Jota 2, 32, Thiago Alcontara 37, Van Dijk 52) Southampton 0. Att: 53,040

DECEMBER 2021

1   Everton 1 (Gray 38) Liverpool 4 (Henderson 9, Salah 19, 64, Diogo Jota 79). Att: 39,641

4   Wolves 0 Liverpool 1 (Origi 90+4). Att: 30,729

11   Liverpool 1 (Salah 67 pen) Aston Villa 0. Att: 53,093

16   Liverpool 3 (Diogo Jota 21, Salah 25, Alexander-Arnold 87) Newcastle 1 (Shelvey 7). Att: 52,951

19   Tottenham 2 (Kane 13, Son-Heung-min 74) Liverpool 2 (Diogo Jota 35, Robertson 69). Att: 45,421

28   Leicester 1 (Lookman 59) Liverpool 0. Att: 32,230

JANUARY 2022

2   Chelsea 2 (Kovacic 42, Pulisic 45) Liverpool 2 (Mane 9, Salah 26). Att: 40,072

16   Liverpool 3 (Fabinho 44, Oxlade-Chamberlain 69, Minamino 77) Brentford 0. Att: 52,824

23   Crystal Palace 1 (Edouard 55) Liverpool 3 (Van Dijk 8, Oxlade-Chamberlain 32, Fabinho 89 pen). Att: 25,002

FEBRUARY 2022

10   Liverpool 2 (Diogo Jota 34, 87) Leicester 0. Att: 53,050

13   Burnley 0 Liverpool 1 (Fabinho 40). Att: 21,239

19   Liverpool 3 (Mane 64, Salah 67, Diaz 81) Norwich 1 (Rashica 48). Att: 53,135

23   Liverpool 6 (Salah 15 pen, 35 pen, Matip 30, Mane 80, 90, Van Dijk 90+3) Leeds 0. Att: 53,018

MARCH 2022

5   Liverpool 1 (Mane 27) West Ham 0. Att: 53,059

12   Brighton 0 Liverpool 2 (Diaz 19, Salah 61 pen). Att: 31,474

16   Arsenal 0 Liverpool 2 (Diogo Jota 54, Firmino 62). Att: 59,968

APRIL 2022

2   Liverpool 2 (Diogo Jota 22, Fabinho 89 pen) Watford 0. Att: 53,104

10   Manchester City 2 (De Bruyne 5, Gabriel Jesus 37) Liverpool 2 (Diogo Jota 13, Mane 46). Att: 53,197

19   Liverpool 4 (Diaz 5, Salah 22, 85, Mane 68) Manchester Utd 0. Att: 53,394

24   Liverpool 2 (Robertson 52, Origi 85) Everton 0. Att: 52,852

30   Newcastle 0 Liverpool 1 (Keita 19). Att: 52,281

MAY 2022

7   Liverpool 1 (Diaz 74) Tottenham 1 (Son Heung-min 56). Att: 53,177

10   Aston Villa 1 (Douglas Luiz 3) Liverpool 2 (Matip 6, Mane 65). Att: 41,919

17   Southampton 1 (Redmond 13) Liverpool 2 (Minamino 27, Matip 67). Att: 31,588

22   Liverpool 3 (Mane 24, Salah 84, Robertson 89) Wolves 1 (Pedro Neto 3). Att: 53,097

THE THINGS THEY SAY ...

'It's the greatest result in the history of Welsh football, what dreams are made of' – **Gareth Bale** celebrates his country's first World Cup for 64 years after the play-off win over Ukraine.

'I'm lost for words. There is silence in the dressing room. We did everything we could to win the match and I want the people of Ukraine to remember our team, our efforts' – **Oleksandr Petrakov**, Ukraine coach.

ENGLISH FOOTBALL LEAGUE PLAY-OFFS 2022

Nottingham Forest regained what Steve Cooper insisted was their rightful place in the top-flight with an outstanding performance during the course of the season – followed by a pragmatic display at Wembley to make sure it didn't go to waste. In a tight, tense match of few clear-cut chances, Forest were not at their best. But its big moments all went in their favour. They were gifted an own goal by Levi Colwill, then given the benefit of the doubt by referee Jon Moss, whose two crucial penalty box decisions could easily have gone against them. Moss, in his final match before retiring, turned down Huddersfield appeals after Harry Toffolo and Lewis O'Brien went to ground under challenges which VAR, operating for the first time at this level, declined to pursue. Both were borderline cases, with Forest under considerable pressure after having the better of their first 45 minutes. But there was no argument about the size of Cooper's achievement in restoring Premier League football to the City Ground after a break of 23 years. The 14th different manager there in a decade said the club was 'back where it belongs' after his players resurrected a campaign which had relegation, rather than promotion, written all over it when the opening seven matches yielded a single point. A disappointed Carlos Corberan also came away with plenty of plaudits for making Huddersfield a force to be reckoned with after finishing fifth from bottom in 2021. So did Alex Neil for awakening sleeping giants **Sunderland**, who had 46,000 supporters at Wembley to see Ross Stewart, with his 26th goal of the season, and Elliot Embleton deliver a 2-0 win over Wycombe in the League One Final. Darrell Clarke, too, was the centre of attention as **Port Vale** defeated Mansfield 3-0 in an emotional League Two decider, the manager having lost his eldest daughter Ellie during the season.

CHAMPIONSHIP SEMI-FINALS, FIRST LEG

Luton 1 (Bradley 31) **Huddersfield** 1 (Sinani). Att: 10,005. **Sheffield Utd** 1 (Berge 90) **Nottm Forest** 2 (Colback 10, Johnson 71). Att: 30,225.

LEAGUE ONE
Sunderland 1 (Stewart 45) **Sheffield Wed** 0. Att: 44,742 (record). **Wycombe** 2 (Tafazolli 38, Vokes 82) **MK Dons** 0. Att: 8,987

LEAGUE TWO
Mansfield 2 (Oates 13, Bowery 32) **Northampton** 1 (Koiki 61). Att: 7,469. **Swindon** 2 (McKirdy 26, 68) **Port Vale** 1 (Wilson 83). Att: 14,086

SECOND LEG

CHAMPIONSHIP
Huddersfield 1 (Rhodes 82) **Luton** 0. Att: 23,407 (**Huddersfield** won 2-1 on agg). **Nottm Forest** 1 (Johnson 19) **Sheffield Utd** 2 (Gibbs-White 47, Fleck 75). Att: 29,015 (aet, agg 3-3, Nottm Forest won 3-2 on pens)

LEAGUE ONE
MK Dons 1 (Parrott26) **Wycombe** 0. Att: 13,012 (Wycombe won 2-1 on agg). **Sheffield Wed** 1 (Gregory 74) **Sunderland** 1 (Roberts 90+3). Att: 32,978 (Sunderland won 2-1 on agg)

LEAGUE TWO
Northampton 0 **Mansfield** 1 (McLaughlin 32). Att: 7,619 (Mansfield won 3-1 on agg). **Port Vale** 1 (Wilson 8) **Swindon** 0. Att: 11,669 (aet, agg 2-2, Port Vale won 6-5 on pens)

FINALS

CHAMPIONSHIP – MAY 29, 2022
Huddersfield Town 0 **Nottingham Forest** 1 (Colwill 45 og). Att: 80,019 (Wembley)

Huddersfield Town (3-4-2-1): Nicholls, Lees, Sarr (Russell 54), Colwill, Pipa, Hogg (capt), O'Brien, Toffolo, Sinani (Holmes 67), Thomas, Ward (Rhodes 67). **Subs not used**: Blackman, Pearson, Anjorin, Turton. **Booked**: Toffolo. **Manager**: Carlos Corberan
Nottingham Forest (3-4-1-2): Samba (Horvath 90), Worrall (capt), Cook, McKenna, Spence, Yates, Garner, Colback, Zinckernagel (Lowe 74), Johnson, Davis (Surridge 66). **Subs not used**: Figueiredo, Mighten, Cafu, Lolley. **Booked**: Zinckernagel. **Manager**: Steve Cooper
Referee: Jon Moss (Co Durham)). **Half-time**: 0-1

LEAGUE ONE – MAY 21, 2022
Sunderland 2 (Embleton 12, Stewart 79) **Wycombe Wanderers** 0. Att: 72,332 (Wembley)
Sunderland (4-2-3-1): Patterson, Gooch, Wright, Batth, Cirkin, Evans (capt), O'Nien, Roberts, Pritchard (Doyle 81), Embleton (Clarke 61), R Stewart (Broadhead 88). **Subs not used**: Hoffman, Neil, Matete, McGeady. **Booked**: Cirkin, Pritchard. **Manager**: Alex Neil
Wycombe Wanderers (4-2-3-1): Stockdale, McCarthy, A Stewart, Tafazolli, Jacobson (capt), Scowen, Horgan (Wing 55), McCleary, Gape (Akinfenwa 75), Obita (Hanlan 65), Vokes. **Subs not used**: Dickinson, Grimmer, Wheeler, Forino. **Manager**: Gareth Ainsworth
Referee: Simon Hooper (Wiltshire). **Half-time**: 1-0

LEAGUE TWO – MAY 28, 2022
Mansfield Town 0 **Port Vale** 3 (Harratt 20, Wilson 24, Benning 85). Att: 37,303 (Wembley)
Mansfield Town (4-2-3-1): Bishop, Hewitt, Perch, Hawkins, McLaughlin, O'Toole, Longstaff (Maris 65), Quinn, Oates, Murphy (Lapslie 54), Bowery. **Subs not used**: Stech, Clarke, Wallace, Stirk, Akins. **Booked**: Hawkins, Hewitt, Perch. **Sent off**: Hawkins (35). **Manager**: Nigel Clough
Port Vale (3-4-2-1): Stone, Gibbons, Smith, Hall, Worrall (Martin 87), Pett, Taylor (Charsley 67), Benning, Garrity, Harratt (Proctor 77), Wilson. **Subs not used**: Covolan, Robinson, Amoo, Edmondson. **Manager**: Darrell Clarke
Referee: Jarred Gillett (Australia). **Half-time**: 0-2

PLAY-OFF FINALS – HOME & AWAY

1987: Divs 1/2: Charlton beat Leeds 2-1 in replay (Birmingham) after 1-1 agg (1-0h, 0-1a). Charlton remained in Div 1 Losing semi-finalists: Ipswich and Oldham. **Divs 2/3: Swindon** beat Gillingham 2-0 in replay (Crystal Palace) after 2-2 agg (0-1a, 2-1h). Swindon promoted to Div 2. Losing semi-finalists: Sunderland and Wigan; Sunderland relegated to Div 3. **Divs 3/4: Aldershot** beat Wolves 3-0 on agg (2-0h, 1-0a) and promoted to Div 3. Losing semi-finalists: Bolton and Colchester; Bolton relegated to Div 4

1988: Divs 1/2: Middlesbrough beat Chelsea 2-1 on agg (2-0h, 0-1a) and promoted to Div 1; Chelsea relegated to Div 2. Losing semi-finalists: Blackburn and Bradford City. **Divs 2/3: Walsall** beat Bristol City 4-0 in replay (h) after 3-3 agg (3-1a, 0-2h) and promoted to Div 2. Losing semi-finalists: Sheffield Utd and Notts County; Sheffield Utd relegated to Div 3. **Divs 3/4: Swansea** beat Torquay 5-4 on agg (2-1h, 3-3a) and promoted to Div 3. Losing semi-finalists: Rotherham and Scunthorpe.; Rotherham relegated to Div 4

1989: Div 2: Crystal Palace beat Blackburn 4-3 on agg (1-3a, 3-0h). Losing semi-finalists: Watford and Swindon. **Div 3: Port Vale** beat Bristol Rovers 2-1 on agg (1-1a, 1-0h). Losing semi-finalists: Fulham and Preston **Div.4: Leyton Orient** beat Wrexham 2-1 on agg (0-0a, 2-1h). Losing semi-finalists: Scarborough and Scunthorpe

PLAY-OFF FINALS AT WEMBLEY

1990: Div 2: Swindon 1 Sunderland 0 (att: 72,873). Swindon promoted, then demoted for financial irregularities; Sunderland promoted. Losing semi-finalists: Blackburn and Newcastle Utd **Div 3: Notts County** 2 Tranmere 0 (att: 29,252). Losing semi-finalists: Bolton and Bury.

Div 4: Cambridge Utd 1 Chesterfield 0 (att: 26,404). Losing semi-finalists: Maidstone and Stockport County

1991: Div 2: Notts County 3 Brighton 1 (att: 59,940). Losing semi-finalists: Middlesbrough and Millwall. **Div 3: Tranmere** 1 Bolton 0 (att: 30,217). Losing semi-finalists: Brentford and Bury. **Div 4: Torquay** 2 Blackpool 2 – Torquay won 5-4 on pens (att: 21,615). Losing semi-finalists: Burnley and Scunthorpe

1992: Div 2: Blackburn 1 Leicester 0 (att: 68,147). Losing semi-finalists: Derby and Cambridge Utd. **Div 3: Peterborough** 2 Stockport 1 (att: 35,087). Losing semi-finalists: Huddersfield and Stoke. **Div 4: Blackpool** 1 Scunthorpe 1 aet, Blackpool won 4-3 on pens (att: 22,741). Losing semi-finalists: Barnet and Crewe

1993: Div 1: Swindon 4 Leicester 3 (att: 73,802). Losing semi-finalists: Portsmouth and Tranmere. **Div 2: WBA** 3 Port Vale 0 (att: 53,471). Losing semi-finalists: Stockport and Swansea. **Div 3: York** 1 Crewe 1 aet, York won 5-3 on pens (att: 22,416). Losing semi-finalists: Bury and Walsall

1994: Div 1: Leicester 2 Derby 1 (att: 73,671). Losing semi-finalists: Millwall and Tranmere. **Div 2: Burnley** 2 Stockport 1 (att: 44,806). Losing semi-finalists: Plymouth Argyle and York. **Div 3: Wycombe** 4 Preston 2 (att: 40,109). Losing semi-finalists: Carlisle and Torquay

1995: Div 1: Bolton 4 Reading 3 (att: 64,107). Losing semi-finalists: Tranmere and Wolves. **Div 2: Huddersfield** 2 Bristol Rov 1 (att: 59,175). Losing semi-finalists: Brentford and Crewe. **Div 3: Chesterfield** 2 Bury 0 (att: 22,814). Losing semi-finalists: Mansfield and Preston

1996: Div 1: Leicester 2 Crystal Palace 1 aet (att: 73,573). Losing semi-finalists: Charlton and Stoke. **Div 2: Bradford City** 2 Notts Co 0 (att: 39,972). Losing semi-finalists: Blackpool and Crewe. **Div 3: Plymouth Argyle** 1 Darlington 0 (att: 43,431). Losing semi-finalists: Colchester and Hereford

1997: Div 1: Crystal Palace 1 Sheffield Utd 0 (att: 64,383). Losing semi-finalists: Ipswich and Wolves. **Div 2: Crewe** 1 Brentford 0 (att: 34,149). Losing semi-finalists: Bristol City and Luton. **Div 3: Northampton** 1 Swansea 0 (att: 46,804). Losing semi-finalists: Cardiff and Chester

1998: Div 1: Charlton 4 Sunderland 4 aet, Charlton won 7-6 on pens (att: 77, 739). Losing semi-finalists: Ipswich and Sheffield Utd. **Div 2: Grimsby** 1 Northampton 0 (att: 62,988). Losing semi-finalists: Bristol Rov and Fulham. **Div 3: Colchester** 1 Torquay 0 (att: 19,486). Losing semi-finalists: Barnet and Scarborough

1999: Div 1: Watford 2 Bolton 0 (att: 70,343). Losing semi-finalists: Ipswich and Birmingham. **Div 2: Manchester City** 2 Gillingham 2 aet, Manchester City won 3-1 on pens (att: 76,935). Losing semi-finalists: Preston and Wigan. **Div 3: Scunthorpe** 1 Leyton Orient 0 (att: 36,985). Losing semi-finalists: Rotherham and Swansea

2000: Div 1: Ipswich 4 Barnsley 2 (att: 73,427). Losing semi-finalists: Birmingham and Bolton. **Div 2: Gillingham** 3 Wigan 2 aet (att: 53,764). Losing semi-finalists: Millwall and Stoke. **Div 3: Peterborough** 1 Darlington 0 (att: 33,383). Losing semi-finalists: Barnet and Hartlepool

PLAY-OFF FINALS AT MILLENNIUM STADIUM

2001: Div 1: Bolton 3 Preston 0 (att: 54,328). Losing semi-finalists: Birmingham and WBA. **Div 2: Walsall** 3 Reading 2 aet (att: 50,496). Losing semi-finalists: Stoke and Wigan. **Div 3: Blackpool** 4 Leyton Orient 2 (att: 23,600). Losing semi-finalists: Hartlepool and Hull

2002: Div 1: Birmingham 1 Norwich 1 aet, Birmingham won 4-2 on pens, (att: 71,597). Losing semi-finalists: Millwall and Wolves. **Div 2: Stoke** 2 Brentford 0 (att: 42,523). Losing semi-finalists: Cardiff and Huddersfield. **Div 3: Cheltenham** 3 Rushden & Diamonds 1 (att: 24,368). Losing semi-finalists: Hartlepool and Rochdale

2003: Div 1: Wolves 3 Sheffield Utd 0 (att: 69,473). Losing semi-finalists: Nott'm Forest and Reading. **Div 2: Cardiff** 1 QPR. 0 aet (att: 66,096). Losing semi-finalists: Bristol City and Oldham. **Div 3: Bournemouth** 5 Lincoln 2 (att: 32,148). Losing semi-finalists: Bury and Scunthorpe.

2004: Div 1: Crystal Palace 1 West Ham 0 (att: 72,523). Losing semi-finalists: Ipswich and Sunderland. **Div 2: Brighton** 1 Bristol City 0 (att: 65,167). Losing semi-finalists: Hartlepool and Swindon. **Div 3: Huddersfield** 0 Mansfield 0 aet, Huddersfield won 4-1 on pens (att: 37,298). Losing semi-finalists: Lincoln and Northampton

2005: Championship: West Ham 1 Preston 0 (att: 70,275). Losing semifinalists: Derby Co and Ipswich. **League 1: Sheffield Wed** 4 Hartlepool 2 aet (att: 59,808). Losing semi-finalists: Brentford and Tranmere **League 2: Southend** 2 Lincoln 0 aet (att: 19532). Losing semi-finalists: Macclesfield and Northampton

2006: Championship: Watford 3 Leeds 0 (att: 64,736). Losing semi-finalists: Crystal Palace and Preston. **League 1: Barnsley** 2 Swansea 2 aet (att: 55,419), Barnsley won 4-3 on pens. Losing semi-finalists: Huddersfield and Brentford. **League 2: Cheltenham** 1 Grimsby 0 (att: 29,196). Losing semi-finalists: Wycombe and Lincoln

PLAY-OFF FINALS AT WEMBLEY

2007: Championship: Derby 1 WBA 0 (att: 74,993). Losing semi-finalists: Southampton and Wolves. **League 1: Blackpool** 2 Yeovil 0 (att: 59,313). Losing semi-finalists: Nottm Forest and Oldham. **League 2: Bristol Rov** 3 Shrewsbury 1 (att: 61,589). Losing semi-finalists: Lincoln and MK Dons

2008: Championship: Hull 1 Bristol City 0 (att: 86,703). Losing semi-finalists: Crystal Palace and Watford. **League 1: Doncaster** 1 Leeds 0 (att: 75,132). Losing semi-finalists: Carlisle and Southend. **League 2: Stockport** 3 Rochdale 2 (att: 35,715). Losing semi-finalists: Darlington and Wycombe

2009: Championship: Burnley 1 Sheffield Utd 0 (att: 80,518). Losing semi-finalists: Preston and Reading. **League 1: Scunthorpe** 3 Millwall 2 (att: 59,661). Losing semi-finalists: Leeds and MK Dons. **League 2: Gillingham** 1 Shrewsbury 0 (att: 53,706). Losing semi-finalists: Bury and Rochdale

2010: Championship: Blackpool 3 Cardiff 2 (att: 82,244). Losing semi-finalists: Leicester and Nottm Forest. **League 1: Millwall** 1 Swindon 0 (att:73,108). Losing semi-finalists: Charlton and Huddersfield. **League 2: Dagenham & Redbridge** 3 Rotherham 2 (att: 32,054). Losing semi-finalists: Aldershot and Morecambe

2011: Championship: Swansea 4 Reading 2 (att: 86,581). Losing semi-finalists: Cardiff and Nottm Forest. **League 1: Peterborough** 3 Huddersfield 0 (Old Trafford; att:48,410). Losing semi-finalists: Bournemouth and MK Dons. **League 2: Stevenage** 1 Torquay 0 (Old Trafford, att: 11,484. Losing semi-finalists: Accrington and Shrewsbury

2012: Championship: West Ham 2 Blackpool 1 (att: 78,523). Losing semi-finalists: Birmingham and Cardiff. **League 1: Huddersfield** 0 Sheffield Utd 0 aet, Huddersfield won 8-7 on pens (att: 52,100). Losing semi-finalists: MK Dons and Stevenage. **League 2: Crewe** 2 Cheltenham 0 (att: 24,029). Losing semi-finalists: Southend and Torquay

2013: Championship: Crystal Palace 1 Watford 0 (att: 82,025). Losing semi-finalists: Brighton and Leicester. **League 1: Yeovil** 2 Brentford 1 (att: 41,955). Losing semi-finalists: Sheffield Utd and Swindon. **League 2: Bradford** 3 Northampton 0 (att: 47,127). Losing semi-finalists: Burton and Cheltenham

2014: Championship: QPR 1 Derby 0 (att: 87,348). Losing semi-finalists: Brighton and Wigan. **League 1: Rotherham** 2 Leyton Orient 2 aet, Rotherham won 4-3 on pens (att: 43,401). Losing semi-finalists: Peterborough and Preston. **League 2: Fleetwood** 1 Burton 0 (att: 14,007). Losing semi-finalists: Southend and York

2015: Championship: Norwich 2 Middlesbrough 0 (att: 85,656). Losing semi-finalists: Brentford and Ipswich. **League 1: Preston** 4 Swindon 0 (att: 48,236). Losing semi-finalists: Chesterfield and Sheffield Utd. **League 2: Southend** 1 Wycombe 1 aet, Southend won 7-6 on pens (att: 38,252). Losing semi-finalists: Stevenage and Plymouth

2016: Championship: Hull 1 Sheffield Wed 0 (att 70,189). Losing semi-finalists: Brighton and Derby. **League 1: Barnsley** 3 Millwall 1 (att 51,277). Losing semi-finalists: Bradford and Walsall. **League 2: AFC Wimbledon** 2 Plymouth 0 (att 57,956). Losing semi-finalists: Accrington and Portsmouth)

2017: Championship: Huddersfield 0 Reading 0 aet, Huddersfield won 4-3 on pens (att 76,682). Losing semi-finalists: Fulham and Sheffield Wed. **League 1: Millwall** 1 Bradford 0 (att 53,320. Losing semi-finals: Fleetwood and Scunthorpe. **League 2: Blackpool** 2 Exeter 1 (att 23,380). Losing semi-finalists: Carlisle and Luton

2018: Championship: Fulham 1 Aston Villa 0 (att 85,243). Losing semi-finalists: Derby and Middlesbrough. **League 1: Rotherham** 2 Shrewsbury 1 (att 26,218). Losing semi-finalists: Charlton and Scunthorpe. **League 2: Coventry** 3 Exeter 1. Losing semi-finalists: Lincoln and Notts Co

2019: Championship: Aston Villa 2 Derby 1 (85,826). Losing semi-finalists: Leeds and WBA. **League 1: Charlton** 2 Sunderland 1 (76,155). Losing semi-finalists: Doncaster and Portsmouth. **League 2: Tranmere** 1 Newport 0, aet (25,217 Losing semi-finalists: Forest Green and Mansfield

2020: Championship: Fulham 2 Brentford 1 (no att). Losing semi-finalists: Cardiff and Swansea. **League 1: Wycombe** 2 Oxford 1 (no att). Losing semi-finalists: Fleetwood and Portsmouth. **League 2: Northampton** 4 Exeter 0 (no att). Losing semi-finalists: Cheltenham and Colchester

2021: Championship: Brentford 2 Swansea 0 (11,689). Losing semi-finalists: Barnsley and Bournemouth. **League 1: Blackpool** 2 Lincoln 1 (9,751). Losing semi-finalists: Oxford and Sunderland. **League 2: Morecambe** 1 Newport 0 (9,083). Losing semi-finalists: Forest Green and Tranmere

HISTORY OF THE PLAY-OFFS

Play-off matches were introduced by the Football League to decide final promotion and relegation issues at the end of season 1986-87. A similar series styled 'Test Matches' had operated between Divisions One and Two for six seasons from 1893-98, and was abolished when both divisions were increased from 16 to 18 clubs.

Eighty-eight years later, the play-offs were back in vogue. In the first three seasons (1987-88-89), the Finals were played home-and-away, and since they were made one-off matches in 1990, they have featured regularly in Wembley's spring calendar, until the old stadium closed its doors and the action switched to the Millennium Stadium in Cardiff in 2001.

Through the years, these have been the ups and downs of the play-offs:

1987: Initially, the 12 clubs involved comprised the one that finished directly above those relegated in Divisions One, Two and Three and the three who followed the sides automatically promoted in each section. Two of the home-and-away Finals went to neutral-ground replays, in which **Charlton** clung to First Division status by denying Leeds promotion while **Swindon** beat Gillingham to complete their climb from Fourth Division to Second in successive seasons, via the play-offs, Sunderland fell into the Third and Bolton into Division Four, both for the first time. **Aldershot** went up after finishing only sixth in Division Four; in their Final, they beat Wolves, who had finished nine points higher and missed automatic promotion by one point.

1988: Chelsea were relegated from the First Division after losing on aggregate to **Middlesbrough**, who had finished third in Division Two. So Middlesbrough, managed by Bruce Rioch, completed the rise from Third Division to First in successive seasons, only two years after their very existence had been threatened by the bailiffs. Also promoted via the play-offs: **Walsall** from Division Three and **Swansea** from the Fourth. Relegated, besides Chelsea: Sheffield Utd (to Division Three) and Rotherham (to Division Four).

1989: After two seasons of promotion-relegation play-offs, the system was changed to involve the four clubs who had just missed automatic promotion. That format has remained. Steve Coppell's

Crystal Palace, third in Division Two, returned to the top flight after eight years, beating Blackburn 4-3 on aggregate after extra time. Similarly, **Port Vale** confirmed third place in Division Three with promotion via the play-offs. For **Leyton Orient**, promotion seemed out of the question in Division Four when they stood 15th on March 1. But eight wins and a draw in the last nine home games swept them to sixth in the final table, and two more home victories in the play-offs completed their season in triumph.

1990: The play-off Finals now moved to Wembley over three days of the Spring Holiday week-end. On successive afternoons, **Cambridge Utd** won promotion from Division Four and **Notts Co** from the Third. Then, on Bank Holiday Monday, the biggest crowd for years at a Football League fixture (72,873) saw Ossie Ardiles' **Swindon** beat Sunderland 1-0 to reach the First Division for the first time. A few weeks later, however, Wembley losers **Sunderland** were promoted instead, by default; Swindon were found guilty of "financial irregularities" and stayed in Division Two.

1991: Again, the season's biggest League crowd (59,940) gathered at Wembley for the First Division Final in which **Notts Co** (having missed promotion by one point) still fulfilled their ambition, beating Brighton 3-1. In successive years, County had climbed from Third Division to First via the play-offs – the first club to achieve double promotion by this route. Bolton were denied automatic promotion in Division Three on goal difference, and lost at Wembley to an extra-time goal by **Tranmere**. The Fourth Division Final made history, with Blackpool beaten 5-4 on penalties by **Torquay** – first instance of promotion being decided by a shoot-out. In the table, Blackpool had finished seven points ahead of Torquay.

1992: Wembley that Spring Bank Holiday was the turning point in the history of **Blackburn**. Bolstered by Kenny Dalglish's return to management and owner Jack Walker's millions, they beat Leicester 1-0 by Mike Newell's 45th-minute penalty to achieve their objective – a place in the new Premier League. Newell, who also missed a second-half penalty, had recovered from a broken leg just in time for the play-offs. In the Fourth Division Final **Blackpool** (denied by penalties the previous year) this time won a shoot-out 4-3 against Scunthorpe., who were unlucky in the play-offs for the fourth time in five years. **Peterborough** climbed out of the Third Division for the first time, beating Stockport County 2-1 at Wembley.

1993: The crowd of 73,802 at Wembley to see **Swindon** beat Leicester 4-3 in the First Division Final was 11,000 bigger than that for the FA Cup Final replay between Arsenal and Sheffield Wed. Leicester rallied from three down to 3-3 before Paul Bodin's late penalty wiped away **Swindon**'s bitter memories of three years earlier, when they were denied promotion after winning at Wembley. In the Third Division Final, **York** beat Crewe 5-3 in a shoot-out after a 1-1 draw, and in the Second Division decider, **WBA** beat Port Vale 3-0. That was tough on Vale, who had finished third in the table with 89 points – the highest total never to earn promotion in any division. They had beaten Albion twice in the League, too.

1994: Wembley's record turn-out of 158,586 spectators at the three Finals started with a crowd of 40,109 to see Martin O'Neill's **Wycombe** beat Preston 4-2. They thus climbed from Conference to Second Division with successive promotions. **Burnley**'s 2-1 victory in the Second Division Final was marred by the sending-off of two Stockport players, and in the First Division decider **Leicester** came from behind to beat Derby Co and end the worst Wembley record of any club. They had lost on all six previous appearances there – four times in the FA Cup Final and in the play-offs of 1992 and 1993.

1995: Two months after losing the Coca-Cola Cup Final to Liverpool, Bruce Rioch's **Bolton** were back at Wembley for the First Division play-off Final. From two goals down to Reading in front of a crowd of 64,107, they returned to the top company after 15 years, winning 4-3 with two extra-time goals. **Huddersfield** ended the first season at their new £15m. home with promotion to the First Division via a 2-1 victory against Bristol Rov – manager Neil Warnock's third play-off success (after two with Notts Co). Of the three clubs who missed automatic promotion by one place, only **Chesterfield** achieved it in the play-offs, comfortably beating Bury 2-0.

1996: Under new manager Martin O'Neill (a Wembley play-off winner with Wycombe in 1994), **Leicester** returned to the Premiership a year after leaving it. They had finished fifth in the table, but in the Final came from behind to beat third-placed Crystal Palace by Steve Claridge's shot in the last seconds of extra time. In the Second Division **Bradford City** came sixth, nine points behind Blackpool (3rd), but beat them (from two down in the semi-final first leg) and then clinched promotion by 2-0 v Notts County at Wembley. It was City's greatest day since they won the Cup in 1911. **Plymouth Argyle** beat Darlington in the Third Division Final to earn promotion a year after being relegated. It was manager Neil Warnock's fourth play-off triumph in seven seasons after two with Notts County (1990 and 1991) and a third with Huddersfield in 1995.

1997: High drama at Wembley as **Crystal Palace** left it late against Sheffield Utd in the First Division play-off final. The match was scoreless until the last 10 seconds when David Hopkin lobbed Blades' keeper Simon Tracey from 25 yards to send the Eagles back to the Premiership after two seasons of Nationwide action. In the Second Division play-off final, **Crewe** beat Brentford 1-0 courtesy of a Shaun Smith goal. **Northampton** celebrated their first Wembley appearance with a 1-0 victory over Swansea thanks to John Frain's injury-time free-kick in the Third Division play-off final.

1998: In one of the finest games ever seen at Wembley, **Charlton** eventually triumphed 7-6 on penalties over Sunderland. For Charlton, Wearside-born Clive Mendonca scored a hat-trick and Richard Rufus his first career goal in a match that lurched between joy and despair for both sides as it ended 4-4. Sunderland defender Michael Gray's superb performance ill deserved to end with his weakly struck spot kick being saved by Sasa Ilic. In the Third Division, the penalty spot also had a role to play, as **Colchester**'s David Gregory scored the only goal to defeat Torquay, while in the Second Division a Kevin Donovan goal gave **Grimsby** victory over Northampton.

1999: Elton John, watching via a personal satellite link in Seattle, saw his **Watford** side overcome Bolton 2-0 to reach the Premiership. Against technically superior opponents, Watford prevailed with application and teamwork. They also gave Bolton a lesson in finishing through match-winners by Nick Wright and Allan Smart. **Manchester City** staged a remarkable comeback to win the Second Division Final after trailing to goals by Carl Asaba and Robert Taylor for Gillingham. Kevin Horlock and Paul Dickov scored in stoppage time and City went on to win on penalties. A goal by Spaniard Alex Calvo-Garcia earned **Scunthorpe** a 1-0 success against Leyton Orient in the Third Division Final.

2000: After three successive play-off failures, **Ipswich** finally secured a place in the Premiership. They overcame the injury loss of leading scorer David Johnson to beat Barnsley 4-2 with goals by 36-year-old Tony Mowbray, Marcus Stewart and substitutes Richard Naylor and Martijn Reuser. With six minutes left of extra-time in the Second Division Final, **Gillingham** trailed Wigan 2-1. But headers by 38-year-old player-coach Steve Butler and fellow substitute Andy Thomson gave them a 3-2 victory. Andy Clarke, approaching his 33rd birthday, scored the only goal of the Third Division decider for **Peterborough** against Darlington.

2001: **Bolton**, unsuccessful play-off contenders in the two previous seasons, made no mistake at the third attempt. They flourished in the new surroundings of the Millennium Stadium to beat Preston 3-0 with goals by Gareth Farrelly, Michael Ricketts – his 24th of the season – and Ricardo Gardner to reach the Premiership. **Walsall**, relegated 12 months earlier, scored twice in a three-minute spell of extra time to win 3-2 against Reading in the Second Division Final, while **Blackpool** capped a marked improvement in the second half of the season by overcoming Leyton Orient 4-2 in the Third Division Final.

2002: Holding their nerve to win a penalty shoot-out 4-2, **Birmingham** wiped away the memory of three successive defeats in the semi-finals of the play-offs to return to the top division after an absence of 16 years. Substitute Darren Carter completed a fairy-tale first season as a professional by scoring the fourth spot-kick against Norwich. **Stoke** became the first successful team to come from the south dressing room in 12 finals since football was adopted by the home of Welsh rugby, beating Brentford 2-0 in the Second Division Final with Deon Burton's strike and a Ben Burgess own goal. Julian Alsop's 26th goal of the season helped **Cheltenham** defeat League newcomers Rushden & Diamonds 3-1 in the Third Division decider.

2003: **Wolves** benefactor Sir Jack Hayward finally saw his £60m investment pay dividends when the club he first supported as a boy returned to the top flight after an absence of 19 years by beating Sheffield Utd 3-0. It was also a moment to savour for manager Dave Jones, who was forced to leave his previous club Southampton because of child abuse allegations, which were later found to be groundless. **Cardiff**, away from the game's second tier for 18 years, returned with an extra-time winner from substitute Andy Campbell against QPR after a goalless 90 minutes in the Division Two Final. **Bournemouth**, relegated 12 months earlier, became the first team to score five in the end-of-season deciders, beating Lincoln 5-2 in the Division Three Final.

2004: Three tight, tense Finals produced only two goals, the lowest number since the Play-offs were introduced. One of them, scored by Neil Shipperley, gave **Crystal Palace** victory over West Ham, the much-travelled striker tapping in a rebound after Stephen Bywater parried Andy Johnson's shot. It completed a remarkable transformation for Crystal Palace, who were 19th in the table when Iain Dowie left Oldham to become their manager. **Brighton** made an immediate return to Division One in a poor game against Bristol City which looked set for extra-time until Leon Knight netted his 27th goal of the campaign from the penalty spot after 84 minutes. **Huddersfield** also went back up at the first attempt, winning the Division Three Final in a penalty shoot-out after a goalless 120 minutes against Mansfield.

2005: Goals were few and far between for Bobby Zamora during **West Ham**'s Championship season – but what a difference in the Play-offs. The former Brighton and Tottenham striker scored three times in the 4-2 aggregate win over Ipswich in the semi-finals and was on the mark again with the only goal against Preston at the Millennium Stadium. **Sheffield Wed** were eight minute away from defeat against Hartlepool in the League One decider when Steven MacLean made it 2-2 from the penalty spot and they went on to win 4-2 in extra-time. **Southend**, edged out of an automatic promotion place, won the League Two Final 2-0 against Lincoln, Freddy Eastwood scoring their first in extra-time and making the second for Duncan Jupp. **Carlisle** beat Stevenage 1-0 with a goal by Peter Murphy in the Conference Final to regain their League place 12 months after being relegated.

2006: From the moment Marlon King scored his 22nd goal of the season to set up a 3-0 win over Crystal Palace in the semi-final first leg, **Watford** had the conviction of a team going places. Sure enough, they went on to beat Leeds just as comfortably in the final. Jay DeMerit, who was playing non-league football 18 months earlier, headed his side in front. James Chambers fired in a shot that hit a post and went in off goalkeeper Neil Sullivan. Then Darius Henderson put away a penalty after King was brought down by Shaun Derry, the man whose tackle had ended Boothroyd's playing career at the age of 26. **Barnsley** beat Swansea on penalties in the League One Final, Nick Colgan making the vital save from Alan Tate, while Steve Guinan's goal earned **Cheltenham** a 1-0 win over Grimsby in the League Two Final. **Hereford** returned to the Football League after a nine-year absence with Ryan Green's extra-time winner against Halifax in the Conference Final.

2007: Record crowds, plenty of goals and a return to Wembley for the finals made for some eventful and entertaining matches. Stephen Pearson, signed from Celtic for £650,000 in the January transfer window, took **Derby** back to the Premier League after an absence of five seasons with a 61st minute winner, his first goal for the club, against accounted for West Bromwich Albion. It was third time lucky for manager Billy Davies, who had led Preston into the play-offs, without success, in the two previous seasons. **Blackpool** claimed a place in the game's second tier for the first time for 30 years by beating Yeovil 2-0 – their tenth successive victory in a remarkable end-of-season run. Richard Walker took his tally for the season to 23 with two goals for **Bristol Rov**, who beat Shrewsbury 3-1 in the League Two Final. Sammy McIlroy, who led Macclesfield into the league in 1997, saw his Morecambe side fall behind in the Conference Final against Exeter, but they recovered to win 2-1.

2008: Wembley has produced some unlikely heroes down the years, but rarely one to match 39-year-old Dean Windass. The **Hull** striker took his home-town club into the top-flight for the first time with the only goal of the Championship Final against Bristol City – and it was a goal fit to grace any game. In front of a record crowd for the final of 86,703, Fraizer Campbell, his 20-year-old partner up front, picked out Windass on the edge of the penalty box and a sweetly-struck volley flew into the net. **Doncaster**, who like Hull faced an uncertain future a few years earlier, beat Leeds 1-0 in the League One Final with a header by James Hayer from Brian Stock's corner. Jim Gannon had lost four Wembley finals with **Stockport** as a player, but his first as manager brought a 3-2 win against Rochdale in the League Two Final with goals by Anthony Pilkington and Liam Dickinson and a Nathan Stanton own goal. Exeter's 1-0 win over Cambridge United in the Conference Final took them back into the Football League after an absence of five years.

2009: Delight for Burnley, back in the big time after 33 years thanks to a fine goal from 20 yards by Wade Elliott, and for their town which became the smallest to host Premier League football. Despair for Sheffield Utd, whose bid to regain a top-flight place ended with two players, Jamie Ward and Lee Hendrie, sent off by referee Mike Dean. Martyn Woolford capped a man-of-the-match performance with an 85th minute winner for Scunthorpe, who beat Millwall 3-2 to make an immediate return to the Championship, Matt Sparrow having scored their first two goals. Gillingham also went back up at the first attempt, beating Shrewsbury with Simeon Jackson's header seconds from the end of normal time in the League Two Final. Torquay returned to the Football League after a two-year absence by beating Cambridge United 2-0 in the Conference Final.

2010: Blackpool, under the eccentric yet shrewd Ian Holloway, claimed the big prize two years almost to the day after the manager was sacked from his previous job at Leicester. On a scorching afternoon, with temperatures reaching 106 degrees, they twice came back from a goal down to draw level against Cardiff through Charlie Adam and Gary Taylor-Fletcher, then scored what proved to be the winner through Brett Ormerod at the end of a pulsating first half. **Millwall,** beaten in five previous play-offs, reached the Championship with the only goal of the game against Swindon from captain Paul Robinson. **Dagenham & Redbridge** defeated Rotherham 3-2 in the League Two Final, Jon Nurse scoring the winner 20 minutes from the end. **Oxford** returned to the Football League after an absence of four years with a 3-1 over York in the Conference Final.

2011: Scott Sinclair scored a hat-trick as **Swansea** reached the top flight, just eight years after almost going out of the Football League. Two of his goals came from the penalty spot as Reading were beaten 4-2 in the Championship Final, with Stephen Dobbie netting their other goal. The day after his father's side lost to Barcelona in the Champions League Final, Darren Ferguson led **Peterborough** back to the Championship at the first attempt with goals by Tommy Rowe, Craig Mackail-Smith and Grant McCann in the final 12 minutes against Huddersfield. John Mousinho scored the only one of the League Two Final for **Stevenage,** who won a second successive promotion by beating Torquay. **AFC Wimbledon,** formed by supporters in 2002 after the former FA Cup-winning club relocated to Milton Keynes, completed their rise from the Combined Counties to the Football League by winning a penalty shoot-out against Luton after a goalless draw in the Conference Final.

2012: West Ham were third at the Championship and second best to Blackpool in the final. But they passed the post first at Wembley, thanks to an 87th minute goal from Ricardo Vaz Te which gave Sam Allardyce's side a 2-1 victory. Allardyce brought the Portuguese striker to Upton Park from Barnsley for £500,000 – a fee dwarfed by the millions his goal was worth to the club. Goalkeepers took centre stage in the League One Final, with **Huddersfield** and Sheffield United still locked in a marathon shoot-out after a goalless 120 minutes. Alex Smithies put the 21st penalty past his opposite number Steve Simonsen, who then drove over the crossbar to give Huddersfield victory by 8-7. Nick Powell, 18, lit up the League Two Final with a spectacular volley as **Crewe** beat Cheltenham 2-0. **York** regained a Football League place after an absence of eight years by beating Luton 2-1 in the Conference decider.

2013: Veteran Kevin Phillips, a loser in three previous finals, came off the bench to fire **Crystal Palace** into the Premier League with an extra-time penalty. Wilfried Zaha was brought down by Marco Cassetti and 39-year-old Phillips showed nerves of steel to convert the spot-kick. A goalline clearance by Joel Ward then denied Fernando Forestieri as Watford sought an equaliser. **Yeovil** upset the odds by reaching the Championship for the first time. They defeated Brentford 2-1, Paddy Madden scoring his 23rd goal of the season and on-loan Dan Burn adding the second. **Bradford,** back at Wembley three months after their Capital One Cup adventure, swept aside Northampton 3-0 in the League Two Final with goals from James Hanson, Rory McArdle and Nahki Wells. **Newport** returned to the Football League after a 25-year absence by defeating Wrexham 2-0 in the Conference Final.

2014: An immediate return to the Premier League for **Queens Park Rangers** seemed unlikely when Gary O'Neil was sent off for bringing down Derby's Johnny Russell. There was still more than half-an-hour to go of a match Derby had dominated. But Rangers held on and with 90 minutes nearly up Bobby Zamora punished a mistake by captain Richard Keogh to score the only goal. **Rotherham** retrieved a 2-0 deficit against Leyton Orient with two goals by Alex Revell in the League One Final and won the eventual penalty shoot-out 4-3 for a second successive promotion. **Fleetwood** achieved their sixth promotion in ten seasons with a 1-0 victory over Burton, courtesy of a free-kick from Antoni Sarcevic in the League Two Final. Liam Hughes and Ryan Donaldson were on the mark as **Cambridge United** returned to the Football League after a nine-year absence by beating Gateshead 2-1 in the Conference Final, two months after winning the FA Trophy at Wembley

2015: **Norwich** were rewarded for a flying start with a return to the Premier League at the first attempt. Cameron Jerome put them ahead against Middlesbrough after 12 minutes of the Championship Final and Nathan Redmond made it 2-0 three minutes later, a scoreline they maintained without too many problems. Jermaine Beckford's hat-trick put **Preston** on the way to a record 4-0 victory over Swindon in the League One Final. **Southend**, who like Preston were denied automatic promotion on the final day of the regular season, beat Wycombe 7-6 on penalties after the League Two Final ended 1-1. **Bristol Rovers** were also penalty winners, by 5-3 against Grimsby in the Conference decider, so making an immediate return to the Football League.

2016: A goal worthy of winning any game took Hull back to the Premier League at the first attempt. Mohamed Diame, their French-born Senegal international midfielder, curled a 25-yard shot into the top corner after 72 minues for a 1-0 win over Sheffield Wednesday. Another spectacular goal, by Adam Hammill, helped Barnsley beat Millwall 3-1 on their return to Wembley for the League One Final after winning the Johnstone's Paint Trophy. AFC Wimbledon achieved their sixth promotion since being formed by supporters in 2002, defeating favourites Plymouth 2-0 in the League Two Final. Grimsby ended a six-year absence from the Football League with a 3-1 victory over Forest Green in the National League decider

2017: David Wagner transformed **Huddersfield** from relegation candidates into a Premier League club – with the help of German penalty-taking expertise. After a goalless Championship Play-off Final, they beat Reading 4-3 in a shoot-out clinched by Christopher Schindler'spot-kick. Steve Morison followed up his two goals in **Millwall**'s League One semi-final against Scunthorpe with the only one against Bradford, in the 85th minute at Wembley. Brad Potts and Mark Cullen were on the mark to give **Blackpool** a 2-1 victory over Exeter in the League Two Final. **Forest Green** beat Tranmere 3-1 in the National League Final, on-loan Kaiyne Woolery scoring twice.

2018: **Fulham** overcame the sending-off of central defender Denis Odoi after 70 minutes for a second yellow card to reach the Premier League. They protected the lead established by a goal from captain Tom Cairney, set up by the Championship's Player of the Year, 18-year-old Ryan Sessegnon, to defeat Aston Villa 1-0. There was another captain's performance in the League One Final, Richard Wood scoring both goals in **Rotherham**'s 2-1 win over Shrewsbury. **Coventry** ended years of decline by beating Exeter 3-1 in the League Two Final with goals from Jordan Willis, Jordan Shipley and Jack Grimmer. **Tranmere** had Liam Ridehalgh dismissed after 48 seconds for a two-footed challenge, but were 2-1 winners over Boreham Wood in the National League Final (Andy Cook and James Norwood).

2019: **Aston Villa** made a royal return to the Premier League after a three-year absence by defeating Derby 2-1. Prince William, a supporter of the club, joined the celebrations at Wembley after loanee Anwar El Ghazi and bargain-buy John McGinn scored the goals to complete the club's renaissance under former Brentford manager Dean Smith. **Charlton** recovered from Naby Sarr's bizarre own goal – a back-pass missed by goalkeeper Dillon Phillips – to equalise through Ben Purrington and beat Sunderland with captain Patrick Bauer's goal seconds from time. **Tranmere** made a successful return to the national stadium after winning the National League decider in 2018, scoring the only goal against Newport through Connor Jennings. **Salford**, co-owned by six former Manchester United players, defeated AFC Fylde 3-0 in the National League decider to reach the Football League for the first time.

2020: Full-back Joe Bryan scored both goals as **Fulham** returned to the Premier League at the first attempt with a 2-1 win over Brentford after a goalless 90 minutes in the Championship Final. He deceived goalkeeper David Raya with a low, skidding free-kick, then combined with leading marksman Aleksandar Mitrovic for the second. Henrik Dalsgaard replied in stoppage-time. Two more defenders put unfancied **Wycombe** into the second tier. Anthony Stewart scored from Joe Jacobson's corner and Jacobson converted a penalty to overcome Oxford 2-1 in the League One Final. **Northampton** defeated ten-man Exeter 4-0 in the League Two decider after Dean Moxey was shown a straight red card at 2-0.

2021: Thomas Frank led **Brentford** into the Premier League with a 2-0 victory over Swansea which he believed could inspire more smaller clubs to aim for the top. Frank lost Ollie Watkins and Said Benrahma from the side beaten by Fulham in the 2020 final. But they regrouped and had the match under control with barely 20 minutes gone. Ivan Toney, the Championship's leading scorer, put them ahead from the penalty spot and Emiliano Marcondes finished superbly for the second. Australian midfielder Kenny Dougall, with a single goal to his name in the regular season, scored twice to give **Blackpool** a 2-1 win over Lincoln in the League One decider. **Morecambe** reached the third tier for the first time by beating Newport 1-0 with an extra-time penalty from Carlos Mendes Gomes.

Play-off attendances

1987	20	310,000	2005	15	353,330
1988	19	305,817	2006	15	340,804
1989	18	234,393	2007	15	405,278
1990	15	291,428	2008	15	382,032
1991	15	266,442	2009	15	380,329
1992	15	277,684	2010	15	370,055
1993	15	319,907	2011	15	310,998
1994	15	314,817	2012	15	332,930
1995	15	295,317	2013	15	346,062
1996	15	308,515	2014	15	307,011
1997	15	309,085	2015	15	367,374
1998	15	320,795	2016	15	393,145
1999	15	372,969	2017	15	323,727
2000	15	333,999	2018	15	373,295
2001	15	317,745	2019	15	430,025 (record)
2002	15	327,894	2020		No attendances – Covid
2003	15	374,461	2021		Limited attendances – Covid
2004	15	388,675	2022	15	422,868

THE THINGS THEY SAY ...

'The Champions League Final should be one of the finest spectacles in football and it resulted in one of the worst experiences of many supporters' lives' – **Billy Hogan**, Liverpool chief executive, rejecting UEFA's claim that his club's fans were responsible for ugly scenes at the Stade de France.

'UEFA wishes to sincerely apologise to all spectators who had to experience or witness frightening and distressing events on a night which should have been a celebration of European club football' – **European governing body** backs down six days after the match.

'Where's the final next year? Istanbul? Book the hotel' – **Jurgen Klopp**, Liverpool manager, tells his club's fans their team will be back.

'Four Premier Leagues – these guys are legends, absolutely eternal in this club' – **Pep Guardiola**, Manchester City manager, hails his title-winning players.

'We are honoured to become the new custodians of this club. We are all in 100 per cent – every minute of every match' – **Todd Boehly**, head of the consortium which paid £4.25bn to take over Chelsea.

ENGLISH HONOURS LIST

PREMIER LEAGUE

	First	Pts	Second	Pts	Third	Pts
1992–3a	Manchester Utd	84	Aston Villa	74	Norwich	72
1993–4a	Manchester Utd	92	Blackburn	84	Newcastle	77
1994–5a	Blackburn	89	Manchester Utd	88	Nottm Forest	77
1995–6b	Manchester Utd	82	Newcastle	78	Liverpool	71
1996–7b	Manchester Utd	75	Newcastle	68	Arsenal	68
1997–8b	Arsenal	78	Manchester Utd	77	Liverpool	65
1998–9b	Manchester Utd	79	Arsenal	78	Chelsea	75
1999–00b	Manchester Utd	91	Arsenal	73	Leeds	69
2000–01b	Manchester Utd	80	Arsenal	70	Liverpool	69
2001–02b	Arsenal	87	Liverpool	80	Manchester Utd	77
2002–03b	Manchester Utd	83	Arsenal	78	Newcastle	69
2003–04b	Arsenal	90	Chelsea	79	Manchester Utd	75
2004–05b	Chelsea	95	Arsenal	83	Manchester Utd	77
2005–06b	Chelsea	91	Manchester Utd	83	Liverpool	82
2006–07b	Manchester Utd	89	Chelsea	83	Liverpool	68
2007–08b	Manchester Utd	87	Chelsea	85	Arsenal	83
2008–09b	Manchester Utd	90	Liverpool	86	Chelsea	83
2009–10b	Chelsea	86	Manchester Utd	85	Arsenal	75
2010–11b	Manchester Utd	80	Chelsea	71	Manchester City	71
2011–12b	Manchester City*	89	Manchester Ud	89	Arsenal	70
2012–13b	Manchester Utd	89	Manchester City	78	Chelsea	75
2013–14b	Manchester City	86	Liverpool	84	Chelsea	82
2014–15b	Chelsea	87	Manchester City	79	Arsenal	75
2015–16b	Leicester	81	Arsenal	71	Tottenham	70
2016–17b	Chelsea	93	Tottenham	86	Manchester City	78
2017–18b	Manchester City	100	Manchester Utd	81	Tottenham	77
2018–19b	Manchester City	98	Liverpool	97	Chelsea	72
2019–20b	Liverpool	99	Manchester City	81	Manchester Utd	66
2020–21b	Manchester City	86	Manchester Utd	74	Liverpool	69
2021–22b	Manchester City	93	Liverpool	92	Chelsea	74

* won on goal difference. Maximum points: a, 126; b, 114

FOOTBALL LEAGUE

FIRST DIVISION

1992–3	Newcastle	96	West Ham	88	††Portsmouth	88
1993–4	Crystal Palace	90	Nottm Forest	83	††Millwall	74
1994–5	Middlesbrough	82	††Reading	79	Bolton	77
1995–6	Sunderland	83	Derby	79	††Crystal Palace	75
1996–7	Bolton	98	Barnsley	80	††Wolves	76
1997–8	Nottm Forest	94	Middlesbrough	91	††Sunderland	90
1998–9	Sunderland	105	Bradford City	87	††Ipswich	86
1999–00	Charlton	91	Manchester City	89	Ipswich	87
2000–01	Fulham	101	Blackburn	91	Bolton	87
2001–02	Manchester City	99	WBA	89	††Wolves	86
2002–03	Portsmouth	98	Leicester	92	††Sheffield Utd	80
2003–04	Norwich	94	WBA	86	††Sunderland	79

CHAMPIONSHIP

2004–05	Sunderland	94	Wigan	87	††Ipswich	85
2005–06	Reading	106	Sheffield Utd	90	Watford	81
2006–07	Sunderland	88	Birmingham	86	Derby	84

2007–08	WBA	81	Stoke	79	Hull	75
2008–09	Wolves	90	Birmingham	83	††Sheffield Utd	80
2009–10	Newcastle	102	WBA	91	††Nottm Forest	79
2010–11	QPR	88	Norwich	84	Swansea	80
2011–12	Reading	89	Southampton	88	West Ham	86
2012–13	Cardiff	87	Hull	79	††Watford	77
2013–14	Leicester	102	Burnley	93	††Derby	85
2014–15	Bournemouth	90	Watford	89	Norwich	86
2015–16	Burnley	93	Middlesbrough	89	††Brighton	89
2016–17	Newcastle	94	Brighton	93	††Reading	85
2017–18	Wolves	99	Cardiff	90	Fulham	88
2018–19	Norwich	94	Sheffield Utd	89	††Leeds	83
2019–20	Leeds	93	WBA	83	††Brentford	81
2020–21	Norwich	97	Watford	91	Brentford	87
2021–22	Fulham	90	Bournemouth	88	††Huddersfield	82

Maximum points: 138 ††Not promoted after play–offs

SECOND DIVISION

1992–3	Stoke	93	Bolton	90	††Port Vale	89
1993–4	Reading	89	Port Vale	88	††Plymouth Argyle	85
1994–5	Birmingham	89	††Brentford	85	††Crewe	83
1995–6	Swindon	92	Oxford Utd	83	††Blackpool	82
1996–7	Bury	84	Stockport	82	††Luton	78
1997–8	Watford	88	Bristol City	85	Grimsby	72
1998–9	Fulham	101	Walsall	87	Manchester City	82
1999–00	Preston	95	Burnley	88	Gillingham	85
2000–01	Millwall	93	Rotherham	91	††Reading	86
2001–02	Brighton	90	Reading	84	††Brentford	83
2002–03	Wigan	100	Crewe	86	††Bristol City	83
2003–04	Plymouth Argyle	90	QPR	83	††Bristol City	82

LEAGUE ONE

2004–05	Luton	98	Hull	86	††Tranmere	79
2005–06	Southend	82	Colchester	79	††Brentford	76
2006–07	Scunthorpe	91	Bristol City	85	Blackpool	83
2007–08	Swansea	92	Nottm Forest	82	Doncaster	80
2008–09	Leicester	96	Peterborough	89	††MK Dons	87
2009–10	Norwich	95	Leeds	86	Millwall	85
2010–11	Brighton	95	Southampton	92	††Huddersfield	87
2011–12	Charlton	101	Sheffield Wed	93	††Sheffield Utd	90
2012–13	Doncaster	84	Bournemouth	83	††Brentford	79
2013–14	Wolves	103	Brentford	94	††Leyton Orient	86
2014–15	Bristol City	99	MK Dons	91	Preston	89
2015–16	Wigan	87	Burton	85	††Walsall	84
2016–17	Sheffield Utd	100	Bolton	86	††Scunthorpe	82
2017–18	Wigan	98	Blackburn	96	††Shrewsbury	87
2018–19	Luton	94	Barnsley	91	Charlton	88
2019–20a	Coventry	67	Rotherham	62	Wycombe	59
2020–21	Hull	89	Peterborough	87	Blackpool	80
2021–22	Wigan	92	Rotherham	90	††MK Dons	89

a season abandoned – Covid-19; points-per-game decided final positions
Maximum points: 138 †† Not promoted after play–offs

THIRD DIVISION

1992–3a	Cardiff	83	Wrexham	80	Barnet	79
1993–4a	Shrewsbury	79	Chester	74	Crewe	73
1994–5a	Carlisle	91	Walsall	83	Chesterfield	81
1995–6b	Preston	86	Gillingham	83	Bury	79

1996–7b	Wigan	87	Fulham	87	Carlisle	84
1997–8b	Notts Co	99	Macclesfield	82	Lincoln	75
1998–9b	Brentford	85	Cambridge Utd	81	Cardiff	80
1999–00b	Swansea	85	Rotherham	84	Northampton	82
2000–01b	Brighton	92	Cardiff	82	*Chesterfield	80
2001–02b	Plymouth Argyle	102	Luton	97	Mansfield	79
2002–03b	Rushden & D	87	Hartlepool Utd	85	Wrexham	84
2003–04b	Doncaster	92	Hull	88	Torquay	81

* Deducted 9 points for financial irregularities

LEAGUE TWO

2004–05b	Yeovil	83	Scunthorpe	80	Swansea	80
2005–06b	Carlisle	86	Northampton	83	Leyton Orient	81
2006–07b	Walsall	89	Hartlepool	88	Swindon	85
2007–08b	MK Dons	97	Peterborough	92	Hereford	88
2008–09b	Brentford	85	Exeter	79	Wycombe	78
2009–10b	Notts Co	93	Bournemouth	83	Rochdale	82
2010–11b	Chesterfield	86	Bury	81	Wycombe	80
2011–12b	Swindon	93	Shrewsbury	88	Crawley	84
2012–13b	Gillingham	83	Rotherham	79	Port Vale	78
2013–14b	Chesterfield	84	Scunthorpe	81	Rochdale	81
2014–15b	Burton	94	Shrewsbury	89	Bury	85
2015–16b	Northampton	99	Oxford	86	Bristol Rov	85
2016–17b	Portsmouth	87	Plymouth	87	Doncaster	85
2017–18b	Accrington	93	Luton	88	Wycombe	84
2018–19b	Lincoln	85	Bury	79	MK Dons	79
2019–20c	Swindon	69	Crewe	69	Plymouth	68
2020–21b	Cheltenham	82	Cambridge	80	Bolton	79
2021–22b	Forest Green*	84	Exeter	84	Bristol Rov	80

c season abandoned – Covid 19; points-per-game decided final positions. Won on goal difference
Maximum points: a, 126; b, 138

FOOTBALL LEAGUE 1888–1992

1888–89a	Preston	40	Aston Villa	29	Wolves	28
1889–90a	Preston	33	Everton	31	Blackburn	27
1890–1a	Everton	29	Preston	27	Notts Co	26
1891–2b	Sunderland	42	Preston	37	Bolton	36

OLD FIRST DIVISION

1892–3c	Sunderland	48	Preston	37	Everton	36
1893–4c	Aston Villa	44	Sunderland	38	Derby	36
1894–5c	Sunderland	47	Everton	42	Aston Villa	39
1895–6c	Aston Villa	45	Derby	41	Everton	39
1896–7c	Aston Villa	47	Sheffield Utd	36	Derby	36
1897–8c	Sheffield Utd	42	Sunderland	39	Wolves	35
1898–9d	Aston Villa	45	Liverpool	43	Burnley	39
1899–1900d	Aston Villa	50	Sheffield Utd	48	Sunderland	41
1900–1d	Liverpool	45	Sunderland	43	Notts Co	40
1901–2d	Sunderland	44	Everton	41	Newcastle	37
1902–3d	The Wednesday	42	Aston Villa	41	Sunderland	41
1903–4d	The Wednesday	47	Manchester City	44	Everton	43
1904–5d	Newcastle	48	Everton	47	Manchester City	46
1905–6e	Liverpool	51	Preston	47	The Wednesday	46
1906–7e	Newcastle	51	Bristol City	48	Everton	45
1907–8e	Manchester Utd	52	Aston Villa	43	Manchester City	43
1908–9e	Newcastle	53	Everton	46	Sunderland	44

1909–10e	Aston Villa	53	Liverpool	48	Blackburn	45
1910–11e	Manchester Utd	52	Aston Villa	51	Sunderland	45
1911–12e	Blackburn	49	Everton	46	Newcastle	44
1912–13e	Sunderland	54	Aston Villa	50	Sheffield Wed	49
1913–14e	Blackburn	51	Aston Villa	44	Middlesbrough	43
1914–15e	Everton	46	Oldham	45	Blackburn	43
1919–20f	WBA	60	Burnley	51	Chelsea	49
1920–1f	Burnley	59	Manchester City	54	Bolton	52
1921–2f	Liverpool	57	Tottenham	51	Burnley	49
1922–3f	Liverpool	60	Sunderland	54	Huddersfield	53
1923–4f	*Huddersfield	57	Cardiff	57	Sunderland	53
1924–5f	Huddersfield	58	WBA	56	Bolton	55
1925–6f	Huddersfield	57	Arsenal	52	Sunderland	48
1926–7f	Newcastle	56	Huddersfield	51	Sunderland	49
1927–8f	Everton	53	Huddersfield	51	Leicester	48
1928–9f	Sheffield Wed	52	Leicester	51	Aston Villa	50
1929–30f	Sheffield Wed	60	Derby	50	Manchester City	47
1930–1f	Arsenal	66	Aston Villa	59	Sheffield Wed	52
1931–2f	Everton	56	Arsenal	54	Sheffield Wed	50
1932–3f	Arsenal	58	Aston Villa	54	Sheffield Wed	51
1933–4f	Arsenal	59	Huddersfield	56	Tottenham	49
1934–5f	Arsenal	58	Sunderland	54	Sheffield Wed	49
1935–6f	Sunderland	56	Derby	48	Huddersfield	48
1936–7f	Manchester City	57	Charlton	54	Arsenal	52
1937–8f	Arsenal	52	Wolves	51	Preston	49
1938–9f	Everton	59	Wolves	55	Charlton	50
1946–7f	Liverpool	57	Manchester Utd	56	Wolves	56
1947–8f	Arsenal	59	Manchester Utd	52	Burnley	52
1948–9f	Portsmouth	58	Manchester Utd	53	Derby	53
1949–50f	*Portsmouth	53	Wolves	53	Sunderland	52
1950–1f	Tottenham	60	Manchester Utd	56	Blackpool	50
1951–2f	Manchester Utd	57	Tottenham	53	Arsenal	53
1952–3f	*Arsenal	54	Preston	54	Wolves	51
1953–4f	Wolves	57	WBA	53	Huddersfield	51
1954–5f	Chelsea	52	Wolves	48	Portsmouth	48
1955–6f	Manchester Utd	60	Blackpool	49	Wolves	49
1956–7f	Manchester Utd	64	Tottenham	56	Preston	56
1957–8f	Wolves	64	Preston	59	Tottenham	51
1958–9f	Wolves	61	Manchester Utd	55	Arsenal	50
1959–60f	Burnley	55	Wolves	54	Tottenham	53
1960–1f	Tottenham	66	Sheffield Wed	58	Wolves	57
1961–2f	Ipswich	56	Burnley	53	Tottenham	52
1962–3f	Everton	61	Tottenham	55	Burnley	54
1963–4f	Liverpool	57	Manchester Utd	53	Everton	52
1964–5f	*Manchester Utd	61	Leeds	61	Chelsea	56
1965–6f	Liverpool	61	Leeds	55	Burnley	55
1966–7f	Manchester Utd	60	Nottm Forest	56	Tottenham	56
1967–8f	Manchester City	58	Manchester Utd	56	Liverpool	55
1968–9f	Leeds	67	Liverpool	61	Everton	57
1969–70f	Everton	66	Leeds	57	Chelsea	55
1970–1f	Arsenal	65	Leeds	64	Tottenham	52
1971–2f	Derby	58	Leeds	57	Liverpool	57
1972–3f	Liverpool	60	Arsenal	57	Leeds	53
1973–4f	Leeds	62	Liverpool	57	Derby	48

1974–5f	Derby	53	Liverpool	51	Ipswich	51
1975–6f	Liverpool	60	QPR	59	Manchester Utd	56
1976–7f	Liverpool	57	Manchester City	56	Ipswich	52
1977–8f	Nottm Forest	64	Liverpool	57	Everton	55
1978–9f	Liverpool	68	Nottm Forest	60	WBA	59
1979–80f	Liverpool	60	Manchester Utd	58	Ipswich	53
1980–1f	Aston Villa	60	Ipswich	56	Arsenal	53
1981–2g	Liverpool	87	Ipswich	83	Manchester Utd	78
1982–3g	Liverpool	82	Watford	71	Manchester Utd	70
1983–4g	Liverpool	80	Southampton	77	Nottm Forest	74
1984–5g	Everton	90	Liverpool	77	Tottenham	77
1985–6g	Liverpool	88	Everton	86	West Ham	84
1986–7g	Everton	86	Liverpool	77	Tottenham	71
1987–8h	Liverpool	90	Manchester Utd	81	Nottm Forest	73
1988–9j	††Arsenal	76	Liverpool	76	Nottm Forest	64
1989–90j	Liverpool	79	Aston Villa	70	Tottenham	63
1990–1j	Arsenal	83	Liverpool	76	Crystal Palace	69
1991–2g	Leeds	82	Manchester Utd	78	Sheffield Wed	75

Maximum points: a, 44; b, 52; c, 60; d, 68; e, 76; f, 84; g, 126; h, 120; j, 114
*Won on goal average †Won on goal diff ††Won on goals scored No comp 1915–19 –1939–46

OLD SECOND DIVISION 1892–1992

1892–3a	Small Heath	36	Sheffield Utd	35	Darwen	30
1893–4b	Liverpool	50	Small Heath	42	Notts Co	39
1894–5c	Bury	48	Notts Co	39	Newton Heath	38
1895–6c	*Liverpool	46	Manchester City	46	Grimsby	42
1896–7c	Notts Co	42	Newton Heath	39	Grimsby	38
1897–8c	Burnley	48	Newcastle	45	Manchester City	39
1898–9d	Manchester City	52	Glossop	46	Leicester Fosse	45
1899–1900d	The Wednesday	54	Bolton	52	Small Heath	46
1900–1d	Grimsby	49	Small Heath	48	Burnley	44
1901–2d	WBA	55	Middlesbrough	51	Preston	42
1902–3d	Manchester City	54	Small Heath	51	Woolwich Arsenal	48
1903–4d	Preston	50	Woolwich Arsenal	49	Manchester Utd	48
1904–5d	Liverpool	58	Bolton	56	Manchester Utd	53
1905–6e	Bristol City	66	Manchester Utd	62	Chelsea	53
1906–7e	Nottm Forest	60	Chelsea	57	Leicester Fosse	48
1907–8e	Bradford City	54	Leicester Fosse	52	Oldham	50
1908–9e	Bolton	52	Tottenham	51	WBA	51
1909–10e	Manchester City	54	Oldham	53	Hull	53
1910–11e	WBA	53	Bolton	51	Chelsea	49
1911–12e	*Derby	54	Chelsea	54	Burnley	52
1912–13e	Preston	53	Burnley	50	Birmingham	46
1913–14e	Notts Co	53	Bradford PA	49	Woolwich Arsenal	49
1914–15e	Derby	53	Preston	50	Barnsley	47
1919–20f	Tottenham	70	Huddersfield	64	Birmingham	56
1920–1f	*Birmingham	58	Cardiff	58	Bristol City	51
1921–2f	Nottm Forest	56	Stoke	52	Barnsley	52
1922–3f	Notts Co	53	West Ham	51	Leicester	51
1923–4f	Leeds	54	Bury	51	Derby	51
1924–5f	Leicester	59	Manchester Utd	57	Derby	55
1925–6f	Sheffield Wed	60	Derby	57	Chelsea	52
1926–7f	Middlesbrough	62	Portsmouth	54	Manchester City	54
1927–8f	Manchester City	59	Leeds	57	Chelsea	54
1928–9f	Middlesbrough	55	Grimsby	53	Bradford City	48

1929–30f	Blackpool	58	Chelsea	55	Oldham	53
1930–1f	Everton	61	WBA	54	Tottenham	51
1931–2f	Wolves	56	Leeds	54	Stoke	52
1932–3f	Stoke	56	Tottenham	55	Fulham	50
1933–4f	Grimsby	59	Preston	52	Bolton	51
1934–5f	Brentford	61	Bolton	56	West Ham	56
1935–6f	Manchester Utd	56	Charlton	55	Sheffield Utd	52
1936–7f	Leicester	56	Blackpool	55	Bury	52
1937–8f	Aston Villa	57	Manchester Utd	53	Sheffield Utd	53
1938–9f	Blackburn	55	Sheffield Utd	54	Sheffield Wed	53
1946–7f	Manchester City	62	Burnley	58	Birmingham	55
1947–8f	Birmingham	59	Newcastle	56	Southampton	52
1948–9f	Fulham	57	WBA	56	Southampton	55
1949–50f	Tottenham	61	Sheffield Wed	52	Sheffield Utd	52
1950–1f	Preston	57	Manchester City	52	Cardiff	50
1951–2f	Sheffield Wed	53	Cardiff	51	Birmingham	51
1952–3f	Sheffield Utd	60	Huddersfield	58	Luton	52
1953–4f	*Leicester	56	Everton	56	Blackburn	55
1954–5f	*Birmingham	54	Luton	54	Rotherham	54
1955–6f	Sheffield Wed	55	Leeds	52	Liverpool	48
1956–7f	Leicester	61	Nottm Forest	54	Liverpool	53
1957–8f	West Ham	57	Blackburn	56	Charlton	55
1958–9f	Sheffield Wed	62	Fulham	60	Sheffield Utd	53
1959–60f	Aston Villa	59	Cardiff	58	Liverpool	50
1960–1f	Ipswich	59	Sheffield Utd	58	Liverpool	52
1961–2f	Liverpool	62	Leyton Orient	54	Sunderland	53
1962–3f	Stoke	53	Chelsea	52	Sunderland	52
1963–4f	Leeds	63	Sunderland	61	Preston	56
1964–5f	Newcastle	57	Northampton	56	Bolton	50
1965–6f	Manchester City	59	Southampton	54	Coventry	53
1966–7f	Coventry	59	Wolves	58	Carlisle	52
1967–8f	Ipswich	59	QPR	58	Blackpool	58
1968–9f	Derby	63	Crystal Palace	56	Charlton	50
1969–70f	Huddersfield	60	Blackpool	53	Leicester	51
1970–1f	Leicester	59	Sheffield Utd	56	Cardiff	53
1971–2f	Norwich	57	Birmingham	56	Millwall	55
1972–3f	Burnley	62	QPR	61	Aston Villa	50
1973–4f	Middlesbrough	65	Luton	50	Carlisle	49
1974–5f	Manchester Utd	61	Aston Villa	58	Norwich	53
1975–6f	Sunderland	56	Bristol City	53	WBA	53
1976–7f	Wolves	57	Chelsea	55	Nottm Forest	52
1977–8f	Bolton	58	Southampton	57	Tottenham	56
1978–9f	Crystal Palace	57	Brighton	56	Stoke	56
1979–80f	Leicester	55	Sunderland	54	Birmingham	53
1980–1f	West Ham	66	Notts Co	53	Swansea	50
1981–2g	Luton	88	Watford	80	Norwich	71
1982–3g	QPR	85	Wolves	75	Leicester	70
1983–4g	†Chelsea	88	Sheffield Wed	88	Newcastle	80
1984–5g	Oxford Utd	84	Birmingham	82	Manchester City	74
1985–6g	Norwich	84	Charlton	77	Wimbledon	76
1986–7g	Derby	84	Portsmouth	78	††Oldham	75
1987–8h	Millwall	82	Aston Villa	78	Middlesbrough	78
1988–9j	Chelsea	99	Manchester City	82	Crystal Palace	81
1989–90j	†Leeds	85	Sheffield Utd	85	†† Newcastle	80

| 1990–1j | Oldham | 88 | West Ham | 87 | Sheffield Wed | 82 |
| 1991–2j | Ipswich | 84 | Middlesbrough | 80 | †† Derby | 78 |

Maximum points: *a*, 44; *b*, 56; *c*, 60; *d*, 68; *e*, 76; *f*, 84; *g*, 126; *h*, 132; *j*, 138 * Won on goal average † Won on goal difference †† Not promoted after play-offs

THIRD DIVISION 1958–92

1958–9	Plymouth Argyle	62	Hull	61	Brentford	57
1959–60	Southampton	61	Norwich	59	Shrewsbury	52
1960–1	Bury	68	Walsall	62	QPR	60
1961–2	Portsmouth	65	Grimsby	62	Bournemouth	59
1962–3	Northampton	62	Swindon	58	Port Vale	54
1963–4	*Coventry	60	Crystal Palace	60	Watford	58
1964–5	Carlisle	60	Bristol City	59	Mansfield	59
1965–6	Hull	69	Millwall	65	QPR	57
1966–7	QPR	67	Middlesbrough	55	Watford	54
1967–8	Oxford Utd	57	Bury	56	Shrewsbury	55
1968–9	*Watford	64	Swindon	64	Luton	61
1969–70	Orient	62	Luton	60	Bristol Rov	56
1970–1	Preston	61	Fulham	60	Halifax	56
1971–2	Aston Villa	70	Brighton	65	Bournemouth	62
1972–3	Bolton	61	Notts Co	57	Blackburn	55
1973–4	Oldham	62	Bristol Rov	61	York	61
1974–5	Blackburn	60	Plymouth Argyle	59	Charlton	55
1975–6	Hereford	63	Cardiff	57	Millwall	56
1976–7	Mansfield	64	Brighton	61	Crystal Palace	59
1977–8	Wrexham	61	Cambridge Utd	58	Preston	56
1978–9	Shrewsbury	61	Watford	60	Swansea	60
1979–80	Grimsby	62	Blackburn	59	Sheffield Wed	58
1980–1	Rotherham	61	Barnsley	59	Charlton	59
†1981–2	**Burnley	80	Carlisle	80	Fulham	78
†1982–3	Portsmouth	91	Cardiff	86	Huddersfield	82
†1983–4	Oxford Utd	95	Wimbledon	87	Sheffield Utd	83
†1984–5	Bradford City	94	Millwall	90	Hull	87
†1985–6	Reading	94	Plymouth Argyle	87	Derby	84
†1986–7	Bournemouth	97	Middlesbrough	94	Swindon	87
†1987–8	Sunderland	93	Brighton	84	Walsall	82
†1988–9	Wolves	92	Sheffield Utd	84	Port Vale	84
†1989–90	Bristol Rov	93	Bristol City	91	Notts Co	87
†1990–1	Cambridge Utd	86	Southend	85	Grimsby	83
†1991–2	Brentford	82	Birmingham	81	††Huddersfield	78

* Won on goal average ** Won on goal difference † Maximum points 138 (previously 92) †† Not promoted after play-offs

FOURTH DIVISION 1958–92

1958–9	Port Vale	64	Coventry	60	York	60	Shrewsbury	58
1959–60	Walsall	65	Notts Co	60	Torquay	60	Watford	57
1960–1	Peterborough	66	Crystal Palace	64	Northampton	60	Bradford PA	60
1961–2	Millwall	56	Colchester	55	Wrexham	53	Carlisle	52
1962–3	Brentford	62	Oldham	59	Crewe	59	Mansfield	57
1963–4	*Gillingham	60	Carlisle	60	Workington	59	Exeter	58
1964–5	Brighton	63	Millwall	62	York	62	Oxford Utd	61
1965–6	*Doncaster	59	Darlington	59	Torquay	58	Colchester	56
1966–7	Stockport	64	Southport	59	Barrow	59	Tranmere	58
1967–8	Luton	66	Barnsley	61	Hartlepool Utd	60	Crewe	58
1968–9	Doncaster	59	Halifax	57	Rochdale	56	Bradford City	56
1969–70	Chesterfield	64	Wrexham	61	Swansea	60	Port Vale	59
1970–1	Notts Co	69	Bournemouth	60	Oldham	59	York	56
1971–2	Grimsby	63	Southend	60	Brentford	59	Scunthorpe	57
1972–3	Southport	62	Hereford	58	Cambridge Utd	57	Aldershot	56
1973–4	Peterborough	65	Gillingham	62	Colchester	60	Bury	59

1974–5	Mansfield	68	Shrewsbury	62	Rotherham	58	Chester	57
1975–6	Lincoln	74	Northampton	68	Reading	60	Tranmere	58
1976–7	Cambridge Utd	65	Exeter	62	Colchester	59	Bradford City	59
1977–8	Watford	71	Southend	60	Swansea	56	Brentford	59
1978–9	Reading	65	Grimsby	61	Wimbledon	61	Barnsley	61
1979–80	Huddersfield	66	Walsall	64	Newport	61	Portsmouth	60
1980–1	Southend	67	Lincoln	65	Doncaster	56	Wimbledon	55
†1981–2	Sheffield Utd	96	Bradford City	91	Wigan	91	Bournemouth	88
†1982–3	Wimbledon	98	Hull	90	Port Vale	88	Scunthorpe	83
†1983–4	York	101	Doncaster	85	Reading	82	Bristol City	82
†1984–5	Chesterfield	91	Blackpool	86	Darlington	85	Bury	84
†1985–6	Swindon	102	Chester	84	Mansfield	81	Port Vale	79
†1986–7	Northampton	99	Preston	90	Southend	80	††Wolves	79
†1987–8	Wolves	90	Cardiff	85	Bolton	78	††Scunthorpe	77
†1988–9	Rotherham	82	Tranmere	80	Crewe	78	††Scunthorpe	77
†1989–90	Exeter	89	Grimsby	79	Southend	75	††Stockport	74
†1990–1	Darlington	83	Stockport	82	Hartlepool Utd	82	Peterborough	80
1991–2a	Burnley	83	Rotherham	77	Blackpool	76		

* Won on goal average Maximum points: †, 138; a, 126; previously 92 †† Not promoted after play–offs

THIRD DIVISION – SOUTH 1920–58

1920–1a	Crystal Palace	59	Southampton	54	QPR	53
1921–2a	*Southampton	61	Plymouth Argyle	61	Portsmouth	53
1922–3a	Bristol City	59	Plymouth Argyle	53	Swansea	53
1923–4a	Portsmouth	59	Plymouth Argyle	55	Millwall	54
1924–5a	Swansea	57	Plymouth Argyle	56	Bristol City	53
1925–6a	Reading	57	Plymouth Argyle	56	Millwall	53
1926–7a	Bristol City	62	Plymouth Argyle	60	Millwall	56
1927–8a	Millwall	65	Northampton	55	Plymouth Argyle	53
1928–9a	*Charlton	54	Crystal Palace	54	Northampton	52
1929–30a	Plymouth Argyle	68	Brentford	61	QPR	51
1930–31a	Notts Co	59	Crystal Palace	51	Brentford	50
1931–2a	Fulham	57	Reading	55	Southend	53
1932–3a	Brentford	62	Exeter	58	Norwich	57
1933–4a	Norwich	61	Coventry	54	Reading	54
1934–5a	Charlton	61	Reading	53	Coventry	51
1935–6a	Coventry	57	Luton	56	Reading	54
1936–7a	Luton	58	Notts Co	56	Brighton	53
1937–8a	Millwall	56	Bristol City	55	QPR	53
1938–9a	Newport	55	Crystal Palace	52	Brighton	49
1946–7a	Cardiff	66	QPR	57	Bristol City	51
1947–8a	QPR	61	Bournemouth	57	Walsall	51
1948–9a	Swansea	62	Reading	55	Bournemouth	52
1949–50a	Notts Co	58	Northampton	51	Southend	51
1950–1d	Nottm Forest	70	Norwich	64	Reading	57
1951–2d	Plymouth Argyle	66	Reading	61	Norwich	61
1952–3d	Bristol Rov	64	Millwall	62	Northampton	62
1953–4d	Ipswich	64	Brighton	61	Bristol City	56
1954–5d	Bristol City	70	Leyton Orient	61	Southampton	59
1955–6d	Leyton Orient	66	Brighton	65	Ipswich	64
1956–7d	*Ipswich	59	Torquay	59	Colchester	58
1957–8d	Brighton	60	Brentford	58	Plymouth Argyle	58

THIRD DIVISION – NORTH 1921–58

1921–2b	Stockport	56	Darlington	50	Grimsby	50
1922–3b	Nelson	51	Bradford PA	47	Walsall	46
1923–4a	Wolves	63	Rochdale	62	Chesterfield	54
1924–5a	Darlington	58	Nelson	53	New Brighton	53
1925–6a	Grimsby	61	Bradford PA	60	Rochdale	59

Season						
1926–7a	Stoke	63	Rochdale	58	Bradford PA	57
1927–8a	Bradford PA	63	Lincoln	55	Stockport	54
1928–9a	Bradford City	63	Stockport	62	Wrexham	52
1929–30a	Port Vale	67	Stockport	63	Darlington	50
1930–1a	Chesterfield	58	Lincoln	57	Wrexham	54
1931–2c	*Lincoln	57	Gateshead	57	Chester	50
1932–3a	Hull	59	Wrexham	57	Stockport	54
1933–4a	Barnsley	62	Chesterfield	61	Stockport	59
1934–5a	Doncaster	57	Halifax	55	Chester	54
1935–6a	Chesterfield	60	Chester	55	Tranmere	54
1936–7a	Stockport	60	Lincoln	57	Chester	53
1937–8a	Tranmere	56	Doncaster	54	Hull	53
1938–9a	Barnsley	67	Doncaster	56	Bradford City	52
1946–7a	Doncaster	72	Rotherham	64	Chester	56
1947–8a	Lincoln	60	Rotherham	59	Wrexham	50
1948–9a	Hull	65	Rotherham	62	Doncaster	50
1949–50a	Doncaster	55	Gateshead	53	Rochdale	51
1950–1d	Rotherham	71	Mansfield	64	Carlisle	62
1951–2d	Lincoln	69	Grimsby	66	Stockport	59
1952–3d	Oldham	59	Port Vale	58	Wrexham	56
1953–4d	Port Vale	69	Barnsley	58	Scunthorpe	57
1954–5d	Barnsley	65	Accrington	61	Scunthorpe	58
1955–6d	Grimsby	68	Derby	63	Accrington	59
1956–7d	Derby	63	Hartlepool Utd	59	Accrington	58
1957–8d	Scunthorpe	66	Accrington	59	Bradford City	57

Maximum points: a, 84; b, 76; c, 80; d, 92 * Won on goal average

TITLE WINNERS

PREMIER LEAGUE

Manchester Utd	13
Manchester City	6
Chelsea	5
Arsenal	3
Blackburn	1
Leicester	1
Liverpool	1

CHAMPIONSHIP

Newcastle	2
Norwich	2
Reading	2
Sunderland	2
Wolves	2
Bournemouth	1
Burnley	1
Cardiff	1
Fulham	1
Leeds	1
Leicester	1
QPR	1
WBA	1

DIV 1 (NEW)

Sunderland	2
Bolton	1
Charlton	1
Crystal Palace	1
Fulham	1
Manchester City	1
Middlesbrough	1
Newcastle	1
Norwich	1
Nottm Forest	1
Portsmouth	1

DIV 1 (ORIGINAL)

Liverpool	18
Arsenal	10
Everton	9
Aston Villa	7
Manchester Utd	7
Sunderland	6
Newcastle	4
Sheffield Wed	4
Huddersfield	3
Leeds	3
Wolves	3
Blackburn	2
Burnley	2
Derby	2
Manchester City	2
Portsmouth	2
Preston	2
Tottenham	2
Chelsea	1
Ipswich	1
Nottm Forest	1
Sheffield Utd	1
WBA	1

LEAGUE ONE

Wigan	3
Luton	1
Brighton	1
Bristol City	1
Charlton	1
Coventry	1
Doncaster	1
Hull	1
Leicester	1
Norwich	1
Scunthorpe	1
Sheffield Utd	1
Southend	1
Swansea	1
Wolves	1

DIV 2 (NEW)

Wigan	3
Birmingham	1
Brighton	1
Bury	1
Chesterfield	1
Fulham	1
Lincoln	1
Millwall	1
Plymouth	1
Preston	1
Reading	1
Stoke	1
Swindon	1
Watford	1
Notts Co	1

DIV 2 (ORIGINAL)

Leicester	6
Manchester City	6
Sheffield Wed	5

Birmingham	4	West Ham	2	Sheffield Utd	1
Derby	4	Wolves	2	Sunderland	1
Liverpool	4	Blackburn	1	**LEAGUE TWO**	
Ipswich	3	Blackpool	1	Chesterfield	2
Leeds	3	Bradford City	1	Swindon	2
Middlesbrough	3	Brentford	1	Accrington	1
Notts County	3	Bristol City	1	Brentford	1
Preston	3	Bury	1	Burton	1
Aston Villa	2	Coventry	1	Carlisle	1
Bolton	2	Crystal Palace	1	Cheltenham	1
Burnley	2	Everton	1	Forest Green	1
Chelsea	2	Fulham	1	Gillingham	1
Grimsby	2	Huddersfield	1	Lincoln	1
Manchester Utd	2	Luton	1	MK Dons	1
Norwich	2	Millwall	1	Northampton	1
Nottm Forest	2	Newcastle	1	Notts County	1
Stoke	2	Oldham	1	Portsmouth	1
Tottenham	2	Oxford Utd	1	Walsall	1
WBA	2	QPR	1	Yeovil	1

APPLICATIONS FOR RE-ELECTION (System discontinued 1987)

14	Hartlepool	4	Norwich	2	Oldham
12	Halifax	3	Aldershot	2	QPR
11	Barrow	3	Bradford City	2	Rotherham
11	Southport	3	Crystal Palace	2	Scunthorpe
10	Crewe	3	Doncaster	2	Southend
10	Newport	3	Hereford	2	Watford
10	Rochdale	3	Merthyr	1	Blackpool
8	Darlington	3	Swindon	1	Brighton
8	Exeter	3	Torquay	1	Bristol Rov
7	Chester	3	Tranmere	1	Cambridge Utd
7	Walsall	2	Aberdare	1	Cardiff
7	Workington	2	Ashington	1	Carlisle
7	York	2	Bournemouth	1	Charlton
6	Stockport	2	Brentford	1	Mansfield
5	Accrington	2	Colchester	1	Port Vale
5	Gillingham	2	Durham	1	Preston
5	Lincoln	2	Gateshead	1	Shrewsbury
5	New Brighton	2	Grimsby	1	Swansea
4	Bradford PA	2	Millwall	1	Thames
4	Northampton	2	Nelson	1	Wrexham

RELEGATED CLUBS (TO 1992)

1892–3	In Test matches, Darwen and Sheffield Utd won promotion in place of Accrington and Notts Co
1893–4	Tests, Liverpool and Small Heath won promotion Darwen and Newton Heath relegated
1894–5	After Tests, Bury promoted, Liverpool relegated
1895–6	After Tests, Liverpool promoted, Small Heath relegated
1896–7	After Tests, Notts Co promoted, Burnley relegated
1897–8	Test system abolished after success of Burnley and Stoke, League extended Blackburn and Newcastle elected to First Division

Automatic promotion and relegation introduced

FIRST DIVISION TO SECOND

1898–9	Bolton, Sheffield Wed
1899–00	Burnley, Glossop
1900–1	Preston, WBA
1901–2	Small Heath, Manchester City
1902–3	Grimsby, Bolton
1903–4	Liverpool, WBA
1904–5	League extended Bury and Notts Co, two bottom clubs in First Division, re-elected
1905–6	Nottm Forest, Wolves
1906–7	Derby, Stoke

1907–8	Bolton, Birmingham
1908–9	Manchester City, Leicester Fosse
1909–10	Bolton, Chelsea
1910–11	Bristol City, Nottm Forest
1911–12	Preston, Bury
1912–13	Notts Co, Woolwich Arsenal
1913–14	Preston, Derby
1914–15	Tottenham, *Chelsea
1919–20	Notts Co, Sheffield Wed
1920–1	Derby, Bradford PA
1921–2	Bradford City, Manchester Utd
1922–3	Stoke, Oldham
1923–4	Chelsea, Middlesbrough
1924–5	Preston, Nottm Forest
1925–6	Manchester City, Notts Co
1926–7	Leeds, WBA
1927–8	Tottenham, Middlesbrough
1928–9	Bury, Cardiff
1929–30	Burnley, Everton
1930–1	Leeds, Manchester Utd
1931–2	Grimsby, West Ham
1932–3	Bolton, Blackpool
1933–4	Newcastle, Sheffield Utd
1934–5	Leicester, Tottenham
1935–6	Aston Villa, Blackburn
1936–7	Man§chester Utd, Sheffield Wed
1937–8	Manchester City, WBA
1938–9	Birmingham, Leicester
1946–7	Brentford, Leeds
1947–8	Blackburn, Grimsby
1948–9	Preston, Sheffield Utd
1949–50	Manchester City, Birmingham
1950–1	Sheffield Wed, Everton
1951–2	Huddersfield, Fulham
1952–3	Stoke, Derby
1953–4	Middlesbrough, Liverpool
1954–5	Leicester, Sheffield Wed
1955–6	Huddersfield, Sheffield Utd
1956–7	Charlton, Cardiff
1957–8	Sheffield Wed, Sunderland
1958–9	Portsmouth, Aston Villa
1959–60	Luton, Leeds
1960–61	Preston, Newcastle
1961–2	Chelsea, Cardiff
1962–3	Manchester City, Leyton Orient
1963–4	Bolton, Ipswich
1964–5	Wolves, Birmingham
1965–6	Northampton, Blackburn
1966–7	Aston Villa, Blackpool
1967–8	Fulham, Sheffield Utd
1968–9	Leicester, QPR
1969–70	Sheffield Wed, Sunderland
1970–1	Burnley, Blackpool
1971–2	Nottm Forest, Huddersfield
1972–3	WBA, Crystal Palace
1973–4	Norwich, Manchester Utd, Southampton
1974–5	Chelsea, Luton, Carlisle
1975–6	Sheffield Utd, Burnley, Wolves
1976–7	Tottenham, Stoke, Sunderland
1977–8	Leicester, West Ham, Newcastle
1978–9	QPR, Birmingham, Chelsea
1979–80	Bristol City, Derby, Bolton
1980–1	Norwich, Leicester, Crystal Palace
1981–2	Leeds, Wolves, Middlesbrough
1982–3	Manchester City, Swansea, Brighton
1983–4	Birmingham, Notts Co, Wolves
1984–5	Norwich, Sunderland, Stoke
1985–6	Ipswich, Birmingham, WBA
1986–7	Leicester, Manchester City, Aston Villa
1987–8	Chelsea**, Portsmouth, Watford, Oxford Utd
1988–9	Middlesbrough, West Ham, Newcastle
1989–90	Sheffield Wed, Charlton, Millwall
1990–1	Sunderland, Derby
1991–2	Luton, Notts Co, West Ham

* Subsequently re–elected to First Division when League extended after the war

** Relegated after play–offs

SECOND DIVISION TO THIRD DIVISION

1920–1	Stockport
1921–2	Bradford City, Bristol City
1922–3	Rotherham, Wolves
1923–4	Nelson, Bristol City
1924–5	Crystal Palace, Coventry
1925–6	Stoke, Stockport
1926–7	Darlington, Bradford City
1927–8	Fulham, South Shields
1928–9	Port Vale, Clapton Orient
1929–30	Hull, Notts County
1930–1	Reading, Cardiff
1931–2	Barnsley, Bristol City
1932–3	Chesterfield, Charlton
1933–4	Millwall, Lincoln
1934–5	Oldham, Notts Co
1935–6	Port Vale, Hull
1936–7	Doncaster, Bradford City
1937–8	Barnsley, Stockport
1938–9	Norwich, Tranmere
1946–7	Swansea, Newport
1947–8	Doncaster, Millwall
1948–9	Nottm Forest, Lincoln
1949–50	Plymouth Argyle, Bradford PA
1950–1	Grimsby, Chesterfield
1951–2	Coventry, QPR
1952–3	Southampton, Barnsley
1953–4	Brentford, Oldham
1954–5	Ipswich, Derby
1955–6	Plymouth Argyle, Hull
1956–7	Port Vale, Bury
1957–8	Doncaster, Notts Co
1958–9	Barnsley, Grimsby
1959–60	Bristol City, Hull
1960–1	Lincoln, Portsmouth
1961–2	Brighton, Bristol Rov
1962–3	Walsall, Luton
1963–4	Grimsby, Scunthorpe
1964–5	Swindon, Swansea
1965–6	Middlesbrough, Leyton Orient
1966–7	Northampton, Bury
1967–8	Plymouth Argyle, Rotherham

74

1968–9	Fulham, Bury
1969–70	Preston, Aston Villa
1970–1	Blackburn, Bolton
1971–2	Charlton, Watford
1972–3	Huddersfield, Brighton
1973–4	Crystal Palace, Preston, Swindon
1974–5	Millwall, Cardiff, Sheffield Wed
1975–6	Portsmouth, Oxford Utd, York
1976–7	Carlisle, Plymouth Argyle, Hereford
1977–8	Hull, Mansfield, Blackpool
1978–9	Sheffield Utd, Millwall, Blackburn
1979–80	Fulham, Burnley, Charlton
1980–1	Preston, Bristol City, Bristol Rov
1981–2	Cardiff, Wrexham, Orient
1982–3	Rotherham, Burnley, Bolton
1983–4	Derby, Swansea, Cambridge Utd
1984–5	Notts Co, Cardiff, Wolves
1985–6	Carlisle, Middlesbrough, Fulham
1986–7	Sunderland**, Grimsby, Brighton
1987–8	Sheffield Utd**, Reading, Huddersfield
1988–9	Shrewsbury, Birmingham, Walsall
1989–90	Bournemouth, Bradford City, Stoke
1990–1	WBA, Hull
1991–2	Plymouth Argyle, Brighton, Port Vale

** Relegated after play–offs

THIRD DIVISION TO FOURTH DIVISION

1958–9	Rochdale, Notts Co, Doncaster, Stockport
1959–60	Accrington, Wrexham, Mansfield, York
1960–1	Chesterfield, Colchester, Bradford City, Tranmere
1961–2	Newport, Brentford, Lincoln, Torquay
1962–3	Bradford PA, Brighton, Carlisle, Halifax
1963–4	Millwall, Crewe, Wrexham, Notts Co
1964–5	Luton, Port Vale, Colchester, Barnsley
1965–6	Southend, Exeter, Brentford, York
1966–7	Doncaster, Workington, Darlington, Swansea
1967–8	Scunthorpe, Colchester, Grimsby, Peterborough (demoted)
1968–9	Oldham, Crewe, Hartlepool Utd, Northampton
1969–70	Bournemouth, Southport, Barrow, Stockport
1970–1	Gillingham, Doncaster, Bury, Reading
1971–2	Mansfield, Barnsley, Torquay, Bradford City
1972–3	Scunthorpe, Swansea, Brentford, Rotherham
1973–4	Cambridge Utd, Shrewsbury, Rochdale, Southport
1974–5	Bournemouth, Watford, Tranmere, Huddersfield
1975–6	Aldershot, Colchester, Southend, Halifax
1976–7	Reading, Northampton, Grimsby, York
1977–8	Port Vale, Bradford City, Hereford, Portsmouth
1978–9	Peterborough, Walsall, Tranmere, Lincoln
1979–80	Bury, Southend, Mansfield, Wimbledon
1980–1	Sheffield Utd, Colchester, Blackpool, Hull
1981–2	Wimbledon, Swindon, Bristol City, Chester
1982–3	Reading, Wrexham, Doncaster, Chesterfield
1983–4	Scunthorpe, Southend, Port Vale, Exeter
1984–5	Burnley, Orient, Preston, Cambridge Utd
1985–6	Lincoln, Cardiff, Wolves, Swansea
1986–7	Bolton**, Carlisle, Darlington, Newport
1987–8	Doncaster, York, Grimsby, Rotherham**
1988–9	Southend, Chesterfield, Gillingham, Aldershot
1989–90	Cardiff, Northampton, Blackpool, Walsall
1990–1	Crewe, Rotherham, Mansfield
1991–2	Bury, Shrewsbury, Torquay, Darlington

** Relegated after plays–offs

DEMOTED FROM FOURTH DIVISION TO CONFERENCE

1987	Lincoln
1988	Newport
1989	Darlington
1990	Colchester
1991	No demotion
1992	No demotion

DEMOTED FROM THIRD DIVISION TO CONFERENCE

1993	Halifax
1994–6	No demotion
1997	Hereford
1998	Doncaster
1999	Scarborough
2000	Chester
2001	Barnet
2002	Halifax
2003	Exeter, Shrewsbury
2004	Carlisle, York

DEMOTED FROM LEAGUE TWO TO CONFERENCE/NATIONAL LEAGUE

| 2005 | Kidderminster, Cambridge Utd |

2006	Oxford Utd, Rushden & Diamonds
2007	Boston, Torquay
2008	Mansfield, Wrexham
2009	Chester Luton
2010	Grimsby, Darlington
2011	Lincoln, Stockport
2012	Hereford, Macclesfield
2013	Barnet, Aldershot
2014	Bristol Rov, Torquay
2015	Cheltenham, Tranmere
2016	Dagenham, York
2017	Hartlepool, Leyton Orient
2018	Barnet, Chesterfield
2019	Notts Co, Yeovil
2020	Macclesfield
2021	Southend, Grimsby
2022	Oldham, Scunthorpe

RELEGATED CLUBS (SINCE 1993)

1993
Premier League to Div 1: Crystal Palace, Middlesbrough, Nottm Forest
Div 1 to Div 2: Brentford, Cambridge Utd, Bristol Rov
Div 2 to Div 3: Preston, Mansfield, Wigan, Chester

1994
Premier League to Div 1: Sheffield Utd, Oldham, Swindon
Div 1 to Div 2: Birmingham, Oxford Utd, Peterborough
Div 2 to Div 3: Fulham, Exeter, Hartlepool Utd, Barnet

1995
Premier League to Div 1: Crystal Palace, Norwich, Leicester, Ipswich
Div 1 to Div 2: Swindon, Burnley, Bristol City, Notts Co
Div 2 to Div 3: Cambridge Utd, Plymouth, Cardiff, Chester, Leyton Orient

1996
Premier League to Div 1: Manchester City, QPR, Bolton
Div 1 to Div 2: Millwall, Watford, Luton
Div 2 to Div 3: Carlisle, Swansea, Brighton, Hull

1997
Premier League to Div 1: Sunderland, Middlesbrough, Nottm Forest
Div 1 to Div 2: Grimsby, Oldham, Southend
Div 2 to Div 3: Peterborough, Shrewsbury, Rotherham, Notts Co

1998
Premier League to Div 1: Bolton, Barnsley, Crystal Palace
Div 1 to Div 2: Manchester City, Stoke, Reading
Div 2 to Div 3: Brentford, Plymouth, Carlisle, Southend

1999
Premier League to Div 1: Charlton, Blackburn, Nottm Forest
Div 1 to Div 2: Bury, Oxford Utd, Bristol City
Div 2 to Div 3: York, Northampton, Lincoln, Macclesfield

2000
Premier League to Div 1: Wimbledon, Sheffield Wed, Watford
Div 1 to Div 2: Walsall, Port Vale, Swindon
Div 2 to Div 3: Cardiff, Blackpool, Scunthorpe, Chesterfield

2001
Premier League to Div 1: Manchester City, Coventry, Bradford City
Div 1 to Div 2: Huddersfield, QPR, Tranmere
Div 2 to Div 3: Bristol Rov, Luton, Swansea, Oxford Utd

2002
Premier League to Div 1: Ipswich, Derby, Leicester
Div 1 to Div 2: Crewe, Barnsley, Stockport
Div 2 to Div 3: Bournemouth, Bury, Wrexham, Cambridge Utd

2003
Premier League to Div 1: West Ham, WBA, Sunderland
Div 1 to Div 2: Sheffield Wed, Brighton, Grimsby
Div 2 to Div 3: Cheltenham, Huddersfield, Mansfield, Northampton

2004
Premier League to Div 1: Leicester, Leeds, Wolves
Div 1 to Div 2: Walsall, Bradford City, Wimbledon
Div 2 to Div 3: Grimsby, Rushden & Diamonds, Notts Co, Wycombe

2005
Premier League to Championship: Crystal Palace, Norwich, Southampton
Championship to League 1: Gillingham, Nottm Forest, Rotherham
League 1 to League 2: Torquay, Wrexham, Peterborough, Stockport

2006
Premier League to Championship: Birmingham, WBA, Sunderland
Championship to League 1: Crewe, Millwall, Brighton
League 1 to League 2: Hartlepool Utd, MK Dons, Swindon, Walsall

2007
Premier League to Championship: Sheffield Utd, Charlton, Watford

Championship to League 1: Southend, Luton, Leeds

League 1 to League 2: Chesterfield, Bradford City, Rotherham, Brentford

2008

Premier League to Championship: Reading, Birmingham, Derby

Championship to League 1: Leicester, Scunthorpe, Colchester

League 1 to League 2: Bournemouth, Gillingham, Port Vale, Luton

2009

Premier League to Championship: Newcastle, Middlesbrough, WBA

Championship to League 1: Norwich, Southampton, Charlton

League 1 to League 2: Northampton, Crewe, Cheltenham, Hereford

2010

Premier League to Championship: Burnley, Hull, Portsmouth

Championship to League 1: Sheffield Wed, Plymouth, Peterborough

League 1 to League 2: Gillingham, Wycombe, Southend, Stockport

2011

Premier League to Championship: Birmingham, Blackpool, West Ham

Championship to League 1: Preston, Sheffield Utd, Scunthorpe

League 1 to League 2: Dagenham & Red bridge, Bristol Rov, Plymouth, Swindon

2012

Premier League to Championship: Bolton, Blackburn, Wolves

Championship to League 1: Portsmouth, Coventry, Doncaster

League 1 to League 2: Wycombe, Chesterfield, Exeter, Rochdale

2013

Premier League to Championship: Wigan, Reading, QPR

Championship to League 1: Peterborough, Wolves, Bristol City

League 1 to League 2: Scunthorpe, Bury, Hartlepool, Portsmouth

2014

Premier League to Championship: Norwich, Fulham, Cardiff

Championship to League 1: Doncaster, Barnsley, Yeovil

League 1 to League 2: Tranmere, Carlisle, Shrewsbury, Stevenage

2015

Premier League to Championship: Hull, Burnley QPR

Championship to League 1: Millwall, Wigan, Blackpool

League 1 to League 2: Notts Co, Crawley, Leyton Orient, Yeovil

2016

Premier League to Championship: Newcastle, Norwich, Aston Villa

Championship to League 1: Charlton, MK Dons, Bolton

League 1 to League 2: Doncaster, Blackpool, Colchester, Crewe

2017

Premier League to Championship: Hull, Middlesbrough, Sunderland

Championship to League 1: Blackburn, Wigan, Rotherham

League 1 to League 2: Port Vale, Swindon, Coventry, Chesterfield

2018

Premier League to Championship: Swansea, Stoke, WBA

Championship to League 1: Barnsley, Burton, Sunderland

League 1 to League 2: Oldham, Northampton, MK Dons, Bury

2019

Premier League to Championship: Cardiff, Fulham, Huddersfield

Championship to League 1: Rotherham, Bolton, Ipswich

League 1 to League 2: Plymouth, Walsall, Scunthorpe, Bradford

2020

Premier League to Championship: Bournemouth, Watford, Norwich

Championship to League 1: Charlton, Wigan, Hull

League 1 to League 2: Tranmere, Southend, Bolton

2021

Premier League to Championship: Fulham, WBA, Sheffield Utd

Championship to League 1: Wycombe, Rotherham, Sheffield Wed

League 1 to League 2: Rochdale, Northampton, Swindon, Bristol Rov

2022

Premier League to Championship: Burnley, Watford, Norwich

Championship to League 1: Peterborough, Derby, Barnsley

League 1 to Lague 2: Gillingham, Doncaster, AFC Wimbledon, Crewe

ANNUAL AWARDS

FOOTBALL WRITERS' ASSOCIATION

Footballer of the Year: 1948 Stanley Matthews (Blackpool); **1949** Johnny Carey (Manchester Utd); **1950** Joe Mercer (Arsenal); **1951** Harry Johnston (Blackpool); **1952** Billy Wright (Wolves); **1953** Nat Lofthouse (Bolton); **1954** Tom Finney (Preston); **1955** Don Revie (Manchester City); **1956** Bert Trautmann (Manchester City); **1957** Tom Finney (Preston); **1958** Danny Blanchflower (Tottenham); **1959** Syd Owen (Luton); **1960** Bill Slater (Wolves); **1961** Danny Blanchflower (Tottenham); **1962** Jimmy Adamson (Burnley); **1963** Stanley Matthews (Stoke); **1964** Bobby Moore (West Ham); **1965** Bobby Collins (Leeds); **1966** Bobby Charlton (Manchester Utd); **1967** Jack Charlton (Leeds); **1968** George Best (Manchester Utd); **1969** Tony Book (Manchester City) & Dave Mackay (Derby) – shared; **1970** Billy Bremner (Leeds); **1971** Frank McLintock (Arsenal); **1972** Gordon Banks (Stoke); **1973** Pat Jennings (Tottenham); **1974** Ian Callaghan (Liverpool); **1975** Alan Mullery (Fulham); **1976** Kevin Keegan (Liverpool); **1977** Emlyn Hughes (Liverpool); **1978** Kenny Burns (Nott'm Forest); **1979** Kenny Dalglish (Liverpool); **1980** Terry McDermott (Liverpool); **1981** Frans Thijssen (Ipswich); **1982** Steve Perryman (Tottenham); **1983** Kenny Dalglish (Liverpool); **1984** Ian Rush (Liverpool); **1985** Neville Southall (Everton); **1986** Gary Lineker (Everton); **1987** Clive Allen (Tottenham); **1988** Ian Barnes (Liverpool); **1989** Steve Nicol (Liverpool); Special award to the Liverpool players for the compassion shown to bereaved families after the Hillsborough Disaster; **1990** John Barnes (Liverpool); **1991** Gordon Strachan (Leeds); **1992** Gary Lineker (Tottenham); **1993** Chris Waddle (Sheffield Wed); **1994** Alan Shearer (Blackburn); **1995** Jurgen Klinsmann (Tottenham); **1996** Eric Cantona (Manchester Utd); **1997** Gianfranco Zola (Chelsea); **1998** Dennis Bergkamp (Arsenal); **1999** David Ginola (Tottenham); **2000** Roy Keane (Manchester Utd); **2001** Teddy Sheringham (Manchester Utd); **2002** Robert Pires (Arsenal); **2003** Thierry Henry (Arsenal); **2004** Thierry Henry (Arsenal); **2005** Frank Lampard (Chelsea); **2006** Thierry Henry (Arsenal); **2007** Cristiano Ronaldo (Manchester Utd); **2008** Cristiano Ronaldo (Manchester Utd); **2009** Steven Gerrard (Liverpool); **2010** Wayne Rooney (Manchester Utd); **2011** Scott Parker (West Ham); **2012** Robin van Persie (Arsenal); **2013** Gareth Bale (Tottenham); **2014** Luis Suarez (Liverpool); **2015** Eden Hazard (Chelsea); **2016** Jamie Vardy (Leicester); **2017** N'Golo Kante (Chelsea); **2018** Mohamed Salah (Liverpool); **2019** Raheem Sterling (Manchester City); **2020** Jordan Henderson (Liverpool); **2021** Ruben Dias (Manchester City); **2022** Mohamed Salah (Liverpool)

PROFESSIONAL FOOTBALLERS' ASSOCIATION

Player of the Year: 1974 Norman Hunter (Leeds); **1975** Colin Todd (Derby); **1976** Pat Jennings (Tottenham); **1977** Andy Gray (Aston Villa); **1978** Peter Shilton (Nott'm Forest); **1979** Liam Brady (Arsenal); **1980** Terry McDermott (Liverpool); **1981** John Wark (Ipswich); **1982** Kevin Keegan (Southampton); **1983** Kenny Dalglish (Liverpool); **1984** Ian Rush (Liverpool); **1985** Peter Reid (Everton); **1986** Gary Lineker (Everton); **1987** Clive Allen (Tottenham); **1988** Ian Barnes (Liverpool); **1989** Mark Hughes (Manchester Utd); **1990** David Platt (Aston Villa); **1991** Mark Hughes (Manchester Utd); **1992** Gary Pallister (Manchester Utd); **1993** Paul McGrath (Aston Villa); **1994** Eric Cantona (Manchester Utd); **1995** Alan Shearer (Blackburn); **1996** Les Ferdinand (Newcastle); **1997** Alan Shearer (Newcastle); **1998** Dennis Bergkamp (Arsenal); **1999** David Ginola (Tottenham); **2000** Roy Keane (Manchester Utd); **2001** Teddy Sheringham (Manchester Utd); **2002** Ruud van Nistelrooy (Manchester Utd); **2003** Thierry Henry (Arsenal); **2004** Thierry Henry (Arsenal); **2005** John Terry (Chelsea); **2006** Steven Gerrard (Liverpool); **2007** Cristiano Ronaldo (Manchester Utd); **2008** Cristiano Ronaldo (Manchester Utd); **2009** Ryan Giggs (Manchester Utd); **2010** Wayne Rooney (Manchester Utd); **2011** Gareth Bale (Tottenham); **2012** Robin van Persie (Manchester Utd); **2013** Gareth Bale (Tottenham); **2014** Luis Suarez (Liverpool); **2015** Eden Hazard (Chelsea); **2016** Riyad Mahrez (Leicester); **2017** N'Golo Kante (Chelsea); **2018** Mohamed Salah (Liverpool); **2019** Virgil van Dijk (Liverpool); **2020** Kevin De Bruyne (Manchester City); **2021** Kevin De Bruyne (Manchester City); **2022** Mohamed Salah (Liverpool)

Young Player of the Year: 1974 Kevin Beattie (Ipswich); 1975 Mervyn Day (West Ham); 1976 Peter Barnes (Manchester City); 1977 Andy Gray (Aston Villa); 1978 Tony Woodcock (Nott'm Forest); 1979 Cyrille Regis (WBA); 1980 Glenn Hoddle (Tottenham); 1981 Gary Shaw (Aston Villa); 1982 Steve Moran (Southampton); 1983 Ian Rush (Liverpool); 1984 Paul Walsh (Luton); 1985 Mark Hughes (Manchester Utd); 1986 Tony Cottee (West Ham); 1987 Tony Adams (Arsenal); 1988 Paul Gascoigne (Newcastle); 1989 Paul Merson (Arsenal); 1990 Matthew Le Tissier (Southampton); 1991 Lee Sharpe (Manchester Utd); 1992 Ryan Giggs (Manchester Utd); 1993 Ryan Giggs (Manchester Utd); 1994 Andy Cole (Newcastle); 1995 Robbie Fowler (Liverpool); 1996 Robbie Fowler (Liverpool); 1997 David Beckham (Manchester Utd); 1998 Michael Owen (Liverpool); 1999 Nicolas Anelka (Arsenal); 2000 Harry Kewell (Leeds); 2001 Steven Gerrard (Liverpool); 2002 Craig Bellamy (Newcastle); 2003 Jermaine Jenas (Newcastle); 2004 Scott Parker (Chelsea); 2005 Wayne Rooney (Manchester Utd); 2006 Wayne Rooney (Manchester Utd); 2007 Cristiano Ronaldo (Manchester Utd); 2008 Cesc Fabregas (Arsenal); 2009 Ashley Young (Aston Villa); 2010 James Milner (Aston Villa); 2011 Jack Wilshere (Arsenal); 2012 Kyle Walker (Tottenham); 2013 Gareth Bale (Tottenham); 2014 Eden Hazard (Chelsea); 2015 Harry Kane (Tottenham); 2016 Dele Alli (Tottenham); 2017 Dele Alli (Tottenham); 2018 Leroy Sane (Manchester City); 2019 Raheem Sterling (Manchester City); 2020 Trent Alexander-Arnold (Liverpool); 2021 Phil Foden (Manchester City); 2022 Phil Foden (Manchester City)

Merit Awards: 1974 Bobby Charlton & Cliff Lloyd; 1975 Denis Law; 1976 George Eastham; 1977 Jack Taylor; 1978 Bill Shankly; 1979 Tom Finney; 1980 Sir Matt Busby; 1981 John Trollope; 1982 Joe Mercer; 1983 Bob Paisley; 1984 Bill Nicholson; 1985 Ron Greenwood; 1986 England 1966 World Cup–winning team; 1987 Sir Stanley Matthews; 1988 Billy Bonds; 1989 Nat Lofthouse; 1990 Peter Shilton; 1991 Tommy Hutchison; 1992 Brian Clough; 1993 Manchester Utd; 1968 European Champions; Eusebio; 1994 Billy Bingham; 1995 Gordon Strachan; 1996 Pele; 1997 Peter Beardsley; 1998 Steve Ogrizovic; 1999 Tony Ford; 2000 Gary Mabbutt; 2001 Jimmy Hill; 2002 Niall Quinn; 2003 Sir Bobby Robson; 2004 Dario Gradi; 2005 Shaka Hislop; 2006 George Best; 2007 Sir Alex Ferguson; 2008 Jimmy Armfield; 2009 John McDermott; 2010 Lucas Radebe; 2011 Howard Webb; 2012 Graham Alexander; 2013 Eric Harrison/Manchester Utd Class of '92; 2014 Donald Bell (posthumously; only footballer to win Victoria Cross; World War 1); 2015 Steven Gerrard & Frank Lampard; 2016 Ryan Giggs; 2017 David Beckham; 2018 Cyrille Regis (posthumously); 2019 Steph Houghton; 2020 Marcus Rashford; 2021 Gordon Taylor; 2022 Roy Hodgson, Hope Powell

MANAGER OF THE YEAR 1

(chosen by media and sponsors)

1966 Jock Stein (Celtic); 1967 Jock Stein (Celtic); 1968 Matt Busby (Manchester Utd); 1969 Don Revie (Leeds); 1970 Don Revie (Leeds); 1971 Bertie Mee (Arsenal); 1972 Don Revie (Leeds); 1973 Bill Shankly (Liverpool); 1974 Jack Charlton (Middlesbrough); 1975 Ron Saunders (Aston Villa); 1976 Bob Paisley (Liverpool); 1977 Bob Paisley (Liverpool); 1978 Brian Clough (Nott'm Forest); 1979 Bob Paisley (Liverpool); 1980 Bob Paisley (Liverpool); 1981 Ron Saunders (Aston Villa); 1982 Bob Paisley (Liverpool); 1983 Bob Paisley (Liverpool); 1984 Joe Fagan (Liverpool); 1985 Howard Kendall (Everton); 1986 Kenny Dalglish (Liverpool); 1987 Howard Kendall (Everton); 1988 Kenny Dalglish (Liverpool); 1989 George Graham (Arsenal); 1990 Kenny Dalglish (Liverpool); 1991 George Graham (Arsenal); 1992 Howard Wilkinson (Leeds); 1993 Alex Ferguson (Manchester Utd); 1994 Alex Ferguson (Manchester Utd); 1995 Kenny Dalglish (Blackburn); 1996 Alex Ferguson (Manchester Utd); 1997 Alex Ferguson (Manchester Utd); 1998 Arsene Wenger (Arsenal); 1999 Alex Ferguson (Manchester Utd); 2000 Sir Alex Ferguson (Manchester Utd); 2001 George Burley (Ipswich); 2002 Arsene Wenger (Arsenal); 2003 Sir Alex Ferguson (Manchester Utd); 2004 Arsene Wenger (Arsenal); 2005 Jose Mourinho (Chelsea); 2006 Jose Mourinho (Chelsea); 2007 Sir Alex Ferguson (Manchester Utd); 2008 Sir Alex Ferguson (Manchester Utd); 2009 Sir Alex Ferguson (Manchester Utd); 2010 Harry Redknapp (Tottenham); 2011 Sir Alex Ferguson (Manchester Utd); 2012: Alan Pardew (Newcastle); 2013 Sir Alex Ferguson (Manchester

Utd); **2014** Tony Pulis (Crystal Palace); **2015** Jose Mourinho (Chelsea); **2016** Claudio Ranieri (Leicester); **2017** Antonio Conte (Chelsea); **2018** Pep Guardiola (Manchester City); **2019** Pep Guardiola (Manchester City); **2020** Jurgen Klopp (Liverpool); **2021** Pep Guardiola (Manchester City); **2022** Jurgen Klopp (Liverpool)

MANAGER OF THE YEAR 2

(Chosen by the League Managers' Association)

1993 Dave Bassett (Sheffield Utd); **1994** Joe Kinnear (Wimbledon); **1995** Frank Clark (Nott'm Forest); **1996** Peter Reid (Sunderland); **1997** Danny Wilson (Barnsley); **1998** David Jones (Southampton); **1999** Alex Ferguson (Manchester Utd); **2000** Alan Curbishley (Charlton Athletic); **2001** George Burley (Ipswich); **2002** Arsene Wenger (Arsenal); **2003** David Moyes (Everton); **2004** Arsene Wenger (Arsenal); **2005** David Moyes (Everton); **2006** Steve Coppell (Reading); **2007** Steve Coppell (Reading); **2008** Sir Alex Ferguson (Manchester Utd); **2009** David Moyes (Everton); **2010** Roy Hodgson (Fulham); **2011** Sir Alex Ferguson (Manchester Utd); **2012:** Alan Pardew (Newcastle); **2013** Sir Alex Ferguson (Manchester Utd); **2014** Brendan Rodgers (Liverpool); **2015** Eddie Howe (Bournemouth); **2016** Claudio Ranieri (Leicester); **2017** Antonio Conte (Chelsea); **2018** Pep Guardiola (Manchester City); **2019** Chris Wilder (Sheffield Utd); **2020** Jurgen Klopp (Liverpool); **2021** Pep Guardiola (Manchester City); **2022** Jurgen Klopp (Liverpool)

SCOTTISH FOOTBALL WRITERS' ASSOCIATION

Footballer of the Year: 1965 Billy McNeill (Celtic); **1966** John Greig (Rangers); **1967** Ronnie Simpson (Celtic); **1968** Gordon Wallace (Raith); **1969** Bobby Murdoch (Celtic); **1970** Pat Stanton (Hibernian); **1971** Martin Buchan (Aberdeen); **1972** David Smith (Rangers); **1973** George Connelly (Celtic); **1974** World Cup Squad; **1975** Sandy Jardine (Rangers); **1976** John Greig (Rangers); **1977** Danny McGrain (Celtic); **1978** Derek Johnstone (Rangers); **1979** Andy Ritchie (Morton); **1980** Gordon Strachan (Aberdeen); **1981** Alan Rough (Partick Thistle); **1982** Paul Sturrock (Dundee Utd); **1983** Charlie Nicholas (Celtic); **1984** Willie Miller (Aberdeen); **1985** Hamish McAlpine (Dundee Utd); **1986** Sandy Jardine (Hearts); **1987** Brian McClair (Celtic); **1988** Paul McStay (Celtic); **1989** Richard Gough (Rangers); **1990** Alex McLeish (Aberdeen); **1991** Maurice Malpas (Dundee Utd); **1992** Ally McCoist (Rangers); **1993** Andy Goram (Rangers); **1994** Mark Hateley (Rangers); **1995** Brian Laudrup (Rangers); **1996** Paul Gascoigne (Rangers); **1997** Brian Laudrup (Rangers); **1998** Craig Burley (Celtic); **1999** Henrik Larsson (Celtic); **2000** Barry Ferguson (Rangers); **2001** Henrik Larsson (Celtic); **2002** Paul Lambert (Celtic); **2003** Barry Ferguson (Rangers); **2004** Jackie McNamara (Celtic); **2005** John Hartson (Celtic); **2006** Craig Gordon (Hearts); **2007** Shunsuke Nakamura (Celtic); **2008** Carlos Cuellar (Rangers); **2009** Gary Caldwell (Celtic); **2010** David Weir (Rangers); **2011** Emilio Izaguirre (Celtic); **2012** Charlie Mulgrew (Celtic); **2013** Leigh Griffiths (Hibernian); **2014** Kris Commons (Celtic); **2015** Craig Gordon (Celtic); **2016** Leigh Griffiths (Celtic); **2017** Scott Sinclair (Celtic); **2018** Scott Brown (Celtic); **2019** James Forrest (Celtic); **2020** Odsonne Edouard; **2021** Steven Davis (Rangers); **2022** Craig Gordon (Hearts)

PROFESSIONAL FOOTBALLERS' ASSOCIATION SCOTLAND

Player of the Year: 1978 Derek Johnstone (Rangers); **1979** Paul Hegarty (Dundee Utd); **1980** Davie Provan (Celtic); **1981** Mark McGhee (Aberdeen); **1982** Sandy Clarke (Airdrieonians); **1983** Charlie Nicholas (Celtic); **1984** Willie Miller (Aberdeen); **1985** Jim Duffy (Morton); **1986** Richard Gough (Dundee Utd); **1987** Brian McClair (Celtic); **1988** Paul McStay (Celtic); **1989** Theo Snelders (Aberdeen); **1990** Jim Bett (Aberdeen); **1991** Paul Elliott (Celtic); **1992** Ally McCoist (Rangers); **1993** Andy Goram (Rangers); **1994** Mark Hateley (Rangers); **1995** Brian Laudrup (Rangers); **1996** Paul Gascoigne (Rangers); **1997** Paolo Di Canio (Celtic) **1998** Jackie McNamara (Celtic); **1999** Henrik Larsson (Celtic); **2000** Mark Viduka (Celtic); **2001** Henrik Larsson (Celtic); **2002** Lorenzo Amoruso (Rangers); **2003** Barry Ferguson (Rangers); **2004** Chris Sutton (Celtic); **2005** John Hartson (Celtic) and Fernando Ricksen (Rangers); **2006** Shaun Maloney (Celtic); **2007** Shunsuke Nakamura (Celtic); **2008** Aiden McGeady (Celtic); **2009** Scott Brown (Celtic); **2010** Steven Davis (Rangers); **2011** Emilio Izaguirre (Celtic); **2012** Charlie Mulgrew (Celtic); **2013** Michael Higdon

(Motherwell); **2014** Kris Commons (Celtic); **2015** Stefan Johansen (Celtic); **2016** Leigh Griffiths (Celtic); **2017** Scott Sinclair (Celtic); **2018** Scott Brown (Celtic); **2019** James Forrest (Celtic); **2020** No Award; **2021** James Tavernier (Rangers); **2022** Callum McGregor (Celtic)

Young Player of the Year: 1978 Graeme Payne (Dundee Utd); **1979** Ray Stewart (Dundee Utd); **1980** John McDonald (Rangers); **1981** Charlie Nicholas (Celtic); **1982** Frank McAvennie (St Mirren); **1983** Paul McStay (Celtic); **1984** John Robertson (Hearts); **1985** Craig Levein (Hearts); **1986** Craig Levein (Hearts); **1987** Robert Fleck (Rangers); **1988** John Collins (Hibernian); **1989** Billy McKinlay (Dundee Utd); **1990** Scott Crabbe (Hearts); **1991** Eoin Jess (Aberdeen); **1992** Phil O'Donnell (Motherwell); **1993** Eoin Jess (Aberdeen); **1994** Phil O'Donnell (Motherwell); **1995** Charlie Miller (Rangers); **1996** Jackie McNamara (Celtic); **1997** Robbie Winters (Dundee Utd); **1998** Gary Naysmith (Hearts); **1999** Barry Ferguson (Rangers); **2000** Kenny Miller (Hibernian); **2001** Stilian Petrov (Celtic); **2002** Kevin McNaughton (Aberdeen); **2003** James McFadden (Motherwell); **2004** Stephen Pearson (Celtic); **2005** Derek Riordan (Hibernian); **2006** Shaun Maloney (Celtic); **2007** Steven Naismith (Kilmarnock); **2008** Aiden McGeady (Celtic); **2009** James McCarthy (Hamilton); **2010** Danny Wilson (Rangers); **2011:** David Goodwillie (Dundee Utd); **2012** James Forrest (Celtic); **2013** Leigh Griffiths (Hibernian); **2014** Andy Robertson (Dundee Utd); **2015** Jason Denayer (Celtic); **2016** Kieran Tierney (Celtic); **2017** Kieran Tierney (Celticl); **2018** Kieran Tierney (Celtic); **2019** Ryan Kent (Rangers); **2020** No Award; **2021** David Turnbull (Celtic); **2022** Liel Abada (Celtic)

SCOTTISH MANAGER OF THE YEAR

1987 Jim McLean (Dundee Utd); **1988** Billy McNeill (Celtic); **1989** Graeme Souness (Rangers); **1990** Andy Roxburgh (Scotland); **1991** Alex Totten (St Johnstone); **1992** Walter Smith (Rangers); **1993** Walter Smith (Rangers); **1994** Walter Smith (Rangers); **1995** Jimmy Nicholl (Raith); **1996** Walter Smith (Rangers); **1997** Walter Smith (Rangers); **1998** Wim Jansen (Celtic); **1999** Dick Advocaat (Rangers); **2000** Dick Advocaat (Rangers); **2001** Martin O'Neill (Celtic); **2002** John Lambie (Partick Thistle); **2003** Alex McLeish (Rangers); **2004** Martin O'Neill (Celtic); **2005** Alex McLeish (Rangers); **2006** Gordon Strachan (Celtic); **2007** Gordon Strachan (Celtic); **2008** Billy Reid (Hamilton); **2009** Csaba Laszlo (Hearts); **2010** Walter Smith (Rangers); **2011:** Mixu Paatelainen (Kilmarnock); **2012** Neil Lennon (Celtic); **2013** Neil Lennon (Celtic); **2014** Derek McInnes (Aberdeen); **2015** John Hughes (Inverness); **2016** Mark Warburton (Rangers); **2017** Brendan Rodgers (Celtic); **2018** Jack Ross (St Mirren); **2019** Steve Clarke (Kilmarnock); **2020** Neil Lennon (Celtic); **2021** Stevn Gerrard (Rangers); **2022** Angelos Postecoglou (Celtic)

EUROPEAN FOOTBALLER OF THE YEAR

1956 Stanley Matthews (Blackpool); **1957** Alfredo di Stefano (Real Madrid); **1958** Raymond Kopa (Real Madrid); **1959** Alfredo di Stefano (Real Madrid); **1960** Luis Suarez (Barcelona); **1961** Omar Sivori (Juventus); **1962** Josef Masopust (Dukla Prague); **1963** Lev Yashin (Moscow Dynamo); **1964** Denis Law (Manchester Utd); **1965** Eusebio (Benfica); **1966** Bobby Charlton (Manchester Utd); **1967** Florian Albert (Ferencvaros); **1968** George Best (Manchester Utd); **1969** Gianni Rivera (AC Milan); **1970** Gerd Muller (Bayern Munich); **1971** Johan Cruyff (Ajax); **1972** Franz Beckenbauer (Bayern Munich); **1973** Johan Cruyff (Barcelona); **1974** Johan Cruyff (Barcelona); **1975** Oleg Blokhin (Dynamo Kiev); **1976** Franz Beckenbauer (Bayern Munich); **1977** Allan Simonsen (Borussia Moenchengladbach); **1978** Kevin Keegan (SV Hamburg); **1979** Kevin Keegan (SV Hamburg); **1980** Karl-Heinz Rummenigge (Bayern Munich); **1981** Karl-Heinz Rummenigge (Bayern Munich); **1982** Paolo Rossi (Juventus); **1983** Michel Platini (Juventus); **1984** Michel Platini (Juventus); **1985** Michel Platini (Juventus); **1986** Igor Belanov (Dynamo Kiev); **1987** Ruud Gullit (AC Milan); **1988** Marco van Basten (AC Milan); **1989** Marco van Basten (AC Milan); **1990** Lothar Matthaus (Inter Milan); **1991** Jean-Pierre Papin (Marseille); **1992** Marco van Basten (AC Milan); **1993** Roberto Baggio (Juventus); **1994** Hristo Stoichkov (Barcelóna); **1995** George Weah (AC Milan); **1996** Matthias Sammer (Borussia Dortmund); **1997** Ronaldo (Inter Milan); **1998** Zinedine Zidane (Juventus); **1999** Rivaldo (Barcelona); **2000** Luis Figo (Real Madrid); **2001** Michael Owen (Liverpool); **2002** Ronaldo (Real Madrid); **2003** Pavel Nedved (Juventus); **2004** Andriy Shevchenko (AC Milan); **2005** Ronaldinho (Barcelona); **2006** Fabio Cannavaro (Real

Madrid); **2007** Kaka (AC Milan); **2008** Cristiano Ronaldo (Manchester United); **2009** Lionel Messi (Barcelona)

WORLD FOOTBALLER OF YEAR

1991 Lothar Matthaus (Inter Milan and Germany); **1992** Marco van Basten (AC Milan and Holland); **1993** Roberto Baggio (Juventus and Italy); **1994** Romario (Barcelona and Brazil); **1995** George Weah (AC Milan and Liberia); **1996** Ronaldo (Barcelona and Brazil); **1997** Ronaldo (Inter Milan and Brazil); **1998** Zinedine Zidane (Juventus and France); **1999** Rivaldo (Barcelona and Brazil); **2000** Zinedine Zidane (Juventus and France); **2001** Luis Figo (Real Madrid and Portugal); **2002** Ronaldo (Real Madrid and Brazil); **2003** Zinedine Zidane (Real Madrid and France); **2004** Ronaldinho (Barcelona and Brazil); **2005** Ronaldinho (Barcelona and Brazil); **2006** Fabio Cannavaro (Real Madrid and Italy); **2007** Kaka (AC Milan and Brazil); **2008** Cristiano Ronaldo (Manchester United and Portugal); **2009** Lionel Messi (Barcelona and Argentina)

FIFA BALLON D'OR

(replaces European and World Footballer of the Year)

2010: Lionel Messi (Barcelona). **2011** Lionel Messi (Barcelona); **2012** Lionel Messi (Barcelona); **2013** Cristiano Ronaldo (Real Madrid); **2014:** Cristiano Ronaldo (Real Madrid); **2015** Lionel Messi (Barcelona)

FIFA BEST PLAYER

2016 Cristiano Ronaldo (Real Madrid); **2017** Cristiano Ronaldo (Real Madrid); **2018** Luka Modric (Real Madrid) ; **2019** Lionel Messi (Barcelona)); **2020:** Robert Lewandowski (Bayern Munich); **2021** Robert Lewandowski (Bayern Munich)

FIFA WORLD COACH OF THE YEAR

2010: Jose Mourinho (Inter Milan). **2011** Pep Guardiola (Barcelona); **2012** Vicente del Bosque (Spain); **2013** Jupp Heynckes (Bayern Munich); **2014** Joachim Low (Germany); **2015** Luis Enrique (Barcelona); **2016** Claudio Ranieri (Leicester); **2017** Zinedine Zidane (Real Madrid); **2018** Didier Deschamps (France); **2019** Jurgen Klopp (Liverpool); **2020** Jurgen Klopp (Liverpool); **2021** Thomas Tuchel (Chelsea)

THE THINGS THEY SAY ...

'To go through what I've been through, being back is a wonderful feeling' – **Christian Eriksen** on his comeback for Brentford, eight months after a cardiac arrest in Denmark's opening Euro 2020 match against Finland

'I looked him in the eyes He looked at me. And I said: "Enjoy it. Welcome back"' – **Kasper Hjulmand**, Denmark coach, on Christian Eriksen's return to international football against Holland.

'It was the siren call from a mermaid as the sailor passes by on his ship' – **Roy Hodgson** on his return to management with struggling Watford at the age of 74.

'I thought we could make a difference and help the club out. Unfortunately, we've failed in that respect' – **Roy Hodgson** on Watford relegation from the Premier League.

REVIEWS APPEARANCES, SCORERS 2021–22

(figures in brackets denote appearances as substitute)

PREMIER LEAGUE

ARSENAL

A return to Champions League football beckoned with three matches remaining. Arsenal were four points clear of Tottenham from the same number of matches played after four successive victories and 11 goals scored. Mikel Arteta's side overcame the loss of the injured Thomas Partey and Kieran Tierney to defeat Chelsea, Manchester United, West Ham and Leeds with the confidence to end a four-year exile from Europe's premier competition. Previously, the club stripped Pierre-Emerick Aubameyang of the captaincy for breaches of discipline, then gave him a free transfer to Barcelona. But that confidence suddenly drained away against their north London rivals, who maintained their own late charge with a comprehensive 3-0 victory. And it deserted them completely in a limp performance against rejuvenated Newcastle under Eddie Howe. A 2-0 defeat at St James' Park left them two points adrift and with little hope of Tottenham slipping up at relegated Norwich in the final round of fixtures. Arsenal took care of Everton, fresh from celebrating their survival, but as expected it was not enough. Tottenham also scored five, so fifth place meant Thursday nights in the Europa League, albeit after a season without any European competition for the first time since 1995–96.

Aubameyang P-E	12 (2)	Maitland-Niles A	2 (6)	Ramsdale A	34
Balogun F	1 (1)	Mari P	2	Saka B	36 (2)
Chambers C	2	Martinelli G	21 (8)	Sambi Lokonga A	12 (7)
Elneny M	8 (6)	Nelson R	- (1)	Smith Rowe E	21 (12)
Gabriel	35	Nketiah E	8 (13)	Soares C	16 (5)
Holding R	9 (6)	Nuno Tavares	13 (9)	Tierney K	22
Kolasinac S	1 (1)	Odegaard M	32 (4)	Tomiyasu T	20 (1)
Lacazette A	20 (10)	Partey T	23 (1)	White B	32
Leno B	4	Pepe N	5 (15)	Xhaka G	27

League goals (61): Saka 11, Smith Rowe 10, Odegaard 7, Martinelli 6, Gabriel 5, Nketiah 5, Aubameyang 4, Lacazette 4, Partey 2, Holding 1, Nuno Tavares 1, Pepe 1, Soares 1, Tierney 1, Xhaka 1, Opponents 1

FA Cup goals: None. **League Cup goals** (16): Nketiah 5, Aubameyang 3, Lacazette 2, Pepe 2, Chambers 1, Patino C 1, Saka 1, Smith Rowe 1

Average home league attendance: 59,776

Player of Year: Bukayo Saka

ASTON VILLA

Steven Gerrard's return to the Premier League as Villa manager started well, developed along more modest lines, then became the focus of attention on a dramatic final day of the season. Gerrard insisted that, first and foremost, he wanted his team to finish on a high against Manchester City. But, like everyone else, he knew that could mean delivering the title to his old club Liverpool. When Matty Cash and Philippe Coutinho established a 2-0 lead at the Etihad he looked like having his cake and eating it. Instead, they were overtaken by three goals in five minutes which left City champions for the fourth time in five years and Villa in 14th place, three places and ten points worse off than in 2021. Ahead of a first full season in charge, Gerrard promised to put his own stamp on the club, indicating major changes in personnel, with a first top-half finish since 2011 the minimum target. He left Rangers after breaking Celtic's stranglehold on the Scottish Premiership title the previous season to replace Dean Smith, the division's fifth manager to be sacked in early November following Villa's fifth successive defeat. Four of his first six matches were won and there was another successful sequence in the new year – back-to-back victories over Brighton, Southampton and Leeds. But Villa had a poor record against the leading teams.

Archer C .... - (3)	El Ghazi A 4 (5)	Ramsey J 29 (5)
Bailey L................... 7 (11)	Hause K 4 (3)	Sanson M 3 (7)
Buendia E.............. 22 (13)	Ings D 22 (8)	Steer J 1
Cash M......................38	Iroegbunam T 1 (2)	Targett M 17
Chambers C 9 (2)	Konsa E 29	Traore B 1 (8)
Chrisene B .... - (1)	Martinez E................36	Trezeguet .... - (1)
Chukwuemeka C 2 (10)	McGinn J 35	Tuanzebe A 6 (3)
Countinho P 16 (3)	Mings T 35 (1)	Watkins O.............. 33 (2)
Davis K .... - (1)	Nakamba M.............. 10 (6)	Wesley .... - (1)
Digne L......................16	Olsen R......................1	Young A 10 (14)
Douglas Luiz .... 31(3)	Philogene-Bidace J........ - (1)	

League goals (52): Watkins 11, Ings 7, Ramsey 6, Coutinho 5, Buendia 4, Cash 4, McGinn 3, Douglas Luiz 2, Konsa 2, Bailey 1, Chambers 1, El Ghazi 1, Hause 1, Mings 1, Targett 1, Opponents 2
FA Cup goals: None. **League Cup goals (7):** Archer 4, El Ghazi 2, Guilbert F 1
Average home league attendance: 41,650
Player of Year: Matty Cash

BRENTFORD

The dream became reality as Brentford exceeded all expectations with the help of an emotional return to the game by Christian Eriksen following his dice with death at Euro 2020. Eriksen, who suffered a cardiac arrest during his country's opening match against Finland, chose to join the club's Danish contingent following his release by Inter Milan at a time questions were being asked about their ability to last the course in the Premier League. Brentford defeated Arsenal, in their first top-flight game for 74 years, Wolves, West Ham, Everton and Watford. And approaching the halfway point of the season they were holding their own just below mid-table. Seven defeats in eight matches then resulted in a fall to within three points of the bottom three before Eriksen's first start sparked a 3-1 win over Norwich, with Ivan Toney's hat-trick. He scored his first goal in a remarkable 4-1 victory over Chelsea at Stamford Bridge and with maximum points in five successive fixtures, Brentford reached 40 with a month of the campaign still to play. They finished 13th and would have gone higher had Leeds not come away from the Community Stadium on the final day with the result needed to beat the drop.

Ajer K...................... 23 (1)	Ghoddos S................. 4 (13)	Pinnock E.......................32
Baptiste S............ 9 (13)	Henry R 33 (1)	Raya D 24
Bidstrup M................... - (4)	Janelt V 27 (4)	Roersley M 12 (9)
Canos S 25 (6)	Jansson P.....................37	Sorensen M B 9 (2)
Goode C.................... 4 (2)	Jensen M 19 (12)	Stevens F .... - (1)
Dasilva J 2 (7)	Jorgensen M 6 (2)	Thompson D 2
Eriksen C 10 (1)	Lossl J 2	Toney I....................32 (1)
Fernandez A..................12	Mbeumo B 34 (1)	Wissa Y 12 (18)
Forss M 1 (6)	Norgaard C 35	Young-Coombes N .... - (1)
Fosu-Henry T.............. - (1)	Onyeka F 12 (8)	

League goals (48): Toney 12, Wissa 7, Janelt 4, Mbeumo 4, Canos 3, Henry 3, Jansson 3, Norgaard 3, Ajer 1, Baptiste 1, Eriksen 1, Ghoddos 1, Jorgensen 1, Pinnock 1, Roersley 1, Opponents 2
FA Cup goals (5): Mbeumo 3, Forss 1, Toney 1. **League Cup goals (12):** Forss 5, Wissa 3, Canos 1, Mbeumo 1, Toney 1, Opponents 1
Average home league attendance: 16,899
Player of Year: Christian Norgaard

BRIGHTON AND HOVE ALBION

Brighton overcame two potentially dangerous passages of play to deliver the club's highest Premier League place of ninth and their biggest points total of 51. Graham Potter's side won four of their first five matches to reach the top four, before 11 without a victory provided a sober reminder of the company they were keeping. The second worrying spell came with a comfortable mid-table position apparently secured. Seven games produced a single goal, six defeats and Brighton needed a lift, even though there was no immediate threat coming from teams below them. It was provided by Leandro Trossard and Enock Mwepo, whose goals brought a 2-1 success at the Emirates undermined Arsenal bid for a Champions League place. A week later, they returned to north London to ruin Tottenham's chances of remaining in the top four with the only goal of the game from Trossard. Had Brighton held on to a 2-0 lead against Southampton, there would have been a third successive maximum. But they finished in style, scoring ten goals against Wolves, Manchester United and West Ham to reach ninth – a commendable performance after having their defensive ranks depleted by the loss of Ben White in the summer and Dan Burn during the winter transfer window.

Mac Allister A	22 (11)	Gross P	24 (5)	Richards T	- (2)
Alzate S	5 (4)	Lallana A	18 (6)	Sanchez R	37
Bissouma Y	25 (1)	Lamptey T	16 (14)	Sarmiento J	1 (4)
Burn D	12 (1)	Locadia J	- (1)	Steele J	1
Connolly A	1 (3)	March S	17 (14)	Trossard L	32 (2)
Cucurella M	35	Maupay N	25 (7)	Veltman J	33 (1)
Duffy S	15 (3)	Moder J	19 (9)	Webster A	16 (6)
Dunk L	29	Caicedo M	8	Welbeck D	15 (10)
Ferguson E	- (1)	Mwepu E	12 (6)		

League goals (42): Maupay 8, Trossard 8, Welbeck 6, Mac Allister 5, Gross 2, Mwepu 2, Webster 2, Bissouma 1, Burn 1, Cucurella 1, Duffy 1, Dunk 1, Caicedo 1, Veltman 1, Opponents 2
FA Cup goals (3): Bissouma 1, Maupay 1, Moder 1. **League Cup goals** (6): Connolly 2, Moder 1, Mwepu 1, Webster 1, Zeqiri A 1
Average home league attendance: 30,988
Player of Year: Marc Cucurella

BURNLEY

Burnley gambled by sacking Sean Dyche in the heat of a relegation struggle – and it almost paid off. Caretaker Mike Jackson revived flagging fortunes, despite losing Matej Vydra and Ashley Westwood to injuries. And they went into the last match of the season against rejuvenated Newcastle out of the bottom three on goal difference. Turf Moor was in expectant mood until young defender Nathan Collins needlessly flicked away a corner with his hand. Callum Wilson converted the penalty, added a second and Maxwel Cornet's reply was not enough. Leeds won at Brentford to stay up, Burnley went down after six years in the Premier League to face severe financial implications of life in the Championship. Dyche, appointed in 2012 and the division's longest-serving manager, was seven months into a new four-year contract. He admitted not enough matches had been won, while expressing surprise at the timing of his dismissal. Burnley had been up against it from the start, with a single victory in the first 21 games. They lost Chris Wood to Newcastle in the winter transfer window and his replacement, Holland striker Wout Weghorst from Wolfsburg did little to improve their poor strike rate. Jackson's promotion from coach brought back-to-back successes against Southampton, Wolves and Watford, but his side were back in trouble after losing to Aston Villa and Tottenham.

Barnes A	8 (15)	Cork J	20	Hennessey W	2
Brownhill J	32 (3)	Cornet M	21 (5)	Lennon A	17 (11)
Collins N	18 (1)	Gudmundsson J B	13 (5)	Long K	4 (2)

Lowton M................. 20 (5)	Roberts C................. 19 (2)	Vydra M 5 (17)
McNeil D 35 (3)	Rodriguez J 13 (16)	Weghorst W 17 (3)
Mee B 21	Stephens D 1 (2)	Westwood A 26 (1)
Pieters E................... 8 (4)	Tarkowski J 35	Wood C...........................17
Pope N 36	Taylor C 30 (1)	

League goals (34): Cornet 9, Mee 3, Wood 3, Brownhill 2, Collins 2, Lennon 2, Rodriguez 2, Vydra 2, Weghorst 2, Barnes 1, Cork 1, Lowton 1, Roberts 1, Tarkowski 1, Opponents 2
FA Cup goals (1): Rodriguez 1. **League Cup goals** (4): Rodriguez 4
Average home league attendance: 19,189
Player of Year: Nick Pope

CHELSEA

A season like no other at Stamford Bridge brought the end to the Roman Abramovich era, off the pace in the Premier League, defeat in both domestic cup finals – but success in the World Club Cup. Through it all, manager Thomas Tuchel maintained a calm, dignified presence which drew admiration through the game. Penalties shaped much of what happened on the pitch – victory over Villarreal in the European Super Cup, heartbreak against Liverpool at Wembley in the FA Cup and League Cup. In mid-season, Chelsea defeated Palmeiras of Brazil 2-1 to become world champions with goals from £97m record-buy Romelu Lukaku and Kai Havertz. Towards the end there was an epic Champion League quarter-final against Real Madrid when, against all the odds, a 3-1 loss in the first leg was transformed into a 4-3 overall lead in the Bernabeu before two Karim Benzema goals. Finally, they finished third without ever threatening the supremacy of Manchester City and Liverpool. By then the club was in new hands – an American-Swiss consortium headed by Todd Boehly, co-owner of the Los Angeles Dodgers baseball team. Abramovic was sanctioned following the war in Ukraine for links to Russian leader Vladimir Putin. During his 19 years at the helm there were 19 major trophies. Would that success be continued under the new owners, with the likelihood of big changes in the playing squad?

Arrizabalaga K..................4	James R 22 (4)	Mount M 27 (5)
Azpilicueta C............ 24 (3)	Jorginho 26 (3)	Pulisic C 13 (9)
Barkley R.................... 1 (5)	Kante N 21 (5)	Rudiger A......................34
Chalobah T 17 (3)	Kenedy 1	Sarr M 6 (2)
Chilwell B 6 (1)	Kovacic M 16 (9)	Saul Niguez..............5 (5)
Christensen A........... 17 (2)	Loftus-Cheek R 13 (11)	Thiago Silva...............28 (4)
Emerson .... - (1)	Lukaku R 16 (10)	Werner T ....15.(6)
Havertz K.................. 22 (7)	Marcos Alonso 25 (3)	Ziyech H 14 (9)
Hudson-Odoi C......... 11 (4)	Mendy E........................34	

League goals (76): Mount 11, Havertz 8, Lukaku 8, Jorginho 6, Pulisic 6, James 5, Marcos Alonso 4, Werner 4, Ziyech 4, Chalobah 3, Chilwell 3, Rudiger 3, Thiago Silva 3, Kante 2, Kovacic 2, Azpilicueta 2, Barkley 1, Hudson-Odoi 1, Opponents 1
FA Cup goals (14): Lukaku 3, Werner 2, Ziyech 2, Azpilicueta 1, Christensen 1, Hudson-Odoi 1, Loftus-Cheek 1, Marcos Alonso 1, Mount 1, Saul Niguez 1. **League Cup goals** (7): Havertz 2, Jorginho 1, Rudiger 1, Werner 1, Opponents 2
Champions League goals (21): Werner 4, Havertz 3, Jorginho 2, Lukaku 2, Pulisic 2, Azpilicueta 1, Chalobah 1, Christensen 1, Hudson-Odoi 1, James 1, Mount 1, Rudiger 1, Ziyech 1. **Club World Cup goals** (3): Lukaku 2, Havertz 1. **European Super Cup goals** (1): Ziyech 1
Average home league attendance: 36,424
Player of Year: Mason Mount

CRYSTAL PALACE

An encouraging first season at Selhurst Park for Patrick Vieira ended on a worrying note for the manager and his club. Minutes after Palace had surrendered a 2-0 lead at Everton and lost 3-2 to a side celebrating Premier League survival, Vieira was taunted and abused by a supporter. He responded by kicking out at the offender, prompting an investigation by police and the FA. Fortunately, common sense prevailed, neither taking action against the former Arsenal stalwart, with the FA concentrating its attention on the mass pitch invasion. Palace went on to complete the campaign with a 1-0 victory over Manchester United which moved Palace up to 12th – an improvement of two places and four points on 2021. Vieira, who succeeded Roy Hodgson during the summer, took over a much-changed squad, with nine senior players leaving. In their place was a younger, fresher line-up producing football that was easier on the eye. Conor Gallagher, on loan from Chelsea, earned an England call-up on the back of enterprising performances in midfield, one of them highlighted by a goal in the 2-0 away victory over Manchester City. Gareth Southgate also introduced central defender Marc Guehi, who featured in Palace's run to the semi-finals of the FA Cup with the opening goal in a 4-0 victory over Everton.

Andersen J.............. 32 (2)	Gallagher C............... 33 (1)	Mitchell T.................35 (1)
Ayew J..................... 23 (8)	Guaita V..........................30	Olise M 12 (14)
Benteke C............. 11 (14)	Guehi M..........................36	Rak-Sakyi J 1 (1)
Butland J.................... 8 (1)	Hughes W............. 13 (3)	Riedewald J................ 1 (2)
Clyne N 15 (1)	Kouyate C................. 23 (4)	Schlupp J............20 (12)
Edouard O............. 18 (10)	Mateta J-P............. 13 (9)	Tomkins J................... 6 (2)
Eze E 6 (7)	McArthur J 15 (6)	Ward J 27 (1)
Ferguson N .... - (1)	Milivojevic L 9 (6)	Zaha W 31 (2)

League goals (50): Zaha 14, Gallagher 8, Edouard 6, Mateta 5, Benteke 4, Schlupp 4, Ayew 3, Guehi 2, Olise 2, Eze 1, Tomkins 1
FA Cup goals (10): Guehi 2, Mateta 2, Olise 2, Hughes 1, Kouyate 1, Ridewald 1, Zaha 1.
League Cup goals: None.
Average home league attendance: 24,282
Player of Year: Conor Gallagher

EVERTON

Across Stanley Park, their neighbours had added more silverware to the trophy cabinet. For Everton, celebrations were in marked contrast – the spectre of relegation finally removed on a tumultuous night at Goodison Park. In accordance with a troubled season, they did it the hard way, trailing Crystal Palace 2-0 and facing the prospect of a visit to Arsenal for an all-or-nothing final fixture. Instead, Michael Keane offered hope, Richarlison equalised and Dominic Calvert-Lewin completed the comeback with five minutes of normal time remaining. While all the pent-up frustrations of supporters turned to relief, Frankl Lampard called it one of the best moments of a distinguished career. For Calvert-Lewin it was also a moment to savour after missing half the campaign through injury. But if the contribution of one player stood out it was that of England goalkeeper Jordan Pickford, who made one of saves of the season against Cesar Azpilicueta against Chelsea and had another fine game against Leicester. Without those back-to-back victories, his side could well have gone down. Everton had started promisingly under Rafael Benitez, back in the Premier League after managing in China, with ten points from first four games. But the loss of Calvert-Lewin and, for a while Richarlison, was followed by worrying home defeats by Watford (5-2) and Liverpool (4-1). Benitez was sacked after one win in 13 games. There was no marked improvement under Lampard. They dropped into the bottom three after another defeat by Liverpool and when Jarrad Branthwaite and Salomon Rondon were sent off against Brentford, they were in deep trouble.

Allan 25 (3)	Begovic A 3	Cenk Tosun .... - (1)
Alli D....................... 1 (10)	Branthwaite J............. 4 (2)	Coleman S 30
Andre Gomes.............. 7 (7)	Calvert-Lewin D....... 15 (2)	Davies T 2 (4)

Delph F 8 (3)	Holgate M 23 (2)	Price I .... - (1)
Digne L 13	Iwobi A 22 (6)	Richarlison 28 (2)
Dobbin L .... - (3)	Kean M .... - (1)	Rondon S 8 (12)
Doucoure A 29 (1)	Keane M 31 (1)	Simms E 1
El Ghazi A .... - (2)	Kenny J 11 (4)	Townsend A 17 (4)
Gbamin J-P 1 (2)	Mina Y 11 (2)	Van de Beek D 5 (2)
Godfrey B 23	Mykolenko V 12 (1)	
Gordon A 25 (10)	Onyango T .... - (3)	
Gray D 28 (6)	Pickford J 35	

League goals (43): Richarlison 10, Calvert-Lewin 5, Gray 5, Gordon 4, Keane 3, Townsend 3, Doucoure 2, Holgate 2, Iwobi 2, Branthwaite 1, Coleman 1, Davies 1, Mykolenko 1, Rondon 1, Van de Beek 1, Opponents 1
FA Cup goals (9): Rondon 2, Townsend 2, Andre Gomes 1, Gray 1, Holgate 1, Mina 1, Richarlison 1. **League Cup goals (4):** Townsend 2, Digne 2, Iwobi 1
Average home league attendance: 38,441
Player of Year: Jordan Pickford

LEEDS UNITED

American coach Jesse Marsch stabilised a season spinning out of control at Elland Road, saw his side slide back into trouble, then supervised survival in the final match. Leeds went into it third from bottom on goal difference. They came out with a 2-1 win at Brentford, secured by Jack Harrison's 94th minute goal, to overtake Burnley, beaten by the same scoreline at home to Newcastle. A catalogue of injuries, together with Marcelo Bielsa's declining influence, came to a head with four damaging defeats and 17 goals conceded by Everton, Manchester United, Liverpool and Tottenham. Leeds slipped to within two points of the bottom three and Bielsa, architect of the club's return to the Premier League after a 16-year absence followed by a season of consolidation, was sacked. It was almost a reluctant dismissal in light of what he had achieved and considering the casualty list he faced – Patrick Bamford missing for most of the season, Liam Cooper, Kalvin Phillips and Luke Ayling sidelined for months on end. But with relegation a distinct possibility, the club felt there was no alternative and entrusted Marsch with steering a course to safety. The former RB Leipzig coach, started with two more defeats before Joe Gelhardt's 94th minute winner against Norwich turned the tide. Another stoppage-time goal, from Ayling, completed a recovery from two down to 3-2, then a 3-0 success against Watford gave his new side breathing space.

Ayling L 26	Harrison J 32 (3)	McKinstry S .... - (1)
Bamford P 7 (2)	Helder Costa .... - (1)	Meslier I 38
Bate L 1 (2)	Hjelde L .... - (2)	Phillips K 18 (2)
Cooper L 21	James D 29 (3)	Raphina 34 (1)
Cresswell C 1 (4)	Junior Firpo 19 (5)	Rodrigo 27 (4)
Dallas S 34	Klaesson K .... - (1)	Roberts T 7 (16)
Drameh C 1 (2)	Klich M 26 (7)	Shackleton J 7 (7)
Forshaw A 17 (5)	Koch R 17 (3)	Struijk P 22 (7)
Gelhardt J 5 (15)	Llorente D 28	Summerville C .... - (6)
Greenwood S 1 (6)	McCarron .... - (1)	

League goals (42): Raphina 11, Harrison 8, Rodrigo 6, James 4, Llorente 3, Ayling 2, Bamford 2, Gelhardt 2, Dallas 1, Klich 1, Roberts 1, Struijk 1
FA Cup goals: None. **League Cup goals (3):** Harrison 2, Phillips 1
Average home league attendance: 36,285
Player of Year: Raphina

LEICESTER CITY

A season blighted by injuries left Leicester holding on to a place in the top half of the table and out of two European competitions. Brendan Rodgers had to reshape his defence from the start, with Jonny Evans, Wesley Fofana and James Justin all ruled out for long spells. The manager then had to contend with losing Jamie Vardy for most of the second half of the campaign. Not surprisingly, his side struggled for consistency after victory over Manchester City in the traditional Community Shield opener to the new campaign. They conceded too many goals from set pieces and at no stage came close to threatening the leading group. Leicester's defence of the FA Cup ended with a 4-1 defeat by Nottingham Forest in round four. Failure to qualify from the group stage of the Europa League was followed by a semi-final defeat by Jose Mourinho's Roma in the semi-finals of the inaugural Europa Conference. How much they missed Vardy was evident on his return when he scored four goals in back-to-back victories over Norwich and Watford and another in a 4-1 success against Southampton on the final afternoon.

Albrighton M 11 (6)	Evans J 16 (2)	Schmeichel K 37
Amartey D................ 23 (5)	Fofana W..........................7	Soumare B 12 (7)
Ayoze Perez................ 6 (8)	Iheanacho K 13 (13)	Soyuncu C 28
Barnes H 24 (8)	Justin J 11 (2)	Thomas L 21 (1)
Bertrand R 4	Lookman A 16 (10)	Tielemans Y............... 29 (3)
Brunt L........................ - (1)	Maddison J............... 28 (7)	Vardy J.................... 20 (5)
Castagne T............... 22 (5)	McAteer K .... - (1)	Vestergaard J 6 (4)
Choudhury H............... 4 (2)	Mendy N 12 (2)	Ward D............................ 1
Daka P 13 (10)	Ndidi O 18 (1)	
Dewsbury-Hall K 23 (5)	Ricardo Pereira 13 (1)	

League goals (62): Vardy 15, Maddison 12, Barnes 6, Lookman 6, Tielemans 6, Daka 5, Iheanacho 4, Ayoze Perez 2, Albrighton 1, Castagne 1, Dewsbury-Hall 1, Evans 1, Ricardo Pereira 1, Soyuncu 1
FA Cup goals (5): Albrighton 1, Barnes 1, Iheanacho 1, Maddison 1, Tielemans 1. **League Cup goals** (7): Lookman 2, Vardy 2, Barnes 1, Iheanacho 1, Maddison 1. **Community Shield goals** (1): Iheanacho 1
Europa League goals (12): Daka 5, Amartey 1, Ayoze Perez 1, Barnes 1, Dewsbury-Hall 1, Evans 1, Maddison 1, Ndidi 1. **Europa Conference** goals (13): Maddison 3, Barnes 2, Albrighton 1, Daka 1, Dewsbury-Hall 1, Fofana 1, Iheanacho 1, Ndidi 1, Ricardo Pereira 1, Opponents 1
Average home league attendance: 32,440
Player of Year: James Maddison

LIVERPOOL

Liverpool did all they could to achieve what many felt was impossible – four trophies in a single season. But, in the space of six days, everything conspired against Jurgen Klopp and his players. First, the Premier League title was in their grasp until Manchester City scored three goals in five minutes to retrieve a 2-0 deficit against Aston Villa and retain top spot. Then, an inspired performance by Thibaut Courtois, who denied Mohamed Salah no fewer than six times, enabled Real Madrid to win the Champions League Final on a chaotic night in Paris. Liverpool were left with FA Cup and League Cup successes, both against Chelsea and both on penalties. Klopp won two Manager of the Year awards, Salah had a share of the Golden Boot with Tottenham's Son Heung-min and Alisson a share of the Golden Glove alongside City's Ederson. But these collective and individual honours tended to pale next to finishing runners-up to the two big prizes. Some consolation came with the way they ran City so close after starting the new year 11 points behind with a single game in hand. Ten successive victories and 25 goals scored reduced that deficit to one point and from then on the pair went toe to toe. It remained after a 2-2 draw at the Etihad – arguably the game of the season. Liverpool were then held by Tottenham, City by West Ham. No quarter was asked, none was given.

Alexander-Arnold T 32	Henderson J 29 (6)	Morton T 1 (1)
Alisson 36	Jones C 10 (5)	Origi D ....- (7)
Diaz L............. 11 (2)	Keita N 14 (9)	Oxlade-Chamberlain A .9 (8)
Diogo Jota............... 27 (8)	Kelleher C 2	Robertson A.................. 29
Elliott H.................... 4 (2)	Konate I....................11	Salah M 30 (5)
Fabinho 26 (3)	Mane S 32 (2)	Thiago Alcontara 17 (8)
Firmino R 10 (10)	Matip J 31	Tsimikas K..................9 (4)
Gomez J 4 (4)	Milner J 9 (15)	Van Dijk V 34
Gordon K .... - (1)	Minamino T............. 1 (10)	Williams N..................- (1)

League goals (94): Salah 23, Mane 16, Diogo Jota 15, Fabinho 5, Firmino 5, Diaz 4, Keita 3, Matip 3, Minamino 3, Origi 3, Robertson 3, Van Dijk 3, Alexander-Arnold 2, Henderson 2, Oxlade-Chamberlain 2, Jones 1, Thiago Alcontara 1
FA Cup goals (13): Minamino 3, Diogo Jota 2, Fabinho 2, Mane 2, Elliott 1, Firmino 1, Gordon 1, Konate 1. **League Cup goals** (10): Minamino 4, Diogo Jota 3, Origi 2, Oxlade-Chamberlain 1.
Champions League goals (30): Salah 8, Firmino 5, Mane 5, Diaz 2, Konate 2, Diogo Jota 1, Fabinho 1, Henderson 1, Keita 1, Origi 1, Thiago Alcontara 1, Opponents 2
Average home league attendance:53,096
Player of Year: Mohamed Salah

MANCHESTER CITY

The debate will continue for years to come – was this the most dramatic of Manchester City's last-day-of-the-season title triumphs? Ahead of 2012 when stoppage-time goals by Edin Dzeko and Sergio Aguero against Queens Park Rangers pipped Manchester United at the post on goal difference? More special than 2019, after the leadership had changed hands 32 times over the course of the season, with City coming from behind to beat Brighton to finish a point ahead of Liverpool? This time, two goals by Ilkay Gundogan and one from Rodri in the space of five minutes transformed a 2-0 deficit against Aston Villa, which again edged out Liverpool by the same margin. Each success was remarkable in its own way and it would be no surprise if season 2022-23 produced another thrilling campaign. Pep Guardiola's side scored ten successive victories to go into the new year eight points ahead of Chelsea and nine clear of Liverpool, who had a game in hand. They scored 17 goals in successive matches against Leeds, Newcastle and Leicester and, after extending that run to 12, there seemed no stopping them. Instead, dropped points against Southampton, Tottenham and Crystal Palace enabled Liverpool to close the gap, which eventually became a single point after they were held 2-2 by West Ham in the penultimate fixture. Elsewhere, City's four-year stranglehold on the League Cup was ended by West Ham on penalties, they lost to Liverpool in the semi-finals of the FA Cup and, most damaging, there was the Champions League defeat by Real Madrid after going into the 90th minute of the return match in the Bernabeu two goals ahead on aggregate.

Ake N 10 (4)	Gabriel Jesus 21 (7)	Palmer C......................- (3)
Bernardo Silva.......... 33 (2)	Grealish J.................. 22 (4)	Rodri 33
De Bruyne K.......... 25 (5)	Gundogan I.............. 20 (7)	Ruben Dias.............. 27 (2)
Delap L......................- (1)	Joao Cancelo 36	Steffen Z.........................1
Ederson 37	Kayky.......................... - (1)	Sterling R.................. 23 (7)
Egan-Riley C .... - (1)	Laporte A 33	Stones J 12 (2)
Fernandinho 10 (9)	Mahrez R 15 (13)	Walker K 20
Ferran Torres....................4	McAtee J..................... - (2)	Zinchenko O 10 (5)
Foden P.................. 24 (4)	Mendy B 1	

League goals (99): De Bruyne 15, Sterling 13, Mahrez 11, Foden 9, Gabriel Jesus 8, Gundpgan 8, Bernardo Silva 8, Rodri 7, Laporte 4, Grealish 3, Ake 2, Fernandinho 2, Ferran Torres 2, Ruben Dias 2, Joao Cancelo 1, Stones 1, Opponents 3

FA Cup goals (16): Mahrez 4, Bernardo Silva 2, Grealish 2, Gundogan 2, De Bruyne 1, Foden 1, Gabriel Jesus 1, Palmer 1, Sterling 1, Stones 1. **League Cup goals** (6): Mahrez 2, De Bruyne 1, Ferran Torres 1, Foden 1, Palmer 1
Champions League goals (29): Mahrez 7, Gabriel Jesus 4, Bernardo Silva 3, Foden 3, Sterling 3, De Bruyne 2, Joao Cancelo 2, Ake 1, Grealish 1, Palmer 1, Walker 1, Opponents 1
Average home league attendance: 52,739
Player of Year: Kevin De Bruyne

MANCHESTER UNITED

No club came under more scrutiny than Manchester United during a season of under-achievement. Not even the return of Cristiano Ronaldo as leading scorer could halt their decline after finishing Premier League and Europa League runners-up under Ole Gunnar Solskjaer in 2021. Ronaldo, back at Old Trafford 12 years after leaving for Real Madrid scored 24 goals in all competitions. He also became the first player to score 800 goals at top level with a brace in a 3-2 victory over Arsenal. Questions were asked whether the 36-year-old's singular approach benefited or hindered the players around him. Certainly, without his goals United would probably not even have been able to finish sixth – 35 points behind champions Manchester City. Solskjaer was sacked after they were outplayed at home by Liverpool and Manchester City and lost 4-1 at Watford. Ralph Rangnick, previously head of sports and development at Lokomotiv Moscow and his surprise replacement until the end of the season, failed to effect any improvement. United were knocked out of the FA Cup by Middlesbrough on penalties and went out of the Champions League to Atletico Madrid in the last 16. Ajax coach Erik ten Hag was appointed on a permanent basis, after which a 4-0 defeat at Brighton meant the club's worst-ever Premier League points total – 58.

Alex Telles	18 (3)	Jones P	2 (2)	Rashford M	13 (12)
Bailly E	3 (1)	Lindelof V	26 (2)	Ronaldo C	27 (3)
Bruno Fernandes	35 (1)	Lingard J	2 (14)	Sancho J	20 (9)
Cavani E	7 (8)	Maguire H	28 (2)	Shaw L	19 (1)
Dalot D	19 (5)	Martial A	2 (6)	Shoretire S	- (1)
De Gea D	38	Mata J	2 (5)	Van de Beek D	- (8)
Elanga A	14 (7)	Matic N	16 (7)	Varane R	20 (2)
Fred	24 (4)	McTominay S	28 (2)	Wan-Bissaka A	20
Greenwood M	16 (2)	Mejbri H	1 (1)		
James D	2	Pogba P	16 (4)		

League goals (57): Ronaldo 18, Bruno Fernandez 10, Greenwood 5, Fred 4, Rashford 4, Sancho 3, Cavani 2, Elanga 2, Lingard 2, Maguire 1, Martial 1, McTominay 1, Pogba 1, Varane 1, Van de Beek 1, Opponents 1
FA Cup goals (2): McTominay 1, Sancho 1. **League Cup goals:** None
Champions League goals (12): Ronaldo 6, Alex Telles 1, Elanga 1, Greenwood 1, Maguire 1, Rashford 1, Sancho 1
Average home league attendance: 73,161
Player of Year: David de Gea

NEWCASTLE UNITED

Eddie Howe transformed fortunes at St James' Park armed with a £100m budget from new owners for the winter transfer window. Back in management 15 months after leaving Bournemouth, he signed five players after a Saudi-led consortium paid £305m to bring to an end Mike Ashley's controversial 14 years in control. One of them, Kieran Tripper, delivered an instant dividend with trademark free-kicks in successive victories against Everton and Aston Villa to lift his new side out of the bottom three. The England defender played no further part in the revival because of a broken bone in his left foot, joining long-term casualty Callum Wilson on the sidelines. But Howe, brought in when Steve Bruce was sacked shortly after reaching 1,000 games as a manager, had another player making an instant hit in Bruno Guimaraes. He also successfully switched the midfielder's fellow Brazilian Joelinton to a deeper role and Newcastle continued to flourish. They won six successive home games for the first time since the days of Sir Bobby Robson, establishing a place in the top half of the table when Joelinton doubled his tally for the season with two goals in a 3-0 win at Norwich.

Almiron M............. 19 (11)	Hayden I 12 (2)	Saint-Maximin A 31 (4)
Bruno Guimaraes...... 11 (6)	Hendrick J................. - (3)	Schar F 25
Burn D 16	Manquillo J 15 (4)	Shelvey J................... 22 (2)
Clark C 12 (1)	Joelinton 30 (5)	Targett M 16
Darlow K...........................8	Krafth E 18 (2)	Trippier K 5 (1)
Dubravka M...................26	Lascelles J 22 (4)	Willock J 24 (5)
Dummett P 2 (1)	Lewis J................... 4 (1)	Wilson C 16 (2)
Fernandez F 5 (2)	Longstaff S 15 (9)	Wood C 15 (2)
Fraser R................... 18 (9)	Murphy J 13 (20)	Woodman F 4
Gayle D...................... - (8)	Ritchie M 14 (4)	

League goals (44): Wilson 8, Bruno Guimaraes 5, Saint-Maximin 5, Joelinton 4, Fraser 2, Schar 2, Shelvey 2, Trippier 2, Willock 2, Wood 2, Almiron 1, Hayden 1, Hendrick 1, Manquillo 1, Lascelles 1, Longstaff 1, Murphy 1, Opponents 3
FA Cup goals: None. **League Cup goals:** None
Average home league attendance: 51,487
Player of Year: Joelinton

NORWICH CITY

Norwich spent modestly on their previous Premier League season. This time, the club changed tack by investing £50m in strengthening the squad. They also changed managers, sacking Daniel Farke four months into a four-year-contract after a single win in the opening 11 matches and a 7-0 drubbing by Chelsea. There was no change, however, in what followed – an immediate return to the Championship by a side equally as ill-equipped to meet the demands of the top-flight as the previous one had been. Dean Smith, who replaced Farke eight days after his own dismissal by Aston Villa, made an encouraging start – victory over Southampton and the spoils shared with Wolves and Newcastle. But six successive defeats, without a goal scored, underlined the size of his task. And although United States international Josh Sargent was on the mark twice in a 3-0 success at Watford which lifted his side out of the bottom four, the respite was only brief. Teemu Pukki was again the nearest Norwich came to having anything like a genuine marksman and there was only one more victory to show for the rest of the campaign – 2-0 against Burnley. They went down after losing the return against Villa with four matches remaining, one against Tottenham, who claimed the fourth Champions League place with a 5-0 win at Carrow Road.

Aarons M 32 (2)	Kabak O...........................11	Rowe J...................... - (13)
Byram S 11 (4)	Krul T 29	Rupp L................ 7 (12)
Cantwell T................ 5 (3)	Lees-Melou P............ 27 (6)	Sargent J............ 18 (8)
Dowell K 11 (8)	McLean K 29 (2)	Sorensen J 6 (4)
Giannoulis D 14 (4)	Mumba B .... - (1)	Springett T 1 (2)
Gibson B...................28	Normann M 20 (3)	Tzolis C.................... 3 (11)
Gilmour B 21 (3)	Omobamidele A 4 (1)	Williams B............ 23 (3)
Gunn A...................9	Placheta P 6 (6)	Zimmerman C............ 2 (1)
Hanley G...................33	Pukki T 37	
Idah A 6 (11)	Rashica M 25 (6)	

League goals (23): Pukki 11, Sargent 2, Dowell 1, Hanley 1, Idah 1, Lees-Melou 1, McLean 1, Normann 1, Omobamidele 1, Rashica 1, Opponents 2
FA Cup goals (3): McLean 1, Rashica 1, Rupp 1. **League Cup goals (6):** Sargent 2, Tzolis 2, McLean 1, Rupp 1
Average home league attendance: 26,885
Player of Year: Teemu Pukki

SOUTHAMPTON

Southampton started poorly, finished not much better and could not improve on the previous season's 15th place. In between, sufficient points were accrued to keep a relatively safe distance from the bottom three. A shortage of goals was evident throughout, with only midfielder James Ward-Prowse reaching double figures, thanks to his prowess for set-piece situations. So too was his side's repeated failure to hold on to leading positions, with 29 points dropped. The first of the captain's two goals against Brighton took him to within four of David Beckham's record of 18 successful Premier League free-kicks. Southampton came from 2-0 down in that match, but lost England under-21 full-back Tino Livramento with a knee injury which could keep him out for the remainder of the year. They also excelled with a 3-2 victory at Tottenham, achieved by goals in the final 11 minutes from Mohamed Elyounoussi and Che Adams in a performance Ralph Hasenhuttl rated the best of his tenure as manager. Southampton failed to win any of the first seven games before three 1-0 scorelines against Leeds, Watford and Aston Villa took them clear of trouble. They twice held Manchester City and defeated Arsenal 1-0. But a 6-0 home defeat by Chelsea and a single point from the final six fixtures ruled out any prospect of a mid-table position.

Adams C 23 (7)	Forster F 19	Smallbone W 2 (2)
Armstrong A 17 (6)	Livramento T 25 (3)	Stephens J 9 (2)
Armstrong S 15 (10)	Long S 3 (10)	Tella N 10 (4)
Bednarek J............... 30 (1)	Lyanco 9 (6)	Valery Y.................... 3 (2)
Broja A 21 (11)	McCarthy A.................17	Walcott T................. 5 (4)
Caballero W....................2	Perraud R 18 (2)	Walker-Peters K 29 (3)
Diallo I 10 (13)	Redmond N............. 20 (7)	Ward-Prowse J 36
Djenepo M 5 (7)	Romeu O 34 (2)	
Elyounoussi M......... 23 (7)	Salisu M.................. 33 (1)	

League goals (43): Ward-Prowse 10, Adams 7, Broja 6, Bednarek 4, Elyounousi 4, Armstrong A 2, Armstrong S 2, Romeu 2, Livramento 1, Long 1, Redmond 1, Walker-Peters 1, Opponents 2
FA Cup goals (9): Armstrong S 1, Broja 1, Elyounoussi 1, Long 1, Perraud 1, Redmond 1, Walker-Peters 1, Ward-Prowse 1, Opponents 1. **League Cup goals (11):** Elyounoussi 3, Broja 2, Adams 1, Diallo 1, Redmond 1, Salisu 1, Tella 1, Walker-Peters 1
Average home league attendance: 29,860
Player of Year: James Ward-Prowse

TOTTENHAM HOTSPUR

Antonio Conte was happy to eat his own words after writing off his new club's chances of a Champions League place. Conte insisted they were too inconsistent and it would be a 'miracle' to achieve a top-four place. A run of four defeats in five matches seemed to suggest the manager had got his sums right, with Tottenham seven points adrift. But Son Heung-min struck a rich seam of goals alongside Harry Kane, who proved in a slightly deeper role that he can make them as well as score them. Spurs netted five against Everton and Newcastle and put four past Leeds and Aston Villa – Son scoring a hat-trick at Villa Park. The pair combined for a crucial 3-0 victory over Arsenal, then Kane's winner against relegation-threatened Burnley that left his side in fourth place. two points clear of Arsenal with a superior goal difference, and away to relegated Norwich in the final round of fixtures. A 5-0 victory confirmed it, with two more for Son taking his tally to 23 for a share in the Golden Boot award alongside Liverpool's Mohamed Salah. Conte, a Premier League and FA Cup winner with Chelsea and latterly coach to Inter Milan, came in when Nuno Espirito Santo was sacked four months into the job after supporters turned against him after a 3-0 home defeat by Manchester United.

Alli D........................ 8 (2)	Kane H 36 (1)	Sanchez D................. 17 (6)
Betancur R 16 (1)	Kulusevski D........... 14 (4)	Scarlett D.................... - (1)
Bergwijn S 4 (21)	Lloris H 38	Sessegnon R............. 13 (2)
Davies B 28 (1)	Lo Celso G................. 2 (7)	Skipp O...................... 14 (4)
Dier E...........................35	Lucas Moura........... 19 (15)	Son Heung-min............. 35
Doherty M 9 (6)	Ndombele T............... 6 (3)	Tanganga J 10 (1)
Emerson 26 (5)	Reguilon S 22 (3)	Winks H 9 (10)
Gil B .... - (9)	Rodon J .... - (3)	
Hojbjerg P....................36	Romero C 21 (1)	

League goals (69): Son Heung-min 23, Kane 17, Kulusevski 5, Bergwijn 3, Doherty 2, Hojbjerg 2, Lucas Moura 2, Reguilon 2, Sanchez 2, Alli 1, Davies 1, Emerson Royal 1, Ndombele 1, Romero 1, Opponents 6
FA Cup goals (6): Kane 3, Lucas Moura 1, Winks 1, Opponents 1. **League Cup goals (5):** Lucas Moura 2, Bergwijn 1, Kane 1, Ndombele 1
Europa Conference goals (14): Kane 6, Lo Celso 2, Alli 1, Son Heung-min 1, Hojbjeg 1, Lucas Moura 1, Opponents 2
Average home league attendance: 56,523
Player of Year: Son Heung-min

WATFORD

Claudio Ranieri was unable to weave the magic which made him a legend at Leicester and Roy Hodgson's 46 years in management counted for little as Watford dropped straight back into the Championship. On the way down, the pair shared an unwanted English top-flight record of 11 successive home defeats, with Hodgson, the club's 15th 'permanent' manager in ten years, unable see his team record a single win at Vicarage Road. The 74-year-old came in believing he could bring about some degree of improvement to a side rooted in the bottom three. In truth, Hodgson was on a hiding to nothing in his 17th club appointment until the end of the season. There were victories at Villa Park and Southampton, but Watford never looked like escaping and went down with three fixtures remaining, ironically after losing at Hodgson's former club Crystal Palace. He bowed out gracefully, handing over to Forest Green's League Two title-winner Rob Edwards, the former Wolves and Wales defender. Ranieri had lasted less than four months in the job after taking over from Xisco Munoz, sacked seven games into the season, despite having won promotion in 2021. The Italian supervised handsome success at Everton (5-2), with a hat-trick from Josh King, and 4-1 against Manchester United before the malaise set in and he too was ousted from the game's most precarious managerial position.

Bachmann D..................12	Kabasele C 12 (4)	Ngakia J......................9 (7)
Cathcart C.............. 27 (4)	Kalu S 2 (2)	Etebo P.....................4 (5)
Cleverley T 20 (8)	Kamara H.................. 18 (1)	Rose D........................7 (1)
Deeney T .... - (2)	Kayembe E 9 (4)	Samir 19
Dennis E................. 30 (3)	Kiko.........................., 26 (1)	Sarr I........................21 (1)
Fletcher A.................. - (3)	King J 27 (5)	Sema K......................7 (11)
Foster B....................26	Kucka J.................... 22 (4)	Sierralta F 5
Gosling D...................2 (2)	Louza I...................... 17 (3)	Sissoko M.......................36
Hernandez J.......... 11 (14)	Masina A.................. 13 (2)	Troost-Ekong W 15 (2)
Joao Pedro............. 15 (13)	N'koulou N................ 2 (1)	Tufan O.......................4 (3)

League goals (34): Dennis 10, Hernandez 5, King 5, Sarr 5, Joao Pedro 3, Sissoko 2, Gosling 1, Kamara 1, Kucka 1, Opponents 1
FA Cup goals (1): Joao Pedro 1. **League Cup goals (2):** Fletcher 2
Average home league attendance: 20,590
Player of Year: Hassane Kamara

WEST HAM UNITED

A hitherto successful season for David Moyes and his players ended on a disappointing note. They led through Michail Antonio at Brighton on the final day and looked to be on the way to another campaign in the Europa League after reaching the semi-finals this time. Instead, they conceded three second-half goals, lost the chance to overtake Manchester United in the table and had to be satisfied with a place in the Europa Conference. Moyes reached 1,000 matches as a manager at West Ham made an impression on all fronts, without quite breaking through in any of them. His side were up to third in the Premier League after beating Liverpool 3-2 in early November, held down fourth place in mid-February and remained in contention for a Champions League spot until the final month of the campaign. They ended Manchester City's four-year dominance of the League Cup and reached the fifth round of the FA Cup. But it was in Europe where they excelled. After topping the group, they knocked out Sevilla and Lyon and had high hopes of reaching the final. But a 2-1 home defeat by Eintracht Frankfurt was followed by a 1-0 reversal, in the second leg when Aaron Cresswell was sent off and Moyes shown a red card for kicking the ball at a ball boy.

Antonio M	34 (2)	Diop IO	10 (3)	Ogbonna A	11
Areola A	1	Fabianski L	37	Perkins S	- (1)
Ashby H	- (1)	Fornals P	32 (4)	Rice D	35 (1)
Benrahma S	26 (6)	Fredericks R	3 (4)	Soucek T	34 (1)
Bowen J	34 (2)	Johnson B	16 (4)	Vlasic N	6 (13)
Chesters D	- (1)	Kral A	- (1)	Yarmolenko A	1 (18)
Coufal V	25 (3)	Lanzini M	19 (11)	Zouma K	24
Cresswell A	31	Masuaku A	6 (7)		
Dawson C	30 (4)	Noble M	3 (8)		

League goals (60): Bowen 12, Antonio 10, Benrahma 8, Fornals 6, Lanzini 5, Soucek 5, Cresswell 2, Dawson 2, Johnson 1, Masuaku 1, Noble 1, Ogbonna 1, Rice 1, Vlasic 1, Yarmolenko 1, Zouma 1, Opponents 2
FA Cup goals (5): Bowen 2, Antonio 1, Lanzini 1, Rice 1. **League Cup goals** (2): Bowen 1, Lanzini 1
Europa League goals (18): Benrahma 3, Bowen 3, Rice 3, Antonio 2, Dawson 2, Yarmolenko 2, Diop 1, Noble 1, Soucek 1
Average home league attendance: 59,151
Player of Year: Declan Rice

WOLVERHAMPTON WANDERERS

A late season slump cost Wolves the chance of a place in Europe. Under new manager Bruno Lage, they were handily placed after back-to-back victories over Watford and Everton, then one against Aston Villa to complete the double over their west Midlands rivals. But the failure to win any of the final seven fixtures ruled out any prospect of overhauling two teams immediately above them, Manchester United and West Ham. That sequence included a 5-1 home defeat by Manchester City and a 3-1 loss to Liverpool after taking a third-minute lead through Pedro Neto on the final day of the campaign at Anfield. Former Benfica coach Lage replaced Nuno Espirito Santo, who stepped down in the summer after four years in charge and subsequently had a brief, unsuccessful spell in charge at Tottenham. Wolves started poorly, losing four of the opening five games, but were up and running with successive victories over Southampton, Newcastle and Villa, the latter achieved by goals from Romain Saiss, Conor Coady and Ruben Neves in the final 15 minutes which overturned a 2-0 deficit. Coady also made his mark with a 97th minute equaliser at Stamford Bridge for a 2-2 draw against Chelsea. Wolves finished tenth, an improvement of three places on 2021.

Ait Nouri R.............. 20 (3)	Gibbs-White M............. - (2)	Podence D.............. 15 (11)
Boly W...................10	Hee-Chan Hwang ... 20 (10)	Raul Jimenez...........30 (4)
Campbell C .... - (1)	Hoever K-J 4 (4)	Ruben Neves 31 (2)
Chiquinho 1 (7)	Jonny...................... 10 (3)	Ruddy J 1 (1)
Coady C 38	Jose Sa 37	Saiss R 31
Cundle L................... 2 (2)	Kilman M 30	Tote Gomes 4
Dendoncker L.......... 21 (9)	Joao Moutinho 34 (1)	Traore A 10 (10)
Fabio Silva 6 (16)	Nelson Semedo...............25	Trincao 16 (12)
Fernando Marcal....... 17 (1)	Pedro Neto 5 (8)	

League goals: (38): Raul Jimenez 6, Hee-Chan Hwang 5, Coady 4, Ruben Neves 4, Dendoncker 2, Jonny 2, Joao Moutinho 2, Podence 2, Saiss 2, Trincao 2, Ait Nouri 1, Kilman 1, Pedro Neto 1, Traore 1, Opponents 3
FA Cup goals (3): Podence 2, Nelson Semedo 1. **League Cup goals** (6): Podence 2, Gibbs-White 1, Dendoncker 1, Saiss 1, Trincao 1
Average home league attendance: 30,602
Player of Year: Jose Sa

SKY BET CHAMPIONSHIP

BARNSLEY

Former manager Valerien Ismael cast a shadow throughout the season as Barnsley struggled under two successors and were relegated. Austrian coach Markus Schopp, who took over when Ismael left for West Bromwich Albion after leading the club to the play-offs, was sacked after a single win in 15 league games. His replacement, Sweden under-21 coach Poya Asbaghi, had to wait 12 matches for his first three points – 1-0 against Queens Park Rangers – and by then, his team were six points adrift. They had missed Ismael's leading scorer, Cauley Woodrow, out for four months with an ankle injury. Back-to-back successes against Hull (2-0) and Middlesbrough (3-2) offered some encouragement. But late equalisers conceded to Stoke and Fulham denied Barnsley the chance to build on those two performances. Overall, the division's lowest scoring record proved too big a handicap and they went down, still rooted to the foot of the table, with a fortnight still to play. Asbaghi was replaced by Cheltenham's Michael Duff.

Adeboyejo V 7 (19)	Helik M..........................38	Sibbick T 11 (1)
Andersen M...................28	Helliwell J 1 (1)	Sraha J 2
Bassi A 14 (1)	Hondermarck W 3 (6)	Styles C 40 (3)
Benson J................ 14 (11)	Kitching L 29 (3)	Thompson C ....- (1)
Bremang D.................... - (2)	Leya Iseka A............ 14 (11)	Vita R 18 (1)
Brittain C 34 (2)	Marsh A 2 (2)	Walton J.....................6 (1)
Christie-Davies I 1 (1)	Moon J...................... 18 (7)	Williams B 5
Cole D 8 (16)	Morris C 26 (2)	Williams J 17 (4)
Collins B.......................40	Oduor C 10 (10)	Wolfe M 13 (3)
Frieser D................. 12 (2)	Oulare O.................... - (2)	Woodrow C 25 (3)
Gomes C 28 (3)	Palmer R................... 24 (9)	
Halme A 2 (3)	Quina.........................16	

League goals (33): Morris 7, Woodrow 4, Adeboyejo 3, Leya Iseka 3, Styles 3, Bassi 2, Frieser 2, Quina 2, Andersen 1, Cole 1, Gomes 1, Helik 1, Marsh 1, Palmer 1, Sibbick 1
FA Cup goals (5): Morris 2, Andersen 1, Cole 1, Williams J 1. **League Cup goals:** None
Average home league attendance: 12,824
Player of Year: Brad Collins

BIRMINGHAM CITY

Another poor season came to a head with two damaging defeats over Easter. Birmingham surrendered a two-goal lead to lose 4-2 to Coventry at St Andrew's. Three days later, manager Lee Bowyer called a 6-1 drubbing at Blackpool 'my lowest day in football' and captain Troy Deeney went over to apologise to supporters at the final whistle. The losses dropped Bowyer's side to fifth from bottom after an encouraging start which included a 5-0 victory at Luton. They accumulated 11 points from the opening six games, but then failed to score in six in succession. Back-to-back maximums against Swansea, Middlesbrough and Bristol City looked to have put things right. Instead, a single success in ten, including a 6-2 defeat at Fulham, sent them sliding and they were grateful to have enough points in the bank to keep the bottom three at arm's length. After a sixth successive campaign in the lower reaches of the division, Bowyer was sacked..

Aneke C................... 1 (17)	Graham J 18 (6)	Oakley M...........................2
Bacuna J 16 (1)	Hall G........................ 1 (1)	Pedersen K...................... 37
Bela J 26 (5)	Hernandez O........... 21 (1)	Richards T.................... 2 (4)
Bellingham J............. - (2)	Hogan S................... 28 (8)	Roberts Marc 39
Chong T.................. 18 (2)	Ivan Sanchez I .... - (2)	Roberts Mitchell 1
Colin M................... 31 (2)	James J.................... 13 (6)	Sanderson D............. 14 (1)
Dean H................... 14 (1)	Jeacock Z........................2	Sarkic M 23
Deeney T 15 (6)	Castillo J.................... 1 (2)	Sunjic I....................... 33 (8)
Etheridge N....................21	Jutkiewicz L 17 (19)	Taylor L............................ 14
Friend G 11 (3)	Leko J......................... 1 (3)	Trueman C...................... - (1)
Gardner G 31 (4)	McGree R 10 (3)	Woods R.................... 25 (5)
Gordon N 11	Mengi T 9	

League goals (50): Hogan 10, Gardner 6, Taylor 5, Deeney 4, Hernandez 3, Sunjic 3, Aneke 2, Bacuna 2, Bela 2, Jutkiewicz 2, McGree 2, Pedersen 2, Roberts Marc 2, Chong 1, Colin 1, Gordon 1, James 1, Opponents 1
FA Cup goals: None. **League Cup goals (1):** Oakley 1
Average home league attendance: 16,375
Player of Year: Matija Sarkic

BLACKBURN ROVERS

Ben Brereton Diaz matched Alan Shearer's 1995–96 record of 20 league goals before the turn of the year to set Blackburn on course for a promotion bid. The new Chile international took them level on points with Fulham at the half-way point after a record 7-0 home defeat by the eventual champions was followed by seven wins in the next eight matches. But his goals dried up, an ankle injury kept him out for a month and Rovers dropped out of contention for a top-two place after eight goalless games in nine. By the time Brereton Diaz returned, they were also struggling to maintain a play-off place, with Tony Mowbray admitting they had relied on him too much. A first goal for four months was not enough to prevent defeat by relegation-bound Peterborough and Blackburn finished six points adrift. Mowbray, appointed in February 2017 and the Championship's longest serving manager, left the club at the end of his contract and was replaced by former Newcastle and Denmark forward Jon Dahl Tomasson.

Ayala D.................... 16 (5)	Dack B.......................... - (9)	Khadra R 18 (9)
Brereton Diaz B 34 (3)	Davenport J................ 2 (7)	Lenihan D........................41
Brown J 1	Dolan T.................... 20 (15)	Magloire T.................. 1 (3)
Buckley J 39 (3)	Gallagher S 28 (9)	Markandy D................ - (2)
Butterworth D........... 1 (11)	Giles R 8 (3)	Nyambe R........................31
Carter H................... 5 (4)	Hedges R 4 (7)	Pears A....................... 2 (1)
Chapman H................ - (3)	Johnson B................ 8 (10)	Pickering H................ 31 (1)
Clarkson L................ 4 (3)	Kaminski T 44	Poveda I 4 (6)

Rankin-Costello J........ 6 (4)	Travis L...........................45	Van Hecke J P 30 (1)
Rothwell J................ 36 (5)	Vale J .... - (2)	Zeefuik D.................... 4 (2)
Tayo Edun................. 13 (7)	Wharton S....................30	

League goals (59): Brereton Diaz 22, Gallagher 9, Dolan 4, Khadra 4, Buckley 3, Lenihan 3, Rothwell 3, Ayala 2, Pickering 2, Wharton 2, Dack 1, Poveda 1, Travis 1, Van Hecke 1 Opponents 1
FA Cup goals (2): Ayala 1, Khadra 1. **League Cup goals** (1): Dolan 1
Average home league attendance: 14,218
Player of Year: Jan Paul van Hecke

BLACKPOOL

Play-off winners Blackpool had a satisfactory return to the Championship. Neil Critchley's side took a while to find their feet, but were up and running after defeating the eventually champions Fulham and went on to fare better than the two other promoted teams, Hull and Peterborough. The manager signed a new four-and-a-half-year contract after a spell in the top half of the table, helped by victory at Reading, where a two-goal deficit was overturned in the final 22 minutes by goals from the previous season's leading marksman Jerry Yates (2) and Owen Dale. Blackpool slipped from that position in a run of seven games without a win approaching the midway part of the campaign, but had no worries about dropping into trouble and treated one of their biggest crowds of the season to a 6-1 victory over Birmingham in the penultimate home game, with Jake Beesley scoring twice on his first start. Critchley left to become Steven Gerrard's No. 2 at Aston Villa and was replaced by former Lincoln manager Michael Appleton.

Anderson K 29 (3)	Gretarsson D................ 2 (1)	Mitchell D 6 (7)
Beesley J 4 (2)	Grimshaw D....................26	Moore S .... - (1)
Bowler J 30 (12)	Hamilton C 17 (7)	Robson E 2
Carey S 5 (6)	Husband J................ 28 (3)	Sterling D................ 22 (2)
Casey O 3 (3)	James R 15 (2)	Stewart K 10 (2)
Connolly C 25 (6)	John-Jules T 8 (3)	Thorniley J 12 (2)
Dale O 7 (8)	Keogh R 26 (3)	Virtue M 1 (2)
Dougall K 37 (3)	Kirk C 7 (2)	Ward G...............................4
Ekpiteta M 39 (1)	Lavery S 20 (17)	Wintle R 18
Gabriel J 19 (2)	Madine G 27 (7)	Yates J 23 (16)
Garbutt L 14 (3)	Maxwell C................ 20 (1)	

League goals (54): Madine 9, Lavery 8, Yates 8, Bowler 7, Ekpiteta 5, Anderson 4, Beesley 2, Connolly 2, Dale 2, Hamilton 2, Carey 1, Casey 1, Dougall 1, Husband 1, Opponents 1
FA Cup goals (1): Anderson 1. **League Cup goals** (5): Lavery 2, Anderson 1, Bowler 1, Connolly 1
Average home league attendance: 14,365
Player of Year: Marvin Ekpiteta

BOURNEMOUTH

Dominic Solanke fired the club back to the Premier League under new manager Scott Parker. After a season's absence, they finished runners-up to Parker's former club Fulham, with Solanke's 29 goals second in the scoring charts to the champions' record-breaking Aleksandar Mitrovic. Bournemouth looked as if they might run away with promotion after 15 games unbeaten to start the season. The club-record run, 11 victories and four draws, established a nine-point lead over West Bromwich Albion in third place. It was whittled down when they failed to win any of the next six matches. There was also a wobble in successive games before Easter when Solanke had a rare blank spell and his side were goalless against Albion, Sheffield United and Middlesbrough. Two against Coventry restored order. Then, Wales striker Kieffer Moore made an impact on his return to the side after a broken foot. He scored twice as Bournemouth retrieved a 3-0 deficit at

Swansea for a point and netted the only goal against nearest rivals Nottingham Forest to ensure his side went up. They closed to within two points of the champions after winning the final three matches.

Anthony J 38 (7)	Hill J .... - (1)	Phillips N 17
Billing P 37 (3)	Kelly L 40 (1)	Rogers M 1 (14)
Brady R 2 (4)	Kilkenny G 13 (1)	Rossi Z 3 (1)
Brooks D 7	Laird E 4 (2)	Saydee C .... - (2)
Cahill G 21 (1)	Lerma J 33 (1)	Smith A 20
Cantwell T 8 (3)	Lowe J 9 (25)	Solanke D 46
Christie R 36 (2)	Marcondes E 8 (9)	Stacey J 24 (1)
Cook L 25 (3)	Mepham C 12 (10)	Stanislas J 2 (5)
Cook S 3	Moore K .... - (4)	Travers M 45
Davis L 7 (5)	Nyland O 1	Zemura J 32 (1)
Dembele S 4 (9)	Pearson B 8 (15)	

League goals (74): Solanke 29, Billing 10, Anthony 8, Lowe 7, Moore 4, Christie 3, Zemura 3, Dembele 2, Marcondes 2, Brooks 1, Cook L 1, Kelly 1, Lerma 1, Rogers 1, Opponents 1
FA Cup goals (3): Marcondes 3. **League Cup goals (5):** Brooks 2, Billing 1, Saydee 1, Solanke 1
Average home league attendance: 9,753
Player of Year: Mark Travers

BRISTOL CITY

Andi Weimann made a successful return from injury in a transitional season for the club. The Austria forward scored 22 goals, provided ten assists and started every match after being sidelined for most of the previous campaign. His tally included a hat-trick against Millwall when City included seven Academy graduates. There was also a brace against Barnsley when his side ended 17 matches without a victory at Ashton Gate. Weimann and Chris Martin, who missed only one match, led the way as City were the highest scorers outside the top teams. They also had one of the worst defensive records, keeping only six clean sheets and conceding too many goals in the final ten minutes of matches. That meant no back-to-back wins until 3-1 against relegated Derby followed by a 5-0 success against Hull in the final home match when Weimann and Martin shared four of the goals. City finished 17th, an improvement of two places on 2021.

Atkinson R 29 (5)	James M 31 (2)	Pring C 23 (9)
Baker N 13 (2)	Janneh S .... - (1)	Scott A 35 (3)
Bakinson T 10 (3)	Kalas T 34 (1)	Semenyo A 24 (7)
Bell S 3 (2)	King A 10 (4)	Simpson D 2 (1)
Benarous A 7 (4)	Klose T 18	Tanner G 11 (2)
Bentley D 37 (1)	Martin C 43 (2)	Towler R 1
Conway T .... - (4)	Massego H-N 26 (11)	Weimann A 46
Cundy R 10 (4)	O'Dowda C 16 (4)	Wells N 7 (25)
Dasilva J 28 (8)	O'Leary M 9	Williams J 13 (9)
Idehen D .... - (2)	Palmer K 1 (5)	

League goals (62): Weimann 22, Martin 12, Semenyo 8, Scott 4, Wells 3, Atkinson 2, Baker 1, Bakinson 1, Dasilva 1, James 1, King 1, Klose 1, O'Dowda 1, Palmer 1, Tanner 1, Opponents 2
FA Cup goals: None. **League Cup goals (2):** Janneh 2
Average home league attendance: 19,205
Player of Year: Andi Weimann

CARDIFF CITY

A club-record run of defeats undermined Cardiff's prospects of building on the revival in fortunes under Mick McCarthy the previous season. They started well, with defender Aiden Flint scoring four times in successive matches against Peterborough and Millwall. But eight straight losses cost McCarthy his job after nine months, casting a shadow over the whole campaign and the appointment of coach Steve Morison, initially as caretaker then as permanent manager. Morison began with a point at Stoke, where his side retrieved a three-goal deficit, but for a while, looked as if he might have a struggle against relegation on his hands. Cardiff slid to within three points of the bottom three before victory over Nottingham Forest sparked a sequence of 12 points from five matches which removed that threat. They were victims, however, of another record when a 4-0 home defeat by Swansea followed a 3-0 reversal in the teams' first meeting – the first league double in the history of the South Wales derby. Cardiff finished 18th, down ten places from 2021.

Bacuna L 13 (2)	Evans K 2 (3)	Ng P 39
Bagan J 22 (4)	Flint A 35 (3)	Pack M 23 (1)
Bowen S 3 (1)	Giles R 19 (2)	Phillips D 17
Brown C 5	Harris M 17 (17)	Ralls J 26 (3)
Collins J 13 (13)	Hugill J 17 (1)	Sang T 3
Colwill R 15 (19)	Ikpeazu U 1 (12)	Smithies A 29
Davies I 10 (18)	King E 3 (1)	Vaulks W 23 (13)
Denham O 5	McGuinness M 33 (1)	Watters M 5 (3)
Doughty A 7 (2)	Moore K 15 (7)	Wintle R 20 (3)
Doyle T 17 (2)	Morrison S 16	Zimba C 1
Drameh C 22	Nelson C 30	

League goals (50): Flint 6, Colwill 5, Moore 5, Hugill 4, Bagan 3, Collins 3, Harris 3, Ikpeazu 3, McGuinness 3, Morrison 3, Davies 2, Doyle 2, Vaulks 2, Bacuna 1, Doughty 1, Pack 1, Ralls 1, Watters 1, Opponents 1
FA Cup goals (3): Colwill 1, Davies 1, Harris 1. **League Cup goals** (3): Watkins M 2, Murphy J 1
Average home league attendance: 18,869
Player of Year: Cody Drameh

COVENTRY CITY

Mark Robins and his players won plenty of admirers for an enterprising season which kept them on the fringes of a play-off place until Easter. Their ability to retrieve losing positions and pick up points – many with late goals – was a key asset, typified when turning a two-goal deficit into a 4-2 victory at Birmingham, with Ben Sheaf scoring his first two goals for the club. It followed a 3-1 success at Craven Cottage, where they became the only side to complete the double over champions Fulham, having been 4-1 winners earlier in the campaign. Coventry climbed to within three points of the top six, but missed chances proved costly against Bournemouth, whose own clinical finishing delivered a 3-0 victory on their way back to the Premier League. A goalless draw against West Bromwich Albion put them out of the running, but Robins signed an unspecified contract extension and following Tony Mowbray's departure from Blackburn is now the longest serving Championship manager with five years in the job.

Allen J 29 (9)	Howley R .... - (1)	Rose M 24 (5)
Bidwell J 13 (3)	Hyam D 41 (2)	Sheaf B 33 (4)
Clarke-Salter J 27 (2)	Jones J .... - (9)	Shipley J 8 (3)
Da Costa J 2 (2)	Kane T 23 (6)	Tavares F .... - (7)
Dabo F 26 (3)	Kelly L 8 (8)	Waghorn M 11 (16)
Eccles J 3 (2)	Maatsen I 35 (5)	Walker T 4 (15)
Godden M 17 (7)	McFadzean K 35 (2)	Wilson B 5 (1)
Gyokeres V 41 (4)	Moore S 41	
Hamer G 37 (2)	O'Hare C 43 (2)	

League goals (60): Gyokeres 17, Godden 12, O'Hare 5, Hamer 3, Maatsen 3, McFadzean 3, Hyam 2, Rose 2, Sheaf 2, Walker 2, Allen 1, Kane 1, Shipley 1, Tavares 1, Waghorn 1, Opponents 4

FA Cup goals (2): Gyokeres 1, Hyam 1. **League Cup goals** (1): Walker 1
Average home league attendance: 19,541
Player of Year: Gustavo Hamer

DERBY COUNTY

Derby went down but Wayne Rooney's stock soared in a season which would have tested to the limit an experienced manager, let alone one in his first full season in charge. Rooney never lost faith in his players, nor in his own ability to handle a 12-point deduction for entering administration, nine more for historic breaches of spending rules and the constant threat of the club folding. He also took in his stride the loss of the experienced Phil Jagielka and Graeme Shinnie in the winter transfer window, introducing more young players who contributed to cutting the deficit to eight points, then five. At that point the former Manchester United and England captain declared it would be the biggest achievement of his career were Derby to escape. That they failed to do so was down more to the way struggling Reading responded to another former stalwart for club and country, Paul Ince, who took them clear of trouble in his role as caretaker manager. Derby had one last shot of upsetting all the odds, overcoming champions-elect Fulham, before defeat by QPR sent them down to the third tier for the first time since the 1985–86 season. Rooney resigned in the summer, maintaining the club needs 'fresh energy'.

Aghatise O .... - (3)	Ebosele F 18 (17)	Robinson D..................- (1)
Allsop R.................. 29 (1)	Forsyth C.............. 23 (3)	Roos K 17 (1)
Baldock S 12 (1)	Hutchinson I................. - (1)	Shinnie G..................... 21
Bielik K 12 (3)	Jagielka P......................20	Sibley L 11 (15)
Bird M........................ 41 (1)	Jozwiak K 13 (4)	Stearman R 10 (4)
Buchanan L 24 (6)	Kazim-Richards C 5 (18)	Stretton J 1 (8)
Byrne N..........................41	Knight J 31 (7)	Thompson L 19 (4)
Cashin E 14 (4)	Lawrence T............ 37 (1)	Watson L..................3 (1)
Cybulski B 1 (3)	Morrison R 25 (11)	Williams D..................2 (4)
Davies C 46	Plange L................ 19 (7)	
Ebiowei M............. 11 (5)	Peliza Richards C...... - (1)	

League goals (45): Lawrence 11, Davies 4, Morrison 4, Plange 4, Forsyth 3, Kazim-Richards 3, Baldock 2, Bird 2, Ebosele 2, Knight 2, Bielik 1, Cashin 1, Ebiowei 1, Shinnie 1, Sibley 1, Stretton 1, Opponents 2
FA Cup goals: None. **League Cup goals** (4): Hutchinson 1, Kazim-Richards 1, Morrison 1, Sibley 1
Average home league attendance: 23,010
Player of Year: Curtis Davies

FULHAM

Aleksandar Mitrovic and his team flooded the Championship with goals in an impressive return to the Premier League at the first attempt under new manager Marco Silva. They topped the 100 mark in becoming champions ahead of Bournemouth, with Mitrovic's tally of 43 breaking Guy Whittingham's post-1992 second-tier scoring record. The Serb, who signed a new five-year contract early on, struck hat-tricks against Swansea, West Bromwich Albion and Bristol City and scored a brace in nine other matches His team overwhelmed Blackburn and Reading 7-0, the first to do so away from home in the same season since Liverpool in 1895-96. They repeated that scoreline against Luton to clinch the title in the penultimate fixture, having also hit six against Bristol City and Birmingham and five against Huddersfield and Swansea. Fulham's position was threatened briefly by a run of five games without a win approaching the midway point of the campaign. After that they were always in control. Mitrovic was acclaimed the EFL's top player, his manager having to cede to Nathan Jones's achievement in taking unfancied Luton to the play-offs.

Bryan J................. 13 (2)	Kebano N................. 31 (9)	Rodak M 33
Cairney T 16 (10)	Knockaert A................ - (4)	Muniz R 2 (23)
Carvalho F............... 33 (3)	Mawson A................... 1 (5)	Seri J.......................... 26 (7)
Cavaleiro I.............. 5 (13)	Mitrovic A...................44	Stansfield J ....- (1)
Chalobah N.............. 11 (9)	Odoi D 17 (1)	Tete K 15 (5)
Decordova-Reid B... 26 (15)	Onomah J................. 8 (12)	Tosin Adarabioyo............ 41
Francois T................ 1 (1)	Quina...................... 1 (1)	Williams N..................... 14
Gazzaniga P 13	Ream T.......................46	Wilson H 40 (1)
Hector M 4	Reed H 32 (7)	Zambo F.......................- (3)
Kamara A.................... - (1)	Robinson A............... 33 (3)	

League goals (106): Mitrovic 43, Carvalho 10, Wilson 10, Kebano 9, Decordova-Reid 8, Muniz 5, Cairney 3, Cavaleiro 2, Robinson 2 Tete 2, Tosin Adarabioyo 2, Williams 2, Seri 1, Odoi 1, Onomah 1, Ream 1, Opponents 4
FA Cup goals (2): Carvalho 1, Wilson 1. **League Cup goals** (2): Robinson 1, Stansfield 2
Average home league attendance: 17,774
Player of Year: Aleksandar Mitrovic

HUDDERSFIELD TOWN

Defeat by Nottingham Forest in the Play-off Final took nothing away from considerable progress made under Carlos Corberan. The former right-hand man to Marcelo Bielsa at Leeds experienced an uncomfortable first season in charge, his new team finishing fifth from bottom. But despite minimal investment during the summer, then a 5-1 defeat by Fulham in the first home fixture, Huddersfield soon made an impact. Corberan reshaped his defence, with Levi Colwill on loan from Chelsea a key figure, developed a major threat from set-pieces, which yielded 21 goals, and at the midway point had climbed to sixth. They were briefly in an automatic promotion position behind Fulham before Bournemouth began addressing a backlog of fixtures. After that, they protected third place during a run of 17 games without losing and finished two points ahead of their Wembley opponents. The only goal of a tight match of few chances came two minutes from half-time when Colwill, under pressure, diverted a cross from James Garner into his own net. Huddersfield, second best up to then, had Forest on the defensive after the break without managing an effort on target. They did have two penalty appeals for challenges on Harry Toffolo and Lewis O'Brien, with borderline decisions going against them.

Aarons R...................... - (1)	Lees T...................... 39 (1)	Sarr N...................... 14 (4)
Anjorin F...................... - (7)	Nicholls L...................43	Schofield R...................... 2
Blackman J...................1	O'Brien L...................43	Sinani D................ 31 (8)
Campbell F 4 (15)	Odubeko M................- (6)	Thomas S................ 42 (1)
Colwill L 26 (3)	Pearson M...................37	Toffolo H 40 (2)
Eiting C 1 (4)	Pipa 6 (5)	Turton O................ 25 (15)
High S 14 (9)	Rhodes J 6 (15)	Vallejo A.................. 2 (3)
Hogg J..........................31	Rowe A .... - (1)	Ward D................ 37 (3)
Holmes D 26 (11)	Ruffles J.................... 2 (6)	
Koroma J 19 (15)	Russell J................ 15 (2)	

Play-offs – appearances: Hogg 3, Lees 3, O'Brien 3, Nicholls 3, Sinani 3, Toffolo 3, Ward 3, Holmes 2 (1), Pipa 2 (1), Russell 2 (1), Sarr 2 (1), Colwill 2, Thomas 1 (2), Turton 1, Rhodes – (3)
League goals (64): Ward 14, Sinani 6, Toffolo 6, Holmes 5, Koroma 4, Lees 3, O'Brien 3, Pearson 3, Rhodes 3, Sarr 3, Thomas 3, Colwill 2, Hogg 2, Russell 2, Anjorin 1, Vallejo 1, Opponents 2. **Play-offs – goals** (2): Rhodes 1, Sinani 1
FA Cup goals (4): Holmes 1, Koroma 1, Lees 1, Pearson 1. **League Cup goals** (1): Lees 1
Average home league attendance: 17,352
Player of Year: Lee Nicholls

HULL CITY

Another eventful season on Humberside, following a title-winning return to the Championship, brought a new owner and a new manager to the club. Turkish businessman Acun Ilicali bought it from the Allam family, owners for 12 years and unpopular to the end, and immediately sacked Grant McCann, despite back-to-back victories over promotion-minded Blackburn and Bournemouth. He installed former Rangers, Ajax and Georgia international Shota Arveladze, promising to bring the fans on board for what he predicted would be 'a beautiful journey.' The new man had a successful start, victory over Swansea, but it proved a rare home success. There were six successive defeats at the KCOM Stadium before Cardiff were beaten, a run which could have proved costly without victories away to Peterborough, Coventry and Middlesbrough. Those points gained enabled Hull to keep the bottom three at arm's length, although they will be looking to improve on 19th place in the new season.

Baxter N 16	Hinds J .... - (1)	Mills J..........................- (1)
Bernard D 24 (2)	Honeyman G............ 34 (1)	Moncur G 7 (7)
Cannon A............... 4 (6)	Huddlestone T 4 (7)	Sayyadmanesh A.........6 (6)
Cartwright H............... 1 (1)	Ingram M 29	Scott J ....- (1)
Coyle L 21 (2)	Jarvis W .... - (1)	Slater R 12 (4)
Docherty G............... 31 (9)	Jones A 21 (2)	Smallwood R 40 (2)
Eaves T................... 12 (19)	Jones C .... - (2)	Smith T 7 (16)
Elder C 21 (7)	Lewis-Potter K............46	Walsh L 1 (2)
Emmanuel J............... 3 (3)	Longman R............... 26 (9)	Wilks M 17 (3)
Fleming B 15 (1)	Magennis J 18 (1)	Williams R...................4 (9)
Forss M 5 (6)	Smith M 6 (3)	
Greaves J......................46	McLoughlin S 29 (3)	

League goals (41): Lewis-Potter 12, Eaves 5, Honeyman 5, Longman 4, Wilks 3, Magennis 2, Smallwood 2, Cannon 1, Coyle 1, Forss 1, Jones A 1, Sayyadmanesh 1, Smith 1, Opponents 2
FA Cup goals (2): Longman 1, Smith 1. **League Cup goals** (1): Lewis-Potter 1
Average home league attendance: 12,888
Player of Year: Keane Lewis-Potter

LUTON TOWN

A fairy-tale season carried Luton into the play-offs against all the odds – and they were not far away from extending it to a Wembley final. 'It was like reaching utopia' beamed Nathan Jones, whose side finished sixth in a division packed with big clubs, then stretched Huddersfield all the way in their semi-final. After a 1-1 draw at Kenilworth Road, they had chances to take control of the return, but failed to take them and were punished by a Jordan Rhodes goal eight minutes from time. It was still a remarkable achievement for a club, who were playing non-league football in 2014, then for six successive seasons continued to improve their Football League position. Recognition came with Jones named EFL Championship Manager of the Year, ahead of promotion-winning Marco Silva at Fulham and Bournemouth's Scott Parker. Approaching the midway point of the campaign, Luton were in the bottom half, before a run of 13 matches yielding 29 points launched their challenge. A 7-0 drubbing at Fulham and a spate of injuries, threatened to derail it, with leading scorer Elijah Adebayo hobbling and Jones having to bring in goalkeeper Matt Ingram from Hull on an emergency loan. But they held on thanks to Harry Cornick's winner against Reading and results elsewhere in the final round of fixtures.

Adebayo E............... 38 (2)	Burke R 25 (2)	Ingram M..........................2
Bell A...................... 40 (1)	Campbell A 31 (2)	Isted N 1 (1)
Berry L 10 (3)	Clark J 19 (6)	Jerome C 14 (17)
Bradley S................... 20 (2)	Cornick H 30 (8)	Kioso P...................... 8 (8)
Bree J......................42	Hylton D 5 (12)	Lansbury H 18 (16)

Lockyer T .... 27 (2) Osho G .... 16 (7) Shea J 19
Mendes Gomes C .... 2 (7) Palmer A ....2 Sluga S 19
Muskwe A .... 7 (13) Potts D .... 9 (1) Snodgrass R 4 (4)
Naismith K ....42 Rea G .... 8 (4) Steer J 3
Onyedinma F .... 14 (15) Ruddock P 31 (3)

Play-offs – appearances: Bell 2, Bradley 2, Bree 2, Burke 2, Clark 2, Campbell 2, Cornick 2, Ingram M 2, Naismith 2, Hylton M 2 (1), Jerome 1 (1), Snodgrass 1 (1), Lansbury 1, Adebayo – (1), Lockyer 1 (1), Mendes Gomes – (1)
League goals (63): Adebayo 16, Cornick 12, Berry 6, Campbell 4, Hylton 4, Jerome 3, Onyedinma 3, Bradley 2, Clark 2, Naismith 2, Bell 1, Bree 1, Lockyer 1, Ruddock 1, Opponents 5. **Play-offs – goals** (1): Bradley 1
FA Cup goals (9): Burke 2, Adebayo 1, Berry 1, Cornick 1, Jerome 1, Mendes Gomes 1, Muskwe 1, Naismith 1. **League Cup goals (2):** Jerome 1, Muskwe 1
Average home league attendance: 9,857
Player of Year: Kai Naismith

MIDDLESBROUGH

Chris Wilder took Sheffield United into the Premier League and quickly set about steering Middlesbrough in that direction when taking over at the Riverside from Neil Warnock, dismissed four days after supervising a record 1,602nd English league match. Wilder's first nine games yielded 20 points, lifting his new side from the bottom half of the table to sixth. While not threatening the top two, Fulham and Bournemouth, Middlesbrough looked a decent bet to maintain a play-off place. But after a 4-0 victory at Peterborough with a month of the season remaining, form deserted them, goals dried up and five matches yielded just two points. The sequence included defeats by champions-elect Fulham and in-form Huddersfield and left them five points adrift. There was still a chance that successive wins over Cardiff and Stoke, depending on victory at Preston in the final round of fixtures and results elsewhere going their way. As it was, both Luton and Sheffield United were winners, while a 4-1 defeat at Deepdale, which Wilder admitted was not good enough, proved irrelevant.

Akpom C .... - (1) Fry D .... 32 (1) McNair P 42
Balogun F .... 9 (9) Hall G ....8 Morsy S 3
Bamba S .... 18 (6) Hernandez O .... 9 (8) Olusanya T .... - (3)
Bola M .... 19 (4) Howson J .... 44 (1) Payero M 6 (7)
Boyd-Munce C .... - (1) Ikpeazu U .... 8 (12) Peltier L 17 (4)
Coburn J .... 3 (15) Jones I .... 36 (6) Spence D 2 (1)
Connolly A .... 13 (6) Kokolo W .... - (1) Sporar A 28 (7)
Crooks M ....40 Lea Siliki J .... 3 (8) Tavernier M 43 (1)
Daniels L ....12 Lumley J ....34 Taylor N 14
Dijksteel A ....34 McGree R .... 7 (4) Watmore D 22 (19)

League goals (59): Crooks 10, Sporar 8, Watmore 7, McNair 5, Tavernier 5, Coburn 4, Balogun 3, Connolly 2, Ikpeazu 2, McGree 2, Bola 1, Fry 1, Hernandez 1, Howson 1, Jones 1, Payero 1, Opponents 5
FA Cup goals (5): Boyd-Munce 1, Coburn 1, Crooks 1, Ikpeazu 1, Opponents 1. **League Cup goals:** None
Average home league attendance: 21,825
Player of Year: Jonny Howson

MILLWALL

A season that looked to be drifting along in mid-table following a 3-0 defeat by champions-elect Fulham, took on real significance with a run of five successive victories. Millwall overcame

Cardiff, Queens Park Rangers, Derby, Sheffield United and Reading to close to within three points of a play-off place. Defeating third-place Huddersfield with two goals from Benik Afobe edged them another point nearer. Gary Rowett's side still had it all to do with four other clubs also seeking to break into the top six. But they hung in there, twice coming from behind for a point at Birmingham, then beating Peterborough 3-0 in the final home fixture with Afobe again on the mark. A visit to newly-promoted Bournemouth in the final round of matches represented a tough assignment, but as it turned out a 1-0 loss was rendered irrelevant by victories for the teams within touching distance, Luton and Sheffield United. Ninth place, however, represented a solid season's work in a tough division – two higher than 2021.

Afobe B................... 34 (4)	Freeman L.................. - (1)	Ojo S..................... 12 (6)
Ballard D 30 (1)	Hutchinson S............ 28 (1)	Pearce A 3 (3)
Bennett M.............. 16 (13)	Kieftenbeld M........... 19 (8)	Romeo M 2
Bialkowski B 46	Leonard R 11 (8)	Saville G 34 (3)
Bradshaw T 16 (8)	Lovelace Z.................. - (4)	Smith M................. 6 (15)
Burey T..................... 6 (9)	Mahoney C 1 (7)	Thompson B .... - (2)
Burke O 10 (4)	Malone S................ 36 (3)	Wallace J................. 33 (5)
Cooper J 41 (1)	McNamara D 33 (4)	Wallace M 42
Evans G 12 (11)	Mitchell B 35 (7)	

League goals (53): Afobe 12, Bradshaw 9, Wallace J 6, Cooper 4, Wallace M 4, Bennett 3, Burey 2, Burke 2, Malone 2, McNamara 2, Saville 2, Ballard 1, Evans 1, Smith 1, Opponents 2
FA Cup goals (1): Afobe 1. **League Cup goals** (5): Wallace M 2, Malone 1, Saville 1, Smith 1
Average home league attendance: 12,970
Player of Year: Murray Wallace

NOTTINGHAM FOREST

Steve Cooper led this grand old club back to the Premier League after a 23-year absence with a remarkable, against-the-odds performance by the manager and his players. Rarely can a team have started the season so badly and finished it in front of 80,000 at Wembley with one of the biggest prizes in the game – success in the Play-off Final. When Forest were bottom of the table with a single point from the opening seven matches, such a prospect would have seemed far-fetched. But Cooper picked up the pieces after Chris Hughton was sacked, effected an immediate improvement and, by the time Christmas arrived, they were on the fringes of the top group after a single defeat in his first 15 matches. Forest broke through by beating Blackburn 2-0 and eventually finished fourth, having scored four goals against Reading, Blackpool and West Bromwich Albion, followed by a 5-1 win over Swansea, the side Cooper took to the 2021 final against Brentford. Victory over Huddersfield at Wembley, the club's first appearance there since Brian Clough lost a League Cup Final to Manchester United in 1992, came via Levi Colwill's deflection into his own net from James Garner's cross two minutes from the break. In a tight, tense affair of few clear-cut chances, Forest had the better of the first half, then defended resolutely, while surviving two penalty appeals, to protect their advantage.

Back F...................... 2 (1)	Horvath E 6	Osei-Tutu J 4
Bong G 4 (3)	Joao Carvalho 2 (5)	Panzo J 1,
Cafu 2 (12)	Johnson B 44 (2)	Richardson J.............. – (2)
Colback J 36 (2)	Konate A .... - (1)	Samba B 40
Cook S.................... 13 (1)	Laryea R.................. 1 (4)	Silva X 2 (6)
Davis K 14 (1)	Lolley J 10 (17)	Spence D 38 (17)
Figueiredo T............ 22 (4)	Lowe M 19 (1)	Surridge S 5 (12)
Fornah T ....- (1)	Mbe Soh L.......................2	Taylor..................... 8 (10)
Gabriel J 4	McKenna S.....................45	Worrall J.......................39
Garner J 36 (4)	Mighten A 5 (18)	Yates R 41 (2)
Grabban L 23 (9)	Ojeda B..........................3	Zinckernagel P...........35 (7)

Play-offs – appearances: Colback 3, Cook 3, Garner 3, Johnson 3, McKenna 3, Samba 3, Spence 3, Worrall 3, Yates 3, Zinckernagel 3, Surridge 2 (1), Davis 1 (2), Lolley – (2), Mighten – (1), Horvath – (1), Lowe – (1)
League goals (73): Johnson 16, Grabban 12, Yates 8, Surridge 7, Zinckernagel 6, Davis 5, Garner 4, Colback 3, Taylor 3, McKenna 2, Spence 2, Cafu 1, Lowe 1, Mighten 1, Opponents 2.
Play-offs – goals (4): Johnson 2, Colback 1, Opponents 1
FA Cup goals (7): Grabban 1, Johnson 1, Spence 1, Surridge 1, Worrall 1, Yates 1, Zinckernagel 1. **League Cup goals** (2): Joao Carvalho 2
Average home league attendance: 27,137
Player of Year: Brennan Johnson

PETERBOROUGH UNITED

Darren Ferguson's long-standing affinity with the club came to an end on the way to an immediate return to League One. In his third spell as manager, Ferguson overtook Barry Fry's record of 491 matches in charge. But he was unable to do anything about the team's acute defensive fragility on their travels – apart from bringing in at one stage a psychiatrist to work on what he was convinced was a mental problem, rather than a lack of ability. He resigned in mid-February after a run of nine games without a win and was replaced by Grant McCann, returning for a second tilt at the job after being sacked by Hull. He began with 3-0 defeats by his former team and Huddersfield, either side of Peterborough's first appearance in the fifth round of the FA Cup for 36 years. McCann drew encouragement from the performance in a 2-0 defeat by Manchester City and by a rare away victory against Queens Park Rangers. There were also two wins over Easter, against Blackburn and Barnsley. By then, however, Reading's revival had taken them clear and Peterbrough went down with two matches remaining.

Beevers M.................14	Edwards R.............. 31 (3)	Mumba B 7 (3)
Benda S.......................9	Fernandez E 1	Norburn O 34 (2)
Brown R 5 (3)	Fuchs J.................. 17 (1)	Poku K.....................11 (9)
Burrows H.............. 29 (8)	Grant J.................. 21 (5)	Pym C.............................7
Butler D.............. 19 (3)	Hamilton E............... - (2)	Randell J.................1 (10)
Clarke-Harris J..........32 (9)	Jade-Jones R 6 (12)	Szmodics S 26 (10)
Corbett K.....................1	Kanu I 1 (4)	Taylor Jack 29 (5)
Cornell D.................30	Kent F 33 (1)	Taylor Joseph.............- (4)
Coulson H............... 5 (1)	Knight J 31 (5)	Thompson N.................27
Coventry C 4 (8)	Marriott J.......... 16 (12)	Tomlinson J.............3 (2)
Dembele S 22 (2)	Morton C.................. 3 (4)	Ward J 31 (7)

League goals (43): Clarke-Harris 12, Marriott 9, Szmodics 6, Dembele 5, Burrows 3, Taylor Jack 3, Grant 2, Thompson 1, Opponents 2
FA Cup goals (4): Jade-Jones 1, Mumba 1, Szmodics 1, Ward 1. **League Cup goals:** None
Average home league attendance: 10,089
Player of Year: Ronnie Edwards

PRESTON NORTH END

Indifferent home form hampered Preston for the second successive season – before and after a change of manager. Frankie McAvoy, in charge for seven months following a spell as caretaker, was dismissed approaching the midway point of the season with his side 18th in the table. He was replaced by Plymouth's Ryan Lowe, who won his first two matches against Barnsley and Stoke. Preston also accounted for promotion hopefuls West Bromwich Albion and Bournemouth, but drew 10 matches at Deepdale, following 11 defeats there in the previous campaign and finished in the same position – 13th. At least they bowed out in style with a 4-1 victory over Middlesbrough – best of the campaign – in which leading scorer Emil Riis thought he had scored a hat-trick. Lowe and captain Alan Browne backed up that claim, but one of his efforts was given officially as an own goal. The match marked the end of defender Paul Huntington's ten years at the club, an appearance off the bench bringing his total appearances to 306.

Archer C 18 (2)	Iversen D 45 (1)	Rafferty J 2 (30)
Barkhuizen T 10 (3)	Johnson D 35 (6)	Riis E 38 (6)
Bauer P 34	Ledson R 15 (10)	Rodwell-Grant J ....- (1)
Browne A 35 (4)	Lindsay L 13 (2)	Rudd D 1
Cunningham G 17 (4)	Maguire S 15 (11)	Sinclair S 6 (17)
Diaby B 4 (3)	McCann A 16 (12)	Storey J 15 (2)
Earl J 24 (5)	Murphy J ....- (12)	Whiteman B 42 (2)
Evans C 14 (9)	O'Neill M ....- (3)	Wickham C ....- (1)
Hughes A 40	Olusunde M 1 (1)	Van den Berg S 43 (2)
Huntington P ....- (1)	Potts B 23 (12)	

League goals (52): Riis 16, Archer 7, Johnson 7, Browne 4, Whiteman 4, Bauer 3, Evans 2, Earl 1, Hughes 1, Maguire 1, McCann 1, Potts 1, Van den Berg 1, Opponents 3
FA Cup goals (1): Johnson 1. **League Cup goals** (11): Riis 4, Sinclair 2, Hughes 1, Ledson 1, Maguire 1, Rafferty 1, Van den Berg 1
Average home league attendance: 12,608
Player of Year: Daniel Iversen

QUEENS PARK RANGERS

Mark Warburton's side looked a good bet to sustain a promotion challenge when closing to within two points of second-place Bournemouth in late February. Instead, seven defeats in eight matches – including home losses to Cardiff, Peterborough and Fulham – sent them sliding and left the manager's position under scrutiny. Rangers restored belief by twice coming from behind for a point at Huddersfield, then sent Derby down with an 88th minute winner from Luke Amos. But defeat at Stoke had them six points adrift and with an inferior goal difference to other play-off hopefuls. Warburton left the club, reluctantly, at the end of his contract and was replaced by Michael Beale, Steven Gerrard's No. 2 at Aston Villa.

Adomah A 22 (11)	Dunne J 34 (4)	Marshall D 10 (1)
Amos L 15 (14)	Dykes L 27 (6)	McCallum S 15 (2)
Austin C 15 (19)	Field S 26 (3)	Odubajo M 23 (5)
Ball D 13 (7)	Gray A 13 (15)	Sanderson D 10 (1)
Barbet Y 41	Hendrick J 7 (3)	Thomas G 6 (14)
Chair I 37 (2)	Johansen S 31 (4)	Wallace L: 21
Dickie R 38	Kakay O 4 (9)	Westwood K 6
Dieng T 28	Kelman C ....- (1)	Willock C 33 (2)
Dozzell A 18 (9)	Mahoney M 2	De Wijs J 11 (1)

League goals (60): Gray 10, Chair 9, Dykes 8, Willock 7, Amos 6, Austin 5, Dunne 3, Dickie 3, Adomah 2, Barbet 2, McCallum 2, Ball 1, Johansen 1, Opponents 1
FA Cup goals (1): Dykes 1. **League Cup goals** (5): Austin 2, Dickie 2, Opponents 1
Average home league attendance: 14,437
Player of Year: Chris Willock

READING

Former England midfielder Paul Ince bridged an eight-year gap in his managerial career to lead Reading away from the threat of relegation. They had slipped to within two points of the drop zone on the back of a six-point deduction for breaching EFL spending rules, a 7-0 drubbing by Fulham and a run of seven successive losses. There was also an FA Cup defeat by non-league Kidderminster. Ince came in as caretaker after Veljko Paunovic was sacked and had a double boost – victory in his first match against Birmingham and a scoring return to the side by the previous season's leading marksman, Lucas Joao, out for five months with a hip injury. Against that, Reading conceded four in quick succession to Blackpool and Nottingham Forest. But Ince's son Tom, on loan from Stoke, earned a point at Bournemouth, his side defeated another promotion-chasing team, Sheffield United, then made sure of staying up by coming from 4-1 down to daw 4-4 with Swansea, Tom McIntyre completing the recovery in the fifth minute of stoppage-time. Ince was later confirmed in the job.

Abrefa K .... - (3)	Halilovic A 9 (2)	Ovie Ejaria.............. 21 (5)
Ashcroft T.....................4	Hein K 5	Puscas G .... 17 (8))
Azeez F. 5 (8)	Hoilett J 20 (7)	Rafael Cabral.................. 6
Barker B .... - (4)	Holmes T 27 (5)	Rahman B 29
Bristow E 6	Ince T..........................19	Rinomhota A.............. 19 (1)
Camara M .... - (6)	Laurent J..........................41	Scott R .... - (1)
Carroll A 6 (2)	Lucas Joao 21 (3)	Southwood L.................. 25
Clarke J .... - (12)	McIntyre T.............. 18 (1)	Stickland M.................. - (1)
Dann S 14 (4)	Meite Y 3 (10)	Swift J 36 (2)
Dele-Bashiru T 27 (11)	Moore L..........................17	Tetek D 5 (5)
Drinkwater D 31 (2)	Morrison M......................29	Thomas T........................2
Felipe Araruna.............. (1)	Nyland O..........................10	Yiadom A..........................38

League goals (54): Swift 11, Lucas Joao 10, Dele-Basihru 4, Hoilett 3, Azeez 2, Carroll 2, Clarke 2, Dann 2, Ince 2, Laurent 2, McIntyre 2, Moore 2, Morrison 2, Ovie Ejaria 2, Drinkwater 1, Halilovic 1, Holmes 1, Puscas 1, Yiadom 1, Opponents 1
FA Cup goals (1): Puscas 1. **League Cup goals:** None
Average home league attendance: 13,515
Player of Year: Andy Yiadom

SHEFFIELD UNITED

A stirring comeback in the play-offs was not enough to keep alive Sheffield United's bid for an immediate return to the Premier League. Trailing Nottingham Forest 3-1 on aggregate in the second leg of their semi-final at the City Ground, Paul Heckingbottom's side drew level through Morgan Gibbs-White and John Fleck. And they went close to a winner in extra-time through Iliman Ndiaye, whose volley produced a fine save from Brice Samba. The goalkeeper then denied Ollie Norwood, Conor Hourihane and Gibbs-White in the penalty shoot-out which Forest won 3-2. United's defeat was soured when leading scorer Billy Sharp was left bleeding when attacked by a supporter at the final whistle. They had made little impression in the first half of the season under Slavisa Jokanovic, who was dismissed after six months with his side in the bottom half. Heckingbottom, caretaker after Chris Wilder's departure from Bramall Lane, replaced him and there was a. significant improvement in fortunes, with seven wins in his first nine games. Sharp became the Championship's all-time leading scorer since the division's rebranding in 2004 with his 122nd goal and United confirmed a top-six place by winning their final three games, including 4-0 against champions Fulham.

Baldock G 24 (1)	Fleck J 31 (4)	McGoldrick D 9 (10)
Basham C 24 (4)	Foderingham W 32	Mousset L.................. 4 (3)
Berge S 22 (9)	Freeman L 1 (3)	Ndiaye I.................. 23 (7)
Bogle J 16 (2)	Gibbs-White M 33 (2)	Norrington-Davies R.. 20 (2)
Brewster R 10 (4)	Gordon K 4 (1)	Norwood O 42 (2)
Burke O 2 (1)	Guedioura A .... - (1)	Olsen N..........................11
Goode C 1 (1)	Hourihane C 15 (14)	Osborn B 21 (13)
Davies B 21 (2)	Jebbison D.............. 1 (7)	Osula W.................. - (5)
Egan J..........................46	McBurnie O.............. 9 (19)	Ramsdale A........................2

| Robinson J | 26 (1) | Sharp B | 30 (9) | Uremovic F | 3 |
| Seriki F | 1 | Stevens E | 21 (1) | Verrips M | 1 |

Play-offs – appearances: Basham 2, Berge 2, Egan 2, Fleck 2, Foderingham 2, Gibbs-White 2, Norwood 2, Robinson 2, Ndiaye 2, Baldock 1 (1), Norrington-Davies 1 (1), Osborn 1 (1), Stevens 1, Jebbison – (1), Hourihane – (1)
League goals (63): Sharp 14, Gibbs-White 11, Ndiaye 7, Berge 5, Bogle 3, Brewster 3, Mousset 3, Osborn 3, Robinson 3, Egan 2, McGoldrick 2, Baldock 1, Davies 1, Fleck 1, Hourihane 1, Norwood 1, Stevens 1, Opponents 1. **Play-offs – goals (3):** Berge 1, Fleck 1, Gibbs-White 1
FA Cup goals: None. **League Cup goals (5):** Brewster 1, Freeman 1, McBurnie 1, Sharp 1, Stevens 1
Average home league attendance: 27,611
Player of Year: Morgan Gibbs-White

STOKE CITY

Another indifferent season for Stoke, who finished in the bottom half of the table for the fourth successive season since being relegated from the Premier League in 2018. This time, they were up to third with 21 points from 11 matches, having beaten Nottingham Forest and Huddersfield, two clubs who went on to figure prominently in the promotion race. Michael O'Neill's team maintained a top-six place until mid-way through before falling back and securing just one victory in a run of 12 matches. Things improved when they disrupted the ambitions of Sheffield United and Millwall and confirmed West Bromwich Albion's slide. But these results were not enough to prevent a 14th place finish, unchanged from 2021. Stoke could point to 16 of their 18 defeats inflicted by a single goal margin. At the same time, they dropped too many points from winning positions

Allen J	38 (3)	Fletcher S	16 (19)	Sima A	1 (1)
Baker L	20	Forrester W	3	Smith T	30 (2)
Batth D	10 (1)	Fox M	9 (1)	Souttar H	16
Bonham J	15	Harwood-Bellis T	22	Sparrow T	1
Brown J	38 (7)	Ince T	4 (7)	Surridge S	6 (14)
Bursik J	19	Jagielka P	20	Thompson J	12 (6)
Campbell T	10 (16)	Maja J	9 (6)	Tymon J	44
Chester J	16 (1)	Moore L	4	Vrancic M	24 (6)
Clucas S	16 (9)	Ostigard L	12 (1)	Wilmot B	31 (4)
Davies A	12	Philogene-Bidace J	6 (5)	Wright-Phillips D	6 (4)
Doughty A	- (11)	Powell N	14 (4)		
Duhaney D	3	Sawyers R	19 (6)		

League goals (57): Brown 13, Baker 8, Powell 6, Campbell 4, Fletcher 3, Ince 3, Vrancic 3, Clucas 2, Sawyers 2, Surridge 2, Maja 1, Ostigard 1, Philogene-Bidace 1, Smith 1, Tymon 1, Wilmot 1, Wright-Phillips 1, Opponents 4
FA Cup goals (5): Brown 1, Campbell 1, Ince 1, Maja 1, Tymon 1. **League Cup goals (8):** Surridge 2, Clucas 1, Ince 1, Powell 1, Sawyers 1, Souttar 1, Tymon 1
Average home league attendance: 20,921
Player of Year: Jacob Brown

SWANSEA CITY

A prolific first season for Dutch striker Joel Piroe and history-making wins over Cardiff were offset by points surrendered in the final month of the season which deprived Swansea of the chance of a top-half finish. Piroe's 22 goals ranked him joint third behind Aleksandar Mitrovic and Dominic Solanke in the Championship scoring charts. One of them came in a 3-0 victory over their local rivals which Russell Martin's side followed up with a 4-0 success in the return fixture to record the first-ever league double in the South Wales derby. There should have been another three points in the bag when leading Reading 4-1. Instead, their relegation-threatened opponents retrieved the deficit for a point. Swansea then surrendered a 3-0 lead to promotion-bound Bournemouth before a 5-1 defeat by Nottingham Forest in the penultimate game completed a costly sequence for the club. MK Dons manager Martin came in when Steve Cooper left for Forest during the summer after leading Swansea to the Play-off Final.

Benda S 5	Fisher A 20	Ogbeta N.....................- (2)
Bennett R 16 (2)	Fulton J 8 (10)	Ntcham O............... 20 (17)
Bidwell J.......................16	Grimes M 46	Paterson J 33 (5)
Burns F 3	Hamer B 21	Piroe J 40 (5)
Cabango B 34 (3)	Joseph K .... - (10)	Smith K 21 (14)
Christie C...................23	Laird E 18 (2)	Walsh L 1 (4)
Congreve C............... 2 (3)	Latibeaudiere J 21 (8)	Whittaker M.................- (6)
Cooper B.................. 3 (1)	Lowe J 3 (2)	Williams R.................. 4 (1)
Cullen L.................. 4 (8)	Manning R 34 (4)	Wolf H 18 (1)
Dhanda Y................... 1 (2)	Naughton K 37 (1)	
Downes F 34 (3)	Obafemi M 20 (12)	

League goals (58): Piroe 22, Obafemi 12, Paterson 9, Ntcham 4, Christie 3, Bidwell 2, Manning 2, Wolf 2, Cabango 1, Downes 1
FA Cup goals (2): Piroe 1, Opponents 1. **League Cup goals (7):** Whittaker 3, Cabango 1, Latibeaudiere 1, Piroe 1, Williams D 1
Average home league attendance: 17,389
Player of Year: Joel Piroe

WEST BROMWICH ALBION

Albion disputed the automatic promotion places with Fulham and Bournemouth throughout the first half of the season under new manager Valerien Ismael. Then, a chronic shortage of goals undermined their chances of a swift return to the Premier League, with just seven scored in a run of 12 matches. Ismael, who joined from Barnsley, paid the price for his side falling eight points adrift – sacked seven months into the job. There was no quick fix either from his replacement, the former Newcastle manager Steve Bruce, who had to wait for six games for a first victory – the worst start at any of his previous ten clubs. Albion eventually accounted for champions-elect Fulham and promotion-bound Bournemouth, but defeats to lowly Birmingham and mid-table Stoke ruled out any chance of closing the gap on the play-off places. And a 4-0 beating by Nottingham Forest during which Darnell Furlong was sent off for a second yellow card, cast them further adrift. Albion finished a campaign which had promised so much a distant tenth.

Ajayi S....................... 27 (4)	Fellows T.................... 1 (1)	O'Shea D.................... 12 (2)
Ashworth Z............... - (2)	Furlong D 38 (3)	Phillips M............... 18 (10)
Bartley K 38 (1)	Gardner-Hickman T ... 14 (5)	Reach A 21 (13)
Bryan K 1 (2)	Grant K 41 (3)	Robinson C............... 26 (17)
Button D.......................10	Hugill M 7 (13)	Snodgrass R 4 (2)
Carroll A 11 (4)	Johnstone S.................36	Taylor C......................- (1)
Clarke M.......................33	Kipre C 14 (1)	Townsend C 43
De Castro Q............... - (2)	Livermore J...................37	Tulloch R......................- (2)
Diangana G 22 (19)	Molumby J 17 (14)	Zohore K ....- (2)
Dike D 1 (1)	Mowatt A........................34	

League goals (52): Grant 18, Robinson 7, Mowatt 4, Carroll 3, Phillips 3, Bartley 2, Diangana 2, O'Shea 2, Reach 2, Ajayi 1, Clarke 1, Hugill 1, Kipre 1, Molumby 1, Opponents 4
FA Cup goals (1): Robinson 1. **League Cup goals:** None
Average home league attendance: 21,431
Player of Year: Matt Clarke

SKY BET LEAGUE ONE

ACCRINGTON STANLEY

Accrington overcame a poor disciplinary record to reach the top half of the table. They had eight red cards in the second part of the season, two of them shown to goalkeeper Toby Savin, one for denying Plymouth a goal-scoring chance, the other a month later for handling outside the penalty area against Lincoln. But his side still picked up 12 points from those eight matches, four of them against promotion-chasing opponents. Another sending-off came against Cheltenham when they led 4-2 before conceding goals in the 90th and 96th minutes. Accington also let in four in five other matches and five against Oxford. The biggest success was 5-1 against Fleetwood and there was a solid finish which brought three victories out of five, one of them against AFC Wimbledon, whose relegation was confirmed. Accrington's 4-3 success in that final round of fixtures, after leading 3-0, took them above Charlton into 12th place and reflected an up-and-down campaign.

Adedoyin K 6 (6)	Leigh T 17 (7)	Pell H 26 (11)
Amankwah Y 20 (4)	Lewis M 1 (2)	Perritt H .... - (2)
Bishop C 41	Longelo R 4 (8)	Pritchard J 5 (5)
Burgess C 1	Malcolm J 3 (7)	Rich-Baghuelou J 11 (2)
Butcher M 30 (4)	Mansell L 5 (1)	Rodgers H 20 (2)
Charles D 6	McConville S 45 (1)	Savin T 33
Clark M 25	Morgan D 13 (1)	Sherring S 9 (1)
Conneely S 19 (3)	Mumbongo J 3 (7)	Sykes R 38 (1)
Coyle L 13 (6)	Nolan J 1 (4)	Trafford J 11
Hamilton E 38 (1)	Nottingham M 46	Woods J 1 (2)
Isherwood L 2 (2)	O'Sullivan J 13 (12)	

League Goals (61): Bishop 11, Hamilton 6, Leigh 6, Nottingham 6, Pell 6, Butcher 4, McConville 4, Sykes 3, Mumbongo 2, O'Sullivan 2, Rich-Baghuelou 2, Adedoyin 1, Clark 1, Coyle 1, Longelo 1, Mansell 1, Opponents 4
FA Cup goals (1): Hamilton 1, **League Cup goals** (2): Bishop 1, Charles 1. **League Trophy goals** (12): Bishop 2, Leigh 2, Nottingham 2, Pell 2, Hamilton 1, Malcolm 1, Nolan 1, O'Sullivan 1
Average home league attendance: 2,915
Player of Year: Sean McConville

AFC WIMBLEDON

A late rally staved off the threat of relegation the previous season. This time, there was no escape from a run of 27 matches without a victory – more than twice the club's previous record – which had only one outcome. Thirteen draws and 14 defeats followed a 2-0 win at Accrington on December 7 when Wimbledon were four points clear of trouble. They paid a heavy price for surrendering the lead on numerous occasions – a weakness that continued after a last throw of the dice brought in former Reading manager Mark Bowen when Mark Robinson was sacked with a month of the campaign remaining. Points were dropped in must-win games against Crewe and Fleetwood. There was still one fixture remaining – ironically the return with Accrington. But Wimbledon's inferior goal difference meant that result – a 4-3 defeat – was rendered irrelevant and they finished three points from safety. Bowen declined a permanent position and the club appointed Johnnie Jackson, a fortnight after his dismissal by Charlton.

Ablade T 2 (10)	Brown L 14 (1)	Mebude D 12 (13)
Adjei-Hersey D 1 (1)	Chislett E 11 (18)	Guinness-Walker N ... 20 (8)
Alexander C 21	Cosgrove A 2 (6)	Hartigan A 26 (8)
Assal A 38 (4)	Cosgrove S 13 (2)	Heneghan B 41
Bendle A 1	Csoka D 14 (3)	Kaja E 1 (4)

111

Kalambayi P............. 11 (2) Nightingale W .... 33 (2) Robinson Z 4 (2)
Kalinauskas T............. 1 (1) Osei Yaw D................. 1 (5) Rudoni J.................... 38 (3)
Lawrence H............... 17 (7) Osew P .... 22 (5) Tzanev N 46
Marsh G.................. 21 (6) Palmer O .... 16 (2) Woodyard A....................36
McCormick L............ 34 (6) Pressley A................ 9 (12)

League goals (49): Rudoni 12, Assal 8, McCormick 7, Palmer 5, Nightingale 3, Chislett 2, Mebude 2, Heneghan 2, Pressley 2, Cosgrove A 1, Cosgrove S 1, Guinness-Walker 1, Hartigan 1, Robinson 1, Woodyard 1
FA Cup goals (5): Palmer 3, Assal 2. **League Cup goals** (2): Hartigan 1, Osew 1. **League Trophy goals** (5): Pressley 2, Kalambayi 1, McCormick 1, Nightingale 1
Average home league attendance: 7,690
Player of Year: Jack Rudoni

BOLTON WANDERERS

Ian Evatt's team fell some way short of his early season claim that they could be the best of the bunch in a division packed with big clubs ambitious for a return to the Championship. The manager's pronouncement after a solid start was followed immediately by a single point from a run of five matches, accompanied by a fall into the bottom half of the table. After that, Bolton were always up against it attempting to make up lost ground and re-establish contact with the leading group. A 6-0 drubbing of Sunderland, the club's biggest since leaving Burnden Park in 1997, was a reminder of their potential, highlighting a run of eight wins in ten which took them to within four points of a play-off place. But that was as good as it got. Dropped points at home proved costly and despite finishing with four victories out of five they were still ten points adrift in ninth place.

Afolayan O .... 38 (6) Dixon J..........................23 Morley A.........................21
Aimson W .... 22 (3) Doyle E .... 20 (1) Sadlier K.....................8 (9)
Amaechi X .... 2 (8) Fossey M......................15 Santos R 37
Bakayoko A .... 16 (16) Gilks M ....1 Sarcevic A................ 13 (1)
Baptiste A................ 6 (6) Gordon L................ 10 (3) Senior A...........................2
Bodvarsson J D....... 10 (11) Isgrove L .... 12 (6) Sheehan J 12 (3)
Brockbank H .... 2 (2) John D .... 38 (1) Thomason G 9 (4)
Charles D................ 21 (2) Johnston G .... 38 (5) Trafford J.......................22
Darcy R .... - (1) Jones G .... 28 (1) Williams MJ.............39 (1)
Delfouneso N .... 2 (9) Kachunga E........... 15 (17)
Dempsey K .... 5 (6) Lee K 19 (6)

League goals (74): Afolayan 12, Bakayoko 10, Charles 8, Bodvarsson 7, Doyle 5, Lee 5, John 4, Sadlier 4, Sheehan 4, Sarcevic 3, Johnston 2, Kachunga 2, Aimson 1, Amaechi 1, Baptiste 1, Fossey 1, Morley 1, Thomason 1, Williams 1, Opponents 1
FA Cup goals (5): Kachunga 2, Bakayoko 1, Doyle 1, Opponents 1. **League Cup goals**: None. **League Trophy goals** (11): Afolayan 2, Bakayoko 2, Delfouneso 2, Doyle 2, John 1, Lee 1, Opponents 1
Average home league attendance: 15,439
Player of Year: Dapo Afolayan

BURTON ALBION

Jimmy Floyd Hasselbaink's side looked like building on the momentum of the previous season's impressive recovery from the threat of relegation with a successful start to the new campaign. They won the first three fixtures – two of them against Ipswich and Sunderland, teams fancied to be serious promotion contenders. Instead, Burton failed to win any of the next six and any chance of challenging for a place among the leading group had gone by the half-way stage when they were a dozen points adrift. A top-half finish remained a possibility until nine goals conceded in successive matches against Sheffield Wednesday and Oxford was followed by a club-record-equalling five without scoring. Goals by Cameron Borthwick-Jackson and John Brayford ended that sequence, a 2-0 win also denting Rotherham's title prospects, and Burton finished 16th, the same as in 2021.

Ahadme G.............. 10 (4)	Hemmings K............ 10 (8)	Moult L..................... 3 (7)
Akins L.................. 21 (1)	Holloway A 2 (4)	Niasse O 7 (5)
Blake-Tracy F 5 (2)	Hughes S 21	O'Connor T 17 (1)
Borthwick-Jackson C. 33 (4)	Jebbison D 16 (6)	Oshilaja A........................ 30
Bostwick M 8 (2)	Kokolo W 11 (4)	Patrick O..................... 5 (2)
Brayford J.......................33	Kovar M 6	Powell J 29 (5)
Chapman H.......... 16 (12)	Lakin C 12 (15)	Rowe D .... - (2)
Garratt B.........................40	Leak R 14 (2)	Saydee C 7 (11)
Gilligan C.................. 7 (1)	Maddox J 8 (8)	Shaughnessy C 35 (3)
Guedioura A................ 2 (2)	Mancienne M............ 19 (3)	Smith J 23 (6)
Hamer T.........................45	Morris B 1 (6)	Taylor T 12 (4)

League goals (51): Jebbison 7, Brayford 6, O'Connor 5, Hemmings 4, Smith 4, Ahadme 3, Akins 3, Niasse 3, Powell 3, Shaughnessy 3, Borthwick-Jackson 2, Guedioura 2, Chapman 1, Hamer 1, Hughes 1, Kokolo 1, Lakin 1, Moult 1
FA Cup goals (3): Jebbison 1, Leak 1, Powell 1. **League Cup goals** (1): Opponents 1. **League Trophy goals** (8): Holloway 3, Hemmings 1, Jebbison 1, Lakin 1, Smith 1, Opponents 1
Average home league attendance: 3,229
Player of Year: John Brayford

CAMBRIDGE UNITED

Mark Bonner's promoted side overcame the loss of leading marksman Paul Mullin to consolidate League One status – and enjoy a magical moment in the FA Cup. They joined the ranks of genuine giantkillers by defeating full-strength Newcastle at a sell-out St James' Park with a goal from Joe Ironside and a man-of-the-match performance by goalkeeper Dimitar Mitov. Ironside shared scoring responsibilities with new-signing Sam Smith after 32-goal Mullin rejected a new contract to join ambitious National League club Stockport. And there was another performance for him to savour in the 5-0 defeat of Cheltenham – a perfect hat-trick of left-foot, header and right-foot. Along the way to a mid-table place, Cambridge experienced some difficult defensive performances of their own, conceding six to Sheffield Wednesday and five to Lincoln and Sunderland. But the season was perhaps best captured by an accomplished performance which accounted for champions Wigan 2-1 in their penultimate away fixture.

Bennett L 4 (1)	Lankester J................ 7 (11)	Smith S 34 (12)
Brophy J 40 (3)	Mannion W 2	Taylor G............................ 3
Digby P.................... 43 (1)	Masterson C 15 (1)	Tolaj L..................... - (4)
Dunk H..................... 26 (8)	May A 32 (6)	Tracey S................. 15 (11)
Holy T 2	McKenzie-Lyle K .... - (1)	Weir J 10 (5)
Hoolahan W 20 (6)	Mitov D..........................42	Williams G................... 40
Iredale J 35	O'Neil L 15 (6)	Worman B 8 (5)
Ironside J 34 (4)	Adesope Okedina J.... 27 (3)	Yearn K.......................... - (1)
Jones L...........................25	Sherring S 11 (3)	
Knibbs H 14 (20)	Simper L 2	

League goals (56): Smith 15, Ironside 14, May 5, Knibbs 4, Tracey 2, Brophy 1, Digby 1, Dunk 1, Hoolahan 1, Iredale 1, Lankester 1, O'Neil 1, Weir 1, Williams 1, Worman 1, Opponents 6

FA Cup goals (8): Knibbs 2, Smith 2, Ironside 1, Masterson 1, May 1, Worman 1. **League Cup goals** (1): Williams 1. **League Trophy goals** (10): Smith 4, Knibbs 3, Digby 1, Tracey 1, Yearn 1
Average home league attendance: 5,668
Player of Year: Dimitar Mitov

CHARLTON ATHLETIC

Only goal difference separated Charlton from a play-off place the previous season under Nigel Adkins. This time, there was never a hint of a promotion challenge. Instead, just two wins in the opening 13 games left them third from bottom and cost Adkins his job after seven months as manager. Former Valley midfielder Johnnie Jackson dispelled fears of a relegation struggle with seven wins in ten games as caretaker. A permanent appointment was followed by three successive defeats, dropping his side back into the bottom half of the table. After that, Charlton meandered from week to week, neither threatening the leading group, nor in danger of being dragged back into the danger zone. Victory at promoted Rotherham, followed by a home defeat against lowly Morecambe, summed things up. Jackson's position proved far from permanent – he was dismissed at the end of the season and replaced by Swindon's Ben Garner.

Aneke C 4 (5)	Fraser S 6 (3)	Leko J 15 (10)
Arter H 4	Gilbey A 32 (5)	MacGillivray C 43
Blackett-Taylor C 15 (12)	Gunter C 17 (1)	Matthews A 28
Burstow M 8 (8)	Harness N 1	Morgan A 21 (1)
Campbell T .... - (2)	Henderson S 2	Pearce J 20 (3)
Clare S 31 (5)	Inniss R 12 (3)	Purrington B 24 (3)
Clayden C .... - (2)	Jaiyesimi D 22 (11)	Souare P 7 (2)
Davison J 9 (6)	Castillo J 1 (1)	Stockley J 28 (5)
Dobson G 38	Kanu D .... - (2)	Taylor C 15 (12)
Elerewe A .... - (3)	Kirk C 5 (3)	Washington C 28 (7)
Famewo A 34 (4)	Lavelle S 18 (1)	Watson B 6 (3)
Forster-Caskey J 1 (3)	Lee E 26 (8)	

League goals (55): Stockley 13, Washington 11, Aneke 4, Lee 3, Purrington 3, Blackett-Taylor 2, Burstow 2, Davison 2, Gilbey 2, Jaiyesimi 2, Lavelle 2, Leko 2, Clare 1, Dobson 1, Famewo 1, Inniss 1, Morgan 1, Opponents 2
FA Cup goals 6): Stockley 4, Burstow 1, Davison 1. **League Cup goals:** None. **League Trophy goals** (15): Burstow 3, Stockley 3, Davison 2, Gilbey 1, Blackett-Taylor 1, Lee 1, Leko 1, Pearce 1, Purrington 1, Opponents 1
Average home league attendance: 15,592
Player of Year: George Dobson

CHELTENHAM TOWN

Alfie May took pride of place in a record-breaking season for Michael Duff and his players. May scored 23 goals, third highest tally behind Wigan's Will Keane and Sunderland's Ross Stewart, as Cheltenham achieved their best-ever league placing of 15th in the third tier. The previous season's League Two champions could have gone higher with a better finish than two points from four fixtures. May, however, put the seal on a prolific campaign with both goals against Cambrdge in the final round of matches. It included four in 5-5 draw at Wycombe, where his side came from 3-1 and 5-3 down for a point. They also showed character to draw 4-4 at Accrington courtesy of goals from Callum Wright and Will Boyle in the final six minutes. Those two matches reflected a season in which Cheltenham were the great 'entertainers', with 66 goals scored and 80 conceded. Duff left at the end of it to become Barnsley's new manager. Coach Wade Elliott replaced him

Barkers D 1 (4)	Bonds E 17 (6)	Brown C .... - (3)
Blair M 38 (1)	Boyle W 29 (2)	Chapman E 19 (6)

Colkett C................ 4 (5)	Joseph K................ 13 (6)	Ramsey A 9 (6)
Crowley D 9 (3)	Lloyd G................... 3 (9)	Sercombe L 33 (8)
Etete K.................. 10 (3)	Long S................... 37 (2)	Thomas C 21 (3)
Evans O........................27	May A..................... 40 (6)	Tozer B 2
Flinders S.....................19	N'Lundulu D 4	Vassell K 10 (6)
Freestone L 18 (10)	Norton C 1 (8)	Williams A 10 (13)
Horton G................. 1 (1)	Perry T 5 (5)	Williams B 9 (2)
Hussey C......................23	Pollock M 34	Wright C 29 (5)
Hutchinson R...................6	Raglan C 25 (3)	

League goals (66): May 23, Wright 9, Boyle 4, Joseph 4, Williams A 4, Blair 3, Etete 3, Sercombe 3, Vassell 2, Bonds 1, Freestone 1, Lloyd 1, Long 1, N'Lundulu 1, Perry 1, Pollock 1, Raglan 1, Ramsey 1, Thomas 1, Williams B 1
FA Cup goals (5): Pollock 2, May 1, Williams A 1, Opponents 1. **League Cup goals** (4): May 2, Vassell 2. **League Trophy goals** (2): Chapman 1, Miles F 1
Average home league attendance: 4,239
Player of Year: Alfie May

CREWE ALEXANDRA

David Artell apologised to supporters for a return to League Two in a season spent entirely in the bottom four. Crewe were the first EFL club to be relegated following a 2-0 defeat by fellow-strugglers Doncaster with four matches still to play. They were then 13 points adrift after a run of 15 defeats in 16 games. Artell, appointed in January 2017 and the division's second longest-serving manager to Accrington's John Coleman, was sacked two days later. He was up against it from day one, having lost four key players during the summer, then a single victory to show from the first 17 matches. The only respite came midway through the campaign with three wins in five against Lincoln, Morecambe and Charlton which lifted Crewe off the bottom and took them to within four points of safety. Artell was replaced on a temporary basis by his assistant Alex Morris, who won his first match in charge – 3-1 against AFC Wimbledon who also went down – and was given the job permanently before the end of the campaign.

Adebisi R......................22	Johnson T................ 14 (6)	Onyeka T.....................- (1)
Agyei D...................... 8 (1)	Kashket S................. 15 (3)	Porter C 20 (16)
Ainley C.................. 24 (7)	Knight B 4 (2)	Ramsay K................ 12 (3)
Alebiousu R.....................6	Lawton S .... - (2)	Richards D 32
Bennett J'Neil 8 (1)	Long C 29 (3)	Robertson S.............. 16 (4)
Billington L......................1	Lowery T 31 (1)	Salisbury C...................- (5)
Dale O...........................2	Lundstram J 15 (7)	Sambou B 6 (10)
Daniels D......................11	MacDonald S 2 (1)	Sass-Davies B...........21 (1)
Finney O................ 18 (10)	Mandron M 26 (7)	Tabiner J ....- (1)
Gomes M 4 (4)	McFadzean C 6 (4)	Thomas L 12 (1)
Griffiths R.............. 10 (11)	Murphy L 28 (10)	Uwakwe T.....................7 (1)
Harper R................. 12 (3)	O'Riordan C............... 9 (2)	Williams M 18 (1)
Jaaskelainen W...............14	Offord L 43 (1)	

League goals (37): Long 10, Mandron 7, Porter 6, Lowery 4, Finney 2, Sambou 2, Agyei 1, Bennett 1, Kashket 1, Murphy 1, Robertson 1, Opponents 1
FA Cup goals: None. **League Cup goals** (1): Ainley 1. **League Trophy goals** (10): Mandron 3, Finney 2, Knight 2, Robbins J 1, Robertson 1, Opponents 1
Average home league attendance: 4,523
Player of Year: Tom Lowery

DONCASTER ROVERS

Neither the experienced Richie Wellens nor managerial newcomer Gary McSheffrey could halt Doncaster's decline. One point from the opening six matches bore the hallmarks of a relegation struggle, which continued all season with not a single week's relief from a place in the bottom four. Wellens was sacked after six months in charge with his side second from bottom. Former Coventry and Birmingham midfielder McSheffrey, promoted from managing the club's under-18 team, had the worst possible start – a three-goal lead after half an hour surrendered and a 4-3 defeat inflicted at Morecambe. Beating Sunderland in front of a 38,000 crowd at the Stadium of Light offered hope. But that unlikely 2-1 success, achieved with goals by Reo Griffiths on his debut and Tommy Rowe, was swallowed up by a run of seven successive home defeats which left them six points adrift. Rowe was again on the mark in victory over another side to be relegated, Crewe, but his side's inferior goal difference meant they were effectively down with two games remaining.

Agard K 4 (4)	Gardner D 12 (8)	Odubeko M 8 (8)
Anderson T 19	Greaves A .... - (1)	Olowu J 33 (2)
Barlow A 13 (15)	Griffiths R 12 (4)	Ravenhill L 1 (2)
Blythe B 2	Hasani L 4 (3)	Rowe T 42 (1)
Bogle O 2 (8)	Hiwula J 18 (2)	Seaman C 9 (5)
Bostock J 17 (4)	Horton B 14 (6)	Smith M 37 (6)
Clayton A 9 (3)	Jackson B 12 (2)	Taylor J 2 (1)
Close B 14	John C 2 (3)	Vilca R 7 (3)
Cukur T 10 (11)	Jones L 10	Williams R-S 32
Dahlberg P 18	Knoyle K 42 (3)	Williams E .... - (1)
Dodoo J 26 (7)	Martin J 18 (2)	Younger O 12 (4)
Galbraith E 27 (6)	Mitchell J 18	

League goals (37): Rowe 7, Dodoo 4, Martin 4, Olowu 4, Gardner 3, Griffiths 2, Horton 2, Odubeko 2, Anderson 1, Barlow 1, Bogle 1, Cukur 1, Galbraith 1, Hiwula 1, Knoyle 1, Seaman 1, Vilca 1
FA Cup goals (3): Rowe 2, Horton 1. **League Cup goals**: None. **League Trophy goals** (5): Dodoo 4, Vilca 1
Average home league attendance: 6,906
Player of Year: Tommy Rowe

FLEETWOOD TOWN

Fleetwood preserved League One status under Stephen Crainey – but it was a close thing. His team survived on goal difference in a nail-biting final round of matches when they were one of three teams who could have gone down alongside Crewe, AFC Wimbledon and Doncaster. They were locked on 40 points with Gillingham, with Morecambe on 42. All three were defeated, Fleetwood leading at Bolton, then pegging the home side back to 2-2 before conceding twice in the final ten minutes. But it was enough to stay up on minus-20 after Gillingham lost at home to promoted Rotherham and finished on minus-34. Former Scotland defender Crainey came in as caretaker, then appointed until the end of the season, when Simon Grayson, manager for ten months, was sacked after a run of seven defeats in eight matches. His initial success proved crucial to eventual survival, with points in the bank from four victories and a draw in six matches. Former Celtic captain Scott Brown was the club's choice as the new permanent manager.

Andrew D 39	Butterworth D 5 (7)	Conn-Clarke C .... - (4)
Baggley B 5 (2)	Cairns A 42	Edmondson R 4 (7)
Batty D 23 (7)	Camps C 29 (2)	Garner G 23 (5)
Biggins H 26 (6)	Clark M 8 (2)	Garner J 4 (14)
Boyle D 6 (4)	Clarke T 35	Halliday B 3

Harrison E................ 16 (2)	Johnston C................ 15 (2)	Morton C................ 15 (3)
Harrop J 3 (2)	Jules Z 19 (1)	Nsiala A................. 18 (2)
Hayes C 17 (7)	Lane P.................... 30 (7)	O'Hara K.....................4
Hill J....................13	Macadam H 7 (3)	Pilkington A 9 (17)
Holgate H 5 (1)	Matete A 18 (2)	Rossiter J.....................10
Johnson C 32 (3)	McLaughlin C............ 7 (2)	Thiam C.................. - (3)
Johnson D.....................3	Morris S................ 13 (13)	

League goals (62): Garner G 7, Andrew 6, Harrison 6, Biggins 5, Lane 5, Garner J 4, Johnson C 4, Morton 4, Pilkington 4, Camps 3, Batty 2, Clarke 2, Morris 2, Baggley 1, Butterworth 1, Hayes 1, Hill 1, Johnson D 1, Macadam 1, Matete 1, Opponents 1
FA Cup goals (1): Garner J 1. **League Cup goals** (1): Opponents 1. **League Trophy goals** (8): Morton 3, Edmondson 2, Garner G 1, Matete 1, McMillan M 1
Average home league attendance: 3,228
Player of Year: Paddy Lane

GILLINGHAM

Neil Harris promised a summer clear-out after Gillingham were relegated on the last day of the season. They went down on goal difference, with Harris describing balance, fitness and standards a 'disgrace.' The former Millwall and Cardiff manager took over a side without a win in 14 matches and just beaten 7-2 at home by Oxford. He had had two quick victories against Crewe and Cambridge and accumulated sufficient points to move four clear of the drop zone going into the final month of the campaign. But a goalless draw in a must-win home match against fellow-strugglers Fleetwood was to prove costly. Going into the final round of fixtures, the teams were locked on 40 points, with Crewe, Doncaster and AFC Wimbledon already down. Both were beaten – Gillingham by promoted Rotherham; Fleetwood by Bolton – leaving Gillingham on minus-34 and their rivals on minus-20. Harris had replaced Steve Evans, whose contract was terminated ten matches into that damaging lean run.

Adshead D .... 11(4)	Dickson-Peters T........ 2 (7)	Masterson C 18
Akehurst B................. 2 (3)	Ehmer M 45	McKenzie R.............. 37 (1)
Akinde J 13 (5)	Gale S................. - (1)	O'Keefe S................ 36 (2)
Bennett R 13 (5)	Gbode J .... - (2)	Oliver V................ 38 (1)
Carayol M 16 (6)	Jackson R................ 30 (4)	Phillips D 13 (11)
Chambers J................ 1 (1)	Kelman C 16 (7)	Reeves B 7 (13)
Chapman A ....,........18	Lee O..................... 29 (3)	Sithole G................. 2 (13)
Cumming J 22	Lintott H 2 (4)	Thompson B 17
Dahlberg P.....................6	Lloyd D 19 (8)	Tucker J 44
Dempsey K 21	MacDonald A..................7	Tutonda D 21 (8)

League goals (35): Oliver 10, Lloyd 5, McKenzie 3, Jackson 2, Kelman 2, Reeves 2, Tucker 2, Akinde 1, Carayol 1, Dempsey 1, Lee 1, MacDonald 1, O'Keefe 1, Thompson 1, Opponents 2.
FA Cup goals (1): Sithole 1. **League Cup goals** (3): Olver 1, Phillips 1, Sithole 1. **League Trophy goals** (1): McKenzie
Average home league attendance: 5,139
Player of Year: Stuart O'Keefe

IPSWICH TOWN

Another season of high expectations and modest returns at Portman Road. Paul Cook, like his predecessor Paul Lambert, fell short of pointing the club towards a return to the Championship and was sacked nine months into the job after a goalless draw with Barrow in the FA Cup. Cook was replaced by Manchester United coach Kieran McKenna, whose first match against Wycombe drew a crowd of more than 26,000. He repaired defensive weaknesses to such an extent that Ipswich conceded a single goal in a run of nine matches during which they whittled away a ten-point gap between a play-off place. With attendances continuing to boom, they closed to within three of their target before progress stalled in a home defeat by Cambridge. Further points were dropped over Easter in tough assignments against the top two, Wigan and Rotherham, by which time Ipswich had fallen out of contention. They finished on a high – 4-0 winners against Charlton – but were still well short.

Aluko S.................. 18 (12)	Coulson H 6	Jackson K.................... 7 (5)
Baggott E.............................2	Dobra A.................. 1 (1)	Morsy S...............33 (1)
Bakinson T............... 14 (3)	Donacien J 40 (3)	Norwood J 12 (11)
Barry L 1 (1)	Edmundson G................32	Nsiala A........................10 (1)
Bonne M............. 29 (14)	Edwards K............. 11 (7)	Penney M................. 18 (4)
Burgess C 18 (3)	El Mizouni I................ 3 (2)	Pigott J 10 (12)
Burns W 34 (3)	Evans L 26 (1)	Thompson D 15 (2)
Carroll T 8 (6)	Fraser S 14 (1)	Vincent-Young K 11 (4)
Celina B 23 (9)	Harper R 6 (7)	Walton C 34
Chaplin C............... 24 (15)	Hladky V 12	Woolfenden L............30 (1)
Clements B 4	Humphreys C............... - (2)	

League goals (67): Bonne 12, Burns 12, Chaplin 9, Celina 6, Norwood 6, Aluko 3, Evans 3, Jackson 3, Morsy 3, Bakinson 2, Edmundson 2, Pigott 2, Fraser 1, Penney 1, Opponents 2
FA Cup goals (3): Burns 1, Chaplin 1, El Mizouni 1. **League Cup goals:** None. **League Trophy goals** (5): Jackson 2, Chaplin 1, Norwood 1, Pigott 1
Average home league attendance: 21,779
Player of Year: Wes Burns

LINCOLN CITY

Michael Appleton stepped down as manager after a disappointing follow-up to reaching the Play-off Final in 2021. A season blighted by inconsistency – and injuries – was captured by a 3-0 win over Cheltenham in the penultimate home match followed by a 2-1 defeat against ten-man Accrington. Lincoln were two points off the drop zone on Boxing Day before their best spell of the campaign brought victories over promotion contenders Oxford, Sunderland and Plymouth, with Chris Maguire scoring a hat-trick on his return to the Stadium of Light after being released by the club in the summer. They defeated another fancied side, Sheffield Wednesday with two goals from winter signing John Marquis, but again momentum was not maintained and the season tailed off with Lincoln finishing in lower mid-table. Appleton was replaced by Mark Kennedy, Birmingham's assistant manager and a former Republic of Ireland winger.

Adelakun H............ 10 (13)	House B 2 (4)	Norton-Cuffy B..........13 (4)
Bishop E.................. 28 (8)	Howarth R .... - (4)	Poole R 44
Bramall C 22 (7)	Jackson A................. 23 (2)	Robson J 20 (3)
Bridcutt L........................14	Long S............................1	Sanders M...............5 (14)
Cullen L 13 (7)	Maguire C................. 28 (4)	Scully A 31 (4)
Draper F 3 (5)	Marquis J 17 (3)	Sorenson L 19 (11)
Eyoma T 20 (3)	McGrandles C................39	Tayo Edun 4
Fiorini L 32 (7)	Melbourne M 5 (2)	Walsh J 12
Griffiths J.......................33	Montsma L.....................19	Whittaker M..............17 (3)
Hopper T 14 (6)	N'Lundulu D........... 6 (10)	Wright J 12 (1)

League goals (55): Scully 11, Fiorini 6, Marquis 5, Whittaker 5, Bishop 4, Maguire 4, Adelakun 2, Bramall 2, Hopper 2, McGrandles 2, Cullen 1, Eyoma 1, House 1, Melbourne 1, Montsma 1, N'Lundulu 1, Norton-Cuffy 1, Poole 1, Sorenson 1, Tayo Edun 1, Opponents 2

FA Cup goals (1): Sanders 1. League Cup goals (2): Bishop 1, Hopper 1. League Trophy goals (8): Scully 4, Adelakun 1, Hopper 1, Maguire 1, Montsma 1
Average home league attendance: 8,773
Player of Year: Regan Poole

MILTON KEYNES DONS

No team carried more momentum into the play-offs than MK Dons after a 5-0 victory over Plymouth, with four of the goals scored by Scott Twine, League One's Player of the Year. They had also beaten opponents Wycombe three times in league and cup matches. But it all counted for nothing after the club's fifth semi-final defeat over the years. They were beaten 2-0 in the first leg and had midfielder Josh McEachran shown a second yellow card at 1-0. Troy Parrott's header after 26 minutes of the return match pulled one back, but that was all Liam Manning's side had to show from dominating throughout. Eight victories in nine matches had previously taken Dons to second behind Wigan with a month of the regular season remaining. Successive defeats by Sheffield Wednesday and Oxford set them back, but they were still in contention for automatic promotion going into the final round of fixtures and finished a single point behind runners-up Rotherham. Former West Ham and Ipswich youth coach Manning came in after Russell Martin took over at Swansea six days before the opening day of the campaign.

Baldwin A 4 (5)	Hayden K 13 (2)	O'Hora W 46
Boateng H 9 (20)	Ilunga B .... - (1)	O'Riley M 26
Brown C 1 (5)	Jules Z 6 (1)	Parrott T 34 (7)
Corbeanu T 9 (7)	Kasumu D 12 (11)	Ravizzoli F 1
Coventry C 20	Kemp D .... - (5)	Robson E 16 (2)
Cumming J 21	Kioso P 16 (2)	Twine S 44 (1)
Darling H 40 (1)	Lewington D 42 (2)	Walker L 1
Eisa M 28 (7)	Martin J .... - (5)	Watson T 20 (8)
Fisher A 23	Smith M 2 (2)	Watters M 5 (6)
Harvie D 41	McEachran J........... 24 (11)	Wickham C 2 (11)

Play-offs – appearances: Coventry 2, Cumming 2, Darling 2, Harvie 2, Hayden 2, Lewington 2, O'Hora 2, Twine 2, Parrott 2, Boateng 1 (1), Corbeanu 1, Kasumu 1, McEachran 1, Wickham – (2), Kemp – (1), Watson – (1)
League goals (78): Twine 20, Eisa 12, Parrott 8, Darling 7, O'Riley 7, Watters 5, Kioso 4, Boateng 3, O'Hora 2, Watson 2, Corbeanu 1, Coventry 1, Harvie 1, Hayden 1, Robson 1, Wickham 1, Opponents 2. Play-offs – goals (1): Parrott 1
FA Cup goals (3): Darling 2, Watters 1. League Cup goals: None. League Trophy goals (6): Bird J 1, Boateng 1, Darling 1, Jules 1, Parrott 1, Watters 1
Average home league attendance: 9,412
Player of Year: Scott Twine

MORECAMBE

Derek Adams returned to the club he led to promotion via the play-offs the previous season and achieved success at the opposite end of the table. Morecambe were in danger of dropping straight back to League Two after 12 goals conceded in successive fixtures against Cheltenham, Shrewsbury and Wigan left them in the bottom four with a month remaining. But Cole Stockton sustained his prolific form with goals in three wins out of four against Burton, Oxford and Charlton to give his side sufficient breathing space to survive a tense final round of matches, despite a home defeat by Sunderland. They had two points to spare over Fleetwood and Gillingham, who also lost, with the latter joining Crewe, Doncaster and AFC Wimbledon in going down. Stockton's tally of 23 featured some spectacular goals, including a stoppage-time winner from the centre circle against Fleetwood. Adams, who left the club for Bradford, where he was sacked after eight months, came back after his successor, Stephen Robinson, took over at St Mirren.

Andersson J 13	Gibson L 23 (6)	McPake J 3 (2)
Ayunga J 20 (16)	Gnahoua A 31 (3)	Mellor K 1
Bedeau J 22	Harrison S .... - (3)	Mensah J ....- (1)
Bennett R 11 (1)	Jones C 9 (2)	O'Connor A 39 (1)
Carson T 21	Lavelle S 4 (1)	Obika J 3 (9)
Connolly D 13 (2)	Leigh G 33 (3)	Phillips A 27 (11)
Cooney R 22 (10)	Letheren K 11 (1)	Price F ....- (3)
Delaney R 10 (3)	McCalmont A 18 (8)	Smith A 1
Diagouraga T........... 32 (8)	McDonald W.......... 9 (8)	Stockton C 44
Duffus C 3 (4)	McLaughlin R 18 (1)	Wildig A 16 (6)
Fane O 9 (3)	McLoughlin S 31 (5)	Wootton S 9 (1)

League goals (57): Stockton 23, Ayunga 6, Phillips 6, Gnahoua 5, Diagouraga 2, Leigh 2, O'Connor 2, Obika 2, Wildig 2, Connolly 1, Gibson 1, Jones 1, McCalmont 1, McLoughlin 1, Wootton 1, Opponents 1
FA Cup goals (3): O'Connor 1, Stockton 1, Wildig 1. **League Cup goals** (4): Stockton 2, O'Connor 1, Phillips 1. **League Trophy goals** (2): Jones 1, McLoughlin 1
Average home league attendance: 4,333
Player of Year: Cole Stockton

OXFORD UNITED

Cameron Brannagan's prowess from the penalty spot pointed Oxford towards a third successive play-off place until form dipped at a crucial time. The former Liverpool midfielder became the first player in English football to score four spot-kicks in a single fixture – a 7-2 romp at Gillingham. Brannagan was also on the mark, this time from distance, in follow-up wins over Portsmouth and Charlton, during a purple patch of nine goals in 11 matches which pushed his side up to fourth. But a single point gained from a run of four games – Ipswich, Plymouth, Morecambe and Sunderland – contrasted sharply with how they came through strongly late on in 2021. It left them four points adrift in the scramble for places which left little room for error. There was still a chance after victory over MK Dons in the penultimate home fixture. But despite leading at promotion-bound Rotherham through an early own goal, a 2-1 defeat left them out of contention.

Agyei D.................... - (14)	Gorrin A 11 (2)	O'Donkor G.................- (1)
Baldock S 4 (3)	Hanson J.......................2	Seddon S 35 (1)
Bodin B 14 (7)	Henry J 17 (9)	Stevens J 30
Brannagan C 41	Holland N.............. 21 (14)	Sykes M 36 (4)
Brown C 11 (2)	Kane H 34 (1)	Taylor M 43 (1)
Browne M 2 (3)	Long S 35 (1)	Thorniley J 21
Cooper J .... - (2)	McGuane M 12 (18)	Trueman C.......................2
Eastwood S...............14	McNally L............ 28 (2)	Whyte G 26 (11)
Forde A.................. 10 (3)	Moore E..................31	Williams R 22 (11)
Golding J 1	Mousinho J........... 1 (6)	Winnall S 2 (18)

League goals (82): Taylor 20, Brannagan 14, Sykes 8, Henry 7, Bodin 6, Holland 5, Baldock 4, McNally 4, Seddon 2, Williams 2, Brown 1, Browne 1, Forde 1, Long 1, Moore 1, Whyte 1, Winnall 1, Opponents 3
FA Cup goals (5): Taylor 2, Bodin 1, McGuane 1, Seddon 1. **League Cup goals** (1): Holland 1.
League Trophy goals (5): Agyei 2, Cooper 2, Gorrin 1
Average home league attendance: 8,463
Player of Year: Cameron Brannagan

PLYMOUTH ARGYLE

There was no play-off place for manager Steven Schumacher to celebrate on his 38th birthday. Instead, a 15,000 Home Park crowd were stunned by a 5-0 defeat by MK Dons on the final day of the regular season, which meant that Wycombe, 2-1 winners at Burton, overtook their side for sixth place. Plymouth went into the final month with a seven-point cushion after a run of six matches without conceding a goal, during which Ryan Hardie took his tally to 16 goals. But injuries to key players exposed a lack of depth in their squad at a crucial time when some big clubs were scrambling for places in a highly competitive division. Despite failing to win any of the final five games, Schumacher felt the campaign offered plenty of positives, including a run to the fourth round of the FA Cup and a spirited performance at Stamford Bridge, where Hardie had an extra-time penalty saved, enabling Chelsea to go through 2-1. Schumacher was promoted from assistant manager midway through when Ryan Lowe left to take charge at Preston.

Agard K 3 (9)	Galloway B 12 (2)	Lewis A ....- (1)
Bolton J................. 12 (1)	Garrick J 19 (23)	Mayor D 26 (7)
Broom R 29 (14)	Gillesphey M............. 36 (4)	Randell A................8 (16)
Camara P................. 36 (4)	Grant C 37 (1)	Scarr D 35
Cooper G.................. - (1)	Hardie R 34 (3)	Sessegnon S 6 (4)
Cooper M...................46	Houghton J.................42	Shirley R ....- (3)
Crichlow-Noble R........ 1 (2)	Jenkins-Davies W .... - (1)	Wilson J 42
Edwards J 38 (3)	Jephcott L 27 (13)	
Ennis N 13 (12)	Law R 4 (10)	

League goals (68): Hardie 16, Jephcott 10, Grant 7, Edwards 5, Broom 4, Camara 4, Ennis 4, Garrick 4, Mayor 3, Galloway 2, Scarr 2, Agard 1, Gillesphey 1, Houghton 1, Law 1, Randell 1, Opponents 1.
FA Cup goals (7): Garrick 3, Gillesphey 1, Hardie 1, Jephcott 1, Law 1. **League Cup goals** (5): Hardie 1, Camara 1, Jephcott 1, Shirley 1. **League Trophy goals** (2): Agard 2
Average home league attendance: 13,130
Player of Year: Mike Cooper

PORTSMOUTH

A strong finish was not enough to camouflage another frustrating season at Fratton Park. Portsmouth scored 12 goals in four victories – two against pacemakers Wigan and Rotherham – but still fell well short of a sustained promotion bid. Their new-look squad had started with three victories and approached the midway point of the campaign a single point away from a play-off place. Momentum stalled during an enforced three-week break because of postponements and the new year return brought five games without a win. Portsmouth then took advantage of a run of fixtures against teams in the bottom half of the table to refresh their faltering challenge, before sterner testes against Ipswich, Plymouth, Wyconbe and Bolton proved a different proposition. A single goal from those matches left them with too much ground to make up on the leading group and despite that final flourish they closed ten points adrift in tenth place.

Ahadme G................. 2 (3)	Harness M 39 (1)	Ogilvie C 31 (3)
Azeez M..................... 4 (2)	Harrison E............... 1 (10)	Raggett S 45
Bass A...........................2	Hirst G 27 (13)	Robertson C.............22 (4)
Bazunu G.....................44	Hume D 7 (2)	Romeo M 30 (5)
Brown L 18 (1)	Jacobs M 11 (13)	Thompson L 22 (10)
Carter H......................22	Johnson C .... - (1)	Tunnicliffe R.............21 (9)
Curtis R 37 (6)	Marquis J 15 (4)	Walker T...................9 (6)
Downing P 1 (1)	Mingi J................... - (3)	Williams S...............24 (7)
Freeman K...................19	Morrell J................. 29 (7)	
Hackett-Fairchild R. 16 (11)	O'Brien A 8 (9)	

League goals (68): Hirst 13, Harness 11, Curtis 8, Jacobs 6, Raggett 6, O'Brien 5, Hackett-Fairchild 4, Marquis 4, Brown 3, Robertson 2, Tunnicliffe 2, Carter 1, Ogilvie 1, Thompson 1, Walker 1
FA Cup goals (2): Harness 1, Harrison 1. League Cup goals (1): Hackett-Fairchild 1. League Trophy goals (10): Harrison 3, Curtis 2, Hirst 2, Ahadme 1, Azeez 1, Jacobs 1
Average home league attendance: 15,003
Player of Year: Gavin Bazunu

ROTHERHAM UNITED

There are no half measures with this redoubtable Yorkshire club. They regained a place in the Championship as runners-up to Wigan and have now been promoted to or relegated from the second tier for six successive seasons. Paul Warne and his players also had a League Trophy success at Wembley to celebrate during an eventful season which went to the wire. Rotherham were overtaken at the top after holding down a nine-point lead, established on the back of a club-record 21 games without defeat in all competitions. And there some anxious moments on the final day of the campaign as fast-finishing MK Dons were also in contention for automatic promotion. They were 5-0 winners at Plymouth, while Wigan defeated Shrewsbury 3-0. But, with no margin for error, Rotherham held their nerve – and a one point advantage - to win 2-0 at Gillingham with goals from Rarmani Edmonds-Green and Georgie Kelly on his debut against a side battling to stay up. It had also been touch-and-go in the Trophy decider against League Two newcomers Sutton, who led 2-1 going into stoppage-time before Arsenal loanee Jordi Osei-Tutu equalised and Chiedozie Ogbene and Michael Ihiekwe scored in the extra period for a 4-2 success.

Barlaser D	40 (4)	Kelly G	- (1)	Osei-Tutu J	9 (5)
Edmonds-Green R	26 (2)	Ladapo F	22 (9)	Rathbone O	39 (3)
Ferguson S	25 (7)	Lindsay J	15 (13)	Sadlier K	5 (7)
Grigg W	13 (6)	MacDonald A	3 (4)	Smith M	45
Harding W	32 (6)	Mattock J	10 (10)	Bola T	3 (1)
Ihiekwe M	42	Miller M	11 (12)	Vickers J	20
Johansson V	26	Odofin H	1 (10)	Wiles B	43 (3)
Kayode J	6 (15)	Ogbene C	37 (8)	Wood R	33 (6)

League goals (70): Smith 19, Ladapo 11, Barlaser 9, Wiles 8, Edmonds-Green 3, Ihiekwe 3, Miller 3, Ogbene 3, Grigg 2, Rathbone 2, Ferguson 1, Kayode 1, Kelly 1, Lindsay 1, Sadlier 1, Wood 1, Opponents 1
FA Cup goals (5): Grigg 1, Ihiekwe 1, Ladapo 1, Smith 1, Wiles 1. League Cup goals (1); Sadlier 2. League Trophy goals (26): Smith 5, Sadlier 4, Grigg 3, Ladapo 3, Hull J 2, Harding 1, Ihiekwe 1, Kayode 1, Mattock 1, Miller 1, Odofin 1, Ogbene 1, Osei-Tutu 1, Wiles 1
Average home league attendance: 9,337
Player of Year: Michael Smith

SHEFFIELD WEDNESDAY

Wednesday carried plenty of momentum into their 'heavyweight' play-off semi-final against Sunderland, with six victories in the final eight games of the regular season and eight goals from Lee Gregory during that run, including a hat-trick against Fleetwood. It was anyone's guess who would prevail. Darren Moore's side had won 3-0 at Hillsborough, Sunderland dominated the return 5-0 and the teams were separated by a single point in the final table. Two tight, tense encounters followed – Ross Stewart's winner at the Stadium of Light in front of a record semi-final crowd of nearly 45,000, cancelled out by Gregory's 17th goal in the second leg. Wednesday looked favourites to go on to Wembley, but were caught cold in the third minute of stoppage-time when Patrick Roberts denied them the chance of an immediate return to the Championship. Previously, they had been off the pace at the midway point of the campaign, drawing ten times, then came through strongly, defeating Cambridge 6-0, Burton 5-2 and scoring four against Plymouth, Cheltenham and Portsmouth.

Adeniran D.............. 12 (6)	Gibson L 3 (2)	Mendez-Laing N........12 (6)
Bannan B 45	Green A..........................2	Palmer L 37 (2)
Berahino S........... 13 (16)	Gregory L 31 (5)	Paterson C.............27 (13)
Brennan C.................. 5 (6)	Hunt J 36 (3)	Peacock-Farrell B...........43
Brown J 7 (4)	Hutchinson S.................28	Shodipo O 7 (8)
Byers G..................... 21 (1)	Iorfa D 16 (3)	Sow S 5 (8)
Corbeanu T 6 (7)	John-Jules T .... - (1)	Storey J 19
Dean H..................... 6 (1)	Johnson M 38 (1)	Wildsmith J 3
Dunkley C 15 (6)	Kamberi F 12 (11)	Windass J.................3 (6)
Dele-Bashiru F 16 (8)	Luongo M 23 (2)	Wing L 15 (3)

Play-offs – appearances: Bannan 2, Byers 2, Dean 2, Gregory 2, Hutchinson 2, Johnson 2, Luongo 2, Peacock-Farrell 2, Storey 2, Berahino 1 (1), Palmer 1 (1), Windass 1 (1), Hunt 1, Dele-Bashiru – (1), Mendez-Laing – (1), Paterson – (1).
League goals (78): Gregory 16, Bannan 9, Berahino 8, Byers 6, Paterson 6, Kamberi 4, Windass 4, Adeniran 3, Corbeanu 2, Dunkley 2, Hunt 2, Johnson 2, Mendez-Laing 2, Sow 2, Storey 2, Dele-Bashiru 1, Hutchinson 1, Luongo 1, Palmer 1, Shodipo 1, Opponents 3. **Play-offs – goals** (1): Gregory 1
FA Cup goals: None. **League Cup goals:** None. **League Trophy goals** (9): Sow 2, Adedoyin K 1, Berahino 1, Byers 1, Johnson 1, Kamberi 1, Palmer 1, Wing 1
Average home league attendance: 22,908
Player of Year: Barry Bannan

SHREWSBURY TOWN

Ryan Bowman's 'perfect' hat-trick helped stabilise Shrewsbury after early season problems. They lost the opening four fixtures without a goal scored, the club's worst start for 38 years, and won just three of the first 14 before Bowman set up a confidence-boosting 4-1 victory over Cambridge with a header and strikes with both feet. It came a fortnight after he had to leave the field against Ipswich with heart palpitations and taken to hospital. Bowman was cleared to return with a change of medication and his side eventually cleared a way out of relegation trouble with three wins over Christmas and the new year. They consolidated a position in lower mid-table before pushing to go higher on the back of wins over Morecambe (5-0) and leaders Rotherham away (3-0). But a disappointing finish pushed them back, the final six matches yielding just two points with 14 goals conceded.

Bennett E 42	Flanagan T 13 (1)	Ogbeta N................... 19 (7)
Bloxham T 17 (17)	Fornah T 17 (2)	Pennington M 45
Bowman R 35 (7)	Janneh S.................. 1 (11)	Pierre A............... 15 (10)
Cosgrove S................ 8 (9)	Leahy L 42	Pyke R 4 (12)
Daniels J 9 (12)	Leshabela T................ - (3)	Udoh D 42 (4)
Davis D..........................27	Marosi M.......................46	Vela J.............................36
Ebanks-Landell E...........33	Nurse G 41 (4)	Whalley S 14 (7)

League goals (47): Udoh 13, Bowman 10, Leahy 8, Whalley 4, Pennington 3, Bloxham 2, Cosgrove 2, Vela 2, Bennett 1, Davis 1, Flanagan 1
FA Cup goals (8): Bowman 3, Bloxham 2, Bennett 1, Leahy 1, Udoh 1. **League Cup goals** (2): Udoh 2. **League Trophy goals** (3): Bloxham 1, Lloyd L 1, Pyke 1
Average home league attendance: 6,216
Player of Year: Luke Leahy

SUNDERLAND

The fallen giant finally stirred – backed by massive support – after four frustrating seasons spent in League One. More than 46,000 fans roared their approval at Wembley as Sunderland defeated Wycombe 2-0 in the Play-off Final with goals from Elliot Embleton and Ross Stewart. Embleton, restored to the starting line-up because manager Alex Neil had a hunch he was the right man for the job, and Stewart, with his 26th goal of the season, delivered a deserved victory, their team dominating throughout. The semi-final, against Sheffield Wednesday, had been a much tighter affair. Stewart scored the only goal at the Stadium of Light, watched by a record crowd for that stage of the competition of nearly 45,000, and the return looked to be heading for extra-time when Patrick Roberts equalised on the night in the 93rd minute for a 2-1 aggregate success. Sunderland finished fifth after 13 unbeaten matches at the end of a campaign which had its share of problems. Injuries left Aiden McGeady, Luke O'Nien and Everton loanee Nathan Broadhead out for lengthy spells and Lee Johnson was sacked following a 6-0 defeat at Bolton. It was the first of six games without a win, the last three under Johnson's replacement, former Preston manager Neil. But they were back in business with a 3-0 victory at champions-to-be Wigan and never looked back. Stewart's goals included the perfect hat-trick – left-foot, right-foot, header – in the 5-0 league win over Wednesday.

Alves F	- (3)	Evans C	26 (7)	McGeady A	12 (2)
Batth D	8 (1)	Flanagan T	25	Neill D	31 (8)
Broadhead N	15 (5)	Gooch L	33 (5)	O'Brien A	7 (10)
Burge L	3	Harris W	- (3)	O'Nien L	24 (2)
Cirkin D	31 (3)	Hawkes J	- (1)	Patterson A	20
Clarke J	9 (8)	Hoffmann R-T	23	Pritchard A	25 (11)
Dajaku L	14 (8)	Huggins N	1 (1)	Roberts P	6 (8)
Defoe J	2 (5)	Hume D	- (4)	Stewart R	46
Diamond J	1 (2)	Hume T	3	Winchester C	39 (1)
Doyle C	33 (3)	Kimpioka B	- (2)	Wright B	28 (9)
Embleton E	26 (12)	Matete J	12 (2)	Xhemajli A	3

Play-offs – appearances: Batth 3, Cirkin 3, Evans 3, Gooch 3, O'Nien 3, Patterson 3, Pritchard 3, Roberts 3, Stewart 3, Wright 3, Clarke 2 (1), Embleton 1 (1), Doyle – (3), Broadhead – (2), Matete – (2).
League goals (79): Stewart 24, Broadhead 10, Embleton 8, Dajaku 4, Pritchard 4, McGeady 3, Neill 3, O'Nien 3, Winchester 3, Evans 2, O'Brien 2, Wright 2, Batth 1, Clarke 1, Doyle 1, Flanagan 1, Kimpioka 1, Roberts 1, Opponents 5. **Play-offs – goals (4)**: Stewart 2, Embleton 1, Roberts 1.
FA Cup goals: None. **League Cup goals (8)**: O'Brien 4, Broadhead 2, Hawkes 1, O'Nien 1. **League Trophy goals (5)**: Wearne S 2, Broadhead 1, Dyce T 1, Neill 1
Average home league attendance: 31,426
Player of Year: Ross Stewart

WIGAN ATHLETIC

Leam Richardson dedicated a title-winning return to the Championship to members of staff made redundant when the club faced dark days during the pandemic. Wigan were in administration, faced a second successive relegation and the club's future looked in doubt until the new manager kept them up by a point, backed by new owners. His gesture underlined a remarkable change in fortunes with a rebuilt squad who went toe-to-toe with Rotherham before prevailing on the last day of the season. Will Keane, League One's leading marksman with 26 goals, led the way as his side made full use of games in hand to overtake the nine-point advantage Rotherham established at one point in the campaign. They took over the leadership by beating Accrington 3-0 in the second of nine matches in April, wobbled in the middle of the month – like their rivals – and went into the final round of fixtures also under pressure from fast-finishing MK Dons. All three teams won, with Keane scoring twice, one a penalty, in a 3-0 victory at Shrewsbury to keep Wigan on top and deliver the divisional EFL Manager of the Year award to Richardson.

Aasgaard T	1 (4)	Keane W	43 (1)	Pearce T	9 (7)
Amos B	46	Kerr J	16 (8)	Power M	44
Bayliss T	6 (2)	Lang C	41 (1)	Rea G	1 (2)
Bennett J	10 (1)	Long A	1	Robinson L	1
Cousins J	13 (3)	Magennis J	14 (3)	Shinnie G	6 (4)
Darikwa T	42 (1)	Massey G	9 (24)	Tilt C	18 (2)
Edwards G	9 (21)	McClean J	31 (2)	Watts K	25 (1)
Humphrys S	12 (26)	McGrath J	1 (1)	Whatmough J	46
Jones J	3 (6)	Naylor T	43	Wyke C	15

League goals (82): Keane 26, Lang 15, McClean 9, Humphrys 5, Wyke 5, Magennis 3, Naylor 3, Power 3, Darikwa 2, Tilt 2, Whatmough 2, Aasgaard 1, Bennett 1, Edwards 1, Kerr 1, Massey 1, Opponents 2
FA Cup goals (7): Lang 3, Aasgaard 1, Kerr 1, Power 1, Opponents 1. **League Cup goals** (1): Humphrys 1. **League Trophy goals** (11): Edwards 2, Baningime D 1, Humphrys 1, Keane 1, Long 1, Massey 1, McClean 1, Naylor 1, Power 1 Sze C 1
Average home league attendance: 10,397
Player of Year: Jack Whatmough

WYCOMBE WANDERERS

There was no immediate return to the Championship for Gareth Ainsworth, nor a fairy-tale finish to a 22-year career for Adebayo Akinfenwa. Ainsworth admitted his side could not complain about a 2-0 Play-off Final defeat by Sunderland. They were second best from the start and created little against opponents backed by more than 46,000 fans at Wembley. But Wycombe, one of the minnows in a division packed with big clubs, were able to look back with plenty of satisfaction on going so far. For a while, their manager was bemoaning the possibility of missing out on a top-six place with a likely 80 points. Instead, an unbeaten run of 12 games through to the end of the season sealed sixth, a point behind Sunderland. They had also started well, wining the first six home games for the first time in the club's history. February was tough – a barren five games, including a bizarre 5-5 draw against Cheltenham. But they were back up and running by beating Cambridge 3-0 and went on to reach Wembley on the back of a 2-0 success in the first leg of their semi-final against MK Dons. Akinfenwa came off the bench in that match for his last home appearance, five days before his 40th birthday. Ainsworth also turned to the big man for the final quarter-of-an-hour in the final, but by then Sunderland's control was unshakable.

Akinfenwa A	3 (31)	Jacobson J	40	Stewart A	34 (2)
De Barr T	- (5)	Kaikai S	8 (9)	Stockdale D	46
Forino-Joseph C	13 (2)	McCarthy J	31	Tafazolli R	33
Freeman N	1 (2)	McCleary G	37 (5)	Thompson C	24 (4)
Gape D	7 (3)	Mehmeti A	23 (9)	Vokes S	42 (1)
Grimmer J	23 (3)	Obita J	37 (4)	Wheeler D	8 (22)
Hanlan B	25 (11)	Pendlebury O	3 (1)	Wing L	11 (2)
Horgan P	21 (13)	Scowen J	36 (1)	Young J	- (2)

Play-offs – appearances: Gape 3, Horgan 3, Jacobson 3, McCarthy 3, McCleary 3, Obita 3, Scowen 3, Stewart 3, Stockdale 3, Tafazolli 3, Vokes 3. Akinfenwa – (2), Wheeler – (2), Wing – (2), Grimmer – (1), Hanlan – (1)
League goals (75): Vokes 16, McCleary 11, Mehmeti 7, Hanlan 6, Akinfenwa 5, Obita 5, Tafazolli 4, Jacobson 3, Grimmer 3, Kaikai 2, Pendlebury 2, Stewart 2, Thompson 2, Wheeler 2, Wing 2, Forino-Joseph 1, Horgan 1, McCarthy 1, Scowen 1. Play-offs – goals (2): Tafazolli 1, Vokes 1
FA Cup goals (2): Forino-Joseph 1, Jacobson 1. **League Cup goals** (3): Akinfenwa 1, De Barr 1, Hanlan 1. **League Trophy goals** (2): Hanlan 1, Parsons C 1
Average home league attendance: 5,662
Player of Year: Josh Scowen

SKY BET LEAGUE TWO

BARROW

Phil Brown answered a call to preserve Football League status for the second successive season and this time was successful. Brown had little chance of saving Southend in 2021 with six matches remaining. But with a few weeks' extra time here, he was able to keep Barrow afloat after three successive defeats left them hanging on by goal difference and facing the prospect of all the final six fixtures against clubs with promotion ambitions. They turned the table upside down to give leaders Forest Green a 4-0 drubbing, with three of the goals coming from corners. Three days later, three more points looked to be in the bag until an 89th minute equaliser was conceded at Salford. But the performance was enough to keep momentum going and John Rooney's winner against Sutton took Barrow clear with three to play. Brown was appointed until the end of the campaign when Mark Cooper left after an eight-match touchline ban and £3,000 from the FA for abusive comments, including a reference to gender, made to assistant referee Helen Edwards. The club's permanent replacement was former Halifax manager Pete Wild.

Arthur F..................... 4 (5)	Gordon J 29 (7)	Ntlhe K 3 (2)
Banks O................... 37 (2)	Gotts R 34 (1)	Platt M.................... 24 (4)
Beadling T 10 (2)	Grayson J 23 (3)	Rooney J 19
Brough P 40 (1)	Harris W 5 (4)	Sea D.................... - (10)
Brown C 19 (2)	Holloway A 14	Stevens J 16 (3)
Canavan N 17 (1)	Hutton R 37 (7)	Taylor J 10 (2)
Devitt J...................... - (4)	James L 6 (13)	Wakeling J.................. 2 (2)
Driscoll-Giennon A.... 12 (3)	Jones J.................... 19 (6)	White T................... 23 (4)
Ellis M................... 14 (2)	Jones M 3	Williams G................5 (13)
Farman P....................46	Kay J 20 (14)	Zanzala O................ 15 (4)

League goals (44): Banks 9, Gordon 6, Kay 5, Rooney 5, Holloway 3, Zanzala 3, Gotts 2, Grayson 2, Platt 2, Jones J 1, Sea 1, Stevens 1, Williams 1, Opponents 3
FA Cup goals (10): Banks 2, Stevens 2, Driscoll-Glennon 1, Gordon 1, Gotts 1, Jones J 1, Kay 1, Zanzala 1. **League Cup goals** (1): Sea 1. **League Trophy goals** (4): Arthur 1, Banks 1, Stevens 1, Zanzala 1
Average home league attendance: 3,202
Player of Year: Robbie Gotts

BRADFORD CITY

Mark Hughes, the season's most high-profile appointment, had an immediate taste of the potential on offer at Valley Parade. A crowd of nearly 17,000 welcomed the former Wales and Manchester City manager for his first match against Mansfield. A 2-0 defeat, followed immediately by a 2-1 reversal against Swindon, also showed the size of his task. Hughes pledged to make Bradford 'a team people can be proud to come and watch' and was up and running with victories over leaders Forest Green and Hartlepool. It was a month before he was able to savour a first home success – 2-1 against relegated Scunthorpe with Jamie Walker scoring after 18 seconds. A second followed against Carlisle, watched by more than 18,000, and Bradford closed with three successive wins to finish just below mid-table. Hughes, out of management since being sacked by Southampton in December 2018, replaced Derek Adams, dismissed after seven months in charge, with his side eight points adrift of the play-offs.

Angol L.................... 14 (4)	Cooke C 28 (14)	Delfouneso N 4 (2)
Bass A.....................21	Cousin-Dawson F 8 (3)	Eisa A........................ 1 (3)
Canavan N 17	Crankshaw O .... - (6)	Elliott T 2 (5)
Cook A 35 (4)	Daly M.................... 8 (1)	Evans G 13 (7)

126

Foulds M 18 (5)	O'Donnell R 19	Sutton L 23 (9)
Gillieard A 38 (5)	Pereira D 9 (1)	Threlkeld O 22
Hendrie L 16	Ridehalgh L 28 (1)	Vernam C 19 (9)
Hornby S 6	Robinson T 5 (18)	Walker J.................. 15 (4)
Kelleher F 6 (3)	Scales K .... - (2)	Watt E 41
Lavery C 5 (14)	Songo'o Y 39 (2)	
O'Connor P 45	Staunton R .,................1	

League goals (53): Cook 12, Vernam 8, Angol 6, Walker 4, O'Connor 3, Songo'o 3, Cooke 2, Foulds 2, Robinson 2, Sutton 2, Watt 2, Canavan 1, Daly 1, Evans 1, Gillieard 1, Lavery 1, Pereira 1, Opponents 1
FA Cup goals (1): Angol 1. **League Cup goals** (1): Cooke 1. **League Trophy goals** (1): Robinson 1
Average home league attendance: 15,450
Player of Year: Paudie O'Connor

BRISTOL ROVERS

No-one, least of all Joey Barton and his players, could have banked on the events of a quite remarkable final day of the season. Rovers were preparing for the play-offs, level on points with third-place Northampton but with a much inferior goal difference. Instead, they finished the afternoon relishing League One football after scoring five second-half goals for a 7-0 win over a relegated Scunthorpe side including seven teenagers. That put them on plus 22, the same as Northampton, 3-1 winners at Barrow, along with a better goals-scored record which delivered Barton's first promotion as a manager. Rovers' final goal came from Elliot Anderson, his eighth of an influential winter loan move from Newcastle. He joined a side who had spent the whole of the first half of the campaign in the bottom half of the table, while receiving seven red cards. A run of ten points from four matches in the new year lifted them into the top half. Eight wins and a draw in ten then took them into a challenging position. And a 4-3 victory in the penultimate match at Rochdale, where Aaron Collins completed a hat-trick with a stoppage-time winner, after his side had twice trailed by two goals, cemented their position.

Anderson E 20 (1)	Evans A................... 34 (1)	Martinez P...................- (1)
Anderson H.............. 39 (5)	Finley S 34 (2)	Nicholson S.............. 26 (8)
Anderton N 26 (8)	Grant J 20 (2)	Nolan J ....- (1)
Baldwin J.................... 2 (1)	Hanlan B .... - (1)	Pitman B....................8 (8)
Belshaw J....................42	Hargreaves C 1	Rodman A 3 (1)
Brown J 4 (2)	Harries C 15 (1)	Saunders H 10 (11)
Clarke L...................... 2 (9)	Hoole L 27 (2)	Spence S 1 (5)
Clarke T 5 (2)	Hughes M....................6	Taylor C................... 41 (1)
Collins A 36 (9)	Jaakkola A......................4	Thomas L 10 (18)
Connolly J....................24	Kilgour A 10 (1)	Westbrooke Z.............- (3)
Coutts P 35 (4)	Loft R 2 (11)	Whelan G 19 (12)

League goals (71): Collins 15, Evans 10, Anderson E 8, Anderson H 6, Finley 5, Nicholson 5, Pitman 4, Grant 3, Taylor 3, Clarke L 2, Saunders 2, Anderton 1, Connolly 1, Harries 1, Hoole 1, Kilgour 1, Loft 1, Spence 1, Opponents 1
FA Cup goals (9): Collins 2, Finley 2, Spence 2, Anderton 1, Coutts 1, Evans 1. **League Cup goals**: None. **League Trophy goals** (6): Anderton 1, Jones R 1, Nicholson 1, Saunders 1, Thomas 1, Westbrooke 1
Average home league attendance: 7,512
Player of Year: James Belshaw

CARLISLE UNITED

Paul Simpson returned to Brunton Park 15 years after leaving to take over at Preston and led

Carlisle away from the threat of non-league football. The club's third manager of the season took over a side low on confidence and second from bottom after being overtaken by improving Oldham. Simpson, who achieved back-to-back promotions in his first spell, made club history by winning his first four games – Leyton Orient, Rochdale, Oldham and Northampton. There was a fifth success against Barrow, by which time Carlisle were nine points clear of the drop zone, their fortunes transformed. His appointment, initially until the end of the campaign, became permanent with a three-year contract. Chris Beech had been the first to go, sacked after two wins out of 11 in the opening two months. Former Bristol City manager Keith Millen then delivered an eight-point mid-winter cushion, but he too departed when six matches produced a single point.

Abrahams T.............. 12 (8)	Feeney M 31 (4)	Omotoye T.................. 7 (6)
Alessandra L 15 (9)	Fishburn S 3 (6)	Riley J :.................... 27 (4)
Armer J.................... 39 (2)	Gibson J 33 (6)	Roberts M 3 (3)
Bell L .... - (1)	Guy C.............................34	Senior J 3 (1)
Charters T.................. 1 (8)	Howard M.......................35	Sho-Silva T................. 4 (9)
Clough Z.................. 10 (7)	Jensen L 1	Simeu D........................ 18
Dennis K.................. 12 (5)	Mampala M .... - (8)	Tanner D 5
Devine D.................... 9 (8)	McDonald R 30 (1)	Toure G 1 (4)
Devitt J.................... 4 (3)	Mellish J.........................42	Whelan C 30 (5)
Dickenson B............. 35 (4)	Mellor K 17 (4)	Windsor O 3
Dinzeyi J..........................1	Norman M 10	Young B 7 (7)
Ellis J..............................2	Omari Patrick 22 (2)	

League goals (39): Omari Patrick 9, Gibson 6, Sho-Silva 4, Abrahams 3, Mellish 3, Riley 3, Alessandra 2, Clough 2, Dennis 2, Dickenson 2, Feeney 1, McDonald 1, Windsor 1
FA Cup goals (3): Clough 1, Gibson 1, Young 1. **League Cup goals:** None. **League Trophy goals (8):** Young 2, Abrahams 1, Armer 1, Charters 1, Gibson 1, Mampala 1, Mellor 1
Average home league attendance: 4,966
Player of Year: Mark Howard

COLCHESTER UNITED

Wayne Brown achieved success with the club as a player and made his mark as manager at a difficult time of the season. Five successive mid-winter defeats had left Colchester three points above the drop zone, bringing to an end Hayden Mullins's eight months in charge. Brown, Player of the Year when the club reached the Championship for the first time in 2006, brought about an immediate change of fortune as caretaker with a 3-0 victory at Salford and a single defeat in his first six games. It was not all plain sailing as an eight-point safety net was halved. But victory over promotion contenders Port Vale and Tranmere, the latter with 18-year-old Junior Tchamadeu scoring his first professional goal with a spectacular 95th minute strike, eased the pressure and goals by Freddie Sears and Noah Chilvers at Harrogate took them well clear of the danger zone. They finished 15th, an improvement of five places on 2021, and Brown was confirmed in the job.

Akinde J 6 (9)	Eastman T................ 21 (7)	Nouble F 14 (5)
Andrews C.................. 3 (8)	Edwards O................. 9 (4)	Sarpong-Wiredu B 35 (3)
Bennet K .... - (1)	George S 30	Sears F 43 (2)
Chambers L............... 42 (4)	Hannant L 26 (11)	Skuse C 41
Chilvers N 29 (9)	Hornby S........................8	Smith T.................... 29 (3)
Clampin A.................. 4 (1)	Huws E 10 (2)	Tchamadeu J 21 (5)
Collins T .... - (1)	Ihionvien B.................. - (1)	Tovide S...................... 1 (5)
Cooper C.................... - (1)	Jasper S 11 (7)	Turner J...................... 8 (1)
Coxe C..................... 23 (8)	Judge A.................... 27 (5)	Welch-Hayes M 7 (5)
Dallison T 9	Kenlock M 19 (1)	Wright T...................... 5 (7)
Daniels C 16 (2)	Kennedy G 2 (4)	
Dobra A 7 (4)	McCoulsky S................ - (40	

League goals (48): Sears 14, Chilvers 8, Edwards 3, Judge 3, Kenlock 3, Akinde 2, Jasper 2, Andrews 1, Chambers 1, Cooper 1, Dallison 1, Dobra 1, Eastman 1, Huws 1, Sarpong-Wiredu 1, Smith 1, Tchamadeu 1, Wright 1, Opponents 2
FA Cup goals (5): Sears 2, Jasper 1, McCoulsky 1, Sarpong-Wiredu 1. **League Cup goals**: None.
League Trophy goals (4): Chambers 2, Dobra 1, Sears 1
Average home league attendance: 2,813
Player of Year: Shamal George

CRAWLEY TOWN

The suspension of John Yems put a damper on a season which looked to be finishing on a high on and off the field. It followed allegations of discriminatory behaviour and language against his own players by the 62-year-old manager. The FA opened an investigation over complaints made by the players' union, the PFA, and Yems was then sacked after two-and-a-half-years in charge The decision was made by the club's new owners, an American investment group, which took over a month earlier. Crawley had won for the first time in six matches to climb into the top half of the table. There was also a club record of scoring in 17 successive away games. But three successive defeats followed before they came from 2-0 and 3-2 down for a point away to relegated Oldham in the final round of matches to cement 12th place. Arsenal coach Kevin Betsy took over.

Appiah K............. 17 (9)	Frost T 9 (5)	Nichols T 35 (4)
Ashford S 7 (5)	Gallacher O 1 (2)	Tsaroulla N........... 24 (3)
Bansal-McNulty A 2 (2)	Grego-Cox R 2 (8)	Oteh A 5 (3)
Battle A ....- (1)	Hessenthaler J 31 (1)	Payne J 31 (4)
Craig T 32 (3)	Hutchinson I 11 (8)	Powell J 37
Dallison T 11 (1)	Lynch J............... 21 (3)	Rodari D .... - (1)
Davies A 19 (14)	Marshall M 1 (17)	Tilley J 23 (7)
Ferry W 27 (9)	Matthews S 6 (2)	Tunnicliffe J 17 (1)
Francillette L .... 24(2)	Morris G 46	Watts C .... - (1)
Francomb G 37 (1)	Nadesan A 30 (9)	

League goals (56): Appiah 11, Nichols 10, Nadesan 9, Hessenthaler 4, Tsaroulla 3, Tilley 3, Francomb 2, Hutchinson 2, Lynch 2, Oteh 2, Ashford 1, Craig 1, Ferry 1, Francillette 1, Payne 1, Powell 1, Tunnicliffe 1, Opponents 1
FA Cup goals: None. **League Cup goals** (2): Ashford 1, Davies 1. **League Trophy goals** (1): Appiah 1.
Average home league attendance: 2,277
Player of Year: Glenn Morris

EXETER CITY

Manager Matt Taylor admitted to mixed emotions after a promotion-winning season ended ten seasons in League Two. Exeter finished runners-up to Forest Green, who had a superior goal difference after both teams totalled 84 points. They had the chance of the title going into the final day, leading the table by a single point. Instead, a 1-0 home defeat by Port Vale enabled their rivals to take over with a 2-2 draw in their last fixture at Mansfield. 'We weren't quite good enough on the day, but it's still been an incredible season,' said Taylor. Exeter, beaten in three of the previous five Play-off Finals, laid the foundation with a club-record run of 20 unbeaten matches in all competitions. Six without a win set them back, 19 points accumulated from seven restored momentum. That sequence included a 4-3 success against Harrogate, achieved after trailing 3-1 with 20 minutes left, the winner coming from Jack Sparkes in the fifth minute of stoppage-time. They were up to second after beating Oldham and made sure of promotion in the penultimate home game against Barrow.

Amond P.................. 8 (18)	Brown J 42 (1)	Caprice J 29 (5)
Atangana N.............. 4 (12)	Brown S...................1	Coley J 4 (14)

Collins A	36 (2)	Hartridge A	27 (1)	Rowe C	4 (4)
Daniel C	4	Jay M	41 (4)	Seymour B	1 (5)
Dawson C	45	Key J	44	Sparkes J	15 (6)
Diabate C	16 (2)	Kite H	12 (2)	Stubbs S	21 (1)
Dieng T	39 (3)	Nombe S	19 (9)	Sweeney P	42 (1)
Edwards O	3 (7)	Phillips K	6 (5)	Taylor K	6 (8)
Grounds J	7 (8)	Ray G	18 (1)	Zanzala O	12 (3)

League goals (65): Jay 14, Dieng 12, Nombe 8, Brown J 7, Amond 3, Diabate 2, Grounds 2, Key 2, Phillips 2, Sparkes 2, Stubbs 2, Zanzala 2, Atangana 1, Caprice 1, Kite 1, Ray 1, Taylor 1, Opponents 2
FA Cup goals (4): Nombe 2, Dieng 1, Ray 1. **League Cup goals:** None. **League Trophy goals** (10): Amond 2, Coley 2, Collins 2, Jay 2, Daniel 1, Dieng 1
Average home league attendance: 5,312
Player of Year: Tim Dieng

FOREST GREEN ROVERS

Rob Edwards toasted a title-winning season with his players – and was then at the centre of a public row after leaving to become relegated Watford's new manager. Forest Green owner Dale Vince said his club had been left in the dark over negotiations, adding: 'It takes a bit of the shine off promotion. If there's any kind of karma in football, they will languish in the Championship and we'll meet them there in a year's time.' Former Wolves and Wales defender Edwards led last season's play-off semi-finalists to an 11-point lead at the top on the back of a club-record 19 unbeaten league games. Seven without a win then left them under threat from Exeter, who took over the leadership by a point going into the final round of matches. But they lost at home to Port Vale, while Forest Green twice came from behind for a point at Mansfield with goals from Ebou Adams and Josh March to become champions on goal difference with a club-best 84 points. There was also a record 75 goals – Matt Stevens scoring 23 of them and Jamille Matt 19. Edwards was replaced by Notts County manager Ian Burchnall.

Adams E	33 (4)	Godwin-Malife U	23 (4)	Stevens M	35 (2)
Aitchison J	31 (15)	Hendry R	29 (2)	Stevenson B	39 (2)
Allen T	2 (2)	March J	7 (28)	Sweeney D	20 (16)
Bernard D	29 (5)	Matt J	46	Wilson K	45
Cadden N	44	McAteer K	- (9)	Young J	2 (20)
Cargill B	32 (4)	McGee L	46		
Diallo S	3 (6)	Moore-Taylor J	40		

League goals (75): Stevens 23, Matt 19, Cadden 6, Aitchison 5, March 5, Adams 3, Hendry 3, Wilson 3, Young 3, Moore-Taylor 2, Bernard 1, Sweeney 1, Opponents 1
FA Cup goals (2): Aitchison 1, Stevens 1. **League Cup goals** (3): Aitchison 1, Hendry 1, Matt 1.
League Trophy goals (5): Stevens 3, March 1, Young 1
Average home league attendance: 2,687
Player of Year: Kane Wilson

HARROGATE TOWN

Simon Weaver's 13th season as manager – the club's second in the EFL – proved a mixed affair. It held plenty of promise with a single defeat in the opening 13 matches in all competitions. Harrogate were then holding down second place to Forest Green after beating Scunthorpe 6-1 and were still in a play-off position approaching the half-way point of the campaign. But a 4-1 home defeat by the leaders and a 4-0 reversal against Newport were part of a loss of form which left them in mid-table. Jack Muldoon's hat-trick against Oldham ended a run of four successive defeats. After that, wins were few and far between, although points in the bank insured against dropping into trouble. Weaver was disappointed with 19th position, a fall of two places on 2021, but felt that progress made on and off the field would stand them in good stead.

Armstrong L 45	Hall C 20	Page L 27 (1)
Austerfield J 5 (4)	Ilesanmi E ....- (1)	Pattison A............. 38 (3)
Beck M 5 (8)	Kavanagh C 5 (6)	Power S 8 (18)
Burrell W 44 (1)	Kerry L 12 (11)	Richards L 7 (1)
Cracknell J 5 (1)	Legge L 5 (3)	Sheron N............. 22 (6)
Diamond J 39	McArdle R........... 21 (2)	Smith W 16 (1)
Diarra B 7 (3)	Muldoon J........... 33 (9)	Thomson G........... 44 (2)
Falkingham J 34	Orsi-Dadamo D........ 3 (7)	
Fallowfield R........ 20 (8)	Oxley M 41	

League goals (64): Diamond 13, Armstrong 12, Muldoon 12, Pattison 9, Thomson 5, Burrell 2, Kerry 2, Diarra 1, Kavanagh 1, McArdle 1, Orsi-Dadamo 1, Page 1, Power 1, Smith 1, Opponents 2
FA Cup goals (4): Armstrong 1, Diamond 1, Orsi-Dadamo 1, Power 1. **League Cup goals:** None.
League Trophy goals (8): Orsi-Dadamo 4, Armstrong 1, Kerry 1, Muldoon 1, Pattison 1,
Average home league attendance: 2,301
Player of Year:

HARTLEPOOL UNITED

Hartlepool's return to the Football League after a four-year absence promised a mid-table finish to go with two good Cup runs. But nine matches without a win resulted in a drop to 17th and the dismissal of manager Graeme Lee ahead of the final round of fixtures. Lee, a former defender at the club, had started planning for the new season, believing he was the right man to take the club forward. He had replaced Dave Challinor, who moved to ambitious National League Stockport, six weeks after signing a new three-year contract. Lee won his first two matches, experienced a difficult mid-winter spell, then had a productive run of four wins out of five before his side faltered again. Hartlepool made it to the fourth round of the FA Cup and gave a spirited performance at Selhurst Park before losing 2-0 to Crystal Palace. They overcame three more League One opponents in the League Trophy before losing to another, Rotherham, on penalties in the semi-finals. Paul Hartley, manager of Scottish League One champions Cove, took over.

Bilokapic N 2	Fondop M 3 (5)	Mitchell J 2
Bogle O 19 (1)	Francis-Angol Z 16	Molyneux L 35 (8)
Burey T 5 (2)	Goodwin W 8 (2)	Morris B................. 10
Byrne M 40	Grey J 9 (19)	Odusina T 29 (2)
Carver M 6 (11)	Hendrie L 7	Ogle R 8 (10)
Cook J............... 1 (3)	Holohan G 12 (6)	Olomola O........... 6 (6)
Cullen M 11 (6)	Hull J................... 5 (2)	Shelton M 27 (6)
Daly M 15 (4)	Jones E.....................3	Smith M 4 (3)
Featherstone N 40	Killip B 42	Sterry J................. 37
Ferguson J 41 (1)	Lawlor J ....- (1)	Crawford T 22 (6)
Fletcher I 3 (11)	Liddle G 29 (3)	White J...........9 (6)

League goals (44): Molyneux 8, Bogle 5, Featherstone 5, Cullen 4, Ferguson 4, Burey 3, Daly 2, Holohan 2, Sterry 2, Byrne 1, Crawford 1, Fletcher 1, Goodwin 1, Grey 1, Morris 1, Shelton 1, Opponents 2
FA Cup goals (6): Cullen 2, Ferguson 1, Grey 1, Molyneux 1, Opponents 1. **League Cup goals:** None. **League Trophy goals (14):** Daly 5, Molyneux 3, Grey 2, Goodwin 1, Olomola 1, Shelton 1, Opponents 1
Average home league attendance: 5,195
Player of Year: Luke Molyneux

LEYTON ORIENT

Orient flourished, faltered then found their touch again in a see-saw season. Aaron Drinan's hat-trick against Hartlepool (5-0) and 4-1 victories over Sutton and Swindon lifted them into a play-off place, raising hopes of a sustained promotion challenge. Instead, Kenny Jackett's side managed just two points and two goals from a run of ten games amid a Covid-enforced month's break. His side dropped to the lower reaches of the division and Jackett was dismissed after nine months in charge. His replacement, former Salford and Doncaster manager Richie Wellens, steadied the ship, with the help of six goals in seven matches from Ruel Sotiriou. He got another in a 3-0 victory over Scunthorpe, who were relegated as a result, while central defender Omar Beckles netted twice to dent Swindon's promotion chances. But Orient finished with successive home defeats by Northampton and Tranmere and closed in 13th, two places worse off than in 2021.

Archibald T 35 (3)	Kyprianou H............ 31 (7)	Reilly C...................... - (4)
Beckles O 44	Mitchell A................ 23 (3)	Smith H................. 31 (10)
Brown J 6 (5)	Moss D 3 (1)	Smyth P 14 (10)
Clay C 14 (5)	Nkrumah D .... - (3)	Sotiriou R 19 (15)
Coleman E 12 (3)	Nouble F.................... 3 (5)	Sweeney J................. 3 (2)
Drinan A 36 (4)	Obiero Z 1	Tanga J...................... - (1)
Happe D 11 (1)	Ogie S 29 (5)	Thompson A..................14
James T....................21	Omotoye T 1 (3)	Vigouroux L..................46
Kemp D 15 (4)	Pratley D................ 34 (5)	Wood C................... 29 (3)
Khan O 17 (3)	Ray G 8 (1)	Young M 6 (8)

League goals (62): Drinan 13, Smith 13, Sotiriou 9, Archibald 8, Beckles 5, James 4, Smyth 3, Brown 1, Clay 1, Coleman 1, Khan 1, Pratley 1, Opponents 2
FA Cup goals (5): Drinan 2, Smith 2, Beckles 1. **League Cup goals** (1): Drinan 1. **League Trophy goals** (6): Sotiriou 2, Happe 1, Kemp 1, Papadopoulos A 1, Smyth 1
Average home league attendance: 5,116
Player of Year: Theo Archibald

MANSFIELD TOWN

Nigel Clough's side delivered one of the comebacks of the season on the way to reaching the play-offs. They defeated Northampton 3-1 on aggregate in the semi-finals, but were second best at Wembley, missing two gilt-edged chances in the first half and losing 3-0 to Port Vale, managed by Mansfield-born Darrell Clarke, who also had Oli Hawkins sent off for two yellow cards at 2-0 and Clough admitted; 'We didn't do ourselves justice.' Consolation came in the way Mansfield overcame a run of 12 matches without a win which left them second from bottom. They then won 11 of the next 12 and followed that with a club-record 11th straight home success – 1-0 against Northampton. The transformation was rewarded with fifth in the table, a single point away from an automatic promotion place. A brief loss of momentum in a tightly-packed promotion race halted the revival, but Manfield came again and clinched the final play-off place with a 2-2 draw in the final fixture against Forest Green, whose point made them champions.

Akins L. 15 (4)	Hawkins O 39 (2)	O'Toole J-J 25 (2)
Bishop N................. 46	Hewitt E.............. 40 (3)	Oates R 34 (4)
Bowery J 25 (15)	Johnson D............ 9 (13)	Perch J................ 15 (5)
Burke R 1 (3)	Lapslie G 21 (11)	Quinn S 36
Charsley H 10 (6)	Law J................... 1 (4)	Rawson F 23 (7)
Clarke J 3 (1)	Longstaff M 16	Sinclair T 1 (13)
Clarke O 24 (2)	Maris G 31 (7)	Stirk R 23 (8)
Forrester W 2 (2)	McLaughlin S 42 (1)	Wallace K 3 (14)
Gale J...................- (3)	Murphy J 14	Ward K .... - (2)
Gordon K 6 (1)	Nartey R................. 2 (1)	

Play-offs – appearances: Bishop 3, Bowery 3, Hawkins 3, McLaughlin 3, O'Toole 3, Oates 3, Perch 3, Quinn 3, Longstaff 2, Hewitt 2, Murphy 2, Akins 1 (1), Maris 1 (1), Wallace 1 (1), Lapslie – (2), Clarke O – (1)
League goals (67): Oates 9, Bowery 8, Hawkins 7, McLaughlin 7, Longstaff 6, Clarke O 4, Johnson 4, Lapslie 4, Maris 3, Charsley 2, O'Toole 2, Stirk 2, Akins 1, Hewitt 1, Murphy 1, Perch 1, Quinn 1, Rawson 1, Opponents 3. **Play-offs – goals (3)**: Bowery 1, McLaughlin 1, Oates 1
FA Cup goals (6): Lapslie 2, Oates 2, Forrester 1, Hawkins 1. **League Cup goals**: None. **League Trophy goals (8)**: Johnson 3, Caine N 1, Lapslie 1, O'Toole 1, Quinn 1, Sinclair 1
Average home league attendance: 5,153
Player of Year: Stephen McLaughlin

NEWPORT COUNTY

Dominic Telford's prolific season was not enough to fire Newport towards a second successive play-off place. League Two's leading marksman became the club's first player to score 20 league goals since John Aldridge in season 1983–84. With two months of the season to play he had 25 on the board, including a hat-trick against Stevenage and a brace in six other games. His team, under James Rowberry, climbed to third. But Telford hit a barren patch and by the time of his next goal, against Colchester, they were four points adrift, having a single win to show from a run of seven games. It was not enough to keep pace with rivals scrambling to join the leading group and they finished well adrift. Cardiff coach and boyhood fan Rowberry took over when Mike Flynn stepped down after four years as manager, the club's most successful period since returning to the Football League.

Abraham T	3 (9)	Demetriou M	39	Missilou C	2 (2)
Azaz F	34 (8)	Dolan M	25 (8)	Norman C	45 (1)
Baker-Richardson C	25 (6)	Ellison K	1 (9)	Pask J	10
Bennett S	31 (6)	Farquharson P	6 (4)	Street R	11 (7)
Bright H	- (1)	Fisher A	8 (14)	Telford D	35 (2)
Cain J	16 (9)	Greenidge J	- (1)	Townsend N	19
Clarke J	33 (2)	Haynes R	29 (5)	Upson E	15 (1)
Collins L	4 (13)	Hylton J	3 (1)	Waite J	9 (7)
Cooper O	28 (5)	Lewis A	20 (7)	Willmott R	26 (4)
Day J	27	Livermore A	2 (1)		

League goals (67); Telford 25, Baker-Richardson 8, Azaz 7, Demetriou 4, Haynes 3, Willmott 3, Dolan 2, Street 2, Waite 2, Bennett 1, Clarke 1, Collins 1, Cooper 1, Ellison 1, Fisher 1, Lewis 1, Norman 1, Opponents 3
FA Cup goals: None. **League Cup goals (1)**: Abraham 1. **League Trophy goals (5)**: Abraham 2, Fisher 1, Greenidge 1, Telford 1
Average home league attendance: 4,333
Player of Year: Dom Telford

NORTHAMPTON TOWN

So near, yet so far. With just 45 minutes of the season remaining, Northampton were poised for a return to League One at the first time of asking in the third automatic promotion place. Level on points with Bristol Rovers, they led 3-1 at Barrow to maintain a superior goal difference of five on their rivals, who were 2-0 ahead against Scunthorpe at the break. Instead, Rovers stretched the lead to a 7-0 against a side including seven teenagers to finish with an identical record – and they went up having scored more goals than Northampton over the course of the campaign. Jon Brady's shell-shocked players faced Mansfield in the play-offs, lost the first leg 2-1 after strong penalty appeals either side of half-time were turned down. The manager insisted it had still been a good season. But the disappointment was palpable for a team who kept 22 clean sheets and accumulated 12 goals in four games in the final month to establish and maintain third place, having kept up an impressive record of scoring from set pieces.

Abimbola P ....- (1)	Horsfall F 45	Mills J................ 10 (7)
Appere L 16 (2)	Hoskins S 44	Nelson S 1 (1)
Ashley-Seal B............ 1 (8)	Kabamba N 6 (15)	Pinnock M 44 (2)
Connolly D 3 (14)	Kanu I................... 1 (5)	Pollock S................ 1 (1)
Dyche M 1	Koiki A 37 (5)	Revan D................ 1 (2)
Eppiah J 8 (5)	Lewis P............... 37 (2)	Roberts L 46
Etete K............... 15 (3)	Lubula B 5 (9)	Rose D 14 (22)
Flores J 6 (5)	Magloire T............ 8 (2)	Sowerby J 34
Guthrie J 44	McGowan A 42	Zimba C............... 2 (10)
Harriman M.............- (5)	McWilliams S 34 (2)	

Play-offs – appearances: Appere 2, Guthrie 2, Horsfall 2, Hoskins 2, Koiki 2, McWilliams 2, Mills 2, Pinnock 2, Sowerby 2, Eppiah 1 (1), Kanu 1, Maxted J 1, Roberts 1, Rose – (2), Zimba – (1)
League goals (60): Hoskins 13, Horsfall 9, Pinnock 9, Guthrie 8, Lewis 6, Appere 3, Etete 3, Ashley-Seal 2, Eppiah 2, McGowan 2, Rose 1, Sowerby 1, Zimba 1. **Play-offs – goals (1)**: Koiki 1
FA Cup goals (3): Etete 1, Lewis 1, Rose 1. **League Cup goals** (2): Etete 2. **League Trophy goals** (3): Connolly 1, Kabamba 1, Pollock 1
Average home league attendance: 5,356
Player of Year: Liam Roberts

OLDHAM ATHLETIC

A dark day for the club reached a new low when angry supporters invaded the pitch as 115 years in the Football League came to an end. Referee Bobby Madley took the players off 14 minutes from the end of a 2-1 home defeat by Salford which meant Oldham became the first former Premier League club to drop into non-league football, having been part of its inaugural season in 1992-93 The fans, protesting at owner Abdallah Lemsagam, ignored pleas from manager John Sheridan to clear the pitch and the match was eventually completed in an empty stadium. Sheridan, in his sixth spell in charge at Boundary Park – four permanent and two in a caretaker role – supervised eight points from his first four games following the dismissal of Keith Curle eight months into the job. But six successive defeats undermined that recovery and victory at Stevenage in a relegation 'six-pointer' was not enough to kick-start another revival. Oldham went down seven points adrift with two fixtures remaining. Sheridan agreed to stay with a contract until the summer of 2023

Adams N 31 (5)	Fage D 10 (4)	Missilou C............... 18 (2)
Bahamboula D....... 25 (5)	Fondop M 1 (1)	Modi I................... - (2)
Bettache F............. 5 (5)	Hart S 30 (1)	Obadeyi T.............. 4 (4)
Blyth J 1 (2)	Hopcutt J 6 (10)	Piergianni C............... 40
Bowden J 14 (3)	Hope H 29 (10)	Rogers D 22
Cisse O 8	Hunt A 7 (6)	Sheehan A 5 (1)
Clarke J 40	Jameson K 6 (5)	Stobbs J 17 (13)
Couto B 15 (4)	Keillor-Dunn D 43 (3)	Sutton W................... 9
Da Silva V.............- (3)	Leutwiler J 22	Vaughan H 7 (16)
Dearnley Z 7 (5)	Luamba J 9 (6)	Walker L 2
Diarra R................ 9 (3)	McGahey H................ 25	Whelan C 39 (4)

League goals (46): Keillor-Dunn 15, Hope 5, Bahamboula 3, Piergianni 3, Fondop 2, Luamba 2, Missilou 2, Stobbs 2, Sutton 2, Bowden 1, Clarke 1, Couto 1, Hart 1, Hopcutt 1, Vaughan 1, Whelan 1, Opponents 3
FA Cup goals (2): Keillor-Dunn 1, McGahey 1. **League Cup goals** (2): Bahamboula 1, Opponents 1. **League Trophy goals** (6): Dearnley 3, Keillor-Dunn 1, Piergianni 1, Vaughan 1
Average home league attendance: 4,961
Player of Year: Davis Keillor-Dunn

PORT VALE

An emotional Darrell Clarke dedicated Port Vale's 3-0 Play-off Final victory over Mansfield to his 18-year-old eldest daughter Ellie, who died in February. 'I think she was up there kicking every ball for me today, said the Mansfield-born manager, who took a six-week break from football afterwards. A single point separated the teams at the end of the regular season, but Vale dominated at Wembley. Kian Harratt and James Wilson scored in the opening 24 minutes, Mansfield had Oli Hawkins sent off for two yellow cards and Mal Benning completed their success five minutes from the end. Former Manchester United striker Wilson also netted twice in the semi-final victory over Swindon, settled 6-5 on penalties after a 2-2 aggregate result. Vale failed to win any of their opening four games, quickly made up ground, then had momentum interrupted by a month without a fixture caused by postponements. With assistant manager Andy Crosby in charge in Clarke's absence, they regained a play-off place with three wins in eight days against Crawley, Mansfield and Bradford and went on to confirm it with Wilson's winner on the final day against Exeter which deprived the home side of the title. Clarke signed a new contract through to 2027.

Amoo D 7 (20)	Gibbons J 19 (4)	Pett T 39
Bailey E................- (1)	Hall C 24	Politic D 5 (5)
Benning M 17 (9)	Harratt K 5 (14)	Proctor J 24 (7)
Burgess S.............- (2)	Holy T 9	Robinson S .... - (1)
Cass L.............. 16 (3)	Hurst A ....- (1)	Rodney D 9 (5)
Charsley H 13 (7)	Hussey C 15 (4)	Smith N.................. 44
Conlon T 17 (1)	Johnson R............. 3 (1)	Stone A 16 (2)
Cooper J 4 (2)	Jones D 20 (2)	Taylor J............... 1 (10)
Covolan L 21	Legge L 4 (1)	Walker B 24 (4)
Edmondson R........ 9 (10)	Lloyd G 1 (6)	Wilson J.............. 38 (3)
Garrity B 42 (1)	Martin A 21 (8)	Worrall D 39 (2)

Play-offs – appearances: Garrity 3, Gibbons 3, Hall 3, Pett 3, Smith 3, Stone 3, Wilson 3, Worrall 3, Benning 2 (1), Taylor 2 (1), Harratt 2, Charsley 1 (2), Edmondson 1 (1), Martin 1 (1), Proctor – (2),
League goals (67): Garrity 12, Proctor 12, Wilson 9, Worrall 4, Conlon 3, Edmondson 3, Harratt 3, Amoo 2, Gibbons 2, Hall 2, Martin 2, Pett 2, Politic 2, Smith 2, Benning 1, Charsley 1, Rodney 1, Walker 1, Opponents 3. **Play-offs – goals (5)**: Wilson 3, Benning 1, Harratt 1
FA Cup goals (8): Wilson 3, Politic 2, Cass 1, Harratt 1, Lloyd 1. **League Cup goals (1)**: Proctor 1. **League Trophy goals (9)**: Amoo 2, Benning 1, Conlon 1, Lloyd 1, Martin 1, Politic 1, Taylor 1, Opponents 1
Average home league attendance: 6,104
Player of Year: James Wilson

ROCHDALE

Robbie Stockdale's first managerial appointment got off to a solid start with victories over three teams who would go on to challenge for promotion – Northampton, Port Vale and Tranmere. They took his side into the leading group with 12 points accumulated from the opening eight matches. But things got tougher for the former Middlesbrough and Scotland defender after that initial flourish. Rochdale spent most of the time in the bottom half of the table, showing few signs of working their way back up, nor in danger of dropping into relegation trouble. After completing a league double over Northampton, they slipped to fifth from bottom with only two points from a run of seven games. There was improvement with home wins over Carlisle, Walsall and Hartlepool and victory at Newport in the final fixture.

Andrews J.............. 7 (10)	Done M.............. 13 (12)	McNulty J.............. 9 (3)
Ball J 11	Dooley S.............. 30 (8)	Morley A 19 (2)
Beesley J................ 21	Dorsett J 36 (1)	Newby A 27 (9)
Brierley E 2	Downing P 10	O'Connell E 45
Broadbent G 13 (8)	Eastwood J 2	O'Keefe C 39 (4)
Campbell T 13	Graham S 11 (1)	Odoh A............17 (15)
Cashman D 9 (14)	Grant C............. 21 (12)	Taylor M............. 19 (3)
Charman L........... 10 (9)	Kelly L 24 (6)	White A 7 (5)
Clark M 22 (1)	Keohane J............ 25 (1)	
Coleman J 19	Lynch J.................. 25	

League goals (51): Beesley 9, Newby 6, Kelly 5, Grant 4, Andrews 3, Ball 3, Odoh 3, Taylor 3, Campbell 2, Cashman 2, Charman 2, Keohane 2, O'Keefe 2, Broadbent 1, Clark 1, Done 1, Morley 1, O'Connell 1
FA Cup goals (4): Andrews 1, Beesley 1, Morley 1, O'Keefe 1. **League Cup goals (3):** Beesley 2, Cashman 1. **League Trophy goals (4):** O'Keefe 2, Andrews 1, Kelly 1
Average home league attendance: 2,914
Player of Year: Eoghan O'Connell

SALFORD CITY

Salford struck a purple patch at a crucial time of the season to raise hopes of a play-off place. Momentum had been building with the arrival of Matt Smith from Millwall and came to a head with Brandon Thomas-Asante's hat-trick against Scunthorpe. It sparked a run of five wins in six matches – 11 unbeaten in all – which closed a ten-point deficit on the leading group to just one. A pair of 1-0 defeats inflicted by two of those teams, Port Vale and Bristol Rovers, set them back. So too did a 2-2 home draw against lowly Barrow when it needed an 89th minute goal by substitute Ian Henderson to prevent another loss. Jordan Turnbull's header after 90 seconds against Mansfield revived their chances of carrying the challenge into the final round of fixtures. But another 2-2 scoreline meant 70 points was not enough and Salford finished with that total in tenth place – two lower than 2021 – after a 4-2 defeat at Stevenage. Gary Bowyer was sacked 12 months into a two-year-contract and replaced by Manchester United under-23 coach Neil Wood – the club's fifth manager since promotion to the Football League in 2019.

Bolton L 2 (13)	Kelly S 18 (3)	Ripley C....................7
Burgess L ....- (1)	King T..................... 36	Shephard L 30 (5)
Dackers M ....- (1)	Loughlin L .... – (3)	Smith M 21
D'Mani Mellor ....- (3)	Love D............. 19 (6)	Thomas-Asante B 34 (5)
Eastham A 28	Lowe J..................... 45	Touray I 25 (2)
Elliott T 11 (8)	Lund M............. 33 (7)	Turnbull J 36 (1)
Fielding F...................2	McAleny C 14 (10)	Vassell T 24 (3)
Golden T ....-(2)	Morris J 21	Watson R................. 23
Henderson I 7 (8)	Ndaba C................. 29	Willock M 6 (6)
Hunter A 23 (10)	N'Mai K 1 (6)	Wright T............7 (9)
Jeacock Z..................1	Oteh A............3 (7)	

League goals (60): Thomas-Asante 11, Lund 7, Smith 7, Elliott 4, Watson 4, Henderson 3, Shephard 3, Turnbull 3, Eastham 2, Lowe 2, McAleny 2, Ndaba 2, Willock 2, Hunter 1, Kelly 1, Morris 1, Oteh 1, Vassell 1, Wright 1, Opponents 2
FA Cup goals (1): Turnbull 1. **League Cup goals (3):** Morris 2, Turnbull 1. **League Trophy goals (5):** Thomas-Asante 2, Oteh 1, Touray 1, Turnbull 1
Average home league attendance: 2,152
Player of Year: Corrie Ndaba

SCUNTHORPE UNITED

Seventy-two years in the Football League came to an end for a club who had two spells in the Championship between 2007–11. Scunthope spent significantly in an effort to recapture those heady days, reaching the League One play-offs in 2018 when losing to Rotherham in the semifinals. They went down the following season, were clinging on in 2021 and this time there was no escape after a single victory in the first 13 matches. The club, now under a transfer embargo, turned to the experienced Keith Hill after sacking manager Neil Cox and began 2022 with an encouraging victory at Oldham thanks to two goals from Ryan Loft. He was sold to Bristol Rovers shortly afterwards and it was all downhill after that. When relegation was confirmed by a 3-0 defeat against Leyton Orient with four fixtures still to play, Scunthorpe had one win to show from a run of 20 games. That run reached 24 by the final day when a team including seven teenagers lost 7-0 to promoted Bristol Rovers. By then the club were looking for new owners after the resignation of chairman Peter Swann.

Beestin A 24 (14)	Jarvis A................. 11 (8)	Perry A 12 (2)
Bilson T...................... 1	Jessop H ....- (2)	Pugh T 18 (6)
Bunn H 10 (10)	Dunnwald K ....- (1)	Pyke R 6 (4)
Burns S 11 (4)	Kenyon A 6 (1)	Rowe J 34 (4)
Cribb H 7 (1)	Lewis H 6 (5)	Scrimshaw J 13 (4)
Davis H 14	Lobley O................. 1	Shrimpton F 3 (1)
Delaney R 18	Loft R 12 (3)	Sinclair T 10 (4)
Feeney L 17 (2)	Matheson L 11 (2)	Taft G 33 (1)
Foster O.................. 2	Millen R 19 (1)	Thompson L 13 (1)
Gallimore D 7 (4)	Moore-Billam J........ 3 (3)	Watson R 40 (1)
Grant A 12 (1)	Nuttall J............. 13 (3)	Wilson C 4 (4)
Green D 11 (5)	O'Hara K 3	Wood H 7 (3)
Hackney H 20 (8)	O'Malley M 20 (5)	Young E 5 (1)
Hallam J ....- (8)	O'Neill T 1 (3)	
Hippolyte M 19 (3)	Onariase E 29 (1)	

League goals (29): Hippolyte 4, Loft 4, Scrimshaw 3, Burns 2, Davis 2, Jarvis 2, Nuttall 2, Onariase 2, Beestin 1, Bunn 1, Rowe 1, Taft 1, Wilson 1, Opponents 3
FA Cup goals: None. **League Cup goals**: None. **League Trophy goals** (3): Loft 2, Scrimshaw 1
Average home league attendance: 2,781
Player of Year: Rory Watson

STEVENAGE

Stevenage struck lucky with their third manager of a testing season in which the threat of relegation was becoming more acute. Eight games remained when Steve Evans took over a side struggling to put an end to a run of nine without a win. It was his seventh club appointment, the latest at Gillingham, and there was no immediate fix. Defeats by promotion-chasing Exeter and fellow-strugglers Oldham, in a potential 'six-pointer', in his first two matches left his new club second from bottom, three points adrift. But wins over Colchester and Rochdale, then a point at relegated Scunthorpe, transformed their fortunes. And two goals by Luke Norris, one a penalty, in the penultimate home fixture accounted for Tranmere 2-0 to complete the recovery. Stevenage also finished on a high – 4-2 winners against Salford – before Evans began a complete overhaul of the squad he inherited. Previously, Alex Revell was sacked after one league win in 14 and Paul Tisdale lost his job after just three-and-a-half months.

Anang J 13	Bastien S...........................1	Clements B 4
Andrade B.............. 13 (14)	Bostwick M 14	Cochrane O 1
Barry B 6 (6)	Carter C 4 (16)	Coker B 36

Cuthbert S 39	Osborne E.............. 10 (4)	Taylor J........................42
Daly J.................... 2 (13)	Prosser L 23 (4)	Tinubu S................... - (1)
Lines C 22 (9)	Pym C 23	Upson E 10 (5)
List E 34 (3)	Read A 9 (10)	VanCouten T............ 36 (2)
Marshall R 2 (3)	Reeves J 27	Walker L.................... - (1)
Melbourne M 4 (3)	Reid J 26 (12)	Westbrooke Z 11 (1)
Norris L 35 (8)	Smith A..........................9	Wildin L................ 38 (2)
O'Neill L 10 (2)	Smith J 2 (1)	

League goals (45): Norris 13, List 9, Reid 6, Cuthbert 3, Lines 3, Taylor 3, Reeves 2, Bostwick 1, Coker 1, Prosser 1, Read 1, Opponents 2
FA Cup goals (4): Barry 1, List 1, Norris 1, Reid 1. **League Cup goals** (4): List 2, Coker 1, Reid 1.
League Trophy goals (6): Daly 1, List 1, Marshall 1, Norris 1, Reid 1, Opponents 1
Average home league attendance: 2,850
Player of Year: Luke Norris

SUTTON UNITED

What a first season in the Football League for Sutton, who were just a point away from the play-offs and came within seconds of lifting the League Trophy. Manager Matt Gray said he was so proud of the players who exceeded all expectations by going so close. After a testing start, two points from the opening four fixtures, six wins in the next seven had them up and running, including a 4-3 success against Port Vale after trailing 2-0 and 3-2. They were third at the midway point on the back of a ten-match unbeaten run, wobbled after reaching Wembley on penalties against Wigan, then made up ground to go into the final round of fixtures breathing down the necks of the teams above them. Sutton were 2-0 winners at Harrogate, but Swindon, Port Vale and Mansfield all did enough to hold their ground and go forward to the knockout phase. The League Trophy beckoned when goals by Donovan Wilson and captain Craig Eastmond established a 2-1 lead going into stoppage-time. Rotherham's equaliser came in the 95th minute and the League One runners-up went on to prevail 4-2 in extra-time.

Ajiboye D 42 (1)	Eastmond C 31	Randall W...........18 (10)
Barden J 18 (3)	Goodliffe B 43	Rowe C............... 12 (5)
Beautyman H 12 (7)	John L....................36	Sho-Silva T 4 (3)
Bennett R 22 (16)	Korboa R 3 (11)	Smith A 28 (5)
Boldewijn E 27 (12)	Kouassi K ....- (4)	Wilson D 23 (15)
Bouzanis D 44	Lovatt A 3	Wyatt B 13 (3)
Bugiel O 27 (12)	Milsom R 37 (1)	Kizzi J.............. 31 (1)
Davis K 12 (8)	Nelson S 2	
Dundas C ....- (4)	Olaofe I 18 (9)	

League goals (69): Ajiboye 8, Olaofe 8, Smith 8, Milsom 7, Bennett 6, Kizzi 6, Bugiel 4, Randall 4, Wilson 4, Goodliffe 3, Beautyman 2, Boldewijn 2, Korboa 2, Davis 1, Eastmond 1, John 1, Rowe 1, Opponents 1
FA Cup goals (2): Randall 2. **League Cup goals** (2): Rowe 1, Wilson 1. **League Trophy goals** (12): Wilson 3, Eastmond 2, John 1, Korboa 1, Olaofe 1, Randall 1, Sho-Silva 1, Smith 1, Opponents 1
Average home league attendance: 3,088
Player of Year: Ben Goodliffe

SWINDON TOWN

Swindon came within penalties of a place at Wembley after a transformation in fortunes described by manager Ben Garner as a 'miracle.' Two goals by leading scorer Harry McKirdy established a 2-1 lead in the first leg of their play-of semi-final against Port Vale, who brough the aggregate score level in the return match. Josh Davison missed a chance to win it in the shoot-out, then Ellis Iandolo, their longest-serving player, fired over to give Vale a 6-5 victory. Swindon exceeded all expectations by finishing the regular season in sixth place. There were fears for the future of the club after relegation in 2021, a transfer embargo and only a handful of senior players signed ahead of pre-season friendlies. Instead, they won more matches – 13 – away from home than any team in the division, remaining in touch with the leading group before a strong finish brought its reward. Swindon bridged a four-point deficit with five victories and 14 goals scored in in the final six fixtures. McKirdy's tally of 19 included four in the 5-2 win over Northampton. Garner took over at Charlton in the summer and was replaced by assistant manager Scott Lindsey.

Aguiar R 8 (8)	Gladwin B 23 (13)	Parsons H 1 (14)
Barry L 12 (2)	Grant A.............................5	Payne J................. 31 (4)
Baudry M................. 13 (2)	Hayden K................. 16 (2)	Reed L 39
Conroy D........................35	Hunt R 35 (2)	Simpson T 24 (1)
Cooper B........................8	Iandolo E 39 (5)	Tomlinson J.................10
Crichlow-Noble R...... 15 (3)	Lyden J.................. 5 (5)	Ward L.........................9
Davison J........................21	McKirdy H 32 (3)	Williams 24 (16)
East R 5 (11)	Mitchell-Lawson J.... 2 (22)	Wollacott J....................37
Egbo M......................6(3)	O'Brien J 16 (3)	
Gilbert A.................. 5 (3)	Odimayo A 30 (5)	

Play-offs – appearances: Barry 2, Baudry 2, Conroy 2, Davison 2, Egbo 2, Iandolo 2, McKirdy 2, Payne 2, Reed 2, Ward 2, Williams 2, Gladwin – (2), O'Brien – (2), Odimayo – (1)
League goals (77): McKirdy 19, Payne 13, Davison 9, Simpson 9, Barry 6, Gladwin 5, Williams 5, Aguiar 2, Reed 2, Baudry 1, Conroy 1, Crichlow-Noble 1, Iandolo 1, Tomlinson 1, Opponents 2. **Play-offs – goals** (2): McKirdy 2
FA Cup goals (6): Reed 2, Simpson 2, Hayden 1, McKirdy 1. **League Cup goals:** None. **League Trophy goals** (7): Crichlow-Noble 1, Dabre M 1, Lyden 1, McKirdy 1, Mitchell-Lawson 1, Opponents 2
Average home league attendance: 9,603
Player of Year: Harry McKirdy

TRANMERE ROVERS

No team had a better home record than Tranmere. They recorded 16 victories which would secured a play-off place had there been even a minimal improvement in form away from Prenton Park. Instead, they missed out by two points at the end of Micky Mellon's first season back at the club after a spell in the Scottish Premiership with Dundee United. His side were up to fourth, a single point shy of an automatic promotion place, before five matches without a win left them playing catch-up. Particularly costly was a 2-2 draw at home to Carlisle on a bad-tempered afternoon when they had Calum MacDonald and Kieron Morris both sent off and conceded an equaliser in the seventh minute of stoppage-time. A week later they were held again, this time by Bristol Rovers, and despite beating runners-up Exeter 2-0, the damage had been done. There was still a slim chance in the final programme of fixtures, but it depended on results elsewhere going in their favour and a Kane Hemmings winner at Leyton Orient, on its own, was not enough.

Burton J 1	Glatzel P 10 (6)	McPake J 10 (4)
Clarke P....................... 46	Hawkes J 28 (7)	Merrie C.................7 (8)
Dacres-Cogley J......... 45	Hemmings K 22	Morris K 34 (3)
Davies T 36	Jolley C................. 10 (2)	Murphy J....................17
Dieseruvwe E 4 (2)	Knight-Percival N 14 (2)	Nevitt E 31 (9)
Doohan R 29 (1)	MacDonald C............. 34	O'Connor L............ 26 (5)
Duffy M 1 (2)	Maguire – (1)	Spearing J 27 (5)
Feeney L............... 10 (9)	Maynard N 3 (7)	Warrington L 17
Foley S............... 20 (19)	McManaman C......18 (11)	Watson R............. 6 (10)

League goals (53): Hemmings 8, Nevitt 7, Hawkes 6, Morris 5, Clarke 4, Glatzel 4, Jolley 4, Spearing 3, McManaman 2, Dacres-Cogley 1, Davies 1, Foley 1, MacDonald 1, Maynard 1, McPake 1, Warrington 1, Watson 1, Opponents 2
FA Cup goals (1): McManaman 1. **League Cup goals** (2): Foley 1, Nevitt 1. **League Trophy goals** (10): Maynard 4, Foley 2, Glatzel 2, Walker S 1, Watson 1
Average home league attendance: 6,872
Player of Year: Elliott Nevitt

WALSALL

Walsall recovered from an uncertain start – one point from four matches – to approach the halfway point of the season sitting comfortably in mid-table. Seven successive defeats then sent them sliding and Matt Taylor, in charge for nine months, was dismissed with his team fourth from bottom. Mike Flynn, who stepped down at Newport earlier in the campaign after four years at the club, returned to management with a victory over runaway leaders Forest Green, courtesy of George Miller's goal. A 5-0 drubbing at Swindon followed, then a 3-1 win over Hartlepool with Miller on the mark twice. Walsall defeated two more teams aiming for promotion, Sutton and Port Vale, to help towards a 16th place finish, three higher than 2021. But they were second best in the return fixture against Swindon, who scored three times in the first half on the final day to reach the play-offs.

Daniels D 18	Miller G 36 (5)	Sadler M .... - (1)
Devine R 8	Mills Z................. 5 (4)	Shade T 26 (13)
Earing J 42 (3)	Monthe E............. 36 (1)	Shaw J .... - (2)
Khan O................. 5 (2)	Osadebe E 35 (8)	Taylor A 8 (3)
Kiernan B 28 (9)	Perry S 7 (13)	Tomlin L 1 (4)
Kinsella L........... 27 (5)	Phillips K 15 (11)	Ward S 26 (1)
Labadie J 32 (3)	Rodney D............ 2 (12)	White H 41 (1)
Leak T 5 (1)	Rose J................. 3	Wilkinson C 28 (5)
Menayesse R........ 29 (4)	Rushworth C 43	Willock S............... - (2)

League goals (47): Miller 12, Wilkinson 10, Kiernan 5, Earing 4, Phillips 4, Osadebe 3, Khan 2, Shade 2, Daniels 1, Menayesse 1, Perry 1, Taylor 1, Opponents 1
FA Cup goals (2): Kiernan 1, Osadebe 1. **League Cup goals**: None. **League Trophy goals** (2): Osadebe 1, Phillips 1
Average home league attendance: 5,067
Player of Year: Liam Kinsella

LEAGUE CLUB MANAGERS 2022–23

Figure in brackets = number of managerial changes at club since the War. †Second spell at club

PREMIER LEAGUE

Arsenal (13)	Mikel Arteta	December 2019
Aston Villa (28)	Steven Gerrard	November 2021
Bournemouth (27)	Scott Parker	June 2021
Brentford (34)	Thomas Frank	October 2018
Brighton (34)	Graham Potter	May 2019
Chelsea (32)	Thomas Tuchel	January 2021
Crystal Palace (44)	Patrick Vieira	July 2021
Everton (23)	Frank Lampard	January 2022
Fulham (35)	Marco Silva	July 2021
Leeds (34)	Jesse Marsch	February 2022
Leicester (31)	Brendan Rodgers	February 2019
Liverpool (14)	Jurgen Klopp	October 2015
Manchester City (30)	Pep Guardiola	May 2016

Manchester Utd (14)	Erik ten Hag	April 2022
Newcastle (29)	Eddie Howe	November 2021
Nottm Forest (29)	Steve Cooper	September 2021
Southampton (29)	Ralph Hasenhuttl	December 2018
Tottenham (26)	Antonio Conte	November 2021
West Ham (17)	David Moyes †	December 2019
Wolves (28)	Bruno Lage	June 2021

CHAMPIONSHIP

Birmingham (33)	John Eustace	July 2022
Blackburn (32)	Jon Dahl Tomasson	June 2022
Blackpool (35)	Michael Appleton	June 2022
Bristol City (28)	Nigel Pearson	February 2021
Burnley (25)	Vincent Kompany	June 2022
Cardiff (34)	Steve Morison	November 2021
Coventry (35)	Mark Robins	March 2017
Huddersfield (31)		
Hull (32)	Shota Arveladze	January 2022
Luton (4)	Nathan Jones †	May 2020
Middlesbrough (25)	Chris Wilder	November 2021
Millwall (32)	Gary Rowett	October 2019
Norwich (30)	Dean Smith	November 2021
Preston (31)	Ryan Lowe	December 2021
QPR (37)	Michael Beale	June 2022
Reading (27)	Paul Ince	May 2022
Rotherham (28)	Paul Warne	April 2017
Sheffield Utd (40)	Paul Heckingbottom	November 2021
Stoke (27)	Michael O'Neill	November 2019
Sunderland (35)	Alex Neil	February 2022
Swansea (39)	Russell Martin	July 2021
Watford (41)	Rob Edwards	May 2022
WBA (38)	Steve Bruce	February 2022
Wigan (26)	Leam Richardson	April 2021

Number of changes since elected to Football League: Wigan 1978. Since returning: Luton 2014

LEAGUE ONE

Accrington (4)	John Coleman	September 2014
Barnsley (32)	Michael Duff	June 2022
Bolton (25)	Ian Evatt	July 2020
Bristol Rov (4)	Joey Barton	February 2021
Burton (5)	Jimmy Floyd Hasselbaink †	January 2021
Cambridge (4)	Mark Bonner	March 2020
Charlton (28)	Ben Garner	June 2022
Cheltenham (2)	Wade Elliott	June 2022
Derby (30)	Liam Rosenior (interim)	June 2022
Exeter (1)	Matt Taylor	June 2018
Fleetwood (8)	Scott Brown	May 2022
Forest Green (2)	Ian Burchnall	May 2022
Ipswich (17)	Kieran McKenna	December 2021
Lincoln (2)	Mark Kennedy	May 2022
MK Dons (20)	Liam Manning	August 2021
Morecambe (4)	Derek Adams †	February 2022
Oxford (4)	Karl Robinson	March 2018
Peterborough (33)	Grant McCann †	February 2022
Plymouth (36)	Steven Schumacher	December 2021
Portsmouth (35)	Danny Cowley	March 2021
Port Vale (29)	Darrell Clarke	February 2021
Sheffield Wed (34)	Darren Moore	March 2021

Shrewsbury (8)	Steve Cotterill	November 2020
Wycombe (10)	Gareth Ainsworth	November 2012

Number of changes since elected to Football League: Peterborough 1960, Wycombe 1993, Morecambe 2007, Burton 2009, Fleetwood 2012., Forest Green 2017. Since returning: Shrewsbury 2004, Exeter 2008, Accrington 2006, Oxford 2010, Cambridge 2014, Bristol Rov 2015, Cheltenham 2016, Lincoln 2017

LEAGUE TWO

AFC Wimbledon (5)	Johnnie Jackson	May 2022
Barrow (4)	Pete Wild	May 2022
Bradford (42)	Mark Hughes	February 2022
Carlisle (10)	Paul Simpson †	February 2022
Colchester (32)	Wayne Brown	May 2022
Crawley (10)	Kevin Betsy	June 2022
Crewe (23)	Alex Morris	April 2022
Doncaster (9)	Gary McSheffrey	December 2021
Gillingham (28)	Neil Harris	January 2022
Grimsby (-)	Paul Hurst †	December 2020
Hartlepool (1)	Paul Hartley	June 2022
Harrogate (-)	Simon Weaver	May 2009
Leyton Orient (4)	Richie Wellens	March 2022
Mansfield (6)	Nigel Clough	November 2020
Newport (6)	James Rowberry	October 2021
Northampton (37)	Jon Brady	May 2021
Rochdale (34)	Robbie Stockdale	July 2021
Salford (3)	Neil Wood	May 2022
Stockport (-)	Dave Challinor	November 2021
Sutton (-)	Matt Gray	May 2019
Swindon (37)	Scott Lindsey	June 2022
Stevenage (9)	Steve Evans	March 2022
Tranmere (3)	Micky Mellon †	May 2021
Walsall (40)	Mike Flynn	February 2022

†Second spell as manager. Number of changes since elected to Football League: Stevenage 2010, Crawley 2011, Salford 2019, Harrogate 2020, Sutton 2021. Since returning: Colchester 1992, Carlisle 2005, Mansfield 2013, Newport 2013, Tranmere 2018, Leyton Orient 2019, Barrow 2020, Hartlepool 2021, Grimsby 2022, Stockport 2022

MANAGERIAL CHANGES 2021–22

PREMIER LEAGUE

Aston Villa:	Out – Dean Smith (Nov 2021); In – Steven Gerrard
Burnley:	Out – Sean Dyche (Apr 2022); In – Vincent Kompany
Everton:	Out – Rafael Benitez (Jan 2022); In – Frank Lampard
Leeds:	Out – Marcelo Bielsa (Feb 2022); In – Jesse Marsch
Manchester Utd:	Out – Ole Gunnar Solskjaer (Nov 2021); In – Ralf Rangnick (Out May 2022); In – Erik ten Hag
Newcastle:	Out – Steve Bruce (Oct 2021); In – Eddie Howe
Norwich:	Out – Daniel Farke (Nov 2021); In – Dean Smith
Tottenham:	Out – Nuno Espirito Santo (Oct 2021); In – Antonio Conte
Watford:	Out – Xisco Munoz (Oct 2021); In -Claudio Ranieri (Out Jan 2022); In – Roy Hodgson (Out May 2022); In – Rob Edwards

CHAMPIONSHIP

Barnsley:	Out – Markus Schlupp (Nov 2021); In – Poya Asbaghi (Out May 2022); In – Michael Duff

Birmingham:	Out – Lee Bowyer (Jul 2022); In – John Eustace
Blackburn:	Out – Tony Mowbray (May 2022); In – Jon Dahl Tomason
Blackpool:	Out – Neil Critchley (Jun 2022); In – Michael Appleton
Cardiff:	Out – Mick McCarthy (Oct 2021); In – Steve Morison
Derby	Out – Wayne Rooney June 2022; In – Liam Rosenior (interim)
Huddersfield:	Out – Carlos Corberan (Jul 2022)
Hull	Out – Grant McCann (Jan 2022); In – Shota Arveladze
Middlesbrough:	Out – Neil Warnock (Nov 2021); In – Chris Wilder
Nottm Forest:	Out – Chris Hughton (Sep 2021); In – Steve Cooper
Peterborough:	Out – Darren Ferguson (Feb 2022); In – Grant McCann
Preston:	Out – Frankie McAvoy (Dec 2021); In - Ryan Lowe
QPR:	Out – Mark Warburton (May 2022); In – Michael Beale
Reading	Out – Veljko Paunovic (Feb 2022); In – Paul Ince
Sheffield Utd:	Out – Slavisa Jokanovic (Nov 2021); In – Paul Heckingbottom
Swansea:	Out – Steve Cooper (Jul 2021); In – Russell Martin
WBA:	Out – Valerien Ismael (Feb 2022); In – Steve Bruce

LEAGUE ONE

AFC Wimbledon:	Out – Mark Robinson (Mar 2022); In – Johnnie Jackson
Charlton:	Out – Nigel Adkins (Oct 2021); In – Johnnie Jackson (Out May 2022); In – Ben Garner
Cheltenham:	Out – Michael Duff (Jun 2022); In – Wade Elliott
Crewe:	Out – David Artell (Apr 2022); In – Alex Morris
Doncaster:	Out – Richie Wellens (Dec 2021); In – Gary McSheffrey
Fleetwood:	Out – Simon Grayson (Nov 2021); In – Stephen Crainey (Out May 2022); In – Scott Brown
Gillingham:	Out – Steve Evans (Jan 2022); In – Neil Harris
Ipswich:	Out – Paul Cook (Dec 2021); In – Kieran McKenna
MK Dons:	Out – Russell Martin (Aug 2021); In – Liam Manning
Morecambe:	Out – Stephen Robinson (Feb 2022); In – Derek Adams
Plymouth:	Out – Ryan Lowe (Dec 2021); In – Steven Schumacher
Sunderland:	Out – Lee Johnson (Jan 2022); In – Alex Neil

LEAGUE TWO

Barrow:	Out – Mark Cooper (Mar 2022); In – Pete Wild
Bradford:	Out – Derek Adams (Feb 2022); In – Mark Hughes
Carlisle:	Out – Chris Beech (Oct 2021); In – Keith Millen (Out Feb 2022); In – Paul Simpson
Colchester:	Out – Hayden Mullins (Jan 2022); In – Wayne Brown
Crawley:	Out – John Yems (May 2022); In – Kevin Betsy
Forest Green:	Out – Rob Edwards (May 2022); In – Ian Burchnall
Hartlepool:	Out – Dave Challinor (Nov 2021); In – Graeme Lee (Out May 2022); In – Paul Hartley
Leyton Orient:	Out – Kenny Jackett (Feb 2022); In – Richie Wellens
Newport:	Out – Mike Flynn (Oct 2021); In – James Rowberry
Oldham:	Out – Keith Curle (Nov 2021); In – John Sheridan
Salford:	Out – Gary Bowyer (May 2022); In – Neil Wood
Scunthorpe:	Out – Neil Cox (Nov 2021); In – Keith Hill
Stevenage:	Out – Alex Revell (Nov 2021); In – Paul Tisdale (Out Mar 2022); In – Steve Evans
Swindon:	Out – Ben Garner (Jun 2022); In – Scott Lindsey
Walsall:	Out – Matt Taylor (Feb 2022); In – Mike Flynn

EMIRATES FA CUP 2021–22

FIRST ROUND

Stockport and St Albans take pride of place in a programme which sees most non-league clubs bow out to higher-grade opposition. Stockport, trailing Bolton 3-1 in a replay, level through Scott Quigley and Ashley Palmer. Quigley adds a second in extra-time, then Ollie Crankshaw seals victory, losing his shirt in the celebrations and having to wear a replacement for the final seconds. St Albans overcome League Two leaders Forest Green with goals by Mitchell Weiss, Zane Banton and the clincher from Shaun Jeffers. Bristol Rovers, 3-1 down to Oxford in extra-time, score three times in eight minutes through Sion Spence (2) and Aaron Collins to reach round two. Mansfield repeat the previous season's 1-0 victory at Sunderland, with Ryan Oates on the mark, while James Wilson's hat-trick sparks a handsome success for Port Vale against Accrington. For goals, the tie of the round is at Halifax, whose manager Pete Wild watches his side 'go from the sublime to the ridiculous' when defeating National League rivals Maidenhead 7-4. The most heated involves Exeter, who are ordered by the FA to play a third match against Bradford after fielding an illegal sixth substitute on the way to a 3-0 victory in the teams' first replay. Bradford, unhappy with that decision, finally go out 2-1.

AFC Wimbledon 1 Guiseley 0	Portsmouth 1 Harrow 0
Banbury 0 Barrow 4	Rochdale 1 Notts Co 1
Bolton 2 Stockport 2	Rotherham 3 Bromley 0
Boreham Wood 2 Eastleigh 0	Scunthorpe 0 Doncaster 1
Bradford 1 Exeter 1	Sheffield Wed 0 Plymouth 0
Carlisle 2 Horsham 0	St Albans 3 Forest Green 2
Charlton 4 Havant 0	Stratford 1 Shrewsbury 5
Chesterfield 3 Southend 1	Sudbury 0 Colchester 4
Crawley 0 Tranmere 1	Sunderland 0 Mansfield 1
Crewe 0 Swindon 3	Wigan 0 Solihull 1
Dagenham & Redbridge 0 Salford 1	Yate 0 Yeovil 5
FC Halifax 7 Maidenhead 4	York 0 Buxton 1
Fleetwood 1 Burton 2	**Replays**
Gateshead 2 Altrincham 2	Altrincham 2 Gateshead 3
Gillingham 1 Cheltenham 1	Bristol Rov 4 Oxford 3 (aet)
Harrogate 2 Wrexham 1	Cambridge 3 Northampton 1
Hartlepool 2 Wycombe 2	Cheltenham 1 Gillingham 0
Hayes 0 Sutton 1	*Exeter 3 Bradford 0 (aet)
Ipswich 1 Oldham 1	Exeter 2 Bradford 1
Kidderminster 1 Grimsby 0	Notts Co 1 Rochdale 0
King's Lynn 0 Walsall 1	Oldham 1 Ipswich 2
Leyton Orient 1 Ebbsfleet 0	Plymouth 0 Sheffield Wed 0
Lincoln 1 Bowers & Pitsea 0	Solihull 1 Wigan 2 (aet)
MK Dons 2 Stevenage 2	Stevenage 2 MK Dons 1 (aet)
Morecambe 1 Newport 0	Stockport 5 Bolton 3 (aet)
Northampton 2 Cambridge 2	Wycombe 0 Hartlepool 1
Oxford 2 Bristol Rov 2	*Exeter ordered to replay tie
Port Vale 5 Accrington 1	– rule infringement

SECOND ROUND

Managers Graeme Lee and Paul Cook experience contrasting fortunes. Hartlepool, who have Lee in charge for the first time after succeeding Dave Challinor, win at Lincoln with Lewis Fiorini's own goal. Cook is sacked after Ipswich's goalless draw at home to Barrow, who go through 2-0 in the replay. Former Chelsea youngster Charlie Wakefield sends Yeovil into round three with the only goal against Stevenage. They are joined by National League rivals Chesterfield, who put out Salford, thanks to goals from Liam Mandeville and Jim Kellermann, and are rewarded with a plum tie against Chelsea at Stamford Bridge.

AFC Wimbledon 4 Cheltenham 3
Boreham Wood 4 St Albans 0
Bristol Rov 2 Sutton 1
Burton 1 Port Vale 2
Buxton 0 Morecambe 1
Cambridge 2 Exeter 1
Carlisle 1 Shrewsbury 2
Colchester 1 Wigan 2
Doncaster 2 Mansfield 3
Gateshead 0 Charlton 2
Ipswich 0 Barrow 0

Kidderminster 2 FC Halifax 0
Leyton Orient 4 Tranmere 0
Lincoln 0 Hartlepool 1
Portsmouth 1 Harrogate 2
Rochdale 1 Plymouth 2
Rotherham 1 Stockport 0
Salford 0 Chesterfield 2
Walsall 1 Swindon 2
Yeovil 1 Stevenage 0
Replay
Barrow 2 Ipswich 0

THIRD ROUND

Cambridge join the ranks of genuine giant-killers by defeating full-strength Newcastle at a sell-out St James' Park. Joe Ironside scores the only goal and Dimitar Mitov earns man-of-the-match honours with some fine saves. Kidderminster, the lowest-ranked club left in the competition are rewarded with a home tie against West Ham after coming from behind to overcome Reading with goals from Sam Austin and Amari Morgan-Smith. The National League North side hold on through 13 minutes of stoppage-time, caused by a dislocated knee sustained by Reading's Felipe Araruna and flares thrown from the crowd. Boreham Wood also overcome EFL opponents, goals by Tyrone Marsh and substitute Adrian Clifton accounting for AFC Wimbledon. Three more underdogs enjoy special moments before bowing out. Morecambe lead through Anthony O'Connor at Tottenham and hold on until the final quarter-of-an-hour. Daniel Udoh puts Shrewsbury ahead at Anfield before Liverpool assume control. And Akwasi Asante scores a consolation in front of 6,000 Chesterfield fans at Stamford Bridge. Hard-luck story belongs to Mansfield, who retrieve a 2-0 deficit against Middlesbrough, but lose to Elliott Hewitt's 95th minute own goal. Barrow, despite playing for more than an hour with ten men after Tom Beadling's dismissal, also go close at Barnsley who need an extra-time Carlton Morris goal to settle a nine-goal thriller. Emiliano Marcondes, for Bournemouth at Yeovil, and Brentford's Bryan Mbeumo against Port Vale, score hat-tricks. History is made at St Andrew's, where Rebecca Welch makes her mark as the first female referee for a third-round tie by sending off Birmingham's George Friend for a second bookable offence.

Barnsley 5 Barrow 4 (aet)
Birmingham 0 Plymouth 1 (aet)
Boreham Wood 2 AFC Wimbledon 0
Bristol City 0 Fulham 1 (aet)
Burnley 1 Huddersfield 2
Cardiff 2 Preston 1 (aet)
Charlton 0 Norwich 1
Chelsea 5 Chesterfield 1
Coventry 1 Derby 0
Hartlepool 2 Blackpool 1
Hull 2 Everton 3 (aet)
Kidderminster 2 Reading 1
Leicester 4 Watford 1
Liverpool 4 Shrewsbury 1
Luton 4 Harrogate 0
Manchester Utd 1 Aston Villa 0
Mansfield 2 Middlesbrough 3

Millwall 1 Crystal Palace 2
Newcastle 0 Cambridge 1
Nottm Forest 1 Arsenal 0
Peterborough 2 Bristol Rov 1
Port Vale 1 Brentford 4
QPR 1 Rotherham 1
(aet, QPR won 8-7 on pens)
Stoke 2 Leyton Orient 0
Swansea 2 Southampton 3 (aet)
Swindon 1 Manchester City 4
Tottenham 3 Morecambe 1
WBA 1 Brighton 2 (aet)
West Ham 2 Leeds 0
Wigan 3 Blackburn 1
Wolves 3 Sheffield Utd 0
Yeovil 1 Bournemouth 3

FOURTH ROUND

So near, yet so far. Kidderminster are on the brink of one of the biggest upsets in FA Cup history when leading West Ham through Alex Penny. They hold on to the full-back's 19th minute goal until the second minute of stoppage-time when England midfielder Declan Rice equalises. With a penalty shoot-out beckoning, the sixth-tier side are denied again when Jarrod Bowen adds a second with virtually the last kick of extra-time. Boreham Wood keep the non-league flag flying, reaching the last 16 for the first time by winning at Bournemouth with a goal from 37-year-old Mark Ricketts. Third-round heroes Cambridge bow out, against Luton. So do holders Leicester as Nottingham Forest follow their victory over Arsenal with another impressive performance. Plymouth also rise to the occasion, threatening to take Chelsea to penalties at Stamford Bridge until Ryan Hardie has an extra-time spot-kick saved. Everton mark Frank Lampard's first match as manager with victory over Brentford. Manchester United are beaten on penalties by Middlesbrough at Old Trafford.

Bournemouth 0 Boreham Wood 1	Manchester Utd 1 Middlesbrough 1
Cambridge 0 Luton 3	(aet, Middlesbrough won 8-7 on pens)
Chelsea 2 Plymouth 1	Nottm Forest 4 Leicester 1
Crystal Palace 2 Hartlepool 0	Peterborough 2 QPR 0
Everton 4 Brentford 1	Southampton 2 Coventry 1
Huddersfield 1 Barnsley 0	Stoke 2 Wigan 0
Kidderminster 1 West Ham 2 (aet)	Tottenham 3 Brighton 1
Liverpool 3 Cardiff 1	Wolves 0 Norwich 1
Manchester City 4 Fulham 1	

FIFTH ROUND

Middlesbrough continue to prosper under Chris Wilder. In front of a sell-out Riverside crowd, 19-year-old substitute Josh Coburn scores an extra-time winner to condemn Tottenham to another season without a trophy. On the night Roman Abramovich put the club up for sale, Chelsea twice come from behind to defeat Luton with a goal from Romelu Lukaku. Everton are also made to work to end the run of Boreham Wood, who share a goalless first half before bowing to a brace by Salomon Rondon.

Crystal Palace 2 Stoke 1	Middlesbrough 1 Tottenham 0 (aet)
Everton 2 Boreham Wood 0	Nottm Forest 2 Huddersfield 1
Liverpool 2 Norwich 1	Peterborough 0 Manchester City 2
Luton 2 **Chelsea** 3	Southampton 3 West Ham 1

SIXTH ROUND

Marc Guehi celebrates his England call-up by putting Crystal Palace on the way to an emphatic win over Frank Lampard's struggling side with a header from Michael Olise's corner. Manchester City also score four at St Mary's – the pick of bunch a sweet strike from Phil Foden. Chelsea, showing no signs being affected by turbulent issues off the field, end Middlesbrough's eye-catching run. Nottingham Forest prove a handful for Liverpool before Diogo Jota's decisive intervention 12 minutes from the end of normal time.

Middlesbrough 0 **Chelsea** 2	Nottm Forest 0 **Liverpool** 1
Crystal Palace 4 Everton 0	Southampton 1 Manchester City 4

SEMI-FINALS (both at Wembley)

Liverpool overwhelm Manchester City with goals from Ibrahima Konate and Sadio Mane in the opening 17 minutes and a third from Mane on the stroke of half-time. Jack Grealish pulls one back two minutes after the break, but his side's improvement is not enough to alter the outcome, with Bernardo Silva's effort coming in stoppage-time. Crystal Palace hold their own for more than an hour before Ruben Loftus-Cheek and Mason Mount make the breakthrough to send Chelsea back to Wembley.

Chelsea 2 Crystal Palace 0   **Liverpool** 3 Manchester City 2

FINAL

They could not be separated in two Premier League meetings. The League Cup Final was goalless after extra-time. So was this one. The two clubs even finished with two trophies each. Such was the intensity of the rivalry between Liverpool and Chelsea over the course of the season. In boxing terms, Jurgen Klopp's side earned a unanimous points verdict, their two Wembley successes taking pride of place over Chelsea's victories in the Club World Cup and the less prestigious UEFA Super Cup. But Klopp was no less complimentary about Thomas Tuchel's team. 'We are mentality monsters, but so were the team who play in blue,' he said. 'The margins are so small.' Liverpool had the better of things here, despite losing Mohamed Salah with a groin injury after 35 minutes. The outstanding Luis Diaz and Andrew Robertson struck the woodwork. For Chelsea, Marcos Alonso hit a post and was also denied by Alisson. Liverpool's goalkeeper made the shoot-out's crucial save, from Mason Mount, giving Greece full-back Kostas Tsimikas the chance to win it, which he confidently accepted. For Mount, it was a sixth successive Wembley defeat for club and country. For his England team-mate Trent Alexander-Arnold, at the age of 23, there was the distinction of having lifted six major trophies available to English clubs.

CHELSEA 0 LIVERPOOL 0 – aet, Liverpool won 6-5 on pens
Wembley (84,897); May 14, 2022
Chelsea (3-4-2-1): Mendy, Chalobah (Azpilicueta, capt, 105), Thiago Silva, Rudiger, James, Jorginho, Kovacic (Kante 66), Marcos Alonso, Mount, Pulisic (Loftus-Cheek 105, Barkley 120), Lukaku (Ziyech 85). **Subs not used:** Arrizabalaga, Werner, Saul. **Booked:** James. **Manager:** Thomas Tuchel
Liverpool (4-3-3): Alisson, Alexander-Arnold, Konate, Van Dijk (Matip 90), Robertson (Tsimikas 111), Keita (Milner 74), Henderson (capt), Thiago Alcantara, Salah (Diogo Jota 33), Mane, Diaz (Firmino 98). **Subs not used:** Kelleher, Gomez, Jones, Origi. **Manager:** Jurgen Klopp
Referee: Craig Pawson (South Yorks)
Penalty shoot-out: Chelsea scored – Marcos Alonso, James, Barkley, Jorginho, Ziyech; missed – Azpilicueta, saved – Mount. Liverpool scored – Milner, Thiago Alcantara, Firmino, Alexander-Arnold, Diogo Jota, Tsimikas; saved - Mane

HOW THEY REACHED THE FINAL

Chelsea
Round 3: 5-1 home to Chesterfield (Werner, Hudson-Odoi, Lukaku, Christensen, Ziyech pen)
Round 4: 2-1 home to Plymouth (Azpilicueta, Marcos Alonso) - aet
Round 5: 3-2 away to Luton (Saul, Werner, Lukaku)
Quarter-finals: 2-0 away to Middlesbrough (Lukaku, Ziyech)
Semi-finals: 2-0 v Crystal Palace (Loftus-Cheek, Mount)

Liverpool
Round 3: 4-1 home to Shrewsbury (Gordon, Fabinho 44 pen, 90, Firmino 78)
Round 4: 3-1 home to Cardiff (Diogo Jota, Minamino, Elliott)
Round 5: 2-1 home to Norwich (Minamino 2)
Quarter-finals: 1-0 away to Nottingham Forest (Diogo Jota)
Semi-finals: 3-2 v Manchester City (Mane 2, Konate)

Leading scorers: 4 Mahrez (Manchester City), Stockley (Charlton); 3 Bowman (Shrewsbury), Garrick (Plymouth), Kane (Tottenham), Lang (Wigan), Lukaku (Chelsea), Marcondes (Bournemouth), Mbeumo (Brentford), Minamino (Liverpool), Palmer (AFC Wimbledon), Quigley (Stockport), Wilson (Port Vale)

FINAL FACTS AND FIGURES

- Liverpool won the FA Cup for the first time since 2006 when they defeated West Ham 3-1 on penalties after a 3-3 scoreline at the Millennium Stadium in Cardiff. Rafael Benitez was the manager.

- They reached the final in 2012, losing 2-1 to Chelsea. Jordan Henderson was the one survivor of that team.

- Trent Alexander, at the age of 23, won a sixth major trophy – Premier League, FA Cup, League Cup, Champions League, European Super Cup and Club World Cup.

- Jurgen Klopp was the first German manager to lift the FA Cup, at the expense of compatriot Thomas Tuchel.

- Chelsea became the first club in the history of the competition to lose three successive finals, following defeats by Arsenal (2020) and Leicester (2021).

- Mason Mount has now lost all six of his finals at Wembley – three in the FA Cup, one in the League Cup, a Championship play-off with Derby and Euro 2020 with England.

- Thiago Silva, 37, became the oldest outfield player to start an FA Cup Final since Stanley Matthews, 38, with Blackpool in 1953.

FA CUP FINAL SCORES & TEAMS

1872 Wanderers 1 (Betts) Bowen, Alcock, Bonsor, Welch; Betts, Crake, Hooman, Lubbock, Thompson, Vidal, Wollaston. Note: Betts played under the pseudonym 'AH Chequer' on the day of the match **Royal Engineers 0** Capt Merriman; Capt Marindin; Lieut Addison, Lieut Cresswell, Lieut Mitchell, Lieut Renny-Tailyour, Lieut Rich, Lieut George Goodwyn, Lieut Muirhead, Lieut Cotter, Lieut Bogle

1873 Wanderers 2 (Wollaston, Kinnaird) Bowen; Thompson, Welch, Kinnaird, Howell, Wollaston, Sturgis, Rev Stewart, Kenyon-Slaney, Kingsford, Bonsor **Oxford University 0** Kirke-Smith; Leach, Mackarness, Birley, Longman, Chappell-Maddison, Dixon, Paton, Vidal, Sumner, Ottaway. March 29; 3, 000; A Stair

1874 Oxford University 2 (Mackarness, Patton) Neapean; Mackarness, Birley, Green, Vidal, Ottaway, Benson, Patton, Rawson, Chappell-Maddison, Rev Johnson **Royal Engineers 0** Capt Merriman; Major Marindin, Lieut W Addison, Gerald Onslow, Lieut Oliver, Lieut Digby, Lieut Renny-Tailyour, Lieut Rawson, Lieut Blackman Lieut Wood, Lieut von Donop. March 14; 2, 000; A Stair

1875 Royal Engineers 1 (Renny-Tailyour) Capt Merriman; Lieut Sim, Lieut Onslow, Lieut (later Sir) Ruck, Lieut Von Donop, Lieut Wood, Lieut Rawson, Lieut Stafford, Capt Renny-Tailyour, Lieut Mein, Lieut Wingfield-Stratford **Old Etonians 1** (Bonsor) Thompson; Benson, Lubbock, Wilson, Kinnaird, (Sir) Stronge, Patton, Farmer, Bonsor, Ottaway, Kenyon-Slaney. March 13; 2, 000; CW Alcock. aet **Replay – Royal Engineers 2** (Renny-Tailyour, Stafford) Capt Merriman; Lieut Sim, Lieut Onslow, Lieut (later Sir) Ruck, Lieut Von Donop, Lieut Wood, Lieut Rawson, Lieut Stafford, Capt Renny-Tailyour, Lieut Mein, Lieut Wingfield-Stratford **Old Etonians 0** Capt Drummond-Moray; Kinnaird, (Sir) Stronge, Hammond, Lubbock, Patton, Farrer, Bonsor, Lubbock, Wilson, Farmer. March 16; 3, 000; CW Alcock

1876 Wanderers 1 (Edwards) Greig; Stratford, Lindsay, Chappell-Maddison, Birley, Wollaston, C Heron, G Heron, Edwards, Kenrick, Hughes **Old Etonians 1** (Bonsor) Hogg; Rev Welldon, Lyttleton, Thompson, Kinnaird, Meysey, Kenyon-Slaney, Lyttleton, Sturgis, Bonsor, Allene. March 11; 3, 500; WS Rawson aet **Replay – Wanderers 3** (Wollaston, Hughes 2) Greig; Stratford, Lindsay, Chappel-Maddison, Birley, Wollaston, C Heron, G Heron, Edwards, Kenrick, Hughes **Old Etonians 0** Hogg, Lubbock, Lyttleton, Farrer, Kinnaird, (Sir) Stronge, Kenyon-Slaney, Lyttleton, Sturgis, Bonsor, Allene. March 18; 1, 500; WS Rawson

1877 Wanderers 2 (Kenrick, Lindsay) Kinnaird; Birley, Denton, Green, Heron, Hughes, Kenrick, Lindsay,

Stratford, Wace, Wollaston **Oxford University 1** (Kinnaird og) Allington; Bain, Dunnell, Rev Savory, Todd, Waddington, Rev Fernandez, Otter, Parry, Rawson. March 24; 3, 000; SH Wright, aet

1878 Wanderers 3 (Kinnaird, Kenrick 2) (Sir) Kirkpatrick; Stratford, Lindsay, Kinnaird, Green, Wollaston, Heron, Wylie, Wace, Denton, Kenrick **Royal Engineers 1** (Morris) Friend; Cowan, (Sir) Morris, Mayne, Heath, Haynes, Lindsay, Hedley, (Sir) Bond, Barnet, Ruck. March 23; 4, 500; SR Bastard

1879 Old Etonians 1 (Clerke) Hawtrey; Edward, Bury, Kinnaird, Lubbock, Clerke, Pares, Goodhart, Whitfield, Chevalier, Beaufoy **Clapham Rovers 0** Birkett; Ogilvie, Field, Bailey, Prinsep, Rawson, Stanley, Scott, Bevington, Growse, Keith-Falconer. March 29; 5, 000; CW Alcock

1880 Clapham Rovers 1 (Lloyd-Jones) Birkett; Ogilvie, Field, Weston, Bailey, Stanley, Brougham, Sparkes, Barry, Ram, Lloyd-Jones **Oxford University 0** Parr; Wilson, King, Phillips, Rogers, Heygate, Rev Childs, Eyre, (Dr) Crowdy, Hill, Lubbock. April 10; 6, 000; Major Marindin

1881 Old Carthusians 3 (Page, Wynyard, Parry) Gillett; Norris, (Sir) Colvin, Prinsep, (Sir) Vintcent, Hansell, Richards, Page, Wynyard, Parry, Todd **Old Etonians 0** Rawlinson; Foley, French, Kinnaird, Farrer, Macauley, Goodhart, Whitfield, Novelli, Anderson, Chevallier. April 9; 4, 000; W Pierce-Dix

1882 Old Etonians 1 (Macauley) Rawlinson; French, de Paravicini, Kinnaird, Foley, Novelli, Dunn, Macauley, Goodhart, Chevallier, Anderson **Blackburn Rov 0** Howarth; McIntyre, Suter, Hargreaves, Sharples, Hargreaves, Avery, Brown, Strachan, Douglas, Duckworth. March 25; 6, 500; JC Clegg

1883 Blackburn Olympic 2 (Matthews, Costley) Hacking; Ward, Warburton, Gibson, Astley, Hunter, Dewhurst, Matthews, Wilson, Costley, Yates **Old Etonians 1** (Goodhart) Rawlinson; French, de Paravicini, Kinnaird, Foley, Dunn, Bainbridge, Chevallier, Anderson, Goodhart, Macauley. March 31; 8, 000; Major Marindin, aet

1884 Blackburn Rov 2 (Sowerbutts, Forrest) Arthur; Suter, Beverley, McIntyre, Forrest, Hargreaves, Brown, Inglis Sowerbutts, Douglas, Lofthouse **Queen's Park 1** (Christie) Gillespie; MacDonald, Arnott, Gow, Campbell, Allan, Harrower, (Dr) Smith, Anderson, Watt, Christie. March 29; 4, 000; Major Marindin

1885 Blackburn Rov 2 (Forrest, Brown) Arthur; Turner, Suter, Haworth, McIntyre, Forrest, Sowerbutts, Lofthouse, Douglas, Brown, Fecitt **Queen's Park 0** Gillespie; Arnott, MacLeod, MacDonald, Campbell, Sellar, Anderson, McWhammel, Hamilton, Allan, Gray. April 4; 12, 500; Major Marindin

1886 Blackburn Rov 0 Arthur; Turner, Suter, Heyes, Forrest, McIntyre, Douglas, Strachan, Sowerbutts, Fecitt, Brown **WBA 0** Roberts; Green, Bell, Horton, Perry, Timmins, Woodhall, Green, Bayliss, Loach, Bell. April 3; 15, 000; Major Marindin **Replay – Blackburn Rov 2** (Sowerbutts, Brown) Arthur; Turner, Suter, Walton, Forrest, McIntyre, Douglas, Strachan, Sowerbutts, Fecitt, Brown **WBA 0** Roberts; Green, Bell, Horton, Perry, Timmins, Woodhall, Green, Bayliss, Loach, Bell. April 10; 12, 000; Major Marindin

1887 Aston Villa 2 (Hodgetts, Hunter) Warner; Coulton, Simmonds, Yates, Dawson, Burton, Davis, Albert Brown, Hunter, Vaughton, Hodgetts **WBA 0** Roberts; Green, Aldridge, Horton, Perry, Timmins, Woodhall, Green, Bayliss, Paddock, Pearson. April 2; 15, 500; Major Marindin

1888 WBA 2 (Bayliss), Woodhall) Roberts; Aldridge, Green, Horton, Perry, Timmins, Woodhall, Bassett, Bayliss, Wilson, Pearson **Preston 1** (Dewhurst) Mills-Roberts; Howarth, Holmes, Ross, Russell, Gordon, Ross, Goodall, Dewhurst, Drummond, Graham. March 24; 19, 000; Major Marindin

1889 Preston 3 (Dewhurst, Ross, Thomson) Mills-Roberts; Howarth, Holmes, Drummond, Russell, Graham, Gordon, Goodall, Dewhurst, Thompson, Ross **Wolves 0** Baynton; Baugh, Mason, Fletcher, Allen, Lowder, Hunter, Wykes, Brodie, Wood, Knight. March 30; 22, 000; Major Marindin

1890 Blackburn Rov 6 (Lofthouse, Jack Southworth, Walton, Townley 3) Horne; James Southworth, Forbes, Barton, Dewar, Forrest, Lofthouse, Campbell, Jack Southworth, Walton, Townley **Sheffield Wed 1** (Bennett) Smith; Morley, Brayshaw, Dungworth, Betts, Waller, Ingram, Woolhouse, Bennett, Mumford, Cawley. March 29; 20, 000; Major Marindin

1891 Blackburn Rov 3 (Dewar, Jack Southworth, Townley) Pennington; Brandon, Forbes, Barton, Dewar, Forrest, Lofthouse, Walton, Southworth, Hall, Townley **Notts Co 1** (Oswald) Thraves; Ferguson, Hendry, Osborne, Calderhead, Shelton, McGregor, McInnes Oswald, Locker, Daft. March 21; 23, 000; CJ Hughes

1892 WBA 3 (Geddes, Nicholls, Reynolds) Reader; Nicholson, McCulloch, Reynolds, Perry, Groves, Bassett, McLeod, Nicholls, Pearson, Geddes **Aston Villa 0** Warner; Evans, Cox, Devey, Cowan, Baird,

Athersmith, Devey, Dickson, Hodgetts, Campbell. March 19; 32, 810; JC Clegg

1893 **Wolves 1** (Allen) Rose; Baugh, Swift, Malpass, Allen, Kinsey, Topham, Wykes, Butcher, Griffin, Wood **Everton 0** Williams; Kelso, Howarth, Boyle, Holt, Stewart, Latta, Gordon, Maxwell, Chadwick, Milward. March 25; 45, 000; CJ Hughes

1894 **Notts Co 4** (Watson, Logan 3) Toone; Harper, Hendry, Bramley, Calderhead, Shelton, Watson, Donnelly, Logan Bruce, Daft **Bolton 1** (Cassidy) Sutcliffe; Somerville, Jones , Gardiner, Paton, Hughes, Tannahill, Wilson, Cassidy, Bentley, Dickenson. March 31; 37, 000; CJ Hughes

1895 **Aston Villa 1** (Chatt) Wilkes; Spencer, Welford, Reynolds, Cowan, Russell, Athersmith Chatt, Devey, Hodgetts, Smith **WBA 0** Reader; Williams, Horton, Perry, Higgins, Taggart, Bassett, McLeod, Richards, Hutchinson, Banks. April 20; 42, 560; J Lewis

1896 **Sheffield Wed 2** (Spikesley 2) Massey; Earp, Langley, Brandon, Crawshaw, Petrie, Brash, Brady, Bell, Davis, Spikesley **Wolves 1** (Black) Tennant; Baugh, Dunn, Owen, Malpass, Griffiths, Tonks, Henderson, Beats, Wood, Black. April 18; 48, 836; Lieut Simpson

1897 **Aston Villa 3** (Campbell, Wheldon, Crabtree) Whitehouse; Spencer, Reynolds, Evans, Cowan, Crabtree, Athersmith, Devey, Campbell, Wheldon, Cowan **Everton 2** (Bell, Boyle) Menham; Meechan, Storrier, Boyle, Holt, Stewart, Taylor, Bell, Hartley, Chadwick, Milward. April 10; 65, 891; J Lewis

1898 **Nottm Forest 3** (Capes 2, McPherson) Allsop; Ritchie, Scott, Forman, McPherson, Wragg, McInnes, Richards, Benbow, Capes, Spouncer **Derby 1** (Bloomer) Fryer; Methven, Leiper, Cox, Goodall, Bloomer, Boag, Stevenson, McQueen. April 16; 62, 017; J Lewis

1899 **Sheffield Utd 4** (Bennett, Beers, Almond, Priest) Foulke; Thickett, Boyle, Johnson, Morren, Needham, Bennett, Beers, Hedley, Almond, Priest **Derby 1** (Boag) Fryer; Methven, Staley, Cox, Paterson, May, Arkesden, Bloomer, Boag, McDonald, Allen. April 15; 73, 833; A Scragg

1900 **Bury 4** (McLuckie 2, Wood, Plant) Thompson; Darroch, Davidson, Pray, Leeming, Ross, Richards, Wood, McLuckie, Sagar, Plant **Southampton 0** Robinson; Meechan, Durber, Meston, Chadwick, Petrie, Turner, Yates, Farrell, Wood, Milward. April 21; 68, 945; A Kingscott

1901 **Tottenham 2** (Brown 2) Clawley; Erentz, Tait, Morris, Hughes, Jones, Smith, Cameron, Brown, Copeland, Kirwan **Sheffield Utd 2** (Priest, Bennett) Foulke; Thickett, Boyle, Johnson, Morren, Needham, Bennett, Field, Hedley, Priest, Lipsham. April 20; 110, 820; A Kingscott **Replay – Tottenham 3** (Cameron, Smith, Brown) Clawley; Erentz, Tait, Morris, Hughes, Jones, Smith, Cameron, Brown, Copeland, Kirwan. **Sheffield Utd 1** (Priest) Foulke; Thickett, Boyle, Johnson, Morren, Needham, Bennett, Field, Hedley, Priest, Lipsham. April 27; 20, 470; A Kingscott

1902 **Sheffield Utd 1** (Common) Foulke; Thickett, Boyle, Needham, Wilkinson, Johnson, Bennett, Common, Hedley, Priest, Lipsham **Southampton 1** (Wood) Robinson; Fry, Molyneux, Meston, Bowman, Lee, Turner, Wood Brown, Chadwick, Turner. April 19; 76, 914; T Kirkham. **Replay – Sheffield Utd 2** (Hedley, Barnes) Foulke; Thickett, Boyle, Needham, Wilkinson, Johnson, Barnes, Common, Hedley, Priest, Lipsham **Southampton 1** (Brown) Robinson; Fry, Molyneux, Meston, Bowman, Lee, Turner, Wood, Brown, Chadwick, Turner. April 26; 33, 068; T Kirkham

1903 **Bury 6** (Leeming 2, Ross, Sagar, Wood, Plant) Monteith; Lindsey, McEwen, Johnston, Thorpe, Ross, Richards, Wood, Sagar Leeming, Plant **Derby 0** Fryer; Methven, Morris, Warren, Goodall, May, Warrington, York, Boag, Richards, Davis. April 18; 63, 102; J Adams

1904 **Manchester City 1** (Meredith) Hillman; McMahon, Burgess, Frost, Hynds, Ashworth, Meredith, Livingstone, Gillespie, Turnbull, Booth **Bolton 0** Davies; Brown, Struthers, Clifford, Greenhalgh, Freebairn, Stokes, Marsh, Yenson, White, Taylor. April 23; 61, 374; AJ Barker

1905 **Aston Villa 2** (Hampton 2) George; Spencer, Miles, Pearson, Leake, Windmill, Brawn, Garratty, Hampton, Bache, Hall **Newcastle 0** Lawrence; McCombie, Carr, Gardner, Aitken, McWilliam, Rutherford, Howie, Appleyard, Veitch, Gosnell. April 15; 101, 117; PR Harrower

1906 **Everton 1** (Young) Scott; Crelley, Walter Balmer, Makepeace, Taylor, Abbott, Sharp, Bolton, Young, Settle, Hardman **Newcastle 0** Lawrence; McCombie, Carr, Gardner, Aitken, McWilliam, Rutherford, Howie, Orr, Veitch, Gosnell. April 21; 75, 609; F Kirkham

1907 **Sheffield Wed 2** (Stewart, Simpson) Lyall; Layton, Burton, Brittleton, Crawshaw, Bartlett, Chapman, Bradshaw, Wilson, Stewart, Simpson **Everton 1** (Sharp) Scott; Walter Balmer, Bob Balmer, Makepeace, Taylor, Abbott, Sharp, Bolton, Young, Settle, Hardman. April 20; 84, 594; N Whittaker

1908 **Wolves** 3 (Hunt, Hedley, Harrison) Lunn; Jones, Collins, Rev Hunt, Wooldridge, Bishop, Harrison, Shelton, Hedley, Radford, Pedley **Newcastle** 1 (Howie) Lawrence; McCracken, Pudan, Gardner, Veitch, McWilliam, Rutherford, Howie, Appleyard, Speedie, Wilson. April 25; 74, 697; TP Campbell

1909 **Manchester Utd** 1 (Sandy Turnbull) Moger; Stacey, Hayes, Duckworth, Roberts, Bell, Meredith, Halse, J Turnbull, S Turnbull, Wall **Bristol City** 0 Clay; Annan, Cottle, Hanlin, Wedlock, Spear, Staniforth, Hardy, Gilligan, Burton, Hilton. April 24; 71, 401; J Mason

1910 **Newcastle** 1 (Rutherford) Lawrence; McCracken, Whitson, Veitch, Low, McWilliam, Rutherford, Howie, Higgins, Shepherd, Wilson **Barnsley** 1 (Tufnell) Mearns; Downs, Ness, Glendinning, Boyle, Utley, Tufnell, Lillycrop, Gadsby, Forman, Bartrop. April 23; 77, 747; JT Ibbotson **Replay – Newcastle** 2 (Shepherd 2, 1pen) Lawrence; McCracken, Carr, Veitch, Low, McWilliam, Rutherford, Howie, Higgins, Shepherd, Wilson **Barnsley** 0 Mearns; Downs, Ness, Glendinning, Boyle, Utley, Tufnell, Lillycrop, Gadsby, Forman, Bartrop. April 28; 69, 000; JT Ibbotson

1911 **Bradford City** 0 Mellors; Campbell, Taylor, Robinson, Gildea, McDonald, Logan, Speirs, O'Rourke, Devine, Thompson **Newcastle** 0 Lawrence; McCracken, Whitson, Veitch, Low, Willis, Rutherford, Jobey, Stewart, Higgins, Wilson. April 22; 69, 068; JH Pearson **Replay – Bradford City** 1 (Speirs) Mellors; Campbell, Taylor, Robinson, Torrance, McDonald, Logan, Speirs, O'Rourke, Devine, Thompson **Newcastle** 0 Lawrence; McCracken, Whitson, Veitch, Low, Willis, Rutherford, Jobey, Stewart, Higgins, Wilson. April 26; 58, 000; JH Pearson

1912 **Barnsley** 0 Cooper; Downs, Taylor, Glendinning, Bratley, Utley, Bartrop, Tufnell, Lillycrop, Travers, Moore **WBA** 0 Pearson; Cook, Pennington, Baddeley, Buck, McNeal, Jephcott, Wright, Pailor, Bowser, Shearman. April 20; 54, 556; JR Shumacher **Replay – Barnsley** 1 (Tufnell) Cooper; Downs, Taylor, Glendinning, Bratley, Utley, Bartrop, Harry, Lillycrop, Travers, Jimmy Moore **WBA** 0 Pearson; Cook, Pennington, Baddeley, Buck, McNeal, Jephcott, Wright, Pailor, Bowser, Shearman. April 24; 38, 555; JR Schumacher. aet

1913 **Aston Villa** 1 (Barber) Hardy; Lyons, Weston, Barber, Harrop, Leach, Wallace, Halse, Hampton, Stephenson, Bache **Sunderland** 0 Butler; Gladwin, Ness, Cuggy, Thomson, Low, Mordue, Buchan, Richardson, Holley, Martin. April 19; 120, 081; A Adams

1914 **Burnley** 1 (Freeman) Sewell; Bamford, Taylor, Halley, Boyle, Watson, Nesbit, Lindley, Freeman, Hodgson, Mosscrop **Liverpool** 0 Campbell; Longworth, Pursell, Fairfoul, Ferguson, McKinley, Sheldon, Metcalfe, Miller, Lacey, Nicholl. April 25; 72, 778; HS Bamlett

1915 **Sheffield Utd** 3 (Simmons, Fazackerly, Kitchen) Gough; Cook, English, Sturgess, Brelsford, Utley, Simmons, Fazackerly, Kitchen, Masterman, Evans **Chelsea** 0 Molyneux; Bettridge, Harrow, Taylor, Logan, Walker, Ford, Halse, Thomson, Croal, McNeil. April 24; 49, 557; HH Taylor

1920 **Aston Villa** 1 (Kirton) Hardy; Smart, Weston, Ducat, Barson, Moss, Wallace, Kirton, Walker, Stephenson, Dorrell **Huddersfield** 0 Mutch; Wood, Bullock, Slade, Wilson, Watson, Richardson, Mann, Taylor, Swann, Islip. April 24; 50, 018; JT Howcroft. aet

1921 **Tottenham** 1 (Dimmock) Hunter; Clay, McDonald, Smith, Walters, Grimsdell, Banks, Seed, Cantrell, Bliss, Dimmock **Wolves** 0 George; Woodward, Marshall, Gregory, Hodnett, Riley, Lea, Burrill, Edmonds, Potts, Brooks. April 23; 72, 805; S Davies

1922 **Huddersfield** 1 (Smith pen) Mutch; Wood, Wadsworth, Slade, Wilson, Watson, Richardson, Mann, Islip, Stephenson, Billy Smith **Preston** 0 Mitchell; Hamilton, Doolan, Duxbury, McCall, Williamson, Rawlings, Jefferis, Roberts, Woodhouse, Quinn. April 29; 53, 000; JWP Fowler

1923 **Bolton** 2 (Jack, JR Smith) Pym; Haworth, Finney, Nuttall, Seddon, Jennings, Butler, Jack, JR Smith, Joe Smith, Vizard **West Ham** 0 Hufton; Henderson, Young, Bishop, Kay, Tresadern, Richards, Brown, Watson, Moore, Ruffell. April 28; 126, 047; DH Asson

1924 **Newcastle** 2 (Harris, Seymour) Bradley; Hampson, Hudspeth, Mooney, Spencer, Gibson, Low, Cowan, Harris, McDonald, Seymour **Aston Villa** 0 Jackson; Smart, Mort, Moss, Milne, Blackburn, York, Kirton, Capewell, Walker, Dorrell. April 26; 91, 695; WE Russell

1925 **Sheffield Utd** 1 (Tunstall) Sutcliffe; Cook, Milton, Pantling, King, Green, Mercer, Boyle, Johnson, Gillespie, Tunstall **Cardiff** 0 Farquharson; Nelson, Blair, Wake, Keenor, Hardy, Davies, Gill, Nicholson, Beadles, Evans. April 25; 91, 763; GN Watson

1926 **Bolton** 1 (Jack) Pym; Haworth, Greenhalgh, Nuttall, Seddon, Jennings, Butler, JR Smith, Jack,

Joe Smith, Vizard **Manchester City 0** Goodchild; Cookson, McCloy, Pringle, Cowan, McMullan, Austin, Browell, Roberts, Johnson, Hicks. April 24; 91, 447; I Baker

1927 Cardiff 1 (Ferguson) Farquharson; Nelson, Watson, Keenor, Sloan, Hardy, Curtis, Irving, Ferguson, Davies, McLachlan **Arsenal 0** Lewis; Parker, Kennedy, Baker, Butler, John, Hulme, Buchan, Brain, Blythe, Hoar. April 23; 91, 206; WF Bunnell

1928 Blackburn 3 (Roscamp 2, McLean) Crawford; Hutton, Jones, Healless, Rankin, Campbell, Thornewell, Puddefoot, Roscamp, McLean, Rigby **Huddersfield 1** (Jackson) Mercer; Goodall, Barkas, Redfern, Wilson, Steele, Jackson, Kelly, Brown, Stephenson, Smith. April 21; 92, 041; TG Bryan

1929 Bolton 2 (Butler, Blackmore) Pym; Haworth, Finney, Kean, Seddon, Nuttall, Butler, McClelland, Blackmore, Gibson, Cook **Portsmouth 0** Gilfillan; Mackie, Bell, Nichol, McIlwaine, Thackeray, Forward, Smith, Weddle, Watson, Cook. April 27; 92, 576; A Josephs

1930 Arsenal 2 (James, Lambert) Preedy; Parker, Hapgood, Baker, Seddon, John, Hulme, Jack, Lambert, James, Bastin **Huddersfield 0** Turner; Goodall, Spence, Naylor, Wilson, Campbell, Jackson, Kelly, Davies, Raw, Smith. April 26; 92, 488; T Crew

1931 WBA 2 (WG Richardson 2) Pearson; Shaw, Trentham, Magee, Bill Richardson, Edwards, Glidden, Carter, WG Richardson, Sandford, Wood **Birmingham 1** (Bradford) Hibbs; Liddell, Barkas, Cringan, Morrall, Leslie, Briggs, Crosbie, Bradford, Gregg, Curtis. April 25; 92, 406; AH Kingscott

1932 Newcastle 2 (Allen 2) McInroy; Nelson, Fairhurst, McKenzie, Davidson, Weaver, Boyd, Richardson, Allen, McMenemy, Lang **Arsenal 1** (John) Moss; Parker, Hapgood, Jones, Roberts, Male, Hulme, Jack, Lambert, Bastin, John. April 23; 92, 298; WP Harper

1933 Everton 3 (Stein, Dean, Dunn) Sagar; Cook, Cresswell, Britton, White, Thomson, Geldard, Dunn, Dean, Johnson, Stein **Manchester City 0** Langford; Cann, Dale, Busby, Cowan, Bray, Toseland, Marshall, Herd, McMullan, Eric Brook. April 29; 92, 950; E Wood

1934 Manchester City 2 (Tilson 2) Swift; Barnett, Dale, Busby, Cowan, Bray, Toseland, Marshall, Tilson, Herd, Brook **Portsmouth 1** (Rutherford) Gilfillan; Mackie, Smith, Nichol, Allen, Thackeray, Worrall, Smith, Weddle, Easson, Rutherford. April 28; 93, 258; Stanley Rous

1935 Sheffield Wed 4 (Rimmer 2, Palethorpe, Hooper) Brown; Nibloe, Catlin, Sharp, Millership, Burrows, Hooper, Surtees, Palethorpe, Starling, Rimmer **WBA 2** (Boyes, Sandford) Pearson; Shaw, Trentham, Murphy, Bill Richardson, Edwards, Glidden, Carter, WG Richardson, Sandford, Wally. April 27; 93, 204; AE Fogg

1936 Arsenal 1 (Drake) Wilson; Male, Hapgood, Crayston, Roberts, Copping, Hulme, Bowden, Drake, James, Bastin **Sheffield Utd 0** Smith; Hooper, Wilkinson, Jackson, Johnson, McPherson, Barton, Barclay, Dodds, Pickering, Williams. April 25; 93, 384; H Nattrass

1937 Sunderland 3 (Gurney, Carter, Burbanks) Mapson; Gorman, Hall, Thomson, Johnston, McNab, Duns, Carter, Gurney, Gallacher, Burbanks **Preston 1** (Frank O'Donnell) Burns; Gallimore, Andy Beattie, Shankly, Tremelling, Milne, Dougal, Beresford, Frank O'Donnell, Fagan, Hugh O'Donnell. May 1; 93, 495; RG Rudd

1938 Preston 1 (Mutch pen) Holdcroft; Gallimore, Andy Beattie, Shankly, Smith, Batey, Watmough, Mutch, Maxwell, Bob Beattie, Hugh O'Donnell **Huddersfield 0** Hesford; Craig, Mountford, Willingham, Young, Boot, Hulme, Issac, MacFadyen, Barclay, Beasley. April 30; 93, 497; AJ Jewell. aet

1939 Portsmouth 4 (Parker 2, Barlow, Anderson) Walker; Morgan, Rochford, Guthrie, Rowe, Wharton, Worrall, McAlinden, Anderson, Barlow, Parker **Wolves 1** (Dorsett) Scott; Morris, Taylor, Galley, Cullis, Gardiner, Burton, McIntosh, Westcott, Dorsett, Maguire. April 29; 99, 370; T Thompson

1946 Derby 4 (Stamps 2, Doherty, Bert Turner og) Woodley; Nicholas, Howe, Bullions, Leuty, Musson, Harrison, Carter, Stamps, Doherty, Duncan **Charlton Athletic 1** (Bert Turner) Bartram; Phipps, Shreeve, Bert Turner, Oakes, Johnson, Fell, Brown, Arthur Turner, Welsh, Duffy. April 27; 98, 000; ED Smith. aet

1947 Charlton Athletic 1 (Duffy) Bartram; Croker, Shreeve, Johnson, Phipps, Whittaker, Hurst, Dawson, Robinson, Welsh, Duffy **Burnley 0** Strong; Woodruff, Mather, Attwell, Brown, Bray, Chew, Morris, Harrison, Potts, Kippax. April 26; 99, 000; JM Wiltshire. aet

1948 Manchester Utd 4 (Rowley 2, Pearson, Anderson) Crompton; Carey, Aston, Anderson, Chilton, Cockburn, Delaney, Morris, Rowley, Pearson, Mitten **Blackpool 2** (Shimwell pen, Mortensen) Robinson;

Shimwell, Crosland, Johnston, Hayward, Kelly, Matthews, Munro, Mortensen, Dick, Rickett. April 24; 99, 000; CJ Barrick

1949 Wolves 3 (Pye 2, Smyth) Williams; Pritchard, Springthorpe Crook, Shorthouse, Wright, Hancocks, Smyth, Pye, Dunn, Mullen **Leicester** 1 (Griffiths) Bradley; Jelly, Scott, Walter Harrison, Plummer, King, Griffiths, Lee, Jimmy Harrison, Chisholm, Adam. April 30; 99, 500; RA Mortimer

1950 Arsenal 2 (Lewis 2) Swindin; Scott, Barnes, Forbes, Les Compton, Mercer, Cox, Logie, Goring, Lewis, Denis Compton **Liverpool** 0 Sidlow; Lambert, Spicer, Taylor, Hughes, Jones, Payne, Baron, Stubbins, Fagan, Liddell. April 29; 100, 000; H Pearce

1951 Newcastle 2 (Milburn 2) Fairbrother; Cowell, Corbett, Harvey, Brennan, Crowe, Walker, Taylor, Milburn, Jorge Robledo, Mitchell **Blackpool** 0 Farm; Shimwell, Garrett, Johnston, Hayward, Kelly, Matthews, Mudie, Mortensen, Slater, Perry. April 28; 100, 000; W Ling

1952 Newcastle 1 (George Robledo) Simpson; Cowell, McMichael, Harvey, Brennan, Ted Robledo, Walker, Foulkes, Milburn, George Robledo, Mitchell **Arsenal** 0 Swindin; Barnes, Smith, Forbes, Daniel Mercer, Cox, Logie, Holton, Lishman, Roper. May 3; 100, 000; A Ellis

1953 Blackpool 4 (Mortensen 3, Perry) Farm; Shimwell, Garrett, Fenton, Johnston, Robinson, Matthews, Taylor, Mortensen, Mudie, Perry **Bolton** 3 (Lofthouse, Moir, Bell) Hanson; Ball, Ralph Banks, Wheeler, Barrass, Bell, Holden, Moir, Lofthouse, Hassall, Langton. May 2; 100, 000; M Griffiths

1954 WBA 3 (Allen 2 [1pen], Griffin) Sanders; Kennedy, Millard, Dudley, Dugdale, Barlow, Griffin, Ryan, Allen, Nicholls, Lee **Preston** 2 (Morrison, Wayman) Thompson; Cunningham, Walton, Docherty, Marston, Forbes, Finney, Foster, Wayman, Baxter, Morrison. May 1; 100, 000; A Luty

1955 Newcastle 3 (Milburn, Mitchell, Hannah) Simpson; Cowell, Batty, Scoular, Stokoe, Casey, White, Milburn, Keeble, Hannah, Mitchell **Manchester City** 1 (Johnstone) Trautmann; Meadows, Little, Barnes, Ewing, Paul, Spurdle, Hayes, Revie, Johnstone, Fagan. May 7; 100, 000; R Leafe

1956 Manchester City 3 (Hayes, Dyson, Johnstone) Trautmann; Leivers, Little, Barnes, Ewing, Paul, Johnstone, Hayes, Revie, Dyson, Clarke **Birmingham** 1 (Kinsey) Merrick; Hall, Green, Newman, Smith, Boyd, Astall, Kinsey, Brown, Murphy, Govan. May 5; 100, 000; A Bond

1957 Aston Villa 2 (McParland 2) Sims; Lynn, Aldis, Crowther, Dugdale, Saward, Smith, Sewell, Myerscough, Dixon, McParland **Manchester Utd** 1 (Tommy Taylor) Wood; Foulkes, Byrne, Colman, Blanchflower, Edwards, Berry, Whelan, Tommy Taylor, Charlton, Pegg. May 4; 100, 000; F Coultas

1958 Bolton 2 (Lofthouse 2) Hopkinson; Hartle, Tommy Banks, Hennin, Higgins, Edwards, Birch, Stevens, Lofthouse, Parry, Holden **Manchester Utd** 0 Gregg; Foulkes, Greaves, Goodwin, Cope, Crowther, Dawson, Ernie Taylor, Charlton, Viollet, Webster. May 3; 100, 000; J Sherlock

1959 Nottingham Forest 2 (Dwight, Wilson) Thomson; Whare, McDonald, Whitefoot, McKinlay, Burkitt, Dwight, Quigley, Wilson, Gray, Imlach **Luton Town** 1 (Pacey) Baynham; McNally, Hawkes, Groves, Owen, Pacey, Bingham, Brown, Morton, Cummins, Gregory. May 2; 100, 000; J Clough

1960 Wolves 3 (McGrath og, Deeley 2) Finlayson; Showell, Harris, Clamp, Slater, Flowers, Deeley, Stobart, Murray, Broadbent, Horne **Blackburn** 0 Leyland; Bray, Whelan, Clayton, Woods, McGrath, Bimpson, Dobing, Dougan, Douglas, McLeod. May 7; 100, 000; K Howley

1961 Tottenham 2 (Smith, Dyson) Brown; Baker, Henry, Blanchflower, Norman, Mackay, Jones, White, Smith, Allen, Dyson **Leicester** 0 Banks; Chalmers, Norman, McLintock, King, Appleton, Riley, Walsh, McIlmoyle, Keyworth, Cheesebrough. May 6; 100, 000; J Kelly

1962 Tottenham 3 (Greaves, Smith, Blanchflower pen) Brown; Baker, Henry, Blanchflower, Norman, Mackay, Medwin, White, Smith, Greaves, Jones **Burnley** 1 (Robson) Blacklaw; Angus, Elder, Adamson, Cummings, Miller, Connelly, McIlroy, Pointer, Robson, Harris. May 5; 100, 000; J Finney

1963 Manchester Utd 3 (Law, Herd 2) Gaskell; Dunne, Cantwell, Crerand, Foulkes, Setters, Giles, Quixall, Herd, Law, Charlton **Leicester** 1 (Keyworth) Banks; Sjoberg, Norman, McLintock, King, Appleton, Riley, Cross, Keyworth, Gibson, Stringfellow. May 25; 100, 000; K Aston

1964 West Ham 3 (Sissons, Hurst, Boyce) Standen; Bond, Burkett, Bovington, Brown, Moore, Brabrook, Boyce, Byrne, Hurst, Sissons **Preston** 2 (Holden, Dawson) Kelly; Ross, Lawton, Smith, Singleton,

Kendall, Wilson, Ashworth, Dawson, Spavin, Holden. May 2; 100, 000; A Holland

1965 Liverpool 2 (Hunt, St John) Lawrence; Lawler, Byrne, Strong, Yeats, Stevenson, Callaghan, Hunt, St John, Smith, Thompson **Leeds 1** (Bremner) Sprake; Reaney, Bell, Bremner, Charlton, Hunter, Giles, Storrie, Peacock, Collins, Johanneson. May 1; 100, 000; W Clements. aet

1966 Everton 3 (Trebilcock 2, Temple) West; Wright, Wilson, Gabriel, Labone, Harris, Scott, Trebilcock, Young, Harvey, Temple **Sheffield Wed 2** (McCalliog, Ford) Springett; Smith, Megson, Eustace, Ellis, Young, Pugh, Fantham, McCalliog, Ford, Quinn. May 14; 100, 000; JK Taylor

1967 Tottenham 2 (Robertson, Saul) Jennings; Kinnear, Knowles, Mullery, England, Mackay, Robertson, Greaves, Gilzean, Venables, Saul. Unused sub: Jones **Chelsea 1** (Tambling) Bonetti; Allan Harris, McCreadie, Hollins, Hinton, Ron Harris, Cooke, Baldwin, Hateley, Tambling, Boyle. Unused sub: Kirkup. May 20; 100, 000; K Dagnall

1968 WBA 1 (Astle) Osborne; Fraser, Williams, Brown, Talbut, Kaye, Lovett, Collard, Astle Hope, Clark Sub: Clarke rep Kaye 91 **Everton 0** West; Wright, Wilson, Kendall, Labone, Harvey, Husband, Ball, Royle, Hurst, Morrissey. Unused sub: Kenyon. May 18; 100, 000; L Callaghan. aet

1969 Manchester City 1 (Young) Dowd: Book, Pardoe, Doyle, Booth, Oakes, Summerbee, Bell, Lee, Young, Coleman. Unused sub: Connor **Leicester 0** Shilton; Rodrigues, Nish, Roberts, Woollett, Cross, Fern, Gibson, Lochhead, Clarke, Glover. Sub: Manley rep Glover 70. April 26; 100, 000; G McCabe

1970 Chelsea 2 (Houseman, Hutchinson) Bonetti; Webb, McCreadie, Hollins, Dempsey, Ron Harris, Baldwin, Houseman, Osgood, Hutchinson, Cooke. Sub: Hinton rep Harris 91 **Leeds 2** (Charlton, Jones) Sprake; Madeley, Cooper, Bremner, Charlton, Hunter, Lorimer, Clarke, Jones, Giles, Gray Unused sub: Bates. April 11; 100, 000; E Jennings. aet **Replay – Chelsea 2** (Osgood, Webb) Bonetti, Webb, McCreadie, Hollins, Dempsey, Ron Harris, Baldwin, Houseman, Osgood, Hutchinson, Cooke. Sub: Hinton rep Osgood 105 **Leeds 1** (Jones) Harvey; Madeley, Cooper, Bremner, Charlton, Hunter, Lorimer, Clarke, Jones, Giles, Gray Unusued sub: Bates. April 29; 62, 078; E Jennings. aet

1971 Arsenal 2 (Kelly, George) Wilson; Rice, McNab, Storey, McLintock Simpson, Armstrong, Graham, Radford, Kennedy, George. Sub: Kelly rep Storey 70 **Liverpool 1** (Heighway) Clemence; Lawler, Lindsay, Smith, Lloyd, Hughes, Callaghan, Evans, Heighway, Toshack, Hall. Sub: Thompson rep Evans 70. May 8; 100, 000; N Burtenshaw. aet

1972 Leeds 1 (Clarke) Harvey; Reaney, Madeley, Bremner, Charlton, Hunter, Lorimer, Clarke, Jones, Giles, Gray. Unused sub: Bates **Arsenal 0** Barnett; Rice, McNab, Storey, McLintock, Simpson, Armstrong, Ball, George, Radford, Graham. Sub: Kennedy rep Radford 80. May 6; 100, 000; DW Smith

1973 Sunderland 1 (Porterfield) Montgomery; Malone, Guthrie, Horswill, Watson, Pitt, Kerr, Hughes, Halom, Porterfield, Tueart. Unused sub: Young **Leeds 0** Harvey; Reaney, Cherry, Bremner, Madeley, Hunter, Lorimer, Clarke, Jones, Giles, Gray. Sub: Yorath rep Gray 75. May 5; 100, 000; K Burns

1974 Liverpool 3 (Keegan 2, Heighway) Clemence; Smith, Lindsay, Thompson, Cormack, Hughes, Keegan, Hall, Heighway, Toshack, Callaghan. Unused sub: Lawler **Newcastle 0** McFaul; Clark, Kennedy, McDermott, Howard, Moncur, Smith, Cassidy, Macdonald, Tudor, Hibbitt. Sub: Gibb rep Smith 70. May 4; 100, 000; GC Kew

1975 West Ham 2 (Alan Taylor 2) Day; McDowell, Tommy Taylor, Lock, Lampard, Bonds, Paddon, Brooking, Jennings, Alan Taylor, Holland. Unused sub: Gould **Fulham 0** Mellor; Cutbush, Lacy, Moore, Fraser, Mullery, Conway, Slough, Mitchell, Busby, Barrett. Unused sub: Lloyd. May 3; 100, 000; P Partridge

1976 Southampton 1 (Stokes) Turner; Rodrigues, Peach, Holmes, Blyth, Steele, Gilchrist, Channon, Osgood, McCalliog, Stokes. Unused subs: Fisher **Manchester Utd 0** Stepney; Forsyth, Houston, Daly, Brian Greenhoff, Buchan, Coppell, McIlroy, Pearson, Macari, Hill. Sub: McCreery rep Hill 66. May 1; 100, 000; C Thomas

1977 Manchester Utd 2 (Pearson, J Greenhoff) Stepney; Nicholl, Albiston, McIlroy, Brian Greenhoff, Buchan, Coppell, Jimmy Greenhoff, Pearson, Macari, Hill. Sub: McCreery rep Hill 81 **Liverpool 1** (Case) Clemence; Neal, Jones, Smith, Kennedy, Hughes, Keegan, Case, Heighway, Johnson, McDermott. Sub: Callaghan rep Johnson 64. May 21; 100, 000; R Matthewson

1978 Ipswich Town 1 (Osborne) Cooper; Burley, Mills, Talbot, Hunter, Beattie, Osborne, Wark, Mariner, Geddis, Woods. Sub: Lambert rep Osborne 79 **Arsenal 0** Jennings; Rice, Nelson, Price, Young, O'Leary, Brady, Hudson, Macdonald, Stapleton, Sunderland. Sub: Rix rep Brady 65. May 6; 100, 000; D Nippard

1979 **Arsenal 3** (Talbot, Stapleton, Sunderland) Jennings; Rice, Nelson, Talbot, O'Leary, Young, Brady, Sunderland, Stapleton, Price, Rix. Sub: Walford rep Rix 83 **Manchester Utd 2** (McQueen, McIlroy) Bailey; Nicholl, Albiston, McIlroy, McQueen, Buchan, Coppell, Jimmy Greenhoff, Jordan, Macari, Thomas. Unused sub: Brian Greenhoff. May 12; 100, 000; R Challis

1980 **West Ham 1** (Brooking) Parkes; Stewart, Lampard, Bonds, Martin, Devonshire, Allen, Pearson, Cross, Brooking, Pike. Unused sub: Brush **Arsenal 0** Jennings; Rice, Devine, Talbot, O'Leary, Young, Brady, Sunderland, Stapleton, Price, Rix. Sub: Nelson rep Devine 61. May 10; 100, 000; G Courtney

1981 **Tottenham 1** (Hutchison og) Aleksic; Hughton, Miller, Roberts, Perryman, Villa, Ardiles, Archibald, Galvin, Hoddle, Crooks. Sub: Brooke rep Villa 68. **Manchester City 1** (Hutchison) Corrigan; Ranson, McDonald, Reid, Power, Caton, Bennett, Gow, Mackenzie, Hutchison Reeves. Sub: Henry rep Hutchison 82. May 9; 100, 000; K Hackett. aet **Replay – Tottenham 3** (Villa 2, Crooks) Aleksic; Hughton, Miller, Roberts, Perryman, Villa, Ardiles, Archibald, Galvin, Hoddle, Crooks. Unused sub: Brooke **Manchester City 2** (Mackenzie, Reeves pen) Corrigan; Ranson, McDonald, Reid, Power, Caton, Bennett, Gow, Mackenzie, Hutchison Reeves. Sub: Tueart rep McDonald 79. May 14; 92, 000; K Hackett

1982 **Tottenham 1** (Hoddle) Clemence; Hughton, Miller, Price, Hazard, Perryman, Roberts, Archibald, Galvin, Hoddle, Crooks. Sub: Brooke rep Hazard 104 **Queens Park Rangers 1** (Fenwick) Hucker; Fenwick, Gillard, Waddock, Hazell, Roeder, Currie, Flanagan, Allen, Stainrod, Gregory. Sub: Micklewhite rep Allen 50. May 22; 100, 000; C White. aet **Replay – Tottenham 1** (Hoddle pen) Clemence; Hughton, Miller, Price, Hazard, Perryman, Roberts, Archibald, Galvin, Hoddle, Crooks. Sub: Brooke rep Hazard 67 **Queens Park Rangers 0** Hucker; Fenwick, Gillard, Waddock, Hazell, Neill, Currie, Flanagan, Micklewhite, Stainrod, Gregory. Sub: Burke rep Micklewhite 84. May 27; 90, 000; C White

1983 **Manchester Utd 2** (Stapleton, Wilkins) Bailey; Duxbury, Moran, McQueen, Albiston, Davies, Wilkins, Robson, Muhren, Stapleton, Whiteside. Unused sub: Grimes **Brighton 2** (Smith, Stevens) Moseley; Ramsey, Gary A Stevens, Pearce, Gatting, Smillie, Case, Grealish, Howlett, Robinson, Smith. Sub: Ryan rep Ramsey 56. May 21; 100, 000; AW Grey. aet **Replay – Manchester Utd 4** (Robson 2, Whiteside, Muhren pen) Bailey; Duxbury, Moran, McQueen, Albiston, Davies, Wilkins, Robson, Muhren, Stapleton, Whiteside. Unused sub: Grimes **Brighton 0** Moseley; Gary A Stevens, Pearce, Foster, Gatting, Smillie, Case, Grealish, Howlett, Robinson, Smith. Sub: Ryan rep Howlett 74. May 26; 100, 000; AW Grey

1984 **Everton 2** (Sharp, Gray) Southall; Gary M Stevens, Bailey, Ratcliffe, Mountfield, Reid, Steven, Heath, Sharp, Gray, Richardson. Unused sub: Harper **Watford 0** Sherwood; Bardsley, Price, Taylor, Terry, Sinnott, Callaghan, Johnston, Reilly, Jackett, Barnes. Sub: Atkinson rep Price 58. May 19; 100, 000; J Hunting

1985 **Manchester Utd 1** (Whiteside) Bailey; Gidman, Albiston, Whiteside, McGrath, Moran, Robson, Strachan, Hughes, Stapleton, Olsen. Sub: Duxbury rep Albiston 91. Moran sent off 77. **Everton 0** Southall; Gary M Stevens, Van den Hauwe, Ratcliffe, Mountfield, Reid, Steven, Sharp, Gray, Bracewell, Sheedy. Unused sub: Harper. May 18; 100, 000; P Willis. aet

1986 **Liverpool 3** (Rush 2, Johnston) Grobbelaar; Lawrenson, Beglin, Nicol, Whelan, Hansen, Dalglish, Johnston, Rush, Molby, MacDonald. Unused sub: McMahon **Everton 1** (Lineker) Mimms; Gary M Stevens, Van den Hauwe, Ratcliffe, Mountfield, Reid, Steven, Lineker, Sharp, Bracewell, Sheedy. Sub: Heath rep Stevens 65. May 10; 98, 000; A Robinson

1987 **Coventry City 3** (Bennett, Houchen, Mabbutt og) Ogrizovic; Phillips, Downs, McGrath, Kilcline, Peake, Bennett, Gynn, Regis, Houchen, Pickering. Sub: Rodger rep Kilcline 88. Unused sub: Sedgley **Tottenham 2** (Clive Allen, Mabbutt) Clemence; Hughton Thomas, Hodge, Gough, Mabbutt, Clive Allen, Paul Allen, Waddle, Hoddle, Ardiles. Subs: Gary A Stevens rep Ardiles 91; Claesen rep Hughton 97. May 16; 98, 000; N Midgley. aet

1988 **Wimbledon 1** (Sanchez) Beasant; Goodyear, Phelan, Jones, Young, Thorn, Gibson Cork, Fashanu, Sanchez, Wise. Subs: Cunningham rep Cork 56; Scales rep Gibson 63 **Liverpool 0** Grobbelaar; Gillespie, Ablett, Nicol, Spackman, Hansen, Beardsley, Aldridge, Houghton, Barnes, McMahon. Subs: Johnston rep Aldridge 63; Molby rep Spackman 72. May 14; 98, 203; B Hill

1989 **Liverpool 3** (Aldridge, Rush 2) Grobbelaar; Ablett, Staunton, Nichol, Whelan, Hansen, Beardsley, Aldridge Houghton, Barnes, McMahon. Subs: Rush rep Aldridge 72; Venison rep Staunton 91 **Everton 2** (McCall 2) Southall; McDonald, Van den Hauwe, Ratcliffe, Watson, Bracewell, Nevin, Steven, Cottee, Sharp, Sheedy. Subs: McCall rep Bracewell 58; Wilson rep Sheedy 77. May 20; 82, 500; J Worrall. aet

1990 **Manchester Utd 3** (Robson, Hughes 2) Leighton; Ince, Martin, Bruce, Phelan, Pallister, Robson,

Webb, McClair, Hughes, Wallace. Subs: Blackmore rep Martin 88; Robins rep Pallister 93. **Crystal Palace 3** (O'Reilly, Wright 2) Martyn; Pemberton, Shaw, Gray, O'Reilly, Thorn, Barber, Thomas, Bright, Salako, Pardew. Subs: Wright rep Barber 69; Madden rep Gray 117. May 12; 80, 000; A Gunn. aet **Replay – Manchester Utd 1** (Martin) Sealey; Ince, Martin, Bruce, Phelan, Pallister, Robson, Webb, McClair, Hughes, Wallace. Unused subs: Robins, Blackmore **Crystal Palace 0** Martyn; Pemberton, Shaw, Gray, O'Reilly, Thorn, Barber, Thomas, Bright, Salako, Pardew. Subs: Wright rep Barber 64; Madden rep Salako 79. May 17; 80, 000; A Gunn

1991   Tottenham 2 (Stewart, Walker og) Thorstvedt; Edinburgh, Van den Hauwe, Sedgley, Howells, Mabbutt, Stewart, Gascoigne, Samways, Lineker, Paul Allen. Subs: Nayim rep Gascoigne 18; Walsh rep Samways 82. **Nottingham Forest 1** (Pearce) Crossley; Charles, Pearce, Walker, Chettle, Keane, Crosby, Parker, Clough, Glover, Woan. Subs: Hodge rep Woan 62; Laws rep Glover 108. May 18; 80, 000; R Milford. aet

1992   Liverpool 2 (Thomas, Rush) Grobbelaar; Jones, Burrows, Nicol, Molby, Wright, Saunders, Houghton, Rush, McManaman, Thomas. Unused subs: Marsh, Walters **Sunderland 0** Norman; Owers, Ball, Bennett, Rogan, Rush, Bracewell, Davenport, Armstrong, Byrne, Atkinson. Subs: Hardyman rep Rush 69; Hawke rep Armstrong 77. May 9; 80, 000; P Don

1993   Arsenal 1 (Wright) Seaman; Dixon, Winterburn, Linighan, Adams, Jensen, Davis, Parlour, Merson, Campbell, Wright. Subs: Smith rep Parlour 66; O'Leary rep Wright 90. **Sheffield Wed 1** (Hirst) Woods; Nilsson Worthington, Palmer, Hirst, Anderson, Waddle, Warhurst, Bright, Sheridan, Harkes. Subs: Hyde rep Anderson 85; Bart-Williams rep Waddle 112. May 15; 79, 347; K Barratt. aet **Replay – Arsenal 2** (Wright, Linighan) Seaman; Dixon, Winterburn, Linighan, Adams, Jensen, Davis, Smith, Merson, Campbell, Wright. Sub: O'Leary rep Wright 81. **Sheffield Wed 1** (Waddle) Woods; Nilsson, Worthington, Palmer, Hirst, Wilson, Waddle, Warhurst, Bright, Sheridan, Harkes. Subs: Hyde rep Wilson 62; Bart-Williams rep Nilsson 118. May 20; 62, 267; K Barratt. aet

1994   Manchester Utd 4 (Cantona 2 [2pens], Hughes, McClair) Schmeichel; Parker, Bruce, Pallister, Irwin, Kanchelskis, Keane, Ince, Giggs, Cantona, Hughes. Subs: Sharpe rep Irwin 84; McClair rep Kanchelskis 84. Unused sub: Walsh (gk) **Chelsea 0** Kharine; Clarke, Sinclair, Kjeldberg, Johnsen, Burley, Spencer, Newton, Stein, Peacock, Wise Substitutions Hoddle rep Burley 65; Cascarino rep Stein 78. Unused sub: Kevin Hitchcock (gk) May 14; 79, 634; D Elleray

1995   Everton 1 (Rideout) Southall; Jackson, Hinchcliffe, Ablett, Watson, Parkinson, Unsworth, Horne, Stuart, Rideout, Limpar. Subs: Ferguson rep Rideout 51; Amokachi rep Limpar 69. Unused sub: Kearton (gk) **Manchester Utd 0** Schmeichel; Gary Neville, Irwin, Bruce, Sharpe, Pallister, Keane, Ince, Brian McClair, Hughes, Butt. Subs: Giggs rep Bruce 46; Scholes rep Sharpe 72. Unused sub: Gary Walsh (gk) May 20; 79, 592; G Ashby

1996   Manchester Utd 1 (Cantona) Schmeichel; Irwin, Phil Neville, May, Keane, Pallister, Cantona, Beckham, Cole, Butt, Giggs. Subs: Scholes rep Cole 65; Gary Neville rep Beckham 89. Unused sub: Sharpe **Liverpool 0** James; McAteer, Scales, Wright, Babb, Jones, McManaman, Barnes, Redknapp, Collymore, Fowler. Subs: Rush rep Collymore 74; Thomas rep Jones 85. Unused sub: Warner (gk) May 11; 79, 007; D Gallagher

1997   Chelsea 2 (Di Matteo, Newton) Grodas; Petrescu, Minto, Sinclair, Lebouef, Clarke, Zola, Di Matteo, Newton, Hughes, Wise. Sub: Vialli rep Zola 89. Unused subs: Hitchcock (gk), Myers **Middlesbrough 0** Roberts; Blackmore, Fleming, Stamp, Pearson, Festa, Emerson, Mustoe, Ravanelli, Juninho, Hignett. Subs: Beck rep Ravanelli 24; Vickers rep Mustoe 29; Kinder, rep Hignett 74. May 17; 79, 160; S Lodge

1998   Arsenal 2 (Overmars, Anelka) Seaman; Dixon, Winterburn, Vieira, Keown, Adams, Parlour, Anelka, Petit, Wreh, Overmars. Sub: Platt rep Wreh 63. Unused subs: Manninger (gk); Bould, Wright, Grimandi **Newcastle 0** Given; Pistone, Pearce, Batty, Dabizas, Howey, Lee, Barton, Shearer, Ketsbaia, Speed. Subs: Andersson rep Pearce 72; Watson rep Barton 77; Barnes rep Ketsbaia 85. Unused subs: Hislop (gk); Albert. May 16; 79, 183; P Durkin

1999   Manchester Utd 2 (Sheringham, Scholes) Schmeichel; Gary Neville, Johnsen, May, Phil Neville, Beckham, Scholes, Keane, Giggs, Cole, Solskjaer. Subs: Sheringham rep Keane 9; Yorke rep Cole 61; Stam rep Scholes 77. Unused subs: Blomqvist, Van Der Gouw **Newcastle 0** Harper; Griffin, Charvet, Dabizas, Domi, Lee, Hamann, Speed, Solano, Ketsbaia, Shearer. Subs: Ferguson rep Hamann 46; Maric rep Solano 68; Glass rep Ketsbaia 79. Unused subs: Given (gk); Barton. May 22; 79, 101; P Jones

2000   Chelsea 1 (Di Matteo) de Goey; Melchiot Desailly, Lebouef, Babayaro, Di Matteo, Wise, Deschamps, Poyet, Weah, Zola. Subs: Flo rep Weah 87; Morris rep Zola 90. Unused subs: Cudicini (gk), Terry , Harley **Aston Villa 0** James; Ehiogu, Southgate, Barry, Delaney, Taylor, Boateng, Merson,

156

Wright, Dublin, Carbone. Subs: Stone rep Taylor 79; Joachim rep Carbone 79; Hendrie rep Wright 88. Unused subs: Enckelman (gk); Samuel May 20; 78, 217; G Poll

2001 Liverpool 2 (Owen 2) Westerveld; Babbel, Henchoz, Hyypia, Carragher, Murphy, Hamann, Gerrard, Smicer, Heskey, Owen. Subs: McAllister rep Hamann 60; Fowler rep Smicer 77; Berger rep Murphy 77. Unused subs: Arphexad (gk); Vignal **Arsenal 1** (Ljungberg) Seaman; Dixon, Keown, Adams, Cole, Ljungberg, Grimandi, Vieira, Pires, Henry, Wiltord Subs: Parlour rep Wiltord 76; Kanu rep Ljungberg 85; Bergkamp rep Dixon 90. Unused subs: Manninger (gk); Lauren. May 12; 72, 500; S Dunn

2002 Arsenal 2 (Parlour, Ljungberg) Seaman; Lauren, Campbell, Adams, Cole, Parlour, Wiltord, Vieira, Ljungberg, Bergkamp, Henry Subs: Edu rep Bergkamp 72; Kanu rep Henry 81; Keown rep Wiltord 90. Unused subs: Wright (gk); Dixon **Chelsea 0** Cudicini; Melchiot, Desailly, Gallas, Babayaro, Gronkjaer, Lampard, Petit, Le Saux, Floyd Hasselbaink, Gudjohnsen. Subs: Terry rep Babayaro 46; Zola rep Hasselbaink 68; Zenden rep Melchiot 77. Unused subs: de Goey (gk); Jokanovic. May 4; 73, 963; M Riley

2003 Arsenal 1 (Pires) Seaman; Lauren, Luzhny, Keown, Cole, Ljungberg, Parlour, Gilberto, Pires, Bergkamp, Henry. Sub: Wiltord rep Bergkamp 77. Unused subs: Taylor (gk); Kanu, Toure, van Bronckhorst **Southampton 0** Niemi; Baird, Svensson, Lundekvam, Bridge, Telfer, Svensson, Oakley, Marsden, Beattie, Ormerod. Subs: Jones rep Niemi 66; Fernandes rep Baird 87; Tessem rep Svensson 75. Unused subs: Williams, Higginbotham. May 17; 73, 726; G Barber

2004 Manchester Utd 3 (Van Nistelrooy [2, 1 pen], Ronaldo) Howard; Gary Neville, Brown, Silvestre, O'Shea, Fletcher, Keane, Ronaldo, Scholes, Giggs, Van Nistelrooy. Subs: Carroll rep Howard, Butt rep Fletcher, Solskjaer rep Ronaldo 84. Unused subs: P Neville, Djemba-Djemba **Millwall 0** Marshall; Elliott, Lawrence, Ward, Ryan, Wise, Ifill, Cahill, Livermore, Sweeney, Harris. Subs: Cogan rep Ryan, McCammon rep Harris 74 Weston rep Wise 88. Unused subs: Gueret (gk); Dunne. May 22; 71, 350; J Winter

2005 Arsenal 0 Lehmann; Lauren, Toure, Senderos, Cole, Fabregas, Gilberto, Vieira, Pires, Reyes, Bergkamp Subs: Ljungberg rep Bergkamp 65, Van Persie rep Fabregas 86, Edu rep Pires 105. Unused subs: Almunia (gk); Campbell. Reyes sent off 90. **Manchester Utd 0** Carroll; Brown, Ferdinand, Silvestre, O'Shea, Fletcher, Keane, Scholes, Rooney, Van Nistelrooy, Ronaldo. Subs: Fortune rep O'Shea 77, Giggs rep Fletcher 91. Unused subs: Howard (gk); G Neville, Smith. **Arsenal** (Lauren, Ljungberg, van Persie, Cole, Vieira) beat Manchester Utd (van Nistelrooy, Scholes [missed], Ronaldo, Rooney, Keane) 5-4 on penalties. May 21; 71, 876; R Styles

2006 Liverpool 3 (Gerrard 2, Cisse) Reina; Finnan, Carragher, Hyypiä, Riise, Gerrard, Xabi, Sissoko, Kewell, Cisse, Crouch. Subs: Morientes rep Kewell 48; Kromkamp rep Alonso 67, Hamman rep Crouch 71. Unused subs: Dudek (gk); Traoré **West Ham 3** (Ashton, Konchesky, Carragher (og)) Hislop; Scaloni, Ferdinand, Gabbidon, Konchesky, Benayoun, Fletcher, Reo-Coker, Etherington, Ashton, Harewood. Subs: Zamora rep Ashton 71, Dailly rep Fletcher, Sheringham rep Etherington 85. Unused subs: Walker (gk); Collins. **Liverpool** (Hamann, Hyypiä [missed], Gerrard, Riise) beat **West Ham** (Zamora [missed], Sheringham, Konchesky [missed], Ferdinand [missed]) 3-1 on penalties. May 13; 71, 140; A Wiley

2007 Chelsea 1 (Drogba) Cech, Ferreira, Essien, Terry, Bridge, Mikel, Makelele, Lampard, Wright-Phillips, Drogba, Joe Cole Subs: Robben rep J Cole 45, Kalou rep Wright-Phillips 93, A Cole rep Robben 108. Unused subs: Cudicini (gk); Diarra. **Manchester Utd 0** Van der Sar, Brown, Ferdinand, Vidic, Heinze, Fletcher, Scholes, Carrick, Ronaldo, Rooney, Giggs Subs: Smith rep Fletcher 92, O'Shea rep Carrick, Solskjaer rep Giggs 112. Unused subs: Kuszczak (gk); Evra. May 19; 89, 826; S Bennett

2008 Portsmouth 1 (Kanu) James; Johnson, Campbell, Distin, Hreidarsson, Utaka, Muntari, Mendes, Diarra, Kranjcar, Kanu. Subs: Nugent rep Utaka 69, Diop rep Mendes 78, Baros rep Kanu 87. Unused subs: Ashdown (gk); Pamarot. **Cardiff 0** Enckelman; McNaughton, Johnson, Loovens, Capaldi, Whittingham, Rae, McPhail, Ledley, Hasselbaink, Parry. Subs: Ramsey rep Whittingham 62, Thompson rep Hasselbaink 70, Sinclair rep Rae 87. Unused subs: Oakes (gk); Purse. May 17; 89, 874; M Dean

2009 Chelsea 2 (Drogba, Lampard) Cech; Bosingwa, Alex, Terry, Ashley Cole, Essien, Mikel, Lampard, Drogba, Anelka, Malouda. Subs: Ballack rep Essien 61. Unused subs: Hilario (gk), Ivanovic, Di Santo, Kalou, Belletti, Mancienne. **Everton 1** (Saha) Howard; Hibbert, Yobo, Lescott, Baines, Osman, Neville, Cahill, Pienaar, Fellaini, Saha. Subs: Jacobsen rep Hibbert 46, Vaughan rep Saha 77, Gosling rep Osman 83. Unused subs: Nash, Castillo, Rodwell, Baxter. May 30; 89, 391; H Webb

2010 Chelsea 1 (Drogba) Cech; Ivanovic, Alex, Terry, Ashley Cole, Lampard, Ballack, Malouda, Kalou, Drogba, Anelka. Subs: Belletti rep Ballack 44, J Cole rep Kalou 71, Sturridge rep Anelka 90. Unused subs: Hilario (gk), Zhirkov, Paulo Ferreira, Matic. **Portsmouth 0** James; Finnan, Mokoena, Rocha,

Mullins, Dindane, Brown, Diop, Boateng, O'Hara, Piquionne. Subs: Utaka rep Boateng 73, Belhadj rep Mullins 81, Kanu rep Diop 81. Unused subs: Ashdown (gk), Vanden Borre, Hughes, Ben Haim. May 15; 88, 335; C Foy

2011   Manchester City 1 (Y Toure) Hart; Richards, Kompany, Lescott, Kolarov, De Jong, Barry, Silva, Y Toure, Balotelli, Tevez. Subs: Johnson rep Barry73, Zabaleta rep Tevez 87, Vieira rep Silva 90. Unused subs: Given (gk), Boyata, Milner, Dzeko. **Stoke 0** Sorensen; Wilkinson, Shawcross, Huth, Wilson, Pennant, Whelan, Delap, Etherington, Walters, Jones. Subs: Whitehead rep Etherington 62, Carew rep Delap 80, Pugh rep Whelan 84. Unused subs: Nash (gk), Collins, Faye, Diao. May 14; 88, 643; M Atkinson

2012   Chelsea 2 (Ramires, Drogba) Cech; Bosingwa, Ivanovic, Terry, Ashley Cole, Mikel, Lampard, Ramires, Mata, Kalou, Drogba. Subs: Meireles rep Ramires76, Malouda rep Mata 90. Unused subs: Turnbull (gk), Paulo Ferreira, Essien, Torres, Sturridge. **Liverpool 1** (Carroll) Reina; Johnson, Skrtel, Agger, Luis Enrique, Spearing, Bellamy, Henderson, Gerrard, Downing, Suarez. Subs Carroll rep Spearing 55, Kuyt rep Bellamy 78. Unused subs: Doni (gk), Carragher, Kelly, Shelvey, Rodriguez. May 5; 89, 102; P Dowd

2013   Wigan 1 (Watson) Robles; Boyce, Alcaraz, Scharner, McCarthy, McArthur, McManaman, Maloney, Gomez, Espinoza, Kone. Subs: Watson rep Gomez 81. Unused subs: Al Habsi (gk), Caldwell, Golobart, Fyvie, Henriquez, Di Santo. **Manchester City 0** Hart; Zabaleta, Kompany, Nastasic, Clichy, Toure, Barry, Silva, Tevez, Nasri, Aguero. Subs: Milner rep Nasri 54, Rodwell rep Tevez 69, Dzeko rep Barry 90. Unused subs: Pantilimon (gk), Lescott, Kolarov, Garcia. Sent off Zabaleta (84). May 11; 86, 254; A Marriner

2014   Arsenal 3 (Cazorla, Koscielny, Ramsey) Fabianski; Sagna, Koscielny, Mertesacker, Gibbs, Arteta, Ramsey, Cazorla, Ozil, Podolski, Giroud. Subs: Sanogo rep Podolski 61, Rosicky rep Cazorla 106, Wilshire rep Ozil 106. Unused subs: Szczesny (gk), Vermaelen, Monreal, Flamini. **Hull 2** (Chester, Davies) McGregor; Davies, Bruce, Chester, Elmohamady, Livermore, Huddlestone, Meyler, Rosenior, Quinn, Fryatt. Subs: McShane rep Bruce 67, Aluko rep Quinn 71, Boyd rep Rosenior 102. Unused subs: Harper (gk), Figueroa, Koren, Sagbo. May 17; 89, 345; L Probert. aet

2015   Arsenal 4 (Walcott, Sanchez, Mertesacker, Giroud) Szczesny; Bellerin, Koscielny, Mertesacker, Monreal, Coquelin, Cazorla, Ramsey, Ozil, A Sanchez, Walcott. Subs: Wilshere rep Ozil 77, Giroud rep Walcott 77, Oxlade-Chamberlain rep A Sanchez 90. Unused subs: Ospina (gk), Gibbs, Gabriel, Flamini. **Aston Villa 0** Given; Hutton, Okore, Vlaar, Richardson, Cleverley, Westwood, Delph, N'Zogbia, Benteke, Grealish. Subs: Agbonlahor rep N'Zogbia 53, Bacuna rep Richardson 68, C Sanchez rep Westwood 71. Unused subs: Guzan (gk), Baker, Sinclair, Cole. May 30; 89, 283; J Moss

2016   Manchester Utd 2 (Mata, Lingard) De Gea, Valencia, Smalling, Blind, Rojo, Carrick, Rooney, Fellaini, Mata, Martial, Rashford. Subs: Darmian rep Rojo 65, Young rep Rashford 71, Lingard rep Mata 90. Unused subs: Romero, Jones, Herrera, Schneiderlin. Smalling sent off 105 . **Crystal Palace 1** (Puncheon) Hennessey, Ward, Dann, Delaney, Souare, Cabaye, Jedinak, Zaha, McArthur, Bolasie, Wickham. Subs: Puncheon rep Cabaye 72, Gayle rep Wickham 86, Mariappa rep Dann 90 May 21; 88, 619; M Clattenburg

2017   Arsenal 2 (Sanchez, Ramsey) Ospina, Holding, Mertesacker, Monreal, Bellerin, Ramsey, Xhaka, Oxlade-Chamberlain, Sanchez, Ozil, Welbeck. Subs: Giroud rep Welbeck78, Coquelin rep Oxlade-Chamberlain 83, Elneny rep Sanchez 90. Unused subs: Cech (gk), Walcott, Iwobi, Lucas Perez. **Chelsea 1** (Diego Costa) Courtois, Azpilicueta, Luiz, Cahill, Moses, Kante, Matic, Alonso, Pedro, Diego Costa, Hazard. Subs Fabregas rep Matic 62, Willian rep Pedro 72, Batshuayi rep Diego Costa 88. Unused subs: Begovic (gk), Terry, Zouma, Ake, Moses sent off 68. May 27; 89, 472; A Taylor

2018   Chelsea 1 (Hazard pen) Courtois, Azpilicueta, Cahill, Rudiger, Moses, Fabregas, Kante, Bakayoko, Alonso, Hazard, Giroud. Subs: Morata rep Giroud 89, Willian rep Hazard 90. Unused subs: Caballero (gk), Barkley, Pedro, Zappacosta, Chalobah. **Manchester Utd 0** De Gea, Valencia, Smalling, Jones, Young, Herrera, Matic, Pogba, Lingard, Sanchez, Rashford. Subs: Martial rep Lingard 73, Lukaku rep Rashford 73, Mata rep Jones 87. Unused subs: Romero (gk), Bailly, Darmian, McTominay. May 19, 87, 647; M Oliver

2019   Manchester City 6 (Gabriel Jesus 2, Sterling 2, David Silva, De Bruyne) Ederson, Walker, Kompany, Laporte, Zinchenko, Gundogan, David Silva, Bernardo Silva, Mahrez, Gabriel Jesus, Sterling. Subs: De Bruyne rep Mahrez 55, Sane rep Gundogan 73, Stones rep Davi Silva 79. Unused subs:

Muric (gk), Danilo, Otamendi, Aguero. **Watford 0** Gomes, Femenia, Mariappa, Cathcart, Holebas, Hughes, Capoue, Doucoure, Pereyra, Deulofeu, Deeney, Subs: Success rep Pereyra 65, Gray rep Deulofeu 65, Cleverley rep Hughes 73. Unused subs: Foster (gk), Janmaat, Masina, Kabasele. May 18; 85, 854; K Friend

2020 Arsenal 2 (Aubameyang 28 pen, 67) Martinez, Holding, Luiz, Tierney, Bellerin, Ceballos, Xhaka, Maitland-Niles, Pepe, Lacazette, Aubameyang. Subs: Nketiah rep Lacazette 82, Sokratis rep Luiz 88, Kolasinac rep Tierney 90. Unused subs: Macey (gk), Torreira, Nelson, Willock, Smith Rowe, Saka. **Chelsea 1** (Pulisic 5) Caballero, Azpilicueta, Zouma, Rudiger, James, Jorginho, Kovacic, Marcos Alonso, Mount, Pulisic, Giroud. Subs: Christensen rep Azpilicueta 35, Pedro rep Pulisic 49, Hudson-Odoi rep Rudiger 78, Barkley rep Mount 78, Abraham rep Giroud 78. Unused subs: Arrizabalaga (gk), Kante, Tomori, Emerson. August 1; behind closed doors; A Taylor

2021 Leicester 1 (Tielemans) Schmeichel, Fofana, Evans, Soyuncu, Castagne, Tielemans, Ndidi, Thomas, Ayoze Perez, Iheanacho, Vardy. Subs: Albrighton rep Evans, Maddison rep Iheanacho, Morgan rep Thomas, Choudhury rep Ayoze Perez. Unused subs: Ward (gk), Amartey, Ricardo Pereira, N Mendy, Praet. **Chelsea** Arrizabalaga, James, Thiago Silva, Rudiger, Azpilicueta, Kante, Jorginho, Marcos Alonso, Ziyech, Mount, Werner. Subs: Chilwell rep Marcos Alonso, Pulisic rep Ziyech, Havertz rep Jorginho, Hudson-Odoi rep Azpilicueta, Giroud rep Werner. Unused subs: Mendy (gk), Zouma, Gilmour, Emerson. May 15, 21,000, M Oliver

VENUES

Kennington Oval 1872; **Lillie Bridge** 1873; **Kennington Oval** 1874–1892 (1886 replay at the **Racecourse Ground, Derby**); **Fallowfield, Manchester**, 1893; **Goodison Park** 1894; **Crystal Palace** 1895–1914 (1901 replay at **Burnden Park**; 1910 replay at **Goodison Park**; 1911 replay at **Old Trafford**; 1912 replay at **Bramall Lane**);; **Old Trafford** 1915; **Stamford Bridge** 1920–1922; **Wembley** 1923–2000 (1970 replay at **Old Trafford**; all replays from 1981 at **Wembley**); **Millennium Stadium** 2001–2006; **Wembley** 2007–2022

SUMMARY OF FA CUP WINS

Arsenal	14	Sheffield Wed	3	Clapham Rov	1
Manchester Utd	12	West Ham	3	Coventry	1
Tottenham	8	Bury	2	Derby	1
Chelsea	8	Nottm Forest	2	Huddersfield	1
Liverpool	8	Old Etonians	2	Ipswich	1
Aston Villa	7	Portsmouth	2	Leeds	1
Blackburn Rov	6	Preston	2	Leicester	1
Manchester City	6	Sunderland	2	Notts Co	1
Newcastle	6	Barnsley	1	Old Carthusians	1
Everton	5	Blackburn Olympic	1	Oxford University	1
The Wanderers	5	Blackpool	1	Royal Engineers	1
WBA	5	Bradford City	1	Southampton	1
Bolton	4	Burnley	1	Wigan	1
Sheffield Utd	4	Cardiff	1	Wimbledon	1
Wolves	4	Charlton	1		

APPEARANCES IN FINALS (Figures do not include replays)

Arsenal	21	WBA	10	Sheffield Wed	6
Manchester Utd	20	Tottenham	9	Huddersfield	5
Chelsea	16	Blackburn Rov	8	Leicester	5
Liverpool	15	Wolves	8	Portsmouth	5
Everton	13	Bolton	7	The Wanderers*	5
Newcastle	13	Preston	7	West Ham	5
Aston Villa	11	Old Etonians	6	Derby	4
Manchester City	11	Sheffield Utd	6	Leeds	4

Oxford University 4	Clapham Rov..................2	Ipswich* 1
Royal Engineers.............4	Crystal Palace 2	Luton 1
Southampton 4	Notts Co 2	Middlesbrough 1
Sunderland 4	Queen's Park (Glasgow)..2	Millwall 1
Blackpool.....................3	Watford.......................2	Old Carthusians* 1
Burnley 3	Blackburn Olympic*.......1	QPR 1
Cardiff.........................3	Bradford City* 1	Stoke...........................1
Nottm Forest................3	Brighton 1	Wigan 1
Barnsley 2	Bristol City...................1	Wimbledon* 1
Birmingham 2	Coventry*.....................1	(* Denotes undefeated)
Bury* 2	Fulham 1	
Charlton.......................2	Hull 1	

APPEARANCES IN SEMI-FINALS (Figures do not include replays)

31 Manchester Utd; **30** Arsenal; **26** Chelsea, Everton; **25** Liverpool; **21** Aston Villa, Tottenham; **20** WBA; **18** Blackburn; **17** Manchester City, Newcastle; **16** Sheffield Wed; **15** Wolves; **14** Bolton, Sheffield Utd; **13** Derby, Southampton; **12** Nottm Forest, Sunderland; **10** Preston; **9** Birmingham; **8** Burnley, Leeds, Leicester; **7** Huddersfield, Portsmouth, Watford, West Ham; **6** Fulham, Newcastle Old Etonians, Oxford University; **5** *Crystal Palace, Millwall, Notts Co, The Wanderers; **4** Cardiff, Luton, Queen's Park (Glasgow), Royal Engineers, Stoke; **3** Barnsley, Blackwood, Clapham Rov, Ipswich, Middlesbrough, Norwich, Old Carthusians, Oldham, The Swifts; **2** Blackburn Olympic, Brighton, Bristol City, Bury, Charlton, Grimsby, Hull, Reading, Swansea, Swindon, Wigan, Wimbledon; **1** Bradford City, Cambridge University, Chesterfield, Coventry, Crewe, Darwen, Derby Junction, Marlow, Old Harrovians, Orient, Plymouth Argyle, Port Vale, QPR, Rangers (Glasgow), Shropshire Wand, Wycombe, York

(*A previous and different Crystal Palace club also reached the semi-final in season 1871–72)

CARABAO EFL CUP 2021–22

FIRST ROUND

Barrow 1 Scunthorpe 0
Birmingham 1 Colchester 0
Blackburn 1 Morecambe 2
Blackpool 3 Middlesbrough 0
Bolton 0 Barnsley 0
(Bolton won 5-4 on pens)
Bristol Rov 0 Cheltenham 2
Burton 1 Oxford 1
(Oxford won 4-2 on pens)
Cambridge 0 Swindon 0
(Cambridge won 3-1 on pens)
Cardiff 3 Sutton 2
Charlton 0 AFC Wimbledon 1
Coventry 1 Northampton 2
Crawley 2 Gillingham 2
(Gillingham won 10-9 on pens)
Derby 3 Salford 3
(Derby won 5-3 on pens)
Exeter 0 Wycombe 0
(Wycombe won 4-3 on pens)
Forest Green 2 Bristol City 2
(Forest Green won 6-5 on pens)
Harrogate v Rochdale – postponed

(Rochdale awarded a bye)
Hartlepool 0 Crewe 1
Hull 1 Wigan 1
(Wigan won 8-7 on pens)
Ipswich 0 Newport 1
Leyton Orient 1 QPR 1
(QPR won 5-3 on pens)
Mansfield 0 Preston 3
Millwall 2 Portsmouth 1
Nottm Forest 2 Bradford 1
Oldham 2 Tranmere 2
(Oldham won 4-3 on pens)
Peterborough 4 Plymouth 4
Port Vale 1 Sunderland 2
Reading 0 Swansea 3
Rotherham 1 Accrington 2
Sheffield Utd 1 Carlisle 0
Sheffield Wed 0 Huddersfield 0
(Huddersfield won 4-2 on pens)
Shrewsbury 3 Lincoln 2
(Shrewsbury won 4-2 on pens)
Stevenage 2 Luton 2
(Stevenage won 3-0 on pens)

Stoke 2 Fleetwood 1
Walsall 0 Doncaster 0

(Doncaster won 4-3 on pens)

SECOND ROUND

Barrow 0 Aston Villa 6
Birmingham 0 Fulham 2
Blackpool 2 Sunderland 3
Brentford 3 Forest Green 1
Cardiff 0 Brighton 2
Gillingham 1 Cheltenham 1
(Cheltenham won 5-4 on pens)
Huddersfield 1 Everton 2
Leeds 3 Crewe 0
Millwall 3 Cambridge 1
Morecambe 2 Preston 4
Newcastle 0 Burnley 0
(Burnley won 4-3 on pens)
Newport 0 Southampton 8
Northampton 0 AFC Wimbledon 1

Norwich 6 Bournemouth 0
Nottm Forest 0 Wolves 4
Oldham 0 Accrington 0
(Oldham won 5-4 on pens)
QPR 2 Oxford 0
Sheffield Utd 2 Derby 1
Shrewsbury 0 Rochdale 2
Stevenage 2 Wycombe 2
(Wycombe won 5-3 on pens)
Stoke 2 Doncaster 0
Swansea 4 Plymouth 1
Watford 1 Crystal Palace 0
WBA 0 Arsenal 6
Wigan 0 Bolton 0
(Wigan won 5-4 on pens).

THIRD ROUND

Arsenal 3 AFC Wimbledon 0
Brentford 7 Oldham 0
Brighton 2 Swansea 0
Burnley 4 Rochdale 1
Chelsea 1 Aston Villa 1
(Chelsea won 4-3 on perns)
Fulham 0 Leeds 0
(Leeds won 6-5 on pens)
Manchester City 6 Wycombe 1
Manchester Utd 0 West Ham 1
Millwall 0 Leicester 2

Norwich 0 **Liverpool** 3
Preston 4 Cheltenham 1
QPR 2 Everton 2
(QPR won 8-7 on pens)
Sheffield Utd 2 Southampton 2
(Southampton won 4-2 on pens)
Watford 1 Stoke 3
Wigan 0 Sunderland 2
Wolves 2 Tottenham 2
(Tottenham won 3-2 on pens)

FOURTH ROUND

Arsenal 2 Leeds 0
Burnley 0 Tottenham 1
Chelsea 1 Southampton 1
(Chelsea won 4-3 on pens)
Leicester 2 Brighton 2
(Leicester won 4-2 on pens)

Preston 1 **Liverpool** 2
QPR 0 Sunderland 0
(Sunderland won 3-1 on pens)
Stoke 1 Brentford 2
West Ham 0 Manchester City 0
(West Ham won 5-3 on pens)

QUARTER-FINALS

Arsenal 5 Sunderland 1
Brentford 0 **Chelsea** 2
Liverpool 3 Leicester 3

(Liverpool won 5-4 on pens)
Tottenham 2 West Ham 1

SEMI-FINALS (two legs)

Chelsea 2 Tottenham 0
Tottenham 0 **Chelsea** 1

Liverpool 0 Arsenal 0
Arsenal 0 **Liverpool** 2

FINAL

CHELSEA 0 LIVERPOOL 0 (aet, Liverpool won 11-10 on pens)
Wembley (85,512); February 27, 2022

Chelsea (3-4-3): Mendy (Arrizabalaga 120), Chalobah, Thiago Silva, Rudiger, Azpilicueta (capt) (James 57), Kante, Kovacic (Jorginho 105), Marcos Alonso, Pulisic (Werner 73), Havertz, Mount (Lukaku 73). **Subs not used:** Hudson-Odoi, Saul, Loftus-Cheek, Sarr. **Booked:** Kovacic, Kante, Havertz. **Manager:** Thomas Tuchel
Liverpool (4-3-3): Kelleher, Alexander-Arnold, Matip (Konate 91), Van Dijk, Robertson, Henderson (capt) (Elliott 80), Fabinho, Keita (Milner 80), Salah, Mane (Diogo Jota 80), Diaz (Origi 98). **Subs not used:** Alisson, Tsimikas, Minamino, Oxlade-Chamberlain. **Booked:** Alexander-Arnold. **Manager:** Jurgen Klopp
Referee: Stuart Attwell (Warwicks)
Penalty shoot-out: Chelsea – scored: Marcos Alonso, Lukaku, Havertz, James, Jorginho, Rudiger, Kante, Werner, Thiago Silva, Chalobah; missed – Arrizabalaga. **Liverpool** – scored: Milner, Fabinho, Van Dijk, Alexander-Arnold, Salah, Diogo Jota, Origi, Robertson, Elliott, Konate, Kelleher

There has never been a Wembley occasion like it, with Russia's invasion of Ukraine casting a shadow before, during and in the immediate aftermath. On the eve of the final, Wembley lit up the stadium arch in the blue and yellow of the Ukrainian flag. At the same time, Chelsea owner Roman Abramovich was announcing his intention to hand over 'stewardship' to the club's charitable foundation. As the teams walked out, captains Cesar Azpilicueta and Jordan Henderson carried a blue and yellow wreath. Managers Thomas Tuchel and Jurgen Klopp carried it off amid a minute's applause from a packed stadium. Tuchel had admitted that the invasion cast a pall over Stamford Bridge, but in a game bearing no resemblance to the customary dour, defence-dominated goalless draw, his side played with great energy, had three goals disallowed and with steadier finishing would have added the League Cup to their newly acquired World Club title. Liverpool, too, displayed the confidence of a side chasing honours in four directions and had the final say in a marathon penalty shoot-out unprecedented in English top-flight football. It boiled down to the two goalkeepers, both understudies in the Premier League, but this time taking centre stage. Klopp rewarded Caoimhin Kelleher for his performances in earlier rounds with a starting place, the Republic of Ireland international repaying him with some fine saves, followed by his team's final successful spot-kick against Kepa Arrizabalaga, the player brought off the bench a minute from the end of extra-time at Chelsea's specialist penalty saver. The move had not gone to plan and neither did his own effort which sailed over the crossbar to present Liverpool with a record ninth success in the competition, courtesy of an 11-10 scoreline. Two day later, Abramovich bowed to pressure and put his club up for sale – again making no mention of the war.

HOW THEY REACHED THE FINAL

Chelsea
Round 3: 1-1 home to Aston Villa (Werner) – won 4-3 on pens
Round 4: 1-1 home to Southampton (Havertz) – won 4-3 on pens
Quarter-final: 2-0 away to Brentford (Jansson og, Jorginho pen)
Semi-final v Tottenham: first leg, 2-0 home (Havertz, Davies og); second leg, 1-0 away (Rudiger)

Liverpool
Round 3: 3-0 away to Norwich (Minamino 2, Origi)
Round 4: 2-0 away to Preston (Minamino, Origi)
Quarter-final: 3-3 home to Leicester (Oxlade-Chamberlain, Diogo Jota, Minamino) – won 5-4 on pens
Semi-final: v Arsenal: first leg, 0-0 home; second leg, 2-0 away (Diogo Jota 2)

LEAGUE CUP – COMPLETE RESULTS

LEAGUE CUP FINALS

1961* Aston Villa beat Rotherham 3-2 on agg (0-2a, 3-0h)
1962 Norwich beat Rochdale 4-0 on agg (3-0a, 1-0h)
1963 Birmingham beat Aston Villa 3-1 o agg (3-1h, 0-0a)
1964 Leicester beat Stoke 4-3 on agg (1-1a, 3-2h)
1965 Chelsea beat Leicester 3-2 on agg (3-2h, 0-0a)
1966 WBA beat West Ham 5-3 on agg (1-2a, 4-1h)

AT WEMBLEY

1967 QPR 3 WBA 2
1968 Leeds 1 Arsenal 0
1969* Swindon 3 Arsenal 1
1970* Man City 2 WBA 1
1971 Tottenham 2 Aston Villa 0
1972 Stoke 2 Chelsea 1
1973 Tottenham 1 Norwich 0
1974 Wolves 2 Man City 1
1975 Aston Villa 1 Norwich 0
1976 Man City 2 Newcastle 1
1977†* Aston Villa 3 Everton 2 after 0-0 and1-1
1978†† Nottm Forest 1 Liverpool 0 after 0-0
1979 Nottm Forest 3 Southampton 2
1980 Wolves 1 Nottm Forest 0
1981††† Liverpool 2 West Ham 1 (after 1-1)

MILK CUP

1982* Liverpool 3 Tottenham 1
1983* Liverpool 2 Man Utd 1
1984** Liverpool 1 Everton 0 after *0 0 draw
1985 Norwich 1 Sunderland 0
1986 Oxford Utd 3 QPR 0

LITTLEWOODS CUP

1987 Arsenal 2 Liverpool 1
1988 Luton 3 Arsenal 2
1989 Nottm Forest 3 Luton 1
1990 Nottm Forest 1 Oldham 0

RUMBELOWS CUP

1991 Sheffield Wed 1 Man Utd 0
1992 Man Utd 1 Nottm Forest 0

COCA COLA CUP

1993 Arsenal 2 Sheffield Wed 1
1994 Aston Villa 3 Man Utd 1
1995 Liverpool 2 Bolton 1
1996 Aston Villa 3 Leeds 0
1997*** Leicester 1Middlesbrough 0 (after *1-1)
1998 Chelsea 2 Middlesbrough 0

WORTHINGTON CUP (at Millennium Stadium from 2001)

1999 Tottenham 1 Leicester 0
2000 Leicester 2 Tranmere 1
2001 Liverpool 1 Birmingham 1 (Liverpool won 5-4 on pens)
2002 Blackburn 2 Tottenham 1
2003 Liverpool 2 Man Utd 0

CARLING CUP (at Wembley from 2008)

2004 Middlesbrough 2 Bolton 1
2005* Chelsea 3 Liverpool 2
2006 Man Utd 4 Wigan 0
2007 Chelsea 2 Arsenal 1
2008* Tottenham 2 Chelsea 1
2009 Man Utd 0 Tottenham 0 (Man Utd won 4-1 on pens)
2010 Man Utd 2 Aston Villa 1
2011 Birmingham 2 Arsenal 1
2012 Liverpool 2 Cardiff 2 (Liverpool won 3-2 on pens

CAPITAL ONE CUP (at Wembley from 2013)

2013 Swansea 5 Bradford 0
2014 Manchester City 3 Sunderland 1
2015 Chelsea 2 Tottenham 0
2016 Man City 1 Liverpool 1 Man City won 3-1 on pens

* After extra time. † First replay at Hillsborough, second replay at Old Trafford. †† Replayed at Old Trafford. ††† Replayed at Villa Park. ** Replayed at Maine Road. *** Replayed at Hillsborough

EFL CUP (at Wembley from 2017)

2017 Man Utd Utd 3 Southampton 2

CARABAO CUP (at Wembley from 2018)

2018 Man City 3 Arsenal 0
2019 Man City 0 Chelsea 0

	Man City won 4-3 on pens	2022	Chelsea 0 Liverpool 0
2020	Man City 2 Aston Villa 1		(aet, Liverpool won 11-10 on pens)
2021	Manchester City 1 Tottenham 0		

SUMMARY OF LEAGUE CUP WINNERS

Liverpool 9	Arsenal.........................2	Oxford Utd 1
Manchester City...........8	Birmingham 2	QPR.............................. 1
Aston Villa 5	Norwich 2	Sheffield Wed 1
Chelsea 5	Wolves 2	Stoke 1
Manchester Utd...........5	Blackburn 1	Swansea....................... 1
Nottm Forest................4	Leeds. 1	Swindon 1
Tottenham....................4	Luton 1	WBA 1
Leicester......................3	Middlesbrough 1	

LEAGUE CUP FINAL APPEARANCES

13 Liverpool; **10** Chelsea,; **9**, Aston Villa, Manchester City, Manchester Utd; **8** Arsenal, Tottenham **6** Nottm Forest; **5** Leicester; **4** Norwich; **3** Birmingham, Middlesbrough, WBA; **2** Bolton, Everton, Leeds, Luton, QPR, Sheffield Wed, Southampton, Stoke, Sunderland, West Ham, Wolves; **1** Blackburn, Bradford, Cardiff, Newcastle, Oldham, Oxford Utd, Rochdale, Rotherham, Swansea, Swindon, Tranmere, Wigan (Figures do not include replays)

LEAGUE CUP SEMI-FINAL APPEARANCES

19 Tottenham; **18** Liverpool; **16** Arsenal, Manchester Utd; **15** Aston Villa, Chelsea; **13** Manchester City; **9** West Ham; **6** Blackburn, Leicester, Nottm Forest; **5** Birmingham, Everton, Leeds, Middlesbrough, Norwich; **4** Bolton, Burnley, Crystal Palace, Ipswich, Sheffield Wed, Sunderland, WBA; **3** Bristol City, QPR, Southampton, Stoke, Swindon, Wolves; **2** Cardiff, Coventry, Derby, Luton, Oxford Utd, Plymouth, Sheffield Utd, Tranmere, Watford, Wimbledon; **1** Blackpool, Bradford, Brentford, Burton, Bury, Carlisle, Chester, Huddersfield, Hull, Newcastle, Oldham, Peterborough, Rochdale, Rotherham, Shrewsbury, Stockport, Swansea, Walsall, Wigan, Wycombe. (Figures do not include replays)

THE THINGS THEY SAY ...

'Coming on for Manchester United is Charlie Savage. Wow, I never believed I would say those words' – **Robbie Savage**, former Wales midfielder, commentating on his son's debut off the bench in a Champions League match against Young Boys.

'There is no rush (for a return to club management). If, in three years I decided that was it with England, I would still be only 54 with the experience of managing in one of football's most pressurised jobs'- **Gareth Southgate** after signing a new contract to take England beyond the World Cup and Euro 2024

'I'm going to leave by the front door because I think everyone knows I've given everything for the club' – **Ole Gunnar Solskjaer** after being sacked by Manchester United.

'If it is a limitation of their freedom, they might as well argue that it is their right to drink and drive'- **Jurgen Klopp**, Liverpool manager, criticising players refusing to be vaccinated against Covid.

OTHER COMPETITIONS 2021–22

FA COMMUNITY SHIELD

LEICESTER CITY 1 (Iheanacho 89 pen) MANCHESTER CITY 0
Wembley (45,602); August 7, 2021

Leicester City (4-2-3-1): Schmeichel (capt), Ricardo Pereira, Amartey, Soyuncu, Bertrand (Thomas 78), Ndidi, Tielemans (Souhare 72), Ayoze Perez (Albrighton 71), Maddison (Dewsbury-Hall 71), Barnes (Iheanacho 79) Vardy (Daka 71). **Subs not used:** Ward, Benkovic, Choudhury. **Booked:** Bertrand. **Manager:** Brendan Rodgers.

Manchester City (4-3-3): Steffen, Joao Cancelo, Ruben Dias, Ake, Mendy, Palmer (Bernardo Silva 74), Fernandinho (capt), Gundogan (Rodri 65), Mahrez, Ferran Torres (Knight 74), Edozie (Grealish 65). **Subs not used:** Carson, Sandler, Couto, Doyle, Gomes. **Booked:** Fernandinho, Ruben Dias. **Manager:** Pep Guardiola

Referee: Paul Tierney (Lancs). **Half-time:** 0-0

PAPA JOHNS EFL TROPHY

(Three points for a group match win. One point for a drawn game after 90 minutes, then penalties with winners awarded one additional point. Group winners and runners-up through to knockout stage)

NORTHERN SECTION

GROUP A

Carlisle	3	2	1	0	7	3	8
Hartlepool	3	1	2	0	6	5	6
Everton U21	3	1	0	2	1	3	3
Morecambe	3	0	1	2	2	5	1

GROUP B

Tranmere	3	3	0	0	9	3	9
Oldham	3	1	0	2	5	6	3
Salford	3	1	0	2	5	6	3
Leeds U21	3	1	0	2	7	11	3

GROUP C

Crewe	3	3	0	0	6	0	9
Wigan	3	1	1	1	2	2	4
Shrewsbury	3	1	0	2	3	4	3
Wolves U21	3	0	1	2	1	6	2

GROUP D

Bolton	3	3	0	0	10	3	9
Port Vale	3	2	0	1	8	3	6
Rochdale	3	1	0	2	4	4	3
Liverpool U21	3	0	0	3	1	13	0

GROUP E

Rotherham	3	3	0	0	15	1	9
Doncaster	3	2	0	1	5	9	6
Man City U21	3	1	0	2	4	7	3
Scunthorpe	3	0	0	3	3	10	0

GROUP F

Sunderland	3	2	1	0	5	3	7
Lincoln	3	2	0	1	7	4	6
Man Utd U21	3	1	0	2	6	5	3
Bradford	3	0	1	2	1	7	1

GROUP G

Accrington	3	2	1	0	11	3	8
Fleetwood	3	2	0	1	8	6	6
Barrow	3	1	1	1	4	5	4
Leicester U21	3	0	0	3	1	10	0

GROUP H

Sheffield Wed	3	3	0	0	9	1	9
Harrogate	3	2	0	1	5	5	6
Mansfield	3	1	0	2	8	8	3
Newcastle U21	3	0	0	3	3	-8	11

SOUTHERN SECTION

GROUP A

Ipswich	3	1	1	1	3	2	5
Colchester	3	1	1	1	1	1	4
West Ham U21*	3	2	0	1	4	2	3
Gillingham	3	1	0	2	1	4	3

*Deducted 3 pts, ineligible player

GROUP B

Sutton	3	3	0	0	6	0	9
Portsmouth	3	1	0	2	6	7	3
AFC Wimbledon	3	1	0	2	5	6	3
Crystal Palace U21	3	1	0	2	2	6	3

GROUP C

Aston Villa U21	3	3	0	0	11	5	9
MK Dons	3	2	0	1	6	6	6
Burton	3	1	0	2	8	6	3
Wycombe	3	0	0	3	2	10	0

GROUP D

Forest Green	3	1	2	0	5	3	6
Walsall	3	1	1	1	2	3	5
Brighton U21	3	1	1	1	4	4	4
Northampton	3	0	2	1	3	4	3

GROUP E							
Exeter	3	1	2	0	8	6	6
Chelsea U21	3	1	2	0	3	2	6
Bristol Rov	3	1	0	2	6	7	3
Cheltenham	3	0	2	1	2	4	3

GROUP G							
Leyton Orient	3	3	0	0	6	0	9
Charlton	3	2	0	1	10	3	6
Southampton U21	3	1	0	2	5	5	3
Crawley	3	0	0	3	1	14	0

GROUP F							
Swindon	3	3	0	0	6	2	9
Arsenal U21	3	1	1	1	6	6	4
Newport	3	1	0	2	5	5	3
Plymouth	3	0	1	2	2	6	2

GROUP H							
Cambridge	3	2	0	1	5	2	6
Stevenage	3	2	0	1	6	5	6
Tottenham U21	3	1	0	2	6	7	3
Oxford	3	1	0	2	5	8	3

SECOND ROUND

North: Accrington 1 Wigan 1 (Wigan won 5-4 on pens); Bolton 1 Fleetwood 1; Carlisle 1 Lincoln 1 (Carlisle won 4-3 on pens); Crewe 2 Doncaster 0; Rotherham 1 Port Vale 1 (Rotherham won 5-3 on pens); Sheffield Wed 0 Hartlepool 1; Sunderland 0 Oldham 1; Tranmere 1 Harrogate 2

South: Cambridge 2 Walsall 0; Charlton 2 Aston Villa U21 1; Exeter 2 Portsmouth 3; Forest Green 1 Chelsea U21 1 (Chelsea U21 won 4-1 on pens); Ipswich 2 Arsenal U21 2 (Arsenal U21 won 4-3 on pens); Leyton Orient 0 MK Dons 0 (MK Dons won 5-4 on pens); Sutton 0 Stevenage 0 (Sutton won 4-3 on pens); Swindon 1 Colchester 2

THIRD ROUND

Arsenal U21 4 Chelsea U21 1; Cambridge 2 Portsmouth 1; Charlton 1 MK Dons 0; Crewe 2 Rotherham 4; Harrogate 1 Carlisle 0; Hartlepool 1 Bolton 0; Oldham 0 Wigan 6; Sutton 2 Colchester 1

QUARTER-FINALS

Hartlepool 2 Charlton 2 (Hartlepool won 5-4 on pens); Rotherham 1 Cambridge 1 (Rotherham won 7-6 on pens); Sutton 1 Harrogate 0; Wigan 1 Arsenal U21 0

SEMI-FINALS

Hartlepool 2 Rotherham 2 (Rotherham won 5-4 on pens); Wigan 1 Sutton 1 (Sutton won 7-6 on pens

FINAL

ROTHERHAM UNITED 4 (Wiles 42, Osei-Tutu 90+6, Ogbene 96, Ihiekwe 112) SUTTON UNITED 2 (Wilson 30, Eastmond 48) – aet
Wembley (30,688); April 3, 2022

Rotherham United (3-1-4-2): Johansson, Ihiekwe, Wood (capt), Mattock (Ferguson 80), Barlaser (Lindsay (90+4), Ogbene, Rathbone (Harding 60), Wiles, Miller (Osei-Tutu 80), Smith, Kayode (Ladapo 60). **Subs not used:** Chapman, Edmonds-Greene. **Booked:** Wiles. **Manager:** Paul Warne
Sutton United (4-4-2): Bouzanis, Kizzi, Goodliffe (Rowe 73), John, Milsom (Wyatt 82), Ajiboye, Eastmond (capt) (Davis 81), Beautyman, Randall, Bugiel (Bennett 82), Wilson (Olaofe 66). **Subs not used:** Nelson, Boldewijn. **Booked:** John, Kizzi. **Manager:** Matt Gray
Referee: Sebastian Stockbridge (Tyne & Wear). **Half-time:** 1-1

BUILDBASE FA TROPHY

TTHIRD ROUND: AFC Fylde 0 Solihull 1; Aldershot 2 Kingstonian 1; Barnet 2 Boreham Wood 3;

Boston 4 Kidderminster 1; Bradford PA 3 FC Halifax 3 (FC Halifax won 5-3 on pens); Cheshunt 0 Bishop's Stortford 0 (Cheshunt won 4-3 on pens); Chesterfield (withdrew) v Guiseley (w/o); Cray 1 Dartford 3; Curzon Ashton 1 Alfreton 3; Dover 0 Bromley 1; Eastleigh 5 Enfield 0; Farsley Celtic 0 Southport 3; Folkestone 2 Uxbridge 0; Hungerford 0 Weymouth 1; King's Lynn 2 Nantwich 1; Larkhall 2 AFC Totton 1; Maidenhead (withdrew) v Maidstone (w/o) ; Matlock 2 York 1; Morpeth 3 Lancaster 3 (Morpeth won 5-3 on pens); Needham Market 2 Wealdstone 1; Notts Co 2 Altrincham 1; Plymouth Parkway 1 Dulwich Hamlet 1 (Plymouth Parkway won 4-3 on pens); Radcliffe 0 Spennymoor 2; Slough 3 Eastbourne 1; Southend 2 Dorking 1; St Albans 0 Braintree 0 (St Albans won 6-5 on pens); Stockport 4 Grimsby 0; Stourbridge 3 AFC Telford 2; Tonbridge 2 Torquay 1; Truro 1 Dag & Red 1 (Dag & Red won 4-2 on pens); Wrexham 5 Gloucester 0; Yeovil 3 Woking 1

FOURTH ROUND: Aldershot 0 Bromley 2; Alfreton 1 Halifax 1 (Halifax won 3-2 on pens); Boreham Wood 1 Maidstone 1 (Boreham Wood won 5-4 on pens); Dag & Red 2 Southend 0; Dartford 1 Weymouth 0; Morpeth 4 Boston 3; Notts Co 2 Eastleigh 1; Southport 0 Solihull 1; Spennymoor 3 Plymouth Parkway 1; St Albans 0 Cheshunt 3; Stockport 3 Larkhall 0; Stourbridge 0 Guiseley 0 (Stourbridge won 2-0 on pens); Tonbridge 1 King's Lynn 1 (Tonbridge won 5-4 on pens); Wrexham 5 Folkestone 0; Yeovil 1 Needham Market 1 (Needham Market won 8-7 on pens); York 1 Slough 0

FIFTH ROUND: Dag & Red 2 Spennymoor 0; Halifax 1 Notts Co 2; Needham Market 1 Dartford 0; Stockport 1 Cheshunt 0; Stourbridge 0 Solihull 1; Tonbridge 1 Bromley 1 (Bromley won 3-2 on pens); Wrexham 3 Boreham Wood 0; York 3 Morpeth 2

QUARTER-FINALS: Bromley 3 Solihull 1; Dag & Red 1 York 1 (York won 7-6 on pens); Needham Market 0 Stockport 3; Notts Co 1 Wrexham 2

SEMI-FINALS: Bromley 3 York 1; Wrexham 2 Stockport 0

FINAL`

BROMLEY 1 (Cheek 63) WREXHAM 0
Wembley (46,111); May 22, 2022

Bromley (3-4-3): Balcombe, Sowunmi (Partington 46), Webster (capt), Bush, Coulson, Bingham (Trotter 78), Vennings, Forster, Whitely, Cheek (Bloomfield 80), Al-Hamadi. **Subs not used:** Cousins, Alabi, Dennis, Cawley. **Booked:** Vennings. **Manager:** Andy Woodman
Wrexham (5-3-2): Dibble, McAlinden (Hall-Johnson 74), Cleworth, Tozer, O'Connor (Jarvis 74), McFadzean, Davies, J Jones, Young (capt) (Hyde 86), Mullin, Palmer. **Subs not used:** Camp, French, D Jones, Ponticelli. **Manager:** Phil Parkinson
Referee: Tom Bramall. **Half-time:** 0-0

FINALS – RESULTS

Associated Members' Cup

1984	(Hull) Bournemouth 2 Hull 1	

Freight Rover Trophy – Wembley

1985	Wigan 3 Brentford 1
1986	Bristol City 3 Bolton 0
1987	Mansfield 1 Bristol City 1
	(aet; Mansfield won 5-4 on pens)

Sherpa Van Trophy – Wembley

1988	Wolves 2 Burnley 0
1989	Bolton 4 Torquay 1

Leyland Daf Cup – Wembley

1990	Tranmere 2 Bristol Rov 1
1991	Birmingham 3 Tranmere 2

Autoglass Trophy – Wembley

1992	Stoke 1 Stockport 0
1993	Port Vale 2 Stockport 1
1994	Huddersfield 1 Swansea 1
	(aet; Swansea won 3-1 on pens)

Auto Windscreens Shield – Wembley

1995	Birmingham 1 Carlisle 0
	(Birmingham won in sudden-death overtime)

1996	Rotherham 2 Shrewsbury 1
1997	Carlisle 0 Colchester 0
	(aet; Carlisle won 4-3 on pens)
1998	Grimsby 2 Bournemouth 1
	(Grimsby won with golden goal in
	extra-time)
1999	Wigan 1 Millwall 0
2000	Stoke 2 Bristol City 1

LDV Vans Trophy – Millennium Stadium

2001	Port Vale 2 Brentford 1
2002	Blackpool 4 Cambridge Utd 1
2003	Bristol City 2 Carlisle 0
2004	Blackpool 2 Southend 0
2005	Wrexham 2 Southend 0

Football League Trophy – Millennium Stadium

| 2006 | Swansea 2 Carlisle 1 |

Johnstone's Paint Trophy – Wembley

2007	Doncaster 3 Bristol Rov 2 (aet)
	(Millennium Stadium)
2008	MK Dons 2 Grimsby 0
2009	Luton 3 Scunthorpe 2 (aet)
2010	Southampton 4 Carlisle 1
2011	Carlisle 1 Brentford 0
2012	Chesterfield 2 Swindon 0
2013	Crewe 2 Southend 0
2014	Peterborough 3 Chesterfield 1
2015	Bristol City 2 Walsall 0
2016	Barnsley 3 Oxford 2

Checkatrade Trophy – Wembley

2017	Coventry 2 Oxford 1
2018	Lincoln 1 Shrewsbury 0
2019	Portsmouth 2 Sunderland 2
	(aet, Portsmouth won 5-4 on pens)

Papa John's Trophy – Wembley

2020	Salford 0 Portsmouth 0
	(aet, Salford won 4-2 on pens)
2021	Sunderland 1 Tranmere 0
2022	Rotherham 4 Sutton 2 (aet)

FINALS – AT WEMBLEY

Full Members' Cup (Discontinued after 1992)

| 1985–86 | Chelsea 5 Man City 4 |
| 1986–87 | Blackburn 1 Charlton 0 |

Simod Cup

| 1987–88 | Reading 4 Luton 1 |
| 1988–89 | Nottm Forest 4 Everton 3 |

Zenith Data Systems Cup

1989–90	Chelsea 1 Middlesbrough 0
1990–91	Crystal Palace 4 Everton 1
1991–92	Nottm Forest 3 Southampton 2

Anglo-Italian Cup (Discontinued after 1996
* Home club)

1970	*Napoli 0 Swindon 3
1971	*Bologna 1 Blackpool 2 (aet)
1972	*AS Roma 3 Blackpool 1
1973	*Fiorentina 1 Newcastle 2
1993	Derby 1 Cremonese 3 (at Wembley)
1994	Notts Co 0 Brescia 1 (at Wembley)
1995	Ascoli 1 Notts Co 2 (at Wembley)
1996	Port Vale 2 Genoa 5 (at Wembley)

FA Vase

At Wembley (until 2000 and from 2007)

1975	Hoddesdon 2 Epsom & Ewell 1
1976	Billericay 1 Stamford 0*
1977	Billericay 2 Sheffield 1
	(replay Nottingham after a 1-1 at
	Wembley)
1978	Blue Star 2 Barton Rov 1
1979	Billericay 4 Almondsbury Greenway 1
1980	Stamford 2 Guisborough Town 0
1981	Whickham 3 Willenhall 2*
1982	Forest Green 3 Rainworth MF Welfare 0
1983	VS Rugby 1 Halesowen 0
1984	Stansted 3 Stamford 2
1985	Halesowen 3 Fleetwood 1
1986	Halesowen 3 Southall 0
1987	St Helens 3 Warrington 2
1988	Colne Dynamoes 1 Emley 0*
1989	Tamworth 3 Sudbury 0 (replay
	Peterborough after a 1-1 at Wembley)
1990	Yeading 1 Bridlington 0 (replay
	Leeds after 0-0 at Wembley)
1991	Guiseley 3 Gresley Rov 1 (replay
	Bramall Lane Sheffield after a 4-4
	at Wembley)
1992	Wimborne 5 Guiseley 3
1993	Bridlington 1 Tiverton 0
1994	Diss 2 Taunton 1*
1995	Arlesey 2 Oxford City 1
1996	Brigg Town 3 Clitheroe 0
1997	Whitby Town 3 North Ferriby 0
1998	Tiverton 1 Tow Law 0
1999	Tiverton 1 Bedlington 0
2000	Deal 1 Chippenham 0
2001	Taunton 2 Berkhamsted 1 (Villa Park)
2002	Whitley Bay 1 Tiptree 0* (Villa Park)
2003	Brigg 2 AFC Sudbury 1 (Upton Park)
2004	Winchester 2 AFC Sudbury 0
	(St Andrews)
2005	Didcot 3 AFC Sudbury 2
	(White Hart Lane)
2006	Nantwich 3 Hillingdon 1
	(St Andrews)
2007	Truro 3 AFC Totton 1
2008	Kirkham & Wesham (Fylde) 2
	Lowestoft 1

2009	Whitley Bay 2 Glossop 0
2010	Whitley Bay 6 Wroxham 1
2011	Whitley Bay 3 Coalville 2
2012	Dunston 2 West Auckland 0
2013	Spennymoor 2 Tunbridge Wells 1
2014	Sholing 1 West Auckland 0
2015	North Shields 2 Glossop North End 1*
2016	Morpeth 1 Hereford 1
2017	South Shields 4 Cleethorpes 0
2018	Thatcham 1 Stockton 0
2019	Chertsey 3 Cray Valley 1*
2020	Hebburn 3 Consett 2
2021	Warrington Rylands 3 Binfield 2
2022	Newport Pagnall 3 Littlehampton 0
	* After extra-time

FA Trophy Finals
At Wembley

1970	Macclesfield 2 Telford 0
1971	Telford 3 Hillingdon 2
1972	Stafford 3 Barnet 0
1973	Scarborough 2 Wigan 1*
1974	Morecambe 2 Dartford 1
1975	Matlock 4 Scarborough 0
1976	Scarborough 3 Stafford 2*
1977	Scarborough 2 Dag & Red 1
1978	Altrincham 3 Leatherhead 1
1979	Stafford 2 Kettering 0
1980	Dag & Red 2 Mossley 1
1981	Bishop's Stortford 1 Sutton 0
1982	Enfield 1 Altrincham 0*
1983	Telford 2 Northwich 1
1984	Northwich 2 Bangor 1 (replay Stoke after a 1-1 at Wembley)
1985	Wealdstone 2 Boston 1
1986	Altrincham 1 Runcorn 0
1987	Kidderminster 2 Burton 1 (replay WBA after a 0-0 at Wembley)
1988	Enfield 3 Telford 2 (replay WBA after a 0-0 at Wembley)
1989	Telford 1 Macclesfield 0*
1990	Barrow 3 Leek 0
1991	Wycombe 2 Kidderminster 1
1992	Colchester 3 Witton 1
1993	Wycombe 4 Runcorn 1
1994	Woking 2 Runcorn 1
1995	Woking 2 Kidderminster 1
1996	Macclesfield 3 Northwich 1
1997	Woking 1 Dag & Red & Redbridge 0*
1998	Cheltenham 1 Southport 0
1999	Kingstonian 1 Forest Green 0
2000	Kingstonian 3 Kettering 2

At Villa Park

2001	Canvey 1 Forest Green 0
2002	Yeovil 2 Stevenage 0
2003	Burscough 2 Tamworth 1

2004	Hednesford 3 Canvey 2
2005	Grays 1 Hucknall 1* (Grays won 6-5 on pens)

At Upton Park

2006	Grays 2 Woking 0

At Wembley

2007	Stevenage 3 Kidderminster 2
2008	Ebbsfleet 1 Torquay 0
2009	Stevenage 2 York 0
2010	Barrow 2 Stevenage 1*
2011	Darlington 1 Mansfield 0 *
2012	York 2 Newport 0
2013	Wrexham 1 Grimsby 1 * Wrexham won 4-1 on pens)
2014	Cambridge Utd 4 Gosport 0
2015	North Ferriby 3 Wrexham 3* (North Ferriby won 5-4 on pens)
2016	Halifax 1 Grimsby 0
2017	York 3 Macclesfield 2
2018	Brackley 1 Bromley 1
2019	AFC Fylde 1 Leyton Orient 0
2020	Harrogate 1 Concord 0
2021	Hornchurch 3 Hereford 1
2022	Bromley 1 Wrexham 0

(* Brackley won 5-4 on pens)

(*After extra-time)

FA Youth Cup
Aggregate scores

1953	Man Utd 9 Wolves 3
1954	Man Utd 5 Wolves 4
1955	Man Utd 7 WBA 1
1956	Man Utd 4 Chesterfield 3
1957	Man Utd 8 West Ham 2
1958	Wolves 7 Chelsea 6
1959	Blackburn 2 West Ham 1
1960	Chelsea 5 Preston 2
1961	Chelsea 5 Everton 3
1962	Newcastle 2 Wolves 1
1963	West Ham 6 Liverpool 5
1964	Man Utd 5 Swindon 2
1965	Everton 3 Arsenal 2
1966	Arsenal 5 Sunderland 3
1967	Sunderland 2 Birmingham 0
1968	Burnley 3 Coventry 2
1969	Sunderland 6 WBA 3
1970	Tottenham 4 Coventry 3
1971	Arsenal 2 Cardiff 0
1972	Aston Villa 5 Liverpool 2
1973	Ipswich 4 Bristol City 1
1974	Tottenham 2 Huddersfield 1
1975	Ipswich 5 West Ham 1
1976	WBA 5 Wolves 0
1977	Crystal Palace 1 Everton 0

1978	Crystal Palace 1 Aston Villa 0
	one match only
1979	Millwall 2 Man City 0
1980	Aston Villa 3 Man City 2
1981	West Ham 2 Tottenham 1
1982	Watford 7 Man Utd 6
1983	Norwich 6 Everton 5
1984	Everton 4 Stoke 2
1985	Newcastle 4 Watford 1
1986	Man City 3 Man Utd 1
1987	Coventry 2 Charlton 1
1988	Arsenal 6 Doncaster 1
1989	Watford 2 Man City 1
1990	Tottenham 3 Middlesbrough 2
1991	Millwall 3 Sheffield Wed 0
1992	Man Utd 6 Crystal Palace 3
1993	Leeds 4 Man Utd 1
1994	Arsenal 5 Millwall 3
1995	Man Utd 2 Tottenham 2
	Man Utd won 4-3 on pens
1996	Liverpool 4 West Ham 1
1997	Leeds 3 Crystal Palace 1
1998	Everton 5 Blackburn 3
1999	West Ham 9 Coventry 0
2000	Arsenal 5 Coventry 1
2001	Arsenal 6 Blackburn 3

2002	Aston Villa 4 Everton 2
2003	Man Utd 3 Middlesbrough 1
2004	Middlesbrough 4 Aston Villa 0
2005	Ipswich 3 Southampton 2
2006	Liverpool 3 Man City 2
2007	Liverpool 2 Man Utd 2
	Liverpool won 4-3 on pens
2008	Man City 4 Chelsea 2
2009	Arsenal 6 Liverpool 2
2010	Chelsea 3 Aston Villa 2
2011	Man Utd 6 Sheff Utd 3
2012	Chelsea 4 Blackburn 1
2013	Norwich 4 Chelsea 2
2014	Chelsea 7 Fulham 6
2015	Chelsea 5 Man City 2
2016	Chelsea 4 Man City 2
2017	Chelsea 6 Man City 2
2018	Chelsea 7 Arsenal 1
2019	Liverpool 1 Man City 1
	Liverpool won 5-3 on pens,
	one match only
2020	Man City 3 Chelsea 2
	one match only
2021	Aston Villa 2 Liverpool 1
2022	Manchester Utd 3 Nottm Forest 1
	(Record crowd – 67,492)

CHARITY/COMMUNITY SHIELD RESULTS (POST WAR)

CHARITY SHIELD

1948	Arsenal 4 Man Utd 3
1949	Portsmouth *1 Wolves 1
1950	England World Cup XI 4
	FA Canadian Tour Team 2
1951	Tottenham 2 Newcastle 1
1952	Man Utd 4 Newcastle 2
1953	Arsenal 3 Blackpool 1
1954	Wolves *4 WBA 4
1955	Chelsea 3 Newcastle 0
1956	Man Utd 1 Man City 0
1957	Man Utd 4 Aston Villa 0
1958	Bolton 4 Wolves 1
1959	Wolves 3 Nottm Forest 1
1960	Burnley *2 Wolves 2
1961	Tottenham 3 FA XI 2
1962	Tottenham 5 Ipswich Town 1
1963	Everton 4 Man Utd 0
1964	Liverpool *2 West Ham 2
1965	Man Utd *2 Liverpool 2
1966	Liverpool 1 Everton 0
1967	Man Utd *3 Tottenham 3
1968	Man City 6 WBA 1
1969	Leeds 2 Man City 1
1970	Everton 2 Chelsea 1
1971	Leicester 1 Liverpool 0

1972	Man City 1 Aston Villa 0
1973	Burnley 1 Man City 0
1974	Liverpool 1 Leeds 1
	(Liverpool won 6-5 on pens)
1975	Derby Co 2 West Ham 0
1976	Liverpool 1 Southampton 0
1977	Liverpool *0 Man Utd 0
1978	Nottm Forest 5 Ipswich 0
1979	Liverpool 3 Arsenal 1
1980	Liverpool 1 West Ham 0
1981	Aston Villa *2 Tottenham 2
1982	Liverpool 1 Tottenham 0
1983	Man Utd 2 Liverpool 0
1984	Everton 1 Liverpool 0
1985	Everton 2 Man Utd 0
1986	Everton *1 Liverpool 1
1987	Everton 1 Coventry 0
1988	Liverpool 2 Wimbledon 1
1989	Liverpool 1 Arsenal 0
1990	Liverpool *1 Man Utd 1
1991	Arsenal *0 Tottenham 0
1992	Leeds 4 Liverpool 3
1993	Man Utd 1 Arsenal 1
	(Man Utd won 5-4 on pens)
1994	Man Utd 2 Blackburn 0
1995	Everton 1 Blackburn 0
1996	Man Utd 4 Newcastle 0
1997	Man Utd 1 Chelsea 0
	(Man Utd won 4-2 on pens)

1998	Arsenal 3 Man Utd 0
1999	Arsenal 2 Man Utd 1
2000	Chelsea 2 Man Utd 0
2001	Liverpool 2 Man Utd 1

COMMUNITY SHIELD

2002	Arsenal 1 Liverpool 0
2003	Man Utd 1 Arsenal 1
	(Man Utd won 4-3 on pens)
2004	Arsenal 3 Man Utd 1
2005	Chelsea 2 Arsenal 1
2006	Liverpool 2 Chelsea 1
2007	Man Utd 1 Chelsea 1
	(Man Utd won 3-0 on pens)
2008	Man Utd 0 Portsmouth 0
	(Man Utd won 3-1 on pens)
2009	Chelsea 2 Man Utd 2
	(Chelsea won 4-1 on pens)

2010	Man Utd 3 Chelsea 1
2011	Man Utd 3 Man City 2
2012	Man City 3 Chelsea 2
2013	Man Utd 2 Wigan 0
2014	Arsenal 3 Man City 0
2015	Arsenal 1 Chelsea 0
2016	Man Utd 2 Leicester 1
2017	Arsenal 1 Chelsea 1
	(Arsenal won 4-1 on pens)
2018	Man City 2 Chelsea 0
2019	Man City 1 Liverpool 1
	(Man City won 5 -4 on pens)
2020	Arsenal 1 Liverpool 1
	(Arsenal won 5 -4 on pens)
2022	Leicester 1 Manchester City 0

(Fixture played at Wembley 1974–2000 and from 2007); Millennium Stadium 2001–06; Villa Park 2012) * Trophy shared

FOOTBALL'S CHANGING HOMES

Manchester United expect to have design plans in place for a new-look Old Trafford early in the new season. After considering various options, including building a new stadium on the same site, the club decided on a major redevelopment of the second biggest ground in the country after Wembley. Reports suggest it could involve expanding the Sir Bobby Charlton Stand, providing 15,000 new seats and boosting capacity to around 88, 000. United already have more than 50,000 season-ticket holders, with double that on a waiting list. **Leicester City** are still hoping for an expansion of the King Power Stadium to be ready by the summer of 2024, despite two planning delays. The new East Stand would raise capacity from 32,000 to 40,000, with the scheme also involving an indoor arena, hotel and new homes. The local council says delays for 'large and complex projects' are not out of the ordinary. **West Ham United** have confirmed an increase in capacity from 60,000 to 62,500 for the London Stadium, along with reconfiguration of the West Stand's lower tier to bring spectators closer to the pitch. The club says it would develop a 'more traditional football stadium layout.'

THE THINGS THEY SAY ...

'It's unfair to describe this as stepping-stone. I am honoured to be here' – **Steven Gerrard**, Aston Villa's new manager, denying he is just biding his time before the Liverpool job becomes vacant.

'It would be naïve and stupid to think I am better than League One. I'm more than prepared to help us get out of that league' – **Wayne Rooney**, Derby manager, after a total of 21 points deducted condemned his club to relegation from the Championship.

'A resignation from the football elite' – **Spanish newspaper** headline after Barcelona failed to qualify from the Champions League group stage for the first time in 21 years.

SCOTTISH TABLES 2021–2022

PREMIERSHIP

		P	W	D	L	F	A	W	D	L	F	A	Gd	Pts
1	Celtic	38	16	3	0	55	6	13	3	3	37	16	70	93
2	Rangers	38	14	4	1	40	12	13	4	2	40	19	49	89
3	Hearts	38	11	4	4	32	16	6	6	7	22	28	10	61
4	Dundee Utd	38	8	4	7	21	23	4	8	7	16	21	-7	48
5	Motherwell	38	9	4	6	26	28	3	6	10	16	33	-19	46
6	Ross Co	38	5	5	7	28	30	5	4	10	19	31	-14	41
7	Livingston	38	7	5	7	22	23	6	5	8	19	23	-5	49
8	Hibernian	38	7	7	5	22	16	4	5	10	16	26	-4	45
9	St.Mirren	38	4	8	7	14	20	6	6	7	19	31	-18	44
10	Aberdeen	38	8	5	6	25	19	2	6	11	16	27	-5	41
11	St.Johnstone	38	5	5	9	15	21	3	6	10	9	30	-27	35
12	Dundee	38	4	7	8	20	29	2	4	13	14	35	-30	29

Celtic into Champions League group stage, Rangers into third qualifying round; Hearts into Europa League play-off round; Dundee Utd into Europa Conference third qualifying round, Motherwell into second qualifying round

Play-offs (on agg): **Quarter-final:** Inverness 3 Partick 1. **Semi-final:** Inverness 0 Arbroath 0 – aet, Inverness won 5-3 on pens. **Final:** St Johnstone 6 Inverness 2

Player of Year: Callum McGregor (Celtic). **Manager of Year:** Angelod Postecoglou (Celtic)

Team of Year: Gordon (Hearts), Tavernier (Rangers), Carter-Vickers (Celtic), Souttar (Hearts), Juranovic (Celtic), Rogic (Celtic), McGregor (Celtic), Charles-Cook (Ross Co), Jota (Celtic), Morelos (Rangers), Furuhashi (Celtic)

Leading league scorers: 13 Charles-Cook (Ross Co), Giakoumakis (Celtic); 12 Furuhashi (Celtic); 11 Anderson (Livingston), Ferguson (Aberdeen), Morelos (Rangers); 10 Abada (Celtic), Boyce (Hearts), Jota (Celtic), Ramirez (Aberden), Roofe (Rangers)

CHAMPIONSHIP

		P	W	D	L	F	A	W	D	L	F	A	Gd	Pts
1	Kilmarnock	36	12	1	5	28	14	8	6	4	22	13	23	67
2	Arbroath	36	9	8	1	32	14	8	6	4	22	14	26	65
3	Inverness	36	10	3	5	30	17	6	8	4	23	17	19	59
4	Partick	36	9	4	5	17	13	5	6	7	29	27	6	52
5	Raith	36	5	8	5	23	26	7	6	5	21	18	0	50
6	Hamilton	36	5	5	8	16	28	5	7	6	22	25	-15	42
7	Morton	36	3	9	6	23	27	6	4	8	13	20	-11	40
8	Ayr	36	5	7	6	21	25	4	5	9	18	27	-13	39
9	Dunfermline	36	5	8	5	22	24	2	6	10	14	29	-17	35
10	Queen of Sth	36	4	5	9	13	19	4	4	10	23	35	-18	33

Play-offs (on agg): **Semi-finals:** Airdrieonians 6 Montrose 5 (aet); Queen's Park 1 Dunfermline 0. **Final:** Queen's Park 3 Airdrieonians 2 (aet)

Player of Year: Michael McKenna (Arbroath). **Manager of Year:** Dick Campbell (Arbroath)

Team of Year: Hemming (Kilmarnock), Little (Arbroath), Mayo (Partick), Deas (Inverness), Holt (Partick), Murray (Partick), McKenna (Arbroath), Tiffoney (Partick), McKay (Inverness), Graham (Partick), Lafferty (Kilmarnock)

Leading league scorers: 15 McKenna (Arbroath); 14 Shaw (Kilmarnock); 13 Graham (Partick); 11 Adeloye (Ayr); 10 Sutherland (Inverness); 9 McKay (Inverness), Ryan (Hamilton); 8 Connolly (Raith), Lafferty (Kilmarnock), Moyo (Hamilton), Zanatta (Raith)

LEAGUE ONE

			Home				Away					
		P	W	D	L	F	A	W	D	L	F	A	Gd	Pts
1	Cove	36	13	5	0	43	13	10	5	3	30	19	41	79
2	Airdrieonians	36	12	3	3	36	21	9	6	3	32	16	31	72
3	Montrose	36	6	9	3	25	20	9	5	4	28	16	17	59
4	Queen's Park*	36	8	8	2	29	15	3	10	5	22	21	15	51
5	Alloa	36	6	4	8	26	30	6	5	7	23	27	-8	45
6	Falkirk	36	5	3	10	23	31	7	5	6	26	24	-6	44
7	Peterhead	36	8	4	6	24	17	3	5	10	22	34	-5	42
8	Clyde	36	6	5	7	23	36	3	7	8	16	26	-23	39
9	Dumbarton	36	3	6	9	21	31	6	1	11	27	40	-23	34
10	East Fife	36	4	5	9	17	26	1	3	14	14	44	-39	23

*also promoted

Play-offs (on agg): **Semi-finals:** Edinburgh City 5 Dumbarton 2; Annan 2 Forfar 1. **Final:** Edinburgh City 3 Annan 2
Player of Year: Dylan Easton (Airdrieonians) **Manager of Year:** Paul Hartley (Cove)
Team of Year: McKenzie (Cove), Ballantyne (Montrose), Fordyce (Airdrieonians), Neill (Cove), Milne (Cove), Yule (Cove), Fyvie (Cove), Frizzell (Airdrieonians), Megginson (Cove), McAllister (Cove), Easton (Airdrieonians)
Leading league scorers: 18 Megginson (Cove); 16 McAllister (Cove); 15 Gallagher (Airdrieonians), Goodwillie (Clyde), Webster (Montrose); 14 Henderson (Alloa); 12 McLean (Peterhead), Smith (Airdrieonians)

LEAGUE TWO

			Home				Away					
		P	W	D	L	F	A	W	D	L	F	A	Gd	Pts
1	Kelty	36	13	5	0	36	12	11	4	3	32	16	40	81
2	Forfar	36	10	5	3	34	17	6	7	5	23	19	21	60
3	Annan	36	7	4	7	33	29	11	1	6	31	22	13	59
4	Edinburgh City*	36	7	5	6	23	25	7	5	6	20	24	-6	52
5	Stenhousemuir	36	5	4	9	22	27	8	6	4	25	19	1	49
6	Stranraer	36	6	4	8	18	26	7	4	7	32	28	-4	47
7	Stirling	36	6	2	10	22	26	5	7	6	19	20	-5	42
8	Albion	36	5	5	8	17	26	5	4	9	20	32	-21	39
9	Elgin	36	6	6	6	20	21	3	4	11	13	30	-18	37
10	Cowdenbeath	36	3	5	10	13	21	4	3	11	15	28	-21	29

*also promoted

Pyramid play-offs (on agg): **Semi-final** Bonnyrigg 3 Fraserburgh 2. **Final:** Bonnyrigg 4 Cowdenbeath 0
Player of Year: Joe Cardle (Kelty). **Manager of Year:** Kevin Thomson (Kelty)
Team of Year: Jamieson (Kelty), Meechan (Forfar), Munro (Forfar), O'Ware (Kelty), Forster (Kelty), Barjonas (Kelty), Moxon (Annan), Cardle (Kelty), Orr (Stenhousemuir), Austin (Kelty), Hester (Elgin)
Leading league scorers: 17 Austin (Kelty); 13 Hester (Elgin), Orr (Stenhousemuir), Wallace (Annan); 12 Cardle (Kelty), Goss (Annan); 11 Carrick (Stirling), McCluskey (Forfar)

SCOTTISH LEAGUE RESULTS 2021–2022

PREMIERSHIP

	Aberdeen	Celtic	Dundee	Dundee Utd	Hearts	Hibernian	Livingston	Motherwell	Rangers	Ross Co	St Johnstone	St Mirren
Aberdeen	—	1-2	2-1	2-0	2-1	1-0	2-0	0-2	1-1	1-1	0-1	4-1
	—	2-3	1-0	1-1		3-1	1-2			0-1	1-1	0-0
Celtic	2-1	—	6-0	1-1	1-0	2-0	0-0	1-0	3-0	3-0	2-0	6-0
		—	3-2	1-0	4-1			6-0	1-1	4-0	7-0	2-0
Dundee	2-1	2-4	—	0-0	0-1	2-2	0-0	3-0	0-1	0-5	1-0	2-2
	2-2		—			0-0	0-4		1-2	1-2	1-1	0-1
			—			3-1						
Dundee Utd	1-0	0-3	1-0	—	0-2	1-3	0-1	2-1	1-0	1-0	0-1	1-2
		1-1	2-2	—	2-2			2-0	1-1	2-1		
				—	2-3			1-0				
Hearts	1-1	2-1	1-1	5-2	—	0-0	3-0	2-0	0-2	2-1	2-0	2-0
	2-0	1-2	1-2		—	3-1	2-0	2-0	1-3	0-0		
Hibernian	1-0	1-3	1-0	0-3	0-0	—	2-0	1-1	0-1	3-0	1-0	2-2
	1-1	0-0		1-1		—	2-3			2-0	0-0	0-1
						—					4-0	
Livingston	1-2	1-0	2-0	1-1	0-1	1-0	—	1-2	1-3	1-1	1-2	0-1
	2-1	1-3	2-1	2-1		1-0	—	2-2			1-1	1-1
Motherwell	2-0	0-2	1-0	1-0	2-0	2-3	2-1	—	1-6	2-1	2-0	2-2
	1-1	0-4	1-1		2-1	0-0		—	1-3	0-1		4-2
Rangers	2-2	1-0	3-0	1-0	1-1	2-1	3-0	1-1	—	4-2	2-0	2-0
	1-0	1-2		2-0	5-0	2-0	1-0	2-2	—	4-1		
Ross Co	1-1	1-2	3-2	1-1	2-2	1-0	2-3	3-1	2-4	—	0-0	2-3
		0-2	1-2	1-1		1-1	0-1	3-3		—	3-1	1-0
St Johnstone	0-1	1-3	3-1	0-1	1-1	1-2	0-3	1-1	1-2	1-2	—	0-0
	1-0		0-0	0-0	2-1		1-0	2-1	0-1		—	0-1
St Mirren	3-2	0-0	0-1	0-0	1-2	1-1	1-1	1-1	1-2	0-0	0-0	—
	1-0		2-0	1-2	0-2	0-1	0-0		0-4		2-1	—

CHAMPIONSHIP

	Arbroath	Ayr	Dunfermline	Greenock	Hamilton	Inverness	Kilmarnock	Partick	Queen of South	Raith
Arbroath	—	1-1	4-2	2-1	4-0	0-1	0-0	3-1	1-1	0-0
	—	1-0	1-0	3-0	2-2	0-0	1-0	1-1	5-1	3-3
Ayr	2-2	—	3-1	0-0	1-1	2-2	0-1	0-4	2-1	0-2
	1-0	—	1-1	0-2	1-1	2-2	1-3	3-1	0-1	2-0
Dunfermline	0-3	3-0	—	1-3	0-0	0-0	2-2	0-3	3-3	1-1
	0-3	2-1	—	1-1	1-0	1-1	0-0	4-1	1-2	2-0
Greenock	2-2	2-2	2-2	—	1-1	1-6	0-2	0-0	2-3	0-1
	0-0	1-1	5-0	—	0-1	0-1	1-1	2-1	2-1	2-2
Hamilton	1-1	0-2	1-0	0-1	—	2-1	0-2	1-6	1-0	0-3
	0-1	1-1	2-2	1-0	—	1-1	2-3	2-2	1-0	0-2
Inverness	0-1	1-0	1-2	2-0	1-2	—	1-0	3-1	2-1	1-0
	3-0	1-2	2-0	0-1	4-0	—	2-1	3-3	2-2	1-1
Kilmarnock	0-1	2-0	2-1	1-0	2-1	0-1	—	0-1	4-0	1-3
	2-1	1-2	2-0	1-1	2-0	1-0	—	2-1	2-1	3-0
Partick	0-2	4-0	0-0	3-0	1-0	0-0	0-2	—	3-2	1-0
	0-0	1-0	1-0	0-1	0-4	1-0	1-1	—	1-0	0-1
Queen of Sth	0-2	3-0	1-0	0-0	1-2	1-2	0-1	0-0	—	1-1
	0-0	1-1	0-2	3-0	0-3	2-1	0-2	0-1	—	0-1
Raith	2-1	2-1	1-1	2-1	4-4	1-1	1-0	3-2	0-1	—
	1-2	0-4	0-0	0-1	0-0	2-3	1-1	0-0	3-3	—

LEAGUE ONE

	Airdrieonians	Alloa	Clyde	Cove	Dumbarton	East Fife	Falkirk	Montrose	Peterhead	Queen's Park
Airdrieonians	—	2-1	2-1	0-2	3-2	3-0	1-2	0-3	3-1	1-0
	—	3-1	1-1	1-1	3-2	3-0	3-2	4-1	1-1	2-0
Alloa	2-1	—	0-1	1-3	1-2	3-1	2-0	2-2	2-4	1-1
	0-2	—	1-0	2-2	2-3	1-3	0-3	4-1	1-0	1-1
Clyde	2-2	2-1	—	2-1	0-3	3-1	1-3	0-5	2-2	2-2
	0-5	2-1	—	0-1	1-3	2-0	1-1	2-1	0-3	1-1
Cove	1-0	3-0	3-0	—	2-0	5-2	1-1	1-1	3-0	3-3
	1-1	3-0	4-1	—	1-0	4-2	2-0	1-0	5-2	0-0
Dumbarton	2-2	1-1	1-1	1-3	—	5-0	0-3	1-3	2-3	0-3
	0-1	1-2	2-1	2-2	—	2-0	0-2	0-0	1-1	0-3
East Fife	0-1	1-1	0-2	4-2	2-1	—	0-2	0-2	3-0	1-1
	0-2	0-3	0-0	2-3	2-0	—	1-3	0-2	0-0	1-1
Falkirk	0-3	1-1	3-0	0-3	1-2	2-1	—	0-1	2-1	0-1
	1-4	1-2	1-2	0-2	6-2	3-1	—	0-3	1-1	1-1
Montrose	2-1	0-2	2-2	0-0	1-2	4-1	2-2	—	1-0	1-1
	2-2	1-1	1-1	1-2	1-1	0-0	2-1	—	2-0	2-1
Peterhead	2-3	2-0	3-2	0-1	5-0	1-1	0-0	0-0	—	2-1
	0-1	0-1	1-1	0-1	4-3	1-0	1-0	0-1	—	2-1
Queen's Park	0-0	3-4	0-0	2-0	3-0	1-1	6-0	1-1	3-2	—
	1-1	1-1	1-0	1-1	2-1	1-0	1-1	0-1	2-1	—

LEAGUE TWO

	Albion	Annan	Cowdenbeath	Edinburgh City	Elgin	Forfar	Kelty	Stenhousemuir	Stirling	Stranraer
Albion	—	0-1	2-1	2-0	2-0	2-3	0-3	2-2	1-0	3-2
	—	1-4	0-1	0-1	0-0	0-0	0-0	1-2	1-1	0-5
Annan	1-1	—	1-0	1-3	4-1	0-2	5-1	1-2	3-1	2-2
	2-4	—	2-3	2-1	2-1	2-2	1-2	0-2	0-0	4-1
Cowdenbeath	0-0	1-3	—	1-2	3-1	1-1	0-1	0-2	1-0	1-2
	0-1	1-3	—	0-0	2-0	1-2	0-1	1-1	0-0	0-1
Edinburgh City	0-4	0-1	1-1	—	2-0	0-4	2-3	1-0	2-2	3-1
	1-2	2-1	1-0	—	2-2	2-0	1-1	1-1	1-0	1-2
Elgin	3-0	0-2	1-0	1-1	—	1-1	2-0	2-2	0-2	1-1
	1-1	0-2	1-4	2-0	—	1-0	0-0	0-2	3-1	1-2
Forfar	3-1	2-0	3-0	2-0	2-1	—	2-2	3-4	2-0	1-1
	2-0	5-1	1-1	2-3	0-0	—	1-0	0-0	0-1	3-2
Kelty	6-1	2-1	2-0	1-0	1-1	1-0	—	2-0	1-1	1-0
	3-1	3-1	1-0	2-2	4-0	1-1	—	1-0	1-1	3-2
Stenhousemuir	3-1	2-0	1-1	2-2	1-2	1-1	1-4	—	0-1	1-4
	4-1	0-1	0-2	0-0	2-1	2-0	0-1	—	1-2	1-3
Stirling	2-1	2-3	4-0	1-2	0-1	1-0	1-3	1-3	—	1-1
	0-1	0-3	2-1	5-0	0-2	1-1	0-3	0-1	—	1-0
Stranraer	1-0	0-3	2-0	0-1	1-0	2-3	0-4	2-0	0-3	—
	0-0	1-1	3-0	0-2	2-0	0-2	0-3	1-1	3-3	—

NEW-LOOK CELTIC BACK ON TOP

Celtic went into the new season with a little-known new manager, an untested new strike force and in the unfamiliar position of being Scottish Premiership underdogs. It remained that way even when Steven Gerrard left Rangers in mid-November, after three-and-a-half years in charge, to take over at Aston Villa. If anything, the Ibrox club had a stronger case for retaining the title with a six-point lead at the winter break. Instead, the appointment of Angelos Postecoglou, three months after Neil Lennon's resignation, proved a masterstroke. The former coach to the Australia national team and the Japanese club Yokohama Marinos led his side back into contention, before the balance of power shifted in the space of a pivotal few days. Israel international Liel Abada scored a last-minute winner against Dundee United and was on the mark again as Rangers were swept aside 3-0. Once back on top, Celtic never wavered. Despite missing half the season with injuries Japan forward Kyogo Furuhashi maintained an impressive goals ratio, alongside Greece international Georgios Giakoumakis. Another Old Firm victory, this time 2-1, underlined their superiority and Callum McGregor, Scotland's Player of the Year, lifted the trophy with his side four points clear.

Celtic also won the League Cup, Furuhashi scoring both goals in the final against Hibernian. But they lost to Giovanni van Bronckhorst's team in the semi-finals of the Scottish Cup, before results in Europe were again best forgotten – defeat by the Danish side Midtjylland in the second qualifying round of the Champions League, failure to progress from their Europa League group and embarrassed by the Norwegian champions Bodo/Glimt in the inaugural Europa Conference. In sharp contrast, Rangers reached the Europa League Final after finishing second in their group, then defeating Borussia Dortmund, Red Star Belgrade, Sporting Braga and RB Leipzig in the knockout rounds. Captain James Tavernier, despite his defensive responsibilities, was the competition's leading scorer with seven goals, but his side fell at the final hurdle, beaten 5-4 on penalties by Eintracht Frankfurt in Seville after a 1-1 scoreline at the end of 120 minutes. Three days later, the pain was eased by a 2-0 success against Hearts in the Scottish Cup Final, courtesy of extra-times goals from substitutes Ryan Jack and Scott Wright.

HOW CELTIC REGAINED THE TITLE

JULY 2021

31   Hearts 2 (Mackay-Steven 8, Souttar 89) Celtic 1 (Ralston54). Att: 5,272

AUGUST 2021

8   Celtic 6 (Furuhashi 20, 25, 67, Rogic 49, Ralston 84, Edouard 90 pen). Att: 19,660
21   Celtic 6 (Abada 17, 22, Turnbull 28, 44, 84, Edouard 62) St Mirren 0. Att: 56,052
28   Rangers 1 (Helander 66) Celtic 0. Att: 49,402

SEPTEMBER 2021

11   Celtic 3 (Carter-Vickers 64, Ajeti 70, 85) Ross Co 0. Att: 56,511
18   Livingston 1 (Shinnie 25) Celtic 0. Att: 8,573
25   Celtic 1 (Abada 16) Dundee Utd 1 (Harkes 18). Att: 56,403

OCTOBER 2021

3   Aberdeen 1 (Ferguson 56) Celtic 2 (Furuhashi 11, Jota 84). Att: 14,522
16   Motherwell 0 Celtic 2 (Jota 17, Turnbull 52). Att: 8,446
23   Celtic 2 (Giakoumakis 34, Juranovic 80 pen) St Johnstone 0. Att: 57,434
27   Hibernian 1 (Boyle 37) Celtic 3 (Ralston 10, Carter-Vickers 14, Furuhashi 30). Att: 17,580
30   Celtic 0 Livingston 0. Att: 57,388

NOVEMBER 2021

6   Dundee 2 (Mullen 23, Ashcroft 67) Celtic 4 (Jota 8, 47, Furuhashi 20, 50). Att: 8,604
28   Celtic 2 (Jota 20, McGregor 60) Aberdeen 1 (Ferguson 33 pen). Att: 58,469

DECEMBER 2021

2   Celtic 1 (Furuhashi 33) Hearts 0. Att: 57,578
5   Dundee Utd 0 Celtic 3 (Rogic 19, Turnbull 40, Scales 81). Att: 8,311
12   Celtic 1 (Rogic 45) Motherwell 0. Att: 57,705
15   Ross Co 1 (Baldwin 57) Celtic 2 (Abada 21, Ralston 90+7). Att: 5,592
22   St Mirren 0 Celtic 0. Att: 6,596
26   St Johnstone 1 (Kane 69) Celtic 3 (Abada 9, 22, Bitton 82). Att: 500

JANUARY 2022

17   Celtic 2 (Maeda 4, Juranovic 25 pen) Hibernian 0. Att: 58,296
26   Hearts 1 (Boyce 62) Celtic 2 (Hatate 27, Giakoumakis 35). Att: 17,967
29   Celtic 1 (Abada 90) Dundee Utd 0. Att: 58,188

FEBRUARY 2022

2   Celtic 3 (Hatate 5, 42, Abada 44) Rangers 0. Att: 59,077
6   Motherwell 0 Celtic 4 (Abada 28, Rogic 31, 45, Maeda 71). Att: 7,421
9   Aberdeen 2 (Ramirez 56, Ferguson 61) Celtic 3 (Jota 17, 62, O'Riley 20). Att: 15,291
20   Celtic 3 (Giakoumakis 34, 38, 86) Dundee 2 (Mullen 26, Sweeney 60). Att: 58,030
27   Hibernian 0 Celtic 0. Att: 17,374

MARCH 2022

2   Celtic 2 (Carter-Vickers 55, McGregor 81) St Mirren 0. Att: 57,360
6   Livingston 1 (Shinnie 56) Celtic 3 (Maeda 17, Devlin 46 og, Forrest 55). Att: 8,922
19   Celtic 4 (Giakoumakis 11, 18, 61 pen, Maeda 26) Ross Co 0. Att: 58,432

APRIL 2022

3   Rangers 1 (Ramsey 3) Celtic 2 (Rogic 7, Carter-Vickers 43). Att: 50,023
9   Celtic 7 (Hatate 8, Giakoumakis 22, Maeda 36, Juranovic 52 pen, O'Riley 70, 73, Abada 78). Att: 58,321
24   Ross Co 0 Celtic 2 (Furuhaashi 12, Jota 87). Att: 6,698

MAY 2022

1   Celtic 1 (Jota 21) Rangers 1 (Sakala 67). Att: 58,247
7   Celtic 4 (Maeda 30, Furuhashi 37, O'Riley 69, Giakoumakis 90) Hearts 1 (Simms 3). Att: 58,554
11   Dundee Utd 1 (Levitt 72) Celtic 1 (Giakoumakis 53). Att: 9,401 (Celtic clinch title)
14   Celtic 6 (Furuhashi 21, 43, Turnbull 40, Jota 59, Giakoumakis 68, 90+1) Motherwell 0. Att: 58,953

SCOTTISH HONOURS LIST

PREMIER DIVISION

	First	Pts	Second	Pts	Third	Pts
1975–6	Rangers	54	Celtic	48	Hibernian	43
1976–7	Celtic	55	Rangers	46	Aberdeen	43
1977–8	Rangers	55	Aberdeen	53	Dundee Utd	40
1978–9	Celtic	48	Rangers	45	Dundee Utd	44
1979–80	Aberdeen	48	Celtic	47	St Mirren	42
1980–81	Celtic	56	Aberdeen	49	Rangers	44
1981–2	Celtic	55	Aberdeen	53	Rangers	43
1982–3	Dundee Utd	56	Celtic	55	Aberdeen	55
1983–4	Aberdeen	57	Celtic	50	Dundee Utd	47
1984–5	Aberdeen	59	Celtic	52	Dundee Utd	47
1985–6	*Celtic	50	Hearts	50	Dundee Utd	47
1986–7	Rangers	69	Celtic	63	Dundee Utd	60
1987–8	Celtic	72	Hearts	62	Rangers	60
1988–9	Rangers	56	Aberdeen	50	Celtic	46
1989–90	Rangers	51	Aberdeen	44	Hearts	44
1990–1	Rangers	55	Aberdeen	53	Celtic	41
1991–2	Rangers	72	Hearts	63	Celtic	62
1992–3	Rangers	73	Aberdeen	64	Celtic	60
1993–4	Rangers	58	Aberdeen	55	Motherwell	54
1994–5	Rangers	69	Motherwell	54	Hibernian	53
1995–6	Rangers	87	Celtic	83	Aberdeen	55
1996–7	Rangers	80	Celtic	75	Dundee Utd	60
1997–8	Celtic	74	Rangers	72	Hearts	67

PREMIER LEAGUE

	First	Pts	Second	Pts	Third	Pts
1998–99	Rangers	77	Celtic	71	St Johnstone	57
1999–2000	Rangers	90	Celtic	69	Hearts	54
2000–01	Celtic	97	Rangers	82	Hibernian	66
2001–02	Celtic	103	Rangers	85	Livingston	58
2002–03	*Rangers	97	Celtic	97	Hearts	63
2003–04	Celtic	98	Rangers	81	Hearts	68
2004–05	Rangers	93	Celtic	92	Hibernian	61
2005–06	Celtic	91	Hearts	74	Rangers	73
2006–07	Celtic	84	Rangers	72	Aberdeen	65
2007–08	Celtic	89	Rangers	86	Motherwell	60
2008–09	Rangers	86	Celtic	82	Hearts	59
2009–10	Rangers	87	Celtic	81	Dundee Utd	63
2010–11	Rangers	93	Celtic	92	Hearts	63
2011–12	Celtic	93	**Rangers	73	Motherwell	62
2012–13	Celtic	79	Motherwell	63	St Johnstone	56

Maximum points: 72 except 1986–8, 1991–4 (88), 1994–2000 (108), 2001–10 (114)
* Won on goal difference. **Deducted 10 pts for administration

PREMIERSHIP

	First	Pts	Second	Pts	Third	Pts
2013–14	Celtic	99	Motherwell	70	Aberdeen	68
2014–15	Celtic	92	Aberdeen	75	Inverness	65
2015–16	Celtic	86	Aberdeen	71	Hearts	65
2016–17	Celtic	106	Aberdeen	76	Rangers	67
2017–18	Celtic	82	Aberdeen	73	Rangers	70
2018–19	Celtic	87	Rangers	78	Kilmarnock	67
2019–20C	Celtic	80	Rangers	67	Motherwell	46
2020–21	Rangers	102	Celtic	77	Hibernian	63
2021–22	Celtic	93	Rangers	89	Hearts	61

C Season curtailed – COVID-19

FIRST DIVISION (Scottish Championship until 1975–76)

	First	Pts	Second	Pts	Third	Pts
1890–1a	††Dumbarton	29	Rangers	29	Celtic	24
1891–2b	Dumbarton	37	Celtic	35	Hearts	30
1892–3a	Celtic	29	Rangers	28	St Mirren	23
1893–4a	Celtic	29	Hearts	26	St Bernard's	22
1894–5a	Hearts	31	Celtic	26	Rangers	21
1895–6a	Celtic	30	Rangers	26	Hibernian	24
1896–7a	Hearts	28	Hibernian	26	Rangers	25
1897–8a	Celtic	33	Rangers	29	Hibernian	22
1898–9a	Rangers	36	Hearts	26	Celtic	24
1899–1900a	Rangers	32	Celtic	25	Hibernian	24
1900–1c	Rangers	35	Celtic	29	Hibernian	25
1901–2a	Rangers	28	Celtic	26	Hearts	22
1902–3b	Hibernian	37	Dundee	31	Rangers	29
1903–4d	Third Lanark	43	Hearts	39	Rangers	38
1904–5a	†Celtic	41	Rangers	41	Third Lanark	35
1905–6a	Celtic	46	Hearts	39	Rangers	38
1906–7f	Celtic	55	Dundee	48	Rangers	45
1907–8f	Celtic	55	Falkirk	51	Rangers	50
1908–9f	Celtic	51	Dundee	50	Clyde	48
1909–10f	Celtic	54	Falkirk	52	Rangers	49
1910–11f	Rangers	52	Aberdeen	48	Falkirk	44
1911–12f	Rangers	51	Celtic	45	Clyde	42
1912–13f	Rangers	53	Celtic	49	Hearts	41
1913–14g	Celtic	65	Rangers	59	Hearts	54
1914–15g	Celtic	65	Hearts	61	Rangers	50
1915–16g	Celtic	67	Rangers	56	Morton	51
1916–17g	Celtic	64	Morton	54	Rangers	53
1917–18f	Rangers	56	Celtic	55	Kilmarnock	43
1918–19f	Celtic	58	Rangers	57	Morton	47
1919–20h	Rangers	71	Celtic	68	Motherwell	57
1920–1h	Rangers	76	Celtic	66	Hearts	56
1921–2h	Celtic	67	Rangers	66	Raith	56
1922–3g	Rangers	55	Airdrieonians	50	Celtic	46
1923–4g	Rangers	59	Airdrieonians	50	Celtic	41
1924–5g	Rangers	60	Airdrieonians	57	Hibernian	52
1925–6g	Celtic	58	Airdrieonians	50	Hearts	50
1926–7g	Rangers	56	Motherwell	51	Celtic	49
1927–8g	Rangers	60	Celtic	55	Motherwell	55
1928–9g	Rangers	67	Celtic	51	Motherwell	50
1929–30g	Rangers	60	Motherwell	55	Aberdeen	53
1930–1g	Rangers	60	Celtic	58	Motherwell	56
1931–2g	Motherwell	66	Rangers	61	Celtic	48
1932–3g	Rangers	62	Motherwell	59	Hearts	50
1933–4g	Rangers	66	Motherwell	62	Celtic	47
1934–5g	Rangers	55	Celtic	52	Hearts	50
1935–6g	Celtic	68	Rangers	61	Aberdeen	61
1936–7g	Rangers	61	Aberdeen	54	Celtic	52
1937–8g	Celtic	61	Hearts	58	Rangers	49
1938–9f	Rangers	59	Celtic	48	Aberdeen	46
1946–7f	Rangers	46	Hibernian	44	Aberdeen	39
1947–8g	Hibernian	48	Rangers	46	Partick	46
1948–9i	Rangers	46	Dundee	45	Hibernian	39
1949–50i	Rangers	50	Hibernian	49	Hearts	43
1950–1i	Hibernian	48	Rangers	38	Dundee	38
1951–2i	Hibernian	45	Rangers	41	East Fife	37
1952–3i	*Rangers	43	Hibernian	43	East Fife	39
1953–4i	Celtic	43	Hearts	38	Partick	35

181

	First	Pts	Second	Pts	Third	Pts
1954–5f	Aberdeen	49	Celtic	46	Rangers	41
1955–6f	Rangers	52	Aberdeen	46	Hearts	45
1956–7f	Rangers	55	Hearts	53	Kilmarnock	42
1957–8f	Hearts	62	Rangers	49	Celtic	46
1958–9f	Rangers	50	Hearts	48	Motherwell	44
1959–60f	Hearts	54	Kilmarnock	50	Rangers	42
1960–1f	Rangers	51	Kilmarnock	50	Third Lanark	42
1961–2f	Dundee	54	Rangers	51	Celtic	46
1962–3f	Rangers	57	Kilmarnock	48	Partick	46
1963–4f	Rangers	55	Kilmarnock	49	Celtic	47
1964–5f	*Kilmarnock	50	Hearts	50	Dunfermline	49
1965–6f	Celtic	57	Rangers	55	Kilmarnock	45
1966–7f	Celtic	58	Rangers	55	Clyde	46
1967–8f	Celtic	63	Rangers	61	Hibernian	45
1968–9f	Celtic	54	Rangers	49	Dunfermline	45
1969–70f	Celtic	57	Rangers	45	Hibernian	44
1970–1f	Celtic	56	Aberdeen	54	St Johnstone	44
1971–2f	Celtic	60	Aberdeen	50	Rangers	44
1972–3f	Celtic	57	Rangers	56	Hibernian	45
1973–4f	Celtic	53	Hibernian	49	Rangers	48
1974–5f	Rangers	56	Hibernian	49	Celtic	45

*Won on goal average †Won on deciding match ††Title shared. Competition suspended 1940–46 (Second World War)

SCOTTISH TITLE WINS

Rangers *55	Hibernian 4	Kilmarnock 1
Celtic 52	Dumbarton *2	Motherwell 1
Aberdeen 4	Dundee 1	Third Lanark 1
Hearts 4	Dundee Utd 1	(*Incl 1 shared)

FIRST DIVISION (Since formation of Premier Division)

	First	Pts	Second	Pts	Third	Pts
1975–6d	Partick	41	Kilmarnock	35	Montrose	30
1976–7j	St Mirren	62	Clydebank	58	Dundee	51
1977–8j	*Morton	58	Hearts	58	Dundee	57
1978–9j	Dundee	55	Kilmarnock	54	Clydebank	54
1979–80j	Hearts	53	Airdrieonians	51	Ayr	44
1980–1j	Hibernian	57	Dundee	52	St Johnstone	51
1981–2j	Motherwell	61	Kilmarnock	51	Hearts	50
1982–3j	St Johnstone	55	Hearts	54	Clydebank	50
1983–4j	Morton	54	Dumbarton	51	Partick	46
1984–5j	Motherwell	50	Clydebank	48	Falkirk	45
1985–6j	Hamilton	56	Falkirk	45	Kilmarnock	44
1986–7k	Morton	57	Dunfermline	56	Dumbarton	53
1987–8k	Hamilton	56	Meadowbank	52	Clydebank	49
1988–9j	Dunfermline	54	Falkirk	52	Clydebank	48
1989–90j	St Johnstone	58	Airdrieonians	54	Clydebank	44
1990–1j	Falkirk	54	Airdrieonians	53	Dundee	52
1991–2k	Dundee	58	Partick	57	Hamilton	57
1992–3k	Raith	65	Kilmarnock	54	Dunfermline	52
1993–4k	Falkirk	66	Dunfermline	65	Airdrieonians	54
1994–5l	Raith	69	Dunfermline	68	Dundee	68
1995–6l	Dunfermline	71	Dundee Utd	67	Morton	67
1996–7l	St Johnstone	80	Airdrieonians	60	Dundee	58
1997–8l	Dundee	70	Falkirk	65	Raith	60
1998–9l	Hibernian	89	Falkirk	66	Ayr	62
1999–2000l	St Mirren	76	Dunfermline	71	Falkirk	68
2000–01l	Livingston	76	Ayr	69	Falkirk	56
2001–02l	Partick	66	Airdie	56	Ayr	52

2002–03l	Falkirk	81	Clyde	72	St Johnstone	67
2003–04l	Inverness	70	Clyde	69	St Johnstone	57
2004–05l	Falkirk	75	St Mirren	60	Clyde	60
2005–06l	St Mirren	76	St Johnstone	66	Hamilton	59
2006–07l	Gretna	66	St Johnstone	66	Dundee	53
2007–08l	Hamilton	76	Dundee	69	St Johnstone	58
2008–09l	St Johnstone	65	Partick	55	Dunfermline	51
2009–10l	Inverness	73	Dundee	61	Dunfermline	58
2010–11l	Dunfermline	70	Raith	60	Falkirk	58
2011–12l	Ross	79	Dundee	55	Falkirk	52
2012–13l	Partick	78	Morton	67	Falkirk	53

CHAMPIONSHIP

	First	Pts	Second	Pts	Third	Pts
2013–14l	Dundee	69	Hamilton	67	Falkirk	66
2014–15l	Hearts	91	Hibernian	70	Rangers	67
2015–16l	Rangers	81	Falkirk	70	Hibernian	70
2016–17l	Hibernian	71	Falkirk	60	Dundee Utd	57
2017–18l	St Mirren	74	Livingston	62	Dundee Utd	61
2018–19l	Ross Co	71	Dundee Utd	65	Inverness	56
2019–20C	Dundee Utd	59	Inverness	45	Dundee	41
2020–21m	Hearts	57	Dundee	45	Raith	43
2021–22 l	Kilmarnock	67	Arbroath	65	Inverness	59

C Season curtailed – COVID-19
Maximum points: a, 36; b, 44; c, 40; d 52; e, 60; f, 68; g, 76; h, 84; i, 60; j, 78; k, 88; l, 108;m, 81
*Won on goal difference

SECOND DIVISION

1921–2a	Alloa	60	Cowdenbeath	47	Armadale	45
1922–3a	Queen's Park	57	Clydebank	52	St Johnstone	50
1923–4a	St Johnstone	56	Cowdenbeath	55	Bathgate	44
1924–5a	Dundee Utd	50	Clydebank	48	Clyde	47
1925–6a	Dunfermline	59	Clyde	53	Ayr	52
1926–7a	Bo'ness	56	Raith	49	Clydebank	45
1927–8a	Ayr	54	Third Lanark	45	King'sPark	44
1928–9b	Dundee Utd	51	Morton	50	Arbroath	47
1929–30a	*LeithAthletic	57	East Fife	57	Albion	54
1930–1a	Third Lanark	61	Dundee Utd	50	Dunfermline	47
1931–2a	*E Stirling	55	St Johnstone	55	Stenhousemuir	46
1932–3c	Hibernian	55	Queen of South	49	Dunfermline	47
1933–4c	Albion	45	Dunfermline	44	Arbroath	44
1934–5c	Third Lanark	52	Arbroath	50	St Bernard's	47
1935–6c	Falkirk	59	St Mirren	52	Morton	48
1936–7c	Ayr	54	Morton	51	St Bernard's	48
1937–8c	Raith	59	Albion	48	Airdrieonians	47
1938–9c	Cowdenbeath	60	Alloa	48	East Fife	48
1946–7d	Dundee Utd	45	Airdrieonians	42	East Fife	31
1947–8e	East Fife	53	Albion	42	Hamilton	40
1948–9e	*Raith	42	Stirling	42	Airdrieonians	41
1949–50e	Morton	47	Airdrieonians	44	St Johnstone	36
1950–1e	*Queen of South	45	Stirling	45	Ayr	36
1951–2e	Clyde	44	Falkirk	43	Ayr	36
1952–3	E Stirling	44	Hamilton	43	Queen's Park	37
1953–4e	Motherwell	45	Kilmarnock	42	Third Lanark	36
1954–5e	Airdrieonians	46	Dunfermline	42	Hamilton	39
1955–6b	Queen's Park	54	Ayr	51	St Johnstone	49
1956–7b	Clyde	64	Third Lanark	51	Cowdenbeath	45
1957–8b	Stirling	55	Dunfermline	53	Arbroath	47

1958-9b	Ayr	60	Arbroath	51	Stenhousemuir	46
1959-60b	St Johnstone	53	Dundee Utd	50	Queen of South	49
1960-1b	Stirling	55	Falkirk	54	Stenhousemuir	50
1961-2b	Clyde	54	Queen of South	53	Morton	44
1962-3b	St Johnstone	55	E Stirling	49	Morton	48
1963-4b	Morton	67	Clyde	53	Arbroath	46
1964-5b	Stirling	59	Hamilton	50	Queen of South	48
1965-6b	Ayr	53	Airdrieonians	50	Queen of South	47
1966-7b	Morton	69	Raith	58	Arbroath	57
1967-8b	St Mirren	62	Arbroath	53	East Fife	49
1968-9b	Motherwell	64	Ayr	53	East Fife	48
1969-70b	Falkirk	56	Cowdenbeath	55	Queen of South	50
1970-1b	Partick	56	East Fife	51	Arbroath	46
1971-2b	*Dumbarton	52	Arbroath	52	Stirling	50
1972-3b	Clyde	56	Dunfermline	52	Raith	47
1973-4b	Airdrieonians	60	Kilmarnock	58	Hamilton	55
1974-5b	Falkirk	54	Queen of South	53	Montrose	53

SECOND DIVISION (MODERN)

1975-6d	*Clydebank	40	Raith	40	Alloa	35
1976-7f	Stirling	55	Alloa	51	Dunfermline	50
1977-8f	*Clyde	53	Raith	53	Dunfermline	48
1978-9f	Berwick	54	Dunfermline	52	Falkirk	50
1979-80f	Falkirk	50	E Stirling	49	Forfar	46
1980-1f	Queen's Park	50	Queen of South	46	Cowdenbeath	45
1981-2f	Clyde	59	Alloa	50	Arbroath	50
1982-3f	Brechin	55	Meadowbank	54	Arbroath	49
1983-4f	Forfar	63	East Fife	47	Berwick	43
1984-5f	Montrose	53	Alloa	50	Dunfermline	49
1985-6f	Dunfermline	57	Queen of South	55	Meadowbank	49
1986-7f	Meadowbank	55	Raith	52	Stirling	52
1987-8f	Ayr	61	St Johnstone	59	Queen's Park	51
1988-9f	Albion	50	Alloa	45	Brechin	43
1989-90f	Brechin	49	Kilmarnock	48	Stirling	47
1990-1f	Stirling	54	Montrose	46	Cowdenbeath	45
1991-2f	Dumbarton	52	Cowdenbeath	51	Alloa	50
1992-3f	Clyde	54	Brechin	53	Stranraer	53
1993-4f	Stranraer	56	Berwick	48	Stenhousemuir	47
1994-5g	Morton	64	Dumbarton	60	Stirling	58
1995-6g	Stirling	81	East Fife	67	Berwick	60
1996-7g	Ayr	77	Hamilton	74	Livingston	64
1997-8g	Stranraer	61	Clydebank	60	Livingston	59
1998-9g	Livingston	77	Inverness	72	Clyde	53
1999-2000g	Clyde	65	Alloa	64	Ross Co	62
2000-01g	Partick	75	Arbroath	58	Berwick	54
2001-02g	Queen of South	67	Alloa	59	Forfar Athletic	53
2002-03g	Raith	59	Brechin	55	Airdrie	54
2003-04g	Airdrie	70	Hamilton	62	Dumbarton	60
2004-05g	Brechin	72	Stranraer	63	Morton	62
2005-06g	Gretna	88	Morton	70	Peterhead	57
2006-07g	Morton	77	Stirling	69	Raith	62
2007-08g	Ross	73	Airdrie	66	Raith	60
2008-09g	Raith	76	Ayr	74	Brechin	62
2009-10g	*Stirling	65	Alloa	65	Cowdenbeath	59
2010-11g	Livingston	82	*Ayr	59	Forfar	59
2011-12g	Cowdenbeath	71	Arbroath	63	Dumbarton	58
2012-13g	Queen of South	92	Alloa	67	Brechin	61

LEAGUE ONE

	First	Pts	Second	Pts	Third	Pts
2013–14g	Rangers	102	Dunfermline	63	Stranraer	51
2014–15g	Morton	69	Stranraer	67	Forfar	66
2015–16g	Dunfermline	79	Ayr	61	Peterhead	59
2016–17g	Livingston	81	Alloa	62	Aidrieonians	52
2017–18g	Ayr	76	Raith	75	Alloa	60
2018–19g	Arbroath	70	Forfar	63	Raith	60
2019–20C	Raith	53	Falkirk	52	Airdrieonians	48
2020–21h	Partick	40	Airdrieonians	38	Cove	36
2021–22 g	Cove	79	Airdrieonians	72	Montrose	59

C Season curtailed – COVID-19
Maximum points: a, 76; b, 72; c, 68; d, 52e, 60; f, 78; g, 108;h,66 *Won on goal average/goal difference

THIRD DIVISION (MODERN)

	First	Pts	Second	Pts	Third	Pts
1994–5	Forfar	80	Montrose	67	Ross Co	60
1995–6	Livingston	72	Brechin	63	Caledonian Th	57
1996–7	Inverness	76	Forfar	67	Ross Co	77
1997–8	Alloa	76	Arbroath	68	Ross Co	67
1998–9	Ross Co	77	Stenhousemuir	64	Brechin	59
1999–2000	Queen's Park	69	Berwick	66	Forfar	61
2000–01	*Hamilton	76	Cowdenbeath	76	Brechin	72
2001–02	Brechin	73	Dumbarton	61	Albion	59
2002–03	Morton	72	East Fife	71	Albion	70
2003–04	Stranraer	79	Stirling	77	Gretna	68
2004–05	Gretna	98	Peterhead	78	Cowdenbeath	51
2005–06	*Cowdenbeath	76	Berwick	76	Stenhousemuir	73
2006–07	Berwick	75	Arbroath	70	Queen's Park	68
2007–08	East Fife	88	Stranraer	65	Montrose	59
2008–09	Dumbarton	67	Cowdenbeath	63	East Stirling	61
2009–10	Livingston	78	Forfar	63	East Stirling	61
2010–11	Arbroath	66	Albion	61	Queen's Park	59
2011–12	Alloa	77	Queen's Park	63	Stranraer	58
2012–13	Rangers	83	Peterhead	59	Queen's Park	56

LEAGUE TWO

	First	Pts	Second	Pts	Third	Pts
2013–14	Peterhead	76	Annan	63	Stirling	58
2014–15	Albion	71	Queen's Park	61	Arbroath	56
2015–16	East Fife	62	Elgin	59	Clyde	57
2016–17	Arbroath	66	Forfar	64	Annan	58
2017–18	Montrose	77	Peterhead	76	Stirling	55
2018–19	Peterhead	79	Clyde	74	Edinburgh City	67
2019–20C	Cove	68	Edinburgh City	55	Elgin	43
2020–21	Queen's Park	54	Edinburgh City	38	Elgin	38
2021–22	Kelty	81	Forfar	60	Annan	59

C Season curtailed – COVID-19. Maximum points: 108 (66 in 2020–21). * Won on goal difference

RELEGATED FROM PREMIER DIVISION/PREMIER LEAGUE/PREMIERSHIP

1975–6	Dundee,	St Johnstone	1985–6	No relegation
1976–7	Kilmarnock,	Hearts	1986–7	Clydebank, Hamilton
1977–8	Ayr,	Clydebank	1987–8	Falkirk, Dunfermline, Morton
1978–9	Hearts,	Motherwell	1988–9	Hamilton
1979–80	Dundee,	Hibernian	1989–90	Dundee
1980–1	Kilmarnock,	Hearts	1990–1	No relegation
1981–2	Partick,	Airdrieonians	1991–2	St Mirren, Dunfermline
1982–3	Morton,	Kilmarnock	1992–3	Falkirk, Airdrieonians
1983–4	St Johnstone,	Motherwell	1993–4	St J'stone, Raith, Dundee
1984–5	Dumbarton,	Morton	1994–5	Dundee Utd

1995–6	Falkirk, Partick		2010–11	Hamilton
1996–7	Raith		2011–12	Dunfermline, *Rangers
1997–8	Hibernian		2012–13	Dundee
1998–9	Dunfermline		2013–14	Hibernian, **Hearts
1999–2000	No relegation		2014–15	St Mirren
2000–01	St Mirren		2015–16	Dundee Utd
2001–02	St Johnstone		2016–17	Inverness
2002–03	No relegation		2017–18	Partick, Ross Co
2003–04	Partick		2018–19	Dundee
2004–05	Dundee		2019–20	Hearts
2005–06	Livingston		2020–21	Kilmarnock, Hamilton
2006–07	Dunfermline		2021–22	Dundee
2007–08	Gretna			
2008–09	Inverness			
2009–10	Falkirk			

*Following administration, liquidation and new club formed. **Deducted 15 points for administration

RELEGATED FROM FIRST DIVISION/CHAMPIONSHIP

1975–6	Dunfermline, Clyde		1999–2000	Clydebank
1976–7	Raith, Falkirk		2000–01	Morton, Alloa
1977–8	Alloa, East Fife		2001–02	Raith
1978–9	Montrose, Queen of South		2002–03	Alloa Athletic, Arbroath
1979–80	Arbroath, Clyde		2003–04	Ayr, Brechin
1980–1	Stirling, Berwick		2004–05	Partick, Raith
1981–2	E Stirling, Queen of South		2005–06	Brechin, Stranraer
1982–3	Dunfermline, Queen's Park		2006–07	Airdrie Utd, Ross Co
1983–4	Raith, Alloa		2007–08	Stirling
1984–5	Meadowbank, St Johnstone		2008–09	*Livingston, Clyde
1985–6	Ayr, Alloa		2009–10	Airdrie, Ayr
1986–7	Brechin, Montrose		2010–11	Cowdenbeath, Stirling
1987–8	East Fife, Dumbarton		2011–12	Ayr, Queen of South
1988–9	Kilmarnock, Queen of South		2012–13	Dunfermline, Airdrie
1989–90	Albion, Alloa		2013–14	Morton
1990–1	Clyde, Brechin		2014–15	Cowdenbeath
1991–2	Montrose, Forfar		2015–16	Livingston, Alloa
1992–3	Meadowbank, Cowdenbeath		2016–17	Raith, Ayr
1993–4	Dumbarton, Stirling, Clyde,		2017–18	Dumbarton, Brechin
	Morton, Brechin		2018–19	Falkirk
1994–5	Ayr, Stranraer		2019–20	Partick
1995–6	Hamilton, Dumbarton		2020–21	Alloa
1996–7	Clydebank, East Fife		2021–22	Dunfermline, Queen of South
1997–8	Partick, Stirling		*relegated to Division Three for breaching insolvency	
1998–9	Hamilton, Stranraer		rules	

RELEGATED FROM SECOND DIVISION/LEAGUE ONE

1993–4	Alloa, Forfar, E Stirling,		2007–08	Cowdenbeath, Berwick
	Montrose, Queen's Park,		2008–09	Queen's Park, Stranraer
	Arbroath, Albion,		2009–10	Arbroath, Clyde
	Cowdenbeath		2010–11	Alloa, Peterhead
1994–5	Meadowbank, Brechin		2011–12	Stirling
1995–6	Forfar, Montrose		2012–13	Albion
1996–7	Dumbarton, Berwick		2013–14	East Fife, Arbroath
1997–8	Stenhousemuir, Brechin		2014–15	Stirling
1998–9	East Fife, Forfar		2015–16	Cowdenbeath, Forfar
1999–2000	Hamilton		2016–17	Peterhead, Stenhousemuir
2000–01	Queen's Park, Stirling		2017–18	Queen's Park, Albion
2001–02	Morton		2018–19	Stenhousemuir, Brechin
2002–03	Stranraer, Cowdenbeath		2019–20	Stranraer
2003–04	East Fife, Stenhousemuir		2020–21	Forfar
2004–05	Arbroath, Berwick		2021–22	Dumbarton, East Fife
2005–06	Dumbarton			
2006–07	Stranraer, Forfar			

RELEGATED FROM LEAGUE TWO

2015–16	East Stirling		2019–20	No relegation
2018–19	Berwick		2020–21	Brechin
			2021–22	Cowdenbeath

SCOTTISH PREMIERSHIP 2021–2022
(appearances and scorers)

ABERDEEN

Barron C 13	Hayes J 28 (7)	Ojo F 26 (4)
Bates D 32 (1)	Hedges R 16	Polvara D 3 (2)
Besuijen V 15 (1)	Jenks R 7 (11)	Ramirez C 33 (3)
Brown S.................. 23 (1)	Kennedy M 3 (5)	Ramsey C 20 (4)
Campbell D.............. 7 (5)	Lewis J 34	McCrorie R 30
Considine A.............. 3 (1)	Longstaff M 3 (2)	Ruth M 1 (2)
Emmanuel-Thomas J... 7 (8)	MacKenzie J 14 (6)	Samuels A...................3 (4)
Ferguson L................36	McGeouch D 8 (6)	Watkins M 16 (5)
Gallagher D............. 20 (2)	McGinn N.................. 1 (8)	Woods G.......................... 4
Gurr J 3 (1)	McLennan C 5 (14)	
Harvey L: .... - (1)	Montgomery A............. 4 (3)	

League goals (41): Ferguson 11, Ramirez 10, Watkins 3, Bates 2, Besuijen 2, Brown 2, Hayes 2, Hedges 2, Jenks 2, MacKenzie 1, Ramsey 1, McCrorie 1, Ojo 1, Opponents 1
Scottish Cup goals (4): Ramirez 2, Ferguson 1, Hedges 1. **League Cup goals (1):** Emmanuel-Thomas 1
Europa Conference scorers (11): Ferguson 4, Ramirez 3, Hedges 2, Considine 1, McLennan 1
Player of Year: Ross McCrorie

CELTIC

Abada L.................. 24 (12)	Furuhashi K.............. 16 (4)	Montgomery A..............2 (6)
Ajeti A 3 (4)	Giakoumakis G.......... 11 (10)	O'Riley M 10 (6)
Bain S.........................2	Hart J 35	Ralston A 25 (3)
Barkas V 1	Hatate R 15 (2)	Rogic T 20 (12)
Biton N............. 11 (13)	Ideguchi Y................. - (3)	Scales L 4 (1)
Bolingoli B.....................2	Johnston M 3 (9)	Shaw L.......................- (1)
Carter-Vickers C.............33	Jota 25 (4)	Soro I..........................1 (7)
Christie R 3 (1)	Juranovic J 23 (3)	Starfelt C 34
Dembele K .... - (1)	Maeda D 14 (2)	Taylor G....................22 (2)
Doak B .... - (2)	McCarthy J 4 (6)	Turnbull D 20 (5)
Edouard O................. 3 (1)	McGregor C 33	Welsh S.......................9 (1)
Forrest J 9 (1)	Moffat C 1 (1)	

League goals (92): Giakoumakis 13, Furuhashi 12, Abada 10, Jota 10, Maeda 6, Rogic 6, Turnbull 6, Carter-Vickers 4, Hatate 4, O'Riley 4, Ralston 4, Juranovic 3, Ajeti 2, Edouard 2, McGregor 2, Biton 1, Forrest 1, Scales 1
Scottish Cup goals (10): Giakoumakis 4, Abada 1, Biton 1, Maeda 1, McGregor 1, Scales 1, Taylor 1. **League Cup goals (9):** Furuhashi 3, Abada 1, Edouard 1, Forest 1, Jota 1, Turnbull 1, Welsh 1
Champions League goals (2): Abada 1, McGregor 1. **Europa League goals (23):** Furuhashi 5, Turnbull 3, Abada 2, Forrest 2, Jota 2, Juranovic 2, Ajeti 1, Christie 1, Henderson E 1, Ralston 1, Welsh 1, Opponents 2. **Europa Conference goals (1):** Maeda 1
Player of Year: Callum McGregor

DUNDEE

Adam C 21 (6)	Byrne S 21 (3)	Daley-Campbell V 5 (4)
Anderson M.............. 28 (5)	Chapman J................. - (2)	Elliott C....................9 (4)
Ashcroft L 15 (1)	Cummings J............... 4 (1)	Fontaine L 15 (4)

Griffiths L 9 (6)	McDaid D 3 (4)	Panter C 1
Jakubiak A 2 (5)	McGhee J 30 (4)	Robertson F 1 (1)
Kerr C.............................35	McGinn N 8 (7)	Rossi Z 3
Lawlor I 8	McGowan P 23 (5)	Rudden Z................. 8 (5)
Legzdins A 24	McMullan P 34 (2)	Sharp H 1
Marshall J 29 (1)	Mullen D................. 19 (6)	Sheridan C................ 2 (7)
McCowan L 17 (12)	Mulligan J 5 (6)	Sweeney R 33 (2)

League goals (34): Mullen 7, McCowan 4, Cummings 3, Sweeney 3, Adam 2, Griffiths 2, Mulligan 2, Anderson 1, Ashcroft 1, Elliott 1, Marshall 1, McGhee 1, McGinn 1, McGowan 1, McMullen 1, Rudden 1, Opponents 2
Scottish Cup goals (4): Adam 1, Griffiths 1, McGinn 1, Mulligan 1. **League Cup goals (12):** Cummings 3, McMullan 2, Adam 1, Ashcroft 1, Elliott 1, Jakubiak 1, McCowan 1, McGowan 1, Panter 1
Player of Year: Ryan Sweeney

DUNDEE UNITED

Akinola T 1	Graham R................. 13 (2)	Niskanen I................25 (8)
Anim Cudjoe M........... 1 (1)	Harkes I 27 (1)	Pawlett P 19 (3)
Appere L 4 (9)	Hoti F 2 (3)	Reynolds M 1
Biamou M ....- (3)	Levitt D 23 (2)	Robson J 4
Butcher C 14 (3)	Macleod R 1 (2)	Shankland L 1
Carson T...........................4	McDonald K 6 (3)	Siegrist B 34
Chalmer L 2 (3)	McMinn S 25 (4)	Smith K 3 (2)
Clark N 26 (11)	McNulty M 16 (3)	Smith L 19 (1)
Connolly M ....- (1)	Meekison A............... 7 (2)	Sporle A 7 (9)
Edwards R 36	Mochrie C................ 4 (5)	Thomson M 1
Freeman K 17 (6)	Moore C 1	Watson D................. 2 (4)
Fuchs L.................... 16 (2)	Mulgrew C 30 (1)	Watt T.................. 15 (2)
Glass D.................... 6 (4)	Neilson L 5 (1)	

League goals (37): Clark 8, Levitt 5, Edwards 4, Harkes 3, Graham 2, McNulty 2, Mulgrew 2, Pawlett 2, Smith L 2, Appere 1, Freeman 1, Glass 1, Niskanen 1, Robson 1, Watt 1, Opponents 1
Scottish Cup goals (3): Harkes 1, Levitt 1, McNulty 1. **League Cup goals (11):** Pawlett 3, Shankland 3, Clark 2, Freeman 1, Mochrie 1, Mulgrew 1
Player of Year: Ian Harkes

HEARTS

Atkinson N.............. 23 (2)	Halliday A.............. 15 (12)	Sibbick T................ 11 (3)
Baningime B 23 (1)	Haring P 20 (11)	Simms E.................... 11 (5)
Boyce L 29 (2)	Henderson E .... - (2)	Smith M 19 (1)
Cochrane A 25 (6)	Kingsley S 31 (2)	Souttar J 26 (1)
Devlin C.................... 23 (2)	Kirk M ....- (1)	Stewart R..........................2
Ginnelly J 16 (15)	Mackay-Steven G.... 19 (13)	Thomas M...................- (2)
Gnanduillet A 3 (11)	McEneff A.................. 7 (7)	Walker J...................- (4)
Gordon C.......................36	McKay B 30 (3)	Woodburn B 16 (12)
Halkett C 27 (1)	Moore T................. 16 (6)	

League goals (54): Boyce 10, Kingsley 6, Ginnelly 5, Simms 5, Halliday 4, Souttar 4, Woodburn 3, Cochrane 2, Halkett 2, Mackay-Steven 2, McKay 2, Smith 2, Atkinson 1, Baningime 1, Devlin 1, Gnanduillet 1, Haring 1, McEneff 1, Walker 1
Scottish Cup goals (11): Boyce 2, Haring 2, Simms 2, Baningime 1, Cochrane 1, Halliday 1, Kingsley 1, McEneff 1. **League Cup goals (10):** Boyce 4, Mackay-Steven 2, Halliday 1, McEneff

1, Pollock F 1, Walker 1
Player of Year: Craig Gordon

HIBERNIAN

Aiken M .... - (1)	Gogic A 4 (5)	McGregor D 6 (5)
Allan S 4 (13)	Gullan J 2 (4)	Melkersen E 7 (3)
Blaney J .... - (1)	Hamilton R .... - (1)	Mitchell D 3 (3)
Boyle M 20	Hanlon P 23 (1)	Mueller C 5 (6)
Bradley S .... - (1)	Hauge R .... - (2)	Murphy J 8 (10)
Bushiri R 12 (2)	Henderson E 10 (6)	Newell J 27
Cadden C 28	Jasper S 5 (8)	Nisbet K 26
Campbell J 20 (6)	Dabrowski K 6	O'Connor J .... - (1)
Clarke H 7	MacIntyre O .... - (1)	Porteous R 29
Delferriere A .... - (1)	Macey M 32	Scott J 7 (9)
Doidge C 6 (11)	Mackay D .... - (2)	Stevenson L 19 (4)
Doig J 31 (3)	Magennis K 7	Wood N 1
Doyle-Hayes J 31 (3)	McGinn P 25	Wright D 7 (10)

League goals (38): Boyle 7, Nisbet 5, Scott 4, McGinn 3, Cadden 2, Doidge 2, Doyle-Hayes 2, Magennis 2, Murphy 2, Porteous 2, Campbell 1, Clarke 1, Henderson 1, Mitchell 1, Wright 1, Opponents 2
Scottish Cup goals (7): Melkersen 2, Nisbet 2, Cadden 1, Mitchell 1, Mueller 1. **League Cup goals** (9): Boyle 4, Allan 1, Hanlon 1, Magennis 1, Newell 1, Nisbet 1
Europa Conference goals (7): Boyle 3, Mackay 1, Magennis 1, Murphy 1, Nisbet 1
Player of Year: Chris Cadden

LIVINGSTON

Anderson B 20 (8)	Kelly S 9 (6)	Parkes T 6 (2)
Bailey O 22 (9)	Konovalov I 3	Penrice J 24 (2)
Boyes M 4 (5)	Lewis A 6 (3)	Pittman S 22 (6)
Chukwuemeka C 1 (7)	Longridge J 9 (7)	Reilly G .... - (1)
Devlin N 34 (3)	Maley G .... - (1)	Shinnie A 18 (12)
Fitzwater J 38	McMillan J 11 (5)	Sibbald C 10 (4)
Forrest A 26 (10)	Montano C 7 (7)	Soto S 2 (10)
Hamilton J .... - (8)	Nouble J 13 (3)	Stryjek M 35
Holt J 37	Obileye A 32 (2)	Williamson B 4 (1)
Jacobs K .... - (2)	Omeonga S 25 (2)	
Kabia J .... - (2)	Panayiotou H .... - (4)	

League goals (41): Anderson 11, Forrest 6, Obileye 4, Pittman 4, Bailey 3, Fitzwater 3, Shinnie 3, Devlin 2, Holt 1, McMillan 1, Parkes 1, Opponents 2
Scottish Cup goals (1): Obileye 1. **League Cup goals** (8): Anderson 2, Forrest 1, Longridge 1, Obileye 1, Parkes 1, Sibbald 1, Opponents 1
Player of Year: Max Stryjek

MOTHERWELL

Amaluzor J 2 (8)	Grimshaw L 10 (4)	McGinley N 22 (2)
Carroll J 19 (6)	Johansen J 21 (1)	Mugabi B 29 (2)
Cornelius D 10 (2)	Kelly L 38	Nirennold V 1 (2)
Donnelly L 16 (7)	Lamie R 20 (5)	O'Connor D .... - (1)
Efford J 11 (3)	Lawless S .... - (2)	O'Donnell S 26 (2)
Goss S 26 (3)	Maguire B 11 (2)	O'Hara M 14 (5)

189

Ojala J..................... 18 (3) Shields C................. 17 (8) Watt T 18 (1)
Roberts J................. 7 (11) Slattery C................. 27 (4) Woolery K 24 (7)
Shaw L .... 2 (5) Tierney R .... 5 (9) Van Veen K 24 (8)

League goals (42): Watt 9, Van Veen 9, Lamie 3, Cornelius 2, Efford 2, Mugabi 2, Roberts 2, Shields 2, Slattery 2, Tierney 2, Woolery 2, Goss 1, Grimshaw 1, O'Hara 1, Ojala 1, Opponents 1
Scottish Cup goals (5): Van Veen 2, Donnelly 1, Efford 1, Shields 1. **League Cup goals** (6): Amaluzor 1, Lamie 1, Lawless 1, Maguire 1, Watt 1, Woolery 1
Player of Year: Liam Kelly

RANGERS

Arfield S .... 18 (11) Helander F ....6 McLaughlan J................... 8
Aribo J..................... 31 (3) Itten C .... 3 (3) Morelos A................. 25 (1)
Bacuna J .... 1 (5) Jack R .... 4 (5) Patterson N 2 (4)
Balogun L................ 17 (4) Kamara G .... 28 (3) Ramsey A....................5 (2)
Barisic B................. 22 (1) Kent R ....26 Roofe K...................9 (12)
Bassey C................ 28 (1) King L:.................... 2 (2) Sakala F................13 (17)
Davis S .... 13 (5) Lowry A .... 3 (1) Sands J....................5 (2)
Defoe J.................... - (2) Lundstran J .... 18 (9) Simpson J 1 (3)
Devine A................. 1 (1) McCann C .... - (2) Tavernier J...................35
Diallo A .... 4 (6) McCrorie R ....1 Weston T....................- (1)
Goldson C.....................36 McGregor A ....29 Wright S...................9 (10)
Hagi I.............................15 McKinnon C .... - (1)

League goals (80): Morelos 11, Roofe 10, Sakala 9, Tavernier 9, Aribo 8, Arfield 4, Wright 4, Diallo 3, Goldson 3, Kamara 3, Hagi 2, Kent 2, Ramsey 2, Bacuna 1, Helander 1, Itten 1, Lowry 1, Lundstram 1, McKinnon 1, Opponents 4
Scottish Cup goals (14): Sakala 3, Tavernier 2, Arfield 1 Goldson 1, Helander 1, Itten 1, Jack 1, Lowry 1, Roofe 1, Wright 1, Opponents 1. **League Cup goals** (8): Roofe 3, Arfield 1, Hagi 1, Lundstram 1, Morelos, Wright 1
Champions League goals (2): Davis 1, Morelos 1. **Europa League goals** (24) : Tavernier 7, Morelos 5, Balogun 2, Lundstram 2, Roofe 2, Aribo 1, Hagi 1, Kamara 1, Kent 1, Wright 1, Opponents 1
Player of Year: Alfredo Morelos

ROSS COUNTY

Baldwin J................. 27 (3) Iacovitti A......................31 Samuel D 9 (19)
Paton B .... 6 (4) Laidlaw R......................20 Shaw O ....- (1)
Burroughs J............. 7 (10) Mackinnon A .... 1 (2) Sims J ....- (1)
Callachan R .... 33 (2) Maynard-Brewer A........17 Spittal B 27 (7)
Cancola D .... 12 (6) Munro R............................1 Tillson J 29 (3)
Charles-Cook R........ 36 (1) Paton H .... 23 (8) Vokins J 19 (1)
Clarke H .... 15 (2) Ramsay K .... 5 (3) Watson K...............13 (11)
Donaldson C......................2 Randall C .... 27 (2) White J 31 (7)
Drysdale D .... 3 (2) Robertson A................... - (3) Wright M...................- (4)
Hungbo J............... 21 (12) Samuel A 3 (2)

League goals (47): Charles-Cook 13, Hungbo 7, Spittal 5, White 5, Callachan 4, Clarke 3, Baldwin 2, Iacovitti 2, Cancola 1, Ramsay 1, Samuel D 1, Wright 1, Opponents 2
Scottish Cup goals: None. **League Cup goals** (5): Iacovitti 2, Spittal 2, White 1
Player of Year: Regan Charles-Cook

ST JOHNSTONE

Ambrose E 4 (2)	Dendoncker L 5 (1)	McCann A 4
Bair T .... - (7)	Devine R 4 (2)	McCart J 37
Booth C 25 (2)	Gallacher T 7 (2)	Middleton G 16 (12)
Brown J 16 (6)	Gilmour C 1 (5)	Muller H 7 (1)
Bryson C 8 (1)	Gordon L 30 (1)	Northcott J 1
Butterfield J 12 (6)	Hallberg M 14	O'Halloran M 13 (8)
Ciftci N. 8 (3)	Hendry C 18 (1)	Parish E 6 (1)
Clark Z 32	Kane C 12 (6)	Rooney S 22 (1)
Craigh L 9 (7)	Kerr J 3	Sang T 7 (2)
Crawford A 24 (4)	MacPherson C 11 (9)	Solomon-Otabor V 2 (5)
Cleary D 15	Mahon J 1 (2)	Vertainen E 3 (4)
Davidson M 19 (4)	May S 13 (17)	Wotherspoon D 9 (1)

League goals (24): Hendry 8, Crawford 3, Kane 3, May 2, Butterfield 1, Gordon 1, McCart 1, Middleton 1, O'Halloran 1, Rooney 1, Opponents 4. **Play-offs – goals** (6): Rooney 2, Hallberg 1, Hendry 1, MacPherson 1, May 1
Scottish Cup goals: None. **League Cup goals** (4): Crawford 1, McCart 1, Middleton 1, Rooney 1
Europa Conference goals (3): Kerr 1, O'Halloran 1, Opponents 1. **Europa Conference goals** (1): Kane 1
Player of Year: Zander Clark

ST MIRREN

Alnwick J 33	Greive A 9 (8)	Millar M 9 (3)
Brophy E 23 (8)	Henderson J 11 (8)	Offord K 1 (1)
Dennis K 1 (12)	Jones J 10 (1)	Power A 32 (2)
Dunne C 21 (1)	Kiltie G 19 (6)	Reid D 3
Erhahon E 14 (9)	Lyness D 5 (1)	Ronan C 26 (1)
Erwin L .... - (3)	MacPherson C .... - (2)	Shaughnessy J 36
Flynn R 10 (13)	Main C 16 (15)	Tait R 21 (6)
Fraser M 35 (1)	McAllister K 3 (8)	Tanser S 30 (1)
Gilmartin A .... - (1)	McCarthy C 20 (2)	
Gogic A 12 (1)	McGrath J 18	

League goals (33): Brophy 7, Ronan 7, Shaughnessy 3, Greive 2, Henderson 2, Kiltie 2, Main 2, McGrath 2, Tanser 2, Erhahon 1, Fraser 1, Gogic 1, McCarthy 1,
Scottish Cup goals (8): Kiltie 3, Brophy 1, Greive 1, Jones 1, McAllister 1, Ronan 1. **League Cup goals** (7): Main 2, Dennis 1, Erwin 1, McCarthy 1, McGrath 1, Shaughnessy 1
Player of Year: Connor Ronan

THE THINGS THEY SAY ...

'Absolutely mental' – **Cameron Brannagan** on his history-making four successful penalties in Oxford's 7-2 win at Gillingham.

'Massive respect to them. They were excellent' – **Declan Rice**, England midfielder, after West Ham came within two minutes of FA Cup defeat by sixth-tier Kidderminster.

PREMIER SPORTS LEAGUE CUP 2021–22

Teams awarded three points for group win, one point for drawn match after 90 minutes, then penalties with winners awarded one additional point. Eight group winners and three best runners-up to knockout stage to join five teams competing in Europe – Rangers, Celtic, Hibernian, Aberdeen, St Johnstone.

GROUP A

	P	W	D	L	F	A	Pts
Hearts Q	4	4	0	0	8	0	12
Stirling	4	2	1	1	8	7	8
Inverness	4	1	1	2	5	6	4
Cove	4	1	0	3	6	10	3
Peterhead	4	1	0	3	4	8	3

GROUP B

Dundee Utd Q	4	4	0	0	9	1	12
Arbroath Q	4	3	0	1	6	3	9
Kelty	4	2	0	2	8	5	6
Elgin	4	1	0	3	5	12	3
East Fife	4	0	0	4	2	9	0

GROUP C

Dundee Q	4	4	0	0	14	2	12
Forfar	4	2	1	1	6	5	8
Ross Co	4	2	0	2	5	7	6
Montrose	4	1	1	2	4	6	4
Brora	4	0	0	4	0	9	0

GROUP D

Raith Q	4	2	2	0	5	0	9
Livingston Q	4	2	1	1	7	3	8
Cowdenbeath	4	2	0	2	5	6	6
Alloa	4	1	1	2	2	3	4
Brechin	4	1	0	3	3	10	3

GROUP E

Ayr Q	4	3	1	0	7	0	10
Hamilton	4	2	1	1	5	4	8
Albion	4	0	3	1	4	8	5
Edinburgh City	4	1	1	2	4	5	4
Falkirk	4	1	0	3	6	9	3

GROUP F

Motherwell Q	4	3	0	1	6	4	9
Queen's Park	4	2	1	1	3	2	7
Queen of South	4	2	0	2	9	6	6
Airdrieonians	4	1	2	1	4	5	6
Annan	4	0	1	3	3	8	2

GROUP G

Kilmarnock Q	4	2	1	1	5	6	8
Stranraer	4	2	0	2	5	3	6
Morton	4	1	2	1	3	5	6
East Kilbride	4	1	2	1	5	3	5
Clyde	4	1	1	2	5	6	5

GROUP H

St Mirren Q	4	4	0	0	9	1	12
Dunfermline Q	4	3	0	1	13	5	9
Partick	4	2	0	2	6	7	6
Stenhousemuir	4	1	0	3	5	10	3
Dumbarton	4	0	0	4	2	12	0

SECOND ROUND: Arbroath 2 St Johnstone 2 (aet, St Johnstone won 3-2 on pens); Ayr 1 Dundee Utd 1 (aet, Dundee Utd won 4-3 on pens); Celtic 3 Hearts 2; Dundee 1 Motherwell 0; Hibernian 2 Kilmarnock 0; Livingston 1 St Mirren 1 (aet, Livingston won 4-3 on pens); Raith 2 Aberdeen 1; Rangers 5 Dunfermline 0; **Quarter-finals:** Celtic 3 Raith 0; Dundee 0 St Johnstone 2; Dundee Utd 1 Hibernian 3; Rangers 2 Livingston 0. **Semi-finals** (both at Hampden Park): Celtic 1 St Johnstone 0; Rangers 1 Hibernian 3

FINAL
HIBERNIAN 1 (Hanlon 51) CELTIC 2 (Furuhashi 52, 72)
Hampden Park (48,540); December 19, 2021

Hibernian (4-2-3-1): Macey, McGinn, Porteous, Hanlon (capt), Stevenson (Doig 81), Newell, Doyle-Hayes, Boyle, Campbell (Allan 73), Murphy (Doidge 81), Nisbet. **Subs not used:** Dabrowski, Wright, Gogic, D McGregor, Scott, Cadden. **Booked:** Doyle-Hayes, Nisbet, McGinn. **Manager** (interim): David Gray

Celtic (4-1-4-1): Hart, Juranovic, Carter-Vickers, Starfelt, Taylor (Ralston 75), C McGregor (capt), Abada, Rogic, Turnbull (Bitton 27), Johnston (Scales 83), Furuhashi (Moffat 83). **Subs not used:** Bain, McCarthy, Shaw, Montgomery, Welsh. **Booked:** Juranovic, Johnston. **Manager:** Angelos Postecoglou

Referee: John Beaton. **Half-time:** 0-0. **Referee:** W Collum. **Half-time:** 0-1

SCOTTISH LEAGUE CUP FINALS

1946 Aberdeen 3 Rangers 2
(unofficial competition)
1947 Rangers 4 Aberdeen 0
1948 East Fife 4 Falkirk 1 after 0-0
1949 Rangers 2 Raith Rov 0
1950 East Fife 3 Dunfermline 0
1951 Motherwell 3 Hibernian 0
1952 Dundee 3 Rangers 2
1953 Dundee 2 Kilmarnock 0
1954 East Fife 3 Partick 2
1955 Hearts 4 Motherwell 2
1956 Aberdeen 2 St Mirren 1
1957 Celtic 3 Partick 0 after 0-0
1958 Celtic 7 Rangers 1
1959 Hearts 5 Partick 1
1960 Hearts 2 Third Lanark 1
1961 Rangers 2 Kilmarnock 0
1962 Rangers 3 Hearts 1 after 1-1
1963 Hearts 1 Kilmarnock 0
1964 Rangers 5 Morton 0
1965 Rangers 2 Celtic 1
1966 Celtic 2 Rangers 1
1967 Celtic 1 Rangers 0
1968 Celtic 5 Dundee 3
1969 Celtic 6 Hibernian 2
1970 Celtic 1 St Johnstone 0
1971 Rangers 1 Celtic 0
1972 Partick 4 Celtic 1
1973 Hibernian 2 Celtic 1
1974 Dundee 1 Celtic 0
1975 Celtic 6 Hibernian 3
1976 Rangers 1 Celtic 0
1977† Aberdeen 2 Celtic 1
1978† Rangers 2 Celtic 1
1979 Rangers 2 Aberdeen 1
1980 Dundee Utd 3 Aberdeen 0 after 0-0
1981 Dundee Utd 3 Dundee 0
1982 Rangers 2 Dundee Utd 1
1983 Celtic 2 Rangers 1
1984† Rangers 3 Celtic 2
1985 Rangers 1 Dundee Utd 0
1986 Aberdeen 3 Hibernian 0

1987 Rangers 2 Celtic 1
1988† Rangers 5 Aberdeen 3 on pens
after 3-3
1989 Rangers 3 Aberdeen 2
1990† Aberdeen 2 Rangers 1
1991† Rangers 2 Celtic 1
1992 Hibernian 2 Dunfermline 0
1993† Rangers 2 Aberdeen 1
1994 Rangers 2 Hibernian 1
1995 Raith Rov 6 Celtic 5 on pens after 2-2
1996 Aberdeen 2 Dundee 0
1997 Rangers 4 Hearts 3
1998 Celtic 3 Dundee Utd 0
1999 Rangers 2 St Johnstone 1
2000 Celtic 2 Aberdeen 0
2001 Celtic 3 Kilmarnock 0
2002 Rangers 4 Ayr 0
2003 Rangers 2 Celtic 1
2004 Livingston 2 Hibernian 0
2005 Rangers 5 Motherwell 1
2006 Celtic 3 Dunfermline 0
2007 Hibernian 5 Kilmarnock 1
2008 Rangers 3 Dundee Utd 2 on pens
after 2-2
2009† Celtic 2 Rangers 0
2010 Rangers 1 St Mirren 0
2011† Rangers 2 Celtic 1
2012 Kilmarnock 1 Celtic 0
2013 St Mirren 3 Hearts 2
2014 Aberdeen Inverness 0-0
Aberdeen won 4-2 on pens
2015 Celtic 2 Dundee Utd 0
2016 Ross Co 2 Hibernian 1
2017 Celtic 3 Aberdeen 0
2018 Celtic 2 Motherwell 0
2019 Celtic 1 Aberdeen 0
2020 Celtic 1 Rangers 0
2021 St Johnstone 1 Livingston 0
2022 Celtic 2 Hibernian 1
† After extra time

SUMMARY OF SCOTTISH LEAGUE CUP WINNERS

Rangers 27	Hibernian 3	Raith 1
Celtic 20	Dundee Utd 2	Ross Co 1
Aberdeen 6	Kilmarnock 1	St Johnstone 1
Hearts 4	Livingston 1	St Mirren 1
Dundee.............. 3	Motherwell 1	
East Fife............ 3	Partick.................... 1	

SCOTTISH FA CUP 2021–22

FIRST ROUND

Banks O'Dee 1 Turriff 0
Berwick 2 Gretna 1
Blackburn 1 Rothes 2
Brechin 5 Vale of Leithen 0
Broomhill 6 Glasgow Univ 0
Caledonian 0 Stirling Univ 1
Clachnacuddin 1 Dunipace 2
Clydebank 7 Dalkeith 0
Coldstream 1 East Kilbride 10
Cumbernauld 1 Buckie 1
Deveronvale 2 Haddington 2
Dunbar 2 Camelon 0
East Stirling 3 Fort William 0
Formartine 2 Cumnock 2
Forres 0 Bonnyrigg 2
Fraserburgh 1 Sauchie 2
Golspie 0 Civil Service 3
Huntly 3 Hill of Beath 0
Inverurie 0 Jeanfield 3

Irvine 1 Auchinleck 3
Keith 1 Darvel 2
Lossiemouth 0 Preston 3
Lothian 2 Edinburgh Univ 2
Nairn 4 Strathspey 0
Newtongrange 1 Dalbeattie 1
Penicuik 1 Tranent 3
Spartans 0 Gala 1
Tynecastle 0 Brora 6
Wick 2 Bo'ness 2
Wigtown 0 St Cuthbert 8
Replays
Bo'ness 4 Wick 1
Buckie 4 Cumbernauld 1
Cumnock 1 Formartine 5
Dalbeattie 3 Newtongrange 1
Edinburgh Univ 0 Lothian 3
Haddington 1 Deveronvale 1
(Haddington won 5-3 on pens

SECOND ROUND

Annan 3 Jeanfield 1
Banks O'Dee 5 Nairn 0
Berwick 1 Stirling 2
Brechin 2 Haddington 1
Broomhill 0 Tranent 2
Brora 0 Albion 0
Clydebank 1 Elgin 1
Cowdenbeath 2 Civil Service 4
Dalbeattie 0 Rothes 0
Dunbar 1 Lothian 1
East Kilbride 4 Univ of Stirling 0
East Stirling 0 Bonnyrigg 3
Edinburgh City 2 Bo'ness 1

Formartine 0 Forfar 2
Kelty 4 Buckie 1
Preston 0 Auchinleck 2
Sauchie 2 Dunipace 1
St Cuthbert 1 Gala 3
Stenhousemuir 4 Huntly 1
Stranraer 0 Darvel 1
Replays
Albion 1 Brora 0
Elgin 1 Clydebank 2
Lothian 2 Dunbar 1
Rothes 0 Dalbeattie 1

THIRD ROUND

Alloa 5 Bonnyrigg 0
Arbroath 3 Forfar 0
Auchinleck 1 Hamilton 0
Ayr 2 Albion 1
Banks O'Dee 2 East Fife 1
Brechin 1 Darvel 1
Civil Service 0 Peterhead 3
Clydebank 2 Clyde 0
Cove 2 Queen of South 2
Dalbeattie 1 East Kilbride 2
Dumbarton 3 Sauchie 1
Falkirk 1 Raith 2
Gala 0 Annan 1
Inverness 1 Morton 1

Kelty 0 Montrose 0
Lothian 1 Edinburgh City 2
Partick 1 Dunfermline 0
Queen's Park 0 Kilmarnock 1
Stenhousemuir 0 Airdrieonians 2
Stirling 4 Tranent 0
Replays
Darvel 2 Brechin 2
(Darvel won 5-4 on pens)
Montrose 1 Kelty 1
(Kelty won 3-1 on pens)
Morton 1 Inverness 1
(Morton won 5-4 on pens)
Queen of South 0 Cove 3

FOURTH ROUND

Aberdeen 3 Edinburgh City 0
Alloa 1 Celtic 2
Arbroath 3 Darvel 0

Auchinleck 0 Hearts 5
Ayr 0 St Mirren 2
Banks O'Dee 0 Raith 3

Clydebank 3 Annan 4 (aet)
Dumbarton 0 Dundee 1
Hibernian 1 Cove 1
Kelty 1 St Johnstone 0 (aet)
Kilmarnock1 Dundee Utd 2 (aet)

Livingston 1 Ross Co 0
Motherwell 2 Morton 1 (aet)
Partick 1 Airdrieonians 0
Peterhead 2 East Kilbride 2
(aet, Peterhead won 5-3 on pens)

FIFTH ROUND

Rangers 4 Stirling 0

Annan 0 Rangers 3
Arbroath 1 Hibernian 3
Celtic 4 Raith 0

Hearts 0 Livingston 0
(aet, Hearts won 4-3 on pens)
Motherwell 2 Aberdeen 1
Partick 0 Dundee Utd 1
Peterhead 0 Dundee 3

QUARTER-FINALS

Dundee 0 Rangers 3
Dundee Utd 0 Celtic 3

Hearts 4 St Mirren 2
Motherwell 1 Hibernian 2

SEMI-FINALS

Celtic 1 Rangers 2 (aet)

Hearts 2 Hibernian 1

FINAL

RANGERS 2 (Jack 94, Wright 97) HEARTS 0 - aet
Hampden Park (50,319); May 21, 2022
Rangers (4-3-3): McLaughlin (McGregor 119), Tavernier (capt), Goldson, Balogun, Bassey, Davis (Jack 81), Lundstram, Arfield (Kamara 81), Diallo (Wright 63), Aribo (Sakala 106), Kent. **Subs not used:** Itten, Ramsey, Sands, Roofe, King, Lowry. **Booked:** Diallo. **Manager:** Giovanni van Bronckhorst
Hearts (3-4-1-2): Gordon (capt), Souttar, Halkett, Kingsley, Atkinson, Haring, Devlin (McEneff 105), Cochrane (Mackay-Steven 100), Boyce (Halliday 76), Simms, McKay (Ginnelly 82). **Subs not used:** Stewart, Smith, Woodburn, Moore, Sibbick. **Booked:** Haring, Halkett. **Manager:** Robbie Neilson
Referee: William Collum. **Half-time:** 0-0

SCOTTISH FA CUP FINALS

St Mirren 4 Kelty 0

1874	Queen's Park 2 Clydesdale 0
1875	Queen's Park 3 Renton 0
1876	Queen's Park 2 Third Lanark 0 after 1-1
1877	Vale of Leven 3 Rangers 2 after 0-0, 1-1 draws
1878	Vale of Leven 1 Third Lanark 0
1879	Vale of Leven Cup awarded Rangers withdrew after 1-1
1880	Queen's Park 3 Thornlibank 0
1881	Queen's Park 3 Dumbarton 1
1882	Queen's Park 4 Dumbarton 1after 2-2
1883	Dumbarton 2 Vale of Leven 1 after 2-2
1884	Queen's Park Cup awarded Vale of Leven withdrew from Final
1885	Renton 3 Vale of Leven 1 after 0-0
1886	Queen's Park 3 Renton 1
1887	Hibernian 2 Dumbarton 1
1888	Renton 6 Cambuslang 1
1889	Third Lanark 2 Celtic 1
1890	Queen's Park 2 Vale of Leven 1 after 1-1
1891	Hearts 1 Dumbarton 0
1892	Celtic 5 Queen's Park 1

1893	Queen's Park 2 Celtic 1
1894	Rangers 3 Celtic 1
1895	StBernard's 2 Renton 1
1896	Hearts 3 Hibernian 1
1897	Rangers 5 Dumbarton 1
1898	Rangers 2 Kilmarnock 0
1899	Celtic 2 Rangers 0
1900	Celtic 4 Queen's Park 3
1901	Hearts 4 Celtic 3
1902	Hibernian 1 Celtic 0
1903	Rangers 2 Hearts 0 after 0-0, 1-1
1904	Celtic 3 Rangers 2
1905	Third Lanark 3 Rangers 1 after 0 0
1906	Hearts 1 Third Lanark 0
1907	Celtic 3 Hearts 0
1908	Celtic 5 St Mirren 1
1909	Cup because withheld of riot after two drawn games (2-2, 1-1) final between Celtic and Rangers
1910	Dundee 2 Clyde 1 after 2-2, 0-0
1911	Celtic 2 Hamilton 0 after 0-0
1912	Celtic 2 Clyde 0
1913	Falkirk 2 Raith 0
1914	Celtic 4 Hibernian 1 after 0-0

1915–19 No competition World War I	1975 Celtic 3 Airdrieonians 1
1920 Kilmarnock 3 Albion 2	1976 Rangers 3 Hearts 1
1921 Partick 1 Rangers 0	1977 Celtic 1 Rangers 0
1922 Morton 1 Rangers 0	1978 Rangers 2 Aberdeen 1
1923 Celtic 1 Hibernian 0	1979† Rangers 3 Hibernian 2 after 0-0,0-0
1924 Airdrieonians 2 Hibernian 0	1980† Celtic 1 Rangers 0
1925 Celtic 2 Dundee 1	1981 Rangers 4 Dundee Utd 1 after 0-0
1926 St Mirren 2 Celtic 0	1982† Aberdeen 4 Rangers 1
1927 Celtic 3 East Fife 1	1983† Aberdeen 1 Rangers 0
1928 Rangers 4 Celtic 0	1984† Aberdeen 2 Celtic 1
1929 Kilmarnock 2 Rangers 0	1985 Celtic 2 Dundee Utd 1
1930 Rangers 2 Partick 1 after 0-0	1986 Aberdeen 3 Hearts 0
1931 Celtic 4 Motherwell 2 after 2-2	1987† St Mirren 1 Dundee Utd 0
1932 Rangers 3 Kilmarnock 0 after 1-1	1988 Celtic 2 Dundee Utd 1
1933 Celtic 1 Motherwell 0	1989 Celtic 1 Rangers 0
1934 Rangers 5 St Mirren 0	1990† Aberdeen 9 Celtic 8 on pens after 0-0
1935 Rangers 2 Hamilton 1	1991† Motherwell 4 Dundee Utd 3
1936 Rangers 1 Third Lanark 0	1992 Rangers 2 Airdrieonians 1
1937 Celtic 2 Aberdeen 1	1993 Rangers 2 Aberdeen 1
1938 East Fife 4 Kilmarnock 2 after 1-1	1994 Dundee Utd 1 Rangers 0
1939 Clyde 4 Motherwell 0	1995 Celtic 1 Airdrieonians 0
1940–6 No competition World War II	1996 Rangers 5 Hearts 1
1947 Aberdeen 2 Hibernian 1	1997 Kilmarnock 1 Falkirk 0
1948† Rangers 1 Morton 0 after 1-1	1998 Hearts 2 Rangers 1
1949 Rangers 4 Clyde 1	1999 Rangers 1 Celtic 0
1950 Rangers 3 East Fife 0	2000 Rangers 4 Aberdeen 0
1951 Celtic 1 Motherwell 0	2001 Celtic 3 Hibernian 0
1952 Motherwell 4 Dundee 0	2002 Rangers 3 Celtic 2
1953 Rangers 1 Aberdeen 0 after 1-1	2003 Rangers 1 Dundee 0
1954 Celtic 2 Aberdeen 1	2004 Celtic 3 Dunfermline 1
1955 Clyde 1 Celtic 0 after 1-1	2005 Celtic 1 DundeeUtd 0
1956 Hearts 3 Celtic 1	2006† Hearts 4 Gretna 2 on pens after 1-1
1957† Falkirk 2 Kilmarnock 1 after 1-1	2007 Celtic 1 Dunfermline 0
1958 Clyde 1 Hibernian 0	2008 Rangers 3 Queen of the South 2
1959 St Mirren 3 Aberdeen 1	2009 Rangers 1 Falkirk 0
1960 Rangers 2 Kilmarnock 0	2010 DundeeUtd RossCo 3 0
1961 Dunfermline 2 Celtic 0 after 0-0	2011 Celtic 3 Motherwell 0
1962 Rangers 2 St Mirren 0	2012 Hearts 5 Hibernian 1
1963 Rangers 3 Celtic 0 after 1-1	2013 Celtic 3 Hibernian 0
1964 Rangers 3 Dundee 1	2014 StJohnstone 2 Dundee Utd 0
1965 Celtic 3 Dunfermline 2	2015 Inverness 2 Falkirk 1
1966 Rangers 1 Celtic 0 after 0-0	2016 Hibernian 3 Rangers 2
1967 Celtic 2 Aberdeen 0	2017 Celtic 2 Aberdeen 1
1968 Dunfermline 3 Hearts 1	2018 Celtic 2 Motherwell 0
1969 Celtic 4 Rangers 0	2019 Celtic 2 Hearts 1
1970 Aberdeen 3 Celtic 1	2020 Celtic 4 Hearts 3 on pens after 3-3
1971 Celtic 2 Rangers 1 after 1-1	2021 St Johnstone 1 Hibernian 0
1972 Celtic 6 Hibernian 1	2022 †Rangers 2 Hearts 0
1973 Rangers 3 Celtic 2	† After extra time
1974 Celtic 3 DundeeUtd 0	

SUMMARY OF SCOTTISH CUP WINNERS

Celtic 40, Rangers 34, Queen's Park 10, Hearts 8, Aberdeen 7, Clyde 3, Hibernian 3, Kilmarnock 3, St Mirren 3, Vale of Leven 3, Dundee Utd 2, Dunfermline 2, Falkirk 2, Motherwell 2, Renton 2, St Johnstone 2, Third Lanark 2, Airdrieonians 1, Dumbarton 1, Dundee 1, East Fife 1, Inverness 1, Morton 1, Partick 1, St Bernard's 1

VANARAMA NATIONAL LEAGUE 2021–2022

		P	W	D	L	F	A						GD	Pts
1	Stockport	44	15	3	4	44	17	15	1	6	43	21	49	94
2	Wrexham	44	15	6	1	47	18	11	4	7	44	28	45	88
3	Solihull	44	14	5	3	51	24	11	4	7	32	21	38	87
4	Halifax	44	17	2	3	37	11	8	7	7	25	24	27	84
5	Notts Co	44	15	5	2	47	22	9	5	8	34	30	29	82
6	Grimsby*	44	15	2	5	38	19	8	6	8	30	27	22	77
7	Chesterfield	44	11	4	7	36	26	9	7	6	33	25	18	74
8	Dag & Red	44	10	6	6	46	29	12	1	9	34	24	27	73
9	Boreham Wood	44	11	8	3	28	14	7	5	10	21	26	9	67
10	Bromley	44	11	7	4	36	23	7	6	9	25	30	8	67
11	Torquay	44	11	6	5	39	23	7	6	9	27	31	12	66
12	Yeovil	44	7	7	8	20	25	8	7	7	23	21	-3	59
13	Southend	44	10	5	7	26	19	6	5	11	19	34	-16	58
14	Altrincham	44	10	4	8	39	27	5	6	11	23	42	-7	55
15	Woking	44	8	0	14	28	36	8	5	9	31	25	-2	53
16	Wealdstone	44	8	7	7	24	24	6	4	12	27	41	-14	53
17	Maidenhead	44	9	5	8	32	35	4	7	11	16	32	-19	51
18	Barnet	44	6	6	10	28	42	7	5	10	31	47	-30	50
19	Eastleigh	44	8	6	8	33	33	4	4	14	19	41	-22	46
20	Aldershot	44	4	5	13	19	40	7	5	10	27	33	-27	43
21	King's Lynn	44	4	1	4	22	38	4	6	12	25	41	-32	34
22	Weymouth	44	3	7	12	21	38	3	3	16	19	50	-48	28
23	Dover	44	1	3	18	13	41	1	4	17	24	60	-64	1

Dover deducted 12 pts for failing to complete 2020-21 season

Play-offs (one match): **Quarter-finals:** Halifax 1 Chesterfield 2, Notts Co 1 Grimsby 2 (aet). **Semi-finals:** Solihull 3 Chesterfield 1, Wrexham 4 Grimsby 5, (aet). **Final:** Grimsby 2 Solihull 1 (aet)

Leading scorers: 26 Mullin (Wrexham); 24 Tshimanga (Chesterfield); 23 Madden (Stockport); 19 Dallas (Solihull), Rodrigues (Notts Co), Wootton (Notts Co); 18 McCallum (Dag & Red), Sbarra (Solihull), Waters (Halifax)

Player of Year: Paul Mullin (Wrexham). **Manager of Year**: Dave Challinor (Stockport)

Team of Year: Johnson (Halifax), Richardson (Notts Co), Palmer (Stockport), Hayden (Wrexham), Boyes (Solihull), Sbarra (Solihull), Davies (Wrexham), Rodrigues (Notts Co), Tshimanga (Chesterfield), Mullin (Wrexham), Madden (Stockport)

CHAMPIONS

1979–80	Altrincham	1995–96	Stevenage	2011–2012*	Fleetwood
1980–81	Altrincham	1996–97*	Macclesfield	2012–13*	Mansfield
1981–82	Runcorn	1997–98*	Halifax	2013–14*	Luton
1982–83	Enfield	1998–99*	Cheltenham	2014–15*	Barnet
1983–84	Maidstone	1999–2000*	Kidderminster	2015–16*	Cheltenham
1984–85	Wealdstone	2000–01*	Rushden	2016–17*	Lincoln
1985–86	Enfield	2001–02*	Boston	2017–18*	Macclesfield
1986–87*	Scarborough	2002–03*	Yeovil	2018–19*	Leyton Orient
1987–88*	Lincoln	2003–04*	Chester	2019–20*	Barrow
1988–89*	Maidstone	2004–05*	Barnet	2020–21*	Sutton
1989–90*	Darlington	2005–06*	Accrington	2021–22*	Stockport
1990–91*	Barnet	2006–07*	Dagenham	*Promoted to Football League
1991–92*	Colchester	2007–08*	Aldershot	
1992–93*	Wycombe	2008–09*	Burton	Record attendance – 12,843 Notts
1993–94	Kidderminster	2009–10*	Stevenage	Co v Solihull, Nov 15, 2021
1994–95	Macclesfield	2010–11*	Crawley	

VANARAMA NATIONAL LEAGUE RESULTS 2021–2022

	Aldershot	Altrincham	Barnet	Boreham W	Bromley	Chesterfield	Dag&Red	Dover	Eastleigh	Grimsby	Halifax	King's Lynn	Maidenhead	Notts Co	Solihull	Southend	Stockport	Torquay	Wealdstone	Weymouth	Woking	Wrexham	Yeovil
Aldershot	—	2-2	1-3	2-1	2-3	0-2	0-2	0-0	0-2	2-1	0-1	3-1	1-1	1-3	1-2	1-1	0-2	1-0	1-3	0-2	1-1	0-5	1-2
Altrincham	1-0	—	1-1	2-0	0-0	1-0	2-3	7-3	4-0	2-3	2-0	4-1	2-0	1-0	5-1	2-0	1-4	1-2	4-2	5-0	2-2	0-2	0-1
Barnet	1-0	1-1	—	2-4	2-4	1-0	3-0	6-0	4-0	2-3	3-2	2-0	1-2	0-5	1-2	1-2	1-3	1-2	1-3	3-1	0-3	0-3	2-2
Boreham W	1-0	2-0	2-4	—	2-0	4-2	0-2	1-2	1-0	0-0	2-0	0-1	4-0	1-1	0-3	1-0	0-0	2-0	0-1	1-1	1-1	2-2	2-1
Bromley	1-1	2-3	2-2	2-3	—	4-2	2-1	1-0	3-0	3-1	0-0	3-2	0-0	1-0	0-1	1-1	1-3	2-0	3-2	3-0	0-1	1-1	1-2
Chesterfield	0-0	4-2	7-3	2-1	4-2	—	2-1	3-2	3-0	1-4	1-1	3-0	0-0	1-0	2-3	3-0	0-2	4-0	2-0	4-0	0-0	0-0	1-0
Dag & Red	1-2	2-3	7-3	0-0	4-2	2-1	—	3-1	1-0	1-2	1-3	3-0	0-2	1-2	5-1	2-0	0-2	2-0	2-0	2-2	0-0	3-0	1-0
Dover	1-2	0-1	0-1	0-2	2-1	0-1	0-2	—	3-1	0-1	1-3	0-1	3-0	0-3	1-0	2-5	0-1	1-3	2-3	4-2	1-4	0-1	0-1
Eastleigh	0-3	2-3	2-3	0-2	0-1	2-1	2-1	4-1	—	4-4	1-2	3-3	1-3	2-0	0-0	0-1	2-5	1-3	2-3	1-2	3-2	1-4	0-2
Grimsby	3-1	0-2	2-0	1-0	1-0	0-1	1-0	6-0	4-0	—	2-0	2-2	1-2	0-0	4-0	3-0	0-1	1-3	4-1	3-2	1-0	0-2	0-0
Halifax	1-1	1-0	4-3	0-1	1-0	2-0	1-0	6-0	4-0	1-1	—	0-0	1-2	3-2	0-0	3-1	0-2	2-0	2-1	2-0	2-1	1-2	2-0
King's Lynn	0-1	2-0	2-0	0-1	0-1	1-1	0-1	2-0	3-3	0-1	2-0	—	2-0	1-3	0-1	2-1	1-1	2-3	0-1	2-1	1-2	1-0	2-2
Maidenhead	2-2	0-0	1-2	3-2	1-1	1-1	1-4	6-0	2-2	1-1	0-0	1-4	—	2-1	0-2	2-0	0-2	3-4	0-2	2-0	3-2	2-6	1-1
Notts Co	3-2	5-0	6-1	3-0	1-1	0-2	3-1	2-1	2-2	3-1	2-4	2-3	3-3	—	2-0	4-1	0-3	2-1	1-1	3-1	1-4	2-2	1-1
Solihull	2-1	5-0	1-1	6-1	1-1	3-1	1-0	2-0	2-0	0-1	0-1	2-0	1-1	4-1	—	2-0	0-2	1-0	1-1	2-0	0-2	2-0	1-1
Southend	2-3	2-0	2-0	2-1	0-0	2-0	0-0	2-1	5-3	1-0	1-0	5-0	1-1	0-0	1-1	—	0-1	0-1	4-2	3-4	0-4	2-2	2-1
Stockport	4-0	1-3	2-0	1-0	1-2	0-2	0-4	4-1	3-0	0-3	2-0	5-1	0-0	0-0	1-0	0-1	—	1-0	0-0	1-1	2-1	0-3	0-3
Torquay	2-2	5-0	1-2	2-0	1-1	1-2	1-2	2-1	2-2	2-1	1-2	2-1	1-1	2-1	2-1	1-0	2-1	—	5-0	1-0	2-3	2-2	1-0
Wealdstone	0-1	1-3	2-0	0-3	1-2	1-1	1-2	2-1	0-1	1-1	0-1	0-0	3-1	0-0	2-4	1-1	1-4	0-1	—	5-0	1-2	1-2	0-0
Weymouth	2-2	1-3	1-0	2-0	1-2	1-2	1-2	2-1	1-1	1-2	2-2	1-1	1-0	0-1	1-1	1-1	1-4	3-2	1-1	—	3-2	1-6	2-1
Woking	4-1	2-2	0-3	1-1	0-1	0-0	0-0	1-1	2-3	1-0	2-1	1-2	3-2	1-4	0-2	0-4	2-1	2-3	1-2	2-0	—	2-1	2-1
Wrexham	4-0	0-1	0-3	4-2	2-0	1-1	1-0	6-5	3-2	2-0	1-1	3-0	1-1	1-1	1-1	2-3	3-0	2-2	2-1	2-1	1-0	—	2-0
Yeovil	0-2	1-1	1-0	2-2	0-2	0-3	1-1	1-1	2-1	1-2	1-0	2-0	0-0	0-2	0-1	2-0	2-1	1-2	1-2	1-1	2-0	1-2	—

VANARAMA NATIONAL LEAGUE NORTH

		P	W	D	L	F	A	GD	PTS
1	Gateshead FC	42	29	7	6	99	47	52	94
2	Brackley	42	25	12	5	53	23	30	87
3	AFC Fylde	42	24	8	10	68	37	31	80
4	Kidderminster	42	21	11	10	72	35	37	74
5	York*	42	19	9	14	58	50	8	66
6	Chorley	42	17	14	11	62	49	13	65
7	Boston	42	18	9	15	63	57	6	63
8	Kettering	42	16	13	13	54	48	6	61
9	Alfreton	42	17	10	15	58	59	-1	61
10	Spennymoor	42	17	9	16	55	51	4	60
11	Southport	42	14	15	13	60	55	5	57
12	Hereford	42	15	10	17	51	52	-1	55
13	Darlington	42	14	11	17	57	58	-1	53
14	Curzon	42	13	13	16	51	63	-12	52
15	Leamington	42	12	12	18	39	47	-8	48
16	Chester	42	12	11	19	70	71	-1	47
17	Gloucester	42	10	16	16	47	60	-13	46
18	Bradford PA	42	11	11	20	46	70	-24	44
19	Blyth	42	12	7	23	41	76	-35	43
20	Telford	42	7	16	19	48	65	-17	37
21	Farsley	42	9	10	23	37	78	-41	37
22	Guiseley	42	9	8	25	31	69	-38	35

*also promoted. **Play-off Final:** York 2 Boston 0

VANARAMA NATIONAL LEAGUE SOUTH

		P	W	D	L	F	A	GD	PTS
1	Maidstone	40	27	6	7	80	38	42	87
2	Dorking*	40	25	6	9	101	53	48	81
3	Ebbsfleet	40	24	4	12	78	53	25	76
4	Dartford	40	21	11	8	75	42	33	74
5	Oxford	40	19	12	9	71	46	25	69
6	Eastbourne	40	17	9	14	73	67	6	60
7	Chippenham	40	16	11	13	61	50	11	59
8	Havant & W.	40	15	12	13	58	55	3	57
9	St Albans	40	15	7	18	55	58	-3	52
10	Dulwich	40	13	12	15	63	60	3	51
11	Hampton & R.	40	14	9	17	56	56	0	51
12	Hungerford	40	15	4	21	59	68	-9	49
13	Slough	40	12	13	15	51	69	-18	49
14	Concord	40	13	10	17	53	72	-19	49
15	Hemel H	40	13	9	18	49	72	-23	48
16	Tonbridge	40	11	12	17	43	53	-10	45
17	Braintree	40	11	12	17	38	54	-16	45
18	Bath	40	13	6	21	45	68	-23	45
19	Chelmsford	40	9	14	17	46	53	-7	41
20	Welling	40	10	8	22	46	87	-41	38
21	Billericay	40	9	9	22	41	68	-27	36

*also promoted. **Play-off Final:** Dorking 3 Ebbsfleet 2 (aet)

OTHER LEAGUES 2021–22

JD WELSH PREMIER LEAGUE

	P	W	D	L	F	A	GD	PTS
New Saints	32	25	5	2	86	26	60	80
Bala	32	16	11	5	67	37	30	59
Newtown	32	15	6	11	50	35	15	51
Caernarfon	32	13	4	15	46	53	-7	43
Flint	32	12	6	14	51	53	-2	42
Penybont	32	10	10	12	49	57	-8	40
Cardiff Met	32	10	12	10	35	38	-3	42
Aberystwyth	32	11	7	14	38	45	-7	40
Connah's Quay	32	15	11	6	44	18	26	38
Haverfordwest	32	10	8	14	45	46	-1	38
Barry	32	8	7	17	31	47	-16	31
Cefn Druids	32	2	3	27	22	109	-87	9

Connor's Quay deducted 18 points for ineligible players
Welsh Cup Final: New Saints 3 Penybont 2 – Cardiff City Stadium (2,417). **Welsh League Cup Final**: Connah's Quay 0 Cardiff Met 0 (Connah's Quay won 10-9 on pens)

ISTHMIAN LEAGUE

Worthing	42	31	4	7	100	45	55	97
Bishop's Stortford	42	25	12	5	89	33	56	87
Enfield	42	26	6	10	91	57	34	84
Hornchurch	42	25	6	11	89	42	47	81
Cheshunt*	42	22	10	10	71	40	31	76
Folkestone	42	20	12	10	85	62	23	72
Lewes	42	20	10	12	89	63	26	70
Margate	42	19	8	15	60	62	-2	65
Bognor Regis	42	15	14	13	62	58	4	59
Kingstonian	42	17	8	17	68	71	-3	59
Horsham	42	16	9	17	66	58	8	57
Carshalton	42	15	12	15	65	57	8	57
Potters Bar	42	16	5	21	54	74	-20	53
Corinthian Cas	42	13	13	16	51	58	-7	49
Wingate& Finchley	42	13	10	19	60	74	-14	49
Bowers & Pitsea	42	12	9	21	54	72	-18	45
Haringey	42	9	15	18	57	81	-24	42
Brightlingsea	42	11	6	25	44	92	-48	39
Cray	42	10	9	23	64	85	-21	36
Leatherhead	42	9	9	24	43	83	-40	36
East Thurrock	42	9	8	25	44	98	-54	35
Merstham	42	10	3	29	43	84	-41	33

*Also promoted
Corinthian Cas and Cray deducted 3pts
Play-off Final: Cheshunt 2 Hornchurch 1

NORTHERN LEAGUE PREMIER

	P	W	D	L	F	A	GD	Pts
Buxton	42	23	12	7	80	38	42	81
South Shields	42	23	9	10	71	40	31	78
Scarborough*	42	21	11	10	61	48	13	74
Matlock	42	21	10	11	59	36	23	72
Warrington	42	20	11	11	67	47	20	71
Bamber Bridge	42	21	6	15	67	59	8	69
Whitby	42	19	9	14	57	50	7	66
Stafford	42	15	16	11	55	39	16	61
Utd Manchester	42	18	7	17	66	57	9	61
Morpeth	42	17	10	15	67	59	8	61
Lancaster	42	17	5	20	44	51	-7	56
Mickleover	42	15	10	17	54	65	-11	55
Nantwich	42	14	10	18	46	52	-6	52
Stalybridge	42	15	7	20	51	59	-8	52
Ashton	42	13	12	17	50	59	-9	51
Radcliffe	42	15	6	21	56	73	-17	51
Gainsborough	42	12	14	16	40	52	-12	50
Hyde	42	14	8	20	52	65	-13	50
Atherton	42	13	9	20	34	45	-11	48
Basford	42	12	9	21	32	49	-17	45
Witton	42	12	7	23	48	78	-30	43
Grantham	42	8	10	24	45	81	-36	34

*Also promoted

Play-off Final: Scarborough 2 Warrington 1

SOUTHERN LEAGUE PREMIER SOUTH

Taunton	42	28	7	7	83	42	41	91
Hayes &Yeading	42	26	8	8	100	39	61	86
Farnborough*	42	26	7	9	73	44	29	85
Met Police	42	24	9	9	72	46	26	81
Weston SM	42	23	9	10	72	41	31	78
Chesham	42	22	11	9	80	50	30	77
Yate	42	21	9	12	66	48	18	72
Truro	42	20	10	12	62	54	8	70
Gosport	42	19	9	14	65	56	9	66
Poole	42	19	7	16	74	69	5	64
Walton Cas	42	16	10	16	53	61	-8	58
Swindon Super	42	16	9	17	63	63	0	57
Tiverton	42	15	8	19	61	63	-2	53
Harrow	42	15	7	20	62	77	-15	52
Salisbury	42	13	9	20	49	75	-26	48
Hendon	42	14	5	23	58	70	-12	47
Beaconsfield	42	13	7	22	70	92	-22	46
Hartley Wintney	42	13	5	24	56	75	-19	44
Dorchester	42	12	5	25	41	58	-17	41
Kings Langley	42	9	10	23	49	68	-19	37
Merthy	42	6	8	28	47	94	-47	26
Wimborne	42	4	7	31	35	106	-71	19

*Also promoted

Play-off Final: Farnborough 2 Hayes & Yeading 1

SOUTHERN LEAGUE PREMIER SOUTH CENTRAL

Banbury	40	32	6	2	92	32	60	102
Peterborough Spts*	40	24	7	9	94	46	48	79
Coalville	40	23	9	8	86	47	39	78
Rushall	40	20	9	11	80	54	26	69
Alvechurch	40	18	11	11	57	41	16	65
Rushden	40	19	8	13	57	49	8	65
Leiston	40	18	6	16	59	65	-6	60
Royston	40	17	8	15	65	51	14	59
Hednesford	40	14	12	14	66	64	2	54
Tamworth	40	14	12	14	58	58	0	54
Stourbridge	40	15	8	17	61	71	-10	53
Needham Market	40	12	13	15	66	69	-3	49
Stratford	40	13	8	19	48	70	-22	47
St Ives	40	13	8	19	57	90	-33	47
Redditch	40	11	12	17	38	50	-12	45
Nuneaton	40	11	10	19	51	62	-11	42
Hitchin	40	11	9	20	47	58	-11	42
Bromsgrove	40	10	12	18	36	59	-23	42
Barwell	40	10	11	19	57	78	-21	41
Biggleswade	40	7	13	20	47	64	-17	34
Lowestoft	40	9	6	25	49	93	-44	33

*Also promoted
Play-off Final: Peterborough Spts 2 Coalville 0

HIGHLAND LEAGUE

Fraserburgh	34	30	2	2	135	24	111	92
Buckie	34	29	2	3	127	21	106	89
Brechin	34	28	1	5	102	27	75	85
Brora	34	25	2	7	117	36	81	77
Rothes	34	21	6	7	75	31	44	69
Formartine	34	21	6	7	80	46	34	69
Inverurie	34	19	6	9	77	47	30	63
Nairn	34	11	6	17	61	70	-9	39
Wick	34	10	9	15	55	85	-30	39
Huntly	34	10	7	17	53	67	-14	37
Clachnacuddin	34	10	7	17	51	80	-29	37
Forres	34	8	10	16	45	80	-35	34
Keith	34	10	4	20	36	88	-52	34
Deveronvale	34	9	5	20	55	94	-39	32
Lossiemouth	34	8	6	20	32	83	-51	30
Strathspey	34	5	5	24	47	114	-67	20
Turriff	34	4	6	24	41	96	-55	18
Fort William	34	1	4	29	34	134	-100	7

LOWLAND LEAGUE

Bonnyrigg	34	28	3	3	92	28	64	87
Rangers 11	34	24	1	9	105	42	63	73
Celtic 11	34	23	4	7	82	30	52	73
East Kilbride	34	22	5	7	92	40	52	71
Spartans	34	20	6	8	69	45	24	66
East Stirling	34	15	11	8	61	36	25	56
Strollers	34	17	5	12	66	53	13	56
Berwick	34	17	3	14	75	46	29	54
Caledonian	34	15	8	11	69	48	21	53
Stirling Univ	34	13	6	15	66	68	-2	45
Bo'ness	34	13	6	15	54	60	-6	45
Dalbeattie	34	14	1	19	53	65	-12	43
Gala	34	11	4	19	54	66	-12	37
Cumbernauld	34	10	5	19	53	73	-20	35
Broomhill	34	10	4	20	42	66	-24	34
Edinburgh Univ	34	8	7	19	54	92	-38	31
Gretna	34	2	5	27	36	109	-73	11
Vale of Leithen	34	1	2	31	10	166	-156	5

Inter-league Play-off (on agg): Bonnyrigg 3 Fraserburgh 2

PREMIER LEAGUE UNDER 23

DIVISION ONE

Manchester City	26	16	6	4	65	32	33	54
West Ham	26	15	3	8	59	39	20	48
Arsenal	26	10	11	5	56	48	8	41
Liverpool	26	11	7	8	47	37	10	40
Crystal Palace	26	12	3	11	54	50	4	39
Manchester Utd	26	11	6	9	46	43	3	39
Tottenham,	26	10	7	9	49	45	4	37
Leicester	26	10	7	9	38	53	-15	37
Blackburn	26	9	8	9	50	56	-6	35
Brighton	26	9	7	10	41	41	0	34
Everton	26	8	5	13	33	54	-21	29
Chelsea	26	7	7	12	39	47	-8	28
Leeds	26	7	6	13	44	49	-5	27
Derby	26	4	3	19	31	58	-27	15

DIVISION TWO

Fulham	26	20	2	4	64	27	37	62
Wolves*	26	14	5	7	46	37	9	47
Stoke	26	12	7	7	34	36	-2	43
Nottm Forest	26	12	6	8	52	31	21	42
Norwich	26	12	3	11	64	52	12	39
Burnley	26	11	6	9	46	39	7	39
Southampton	26	12	3	11	45	42	3	39
Newcastle	26	12	2	12	51	56	-5	38
WBA	26	10	5	11	44	54	-10	35
Aston Villa	26	9	5	12	53	51	2	32
Birmingham	26	7	5	14	34	51	-17	26
Middlesbrough	26	8	2	16	31	50	-19	26
Sunderland	26	7	3	16	35	49	-14	24
Reading	26	5	8	13	32	56	-24	23

*Also promoted)
Play-off Final: Wolves 2 Stoke 0

RECORD TITLE SUCCESS FOR CHELSEA WOMEN

On a dramatic final day of the season echoing the men's game, Chelsea came from behind to win a record third successive Super League title. They twice trailed Manchester United to goals from Martha Thomas and Ella Toone. Erin Cuthbert cancelled out the first, then Emma Hayes's side scored twice in five minutes after the interval through Sam Kerr and Guro Reiten. And with second-place Arsenal leading at West Ham, Kerr made it 4-2 with another eye-catching volley to keep Chelsea a point ahead of their rivals. It was their sixth title overall and they completed the Double by beating Manchester City 3-2 in the FA Cup Final with Kerr's extra-time goal watched by a record crowd of 49,094 at Wembley. She swept the board in the domestic end-of-season awards. So did Hayes, who was also named FIFA's top coach and received an OBE in the New Year Honours for her work promoting women's football. Manchester City turned the tables in the League Cup Final with three second-half goals, two from Caroline Weir, for a 3-1 success. In the Champions League, Chelsea fell short again. They topped their group going into the final fixture, but a 4-0 defeat by Wolfsburg meant third place behind the German side and Juventus.

SUPER LEAGUE

	P	W	D	L	F	A	GD	Pts
Chelsea	22	18	2	2	62	11	51	56
Arsenal	22	17	4	1	65	10	55	55
Manchester City	22	15	2	5	60	22	38	47
Manchester Utd	22	12	6	4	45	22	23	42
Tottenham	22	9	5	8	24	23	1	32
West Ham	22	7	6	9	23	33	-10	27
Brighton	22	8	2	12	24	38	-14	26
Reading	22	7	4	11	21	40	-19	25
Aston Villa	22	6	3	13	13	40	-27	21
Everton	22	5	5	12	18	41	-23	20
Leicester	22	4	1	17	14	53	-39	13
Birmingham	22	3	2	17	15	51	-36	11

CHAMPIONSHIP

	P	W	D	L	F	A	GD	Pts
Liverpool	22	16	4	2	49	11	38	52
London City	22	13	2	7	35	22	13	41
Bristol City	22	11	4	7	43	28	15	37
Crystal Palace	22	11	4	7	35	39	-4	37
Charlton	22	10	4	8	27	18	9	34
Durham	22	10	4	8	30	28	2	34
Sheffield Utd	22	9	6	7	34	31	3	33
Lewes	22	9	2	11	23	24	-1	29
Sunderland	22	6	6	10	23	32	-9	24
Blackburn	22	5	2	15	17	41	-24	17
Coventry	22	5	7	10	18	32	-14	12
Watford	22	2	5	15	18	46	-28	11

Leading scorers: 20 Kerr (Chelsea); 14 Miedema (Arsenal); 11 Mead (Arsenal); 10 Hemp (Manchester City); 9 Russo (Manchester Utd), Shaw (Manchester City); 8 England (Chelsea), Galton (Manchester Utd), Stanway (Manchester City); 7 Reiten (Chelsea), Toone (Manchester Utd)
PFA Team of the Season: Berger (Chelsea), Battle (Manchester Utd), Bright (Chelsea), Williamson (Arsenal), Greenwood (Manchester City), Reiten (Chelsea), Weir (Manchester City), Little (Arsenal), Miedema (Arsenal), Kerr (Chelsea), Hemp (Manchester City)

IRISH FOOTBALL 2021–22

SSE AIRTRICITY LEAGUE OF IRELAND

PREMIER DIVISION

	P	W	D	L	F	A	Pts
Shamrock Rov	36	24	6	6	59	28	78
St Patrick's Ath	36	18	8	10	56	42	62
Sligo Rov	36	16	9	11	43	32	57
Derry City	36	14	12	10	49	42	54
Bohemians	36	14	10	12	60	46	52
Dundalk	36	13	9	14	44	46	48
Drogheda	36	12	8	16	45	43	44
Finn Harps	36	11	11	14	44	52	44
Waterford	36	12	6	18	36	56	42R
Longford	36	2	9	25	22	71	15R

Leading scorer: 21 Georgie Kelly (Bohemians). **Player of Year:** Georgie Kelly (Bohemians). **Young Player of Year:** Dawson Devoy (Bohemians). **Goalkeeper of Year:** Vitezslav Jaros (St Patrick's Ath). **Personality of Year:** Stephen Bradley (Shamrock Rov)

FIRST DIVISION

Shelbourne	27	16	9	2	49	23	57P
Galway	27	15	6	6	39	25	51
UCD	27	13	7	7	55	38	46P
Treaty Utd	27	11	9	7	36	27	42
Bray Wdrs	27	9	10	8	36	31	37
Cork City	27	8	9	10	37	28	33
Athlone	27	9	6	12	32	43	33
Cobh	27	8	4	15	25	46	28
Cabinteely	27	8	1	18	26	47	25
Wexford	27	6	3	18	29	56	21

Leading scorer: 22 Colm Whelan (UCD). **Player of Year:** Ryan Brennan (Shelbourne)

Extra.ie FAI CUP FINAL

Bohemians 1 (Feely) **St Patrick's Ath** 1 (Forrester) – aet, St Patrick's Ath won 4-3 on pens, Aviva Stadium, Dublin, November 28, 2021
Bohemians: Talbot, Lyons, Cornwall, D Kelly (Feely), Wilson, Burt, (Ward), Coote (Mallon), Buckley (Levingston),Tierney, Devoy, G Kelly (Omochere)
St Patrick's Ath: Jaros, Bone (Hickman), Barrett (Abankwah), Desmond, Bermingham, Lennon, Benson, Forrester, Smith (McClelland), Lewis (Coughlan), Burns.
Referee: R Hennessy (Limerick)

DANSKE BANK PREMIERSHIP

Linfield	38	24	11	3	67	24	83
Cliftonville	38	24	10	4	61	29	82
Glentoran	38	21	8	9	68	44	71
Crusaders	38	21	5	12	60	36	68
Larne	38	17	11	10	61	39	62
Coleraine	38	14	9	15	55	45	51
Glenavon	38	15	9	14	54	50	54
Ballymena	38	16	5	17	46	52	53
Dungannon	38	11	2	25	46	86	35
Carrick	38	9	7	22	41	67	34
Portadown	38	5	10	23	29	72	25
Warrenpoint	38	6	3	29	35	79	21

(League divided after 33 games)
Leading scorer: 25 Jay Donnelly (Glentoran). **Player of Year:** Chris Shields (Linfield). **Manager of Year:** David Healy (Linfield). **Young Player of Year:** Luke Turner (Cliftonville)

LOUGH 41 CHAMPIONSHIP

Section A

Newry City	38	22	7	9	70	32	73
Annagh	38	20	7	11	73	64	67
Loughgall	38	19	6	13	68	41	63
Ballinamallard	38	17	9	12	69	56	60
H&W Welders	38	18	5	15	62	57	59
Dergview	38	14	13	11	57	53	55

Section B

Ards	38	16	7	15	64	55	55
Dundela	38	15	8	15	65	56	53
Institute	38	13	6	19	44	71	45
Ballyclare	38	11	9	18	51	72	42
Knockbreda	38	8	10	20	61	94	34
Queen's	38	8	7	23	37	70	31

Leading scorer: 19 B J Banda (Ballinamallard) and Michael McLellan (H&W Welders).
Player of Year: Noel Healy (Newry City)

SAMUEL GELSTON WHISKEY IRISH CUP FINAL

Crusaders 2 (Robinson, McMurray) **Ballymena Utd** 1 (Weir og)- aet,Windsor Park, Belfast, May 7, 2022
Crusaders: Tuffey, Forsythe, O'Rourke, Burns (Doyle), Larmour (Wilson), Weir (Robinson), Lowry (Owens), Clarke (McMurray), Lecky, (Caddell), Kennedy, Heatley
Ballymena Utd: Williamson, McGrory, Graham, Keeley (Loughran), Redman, Millar, McCullough, Barr (McElroy), Parkhouse (Kane), Waide (Plaice), Kelly (Henderson).
Referee: T. Clarke (Belfast)

BETMCLEAN LEAGUE CUP FINAL

Cliftonville 4 (Gormley 2, O'Neill 2) **Coleraine** 3 (Shevlin, Lowry, Allen) – aet,
Windsor Park, Belfast, March 12, 2022

COUNTY ANTRIM SHIELD FINAL

Larne 1 (Cosgrove) **Linfield** 0, Seaview, Belfast, January 11, 2022

UEFA CHAMPIONS LEAGUE 2021–22

FIRST QUALIFYING ROUND, FIRST LEG

Slovan Bratislava 2 (Ratao 28, 47) **Shamrock Rov** 0. Att: 500. **Connah's Quay** 2 (Curran 19, Horan 79) Alashkert 2 (Khurtsidze 21, 44). Att: 145. Zalgiris 3 (Videmont 38, Kis 45 pen, Johns 66 og) **Linfield** 1 (Manzinga 54). Att: 1,500

SECOND LEG

Alashkert 1 (Bezecourt 112) **Connah's Quay** 0. Att: 4,000 (aet, Alashkert won 3-2 on agg.) **Linfield** 1 (Shields 66 pen) Zalgiris 2 (Mikoliunas 17, Onzai 44). Att: 888 (Zalgiris won 5-2 on agg). **Shamrock Rov** 2 (Burke 16 pen, Towell 64) Slovan Bratislava 1 (Weiss 72). Att: 1,500 (Slovan Bratislava won 3-2 on agg)

ON AGGREGATE

CFR Cluj 4 Borac Banja 3; Dinamo Zagreb 5 Valur 2; Ferencvaros 6 Prishtina 1; Flora Tallinn 5 Hibernians 0; HJK Helsinki 7 Buducnost 1; Legia Warsaw 5, Bodo Glimt 2; Lincoln Red Imps 7 Fola Esch 2; Kairat Almaty 3 Maccabi Haifa 1; Ludogorets 2 Shakhtyor 0; Malmo 2 Riga 1; Mura 6 Shkendija 0; Neftchi Baku 4 Dinamo Tbilisi 2; Sheriff Tiraspol 5 Teuta Durres 0

SECOND QUALIFYING ROUND, FIRST LEG

Celtic 1 (Abada 39) Midtjylland 1 (Evander 66). Att: 9,000

SECOND LEG

Midtjylland 2 (Mabil 61, Onyedike 94) **Celtic** 1 (McGregor 48). Att: 4,890 (aet, Midtjylland won 3-2 on agg)

ON AGGREGATE

CFR Cluj 4 Lincoln Red Imps 1; Dinamo Zagreb 3 Omonia Nicosia 0; Ferencvaros 5 Zalgiris 1; Legia Warsaw 3 Flora Tallin 1; Ludogorets 3 Mura 1; Malmo 4 HJK Helsinki 3; Olympiacos 2 Neftchi Baku 0; PSV Eindhoven 7 Galatasaray 2; Red Star Belgrade 6 Kairat Almaty 2; Sheriff Tiraspol 4 Alashkert 1; Sparta Prague 3 Rapid Vienna 2; Young Boys 3 Slovan Bratislava 2

THIRD QUALIFYING ROUND, FIRST LEG

Malmo 2 (Rieks 48, Birmancevic 50) **Rangers** 1 (Davis 90). Att: 5,820

SECOND LEG

Rangers 1 (Morelos 19) Malmo 2 (Colak 54, 58). Att: 47,021 (Malmo won 4-2 on agg)

ON AGGREGATE

Benfica 4 Spartak Moscow 0; Dinamo Zagreb 2 Legia Warsaw 1; Ferencvaros 2 Slavia Prague 1; Ludogorets 3 Olympiacos 3 (aet, Ludogorets won 4-1 on pens); Monaco 5 Sparta Prague 1; PSV Eindhoven 4 Midtjylland 0; Shakhtar Donetsk 4 Genk 2; Sheriff Tiraspol 2 Red Star Belgrade 1; Young Boys 4 CFR Cluj 2

PLAY-OFFS, ON AGGREGATE

Benfica 2 PSV Eindhoven 1; Malmo 3 Ludogorets 2; RB Salzburg 4 Brondby 2; Shakhtar Donetsk 3 Monaco 2; Sheriff Tiraspol 3 Dinamo Zagreb 0; Young Boys 6 Ferencvaros 4

GROUP A

September 15, 2021
Club Bruges 1 (Vanaken 27) **Paris SG** 1 (Ander Herrera 15). Att: 27,546
Manchester City 6 (Ake 16, Mukiele 28 og, Mahrez 45 pen, Grealish 56, Joao Cancelo 75, Gabriel Jesus 85) **RB Leipzig** 3 (Nkunku 42, 51, 73). Att: 38,062
Manchester City (4-3-3): Ederson, Joao Cancelo, Ruben Dias, Ake, Zinchenko, De Bruyne (Foden 71), Rodri (Fernandinho 59), Bernardo Silva (Gundogan 59), Mahrez, Ferran Torres (Sterling 72), Grealish (Gabriel Jesus 81). **Booked**: Zinchenko

September 28, 2021
Paris SG 2 (Gueye 8, Messi 74) **Manchester City** 0. Att: 37,350
Manchester City (4-2-3-1): Ederson, Walker, Ruben Dias, Laporte, Joao Cancelo, Bernardo Silva, Rodri, Mahrez, De Bruyne, Grealish (Foden 68), Sterling (Gabriel Jesus 78). **Booked**: Joao Cancelo, De Bruyne.
RB Leipzig 1 (Nkunku 5) **Club Bruges** 2 (Vanaken 22, Rits 41). Att: 23,500

October 19, 2021
Club Bruges 1 (Vanaken 81) **Manchester City** 5 (Joao Cancelo 30, Mahrez 43 pen, 84, Walker 53, Palmer 67). Att: 24,915
Manchester City (4-3-3): Ederson, Walker, Ruben Dias, Laporte (Ake 57), Joao Cancelo, Bernardo Silva (Gundogan 57), Rodri (Fernandinho 71), De Bruyne (Palmer 65), Mahrez, Foden (Sterling 64), Grealish. **Booked**: Laporte
Paris SG 3 (Mbappe 9, Messi 67, 74 pen) **RB Leipzig** 2 (Andre Silva 28, Mukiele 57). Att: 47,359

November 3, 2021
Manchester City 4 (Foden 15, Mahrez 54, Sterling 72, Gabriel Jesus 90+2) **Club Bruges** 1 (Stones 17 og). Att: 50,228
Manchester City (4-3-3): Ederson, Walker (Zinchenko 80), Stones, Laporte, Joao Cancelo, Bernardo Silva (De Bruyne 75), Rodri, Gundogan, Mahrez (Sterling 69), Foden (Palmer 80), Grealish (Gabriel Jesus 68)
RB Leipzig 2 (Nkunku 8, Szoboszlai 90+2 pen) **Paris SG** 2 (Wijnaldum 22, 39). Att: 47,359

November 24, 2021
Club Bruges 0 **RB Leipzig** 5 (Nkunku 12, 90+3, Forsberg 17 pen, 45, Andre Silva 26). Att: 24,072
Manchester City 2 (Sterling 63, Gabriel Jesus 76) **Paris SG** 1 (Mbappe 50), Att: 52,030
Manchester City (4-3-3): Ederson, Walker, Stones, Ruben Dias, Joao Cancelo, Rodri, Gundogan, Zinchenko (Gabriel Jesus 54), Mahrez, Bernardo Silva, Sterling **Booked**: Rodri, Joao Cancelo, Gabriel Jesus

December 7, 2021
Paris SG 4 (Mbappe 2, 7, Messi 38, 76 pen) **Club Bruges** 0. Att: 47,492
RB Leipzig 2 (Szoboszlai 24, Andre Silva 71) **Manchester City** 1 (Mahrez 76) – played behind closed doors
Manchester City (4-3-3): Steffen, Walker, Stones, Ake (Ruben Dias 87), Zinchenko, De Bruyne (Palmer 87), Fernandinho, Gundogan, Mahrez, Grealish, Foden (Sterling 46). **Booked**: De Bruyne, Stones. **Sent off**: Walker (82)

	P	W	D	L	F	A	Pts
Manchester City Q	6	4	0	2	18	10	12
Paris SG Q	6	3	2	1	13	8	11
RB Leipzig	6	2	1	3	15	14	7
Club Bruges	6	1	1	4	6	20	4

GROUP B

September 15, 2021

Atletico Madrid 0 **Porto** 0. Att: 40,098

Liverpool 3 (Tomori 9 og, Salah 48, Henderson 69) **AC Milan** 2 (Rebic 42, Diaz 44). Att: 51,445
Liverpool (4-3-3): Alisson, Alexander-Arnold, Matip, Gomez, Robertson, Henderson (Milner 84), Fabinho, Keita (Thiago Alcantara 71), Salah (Oxlade-Chamberlain 84), Origi (Mane 63), Diogo Jota (Jones 71). **Booked**: Milner

September 28, 2021

AC Milan 1 (Leao 20) **Atletico Madrid** 2 (Griezmann 84, Suarez 90+7 pen). Att: 35,374
Porto 1 (Taremi 75) **Liverpool** 5 (Salah 18, 60, Mane 45, Firmino 77, 81). Att: 23,520
Liverpool (4-3-3): Alisson, Milner (Gomez 66), Matip, Van Dijk, Robertson, Henderson (Oxlade-Chamberlain 73), Fabinho, Jones, Salah (Firmino 67), Diogo Jota (Origi 88), Mane (Minamino 67)

October 19, 2021

Atletico Madrid 2 (Griezmann 20, 34) **Liverpool** 3 (Salah 8, 78 pen, Keita 13). Att: 60,725
Liverpool (4-3-3): Alisson, Alexander-Arnold (Gomez 85), Matip, Van Dijk, Robertson, Milner (Oxlade-Chamberlain 62), Henderson, Keita (Fabinho 46), Salah (N Williams (90+2), Firmino, Mane (Diogo Jota 62). **Booked**: Milner, Alexander-Arnold
Porto 1 (Diaz 65) **AC Milan** 0. Att: 32,130

November 3, 2021

AC Milan 1 (Mbemba 61 og) **Porto** 1 (Diaz 6). Att: 39,675
Liverpool 2 (Diogo Jota 13, Mane 21) **Atletico Madrid** 0. Att: 51,347
Liverpool (4-3-3): Alisson, Alexander-Arnold (Phillips 90+3), Van Dijk, Matip, Tsimikas, Henderson, Fabinho (Thiago Alcantara 60), Oxlade-Chamberlain, Salah, Diogo Jota, Mane (Firmino 46, Origi 78). **Booked**: Mane, Diogo Jota, Matip

November 24, 2021

Atletico Madrid 0 **AC Milan** 1 (Messias 87). Att: 61,019
Liverpool 2 (Thiago Alcantara 52, Salah 70) **Porto** 0. Att: 52,209
Liverpool (4-3-3): Alisson, N Williams, Matip, Konate, Phillips, Tsimikas (Robertson 64), Oxlade-Chamberlain (Milner 82), Morton, Thiago Alcontara (Henderson 63), Salah (Fabinho 71), Minamino, Mane (Origi 72). **Booked**: Konate, Milner

December 7, 2021

AC Milan 1 (Tomori 29) **Liverpool** 2 (Salah 36, Origi 55). Att: 56,237
Liverpool (4-3-3): Alisson, N Williams (Bradley 90+2), Konate, Phillips, Tsimikas, Oxlade-Chamberlain, Morton, Minamino (Woltman 90+2), Salah (Keita 64), Origi (Fabinho 80), Mane (Gomez 65)
Porto 1 (Oliveira 90+6 pen) **Atletico Madrid** 3 (Griezmann 56, Correa 90, De Paul 90+2). Att: 38,830

Liverpool Q	6	6	0	0	17	6	18
Atletico Madrid Q	6	2	1	3	7	8	7
Porto	6	1	2	3	4	11	5
AC Milan	6	1	1	4	6	9	4

GROUP C

September 15, 2021

Besiktas 1 (Montero 90) **Borussia Dortmund** 2 (Bellingham 20, Haaland 45). Att: 22,445
Sporting 1 (Paulinho 33) **Ajax** 5 (Haller 2, 9, 51, 63, Berghuis 39). Att: 20,382

September 28, 2021
Ajax 2 (Berghuis 17, Haller 43) **Besiktas** 0. Att: 52,628
Borussia Dortmund 1 (Malen 37) **Sporting** 0. Att: 25,000

October 19, 2021
Ajax 4 (Reus 11 og, Blind 25, Antony 57, Haller 72) **Borussia Dortmund** 0. Att:54,029
Besiktas 1 (Larin 24) **Sporting** 4 (Coates 15, 27, Sarabia 44 pen, Paulinho 89). Att:22,936

November 3, 2021
Borussia Dortmund 1 (Reus 37 pen) **Ajax** 3 (Tadic 72, Haller 83, Klassen 90+3). Att: 54,820
Sporting 4 (Goncalves 31 pen, 38, Paulinho 38, Sarabia 56) **Besiktas** 0. Att: 40,835

November 24, 2021
Besiktas 1 (Ghezzal 22 pen) **Ajax** 2 (Haller 54, 69). Att: 11,712
Sporting 3 (Goncalves 30, 39, Porro 81) **Borussia Dortmund** 1 (Malen 90+3). Att: 41,341

December 7, 2021
Ajax 4 (Haller 8 pen, Antony 42, Neres 58, Berghuis 62) **Sporting** 2 (Nuno Santos 22, Tabata 78) – played behind closed doors
Borussia Dortmund 5 (Malen 29, Reus 45 pen, 53, Haaland 68, 81) **Besiktas** 0. Att: 15,000

Ajax Q	6	6	0	0	20	5	18
Sporting Q	6	3	0	3	14	12	9
Borussia Dortmund	6	3	0	3	10	11	9
Besiktas	6	0	0	6	3	19	0

GROUP D

September15, 2021
Inter Milan 0 **Real Madrid** 1 (Rodrygo 89). Att: 37,082
Sheriff Tiraspol 2 (Traore 16, Yansane 62) **Shakhtar Donetsk** 0. Att: 5,205

September 28, 2021
Real Madrid 1 (Benzema 65 pen) **Sheriff Tiraspol** 2 (Yakhshiboev 25, Thill 89). Att: 24,522
Shakhtar Donetsk 0 **Inter Milan** 0. Att: 26,170

October 19, 2021
Inter Milan 3 (Dzeko 34, Vidal 58, De Vrij 67) **Sheriff Tiraspol** 1 (Thill 52). Att: 43,305
Shakhtar Donetsk 0 **Real Madrid** 5 (Kyrvsov 37 og, Vinicius Junior 51, 56, Rodrygo 55, Benzema 90+1). Att: 34,037

November 3, 2021
Real Madrid 2 (Benzema 14, 61) **Shakhtar Donetsk** 1 (Fernando 39). Att: 38,105
Sheriff Tiraspol 1 (Traore 90+1) **Inter Milan** 3 (Brozovic 54, Skriniar 66, Sanchez 82). Att: 5,930

November 24, 2021
Inter Milan 2 (Dzeko 61, 67) **Shakhtar Donetsk** 0. Att: 46,225
Sheriff Tiraspol 0 **Real Madrid** 3 (Alaba 30, Kroos 45, Benzema 55). Att: 5,932

December 7, 2021
Real Madrid 2 (Kroos 17, Marco Asensio 79) **Inter Milan** 0. Att: 46,887
Shakhtar Donetsk 1 (Fernando 42) **Sheriff Tiraspol** 1 (Nikolov 90+3). Att: 6,841

Real Madrid Q	6	5	0	1	14	3	15
Inter Milan Q	6	3	1	2	8	5	10
Sheriff Tiraspol	6	2	1	3	7	11	7
Shakhtar Donetsk	6	0	2	4	2	12	2

GROUP E

September 14, 2021
Barcelona 0 **Bayern Munich** 3 (Muller 34, Lewandowski 56, 85). Att: 39,737
Dynamo Kiev 0 **Benfica** 0. Att: 21,657

September 29, 2021
Bayern Munich 5 (Lewandowski 12 pen, 27, Gnabry 68, Sane 74, Choupo-Moting 87)
Dynamo Kiev 0. Att: 25,000
Benfica 3 (Nunez 3, 79 pen, Rafa Silva 69) **Barcelona** 0. Att: 29,454

October 20, 2021
Barcelona 1 (Pique 36) **Dynamo Kiev** 0. Att: 45,968
Benfica 0 **Bayern Munich** 4 (Sane 70, 84, Sousa Everton 80 og, Lewandowski 82). Att: 55,201

November 2, 2021
Bayern Munich 5 (Lewandowski 26, 61, 84, Gnabry 32, Sane 49) **Benfica** 2 (Morato 38, Nunez 74). Att: 50,000
Dynamo Kiev 0 **Barcelona** 1 (Fati 70). Att: 31,378

November 23, 2021
Barcelona 0 **Benfica** 0. Att: 49,952
Dynamo Kiev 1 (Harmash 70) **Bayern Munich** 2 (Lewandowski 14, Coman 42). Att: 28,732

December 8, 2021
Bayern Munich 3 (Muller 34, Sane 43, Musiala 62) **Barcelona** 0 – played behind closed doors
Benfica 2 (Yaremchuk 16, Gilberto 22) **Dynamo Kiev** 0. Att: 36,591

Bayern Munich Q	6	6	0	0	22	3	18
Benfica Q	6	2	2	2	7	9	8
Barcelona	6	2	1	3	2	9	7
Dynamo Kiev	6	0	1	5	1	11	1

GROUP F

September 14, 2021
Villarreal 2 (Trigueros 39, Danjuma 73) **Atalanta** 2 (Freuler 6, Gosens 83). Att: 12,916
Young Boys 2 (Ngamaleu 66, Siebatcheu 90+5) **Manchester Utd** 1 (Ronaldo 13). Att: 31,120
Manchester Utd (4-2-3-1): De Gea, Wan-Bissaka, Lindelof, Maguire, Shaw, Van de Beek (Varane 46), Fred (Martial 89), Sancho (Dalot 37), Bruno Fernandes (Matic 72), Pogba, Ronaldo (Lingard 72). **Booked**: Varane. **Sent off**: Wan-Bissaka (35)

September 29, 2021
Atalanta 1 (Pessina 68) **Young Boys** 0. Att: 8,536
Manchester Utd 2 (Telles 60, Ronaldo 90+5) **Villarreal** 1 (Alcacer 53). Att: 73,130
Manchester Utd (4-1-4-1): De Gea, Dalot, Varane, Lindelof. Telles (Fred 89), McTominay, Greenwood (Lingard 89), Bruno Fernandes, Pogba (Cavani 75), Sancho (Matic 75), Ronaldo. **Booked**: Greenwood, Telles, Ronaldo

October 20, 2021
Manchester Utd 3 (Rashford 53, Maguire 75, Ronaldo 80) **Atalanta** 2 (Pasalic 15, Demiral 29). Att: 72,279
Manchester Utd (4-2-3-1): De Gea, Wan-Bissaka, Lindelof, Maguire, Shaw, McTominay (Pogba 66), Fred (Matic 88), Greenwood (Sancho 73), Bruno Fernandes, Rashford (Cavani 66), Ronaldo. **Booked**: Shaw, Matic, Cavani
Young Boys 1 (Elia 77) **Villarreal** 4 (Pino 6, Gerard 16, Moreno 88, Chukwueze 90+2). Att: 27,398

November 2, 2021
Atalanta 2 (Ilicic 12, Zapata 56) **Manchester Utd** 2 (Ronaldo 45, 90+2). Att: 14,443
Manchester Utd (3-4-2-1): De Gea, Bailly, Varane (Greenwood 38), Maguire, Wan-Bissaka, Pogba (Matic 69), McTominay (Sancho 87), Shaw, Bruno Fernandes (Van de Beek 87), Rashford (Cavani 69), Ronaldo. **Booked**: McTominay
Villarreal 2 (Capoue 36, Danjuma 89) **Young Boys** 0. Att: 14,890

November 23, 2021
Villarreal 0 **Manchester Utd** 2 (Ronaldo 78, Sancho 90). Att: 20,875
Manchester Utd (4-2-3-1): De Gea, Wan-Bissaka, Lindelof, Maguire, Telles, Fred, McTominay, Sancho (Mata 90+3), Van De Beek (Bruno Fernandes 66), Martial (Rashford 66), Ronaldo (Matic 90+1). **Booked**: Van de Beek
Young Boys 3 (Siebatcheu 39, Sierro 80, Hefti 84) **Atalanta** 3 (Zapata 10, Palomino 51, Muriel 87). Att: 31,120

December 8, 2021
Manchester Utd 1 (Greenwood 9) **Young Boys** 1 (Rieder 42). Att: 73,156
Manchester Utd (4-2-2-2): Henderson (Heaton 68) Wan-Bissaka, Bailly, Matic, Shaw (Mengi 61), Van de Beek, Mata (Savage 89). Diallo (Shoretire 68), Lingard (Iqbal 89) Greenwood, Elanga. **Booked**: Shoretire

December 9, 2021
Atalanta 2 (Malinovskyi 71, Zapata 80) **Villarreal** 3 (Danjuma 3, 51, Capoue 52). Att: 11,690

Manchester Utd Q	6	3	2	1	11	8	11
Villarreal Q	6	3	1	2	12	9	10
Atalanta	6	1	3	2	12	13	6
Young Boys	6	1	2	3	7	12	5

GROUP G

September 14, 2021
Lille 0 **Wolfsburg** 0. Att: 34,314
Sevilla 1 (Rakitic 42 pen) **RB Salzburg** 1 (Sucic 21 pen). Att: 18,373

September 29, 2021
RB Salzburg 2 (Adeyimi, 35 pen, 53 pen) **Lille** 1 (Yilmaz 62). Att: 24,207
Wolfsburg 1 (Steffen 48) **Sevilla** 1 (Rakitic 86 pen). Att: 11,733

October 20,2021
Lille 0 **Sevilla** 0. Att: 34,362
RB Salzburg 3 (Adeyemi 3, Okafor 65, 77). **Wolfsburg** 1 (Nmecha 15). Att: 29,520

November 2, 2021
Sevilla 1 (Ocampos 15) **Lille** 2 (David 43 pen, Ikone 51). Att: 29,369
Wolfsburg 2 (Baku 3, Nmecha 60) **RB Salzburg** 1 (Wober 30). Att: 16,112

November 23, 2021
Lille 1 (David 31) **RB Salzburg** 0. Att: 24,207
Sevilla 2 (Jordan 12, Mir 90+7) **Wolfsburg** 0. Att: 28,663

December 8, 2021
RB Salzburg 1 (Okafor 50) **Sevilla** 0 – played behind closed doors
Wolfsburg 1 (Steffen 89) **Lille** 3 (Yilmaz 11, David 72, Gomes 78). Att: 6,544

	P	W	D	L	F	A	Pts
Lille Q	6	3	2	1	7	4	11
RB Salzburg Q	6	3	1	2	8	6	10
Sevilla	6	1	3	2	5	5	6
Wolfsburg	6	1	2	3	5	10	5

GROUP H

September 14, 2021
Chelsea 1 (Lukaku 69) **Zenit St Petersburg** 0. Att: 39,252
Chelsea (3-4-2-1): Mendy, Azpilicueta, Thiago Silva 83), Christensen, Rudiger, James, Jorginho, Kovacic, Marcos Alonso (Chilwell 83), Ziyech (Havertz 63), Mount (Loftus-Cheek 90+3), Lukaku. **Booked**: Azpilicueta
Malmo 0 **Juventus** 3 (Alex Sandro 23, Dybala 45 pen, Alvaro Morata 45). Att: 5,832

September 29, 2021
Juventus 1 (Chiesa 46) **Chelsea** 0. Att: 19,934
Chelsea (3-4-2-1): Mendy, Christensen (Barkley 75), Thiago Silva, Rudiger, Azpilicueta (Loftus-Cheek 62), Jorginho (Chalobah 62), Kovacic, Marcos Alonso (Chilwell 46), Ziyech (Hudson-Odoi 62), Havertz, Lukaku. **Booked**: Ziyech, Marcos Alonso, Rudiger
Zenit St Petersburg 4 (Claudinho 9, Kuzyaev 49, Sutormin 80, Wendel 90+4) **Malmo** 0. Att: 15,339

October 20, 2021
Chelsea 4 (Christensen 9, Jorginho 21 pen, 57 pen, Havertz 48) **Malmo** 0. Att: 39,095
Chelsea (3-4-2-1): Mendy, Christensen, Thiago Silva, Rudiger, Azpilicueta (James 66), Kante (Niguez 65), Jorginho, Chilwell (Marcos Alonso 66), Mount, Werner (Hudson-Odoi 44), Lukaku (Havertz 23)
Zenit St Petersburg 0 **Juventus** 1 (Kulusevski 86). Att: 18,717

November 2, 2021
Juventus 4 (Dybala 11, 58 pen, Chiesa 73, Alvaro Morata 82) **Zenit St Petersburg** 2 (Bonucci 26 og, Azmoun 90+2). Att: 20,053
Malmo 0 **Chelsea** 1 (Ziyech 56). Att: 19,551
Chelsea (3-4-2-1): Mendy, Christensen, Thiago Silva, Rudiger, Azpilicueta, Loftus-Cheek, Jorginho, Marcos Alonso, Ziyech (Barkley 74), Hudson-Odoi (Pulisic 74), Havertz. **Booked**: Thiago Silva, Loftus-Cheek

November 23, 2021
Chelsea 4 (Chalobah 25, James 56, Hudson-Odoi 58, Werner 90+5) **Juventus** 0. Att: 39,513
Chelsea (3-4-2-1): Mendy, Chalobah, Thiago Silva, Rudiger, James, Kante (Loftus-Cheek 37), Jorginho (Saul 76), Chilwell (Azpilicueta 71), Ziyech, Hudson-Odoi (Mount 76), Pulisic (Werner 72)
Malmo 1 (Rieks 28) **Zenit St Petersburg** 1 (Rakitskiy 90+2 pen). Att: 15,520

December 8, 2021
Juventus 1 (Kean 18) **Malmo** 0. Att: 17,501

Zenit St Petersburg 3 (Claudinho 38, Azmoun 41, Ozdoev 90+4) **Chelsea** 3 (Werner 2, 85, Lukaku 62). Att: 29, 349
Chelsea (3-4-1-2): Arrizabalaga, Azpilicueta, Christensen, Sarr, Hudson-Odoi (Pulisic 65), James, Barkley (Ziyech 65), Saul (Marcos Alonso 75), Mount, Lukaku (Havertz 75), Werner. **Booked:** Hudson-Odoi

	P	W	D	L	F	A	Pts
Juventus Q	6	5	0	1	10	6	15
Chelsea Q	6	4	1	1	13	4	13
Zenit St Petersburg	6	1	2	3	10	10	5
Malmo	6	0	1	5	1	14	1

ROUND OF 16, FIRST LEG

February 15, 2022
Paris SG 1 (Mbappe 90+4) **Real Madrid** 0. Att: 47,443
Sporting 0 **Manchester City** 5 (Mahrez 7, Bernardo Silva 17, 44, Foden 32, Sterling 58). Att: 48,129
Manchester City (4-3-3): Ederson, Stones (Zinchenko 61), Ruben Dias, Laporte (Ake 84), Joao Cancelo, Bernardo Silva (Delap 84), Rodri (Fernandinho 73), De Bruyne, Mahrez, Foden (Gundogan 61), Sterling. **Booked:** Gundogan

February 16, 2022
Inter Milan 0 **Liverpool** 2 (Firmino 75, Salah 83). Att: 37,918
Liverpool (4-3-3): Alisson, Alexander-Arnold, Konate, Van Dijk, Robertson, Thiago Alcantara (Milner 86), Fabinho (Henderson 59), Elliott (Keita 59), Salah, Diogo Jota (Firmino 46), Mane
RB Salzburg 1 (Adamu 21) **Bayern Munich** 1 (Coman 90). Att: 29,520

February 22, 2022
Chelsea 2 (Havertz 8, Pulisic 63) **Lille** 0. Att: 38,832
Chelsea (3-4-3): Mendy, Christensen, Thiago Silva, Rudiger, Azpilicueta, Kante, Kovacic (Loftus-Cheek 51), Marcos Alonso (Sarr 80), Ziyech (Saul 60), Havertz, Pulisic (Werner 80). **Booked:** Loftus-Cheek
Villarreal 1 (Parejo 66) **Juventus** 1 (Vlahovic 10). Att: 17,686

February 23, 2022
Atletico Madrid 1 (Joao Felix 7) **Manchester Utd** 1 (Elanga 80). Att: 63,273
Manchester Utd (4-2-3-1): De Gea, Lindelof (Wan-Bissaka 66), Varane, Maguire, Shaw (Telles 67), Fred, Pogba (Matic 66), Rashford (Elanga 75), Bruno Fernandes, Sancho (Lingard 82), Ronaldo. **Booked:** Shaw, Lindelof, Rashford, Fred, Telles
Benfica 2 (Haller 26 og, Yaremchuk 72) **Ajax** 2 (Tadic 18, Haller 29). Att: 54,780

SECOND LEG

March 8, 2022
Bayern Munich 7 (Lewandowski 12 pen, 21 pen, 23, Gnabry 31, Muller 54, 83, Sane 85)
RB Salzburg 1 (Kjaergaard 70). Att: 25,000 (Bayern Munich won 8-2 on agg)
Liverpool 0 **Inter Milan** 1 (Martinez 61). Att: 51,747 (Liverpool won 2-1 on agg)
Liverpool (4-3-3): Alisson, Alexander-Arnold, Matip, Van Dijk, Robertson, Jones (Keita 64), Fabinho, Thiago Alcantara (Henderson 64), Salah, Diogo Jota (Diaz 83), Mane. **Booked:** Diogo Jota, Robertson, Mane

March 9, 2022
Manchester City 0 **Sporting** 0. Att: 51,213 (Manchester City won 5-0 on agg)
Manchester City (4-3-3): Ederson (Carson 73), Egan-Riley, Stones, Laporte (Mbete 84),

Zinchenko, Bernardo Silva (Mahrez 46), Fernandinho, Gundogan, Gabriel Jesus, Foden (McAtee 46), Sterling. **Booked**: Gabriel Jesus
Real Madrid 3 (Benzema 61, 76, 78) **Paris SG** 1 (Mbappe 39). Att: 59,895 (Real Madrid won 3-2 on agg)

March 15, 2022
Ajax 0 **Benfica** 1 (Nunez 77). Att: 54,066 (Benfica won 3-2 on agg)
Manchester Utd 0 **Atletico Madrid** 1 (Lodi). Att: 73,008 (Atletico Madrid won 2-1 on agg
Manchester Utd (4-2-3-1): De Gea, Dalot, Varane, Maguire (Mata 84), Telles, McTominay (Matic 67), Fred (Cavani 75), Bruno Fernandes (Pogba 67), Elanga (Rashford 67), Sancho, Ronaldo. **Booked**: Dalot, Matic

March 16, 2002
Juventus 0 **Villarreal** 3 (Gerard 78 pen, Torres 85, Danjuma 90 pen). Att: 30,385 (Villarreal won 4-1 on agg)
Lille 1 (Yilmaz 38 pen) **Chelsea** 2 (Pulisic 45, Azpilicueta 71 pen). Att: 49.048 (Chelsea won 4-1 on agg)
Chelsea (3-5-2): Mendy, Christensen (Chalobah 33), Thiago Silva, Rudiger, Azpilicueta, Kante, Jorginho (Loftus-Cheek 74), Kovacic (Mount 46), Marcos Alonso, Havertz (Ziyech 83), Pulisic (Lukaku 74). **Booked**: Chalobah

QUARTER-FINALS, FIRST LEG

April 5, 2022
Benfica 1 (Nunez 49) **Liverpool** 3 (Konate 17, Mane 34, Diaz 87). Att: 59,633
Liverpool (4-3-3): Alisson, Alexander-Arnold (Gomez 89), Konate, Van Dijk, Robertson, Keita (Milner 89), Fabinho, Thiago Alcontara (Henderson 61), Salah (Firmino 61), Mane (Diogo Jota 61), Diaz. **Booked**: Thiago Alcontara
Manchester City 1 (De Bruyne 70) **Atletico Madrid** 0. Att: 52,018
Manchester City (4-3-3): Ederson, Joao Cancelo, Stones, Laporte, Ake, De Bruyne, Rodri, Gundogan (Grealish 68), Mahrez (Foden 68), Bernardo Silva, Sterling (Gabriel Jesus 68). **Booked**: Gabriel Jesus, Ederson

April 6, 2022
Chelsea 1 (Havertz 40) **Real Madrid** 3 (Benzema 21, 24, 46). Att: 38,689
Chelsea (3-4-2-1): Mendy, Christensen (Kovacic 46), Thiago Silva, Rudiger, James, Kante (Ziyech 46), Jorginho (Loftus-Cheek 64), Azpilicueta, Mount, Pulisic (Lukaku 64), Havertz. **Booked**: Rudiger
Villarreal 1 (Danjuma 8) **Bayern Munich** 0. Att: 21,626

SECOND LEG

April 12, 2022
Bayern Munich 1 (Lewandowski 52) **Villarreal** 1 (Chukwueze 88). Att: 70,000 (Villarreal won 2-1 on agg)
Real Madrid 2 (Rodrygo 80, Benzema 96) **Chelsea** 3 (Mount 15, Rudiger 51, Werner 75). Att: 59,839 (aet, Real Madrid won 5-4 on agg)
Chelsea (4-3-3): Mendy, James, Thiago Silva, Rudiger, Marcos Alonso, Kante (Ziyech 100), Loftus-Cheek (Saul 105), Kovacic (Jorginho 105), Mount, Werner (Pulisic 83), Havertz. **Booked**: James, Ziyech, Havertz

April 13, 2022
Atletico Madrid 0 **Manchester City** 0. Att: 65,765 (Manchester City won 1-0 on agg)
Manchester City (4-1-4-1): Ederson, Walker (Ake 73), Stones, Laporte, Joao Cancelo, Rodri, Mahrez, Gundogan, De Bruyne (Sterling 65), Bernardo Silva (Fernandinho 79), Foden

Booked: Rodri, Ake, Mahrez, Foden, Joao Cancelo
Liverpool 3 (Konate 21, Firmino 55, 65) **Benfica** 3 (Ramos 32, Yaremchuk 73, Nunez 82).
Att: 51,373 (Liverpool won 6-4 on agg)
Liverpool (4-3-3): Alisson, Gomez, Konate, Matip, Tsimikas, Keita, Henderson (Fabinho 58), Milner (Thiago Alcontara 58), Diaz (Mane 66), Firmino (Origi 90+1), Diogo Jota (Salah 57)

SEMI-FINALS, FIRST LEG

April 26, 2022
Manchester City 4 (De Bruyne 2, Gabriel Jesus 11, Foden 53, Bernardo Silva 74) **Real Madrid** 3 (Benzema 33, 82 pen, Vinicius Junior 55). Att: 52,217
Manchester City (4-3-3): Ederson, Stones (Fernandinho 36), Días, Laporte, Zinchenko, Bernardo Silva, Rodri, De Bruyne, Mahrez, Gabriel Jesus (Sterling 83), Foden. **Booked**: Fernandinho

April 27, 2022
Liverpool 2 (Estupinan 53 og, Mane 55) **Villarreal** 0. Att: 51,586
Liverpool (4-3-3): Alisson, Alexander-Arnold (Gomez 81), Konate, Van Dijk, Robertson, Henderson (Keita 72), Fabinho, Thiago Alcontara, Salah, Mane (Jota 73), Diaz (Origi 81).
Booked: Van Dijk

SECOND LEG

May 3, 2022
Villarreal 2 (Dia 3, Coquelin 41) **Liverpool** 3 (Fabinho 62, Diaz 67, Mane 74). Att: 21,872
(Liverpool won 5-2 on agg)
Liverpool (4-3-3): Alisson, Alexander-Arnold, Konate, Van Dijk, Robertson (Tsimikas 80), Keita (Henderson 79), Fabinho (Milner 84), Thiago Alcontara (Jones 80), Salah, Diogo Jota (Diaz 46), Mane. **Booked**: Alexander-Arnold

May 4, 2022
Real Madrid 3 (Rodrygo 90, 90+1, Benzema 95 pen) **Manchester City** 1 (Mahrez 73). Att: 61,416 (aet, Real Madrid won 6-5 on agg)
Manchester City (4-3-3): Ederson, Walker (Zinchenko 70), Ruben Dias, Laporte, Joao Cancelo, Bernardo Silva, Rodri (Sterling 99), De Bruyne (Gundogan 78), Mahrez (Fernandinho 85), Gabriel Jesus, Foden. **Booked**: Laporte, Sterling, Zinchenko

FINAL
LIVERPOOL 0 REAL MADRID 1 (Vinicius Junior 59)
Stade de France (71,000): May 28, 2022
Liverpool (4-3-3): Alisson, Alexander-Arnold, Konate, Van Dijk, Robertson, Henderson (capt) (Keita 77), Fabinho, Thiago Alcontara (Firmino 77), Salah, Mane, Diaz (Diogo Jota 65). **Subs not used**: Kelleher, Milner, Gomez, Oxlade-Chamberlain, Jones, Minamino, Tsimikas, Matip, Elliott
Booked: Fabinho. **Manager**: Jurgen Klopp
Real Madrid (4-3-3): Courtois, Dani Carvajal, Eder Militao, Alaba, Mendy. Modric (Dani Ceballos 90), Casemiro, Kroos, Valverde (Camavinga 85), Benzema (capt), Vinicius Junior (Rodrygo 90). **Subs not used**: Lunin, Nacho, Marcelo, Hazard, Marco Asensio, Lucas Vazquez, Bale, Isco, Mariano. **Coach**: Carlo Ancelotti
Referee: Clement Turpin (France). **Half-time**: 0-0

Jurgen Klopp urged Liverpool supporters to start booking their tickets for the 2023 Champions League Final in Istanbul after this crushing defeat. A show of bravado? An attempt to lift the spirits of his beaten team? Or a genuine belief that they have the confidence and capacity to do it all over again? Probably all three from a manager whose mental strength and motivational powers have served this club so successfully – and who signed a new contract a month before the final taking him through to 2026 at Anfield. Liverpool succumbed to a sudden burst of goals by Manchester City against Aston Villa on the final afternoon of the Premier League season. Here, on a night when UEFA and the French police stood accused of being responsible for ugly, chaotic scenes outside the stadium which delayed the kick-off, they were denied by an outstanding performance by Thibaut Courtois. The former Chelsea goalkeeper followed his man of-the-match performance by claiming he has not been shown, in some quarters, the respect he felt he deserved. If so, nine saves in the Stade de France, six of them to thwart and frustrate Mohamed Salah, should have set the record straight. There is not too much more a team can do when faced with such an imposing barrier. Klopp, however, will have pondered at length Real's winning goal, how it came about and how to prevent a recurrence. The young Brazilian Vinicius Junior, an influential part of their semi-final victory over Manchester City in a match that will live long in the memory, should not have been able to steal in unmarked at the far post to score, however measured and threatening Federico Valverde's cross had been.

Leading scorers: 15 Benzema (Real Madrid); 13 Lewandowski (Bayern Munich); 11 Haller (Ajax); 8 Salah (Liverpool); 7 Mahrez (Manchester City), Nkunku (RB Leipzig); 6 Danjuma (Villarreal), Mbappe (Paris SG), Nunez (Benfica), Ronaldo (Manchester Utd), Sane (Bayern Munich)

FACTS AND FIGURES

- Carlo Ancelotti became the first coach to win the Champions League four times – twice with AC Milan, twice with Real Madrid.

- Real's Karim Benzema, Dani Carvajal and Luka Modric lifted the trophy for the fifth time. Real's Franciso Gento won it six times as the European Cup.

- Karim Benzema was named Champions League Player of the Year after scoring 15 goals – four of them against Chelsea in the quarter-finals and three when beating Manchester City in the semi-finals.

- It was the Spanish champions' 14th success in the competition – eight as Champions League winners, six in the European Cup.

- This was Liverpool's fourth defeat in the final, having lost previously to Real, AC Milan and Juventus. They have been winners on six occasions.

- Liverpool won all six group matches, the third club to do so and reach the final after AC Milan and Bayern Munich.

EUROPEAN CUP/CHAMPIONS LEAGUE FINALS

1956	Real Madrid 4 Reims 3 (Paris)
1957	Real Madrid 2 Fiorentina 0 (Madrid)
1958†	Real Madrid 3 AC Milan 2 (Brussels)
1959	Real Madrid 2 Reims 0 (Stuttgart)
1960	Real Madrid 7 Eintracht Frankfurt 3 (Glasgow)
1961	Benfica 3 Barcelona 2 (Berne)
1962	Benfica 5 Real Madrid 3 (Amsterdam)
1963	AC Milan 2 Benfica 1 (Wembley)
1964	Inter Milan 3 Real Madrid 1 (Vienna)
1965	Inter Milan 1 Benfica 0 (Milan)
1966	Real Madrid 2 Partizan Belgrade 1 (Brussels)
1967	Celtic 2 Inter Milan 1 (Lisbon)
1968†	Manchester Utd 4 Benfica 1 (Wembley)
1969	AC Milan 4 Ajax 1 (Madrid)

1970†	Feyenoord 2 Celtic 1 (Milan)
1971	Ajax 2 Panathinaikos 0 (Wembley)
1972	Ajax 2 Inter Milan 0 (Rotterdam)
1973	Ajax 1 Juventus 0 (Belgrade)
1974	Bayern Munich 4 Atletico Madrid 0 (replay Brussels after a 1-1 draw Brussels)
1975	Bayern Munich 2 Leeds Utd 0 (Paris)
1976	Bayern Munich 1 St. Etienne 0 (Glasgow)
1977	Liverpool 3 Borussia Moenchengladbach 1 (Rome)
1978	Liverpool 1 Brugge 0 (Wembley)
1979	Nottm Forest 1 Malmo 0 (Munich)
1980	Nottm Forest 1 Hamburg 0 (Madrid)
1981	Liverpool 1 Real Madrid 0 (Paris)
1982	Aston Villa 1 Bayern Munich 0 (Rotterdam)
1983	SV Hamburg 1 Juventus 0 (Athens)
1984†	Liverpool 1 AS Roma 1 (Liverpool won 4-2 on penalties) (Rome)
1985	Juventus 1 Liverpool 0 (Brussels)
1986†	Steaua Bucharest 0 Barcelona 0 (Steaua won 2-0 on penalties) (Seville)
1987	Porto 2 Bayern Munich 1 (Vienna)
1988†	PSV Eindhoven 0 Benfica 0 (PSV won 6-5 on penalties) (Stuttgart)
1989	AC Milan 4 Steaua Bucharest 0 (Barcelona)
1990	AC Milan 1 Benfica 0 (Vienna)
1991†	Red Star Belgrade 0 Marseille 0 (Red Star won 5-3 on penalties) (Bari)
1992	Barcelona 1 Sampdoria 0 (Wembley)
1993	Marseille 1 AC Milan 0 (Munich)
1994	AC Milan 4 Barcelona 0 (Athens)
1995	Ajax 1 AC Milan 0 (Vienna)
1996†	Juventus 1 Ajax 1 (Juventus won 4-2 on penalties) (Rome)
1997	Borussia Dortmund 3 Juventus 1 (Munich)
1998	Real Madrid 1 Juventus 0 (Amsterdam)
1999	Manchester Utd 2 Bayern Munich 1 (Barcelona)
2000	Real Madrid 3 Valencia 0 (Paris)
2001	Bayern Munich 1 Valencia 1 (Bayern Munich won 5-4 on penalties) (Milan)
2002	Real Madrid 2 Bayer Leverkusen 1 (Glasgow)
2003†	AC Milan 0 Juventus 0 (AC Milan won 3-2 on penalties) (Manchester)
2004	FC Porto 3 Monaco 0 (Gelsenkirchen)
2005†	Liverpool 3 AC Milan 3 (Liverpool won 3-2 on penalties) (Istanbul)
2006	Barcelona 2 Arsenal 1 (Paris)
2007	AC Milan 2 Liverpool 1 (Athens)
2008†	Manchester Utd 1 Chelsea 1 (Manchester Utd won 6-5 on penalties) (Moscow)
2009	Barcelona 2 Manchester Utd 0 (Rome)
2010	Inter Milan 2 Bayern Munich 0 (Madrid)
2011	Barcelona 3 Manchester Utd 1 (Wembley)
2012†	Chelsea 1 Bayern Munich 1 (Chelsea won 4-3 on pens) (Munich)
2013	Bayern Munich 2 Borussia Dortmund 1 (Wembley)
2014†	Real Madrid 4 Atletico Madrid 1 (Lisbon)
2015	Barcelona 3 Juventus 1 (Berlin)
2016	Real Madrid 1 Atletico Madrid 1 (Real Madrid won 5-3 on pens) (Milan)
2017	Real Madrid 4 Juventus 1 (Cardiff)
2018	Real Madrid 3 Liverpool 1 (Kiev)† aet
2019	Liverpool 2 Tottenham 0 (Madrid)
2020	Bayern Munich 1 Paris Saint-Germain 0 (Lisbon)
2021	Chelsea 1 Manchester City 0 (Porto)
2022	Real Madrid 1 Liverpool 0 (Paris)

● **C**hampions League since 1993. † after extra time

UEFA EUROPA LEAGUE 2021–22

THIRD QUALIFYING ROUND (selected results)
FIRST LEG

Galatasaray 1 (Boey 61) **St Johnstone** 1 (Kerr 59 pen). Att: 6,216. Jablonec 2 (Pilar 18, Malinsky 86) **Celtic** 4 (Abada 13, Furuhashi 17, Forrest 65, Christie 90). Att: 4,805

SECOND LEG

Celtic 3 (Turnbull 26, 56, Forrest 73) Jablonec 0. Att: 50,076 (Celtic won 7-2 on agg). **St Johnstone** 2 (Cipe 37 og, O'Halloran 90+3) Galatasaray 4 (Diagne 30, Akturkoglu 65, Feghouli 71, Killinc 90+2). Att: 9,106 (Galatasaray won 5-3 on agg)

QUALIFYTING PLAY-OFF ROUND (selected results)
FIRST LEG

Celtic 2 (Furuhashi 13, Forrest 62) Alkmaar 0. Att 52,916. **Rangers** 1 (Morelos 68) Alashkert 0. Att: 42,649

SECOND LEG

Alkmaar 2 (Aboukhial 7, Starfelt 27 og) **Celtic** 1 (Furuhashi 4). Att: 10,041 (Celtic won 3-2 on agg). Alashkert 0 **Rangers** 0. Att: 6,800 (Rangers won 1-0 on agg)

ON AGGREGATE

Fenerbahce 6 HJK Helsinki 2; Galatasary 3 Randers 2; Legia Warsaw 4 Slavia Prague 3; Olympiacos 5 Slovan Bratislava 2; Rapid Vienna 6 Zorya Luhansk 2; Red Star Belgrade 6 CFR Cluj 1; Royal Antwerp 4 Omonia Nicosia 4 (aet, Royal Antwerp won 3-2 on pens). Sturm Graz 5 Mura 1

GROUP A

Match-day 1: Brondby 0 Sparta Prague 0. Att: 18,867. **Rangers** 0 Lyon 2 (Ekambi 23, Tavernier 55 og). Att: 44,906
Match-day 2: Lyon 3 (Ekambi 64, 71, Aouar 86) Brondby 0. Att: 25,466. Sparta Prague 1 (Hancko 29) **Rangers** 0. Att: 10,879
Match-day 3: **Rangers** 2 (Balogun 18, Roofe 30) Brondby 0. Att: 46, 842. Sparta Prague 3 (Haraslin 4, 19, Krejci 90+6) Lyon 4 (Ekambi 42, 88, Aouar 53, De Lima 67). Att: 12,427
Match-day 4: Brondby 1 (Balogun 45 og) **Rangers** 1 (Hagi 77). Att: 20,462. Lyon 3 (Slimani 61, 63, Ekambi 90+2) Sparta Prague 0. Att: 12,427
Match-day 5: Brondby 1 (Uhre 50) Lyon 3 (Cherki 57, 66, Slimani 76). Att: 16,645. **Rangers** 2 (Morelos 15, 48) Sparta Prague 0. Att: 48,370
Match-day 6: Lyon 1 (Bassey 48 og) **Rangers** 1 (Wright 41). Att: 26,842. Sparta Prague 2 (Hancko 43, Hlozek 49) Brondby 0. Att: 976

	P	W	D	L	F	A	Pts
Lyon Q	6	5	1	0	16	5	16
Rangers Q	6	2	2	2	6	5	8
Sparta Prague	6	2	1	3	6	9	7
Brondby	6	0	2	4	2	11	2

GROUP B

Match-day 1: Monaco 1 (Diatta 66) Sturm Graz 0. Att: 2,941. PSV Eindhoven 2 (Gotze 31, Gakpo 54) Real Sociedad 2 (Januzaj 33, Isak 39). Att: 23,135
Match-day 2: Real Sociedad 1 (Merino 53) Monaco 1 (Disasi 16). Att: 23,765. Sturm Graz 1 (Stankovic 55) PSV Eindhoven 4 (Sangare 32, Zahavi 51, Max 74, Vertessen 78). Att: 15,026
Match-day 3: PSV Eindhoven 1 (Gakpo 59) Monaco 2 (Boadu 19, Diop 89). Att: 30,000. Sturm Graz 0 Real Sociedad 1 (Isak 68). Att: 14,809
Match-day 4: Monaco 0 PSV Eindhoven 0. Att: 5,840. Real Sociedad 1 (Sorloth 53) Sturm Graz 1 (Jantscher 38). Att: 14,809
Match-day 5: Monaco 2 (Volland 28, Fofana 37) Real Sociedad 1 (Isak 36). Att: 3,834. PSV Eindhoven 2 (Alves Morais 45, Tue Na Bangna 55) Sturm Graz 0 – played behind closed doors
Match-day 6: Real Sociedad 3 (Oyarzabal 43 pen, 62, Sorloth 90+3) PSV Eindhoven 0. Att: 24,940. Sturm Graz 1 (Jantscher 6 pen) Monaco 1 (Volland 1) – played behind closed doors

Monaco Q	6	3	3	0	7	4	12
Real Sociedad	6	2	3	1	9	6	9
PSV Eindhoven	6	2	2	2	9	8	8
Sturm Graz	6	0	2	4	3	10	2

GROUP C

Match-day 1: **Leicester** 2 (Ayoze Perez 9, Barnes 64) Napoli 2 (Osimhen 69, 87). Att: 29,579. Spartak Moscow 0 Legia Warsaw 1 (Kastrati 90+1). Att: 6,832
Match-day 2: Legia Warsaw 1 (Emrell 31) **Leicester** 0. Att: 27,087. Napoli 2 (Elmas 1, Osimhen 90+4) Spartak Moscow 3 (Promes 55, 90, Ignatov 80). Att: 13,373
Match-day 3: Napoli 3 (Insigne 76, Osimhen 80, Politano 90+5) Legia Warsaw 0. Att: 10,346. Spartak Moscow 3 (Sobolev 11, 86, Larsson 44) **Leicester** 4 (Daka 45, 48, 54, 78). Att: 11,366
Match-day 4: Legia Warsaw 1 (Emreli 10) Napoli 4 (Zielinski 51 pen, Mertens 75 pen, Lozano 78, Ounas 90). Att: 25,706. **Leicester** 1 (Amartey 54) Spartak Moscow 1 (Moses 51). Att: 30,222
Match-day 5: **Leicester** 3 (Daka 11, Maddison 21, Ndidi 33) Legia Warsaw 1 (Mladenovic 26). Att: 30,658. Spartak Moscow 2 (Sobolev 3 pen, 28) Napoli 1 (Elms 64). Att: 10,852
Match-day 6: Legia Warsaw 0 Spartak Moscow 1 (Bakaev 17). Att: 21,629. Napoli 3 (Ounas 4, Elmas 24, 53) **Leicester** 2 (Evans 27, Dewsbury-Hall 33). Att: 14,646

Spartak Moscow Q	6	3	1	2	10	9	10
Napoli	6	3	1	2	15	10	10
Leicester	6	2	2	2	12	11	8
Legia Warsaw	6	2	0	4	4	11	6

GROUP D

Match-day 1: Eintracht Frankfurt 1 (Lammers 41) Fenerbahce 1 (Ozil 10). Att: 25,000. Olympiacos 2 (El Arabi 52, Reabciuk 87) Royal Antwerp 1 (Samatta 74). Att: 15,615
Match-day 2: Antwerp 0 Eintracht Frankfurt 1 (Paciencia 90+1 pen). Att: 13,193. Fenerbahce 0 Olympiacos 3 (Dos Santos 6, Masouras 62, 68). Att: 22,160
Match-day 3: Eintracht Frankfurt 3 (Borre 26 pen, Toure 45, Kamada 59) Olympiacos 1 (El-Arabi 30 pen). Att: 35,000. Fenerbahce 2 (Valencia 20 pen, 45) Royal Antwerp 2 (Samatta 2, Gerkens 62). Att: 16,629
Match-day 4: Olympiacos 1 (El-Arabi 12) Eintracht Frankfurt 2 (Kamada 17, Hauge 90+1). Att: 23,050. Royal Antwerp 0 Fenerbahce 3 (Yandas 9, Meyer 16, Berisha 29). Att: 16,629
Match-day 5: Eintracht Frankfurt 2 (Kamada 12, (Paciencia 90+4) Royal Antwerp 2

(Nainggolan 33, Samatta 88). Att: 30,045. Olympiacos 1 (Francisco Soares 89) Fenerbahce
0. Att: 22,405.
Match-day 6: Fenerbahce 1 (Berisha 42) Eintracht Frankfurt 1 (Sow 29). Att: 8,932. Royal
Antwerp 1 (Balikwisha 6) Olympiacos 0. Att: 7,992

Eintracht Frankfurt Q	6	3	3	0	10	6	12
Olympiacos	6	3	0	3	8	7	9
Fenerbahce	6	1	3	2	7	8	6
Royal Antwerp	6	1	2	3	6	10	5

GROUP E

Match-day 1: Galatasaray 1 (Strakosha 66 og) Lazio 0. Att: 15,353. Lokomotiv Moscow 1
(Anjorin 89) Marseille 1 (Under 59 pen). Att: 8,100
Match-day 2: Lazio 2 (Basic 13, Patric 38) Lokomotiv Moscow 0. Att: 6,767. Marseille 0
Galatasaray 0. Att: 49,870
Match-day 3: Lazio 0 Marseille 0. Att: 8,329. Lokomotiv Moscow 0 Galatasaray 1 (Akturkoglu
82). Att: 8,100
Match-day 4: Galatasaray 1 (Feghouli 43) Lokomotiv Moscow 1 (Kamano 72). Att: 8,100.
Marseille 2 (Milik 33 pen, Payet 82) Lazio 2 (Felipe Anderson 45, Immobile 49). Att: 59,163
Match-day 5: Galatasaray 4 (Cicaldau 12, Caleta-Car 30 og, Feghouli 64, Babel 83) Marseille
2 (Milik 68, 85). Att: 39,758. Lokomotiv Moscow 0 Lazio 3 (Immobile 56 pen, 63 pen. Pedro
87). Att: 8,100
Match-day 6: Lazio 0 Galatasaray 0. Att:13.178. Marseille 1 (Milik 35) Lokomotiv Moscow 0.
Att: 42,614

Galatasaray Q	6	3	3	0	7	3	12
Lazio	6	2	3	1	7	3	9
Marseille	6	1	4	1	6	7	7
Lokomotiv Moscow	6	0	2	4	2	9	2

GROUP F

Match-day 1: Red Star Belgrade 2 (Rodic 74, Katai 85 pen) Sporting Braga 1 (Galeno 76).
Att: 24,671. Midtjylland 1 (Isaksen 3) Ludogorets 1 (Despodov 32). Att: 6,568
Match-day 2: Ludogorets 0 Red Star Belgrade 1 (Kanga 64). Att: 3,078. Sporting Braga 3
(Galeno 55 pen, 90+5, Horta 62) Midtjylland 1 (Da Silva Ferreira 19 pen). Att: 5,449.
Match-day 3: Ludogorets 0 Sporting Braga 1 (Horta 7). Att: 2,280. Midtjylland 1 (Dyhr 78)
Red Star Belgrade 1 (Ivanic 58). Att: 8,438.
Match-day 4: Red Star Belgrade 0 Midtjylland 1 (Da Silva Ferreira 56). Att: 23,070. Sporting
Braga 4 (Al Musrati 25, Medeiros 37, Galeno 40, Gonzales 73) Ludogorets 2 (Sotiriou 33,
Plastun 75). Att: 6,221
Match-day 5: Midtjylland 3 (Sviatchenko 2, Isaksen 48, Da Silva Ferreira 90+2 pen) Sporting
Braga 2 (Horta 43, Galeno 85). Att: 7,189. Red Star Belgrade 1 (Ivanic 57) Ludogorets 0.
Att: 11,252
Match-day 6: Ludogorets 0 Midtjylland 0. Att: 556. Sporting Braga 1 (Galeno 52 pen) Red
Star Belgrade 1 (Katai 70 pen). Att: 5,344

Red Star Belgarde Q	6	3	2	1	6	4	11
Sporting Braga Q	6	3	1	2	12	9	10
Midtjylland	6	2	3	1	7	7	9
Ludogorets	6	0	2	4	3	8	2

GROUP G

Match-day 1: Bayer Leverkusen 2 (Palacios 37, Wirtz 69) Ferencvaros 1 (Mmaee 8). Att: 11,013. Real Betis 4 (Miranda 32, Juanmi 34, 53, Iglesias 50) **Celtic** 3 (Ajeti 13, Juranovic 27 pen, Ralston 87). Att: 30,893
Match-day 2: Celtic 0 Bayer Leverkusen 4 (Hincaple 25, Wirtz 35, Alario 58 pen, Adli 90). Att: 55,436. Ferencvaros 1 (Uzuni 44) Real Betis 3 (Fekir 17, Wingo 75 og, Tello 90+5). Att: 16,579
Match-day 3: Celtic 2 (Furuhashi 57, Vecsel 81 og) Ferencvaros 0. Att:50,427. Real Betis 1 (Iglesias 75 pen) Bayer Leverkusen 1 (Andrich 82). Att: 39,230
Match-day 4: Bayer Leverkusen 4 (Diaby 42, 52, Wirtz 86, Amiri 90) Real Betis 0. Att: 15,208. Ferencvaros 2 (Juranovic 11 og, Uzuni 86) **Celtic** 3 (Furuhashi 3, Neves Filipe 23, Abada 60). Att: 16,501
Match-day 5: Bayer Leverkusen 3 (Andrich 16, 82, Diaby 87) **Celtic** 2 (Juranovic 40 pen, Neves Filipe 56). Att: 19,830. Real Betis 2 (Tello 5, Canales 52) Ferencvaros 0. Att: 30,137
Match-day 6: **Celtic** 3 (Welsh 3, Henderson 72, Turnbull 78 pen) Real Betis 2 (Bain 69 og, Iglesias 74). Att: 54,548. Ferencvaros 1 (Laidouni 82) Bayer Leverkusen 0. Att: 12,127

Bayer Leverkusen Q	6	4	1	1	14	5	13
Real Betis Q	6	3	1	2	12	12	10
Celtic	6	3	0	3	13	15	9
Ferencvaros	6	1	0	5	5	12	3

GROUP H

Match-day 1: Dinamo Zagreb 0 **West Ham** 2 (Antonio 21, Rice 50). Att: 12,344. Rapid Vienna 0 Genk 1 (Onuachu 90+2). Att: 18,400
Match-day 2: Genk 0 Dinamo Zagreb 3 (Ivanusec 10, Petkovic 45 pen, 66 pen). Att: 11,262. **West Ham** 2 (Rice 29, Benrahma 90+4) Rapid Vienna 0. Att: 50,004
Match-day 3: Rapid Vienna 2 (Grull 9, Hofmann 34) Dinamo Zagreb 1 (Orsic 240. Att: 22,300. **West Ham** 3 (Dawson 57, Diop 57, Bowen 58) Genk 0. Att: 45,980
Match-day 4: Genk 2 (Paintsil 4, Soucek 87 og) **West Ham** 2 (Benrahma12, 82). Att: 12,239. Dinamo Zagreb 3 (Petkovic 12, Andric 34, Sutalo 83) Rapid Vienna 1 (Knasmullner 8). Att: 7,835
Match-day 5: Dinamo Zagreb 1 (Menalo 35) Genk 1 (Ugbo 45). Att: 6,892. Rapid Vienna 0 **West Ham** 2 (Yarmolenko 39, Noble 45 pen) – played behind closed doors
Match-day 6: Genk 0 Rapid Vienna 1 (Ljubicic 29). Att: 10.018. **West Ham** 0 Dinamo Zagreb 1 (Orsic 3). Att: 49,401

West Ham Q	6	4	1	1	11	3	13
Dinamo Zagreb	6	3	1	2	9	6	10
Rapid Vienna	6	2	0	4	4	9	6
Genk	6	1	2	3	4	10	5

KNOCKOUT PLAY-OFFS, FIRST LEG

(Eight Europa League group runners-up, eight third-ranked teams from Champions League group stage)

Atalanta 2 (Djimsiti 61, 63) Olympiacos 1 (Tiquinho Soares 16). Att: 9,448. Barcelona 1 (Ferran Torres 59 pen) Napoli 1 (Zielinski 29). Att: 73,525. Borussia Dortmund 2 (Bellingham 51, Guerreiro 82) **Rangers** 4 (Tavernier 38 pen, Morelos 41, Lundstram 49, Zagadou 54 og). Att: 10,000. Porto 2 (Martinez 37, 49) Lazio 1 (Zaccagni 23). Att: 32,929
RB Leipzig 2 (Nkunku 30, Forsberg 82 pen) Real Sociedad 2 (Le Normand 8, Oyarzabal 64

pen). Att: 21,113. Sevilla 3 (Rakitic 13 pen, Ocampos 44, Martial 45) Dinamo Zagreb 1 (Orsic 41). Att: 28,372. Sheriff Tiraspol 2 (Thill 43 pen, Traore 82) Sporting Braga 0. Att: 3,062. Zenit St Petersburg 2 (Dzyuba 25, Malcom 28) Real Betis 3 (Rodriguez 8, Willian Jose 18, Guardado 41). Att: 28,936

SECOND LEG

Braga 2 (Medeiros 17, Horta 43) Sheriff Tiraspol 0. Att: 9,423 (aet, agg 2-2, Sporting Braga won 3-2 on pens). Dinamo Zagreb 1 (Orsic 65 pen) Sevilla 0. Att: 28,372 (Sevilla won 3-2 on agg). Lazio 2 (Immobile 19, Cataldi 90+4) Porto 2 (Taremi 31 pen, Uribe 68). Att: 24,948 (Porto won 4-3 on agg). Napoli 2 (Insigne 23 pen, Politano 87) Barcelona 4 (Jordi Alba 8, De Jong 13, Pique 45, Aubameyang 59). Att: 37,858 (Barcelona won 5-3 on agg)
Olympiacos 0 Atalanta 3 (Maehle 40, Malinovskiy 66, 69). Att: 15,835 (Atalanta won 5-1 on agg). Rangers 2 (Tavernier 22 pen, 57) Borussia Dortmund 2 (Bellingham 31 Malen 42). Att: 47,709 (Rangers won 6-4 on agg). Real Betis 0 Zenit St Petersburg 0. Att: 28,936 (Real Betis won 3-2 on agg). Real Sociedad 1 (Zubimendi 65) RB Leipzig 3 (Orban 39, Andre Silva 59, Forsberg 89 pen). Att: 30,118 (RB Leipzig won 5-3 on agg)

ROUND OF 16, FIRST LEG

Atalanta 3 (Malinivskiy 23, Muriel 25, 49) Bayer Leverkusen 2 (Aranguiz 11, Diaby 63. Att: 13,134. Barcelona 0 Galatasaray 0. Att: 61,740. Braga 2 (Ruiz 3, Oliveira 89) Monaco 0. Att: 10,228. Porto 0 Lyon 1 (Lucas Paqueta 59). Att: 26,309. Rangers 3 (Tavernier 11 pen, Morelos 15. Balogun 51) Red Star Belgrade 0. Att: 48,589. Real Betis 1 (Fekir 30) Eintracht Frankfurt 2 (Kostic 14, Kamada 32). Att: 36,574. Sevilla 1 (El-Haddadi 60) West Ham 0. Att: 34,728. RB Leipzig v Spartak Moscow – cancelled, Spartak Moscow eliminated

SECOND LEG

Bayer Leverkusen 0 Atalanta 1 (Boga 90+1). Att: 19,871 (Atalanta won 4-2 on agg). Eintracht Frankfurt 1 (Rodriguez 120+1) Real Betis 1 (Iglesias 90). Att: 25,000 (aet, Eintracht Frankfurt won 3-2 on agg). Galatasaray 1 (Teixeira 28) Barcelona 2 (Lopez 37, Aubameyang 49). Att: 50,110 (Barcelona won 2-1 on agg). Lyon 1 (Dembele 13 Porto 1 (Aquino Cossa 27). Att: 54,551 (Lyon won 2-1 on agg). Monaco 1 (Disasi 90) Sporting Braga 1 (Ruiz 19). Att: 3,892 (Sporting Braga won 3-1 on agg). Red Star Belgrade 2 (Ivanic 10, Ben Nabouhane 90+3 pen) Rangers 1 (Kent 56). Att: 47,024 (Rangers won 4-2 on agg). West Ham 2 (Soucek 39, Yarmolenko 112). Att: 59,981 (aet, West Ham won 2-1 on agg)

QUARTER-FINALS, FIRST LEG

Sporting Braga 1 (Ruiz 40) Rangers 0. Att: 20,331. Eintracht Frankfurt 1 (Knauff 48) Barcelona 1 (Torres 66). Att: 48,000. RB Leipzig 1 (Zappacosta 58 og) Atalanta 1 (Muriel 17). Att: 36,029. West Ham 1 (Bowen 52) Lyon 1 (Ndombele 66). Attr: 59,978

SECOND LEG

Atalanta 0 RB Leipzig 2 (Nkunku 18, 87 pen). Att: 17,905 (RB Leipzig won 3-1 on agg). Barcelona 2 (Busquets 90+1, Depay 90+11 pen) Eintracht Frankfurt 3 (Kostic 4 pen, 67, Borre 36). Att: 79,468 (Eintract Frankfurt won 4-3 on agg). Lyon 0 West Ham 3 (Dawson 38, Rice 44, Bowen 48). Att: 50,065 (West Ham won 4-1 on agg). Rangers 3 (Tavernier 2, 44 pen, Roofe 101) Sporting Braga 1 (Carmo 83). Att: 48,894 (aet, Rangers won 3-2 on agg)

SEMI-FINALS, FIRST LEG

RB Leipzig 1 (Angelino 85) Rangers 0. Att: 40,303. West Ham 1 (Antonio 21) Eintracht Frankfurt 2 (Knauff 1, Kamada 54). Att: 59,980

SECOND LEG

Eintracht Frankfurt 1 (Borre 26) **West Ham** 0. Att: 48,000 (Eintracht Frankfurt won 3-1 on agg). **Rangers** 3 (Tavernier 18, Kamara 24, Lundstram 80) RB Leipzig 1 (Nkunku 70). Att: 49,397 (Rangers won 3-2 on gg)

FINAL

EINTRACHT FRANKFURT 1 (Borre 69) RANGERS 1 (Aribo 57) – aet, Eintracht Frankfurt won 5-4 on pens
Estadio Ramon Sanchez, Seville (38,84); May 18, 2022
Eintracht Frankfurt (3-4-2-1): Trapp, Toure, Tuta (Hasebe 58), Ndicka (Lenz 101), Knauff, Rode (capt) (Jakic 90), Sow (Hrustic 105), Kostic, Lindstrom (Hauge 71), Kamada, Borre. **Subs not used:** Grahl, Lammers, Ache, Chandler, Da Costa, Barkok, Mendes Paciencia. **Coach:** Oliver Glasner
Rangers (4-3-3): McGregor, Tavernier (capt), Goldson, Bassey, Barisic (Roofe 117), Jack (Davis 74), Lundstram, Kamara (Arfield 90), Wright (Sakala 74, Ramsey 117), Aribo (Sands 101), Kent. **Subs not used:** McCrorie, McLaughlin, Diallo, Balogun, King, Lowry. **Booked:** Aribo, Wright. **Manager:** Giovanni van Bronckhorst
Referee: Slavko Vincic (Slovenia). **Half-time:** 0-0
Penalty shoot-out: Eintracht Frankfurt scored – Lenz, Hrustic, Kamada, Kostic, Borre. **Rangers** scored – Tavernier, Davis, Arfield, Roofe; saved – Ramsey

A first European trophy for 50 years beckoned twice for Rangers in the searing heat of Seville. First, Joe Aribo took advantage of a defensive mistake with a cool finish to put them ahead after 57 minutes with his first goal in the competition. Then, a minute from the end of extra-time, Ryan Kent was denied by Kevin Trapp after Kemar Roofe's pull-back. The goalkeeper also made the decisive intervention in the penalty shoot-out, saving a hesitant effort from Aaron Ramsey after the loan-loan Juventus midfielder came off the bench specifically to take a spot-kick. That presented Colombian striker Rafael Borre with the chance to add to his earlier equaliser. His delivery, hard and high, left Rangers still without success since a Cup-Winners' Cup victory over Moscow Dynamo in 1972. Some consolation for the team, and an estimated 100,000 supporters in the city, came with a superb run to the final and the seven goals which made their captain, James Tavernier, the leading scorer in the competition. There was also a classy, complimentary message from the German club for 'a passionate and fair match' and good luck in the Scottish Cup Final against Hearts. That, too, went to extra-time, with Rangers beating Hearts 2-0

Leading scorers: 7 Tavernier (Rangers); 6 Ekambi (Lyon), Galeno (Porto/Braga); 5 Daka (Leicester), Kamada (Eintracht Frankfurt); 4 Borre (Frankfurth), Morelos (Rangers)

EUROPA CONFERENCE LEAGUE 2021–22

FIRST QUALIFYING ROUND, FIRST LEG (selected results)

Bala 0 Larne 1 (McDaid 2). Att: 197. **Dundalk** 4 (Duffy 34, McMillan 39, Patching 62, Han Jeong-woo 90+4) **Newtown** 0. Att: 120. **Glentoran** 1 (McDonagh 82) **New Saints** 1 (Smith 13). Att: 1,021. Hafnarfjordur 1 (Lennon 85) **Sligo** 0. Att: 412. Stjarnan 1 (Atlason 24) **Bohemians** 1 (Tierney 62). Att: 720. Velez Mostar 2 (Brandao 37 pen, 66 pen) **Coleraine** 1 (Doherty 9). Att: 5,000

SECOND LEG

Bohemians 3 (Kelly 34, 54, Burt 75) Stjarnan 0. Att: 6,000 (Bohemians won 4-1 on agg). **Coleraine** 1 (Shevlin 33) Velez Mostar 2 (Brandao 54, Andusic 71). Att: 500 (Velez won 4-2 on agg). **Larne** 1 (Hale 84) Bala 0. Att: 850 (Larne won 2-0 on agg). New Saints 2 (McManus

26 pen, Smith 27) **Glentoran** 0. Att: 198 (New Saints won 3-1 on agg). **Newtown** 0 **Dundalk** 1 (Duffy 52). Att: 174 (Dundalk won 4-0 on agg). **Sligo** 1 (Kenny 84 pen) Hafnarfjordur 2 (Lennon 44, 49 pen). Att: 400 (Hafnarfjordur won 3-1 on agg)

SECOND QUALIFYING ROUND, FIRST LEG (selected results)

Aberdeen 5 (Considine 28, Ferguson 44 pen, 53, Ramirez 83, McLennan 90+3) Hacken 1 (Jeremejeff 59). Att: 5,665. **Dundalk** 2 (Patching 3, McMillan 27) Levadia 2 (Vastsuk 1, 19). Att: 880. Dudelange 0 **Bohemians** 1 (Tierney 11). Att: 625. **Hibernian** 3 (Boyle 14 pen, 47, Nisbet 81) Santa Coloma 0. Att: 4,697. Kauno Zalgiris 0 **New Saints** (Smith 8, D Davies 34, 38, McManus 40, Williams 87). Att: 550. **Larne** 2 (McDaid 3, Jarvis 30) Aarhus 1 (Ammitzboll 85). Att: 850. **Linfield** 4 (Newberry 2, Manzinga 25, Mulgrew 75, Callacher 90+2) Borac Banja 0. Att: 995. Prishtina 4 (Bekteshi 41, John 53, 90+4, Krasniqi 78) **Connah's Quay** 1 (Moore 75). Att: 1,268

SECOND LEG

Arahus 1 (Olsen 73 pen) **Larne** 1 (Hale 45). Att: 5,170 (Larne won 3-2 on agg). **Bohemians** 3 (Cornwall 34, G Kelly 68, 73) Dudelange 0. Att: 6,500 (Bohemians won 4-0 on agg). Borac Banja 0 **Linfield** 0. Att: 5,208 (Linfield won 4-0 on agg). **Connah's Quay** 4 (Insall 3, 57, Horan 47, Morris 82 pen) Prishtina 2 (Krasniqi 29, 36). Att: 108 (Prishtina won 6-5 on agg). Hacken 2 (Olsson 51, Bengtsson 68 pen) **Aberdeen** 0. Att: 823 (Aberdeen won 5-3 on agg). Levadia 1 (Agyiri 17) **Dundalk** 2 (McMillan 44, Patching 90+2). Att: 1,875 (Dundalk won 4-3 on agg). **New Saints** 5 (Redmond 13, Robles 20, McManus 25, Smith 69, D Davies 74) Kauno Zalgiris 1 (Michael 85). Att: 362 (New Saints won 10-1 on agg). Santa Coloma 1 (Lopez 70) **Hibernian** 2 (Murphy 73, Mackay 76). Att: 120 (Hibernian won 5-1 on agg

THIRD QUALIFYING ROUND, FIRST LEG (selected results)

Bohemians 2 (Coote 23, 52) PAOK Salonika 1 (Nelson Oliveria 77). Att: 6,500. Breidablik 2 (Eyjolfsson 16, Vihjalmsson 43 pen) **Aberdeen** 3 (Ramirez 3, 49, Ferguson 11). Att: 1,197. **Hibernian** 2 (Boyle 67) Rijeka 1 (Ampem 61). Att: 2,227. **Linfield** 1 (Chadwick 9) Fola Esch 2 (Bensi 69, Caron 88). Att: 2,227. **New Saints** 4 (Hudson 19, McManus 30 pen, 51 pen, 76) Viktoria Plzen 2 (Beauguel 89, Ba Loua 90 +5). Att: 345. Pacos de Ferreira 4 (Denilson 44, 70, Eustaquio 73, Ze Uilton 90) **Larne** 0. Att: 1,577. **Shamrock Rov** 1 (Emakhu 90 +1) Teuta Durres 0. Att: 1,500. Vitesse 2 (Bero 20, Openda 88) **Dundalk** 2 (McEleney 65, 76). Att: 8,756

SECOND LEG

Aberdeen 2 (Hedges 47, 70) Breidablik 1 (Eyjolfsson 59). Att: 15,107 (Aberdeen won 5-3 on agg). **Dundalk** 1 (Hoban 71 pen) Vitesse 2 (Bero 27, Gboho 38). At: 1,475 (Vitesse won 4-3 on agg). Fola Esch 2 (Ramirez 69, Parreira 90+3 pen) **Linfield** 1 (Roscoe-Byrne 89). Att: 730 (Fola Esch won 4-2 on agg). **Larne** 1 (Randall 83) Pacos de Ferreira 0. Att: 1,150 (Pacos de Ferreira won 4-1 on agg). PAOK Salonika 2 (Schwab 4, Bisewar 28) **Bohemians** 0 – behind closed doors (PAOK Salonika won 3-2 on agg) Rijeka 4 (Pavicic 36, Abass 68, McGinn 72 og, Busnja 90+3) **Hibernian** 1 (Magennis 56). Att: 4,077 (Rijeka won 5-2 on agg). Teuta Durres 0 **Shamrock Rov** 2 (Gaffney 20, 62). Att: 310 (Shamrock Rov won 3-0 on agg). Viktoria Plzen 3 (Bucha 56, Chory 85, Beauguel 90+1) **New Saints** 1 (Robles 4). Att: 6,079 (aet, agg 5-5, Viktoria Plzen won 4-1 on pens)

QUALIFYING PLAY-OFF ROUND, FIRST LEG (selected results)

Flora Tallin 4 (Zenjov 13, Miller 27, 87, Sappinen 76) **Shamrock Rov** 2 (Burke 44, Scales 86). Att: 1,129. LASK 1 (Karamoko 60 pen) **St Johnstone** 1 (Kane 17). Att: 550. Pacos de Ferreira 1 (Lucas Silva 45) **Tottenham** 0. Att: 2,284. Qarabag 1 (Romero 30) **Aberdeen** 0. Att: 9,756

SECOND LEG

Aberdeen 1 (Ferguson 90+2 pen) Qarabag 3 (Bayramov 8, Kady 18, Zoubir 72). Att: 15,533 (Qarabag won 4-1 on agg). **Shamrock Rov** 0 Flora Tallinn 1 (Sappinen 57). Att: 3,500 (Flora Tallinn won 5-2 on agg). **St Johnstone** 0 LASK 2 (Balic 72, Raguz 85 pen). Att: 8,845 (LASK won 3-1 on agg). **Tottenham** 3 (Kane 9, 35, Lo Celso 70) Pacos de Ferreira 0. Att: 30,215 (Tottenham won 3-1 on agg)

GROUPS

Winners through to last 16. Runners-up into knockout round with third-ranked teams from Europa League

GROUP A

	P	W	D	L	F	A	Pts
LASK	6	5	1	0	12	1	16
Maccabi Tel Aviv	6	3	2	1	14	4	11
HJK Helsinki	6	2	0	4	5	15	6
Alashkert	6	0	1	5	4	15	1

GROUP B

Gent	6	4	1	1	6	2	13
Partizan Belgrade	6	2	2	2	6	4	8
Anorthosis Famagusta	6	1	3	2	6	9	6
Flora Tallinn	6	1	2	3	5	8	5

GROUP C

Roma	6	4	1	1	18	11	13
Bodo/Glimt	6	3	3	0	14	5	12
Zorya Luhansk	6	2	1	3	5	11	7
CSKA Sofia	6	0	1	5	3	13	1

GROUP D

Alkmaar	6	4	2	0	8	3	14
Randers	6	1	4	1	9	9	7
Jablonec	6	1	3	2	6	8	6
CFR Cluj	6	1	1	4	4	7	4

GROUP E

Feyenoord	6	4	2	0	11	6	14
Slavia Prague	6	2	2	2	8	7	8
Union Berlin	6	2	1	3	8	9	7
Maccabi Haifa	6	1	1	4	2	7	4

GROUP F

Copenhagen	6	5	0	1	15	5	15
PAOK Salonika	6	3	2	1	8	4	11
Slovan Bratislava	6	2	2	2	8	7	8
Lincoln Red Imps	6	0	0	6	2	17	0

GROUP G

Rennes	6	4	2	0	13	7	14
Vitesse	6	3	1	2	12	9	10
Tottenham	6	2	1	3	11	11	7
Mura	6	1	0	5	5	14	3

Match-day 1: Mura 0 Vitesse 2. Rennes 2 (Tait 23, Laborde 71) **Tottenham** 2 (Bade 11og, Hojbjerg 76). Att: 22,000

Match-day 2: **Tottenham** 5 (Alli 4 pen, Lo Celso 8, Kane 68, 77, 88) Mura 1 (Kous 52). Att: 25,121. Vitesse 1 Rennes 2

Match-day 3: Mura 1 Rennes 2. Vitesse 1 (Wittek 78) **Tottenham** 0. Att: 23,931

Match-day 4: Rennes 1 Mura 0. **Tottenham** 3 (Son Heung-min 14, Lucas Moura 22, Rasmussen 28 og) Vitesse 2 (Rasmussen 32, Bero 39). Att: 36,312

Match-day 5: Mura 2 (Horvat 11, Marosa 90+4) **Tottenham** 1 (Kane 72). Att: 6,100. Rennes 3 Vitesse 3

Match-day 6: **Tottenham** 0 Rennes 3 (Tottenham forfeited match after Covid postponement); Vitessse 3 Mura 1

GROUP H

Basle	6	4	2	0	14	6	14
Qarabag	6	3	2	1	10	8	11
Omonia Nicosia	6	0	4	2	5	10	4
Kairat	6	0	2	4	6	11	2

PLAY-OFFS, FIRST LEG

Celtic 1 (Maeda 79) Bodo/Glimt 3 (Espejord 6, Pellegrino 55, Vetlesen 81). Att: 54,926

Leicester 4 (Ndidi 23, Barnes 49, Daka 54, Dewsbury-Hall 74) Randers 1 (Hammershoj-Mistrati 45). Att: 25,242

SECOND LEG

Bodo/Glimt 2 (Solbakken 9, Vetlesen 69) **Celtic** 0. Att: 5,810 (Bodo/Glimt won 5-1 on agg). Randers 1 (Odey 84) **Leicester** 3 (Barnes 2, Maddison 70, 74). Att: 8,948 (Leicester won 7-2 on agg)

ON AGGREGATE

Marseille 6 Qarabag 1; PAOK Salonika 2 Midtjylland 2 (aet, PAOK Salonika won 5-3 on pens); Partizan Belgrade 3 Sparta Prague 1; PSV Eindhoven 2 Maccabi Tel Aviv 1; Slavia Prague 6 Fenerbahce 4; Vitesse Arnhem 3 Rapid Vienna 2

ROUND OF 16

First leg: Leicester 2 (Albrighton 30, Iheanacho 90+3) Rennes 0. Att: 25,848. **Second leg:** Rennes 2 (Bourigeaud 8, Tait 76) **Leicester** 1 (Fofana 51). Att: 27,660 (Leicester won 3-2 on agg)

ON AGGREGATE

Bodo/Glimt 4 Alkmaar 3; Feyenoord 8 Partizan Belgrade 3; Marseille 4 Basle 2; PAOK Salonika 3 Gent 1; PSV Eindhoven 8 Copenhagen 4; Roma 2 Vitesse 1; Slavia Prague 7 LASK 5

QUARTER-FINALS

First leg: Leicester 0 PSV Eindhoven 0. Att: 31,327. **Second leg:** PSV Eindhoven 1 (Zahavi 27) **Leicester** 2 (Maddison 77, Pereira 88). Att: 35,000 (Leicester won 2-1 on agg)

ON AGGREGATE

Marseille 3 PAOK Salonika 1; Roma 5 Bodo/Glimt 1; Feyenoord 6 Slavia Prague 4

SEMI-FINALS, FIRST LEG

Feyenoord 3 (Dessers 18, 46, Sinisterra 20) Marseille 2 (Dieng 28, Gerson 40). Att: 24,500.
Leicester 1 (Mancini 67 og) Roma 1 (Pellegrini 15). Att : 31,659

SECOND LEG

Marseille 0 Feyenoord 0. Att: 49,315 (Feyenoord won 3-2 on agg). Roma 1 (Abraham 11)
Leicester 0. Att: 63,940 (Roma won 2-1 on agg)

FINAL

Roma 1 (Zaniolo 32) **Feynoord** 0 – Air Albania Stadium, Tirana (19,597) – May 25, 2022

Leading scorers: 10 Dessers (Feyenoord); 9 Abraham (Roma); 6 Sinisterra (Feyenoord), Yitra
Sor (Slavia Prague), Solbakken (Bodo/Glimt)

EUROPEAN SUPER CUP 2021

CHELSEA 1 (Ziyech 28) VILLARREAL 1 (Gerard Moreno 74) – aet, Chelsea won 6-5 on pens
Windsor Park, Belfast, August 11, 2021
Chelea (3-4-2-1): Mendy (Arrizabalaga 119), Chalobah, Zouma (Christensen 66), Rudiger,
Hudson-Odoi (Azpilicueta, capt, 82), Kante (Jorginho 65), Kovacic, Marcos Alonso, Ziyech
(Pulisic 43), Havertz, Werner (Mount 65). **Subs not used**: Abraham, Chilwell, Emerson, James,
Loftus-Cheek, Thiago Silva. **Booked**: Rudiger, Arrizabalaga. **Manager**: Thomas Tuchel
Villarreal (4-4-2): Asenjo, Foyth, Albiol (capt), Pau Torres, Pedraza (Estupinan 58), Pino
(Mandi 90), Trigueros (Moi Gomez 70), Capoue (Gaspar 70), Alberto Moreno (Manu 85),
Gerard Moreno, Dia (Dani Raba 86). **Subs not used**: Rulli, Alcacer, Cuenca, Iborra, Nino,
Pena, **Booked**: Pino. **Coach**: Unai Emery
Penalty shoot-out: Chelsea – scored: Azpilicueta, Marcos Alonso, Mount, Jorginho, Pulisic,
Rudiger; missed – Havertz. **Villarreal** – scored: Gerard Moreno, Estupinan, Moi Gomez, Dani
Raba, Foyth; missed – Mandi, Albiol
Referee: Sergey Karasev (Russia). **Half-time**: 1-0

CLUB WORLD CUP – UAE

SEMI-FINALS

Al Hilal (Saudi Arabia) 0 **Chelsea** 1 (Lukaku 32). Att: 19,175. **Palmeiras** (Brazil) 2 (Raphael
Veiga 39, Dudu 49) **Al Ahly** (Egypt) 0. Att: 11,902

FINAL

CHELSEA 2 (Lukaku 54, Havertz 117 pen) PALMEIRAS 1 (Raphael Veiga 64 pen) (aet)
Mohamed Bin Zayed Stadium, Abu Dhabi (32,871); February 12, 2022
Chelsea (3-4-2-1): Mendy, Christensen (Sarr 90), Thiago Silva, Rudiger, Azpilicueta (capt),
Kante, Kovacic (Ziyech 90), Hudson-Odoi (Saul 77), Mount (Pulisic 31), Havertz, Lukaku
(Werner 76). **Subs not used**: Arrizabalaga, Bettinelli, Marcos Alonso, Kenedy, Jorginho,
Barkley. **Booked**: Havertz. **Manager**: Thomas Tuchel
Palmeiras (5-4-1): Weverton, Marcos Rocha (Deyverson 118), Gustavo Gomez, Luan, Joaquin
Piquerez, Gustavo Scarpa, Rony (Wesley 77), Danilo, Ze Rafael (Jailson 60), Dudu (Rafael
Navarro 103), Raphael Veiga (Atuesta 78). **Subs not used**: Marcelo Lomba, Mateus, Kuscevic,
Jorge, Mayke, Breno Lopes, Murilo. **Booked**: Raphael Veiga, Wesley, Luan, Atuesta. **Sent off**:

Luan (120+6). **Coach**: Abel Ferreira
Referee: Chris Beath (Australia). **Half-time**: 0-0

Roman Abramovich made his final public appearance as Chelsea owner as they joined Manchester United and Liverpool in become world champions with an extra-time penalty from Kai Havertz. Abramovich watched the final in Abu Dhabi, raised the trophy and congratulated manager Thomas Tuchel and the players. A month later, he was sanctioned by the Government following Russia's invasion of Ukraine and the club went to an American-Swiss consortium headed by businessman Todd Boehly. Attacking midfielder Havertz followed his match-winning goal against Manchester City in the previous season's Champions League Final after Brazilian defender Luan Garcia handled. Chelsea had taken the lead with Romelu Lukaku's header from a Callum Hudson-Odoi cross and Palmeiras levelled with another penalty after Thiago Silva handled. Lukaku was also on the mark with the winner in the semi-final against Saudi Arabian side Al Hilal.

UEFA CUP FINALS

1972	Tottenham beat Wolves 3-2 on agg (2-1a, 1-1h)
1973	Liverpool beat Borussia Moenchengladbach 3-2 on agg (3-0h, 0-2a)
1974	Feyenoord beat Tottenham 4-2 on agg (2-2a, 2-0h)
1975	Borussia Moenchengladbach beat Twente Enschede 5-1 on agg (0-0h, 5-1a)
1976	Liverpool beat Brugge 4-3 on agg (3-2h, 1-1a)
1977	Juventus beat Atletico Bilbao on away goals after 2-2 agg (1-0h, 1-2a)
1978	PSV Eindhoven beat Bastia 3-0 on agg (0-0a, 3-0h)
1979	Borussia Moenchengladbach beat Red Star Belgrade 2-1 on agg (1-1a, 1-0h)
1980	Eintracht Frankfurt beat Borussia Moenchengladbach on away goals after 3-3 agg (2-3a, 1-0h)
1981	Ipswich Town beat AZ 67 Alkmaar 5-4 on agg (3-0h, 2-4a)
1982	IFK Gothenburg beat SV Hamburg 4-0 on agg (1-0h, 3-0a)
1983	Anderlecht beat Benfica 2-1 on agg (1-0h, 1-1a)
1984	Tottenham beat Anderlecht 4-3 on penalties after 2-2 agg (1-1a, 1-1h)
1985	Real Madrid beat Videoton 3-1 on agg (3-0a, 0-1h)
1986	Real Madrid beat Cologne 5-3 on agg (5-1h, 0-2a)
1987	IFK Gothenburg beat Dundee Utd 2-1 on agg (1-0h, 1-1a)
1988	Bayer Leverkusen beat Espanol 3-2 on penalties after 3-3 agg (0-3a, 3-0h)
1989	Napoli beat VfB Stuttgart 5-4 on agg (2-1h, 3-3a)
1990	Juventus beat Fiorentina 3-1 on agg (3-1h, 0-0a)
1991	Inter Milan beat AS Roma 2-1 on agg (2-0h, 0-1a)
1992	Ajax beat Torino on away goals after 2-2 agg (2-2a, 0-0h)
1993	Juventus beat Borussia Dortmund 6-1 on agg (3-1a, 3-0h)
1994	Inter Milan beat Salzburg 2-0 on agg (1-0a, 1-0h)
1995	Parma beat Juventus 2-1 on agg (1-0h, 1-1a)
1996	Bayern Munich beat Bordeaux 5-1 on agg (2-0h, 3-1a)
1997	FC Schalke beat Inter Milan 4-1 on penalties after 1-1 agg (1-0h, 0-1a)
1998	Inter Milan beat Lazio 3-0 (one match) – Paris
1999	Parma beat Marseille 3-0 (one match) – Moscow
2000	Galatasaray beat Arsenal 4-1 on penalties after 0-0 (one match) – Copenhagen
2001	Liverpool beat Alaves 5-4 on golden goal (one match) – Dortmund
2002	Feyenoord beat Borussia Dortmund 3-2 (one match) – Rotterdam
2003	FC Porto beat Celtic 3-2 on silver goal (one match) – Seville
2004	Valencia beat Marseille 2-0 (one match) – Gothenburg
2005	CSKA Moscow beat Sporting Lisbon 3-1 (one match) – Lisbon
2006	Sevilla beat Middlesbrough 4-0 (one match) – Eindhoven
2007	Sevilla beat Espanyol 3-1 on penalties after 2-2 (one match) – Hampden Park
2008	Zenit St Petersburg beat Rangers 2-0 (one match) – City of Manchester Stadium
2009†	Shakhtar Donetsk beat Werder Bremen 2-1 (one match) – Istanbul

EUROPA LEAGUE FINALS

2010† Atletico Madrid 2 Fulham 1 – Hamburg
2011 Porto 1 Braga 0 – Dublin
2012 Atletico Madrid 3 Athletic Bilbao 0 – Bucharest
2013 Chelsea 2 Benfica 1 – Amsterdam
2014 Sevilla 4 Benfica 2 on penalties after 0-0 – Turin
2015 Sevilla 3 Dnipro 2 – Warsaw
2016 Sevilla 3 Liverpool 1 – Basle
2017 Manchester Utd 2 Ajax 0 – Stockholm
2018 Atletico Madrid 3 Marseille 0 – Lyon
2019 Chelsea 4 Arsenal 1 – Baku
2020 Sevilla 3 Inter Milan 2 - Cologne
2021 Villarreal 1 Manchester Utd 1 (Villarreal won 11-10 on pens– Gdansk
2022† Eintracht Frankfurt 1 Rangers 1 (one match – Seville)
Eintracht Frankfurt won 5-4 on penalties
(† After extra-time)

FAIRS CUP FINALS
(As UEFA Cup previously known)

1958 Barcelona beat London 8-2 on agg (2-2a, 6-0h)
1960 Barcelona beat Birmingham 4-1 on agg (0-0a, 4-1h)
1961 AS Roma beat Birmingham City 4-2 on agg (2-2a, 2-0h)
1962 Valencia beat Barcelona 7-3 on agg (6-2h, 1-1a)
1963 Valencia beat Dynamo Zagreb 4-1 on agg (2-1a, 2-0h)
1964 Real Zaragoza beat Valencia 2-1 (Barcelona)
1965 Ferencvaros beat Juventus 1-0 (Turin)
1966 Barcelona beat Real Zaragoza 4-3 on agg (0-1h, 4-2a)
1967 Dinamo Zagreb beat Leeds Utd 2-0 on agg (2-0h, 0-0a)
1968 Leeds Utd beat Ferencvaros 1-0 on agg (1-0h, 0-0a)
1969 Newcastle Utd beat Ujpest Dozsa 6-2 on agg (3-0h, 3-2a)
1970 Arsenal beat Anderlecht 4-3 on agg (1-3a, 3-0h)
1971 Leeds Utd beat Juventus on away goals after 3-3 agg (2-2a, 1-1h)

CUP-WINNERS' CUP FINALS

1961 Fiorentina beat Rangers 4-1 on agg (2-0, 2-1) – Stuttgart
1962 Atletico Madrid 3 Fiorentina 0 – Stuttgart after 1-1 – Glasgow
1963 Tottenham 5 Atletico Madrid 1 – Rotterdam
1964 Sporting Lisbon 1 MTK Budapest 0 – Antwerp after 3-3, Brussels
1965 West Ham 2 Munich 1860 0 – Wembley
1966† Borussia Dortmund 2 Liverpool 1 – Glasgow
1967† Bayern Munich 1 Rangers 0 – Nuremberg
1968 AC Milan 2 SV Hamburg 0 – Rotterdam
1969 Slovan Bratislava 3 Barcelona 2 – Basle
1970 Manchester City 2 Gornik Zabrze 1 – Vienna
1971† Chelsea 2 Real Madrid 1 – Piraeus   after 1-1 – Piraeus
1972 Rangers 3 Moscow Dynamo 2 – Barcelona
1973 AC Milan 1 Leeds 0 – Salonika
1974 Magdeburg 2 AC Milan 0 – Rotterdam
1975 Dynamo Kiev 3 Ferencvaros 0 – Basle
1976 Anderlecht 4 West Ham 2 – Brussels
1977 SV Hamburg 2 Anderlecht 0 – Amsterdam

1978	Anderlecht 4 Austria WAC 0 – Paris
1979†	Barcelona 4 Fortuna Dusseldorf 3 – Basle
1980†	Valencia 0 Arsenal 0 – Brussels
	Valencia won 5-4 on pen
1981	Dinamo Tbilisi 2 Carl Zeiss Jena 1 – Dusseldorf
1982	Barcelona 2 Standard Liege 1 – Barcelona
1983†	Aberdeen 2 Real Madrid 1 – Gothenburg
1984	Juventus 2 Porto 1 – Basle
1985	Everton 3 Rapid Vienna 1 – Rotterdam
1986	Dynamo Kiev 3 Atletico Madrid 0 – Lyon
1987	Ajax 1 Lokomotiv Leipzig 0 – Athens
1988	Mechelen 1 Ajax 0 – Strasbourg
1989	Barcelona 2 Sampdoria 0 – Berne
1990	Sampdoria 2 Anderlecht 0 – Gothenburg
1991	Manchester Utd 2 Barcelona 1 – Rotterdam
1992	Werder Bremen 2 Monaco 0 – Lisbon
1993	Parma 3 Royal Antwerp 1 – Wembley
1994	Arsenal 1 Parma 0 – Copenhagen
1995†	Real Zaragoza 2 Arsenal 1 – Paris
1996	Paris St Germain 1 Rapid Vienna 0 – Brussels
1997	Barcelona 1 Paris St Germain 0 – Rotterdam
1998	Chelsea 1 VfB Stuttgart 0 – Stockholm
1999	Lazio 2 Real Mallorca 1 – Villa Park, Birmingham

(† After extra time)

EUROPEAN SUPER CUP RESULTS

1972*	Ajax beat Rangers 6-3 on agg (3-1, 3-2)
1973	Ajax beat AC Milan 6-1 on agg (0-1, 6-0)
1974	Bayern Munich and Magdeburg did not play
1975	Dynamo Kiev beat Bayern Munich 3-0 on agg (1-0, 2-0)
1976	Anderlecht beat Bayern Munich 5-3 on agg (1-2, 4-1)
1977	Liverpool beat Hamburg 7-1 on agg (1-1, 6-0)
1978	Anderlecht beat Liverpool 4-3 on agg (3-1, 1-2)
1979	Nottm Forest beat Barcelona 2-1 on agg (1-0, 1-1)
1980	Valencia beat Nottm Forest on away goal after 2-2 agg (1-2, 1-0)
1981	Liverpool and Dinamo Tbilisi did not play
1982	Aston Villa beat Barcelona 3-1 on agg (0-1, 3-0 aet)
1983	Aberdeen beat Hamburg 2-0 on agg (0-0, 2-0)
1984	Juventus beat Liverpool 2-0 – one match (Turin)
1985	Juventus and Everton did not play
1986	Steaua Bucharest beat Dynamo Kiev 1-0 – one match (Monaco)
1987	Porto beat Ajax 2-0 on agg (1-0, 1-0)
1988	Mechelen beat PSV Eindhoven 3-1 on agg (3-0, 0-1)
1989	AC Milan beat Barcelona 2-1 on agg (1-1, 1-0)
1990	AC Milan beat Sampdoria 3-1 on agg (1-1, 2-0)
1991	Manchester Utd beat Red Star Belgrade 1-0 – one match (Old Trafford)
1992	Barcelona beat Werder Bremen 3-2 on agg (1-1, 2-1)
1993	Parma beat AC Milan 2-1 on agg (0-1, 2-0 aet)
1994	AC Milan beat Arsenal 2-0 on agg (0-0, 2-0)
1995	Ajax beat Real Zaragoza 5-1 on agg (1-1, 4-0)
1996	Juventus beat Paris St Germain 9-2 on agg (6-1, 3-1)
1997	Barcelona beat Borussia Dortmund 3-1 on agg (2-0, 1-1)
1998	Chelsea 1 Real Madrid 0 (Monaco)
1999	Lazio 1 Manchester Utd 0 (Monaco)

2000	Galatasaray 2 Real Madrid 1 – aet, golden goal (Monaco)
2001	Liverpool 3 Bayern Munich 2 (Monaco)
2002	Real Madrid 3 Feyenoord 1 (Monaco)
2003	AC Milan 1 Porto 0 (Monaco)
2004	Valencia 2 Porto 1 (Monaco)
2005	Liverpool 3 CSKA Moscow 1 – aet (Monaco)
2006	Sevilla 3 Barcelona 0 (Monaco)
2007	AC Milan 3 Sevilla 1 (Monaco)
2008	Zenit St Petersburg 2 Manchester Utd 1 (Monaco)
2009	Barcelona 1 Shakhtar Donetsk 0 – aet (Monaco)
2010	Atletico Madrid 2 Inter Milan 0 (Monaco)
2011	Barcelona 2 Porto 0 (Monaco)
2012	Atletico Madrid 4 Chelsea 1 (Monaco)
2013	Bayern Munich 5 Chelsea 4 on pens, aet – 2-2 (Prague)
2014	Real Madrid 2 Sevilla 0 (Cardiff)
2015	Barcelona 5 Sevilla 4 – aet (Tbilisi)
2016	Real Madrid 3 Sevilla 2 – aet (Trondheim)
2017	Real Madrid 2 Manchester Utd 1 (Skopje)
2018	Atletico Madrid 4 Real Madrid 2 (Tallinn)
2019	Liverpool 5 Chelsea 4 on pens, aet – 2-2 (Istanbul)
2020	Bayern Munich 2 Sevilla 1 (Budapest)
2021	Chelsea 6 Villarreal 5 on pens aet 1-1(Belfast)

*not recognised by UEFA; from 1998 one match

INTER-CONTINENTAL CUP

Year	Winners	Runners-up	Score
1960	Real Madrid (Spa)	Penarol (Uru)	0-0 5-1
1961	Penarol (Uru)	Benfica (Por)	0-1 2-1 5-0
1962	Santos (Bra)	Benfica (Por)	3-2 5-2
1963	Santos (Bra)	AC Milan (Ita)	2-4 4-2 1-0
1964	Inter Milan (Ita)	Independiente (Arg)	0-1 2-0 1-0
1965	Inter Milan (Ita)	Independiente (Arg)	3-0 0-0
1966	Penarol (Uru)	Real Madrid (Spa)	2-0 2-0
1967	Racing (Arg)	Celtic	0-1 2-1 1-0
1968	Estudiantes (Arg)	Manchester Utd	1-0 1-1
1969	AC Milan (Ita)	Estudiantes (Arg)	3-0 1-2
1970	Feyenoord (Hol)	Estudiantes (Arg)	2-2 1-0
1971	Nacional (Uru)	Panathanaikos (Gre)	*1-1 2-1
1972	Ajax (Hol)	Independiente (Arg)	1-1 3-0
1973	Independiente (Arg)	Juventus* (Ita)	1-0 #
1974	Atletico Madrid (Spa)*	Independiente (Arg)	0-1 2-0
1975	Not played		
1976	Bayern Munich (WGer)	Cruzeiro (Bra)	2-0 0-0
1977	Boca Juniors (Arg)	Borussia Mönchengladbach* (WGer)	2-2 3-0
1978	Not played		
1979	Olimpia Asuncion (Par)	Malmö* (Swe)	1-0 2-1
1980	Nacional (Arg)	Nott'm Forest	1-0
1981	Flamengo (Bra)	Liverpool	3-0
1982	Penarol (Uru)	Aston Villa	2-0
1983	Porto Alegre (Bra)	SV Hamburg (WGer)	2-1
1984	Independiente (Arg)	Liverpool	1-0
1985	Juventus (Ita)	Argentinos Juniors (Arg)	2-2 (aet)

(Juventus won 4-2 on penalties)

1986	River Plate (Arg)	Steaua Bucharest (Rom)	1-0
1987	Porto (Por)	Penarol (Uru)	2-1 (aet)
1988	Nacional (Uru)	PSV Eindhoven (Hol)	1-1 (aet)
		(Nacional won 7-6 on penalties)	
1989	AC Milan (Ita)	Nacional (Col)	1-0 (aet)
1990	AC Milan (Ita)	Olimpia Asuncion (Par)	3-0
1991	Red Star (Yug)	Colo Colo (Chi)	3-0
1992	Sao Paulo (Bra)	Barcelona (Spa)	2-1
1993	Sao Paulo (Bra)	AC Milan (Ita)	3-2
1994	Velez Sarsfield (Arg)	AC Milan (Ita)	2-0
1995	Ajax (Hol)	Gremio (Bra)	0-0 (aet)
		(Ajax won 4-3 on penalties)	
1996	Juventus (Ita)	River Plate (Arg)	1-0
1997	Borussia Dortmund (Ger)	Cruzeiro (Arg)	2-0
1998	Real Madrid (Spa)	Vasco da Gama (Bra)	2-1
1999	Manchester Utd	Palmeiras (Bra)	1-0
2000	Boca Juniors (Arg)	Real Madrid (Spa)	2-1
2001	Bayern Munich (Ger)	Boca Juniors (Arg)	1-0
2002	Real Madrid (Spa)	Olimpia Ascuncion (Par)	2-0
2003	Boca Juniors (Arg)	AC Milan (Ita)	1-1
	(Boca Juniors won 3-1 on penalties)		
2004	FC Porto (Por)	Caldas (Col)	0-0
	(FC Porto won 8-7 on penalties)		

Played as a single match in Japan since 1980
* European Cup runners-up # One match only
Summary: 43 contests; South America 22 wins, Europe 23 wins

CLUB WORLD CHAMPIONSHIP

2005	Sao Paulo (Bra) 1 Liverpool 0
2006	Internacional (Bra) 1 Barcelona (Spa) 0
2007	AC Milan (Ita) 4 Boca Juniors (Arg) 2

CLUB WORLD CUP

2008	Manchester Utd 1 Liga de Quito (Ecu) 0
2009	Barcelona 2 Estudiantes (Arg) 1 (aet)
2010	Inter Milan (Ita) 3 TP Mazembe (DR Congo) 0
2011	Barcelona 4 Santos (Bra) 0
2012	Corinthians (Bra) 1 Chelsea 0
2013	Bayern Munich (Ger) 2 Raja Casablanca (Mar) 0
2014	Real Madrid (Spa) 2 San Lorenzo (Arg) 0
2015	Barcelona 3 River Plate (Arg) 0
2016	Real Madrid 4 Kashima Antlers (Jap) 2 (aet)
2017	Real Madrid 1 Gremio (Bra) 0
2018	Real Madrid 4 Al AIN (UAE) 1
2019	Liverpool 1 Flamengo (Bra) 0 (aet)
2020	Bayern Munich (Ger) 1 Tigres (Mex) 0
2021	Chelsea 2 Palmeiras (Bra) 1

EUROPEAN TABLES 2021–2022

FRANCE – LIGUE 1

	P	W	D	L	F	A	GD	Pts
Paris SG	38	26	8	4	90	36	54	86
Marseille	38	21	8	9	63	38	25	71
Monaco	38	20	9	9	65	40	25	69
Rennes	38	20	6	12	82	40	42	66
Nice	38	20	7	11	52	36	16	66
Strasbourg	38	17	12	9	60	43	17	63
Lens	38	17	11	10	62	48	14	62
Lyon	38	17	11	10	66	51	15	61
Nantes	38	15	10	13	55	48	7	55
Lille	38	14	13	11	48	48	0	55
Brest	38	13	9	16	49	57	-8	48
Reims	38	11	13	14	43	44	-1	46
Montpellier	38	12	7	19	49	61	-12	43
Angers	38	10	11	17	44	55	-11	41
Troyes	38	9	11	18	37	53	-16	38
Lorient	38	8	12	18	35	63	-28	36
Clermont	38	9	9	20	38	69	-31	36
St Etienne	38	7	11	20	42	77	-35	32
Metz	38	6	13	19	35	69	-34	31
Bordeaux	38	6	13	19	52	91	-39	31

Lyon deducted one point – crowd trouble

Leading scorers: 28 Mbappe (Paris SG); 25 Ben Yedder (Monaco); 21 Dembele (Lyon), Terrier (Rennes); 18 Delort (Montpellier/Nice); 15 David (Lille), Laborde (Montpellier/Rennes); 14 Bayo (Clermont); 13 Neymar (Paris SG)
Cup Final: Nantes 1 (Blas 47 pen) Nice 0

HOLLAND – EREDIVISIE

Ajax	34	26	5	3	98	19	79	83
PSV Eindhoven	34	26	3	5	86	42	44	81
Feyenoord	34	22	5	7	76	34	42	71
Twente	34	20	8	6	55	37	18	68
Alkmaar	34	18	7	9	64	44	20	61
Vitesse Arnhem	34	15	6	13	42	51	-9	51
Utrecht	34	12	11	11	51	46	5	47
Heerenveen	34	11	8	15	37	50	-13	41
Cambuur	34	11	6	17	53	70	-17	39
Waalwijk	34	9	11	14	40	51	-11	38
NEC	34	10	8	16	38	52	-14	38
Groningen	34	9	9	16	41	55	-14	36
Go Ahead	34	10	6	18	37	51	-14	36
Sparta Rotterdam	34	8	11	15	30	48	-18	35
Fortuna Sittard	34	10	5	19	36	67	-31	35
Heracles	34	9	7	18	33	49	-16	34
Willem	34	9	6	19	32	57	-25	33
Zwolle	34	7	6	21	26	52	-26	27

Leading scorers: 21 Haller (Ajax); 18 Openda (Vitesse Arnhem); 16 Van Wolfswinkel (Twente), Pavlidis (Alkmaar); 15 Karlsson (Alkmaar), Til (Feyenoord); 14 Strand Larsen (Groningen); 13 Tadic (Ajax), Linssen (Feyenoord)
Cup Final: PSV Eindhoven 2 (Gutierrez 48, Gakpo 50) Ajax 1 (Gravenberch 23)

GERMANY – BUNDESLIGA

Bayern Munich	34	24	5	5	97	37	60	77
Borussia Dortmund	34	22	3	9	85	52	33	69
Bayer Leverkusen	34	19	7	8	80	47	33	64
RB Leipzig	34	17	7	10	72	37	35	58
Union Berlin	34	16	9	9	50	44	6	57
Freiburg	34	15	10	9	58	46	12	55
Cologne	34	14	10	10	52	49	3	52
Mainz	34	13	7	14	50	45	5	46
Hoffenheim	34	13	7	14	58	60	-2	46
Borussia M'Gladbach	34	12	9	13	54	61	-7	45
Eintracht Frankfurt	34	10	12	12	45	59	-4	42
Wolfsburg	34	12	6	16	43	54	-11	42
Bochum	34	12	6	16	38	52	-14	42
Augsburg	34	10	8	16	39	56	-17	38
Stuttgart	34	7	12	15	41	59	-18	33
Hertha Berlin	34	9	6	19	37	71	-34	33
Arminia Bielefeld	34	5	13	16	27	53	-26	28
Greuther Furth	34	3	9	22	28	82	-54	18

Leading scorers: 35 Lewandowski (Bayern Munich); 24 Schick (Bayer Leverkusen); 22 Haaland (Borussia Dortmund); 20 Modeste (Cologne), Nkunku (RB Leipzig); 15 Awoniyi (Union Berlin); 14 Gnabry (Bayern Munich); 13 Diaby (Bayer Leverkusen); 12 Hofmann (Borussia M'gladbach), Kruse (Union Berlin/Wolfsburg)
Cup Final: RB Leipzig 1 (Nkunku 76) Freiburg 1 (Eggestein 19) – aet, RB Leipzig won 4-2 on pens

ITALY – SERIE A

AC Milan	38	26	8	4	69	31	38	86
Inter Milan	38	25	9	4	84	32	52	84
Napoli	38	24	7	7	74	31	43	79
Juventus	38	20	10	8	57	37	20	70
Lazio	38	18	10	10	77	58	19	64
Roma	38	18	9	11	59	43	16	63
Fiorentina	38	19	5	14	59	51	8	62
Atalanta	38	16	11	11	65	48	17	59
Verona	38	14	11	13	65	59	6	53
Torino	38	13	11	14	46	41	5	50
Sassuolo	38	13	11	14	64	66	-2	50
Udinese	38	11	14	13	61	58	3	47
Bologna	38	12	10	16	44	55	-11	46
Empoli	38	10	11	17	50	70	-20	41
Sampdoria	38	10	6	22	46	63	-17	36
Spezia	38	10	6	22	41	71	-30	36
Salernitana	38	7	10	21	33	78	-45	31
Cagliari	36	6	12	20	34	68	-34	30
Genoa	38	4	16	18	27	60	-33	28
Venezia	38	6	9	23	34	69	-35	24

Leading scorers: 27 Immobile (Lazio); 24 Vlahovic (Fiorentina/Juventus); 21 Martinez (Inter Milan); 17 Abraham (Roma), Simeone (Cagliari/Verona); 16 Scamacca (Sassuolo); 15 Berardi (Sassuolo); 14 Arnautovic (Bologna), Osimhen (Napoli)
Cup Final: Inter Milan 4 (Barella 6, Calhanoglu 80 pen, Perisic 99 pen, 102) Juventus 2 (Alex Sandro 50, Vlahovic 52) – aet

PORTUGAL – PRIMEIRA LIGA

Porto	34	29	4	1	86	22	64	91
Sporting Lisbon	34	27	4	3	73	23	50	85
Benfica	34	23	5	6	78	30	48	74
Sporting Braga	34	19	8	7	52	31	21	65
Gil Vicente	34	13	12	9	47	42	5	51
Guimaraes	34	13	9	12	50	41	9	48
Santa Clara	34	9	13	12	38	54	-16	40
Famalicao	34	9	12	13	45	51	-6	39
Estoril	34	9	12	13	36	43	-7	39
Maritimo	34	9	11	14	39	44	-5	38
Pacos Ferreira	34	9	11	14	29	44	-15	38
Boavista	34	7	17	10	39	52	-13	38
Portimonense	34	10	8	16	31	45	-14	38
Vizela	34	7	12	15	37	58	-21	33
Arouca	34	7	10	17	30	54	-24	31
Moreirense	34	7	8	19	33	51	-18	29
Tondela	34	7	7	20	41	67	-26	28
Belenenses	34	5	11	18	23	55	-32	26

Leading scorers: 26 Nunez (Benfica); 20 Taremi (Porto); 19 Horta (Sporting Braga); 16 Navarro (Gil Vicente); 15 Estupinan (Guimaraes), Sarabia (Sporting Lisbon); 14 Banza (Famalicao). Evanilson (Porto), Diaz (Porto)
Cup Final: Porto 3 (Taremi 22 pen, 74, Vitinha 52) Tondela 1 (Borges 73)

SPAIN – LA LIGA

Real Madrid	38	26	8	4	80	31	49	86
Barcelona	38	21	10	7	68	38	30	73
Atletico Madrid	38	21	8	9	65	43	22	71
Sevilla	38	18	16	4	53	30	23	70
Real Betis	38	19	8	11	62	40	22	65
Real Sociedad	38	17	11	10	40	37	3	62
Villarreal	38	16	11	11	63	37	26	59
Athletic Bilbao	38	14	13	11	43	36	7	55
Valencia	38	11	15	12	48	53	-5	48
Osasuna	38	12	11	15	37	51	-14	47
Celta Vigo	38	12	10	16	43	43	0	46
Rayo Vallecano	38	11	9	18	39	50	-11	42
Elche	38	11	9	18	40	52	-12	42
Espanyol	38	10	12	16	40	53	-13	42
Getafe	38	8	15	15	33	41	-8	39
Mallorca	38	10	9	19	36	63	-27	39
Cadiz	38	8	15	15	35	51	-16	39
Granada	38	8	14	16	44	61	-17	38
Levante	38	8	11	19	51	76	-25	35
Alaves	38	8	7	23	31	65	-34	31

Leading scorers: 27 Benzema (Real Madrid); 18 Aspas (Celta Vigo); 17 De Tomas (Espanyol/Barcelona), Vinicus Junior (Real Madrid); 16 Juanmi (Real Betis), Unal (Getafe); 14 Joselu (Alaves)
Cup Final: Real Betis 1 (Iglesias 11) Valencia 1 (Duro 30) – aet, Real Betis won 5-4 on pens

BRITISH AND IRISH INTERNATIONALS
2021–22
(*denotes new cap)

WORLD CUP 2022 QUALIFIYING – EUROPE

GROUP A

PORTUGAL 2 (Cristiano Ronaldo 89, 90+6) REPUBLIC OF IRELAND 1 (Egan 45)
Faro (7,831); September 1, 2021
Portugal (4-3-3); Rui Patricio, Joao Cancelo (Goncalo Guedes 82), Pepe, Ruben Días, Raphael Guerreiro (Nuno Mendes 62), Bernardo Silva, Palhinha (Joao Moutinho 73), Bruno Fernandes (Joao Mario 62), Diogo Jota, Cristiano Ronaldo, Rafa Silva (Andre Silva 46). **Booked**: Cristiano Ronaldo
Republic of Ireland (3-4-2-1): Bazunu, O'Shea (*Omobamidele 36), Duffy, Egan, Coleman, Hendrick, Cullen, Doherty, McGrath (Molumby 90), Connolly (McClean 72), Idah (J Collins 90). **Booked**: Hendrick, O'Shea, Connolly, Doherty
Referee: Matej Jug (Slovenia). **Half-time**: 0-1

REPUBLIC OF IRELAND 1 (Duffy 87) AZERBAIJAN 1 (Mahmudov 45)
Aviva Stadium (21,287); September 4, 2021
Republic of Ireland (3-4-2-1): Bazunu, Coleman, Duffy, Egan, Doherty (J Collins 80), Molumby (Hourihane 63), Cullen (Browne 88), McClean, Parrott (Robinson 63), Connolly (Horgan 46), Idah. **Booked**: Molumby, Browne
Azerbaijan (4-3-3): Mahammadaliyev, Medvedev (Huseynov 70), Badalov, Haghverdi, Krivotsyuk, Mahmudov, Qarayev, Bayramov (Salahli 70), Alaskarov (Akmedzade 70), Emreli (Sheydayev 79), Ozobic (Nuriiev 79). **Booked**: Krivotsyuk, Mahmudov
Referee: Jerome Brisard (France). **Half-time**: 0-1

REPUBLIC OF IRELAND 1 (Milenkovic 86 og) SERBIA 1 (Milinkovic-Savic 20)
Aviva Stadium (25,415); September 7, 2021
Republic of Ireland (3-5-1-1): Bazunu, Omobamidele, Duffy, Egan, Doherty, McGrath (Horgan 66), Cullen (Molumby 66), Hendrick (Hourihane 78), McClean, Browne (Robinson 57), Idah (J Collins 78). **Booked**: Idah, Browne, Molumby
Serbia (3-4-1-2): Rajkovic, Milenkovic, Veljkovic, Pavlovic, Djuricic (Radonjic 71), Milinkovic-Savic, Gudelj, Kostic (Lazovic 87), Tadic (Maksimovic 82), Vlahovic (Jovic 71), Mitrovic. **Booked**: Djurici, Radonjic
Referee: Jose Maria Sanchez (Spain). **Half-time**: 0-1

AZERBAIJAN 0 REPUBLIC OF IRELAND 3 (Robinson 7, 39, Ogbene 90)
Baku (6,852); October 9, 2021
Azerbaijan (5-4-1): Mahammadaliyev, Huseynov, Medvedev, Haghverdi, Krivoysyuk (Dadashov 79), Bayramov (Abdullayev 63), Alasgarov (Sheydayev 63), Mahmudov (Sadikhov 87), Qarayev, Ozobic, Emreli
Republic of Ireland (3-4-2-1): Bazunu, Omobamidele, Duffy, Egan, Doherty, Cullen (Hourihane 90+3), Hendrick, McClean, Robinson (Parrott 90+3), Horgan (McGrath 46), Idah (Ogbene 59). **Booked**: Egan
Referee: Espen Eskas (Norway). **Half-time**: 0-2

REPUBLIC OF IRELAND 0 PORTUGAL 0
Aviva Stadium (50,737); November 11, 2021
Republic of Ireland (3-4-3): Bazunu, Coleman, Duffy, Egan, Doherty, Hendrick (Hourihane

78), Cullen, Stevens (McClean 78), Ogbene (*Keane 90+1), Robinson, McGrath (Idah 60).
Booked: Ogbene, Coleman, Robinson
Portugal (4-3-3):Rui Patricio, Nelson Semedo, Pepe, Danilo Pereira, Diogo Dalot, Palhinha, Matheus Nunes (Joao Mountinho 55), Bruno Fernandes (Renato Sanchez 74), Goncarlo Guedes (Rafael Leao 55, Jose Fonte 83), Andre Silva (Joao Felix 74), Cristiano Ronaldo.
Booked: Danilo Pereira, Pepe. **Sent off:** Pepe (81)
Referee: Jesus Gil Manzano (Spain)

LUXEMBOURG 0 REPUBLIC OF IRELAND 3 (Duffy 67, Ogbene 75, Robinson 88)
Stade de Luxembourg (9,268); November 14, 2021
Luxemboug (4-1-4-1): Schon, Jans, Chanot, Selimovic, Punto, Martins (S Thill 86), Sinani, Barreiro, O Thill, Borges Sanches (Deville 51), Rodrigues. **Booked:** Selimovic, Martins, Jans, Chanot
Republic of Ireland (3-4-2-1): Bazunu, Coleman, Duffy, Egan, Doherty, Hendrick, Cullen (Hourihane 89), McClean, Ogbene (Browne 81), Robinson (Omobamidele 89), Idah (Knight 61). **Booked:** Cullen, Duffy, Knight, Browne
Referee: Tamas Bognar (Hungary). **Half-time:** 0-0

GROUP C

LITHUANIA 1 (Baravykas 55) NORTHERN IRELAND 4 (Ballard 20, Washington 52 pen, Lavery 67, McNair 82 pen)
Vilnius (1,612); September 2, 2021
Lithuania (4-2-3-1): Setkus, Baravykas, Satkus, Utkus, Slavickas (Barauskas 74), Megelaitis, Verbickas (Uzela 80), Novikovas, Chernych (Jankauskas 80). Lasickas, Dubickas (Kazlauskas 74). **Booked:** Utkus, Megelaitis, Slavickas, Barauskas
Northern Ireland (3-5-2): Peacock-Farrell, McNair, Cathcart, Ballard, Smith (Flanagan 89), McCann, Davis, Thompson (McCalmont 83), Lewis, Washington (Jones 83), Lavery (Lafferty 83). **Booked:** Washington, McNair
Referee: Stephanie Frappart (France). **Half-time:** 0-1

NORTHERN IRELAND 0 SWITZERLAND 0
Windsor Park (15,660); September 8, 2021
Northern Ireland (5-3-2): Peacock-Farrell, Smith (Bradley 68), Brown, Ballard, Cathcart, Lewis, McCann, Davis, Thompson (Saville 74), Washington (Charles 68), Lavery (Jones 86). **Booked:** Smith, Lewis, Brown
Switzerland (4-3-2-1): Sommer, Widmer (Lotomba 87), Akanji, Elvedi, Rodriguez, Freuler, Frei (Steffen 60), Zakaria (Aebischer 86), Fassnacht (Zuber 59), Vargas, Seferovic (Zeqiri 77). **Booked:** Frei, Zakaria
Referee: Harald Lechner (Austria)

SWITZERLAND 2 (Zuber 45, Fassnacht 90+1) NORTHERN IRELAND 0
Geneva (19,129); October 9, 2021
Switzerland (4-2-3-1): Sommer, Mbabu (Widmer 81), Akanji (Schar 53), Elvedi, Rodriguez, Zakaria, Freuler, Steffen, Shaqiri, Zuber (Fassnacht 81), Embolo. **Booked:** Zakaria
Northern Ireland (5-4-1): Peacock-Farrell, McNair, Ballard, Cathcart, Brown (Feguson 80), Lewis, Dallas (Bradley 86), Davis, Thompson (Jones 80), Saville, Washington (Magennis 62). **Booked:** Lewis, Bradley, Magennis. **Sent off:** Lewis (37)
Referee: Slavko Vincic (Slovenia). **Half-time:** 1-0

BULGARIA 2 (Nedelev 53, 63) NORTHERN IRELAND 1 (Washington 35)
Sofia (822); October 12, 2021
Bulgaria (4-3-1-2): Karadzhov, Turitsov, P Hristov, A Hristov, Velkovski, R Tsonev (I Iliev 46), Chochev, Nedelev (Yankov 73), B Tsonev (Malinov 73), A Iliev (Krastev 79), Despodov (Bozhikov 90+2). **Booked:** Malinov

Northern Ireland (5-3-2): Peacock-Farrell, Bradley (Jones 68), Ballard (McGinn 82), Cathcart, Flanagan, Ferguson, McNair, Davis, Thompson, Washington (D Charles 82), Magennis (Dallas 67). **Booked:** Ballard, Dallas
Referee: Aleksei Kulbakov (Belarus). **Half-time:** 0-1

NORTHERN IRELAND 1 (Satkus 17 og) LITHUANIA 0
Windsor Park (14,336); November 12, 2021

Northern Ireland (3-5-2): Peacock-Farrell, McNair, J Evans, Cathcart, Dallas, McCann, Davis, Saville (C Evans 70), Ferguson (Lewis 70), Magennis (*Taylor 78), Washington (Jones 88)
Lithuania (4-2-3-1): Setkus, Vaitkunas, Satkus, Dapkus (Gaspuitis 75), Megelaitis (Armanvicius 86), Barauskas, Chernych, Lasickas, Verbickas (Simkus 86), Novikovas, Laukzemis (Kazlaustas 80). **Booked:** Barauskas
Referee: Istvan Vad (Huingary). **Half-time:** 1-0

NORTHERN IRELAND 0 ITALY 0
Windsor Park (15,969); November 15, 2021

Northern Ireland (5-3-2): Peacock-Farrell, Dallas, Flanagan, J Evans, Cathcart, Lewis, McCann, Davis, Saville (C Evans 72), Whyte (Washington 72), Magennis. **Booked:** Magennis, Peacock-Farrell
Italy (4-3-3): Donnarumma, Di Lorenzo, Bonucci, Acerbi, Emerson (Scamacca 80), Tonali (Cristante 46), Jorginho (Locatelli 68), Barella (Belotti 64), Berardi, Insigne (Bernardeschi 68), Chiesa. **Booked;** Tonali, Donnarumma
Referee: Istvan Kovacs (Romania)

GROUP E

BELARUS 2 (Lisakovich 29 pen Sedko 30) WALES 3 (Bale 5 pen, 69 pen, 90+3)
Kazan, Russia; September 5, 2021

Belarus (5-4-1): Chernik, Begunov, Khadarevich, Shetsov, Sachivko. Zolotov, Ebong (Podstrelov 73), Kilmovich, Bykov, Sedko (Yuzepchuk 73), Lisakovich (Skavysh 90). **Booked:** Chernik, Bykov
Wales (4-2-3-1): Ward, Gunter, Mepham, J Lawrence, B Davies, Allen, Morrell, Bale, Johnson (J Williams 63), James, Colwill (*Harris 57). **Booked:** Gunter
Referee: Giorgi Kruasvili (Georgia). **Half-time:** 2-1
(Played in Kazan, Russia, behind closed doors – sanctions against Belarus

WALES 0 ESTONIA 0
Cardiff City Stadium (21,624); September 8, 2021

Wales (4-3-3): Ward, Gunter, Mepham, Ampadu, B Davies, Allen, Morrell, Wilson (J Williams 37), Bale, T Roberts (Harris 63), James. **Booked:** Morrell
Estonia (5-3-2): Hein, Puri (Lilander 30), Paskotsi (Lukka 86), Kuusk, Mets, Pikk, Vassiljev, Kreida (Poom 86), Kait, Anier (Sinyavskiy 71), Sappinen (Sorga 71). **Booked:** Puri, Kreida
Referee: Ruddy Buquet (France)

CZECH REPUBLIC 2 (Pesek 38, Ward 49 og) WALES 2 (Ramsey 36, James 69)
Prague (16,856); October 8, 2021

Czech Republic (4-2-3-1): Vaclik, Mateju, Celustka, Kalas, Novak (Wiesner 83), Kral (Kuchta 83), Soucek, Pesek (Vydra 77), Barak (Sadilek 77), Hlozek (Zmrhal 90), Schick. **Booked:** Barak, Sadilek
Wales (5-3-2): Ward, Gunter (C Roberts 60), Mepham (T Roberts 86), Rodon, Ampadu, N Williams (*Thomas 76), Allen, Morrell (Wilson 60), Ramsey, James, Moore. **Booked:** Ramsey, Ampadu, Moore
Referee: Deniz Aytekin (Germany). **Half-time:** 1-1

ESTONIA 0 WALES 1 (Moore 12)
Tallinn (5,118); October 11, 2021

Estonia (5-3-2): Hein, Teniste (Ojama 75), Paskotsi, Tamm, Kuusk, Pikk (Sinyavskiy 57), Poom, Mets, Kait (Kallaste 82), Zenjov (Vastsuk 82), Sorga (Kirss 81). **Booked**: Pikk, Kait, Kuusk
Wales (3-5-2): Ward, Mepham, Rodon, Ampadu, C Roberts (Gunter 83), Ramsey (Morrell 80), Allen, Wilson (Johnson 83), Thomas, James, Moore (Harris 71). **Booked**: Wilson, Thomas, Moore, Allen
Referee: Sandro Scharer (Switzerland). **Half-time**: 0-1

WALES 5 (Ramsey 2, 50 pen, N Williams 20, B Davies 77, C Roberts 89) BELARUS 1
(Kontsevoi 87)
Cardiff City Stadium (27,152); November 13, 2021

Wales (4-4-2): Ward (Hennessey 90+1), Ampadu, Rodon, B Davies, N Williams, C Roberts, Ramsey (Morrell 71), Allen, Wilson, Bale (Johnson 46), James (T Roberts 76). **Booked**: Ampadu
Belarus (3-5-2): Chernik, Zolotov, Shvestov, Naumov, Yudenkov (Kontsevoi 82), Pechenin, Klimovich (Ebong 71), Yablonski, Selyava, Sedko (Antilevski 60), Lisakovich (Bakhar 81). **Booked**: Zolotov, Antilevski, Ebong
Referee: Maurizio Mariani (Italy). **Half-time**: 2-0
(Gareth Bale's 100th Wales cap)

WALES 1 (Moore 32) BELGIUM 1 (De Bruyne 12)
Cardiff City Stadium (32,343); November 16, 2021

Wales (5-4-1): Ward, C Roberts, Mepham, Rodon, B Davies, N Williams, Morrell, Ramsey (Johnson 90+3), Allen, James, Moore. **Booked**: Morrell, Moore
Belgium (3-4-1-2): Casteels, Castagne (Dendoncker 59), Boyata, Theate (Vertonghen 85), Meunier (Trossard 85), Witsel, Vanaken, T Hazard, De Bruyne, De Ketelaere (Saelemaekers 58), Origi (Vanzeir 59). **Booked**: T Hazard, Saelemaekers, Dendoncker
Referee: Artur Dias (Portugal). **Half-time**: 1-1

GROUP F

DENMARK 2 (Wass 14, Maehle 15) SCOTLAND 0
Copenhagen (34,562); September 1, 2021

Denmark (5-4-1): Schmeichel, Wass (Stryger Larsen 85), Andersen, Kjaer, Christensen, Maehle, Skov Olsen (Daramy 85), Hojbjerg, Delaney (Norgaard 85), Damsgaard (Lindstrom 90+4), Poulsen (Wind 68)
Scotland (3-5-2): Gordon, Hanley, Cooper, McKenna (Dykes 46), Robertson, Gilmour (*Ferguson 90+1), McLean (Turnbull 85), McGregor, Tierney, Fraser, Adams (Christie 71). **Referee**: Ovidiu Hategan (Romania). **Half-time**: 2-0

SCOTLAND 1 (Dykes 14) MOLDOVA 0
Hampden Park (40,869); September 4, 2021

Scotland (3-4-1-2): Gordon, Hendry, Hanley, Tierney, Patterson, Gilmour (McLean 73) (McGregor 65), Robertson (Cooper 74), Christie, Dykes (Turnbull 85), Nisbet (Adams 65)
Moldova (3-5-2): Avram, Potirnche, Bolohan, Armas, Jardan, Platica, Rata, Ionita (Clescenco 90+4) Reabciuk, Ghecev (Dros 46), Ginsari (Spataru 88). **Booked**: Ionita
Referee: Lawrence Visser (Belgium). **Half-time**: 1-0

AUSTRIA 0 SCOTLAND 1 (Dykes 30 pen)
Vienna (18,800); September 7, 2021

Austria (4-2-3-1): Bachmann, Trimmel, Dragovic, Hinteregger, Alaba, Ilsanker (Gregoritsch 56), Grillitsch (Ulmer 77), Laimer (Kara 88), Schaub (Demir 77), Baumgartner, Arnautovic. **Booked**: Hinteregger, Dragovic

Scotland (3-4-1-2): Gordon, Hendry, Hanley, Tierney, O'Donnell (*P McGinn 77), Gilmour (Ferguson 88), McGregor, Robertson, J McGinn, Adams (Nisbet 88), Dykes (Christie 71). **Booked**: Adams, Hanley
Referee: Georgi Kabakov (Bulgaria). **Half-time**: 0-1

SCOTLAND 3 (J McGinn 30, Dykes 57, McTominay 90+4) ISRAEL 2 (Zahavi 5, Dabbur 32)
Hampden Park (50,585); October 9, 2021

Scotland (3-5-2): Gordon, McTominay, Hendry, Tierney, Patterson, J McGinn, Gilmour (Cooper 90+5), McGregor, Robertson, Adams (Christie 68), Dykes. **Booked**: J McGinn, Robertson, Gilmour, Patterson
Israel (3-4-2-1): Marciano, Abaid, Bitton, Arad, Dasa, Peretz, Natcho (Glazer 66), Menachem (Davidzada 87), Dabbur (Weissman 66), Solomon, Zahavi. **Booked**: Natcho, Zahavi, Bitton
Referee: Szymon Marciniak (Poland). **Half-time**: 1-2

FAROE ISLANDS 0 SCOTLAND 1 (Dykes 86)
Torshavn (4,233); October 12, 2021

Faroe Islands (3-4-3): Gestsson, Faero, Vatnsdal (Askham 59), Nattestad, Rolantsson, Vatnhamar, H Olsen, Davidsen (Knudsen 59), Hansson (Frederiksen 90+1), Edmundsson (A Olsen 90+5), Jonsson. **Booked**: H Olsen
Scotland (3-4-3): Gordon, Hendry (McGregor 68), Hanley, Tierney, Fraser (Patterson 83), McTominay, Gilmour (Cooper 89), Robertson, J McGinn, Christie (Nisbet 83), Dykes. **Booked**: Christie, Dykes, McTominay.
Referee: Meteg Jug (Slovenia). **Half-time**: 0-0

MOLDOVA 0 SCOTLAND 2 (Patterson 38, Adams 65)
Chisinau (3,642); November 12, 2021

Moldova (3-5-2): Namasco, Jardan, Posmac, Bolohan (Rozgoniuc 62), Revenco, Rata, Dros (Bogaciuc 61), Ionita, Marandici (Iosipoi 71), Nicolaescu (Puntus 71), Ginsari (Cojocaru 61). **Booked**: Bolohan, Marandici, Ionita, Puntus, Rata
Scotland (3-4-2-1): Gordon, Hendry, Cooper, Tierney, Patterson, Gilmour (McLean 85), McGregor, Robertson, J McGinn (Turnbull 90), Armstrong (Nisbet 75), Adams (*Brown 85) **Booked**: Patterson
Referee: Srdjan Jovanovic (Serbia). **Half-time**: 0-1

SCOTLAND 2 (Souttar 35, Adams 86) DENMARK 0
Hampden Park (49,527); November 15, 2021

Scotland (3-4-2-1): Gordon, Souttar, Cooper, Tierney (*Ralston 87), O'Donnell, Gilmour (McLean 73), McGregor, Robertson (McKenna 79), J McGinn, Christie (Armstrong 80), Adams (Brown 90)
Denmark (3-4-3): Schmeichel, Christensen, Kjaer, Vestergaard, Kristenen (Bah 81), Wass (Dreyer 81), Jonsson (Stage 56), Maehle, Skov Olsen, Cornelius (Uhre 71), Buun Larsen (Sisto 56). **Booked**: Schmeichel
Referee: Alejandro Hernandez (Spain). **Half-time**: 1-0

GROUP I

HUNGARY 0 ENGLAND 4 (Sterling 55, Kane 63, Maguire 69, Rice 87)
Budapest (58,260); September 2, 2021

Hungary (3-4-2-1): Gulasci, Kecskes, Orban, Attila Szalai, Bolla (Varga 70), Kleinheisler (Gazdag 82), Schafer, Fiola, Salai (Sallai 66), Szoboszlai, Adam Szalai. **Booked**: Bolla, Orban, Gazdag
England (4-2-3-1): Pickford, Walker, Stones, Maguire, Shaw, Phillips, Rice (Henderson 88), Sterling, Mount (Lingard 84), Grealish (Saka 88), Kane. **Booked**: Rice, Sterling
Referee: Cunyet Cakir (Turkey). **Half-time**: 0-0

ENGLAND 4 (Lingard 18, 78, Kane 72 pen, Saka 85) ANDORRA 0
Wembley (67,171); September 5, 2021

England (4-3-3): Johnstone, James (Grealish 62), Coady, Mings, Trippier, Alexander-Arnold, Henderson, Bellingham (Mount 62), Lingard, *Bamford (Kane 62), Saka. **Booked**: Mings
Andorra (5-4-1): Gomes, Jesus Rubio, C Garcia, Vales, Llovera, San Nicolas (Cervos 86), Clemente (Martinez 75), Rebes, Vieira (Lima 86), Jordi Rubio (M Garcia 74), Sanchez (Cucu 66). **Booked**: Vales, Rebes, Jordi Rubio, C Garcia, Cucu, Jesus Rubio
Referee: Anastasios Papapetrou (Greece). **Half-time**: 1-0

POLAND 1 (Szymanski 90+2) ENGLAND 1 (Kane 72)
Warsaw (56,212); September 8, 2021

Poland (3-1-4-2): Szczesny, Dawidowicz, Glik (Helik 80), Bednarek, Krychowiak (Szymanski 68), Jozwiak (Frankowski 80), Linetty, Moder, Puchacz (Rybus 80), Buksa (Swiderski 63), Lewandowski. **Booked**: Glik, Krychowiak, Puchacz, Linetty, Szymanski
England (4-2-3-1): Pickford, Walker, Stones, Maguire, Shaw, Phillips, Rice, Sterling, Mount, Grealish, Kane. **Booked**: Phillips, Maguire
Referee: Daniel Siebert (Germany). **Half-time**: 0-0

ANDORRA 0 ENGLAND 5 (Chilwell 17, Saka 40, Abraham 59, Ward-Prowse 79, Grealish 86)
La Vella (2,285); October 9, 2021

Andorra (5-4-1): Gomes, Chus Rubio, C Garcia (Lima 31, E Garcia 63), Vales, Llovera, M Garcia, Martinez (Alaez 64), Rebes, Vieira, Jordi Rubio (Cervos 82), Sanchez (Cucu 64). **Booked**: Martinez, Rebes
England (4-3-3): Johnstone, Trippier, Stones (Tomori 60), Coady, Chilwell, Lingard (Mount 73), Ward-Prowse, Foden, Saka, Abraham (Watkins 80), Sancho (Grealish 63). **Booked**: Stones, Sancho, Coady
Referee: Kateryna Monzul (Ukraine). **Half-time**: 0-2

ENGLAND 1 (Stones 37) HUNGARY 1 (Sallai 24 pen)
Wembley (69,380); October 12, 2021

England (4-3-3): Pickford, Walker, Stones, Mings, Shaw, Mount, Rice, Foden, Sterling (Henderson 76), Kane (Abraham 76) (Watkins 90+2), Grealish (Saka 62). **Booked**: Shaw
Hungary (3-4-2-1): Gulacsi, Lang, Kecskes, Attila Szalai, Nego (Bolla 90+3), Nagy, Schafer (Vecsei 79), Nagy, Sallai (Hahn 79), Szoboszlai (Nikolic 90+2), Schon (Holender 68). **Booked**: Schafer, Szoboszlai
Referee: Alejandro Hernandez (Spain). **Half-time**: 1-1

ENGLAND 5 (Maguire 9, Kane 18, 33, 45, Henderson 28) ALBANIA 0
Wembley (80,366); November 12, 2021

England (3-4-3): Pickford, Walker, Stones, Maguire, James (Alexander-Arnold 77), Henderson, Phillips (Bellingham 63), Chilwell, Foden (Grealish 63), Kane (Abraham 63), Sterling (*Smith Rowe 77)
Albania (3-4-3): Strakosha, Ismajli, Kumbulla (Dermaku 17), Veseli, Hysaj, Gjasula, Bare (Laci 12), Trashi (Mihaj 46), Uzuni (Roshi 87), Cikalleshi, Bajrami (Ramadani 46). **Booked**: Gjasula, Cikalleshi, Ismajli
Referee: Ruddy Buquet (France). **Half-time**: 5-0

SAN MARINO 0 ENGLAND 10 (Maguire 6, Fabbri 15 og, Kane 27 pen, 31, 39 pen, 42, Smith Rowe 58, Mings 69, Abraham 78, Saka 79)
Serravalle (2,775); November 15, 2021

San Marino (3-5-2): Benedettini, Battistini, Fabbri (Conti 80), Rossi, Tomassini (Vitaioli 46), Lunadei (Grandoni 74), E Golinucci, Mularoni, D'Addario (Censoni 46), Nanni, Hirsch (A Golinucci 46). **Booked**: Tomassini, Rossi, D'Addario, Battistini. **Sent off**: Rossi (67)
England (3-4-3): *Ramsdale, Maguire (Chilwell 46), Coady, Mings, Alexander-Arnold,

Bellingham, (*Gallagher 46), Phillips, Saka, Foden (Abraham 46), Kane (James 62), Smith Rowe (Stones 73). **Booked**: Abraham
Referee: Rade Obrenovic (Slovenia), **Half-time**: 6-0

QUALIFYING PLAY-OFF, SEMI-FINALS

WALES 2 (Bale 25, 51) AUSTRIA 1 (Sabitzer 64)
Cardiff City Stadium (32,053); March 24, 2022
Wales (3-4-3): Hennessey, Ampadu, Rodon, B Davies, C Roberts, Ramsey, Allen, Wilson, N Williams, James (Johnson 88), Bale (Mepham 90+3). **Booked**: Wilson, N Williams
Austria (4-2-3-1): Lindner, Lainer (Gregoritsch 88), Dragovic, Hinteregger, Alaba, Laimer (Kalajdzic 55), Schlager (Lazaro 77), Seiwald, Baumgartner (Weimann 77), Sabitzer, Arnautovic. **Booked**: Baumgartner, Lainer
Referee: Szymon Marciniak (Poland). **Half-time**: 1-0

SCOTLAND 1 (McGregor 79) UKRAINE 3 (Yarmolenko 33, Yaremchuk 49, Dovbyk 90+5)
Hampden Park (49,772); June 1, 2022
Scotland (3-4-1-2): Gordon, McTominay, Hanley, Cooper (Hendry 67), Hickey, Gilmour (S Armstrong 67), McGregor, Robertson, McGinn, Adams, Dykes (Christie 46). **Booked**: Dykes, McGinn
Ukraine (4-1-4-1): Bushchan, Karavaev, Zabarnyi, Matviyenko, Mykolenko, Stepanenko (Sydorchuk 90+3), Yarmolenko (Zubkov 77), Malinovskyi (Shaparenko 71), Zinchenko, Tsygankov (Mudryk 71), Yaremchuk (Dovbyk 77). **Booked**: Yaremchuk, Malinovskyi, Shaparenko
Referee: Danny Makkelie (Holland). **Half-time**: 0-1

FINAL

WALES 1 (Yarmolenko og 34) UKRAINE 0
Cardiff City Stadium (33,280); June 5, 2022
Wales (3-4-3): Hennessey, Ampadu, Rodon, B Davies, C Roberts, Allen, Ramsey, N Williams (Norrington-Davies 90+3), Bale (Wilson 83), Moore, James (Johnson 71). **Booked**: Allen, James
Ukraine (4-1-4-1): Bushchan, Karavaev, Zabarnyi, Matviyenko, Mykolenko, Stepanenko (Sydorchuk 70), Yarmolenko, Malinovskyi, Zinchenko, Tsygankov (Mudryk 77), Yaremchuk (Dovbyk 77). **Booked**: Mykolenko, Mudryk
Referee: Antonio Lahoz (Spain). **Half-time**: 1-0

NATIONS LEAGUE

GROUP A3

HUNGARY 1 (Szoboszlai 66 pen) ENGLAND 0
Budapest (26,935); June 4, 2022
Hungary (3-4-1-2): Gulacsi, Lang, Orban, Attila Szalai, Bego, A Nagy (Styles 82), Schafer, Z Nagy (Vecei 88), Sallai (Kleinheisler 71), Szoboszlai (Fiola 82), Adam Szalai (Adam 88). **Booked**: Schafer
England (3-4-3): Pickford, Walker (Stones 62), Coady (Phillips 79), Maguire, Alexander-Arnold (James 62), Bellingham, Rice, *Justin (Saka 45), *Bowen, Kane, Mount (Grealish 62). **Booked**: Coady, James
Referee: Artur Dias (Portugal). **Half-time**: 0-0

GERMANY 1 (Hofmann 51) ENGLAND 1 (Kane 88 pen)
Munich (66,289); June 7, 2022

Germany (3-4-2-1): Neuer, Klostermann, Rudiger, Schlotterbeck, Hofmann (Gnabry 65), Kimmich, Gundogan (Sane 83), Raum, Muller (Goretzka 76), Musiala (Werner 65), Havertz. **Booked**: Schlotterbeck)

England (4-2-3-1): Pickford, Walker, Stones, Maguire, Trippier, Rice, Phillips (Bellingham 14), Saka (Bowen 80), Mount (Grealish 73), Sterling, Kane

Referee: Carlos del Cerro Grande (Spain). **Half-time**: 0-0

ENGLAND 0 ITALY 0
Molineux (1,782); June 11, 2022

England (4-2-3-1): Ramsdale, James, Maguire, Tomori (Guehi 88), Trippier, Ward-Prowse, Rice (Phillips 65), Sterling (Saka 79), Mount (Bowen 65), Grealish, Abraham (Kane 65). **Booked**: Grealish, Ward-Prowse

Italy (4-3-3): Donnarumma, Di Lorenzo, Gatti, Acerbi, Dimarco (Florenzi 87), Frattesi, Locatelli (Gnonto 64), Tonali, Pessina (Cristante 88), Scamacca (Raspadori 77), Pellegrinio (Esposito 64). **Booked**: Locatelli, Gatti, Tonali

Referee: Szymon Marciniak (Poland)

(restricted attendance – previous crowd trouble)

ENGLAND 0 HUNGARY 4 (Sallai 16, 70, Z Nagy 80, Gazdag 89)
Molineux (28,839); June 14, 2022

England (4-3-3): Ramsdale, Walker, Stones, Guehi, James, Gallagher (Mount 56), Phillips, Bellingham (Foden 68), Bowen (Sterling 46), Kane, Saka (Maguire 85). **Booked**: Stones, Walker. **Sent off**: Stones (82)

Hungary (3-4-2-1): Dibusz, Lang, Orban, Attila Szalai, Fiola, Schafer. Styles (A Nagy 55), Z Nagy, Sallai (Nego 78), Szoboszlai (Gazdag 56), Adam Szalai (Adam 68). **Booked**: Z Nagy

Referee: Clement Turpin (France). **Half-time**: 0-1

	P	W	D	L	F	A	Pts
Hungary	4	2	1	1	7	3	7
Germany	4	1	3	0	8	5	6
Italy	4	1	2	1	5	7	5
England	4	0	2	2	1	6	2

GROUP A4

POLAND 2 ((Kaminski 72, Swiderski 85) WALES 1 (J Williams 52)
Wroclaw (35,214); June 1, 2022

Poland (4-3-1-2): Grabara, Bereszynski, Glik, Bednarek, Pushacz (Zalewski 74), Klich (Zurkowski 60), Krychowiak (Grosicki 81), Goralski (Kaminski 60), Zielinski, Lewandowski, Buksa. **Booked**: Bereszynski

Wales (3-4-2-1): Ward (Hennessey 46), Gunter, Mepham, Norrington-Davies, Smith, Levitt, Morrell, J Williams (Thomas 77), *Burns (N Williams 62), Moore (Harris 46), James (Matondo 46). **Booked**: Morrell, Norrington-Davies

Referee: Rade Obrenovic (Slovenia). **Half-time**: 0-0

WALES 1 (Norrington-Davies 90+2) HOLLAND 2 (Koopmeiners 50, Weghorst 90+4)
Cardiff City Stadium (23,395); June 8, 2022

Wales (5-3-2): Ward (A Davies 46), C Roberts, Mepham, Rodon, B Davies, Norrington-Davies, Levitt (Smith 68), Morrell (Colwill 60), Wilson, Johnson (Bale 77), James (Matondo 77)

Holland (3-4-2-1): Flekken, Teze, De Vrij, De Ligt (Martins Indi 84), Hateboer, Koopmeiners, Schouten (De Jong 67), Malacia, Lang (Til 90+1). Gakpo (Bergwijn 67), Weghorst. **Booked**: Teze

Referee: Glenn Nyberg (Sweden). **Half-time**: 0-0

WALES 1 (Johnson 80) BELGIUM 1 (Tielemans 50)
Cardiff City Stadium (27,188); June 11, 2022

Wales (3-1-4-2): Hennessey, Mepham, Rodon, B Davies (Colwill 73), Ampadu, C Roberts (Norrington-Davies 61), Allen (Ramsey 38), Wilson (Burns 73), N Williams, Bale (Johnson 73), James. **Booked**: Rodon, Norrington-Davies
Belgium (3-4-3): Casteels, Dendoncker, Boyata, Theate, Meunier, Witsel (Openda 90+3), Tielemans, Carrasco (T Hazard 61), De Bruyne (E Hazard 72), Trossard (Praet 72), Batshuayi. **Booked**: Carrasco, Theate
Referee: Benoit Bastien (France). **Half-time**: 0-0

HOLLAND 3 (Lang 17, Gakpo 23, Depay 90+3) WALES 2 (Johnson 26, Bale 90+2 pen)
Rotterdam (37,247); June 14, 2022

Holland (3-4-2-1): Cillessen, Teze (De Vrij 46), De Ligt, Martins Indi, Hateboer (Dumfries 46), Koopmeiners, De Jong, Malacia, Gakpo, Janssen (Depay 73), Lang (Bergwijn 73). **Booked**: Martins Indi, Koopmeiners
Wales (5-3-2): Hennessey. Thomas, Mepham, Rodon (Gunter 67), B Davies, Burns (C Roberts 46), Smith (Ramsey 63), Ampadu, Wilson, Johnson, James (Bale 70). **Booked**: Mepham, Ampadu, C Roberts
Referee: Haratiu Fesnic (Romania). **Half-time**: 2-1

Holland	4	3	1	0	11	6	10
Belgium	4	2	1	1	9	6	7
Poland	4	1	1	2	5	10	4
Wales	4	0	1	3	5	8	1

GROUP B1

ARMENIA 1 (Spertsyan 74) REPUBLIC OF IRELAND 0
Yerevan (10,600); June 4, 2022

Armenia (5-3-2): Yurchenko, Hambardzumyan, Mkoyan, Haroyan, A Hovhannisyan (Mkrtchyan 61), K Hovhannisyan, Bayramyan, Grigoryan, Spertsyan, Barseghyan (Dashyan 88), Bichakhchyan (Adamyan 55). **Booked**: Mkrtchyan
Republic of Ireland (3-4-3): Kelleher, N Collins, Duffy, Egan, Coleman (Keane 80), Hendrick, Cullen (Browne 80), Stevens (McClean 72), Ogbene, Robinson (Knight 72), Parrott (Obafemi 65). **Booked**: Duffy, Hendrick
Referee: Radu Petrescu (Romania). **Half-time**: 0-0

SCOTLAND 2 (Ralston 28, McKenna 40) ARMENIA 0
Hampden Park (38,627); June 8, 2022

Scotland (3-4-3): Gordon, Souttar, Hendry, McKenna, Ralston (Patterson 76), J McGinn, McGregor, Robertson (Hickey 76), Armstrong (McTominay 76), Adams (Brown 87), Christie (*Stewart 87). **Booked**: McGregor
Armenia (4-3-2-1): Yurchenko, Hambardzumyan, Mikoyan, Haroyan, A Hovhannisyan, Bayramyan (Dashyan 89), Grigoryan (Angulo 46), Spertsyan (Udo 71), Barseghyan, K Hovhannisyan (Voskanyan 46), Adamyan (Bichakhchyan 46). **Booked**: Haroyan, Spertsyan, Angulo
Referee: Sebastian Gishamer (Austria). **Half-time**: 2-0

REPUBLIC OF IRELAND 0 UKRAINE 1 (Tsygankov 47)
Aviva Stadium (40,111); June 8, 2002

Republic of Ireland (3-4-3): Kelleher, N Collins, Duffy, Egan (O'Shea 62), Christie (Browne 69), Hendrick, Cullen, Stevens (McClean 69), Robinson (Obafemi 69), Ogbene (*Hamilton 78), Knight. **Booked**: Cullen
Ukraine (3-4-2-1): Lunin, Popov, Bondar, Syrota, Kacharaba (Karavayev 72), Sydorchuk (Ignatenko 88), Shaparenko, Mykolenko, Zubkov (Tsygankov 46), Mudryk (Pikhalyonok 72),

Dovbyk (Sikan 80). **Booked:** Mykolenko
Referee: Filip Glova (Slovakia. **Half-time:** 0-0

REPUBLIC OF IRELAND 3 (Browne 20, Parrott 28, Obafemi 51) SCOTLAND 0
Aviva Stadium (46,927); June 11, 2022
Republic of Ireland (3-1-4-2): Kelleher, N Collins, Duffy, Egan, Cullen, Browne, Molumby (Hendrick 81), Knight (Hourihane 71), McClean, Obafemi (Hogan 56), Parrott (Robinson 84). **Booked:** Duffy, Robinson
Scotland (3-4-2-1): Gordon, Hendry (Gilmour 46), Hanley, McKenna (Souttar 74), Ralston, McTominay, McGregor, Robertson, J McGinn (Armstrong 59), Christie (Brown 59), Adams (Stewart 59). **Booked:** Christie
Referee: Marco Di Bello (Italy). **Half-time:** 2-0

ARMENIA 1 (Bichakhchyan 6) SCOTLAND 4 (Armstrong 14, 45, J McGinn 50, Adams 53)
Yerevan (13,500); June 14, 2022
Armenia (5-3-2): Yurchenko, Dashyan, Hambartsumyan, Haroyan, Mkoyan, A Hovhannisyan, Grigoryan (Mkrtchyan 46), Spertsyan (Wbeymar 58), Bayramyan (K Hovhannisyan 59), Barseghyan (Serobyan 84), Bichakhchyan (Udo 59). **Booked:** Haroyan, Hambartsumyan, A Hovhannisyan, Spertsyan. **Sent off:** A Hovhannisyan (44), K Hovhannisyan (90+1)
Scotland (3-4-2-1): Gordon, McTominay, Hanley (*Campbell 85), Hendry, Patterson (Ralston 64), Gilmour (Ferguson 63), McGregor, Taylor, J McGinn (Turnbull 64), Armstrong, Adams (Brown 74). **Booked:** Adams, McTominay
Referee: Nikola Dabanovic (Montenegro). **Half-time:** 1-2

UKRAINE 1 (Dovbyk 47) REPUBLIC OF IRELAND 1 (N Collins 31)
Lodz, Poland (10,641); June 14, 2022
Ukraine (4-3-3): Riznyk, Karavaev, Zabarnyi, Matvienko (Popov 72), Mykolenko, Malinovskyi (Mudryk 28), Sydorchuk, Zinchenko, Yarmolenko, Dovbyk (Sikan 73), Shaparenko. **Booked:** Zabarnyi, Yarmolenko, Zinchenko
Republic of Ireland (5-3-2): Kelleher, Browne, Lenihan, N Collins, O'Shea, McClean, Molumby (Hendrick 67), Cullen, Knight (Hourihane 80), Parrott (Ogbene 80), Hogan (Robinson 56). **Booked:** Browne, Lenihan
Referee: Ali Palabiyik (Turkey), **Half-time:** 0-1

Ukraine	3	2	1	0	5	1	7
Scotland	3	2	0	1	6	4	6
Republic of Ireland	4	1	1	2	4	3	4
Armenia	4	1	0	3	2	9	3

GROUP C2

NORTHERN IRELAND 0 GREECE 1 (Bakasetas 39)
Windsor Park (16,977); June 2, 2022
Northern Ireland (5-3-2): Peacock-Farrell, Bradley (McGinn 62), McNair, J Evans, Ballard, Lane (Hume 78), McCann, Davis, Saville (*S Charles 79), Lavery (Lafferty 62), Whyte. **Booked:** Whyte, McNair
Greece (4-2-3-1): Vlachodimos, Rota (Baldock 90+2), Mavroponas, Hatzidiakos, Tsimikas, Siopis (Tzavellas 82), Bouchalakis, Limnios (Pavlidis 69), Bakasetas (Kourbelis 69), Mantalos, Giakoumakis (Chatzigiovanis 69). **Booked:** Tzavellas, Mantalos
Referee: Erik Lambrechts (Belgium). **Half-time:** 0-1

CYPRUS 0 NORTHERN IRELAND 0
Larnaca (1,663); June 5, 2022
Cyprus (3-5-2): Michal, Katelaris (Panagiotou 46), Gogic, Correa, Pittas, Loizou (Tzionis 56), Artymatas, Kastanos (Papoulis 66), Ioannou, Christofi, Sotiriou. **Booked:** Kastanos

Northern Ireland (4-3-3): Peacock-Farrell, McNair, J Evans, Brown, Lane (*Spencer 64), S Charles (Donnelly 64), Davis (Lavery 71), Saville (McCann 71), McGinn, Lafferty, Whyte (*McMenamin 64). **Booked:** J Evans, Donnelly
Referee: Enea Jorgki (Albania)

KOSOVO 3 (Muriqi 9 pen, 52, Bytyqi 19) NORTHERN IRELAND 2 (Lavery 45, Ballard 83)
Pristina (11,700); June 9, 2022

Kosovo (4-3-3): Ujkani, Kastati, Rrahmani, Kryeziu, Rrudhani (Fazliji 75), Berisha (Domgjoni 79), Dresevic, Muslija, Rashica (Sahiti 89), Muriqi, Bytyqi. **Booked:** Dresevic, Kastrati, Fazliji
Northern Ireland (4-1-4-1): Peacock-Farrell, Spencer (Bradley 86), Ballard, J Evans, Brown, Lavery (Whyte 68), Davis, Saville (Thompson 73), McMenamin, McCann (S Charles 68), Lafferty (D Charles 68). **Booked:** Lavery, Thompson
Referee: Jakob Kehlet (Denmark). **Half-time:** 2-1

NORTHERN IRELAND 2 (McNair 71, J Evans 90+3) CYPRUS 2 (Kakoullis 32, 51)
Windsor Park (16,454); June 12, 2022

Northern Ireland (4-1-4-1): Carson, Spencer (Bradley 69), Ballard, J Evans, Brown, Davis, Lavery (Whyte 59), McNair, S Charles (Thompson 59), McMenamin (McGinn 69), Lafferty (D Charles 69). **Booked:** Davis:
Cyprus (3-4-2-1): Christadoulou, Artymatos, Gogic, Laifis (Ioannou 69), Pittas (Panayiotpou 46), Kryiakou, Kastanos, Panagiotou, Christofi, Tzionis (Papoulis 58), Kakoullis (Katelaris 78). **Booked:** Laifis
Referee: Ricardo De Burgos (Spain). **Half-time:** 0-2

Greece	4	4	0	0	7	0	12
Kosovo	4	2	0	2	5	5	6
Northern Ireland	4	0	2	2	4	6	2
Cyprus	4	0	2	2	2	7	2

FRIENDLY INTERNATIONALS

FINLAND 0 WALES 0
Helsinki (4,357); September 1, 2021

Finland (4-4-2): Eriksson, Raitala (Alho 73), Toivio, Ivanov, Hamalainen, Hostikka (Soiri 64), Kairinen, Kamara, Assehnoun (Nissila 46), Forss (Pohjanpalo 73), Jensen (Taylor 640. **Booked:** Kamara
Wales (3-5-2): Ward (Hennessey 46), Ampadu (Woodburn 73), Lockyer, J Lawrence (Davies 46), Levitt, Smith, J Williams (Sheehan 63), Wilson, Norrington-Davies, Johnson (Colwill 63), T Roberts (Bale 83). **Booked:** Sheehan
Referee: Kristo Tohver (Sweden)

ESTONIA 0 NORTHERN IRELAND 1 (Ferguson 75)
Tallin (2,524); September 5, 2021

Estonia (3-1-4-2): Igonen, Lukka, Kuusk, Paskotsi, Kreida (Mets 46), Lilander (Puri 46), Poom, Vassiljev (Kait 46), Sinyavskiy (Kirss 80), Sappinen (Anier 46), Sorga (Zenjov 76). **Booked:** Vassiljev, Zenjov
Northern Ireland (4-2-3-1): Carson (Hazard 63), McNair, Flanagan, Brown, Lewis (Ferguson 55), Donnelly (Bradley 63), McCalmont, Whyte, Jones, McGinn, Lafferty (D Charles 55). **Booked:** Charles, Bradley
Referee: Mads Kristoffersen (Denmark). **Half-time:** 0-0

REPUBLIC OF IRELAND 4 (Robinson 4, 13 pen, 53, Duffy 59) Qatar 0
Aviva Stadium (25,000); October 12, 2021

Republic of Ireland (3-4-3): Kelleher, Omobamidele, Duffy (*N Collins 76), Egan, Doherty (Christie 46), Hendrick, Hourihane (Arter 87), Stevens, Ogbene (Knight 68), Robinson (Parrott 76), McGrath (J Collins 87)
Qatar (3-5-2): Barsham, Odeh, Al Rawi, Fadlalla, Carvalho, Al Haydos, Boudiaf, Mohammed (Madibo 73), Ahmed, Abdullah (Abdelmotaal 73), Afif. **Booked:** Madibo
Referee: Keith Kennedy (Northern Ireland). **Half-time:** 2-0

SCOTLAND 1 (Tierney 67) POLAND 1 (Piatek 90+4 pen)
Hampden Park (39,090); March 24, 2022

Scotland (3-4-2-1): Gordon, McTominay, Hanley, Tierney, Patterson (O'Donnell 66), Gilmour (McLean 77), McGregor (Jack 77), Taylor (*Hickey 66), McGinn, Christie (Armstrong 77), Adams (Brown 90)
Poland (3-4-3): Skorupski, Salamon (Bielik 44), Glik, Bednarek (Buksa 83), Cash, Zurkowski, Krychowiak (Szymanski 61), Reca, Zielinski (Grosicki 71), Milik (Piatek 27), Moder. **Booked:** Reca
Referee: Robert Hennessy (Republic of Ireland). **Half-time:** 0-0

LUXEMBOURG 1 (M Martins 58) NORTHERN IRELAND 3 (Magennis 16, Davis 83, Whyte 85)
Stade de Luxembourg (4,540); March 25, 2022

Luxembourg (4-3-3): Moris, Jans, Chanot, Carlson (Mahmutovic 46), Pinto (Olesen 74), M Martins, C Martins, Barreiro (S Thill 84), Sinani (Deville 88), O Thill (V Thill 70), Rodrigues (Sanches 84). **Booked:** Chanot, Barreiro
Northern Ireland (3-5-2): Hazard (*Southwood 46), Flanagan, J Evans (Brown 63), Cathcart, Dallas (McGinn 79), Thompson (Davis 63), C Evans, Saville, Ferguson, Magennis (D Charles 63), Lavery (Whyte 63). **Booked:** Charles
Referee: Daniel Schlager (Germany). **Half-time:** 0-1

ENGLAND 2 (Shaw 45, Kane 78 pen) SWITZERLAND 1 (Embolo 22)
Wembley (78,881); March 26, 2022

England (3-4-2-1): Pickford, White, Coady, *Guehi, *Walker-Peters (Sterling 62), Henderson, *Gallagher (Rice 61), Shaw (*Mitchell 61), Foden (Bellingham 80), Mount (Grealish 62), Kane (Watkins 89)
Switzerland (4-2-3-1): Omlin, Widmer (Mbabu 36), Akanji, Frei, Rodriguez, Freuler (Zuber 62), Xhaka, Steffan (Zeqiri 63), Shaqiri (Aebischer 80), Vargas (Sow 63), Embolo (Gavranovic 80)
Referee: Andreas Ekberg (Sweden). **Half-time:** 1-1

REPUBLIC OF IRELAND 2 (Ogbene 35, Browne 86) BELGIUM 2 (Batshuayi 12, Vanaken 58)
Aviva Stadium (48,808); March 26, 2022

Republic of Ireland (3-4-3): Kelleher, Coleman, Duffy, Egan, Doherty, Cullen, Hendrick (Browne 75), McClean (Manning 80), Ogbene, Robinson (Parrott 90+2), Knight (Keane 75)
Belgium (3-4-3): Mignolet, Denayer, Boyata, Theate (Mangala 75), Saelemakers (Foket 46), Dendoncker, Tielemans, T Hazard, De Ketalaere (Januzaj 75), Batshuayi (Benteke 84), Vanaken
Referee: Nick Walsh (Scotland). **Half-time:** 1-1

ENGLAND 3 (Watkins 30, Sterling 45, Mings 90+3) IVORY COAST 0
Wembley (73,405); March 29, 2022

England (4-2-3-1): Pope, White (Walker-Peters 46), Maguire, Mings, Mitchell (Shaw 62), Ward-Prowse (Gallagher 79), Rice, Sterling (Foden 62), Bellingham, Grealish (Smith Rowe 62), Watkins (Kane 62)
Ivory Coast (4-2-3-1): Sangare, Aurier, Bailly (Agbadou 46), Deli, Kamara, Kessie, Seri (Akouokou 90+3), Pepe (Boly 46), Gradel (Coulibaly 46), Cornet (Konan 63), Haller (Boli 85). **Booked:** Aurier, Seri. **Sent off:** Aurier (40)
Referee: Erik Lambrechts (Belgium). **Half-time:** 1-0

AUSTRIA 2 (Gregoritsch 75, Schopf 82) SCOTLAND 2 (Hendry 28, McGinn 56)
Vienna (6,600); March 29, 2022

Austria (3-4-3): Bachmann (Pentz 87), Ilsanker (Weimann 74), Dragovic, Hinteregger, Lazaro, Lainer (Grull 60), Sabitzer, Ulmer (Ullmann 87), Baumgartner (Schopf 59), Kalajdzic (Gregoritsch 74), Arnautovioc

Scotland (3-4-2-1): Gordon, Hendry, Hanley, Tierney, Patterson (O'Donnell 58), Ferguson (Gilmour 77), Jack (McTominay 58), Robertson (Hickey 58), McGinn, Armstrong (Christie 77), Adams (Dykes 66)

Referee: Tamas Bognar (Hungary). **Half-time:** 0-1

WALES 1 (Colwill 34) CZECH REPUBLIC 1 (Soucek 32)
Cardiff City Stadium (12,906); March 29, 2022

Wales (3-4-1-2): Hennessey (A Davies 61), Gunter (Rodon 61), Mepham, Cabango, Thomas, Vaulks (Ampadu 61), Morrell, Norrington-Davies, Colwill (Harris 81), Johnson (Bale 81), Matondo (J Williams 71)

Czech Republic (3-5-1-1): Stanek (Vaclik 46), Zima, Petrasek, Brabec, Masopust (Jankto 63), Lingr (Hlozek 81), Soucek, Sadilek (Barak 63), Zeleny, Pesek (Sykora 46), Kuchta (Jurecka 46)

Referee: Paul Tierney (England). **Half-time:** 1-1

Wayne Hennessey's 100th Wales cap

NORTHERN IRELAND 0 HUNGARY 1 (Sallai 55)
Windsor Park (18,000); March 29, 2022

Northern Ireland (3-4-3): Peacock-Farrell, Ballard (*Hume 83), Cathcart, Brown, McNair, McCann, Davis (Saville 61), *Lane (Dallas 61), Whyte (Thompson 68), Magennis (D Charles 46), McGinn (Lavery 68). **Booked:** Cathcart, Davis, Saville, Dallas

Hungary (3-4-2-1): Dibusz, Lang (Kecskes 82), Orban, Fiola, Nego (Bolla 82), Schafer, Styles (Vecsei 82), Z Nagy, Sallai (Gazdag 72), Szoboszlai (A Nagy 66), Szalai (Adam 73). **Booked:** Sallai, Lang, Nagy

Referee: Robert Harvey (Republic of Ireland). **Half-time:** 0-0

REPUBLIC OF IRELAND 1 (Parrott 90+7) LITHUANIA 0
Aviva Stadium (30,686); March 29, 2022

Republic of Ireland (3-4-3): Kelleher, N Collins, Egan, O'Shea (McClean 62), Doherty, Browne (Hendrick 81), Hourihane, Manning, Ogbene (Knight 81), Keane (Parrott 62), Robinson (Hogan 77)

Lithuania (5-4-1): Bartkus, Baravykas, Satkus, L Klimavicius (Kruzikas 60), Vaitkunas, Milasius (Kazlauskas 46), Lasiskas (Sirvys 82), Utkus, Slivka, Chernykh (Sirgedas 86), A Klimavicius. **Booked:** Slivka, Chernykh

Referee: Bram Van Driessche (Belgium). **Half-time:** 0-0

OTHER BRITISH & IRISH INTERNATIONAL RESULTS

ENGLAND

v ALBANIA

1989	Tirana (WC)	2	0
1989	Wembley (WC)	5	0
2001	Tirana (WC)	3	1
2001	Newcastle (WC)	2	0
2021	Tirana (WC)	2	0
2021	Wembley (WC)	5	0

v ALGERIA

2010	Cape Town (WC)	0	0

v ANDORRA

2006	Old Trafford (EC)	5	0
2007	Barcelona (EC)	3	0
2008	Barcelona (WC)	2	0
2009	Wembley (WC)	6	0
2021	Wembley (WC)	4	0
2021	La Vella (WC)	5	0

v ARGENTINA

1951	Wembley	2	1
1953*	Buenos Aires	0	0
1962	Rancagua (WC)	3	1
1964	Rio de Janeiro	0	1
1966	Wembley (WC)	1	0
1974	Wembley	2	2
1977	Buenos Aires	1	1
1980	Wembley	3	1
1986	Mexico City (WC)	1	2
1991	Wembley	2	2
1998†	St Etienne (WC)	2	2
2000	Wembley	0	0
2002	Sapporo (WC)	1	0
2005	Geneva	3	2

(*Abandoned after 21 mins – rain)

(† England lost 3-4 on pens)

v AUSTRALIA

1980	Sydney	2	1
1983	Sydney	0	0
1983	Brisbane	1	0
1983	Melbourne	1	1
1991	Sydney	1	0
2003	West Ham	1	3
2016	Sunderland	2	1

v AUSTRIA

1908	Vienna	6	1
1908	Vienna	11	1
1909	Vienna	8	1
1930	Vienna	0	0
1932	Stamford Bridge	4	3
1936	Vienna	1	2
1951	Wembley	2	2
1952	Vienna	3	2
1958	Boras (WC)	2	2
1961	Vienna	1	3
1962	Wembley	3	1
1965	Wembley	2	3
1967	Vienna	1	0
1973	Wembley	7	0
1979	Vienna	3	4
2004	Vienna (WC)	2	2
2005	Old Trafford (WC)	1	0
2007	Vienna	1	0
2021	Middlesbrough	1	0

v AZERBAIJAN

2004	Baku (WC)	1	0
2005	Newcastle (WC)	2	0

v BELARUS

2008	Minsk (WC)	3	1
2009	Wembley (WC)	3	0

v BELGIUM

1921	Brussels	2	0
1923	Highbury	6	1
1923	Antwerp	2	2
1924	West Bromwich	4	0
1926	Antwerp	5	3
1927	Brussels	9	1
1928	Antwerp	3	1
1929	Brussels	5	1
1931	Brussels	4	1
1936	Brussels	2	3
1947	Brussels	5	2
1950	Brussels	4	1
1952	Wembley	5	0
1954	Basle (WC)	4	4
1964	Wembley	2	2
1970	Brussels	3	1
1980	Turin (EC)	1	1
1990	Bologna (WC)	1	0
1998*	Casablanca	0	0
1999	Sunderland	2	1
2012	Wembley	1	0
2018	Kaliningrad (WC)	0	1
2018	St Petersburg (WC)	0	2
2020	Wembley (NL)	2	1
2020	Leuven (NL)	0	2

(*England lost 3-4 on pens)

v BOHEMIA
1908	Prague	4	0

v BRAZIL
1956	Wembley	4	2
1958	Gothenburg (WC)	0	0
1959	Rio de Janeiro	0	2
1962	Vina del Mar (WC)	1	3
1963	Wembley	1	1
1964	Rio de Janeiro	1	5
1969	Rio de Janeiro	1	2
1970	Guadalajara (WC)	0	1
1976	Los Angeles	0	1
1977	Rio de Janeiro	0	0
1978	Wembley	1	1
1981	Wembley	0	1
1984	Rio de Janeiro	2	0
1987	Wembley	1	1
1990	Wembley	1	0
1992	Wembley	1	1
1993	Washington	1	1
1995	Wembley	1	3
1997	Paris (TF)	0	1
2000	Wembley	1	1
2002	Shizuoka (WC)	1	2
2007	Wembley	1	1
2009	Doha	0	1
2013	Wembley	2	1
2013	Rio de Janeiro	2	2
2017	Wembley	0	0

v BULGARIA
1962	Rancagua (WC)	0	0
1968	Wembley	1	1
1974	Sofia	1	0
1979	Sofia (EC)	3	0
1979	Wembley (EC)	2	0
1996	Wembley	1	0
1998	Wembley (EC)	0	0
1999	Sofia (EC)	1	1
2010	Wembley (EC)	4	0
2011	Sofia (EC)	3	0
2019	Wembley (EC)	4	0
2019	Sofia (EC)	6	0

v CAMEROON
1990	Naples (WC)	3	2
1991	Wembley	2	0
1997	Wembley	2	0
2002	Kobe (Japan)	2	2

v CANADA
1986	Vancouver	1	0

v CHILE
1950	Rio de Janeiro (WC)	2	0
1953	Santiago	2	1
1984	Santiago	0	0
1989	Wembley	0	0
1998	Wembley	0	2
2013	Wembley	0	2

v CHINA
1996	Beijing	3	0

v CIS
(formerly Soviet Union)
1992	Moscow	2	2

v COLOMBIA
1970	Bogota	4	0
1988	Wembley	1	1
1995	Wembley	0	0
1998	Lens (WC)	2	0
2005	New York	3	2
2018+	Moscow (WC)	1	1
(† England won 4-3 on pens)			

v COSTA RICA
2014	Belo Horizonte (WC)	0	0
2018	Leeds	2	0

v CROATIA
1995	Wembley	0	0
2003	Ipswich	3	1
2004	Lisbon (EC)	4	2
2006	Zagreb (EC)	0	2
2007	Wembley (EC)	2	3
2008	Zagreb (WC)	4	1
2009	Wembley (WC)	5	1
2018	Moscow (WC)	1	2
2018	Rijeka (NL)	0	0
2018	Wembley (NL)	2	1
2021	Wembley (EC)	1	0

v CYPRUS
1975	Wembley (EC)	5	0
1975	Limassol (EC)	1	0

v CZECH REPUBLIC
1998	Wembley	2	0
2008	Wembley	2	2
2019	Wembley (EC)	5	0
2019	Prague (EC)	1	2
2021	Wembley (EC)	1	0

v CZECHOSLOVAKIA
1934	Prague	1	2
1937	White Hart Lane	5	4

1963	Bratislava	4	2
1966	Wembley	0	0
1970	Guadalajara (WC)	1	0
1973	Prague	1	1
1974	Wembley (EC)	3	0
1975*	Bratislava (EC)	1	2
1978	Wembley (EC)	1	0
1982	Bilbao (WC)	2	0
1990	Wembley	4	2
1992	Prague	2	2

(* Aband 0-0, 17 mins prev day – fog)

v DENMARK

1948	Copenhagen	0	0
1955	Copenhagen	5	1
1956	W'hampton (WC)	5	2
1957	Copenhagen (WC)	4	1
1966	Copenhagen	2	0
1978	Copenhagen (EC)	4	3
1979	Wembley (EC)	1	0
1982	Copenhagen (EC)	2	2
1983	Wembley (EC)	0	1
1988	Wembley	1	0
1989	Copenhagen	1	1
1990	Wembley	1	0
1992	Malmo (EC)	0	0
1994	Wembley	1	0
2002	Niigata (WC)	3	0
2003	Old Trafford	2	3
2005	Copenhagen	1	4
2011	Copenhagen	2	1
2014	Wembley	1	0
2020	Copenhagen (NL)	0	0
2020	Wembley (NL)	0	1
2021	Wembley (EC)	2	1

v EAST GERMANY

1963	Leipzig	2	1
1970	Wembley	3	1
1974	Leipzig	1	1
1984	Wembley	1	0

v ECUADOR

1970	Quito	2	0
2006	Stuttgart (WC)	1	0
2014	Miami	2	2

v EGYPT

1986	Cairo	4	0
1990	Cagliari (WC)	1	0
2010	Wembley	3	1

v ESTONIA

2007	Tallinn (EC)	3	0

2007	Wembley (EC)	3	0
2014	Tallinn (EC)	1	0
2015	Wembley (EC)	2	0

v FIFA

1938	Highbury	3	0
1953	Wembley	4	4
1963	Wembley	2	1

v FINLAND

1937	Helsinki	8	0
1956	Helsinki	5	1
1966	Helsinki	3	0
1976	Helsinki (WC)	4	1
1976	Wembley (WC)	2	1
1982	Helsinki	4	1
1984	Wembley (WC)	5	0
1985	Helsinki (WC)	1	1
1992	Helsinki	2	1
2000	Helsinki (WC)	0	0
2001	Liverpool (WC)	2	1

v FRANCE

1923	Paris	4	1
1924	Paris	3	1
1925	Paris	3	2
1927	Paris	6	0
1928	Paris	5	1
1929	Paris	4	1
1931	Paris	2	5
1933	White Hart Lane	4	1
1938	Paris	4	2
1947	Highbury	3	0
1949	Paris	3	1
1951	Highbury	2	2
1955	Paris	0	1
1957	Wembley	4	0
1962	Hillsborough (EC)	1	1
1963	Paris (EC)	2	5
1966	Wembley (WC)	2	0
1969	Wembley	5	0
1982	Bilbao (WC)	3	1
1984	Paris	0	2
1992	Wembley	2	0
1992	Malmo (EC)	0	0
1997	Montpellier (TF)	1	0
1999	Wembley	0	2
2000	Paris	1	1
2004	Lisbon (EC)	1	2
2008	Paris	0	1
2010	Wembley	1	2
2012	Donetsk (EC)	1	1
2015	Wembley	2	0
2017	Paris	2	3

v GEORGIA

1996	Tbilisi (WC)	2	0
1997	Wembley (WC)	2	0

v GERMANY/WEST GERMANY

1930	Berlin	3	3
1935	White Hart Lane	3	0
1938	Berlin	6	3
1954	Wembley	3	1
1956	Berlin	3	1
1965	Nuremberg	1	0
1966	Wembley	1	0
1966	Wembley (WCF)	4	2
1968	Hanover	0	1
1970	Leon (WC)	2	3
1972	Wembley (EC)	1	3
1972	Berlin (EC)	0	0
1975	Wembley	2	0
1978	Munich	1	2
1982	Madrid (WC)	0	0
1982	Wembley	1	2
1985	Mexico City	3	0
1987	Dusseldorf	1	3
1990*	Turin (WC)	1	1
1991	Wembley	0	1
1993	Detroit	1	2
1996†	Wembley (EC)	1	1
2000	Charleroi (EC)	1	0
2000	Wembley (WC)	0	1
2001	Munich (WC)	5	1
2007	Wembley	1	2
2008	Berlin	2	1
2010	Bloemfontein (WC)	1	4
2012	Donetsk (EC)	1	1
2013	Wembley	0	1
2016	Berlin	3	2
2017	Dortmund	0	1
2017	Wembley	0	0
2021	Wembley	2	0
2022	Munich (NL)	1	1

(*England lost 3-4 on pens)
(† England lost 5-6 on pens)

v GHANA

2011	Wembley	1	1

v GREECE

1971	Wembley (EC)	3	0
1971	Athens (EC)	2	0
1982	Salonika (EC)	3	0
1983	Wembley (EC)	0	0
1989	Athens	2	1
1994	Wembley	5	0
2001	Athens (WC)	2	0

2001	Old Trafford (WC)	2	2
2006	Old Trafford	4	0

v HOLLAND

1935	Amsterdam	1	0
1946	Huddersfield	8	2
1964	Amsterdam	1	1
1969	Amsterdam	1	0
1970	Wembley	0	0
1977	Wembley	0	2
1982	Wembley	2	0
1988	Wembley	2	2
1988	Dusseldorf (EC)	1	3
1990	Cagliari (WC)	0	0
1993	Wembley (WC)	2	2
1993	Rotterdam (WC)	0	2
1996	Wembley (EC)	4	1
2001	White Hart Lane	0	2
2002	Amsterdam	1	1
2005	Villa Park	0	0
2006	Amsterdam	1	1
2009	Amsterdam	2	2
2012	Wembley	2	3
2016	Wembley	1	2
2018	Amsterdam	1	0
2019	Guimaraes (NL)	1	3

v HONDURAS

2014	Miami	0	0

v HUNGARY

1908	Budapest	7	0
1909	Budapest	4	2
1909	Budapest	8	2
1934	Budapest	1	2
1936	Highbury	6	2
1953	Wembley	3	6
1954	Budapest	1	7
1960	Budapest	0	2
1962	Rancagua (WC)	1	2
1965	Wembley	1	0
1978	Wembley	4	1
1981	Budapest (WC)	3	1
1981	Wembley (WC)	1	0
1983	Wembley (EC)	2	0
1983	Budapest (EC)	3	0
1988	Budapest	0	0
1990	Wembley	1	0
1992	Budapest	1	0
1996	Wembley	3	0
1999	Budapest	1	1
2006	Old Trafford	3	1
2010	Wembley	2	1
2021	Budapest (WC)	4	0

2021	Wembley WC)	1	1
2022	Budapest (NL	0	1
2022	Wolverhampton (NL)	0	4

v ICELAND

1982	Reykjavik	1	1
2004	City of Manchester	6	1
2016	Nice (EC)	1	2
2020	Reykjavik (NL)	1	0
2020	Wembley (NL)	4	0

v ISRAEL

1986	Tel Aviv	2	1
1988	Tel Aviv	0	0
2006	Tel Aviv (EC)	0	0
2007	Wembley (EC)	3	0

v ITALY

1933	Rome	1	1
1934	Highbury	3	2
1939	Milan	2	2
1948	Turin	4	0
1949	White Hart Lane	2	0
1952	Florence	1	1
1959	Wembley	2	2
1961	Rome	3	2
1973	Turin	0	2
1973	Wembley	0	1
1976	New York	3	2
1976	Rome (WC)	0	2
1977	Wembley (WC)	2	0
1980	Turin (EC)	0	1
1985	Mexico City	1	2
1989	Wembley	0	0
1990	Bari (WC)	1	2
1996	Wembley (WC)	0	1
1997	Nantes (TF)	2	0
1997	Rome (WC)	0	0
2000	Turin	0	1
2002	Leeds	1	2
2012*	Kiev (EC)	0	0
2012	Berne	2	1
2014	Manaus (WC)	1	2
2015	Turin	1	1
2018	Wembley	1	1
2021**	Wembley (EC)	1	1
2022	Wolverhampton (NL)	0	0

(*England lost 2-4 on pens)
(*England lost 2-3 on pens)

v IVORY COAST

| 2022 | Wembley | 3 | 0 |

v JAMAICA

| 2006 | Old Trafford | 6 | 0 |

v JAPAN

1995	Wembley	2	1
2004	City of Manchester	1	1
2010	Graz	2	1

v KAZAKHSTAN

| 2008 | Wembley (WC) | 5 | 1 |
| 2009 | Almaty (WC) | 4 | 0 |

v KOSOVO

| 2019 | Southampton (EC) | 5 | 3 |
| 2019 | Pristina (EC) | 4 | 0 |

v KUWAIT

| 1982 | Bilbao (WC) | 1 | 0 |

v LIECHTENSTEIN

| 2003 | Vaduz (EC) | 2 | 0 |
| 2003 | Old Trafford (EC) | 2 | 0 |

v LITHUANIA

2015	Wembley (EC)	4	0
2015	Vilnius (EC)	3	0
2017	Wembley (WC)	2	0
2017	Vilnius (WC)	1	0

v LUXEMBOURG

1927	Luxembourg	5	2
1960	Luxembourg (WC)	9	0
1961	Highbury (WC)	4	1
1977	Wembley (WC)	5	0
1977	Luxembourg (WC)	2	0
1982	Wembley (EC)	9	0
1983	Luxembourg (EC)	4	0
1998	Luxembourg (EC)	3	0
1999	Wembley (EC)	6	0

v MACEDONIA

2002	Southampton (EC)	2	2
2003	Skopje (EC)	2	1
2006	Skopje (EC)	1	0
2006	Old Trafford (EC)	0	0

v MALAYSIA

| 1991 | Kuala Lumpur | 4 | 2 |

v MALTA

1971	Valletta (EC)	1	0
1971	Wembley (EC)	5	0
2000	Valletta	2	1
2016	Wembley (WC)	2	0
2017	Ta'Qali (WC)	4	0

v MEXICO

1959	Mexico City	1	2
1961	Wembley	8	0
1966	Wembley (WC)	2	0
1969	Mexico City	0	0
1985	Mexico City	0	1
1986	Los Angeles	3	0
1997	Wembley	2	0
2001	Derby	4	0
2010	Wembley	3	1

v MOLDOVA

1996	Kishinev	3	0
1997	Wembley (WC)	4	0
2012	Chisinu (WC)	5	0
2013	Wembley (WC)	4	0

v MONTENEGRO

2010	Wembley (EC)	0	0
2011	Podgorica (EC)	2	2
2013	Podgorica (WC)	1	1
2013	Wembley (WC)	4	1
2019	Podgorica (EC)	5	1
2019	Wembley (EC)	7	0
(England's 1,000th international)			

v MOROCCO

1986	Monterrey (WC)	0	0
1998	Casablanca	1	0

v NEW ZEALAND

1991	Auckland	1	0
1991	Wellington	2	0

v NIGERIA

1994	Wembley	1	0
2002	Osaka (WC)	0	0
2018	Wembley	2	1

v NORWAY

1937	Oslo	6	0
1938	Newcastle	4	0
1949	Oslo	4	1
1966	Oslo	6	1
1980	Wembley (WC)	4	0
1981	Oslo (WC)	1	2
1992	Wembley (WC)	1	1
1993	Oslo (WC)	0	2
1994	Wembley	0	0
1995	Oslo	0	0
2012	Oslo	1	0
2014	Wembley	1	0

v PANAMA

2018	Nizhny Novgorod (WC)	6	1

v PARAGUAY

1986	Mexico City (WC)	3	0
2002	Anfield	4	0
2006	Frankfurt (WC)	1	0

v PERU

1959	Lima	1	4
1961	Lima	4	0
2014	Wembley	3	0

v POLAND

1966	Goodison Park	1	1
1966	Chorzow	1	0
1973	Chorzow (WC)	0	2
1973	Wembley (WC)	1	1
1986	Monterrey (WC)	3	0
1989	Wembley (WC)	3	0
1989	Katowice (WC)	0	0
1990	Wembley (EC)	2	0
1991	Poznan (EC)	1	1
1993	Chorzow (WC)	1	1
1993	Wembley (WC)	3	0
1996	Wembley (WC)	2	1
1997	Katowice (WC)	2	0
1999	Wembley (EC)	3	1
1999	Warsaw (EC)	0	0
2004	Katowice (WC)	2	1
2005	Old Trafford (WC)	2	1
2012	Warsaw (WC)	1	1
2013	Wembley (WC)	2	0
2021	Wembley (WC)	2	1
2021	Warsaw (WC)	1	1

v PORTUGAL

1947	Lisbon	10	0
1950	Lisbon	5	3
1951	Goodison Park	5	2
1955	Oporto	1	3
1958	Wembley	2	1
1961	Lisbon (WC)	1	1
1961	Wembley (WC)	2	0
1964	Lisbon	4	3
1964	Sao Paulo	1	1
1966	Wembley (WC)	2	1
1969	Wembley	1	0
1974	Lisbon	0	0
1974	Wembley (EC)	0	0
1975	Lisbon (EC)	1	1
1986	Monterrey (WC)	0	1
1995	Wembley	1	1

1998	Wembley	3	0
2000	Eindhoven (EC)	2	3
2002	Villa Park	1	1
2004	Faro	1	1
2004*	Lisbon (EC)	2	2
2006†	Gelsenkirchen (WC)	0	0
2016	Wembley	1	0

(† England lost 1–3 on pens)
(*England lost 5–6 on pens)

v REPUBLIC OF IRELAND

1946	Dublin	1	0
1949	Goodison Park	0	2
1957	Wembley (WC)	5	1
1957	Dublin (WC)	1	1
1964	Dublin	3	1
1977	Wembley	1	1
1978	Dublin (EC)	1	1
1980	Wembley (EC)	2	0
1985	Wembley	2	1
1988	Stuttgart (EC)	0	1
1990	Cagliari (WC)	1	1
1990	Dublin (EC)	1	1
1991	Wembley (EC)	1	1
1995*	Dublin	0	1
2013	Wembley	1	1
2015	Dublin	0	0
2020	Wembley	3	0

(*Abandoned 27 mins – crowd riot)

v ROMANIA

1939	Bucharest	2	0
1968	Bucharest	0	0
1969	Wembley	1	1
1970	Guadalajara (WC)	1	0
1980	Bucharest (WC)	1	2
1981	Wembley (WC)	0	0
1985	Bucharest (WC)	0	0
1985	Wembley (WC)	1	1
1994	Wembley	1	1
1998	Toulouse (WC)	1	2
2000	Charleroi (EC)	2	3
2021	Middlesbrough	1	0

v RUSSIA

2007	Wembley (EC)	3	0
2007	Moscow (EC)	1	2
2016	Marseille (EC)	1	1

v SAN MARINO

1992	Wembley (WC)	6	0
1993	Bologna (WC)	7	1
2012	Wembley (WC)	5	0

2013	Serravalle (WC)	8	0
2014	Wembley (EC)	5	0
2015	Serravalle (EC)	6	0
2021	Wembley (WC)	5	0
2021	Serravalle (WC)	10	0

v SAUDI ARABIA

1988	Riyadh	1	1
1998	Wembley	0	0

v SERBIA-MONTENEGRO

2003	Leicester	2	1

v SLOVAKIA

2002	Bratislava (EC)	2	1
2003	Middlesbrough (EC)	2	1
2009	Wembley	4	0
2016	St Etienne (EC)	0	0
2016	Trnava (WC)	1	0
2017	Wembley (WC)	2	1

v SLOVENIA

2009	Wembley	2	1
2010	Port Elizabeth (WC)	1	0
2014	Wembley (EC)	3	1
2015	Ljubljana (EC)	3	2
2016	Ljubljana (WC)	0	0
2017	Wembley (WC)	1	0

v SOUTH AFRICA

1997	Old Trafford	2	1
2003	Durban	2	1

v SOUTH KOREA

2002	Seoguipo	1	1

v SOVIET UNION (see also CIS)

1958	Moscow	1	1
1958	Gothenburg (WC)	2	2
1958	Gothenburg (WC)	0	1
1958	Wembley	5	0
1967	Wembley	2	2
1968	Rome (EC)	2	0
1973	Moscow	2	1
1984	Wembley	0	2
1986	Tbilisi	1	0
1988	Frankfurt (EC)	1	3
1991	Wembley	3	1

v SPAIN

1929	Madrid	3	4
1931	Highbury	7	1
1950	Rio de Janeiro (WC)	0	1

1955	Madrid	1	1
1955	Wembley	4	1
1960	Madrid	0	3
1960	Wembley	4	2
1965	Madrid	2	0
1967	Wembley	2	0
1968	Wembley (EC)	1	0
1968	Madrid (EC)	2	1
1980	Barcelona	2	0
1980	Naples (EC)	2	1
1981	Wembley	1	2
1982	Madrid (WC)	0	0
1987	Madrid	4	2
1992	Santander	0	1
1996*	Wembley (EC)	0	0
2001	Villa Park	3	0
2004	Madrid	0	1
2007	Old Trafford	0	1
2009	Seville	0	2
2011	Wembley	1	0
2015	Alicante	0	2
2016	Wembley	2	2

(*England won 4-2 on pens)

2018	Wembley (NL)	1	2
2018	Seville (NL)	3	2

v SWEDEN

1923	Stockholm	4	2
1923	Stockholm	3	1
1937	Stockholm	4	0
1948	Highbury	4	2
1949	Stockholm	1	3
1956	Stockholm	0	0
1959	Wembley	2	3
1965	Gothenburg	2	1
1968	Wembley	3	1
1979	Stockholm	0	0
1986	Stockholm	0	1
1988	Wembley (WC)	0	0
1989	Stockholm (WC)	0	0
1992	Stockholm (EC)	1	2
1995	Leeds	3	3
1998	Stockholm (EC)	1	2
1999	Wembley (EC)	0	0
2001	Old Trafford	1	1
2002	Saitama (WC)	1	1
2004	Gothenburg	0	1
2006	Cologne (WC)	2	2
2011	Wembley	1	0
2012	Kiev (EC)	3	2
2012	Stockholm	2	4
2018	Samara (WC)	2	0

v SWITZERLAND

1933	Berne	4	0
1938	Zurich	1	2
1947	Zurich	0	1
1949	Highbury	6	0
1952	Zurich	3	0
1954	Berne (WC)	2	0
1962	Wembley	3	1
1963	Basle	8	1
1971	Basle (EC)	3	2
1971	Wembley (EC)	1	1
1975	Basle	2	1
1977	Wembley	0	0
1980	Wembley (WC)	2	1
1981	Basle (WC)	1	2
1988	Lausanne	1	0
1995	Wembley	3	1
1996	Wembley (EC)	1	1
1998	Berne	1	1
2004	Coimbra (EC)	3	0
2008	Wembley	2	1
2010	Basle (EC)	3	1
2011	Wembley (EC)	2	2
2014	Basle (EC)	2	0
2015	Wembley (EC)	2	0
2018	Leicester	1	0
2019*	Guimaraes (NL)	0	0
2022	Wembley	2	1

(* England won 6-5 on pens)

v TRINIDAD & TOBAGO

2006	Nuremberg (WC)	2	0
2008	Port of Spain	3	0

v TUNISIA

1990	Tunis	1	1
1998	Marseille (WC)	2	0
2018	Volgograd (WC)	2	1

v TURKEY

1984	Istanbul (WC)	8	0
1985	Wembley (WC)	5	0
1987	Izmir (EC)	0	0
1987	Wembley (EC)	8	0
1991	Izmir (EC)	1	0
1991	Wembley (EC)	1	0
1992	Wembley (WC)	4	0
1993	Izmir (WC)	2	0
2003	Sunderland (EC)	2	0
2003	Istanbul (EC)	0	0
2016	Etihad Stadium	2	1

v UKRAINE

2000	Wembley	2	0
2004	Newcastle	3	0
2009	Wembley (WC)	2	1
2009	Dnipropetrovski (WC)	0	1
2012	Donetsk (EC)	1	0
2012	Wembley (WC)	1	1
2013	Kiev (WC)	0	0
2012	Rome (EC)	4	0

v URUGUAY

1953	Montevideo	1	2
1954	Basle (WC)	2	4
1964	Wembley	2	1
1966	Wembley (WC)	0	0
1969	Montevideo	2	1
1977	Montevideo	0	0
1984	Montevideo	0	2
1990	Wembley	1	2
1995	Wembley	0	0
2006	Anfield	2	1
2014	Sao Paulo (WC)	1	2

v USA

1950	Belo Horizonte (WC)	0	1
1953	New York	6	3
1959	Los Angeles	8	1
1964	New York	10	0
1985	Los Angeles	5	0
1993	Boston	0	2
1994	Wembley	2	0
2005	Chicago	2	1
2008	Wembley	2	0
2010	Rustenburg (WC)	1	1
2018	Wembley	3	0

v YUGOSLAVIA

1939	Belgrade	1	2
1950	Highbury	2	2
1954	Belgrade	0	1
1956	Wembley	3	0
1958	Belgrade	0	5
1960	Wembley	3	3
1965	Belgrade	1	1
1966	Wembley	2	0
1968	Florence (EC)	0	1
1972	Wembley	1	1
1974	Belgrade	2	2
1986	Wembley (EC)	2	0
1987	Belgrade (EC)	4	1
1989	Wembley	2	1

ENGLAND'S RECORD England's first international was a 0-0 draw against Scotland in Glasgow, on the West of Scotland cricket ground, Partick, on November 30, 1872 The 1,000th was a 7-0 win over Montenegro at Wembley on November 14, 2019. Their complete record at the start of 2020–21 is:

P	W	D	L	F	A
1034	592	249	193	2270	999

ENGLAND B

1937	Stockholm	4	0
1948	Highbury	4	2
1949	Stockholm	1	3
1956	Stockholm	0	0
1959	Wembley	2	3
1965	Gothenburg	2	1
1968	Wembley	3	1
1979	Stockholm	0	0
1986	Stockholm	0	1
1988	Wembley (WC)	0	0
1989	Stockholm (WC)	0	0
1992	Stockholm (EC)	1	2
1995	Leeds	3	3
1998	Stockholm (EC)	1	2
1999	Wembley (EC)	0	0
2001	Old Trafford	1	1
2002	Saitama (WC)	1	1
2004	Gothenburg	0	1
2006	Cologne (WC)	2	2
1949	Finland (A)	4	0
1949	Holland (A)	4	0
1950	Italy (A)	0	5
1950	Holland (H)	1	0
1950	Holland (A)	0	3
1950	Luxembourg (A)	2	1
1950	Switzerland (H)	5	0
1952	Holland (A)	1	0
1952	France (A)	1	7
1953	Scotland (A)	2	2
1954	Scotland (H)	1	1
1954	Germany (A)	4	0
1954	Yugoslavia (A)	1	2
1954	Switzerland (A)	0	2
1955	Germany (H)	1	1
1955	Yugoslavia (H)	5	1
1956	Switzerland (H)	4	1
1956	Scotland (A)	2	2
1957	Scotland (H)	4	1
1978	W Germany (A)	2	1
1978	Czechoslovakia (A)	1	0
1978	Singapore (A)	8	0
1978	Malaysia (A)	1	1
1978	N Zealand (A)	4	0

1978	N Zealand (A)	3	1
1978	N Zealand (A)	4	0
1979	Austria (A)	1	0
1979	N Zealand (H)	4	1
1980	USA (H)	1	0
1980	Spain (H)	1	0
1980	Australia (H)	1	0
1981	Spain (A)	2	3
1984	N Zealand (H)	2	0
1987	Malta (A)	2	0
1989	Switzerland (A)	2	0
1989	Iceland (A) .	2	0
1989	Norway (A)	1	0
1989	Italy (H)	1	1
1989	Yugoslavia (H)	2	1
1990	Rep of Ireland (A)	1	4
1990	Czechoslovakia (H)	2	0
1990	Algeria (A)	0	0
1991	Wales (A)	1	0
1991	Iceland (H)	1	0
1991	Switzerland (H)	2	1
1991	Spanish XI (A)	1	0
1992	France (H)	3	0
1992	Czechoslovakia (A)	1	0
1992	CIS (A)	1	1
1994	N Ireland (H)	4	2
1995	Rep of Ireland (H)	2	0
1998	Chile (H)	1	2
1998	Russia (H)	4	1
2006	Belarus (H)	1	2
2007	Albania	3	1

GB v REST OF EUROPE

1947	at Glsagow	6-1
1955	at Belfast	1-4

SCOTLAND

v ALBANIA

2018	Glasgow (NL)	2	0
2018	Shkoder (NL)	4	0

v ARGENTINA

1977	Buenos Aires	1	1
1979	Glasgow	1	3
1990	Glasgow	1	0
2008	Glasgow	0	1

v ARMENIA

2022	Glasgow (NL)	2	0
2022	Yerevan (NL)	4	1

v AUSTRALIA

1985*	Glasgow (WC)	2	0

1985*	Melbourne (WC)	0	0
1996	Glasgow	1	0
2000	Glasgow	0	2
2012	Edinburgh	3	1
(* World Cup play-off)			

v AUSTRIA

1931	Vienna	0	5
1933	Glasgow	2	2
1937	Vienna	1	1
1950	Glasgow	0	1
1951	Vienna	0	4
1954	Zurich (WC)	0	1
1955	Vienna	4	1
1956	Glasgow	1	1
1960	Vienna	1	4
1963*	Glasgow	4	1
1968	Glasgow (WC)	2	1
1969	Vienna (WC)	0	2
1978	Vienna (EC)	2	3
1979	Glasgow (EC)	1	1
1994	Vienna	2	1
1996	Vienna (WC)	0	0
1997	Glasgow (WC)	2	0
(* Abandoned after 79 minutes)			
2003	Glasgow	0	2
2005	Graz	2	2
2007	Vienna	1	0
2021	Glasgow (WC)	2	2
2021	Vienna (WC)	1	0
2022	Vienna	2	2

v BELARUS

1997	Minsk (WC)	1	0
1997	Aberdeen (WC)	4	1
2005	Minsk (WC)	0	0
2005	Glasgow (WC)	0	1

v BELGIUM

1947	Brussels	1	2
1948	Glasgow	2	0
1951	Brussels	5	0
1971	Liege (EC)	0	3
1971	Aberdeen (EC)	1	0
1974	Brugge	1	2
1979	Brussels (EC)	0	2
1979	Glasgow (EC)	1	3
1982	Brussels (EC)	2	3
1983	Glasgow (EC)	1	1
1987	Brussels (EC)	1	4
1987	Glasgow (EC)	2	0
2001	Glasgow (WC)	2	2
2001	Brussels (WC)	0	2
2012	Brussels (WC)	0	2

2013	Glasgow (WC)	0	2
2018	Glasgow	0	4
2019	Brussels (EC)	0	3
2019	Glasgow (EC)	0	4

v BOSNIA

| 1999 | Sarajevo (EC) | 2 | 1 |
| 1999 | Glasgow (EC) | 1 | 0 |

v BRAZIL

1966	Glasgow	1	1
1972	Rio de Janeiro	0	1
1973	Glasgow	0	1
1974	Frankfurt (WC)	0	0
1977	Rio de Janeiro	0	2
1982	Seville (WC)	1	4
1987	Glasgow	0	2
1990	Turin (WC)	0	1
1998	St Denis (WC)	1	2
2011	Arsenal	0	2

v BULGARIA

1978	Glasgow	2	1
1986	Glasgow (EC)	0	0
1987	Sofia (EC)	1	0
1990	Sofia (EC)	1	1
1991	Glasgow (EC)	1	1
2006	Kobe	5	1

v CANADA

1983	Vancouver	2	0
1983	Edmonton	3	0
1983	Toronto	2	0
1992	Toronto	3	1
2002	Edinburgh	3	1
2017	Edinburgh	1	1

v CHILE

| 1977 | Santiago | 4 | 2 |
| 1989 | Glasgow | 2 | 0 |

v CIS (formerly Soviet Union)

| 1992 | Norrkoping (EC) | 3 | 0 |

v COLOMBIA

1988	Glasgow	0	0
1996	Miami	0	1
1998	New York	2	2

v COSTA RICA

| 1990 | Genoa (WC) | 0 | 1 |
| 2018 | Glasgow | 0 | 1 |

v CROATIA

| 2000 | Zagreb (WC) | 1 | 1 |
| 2001 | Glasgow (WC) | 0 | 0 |

v CYPRUS

1968	Nicosia (WC)	5	0
1969	Glasgow (WC)	8	0
1989	Limassol (WC)	3	2
1989	Glasgow (WC)	2	1
2011	Larnaca	2	1
2019	Glasgow (EC)	2	1
2019	Nicosia (EC)	2	1

v CZECH REPUBLIC

1999	Glasgow (EC)	1	2
1999	Prague (EC)	2	3
2008	Prague	1	3
2010	Glasgow	1	0
2010	Prague (EC)	0	1
2011	Glasgow (EC)	2	2
2016	Prague	1	0
2020	Olomouc (NL)	2	1
2020	Glasgow (NL)	1	0
2021	Glasgow (EC)	0	2

v CZECHOSLOVAKIA

1937	Prague	3	1
1937	Glasgow	5	0
1961	Bratislava (WC)	0	4
1961	Glasgow (WC)	3	2
1961*	Brussels (WC)	2	4
1972	Porto Alegre	0	0
1973	Glasgow (WC)	2	1
1973	Bratislava (WC)	0	1
1976	Prague (WC)	0	2
1977	Glasgow (WC)	3	1
(*World Cup play-off)

v DENMARK

1951	Glasgow	3	1
1952	Copenhagen	2	1
1968	Copenhagen	1	0
1970	Glasgow (EC)	1	0
1971	Copenhagen (EC)	0	1
1972	Copenhagen (WC)	4	1
1972	Glasgow (WC)	2	0
1975	Copenhagen (EC)	1	0
1975	Glasgow (EC)	3	1
1986	Neza (WC)	0	1
1996	Copenhagen	0	2
1998	Glasgow	0	1
2002	Glasgow	0	1
2004	Copenhagen	0	1
2011	Glasgow	2	1

2016	Glasgow	1	0
2021	Copenhagen (WC)	0	2
2021	Glasgow (WC)	2	0

v EAST GERMANY
1974	Glasgow	3	0
1977	East Berlin	0	1
1982	Glasgow (EC)	2	0
1983	Halle (EC)	1	2
1986	Glasgow	0	0
1990	Glasgow	0	1

v ECUADOR
| 1995 | Toyama, Japan | 2 | 1 |

v EGYPT
| 1990 | Aberdeen | 1 | 3 |

v ESTONIA
1993	Tallinn (WC)	3	0
1993	Aberdeen	3	1
1996	Tallinn (WC)		
*No result			
1997	Monaco (WC)	0	0
1997	Kilmarnock (WC)	2	0
1998	Edinburgh (EC)	3	2
1999	Tallinn (EC)	0	0
(* Estonia absent)			
2004	Tallinn	1	0
2013	Aberdeen	1	0

v FAROE ISLANDS
1994	Glasgow (EC)	5	1
1995	Toftir (EC)	2	0
1998	Aberdeen (EC)	2	1
1999	Toftir (EC)	1	1
2002	Toftir (EC)	2	2
2003	Glasgow (EC)	3	1
2006	Glasgow (EC)	6	0
2007	Toftir (EC)	2	0
2010	Aberdeen	3	0
2021	Glasgow (WC)	4	0
2021	Torshavn (WC)	1	0

v FINLAND
1954	Helsinki	2	1
1964	Glasgow (WC)	3	1
1965	Helsinki (WC)	2	1
1976	Glasgow	6	0
1992	Glasgow	1	1
1994	Helsinki (EC)	2	0
1995	Glasgow (EC)	1	0
1998	Edinburgh	1	1

v FRANCE
1930	Paris	2	0
1932	Paris	3	1
1948	Paris	0	3
1949	Glasgow	2	0
1950	Paris	1	0
1951	Glasgow	1	0
1958	Orebro (WC)	1	2
1984	Marseilles	0	2
1989	Glasgow (WC)	2	0
1990	Paris (WC)	0	3
1997	St Etienne	1	2
2000	Glasgow	0	2
2002	Paris	0	5
2006	Glasgow (EC)	1	0
2007	Paris (EC)	1	0
2016	Metz	0	3

v GEORGIA
2007	Glasgow (EC)	2	1
2007	Tbilisi (EC)	0	2
2014	Glasgow (EC)	1	0
2015	Tbilisi (EC)	0	1

v GERMANY/WEST GERMANY
1929	Berlin	1	1
1936	Glasgow	2	0
1957	Stuttgart	3	1
1959	Glasgow	3	2
1964	Hanover	2	2
1969	Glasgow (WC)	1	1
1969	Hamburg (WC)	2	3
1973	Glasgow	1	1
1974	Frankfurt	1	2
1986	Queretaro (WC)	1	2
1992	Norrkoping (EC)	0	2
1993	Glasgow	0	1
1999	Bremen	1	0
2003	Glasgow (EC)	1	1
2003	Dortmund (EC)	1	2
2014	Dortmund (EC)	1	2
2015	Glasgow (EC)	2	3

v GIBRALTAR
| 2015 | Glasgow (EC) | 6 | 1 |
| 2015 | Faro (EC) | 6 | 0 |

v GREECE
| 1994 | Athens (EC) | 0 | 1 |
| 1995 | Glasgow | 1 | 0 |

v HOLLAND
1929	Amsterdam	2	0
1938	Amsterdam	3	1
1959	Amsterdam	2	1

1966	Glasgow	0	3
1968	Amsterdam	0	0
1971	Amsterdam	1	2
1978	Mendoza (WC)	3	2
1982	Glasgow	2	1
1986	Eindhoven	0	0
1992	Gothenburg (EC)	0	1
1994	Glasgow	0	1
1994	Utrecht	1	3
1996	Birmingham (EC)	0	0
2000	Arnhem	0	0
2003*	Glasgow (EC)	1	0
2003*	Amsterdam (EC)	0	6
2009	Amsterdam (WC)	0	3
2009	Glasgow (WC)	0	1
2017	Aberdeen	0	1
2021	Algarve	2	2
(*Qual Round play-off)			

v HUNGARY

1938	Glasgow	3	1
1955	Glasgow	2	4
1955	Budapest	1	3
1958	Glasgow	1	1
1960	Budapest	3	3
1980	Budapest	1	3
1987	Glasgow	2	0
2004	Glasgow	0	3
2018	Budapest	1	0

v ICELAND

1984	Glasgow (WC)	3	0
1985	Reykjavik (WC)	1	0
2002	Reykjavik (EC)	2	0
2003	Glasgow (EC)	2	1
2008	Reykjavik (WC)	2	1
2009	Glasgow (WC)	2	1

v IRAN

1978	Cordoba (WC)	1	1

v ISRAEL

1981	Tel Aviv (WC)	1	0
1981	Glasgow (WC)	3	1
1986	Tel Aviv	1	0
2018	Haifa (NL)	1	2
2018	Glasgow (NL)	3	2
2020	Glasgow (NL)	1	1
2020*	Glasgow (EC)	0	0
2020	Netanya (NL)	0	1
2021	Tel Aviv (WC)	1	1
2021	Glasgow (WC)	3	2
(*Scotland won 5-3 on pens)			

v ITALY

1931	Rome	0	3

1965	Glasgow (WC)	1	0
1965	Naples (WC)	0	3
1988	Perugia	0	2
1992	Glasgow (WC)	0	0
1993	Rome (WC)	1	3
2005	Milan (WC)	0	2
2005	Glasgow (WC)	1	1
2007	Bari (EC)	0	2
2007	Glasgow (EC)	1	2
2016	Ta'Qali	0	1

v JAPAN

1995	Hiroshima	0	0
2006	Saitama	0	0
2009	Yokohama	0	2

v KAZAKHSTAN

2019	Astana (EC)	0	3
2019	Glasgow (EC)	3	1

v LATVIA

1996	Riga (WC)	2	0
1997	Glasgow (WC)	2	0
2000	Riga (WC)	1	0
2001	Glasgow (WC)	2	1

v LIECHTENSTEIN

2010	Glasgow (EC)	2	1
2011	Vaduz (EC)	1	0

v LITHUANIA

1998	Vilnius (EC)	0	0
1999	Glasgow (EC)	3	0
2003	Kaunus (EC)	0	1
2003	Glasgow (EC)	1	0
2006	Kaunas (EC)	2	1
2007	Glasgow (EC)	3	1
2010	Kaunas (EC)	0	0
2011	Glasgow (EC)	1	0
2016	Glasgow (WC)	1	1
2017	Vilnius (WC)	3	0

v LUXEMBOURG

1947	Luxembourg	6	0
1986	Glasgow (EC)	3	0
1987	Esch (EC)	0	0
2012	Josy Barthel	2	1
2021	Luxembourg	1	0

v MACEDONIA

2008	Skopje (WC)	0	1
2009	Glasgow (WC)	2	0
2012	Glasgow (WC)	1	1
2013	Skopje (WC)	2	1

v MALTA

1988	Valletta	1	1

1990	Valletta	2	1
1993	Glasgow (WC)	3	0
1993	Valletta (WC)	2	0
1997	Valletta	3	2
2016	Ta'Qali (WC)	5	1
2017	Glasgow (WC)	2	0

v MEXICO
| 2018 | Mexico City | 0 | 1 |

v MOLDOVA
2004	Chisinau (WC)	1	1
2005	Glasgow (WC)	2	0
2021	Glasgow (WC)	1	0
2021	Chisinau (WC)	2	0

v MOROCCO
| 1998 | St Etienne (WC) | 0 | 3 |

v NEW ZEALAND
| 1982 | Malaga (WC) | 5 | 2 |
| 2003 | Edinburgh | 1 | 1 |

v NIGERIA
| 2002 | Aberdeen | 1 | 2 |
| 2014 | Fulham | 2 | 2 |

v NORWAY
1929	Bergen	7	3
1954	Glasgow	1	0
1954	Oslo	1	1
1963	Bergen	3	4
1963	Glasgow	6	1
1974	Oslo	2	1
1978	Glasgow (EC)	3	2
1979	Oslo (EC)	4	0
1988	Oslo (WC)	2	1
1989	Glasgow (WC)	1	1
1992	Oslo	0	0
1998	Bordeaux (WC)	1	1
2003	Oslo	0	0
2004	Glasgow (WC)	0	1
2005	Oslo (WC)	2	1
2008	Glasgow (WC)	0	0
2009	Oslo (WC)	0	4
2013	Molde	1	0

v PARAGUAY
| 1958 | Norrkoping (WC) | 2 | 3 |

v PERU
1972	Glasgow	2	0
1978	Cordoba (WC)	1	3
1979	Glasgow	1	1
2018	Lima	0	2

v POLAND
1958	Warsaw	2	1
1960	Glasgow	2	3
1965	Chorzow (WC)	1	1
1965	Glasgow (WC)	1	2
1980	Poznan	0	1
1990	Glasgow	1	1
2001	Bydgoszcz	1	1
2014	Warsaw	1	0
2014	Warsaw (EC)	2	2
2015	Glasgow (EC)	2	2
2022	Glasgow	1	1

v PORTUGAL
1950	Lisbon	2	2
1955	Glasgow	3	0
1959	Lisbon	0	1
1966	Glasgow	0	1
1971	Lisbon (EC)	0	2
1971	Glasgow (EC)	2	1
1975	Glasgow	1	0
1978	Lisbon (EC)	0	1
1980	Glasgow (EC)	4	1
1980	Glasgow (WC)	0	0
1981	Lisbon (WC)	1	2
1992	Glasgow (WC)	0	0
1993	Lisbon (WC)	0	5
2002	Braga	0	2
2018	Glasgow	1	3

v QATAR
| 2015 | Edinburgh | 1 | 0 |

v REPUBLIC OF IRELAND
1961	Glasgow (WC)	4	1
1961	Dublin (WC)	3	0
1963	Dublin	0	1
1969	Dublin	1	1
1986	Dublin (EC)	0	0
1987	Glasgow (EC)	0	1
2000	Dublin	2	1
2003	Glasgow (EC)	0	2
2011	Dublin (CC)	0	1
2014	Glasgow (EC)	1	0
2015	Dublin (EC)	1	1
2022	Dublin (NL)	0	3

v ROMANIA
1975	Bucharest (EC)	1	1
1975	Glasgow (EC)	1	1
1986	Glasgow	3	0
1990	Glasgow (EC)	2	1
1991	Bucharest (EC)	0	1
2004	Glasgow	1	2

v RUSSIA

1994	Glasgow (EC)	1	1
1995	Moscow (EC)	0	0
2019	Glasgow (EC)	1	2
2019	Moscow (EC)	0	4

v SAN MARINO

1991	Serravalle (EC)	2	0
1991	Glasgow (EC)	4	0
1995	Serravalle (EC)	2	0
1995	Glasgow (EC)	5	0
2000	Serravalle (WC)	2	0
2001	Glasgow (WC)	4	0
2019	Serravalle (EC)	2	0
2019	Glasgow (EC)	6	0

v SAUDI ARABIA

1988	Riyadh	2	2

v SERBIA

2012	Glasgow (WC)	0	0
2013	Novi Sad (WC)	0	2
2020*	Belgrade (EC)	1	1

(Scotland won 5-4 on pens)

v SLOVAKIA

2016	Trnava (WC)	0	3
2017	Glasgow (WC)	1	0
2020	Glasgow (NL)	1	0
2020	Trnova (NL)	0	1

v SLOVENIA

2004	Glasgow (WC)	0	0
2005	Celje (WC)	3	0
2012	Koper	1	1
2017	Glasgow (WC)	1	0
2017	Ljubljana (WC)	2	2

v SOUTH AFRICA

2002	Hong Kong	0	2
2007	Aberdeen	1	0

v SOUTH KOREA

2002	Busan	1	4

v SOVIET UNION (see also CIS and RUSSIA)

1967	Glasgow	0	2
1971	Moscow	0	1
1982	Malaga (WC)	2	2
1991	Glasgow	0	1

v SPAIN

1957	Glasgow (WC)	4	2
1957	Madrid (WC)	1	4
1963	Madrid	6	2
1965	Glasgow	0	0
1975	Glasgow (EC)	1	2
1975	Valencia (EC)	1	1
1982	Valencia	0	3
1985	Glasgow (WC)	3	1
1985	Seville (WC)	0	1
1988	Madrid	0	0
2004*	Valencia	1	1

(*Abandoned after 59 mins – floodlight failure)

2010	Glasgow (EC)	2	3
2011	Alicante (EC)	1	3

v SWEDEN

1952	Stockholm	1	3
1953	Glasgow	1	2
1975	Gothenburg	1	1
1977	Glasgow	3	1
1980	Stockholm (WC)	1	0
1981	Glasgow (WC)	2	0
1990	Genoa (WC)	2	1
1995	Solna	0	2
1996	Glasgow (WC)	1	0
1997	Gothenburg (WC)	1	2
2004	Edinburgh	1	4
2010	Stockholm	0	3

v SWITZERLAND

1931	Geneva	3	2
1948	Berne	1	2
1950	Glasgow	3	1
1957	Basle (WC)	2	1
1957	Glasgow (WC)	3	2
1973	Berne	0	1
1976	Glasgow	1	0
1982	Berne (EC)	0	2
1983	Glasgow (EC)	2	2
1990	Glasgow (EC)	2	1
1991	Berne (EC)	2	2
1992	Berne (WC)	1	3
1993	Aberdeen (WC)	1	1
1996	Birmingham (EC)	1	0
2006	Glasgow	1	3

v TRINIDAD & TOBAGO

2004	Hibernian	4	1

v TURKEY

1960	Ankara	2	4

v UKRAINE

2006	Kiev (EC)	0	2
2007	Glasgow (EC)	3	1
2022	Glasgow (WC)	1	3

v USA

1952	Glasgow	6	0
1992	Denver	1	0
1996	New Britain, Conn	1	2
1998	Washington	0	0
2005	Glasgow	1	1
2012	Jacksonville	1	5
2013	Glasgow	0	0

v URUGUAY

1954	Basle (WC)	0	7
1962	Glasgow	2	3
1983	Glasgow	2	0
1986	Neza (WC)	0	0

v YUGOSLAVIA

1955	Belgrade	2	2
1956	Glasgow	2	0
1958	Vaasteras (WC)	1	1
1972	Belo Horizonte	2	2
1974	Frankfurt (WC)	1	1
1984	Glasgow	6	1
1988	Glasgow (WC)	1	1
1989	Zagreb (WC)	1	3

v ZAIRE

1974	Dortmund (WC)	2	0

WALES

v ALBANIA

1994	Cardiff (EC)	2	0
1995	Tirana (EC)	1	1
2018	Elbasan	0	1
2021	Cardiff	0	0

v ANDORRA

2014	La Vella (EC)	2	1
2015	Cardiff (EC)	2	0

v ARGENTINA

1992	Gifu (Japan)	0	1
2002	Cardiff	1	1

v ARMENIA

2001	Yerevan (WC)	2	2
2001	Cardiff (WC)	0	0

v AUSTRALIA

2011	Cardiff	1	2

v AUSTRIA

1954	Vienna	0	2
1955	Wrexham	1	2
1975	Vienna (EC)	1	2
1975	Wrexham (EC)	1	0
1992	Vienna	1	1
2005	Cardiff	0	2
2005	Vienna	0	1
2013	Swansea	2	1
2016	Vienna (WC)	2	2
2017	Cardiff (WC)	1	0
2022	Austria (WC)	2	1

v AZERBAIJAN

2002	Baku (EC)	2	0
2003	Cardiff (EC)	4	0
2004	Baku (WC)	1	1
2005	Cardiff (WC)	2	0
2008	Cardiff (WC)	1	0
2009	Baku (WC)	1	0
2019	Cardiff (EC)	2	1
2019	Baku (EC)	2	0

v BELARUS

1998	Cardiff (EC)	3	2
1999	Minsk (EC)	2	1
2000	Minsk (WC)	1	2
2001	Cardiff (WC)	1	0
2019	Cardiff	1	0
2021	Kazan (WC)	3	2
2021	Cardiff (WC)	5	1

v BELGIUM

1949	Liege	1	3
1949	Cardiff	5	1
1990	Cardiff (EC)	3	1
1991	Brussels (EC)	1	1
1992	Brussels (WC)	0	2
1993	Cardiff (WC)	2	0
1997	Cardiff (WC)	1	2
1997	Brussels (WC)	2	3
2012	Cardiff (WC)	0	2
2013	Brussels (WC)	1	1
2014	Brussels (EC)	0	0
2015	Cardiff (EC)	1	0
2016	Lille (EC)	3	1
2021	Leuven (WC)	1	3
2021	Cardiff (WC)	1	1
2021	Cardiff (NL)	1	1

v BOSNIA-HERZEGOVINA

2003	Cardiff	2	2
2012	Llanelli	0	2
2014	Cardiff (EC)	0	0
2015	Zenica (EC)	0	2

v BRAZIL

1958	Gothenburg (WC)	0	1
1962	Rio de Janeiro	1	3
1962	Sao Paulo	1	3

1966	Rio de Janeiro	1	3
1966	Belo Horizonte	0	1
1983	Cardiff	1	1
1991	Cardiff	1	0
1997	Brasilia	0	3
2000	Cardiff	0	3
2006	White Hart Lane	0	2

v BULGARIA

1983	Wrexham (EC)	1	0
1983	Sofia (EC)	0	1
1994	Cardiff (EC)	0	3
1995	Sofia (EC)	1	3
2006	Swansea	0	0
2007	Bourgas	1	0
2010	Cardiff (EC)	0	1
2011	Sofia (EC)	1	0
2020	Cardiff (NL)	1	0
2020	Sofia (NL)	1	0

v CANADA

1986	Toronto	0	2
1986	Vancouver	3	0
2004	Wrexham	1	0

v CHILE

1966	Santiago	0	2

v CHINA

2018	Nanning	6	0

v COSTA RICA

1990	Cardiff	1	0
2012	Cardiff	0	1

v CROATIA

2002	Varazdin	1	1
2010	Osijek	0	2
2012	Osijek (WC)	0	2
2013	Swansea (WC)	1	2
2019	Osijek (EC)	1	2
2019	Cardiff (EC)	1	1

v CYPRUS

1992	Limassol (WC)	1	0
1993	Cardiff (WC)	2	0
2005	Limassol	0	1
2006	Cardiff (EC)	3	1
2007	Nicosia (EC)	1	3
2014	Cardiff (EC)	2	1
2015	Nicosia	1	0

v CZECHOSLOVAKIA (see also RCS)

1957	Cardiff (WC)	1	0
1957	Prague (WC)	0	2
1971	Swansea (EC)	1	3

1971	Prague (EC)	0	1
1977	Wrexham (WC)	3	0
1977	Prague (WC)	0	1
1980	Cardiff (WC)	1	0
1981	Prague (WC)	0	2
1987	Wrexham (EC)	1	1
1987	Prague (EC)	0	2

v CZECH REPUBLIC

2002	Cardiff	0	0
2006	Teplice (EC)	1	2
2007	Cardiff (EC)	0	0
2021	Cardiff (WC)	1	0
2021	Prague (WC)	2	2
2022	Cardiff	1	1

v DENMARK

1964	Copenhagen (WC)	0	1
1965	Wrexham (WC)	4	2
1987	Cardiff (EC)	1	0
1987	Copenhagen (EC)	0	1
1990	Copenhagen	0	1
1998	Copenhagen (EC)	2	1
1999	Anfield (EC)	0	2
2008	Copenhagen	1	0
2018	Aarhus (NL)	0	2
2018	Cardiff (NL)	1	2
2021	Amsterdam (EC)	0	4

v EAST GERMANY

1957	Leipzig (WC)	1	2
1957	Cardiff (WC)	4	1
1969	Dresden (WC)	1	2
1969	Cardiff (WC)	1	3

v ESTONIA

1994	Tallinn	2	1
2009	Llanelli	1	0
2021	Cardiff (WC)	0	0
2021	Tallinn (WC)	1	0

v FAROE ISLANDS

1992	Cardiff (WC)	6	0
1993	Toftir (WC)	3	0

v FINLAND

1971	Helsinki (EC)	1	0
1971	Swansea (EC)	3	0
1986	Helsinki (EC)	1	1
1987	Wrexham (EC)	4	0
1988	Swansea (WC)	2	2
1989	Helsinki (WC)	0	1
2000	Cardiff	1	2
2002	Helsinki (EC)	2	0
2003	Cardiff (EC)	1	1
2009	Cardiff (WC)	0	2

2009	Helsinki (WC)	1	2
2013	Cardiff	1	1
2020	Helsinki (NL)	1	0
2020	Cardiff (NL)	3	1
2021	Helsinki	0	0

v FRANCE
1933	Paris	1	1
1939	Paris	1	2
1953	Paris	1	6
1982	Toulouse	1	0
2017	Paris	0	2
2021	Nice	0	3

v GEORGIA
1994	Tbilisi (EC)	0	5
1995	Cardiff (EC)	0	1
2008	Swansea	1	2
2016	Cardiff (WC)	1	1
2017	Tbilisi (WC)	1	0

v GERMANY/WEST GERMANY
1968	Cardiff	1	1
1969	Frankfurt	1	1
1977	Cardiff	0	2
1977	Dortmund	1	1
1979	Wrexham (EC)	0	2
1979	Cologne (EC)	1	5
1989	Cardiff (WC)	0	0
1989	Cologne (WC)	1	2
1991	Cardiff (EC)	1	0
1991	Nuremberg (EC)	1	4
1995	Dusseldorf (EC)	1	1
1995	Cardiff (EC)	1	2
2002	Cardiff	1	0
2007	Cardiff (EC)	0	2
2007	Frankfurt (EC)	0	0
2008	Moenchengladbach (WC)	0	1
2009	Cardiff (WC)	0	2

v GREECE
| 1964 | Athens (WC) | 0 | 2 |
| 1965 | Cardiff (WC) | 4 | 1 |

v HOLLAND
1988	Amsterdam (WC)	0	1
1989	Wrexham (WC)	1	2
1992	Utrecht	0	4
1996	Cardiff (WC)	1	3
1996	Eindhoven (WC)	1	7
2008	Rotterdam	0	2
2014	Amsterdam	0	2
2015	Cardiff	2	3
2022	Cardiff (NL)	1	2
2022	Rotterdam (NL)	2	3

v HUNGARY
1958	Sanviken (WC)	1	1
1958	Stockholm (WC)	2	1
1961	Budapest	2	3
1963	Budapest (EC)	1	3
1963	Cardiff (EC)	1	1
1974	Cardiff (EC)	2	0
1975	Budapest (EC)	2	1
1986	Cardiff	0	3
2004	Budapest	2	1
2005	Cardiff	2	0
2019	Budapest (EC)	0	1
2019	Cardiff (EC)	2	0

v ICELAND
1980	Reykjavik (WC)	4	0
1981	Swansea (WC)	2	2
1984	Reykjavik (WC)	0	1
1984	Cardiff (WC)	2	1
1991	Cardiff	1	0
2008	Reykjavik	1	0
2014	Cardiff	3	1

v IRAN
| 1978 | Tehran | 1 | 0 |

v ISRAEL
1958	Tel Aviv (WC)	2	0
1958	Tel Aviv (WC)	2	0
1984	Tel Aviv	0	0
1989	Tel Aviv	3	3
2015	Haifa (EC)	3	0
2015	Cardiff (EC)	0	0

v ITALY
1965	Florence	1	4
1968	Cardiff (WC)	0	1
1969	Rome (WC)	1	4
1988	Brescia	1	0
1996	Terni	0	3
1998	Anfield (EC)	0	2
1999	Bologna (EC)	0	4
2002	Cardiff (EC)	2	1
2003	Milan (EC)	0	4
2021	Rome (EC)	0	1

v JAMAICA
| 1998 | Cardiff | 0 | 0 |

v JAPAN
| 1992 | Matsuyama | 1 | 0 |

v KUWAIT
| 1977 | Wrexham | 0 | 0 |
| 1977 | Kuwait City | 0 | 0 |

v LATVIA
2004	Riga	2	0

v LIECHTENSTEIN
2006	Wrexham	4	0
2008	Cardiff (WC)	2	0
2009	Vaduz (WC)	2	0

v LUXEMBOURG
1974	Swansea (EC)	5	0
1975	Luxembourg (EC)	3	1
1990	Luxembourg (EC)	1	0
1991	Luxembourg (EC)	1	0
2008	Luxembourg	2	0
2010	Llanelli	5	1

v MACEDONIA
2013	Skopje (WC)	1	2
2013	Cardiff (WC)	1	0

v MALTA
1978	Wrexham (EC)	7	0
1979	Valletta (EC)	2	0
1988	Valletta	3	2
1998	Valletta	3	0

v MEXICO
1958	Stockholm (WC)	1	1
1962	Mexico City	1	2
2012	New York	0	2
2018	Pasadena	0	0
2021	Cardiff	1	0

v MOLDOVA
1994	Kishinev (EC)	2	3
1995	Cardiff (EC)	1	0
2016	Cardiff (WC)	4	0
2017	Chisinau (WC)	2	0

v MONTENEGRO
2009	Podgorica	1	2
2010	Podgorica (EC)	0	1
2011	Cardiff (EC)	2	1

v NEW ZEALAND
2007	Wrexham	2	2

v NORWAY
1982	Swansea (EC)	1	0
1983	Oslo (EC)	0	0
1984	Trondheim	0	1
1985	Wrexham	1	1
1985	Bergen	2	4
1994	Cardiff	1	3
2000	Cardiff (WC)	1	1
2001	Oslo (WC)	2	3
2004	Oslo	0	0
2008	Wrexham	3	0
2011	Cardiff	4	1

v PANAMA
2017	Cardiff	1	1

v PARAGUAY
2006	Cardiff	0	0

v POLAND
1973	Cardiff (WC)	2	0
1973	Katowice (WC)	0	3
1991	Radom	0	0
2000	Warsaw (WC)	0	0
2001	Cardiff (WC)	1	2
2004	Cardiff (WC)	2	3
2005	Warsaw (WC)	0	1
2009	Vila-Real (Por)	0	1
2022	Wroclaw (NL)	1	2

v PORTUGAL
1949	Lisbon	2	3
1951	Cardiff	2	1
2000	Chaves	0	3
2016	Lyon (EC)	0	2

v QATAR
2000	Doha	1	0

v RCS (formerly Czechoslovakia)
1993	Ostrava (WC)	1	1
1993	Cardiff (WC)	2	2

v REPUBLIC OF IRELAND
1960	Dublin	3	2
1979	Swansea	2	1
1981	Dublin	3	1
1986	Dublin	1	0
1990	Dublin	0	1
1991	Wrexham	0	3
1992	Dublin	1	0
1993	Dublin	1	2
1997	Cardiff	0	0
2007	Dublin (EC)	0	1
2007	Cardiff (EC)	2	2
2011	Dublin (CC)	0	3
2013	Cardiff	0	0
2017	Dublin (WC)	0	0
2017	Cardiff (WC)	0	1
2018	Cardiff (NL)	4	1
2018	Dublin (NL)	1	0
2020	Dublin (NL)	0	0
2020	Cardiff (NL)	1	0

v REST OF UNITED KINGDOM
1951	Cardiff	3	2
1969	Cardiff	0	1

v ROMANIA
1970	Cardiff (EC)	0	0
1971	Bucharest (EC)	0	2
1983	Wrexham	5	0
1992	Bucharest (WC)	1	5
1993	Cardiff (WC)	1	2

v RUSSIA (See also Soviet Union)
2003*	Moscow (EC)	0	0
2003*	Cardiff (EC)	0	1
2008	Moscow (WC)	1	2
2009	Cardiff (WC)	1	3
2016	Toulouse (EC)	3	0

(*Qual Round play-offs)

v SAN MARINO
1996	Serravalle (WC)	5	0
1996	Cardiff (WC)	6	0
2007	Cardiff (EC)	3	0
2007	Serravalle (EC)	2	1

v SAUDI ARABIA
1986	Dahran	2	1

v SERBIA
2012	Novi Sad (WC)	1	6
2013	Cardiff (WC)	0	3
2016	Cardiff (WC)	1	1
2017	Belgrade (WC)	1	1

v SERBIA & MONTENEGRO
2003	Belgrade (EC)	0	1
2003	Cardiff (EC)	2	3

v SLOVAKIA
2006	Cardiff (EC)	1	5
2007	Trnava (EC)	5	2
2016	Bordeaux (EC)	2	1
2019	Cardiff (EC)	1	0
2019	Trnava (EC)	1	1

v SLOVENIA
2005	Swansea	0	0

v SOVIET UNION (See also Russia)
1965	Moscow (WC)	1	2
1965	Cardiff (WC)	2	1
1981	Wrexham (WC)	0	0
1981	Tbilisi (WC)	0	3
1987	Swansea	0	0

v SPAIN
1961	Cardiff (WC)	1	2
1961	Madrid (WC)	1	1
1982	Valencia	1	1
1984	Seville (WC)	0	3
1985	Wrexham (WC)	3	0
2018	Cardiff	1	4

v SWEDEN
1958	Stockholm (WC)	0	0
1988	Stockholm	1	4
1989	Wrexham	0	2
1990	Stockholm	2	4
1994	Wrexham	0	2
2010	Swansea	0	1
2016	Stockholm	0	3

v SWITZERLAND
1949	Berne	0	4
1951	Wrexham	3	2
1996	Lugano	0	2
1999	Zurich (EC)	0	2
1999	Wrexham (EC)	0	2
2010	Basle (EC)	1	4
2011	Swansea (EC)	2	0
2021	Baku (EC)	1	1

v TRINIDAD & TOBAGO
2006	Graz	2	1
2019	Wrexham	1	0

v TUNISIA
1998	Tunis	0	4

v TURKEY
1978	Wrexham (EC)	1	0
1979	Izmir (EC)	0	1
1980	Cardiff (WC)	4	0
1981	Ankara (WC)	1	0
1996	Cardiff (WC)	0	0
1997	Istanbul (WC)	4	6
2021	Baku (EC)	2	0

v UKRAINE
2001	Cardiff (WC)	1	1
2001	Kiev (WC)	1	1
2015	Kiev	0	1
2022	Cardiff (WC)	1	0

v URUGUAY
1986	Wrexham	0	0
2018	Nanning	0	1

v USA
2003	San Jose	0	2
2020	Swansea	0	0

v YUGOSLAVIA

1953	Belgrade	2	5
1954	Cardiff	1	3
1976	Zagreb (EC)	0	2
1976	Cardiff (EC)	1	1
1982	Titograd (EC)	4	4
1983	Cardiff (EC)	1	1
1988	Swansea	1	2

NORTHERN IRELAND

v ALBANIA

1965	Belfast (WC)	4	1
1965	Tirana (WC)	1	1
1983	Tirana (EC)	0	0
1983	Belfast (EC)	1	0
1992	Belfast (WC)	3	0
1993	Tirana (WC)	2	1
1996	Belfast (WC)	2	0
1997	Zurich (WC)	0	1
2010	Tirana	0	1

v ALGERIA

1986	Guadalajara (WC)	1	1

v ARGENTINA

1958	Halmstad (WC)	1	3

v ARMENIA

1996	Belfast (WC)	1	1
1997	Yerevan (WC)	0	0
2003	Yerevan (EC)	0	1
2003	Belfast (EC)	0	1

v AUSTRALIA

1980	Sydney	2	1
1980	Melbourne	1	1
1980	Adelaide	2	1

v AUSTRIA

1982	Madrid (WC)	2	2
1982	Vienna (EC)	0	2
1983	Belfast (EC)	3	1
1990	Vienna (EC)	0	0
1991	Belfast (EC)	2	1
1994	Vienna (EC)	2	1
1995	Belfast (EC)	5	3
2004	Belfast (WC)	3	3
2005	Vienna (WC)	0	2
2018	Vienna (NL)	0	1
2018	Belfast(NL)	1	2
2020	Belfast (NL)	0	1
2020	Vienna (NL)	1	2

v AZERBAIJAN

2004	Baku (WC)	0	0
2005	Belfast (WC)	2	0
2012	Belfast (WC)	1	1
2013	Baku (WC)	0	2
2016	Belfast (WC)	4	0
2017	Baku (WC)	1	0

v BARBADOS

2004	Bridgetown	1	1

v BELARUS

2016	Belfast	3	0
2019	Belfast (EC)	2	1
2019	Borisov (EC)	1	0

v BELGIUM

1976	Liege (WC)	0	2
1977	Belfast (WC)	3	0
1997	Belfast	3	0

v BOSNIA-HERZEGOVINA

2018	Belfast (NL)	1	2
2018	Sarajevo (NL)	0	2
2020*	Sarajevo (EC)	1	1

(*Northern Ireland won 4-3 on pens)

v BRAZIL

1986	Guadalajara (WC)	0	3

v BULGARIA

1972	Sofia (WC)	0	3
1973	Sheffield (WC)	0	0
1978	Sofia (EC)	2	0
1979	Belfast (EC)	2	0
2001	Sofia (WC)	3	4
2001	Belfast (WC)	0	1
2008	Belfast	0	1
2021	Belfast (WC)	0	0
2021	Sofia (WC)	1	2

v CANADA

1995	Edmonton	0	2
1999	Belfast	1	1
2005	Belfast	0	1

v CHILE

1989	Belfast	0	1
1995	Edmonton, Canada	0	2
2010	Chillan	0	1
2014	Valparaiso	0	2

v COLOMBIA

1994	Boston, USA	0	2

v COSTA RICA

2018	San Jose	0	3

v CROATIA

2016	Belfast	0	3

v CYPRUS

1971	Nicosia (EC)	3	0
1971	Belfast (EC)	5	0
1973	Nicosia (WC)	0	1
1973	Fulham (WC)	3	0
2002	Belfast	0	0
2014	Nicosia	0	0
2022	Larnaca (NL)	0	0
2022	Belfast (NL)	2	2

v CZECHOSLOVAKIA/CZECH REP

1958	Halmstad (WC)	1	0
1958	Malmo (WC)	2	1
2001	Belfast (WC)	0	1
2001	Teplice (WC)	1	3
2008	Belfast (WC)	0	0
2009	Prague (WC)	0	0
2016	Prague (WC)	0	0
2017	Belfast (WC)	2	0
2019	Prague	3	2

v DENMARK

1978	Belfast (EC)	2	1
1979	Copenhagen (EC)	0	4
1986	Belfast	1	1
1990	Belfast (EC)	1	1
1991	Odense (EC)	1	2
1992	Belfast (WC)	0	1
1993	Copenhagen (WC)	0	1
2000	Belfast (WC)	1	1
2001	Copenhagen (WC)	1	1
2006	Copenhagen (EC)	0	0
2007	Belfast (EC)	2	1

v ESTONIA

2004	Tallinn	1	0
2006	Belfast	1	0
2011	Tallinn (EC)	1	4
2011	Belfast (EC)	1	2
2019	Belfast (EC)	2	0
2019	Tallinn (EC)	2	1
2021	Tallinn	1	0

v FAROE ISLANDS

1991	Belfast (EC)	1	1
1991	Landskrona, Sw (EC)	5	0
2010	Toftir (EC)	1	1
2011	Belfast (EC)	4	0
2014	Belfast (EC)	2	0
2015	Torshavn (EC)	3	1

v FINLAND

1984	Pori (WC)	0	1
1984	Belfast (WC)	2	1
1998	Belfast (EC)	1	0
1999	Helsinki (EC)	1	4
2003	Belfast	0	1
2006	Helsinki	2	1
2012	Belfast	3	3
2015	Belfast (EC)	2	1
2015	Helsinki (EC)	1	1

v FRANCE

1951	Belfast	2	2
1952	Paris	1	3
1958	Norrkoping (WC)	0	4
1982	Paris	0	4
1982	Madrid (WC)	1	4
1986	Paris	0	0
1988	Belfast	0	0
1999	Belfast	0	1

v GEORGIA

2008	Belfast	4	1

v GERMANY/WEST GERMANY

1958	Malmo (WC)	2	2
1960	Belfast (WC)	3	4
1961	Berlin (WC)	1	2
1966	Belfast	0	2
1977	Cologne	0	5
1982	Belfast (EC)	1	0
1983	Hamburg (EC)	1	0
1992	Bremen	1	1
1996	Belfast	1	1
1997	Nuremberg (WC)	1	1
1997	Belfast (WC)	1	3
1999	Belfast (EC)	0	3
1999	Dortmund (EC)	0	4
2005	Belfast	1	4
2016	Paris (EC)	0	1
2016	Hannover (WC)	0	2
2017	Belfast (WC)	1	3
2019	Belfast (EC)	0	2
2019	Frankfurt (EC)	1	6

v GREECE

1961	Athens (WC)	1	2
1961	Belfast (WC)	2	0
1988	Athens	2	3
2003	Belfast (EC)	0	2
2003	Athens (EC)	0	1
2014	Piraeus (EC)	2	0
2015	Belfast (EC)	3	1
2022	Belfast (NL)	0	1

v HOLLAND

1962	Rotterdam	0	4
1965	Belfast (WC)	2	1
1965	Rotterdam (WC)	0	0
1976	Rotterdam (WC)	2	2
1977	Belfast (WC)	0	1
2012	Amsterdam	0	6
2019	Rotterdam (EC)	1	3
2019	Belfast (EC)	0	0

v HONDURAS

1982	Zaragoza (WC)	1	1

v HUNGARY

1988	Budapest (WC)	0	1
1989	Belfast (WC)	1	2
2000	Belfast	0	1
2008	Belfast	0	2
2014	Budapest (EC)	2	1
2015	Belfast (EC)	1	1
2022	Belfast	0	1

v ICELAND

1977	Reykjavik (WC)	0	1
1977	Belfast (WC)	2	0
2000	Reykjavik (WC)	0	1
2001	Belfast (WC)	3	0
2006	Belfast (EC)	0	3
2007	Reykjavik (EC)	1	2

v ISRAEL

1968	Jaffa	3	2
1976	Tel Aviv	1	1
1980	Tel Aviv (WC)	0	0
1981	Belfast (WC)	1	0
1984	Belfast	3	0
1987	Tel Aviv	1	1
2009	Belfast	1	1
2013	Belfast (WC)	0	2
2013	Ramat Gan (WC)	1	1
2018	Belfast	3	0

v ITALY

1957	Rome (WC)	0	1
1957	Belfast	2	2
1958	Belfast (WC)	2	1
1961	Bologna	2	3
1997	Palermo	0	2
2003	Campobasso	0	2
2009	Pisa	0	3
2010	Belfast (EC)	0	0
2011	Pescara (EC)	0	3
2021	Parma (WC)	0	2
2021	Belfast (WC)	0	0

v KOSOVO

2022	Pristina (NL)	2	3

v LATVIA

1993	Riga (WC)	2	1
1993	Belfast (WC)	2	0
1995	Riga (EC)	1	0
1995	Belfast (EC)	1	2
2006	Belfast (EC)	1	0
2007	Riga (EC)	0	1
2015	Belfast	1	0

v LIECHTENSTEIN

1994	Belfast (EC)	4	1
1995	Eschen (EC)	4	0
2002	Vaduz	0	0
2007	Vaduz (EC)	4	1
2007	Belfast (EC)	3	1

v LITHUANIA

1992	Belfast (WC)	2	2
2021	Vilnius WC)	4	1
2021	Belfast (WC)	1	0

v LUXEMBOURG

2000	Luxembourg	3	1
2012	Belfast (WC)	1	1
2013	Luxembourg (WC)	2	3
2019	Belfast	1	0
2022	Luxembourg	3	1

v MALTA

1988	Belfast (WC)	3	0
1989	Valletta (WC)	2	0
2000	Ta'Qali	3	0
2000	Belfast (WC)	1	0
2001	Valletta (WC)	1	0
2005	Valletta	1	1
2013	Ta'Qali	0	0
2021	Klagenfurt	3	0

v MEXICO

1966	Belfast	4	1
1994	Miami	0	3

v MOLDOVA

1998	Belfast (EC)	2	2
1999	Kishinev (EC)	0	0

v MONTENEGRO

2010	Podgorica	0	2

v MOROCCO

1986	Belfast	2	1
2010	Belfast	1	1

v NEW ZEALAND
2017	Belfast	1	0

v NORWAY
1974	Oslo (EC)	1	2
1975	Belfast (EC)	3	0
1990	Belfast	2	3
1996	Belfast	0	2
2001	Belfast	0	4
2004	Belfast	1	4
2012	Belfast	0	3
2017	Belfast (WC)	2	0
2017	Oslo (WC)	0	1
2020	Belfast (NL)	1	5
2020	Oslo (NL)	0	1

v PANAMA
2018	Panama City	0	0

v POLAND
1962	Katowice (EC)	2	0
1962	Belfast (EC)	2	0
1988	Belfast	1	1
1991	Belfast	3	1
2002	Limassol (Cyprus)	1	4
2004	Belfast (WC)	0	3
2005	Warsaw (WC)	0	1
2009	Belfast (WC)	3	2
2009	Chorzow (WC)	1	1
2016	Nice (EC)	0	1

v PORTUGAL
1957	Lisbon (WC)	1	1
1957	Belfast (WC)	3	0
1973	Coventry (WC)	1	1
1973	Lisbon (WC)	1	1
1980	Lisbon (WC)	0	1
1981	Belfast (WC)	1	0
1994	Belfast (EC)	1	2
1995	Oporto (EC)	1	1
1997	Belfast (WC)	0	0
1997	Lisbon (WC)	0	1
2005	Belfast	1	1
2012	Porto (WC)	1	1
2013	Belfast (WC)	2	4

v QATAR
2015	Crewe	1	1

v REPUBLIC OF IRELAND
1978	Dublin (EC)	0	0
1979	Belfast (EC)	1	0
1988	Belfast (WC)	0	0
1989	Dublin (WC)	0	3
1993	Dublin (WC)	0	3
1993	Belfast (WC)	1	1

1994	Belfast (EC)	0	4
1995	Dublin (EC)	1	1
1999	Dublin	1	0
2011	Dublin (CC)	0	5
2018	Dublin	0	0

v ROMANIA
1984	Belfast (WC)	3	2
1985	Bucharest (WC)	1	0
1994	Belfast	2	0
2006	Chicago	0	2
2014	Bucharest (EC)	0	2
2015	Belfast (EC)	0	0
2020	Bucharest (NL)	1	1
2020	Belfast (NL)	1	1

v RUSSIA
2012	Moscow (WC)	0	2
2013	Belfast (WC)	1	0

v SAN MARINO
2008	Belfast (WC)	4	0
2009	Serravalle (WC)	3	0
2016	Belfast (WC)	4	0
2017	Serravalle (WC)	3	0

v SERBIA & MONTENEGRO
2004	Belfast	1	1

v SERBIA
2009	Belfast	0	1
2011	Belgrade (EC)	1	2
2011	Belfast (EC)	0	1

v SLOVAKIA
1998	Belfast	1	0
2008	Bratislava (WC)	1	2
2009	Belfast (WC)	0	2
2016	Trnava	0	0
2020	Belfast (EC)	1	2

v SLOVENIA
2008	Maribor (WC)	0	2
2009	Belfast (WC)	1	0
2010	Maribor (EC)	1	0
2011	Belfast (EC)	0	0
2016	Belfast	1	0

v SOUTH KOREA
2018	Belfast	2	1

v SOVIET UNION
1969	Belfast (WC)	0	0
1969	Moscow (WC)	0	2
1971	Moscow (EC)	0	1
1971	Belfast (EC)	1	1

v SPAIN

1958	Madrid	2	6
1963	Bilbao	1	1
1963	Belfast	0	1
1970	Seville (EC)	0	3
1972	Hull (EC)	1	1
1982	Valencia (WC)	1	0
1985	Palma, Majorca	0	0
1986	Guadalajara (WC)	1	2
1988	Seville (WC)	0	4
1989	Belfast (WC)	0	2
1992	Belfast (WC)	0	0
1993	Seville (WC)	1	3
1998	Santander	1	4
2002	Belfast	0	5
2002	Albacete (EC)	0	3
2003	Belfast (EC)	0	0
2006	Belfast (EC)	3	2
2007	Las Palmas (EC)	0	1

v ST KITTS & NEVIS

2004	Basseterre	2	0

v SWEDEN

1974	Solna (EC)	2	0
1975	Belfast (EC)	1	2
1980	Belfast (WC)	3	0
1981	Stockholm (WC)	0	1
1996	Belfast	1	2
2007	Belfast (EC)	2	1
2007	Stockholm (EC)	1	1

v SWITZERLAND

1964	Belfast (WC)	1	0
1964	Lausanne (WC)	1	2
1998	Belfast	1	0
2004	Zurich	0	0
2010	Basle (EC)	1	4
2017	Belfast (WC)	0	1
2017	Basle (WC)	0	0
2021	Belfast (WC)	0	0
2021	Geneva (WC)	0	2

v THAILAND

1997	Bangkok	0	0

v TRINIDAD & TOBAGO

2004	Port of Spain	3	0

v TURKEY

1968	Belfast (WC)	4	1
1968	Istanbul (WC)	3	0
1983	Belfast (EC)	2	1
1983	Ankara (EC)	0	1
1985	Belfast (WC)	2	0
1985	Izmir (WC)	0	0
1986	Izmir (EC)	0	0
1987	Belfast (EC)	1	0
1998	Istanbul (EC)	0	3
1999	Belfast (EC)	0	3
2010	Connecticut	0	2
2013	Adana	0	1

v UKRAINE

1996	Belfast (WC)	0	1
1997	Kiev (WC)	1	2
2002	Belfast (EC)	0	0
2003	Donetsk (EC)	0	0
2016	Lyon (EC)	2	0
2021	Dnipro	0	1

v URUGUAY

1964	Belfast	3	0
1990	Belfast	1	0
2006	New Jersey	0	1
2014	Montevideo	0	1

v USA

2021	Belfast	1	2

v YUGOSLAVIA

1975	Belfast (EC)	1	0
1975	Belgrade (EC)	0	1
1982	Zaragoza (WC)	0	0
1987	Belfast (EC)	1	2
1987	Sarajevo (EC)	0	3
1990	Belfast (EC)	0	2
1991	Belgrade (EC)	1	4
2000	Belfast	1	2

REPUBLIC OF IRELAND

v ALBANIA

1992	Dublin (WC)	2	0
1993	Tirana (WC)	2	1
2003	Tirana (EC)	0	0
2003	Dublin (EC)	2	1

v ALGERIA

1982	Algiers	0	2
2010	Dublin	3	0

v ANDORRA

2001	Barcelona (WC)	3	0
2001	Dublin (WC)	3	1
2010	Dublin (EC)	3	1
2011	La Vella (EC)	2	0
2021	La Vella	4	1

v ARGENTINA

1951	Dublin	0	1
1979*	Dublin	0	0

1980	Dublin	0	1
1998	Dublin	0	2
2010	Dublin	0	1
(*Not regarded as full Int)			

v ARMENIA
2010	Yerevan (EC)	1	0
2011	Dublin (EC)	2	1
2022	Yerevan (NL)	0	1

v AUSTRALIA
| 2003 | Dublin | 2 | 1 |
| 2009 | Limerick | 0 | 3 |

v AUSTRIA
1952	Vienna	0	6
1953	Dublin	4	0
1958	Vienna	1	3
1962	Dublin	2	3
1963	Vienna (EC)	0	0
1963	Dublin (EC)	3	2
1966	Vienna	0	1
1968	Dublin	2	2
1971	Dublin (EC)	1	4
1971	Linz (EC)	0	6
1995	Dublin (EC)	1	3
1995	Vienna (EC)	1	3
2013	Dublin (WC)	2	2
2013	Vienna (WC)	0	1
2016	Vienna (WC)	1	0
2017	Dublin (WC	1	1

v AZERBAIJAN
| 2021 | Dublin (WC) | 1 | 1 |
| 2021 | Baku (WC) | 3 | 0 |

v BELARUS
| 2016 | Cork | 1 | 2 |

v BELGIUM
1928	Liege	4	2
1929	Dublin	4	0
1930	Brussels	3	1
1934	Dublin (WC)	4	4
1949	Dublin	0	2
1950	Brussels	1	5
1965	Dublin	0	2
1966	Liege	3	2
1980	Dublin (WC)	1	1
1981	Brussels (WC)	0	1
1986	Brussels (EC)	2	2
1987	Dublin (EC)	0	0
1997*	Dublin (WC)	1	1
1997*	Brussels (WC)	1	2
2016	Bordeaux (EC)	0	3

| 2022 | Dublin | 2 | 2 |
| (*World Cup play-off) | | | |

v BOLIVIA
1994	Dublin	1	0
1996	East Rutherford, NJ	3	0
2007	Boston	1	1

v BOSNIA HERZEGOVINA
2012	Dublin	1	0
2015	Zenica (EC)	1	1
2015	Dublin (EC)	2	0

v BRAZIL
1974	Rio de Janeiro	1	2
1982	Uberlandia	0	7
1987	Dublin	1	0
2004	Dublin	0	0
2008	Dublin	0	1
2010	Arsenal	0	2

v BULGARIA
1977	Sofia (WC)	1	2
1977	Dublin (WC)	0	0
1979	Sofia (EC)	0	1
1979	Dublin (EC)	3	0
1987	Sofia (EC)	1	2
1987	Dublin (EC)	2	0
2004	Dublin	1	1
2009	Dublin (WC)	1	1
2009	Sofia (WC)	1	1
2019	Dublin	3	1
2020	Sofia (NL)	1	1
2020	Dublin (NL)	0	0

v CAMEROON
| 2002 | Niigata (WC) | 1 | 1 |

v CANADA
| 2003 | Dublin | 3 | 0 |

v CHILE
1960	Dublin	2	0
1972	Recife	1	2
1974	Santiago	2	1
1982	Santiago	0	1
1991	Dublin	1	1
2006	Dublin	0	1

v CHINA
| 1984 | Sapporo | 1 | 0 |
| 2005 | Dublin | 1 | 0 |

v COLOMBIA
| 2008 | Fulham | 1 | 0 |

v COSTA RICA

2014	Chester, USA	1	1

v CROATIA

1996	Dublin	2	2
1998	Dublin (EC)	2	0
1999	Zagreb (EC)	0	1
2001	Dublin	2	2
2004	Dublin	1	0
2011	Dublin	0	0
2012	Poznan (EC)	1	3

v CYPRUS

1980	Nicosia (WC)	3	2
1980	Dublin (WC)	6	0
2001	Nicosia (WC)	4	0
2001	Dublin (WC)	4	0
2004	Dublin (WC)	3	0
2005	Nicosia (WC)	1	0
2006	Nicosia (EC)	2	5
2007	Dublin (EC)	1	1
2008	Dublin (WC)	1	0
2009	Nicosia (WC)	2	1

v CZECHOSLOVAKIA/CZECH REP

1938	Prague	2	2
1959	Dublin (EC)	2	0
1959	Bratislava (EC)	0	4
1961	Dublin (WC)	1	3
1961	Prague (WC)	1	7
1967	Dublin (EC)	0	2
1967	Prague (EC)	2	1
1969	Dublin (WC)	1	2
1969	Prague (WC)	0	3
1979	Prague	1	4
1981	Dublin	3	1
1986	Reykjavik	1	0
1994	Dublin	1	3
1996	Prague	0	2
1998	Olomouc	1	2
2000	Dublin	3	2
2004	Dublin	2	1
2006	Dublin (EC)	1	1
2007	Prague (EC)	0	1
2012	Dublin	1	1

v DENMARK

1956	Dublin (WC)	2	1
1957	Copenhagen (WC)	2	0
1968*	Dublin (WC)	1	1
1969	Copenhagen (WC)	0	2
1969	Dublin (WC)	1	1
1978	Copenhagen (EC)	3	3
1979	Dublin (EC)	2	0
1984	Copenhagen (WC)	0	3

1985	Dublin (WC)	1	4
1992	Copenhagen (WC)	0	0
1993	Dublin (WC)	1	1
2002	Dublin	3	0
(*Abandoned after 51 mins – fog)			
2007	Aarhus	4	0
2017	Copenhagen (WC)	0	0
2017	Dublin (WC)	1	5
2018	Dublin (NL)	0	0
2018	Aarhus (NL)	0	0
2019	Copenhagen (EC)	1	1
2019	Dublin (EC)	1	1

v ECUADOR

2007	New York	1	1

v EGYPT

1990	Palermo (WC)	0	0

v ESTONIA

2000	Dublin (WC)	2	0
2001	Tallinn (WC)	2	0
2011	Tallinn (EC)	4	0
2011	Dublin (EC)	1	1

v FAROE ISLANDS

2004	Dublin (WC)	2	0
2005	Torshavn (WC)	2	0
2012	Torshavn (WC)	4	1
2013	Dublin (WC)	3	0

v FINLAND

1949	Dublin (WC)	3	0
1949	Helsinki (WC)	1	1
1990	Dublin	1	1
2000	Dublin	3	0
2002	Helsinki	3	0
2020	Dublin (NL)	0	1
2020	Helsinki (NL)	0	1

v FRANCE

1937	Paris	2	0
1952	Dublin	1	1
1953	Dublin (WC)	3	5
1953	Paris (WC)	0	1
1972	Dublin (WC)	2	1
1973	Paris (WC)	1	1
1976	Paris (WC)	0	2
1977	Dublin (WC)	1	0
1980	Paris (WC)	0	2
1981	Dublin (WC)	3	2
1989	Dublin	0	0
2004	Paris (WC)	0	0
2005	Dublin (WC)	0	1
2009	Dublin (WC)	0	1
2009	Paris (WC)	1	1

| 2016 | Lyon (EC) | 1 | 2 |
| 2018 | Paris | 0 | 2 |

v GEORGIA

2002	Tbilisi (EC)	2	1
2003	Dublin (EC)	2	0
2008	Mainz (WC)	2	1
2009	Dublin (WC)	2	1
2013	Dublin	4	0
2014	Tbilisi (EC)	2	1
2015	Dublin (EC)	1	0
2016	Dublin (WC)	1	0
2017	Tbilisi (WC)	1	1
2019	Dublin (EC)	1	0
2019	Tbilisi (EC)	0	0

v GERMANY/WEST GERMANY

1935	Dortmund	1	3
1936	Dublin	5	2
1939	Bremen	1	1
1951	Dublin	3	2
1952	Cologne	0	3
1955	Hamburg	1	2
1956	Dublin	3	0
1960	Dusseldorf	1	0
1966	Dublin	0	4
1970	Berlin	1	2
1975*	Dublin	1	0
1979	Dublin	1	3
1981	Bremen	0	3
1989	Dublin	1	1
1994	Hanover	2	0
2002	Ibaraki (WC)	1	1
2006	Stuttgart (EC)	0	1
2007	Dublin (EC)	0	0
2012	Dublin (WC)	1	6
2013	Cologne (WC)	0	3
2014	Gelsenkirchen (EC)	1	1
2015	Dublin (EC)	1	0

(*v W Germany 'B')

v GIBRALTAR

2014	Dublin (EC)	7	0
2015	Faro (EC)	4	0
2019	Victoria (EC)	1	0
2019	Dublin (EC)	2	0

v GREECE

2000	Dublin	0	1
2002	Athens	0	0
2012	Dublin	0	1

v HOLLAND

1932	Amsterdam	2	0
1934	Amsterdam	2	5
1935	Dublin	3	5
1955	Dublin	1	0
1956	Rotterdam	4	1
1980	Dublin (WC)	2	1
1981	Rotterdam (WC)	2	2
1982	Rotterdam (EC)	1	2
1983	Dublin (EC)	2	3
1988	Gelsenkirchen (EC)	0	1
1990	Palermo (WC)	1	1
1994	Tilburg	1	0
1994	Orlando (WC)	0	2
1995*	Liverpool (EC)	0	2
1996	Rotterdam	1	3
	(*Qual Round play-off)		
2000	Amsterdam (WC)	2	2
2001	Dublin (WC)	1	0
2004	Amsterdam	1	0
2006	Dublin	0	4
2016	Dublin	1	1

v HUNGARY

1934	Dublin	2	4
1936	Budapest	3	3
1936	Budapest	2	3
1939	Cork	2	2
1939	Budapest	2	2
1969	Dublin (WC)	1	2
1969	Budapest (WC)	0	4
1989	Budapest (WC)	0	0
1989	Dublin (WC)	2	0
1992	Gyor	2	1
2012	Budapest	0	0
2021	Budapest	0	0

v ICELAND

1962	Dublin (EC)	4	2
1962	Reykjavik (EC)	1	1
1982	Dublin (EC)	2	0
1983	Reykjavik (EC)	3	0
1986	Reykjavik	2	1
1996	Dublin (WC)	0	0
1997	Reykjavik (WC)	4	2
2017	Dublin	0	1

v IRAN

1972	Recife	2	1
2001*	Dublin (WC)	2	0
2001*	Tehran (WC)	0	1
	(*Qual Round play-off)		

v ISRAEL

| 1984 | Tel Aviv | 0 | 3 |
| 1985 | Tel Aviv | 0 | 0 |

1987	Dublin	5	0
2005	Tel Aviv (WC)	1	1
2005	Dublin (WC)	2	2

v ITALY
1926	Turin	0	3
1927	Dublin	1	2
1970	Florence (EC)	0	3
1971	Dublin (EC)	1	2
1985	Dublin	1	2
1990	Rome (WC)	0	1
1992	Boston, USA	0	2
1994	New York (WC)	1	0
2005	Dublin	1	2
2009	Bari (WC)	1	1
2009	Dublin (WC)	2	2
2011	Liege	2	0
2012	Poznan (EC)	0	2
2014	Fulham	0	0
2016	Lille (EC)	1	0

v JAMAICA
| 2004 | Charlton | 1 | 0 |

v KAZAKHSTAN
| 2012 | Astana (WC) | 2 | 1 |
| 2013 | Dublin (WC) | 3 | 1 |

v LATVIA
1992	Dublin (WC)	4	0
1993	Riga (WC)	2	0
1994	Riga (EC)	3	0
1995	Dublin (EC)	2	1
2013	Dublin	3	0

v LIECHTENSTEIN
1994	Dublin (EC)	4	0
1995	Eschen (EC)	0	0
1996	Eschen (WC)	5	0
1997	Dublin (WC)	5	0

v LITHUANIA
1993	Vilnius (WC)	1	0
1993	Dublin (WC)	2	0
1997	Dublin (WC)	0	0
1997	Zalgiris (WC)	2	1
2022	Dublin	1	0

v LUXEMBOURG
1936	Luxembourg	5	1
1953	Dublin (WC)	4	0
1954	Luxembourg (WC)	1	0
1987	Luxembourg (EC)	2	0
1987	Luxembourg (EC)	2	1
2021	Dublin (WC)	0	1

| 2021 | Luxembourg (WC) | 3 | 0 |

v MACEDONIA
1996	Dublin (WC)	3	0
1997	Skopje (WC)	2	3
1999	Dublin (EC)	1	0
1999	Skopje (EC)	1	1
2011	Dublin (EC)	2	1
2011	Skopje (EC)	2	0

v MALTA
1983	Valletta (EC)	1	0
1983	Dublin (EC)	8	0
1989	Dublin (WC)	2	0
1989	Valletta (WC)	2	0
1990	Valletta	3	0
1998	Dublin (EC)	1	0
1999	Valletta (EC)	3	2

v MEXICO
1984	Dublin	0	0
1994	Orlando (WC)	1	2
1996	New Jersey	2	2
1998	Dublin	0	0
2000	Chicago	2	2
2017	New Jersey	1	3

v MOLDOVA
| 2016 | Chisinau (WC) | 3 | 1 |
| 2017 | Dublin (WC) | 2 | 0 |

v MONTENEGRO
| 2008 | Podgorica (WC) | 0 | 0 |
| 2009 | Dublin (WC) | 0 | 0 |

v MOROCCO
| 1990 | Dublin | 1 | 0 |

v NEW ZEALAND
| 2019 | Dublin | 3 | 1 |

v NIGERIA
2002	Dublin	1	2
2004	Charlton	0	3
2009	Fulham	1	1

v NORWAY
1937	Oslo (WC)	2	3
1937	Dublin (WC)	3	3
1950	Dublin	2	2
1951	Oslo	3	2
1954	Dublin	2	1
1955	Oslo	3	1
1960	Dublin	3	1
1964	Oslo	4	1

1973	Oslo	1	1
1976	Dublin	3	0
1978	Oslo	0	0
1984	Oslo (WC)	0	1
1985	Dublin (WC)	0	0
1988	Oslo	0	0
1994	New York (WC)	0	0
2003	Dublin	1	0
2008	Oslo	1	1
2010	Dublin	1	2

v OMAN

2012	Fulham	4	1
2014	Dublin	2	0
2016	Dublin	4	0

v PARAGUAY

1999	Dublin	2	0
2010	Dublin	2	1

v POLAND

1938	Warsaw	0	6
1938	Dublin	3	2
1958	Katowice	2	2
1958	Dublin	2	2
1964	Cracow	1	3
1964	Dublin	3	2
1968	Dublin	2	2
1968	Katowice	0	1
1970	Dublin	1	2
1970	Poznan	0	2
1973	Wroclaw	0	2
1973	Dublin	1	0
1976	Poznan	2	0
1977	Dublin	0	0
1978	Lodz	0	3
1981	Bydgoszcz	0	3
1984	Dublin	0	0
1986	Warsaw	0	1
1988	Dublin	3	1
1991	Dublin (EC)	0	0
1991	Poznan (EC)	3	3
2004	Bydgoszcz	0	0
2008	Dublin	2	3
2013	Dublin	2	0
2013	Poznan	0	0
2015	Dublin (EC)	1	1
2015	Warsaw (EC)	1	2
2018	Wroclaw	1	1

v PORTUGAL

1946	Lisbon	1	3
1947	Dublin	0	2
1948	Lisbon	0	2
1949	Dublin	1	0
1972	Recife	1	2
1992	Boston, USA	2	0
1995	Dublin (EC)	1	0
1995	Lisbon (EC)	0	3
1996	Dublin	0	1
2000	Lisbon (WC)	1	1
2001	Dublin (WC)	1	1
2005	Dublin	1	0
2014	East Rutherford, USA	1	5
2021	Faro (WC)	1	2
2021	Dublin (WC)	0	0

v QATAR

2021	Debrecen	1	1
2021	Dublin	4	0

v ROMANIA

1988	Dublin	2	0
1990*	Genoa	0	0
1997	Bucharest (WC)	0	1
1997	Dublin (WC)	1	1
2004	Dublin	1	0

(*Rep won 5-4 on pens)

v RUSSIA (See also Soviet Union)

1994	Dublin	0	0
1996	Dublin	0	2
2002	Dublin	2	0
2002	Moscow (EC)	2	4
2003	Dublin (EC)	1	1
2010	Dublin (EC)	2	3
2011	Moscow (EC)	0	0

v SAN MARINO

2006	Dublin (EC)	5	0
2007	Rimini (EC)	2	1

v SAUDI ARABIA

2002	Yokohama (WC)	3	0

v SERBIA

2008	Dublin	1	1
2012	Belgrade	0	0
2014	Dublin	1	2
2016	Belgrade (WC)	2	2
2017	Dublin (WC)	0	1
2021	Belgrade (WC)	2	3
2021	Dublin (WC)	1	1

v SLOVAKIA

2007	Dublin (EC)	1	0
2007	Bratislava (EC)	2	2
2010	Zilina (EC)	1	1
2011	Dublin (EC)	0	0

2016	Dublin	2	2
2020*	Bratislava (EC)	0	0
(* Republic of Ireland lost 4-2 on pens)			

v SOUTH AFRICA
| 2000 | New Jersey | 2 | 1 |
| 2009 | Limerick | 1 | 0 |

v SOVIET UNION (See also Russia)
1972	Dublin (WC)	1	2
1973	Moscow (WC)	0	1
1974	Dublin (EC)	3	0
1975	Kiev (EC)	1	2
1984	Dublin (WC)	1	0
1985	Moscow (WC)	0	2
1988	Hanover (EC)	1	1
1990	Dublin	1	0

v SPAIN
1931	Barcelona	1	1
1931	Dublin	0	5
1946	Madrid	1	0
1947	Dublin	3	2
1948	Barcelona	1	2
1949	Dublin	1	4
1952	Madrid	0	6
1955	Dublin	2	2
1964	Seville (EC)	1	5
1964	Dublin (EC)	0	2
1965	Dublin (WC)	1	0
1965	Seville (WC)	1	4
1965	Paris (WC)	0	1
1966	Dublin (EC)	0	0
1966	Valencia (EC)	0	2
1977	Dublin	0	1
1982	Dublin (EC)	3	3
1983	Zaragoza (EC)	0	2
1985	Cork	0	0
1988	Seville (WC)	0	2
1989	Dublin (WC)	1	0
1992	Seville (WC)	0	0
1993	Dublin (WC)	1	3
2002*	Suwon (WC)	1	1
(*Rep lost 3-2 on pens)			
2012	Gdansk (EC)	0	4
2013	New York	0	2

v SWEDEN
1949	Stockholm (WC)	1	3
1949	Dublin (WC)	1	3
1959	Dublin	3	2
1960	Malmo	1	4
1970	Dublin (EC)	1	1
1970	Malmo (EC)	0	1

1999	Dublin	2	0
2006	Dublin	3	0
2013	Stockholm (WC)	0	0
2013	Dublin (WC)	1	2
2016	Paris (EC)	1	1

v SWITZERLAND
1935	Basle	0	1
1936	Dublin	1	0
1937	Berne	1	0
1938	Dublin	4	0
1948	Dublin	0	1
1975	Dublin (EC)	2	1
1975	Berne (EC)	0	1
1980	Dublin	2	0
1985	Dublin (WC)	3	0
1985	Berne (WC)	0	0
1992	Dublin	2	1
2002	Dublin (EC)	1	2
2003	Basle (EC)	0	2
2004	Basle (WC)	1	1
2005	Dublin (WC)	0	0
2016	Dublin	1	0
2019	Dublin (EC)	1	1
2019	Geneva (EC)	0	2

v TRINIDAD & TOBAGO
| 1982 | Port of Spain | 1 | 2 |

v TUNISIA
| 1988 | Dublin | 4 | 0 |

v TURKEY
1966	Dublin (EC)	2	1
1967	Ankara (EC)	1	2
1974	Izmir (EC)	1	1
1975	Dublin (EC)	4	0
1976	Ankara	3	3
1978	Dublin	4	2
1990	Izmir	0	0
1990	Dublin (EC)	5	0
1991	Istanbul (EC)	3	1
1999	Dublin (EC)	1	1
1999	Bursa (EC)	0	0
2003	Dublin	2	2
2014	Dublin	1	2
2018	Antalya	0	1

v UKRAINE
| 2022 | Dublin (NL) | 0 | 1 |
| 2022 | Lodz (NL) | 1 | 1 |

v URUGUAY
| 1974 | Montevideo | 0 | 2 |

1986	Dublin	1	1
2011	Dublin	2	3
2017	Dublin	3	1

v USA

1979	Dublin	3	2
1991	Boston	1	1
1992	Boston	4	1
1992	Washington	1	3
1996	Boston	1	2

2000	Foxboro	1	1
2002	Dublin	2	1
2014	Dublin	4	1
2018	Dublin	2	1

v YUGOSLAVIA

1955	Dublin	1	4
1988	Dublin	2	0
1998	Belgrade (EC)	0	1
1999	Dublin (EC)	2	1

BRITISH AND IRISH INTERNATIONAL APPEARANCES SINCE THE WAR (1946–2022)

(As at start of season 2022-23; in year shown 2022 = 2021–22. *Also a pre-War international player.
Totals include appearances as substitute)

ENGLAND

Agbonlahor G (Aston Villa, 2009–10)	3
Abraham T (Chelsea, Roma, 2018–22)	11
A'Court A (Liverpool, 1958–59)	5
Adams T (Arsenal, 1987–2001)	66
Alexander-Arnold T (Liverpool, 2018–22)	17
Alli D (Tottenham, 2016–18)	37
Allen A (Stoke, 1960)	3
Allen C (QPR, Tottenham, 1984–88)	5
Allen R (WBA, 1952–55)	5
Anderson S (Sunderland, 1962)	2
Anderson V (Nottm Forest, Arsenal, Manchester Utd, 1979–88)	30
Anderton D (Tottenham, 1994–2002)	30
Angus J (Burnley, 1961)	1
Armfield J (Blackpool, 1959–66)	43
Armstrong D (Middlesbrough, Southampton, 1980-4)	3
Armstrong K (Chelsea, 1955)	1
Ashton D (West Ham, 2008)	1
Astall G (Birmingham, 1956)	2
Astle J (WBA, 1969–70)	5
Aston J (Manchester Utd, 1949–51)	17
Atyeo J (Bristol City, 1956–57)	6
Bailey G (Manchester Utd, 1985)	2
Bailey M (Charlton, 1964–5)	2
Baily E (Tottenham, 1950–3)	9
Baines L (Everton, 2010–15)	30
Baker J (Hibernian, Arsenal, 1960–6)	8
Ball A (Blackpool, Everton, Arsenal, 1965–75)	72
Ball M (Everton, 2001)	1
Bamford P (Leeds, 2022)	1
Banks G (Leicester, Stoke, 1963–72)	73
Banks T (Bolton, 1958–59)	6
Bardsley D (QPR, 1993)	2
Barham M (Norwich, 1983)	2
Barkley R (Everton, Chelsea, 2014–20)	33
Barlow R (WBA, 1955)	1
Barmby N (Tottenham, Middlesbrough, Everton, Liverpool, 1995–2002)	23
Barnes H (Leicester, 2021)	1
Barnes J (Watford, Liverpool, 1983–96)	79
Barnes P (Manchester City, WBA, Leeds, 1978–82)	22
Barrass M (Bolton, 1952–53)	3
Barrett E (Oldham, Aston Villa, 1991–93)	3
Barry G (Aston Villa, Manchester City, 2000–12)	53
Barton J (Manchester City, 2007)	1
Barton W (Wimbledon, Newcastle, 1995)	3
Batty D (Leeds, Blackburn, Newcastle, Leeds, 1991–2000)	42
Baynham R (Luton, 1956)	3
Beardsley P (Newcastle, Liverpool, Newcastle, 1986–96)	59
Beasant D (Chelsea, 1990)	2
Beattie J (Southampton, 2003–04)	5
Beattie K (Ipswich, 1975–58)	9
Beckham D (Manchester Utd, Real Madrid, LA Galaxy, AC Milan 1997–2010)	115
Bell C (Manchester City, 1968–76)	48
Bellingham J (Borussia Dortmund, 2021–22)	15
Bent D (Charlton, Tottenham Sunderland, Aston Villa, 2006–12)	13
Bentley D (Blackburn, 2008–09)	7
Bentley R (Chelsea, 1949–55)	12
Berry J (Manchester Utd, 1953–56)	4
Bertrand R (Chelsea, Southampton, 2013–18)	19
Birtles G (Nottm Forest, 1980–81)	3
Blissett L (Watford, AC Milan, 1983–84)	14
Blockley J (Arsenal, 1973)	1
Blunstone F (Chelsea, 1955–57)	5
Bonetti P (Chelsea, 1966–70)	7
Bothroyd J (Cardiff, 2011)	1
Bould S (Arsenal, 1994)	2
Bowen J (West Ham, 2022)	4
Bowles S (QPR, 1974–77)	5
Bowyer L (Leeds, 2003)	1
Boyer P (Norwich, 1976)	1
Brabrook P (Chelsea, 1958–60)	3
Bracewell P (Everton, 1985–86)	3
Bradford G (Bristol Rov, 1956)	1
Bradley W (Manchester Utd, 1959)	3
Bridge W (Southampton, Chelsea, Manchester City 2002–10)	36

Bridges B (Chelsea, 1965–66) 4
Broadbent P (Wolves, 1958–60) 7
Broadis I (Manchester City, Newcastle, 1952–54) 14
Brooking T (West Ham, 1974–82) 47
Brooks J (Tottenham, 1957) 3
Brown A (WBA, 1971) 1
Brown K (West Ham, 1960) 1
Brown W (Manchester Utd, 1999–2010) 23
Bull S (Wolves, 1989–91) 13
Butcher T (Ipswich, Rangers, 1980–90) 77
Butland D (Birmingham, Stoke, 2013–19) 9
Butt N (Manchester Utd, Newcastle, 1997–2005) 39
Byrne G (Liverpool, 1963–66) 2
Byrne J (Crystal Palace, West Ham, 1962–65) 11
Byrne R (Manchester Utd, 1954–58) 33

Cahill G (Bolton, Chelsea, 2011–18) 61
Callaghan I (Liverpool, 1966–78) 4
Calvert-Lewin D (Everton) 2021) 11
Campbell F (Sunderland, 2012) 1
Campbell S (Tottenham, Arsenal, Portsmouth, 1996–2008) 73
Carragher J (Liverpool, 1999–2010) 38
Carrick M (West Ham, Tottenham, Manchester Utd, 2001–16) 34
Carroll A (Newcastle, Liverpool 2011– 13) 9
Carson S (Liverpool, Aston Villa WBA, Bursaspor 2008–12) 4
*Carter H (Derby, 1947) 7
Caulker S (Tottenham, 2013) 1
Chamberlain M (Stoke, 1983–85) 8
Chalobah N (Watford, 2019) 1
Chambers C (Arsenal, 2015) 3
Channon M (Southampton, Manchester City, 1973–78) 46
Charles G (Nottm Forest, 1991) 2
Charlton, J (Leeds, 1965–70) 35
Charlton, R (Manchester Utd, 1958–70) 106
Charnley R (Blackpool, 1963) 1
Cherry T (Leeds, 1976–80) 27
Chilton A (Manchester Utd, 1951–52) 2
Chilwell B (Leicester, Chelsea, 2019–22) 17
Chivers M (Tottenham, 1971–74) 24
Clamp E (Wolves, 1958) 4
Clapton D (Arsenal, 1959) 1
Clarke A (Leeds, 1970–6) 19
Clarke H (Tottenham, 1954) 1
Clayton R (Blackburn, 1956–60) 35
Clemence R (Liverpool, Tottenham, 1973–84) 61
Clement D (QPR, 1976–7) 5
Cleverley T (Manchester Utd, 2013–14) 13
Clough B (Middlesbrough, 1960) 2
Clough N (Nottm Forest, Liverpool, 1989–93) 14
Clyne N (Southampton, Liverpool, 2015–17) 14
Coady C (Wolves, 2021–22) 10
Coates R (Burnley, Tottenham, 1970–71) 4
Cockburn H (Manchester Utd, 1947–52) 13
Cohen G (Fulham, 1964–68) 37
Cole Andy (Manchester Utd, 1995–2002) 15
Cole Ashley (Arsenal, Chelsea, 2001–14) 107
Cole C (West Ham, 2009–10) 7

Cole J (West Ham, Chelsea, 2001–10) 56
Collymore S (Nottm Forest, Aston Villa, 1995–97) 3
Compton L (Arsenal, 1951) 2
Connelly J (Burnley, Manchester Utd,1960–66) 20
Cook L (Bournemouth, 2018) 1
Cooper C (Nottm Forest, 1995) 2
Cooper T (Leeds, 1969–75) 20
Coppell S (Manchester Utd, 1978–83) 42
Cork J (Burnley 2018) 1
Corrigan J (Manchester City, 1976–82) 9
Cottee T (West Ham, Everton, 1987–89) 7
Cowans G (Aston Villa, Bari, Aston Villa, 1983–91) 10
Crawford R (Ipswich, 1962) 2
Cresswell A (West Ham, 2017–18) 3
Crouch P (Southampton, Liverpool, Portsmouth, Tottenham, 2005–11) 42
Crowe C (Wolves, 1963) 1
Cunningham L (WBA, Real Madrid, 1979–81) 6
Curle K (Manchester City, 1992) 3
Currie A (Sheffield Utd, Leeds, 1972–79) 17

Daley T (Aston Villa, 1992) 7
Davenport P (Nottm Forest, 1985) 1
Davies K (Bolton, 2011) 1
Dawson M (Tottenham 2011) 4
Deane B (Sheffield Utd, 1991–93) 3
Deeley N (Wolves, 1959) 2
Defoe J (Tottenham, Portsmouth, Tottenham, Sunderland, 2004–17) 57
Delph F (Aston Villa, Manchester City, 2015–19) 20
Devonshire A (West Ham, 1980–84) 8
Dickinson J (Portsmouth, 1949–57) 48
Dier E (Tottenham, 2016–21) 45
Ditchburn E (Tottenham, 1949–57) 6
Dixon K (Chelsea, 1985–87) 8
Dixon L (Arsenal, 1990–99) 22
Dobson M (Burnley, Everton, 1974–75) 5
Dorigo T (Chelsea, Leeds, 1990–94) 15
Douglas B (Blackburn, 1959–63) 36
Downing S (Middlesbrough, Aston Villa, Liverpool, West Ham, 2005–15) 35
Doyle M (Manchester City, 1976–77) 5
Drinkwater D (Leicester, 2016) 3
Dublin D (Coventry, Aston Villa, 1998–99) 4
Dunk L (Brighton, 2019) 1
Dunn D (Blackburn, 2003) 1
Duxbury, M (Manchester Utd, 1984–85) 10
Dyer K (Newcastle, West Ham, 2000–08) 33

Eastham G (Arsenal, 1963–66) 19
Eckersley W (Blackburn, 1950–54) 17
Edwards, D (Manchester Utd, 1955–58) 18
Ehiogu U (Aston Villa, Middlesbrough, 1996–2002) 4
Ellerington W (Southampton, 1949) 2
Elliott W (Burnley, 1952–53) 5

Fantham J (Sheffield Wed, 1962) 1
Fashanu J (Wimbledon, 1989) 2
Fenwick T (QPR, 1984–88) 20

Johnson S (Derby, 2001) 1
Johnstone S (WBA, 2021–22) 3
Johnston H (Blackpool, 1947–54) 10
Jones M (Leeds, Sheffield Utd, 1965–70) 3
Jones P (Manchester Utd, 2012–18) 27
Jones R (Liverpool, 1992–95) 8
Jones W H (Liverpool, 1950) 2
Justin J (Leicester, 2022) 1

Kane H (Tottenham, 2015–22) 73
Kay A (Everton, 1963) 1
Keane M (Burnley, Everton, 2017–21) 12
Keegan K (Liverpool, Hamburg,
    Southampton, 1973–82) 63
Kelly, M (Liverpool, 2012) 1
Kennedy A (Liverpool, 1984) 2
Kennedy R (Liverpool, 1976–80) 17
Keown M (Everton, Arsenal,
    1992–2002) 43
Kevan D (WBA, 1957–61) 14
Kidd B (Manchester Utd, 1970) 2
King L (Tottenham, 2002–10) 21
Kirkland C (Liverpool, 2007) 1
Knight Z (Fulham, 2005) 2
Knowles C (Tottenham, 1968) 4
Konchesky P (Charlton, 2003–06) 2

Labone B (Everton, 1963–70) 26
Lallana A (Southampton, Liverpool, 2014–18) 34
Lambert R (Southampton, Liverpool, 2014–15) 11
Lampard F Snr (West Ham, 1973–80) 2
Lampard F Jnr (West Ham, Chelsea, 2000–14) 106
Langley J (Fulham, 1958) 3
Langton R (Blackburn, Preston,
    Bolton, 1947–51) 11
Latchford R (Everton, 1978–9) 12
Lawler C (Liverpool, 1971–72) 4
*Lawton T (Chelsea, Notts Co, 1947–49) 15
Lee F (Manchester City, 1969–72) 27
Lee J (Derby, 1951) 1
Lee R (Newcastle, 1995–99) 21
Lee S (Liverpool, 1983–84) 14
Lennon A (Tottenham, 2006–13) 21
Le Saux G (Blackburn, Chelsea, 1994–2001) 36
Lescott J (Everton, Manchester City, 2008–13) 26
Le Tissier M (Southampton, 1994–97) 8
Lindsay A (Liverpool, 1974) 4
Lineker G (Leicester, Everton, Barcelona,
    Tottenham, 1985–92) 80
Lingard J (Manchester Utd, 2017–22) 32
Little B (Aston Villa, 1975) 1
Livermore J (Tottenham, WBA, 2013–18) 7
Lloyd L (Liverpool, Nottm Forest, 1971–80) 4
Lofthouse N (Bolton, 1951–59) 33
Loftus–Cheek R (Chelsea, 2018–19) 10
Lowe E (Aston Villa, 1947) 3

Mabbutt G (Tottenham, 1983–92) 16
Macdonald M (Newcastle, 1972–76) 14
Madeley P (Leeds, 1971–77) 24
Maddison J (Leicester, 2020) 1
Maguire H (Leicester, Manchester Utd, 2018–22) 46

Maitland–Niles A (Arsenal, 2021) 5
Mannion W (Middlesbrough, 1947–52) 26
Mariner P (Ipswich, Arsenal, 1977–85) 35
Marsh R (QPR, Manchester City, 1972–73) 9
Mason R (Tottenham, 2015) 1
Martin A (West Ham, 1981–87) 17
Martyn N (Crystal Palace, Leeds, 1992–2002) 23
Marwood B (Arsenal, 1989) 1
Matthews R (Coventry, 1956–57) 5
*Matthews S (Stoke, Blackpool, 1947–57) 37
McCann G (Sunderland, 2001) 1
McCarthy A (Southampton, 2019) 1
McDermott T (Liverpool, 1978–82) 25
McDonald C (Burnley, 1958–59) 8
McFarland R (Derby, 1971–77) 28
McGarry W (Huddersfield, 1954–56) 4
McGuinness W (Manchester Utd, 1959) 2
McMahon S (Liverpool, 1988–91) 17
McManaman S (Liverpool, Real Madrid,
    1995–2002) 37
McNab R (Arsenal, 1969) 4
McNeil M (Middlesbrough, 1961–62) 9
Meadows J (Manchester City, 1955) 1
Medley L (Tottenham, 1951–52) 6
Melia J (Liverpool, 1963) 2
Merrick G (Birmingham, 1952–54) 23
Merson P (Arsenal, Middlesbrough,
    Aston Villa, 1992–99) 21
Metcalfe V (Huddersfield, 1951) 2
Milburn J (Newcastle, 1949–56) 13
Miller B (Burnley, 1961) 1
Mills D (Leeds, 2001–04) 19
Mills M (Ipswich, 1973–82) 42
Milne G (Liverpool, 1963–65) 14
Milner J (Aston Villa, Manchester City,
    Liverpool, 2010–16) 61
Milton A (Arsenal, 1952) 1
Mings T (Aston Villa, 2020–22) 17
Mitchell T (Crystal Palace, 2022) 2
Moore R (West Ham, 1962–74) 108
Morley A (Aston Villa, 1982–83) 6
Morris J (Derby, 1949–50) 3
Mortensen S (Blackpool, 1947–54) 25
Mount M (Chelsea, 2020–22) 31
Mozley B (Derby, 1950) 3
Mullen J (Wolves, 1947–54) 12
Mullery A (Tottenham, 1965–72) 35
Murphy D (Liverpool, 2002–04) 9

Neal P (Liverpool, 1976–84) 50
Neville G (Manchester Utd, 1995–2009) 85
Neville P (Manchester Utd, Everton,
    1996–2008) 59
Newton K (Blackburn, Everton, 1966–70) 27
Nicholls J (WBA, 1954) 2
Nicholson W (Tottenham, 1951) 1
Nish D (Derby, 1973–74) 5
Norman M (Tottenham, 1962–5) 23
Nugent D (Preston, 2007) 1

O'Grady M (Huddersfield, Leeds, 1963–9) 2
Osgood P (Chelsea, 1970–74) 4

Osman L (Everton, 2013) 2
Osman R (Ipswich, 1980–84) 11
Owen M (Liverpool, Real Madrid,
Newcastle, 1998–2008) 89
Owen S (Luton, 1954) 3
Oxlade–Chamberlain A (Arsenal,
Liverpool, 2012–20) 35

Paine T (Southampton, 1963–66) 19
Pallister G (Middlesbrough, Manchester
Utd 1988–97) 22
Palmer C (Sheffield Wed, 1992–94) 18
Parker P (QPR, Manchester Utd, 1989–94) 19
Parker S (Charlton, Chelsea, Newcastle,
West Ham, Tottenham, 2004–13) 18
Parkes P (QPR, 1974) 1
Parlour R (Arsenal, 1999–2001) 10
Parry R (Bolton, 1960) 2
Peacock A (Middlesbrough, Leeds,
1962–66) 6
Pearce S (Nottm Forest, West Ham,
1987–2000) 78
Pearson Stan (Manchester Utd, 1948–52) 8
Pearson Stuart (Manchester Utd, 1976–78) 15
Pegg D (Manchester Utd, 1957) 1
Pejic M (Stoke, 1974) 4
Perry W (Blackpool, 1956) 3
Perryman S (Tottenham, 1982) 1
Peters M (West Ham, Tottenham, 1966–74) 67
Phelan M (Manchester Utd, 1990) 1
Phillips K (Leeds, 2021–22) 23
Phillips K (Sunderland, 1999–2002) 8
Phillips L (Portsmouth, 1952–55) 3
Pickering F (Everton, 1964–65) 3
Pickering N (Sunderland, 1983) 1
Pickford J (Everton, 2018–22) 45
Pilkington B (Burnley, 1955) 1
Platt D (Aston Villa, Bari, Juventus,
Sampdoria, Arsenal, 1990–96) 62
Pointer R (Burnley, 1962) 3
Pope N (Burnley, 2018–22) 8
Powell C (Charlton, 2001–02) 5
Pye J (Wolves, 1950) 1

Quixall A (Sheffield Wed, 1954–55) 5

Radford J (Arsenal, 1969–72) 2
Ramsdale A (Arsenal, 2022) 1
Ramsey A (Southampton, Tottenham, 1949–54) 32
Rashford M (Manchester Utd, 2016–21) 46
Reaney P (Leeds, 1969–71) 3
Redknapp J (Liverpool, 1996–2000) 17
Redmond N (Southampton 2017) 1
Reeves K (Norwich, Manchester City, 1980) 2
Regis C (WBA, Coventry, 1982–88) 5
Reid P (Everton, 1985–88) 13
Revie D (Manchester City, 1955–57) 6
Rice D (West Ham, 2019–22) 32
Richards, J (Wolves, 1973) 1
Richards M (Manchester City, 2007–12) 13
Richardson K (Aston Villa, 1994) 1
Richardson K (Manchester Utd, 2005–07) 8

Rickaby S (WBA, 1954) 1
Ricketts M (Bolton, 2002) 1
Rimmer J (Arsenal, 1976) 1
Ripley S (Blackburn, 1994–97) 2
Rix G (Arsenal, 1981–84) 17
Robb G (Tottenham, 1954) 1
Roberts G (Tottenham, 1983–84) 6
Robinson P (Leeds, Tottenham, 2003–08) 41
Robson B (WBA, Manchester Utd,
1980–92) 90
Robson R (WBA, 1958–62) 20
Rocastle D (Arsenal, 1989–92) 14
Rodriguez J (Southampton, 2014) 1
Rodwell J (Everton, Manchester City, 2012–13) 3
Rooney W (Everton, Manchester Utd,
DC United, 2003–19) 120
Rose D (Tottenham, 2016–20) 29
Rowley J (Manchester Utd, 1949–52) 6
Royle J (Everton, Manchester City, 1971–77) 6
Ruddock N (Liverpool, 1995) 1
Ruddy J (Norwich, 2013) 1

Sadler D (Manchester Utd, 1968–71) 4
Saka B (Arsenal, 2021–22) 18
Salako J (Crystal Palace, 1991–92) 5
Sancho J (Borussia Dortmund,
Manchester Utd, 2019–22) 23
Sansom K (Crystal Palace, Arsenal, 1979–88) 86
Scales J (Liverpool, 1995) 3
Scholes P (Manchester Utd, 1997–2004) 66
Scott L (Arsenal, 1947–49) 17
Seaman D (QPR, Arsenal, 1989–2003) 75
Sewell J (Sheffield Wed, 1952–54) 6
Shackleton L (Sunderland, 1949–55) 5
Sharpe L (Manchester Utd, 1991–94) 8
Shaw G (Sheffield Utd, 1959–63) 5
Shaw L (Southampton, Manchester Utd,
2014–22) 21
Shawcross, R (Stoke, 2013) 1
Shearer A (Southampton, Blackburn,
Newcastle, 1992–2000) 63
Shellito K (Chelsea, 1963) 1
Shelvey J (Liverpool, Swansea, 2013–16) 6
Sheringham E (Tottenham, Manchester
Utd, Tottenham, 1993–2002) 51
Sherwood T (Tottenham, 1999) 3
Shilton P (Leicester, Stoke, Nottm Forest,
Southampton, Derby, 1971–90) 125
Shimwell E (Blackpool, 1949) 1
Shorey N (Reading, 2007) 2
Sillett P (Chelsea, 1955) 3
Sinclair T (West Ham, Manchester City,
2002–04) 12
Sinton A (QPR, Sheffield Wed,
1992–94) 12
Slater W (Wolves, 1955–60) 12
Smalling C (Manchester Utd, 2012–17) 31
Smith A (Arsenal, 1989–92) 13
Smith A (Leeds, Manchester Utd,
Newcastle, 2001–08) 19
Smith L (Arsenal, 1951–53) 6
Smith R (Tottenham, 1961–64) 15

Smith T (Birmingham, 1960) 2
Smith T (Liverpool, 1971) 1
Smith Rowe E (Arsenal, 2022) 3
Solanke D (Liverpool, 2018) 1
Southgate G (Aston Villa,
    Middlesbrough, 1996–2004) 57
Spink N (Aston Villa, 1983) 1
Springett R (Sheffield Wed, 1960–66) 33
Staniforth R (Huddersfield, 1954–55) 8
Statham D (WBA, 1983) 3
Stein B (Luton, 1984) 1
Stepney A (Manchester Utd, 1968) 1
Sterland M (Sheffield Wed, 1989) 1
Sterling R (Liverpool, Manchester City, 2013–22) 77
Steven T (Everton, Rangers, Marseille,
    1985–92) 36
Stevens G (Everton, Rangers, 1985–92) 46
Stevens G (Tottenham, 1985–86) 7
Stewart P (Tottenham, 1992) 3
Stiles N (Manchester Utd, 1965–70) 28
Stone S (Nottm Forest, 1996) 9
Stones J (Everton, Manchester City, 2014–22) 58
Storey P (Arsenal, 1971–73) 19
Storey-Moore I (Nottm Forest, 1970) 1
Streten B (Luton, 1950) 1
Sturridge D (Chelsea, Liverpool, 2012–18) 26
Summerbee M (Manchester City, 1968–73) 8
Sunderland, A (Arsenal, 1980) 1
Sutton C (Blackburn, 1997) 1
Swan P (Sheffield Wed, 1960–62) 19
Swift F (Manchester City, 1947–79) 19

Talbot B (Ipswich, Arsenal, 1977–80) 6
Tambling R (Chelsea, 1963–66) 3
Tarkowski J (Burnley, 2018–19) 2
Taylor E (Blackpool, 1954) 1
Taylor J (Fulham, 1951) 2
Taylor P (Liverpool, 1948) 3
Taylor P (Crystal Palace, 1976) 4
Taylor T (Manchester Utd, 1953–58) 19
Temple D (Everton, 1965) 1
Terry J (Chelsea, 2003–13) 78
Thomas D (QPR, 1975–76) 8
Thomas D (Coventry, 1983) 2
Thomas G (Crystal Palace, 1991–92) 9
Thomas M (Arsenal, 1989–90) 2
Thompson A (Celtic, 2004) 1
Thompson Peter (Liverpool, 1964–70) 16
Thompson Phil (Liverpool, 1976–83) 42
Thompson T (Aston Villa, Preston, 1952–57) 2
Thomson R (Wolves, 1964–65) 8
Todd C (Derby, 1972–77) 27
Tomori F (Chelsea, 2020–22) 3
Towers A (Sunderland, 1978) 3
Townsend A (Tottenham, Newcastle,
    Crystal Palace, 2014–17) 13
Trippier K (Tottenham, Atletico Madrid,
    Newcastle, 2017–22) 37
Tueart D (Manchester City, 1975–77) 6

Ufton D (Charlton, 1954) 1
Unsworth D (Everton, 1995) 1

Upson M (Birmingham, West Ham, 2003–10) 21
Vardy J (Leicester, 2015–18) 26
Vassell D (Aston Villa, 2002–04) 22
Venables T (Chelsea, 1965) 2
Venison B (Newcastle, 1995) 2
Viljoen C (Ipswich, 1975) 2
Viollet D (Manchester Utd, 1960) 2

Waddle C (Newcastle, Tottenham,
    Marseille, 1985–92) 62
Waiters A (Blackpool, 1964–65) 5
Walcott T (Arsenal, 2006–17) 47
Walker D (Nottm Forest, Sampdoria,
    Sheffield Wed, 1989–94) 59
Walker I (Tottenham, Leicester, 1996–2004) 4
Walker K (Tottenham, Manchester City,
    2012–22) 68
Walker-Peters K (Southampton, 2022) 2
Wallace D (Southampton, 1986) 1
Walsh P (Luton, 1983–4) 5
Walters M (Rangers, 1991) 1
Ward P (Brighton, 1980) 1
Ward T (Derby, 1948) 2
Ward-Prowse J (Southampton, 2017–22) 11
Warnock S (Blackburn, Aston Villa, 2008–11) 2
Watson D (Sunderland, Manchester City,
    Werder Bremen, Southampton,
    Stoke, 1974–82) 65
Watkins O (Aston Villa, 2021–22) 7
Watson D (Norwich, Everton, 1984–8) 12
Watson W (Sunderland, 1950–1) 4
Webb N (Nottm Forest, Manchester
    Utd, 1988–92) 26
Welbeck D (Manchester Utd, Arsenal,
    2011–19) 42
Weller K (Leicester, 1974) 4
West G (Everton, 1969) 3
Wheeler J (Bolton, 1955) 1
White B (Brighton, Arsenal, 2021–22) 4
White D (Manchester City, 1993) 1
Whitworth S (Leicester, 1975–76) 7
Whymark T (Ipswich, 1978) 1
Wignall F (Nottm Forest, 1965) 2
Wilcox J (Blackburn, Leeds, 1996–2000) 3
Wilkins R (Chelsea, Manchester Utd,
    AC Milan, 1976–87) 84
Williams B (Wolves, 1949–56) 24
Williams S (Southampton, 1983–85) 6
Willis A (Tottenham, 1952) 1
Wilshaw D (Wolves, 1954–57) 12
Wilshere J (Arsenal, 2011–16) 34
Wilson C (Bournemouth, 2019–20) 4
Wilson R (Huddersfield, Everton, 1960–8) 63
Winks H (Tottenham, 2018–21) 10
Winterburn N (Arsenal, 1990–93) 2
Wise D (Chelsea, 1991–2001) 21
Withe P (Aston Villa, 1981–85) 11
Wood R (Manchester Utd, 1955–56) 3
Woodcock A (Nottm Forest, Cologne,
    Arsenal, 1977–86) 42
Woodgate J (Leeds, Newcastle, Middlesbrough,
    Tottenham, 1999–2008) 8

Woods C (Norwich, Rangers,
Sheffield Wed, 1984–93) 43
Worthington F (Leicester, 1974–75) 8
Wright I (Crystal Palace, Arsenal, West Ham,
1991–99) 33
Wright M (Southampton, Derby,
Liverpool, 1984–96) 45
Wright R (Ipswich, Arsenal, 2000–02) 2
Wright T (Everton, 1968–70) 11
Wright W (Wolves, 1947–59) 105
Wright–Phillips S (Manchester City,
Chelsea, Manchester City, 2005–11) 36
Young A (Aston Villa, Manchester Utd, 2008–18) 39
Young G (Sheffield Wed, 1965) 1
Young L (Charlton, 2005) 7
Zaha W (Manchester Utd, 2013–14) 2
Zamora R (Fulham, 2011–12) 2

SCOTLAND

Adam C (Rangers, Blackpool, Liverpool,
Stoke, 2007–15) 26
Adams C (Southampton, 2021–22) 19
Aird J (Burnley, 1954) 4
Aitken G (East Fife, 1949–54) 8
Aitken R (Celtic, Newcastle, St Mirren, 1980–92) 57
Albiston A (Manchester Utd, 1982–6) 14
Alexander G (Preston, Burnley, 2002–10) 40
Alexander N (Cardiff, 2006) 2
Allan T (Dundee, 1974) 2
Anderson J (Leicester, 1954) 1
Anderson R (Aberdeen, Sunderland, 2003–08) 11
Anya I (Watford, Derby, 2014–18) 29
Archer J (Millwall, 2018) 1
Archibald S (Aberdeen, Tottenham,
Barcelona, 1980–86) 27
Armstrong S (Celtic, Southampton, 2017–2022) 36
Auld B (Celtic, 1959–60) 3

Bain S (Celtic, 2018–19) 3
Baird H (Airdrie, 1956) 1
Baird S (Rangers, 1957–58) 7
Bannan B (Aston Villa, Crystal Palace,
Sheffield Wed, 2011–18) 27
Bannon E (Dundee Utd, 1980–86) 11
Bardsley P (Sunderland, 2011–14) 13
Barr D (Falkirk, 2009) 1
Bates D (Hamburger, 2019) 4
Bauld W (Hearts, 1950) 3
Baxter J (Rangers, Sunderland, 1961–68) 34
Beattie C (Celtic, WBA, 2006–08) 7
Bell C (Kilmarnock, 2011) 1
Bell W (Leeds, 1966) 2
Bernard P (Oldham, 1995) 2
Berra C (Hearts, Wolves, Ipswich,
Hearts, 2008–18) 41
Bett J (Rangers, Lokeren, Aberdeen, 1982–90) 26
Black E (Metz, 1988) 2
Black I (Southampton, 1948) 1
Black I (Rangers, 2013) 1
Blacklaw A (Burnley, 1963–66) 3
Blackley J (Hibernian, 1974–77) 7
Blair J (Blackpool, 1947) 1

Blyth J (Coventry, 1978) 2
Bone J (Norwich, 1972–73) 2
Booth S (Aberdeen, Borussia Dortmund,
Twente Enschede 1993–2002) 22
Bowman D (Dundee Utd, 1992–94) 6
Boyd G (Peterborough, Hull, 2013–14) 2
Boyd K (Rangers, Middlesbrough, 2006–11) 18
Boyd T (Motherwell, Chelsea, Celtic,
1991–2002) 72
Brand R (Rangers, 1961–62) 8
Brazil A (Ipswich, Tottenham, 1980–83) 13
Bremner D (Hibernian, 1976) 1
Bremner W (Leeds, 1965–76) 54
Brennan F (Newcastle, 1947–54) 7
Bridcutt L (Brighton, Sunderland, 2013–16) 2
Broadfoot K (Rangers, 2009–11) 4
Brogan J (Celtic, 1971) 4
Brophy E (Kilmarnock, 2019) 1
Brown A (East Fife, Blackpool, 1950–54) 13
Brown H (Partick, 1947) 3
Brown J (Cardiff, Stoke, 2022) 5
Brown J (Sheffield Utd, 1975) 1
Brown R (Rangers, 1947–52) 5
Brown S (Hibernian, Celtic, 2007–18) 55
Brown W (Dundee, Tottenham, 1958–66) 28
Brownlie J (Hibernian, 1971–76) 7
Bryson C (Kilmarnock, Derby, 2011–16) 3
Buchan M (Aberdeen, Manchester Utd, 1972–8) 34
Buckley P (Aberdeen, 1954–55) 3
Burchill M (Celtic, 2000) 6
Burke C (Rangers, Birmingham, 2006–14) 7
Burke O (Nottm Forest, Leipzig, WBA, 2016–21) 13
Burley C (Chelsea, Celtic, Derby, 1995–2003) 46
Burley G (Ipswich, 1979–82) 11
Burns F (Manchester Utd, 1970) 1
Burns K (Birmingham, Nottm Forest, 1974–81) 20
Burns T (Celtic, 1981–88) 8

Cadden C (Motherwell, 2018) 2
Caddis P (Birmingham, 2016) 1
Calderwood C (Tottenham, Aston Villa,
1995–2000) 36
Caldow E (Rangers, 1957–63) 40
Cairney T (Fulham, 2017–18) 2
Caldwell G (Newcastle, Sunderland, Hibernian,
Wigan, 2002–13) 55
Caldwell S (Newcastle, Sunderland,
Celtic, Wigan, 2001–11) 12
Callaghan T (Dunfermline, 1970) 2
Cameron C (Hearts, Wolves, 1999–2005) 28
Campbell A (Luton, 2022) 1
Campbell R (Falkirk, Chelsea, 1947–50) 5
Campbell W (Morton, 1947–48) 5
Canero P (Leicester, 2004) 1
Carr W (Coventry, 1970–73) 6
Chalmers S (Celtic, 1965–67) 5
Christie R (Celtic 2018–22) 31
Clark J (Celtic, 1966–67) 4
Clark R (Aberdeen, 1968–73) 17
Clarke S (Chelsea, 1988–94) 6
Clarkson D (Motherwell, 2008–09) 2
Collins J (Hibernian, Celtic, Monaco,
Everton, 1988–2000) 58

Kerr B (Newcastle, 2003–04) 3
Kingsley S (Swansea, 2016) 1
Kyle K (Sunderland, Kilmarnock, 2002–10) 10
Lambert P (Motherwell, Borussia Dortmund,
Celtic, 1995–2003) 40
Law D (Huddersfield, Manchester City,
Torino, Manchester Utd, 1959–74) 55
Lawrence T (Liverpool, 1963–69) 3
Leggat G (Aberdeen, Fulham, 1956–60) 18
Leighton J (Aberdeen, Manchester Utd,
Hibernian, Aberdeen, 1983–99) 91
Lennox R (Celtic, 1967–70) 10
Leslie L (Airdrie, 1961) 5
Levein C (Hearts, 1990–95) 16
Liddell W (Liverpool, 1947–55) 28
Linwood A (Clyde, 1950) 1
Little R (Rangers, 1953) 1
Logie J (Arsenal, 1953) 1
Long H (Clyde, 1947) 1
Lorimer P (Leeds, 1970–76) 21

Macari L (Celtic, Manchester Utd, 1972–78) 24
Macaulay A (Brentford, Arsenal, 1947–48) 7
MacDonald A (Rangers, 1976) 1
MacDougall E (Norwich, 1975–76) 7
Mackail-Smith C (Peterborough, Brighton
2011–12) 7
MacKay D (Celtic, 1959–62) 14
Mackay D (Hearts, Tottenham, 1957–66) 22
Mackay G (Hearts, 1988) 4
Mackay M (Norwich, 2004–05) 5
Mackay-Steven G (Dundee Utd, 2014) 2
MacKenzie J (Partick, 1954–56) 9
Mackie J (QPR, 2011–13) 9
MacLeod J (Hibernian, 1961) 4
MacLeod M (Celtic, Borussia Dortmund,
Hibernian, 1985–91) 20
Maguire C (Aberdeen, 2011) 2
Maloney S (Celtic, Aston Villa, Celtic,
Wigan, Chicago, Hull, 2006–16) 47
Malpas M (Dundee Utd, 1984–93) 55
Marshall D (Celtic, Cardiff, Hull,
Derby, 2005–21) 47
Marshall G (Celtic, 1992) 1
Martin B (Motherwell, 1995) 2
Martin C (Derby, 2014–18) 17
Martin F (Aberdeen, 1954–55) 6
Martin N (Hibernian, Sunderland, 1965–66) 3
Martin R (Norwich, 2011–17) 29
Martis J (Motherwell, 1961) 1
Mason J (Third Lanark 1949–51) 7
Masson D (QPR, Derby, 1976–78) 17
Mathers D (Partick, 1954) 1
Matteo D (Leeds, 2001–02) 6
May S (Sheffield Wed, 2015) 1
McAllister B (Wimbledon, 1997) 3
McAllister G (Leicester, Leeds,
Coventry, 1990–99) 57
McAllister J (Livingston, 2004) 1
McArthur J (Wigan, Crystal Palace, 2011–18) 32
McAvennie F (West Ham, Celtic, 1986–88) 5
McBride J (Celtic, 1967) 2

McBurnie O (Swansea, Sheffield Utd, 2018–21) 16
McCall S (Everton, Rangers, 1990–98) 40
McCalliog J (Sheffield Wed, Wolves, 1967–71) 5
McCann N (Hearts, Rangers,
Southampton, 1999–2006) 26
McCann R (Motherwell, 1959–61) 5
McClair B (Celtic, Manchester Utd,
1987–93) 30
McCloy P (Rangers, 1973) 4
McCoist A (Rangers, Kilmarnock,
1986–99) 61
McColl I (Rangers, 1950–58) 14
McCormack R (Motherwell, Cardiff,
Leeds, Fulham, 2008–16) 13
McCreadie E (Chelsea, 1965–9) 23
McCulloch L (Wigan, Rangers, 2005–11) 18
McDonald J (Sunderland, 1956) 2
McDonald K (Fulham, 2018–19) 5
McEveley J (Derby, 2008) 3
McFadden J (Motherwell, Everton,
Birmingham, 2002–11) 48
McFarlane W (Hearts, 1947) 1
McGarr E (Aberdeen, 1970) 2
McGarvey F (Liverpool, Celtic, 1979–84) 7
McGeouch D (Hibernian, 2018) 2
McGhee M (Aberdeen, 1983–84) 4
McGinlay J (Bolton, 1995–97) 13
McGinn J (Hibernian, Aston Villa, 2016–22) 48
McGinn P (Hibernian, 2022) 1
McGrain D (Celtic, 1973–82) 62
McGregor A (Rangers, Besiktas, Hull,
Rangers, 2007–19) 42
McGregor C (Celtic, 2018–22) 46
McGrory J (Kilmarnock, 1965–66) 3
McInally A (Aston Villa, Bayern Munich,
1989–90) 8
McInally J (Dundee Utd, 1987–93) 10
McInnes D (WBA, 2003) 2
McKay B (Rangers, 2016) 1
McKean R (Rangers, 1976) 1
McKenna S (Aberdeen, Nottm Forest,
2018–22) 26
McKimmie S (Aberdeen, 1989–96) 40
McKinlay T (Celtic, 1996–98) 22
McKinlay W (Dundee Utd, Blackburn,
1994–99) 29
McKinnon R (Rangers, 1966–71) 28
McKinnon R (Motherwell, 1994–95) 3
McLaren A (Preston, 1947–48) 4
McLaren A (Hearts, Rangers, 1992–96) 24
McLaren A (Kilmarnock, 2001) 1
McLaughlin J (Hearts, Sunderland, 2018–20) 2
McLean G (Dundee, 1968) 1
McLean K (Aberdeen, Norwich, 2016–22) 25
McLean T (Kilmarnock, Rangers,1969–71) 6
McLeish A (Aberdeen, 1980–93) 77
McLintock F (Leicester, Arsenal,1963–71) 9
McManus S (Celtic, Middlesbrough,2007–11) 26
McMillan I (Airdrie, 1952–61) 6
McNamara J (Celtic, Wolves,1997–2006) 33
McNamee D (Livingston, 2004–06) 4
McNaught W (Raith, 1951–55) 5

Shaw J (Rangers, 1947) 4
Shearer D (Aberdeen, 1994–96) 7
Shearer R (Rangers, 1961) 4
Shinnie A (Inverness, 2013) 1
Shinnie G (Aberdeen, 2018–19) 6
Simpson N (Aberdeen, 1983–88) 5
Simpson R (Celtic, 1967–69) 5
Sinclair J (Leicester, 1966) 1
Smith D (Aberdeen, Rangers, 1966–68) 2
Smith G (Hibernian, 1947–57) 18
Smith H (Hearts, 1988–92) 3
Smith JE (Celtic, 1959) 2
Smith J (Aberdeen, Newcastle, 1968–74) 4
Smith J (Celtic, 2003) - 2
Snodgrass R (Leeds, Norwich,
    West Ham, 2011–20) 28
Souness G (Middlesbrough, Liverpool,
    Sampdoria, Rangers, 1975–86) 54
Souttar J (Hearts, 2019–22) 6
Speedie D (Chelsea, Coventry, 1985–89) 10
Spencer J (Chelsea, QPR, 1995–97) 14
Stanton P (Hibernian, 1966–74) 16
Steel W (Morton, Derby, Dundee, 1947–53) 30
Stein C (Rangers, Coventry, 1969–73) 21
Stephen J (Bradford Park Avenue, 1947–48) 2
Stevenson L (Hibernian, 2018) 1
Stewart D (Leeds, 1978) 1
Stewart J (Kilmarnock, Middlesbrough,
    1977–79) 2
Stewart M (Manchester Utd, Hearts 2002–09) 4
Stewart R (Sunderland, 2022) 2
Stewart R (West Ham, 1981–7) 10
St John I (Motherwell, Liverpool, 1959–65) 21
Stockdale R (Middlesbrough, 2002–03) 5
Strachan G (Aberdeen, Manchester Utd,
    Leeds, 1980–92) 50
Sturrock P (Dundee Utd, 1981–87) 20
Sullivan N (Wimbledon, Tottenham,
    1997–2003) 28

Taylor G (Kilmarnock, Celtic, 2019–22) 7
Teale A (Wigan, Derby, 2006–09) 13
Telfer P (Coventry, 2000) 1
Telfer W (St Mirren, 1954) 1
Thomson K (Rangers, Middlesbrough, 2009–11) 3
Thompson S (Dundee Utd, Rangers,
    2002–05) 16
Thomson W (St Mirren, 1980–84) 7
Thornton W (Rangers, 1947–52) 7
Tierney K (Celtic, Arsenal, 2016–22) 32
Toner W (Kilmarnock, 1959) 2
Turnbull D (Celtic, 2021–22) 5
Turnbull E (Hibernian, 1948–58) 8

Ure I (Dundee, Arsenal, 1962–68) 11

Waddell W (Rangers, 1947–55) 17
Walker A (Celtic, 1988–95) 3
Walker N (Hearts, 1993–96) 2
Wallace I (Coventry, 1978–79) 3
Wallace L (Hearts, Rangers, 2010–17) 10
Wallace R (Preston, 2010) 1

Wallace W (Hearts, Celtic, 1965–69) 7
Wardhaugh J (Hearts, 1955–57) 2
Wark J (Ipswich, Liverpool, 1979–85) 29
Watson J (Motherwell, Huddersfield, 1948–54) 2
Watson R (Motherwell, 1971) 1
Watt T (Charlton, 2016) 1
Webster A (Hearts, Rangers, Hearts, 2003–13) 28
Weir A (Motherwell, 1959–60) 6
Weir D (Hearts, Everton, Rangers,
    1997–2011) 69
Weir P (St Mirren, Aberdeen, 1980–84) 6
White J (Falkirk, Tottenham, 1959–64) 22
Whittaker S (Rangers, Norwich, 2010–16) 31
Whyte D (Celtic, Middlesbrough, Aberdeen,
    1988–99) 12
Wilkie L (Dundee, 2002–03) 11
Williams G (Nottm Forest, 2002–03) 5
Wilson A (Portsmouth, 1954) 1
Wilson D (Liverpool, 2011–12) 5
Wilson D (Rangers, 1961–65) 22
Wilson I (Leicester, Everton, 1987–8) 5
Wilson M (Celtic, 2011) 1
Wilson P (Celtic, 1975) 1
Wilson R (Arsenal, 1972) 2
Wood G (Everton, Arsenal, 1978–82) 4
Woodburn W (Rangers, 1947–52) 24
Wright K (Hibernian, 1992) 1
Wright S (Aberdeen, 1993) 2
Wright T (Sunderland, 1953) 3

Yeats R (Liverpool, 1965–66) 2
Yorston H (Aberdeen, 1955) 1
Young A (Hearts, Everton, 1960–66) 8
Young G (Rangers, 1947–57) 53
Younger T (Hibernian, Liverpool, 1955–58) 24

WALES

Aizlewood M (Charlton, Leeds, Bradford City,
    Bristol City, Cardiff, 1986–95) 39
Allchurch I (Swansea City, Newcastle,
    Cardiff, 1951–66) 68
Allchurch L (Swansea City, Sheffield Utd,
    1955–64) 11
Allen B (Coventry, 1951) 2
Allen J (Swansea, Liverpool, Stoke, 2009–22) 72
Allen M (Watford, Norwich, Millwall,
    Newcastle, 1986–94) 14
Ampadu E (Chelsea 2018–22) 36

Baker C (Cardiff, 1958–62) 7
Baker W (Cardiff, 1948) 1
Bale G (Southampton, Tottenham,
    Real Madrid, 2006–22) 106
Barnard D (Barnsley, Grimsby, 1998–2004) 24
Barnes W (Arsenal, 1948–55) 22
Bellamy C (Norwich, Coventry, Newcastle,
    Blackburn, Liverpool, West Ham,
    Manchester City, Liverpool,
    Cardiff, 1998–2014) 78
Berry G (Wolves, Stoke, 1979–83) 5
Blackmore C (Manchester Utd,
    Middlesbrough, 1985–97) 39

Blake D (Cardiff, Crystal Palace, 2011–13) — 14
Blake N (Sheffield Utd, Bolton, Blackburn,
Wolves, 1994–2004) — 29
Bodin B (Preston, 2018) — 1
Bodin P (Swindon, Crystal Palace,
Swindon, 1990–95) — 23
Bowen D (Arsenal, 1955–59) — 19
Bowen J (Swansea City, Birmingham, 1994–97) — 2
Bowen M (Tottenham, Norwich,
West Ham, 1986–97) — 41
Boyle T (Crystal Palace, 1981) — 2
Bradley M (Walsall, 2010) — 1
Bradshaw T (Walsall, Barnsley, 2016–18) — 3
Brooks D (Sheffield Utd, Bournemouth 2018–21) — 21
Brown J (Gillingham, Blackburn, Aberdeen,
2006–12) — 3
Browning M (Bristol Rov, Huddersfield, 1996–97) — 5
Burgess R (Tottenham, 1947–54) — 32
Burns W (Ipswich, 2022) — 3
Burton A (Norwich, Newcastle, 1963–72) — 9

Cabango B (Swansea, 2021–22) — 4
Cartwright L (Coventry, Wrexham, 1974–79) — 7
Charles Jeremy (Swansea City, QPR,
Oxford Utd, 1981–87) — 19
Charles John (Leeds, Juventus, Cardiff, 1950–65) — 38
Charles M (Swansea City, Arsenal,
Cardiff, 1955–63) — 31
Chester J (Hull, WBA, Aston Villa, 2014–19) — 35
Church S (Reading, Nottm Forest, Charlton,
MK Dons 2009–16) — 38
Clarke R (Manchester City, 1949–56) — 22
Coleman C (Crystal Palace, Blackburn,
Fulham, 1992–2002) — 32
Collins D (Sunderland, Stoke, 2005–11) — 12
Collins J (Cardiff, West Ham, Aston Villa,
West Ham, 2004–17) — 50
Collison J (West Ham, 2008–14) — 17
Colwill R (Cardiff, 2021–22) — 6
Cornforth J (Swansea City, 1995) — 2
Cotterill D (Bristol City, Wigan,
Sheffield Utd, Swansea,
Doncaster, Birmingham, 2006–17) — 24
Coyne D (Tranmere, Grimsby, Leicester,
Burnley, Tranmere, 1996–2008) — 16
Crofts A (Gillingham, Brighton, Norwich,
Brighton, Scunthorpe, 2006–18) — 29
Crossley M (Nottm Forest, Middlesbrough,
Fulham, 1997–2005) — 8
Crowe V (Aston Villa, 1959–63) — 16
Curtis A (Swansea City, Leeds,
Southampton, Cardiff, 1976–87) — 35

Daniel R (Arsenal, Sunderland, 1951–57) — 21
Davies A (Manchester Utd, Newcastle,
Swansea City, Bradford City, 1983–90) — 13
Davies A (Barnsley, Stoke, Sheffield Utd,
2019–22) — 4
Davies A (Yeovil 2006) — 1
Davies B (Swansea, Tottenham, 2013–22) — 74
Davies C (Charlton, 1972) — 1
Davies C (Oxford, Verona, Oldham,

Barnsley, Bolton, 2006–14) — 7
Davies D (Everton, Wrexham,
Swansea City 1975–83) — 52
Davies ER (Newcastle, 1953–58) — 6
Davies G (Fulham, Chelsea,
Manchester City, 1980–86) — 16
Davies RT (Norwich, Southampton,
Portsmouth, 1964–74) — 29
Davies RW (Bolton, Newcastle, Man Utd,
Man City, Blackpool, 1964–74) — 34
Davies S (Manchester Utd, 1996) — 1
Davies S (Tottenham, Everton, Fulham, 2001–10) — 58
Davis G (Wrexham, 1978) — 3
Deacy N (PSV Eindhoven, Beringen,
1977–79) — 12
Delaney M (Aston Villa, 2000–07) — 36
Derrett S (Cardiff, 1969–71) — 4
Dibble A (Luton, Manchester City,
1986–89) — 3
Dorman A (St Mirren, Crystal Palace, 2010–11) — 3
Duffy R (Portsmouth, 2006–08) — 13
Dummett P (Newcastle, 2014–19) — 5
Durban A (Derby, 1966–72) — 27
Dwyer P (Cardiff, 1978–80) — 10

Eardley N (Oldham, Blackpool, 2008–11) — 16
Earnshaw R (Cardiff, WBA, Norwich,
Derby, Nottm Forest, Cardiff, 2002–13) — 59
Easter J (Wycombe, Crystal Palace, Millwall,
2007–14) — 12
Eastwood F (Wolves, Coventry, 2008–11) — 11
Edwards C (Swansea City, 1996) — 1
Edwards D (Luton, Wolves, Reading, 2007–18) — 43
Edwards, G (Birmingham, Cardiff,
1947–50) — 12
Edwards, I (Chester, Wrexham, 1978–80) — 4
Edwards, L (Charlton, 1957) — 2
Edwards, R (Bristol City, 1997–98) — 4
Edwards, R (Aston Villa, Wolves, 2003–07) — 15
Emmanuel W (Bristol City, 1973) — 2
England M (Blackburn, Tottenham, 1962–75) — 44
Evans B (Swansea City, Hereford, 1972–74) — 7
Evans C (Manchester City, Sheffield Utd,
2008–11) — 13
Evans I (Crystal Palace, 1976–78) — 13
Evans L (Wolves, Sheffield Utd, Wigan, 2018–19) — 4
Evans P (Brentford, Bradford City,
2002–03) — 2
Evans R (Swansea City, 1964) — 1
Evans S (Wrexham, 2007–09) — 7

Felgate D (Lincoln, 1984) — 1
Fletcher C (Bournemouth, West Ham,
Crystal Palace, 2004–09) — 36
Flynn B (Burnley, Leeds, 1975–84) — 66
Fon Williams O (Inverness, 2016) — 1
Ford T (Swansea City, Sunderland,
Aston Villa, Cardiff, 1947–57) — 38
Foulkes W (Newcastle, 1952–54) — 11
Freeman K (Sheffield Utd, 2019) — 1
Freestone R (Swansea City, 2000–03) — 1

Gabbidon D (Cardiff, West Ham, QPR, Crystal Palace, 2002–14)   49

Garner G (Leyton Orient, 2006)   1

Giggs R (Manchester Utd, 1992–2007)   64

Giles D (Swansea City, Crystal Palace, 1980–83)   12

Godfrey B (Preston, 1964–65)   3

Goss J (Norwich, 1991–96)   9

Green C (Birmingham, 1965–69)   15

Green R (Wolves, 1998)   2

Griffiths A (Wrexham, 1971–77)   17

Griffiths H (Swansea City, 1953)   1

Griffiths M (Leicester, 1947–54)   11

Gunter C (Cardiff, Tottenham, Nottm Forest, Reading, Charlton, 2007–22)   109

Hall G (Chelsea, 1988–92)   9

Harrington A (Cardiff, 1956–62)   11

Harris C (Leeds, 1976–82)   24

Harris W (Middlesbrough, 1954–58)   6

Hartson J (Arsenal, West Ham, Wimbledon, Coventry, Celtic, 1995–2006)   51

Haworth S (Cardiff, Coventry, 1997–8)   5

Hedges R (Barnsley, 2018–19)   3

Henley A (Blackburn, 2016)   2

Hennessey T (Birmingham, Nottm Forest, Derby, 1962–73)   39

Hennessey W (Wolves, Crystal Palace, Burnley, 2007–22)   104

Hewitt R (Cardiff, 1958)   5

Hill M (Ipswich, 1972)   2

Hockey T (Sheffield Utd, Norwich, Aston Villa, 1972–74)   9

Hodges G (Wimbledon, Newcastle, Watford, Sheffield Utd, 1984–96)   18

Holden A (Chester, 1984)   1

Hole B (Cardiff, Blackburn, Aston Villa, Swansea City, 1963–71)   30

Hollins D (Newcastle, 1962–66)   11

Hopkins J (Fulham, Crystal Palace, 1983–90)   16

Hopkins M (Tottenham, 1956–63)   34

Horne B (Portsmouth, Southampton, Everton, Birmingham, 1988–97)   59

Howells R (Cardiff, 1954)   2

Hughes C (Luton, Wimbledon, 1992–97)   8

Hughes I (Luton, 1951)   4

Hughes M (Manchester Utd, Barcelona, Bayern Munich, Manchester Utd, Chelsea, Southampton, 1984–99)   72

*Hughes W (Birmingham, 1947)   3

Hughes WA (Blackburn, 1949)   5

Humphreys J (Everton, 1947)   1

Huws J (Manchester City, Wigan, Cardiff , 2014–17)   11

Isgrove L (Southampton, 2016)   1

Jackett K (Watford, 1983–88)   31

James D (Swansea, Manchester Utd, Leeds, 2019–22)   36

James EG (Blackpool, 1966–71)   2

James L (Burnley, Derby, QPR, Swansea City, Sunderland, 1972–83)   54

James R (Swansea, Stoke, QPR, Leicester, Swansea, 1979–88)   47

Jarvis A (Hull, 1967)   3

Jenkins S (Swansea, Huddersfield, 1996–2002)   16

John D (Cardiff, Rangers, Swansea, 2014–19)   7

Johnson A (Nottm Forest, WBA, 1999–2005)   15

Johnson B (Nottm Forest, 2021–22)   13

Johnson M (Swansea, 1964)   1

Jones A (Port Vale, Charlton, 1987–90)   6

Jones Barrie (Swansea, Plymouth Argyle, Cardiff, 1963–9)   15

*Jones Bryn (Arsenal, 1947–9)   4

Jones C (Swansea, Tottenham, Fulham, 1954–69)   59

Jones D (Norwich, 1976–80)   8

Jones E (Swansea, Tottenham, 1947–9)   4

Jones J (Liverpool, Wrexham, Chelsea, Huddersfield, 1976–86)   72

Jones K (Aston Villa, 1950)   1

Jones L (Liverpool, Tranmere, 1950)   2

Jones M (Leeds, Leicester, 2000–03)   13

Jones M (Wrexham, 2007–08)   2

Jones P (Stockport, Southampton, Wolves, Millwall, QPR, 1997–2007)   50

Jones R (Sheffield Wed, 1994)   1

*Jones TG (Everton, 1946–49)   13

Jones V (Wimbledon, 1995–97)   9

Jones W (Bristol Rov, 1971)   1

Kelsey J (Arsenal, 1954–62)   41

King A (Leicester, 2009–19)   50

King J (Swansea, 1955)   1

Kinsey N (Norwich, Birmingham, 1951–56)   7

Knill A (Swansea, 1989)   1

Koumas J (Tranmere, WBA, Wigan, 2001–09)   34

Krzywicki R (WBA, Huddersfield, 1970–72)   8

Lambert R (Liverpool, 1947–9)   5

Law B (QPR, 1990)   1

Lawrence J (Anderlecht, St Pauli, 2019–22)   11

Lawrence T (Leicester, Derby, 2016–21)   23

Ledley J (Cardiff, Celtic, Crystal Palace, Derby 2005–2018)   77

Lea C (Ipswich, 1965)   2

Leek K (Leicester, Newcastle, Birmingham, Northampton, 1961–65)   13

Legg A (Birmingham, Cardiff, 1996–2001)   6

Lever A (Leicester, 1953)   1

Levitt D (Manchester Utd, 2021–22)   12

Lewis D (Swansea, 1983)   1

Llewellyn C (Norwich, Wrexham, 1998–2007)   6

Lloyd B (Wrexham, 1976)   3

Lockyer T (Bristol Rov, Charlton, Luton, 2018–22)   14

Lovell S (Crystal Palace, Millwall, 1982–86)   6

Lowndes S (Newport, Millwall, Brighton, Barnsley, 1983–88)   10

Lowrie G (Coventry, Newcastle, 1948–49)   4

Lucas M (Leyton Orient, 1962–63)   4

Rowley T (Tranmere, 1959) 1
Rush I (Liverpool, Juventus, Liverpool, 1980–96) 73

Saunders D (Brighton, Oxford Utd, Derby, Liverpool, Aston Villa, Galatasaray, Nottm Forest, Sheffield Utd, Benfica, Bradford City, 1986–2001) 75
Savage R (Crewe, Leicester, Birmingham, 1996–2005) 39
Sayer D (Cardiff, 1977–8) 7
Scrine F (Swansea, 1950) 2
Sear C (Manchester City, 1963) 1
Sheehan J (Newport, Bolton, 2021–22) 3
Sherwood A (Cardiff, Newport, 1947–57) 41
Shortt W (Plymouth Argyle, 1947–53) 12
Showers D (Cardiff, 1975) 2
Sidlow C (Liverpool, 1947–50) 7
Slatter N (Bristol Rov, Oxford Utd, 1983–89) 22
Smallman D (Wrexham, Everton, 1974–6) 7
Smith M (Manchester City, MK Dons, 2018–22) 18
Southall N (Everton, 1982–97) 92
Speed G (Leeds, Everton, Newcastle, 1990–2004) 85
Sprake G (Leeds, Birmingham, 1964–75) 37
Stansfield F (Cardiff, 1949) 1
Stevenson B (Leeds, Birmingham, 1978–82) 15
Stevenson N (Swansea, 1982–83) 4
Stitfall R (Cardiff, 1953–57) 2
Stock B (Doncaster, 2010–11) 3
Sullivan D (Cardiff, 1953–60) 17
Symons K (Portsmouth, Manchester City, Fulham, Crystal Palace, 1992–2004) 37

Tapscott D (Arsenal, Cardiff, 1954–59) 14
Taylor G (Crystal Palace, Sheffield Utd, Burnley, Nottm Forest, 1996–2005) 15
Taylor J (Reading, 2015) 1
Taylor N (Wrexham, Swansea, Aston Villa, 2010–20) 43
Thatcher B (Leicester, Manchester City, 2004–05) 7
Thomas D (Swansea, 1957–58) 2
Thomas G (Leicester, 2018–19) 3
Thomas M (Wrexham, Manchester Utd, Everton, Brighton, Stoke, Chelsea, WBA, 1977–86) 51
Thomas M (Newcastle, 1987) 1
Thomas R (Swindon, Derby, Cardiff, 1967–78) 50
Thomas S (Huddersfield, 2022) 5
Thomas S (Fulham, 1948–49) 4
Toshack J (Cardiff, Liverpool, Swansea, 1969–80) 40
Trollope P (Derby, Fulham, Northampton, 1997–2003) 9
Tudur Jones O (Swansea, Norwich, Hibernian, 2008–14) 7

Van den Hauwe P (Everton, 1985–89) 13

Vaughan D (Crewe, Real Sociedad, Blackpool, Sunderland, Nottm Forest, 20013–16) 42
Vaughan N (Newport, Cardiff, 1983–85) 10
Vaulks W (Rotherham, Cardiff, 2019–22) 7
Vearncombe G (Cardiff, 1958–61) 2
Vernon R (Blackburn, Everton, Stoke, 1957–68) 32
Villars A (Cardiff, 1974) 3
Vokes S (Wolves, Burnley, Stoke, 2008–20) 64

Walley T (Watford, 1971) 1
Walsh I (Crystal Palace, 1980–82) 18
Ward D (Bristol Rov, Cardiff, 1959–62) 2
Ward D (Notts Co, Nottm Forest, 2000–04) 5
Ward D (Liverpool, Leicester, 2016–22) 26
Watkins M (Norwich, 2018) 2
Webster C (Manchester Utd, 1957–58) 4
Weston R (Arsenal, Cardiff, 2000–05) 7
Williams A (Stockport, Swansea, Everton, 2008–19) 86
Williams A (Reading, Wolves, Reading, 1994–2003) 13
Williams A (Southampton, 1997–98) 2
Williams D (Norwich, 1986–87) 5
Williams G (Cardiff, 1951) 1
Williams G (Derby, Ipswich, 1988–96) 13
Williams G (West Ham, 2006) 2
Williams G (Fulham, 2014–16) 7
Williams GE (WBA, 1960–69) 26
Williams GG (Swansea, 1961–62) 5
Williams HJ (Swansea, 1965–72) 3
Williams HT (Newport, Leeds, 1949–50) 4
Williams J (Crystal Palace, Charlton, Swindon, 2013–22) 33
Williams N (Liverpool, 2021–22) 21
Williams S (WBA, Southampton, 1954–66) 43
Wilson H (Liverpool, Fulham, 2014–21) 39
Wilson J (Bristol City, 2014) 1
Witcomb D (WBA, Sheffield Wed, 1947) 3
Woosnam P (Leyton Orient, West Ham, Aston Villa, 1959–63) 17
Woodburn B (Liverpool, 2018–22) 11

Yorath T (Leeds, Coventry, Tottenham, Vancouver Whitecaps 1970–81) 59
Young E (Wimbledon, Crystal Palace, Wolves, 1990–96) 21

NORTHERN IRELAND

Aherne T (Belfast Celtic, Luton, 1947–50) 4
Anderson T (Manchester Utd, Swindon, Peterborough, 1973–79) 22
Armstrong G (Tottenham, Watford, Real Mallorca, WBA, 1977–86) 63

Baird C (Southampton, Fulham, Burnley, WBA, Derby, 2003–16) 79
Ballard D (Arsenal, 2021–22) 16
Barr H (Linfield, Coventry, 1962–63) 3
Barton A (Preston, 2011) 1
Best G (Manchester Utd, Fulham, 1964–77) 37

Finney T (Sunderland, Cambridge Utd, 1975–80) 14

Flanagan T (Burton, Sunderland, Shrewsbury, 2017–22) 13

Fleming G (Nottm Forest, Manchester City, Barnsley, 1987–95) 31

Forde J (Ards, 1959–61) 4

Galbraith E (Manchester Utd, 2020–21) 2

Gallogly C (Huddersfield, 1951) 2

Garrett R (Stoke, Linfield, 2009–11) 5

Gaston R (Coleraine, 1969) 1

Gault M (Linfield, 2008) 1

Gillespie K (Manchester Utd, Newcastle, Blackburn, Leicester, Sheffield Utd, 1995–2009) 86

Gorman J (Wolves, 2010–12) 9

Gorman W (Brentford, 1947–48) 4

Graham W (Doncaster, 1951–99) 14

Gray P (Luton, Sunderland, Nancy, Burnley, Oxford Utd, 1993–2001) 25

Gregg H (Doncaster, Manchester Utd 1954–64) 25

Griffin D (St Johnstone, Dundee Utd, Stockport, 1996–2004) 29

Grigg W (Walsall, Brentford, Wigan, 2012–19) 10

Hamill R (Glentoran, 1999) 1

Hamilton B (Linfield, Ipswich, Everton, Millwall, Swindon, 1969–80) 50

Hamilton G (Glentoran, Portadown, 2003–08) 5

Hamilton W (QPR, Burnley, Oxford Utd, 1978–86) 41

Harkin J (Southport, Shrewsbury,1968–70) 5

Harvey M (Sunderland, 1961–71) 34

Hatton S (Linfield, 1963) 2

Hazard C (Celtic 2018–22) 4

Healy D (Manchester Utd, Preston, Leeds, Fulham, Sunderland, Rangers, Bury, 2000–13) 95

Healy F (Coleraine, Glentoran, 1982–83) 4

Hegan D (WBA, Wolves, 1970–73) 7

Hill C (Sheffield Utd, Leicester, Trelleborg, Northampton, 1990–99) 27

Hill J (Norwich, Everton, 1959–64) 7

Hinton E (Fulham, Millwall, 1947–51) 7

Hodson L (Watford, MK Dons, Rangers, 2011–18) 24

Holmes S (Wrexham, 2002) 1

Horlock K (Swindon, Manchester City, 1995–2003) 32

Hughes A (Newcastle, Aston Villa, Fulham, QPR, Brighton, Melbourne, Hearts, 1997–2018) 112

Hughes J (Lincoln, 2006) 2

Hughes M (Oldham, 2006) 2

Hughes M (Manchester City, Strasbourg, West Ham, Wimbledon, Crystal Palace, 1992–2005) 71

Hughes P (Bury, 1987) 3

Hughes W (Bolton, 1951) 1

Hume T (Sunderland, 2022) 1

Humphries W (Ards, Coventry, Swansea, 1962–65)14

Hunter A (Blackburn, Ipswich, 1970–80) 53

Hunter B (Wrexham, Reading, 1995–2000) 15

Hunter V (Coleraine, 1962) 2

Ingham M (Sunderland, Wrexham, 2005–07) 3

Irvine R (Linfield, Stoke, 1962–5) 8

Irvine W (Burnley, Preston, Brighton, 1963–72) 23

Jackson T (Everton, Nottm Forest, Manchester Utd, 1969–77) 35

Jamison J (Glentoran, 1976) 1

Jenkins I (Chester, Dundee Utd, 1997–2000) 6

Jennings P (Watford, Tottenham, Arsenal, Tottenham, 1964–86) 119

Johnson D (Blackburn, Birmingham, 1999–2010) 56

Johnston W (Glenavon, Oldham, 1962–66) 2

Jones J (Glenavon, 1956–57) 3

Jones J (Kilmarnock, Rangers, Wigan, 2018–22) 18

Jones S (Crewe, Burnley, 2003–08) 29

Keane T (Swansea, 1949) 1

Kee P (Oxford Utd, Ards, 1990–95) 9

Keith R (Newcastle, 1958–62) 23

Kelly H (Fulham, Southampton, 1950–51) 4

Kelly P (Barnsley, 1950) 1

Kennedy M (Aberdeen, 2021) 3

Kennedy P (Watford, Wigan, 1999–2004) 20

Kirk A (Hearts, Boston, Northampton, Dunfermline, 2000–10) 11

Lafferty D (Burnley, 2012–16) 13

Lafferty K (Burnley, Rangers, Sion, Palermo, Norwich, Hearts, Rangers, Sunderland, Sarpsborg, Reggina, Kilmarnock, 2006–22) 89

Lane P (Fleetwood, 2022) 3

Lavery S (Everton, Linfield, Blackpool 2018–22) 15

Lawrie J (Port Vale, 2009–10) 3

Lawther W (Sunderland, Blackburn, 1960–62) 4

Lennon N (Crewe, Leicester, Celtic, 1994–2002) 40

Lewis J (Norwich, Newcastle, 2018–22) 26

Little A (Rangers, 2009–13) 9

Lockhart N (Linfield, Coventry, Aston Villa, 1947–56) 8

Lomas S (Manchester City, West Ham, 1994–2003) 45

Lund M (Rochdale, 2017) 3

Lutton B (Wolves, West Ham, 1970–4) 6

Magennis J (Cardiff, Aberdeen, Kilmarnock, Charlton, Bolton, Hull, Wigan, 2010–22) 67

Magill E (Arsenal, Brighton, 1962–66) 26

Magilton J (Oxford Utd, Southampton, Sheffield Wed, Ipswich, 1991–2002) 52

Mannus A (Linfield, St Johnstone, 2004–17) 9

Martin C (Glentoran, Leeds, Aston Villa, 1947–50) 6

McAdams W (Manchester City, Bolton, Leeds, 1954–62) 15

*McAlinden J (Portsmouth, Southend, 1947–49) 2

McArdle R (Rochdale, Aberdeen, Bradford, 2010–14) 7

McAuley G (Lincoln, Leicester, Ipswich, WBA, Rangers, 2010–19) 80
McBride S (Glenavon, 1991–92) 4
McCabe J (Leeds, 1949–54) 6
McCalmont A (Leeds, 2020–22) 4
McCann A (St Johnstone, Preston, 2021–22) 14
McCann G (West Ham, Cheltenham, Barnsley, Scunthorpe, Peterborough, 2002–12) 39
McCartan S (Accrington, Bradford, 2017–18) 2
McCarthy J (Port Vale, Birmingham, 1996–2001) 18
McCartney G (Sunderland, West Ham) Sunderland 2002–10) 34
McCavana T (Coleraine, 1954–55) 3
McCleary J (Cliftonville, 1955) 1
McClelland J (Arsenal, Fulham, 1961–67) 6
McClelland J (Mansfield, Rangers, Watford, Leeds, 1980–90) 53
McClelland S (Chelsea, 2021) 1
McCourt F (Manchester City, 1952–53) 6
McCourt P (Rochdale, Celtic, Barnsley, Brighton, Luton, 2002–16) 18
McCoy R (Coleraine, 1987) 1
McCreery D (Manchester Utd, QPR, Tulsa, Newcastle, 1976–90) 67
McCrory S (Southend, 1958) 1
McCullough L (Doncaster, 2014–18) 1
McCullough W (Arsenal, Millwall,1961–67) 10
McCurdy C (Linfield, 1980) 1
McDonald A (QPR, 1986–96) 52
McElhinney G (Bolton, 1984–85) 6
McEvilly L (Rochdale, 2002) 1
McFaul W (Linfield, Newcastle, 1967–74) 6
McGarry J (Cliftonville, 1951) 3
McGaughey M (Linfield, 1985) 1
McGibbon P (Manchester Utd, Wigan, 1995–2000) 7
McGinn N (Derry, Celtic, Aberdeen, Dundee, 2009–22) 73
McGivern R (Manchester City, Hibernian, Port Vale, Shrewsbury, 2009–17) 24
McGovern M (Ross Co, Hamilton, Norwich, 2010–21) 33
McGrath C (Tottenham, Manchester Utd 1974–79) 21
McIlroy J (Burnley, Stoke, 1952–66) 55
McIlroy S (Manchester Utd, Stoke, Manchester City, 1972–87) 88
McKay W (Inverness, Wigan, 2013–16) 11
McKeag W (Glentoran, 1968) 2
McKenna J (Huddersfield, 1950–52) 7
McKenzie R (Airdrie, 1967) 1
McKinney W (Falkirk, 1966) 1
McKnight A (Celtic, West Ham, 1988–89) 10
McLaughlin C (Preston, Fleetwood, Millwall, Sunderland, 2012–21) 43
McLaughlin J (Shrewsbury, Swansea, 1962–66) 12
McLaughlin R (Liverpool, Oldham, 2014–18) 5
McLean B (Motherwell, 2006) 1
McMahon G (Tottenham, Stoke, 1995–98) 17
McMenamin C (Glentoran, 2022) 3

McMichael A (Newcastle, 1950–60) 40
McMillan S (Manchester Utd, 1963) 2
McMordie A (Middlesbrough, 1969–73) 21
McMorran E (Belfast Celtic, Barnsley, Doncaster, 1947–57) 15
McNair P (Manchester Utd, Sunderland, Middlesbrough), 2015–22) 56
McNally B (Shrewsbury, 1987–88) 5
McPake J (Coventry, 2012) 1
McParland P (Aston Villa, Wolves, 1954–62) 34
McQuoid J (Millwall, 2011–12) 5
McVeigh P (Tottenham, Norwich, 1999–2005) 20
Montgomery F (Coleraine, 1955) 1
Moore C (Glentoran, 1949) 1
Moreland V (Derby, 1979–80) 6
Morgan S (Port Vale, Aston Villa, Brighton, Sparta Rotterdam, 1972–99) 18
Morrow S (Arsenal, QPR, 1990–2000) 39
Mulgrew J (Linfield, 2010) 2
Mullan G (Glentoran, 1983) 4
Mulryne P (Manchester Utd, Norwich, 1997–2005) 27
Murdock C (Preston, Hibernian, Crewe, Rotherham, 2000–06) 34

Napier R (Bolton, 1966) 1
Neill T (Arsenal, Hull, 1961–73) 59
Nelson S (Arsenal, Brighton, 1970–82) 51
Nicholl C (Aston Villa, Southampton, Grimsby, 1975–83) 51
Nicholl J (Manchester Utd, Toronto, Sunderland, Rangers, WBA, 1976–86) 73
Nicholson J (Manchester Utd, Huddersfield, 1961–72) 41
Nolan I (Sheffield Wed, Bradford City, Wigan, 1997–2002) 18
Norwood O (Manchester Utd, Huddersfield, Reading, Brighton, Sheffield Utd, 2011–19) 57

O'Boyle G (Dunfermline, St Johnstone, 1994–99) 13
O'Connor M (Crewe, Scunthorpe, Rotherham, 2008–14) 11
O'Doherty A (Coleraine, 1970) 2
O'Driscoll J (Swansea, 1949) 3
O'Kane W (Nottm Forest, 1970–75) 20
O'Neill C (Motherwell, 1989–91) 3
O'Neill J (Sunderland, 1962) 1
O'Neill J (Leicester, 1980–86) 39
O'Neill M (Distillery, Nottm Forest, Norwich, Manchester City, Notts Co, 1972–85) 64
O'Neill M (Newcastle, Dundee Utd, Hibernian, Coventry, 1989–97) 31
Owens J (Crusaders, 2011) 1

Parke J (Linfield, Hibernian, Sunderland, 1964–68) 14
Paterson M (Scunthorpe, Burnley, Huddersfield, 2008–14) 22
Paton P (Dundee Utd, St Johnstone, 2014–17) 4
Patterson D (Crystal Palace, Luton, Dundee Utd, 1994–99) 17

Patterson R (Coleraine, Plymouth, 2010–11) 5
Peacock R (Celtic, Coleraine, 1952–62) 31
Peacock–Farrell B (Leeds, Burnley, 2018–22) 33
Penney S (Brighton, 1985–89) 17
Platt J (Middlesbrough, Ballymena, Coleraine, 1976–86) 23
Quinn J (Blackburn, Swindon, Leicester, Bradford City, West Ham, Bournemouth, Reading, 1985–96) 46
Quinn SJ (Blackpool, WBA, Willem 11, Sheffield Wed, Peterborough, Northampton, 1996–2007) 50

Rafferty P (Linfield, 1979) 1
Ramsey P (Leicester, 1984–89) 14
Reeves B (MK Dons, 2015) 2
Rice P (Arsenal, 1969–80) 49
Robinson S (Bournemouth, Luton, 1997–2008) 7
Rogan A (Celtic, Sunderland, Millwall, 1988–97) 18
Ross W (Newcastle, 1969) 1
Rowland K (West Ham, QPR, 1994–99) 19
Russell A (Linfield, 1947) 1
Ryan R (WBA, 1950) 1

Sanchez L (Wimbledon, 1987–89) 3
Saville G (Millwall, Middlesbrough, Millwall, 2018–22) 40
Scott J (Grimsby, 1958) 2
Scott P (Everton, York, Aldershot, 1976–79) 10
Sharkey P (Ipswich, 1976) 1
Shea C (Manchester City, 2022) 4
Shields J (Southampton, 1957) 1
Shiels D (Hibernian, Doncaster, Kilmarnock, Rangers, 2006–13) 14
Simpson W (Rangers, 1951–59) 12
Sloan D (Oxford Utd, 1969–71) 2
Sloan J (Arsenal, 1947) 1
Sloan T (Manchester Utd, 1979) 3
Smith A (Glentoran, Preston, 2003–05) 18
Smith M (Peterborough, Hearts, 2016–22) 19
Smyth P (QPR, 2018–21) 3
Smyth S (Wolves, Stoke, 1948–52) 9
Smyth W (Distillery, 1949–54) 4
Sonner D (Ipswich, Sheffield Wed, Birmingham, Nottm Forest, Peterborough, 1997–2005) 13
Southwood L (Reading, 2022) 1
Spence D (Bury, Blackpool, Southend, 1975–82) 29
Spencer B (Huddersfield, 2022) 3
Sproule I (Hibernian, 2006–08) 11
*Stevenson A (Everton, 1947–48) 3
Steele J (New York Bulls, 2014) 3
Stewart A (Glentoran, Derby, 1967–69) 7
Stewart D (Hull, 1978) 1
Stewart I (QPR, Newcastle, 1982–87) 31
Stewart T (Linfield, 1961) 1
Taggart G (Barnsley, Bolton, Leicester, 1990–2003) 51
Taylor D (Nottm Forest, 2022) 1

Taylor M (Fulham, Birmingham, 1999–2012) 88
Thompson A (Watford, 2011) 2
Thompson J (Rangers, Blackpool, Stoke, 2018–22) 24
Thompson P (Linfield, 2006–08) 8
Todd S (Burnley, Sheffield Wed, 1966–71) 11
Toner C (Leyton Orient, 2003) 2
Trainor D (Crusaders, 1967) 1
Tuffey J (Partick, Inverness, 2009–11) 8
Tully C (Celtic, 1949–59) 10

Uprichard W (Swindon, Portsmouth, 1952–59) 18

Vassell K (Rotherham, 2019) 2
Vernon J (Belfast Celtic, WBA, 1947–52) 17

Walker J (Doncaster, 1955) 1
Walsh D (WBA, 1947–50) 9
Walsh W (Manchester City, 1948–49) 5
Ward J (Derby, Nottm Forest, 2012–19) 35
Washington C (QPR, Shefield, Hearts, Charlton, 2016–22) 35
Watson P (Distillery, 1971) 1
Webb S (Ross Co, 2006–07) 4
Welsh E (Carlisle, 1966–67) 4
Whiteside N (Manchester Utd, Everton, 1982–90) 38
Whitley Jeff (Manchester City, Sunderland, Cardiff, 1997–2006) 20
Whitley Jim (Manchester City, 1998–2000) 3
Williams M (Chesterfield, Watford, Wimbledon, Stoke, Wimbledon, MK Dons, 1999–2005) 36
Whyte G (Oxford, Cardiff, 2019–22) 27
Williams M (Chesterfield, Watford Wimbledon, Stoke, Wimbledon MK Dons 1999–2005) 36
Williams P (WBA, 1991) 1
Wilson D (Brighton, Luton, Sheffield Wed, 1987–92) 24
Wilson K (Ipswich, Chelsea, Notts Co, Walsall, 1987–95) 42
Wilson S (Glenavon, Falkirk, Dundee, 1962–68) 12
Winchester C (Oldham, 2011) 1
Wood T (Walsall, 1996) 1
Worthington N (Sheffield Wed, Leeds, Stoke, 1984–97) 66
Wright T (Newcastle, Nottm Forest, Reading, Manchester City, 1989–2000) 31

REPUBLIC OF IRELAND

Aherne T (Belfast Celtic, Luton, 1946–54) 16
Aldridge J (Oxford Utd, Liverpool, Real Sociedad, Tranmere, 1986–97) 69
Ambrose P (Shamrock R, 1955–64) 5
Anderson J (Preston, Newcastle, 1980–89) 16
Andrews K (Blackburn, WBA, 2009–13) 35
Arter H (Bournemouth, Nottm Forest, 2015–22) 19
Babb P (Coventry, Liverpool, Sunderland, 1994–2003) 35

300

Duffy B (Shamrock R, 1950) 1
Duffy S (Everton, Blackburn, Brighton, 2014–22) 55
Dunne A (Manchester Utd, Bolton,1962–76) 33
Dunne J (Fulham, 1971) 1
Dunne P (Manchester Utd, 1965–67) 5
Dunne R (Everton, Manchester City, Aston Villa, 2000–14) 80
Dunne S (Luton, 1953–60) 15
Dunne T (St Patrick's, 1956–57) 3
Dunning P (Shelbourne, 1971) 2
Dunphy E (York, Millwall, 1966–71) 23
Dwyer N (West Ham, Swansea, 1960–65) 14

Eccles P (Shamrock R, 1986) 1
Egan J (Brentford, Sheffield Utd, 2017–22) 26
Eglington T (Shamrock R, Everton, 1946–56) 24
Elliot R (Newcastle, 2014–16) 1
Elliott S (Sunderland, 2005–07) 9
Evans M (Southampton, 1997) 1

Fagan E (Shamrock R, 1973) 1
Fagan F (Manchester City, Derby, 1955–61) 8
Fahey K (Birmingham, 2010–13) 16
Fairclough M (Dundalk, 1982) 1
Fallon S (Celtic, 1951–55) 8
Farrell P (Shamrock R, Everton, 1946–57) 28
Farrelly G (Aston Villa, Everton, Bolton, 1996–2000) 6
Finnan S (Fulham, Liverpool, Espanyol 2000–09) 53
Finucane A (Limerick, 1967–72) 11
Fitzgerald F (Waterford, 1955–6) 2
Fitzgerald P (Leeds, 1961–2) 5
Fitzpatrick K (Limerick, 1970) 1
Fitzsimons A (Middlesbrough, Lincoln, 1950–59) 26
Fleming C (Middlesbrough, 1996–8) 10
Fogarty A (Sunderland, Hartlepool Utd, 1960–64) 11
Folan C (Hull, 2009–10) 7
Foley D (Watford, 2000–01) 6
Foley K (Wolves, 2009–11) 8
Foley T (Northampton, 1964–67) 9
Fullam J (Preston, Shamrock R, 1961–70) 11
Forde D (Millwall, 2011–16) 24
Fullam J (Preston, Shamrock, 1961–70) 11

Gallagher C (Celtic, 1967) 2
Gallagher M (Hibernian, 1954) 1
Galvin A (Tottenham, Sheffield Wed, Swindon, 1983–90) 29
Gamble J (Cork City, 2007) 1
Gannon E (Notts Co, Sheffield Wed, Shelbourne, 1949–55) 14
Gannon M (Shelbourne, 1972) 1
Gavin J (Norwich, Tottenham, Norwich, 1950–57) 7
Gibbons A (St Patrick's Ath, 1952–56) 4
Gibson D (Manchester Utd, Everton, 2008–16) 27
Gilbert R (Shamrock R, 1966) 1

Giles C (Doncaster, 1951) 1
Giles J (Manchester Utd, Leeds, WBA, Shamrock R, 1960–79) 59
Given S (Blackburn, Newcastle, Manchester City, Aston Villa, Stoke, 1996–2016) 134
Givens D (Manchester Utd, Luton, QPR, Birmingham, Neuchatel, 1969–82) 56
Gleeson S (Wolves, Birmingham, 2007–17) 4
Glynn D (Drumcondra, 1952–55) 2
Godwin T (Shamrock R, Leicester, Bournemouth, 1949–58) 13
Goodman J (Wimbledon, 1997) 4
Goodwin J (Stockport, 2003) 1
*Gorman W (Brentford, 1947) 2
Grealish A (Orient Luton, Brighton, WBA, 1976–86) 45
Green P (Derby, Leeds, 2010–14) 22
Gregg E (Bohemians, 1978–80) 8
Grimes A (Manchester Utd, Coventry, Luton, 1978–88) 18

Hale A (Aston Villa, Doncaster, Waterford, 1962–72) 14
Hamilton CJ (Blackpool, 2022) 1
Hamilton T (Shamrock R, 1959) 2
Hand E (Portsmouth, 1969–76) 20
Harte I (Leeds, Levante, 1996–2007) 64
Hartnett J (Middlesbrough, 1949–54) 2
Haverty J (Arsenal, Blackburn, Millwall, Celtic, Bristol Rov, Shelbourne, 1956–67) 32
Hayes A (Southampton, 1979) 1
Hayes J (Aberdeen, 2016–17) 4
*Hayes W (Huddersfield, 1947) 2
Hayes W (Limerick, 1949) 1
Healey R (Cardiff, 1977–80) 2
Healy C (Celtic, Sunderland, 2002–04) 13
Heighway S (Liverpool, Minnesota, 1971–82) 34
Henderson B (Drumcondra, 1948) 2
Henderson W (Brighton, Preston, 2006–08) 6
Hendrick J (Derby, Burnley, Newcastle, 2013–22) 74
Hennessy J (Shelbourne, St Patrick's Ath, 1956–69) 5
Herrick J (Cork Hibernian, Shamrock R, 1972–73) 3
Higgins J (Birmingham, 1951) 1
Hogan S (Aston Villa, Birmingham, 2018–22) 11
Holland M (Ipswich, Charlton, 2000–06) 49
Holmes J (Coventry, Tottenham, Vancouver W'caps, 1971–81) 30
Hoolahan W (Blackpool, Norwich, 2008–18) 43
Horgan D (Preston, Hibernian, Wycombe, 2017–22) 17
Houghton R (Oxford Utd, Liverpool, Aston Villa, Crystal Palace, Reading, 1986–97) 73
Hourihane C (Aston Villa, 2017–22) 35
Howlett G (Brighton, 1984) 1
Hughton C (Tottenham, West Ham, 1980–92) 53
Hunt N (Reading, 2009) 2
Hunt S (Reading, Hull, Wolves, 2007–12) 39

Hurley C (Millwall, Sunderland, Bolton, 1957–69) 40

Idah A (Norwich, 2020–22) 13
Ireland S (Manchester City, 2006–08) 6
Irwin D (Manchester Utd, 1991–2000) 56

Judge A (Brentford, Ipswich, 2016–20) 9

Kavanagh G (Stoke, Cardiff, Wigan, 1998–2007) 16
Keane, R (Wolves, Coventry, Inter Milan, Leeds Tottenham, Liverpool, LA Galaxy, 1998–2017) 146
Keane R (Nottm Forest, Manchester Utd, 1991–2006) 67
Keane T (Swansea, 1949) 4
Keane W (Wigan, 2022) 4
Kearin M (Shamrock R, 1972) 1
Kearns F (West Ham, 1954) 1
Kearns M (Oxford Utd, Walsall, Wolves, 1970–80) 18
Kelleher C (Liverpool, 2021–22) 8
Kelly A (Sheffield Utd, Blackburn, 1993–2002) 34
Kelly D (Walsall, West Ham, Leicester, Newcastle, Wolves, Sunderland, Tranmere, 1988–98) 26
Kelly G (Leeds, 1994–2003) 52
Kelly JA (Drumcondra, Preston, 1957–73) 47
Kelly M (Portsmouth, 1988–91) 4
Kelly N (Nottm Forest, 1954) 1
Kelly P (Wolves, 1961–62) 5
Kelly S (Tottenham, Birmingham, Fulham, Reading, 2006–14) 39
Kenna J (Blackburn, 1995–2000) 27
Kennedy M (Portsmouth, 1986) 2
Kennedy M (Liverpool, Wimbledon, Manchester City, Wolves, 1996–2004) 35
Kenny P (Sheffield Utd, 2004–07) 7
Keogh A (Wolves, Millwall, 2007–14) 30
Keogh J (Shamrock R, 1966) 1
Keogh R (Derby, 2013–20) 26
Keogh S (Shamrock R, 1959) 1
Kernaghan A (Middlesbrough, Manchester City, 1993–96) 22
Kiely D (Charlton, WBA, 2000–09) 11
Kiernan F (Shamrock R, Southampton, 1951–2) 5
Kilbane K (WBA, Sunderland, Everton, Wigan, Hull, 1997–2011) 110
Kinnear J (Tottenham, Brighton, 1967–76) 26
Kinsella M (Charlton, Aston Villa, WBA, 1998–2004) 48
Knight J (Derby 2021–22) 15

Langan D (Derby, Birmingham, Oxford Utd, 1978–88) 26
Lapira J (Notre Dame, 2007) 1
Lawler R (Fulham, 1953–56) 8
Lawlor J (Drumcondra, Doncaster, 1949–51) 3
Lawlor M (Shamrock R, 1971–73) 5

Lawrence L (Stoke, Portsmouth, 2009–11) 15
Lawrenson M (Preston, Brighton, Liverpool, 1977–88) 39
Lee A (Rotherham, Cardiff, Ipswich, 2003–07) 10
Leech M (Shamrock R, 1969–73) 8
Lenihan D (Blackburn, 2018–22) 3
Long K (Burnley, 2017–21) 17
Long S (Reading, WBA, Hull, Southampton, 2007–21) 88
Lowry D (St Patrick's Ath, 1962) 1

McAlinden J (Portsmouth, 1946) 2
McAteer J (Bolton, Liverpool, Blackburn, Sunderland, 1994–2004) 52
McCann J (Shamrock R, 1957) 1
McCarthy J (Wigan, Everton, Crystal Palace, 2011–21) 43
McCarthy M (Manchester City, Celtic, Lyon, Millwall, 1984–92) 57
McClean J (Sunderland, Wigan, WBA, Stoke, Wigan, 2012–22) 94
McConville T (Dundalk, Waterford, 1972–73) 6
McDonagh J (Everton, Bolton, Sunderland, Notts Co, 1981–86) 25
McDonagh J (Shamrock R, 1984–85) 3
McEvoy A (Blackburn, 1961–67) 17
McGeady A (Celtic, Spartak Moscow, Everton, Sunderland, 2004–18) 93
McGee P (QPR, Preston, 1978–81) 15
McGoldrick E (Crystal Palace, Arsenal, 1992–95) 15
McGoldrick D (Ipswich, Sheffield Utd, 2015–21) 14
McGowan D (West Ham, 1949) 3
McGowan J (Cork Utd, 1947) 1
McGrath J (St Mirren, Wigan, 2021–22) 6
McGrath M (Blackburn, Bradford PA, 1958–66) 22
McGrath P (Manchester Utd, Aston Villa, Derby, 1985–97) 83
Macken J (Manchester City, 2005) 1
Mackey G (Shamrock R, 1957) 3
McLoughlin A (Swindon, Southampton, Portsmouth, 1990–2000) 42
McMillan W (Belfast Celtic, 1946) 2
McNally B (Luton, 1959–63) 3
McPhail S (Leeds, 2000–04) 10
McShane P (WBA, Sunderland, Hull, Reading, 2006–16) 33
Macken A (Derby, 1977) 1
Madden P (Yeovil, 2014) 1
Maguire S (Preston, 2018–21) 11
Mahon A (Tranmere, 2000) 2
Malone G (Shelbourne, 1949) 1
Mancini T (QPR, Arsenal, 1974–75) 5
Manning R (QPR, Swansea, 2021–22) 6
Martin C (Glentoran, Leeds, Aston Villa, 1946–56) 30
Martin M (Bohemians, Manchester Utd, 1972–83) 52
Maybury, A (Leeds, Hearts, Leicester, 1998–2005) 10
Meagan M (Everton, Huddersfield, Drogheda, 1961–70) 17
Meyler D (Sunderland, Hull, 2013–19) 26

Sheedy K (Everton, Newcastle, 1984–93)	46	Treacy R (WBA, Charlton, Swindon, Preston, Shamrock R, 1966–80)	42
Sheridan C (Celtic, CSKA Sofia, 2010–11)	3	Tuohy L (Shamrock R, Newcastle, Shamrock R, 1956–65)	8
Sheridan J (Leeds, Sheffield Wed, 1988–96)	34	Turner A (Celtic, 1963)	2
Slaven B (Middlesbrough, 1990–93)	7		
Sloan P (Arsenal, 1946)	2	Vernon J (Belfast Celtic, 1946)	2
Smyth M (Shamrock R, 1969)	1		
St Ledger S (Preston, Leicester, 2009–14)	37	Waddock G (QPR, Millwall, 1980–90)	21
Stapleton F (Arsenal, Manchester Utd, Ajax, Derby, Le Havre, Blackburn, 1977–90)	71	Walsh D (WBA, Aston Villa, 1946–54)	20
		Walsh J (Limerick, 1982)	1
Staunton S (Liverpool, Aston Villa, Liverpool, Crystal Palace, Aston Villa, 1989–2002)	102	Walsh M (Blackpool, Everton, QPR, Porto, 1976–85)	21
Stevens E (Sheffield Utd, 2018–22)	25	Walsh M (Everton, Norwich, 1982–83)	4
*Stevenson A (Everton, 1947–49)	6	Walsh W (Manchester City, 1947–50)	9
Stokes A (Sunderland, Celtic, 2007–15)	9	Walters J (Stoke, Burnley, 2011–19)	54
Strahan F (Shelbourne, 1964–65)	5	Ward S (Wolves, Burnley, 2011–19)	50
Swan M (Drumcondra, 1960)	1	Waters J (Grimsby, 1977–80)	2
Synnott N (Shamrock R, 1978–79)	3	Westwood K (Coventry, Sunderland, Sheffield Wed, 2009–17)	21
Taylor T (Waterford, 1959)	1	Whelan G (Stoke, Aston Villa, 2009–20)	91
Thomas P (Waterford, 1974)	2	Whelan R (St Patrick's Ath, 1964)	2
Thompson J (Nottm Forest, 2004)	1	Whelan R (Liverpool, Southend, 1981–95)	53
Townsend A (Norwich, Chelsea, Aston Villa, Middlesbrough, 1989–97)	70	Whelan L (Manchester Utd, 1956–57)	4
		Whittaker R (Chelsea, 1959)	1
Traynor T.(Southampton, 1954–64)	8	Williams D (Blackburn, 2018)	3
Travers M (Bournemouth, 2020–21)	3	Williams S (Millwall, 2018–19)	3
Treacy K (Preston, Burnley 2011–12)	6	Wilson M (Stoke, Bournemouth, 2011–17)	25

INTERNATIONAL GOALSCORERS 1946–2022

(start of season 2022–2023)

ENGLAND

Rooney	53	Woodcock	16	Hoddle	8
Kane	50	Welbeck	16	Kevan	8
Charlton R	49	Scholes	14	Sturridge	8
Lineker	48	Chivers	13	Walcott	8
Greaves	44	Mariner	13	Anderson	7
Owen	40	Smith R	13	Connelly	7
Finney	30	Francis T	12	Coppell	7
Lofthouse	30	Rashford	12	Fowler	7
Shearer	30	Barnes J	11	Heskey	7
Lampard Frank jnr	29	Douglas	11	Maguire	7
Platt	27	Mannion	11	Oxlade-Chamberlain	7
Robson B	26	Sheringham	11	Paine	7
Hurst	24	Clarke A	10	Vardy	7
Mortensen	23	Cole J	10	Young A	7
Crouch	22	Flowers R	10	Barkley	6
Channon	21	Gascoigne	10	Charlton J	6
Gerrard	21	Lee F	10	Lingard	6
Keegan	21	Milburn	10	Macdonald	6
Defoe	20	Wilshaw	10	Mullen	6
Peters	20	Beardsley	9	Rowley	6
Sterling	19	Bell	9	Terry	6
Haynes	18	Bentley	9	Vassell	6
Hunt R	18	Hateley	9	Waddle	6
Beckham	17	Wright I	9	Wright-Phillips S	6
Lawton	16	Ball	8	Adams	5
Taylor T	16	Broadis	8	Atyeo	5
		Byrne J	8	Baily	5

SCOTLAND

WALES

N IRELAND

Healy 36
Lafferty K 20
Clarke............................13
Davis..............................13
Armstrong 12
Dowie 12
Quinn JM 12
Bingham 10
Crossan J 10
McIlroy J 10
McParland 10
Best 9
Magennis 9
McAuley 9
Whiteside 9
Dougan 8
Irvine W 8
O'Neill M (1972–85) 8
McAdams 7
Taggart G 7
Wilson S 7
Gray 6
McLaughlin 6
McNair 6
Nicholson J 6
Washington 6
Wilson K 6
Cush 5
Evans J............................5
Feeney (2002–9)) 5
Hamilton W 5
Hughes M 5
Magilton 5
McIlroy S 5
Simpson 5
Smyth S 5
Walsh D 5
Anderson T 4
Elliott 4
Hamilton B 4
McCann G 4
McGinn 4
McGrath 4
McMorran 4
O'Neill M (1989–96) 4
Quinn SJ 4
Ward 4
Whyte 4
Brotherston 3
Brunt...............................3
Dallas..............................3
Harvey M 3
Lockhart...........................3
Lomas 3
McDonald 3
McMordie 3
Morgan S 3
Mulryne 3

Nicholl C 3
Paterson 3
Spence D 3
Tully 3
Whitley (1997–2006) 3
Ballard 2
Blanchflower D 2
Boyce 2
Casey 2
Cathcart...........................2
Clements 2
Doherty P 2
Evans C 2
Ferguson S 2
Finney 2
Gillespie 2
Grigg 2
Harkin 2
Lavery 2
Lennon 2
McCourt 2
McMahon 2
Neill W 2
O'Neill J 2
Peacock 2
Penney 2
Stewart I 2
Barr 1
Black 1
Blanchflower J 1
Brennan 1
Campbell W 1
Caskey 1
Cassidy 1
Cochrane T 1
Crossan E 1
D'Arcy 1
Doherty L 1
Elder 1
Ferguson W 1
Ferris 1
Griffin 1
Hill C 1
Hughes 1
Humphries 1
Hunter A 1
Hunter B 1
Johnston..........................1
Jones J 1
Jones, S...........................1
McCann A 1
McCartney 1
McClelland (1961) 1
McCrory 1
McCurdy 1
McGarry 1
McLaughlin C 1
Moreland 1
Morrow 1

Murdock 1
Nelson 1
Nicholl J 1
O'Boyle............................1
O'Kane 1
Patterson D 1
Patterson R 1
Rowland 1
Shiels..............................1
Smith M 1
Smyth P 1
Sproule............................1
Stevenson 1
Thompson 1
Walker 1
Welsh 1
Williams 1
Wilson D 1

REP OF IRELAND

Keane Robbie..................68
Quinn N 21
Stapleton 20
Aldridge 19
Cascarino 19
Givens 19
Long S 16
Cantwell 14
Doyle...............................14
Walters 14
Daly 13
Harte 12
McClean 11
Brady L.............................9
Connolly 9
Keane Roy 9
Kelly D 9
Morrison 9
Sheedy 9
Brady R 8
Curtis 8
Duff 8
Dunne R 8
Grealish 8
Kilbane.............................8
McGrath P 8
Staunton 8
Breen G 7
Duffy................................7
Fitzsimons 7
Ringstead 7
Robinson C 7
Townsend 7
Coyne 6
Houghton 6
McEvoy............................6
Martin C 6
Moran 6
Cummins 5
Fagan F 5

HOME INTERNATIONAL RESULTS

Note: In the results that follow, WC = World Cup, EC = European Championship, CC = Carling Cup
TF = Tournoi de France For Northern Ireland read Ireland before 1921

ENGLAND v SCOTLAND
Played 115; England won 49; Ireland 41;
drawn 25 Goals: England 203, Ireland 174

Year	Venue	E	S
1872	Glasgow	0	0
1873	The Oval	4	2
1874	Glasgow	1	2
1875	The Oval	2	2
1876	Glasgow	0	3
1877	The Oval	1	3
1878	Glasgow	2	7
1879	The Oval	5	4
1880	Glasgow	4	5
1881	The Oval	1	6
1882	Glasgow	1	5
1883	Sheffield	2	3
1884	Glasgow	0	1
1885	The Oval	1	1
1886	Glasgow	1	1
1887	Blackburn	2	3
1888	Glasgow	5	0
1889	The Oval	2	3
1890	Glasgow	1	1
1891	Blackburn	2	1
1892	Glasgow	4	1
1893	Richmond	5	2
1894	Glasgow	2	2
1895	Goodison Park	3	0
1896	Glasgow	1	2
1897	Crystal Palace	1	2
1898	Glasgow	3	1
1899	Birmingham	2	1
1900	Glasgow	1	4
1901	Crystal Palace	2	2
1902	Birmingham	2	2
1903	Sheffield	1	2
1904	Glasgow	1	0
1905	Crystal Palace	1	0
1906	Glasgow	1	2
1907	Newcastle	1	1
1908	Glasgow	1	1
1909	Crystal Palace	2	0
1910	Glasgow	0	2
1911	Goodison Park	1	1
1912	Glasgow	1	1
1913	Stamford Bridge	1	0
1914	Glasgow	1	3
1920	Sheffield	5	4
1921	Glasgow	0	3
1922	Birmingham	0	1
1923	Glasgow	2	2
1924	Wembley	1	1
1925	Glasgow	0	2
1926	Manchester	0	1
1927	Glasgow	2	1
1928	Wembley	1	5
1929	Glasgow	0	1
1930	Wembley	5	2
1931	Glasgow	0	2
1932	Wembley	3	0
1933	Glasgow	1	2
1934	Wembley	3	0
1935	Glasgow	0	2
1936	Wembley	1	1
1937	Glasgow	1	3
1938	Wembley	0	1
1939	Glasgow	2	1
1947	Wembley	1	1
1948	Glasgow	2	0
1949	Wembley	1	3
1950	Glasgow (WC)	1	0
1951	Wembley	2	3
1952	Glasgow	2	1
1953	Wembley	2	2
1954	Glasgow (WC)	4	2
1955	Wembley	7	2
1956	Glasgow	1	1
1957	Wembley	2	1
1958	Glasgow	4	0
1959	Wembley	1	0
1960	Glasgow	1	1
1961	Wembley	9	3
1962	Glasgow	0	2
1963	Wembley	1	2
1964	Glasgow	0	1
1965	Wembley	2	2
1966	Glasgow	4	3
1967	Wembley (EC)	2	3
1968	Glasgow (EC)	1	1
1969	Wembley	4	1
1970	Glasgow	0	0
1971	Wembley	3	1
1972	Glasgow	1	0
1973	Glasgow	5	0
1973	Wembley	1	0
1974	Glasgow	0	2
1975	Wembley	5	1
1976	Glasgow	1	2
1977	Wembley	1	2
1978	Glasgow	1	0

1979	Wembley	3	1
1980	Glasgow	2	0
1981	Wembley	0	1
1982	Glasgow	1	0
1983	Wembley	2	0
1984	Glasgow	1	1
1985	Glasgow	0	1
1986	Wembley	2	1
1987	Glasgow	0	0
1988	Wembley	1	0
1989	Glasgow	2	0
1996	Wembley (EC)	2	0
1999	Glasgow (EC)	2	0
1999	Wembley (EC)	0	1
2013	Wembley	3	2
2014	Glasgow	3	1
2016	Wembley (WC)	3	0
2017	Glasgow (WC)	2	2
2021	Wembledy (EC)	0	0

ENGLAND v WALES

Played 103; England won 68; Wales 14; drawn 21; Goals: England 250 Wales 91

Year	Venue	E	W
1879	The Oval	2	1
1880	Wrexham	3	2
1881	Blackburn	0	1
1882	Wrexham	3	5
1883	The Oval	5	0
1884	Wrexham	4	0
1885	Blackburn	1	1
1886	Wrexham	3	1
1887	The Oval	4	0
1888	Crewe	5	1
1889	Stoke	4	1
1890	Wrexham	3	1
1891	Sunderland	4	1
1892	Wrexham	2	0
1893	Stoke	6	0
1894	Wrexham	5	1
1895	Queens Club, London	1	1
1896	Cardiff	9	1
1897	Bramall Lane	4	0
1898	Wrexham	3	0
1899	Bristol	4	0
1900	Cardiff	1	1
1901	Newcastle	6	0
1902	Wrexham	0	0
1903	Portsmouth	2	1
1904	Wrexham	2	2
1905	Anfield	3	1
1906	Cardiff	1	0
1907	Fulham	1	1
1908	Wrexham	7	1
1909	Nottingham	2	0
1910	Cardiff	1	0
1911	Millwall	3	0
1912	Wrexham	2	0
1913	Bristol	4	3
1914	Cardiff	2	0
1920	Highbury	1	2
1921	Cardiff	0	0
1922	Anfield	1	0
1923	Cardiff	2	2
1924	Blackburn	1	2
1925	Swansea	2	1
1926	Selhurst Park	1	3
1927	Wrexham	3	3
1927	Burnley	1	2
1928	Swansea	3	2
1929	Stamford Bridge	6	0
1930	Wrexham	4	0
1931	Anfield	3	1
1932	Wrexham	0	0
1933	Newcastle	1	2
1934	Cardiff	4	0
1935	Wolverhampton	1	2
1936	Cardiff	1	2
1937	Middlesbrough	2	1
1938	Cardiff	2	4
1946	Maine Road	3	0
1947	Cardiff	3	0
1948	Villa Park	1	0
1949	Cardiff (WC)	4	1
1950	Sunderland	4	2
1951	Cardiff	1	1
1952	Wembley	5	2
1953	Cardiff (WC)	4	1
1954	Wembley	3	2
1955	Cardiff	1	2
1956	Wembley	3	1
1957	Cardiff	4	0
1958	Villa Park	2	2
1959	Cardiff	1	1
1960	Wembley	5	1
1961	Cardiff	1	1
1962	Wembley	4	0
1963	Cardiff	4	0
1964	Wembley	2	1
1965	Cardiff	0	0
1966	Wembley (EC)	5	1
1967	Cardiff (EC)	3	0
1969	Wembley	2	1
1970	Cardiff	1	1
1971	Wembley	0	0
1972	Cardiff	3	0
1972	Cardiff (WC)	1	0
1973	Wembley (WC)	1	1
1973	Wembley	3	0
1974	Cardiff	2	0

1975	Wembley	2	2
1976	Wrexham	2	1
1976	Cardiff	1	0
1977	Wembley	0	1
1978	Cardiff	3	1
1979	Wembley	0	0
1980	Wrexham	1	4
1981	Wembley	0	0
1982	Cardiff	1	0
1983	Wembley	2	1
1984	Wrexham	0	1
2004	Old Trafford (WC)	2	0
2005	Cardiff (WC)	1	0
2011	Cardiff (EC)	2	0
2011	Wembley (EC)	1	0
2016	Lens (EC)	2	1
2020	Wembley	3	0

ENGLAND v N IRELAND

Played 98; England won 75; Ireland 7; drawn 16 Goals: England 323, Ireland 81

Year	Venue	E	I
1882	Belfast	13	0
1883	Aigburth, Liverpool	7	0
1884	Belfast	8	1
1885	Whalley Range	4	0
1886	Belfast	6	1
1887	Bramall Lane	7	0
1888	Belfast	5	1
1889	Goodison Park	6	1
1890	Belfast	9	1
1891	Wolverhampton	6	1
1892	Belfast	2	0
1893	Perry Barr	6	1
1894	Belfast	2	2
1895	Derby	9	0
1896	Belfast	2	0
1897	Nottingham	6	0
1898	Belfast	3	2
1899	Sunderland	13	2
1900	Dublin	2	0
1901	Southampton	3	0
1902	Belfast	1	0
1903	Wolverhampton	4	0
1904	Belfast	3	1
1905	Middlesbrough	1	1
1906	Belfast	5	0
1907	Goodison Park	1	0
1908	Belfast	3	1
1909	Bradford PA	4	0
1910	Belfast	1	1
1911	Derby	2	1
1912	Dublin	6	1
1913	Belfast	1	2
1914	Middlesbrough	0	3
1919	Belfast	1	1
1920	Sunderland	2	0
1921	Belfast	1	1
1922	West Bromwich	2	0
1923	Belfast	1	2
1924	Goodison Park	3	1
1925	Belfast	0	0
1926	Anfield	3	3
1927	Belfast	0	2
1928	Goodison Park	2	1
1929	Belfast	3	0
1930	Bramall Lane	5	1
1931	Belfast	6	2
1932	Blackpool	1	0
1933	Belfast	3	0
1935	Goodison Park	2	1
1935	Belfast	3	1
1936	Stoke	3	1
1937	Belfast	5	1
1938	Old Trafford	7	0
1946	Belfast	7	2
1947	Goodison Park	2	2
1948	Belfast	6	2
1949	Maine Road (WC)	9	2
1950	Belfast	4	1
1951	Villa Park	2	0
1952	Belfast	2	2
1953	Goodison Park (WC)	3	1
1954	Belfast	2	0
1955	Wembley	3	0
1956	Belfast	1	1
1957	Wembley	2	3
1958	Belfast	3	3
1959	Wembley	2	1
1960	Belfast	5	2
1961	Wembley	1	1
1962	Belfast	3	1
1963	Wembley	8	3
1964	Belfast	4	3
1965	Wembley	2	1
1966	Belfast (EC)	2	0
1967	Wembley (EC)	2	0
1969	Belfast	3	1
1970	Wembley	3	1
1971	Belfast	1	0
1972	Wembley	0	1
1973	*Goodison Park	2	1
1974	Wembley	1	0
1975	Belfast	0	0
1976	Wembley	4	0
1977	Belfast	2	1
1978	Wembley	1	0
1979	Wembley (EC)	4	0
1979	Belfast	2	0
1979	Belfast (EC)	5	1

1980	Wembley	1	1
1982	Wembley	4	0
1983	Belfast	0	0
1984	Wembley	1	0
1985	Belfast (WC)	1	0
1985	Wembley (WC)	0	0
1986	Wembley (EC)	3	0
1987	Belfast (EC)	2	0
2005	Old Trafford (WC)	4	0
2005	Belfast (WC)	0	1

(*Switched from Belfast because of political situation)

SCOTLAND v WALES

Played 107; Scotland won 61; Wales 23; drawn 23; Goals: Scotland 243, Wales 124

		S	W
1876	Glasgow	4	0
1877	Wrexham	2	0
1878	Glasgow	9	0
1879	Wrexham	3	0
1880	Glasgow	5	1
1881	Wrexham	5	1
1882	Glasgow	5	0
1883	Wrexham	3	0
1884	Glasgow	4	1
1885	Wrexham	8	1
1886	Glasgow	4	1
1887	Wrexham	2	0
1888	Edinburgh	5	1
1889	Wrexham	0	0
1890	Paisley	5	0
1891	Wrexham	4	3
1892	Edinburgh	6	1
1893	Wrexham	8	0
1894	Kilmarnock	5	2
1895	Wrexham	2	2
1896	Dundee	4	0
1897	Wrexham	2	2
1898	Motherwell	5	2
1899	Wrexham	6	0
1900	Aberdeen	5	2
1901	Wrexham	1	1
1902	Greenock	5	1
1903	Cardiff	1	0
1904	Dundee	1	1
1905	Wrexham	1	3
1906	Edinburgh	0	2
1907	Wrexham	0	1
1908	Dundee	2	1
1909	Wrexham	2	3
1910	Kilmarnock	1	0
1911	Cardiff	2	2
1912	Tynecastle	1	0
1913	Wrexham	0	0
1914	Glasgow	0	0
1920	Cardiff	1	1
1921	Aberdeen	2	1
1922	Wrexham	1	2
1923	Paisley	2	0
1924	Cardiff	0	2
1925	Tynecastle	3	1
1926	Cardiff	3	0
1927	Glasgow	3	0
1928	Wrexham	2	2
1929	Glasgow	4	2
1930	Cardiff	4	2
1931	Glasgow	1	1
1932	Wrexham	3	2
1933	Edinburgh	2	5
1934	Cardiff	2	3
1935	Aberdeen	3	2
1936	Cardiff	1	1
1937	Dundee	1	2
1938	Cardiff	1	2
1939	Edinburgh	3	2
1946	Wrexham	1	3
1947	Glasgow	1	2
1948	Cardiff (WC)	3	1
1949	Glasgow	2	0
1950	Cardiff	3	1
1951	Glasgow	0	1
1952	Cardiff (WC)	2	1
1953	Glasgow	3	3
1954	Cardiff	1	0
1955	Glasgow	2	0
1956	Cardiff	2	2
1957	Glasgow	1	1
1958	Cardiff	3	0
1959	Glasgow	1	1
1960	Cardiff	0	2
1961	Glasgow	2	0
1962	Cardiff	3	2
1963	Glasgow	2	1
1964	Cardiff	2	3
1965	Glasgow (EC)	4	1
1966	Cardiff (EC)	1	1
1967	Glasgow	3	2
1969	Wrexham	5	3
1970	Glasgow	0	0
1971	Cardiff	0	0
1972	Glasgow	1	0
1973	Wrexham	2	0
1974	Glasgow	2	0
1975	Cardiff	2	2
1976	Glasgow	3	1
1977	Glasgow (WC)	1	0
1977	Wrexham	0	0
1977	Anfield (WC)	2	0
1978	Glasgow	1	1

Year	Venue	S	I
1979	Cardiff	0	3
1980	Glasgow	1	0
1981	Swansea	0	2
1982	Glasgow	1	0
1983	Cardiff	2	0
1984	Glasgow	2	1
1985	Glasgow (WC)	0	1
1985	Cardiff (WC)	1	1
1997	Kilmarnock	0	1
2004	Cardiff	0	4
2009	Cardiff	0	3
2011	Dublin (CC)	3	1
2012	Cardiff (WC)	1	2
2013	Glasgow (WC	1	2

SCOTLAND v NORTHERN IRELAND

Played 96; Scotland won 64; Northern Ireland 15; drawn 17; Goals: Scotland 258, Northern Ireland 80

Year	Venue	S	I
1884	Belfast	5	0
1885	Glasgow	8	2
1886	Belfast	7	2
1887	Belfast	4	1
1888	Belfast	10	2
1889	Glasgow	7	0
1890	Belfast	4	1
1891	Glasgow	2	1
1892	Belfast	3	2
1893	Glasgow	6	1
1894	Belfast	2	1
1895	Glasgow	3	1
1896	Belfast	3	3
1897	Glasgow	5	1
1898	Belfast	3	0
1899	Glasgow	9	1
1900	Belfast	3	0
1901	Glasgow	11	0
1902	Belfast	5	1
1902	Belfast	3	0
1903	Glasgow	0	2
1904	Dublin	1	1
1905	Glasgow	4	0
1906	Dublin	1	0
1907	Glasgow	3	0
1908	Dublin	5	0
1909	Glasgow	5	0
1910	Belfast	0	1
1911	Glasgow	2	0
1912	Belfast	4	1
1913	Dublin	2	1
1914	Belfast	1	1
1920	Glasgow	3	0
1921	Belfast	2	0
1922	Glasgow	2	1
1923	Belfast	1	0
1924	Glasgow	2	0
1925	Belfast	3	0
1926	Glasgow	4	0
1927	Belfast	2	0
1928	Glasgow	0	1
1929	Belfast	7	3
1930	Glasgow	3	1
1931	Belfast	0	0
1932	Glasgow	3	1
1933	Belfast	4	0
1934	Glasgow	1	2
1935	Belfast	1	2
1936	Edinburgh	2	1
1937	Belfast	3	1
1938	Aberdeen	1	1
1939	Belfast	2	0
1946	Glasgow	0	0
1947	Belfast	0	2
1948	Glasgow	3	2
1949	Belfast	8	2
1950	Glasgow	6	1
1951	Belfast	3	0
1952	Glasgow	1	1
1953	Belfast	3	1
1954	Glasgow	2	2
1955	Belfast	1	2
1956	Glasgow	1	0
1957	Belfast	1	1
1958	Glasgow	2	2
1959	Belfast	4	0
1960	Glasgow	5	1
1961	Belfast	6	1
1962	Glasgow	5	1
1963	Belfast	1	2
1964	Glasgow	3	2
1965	Belfast	2	3
1966	Glasgow	2	1
1967	Belfast	0	1
1969	Glasgow	1	1
1970	Belfast	1	0
1971	Glasgow	0	1
1972	Glasgow	2	0
1973	Glasgow	1	2
1974	Glasgow	0	1
1975	Glasgow	3	0
1976	Glasgow	3	0
1977	Glasgow	3	0
1978	Glasgow	1	1
1979	Glasgow	1	0
1980	Belfast	0	1
1981	Glasgow (WC)	1	1
1981	Glasgow	2	0
1981	Belfast (WC)	0	0
1982	Belfast	1	1
1983	Glasgow	0	0

1984	Belfast	0	2
1992	Glasgow	1	0
2008	Glasgow	0	0
2011	Dublin (CC)	3	0
2015	Glasgow	1	0

WALES v NORTHERN IRELAND

Played 97; Wales won 45; Northern Ireland won 27; drawn 25; Goals: Wales 191 Northern Ireland 132

Year	Venue	W	
1882	Wrexham	7	1
1883	Belfast	1	1
1884	Wrexham	6	0
1885	Belfast	8	2
1886	Wrexham	5	0
1887	Belfast	1	4
1888	Wrexham	11	0
1889	Belfast	3	1
1890	Shrewsbury	5	2
1891	Belfast	2	7
1892	Bangor	1	1
1893	Belfast	3	4
1894	Swansea	4	1
1895	Belfast	2	2
1896	Wrexham	6	1
1897	Belfast	3	4
1898	Llandudno	0	1
1899	Belfast	0	1
1900	Llandudno	2	0
1901	Belfast	1	0
1902	Cardiff	0	3
1903	Belfast	0	2
1904	Bangor	0	1
1905	Belfast	2	2
1906	Wrexham	4	4
1907	Belfast	3	2
1908	Aberdare	0	1
1909	Belfast	3	2
1910	Wrexham	4	1
1911	Belfast	2	1
1912	Cardiff	2	3
1913	Belfast	1	0
1914	Wrexham	1	2
1920	Belfast	2	2
1921	Swansea	2	1
1922	Belfast	1	1
1923	Wrexham	0	3
1924	Belfast	1	0
1925	Wrexham	0	0
1926	Belfast	0	3
1927	Cardiff	2	2
1928	Belfast	2	1
1929	Wrexham	2	2
1930	Belfast	0	7
1931	Wrexham	3	2
1932	Belfast	0	4
1933	Wrexham	4	1
1934	Belfast	1	1
1935	Wrexham	3	1
1936	Belfast	2	3
1937	Wrexham	4	1
1938	Belfast	0	1
1939	Wrexham	3	1
1947	Belfast	1	2
1948	Wrexham	2	0
1949	Belfast	2	0
1950	Wrexham (WC)	0	0
1951	Belfast	2	1
1952	Swansea	3	0
1953	Belfast	3	2
1954	Wrexham (WC)	1	2
1955	Belfast	3	2
1956	Cardiff	1	1
1957	Belfast	0	0
1958	Cardiff	1	1
1959	Belfast	1	4
1960	Wrexham	3	2
1961	Belfast	5	1
1962	Cardiff	4	0
1963	Belfast	4	1
1964	Swansea	2	3
1965	Belfast	5	0
1966	Cardiff	1	4
1967	Belfast (EC)	0	0
1968	Wrexham (EC)	2	0
1969	Belfast	0	0
1970	Swansea	1	0
1971	Belfast	0	1
1972	Wrexham	0	0
1973	*Goodison Park	0	1
1974	Wrexham	1	0
1975	Belfast	0	1
1976	Swansea	1	0
1977	Belfast	1	1
1978	Wrexham	1	0
1979	Belfast	1	1
1980	Cardiff	0	1
1982	Wrexham	3	0
1983	Belfast	1	0
1984	Swansea	1	1
2004	Cardiff (WC)	2	2
2005	Belfast (WC)	3	2
2007	Belfast	0	0
2008	Glasgow	0	0
2011	Dublin (CC)	2	0
2016	Cardiff	1	1
2016	Paris (EC)	1	0

(*Switched from Belfast because of political situation)

EUROPEAN TITLE FOR YOUNG ENGLAND

Harry Kane sent a message of congratulations to the England under-19 team who came from behind to become European champions in Slovakia. They trailed Israel at half-time, equalised through Manchester City's Callum Doyle, then scored twice in extra-time to win 3-1. Midfielder Carney Chukwuemeka, who made 12 Premier League appearances for Aston Villa during the season, put them ahead and club-mate Aaron Ramsey made sure four minute from the end. They were also behind in the semi-final against Italy, before goals by Bristol City's Alex Scott and Liverpool's Jarell Quansah secured a 2-1 victory. It was England's second success in five years, having won the 2017 title with a side which included Chelsea's Mason Mount and Aaron Ramsdale, now with Arsenal.

GROUP A

	P	W	D	L	F	A	Pts
France	3	3	0	0	11	2	9
Italy	3	2	0	1	4	5	6
Slovakia	3	1	0	2	1	6	3
Romania	3	0	0	3	2	5	0

GROUP B

	P	W	D	L	F	A	Pts
England	3	3	0	0	7	0	9
Israel	3	1	1	1	6	5	4
Austria	3	1	0	2	5	8	3
Serbia	3	0	1	2	4	9	1

Match-day 1: England 2 (Chukwuemeka 43, Devine 65) Austria 0; Serbia 2 Israel 2
Match-day 2: England 4 (Scarlett 5, 40, Chukwuemeka 68, Jebbison 90+1) Serbia 0; Israel. 4 Austria 2
Match-day 3: Israel 0 England 1 (Delap 6); Austria 3 Serbia 2
Semi-finals: England 2 (Scott 58, Quansah 82) Italy 1 (Miretti 12 pen); France 1 Israel 2

FINAL
Israel 1 (Gloch 40) England 3 (Doyle 52, Chukwuemeka 108, Ramsey 116) aet – Trnava, July 1, 2022
England (3-4-1-2): Cox, Edwards, Quansah, Doyle, Oyegoke (Norton-Cuffy 73), Scott (Iroegbunam 73), Chukwuemeka, Vale (capt), Devine (Chambers 85), Scarlett (Delap 105), Bynoe-Gittens (Ramsey 58). **Booked:** Edwards, Doyle, Scott, Norton-Cuffy, Iroegbunam, Chukwuemeka. **Coach:** Ian Foster

England squad: Cox (Brentford), Davies (Liverpool), Sharman-Lowe (Chelsea); Chambers (Liverpool), Doyle (Manchester City), Edwards (Peterborough), Humphreys (Chelsea), Norton-Cuffy (Arsenal), Oyegoke (Brentford), Quansah (Liverpool); Chukwuemeka (Aston Villa), Devine (Tottenham), Bynoe-Gittens (Borussia Dortmund), Iling-Junior (Juventus), Iroegbunam (Aston Villa), Ramsey (Aston Villa), Scott (Bristol City), Vale (Chelsea); Delap (Manchester City), Jebbison (Sheffield Utd), Scarlett (Tottenham).

BRITISH AND IRISH UNDER 21 INTERNATIONALS 2021–22

EUROPEAN CHAMPIONSHIP QUALIFYING

GROUP 3

MALTA 4 NORTHERN IRELAND 1
Ta'Qali (184); September 3, 2021
Northern Ireland: Hughes, Hume, Donnelly, Scott (Anderson 85), S McClelland (K McClelland 46), Balmer, Boyd-Munce (Smyth 46), Galbraith, Johnston (Conn 85), Waide, Crowe (Lane 46). **Booked:** Balmer, Galbraith
Scorers – Malta: Engerer (24), Veselji (36, 40 pen), Attard (84). **Northern Ireland:** Lane (56). **Half-time:** 3-0

NORTHERN IRELAND 1 SLOVAKIA 0
Mourneview Park, Lurgan (397); September 7, 2021
Northern Ireland: Hughes, Donnelly, Hume, Balmer, S McClelland, Lane, Scott (Cousin-Dawson 90+3), Galbraith, Conn-Clarke (Johnston 90+3), Boyd-Munce (Smyth 82), Waide (Palmer 82). **Booked:** Conn-Clarke
Scorer – Northern Ireland: Galbraith (54 pen). **Half-time:** 0-0

RUSSIA 1 NORTHERN IRELAND 0
Khimki (250); October 8, 2021
Northern Ireland: Webber, Hume, Donnelly, Balmer, S McClelland, McCalmont, Galbraith, Scott (Cousin- Dawson 79), Conn-Clarke (Boyd-Munce 63), Waide (O'Neill 63), Lane (McGovern 79). **Booked:** Hume
Scorer – Russia: Prokhin (16). **Half-time:** 1-0
(Match void – Russia expelled)

SPAIN 3 NORTHERN IRELAND 0
Seville (2,632); October 12, 2021
Northern Ireland: Webber, Balmer (K McClelland 67), S McClelland, Donnelly, Hume, Galbraith, Boyd-Munce, Scott (Cousin-Dawson 46), Waide (O'Neill 67), Conn-Clarke (Smyth 46), Lane (McGovern 67). **Booked:** Donnelly, O'Neill, Cousin-Dawson
Scorers – Spain: Sergio Gomez (26, 32), Ruiz (56). **Half-time:** 2-0

NORTHERN IRELAND 4 LITHUANIA 0
Showgrounds, Ballymena (324); November 12, 2021
Northern Ireland: Hughes, Hume, Balmer, Cousin-Dawson, Donnelly (Charles 82), Smyth, McCalmont, Boyd-Munce (Conn-Clarke 71), Waide (Johnston 82), Lane (Scott 90+1), O'Neill (McGovern 71). **Booked:** Boyd-Munce, O'Neill, Lane
Scorers – Northern Ireland: McCalmont (8, 75), O'Neill (43 pen), Conn-Clarke (87). **Half-time:** 2-0

NORTHERN IRELAND 0 MALTA 2
Mourneview Park, Lurgan (347); November 16, 2021
Northern Ireland: Hughes, Hume, Smyth (Boyd-Munce 71), Balmer, Donnelly, Galbraith, McCalmont, Cousin-Dawson, Taylor, Lane (McGovern 71), O'Neill (Waide 71). **Sent off:** Hume (32)
Scorers – Malta: Grima (49), Zammit (89). **Half-time:** 0-0

SLOVAKIA 2 NORTHERN IRELAND 1
Zilina (1,377); March 25, 2022

Northern Ireland: Webber, Charles, Balmer (Price 86), Donnelly, Stewart (Baggley 86), Galbraith, Johnston (Scott 65), McCann, McKee, McCalmont, Taylor (McGovern 70). **Booked**: Balmer, Charles, McCalmont

Scorers – Slovakia: Trusa (37), Kadak (86 pen). **Northern Ireland**: Johnston (61). **Half-time**: 1-0

NORTHERN IRELAND 0 SPAIN 6
Inver Park, Larne (1,100); June 3, 2022

Northern Ireland: Mee, Scott, McClelland, Donnelly, Stewart, Galbraith (Boyle 77), Balmer, Allen (McGuckin 59), McKee (McGovern 59), Taylor (Baggley 59), Devlin (Smyth 59). **Booked**: Balmer, McGuckin

Scorers – Spain: Ruiz (22), Gil (50, 61), Miranda (64), Riquelme (75), Gomez (87). **Half-time**: 0-1

LITHUANIA 1 NORTHERN IRELAND 1
Alytus (374); June 7, 2022

Northern Ireland: Mee, McClelland, Smyth, Donnelly, Scott, Allen, Galbraith (Boyle 81), Stewart, Baggley (Devlin 82), Taylor (McGovern 75), McKee. **Booked**: Galbraith, Devlin, McKee (McGuckin 81)

Scorers – Lithuania: Tutyskinas (90+6). **Northern Ireland**: Taylor (17). **Half-time**: 0-1

	P	W	D	L	F	A	GD	Pts
Spain Q	8	8	0	0	37	5	32	24
Slovakia	8	5	0	3	18	10	8	15
Lithuania	8	2	1	5	7	22	-15	7
Northern Ireland	8	2	1	5	8	18	-10	7
Malta	8	2	0	6	10	25	-15	6

Russia expelled

GROUP 5

BULGARIA 0 WALES 4
Sofia (425); September 7, 2021

Wales: Barden, Stevens, Sass-Davies, Boyes, Jones, Pearson (Huggins 79), Bowen, Williams, Adams (Beck 79), Vale (Davies 83), Hughes. **Booked**: Jones, Adams, Bowen

Scorers – Wales: Vale (27, 50, 73), Sass-Davies (42). **Half-time**: 0-2

MOLDOVA 1 WALES 0
Orhei (220); October 8, 2021

Wales: Ratcliffe, Stevens, Cooper, Boyes, Beck, Pearson (Jephcott 67), Williams, Bowen (Sass-Davies 90+4), Adams, Vale, Hughes. **Booked**: Stevens, Boyes

Scorer – Moldova: Ieseanu (20). **Half-time**: 1-0

HOLLAND 5 WALES 0
Nijmegen (3,082); October 12, 2021

Wales: Ratcliffe, Stevens, Sass-Davies, Cooper, Jones, Pearson (Beck 70), Taylor, Williams (Hammond 84), Adams, Hughes (Spence 59), Jephcott (Vale 59). **Booked**: Cooper

Scorers – Holland: Ekkelenkamp (7, 53), Botman (35), Stevens (48 og), Redan (50). **Half-time**: 2-0

GIBRALTAR 0 WALES 7
Victoria Stadium (334); November 12, 2021

Wales: Ratcliffe, Astley, Sass-Davies, Cooper (Boyes 59), Beck, Taylor, Pearson (Davies 59),

Williams, (King 77), Vale, Adams (Hughes 70), Jephcott. **Booked**: Jephcott, Pearson
Scorers – Wales: Beck (13), Adams (16 pen, 51), Jephcott (33), Williams (71), Taylor (84), Astley (88). **Half-time**: 3-0

WALES 0 SWITZERLAND 1
Rodney Parade, Newport (237); November 16, 2021
Wales: Ratcliffe, Astley, Sass-Davies, Cooper, Beck, Adams (Jones 74), Williams, Taylor, Pearson, Jephcott (Hughes 81), Vale (Davies 75). **Booked**: Astley, Beck, Taylor, Williams, Cooper
Scorer – Switzerland: Mambimbi (53). **Half-time**: 0-0

SWITZERLAND 5 WALES 1
Lausanne (6,618): March 25, 2022
Wales: Shepperd, Stevens, Astley, Jones, Boyes, Pearson, Williams, Taylor (King 81), Adams (Hughes 69), Jephcott (Vale 46), Davies
Scorers – Switzerland: Mambimbi (12), Ndoye (14, 47), Amdouni (20, 56). **Wales**: Adams (46). **Half-time**: 3-0

WALES 1 BULGARIA 1
Rodney Parade, Newport (210); March 29, 2022
Wales: Shepperd, Stevens, Boyes, Astley, Jones, Pearson (Popov 81), Taylor, Williams (King 86), Thorpe (Hughes 67), Davies, Vale. **Booked**: Williams, Jones, Taylor
Scorers – Wales: Pearson (63). **Bulgaria** (Nikolov 60). **Half-time**: 0-0

WALES 0 HOLLAND 1
Parc y Scarlets, Llanelli (161); June 11, 2022
Wales: Shepperd, Stevens, Astley, Turns, Beck, Pearson (Adams 75), Taylor, King, Thorpe (Jones 65), Hughes (Hammond 80), Jephcott (Popov 65). **Booked**: Turns, Hughes
Scorer – Holland: Geetruida (86). **Half-time**: 0-0

WALES 2 GIBRALTAR 0
Parc y Scarlets, Llanelli (250); June 14, 2022
Wales: Webb, Beck, Connolly, Astley, Stevens (Hoole 75), Adams (Ashworth 81), King (Popov 68), Hammond (Sparrow 75), Hughes, Jephcott, Pearson (Jones 68)
Scorers: Adams (1), Hammond (53). **Half-time**: 1-0

Holland Q	10	8	2	0	32	3	29	26
Switzerland Q	10	7	2	1	22	6	16	23
Moldova	10	3	3	4	7	12	-5	12
Wales	10	3	2	5	15	14	1	11
Bulgaria	10	2	4	4	10	11	-1	10
Gibraltar	10	0	1	9	1	41	-40	1

GROUP 6
BOSNIA-HERZEGOVINA 0 REPUBLIC OF IRELAND 2
Zenica (120); September 3, 2021
Republic of Ireland: Maher, Lyons, O'Brien, McEntee, Ferry (O'Connor 83), Kilkenny, Coventry (Johansson 88), Tierney, Watson (Noss 80), Kayode (Ferguson 83), Wright. **Booked**: Kilkenny, Ferry, Tierney, Ferguson
Scorers – Republic of Ireland: Wright (52 pen), Coventry (73). **Half-time**: 0-0

LUXEMBOURG 1 REPUBLIC OF IRELAND 1
Dudelange (278); September 7, 2021

Republic of Ireland: Maher, O'Connor, McEntree, O'Brien, Bagan, Coventry (Johansson 81), Kilkenny, Wright, Devoy (Noss 81), Ferry (Moran 67), Ferguson (Whelan 67). **Booked**: Coventry, Wright

Scorers – Luxembourg: Kuete (84 pen). **Republic of Ireland**: Whelan (69). **Half-time**: 0-0

REPUBLIC OF IRELAND 2 LUXEMBOURG 0
Tallaght Stadium, Dublin (1,426); October 8, 2021

Republic of Ireland: Maher, O'Connor, O'Brien, McGuinness, Bagan, Tierney (Noss 70), Kilkenny (Devoy 87), Coventry, Kerrigan (Gilbert 87), Kayode (Ferguson 70), Wright (Moran 90+3). **Booked**: McGuinness, Wright

Scorers – Republic of Ireland: Kayode (18), Coventry (64 pen). **Half-time**: 1-0

MONTENEGRO 2 REPUBLIC OF IRELAND 1
Podgorica (278); October 12, 2021

Republic of Ireland: Maher, O'Connor, McGuinness, O'Brien, Bagan, Kilkenny (Kayode 77), Tierney (Devoy 77), Coventry, Gilbert (O'Neill 60), Ferguson (Whelan 60), Ferry. **Booked**: McGuinness, Tierney, Kayode, Coventry

Scorers – Montenegro: Krstovic (4), Vukcevic (9). **Republic of Ireland**: McGuinness (74). **Half-time**: 2-0

REPUBLIC OF IRELAND 0 ITALY 2
Tallaght Stadium, Dublin (2,161); November 12, 2021

Republic of Ireland: Maher, O'Connor, O'Brien, McGuinness, Bagan, Kilkenny (Devoy 76), Coventry, Smallbone (Tierney 76), Noss (Ebosele 56), Wright, Whelan (Kayode 56)

Scorers – Italy: Lucca (30), Cancellieri (90). **Half-time**: 0-1

REPUBLIC OF IRELAND 1 SWEDEN 0
Tallaght Stadium, Dublin (1,535); November 16, 2021

Republic of Ireland: Maher, O'Brien, McGuinness, Bagan, O'Connor, Kilkenny, Coventry, Wright (O'Neill 84), Smallbone (Noss 84), Tierney (Ferry 68), Kayode (Ferguson 76). **Booked**: O'Brien, Smallbone

Scorer – Republic of Ireland: O'Neill (90+2). **Half-time**: 0-0

SWEDEN 0 REPUBLIC OF IRELAND 2
Boras (1,645); March 29, 2022

Republic of Ireland: Maher, McEntee, O'Brien, McGuinness, Bagan, Coventry, O'Connor, Kilkenny, Tierney, Odubeko (Kayode 70), O'Neill (Wright 64). **Booked**: Odubeko, Kilkenny, Maher

Scorers – Republic of Ireland: Tierney (12), Wright (88). **Half-time**: 0-1

REPUBLIC OF IRELAND 3 BOSNIA-HERZEGOVINA 0
Tallaght Stadium, Dublin (3,057); June 3, 2022

Republic of Ireland: Maher, O'Connor, McEntee (O'Brien 53), McGuinness, Bagan, Coventry, Kilkenny (Devoy 79), Smallbone, Tierney (O'Neill 63), Odubeko (Ferguson 63), Wright.

Scorers – Republic of Ireland: Smallbone (16, 81), Odubeko (63). **Half-time**: 1-0

REPUBLIC OF IRELAND 3 MONTENEGRO 1
Tallaght Stadium, Dublin (3,126); June 6, 2022

Republic of Ireland: Maher, O'Connor, Cashin, McGuinness, Adaramola (Lyons 84), Smallbone, Nos (Kilkenny 63), Coventry, Wright; Kerrigan, Kayode (Ferguson 63). **Booked**: Smallbone

Scorers – Republic of Ireland: Smallbone (41), Kerrigan (57), Wright (67). **Montenegro**: Dukanovic (76). **Half-time**: 1-0.

ITALY 4 REPUBLIC OF IRELAND 1
Ascoli (4,450); June 14, 2022
Republic of Ireland: Maher, O'Connor, Cashin (O'Brien 83), McGuinness, Bagan (Lyons 46), Coventry, Kilkenny (Odubeko 62), Kerrigan (Noss 62), Smallbone, Wright, Ferguson (Kayode 74). **Booked**: McGuinness
Scorers — Italy: Rovella (20 pen), Cambiaghi (35), Pellegri (46), Quagliata (85). **Republic of Ireland**: Coventry (61 pen). **Half-time**: 2-0

Italy Q	10	7	3	0	19	5	14	24
Republic of Ireland	10	6	1	3	16	10	6	19
Sweden	10	5	3	2	22	8	14	18
Bosnia-Herz	10	3	2	5	9	16	-7	11
Montenegro	10	3	2	5	14	17	-3	11
Luxembourg	10	0	1	9	2	26	-24	1

(Republic of Ireland through to play-offs)

GROUP 7

ENGLAND 2 KOSOVO 0
Stadium mk (5,781); September 7, 2021
England: Bursik, Aarons, Guehi, Harwood-Bellis, Thomas, Skipp (Doyle 82), Garner, Madueke (Livramento 82), Gallagher, Palmer (John-Jules 72), Brewster (Balogun 65)
Scorers — England: Brewster (10 pen), Palmer (26). **Half-time**: 2-0

SLOVENIA 2 ENGLAND 2
Celje (457); October 7, 2021
England: Bursik, Aarons (Livramento 62), Guehi, Harwood-Bellis, Thomas, Skipp, Gallagher, Ramsey, Smith-Rowe, Brewster (Balogun 69), Palmer (John-Jules 69). **Booked**: Aarons
Scorers — Slovenia: Spanring (50), Stojinovic (66). **England**: Gallagher (5), Palmer (14). **Half-time**: 0-2

ANDORRA 0 ENGLAND 1
La Vella (572); October 11, 2021
England: Green, Livramento, Guehi, Harwood-Bellis, Thomas, Gallagher, Doyle, Garner (Jones 57), Palmer (Gomes 65), Brewster, Smith Rowe (Balogun 90). **Booked**: Brewster, Thomas. **Sent off**: Brewster (55)
Scorer — England: Smith Rowe (67). **Half-time**: 0-0

ENGLAND 3 CZECH REPUBLIC 1
Turf Moor, Burnley (6,507), November 11, 2021
England: Bursik, Aarons, Guehi, Harwood-Bellis, Thomas, Skipp, Ramsey, Gallagher (Cresswell 89), Palmer (Gomes 73), Balogun (Gibbs-White 77), Gordon. **Booked**: Aarons, Thomas
Scorers — England: Gordon (4, 11), Balogun (30). **Czech Republic**: Karabec (40 pen). **Half-time**: 3-1

ENGLAND 4 ANDORRA 1
Vitality Stadium, Bournemouth (8,852); March 25, 2022
England: Bursik, Livramento, Harwood-Bellis, Colwill, Thomas, Gibbs-White (Jones 62), Doyle, Ramsey (Gomes 82), Elliott, Balogun, Madueke (Gordon 71).
Scorers — England: Balogun (6), Ramsey (34), Gibbs-White (53), Gordon (88). **Andorra**: Rosas Ubach (62). **Half-time**: 2-0

ALBANIA 0 ENGLAND 3
Elbasan (600); March 29, 2022
England: Bursik, Livramento (Spence 56), Harwood-Bellis, Colwill, Johnson, Garner, Jones, Madueke (Lewis-Potter 82), Gibbs-White (Gomes 76), Gordon, Balogun. **Booked**: Johnson
Scorers — England: Balogun (47, 61), Jones 51). **Half-time**: 0-0

CZECH REPUBLIC 1 ENGLAND 2
Prague (5,654); June 3, 2022
England: Bursik, Aarons, Cresswell, Harwood-Bellis, Johnson, Jones, Garner, Ramsey, Gibbs-White (Gomes 82), Balogun (Archer 68), Smith Rowe (Gordon 65). **Booked**: Harwood-Bellis, Gibbs-White, Bursik
Scorers – Czech Republic: Fila (87). **England**: Smith Rowe (22), Ramsey (46). **Half-time**: 0-1

ENGLAND 3 ALBANIA 0
Technique Stadium, Chesterfield (4,422); June 7, 2022
England: Bursik, Spence, Cresswell, Harwood-Bellis, Johnson (Thomas 83), Jones (Garner 73), Smith Rowe (Gibbs-White 61), Doyle, Gomes, Balogun (Archer 73), Gordon (Lewis-Potter 83). **Booked**: Balogun, Doyle
Scorers – England: Balogun (44, 66), Archer (77). **Half-time**: 1-0

KOSOVO 0 ENGLAND 5
Pristina (3,900); June 10, 2022
England: Trafford, Aarons, Hill, Harwood-Bellis (Cresswell 46), Thomas, Elliott (McAtee 72), Doyle, Ramsey, Lewis-Potter, Archer (Balogun 73), Gordon (Gomes 56)
Scorers – England: Lewis-Potter (2), Gordon (13), Archer (52, 71), Krasniqi (84 og). **Half-time**: 0-2

ENGLAND 1 SLOVENIA 2
John Smith's Stadium, Huddersfield (5,236); June 13, 2022
England: Bursik, Spence (Aarons 61), Cresswell, Harwood-Bellis, Johnson, Ramsey (Elliott 61), Garner (Lewis-Potter 74), Jones, Gibbs-White, Balogun (Archer 61), Smith Rowe (Gomes 78). **Booked**: Cresswell, Gibbs-White, Garner, Aarons, Elliott, Gomes
Goals – England: Archer (90+1). **Slovenia**: Spence (1 og), Zabukovnik 64). **Half-time**: 0-1

England Q	10	8	1	1	26	7	19	25
Czech Republic	10	7	1	2	23	6	17	22
Slovenia	10	4	4	2	11	7	4	16
Kosovo	10	3	3	4	8	13	-5	12
Albania	10	3	1	6	9	17	-8	10
Andorra	10	0	0	10	1	28	-27	0

GROUP 9

TURKEY 1 SCOTLAND 1
Bursa (1,042); September 7, 2021
Scotland: Sinclair, Mayo, Welsh, Doig, Ramsay, Williamson, Middleton, Kelly, Kennedy (Rudden 63), Scott (Anderson 76), Montgomery (Mackay 71). **Booked**: Montgomery, Doig, Williamson
Scorers – Turkey: Destan (75). **Scotland**: Middleton (9). **Half-time**: 0-1

SCOTLAND 0 DENMARK 1
Tynecastle Park, Edinburgh (1,473); October 7, 2021
Scotland: Slicker, Ashby, Welsh, Mayo, Doig (Banks 72), Burroughs, Kelly (High 76), Williamson (Leonard 72), Fiorini, Montgomery (Mebude 56), Middleton. **Booked**: Fiorini, Mebude
Scorer – Denmark: Isaksen (13). **Half-time**: 0-1

SCOTLAND 2 KAZAKHSTAN 1
Tannadice Park, Dundee (1,221): November 12, 2021
Scotland: Mair, Ashby (Burroughs 79), Welsh, Mayo, Doig, Kelly (Williamson 79), High, Fiorini (Clayton 90), Leonard, Mebude (Banks 79), Middleton, **Booked**: Mebude
Scorers – Scotland: Fiorini (28), Middleton (66). **Kazakhstan**: Samorodov (71). **Half-time**: 1-0

322

SCOTLAND 0 BELGIUM 2
Tannadice Park, Dundee (2,304); November 16, 2021

Scotland: Slicker, Burroughs, Welsh (Montgomery 86), Mayo, Doig (Clayton 46), Williamson, High, Kelly (Banks 86), Leonard, Middleton (Mebude 60), Fiorini. **Booked:** Doig, Mayo, Kelly, Williamson, Mebude

Scorers – Belgium: Openda (40 pen), Raskin (87). **Half-time:** 0-1

SCOTLAND 0 TURKEY 2
Tynecastle Park, Edinburgh (2,068); March 25, 2022

Scotland: Slicker, Ramsay, Welsh, Mayo, Doig, Banks (Rudden 46), Williamson (Smith 81), High (Campbell 46), Leonard (Barron 46), Middleton, Fiorini (Henderson (77). **Booked:** Leonard, Campbell, Barron, Ramsay

Scorers – Turkey: Bayir (28), Welsh og (70). **Half-time:** 0-1

KAZAKHSTAN 2 SCOTLAND 2
Almaty (400); March 29, 2022

Scotland: Slicker, Ramsay (Banks 69), Welsh (Clayton 57), Graham, Doig, Barron, Mayo, Campbell, Leonard, Middleton, Burroughs (High 74). **Booked:** Barron, Welsh, Burroughs, Doig, Slicker

Scorers – Kazakhstan: Seydakhmet (71 pen), Zhumabek (90+5). **Scotland:** Graham (26), Clayton (58). **Half-time:** 0-1

BELGIUM 0 SCOTLAND 0
Sint-Truiden (1,248); June 5, 2022

Scotland: Sinclair, Welsh (Clayton 84), Mayo, Graham, Freeman, Barron, High, Burroughs, Mebude (Mulligan 88), Leonard (Kelly 71), Anderson. **Booked:** Mayo, Barron

DENMARK 1 SCOTLAND 1
Velje (2,151); June 10, 2022

Scotland: Sinclair, Freeman, Welsh, Mayo, Graham, Burroughs (King 80), Kelly, High, Mulligan, Leonard (Smith 64), Mebude. **Booked:** Mulligan

Scorers – Denmark: Kjaergaard (70). **Scotland:** Kelly (45). **Half-time:** 0-1

Belgium Q	8	6	2	0	14	2	12	20
Denmark	8	5	2	1	12	6	6	17
Turkey	8	2	2	4	7	11	-4	8
Scotland	8	1	4	3	6	10	-4	7
Kazakhstan	8	0	2	6	4	14	-10	2

FRIENDLY INTERNATIONAL

GEORGIA 3 ENGLAND 2
Batumi (600); November 16, 2021

England: Green, Drameh (Aarons 77), Cresswell, Mola, Thomas (Guehi 77), Garner (Skipp 77), Doyle, Gibbs-White (Ramsey 66), Gomes (Gordon 67), Balogun (S Greenwood 36), Brewster (Harwood-Bellis 71). **Booked:** Cresswell, Garner

Scorers – Georgia: Guliashvili (24, 46), Gocholeishvili (65). **England:** S Greenwood (81), Guehi (90+4). **Half-time:** 1-0

TRANSFER TRAIL

Player	From	To	Date	£
Philippe Coutinho	Liverpool	Barcelona	1/18	142,000,000
Jack Grealish	Aston Villa	Manchester City	8/21	100,000,000
Romelu Lukaku	Inter Milan	Chelses	8/21	97,500,000
Paul Pogba	Juventus	Manchester Utd	8/16	89,300,000
Eden Hazard	Chelsea	Real Madrid	6/19	89,000,000
Gareth Bale	Tottenham	Real Madrid	8/13	85,300,000
Cristiano Ronaldo	Manchester Utd	Real Madrid	7/09	80,000,000
Harry Maguire	Leicester	Manchester Utd	8/19	80,000,000
Romelu Lukaku	Everton	Manchester Utd	7/17	75,000,000
Virgil van Dijk	Southampton	Liverpool	1/18	75,000,000
Romelu Lukaku	Manchester Utd	Inter Milan	8/19	74,000,000
Jadon Sancho	Borussia Dortmund	Manchester Utd	7/21	73,000,000
Nicolas Pepe	Lille	Arsenal	8/19	72,000,000
Kepa Arrizabalaga	Athletic Bilbao	Chelsea	8/18	71,600,000
Kai Havertz	Bayer Leverekusen	Chelsea	9/20	71,000,000
Luis Suarez	Liverpool	Barcelona	7/14	65,000,000
Alisson	Roma	Liverpool	7/18	65,000,000
Ruben Dias	Benfica	Manchester City	9/20	65,000,000
Darwin Nunez	Benfica	Liverpool	6/22	64,000,000
Rodri	Atletico Madrid	Manchester City	7/19	62,800,000
Riyad Mahrez	Leicester	Manchester City	7/18	60,000,000
Joao Cancelo	Juventus	Manchester City	8/19	60,000,000
Richarlison	Everton	Tottenham	6/22	60,000,000
Angel di Maria	Real Madrid	Manchester Utd	8/14	59,700,000
Alvaro Morata	Chelsea	Atletico Madrid	7/20	58,300,000
Christian Pulisic	Borussia Dortmund	Chelsea	7/19	58,000,000
Alvaro Morata	Real Madrid	Chelsea	7/17	57,200,000
Diego Costa	Chelsea	Atletico Madrid	1/18	57,000,000
Aymeric Laporte	Athletic Bilbao	Manchester City	1/18	57,000,000
Pierre-Emerick Aubameyang	Borussia Dortmund	Arsenal	1/18	56,000,000
Kevin De Bruyne	Wolfsburg	Manchester City	8/15	54,500,000
Tanguy Ndombele	Lyon	Tottenham	7/19	53,800,000
Oscar	Chelsea	Shanghai Shenhua	1/17	52,000,000
Benjamin Mendy	Monaco	Manchester City	7/17	52,000,000
Fred	Shaktar Donetsk	Manchester Utd	6/18	52,000,000
Erling Haaland	Borussia Dortmund	Manchester City	6/22	51,200,000
Fernando Torres	Liverpool	Chelsea	1/11	50,000,000
David Luiz	Chelsea	Paris SG	6/14	50,000,000
Jorginho	Napoli	Chelsea	7/18	50,000,000
Aaron Wan-Bissaka	Crystal Palace	Manchester Utd	6/19	50,000,000
Ben White	Brighton	Arsenal	7/21	50,000,000
Raheem Sterling	Liverpool	Manchester City	7/15	49,000,000
Naby Keita	Leipzig	Liverpool	7/18	48,000,000
John Stones	Everton	Manchester City	8/16	47,500,000
Cristian Romero	Atalanta	Tottenham	8/21	47,500,000
Bruno Fernandes	Sporting Lisbon	Manchester Utd	1/20	47,000,000
Alexandre Lacazette	Lyon	Arsenal	7/17	46,500,000
Gylfi Sigurdsson	Swansea	Everton	8/17	45,000,000
Kyle Walker	Tottenham	Manchester City	7/17	45,000,000
Sebastien Haller	Eintracht Frankfurt	West Ham	7/19	45,000,000
Ben Chilwell	Leicester	Chelsea	8/20	45,000,000

Kalvin Phillips	Leeds	Manchester City	7/22	45,000,000
Gabriel Jesus	Manchester City	Arsenal	7/22	45,000,000
Leroy Sane	Manchester City	Bayern Munich	7/20	44,700,000
Angel di Maria	Manchester Utd	Paris SG	8/15	44,300,000
Fabinho	Monaco	Liverpool	5/8	43,700,000
Bernardo Silva	Monaco	Manchester City	6/17	43,000,000
Mesut Ozil	Real Madrid	Arsenal	9/13	42,400,000
Davinson Sanchez	Ajax	Tottenham	8/17	42,000,000
Diogo Jota	Wolves	Liverpool	9/20	41,000,000
Nemanja Matic	Chelsea	Manchester Utd	7/17	40,000,000
Richarlison	Watford	Everton	7/18	40,000,000
Youri Tielemans	Monaco	Leicester	7/19	40,000,000
Mateo Kovacic	Real Madrid	Chelsea	7/19	40,000,000
Nathan Ake	Bournemouth	Manchester City	8/20	40,000,000
Joelinton	Hoffenheim	Newcastle	7/19	40,000,000
Tiemoue Bakayoko	Monaco	Chelsea	7/17	39,700,000
Sergio Aguero	Atletico Madrid	Manchester City	7/11	38,500,000
Thibaut Courtois	Chelsea	Real Madrid	8/18	38,000,000
Hakim Ziyech	Ajax	Chelsea	6/00	37,800,000
Amad Diallo	Atalanta	Manchester Utd	1/21	37,200,000
Juan Mata	Chelsea	Manchester Utd	1/14	37,100,000
Leroy Sane	Schalke	Manchester City	7/16	37,000,000
Anthony Martial	Monaco	Manchester Utd	9/15	36,000,000
Felipe Anderson	Lazio	West Ham	7/18	36,000,000
Fabio Silva	Porto	Wolves	9/20	35,600,000
Sadio Mane	Liverpool	Bayern Munich	6/22	35,100,000
Andy Carroll	Newcastle	Liverpool	1/11	35,000,000
Cesc Fabregas	Arsenal	Barcelona	8/11	35,000,000
Alexis Sanchez	Barcelona	Arsenal	7/14	35,000,000
Granit Xhaka	Borussia M'gladbach	Arsenal	6/16	35,000,000
Shkodran Mustafi	Valencia	Arsenal	8/16	35,000,000
Alex Oxlade-Chamberlain	Arsenal	Liverpool	8/17	35,000,000
Danny Drinkwater	Leicester	Chelsea	8/17	35,000,000
Donny van de Beek	Ajax	Manchester Utd	9/20	35,000,000
Ibrahima Konate	RB Leipzig	Liverpool	6/21	35,000,000
Ederson	Benfica	Manchester City	6/17	34,900,000
Mohamed Salah	Roma	Liverpool	7/17	34,300,000
Fabio Vieira	Porto	Arsenal	5/22	34,200,000
Danilo	Manchester City	Juventus	8/19	34,100,000
Sadio Mane	Southampton	Liverpool	6/16	34,000,000
Raphael Varane	Real Madrid	Manchester Utd	8/21	34,000,000
Tammy Abraham	Chelsea	Roma	8/21	34,000,000
Michy Batshuayi	Marseille	Chelsea	7/16	33,000,000
Emiliano Buendia	Norwich	Aston Villa	6/21	33,000,000
Sven Botman	Lille	Newcastle	6/22	33,000,000
Robinho	Real Madrid	Manchester City	9/08	32,500,000
Christian Benteke	Aston Villa	Liverpool	7/15	32,500,000
Eden Hazard	Lille	Chelsea	6/12	32,000,000
Diego Costa	Atletico Madrid	Chelsea	7/14	32,000,000
N'Golo Kante	Leicester	Chelsea	7/16	32,000,000
David Luiz	Paris SG	Chelsea	8/16	32,000,000
Eliaquim Mangala	Porto	Manchester City	8/14	31,900,000
Wesley Fofana	St Etienne	Leicester	10/20	31,500,000
Nayef Aguerd	Rennes	West Ham	6/22	31,500,000

Ismaila Sarr	Rennes	Watford	8/19	31,000,000
Dimitar Berbatov	Tottenham	Manchester Utd	9/08	30,750,000
Victor Lindelof	Benfica	Manchester Utd	6/17	30,700,000
Andriy Shevchenko	AC Milan	Chelsea	5/06	30,800,000
Xabi Alonso	Liverpool	Real Madrid	8/09	30,000,000
Fernandinho	Shakhtar Donetsk	Manchester City	6/13	30,000,000
Willian	Anzhi Makhachkala	Chelsea	8/13	30,000,000
Erik Lamela	Roma	Tottenham	8/13	30,000,000
Luke Shaw	Southampton	Manchester Utd	6/14	30,000,000
Eric Bailly	Villarreal	Manchester Utd	6/16	30,000,000
Moussa Sissoko	Newcastle	Tottenham,	8/16	30,000,000
Ayoze Perez	Newcastle	Leicester	7/19	30,000,000
Idrissa Gueye	Everton	Paris SG	7/19	30,000,000
Martin Odegaard	Real Madrid	Arsenal	8/21	30,000,000

BRITISH RECORD TRANSFERS FROM FIRST £1,000 DEAL

Player	From	To	Date	£
Alf Common	Sunderland	Middlesbrough	2/1905	1,000
Syd Puddefoot	West Ham	Falkirk	2/22	5,000
Warney Cresswell	South Shields	Sunderland	3/22	5,500
Bob Kelly	Burnley	Sunderland	12/25	6,500
David Jack	Bolton	Arsenal	10/28	10,890
Bryn Jones	Wolves	Arsenal	8/38	14,500
Billy Steel	Morton	Derby	9/47	15,000
Tommy Lawton	Chelsea	Notts Co	11/47	20,000
Len Shackleton	Newcastle	Sunderland	2/48	20,500
Johnny Morris	Manchester Utd	Derby	2/49	24,000
Eddie Quigley	Sheffield Wed	Preston	12/49	26,500
Trevor Ford	Aston Villa	Sunderland	10/50	30,000
Jackie Sewell	Notts Co	Sheffield Wed	3/51	34,500
Eddie Firmani	Charlton	Sampdoria	7/55	35,000
John Charles	Leeds	Juventus	4/57	65,000
Denis Law	Manchester City	Torino	6/61	100,000
Denis Law	Torino	Manchester Utd	7/62	115,000
Allan Clarke	Fulham	Leicester	6/68	150,000
Allan Clarke	Leicester	Leeds	6/69	165,000
Martin Peters	West Ham	Tottenham	3/70	200,000
Alan Ball	Everton	Arsenal	12/71	220,000
David Nish	Leicester	Derby	8/72	250,000
Bob Latchford	Birmingham	Everton	2/74	350,000
Graeme Souness	Middlesbrough	Liverpool	1/78	352,000
Kevin Keegan	Liverpool	Hamburg	6/77	500,000
David Mills	Middlesbrough	WBA	1/79	516,000
Trevor Francis	Birmingham	Nottm Forest	2/79	1,180,000
Steve Daley	Wolves	Manchester City	9/79	1,450,000
Andy Gray	Aston Villa	Wolves	9/79	1,469,000
Bryan Robson	WBA	Manchester Utd	10/81	1,500,000
Ray Wilkins	Manchester Utd	AC Milan	5/84	1,500,000
Mark Hughes	Manchester Utd	Barcelona	5/86	2,300,000
Ian Rush	Liverpool	Juventus	6/87	3,200,000
Chris Waddle	Tottenham	Marseille	7/89	4,250,000
David Platt	Aston Villa	Bari	7/91	5,500,000
Paul Gascoigne	Tottenham	Lazio	6/92	5,500,000

Andy Cole	Newcastle	Manchester Utd	1/95	7,000,000
Dennis Bergkamp	Inter Milan	Arsenal	6/95	7,500,000
Stan Collymore	Nottm Forest	Liverpool	6/95	8,500,000
Alan Shearer	Blackburn	Newcastle	7/96	15,000,000
Nicolas Anelka	Arsenal	Real Madrid	8/99	22,500,000
Juan Sebastian Veron	Lazio	Manchester Utd	7/01	28,100,000
Rio Ferdinand	Leeds	Manchester Utd	7/02	29,100,000
Andriy Shevchenko	AC Milan	Chelsea	5/06	30,800,000
Robinho	Real Madrid	Manchester City	9/08	32,500,000
Cristiano Ronaldo	Manchester Utd	Real Madrid	7/09	80,000,000
Gareth Bale	Tottenham	Real Madrid	9/13	85,300,000
Paul Pogba	Juventus	Manchester Utd	8/16	89,300,000
Philippe Coutinho	Liverpool	Barcelona	1/18	142,000,000

• World's first £1m transfer: GuiseppeSavoldi, Bologna to Napoli, July 1975

TOP FOREIGN SIGNINGS

Player	From	To	Date	£
Neymar	Barcelona	Paris SG	8/17	198,000,000
Kylian Mbappe	Monaco	Paris SG	8/17	165,700,000
Ousmane Dembele	Borussia Dortmund	Barcelona	8/17	134,000,000
Joao Felix	Benfica	Atletico Madrid	7/19	113,000,000
Antoine Griezmann	Atletico Madrid	Barcelona	7/19	107,000,000
Cristiano Ronaldo	Real Madrid	Juventus	7/18	99,200,000
Gonzalo Higuain	Napoli	Juventus	7/16	75,300,000
Aurelien Tchouameni	Monaco	Real Madrid	6/22	68,300,000
Lucas Hernandez	Atletico Madrid	Bayern Munich	7/19	68,000,000
Matthijs de Ligt	Ajax	Juventus	7/19	67,500,000
Arthur	Barcelona	Juventus	7/20	66,000,000
Frenkie de Jong	Ajax	Barcelona	1/19	65,000,000
Luka Jovic	Eintracht Frankfurt	Real Madrid	6/19	62,000,000
Zlatan Ibrahimovic	Inter Milan	Barcelona	7/09	60,300,000
James Rodriguez	Monaco	Real Madrid	7/14	60,000,000
Kaka	AC Milan	Real Madrid	6/08	56,000,000

WORLD'S MOST EXPENSIVE TEENAGER
£165,700,000: Kylian Mbappe, 19, Monaco to Paris SG, August 2017

WORLD RECORD FOR 16-YEAR-OLD
£39,600,000: Vinicius Junior, Flamengo to Real Madrid, July 2018

RECORD TRIBUNAL FEE
£6.5m: Danny Ings, Burnley to Liverpool, Jun 2016

RECORD FEE BETWEEN SCOTTISH CLUBS
£4.4m: Scott Brown, Hibernian to Celtic, May 2007

RECORD NON-LEAGUE FEE
£1m: Jamie Vardy, Fleetwood to Leicester, May 2012

RECORD FEE BETWEEN NON-LEAGUE CLUBS
£275,000: Richard Brodie, York to Crawley, Aug 2010

MILESTONES

1848 First code of rules compiled at Cambridge University.

1857 Sheffield FC, world's oldest football club, formed.

1862 Notts Co (oldest League club) formed.

1863 Football Association founded – their first rules of game agreed.

1871 FA Cup introduced.

1872 First official International: Scotland 0 England 0. Corner-kick introduced.

1873 Scottish FA formed; Scottish Cup introduced.

1874 Shinguards introduced.

1875 Crossbar introduced (replacing tape).

1876 FA of Wales formed.

1877 Welsh Cup introduced.

1878 Referee's whistle first used.

1880 Irish FA founded; Irish Cup introduced.

1883 Two-handed throw-in introduced.

1885 Record first-class score (Arbroath 36 Bon Accord 0 – Scottish Cup). Professionalism legalised.

1886 International Board formed.

1887 Record FA Cup score (Preston 26 Hyde 0).

1888 Football League founded by William McGregor. First matches on Sept 8.

1889 Preston win Cup and League (first club to complete Double).

1890 Scottish League and Irish League formed.

1891 Goal-nets introduced. Penalty-kick introduced.

1892 Inter-League games began. Football League Second Division formed.

1893 FA Amateur Cup launched.

1894 Southern League formed.

1895 FA Cup stolen from Birmingham shop window – never recovered.

1897 First Players' Union formed. Aston Villa win Cup and League.

1898 Promotion and relegation introduced.

1901 Maximum wage rule in force (£4 a week). Tottenham first professional club to take FA Cup south. First six-figure attendance (110,802) at FA Cup Final.

1902 Ibrox Park disaster (25 killed). Welsh League formed.

1904 FIFA founded (7 member countries).

1905 First £1,000 transfer (Alf Common, Sunderland to Middlesbrough).

1907 Players' Union revived.

1908 Transfer fee limit (£350) fixed in January and withdrawn in April.

1911 New FA Cup trophy – in use to 1991. Transfer deadline introduced.

1914 King George V first reigning monarch to attend FA Cup Final.

1916 Entertainment Tax introduced.

1919 League extended to 44 clubs.

1920 Third Division (South) formed.

1921 Third Division (North) formed.

1922 Scottish League (Div II) introduced.

1923 Beginning of football pools. First Wembley Cup Final.

1924 First International at Wembley (England 1 Scotland 1). Rule change allows goals to be scored direct from corner-kicks.

1925 New offside law.

1926 Huddersfield complete first League Championship hat-trick.

1927 First League match broadcast (radio): Arsenal v Sheffield United. First radio broadcast of Cup Final (winners Cardiff City). Charles Clegg, president of FA, becomes first knight of football.

1928 First £10,000 transfer – David Jack (Bolton to Arsenal). WR ('Dixie') Dean (Everton) creates League record – 60 goals in season. Britain withdraws from FIFA

1930 Uruguay first winners of World Cup.

1931 WBA win Cup and promotion.

1933 Players numbered for first time in Cup Final (1-22).

1934 Sir Frederick Wall retires as FA secretary; successor Stanley Rous. Death of Herbert Chapman (Arsenal manager).

1935 Arsenal equal Huddersfield's Championship hat-trick record. Official two-referee trials.

1936 Joe Payne's 10-goal League record (Luton 12 Bristol Rov 0).

1937 British record attendance: 149,547 at Scotland v England match.

1938 First live TV transmission of FA Cup Final. Football League 50th Jubilee. New pitch marking – arc on edge of penalty-area. Laws of Game re-drafted by Stanley Rous. Arsenal pay record £14,500 fee for Bryn Jones (Wolves).

1939 Compulsory numbering of players in Football League. First six-figure attendance for League match (Rangers v Celtic 118,567). All normal competitions suspended for duration of Second World War.

1945 Scottish League Cup introduced.

1946 British associations rejoin FIFA. Bolton disaster (33 killed) during FA Cup tie with Stoke. Walter Winterbottom appointed England's first director of coaching.

1947 Great Britain beat Rest of Europe 6-1 at Hampden Park, Glasgow. First £20,000 transfer – Tommy Lawton, Chelsea to Notts Co

1949 Stanley Rous, secretary FA, knighted. England's first home defeat outside British Champ. (0-2 v Eire).

1950 Football League extended from 88 to 92 clubs. World record crowd (203,500) at World Cup Final, Brazil v Uruguay, in Rio. Scotland's first home defeat by foreign team (0-1 v Austria).

1951 White ball comes into official use.

1952 Newcastle first club to win FA Cup at Wembley in successive seasons.

1953 England's first Wembley defeat by foreign opponents (3-6 v Hungary).

1954 Hungary beat England 7-1 in Budapest.

1955 First FA Cup match under floodlights (prelim round replay): Kidderminster v Brierley Hill Alliance.

1956 First FA Cup ties under floodlights in competition proper. First League match by floodlight (Portsmouth v Newcastle). Real Madrid win the first European Cup.

1957 Last full Football League programme on Christmas Day. Entertainment Tax withdrawn.

1958 Manchester United air crash at Munich. League re-structured into four divisions.

1960 Record transfer fee: £55,000 for Denis Law (Huddersfield to Manchester City). Wolves win Cup, miss Double and Championship hat-trick by one goal. FA recognise Sunday football. Football League Cup launched.

1961 Tottenham complete the first Championship–FA Cup double this century. Maximum wage (£20 a week) abolished in High Court challenge by George Eastham. First British £100-a-week wage paid (by Fulham to Johnny Haynes). First £100,000 British transfer – Denis Law, Manchester City to Torino. Sir Stanley Rous elected president of FIFA

1962 Manchester United raise record British transfer fee to £115,000 for Denis Law.

1963 FA Centenary. Season extended to end of May due to severe winter. First pools panel. English "retain and transfer" system ruled illegal in High Court test case.

1964 Rangers' second great hat-trick – Scottish Cup, League Cup and League. Football League and Scottish League guaranteed £500,000 a year in new fixtures copyright agreement with Pools. First televised 'Match of the Day' (BBC2): Liverpool 3 Arsenal 2.

1965 Bribes scandal – ten players jailed (and banned for life by FA) for match-fixing 1960–63. Stanley Matthews knighted in farewell season. Arthur Rowley (Shrewsbury) retires with record of 434 League goals. Substitutes allowed for injured players in Football League matches (one per team).

1966 England win World Cup (Wembley).

1967 Alf Ramsey, England manager, knighted; OBE for captain Bobby Moore. Celtic become first

British team to win European Cup. First substitutes allowed in FA Cup Final (Tottenham v Chelsea) but not used.

1968 First FA Cup Final televised live in colour (BBC2 – WBA v Everton). Manchester United first English club to win European Cup.

1970 FIFA/UEFA approve penalty shoot-out in deadlocked ties.

1971 Arsenal win League Championship and FA Cup. Sixty-six supporters die in the Ibrox Stadium disaster.

1973 Football League introduce 3-up, 3-down promotion/relegation between Divisions 1, 2 and 3 and 4-up, 4-down between Divisions 3 and 4.

1974 First FA Cup ties played on Sunday. League football played on Sunday for first time. Last FA Amateur Cup Final. Joao Havelange (Brazil) succeeds Sir Stanley Rous as FIFA president.

1975 Scottish Premier Division introduced.

1976 Football League introduce goal difference (replacing goal average) and red/yellow cards.

1977 Liverpool achieve the double of League Championship and European Cup. Don Revie defects to United Arab Emirates when England manager – successor Ron Greenwood.

1978 Freedom of contract for players accepted by Football League. PFA lifts ban on foreign players in English football. Viv Anderson (Nottm Forest) first black player to win a full England cap.

1979 First all-British £500,000 transfer – David Mills, Middlesbrough to WBA. First British million pound transfer (Trevor Francis – Birmingham to Nottm Forest). Andy Gray moves from Aston Villa to Wolves for a record £1,469,000 fee.

1981 Tottenham win 100th FA Cup Final. Liverpool first British side to win European Cup three times. Three points for a win introduced by Football League. Death of Bill Shankly, manager–legend of Liverpool 1959–74. Record British transfer – Bryan Robson (WBA to Manchester United), £1,500,000.

1982 Aston Villa become sixth consecutive English winners of European Cup. Tottenham retain FA Cup – first club to do so since Tottenham 1961 and 1962. Football.

1983 Liverpool complete League Championship–Milk Cup double for second year running. Manager Bob Paisley retires. Aberdeen first club to do Cup-Winners' Cup and domestic Cup double. Football League clubs vote to keep own match receipts. Football League agree two-year contract for live TV coverage of ten matches per season (5 Friday night, BBC, 5 Sunday afternoon, ITV).

1984 Aberdeen take Scottish Cup for third successive season, win Scottish Championship, too. Tottenham win UEFA Cup on penalty shoot-out. Liverpool win European Cup on penalty shoot-out to complete unique treble with Milk Cup and League title (as well as Championship hat-trick). N Ireland win the final British Championship. France win European Championship – their first honour. Britain's biggest score this century: Stirling Alb 20 Selkirk 0 (Scottish Cup).

1985 Bradford City fire disaster – 56 killed. First £1m receipts from match in Britain (FA Cup Final). Kevin Moran (Manchester United) first player to be sent off in FA Cup Final. Celtic win 100th Scottish FA Cup Final. European Cup Final horror (Liverpool v Juventus, riot in Brussels) 39 die. UEFA ban all English clubs indefinitely from European competitions. No TV coverage at start of League season – first time since 1963 (resumption delayed until January 1986). Sept: first ground-sharing in League history – Charlton Athletic move from The Valley to Selhurst Park (Crystal Palace).

1986 Liverpool complete League and Cup double in player-manager Kenny Dalglish's first season in charge. Swindon (4th Div Champions) set League points record (102). League approve reduction of First Division to 20 clubs by 1988. Two substitutes in FA Cup and League (Littlewoods) Cup. Two-season League/TV deal (£6.2m):- BBC and ITV each show seven live League matches per season, League Cup semi-finals and Final. Luton first club to ban all visiting supporters; as sequel are themselves banned from League Cup. Oldham and Preston install artificial pitches, making four in Football League (following QPR and Luton).

1987 League introduce play-off matches to decide final promotion/relegation places in all divisions. Re-election abolished – bottom club in Div 4 replaced by winners of GM

Vauxhall Conference. Two substitutes approved for Football League 1987–8. Red and yellow disciplinary cards (scrapped 1981) re-introduced by League and FA Football League sponsored by Barclays. First Div reduced to 21 clubs.

1988 Football League Centenary. First Division reduced to 20 clubs.

1989: Soccer gets £74m TV deal: £44m over 4 years, ITV; £30m over 5 years, BBC/BSB. Hillsborough disaster: 95 die at FA Cup semi-final (Liverpool v Nottm Forest). Arsenal win closest-ever Championship with last kick.

1990 Both FA Cup semi-finals played on Sunday and televised live. Play-off finals move to Wembley; Swindon win place in Div 1, then relegated back to Div 2 (breach of financial regulations) – Sunderland promoted instead. Peter Shilton retires as England goalkeeper with 125 caps (world record). Graham Taylor (Aston Villa) succeeds Bobby Robson as England manager. English clubs back in Europe (Manchester United and Aston Villa) after 5-year exile.

1991 First FA Cup semi-final at Wembley (Tottenham 3 Arsenal 1). Bert Millichip (FA chairman) and Philip Carter (Everton chairman) knighted. End of artificial pitches in Div 1 (Luton, Oldham). Scottish League reverts to 12-12-14 format (as in 1987–8). Penalty shoot-out introduced to decide FA Cup ties level after one replay.

1992 FA launch Premier League (22 clubs). Football League reduced to three divisions (71 clubs). Record TV-sport deal: BSkyB/BBC to pay £304m for 5-year coverage of Premier League. ITV do £40m, 4-year deal with Football League. FIFA approve new back-pass rule (goalkeeper must not handle ball kicked to him by team-mate).

1993 For first time both FA Cup semi-finals at Wembley (Sat, Sun). Arsenal first club to complete League Cup/FA Cup double. FA in record British sports sponsorship deal (£12m over 4 years) with brewers Bass for FA Carling Premiership, from Aug. Brian Clough retires after 18 years as Nottm Forest manager; as does Jim McLean (21 years manager of Dundee Utd). Premier League introduce squad numbers with players' names on shirts. Graham Taylor resigns as England manager after World Cup exit. Bobby Moore (51), England World Cup winning captain, dies.

1994 Death of Sir Matt Busby. Terry Venables appointed England coach. Last artificial pitch in English football goes – Preston revert to grass, summer 1994. Bobby Charlton knighted. Scottish League format changes to four divisions of ten clubs. FA announce first sponsorship of FA Cup – Littlewoods Pools (4-year, £14m deal, plus £6m for Charity Shield.

1995 First England match abandoned through crowd trouble (v Republic of Ireland, Dublin). Premiership reduced to 20 clubs. Starting season 1995–6, teams allowed to use 3 substitutes per match, not necessarily including a goalkeeper. European Court of Justice upholds Bosman ruling, barring transfer fees for players out of contract and removing limit on number of foreign players clubs can field.

1996 Death of Bob Paisley (77), ex-Liverpool, most successful manager in English Football. FA appoint Chelsea manager Glenn Hoddle to succeed Terry Venables as England coach after Euro 96. Manchester United first English club to achieve Double twice (and in 3 seasons). Football League completes £125m, 5-year TV deal with BSkyB starting 1996–7. England stage European Championship, reach semi-finals, lose on pens to tournament winners Germany. Linesmen become known as 'referees' assistants'. Alan Shearer football's first £15m player (Blackburn to Newcastle). Peter Shilton first player to make 1,000 League appearances.

1997 Howard Wilkinson appointed English football's first technical director. England's first home defeat in World Cup (0-1 v Italy). Ruud Gullit (Chelsea) first foreign coach to win FA Cup. Rangers equal Celtic's record of 9 successive League titles. Manchester United win Premier League for fourth time in 5 seasons. New record World Cup score: Iran 17, Maldives 0 (qualifying round). Season 1997–8 starts Premiership's record £36m, 4-year sponsorship extension with brewers Bass (Carling).

1998 In French manager Arsene Wenger's second season at Highbury, Arsenal become second English club to complete the Double twice. In breakaway from Scottish League, top ten clubs form new Premiership under SFA, starting season 1998-9. Football League celebrates its 100th season, 1998-9. New FA Cup sponsors – French insurance giants AXA (25m, 4-year deal).

1999 FA buy Wembley Stadium (£103m) for £320m, plan rebuilding (Aug 2000–March 2003) as new national stadium. Scotland's new Premier League takes 3-week mid-season break in January. Sky screen Oxford Utd v Sunderland (Div 1) as first pay-per-view match on TV. FA sack England coach Glenn Hoddle; Fulham's Kevin Keegan replaces him. Sir Alf Ramsey, England's World Cup-winning manager, dies aged 79. With effect 1999, FA Cup Final to be decided on day (via penalties, if necessary). Hampden Park re-opens for Scottish Cup Final after £63m refit. Alex Ferguson knighted after Manchester United complete Premiership, FA Cup, European Cup treble. End of Cup-Winners' Cup (merged into 121-club UEFA Cup). FA allow holders Manchester United to withdraw from FA Cup to participate in FIFA's inaugural World Club Championship. Chelsea first British club to field an all-foreign line-up – at Southampton (Prem). FA vote in favour of streamlined 14-man board of directors to replace its 92-member council.

2000 Wales move to Cardiff's £125m Millennium Stadium (v Finland). Brent Council approve plans for new £475m Wembley Stadium (completion target spring 2003); demolition of old stadium to begin after England v Germany (World Cup qual.). FA Premiership and Nationwide League to introduce (season 2000–01) rule whereby referees advance free-kick by 10 yards and caution player who shows dissent, delays kick or fails to retreat 10 yards. Scottish football increased to 42 League clubs in 2000–01 (12 in Premier League and 3 divisions of ten; Peterhead and Elgin elected from Highland League). France win European Championship – first time a major international tournament has been jointly hosted (Holland/ Belgium). England manager Kevin Keegan resigns after World Cup defeat by Germany in Wembley's last International. Sven-Goran Eriksson agrees to succeed him.

2001 Scottish Premier League experiment with split into two after 33 matches. ITV, after winning auction against BBC's Match of the Day, begin £183m, 3-season contract for highlights of Premiership matches; BSkyB's live coverage (66 matches per season) for next 3 years will cost £1.1bn. BBC and BSkyB pay £400m (3-year contract) for live coverage of FA Cup and England home matches. ITV and Ondigital pay £315m to screen Nationwide League and Worthington Cup matches. In new charter for referees, top men can earn up to £60,000 a season in Premiership. Real Madrid break world transfer record, buying Zinedine Zidane from Juventus for £47.2m. FA introduce prize money, round by round, in FA Cup.

2002 Scotland appoint their first foreign manager, Germany's former national coach Bertie Vogts replacing Craig Brown. Collapse of ITV Digital deal, with Football League owed £178m, threatens lower-division clubs. Bobby Robson knighted. New record British transfer and world record for defender, £29.1m Rio Ferdinand (Leeds to Manchester United). Transfer window introduced to British football. FA Charity Shield renamed FA Community Shield. After 2-year delay, demolition of Wembley Stadium begins. October:

2003 FA Cup draw (from 4th Round) reverts to Monday lunchtime. Scottish Premier League decide to end mid-winter shut-down. For first time, two Football League clubs demoted (replaced by two from Conference). July: David Beckham becomes record British export (Manchester United to Real Madrid, £23.3m). Biggest takeover in British football history – Roman Abramovich buys control of Chelsea for £150m Wimbledon become England's first franchised club in 68-mile move to Milton Keynes.

2004 Arsenal first club to win Premiership with unbeaten record.. Trevor Brooking knighted. Wimbledon change name to Milton Keynes Dons. Greece beat hosts Portugal to win European Championship as biggest outsiders (80-1 at start). Div 1 rebranded as Football League Championship, with 2nd and 3rd Divisions, becoming Leagues 1 and 2. All-time League record of 49 unbeaten Premiership matches set by Arsenal.

2005 Liverpool lift European Cup on penalties after trailing 0-3 in Champions League Final. Wigan, a League club since only 1978, promoted to Premiership. In new record British-club take-over, American tycoon Malcolm Glazer buys Manchester United for £790m George Best dies aged 59.

2006 Steve Staunton succeeds Brian Kerr as Republic of Ireland manager. Sven-Goran Eriksson steps down as England coach. Steve McClaren replaces him. The Premier League announce a new 3-year TV deal worth £1.7 billion under which Sky lose their monopoly of coverage.

2007 Walter Smith resigns as Scotland manager to return to Rangers and is replaced by Alex McLeish. The new £800m Wembley Stadium is completed. World Cup-winner Alan Ball dies aged 61. Lawrie Sanchez resigns as Northern Ireland manager to take over at Fulham. Nigel Worthington succeeds him. Steve McClaren is sacked after England fail to qualify for the European Championship Finals and is replaced by Fabio Capello. The Republic of Ireland's Steve Staunton also goes. Scotland's Alex McLeish resigns to become Birmingham manager.

2008 The Republic of Ireland follow England's lead in appointing an Italian coach – Giovanni Trapattoni. George Burley leaves Southampton to become Scotland manager. Manchester United beat Chelsea in the first all-English Champions League Final.

2009 Sky secure the rights to five of the six Premier League packages from 2010–13 with a bid of £1.6bn. David Beckham breaks Bobby Moore's record number of caps for an England outfield player with his 109th appearance. A British league record for not conceding a goal ends on 1,311 minutes for Manchester United's Edwin van der Sar. AC Milan's Kaka moves to Real Madrid for a world record fee of £56m. Nine days later, Manchester United agree to sell Cristiano Ronaldo to Real for £80m. Sir Bobby Robson dies aged 76. Shay Given and Kevin Kilbane win their 100th caps for the Republic of Ireland. The Premier League vote for clubs to have eight home-grown players in their squads. George Burley is sacked as Scotland manager and replaced by Craig Levein.

2010 Portsmouth become the first Premier League club to go into administration. John Toshack resigns as Wales manager and is replaced by former captain Gary Speed. England are humiliated in the vote for the 2018 World Cup which goes to Russia, with the 2022 tournament awarded to Qatar.

2011 Seven club managers are sacked in a week. The transfer record between British clubs is broken twice in a day, with Liverpool buying Newcastle's Andy Carroll for £35m and selling Fernando Torres to Chelsea for £50m. Football League clubs vote to reduce the number of substitutes from seven to five. Nigel Worthington steps down as Northern Ireland manager and is succeeded by Michael O'Neill. Sir Alex Ferguson completes 25 years as Manchester United manager. Huddersfield set a Football League record of 43 successive unbeaten league games. Football mourns Gary Speed after the Wales manager is found dead at his home.

2012 Chris Coleman is appointed the new Wales manager. Fabio Capello resigns as manager after John Terry is stripped of the England captaincy for the second time. Roy Hodgson takes over. Rangers are forced into liquidation by crippling debts and a newly-formed club are demoted from the Scottish Premier League to Division Three. Manchester City become champions for the first time since 1968 after the tightest finish to a Premier League season. Chelsea win a penalty shoot-out against Bayern Munich in the Champions League Final. Steven Gerrard (England) and Damien Duff (Republic of Ireland) win their 100th caps. The FA's new £120m National Football Centre at Burton upon Trent is opened. Scotland manager Craig Levein is sacked.

2013 Gordon Strachan is appointed Scotland manager. FIFA and the Premier League announce the introduction of goal-line technology. Sir Alex Ferguson retires after 26 years as Manchester United manager. Wigan become the first club to lift the FA Cup and be relegated in the same season. Chelsea win the Europa League. Ashley Cole and Frank Lampard win their 100th England caps. Robbie Keane becomes the most capped player in the British Isles on his 126th appearance for the Republic of Ireland. Scottish Football League clubs agree to merge with the Scottish Premier League. Real Madrid sign Tottenham's Gareth Bale for a world record £85.3m. Giovanni Trapatonni is replaced as Republic of Ireland manager by Martin O'Neill.

2014 Sir Tom Finney dies aged 91. England experience their worst-ever World Cup, finishing bottom the group with a single point. Germany record one of the most remarkable scorelines in World Cup history – 7-1 against Brazil in the semi-finals. England's Wayne

Rooney and the Republic of Ireland's John O'Shea win their 100th caps.

2015 The Premier League sell live TV rights for 2016-19 to Sky and BT for a record £5.13bn. FIFA president Sepp Blatter resigns as a bribery and corruption scandal engulfs the world governing body. Blatter and suspended UEFA president Michel Platini are banned for eight years, reduced on appeal to six years.

2016 An inquest jury rules that the 96 Liverpool fans who died in the Hillsborough disaster of 1989 were unlawfully killed. Leicester, 5,000-1 outsiders become Premier League champions in one of the game's biggest-ever surprises. Aaron Hughes wins his 100th cap for Northern Ireland. FA Cup quarter-final replays are scrapped. England manager Roy Hodgson resigns. He is replaced by Sam Allardyce, who is forced out after one match for 'inappropriate conduct' and succeeded by Gareth Southgate.

2017 Paris Saint-Germain sign Barcelona's Neymar for a world record £198m. Managers Gordon Strachan (Scotland) and Chris Coleman (Wales) resign. Steven Davis reaches a century of Northern Ireland caps. Manchester United win the Europa League. Celtic are champions without losing a game. Arsenal win a record 13th FA Cup, Arsene Wenger for a record seventh time. Wayne Rooney retires from international football as England's record scorer with 53 goals.

2018 Manchester City become the first English champions to total 100 points. Celtic are the first in Scotland to win back-to-back domestic trebles. Alex McLeish (Scotland) and Ryan Giggs (Wales) are appointed. Arsene Wenger leaves Arsenal after 22 years as manager. A helicopter crash outside Leicester's King Power Stadium claims the lives of club owner Vichai Srivaddhanaprabha, the pilot and three others on board. Martin O'Neill is sacked as Republic of Ireland manager and replaced by Mick McCarthy, his second time in charge.

2019 World Cup-winner Gordon Banks dies aged 81. Tottenham open their new £1bn stadium. Manchester City achieve an unprecedented domestic treble. Celtic also make history with a third successive Scottish treble. Scotland manager Alex McLeish is sacked and replaced by Kilmarnock's Steve Clarke. For the first time, English clubs occupy all four places in the European finals - Liverpool defeating Tottenham in the Champions League and Chelsea beating Arsenal to win the Europa League. Bury are expelled from the EFL for financial mismanagement. England play their 1,000th international, against Montenegro. World Cup winner Martin Peters dies aged 76.

2020 Coronavirus forces the English League's One and Two and all four Scottish divisions to be abandoned, with a points-per-game system settling promotion and relegation issues, The Premier League and Championship complete the season, after a three-month break, with Liverpool title winners for the first time since 1990. Euro 2020 is postponed for a year. England lose two more World Cup winners - Jack Charlton (85) and Nobby Stiles (78). FA Cup replays are scrapped. Ian Baraclough succeeds Michael O'Neill as Northern Ireland manager. Stephen Kenny replaces Mick McCarthy in charge of the Republic of Ireland.

2021 Northern Ireland captain Steven Davis becomes Britain's most capped player, overtaking Peter Shilton's record of 125. Chelsea win the Champions League. Rangers deny Celtic a tenth successive Scottish title. Cristiano Ronaldo becomes the highest scorer in international football with his 111th goal for Portugal.

2022 Russian teams are banned from international and club competitions following the invasion of Ukraine. An American-Swiss consortium pays £4.25bn to take over Chelsea. Wales qualify for their first World Cup for 64 years.

FINAL WHISTLE – OBITUARIES 2021–22

JULY 2021

TERRY COOPER, 77, scored the goal that launched a golden era for Leeds and helped establish him as arguably the club's finest left-back. It brought victory over Arsenal in the 1968 League Cup Final and was followed by the League title when his side under Don Revie finished ahead of Liverpool and Everton. Cooper twice won the Fairs Cup – forerunner of the UEFA Cup – against Ferencvaros and Juventus. He also played in the 1970 FA Cup Final, won by Chelsea, but missed two more against Arsenal and Sunderland with a broken leg. After 351 appearances, Cooper joined Jack Charlton's Middlesbrough, then had spells with Bristol City (twice), Bristol Rovers and Doncaster. He won 20 England caps and won praise from Pele for his performances at the 1970 World Cup. His managerial career embraced the two Bristol clubs, Birmingham and Exeter (twice). After that he scouted for Southampton. His death marked a sad 15 months for Leeds, with Charlton, Norman Hunter, Peter Lorimer and Trevor Cherry also passing away.

MIKE SMITH, 83, became the first non-Welshman to manage the national team and the first to be in charge full-time. He succeeded Dave Bowen in 1974 and led the team to the quarter-finals of the European Championship two years later when they topped a group including Hungary and Austria. Wales lost 3-1 on aggregate in the last eight to Yugoslavia – the last time that format was used – after conceding a controversial penalty in the second leg at Ninian Park. They failed to qualify for the 1978 World Cup following a 2-0 defeat by Scotland in a 'home' game at Anfield. Smith, who played as an amateur for Corinthian Casuals, left to manage Hull, then took Egypt to victory in the 1986 African Cup on Nations. He had a second spell as Wales manager between 1994–95.

MICK BATES, 73, had to compete with Billy Bremner and Johnny Giles for a place in the Leeds midfield during the most successful period in the club's history. It brought two League titles, the FA Cup, League Cup and two Inter-Cities Fairs Cup successes – and Bates often had to play a supporting role. But he remained loyal during 14 years at Elland Road, making 191 appearances and scoring in the victory over Juventus in the 1971 final of the Fairs Cup – forerunner of the UEFA Cup. Along with members of Don Revie's squad, Bates was awarded the Freedom of the City by Leeds Council as part of the club's 2019 Centenary celebrations. He also had spells with Walsall, Bradford City and Doncaster before retiring in 1981.

GEORGE CURTIS, 82, played a major role in two memorable periods for Coventry. As a player, he made 543 appearances between 1955–69 – a record surpassed only by goalkeeper Steve Ogrizovic. The captain and tough-tackling centre-half helped the club's rise, under Jimmy Hill, from the old fourth division to the top-flight. After a spell with Aston Villa and retirement, he became commercial manager and later managing director. He also co-managed the team, alongside John Sillett, to FA Cup success – a 3-2 victory over Tottenham at Wembley in 1987.

PETER WILLIS, 83, was the first referee to show a red card in an FA Cup Final, dismissing Manchester United's Kevin Moran against Everton at Wembley in 1985. He officiated from 1972–86, taking charge of the 1982 Liverpool–Tottenham League Cup Final, and was president of the Referees' Association for 18 years. Willis, from County Durham, was restricted to Newcastle reserves as a player and chose a career with the police.

ERNIE MOSS, 71, made 850 appearances and scored 284 goals in a 20-year career with nine clubs. It began in 1968 at home-town Chesterfield and the centre-forward had two further spells there, during which they were twice champions of Division Four. His tally was a club-record 192 goals in 539 matches. Moss helped Port Vale and Doncaster to promotion from that division and also played for Peterborough, Mansfield, Lincoln, Stockport, Scarborough and Rochdale. He then had 15 years managing non-league clubs.

ALLY DAWSON, 63 joined Rangers straight from school at 16, made his debut in 1975 and went on to win six honours during 12 seasons at the club. There were two Scottish Cups and four League Cups included in 315 appearances under Jock Wallace twice, John Greig and latterly Graeme Souness. Dawson, a defender who won five Scotland caps, also played for Blackburn and Airdrieonians and managed Hamilton to the Division Three title in season 2000–01.

DAVE DUNMORE, 87, earned a move to Tottenham in 1954 with his goal-scoring record at York. National Service and the arrival of Bobby Smith limited his chances, although the centre-forward still netted 26 goals in 81 appearances. Dunmore moved to West Ham, then helped Leyton Orient stave off the threat of relegation, before playing a key role in the club's promotion to the First Division – their only season in the top-flight – as runners up to Liverpool in 1961–62. He returned to York in 1965 and finished with a Football League tally of 132 goals in 369 appearances.

KEITH BAMBRIDGE, 85, played a leading role in Rotherham reaching the inaugural League Cup Final in 1960–61. His team won the first leg against Aston Villa 2-0 and lost 3-0 after extra-time in the return match. The left-winger spent eight years at Millmoor, played for Darlington and became the first substitute used by Halifax.

TOMMY LEISHMAN, 83, helped St Mirren beat Aberdeen 3-1 in the 1959 Scottish Cup Final to earn a £10,000 move to Liverpool. The wing-half missed only one match as Bill Shankly's side returned to the top-flight at Division Two champions in season 1961–62. But his appearances there were restricted and a move to Hibernian was followed by a player-manager role with Linfield, which included reaching the quarter-finals of the European Cup. Leishman later had a spell with Stranraer.

JEFF BARMBY, 78, played a handful of games for York before making his name in non-league football with nearly 400 appearances for Scarborough. His goals helped the club reach the FA Trophy Final four times – three of them victories against Wigan (1973), Stafford (1976) and Dagenham (1977). His son, Nick Barmby, won 23 England caps.

DEREK TOMKINSON, 90, started as an amateur with Port Vale in 1949, returned as a professional after a spell with Burton and was part of the Third Division North title-winning side in season 1953–54. The inside-forward also played for Crewe, Macclesfield and Altrincham.

ANDY HIGGINS, 61, began his career with Chesterfield in 1978 and had two spells under manager John McGrath at Port Vale and Chester. The defender also played for Hartlepool and Rochdale.

AUGUST 2021

GERD MULLER, 75, was one of the world's great strikers. He scored 68 goals in 62 appearances for West Germany, including the winner in the 1974 World Cup Final against Holland. Four years earlier, Muller completed their comeback from 2-0 down to a 3-2 quarter-final victory over England in Mexico, finished that tournament as top scorer with ten goals and the same year was named Europe's top player. Short, squat and nicknamed Der Bomber, he also netted twice in a 3-0 victory over the Soviet Union in the 1972 European Championship Final. At club level, the Bayern Munich star scored 547 goals in 594 competitive matches over 15 years, winning four Bundesliga titles and three European Cups. Another Bayern great, Karl-Heinz Rummenigge described him as 'the Muhammad Ali of the penalty box.' Muller played three seasons in the United States before retiring in 1982.

EDDIE PRESLAND, 78, was an all-round sportsman who played at full-back for West Ham and Crystal Palace and county cricket for Essex. He scored on his West Ham debut against Liverpool in 1965 – a 2-1 victory in which Geoff Hust netted the winner. Presland, best man at Hurst's wedding, moved to Crystal Palace after being replaced by Martin Peters. He also had a spell with Colchester, managed Dagenham to the 1980 FA Trophy and served Tottenham as chief scout. In the summer, he made 30 first-class appearances for Essex.

PETER MCNAMEE, 86, scored the goal which gave Peterborough a 2-1 win over Arsenal in the fourth round of the 1964–65 FA Cup, watched by a 30,000 crowd at London Road. He made 331 appearances in ten years at the club during their Midland League days, then when elected to the Football League in 1960. The right-winger also played for Notts County.

JOHNNY WILLIAMSON, 92, paved the way for the deep-lying centre-forward role pioneered by Don Revie at Manchester City following England's 6-3 defeat by Hungary at Wembley in 1953. It was a variation of the tactic used by Nandor Hidegkuti, scorer of three of Hungary's goals. Williamson, in conjunction with wing-half Ken Barnes, implemented the system in City's reserve side and Revie adopted it in a manner comparable to today's false No 9 position. Williamson spent five years at the club and also played for Blackburn.

ROBBIE COOKE, 64, helped Mansfield to the Division Three title in season 1976–77 and scored 57 goals in back-to-back campaigns with Peterborough. He also played for Luton, Cambridge, Brentford and Millwall and was part of non-league Kettering's FA Cup run to the fourth round in 1989.

ARTHUR SMITH, 106, was thought to be the oldest surviving Football League player. The winger signed as an amateur with Bury in 1934, turned professional the following year and moved to Leicester in 1938. His career was cut short by the advent of the Second World War.

SAM OJI, 35, started his career in the youth ranks at Arsenal in 2004 and had spells with Birmingham, Doncaster, Bristol Rovers, Leyton Orient and Hereford. The defender also played for Ljungskile in Sweden, Irish sides Limerick and Galway and for domestic non-league teams.

GERRY JONES, 75, was a left-winger who spent three seasons at Stoke in the mid-1960s without establishing a regular first-team place, then played for non-league Stafford and Macclesfield.

SEPTEMBER 2021

JIMMY GREAVES, 81, stands unchallenged as the greatest goalscorer in English top-flight football. Between 1957 and 1971, he accumulated 357 First Division goals for Chelsea, Tottenham and West Ham with the nerveless, elegant finishing of a natural marksman – a record complemented by his tally in an England shirt. Greaves started out with one against Tottenham on his Chelsea debut at the age of 17 and finished four years at Stamford Bridge with four against Nottingham Forest in 1961. He was sold for financial reasons for £80,000 to AC Milan, where an unhappy eight months ended when Bill Nicholson paid £99,999 to bring him to Tottenham – shaving one pound off the fee to spare him the burden of being a £100,000 player. A debut hat-trick against Blackpool paved the way for a golden era at White Hart Lane. It embraced FA Cup Final victories over Burnley and Chelsea, a 5-1 win over Atletico Madrid in the Cup Winners' Cup – Britain's first European trophy – and a club-record 266 goals in 379 games in all competitions. His international career also flourished until a gashed leg in England's third group match against France at the 1966 World Cup opened the way for Geoff Hurst to take his place and retain it all the way to victory over West Germany in the final at Wembley. Greaves, bitterly disappointed to miss out, netted a record six England hat-tricks and 44 goals in 57 internationals. His Tottenham career ended on a sour note with what he felt was an enforced move to West Ham. He retired from the professional game in 1971 with 464 goals in 659 appearances for club and country, then had spells with a number of non-league clubs, including Barnet. By then, he had a drink problem which threatened his marriage. Greaves eventually overcame it, forged a new career as a sporting pundit and enjoyed seven years on ITV alongside Ian St John on the popular *Saint and Greavsie* show. In 2015 he had a stroke. In 2020 he was awarded an MBE and there were many who believed he deserved a bigger honour. On the day he died, Tottenham and Chelsea players and fans united in tribute before the clubs' Premier League match at the Tottenham Hotspur Stadium.

ROGER HUNT, 83, was a World Cup winner with England and a record league scorer for Liverpool – a modest, quiet man respected throughout the game for an outstanding career for club and country. He may have been overshadowed by the aura surrounding players like Bobby Moore, Bobby Charlton and Geoff Hurst, but there was no doubting his contribution to the success of Alf Ramsey's team in 1966. Hunt played in every game, scored twice against France, once against Mexico in the group stage, and Hurst lauded the role his strike partner played in that match-winning hat-trick at Wembley. He also featured in the final's defining moment when Hurst's shot bounced down off the crossbar for England's third goal, wheeling away in celebration convinced the ball had crossed the line. Hunt scored 18 times in 34 internationals after making his debut in 1962, at a time when Liverpool were in the second tier. Under Bill Shankly, he sparked the club's promotion with 41 goals in as many games and was then part of First Division title-winning sides in 1964 and 1966, either side of an FA Cup success against Leeds when his header paved the way for a 2-1 victory over Leeds. Christened 'Sir Roger' by Anfield's Kop, he scored a club-best 244 league goals and ranked second to Ian Rush with 285 in 492 appearances in all competitions during the course of 11 years. He left in 1969 for Bolton, scoring 24 goals in 76 appearances over three seasons, and also had a spell for Hellenic in South Africa. In 2000, he was made an MBE. His passing left just three survivors of the team of 66 – Charlton, Hurst and George Cohen.

LEN ASHURST, 82, had a distinguished career as a player and manager. He made 458 appearances for Sunderland between 1958–70, a record for an outfield player with only goalkeeper Jim Montgomery featuring in more matches for the club. The full-back was an ever-present in the side that brought top-flight football back to Roker Park by finishing runners-up to Leeds in the old Second Division in season 1963–64. Ashurst also played for and managed Hartlepool on the way to a 20-year managerial career during which he took Sunderland to the 1985 League Cup Final which they lost 1-0 to Norwich. It spanned more than 1,000 matches, brought promotion in the first of two spells at Cardiff and at Newport. He also took charge of Gillingham and Shefield Wednesday and coached in Qatar, Kuwait and Malaysia.

TONY SCOTT, 80, came through the ranks at West Ham, alongside Bobby Moore, and made his senior debut against Chelsea in 1960. The England youth international left-winger stayed for five years before a £25,000 move to Aston Villa, then played under former West Ham stalwarts Frank O'Farrell, at Torquay, and John Bond, at Bournemouth. Scott's 14-year career ended through injury at Exeter after 333 Football League games. He went into coaching and worked alongside Bond again, this time at Manchester City.

TERRY LONG, 86, spent almost his entire career with Crystal Palace, making 480 appearances between 1955–70, and ranks second in the club's all-time list behind Jim Cannon (663). His tally included a run of 214 consecutive matches. The wing-half, who started in the youth ranks at Arsenal, then joined non-league Wycombe, featured in two promotions. Palace were Division Four runners up in 1961 and second again in the Third Division three years later. Long also made two appearances in the 1968–69 season when they reached the old First Division. He was later assistant manager to Bert Head, then No 2 at Millwall.

MARTIN BURLEIGH, 70, made his debut for Newcastle against Leeds in 1970. The goalkeeper then had to wait more than 12 months for another senior appearance and spent most of his six years at the club as understudy to Northern Ireland international Willie McFaul. He later had two spells with Darlington and also played for Carlisle and Hartlepool.

ALAN WOODS, 84, was an England youth international wing-half who began his career with Tottenham, playing a handful of senior games before moving to Swansea. He then scored on his debut for York against Millwall and went on to make 259 appearances for the club between 1960–67.

ALAN FOX, 85, made 412 appearances for Wrexham between 1954–65. The most notable was against Manchester United in 1957 in front of the club's record attendance at the Racecourse Ground– 34,445 – for an FA Cup fourth round tie which Unted won 5-0. Fox, a Wales under-23 international centre-half, was part of the 1961–62 Fourth Division promotion-winning side. He later played for Hartlepool, Bradford City and the Irish club Dundalk.

RAY RUFFETT, 97, was Cambridge United's oldest surviving former player. The wing-half and captain made 200 appearances between 1950–55 during the club's non-league days. He was previously with home-town Luton, but lost the chance of a Football League career there when sustaining a serious knee injury on his senior debut against Bury.

IAN RIDDELL, 83, played for Berwick Rangers in their famous 1-0 victory over Rangers in a Scottish Cup first round tie in 1967. The Scottish under-23 international left-back joined the club from St Mirren, where he spent eight years.

SID WATSON, 93, was the second oldest surviving Mansfield player. He signed as a part-timer in 1948, turned professional the following year and made 307 appearances in 12 years at the club, initially as an inside-forward, then at wing-half.

OCTOBER 2021

WALTER SMITH, 73 was one of Scotland's most successful club managers. In two spells at Rangers, he achieved legendary status with ten Premier titles, five Scottish Cups and six League Cup victories. One of many tributes came from arch-rivals Celtic, with senior officials laying a wreath outside Ibrox Stadium. Smith moved into coaching when his playing career at Dundee United and Dumbarton was ended by a pelvic injury. He was in charge of Scotland's under-18 and under-21-squads, assisted national team manager Alex Ferguson at the 1986 World Cup in Mexico and was No 2 to Graeme Souness at Rangers. Succeeding Souness in 1991, he won the latter seven of their nine-a-a-row titles. After four years at Everton and two in charge of the national team, he returned to Ibrox, delivering three more titles and a UEFA Cup Final appearance against Zenit St Petersburg (0-2). Smith won ten Manager of the Year awards and was awarded an OBE. He retired in 2011 after 810 matches for club and country, then served as a non-executive director and briefly as chairman.

FREDDIE HILL, 81, developed into one of the most skilful and entertaining players in Bolton's history. The inside-forward came through the youth ranks, established himself during the season after they won the FA Cup in 1958 and made 412 appearances in 12 years at the club. During that time, a move to Bill Shankly's Liverpool fell through when a medical showed high blood pressure. Hill was top scorer in the 1961–62 season and remains the last Bolton player to score a top-flight hat-trick – against Sheffield United in 1963. He was capped twice by Walter Winterbottom, but was ignored when Alf Ramsey took over as England manager with an aversion to wide players. A move to Halifax was followed by a return to Division One with Manchester City, alongside former team-mates Francis Lee and Wyn Davies, then on to Peterborough.

GEORGE KINNELL, 83, filled several positions during his career – full-back, wing-half, centre-half and occasionally in attack. He joined Stoke from Aberdeen for £35,000 and featured in the 1964 League Cup Final won 4-3 on aggregate by Leicester. Kinnell later played for Oldham, Sunderland and Middlesbrough, along with spells in Canada and Australia.

TERRY EADES, 77, joined Cambridge United from Southern League rivals Chelmsford in 1969, helped the club achieve Football League status and went on to make 366 appearances in nine years at the club. The centre-half also had a spell at Watford and later managed Histon.

BILLY LAMONT, 85, was involved with seven Scottish clubs during a 37-year career as player and manager. He kept goal for Albion and Hamilton, led Falkirk into the Premier Division as manager in season 1985–86 and gained promotion with from Division Two with East Stirling and Dumbarton. He also took charge of Partick and Alloa.

PAUL LINGER, 46, came through the youth ranks at Charlton and spent four years in the senior squad. The midfielder joined Lyton Orient in 1997, then played for Brighton before moving into non-league football. He died of cancer.

TREVOR HEMMINGS, 86, had a 48-year association with Preston. He joined the board of directors as vice-chairman in 1973 and bought a controlling interest in the summer of 2010 after the club received a winding-up petition. The businessman was also a leading racehorse owner, with three Grand National winners.

BRIAN SHERRATT, 77, helped Oxford win the Third Division title in season 1967–68 when they finished a point ahead of Bury. The goalkeeper joined the club from Stoke and also played for Nottingham Forest, Barnsley and Colchester.

ANDY PORTER, 84, was part of Watford's Fourth Division promotion-winning squad in season 1959–60. The wing-half helped them become established in Division Three, then played non-league football.

NOVEMBER 2021

RAY KENNEDY, 70, was one of the most successful players of his generation – part of the Double-winning Arsenal side of 1970–71, followed by a key role in Liverpool's domestic and European dominance under Bob Paisley. Kennedy was deemed not good enough as a youngster and released at Port Vale by Sir Stanley Matthews. But he made great strides at Highbury, forming a formidable strike partnership with John Radford which delivered the First Division title, a point clear of Leeds, and a 2-1 FA Cup success against Liverpool at Wembley five days later. After 213 appearances and 71 goals for the club, a £200,000 transfer took him to Anfield in 1974 on the day Bill Shankly resigned as manager. Paisley, noting the new signing had great vision and touch in addition to physical strength, transformed him into a hugely influential midfielder. Liverpool were champions five times in seven seasons. Kennedy also featured in three European Cup triumphs, UEFA Cup and European Super Cup victories and a League Cup win. There were also 17 England caps, under Don Revie and Ron Greenwood, although he never fully transferred his club form to the international stage. In 1982, after 393 Liverpool appearances and 72 goals, he joined former team-mate John Toshack at Swansea, where his form began to suffer from the early stages of Parkinson's disease. Kennedy returned to his native north-east to play for Hartlepool, completing a domestic career spanning 681 matches. He also had a brief spell as player-manager of the Cypriot club Pezoporikos. Liverpool and Arsenal played a testimonial game in his honour at Highbury in 1991. Later, he sold medals and caps to help pay for care.

RON FLOWERS, 87, enjoyed success for club and country – winning three top-flight titles with Wolves and making 49 appearances for England. He was a non-playing member of Alf Ramsey's 1966 World Cup squad and joined others in eventually receiving a medal from FIFA in 2009. In the previous tournament in Chile, the wing-half scored penalties in group matches against Hungary and Argentina, with six of his ten international goals coming from the spot. He helped Wolves become First Division champions for the first time in 1954. They were title winners again in 1958 and 1959 and twice finished runners-up. Flowers also featured in their 3-0 victory over Blackburn in the 1960 FA Cup Final and made 515 appearances in 15 years at the club after starting out in the youth ranks of home-town team Doncaster. Later, he was player-manager at Northampton. In the 2021 New Year Honours, he and Jimmy Greaves received MBEs, the last surviving members of that victorious World Cup squad still to be honoured.

BERTIE AULD, 83, crowned a trophy-laden career at Celtic with the European Cup in 1967. He was part of the team known as the 'Lisbon Lions' that became the first British holders by beating Inter Milan 2-1 in the Portuguese capital under Jock Stein. In his second spell at Parkhead, Celtic reached the 1970 final, losing 2-1 to Feyenoord. Auld won five domestic titles, three Scottish Cups and four League Cups in 283 appearances for the club featuring 85 goals. He helped Birmingham defeat Aston Villa to win the English League Cup and reach the final of the Inter-Cities Fairs Cup, forerunner of the UEFA Cup, against Roma. As a manager, he won Scotland's second tier with Partick and Hibernian and also had spells in charge of Hamilton and Dumbarton.

JOHN SILLETT, 85, led Coventry to victory against the odds in the 1987 FA Cup Final – their first major trophy. His side defeated favourites Tottenham 3-2 with goals by Dave Bennett and Keith Houchen, followed by Gary Mabbutt's own goal in extra-time. Sillett was joint-manager alongside George Curtis before taking sole charge the following season. He previously managed Hereford and returned there after being replaced at Highfield Road by Terry Butcher in 1990. Sillett previously played for the club after winning the old First Division title with Chelsea in 1955. Jimmy Hill made the full-back his first signing as manager and he was part of the Third Division title-winning team in 1964. He also played for Plymouth. His association with Coventry was marked by a life presidency in 2011.

FRANK BURROWS, 77, was part of one of the biggest upsets in the history of the League Cup. The centre-half helped Third Division Swindon lift the trophy in 1969 when they defeated Arsenal 3-1 in the final with two extra-time goals from Don Rogers. He joined the club from Scunthorpe, after starting out at Raith Rovers, and later enjoyed a successful managerial career. Burrows won two promotions in two spells with Cardiff, took Portsmouth up and led Swansea to success in the 1994 League Trophy. He was then involved in two promotions to the Premier League as Gary Megson's assistant at West Bromwich Albion. There were also spells on the coaching staff at West Ham, Sunderland and Leicester.

JOHN SEWELL, 85, led Crystal Palace into the old First Division for the first time when they finished runners-up to Derby in season 1968–69. The captain featured in their next two campaigns in the top flight, spending eight years at the club after signing from Charlton. Sewell, a full-back, had a spell with Leyton Orient, then played and coached in the North American League with St Louis and California.

CLIFF MARSHALL, 66, was among the pioneering black players in English football. He was the first to appear in Everton's first team, making his debut off the bench against Leicester in 1975. The Liverpool-born schoolboy international started for the first time a week later against Birmingham, but was restricted to eight appearances because of a surfeit of talented wingers at the club. He left for Miami in the North American League, returned for a season with Southport and retired at 22.

PHIL DWYER, 68, won ten Wales caps during a record-breaking 16 years with Cardiff. One of two international goals came on his debut against Iran in Tehran in 1978. The defender joined his home-town club in 1969, came through the youth ranks and went on to make 575 appearances. They embraced two promotions from Division Three and three Welsh Cup successes. He ended his career at Rochdale.

JOE LAIDLAW, 71, scored one of the goals which clinched Carlisle's place in the top flight for the first and only time. A 2-0 win over Aston Villa in April 1974 confirmed third place in the old Second Division behind Middlesbrough and Luton. Laidlaw, a £20,000 signing from Middlesbrough, was leading scorer with 12 goals in the club's single season at the top of the English game. He spent four years at Brunton Park before moving to Doncaster, then led Portsmouth to promotion from Division Four in 1979–80. The midfielder also played for Hereford and Mansfield, finishing with 514 appearances in the Football League.

KEITH MORTON, 87, had an eventful six years with Darlington after spells at Crystal Palace and Sunderland. In his first season, he scored in six successive Third Division North matches. In 1957–58, the centre forward netted the third goal as his side drew 3-3 with Chelsea at Stamford Bridge, then won the replay 4-1 to reach the fifth round of the FA Cup. In 1960–61, Darlington were involved in a marathon second round tie with Hull which involved four replays before a 3-0 defeat. That same season, Morton helped them defeat Crystal Palace and West Ham in the League Cup before losing to Bolton in front of a record Feethams crowd of 21,023.

JIMMY KERRAY, 85, joined Newcastle in 1962, after spells with Huddersfield and Raith Rovers, and scored on his debut against Southampton. The inside-forward spent a year at the club before returning to Scotland, where he had a second spell with Dunfermline and subsequently played for St Johnstone, Stirling and Falkirk.

LAURIE SHEFFIELD, 82, began his career in the youth ranks at Bristol Rovers, had three years with Welsh side Barry, then played for seven Football League clubs. In the first of two spells with Doncaster, the centre-forward scored 28 goals in their Division Four title-winning side of season 1965–66. Sheffield joined Norwich the following season, scoring a hat-trick on his debut against Derby, and also served Newport, Rotherham, Oldham, Luton and Peterborough.

LOUIS BIMPSON, 92, played an important part in Blackburn reaching the 1960 FA Cup Final against Wolves. He featured in every tie, scoring against Sunderland in round three and netting twice in the win over Tottenham in round five. His side were beaten 3-0 at Wembley, losing full-back Dave Whelan with a broken leg two minutes before half-time and with substitutes yet to be introduced, played for the rest of the match with ten men. Bimpson, an outside-right, joined the club from Liverpool and went on to have spells with Bournemouth, Rochdale and Wigan.

DOUG COWIE, 95, was the oldest surviving Scotland international. He made his debut against England in 1953, played in the 1954 and 1958 World Cups and won 20 caps. The wing-half and captain spent most of his club career with Dundee, making a record 446 competitive appearances in 16 seasons from 1946. He won back-to-back League Cups against Rangers (3-2) and Kilmarnock (2-0) during one of the most successful periods in the club's history. Cowie also played for Morton and manager Raith Rovers.

JOHNNIE HILLS, 87, played in Tottenham's all-time record victory – 13-2 against Crewe in an FA Cup fourth round replay in 1960. The full-back spent 11 years at the clubs, as an amateur and professional, with first-team opportunities in the league limited by the presence of Alf Ramsey and Peter Baker. He later played for Bristol Rovers and Margate before suffering a serious knee injury.

PETER GREENWOOD, 97, played league football for Chester and county cricket for Lancashire at a time when many sportsmen spent all year earning a living. After playing for Burnley reserves, the centre-forward spent four years at the Sealand Road club which included an FA Cup third round tie against Chelsea in 1952. Greenwood scored in a 2-2 draw at Stamford Bridge and lined up in the replay which Chelsea won 3-2. During the summer of 1950, the right-arm bowler helped Lancashire to a share of the county title with Surrey after both finished with the same points total.

BARRY JACKSON, 83, made 538 Football League and cup appearances for York between 1958–70 – a club record. The centre-half was dropped only once during that time, after a run of 474 games. Jackson, who featured in two Fourth Division promotion-winning teams, played for Scarborough after being released by the club.

JACK VITTY, 98, had spells with Charlton and Brighton before Bill Shankly, then Workington manager, signed him in 1952 for the Third Division North club. The full-back was made captain and went on to make 208 appearances.

ALF PATRICK, 100, was a prolific marksman for home-town club York. In 241 league and cup appearances between 1946–52, the centre-forward netted 117 goals and remains the club's only player to score five in one match. That came in a 6-1 victory over Rotherham in a Third Division North fixture in 1948. After a spell with Scarborough, Patrick returned to Bootham Crescent as trainer and coach.

DECEMBER 2021

JIMMY ROBSON, 82, was part of Burnley's First Division title-winning side in season 1959–60 when they finished a point ahead of Wolves and two clear of Tottenham. The inside-forward also scored the 100th FA Cup Final goal in 1962 when his side lost 3-1 to Tottenham. Robson scored 100 goals in 242 appearances for the club in all competitions and also played for

Blackpool, Barnsley and Bury. After retiring, he coached at Huddersfield and Rochdale, then returned to Turf Moor under Stan Ternent, who made him head of the Centre of Excellence.

MARVIN MORGAN, 38, played for five Football League clubs, alongside campaigning against racism and becoming a fashion designer. The striker had spells with Aldershot, Dagenham and Redbridge, Shrewsbury, Plymouth and Hartlepool, together with a dozen non-league sides, the last one Potters Bar in 2020.

GEORGE RYDEN, 81, played in all six of Dundee's ties in the 1963–64 Scottish Cup, including the final which his side lost 3-1 to Rangers watched by a crowd of nearly 121,000 at Hampden Park. The centre-half later played for St Johnstone and Stirling.

STEVE PEPLOW, 72, came through the youth ranks at Liverpool and made two First Division appearances in season 1969–70. The winger had two seasons with Swindon, then brief spells at Nottingham Forest and Mansfield before returning to Merseyside with Tranmere. There, he made 270 appearances, forging a productive attacking alliance with Ronnie Moore which helped bring promotion from Division Four in 1976, Moore scoring 34 goals.

WILLIE MCSEVENEY, 92, was an inside-forward who joined Motherwell from Dunfermline in 1954 and spent a decade at the club. He helped them to a League Cup Final against Hearts, which they lost 4-2, and two Scottish Cup semi-finals. After retiring, he coached the reserves.

TREVOR THOMPSON, 66, began his career with West Bromwich Albion and went on to play for Newport and Lincoln. The full-back also had a spell in the United States with Washington. He later managed Boston.

JANUARY 2022

PETER ROBINSON, 86, played a key role in Liverpool's rise to domestic and European dominance throughout the 1970s and 1980s. The chief executive modernised and streamlined their administrative operations, first as club secretary then as chief executive during 35 years at Anfield. Robinson released successive managers Bill Shankly, Bob Paisley, Joe Fagan and Kenny Dalglish to concentre on achieving success on the pitch. He was instrumental in recruiting players like Dalglish, Kevin Keegan, Ray Clemence, Graeme Souness and John Barnes. By the time he stepped down in 2000, having overseen the appointment of Gerard Houllier as manager, Liverpool had won 29 trophies, including 12 league titles and four European Cups. Robinson and his chairman John Smith were also admired for dealing with the aftermath of the Heysel Stadium and Hillsborough disasters. Robinson joined Liverpool from Brighton, having previously worked at Scunthorpe, Crewe and Stockport.

WIM JANSEN, 75, won the 1997–98 Scottish Premier Division with Celtic in his only season as manager. His team deprived Rangers of a tenth successive title by beating St Johnstone in the final fixture to finish two points ahead of their rivals. They also defeated Dundee United 3-0 to lift the League Cup. Jansen replaced Tommy Burns to become Celtic's first non-British or Irish manager and brought club legend Henrik Larsen to Parkhead. He resigned ten months into a three-year contract over a breakdown in his relationship with owner Fergus McCann and general manager Jock Brown. The Dutchman previously coached Feyenoord, having made more than 500 appearances for them as a player. They embraced four domestic titles, a European Cup success in the 1970 final against Celtic and the UEFA Cup against Tottenham in 1974. He won another title towards the end of his career with Ajax. His 65 caps for Holland included two World Cup Final defeats – 1974 against West Germany and 1978 against Argentina.

FRANCISCO 'PACO' GENTO, 88, achieved legendary status during 18 years with Real Madrid. The left-winger won an unprecedented six European Cups, together with 12 league titles, in 600 appearances after signing from Racing Santander in 1953. His club-record total of 23 trophies was equalled by captain Marcelo in last season's Spanish Super Cup. Gento won

43 caps for Spain, played in the 1962 and 1966 World Cups and became Real's honorary president following the death of the great Alfredo Di Stefano in 2014.

PAUL HINSHELWOOD, 65, was an England under-21 right-back who made 319 senior appearances in ten years at Crystal Palace after coming through the youth ranks alongside brother Martin. He helped them reach the top-flight as Second Division champions under Terry Venables in season 1978–79 and was twice the club's Player of the Year. Hinshelwood was then a Third Division title winner with Oxford, followed by promotion from the same division with Millwall. He also played for Colchester.

JAMIE VINCENT, 46, made 501 appearances for ten clubs after starting his career with Crystal Palace in 1993. He was named in the PFA Division Two team of the year for season 1998–99 when his Bournemouth team-mates included Eddie Howe, now Newcastle's manager. Later, the left back won promotion from League Two with Swindon. He also played for Huddersfield, Portsmouth, Walsall, Derby, Millwall, Yeovil and Aldershot.

LAWRENCE 'LOL' MORGAN, 90, spent a decade with Rotherham and featured in the first League Cup Final which his side lost 3-2 on aggregate to Aston Villa in 1961. The left-back played in all their 50 matches that season, making a total of 326 appearances for his home-town club after starting as an amateur with Sheffield United, then joining Huddersfield. He left Millmoor for Darlington, winning promotion from Division Four in 1966 as player-manager, managed Norwich for three years, then scouted for Tottenham.

JIMMY SMITH, 91, was thought to be Chelsea's oldest surviving player. The winger made his debut against Fulham in 1951 and made 23 appearances for the club. There was strong competition for places and he moved to Leyton Orient in 1955.

JACK FISHER, 96, played alongside twin brother George for Millwall in season 1947–48. He was at left-back and George on the left-wing in two matches in the old Second Division. Jack faced strong competition for his position and moved on to Bournemouth. George, who died in 2015, stayed to make 316 appearances for the club.

KEITH TODD, 80, was part of the Swansea side that reached the FA Cup semi-finals in 1964. They knocked out Sheffield United, Stoke and Liverpool before losing 2-1 to Preston at Villa Park. The centre-forward made 245 appearances for the club between 1959–68, scoring 96 goals. He played for the Wales under-23 team and was among the reserves for a senior international against Russia.

HOWARD RADFORD, 91, made 244 Football League appearances for Bristol Rovers – his only club – between 1951–62. The 5ft 9in goalkeeper was part of the Third Division South title-winning side in his second season. He also played in a remarkable match at Blackburn in 1955 which Rovers lost 8-3 after leading 3-2.

GLYN JONES, 85, was an England youth international inside-forward who began his career with Rotherham in 1953–54, returned to his home-town club after a spell with Sheffield United and also played for Mansfield.

FEBRUARY 2022

STEVE BURTENSHAW, 86, had a 53-year career as player, manager, coach and scout. It began in 1952 at Brighton, where the wing-half made 252 appearances, featured in two lower division title-winning teams and had a testimonial in 1963. He was given his first coaching appointment at the club, followed by a long association with Arsenal, including the caretaker-manager's job following Don Howe's resignation. Burtenshaw was in charge on his own at Sheffield Wednesday and Queens Park Rangers, along with spells at Everton and Manchester City.

JOEY BEAUCHAMP, 50, was a ball boy at Oxford's League Cup Final victory over Queens Park Rangers in 1986, signed youth forms with his home-town club the following year and went on to make 428 appearances in two spells. His first ended with a £1.2m move in 1994 to West Ham, where he was unable to settle and never played a competitive match. The winger joined Swindon for £850,000, returning 15 months later to the Manor Ground, where he helped Oxford win promotion from Division Two in 1996. A toe injury ended his career.

BILLY MCEWAN, 70, played for seven clubs and had six managerial jobs. He began his career with Hibernian, followed by midfield roles at Blackpool, Brighton, Chesterfield Mansfield, Peterborough and Rotherham. He was part of Mansfield's Division Three title-winning team of 1976–77 and won Division Four in his first full season as Rotherham manager (1988–89). McEwan was also in charge at Sheffield United, Darlington, York and Mansfield, along with two spells as Derby caretaker.

ALAN ANDERSON, 82, was one of several players, including Sir Alex Ferguson, finally recognised by Scotland more than half a century after representing their country. He featured in seven matches on a tour of Oceania and Asia in the summer of 1967. Five of them were upgraded to full international status in 2020 and the players received a souvenir cap. Anderson, centre-half and captain, made 475 appearances for Hearts, including season 1964-65 when his side were denied the title by Kilmarnock on goal average and the 1968 Scottish Cup Final against Dunfermline (1-3). He also had spells with Falkirk, Alloa, Millwall and Scunthorpe.

MICK NEWMAN, 89, was the last amateur to play first-team football for West Ham. He made seven appearances after signing from Dagenham, three of them in the 1957–58 season when they became Second Division champions, a point ahead of Blackburn. Newman, an inside-forward who worked in the family dry-cleaning business, returned to non-league with Dartford.

STEVE FINNEY, 48, scored 16 goals in Swindon's Second Division title-winning season of 1995–96. The striker began his career at Preston and also had spells with Manchester City, Cambridge, Carlisle, Leyton Orient, Barrow, Chester and Altrincham. He died after a short illness.

DAVIE CATTANACH, 75, was one of the group of youngsters under Jock Stein at Celtic known as the 'Quality Street Gang,' including Davie Hay, Danny McGrain, Kenny Dalglish and Lou Macari. The wing-half was largely a squad player during six years at the club, but stayed, despite having chances to move on. He joined from Stirling and finished his career in 1974 at home-town Falkirk.

ROY LAMBERT, 88, captained Rotherham in the inaugural League Cup Final which his side lost 3-2 over two legs to Aston Villa in 1961. He featured in every round and made 346 appearances in eight years at the club. Lambert, a wing-half, moved to Barnsley in 1965, but played only a handful of games before a back injury ended his career. He then coached and scouted for Huddersfield.

TREVOR SWIFT, 73, was another Rotherham captain and wing-half stalwart who made 328 appearances across eight years for his home-town club. They included the Fourth Division promotion-winning season of 1974–75. He later played for Worksop.

GEORGE HARRIS, 81, began his Football League career with Newport after starting out at Woking. The winger went on to play for Watford and Reading, then featured in Cambridge's first season in the league – 1970–71.

DOUG BAILLIE, 85, joined Rangers from Airdrieonians in 1960 and was part of their squad in three-winning seasons. The Scotland under-23 international also had spells with Swindon, Third Lanark, Falkirk and Dunfermline. After retiring, he became a reporter for the *Sunday Post* and president of the Scottish Football Writers' Association. His son Lex, also a central defender, was with Celtic St Mirren and Dunfermline.

GEOFF BARKER, 73, was part of Reading's squad that won promotion from Division Four in season 1975–76. The centre-half began his career with home-town club Hull and also played for Southend, Darlington and Grimsby.

ALEX INGRAM, 77, helped Ayr reach Scotland's top division in his first spell after starting his career with Queen's Park. They finished runners-up to Motherwell in the old Second Division under Ally MacLeod in season 1968–69. The centre-forward joined Nottingham Forest the following year for £40,000, returning after one season and going on to make more than 300 appearances for the club.

MARCH 2022

FRANK O'FARRELL, 94, was chosen by Sir Matt Busby to replace him at Manchester United in 1971 after making his name in management by winning promotion with Torquay, then leading Leicester to the Second Division title and to an FA Cup Final. But just as following Sir Alex Ferguson has proved a demanding task at the modern-day Old Trafford, O'Farrell found it hard working in the shadow of a club legend, particularly with an ageing team. United finished eighth in his first season and were third from bottom when he was sacked after 18 months in charge and replaced by Tommy Docherty. He then managed Cardiff, coached Iran and had two further spells at Torquay, retiring as general manager there in 1983. O'Farrell, a wing-half, won nine Republic of Ireland caps while playing for West Ham and Preston.

GORDON LEE, 87, went some way to reviving Everton's fortunes in four-and-a-half-years as manager after succeeding Billy Bingham in 1977. With neighbours Liverpool going from strength to strength, he led them to a League Cup Final which Aston Villa won 3-2 at the third attempt after 0-0 and 1-1 draws. Everton also reached two FA Cup semi-finals and had two top-four finishes in the First Division before he was replaced by Howard Kendall. Lee delivered another League Cup Final with Newcastle, losing to Manchester City, led Blackburn to the Third Division title, won promotion with Fourth Division Port Vale and also managed Preston and the Icelandic club Reykjavik. Highlight of an 11-year playing career at full-back with Villa was victory in the inaugural League Cup Final in 1961 – 3-2 on aggregate against Rotherham. He also played for Shrewsbury.

ANDY LOCHHEAD, 81, accumulated 128 goals in 266 appearances for Burnley between 1960–68. He was the club's last player to score over 100 and the only one to twice net five in a game – against Chelsea and Bournemouth. The Scotland under-23 international centre-forward also scored four against Manchester United. Lochhead then helped Leicester to the 1969 FA Cup against Manchester City (0-1) and was in the Aston Villa side beaten by Tottenham in the League Cup Final two years later. He won the Third Division title with Villa and his next club, Oldham, before finishing his career in the United States with Denver.

TONI MARCHI, 89, was part of Tottenham's Double-winning season of 1960–61, but had to wait for 57 years for a medal. The wing-half made six appearances in the team that topped the old First Division ahead of Sheffield Wednesday and Wolves– not enough for official recognition. In 2018, however, eligibility rules were relaxed and he was presented with a medal at his home by former teammates Cliff Jones and Terry Dyson. Marchi's second spell at the club also included the 1963 European Cup-Winners' Cup Final when he was part of the side that defeated Atletico Madrid 5-1 in Rotterdam to become the first British winners of a major European trophy. Bill Nicholson brought him back to White Hart Lane after spells in Italy with Vincenza and Torino and he made 260 appearances overall for the club. He later managed Northampton and Cambridge City.

TERRY DARRACOTT, 71, chose Everton over Liverpool to sign youth forms and made his senior debut aged 17 when replacing injured World Cup-winning left-back Ray Wilson against Arsenal in 1968. He went on to make 179 appearances for the club, including the 1977 League Cup Final against Aston Villa which they lost 3-2 in a second replay. After playing for Tulsa in the United States, Darracott finished his playing career at Wrexham, then returned to Goodison Park as a coach under managers Howard Kendall and Colin Harvey. He was part of Kenny Dalglish's backroom team when Blackburn won the Premier League in 1994–95, returned to Wrexham as assistant manager and also had spells with Manchester City, Bolton and Hull.

FRANK CONNOR, 86, had three spells with Celtic. The goalkeeper started his career with the club in 1961 and also played for St Mirren, Albion and Cowdenbeath. He was assistant to manager Davie Hay from 1983–86 and caretaker manager following Liam Brady's departure in 1993. O'Connor also had spells as assistant to Jock Wallace at Motherwell, Joe Jordan at Hearts and led Raith to promotion from Division two in 1987.

TOMMY BARNETT, 85, scored the winning goal against Aldershot that clinched promotion from Division Four for Crystal Palace in season 1960–61. The left-winger made 15 senior appearances for the club before a career in non-league football which included a record-breaking 201 goals in 479 appearances for Romford.

IVAN HOLLETT, 81, scored 136 goals in 363 Football League appearances after starting out at Mansfield, where he was part of the team that won promotion back to the Third Division in season 1962–63. The inside-forward also played for Chesterfield, Crewe, Cambridge United and Hereford, then returned to Mansfield in coaching and scouting roles.

BOB TODD, 72, was a winger who began his career as an apprentice at Scunthorpe, had a brief spell with Liverpool, then played for Rotherham, Mansfield and Workington. A subsequent non-league career included the 1975 FA Trophy Final when his team Scarborough lost 4-0 to Matlock.

APRIL 2022

JIMMY HARRIS, 88, had the dubious distinction of scoring a hat-trick for Everton in a match they lost 10-4. It happened in season 1958–59 at White Hart Land against Tottenham, for whom Bobby Smith netted four times. Harris spent nine years at Goodison Park before moving to Birmingham, where he was a League Cup winner against Aston Villa in 1963 (3-1) and a runner-up in the Inter-Cities Fairs Cup against Roma (2-4) in 1961. The centre-forward also had spells with Oldham and Tranmere.

GRAHAM FYFE, 70, was part of Rangers' victorious 1972 European Cup-Winners' Cup squad. He played once in their run to the final, against Sporting Lisbon, and was on the bench when Willie Waddell's side defeated Moscow Dynamo 3-2 to lift the trophy. The winger had seven seasons at the club, also played for Hibernian and Dumbarton and had three years in the American indoor league, latterly with St Louis.

CON SULLIVAN, 93, was Bristol City's oldest living former player. He kept goal for his home-town club for five years before joining Arsenal in 1954, but had his career cut short in 1958 by a shoulder injury.

BERNARD FISHER, 88, joined Hull in 1955, initially as an amateur towards the end of national service, and spent eight seasons at the club. The goalkeeper than had two years with Bradford City before retiring.

NEIL CAMPBELL, 45, was a forward who played for York, Scarborough, Southend, Doncaster and Barrow. He died after being taken ill in a restaurant in Yarm, Teesside.

MAY 2022

BRIAN BEDFORD, 88, scored 25 goals or more in each of his six seasons with Queens Park Rangers. His best was 39 in the 1961–62 campaign when equalling the club's all-time record, which eventually fell to Rodney Marsh five years later with 44. Bedford netted 14 hat-tricks in a total of 180 goals in 284 appearances. The centre-forward started his career at Reading and also had spells with Southampton, Bournemouth, Scunthorpe and Brentford.

NEIL O'DONNELL, 72, helped Norwich reached the top-flight for the first time. He was part of the squad under Ron Saunders that won Division Two, a point ahead of Birmingham, in season 1971–72. The midfielder later played under Len Ashurst at Gillingham and Sheffield Wednesday.

JIMMY WHITEHOUSE, 87, was an inside-forward who scored six goals in Third Division Coventry's FA Cup run of season 1962–63. They reached the quarter-finals before losing to Manchester United, watched by a 44,000 crowd at Highfield Road. Whitehouse, an inside-forward, joined the club from Reading and also played for Millwall.

SYD FARRIMOND, 81, made 404 appearances for Bolton between 1958–70. The England youth international left-back also played for Shrewsbury, Tranmere and Halifax, then coached at Sunderland and Leeds.

DEREK STOKES, 82, had two spells with Bradford City and one with Huddersfield in the 1960s, making a total of 279 appearances and scoring 121 league goals. The England under-23 centre-forward later played in the Irish league with Dundalk and Drogheda.

CRAIG FARRELL, 39, played for the England under-16 team, then came through the youth ranks at Middlesbrough and Leeds. The striker had spells with several Football League and non-league clubs, including Carlisle, Oxford, Exeter and York.

JUNE 2022

BILLY BINGHAM, 90, achieved legendary status by twice guiding Northern Ireland to the World Cup finals. Making the most of limited resources in his second spell in charge of the national team, he took them in 1982 to Spain, where Gerry Armstrong's winner against the hosts remains one of the biggest upsets in the history of the competition. The Irish bowed out at the second group stage after drawing against Austria and losing to France, but returned in Mexico four years later, thanks to victory in Romania and a goalless draw with England at Wembley. This time, there were no heroics at the finals – a draw against Algeria and defeats by Spain and Brazil – for the son of a shipyard worker, who was part of the team under Peter Doherty that reached the quarter-finals in Sweden in 1958. In a 40-year career, Bingham started out at Glentoran and Sunderland, lost the 1959 FA Cup Final with Luton to Nottingham Forest, then won the old First Division with Everton in 1963. There were 56 international caps along the way, before his playing days were cut short by a broken leg at his final club, Port Vale. He then managed Southport, Plymouth, Linfield, Everton and Mansfield, along with clubs in Greece and Saudi Arabia. There was also a brief, unsuccessful return to the international stage coaching Greece. Later, Bingham was Blackpool's director of football and a scout for Burnley.

DAVIE WILSON, 85, won 11 trophies and 22 Scotland caps with the great Rangers team of the early 1960s. The winger shared four league titles, five Scottish Cups and two League Cups and played in both legs of the European Cup-Winners' Cup Final which his side lost 4-1 on aggregate to Fiorentina. Wilson scored 158 goals across 11 seasons at Ibrox, including six in the 7-1 defeat of Falkirk, and netted ten for his country. He later played for Dundee United and Dumbarton, then managed Dumbarton twice and Queen of the South.

BOBBY HOPE, 78, made 409 appearances in 12 years with West Bromwich Albion. They included the 1968 FA Cup Final, in which his side defeated Everton 1-0, and the League Cup success against West Ham, two years earlier, when Albion beat West Ham 5-3 on aggregate over the two legs. Wilson also played for Birmingham, Sheffield Wednesday, along with loan spells at Philadelphia and Dallas in the United States. The midfielder won seven Scotland caps.

COLIN GRAINGER, 89, scored twice on his debut for England in a 4-2 victory over Brazil in a friendly international at Wembley in 1956. It was one of seven caps gained while playing for Sheffield United and Sunderland. In 2007, Grainger welcomed Brazil legend Pele to Bramall Lane for a celebration of the 150th anniversary of Sheffield FC. The outside-left also played for Wrexham, Leeds, Port Vale, Doncaster and Macclesfield. Grainger combined his career with a spell in show business as the 'Singing Winger,' once appearing on a bill with The Beatles.

FRANK CLARKE, 79, was the eldest of five footballing brothers, including former Leeds and England striker Allan Clarke. He played for Shrewsbury, Queens Park Rangers and Ipswich, then helped Carlisle reach the top-flight for the first time, scoring 16 goals in their promotion season of 1973–74.

RONNIE FARMER, 86, joined Coventry from Nottingham Forest and played an important role in their rise to the top-flight with promotion from Division Four in 1959, Division Three (1964) and Division Two (1967). The Guernsey-born wing-half made 318 appearances for the club, had a spell with Notts County and returned to Highfield Road as youth coach, guiding his side to the 1970 FA Youth Cup Final against Tottenham (3-4).

GRAHAM TUTT, 65, came through the youth system at Charlton and made his senior debut against Shrewsbury in 1974 at the age of 17. But the goalkeeper's career in English football was cut short two years later by a head injury sustained against Sunderland. He spent two seasons in South Africa, then played in the United States.

NOEL CAMPBELL, 72, won 11 Republic of Ireland caps while playing for St Patrick's and the German club Fortuna Cologne. The midfielder returned to the League of Ireland with Shamrock Rovers, where he later became assistant manager to Johnny Giles, then succeeded him.

JULY 2022

ANDY GORAM, 58, won ten trophies with Rangers, gained 43 international caps and was the only Scot ever to have played cricket for his country as well. In seven years at Ibrox following a £1m move from Hibernian, the goalkeeper played in five consecutive title-winning teams, three in the Scottish Cup and two in the League Cup. He was also on loan at Manchester United during the run-in to their Premier League success of 2001. Goram also had spells with Oldham, Notts County, Sheffield United, Motherwell, Hamilton, Coventry and Queen of the South, where he won the Challenge Cup to complete a full set of domestic silverware. He was part of Scotland's World Cup squad in 1986 and 1990, but walked out before the 1998 finals because of manager Craig Brown's preference for long-term rival Jim Leighton. At Euro 92 and 96, he was first-choice and in 1993 was voted Player of the Year by the Scottish PFA and the football writers. After retiring, Goram was goalkeeping coach at several clubs, including Motherwell, Hamilton, Dunfermline and Airdrieonians. The left-handed batsman and right-arm medium-pace bowler played for Scotland four times before Rangers manager Walter Smith ordered him to concentrate on football.

DREW BUSBY, 74, made 256 appearances and scored 84 goals for Hearts between 1973–79 following a club record £35,000 move from Airdrieonians. They included the 1976 Scottish Cup Final when his side lost 3-1 to Rangers. The attacking midfielder started his career with Third Lanark and scored the club's last goal, against Dumbarton, before going out of business in 1967. He also had spells with Partick, Barrow, Morton, Toronto in Canada and was player-manager at Queen of the south.

GARY PEARSON, 45, played for Darlington and York after starting out in the youth ranks at Sheffield United. Most of the midfielder's career was spent with non-league clubs in the north-east and he was due to take over as manager of Billingham when he died suddenly.

LEN CASEY, 91, was Chelsea's oldest surviving former player. The wing-half spent four years at the club before joining Plymouth, where he was part of the team that won the Division Three title in season 1958–59, a point ahead of Hull.

CLIVE MIDDLEMASS, 77, played for Workington in the Football League between 1963–70 before having to retire after a car crash. He managed Carlisle for four years and had coaching jobs under David Moyes at Preston and Everton.

RECORDS SECTION

INDEX

GOALSCORING
(†Football League pre-1992–93)

Highest: Arbroath 36 Bon Accord (Aberdeen) 0 in Scottish Cup 1, Sep 12, 1885. On same day, also in Scottish Cup 1, Dundee Harp beat Aberdeen Rov 35-0.

Internationals: France 0 England 15 in Paris, 1906 (Amateur); Ireland 0 England 13 in Belfast Feb 18, 1882 (record in UK); England 9 Scotland 3 at Wembley, Apr 15, 1961; Biggest England win at Wembley: 9-0 v Luxembourg (Euro Champ), Dec 15, 1982.

Other record wins: Scotland: 11-0 v Ireland (Glasgow, Feb 23, 1901); **Northern Ireland:** 7-0 v Wales (Belfast, Feb 1, 1930); **Wales:** 11-0 v Ireland (Wrexham, Mar 3, 1888); **Rep of Ireland:** 8-0 v Malta (Euro Champ, Dublin, Nov 16, 1983).

Record international defeats: England: 1-7 v Hungary (Budapest, May 23, 1954); **Scotland:** 3-9 v England (Wembley, Apr 15, 1961); **Ireland:** 0-13 v England (Belfast, Feb 18, 1882); **Wales:** 0-9 v Scotland (Glasgow, Mar 23, 1878); **Rep of Ireland:** 0-7 v Brazil (Uberlandia, May 27, 1982).

World Cup: Qualifying round – Australia 31 American Samoa 0, world record international score (Apr 11, 2001); Australia 22 Tonga 0 (Apr 9, 2001); Iran 19 Guam 0 (Nov 25, 2000); Maldives 0 Iran 17 (Jun 2, 1997). **Finals – highest scores:** Hungary 10 El Salvador 1 (Spain, Jun 15, 1982); Hungary 9 S Korea 0 (Switzerland, Jun 17, 1954); Yugoslavia 9 Zaire 0 (W Germany, Jun 18, 1974).

European Championship: Qualifying round – highest scorers: San Marino 0 Germany 13 (Serravalle, Sep 6, 2006). **Finals – highest score:** Holland 6 Yugoslavia 1 (quarter-final, Rotterdam, Jun 25, 2000).

Biggest England U-21 win: 9-0 v San Marino (Shrewsbury, Nov 19, 2013).

FA Cup: Preston 26 Hyde 0 1st round, Oct 15, 1887.

League Cup: West Ham 10 Bury 0 (2nd round, 2nd leg, Oct 25, 1983); Liverpool 10 Fulham 0 (2nd round, 1st leg, Sep 23, 1986). **Record aggregates:** Liverpool 13 Fulham 2 (10-0h, 3-2a), Sep 23, Oct 7, 1986; West Ham 12 Bury 1 (2-1a, 10-0h), Oct 4, 25, 1983; Liverpool 11 Exeter 0 (5-0h, 6-0a), Oct 7, 28, 1981.

League Cup – most goals in one match: 12 Reading 5 Arsenal 7 aet (4th round, Oct 30, 2012). Dagenham & Redbridge 6 Brentford 6 aet (Brentford won 4-2 on pens; 1st round, Aug 12, 2014.

Premier League (beginning 1992–93): Manchester Utd 9 Ipswich 0, Mar 4, 1995; Manchester Utd 9 Southampton 0, Feb 2, 2021. **Record away win:** Southampton 0 Leicester 9, Oct 25, 2019.

Highest aggregate scores in Premier League – 11: Portsmouth 7 Reading 4, Sep 29, 2007; **10:** Tottenham 6 Reading 4, Dec 29, 2007; Tottenham 9 Wigan 1, Nov 22, 2009; Manchester Utd 8 Arsenal 2, Aug 28, 2011; Arsenal 7 Newcastle 3, Dec 29, 2012; WBA 5 Manchester Utd 5, May 19, 2013.

Big back-to-back wins: Manchester City became the first Premier League team to score five or more goals in three successive matches in the same season – beating Liverpool 5-0, Watford 6-0 and Crystal Palace 5-0 in September 2017. Chelsea also scored heavily in the last game of the 2009-10 season (Wigan 8-0) and in the first two fixtures of the following campaign (WBA 6-0, Wigan 6-0).

†**Football League (First Division):** Aston Villa 12 Accrington 2, Mar 12, 1892; Tottenham 10 Everton 4, Oct 11, 1958 (highest Div 1 aggregate that century); WBA 12 Darwen 0, Apr 4, 1892; Nottm Forest 12 Leicester Fosse 0, Apr 21, 1909. **Record away win:** Newcastle 1 Sunderland 9, Dec 5, 1908; Cardiff 1 Wolves 9, Sep 3, 1955; Wolves 0 WBA 8, Dec 27, 1893.

New First Division (beginning 1992–93): Bolton 7 Swindon 0, Mar 8, 1997; Sunderland 7 Oxford Utd 0, Sep 19, 1998. **Record away win:** Stoke 0 Birmingham 7, Jan 10, 1998; Oxford Utd 0 Birmingham 7, Dec 12, 1998. **Record aggregate:** Grimsby 6 Burnley 5, Oct 29, 2002; Burnley 4 Watford 7, Apr 5, 2003.

Championship (beginning 2004–05): Birmingham 0 Bournemouth 8, Oct 25, 2014. ; Wigan 8 Hull 0, Jul 14, 2020. **Record away win:** Birmingham 0 Bournemouth 8, Oct 25, 2014. **Record aggregate:** Leeds 4 Preston 6, Sep 29, 2010; Leeds 3 Nottm Forest 7, Mar 20, 2012; Bristol City 5 Hull 5, Apr 21, 2018. Aston Villa 5 Nottm Forest 5, Nov 28, 2018.

†**Second Division:** Newcastle 13 Newport Co 0, Oct 5, 1946; Small Heath 12 Walsall Town Swifts 0, Dec 17, 1892; Darwen 12 Walsall 0, Dec 26, 1896; Woolwich Arsenal 12 Loughborough 0, Mar 12, 1900; Small Heath 12 Doncaster 0, Apr 11, 1903. **Record away win:** *Burslem Port Vale 0 Sheffield Utd 10, Dec 10, 1892. **Record aggregate:** Manchester City 11 Lincoln 3, Mar 23, 1895.

New Second Division (beginning 1992–93): Hartlepool 1 Plymouth Argyle 8, May 7, 1994; Hartlepool 8 Grimsby 1, Sep 12, 2003.

New League 1 (beginning 2004–05): MK Dons 7 Oldham 0, Dec 20, 2014; Oxford 0 Wigan 7, Dec 23, 2017; Peterborough 7 Accrington 0, Mar 27, 2021. **Record aggregate:** Hartlepool 4 Wrexham 6, Mar 5, 2005; Wolves 6 Rotherham 4, Apr 8, 2014; Bristol City 8 Walsall 2, May 3, 2015.

†**Third Division:** Gillingham 10 Chesterfield 0, Sep 5, 1987; Tranmere 9 Accrington 0, Apr 18, 1959; Brentford 9 Wrexham 0, Oct 15, 1963. **Record away win:** Halifax 0 Fulham 8, Sep 16, 1969. **Record aggregate:** Doncaster 7 Reading 5, Sep 25, 1982.

New Third Division (beginning 1992–93): Barnet 1 Peterborough 9, Sep 5, 1998. **Record aggregate:** Hull 7 Swansea 4, Aug 30, 1997.

New League 2 (beginning 2004–05): Peterborough 7 Brentford 0, Nov 24, 2007 Shrewsbury 7 Gillingham 0, Sep 13, 2008; Crewe 7 Barnet 0, Aug 21, 2010; Crewe 8 Cheltenham 1, Apr 2, 2011; Cambridge 7 Morecambe 0, Apr 19, 2016; Luton 7 Cambridge 0, Nov 18, 2017.

Record away win: Boston 0 Grimsby 6, Feb 3, 2007; Macclesfield 0 Darlington 6, Aug 30, 2008; Lincoln 0 Rotherham 6, Mar 25, 2011; Newport 0 Yeovil 6, Sep 15, 2018. **Record aggregate:** Burton 6 Cheltenham 6, Mar 13, 2010; Accrington 7 Gillingham 4, Oct 2, 2010.

†**Third Division (North):** Stockport 13 Halifax 0 (still joint biggest win in Football League – see Div 2) Jan 6, 1934; Tranmere 13 Oldham 4, Dec 26, 1935. (17 is highest Football League aggregate score). **Record away win:** Accrington 0 Barnsley 9, Feb 3, 1934.

†**Third Division (South):** Luton 12 Bristol Rov 0, Apr 13, 1936; Bristol City 9 Gillingham 4, Jan 15, 1927; Gillingham 9 Exeter 4, Jan 7, 1951. **Record away win:** Northampton 0 Walsall 8, Apr 8, 1947.

†**Fourth Division:** Oldham 11 Southport 0, Dec 26, 1962. **Record away win:** Crewe 1 Rotherham 8, Sep 8, 1973. **Record aggregate:** Hartlepool 10 Barrow 1, Apr 4, 1959; Crystal Palace 9 Accrington 2, Aug 20, 1960; Wrexham 10 Hartlepool 1, Mar 3, 1962; Oldham 11 Southport 0, Dec 26, 1962; Torquay 8 Newport 3, Oct 19, 1963; Shrewsbury 7 Doncaster 4, Feb 1, 1975; Barnet 4 Crewe 7, Aug 17, 1991.

Scottish Premier – Highest aggregate: 12: Motherwell 6 Hibernian 6, May 5, 2010; **11:** Celtic 8 Hamilton 3, Jan 3, 1987; Motherwell 5 Aberdeen 6, Oct 20, 1999. **Other highest team scores:** Aberdeen 8 Motherwell 0 (Mar 26, 1979); Hamilton 0 Celtic 8 (Nov 5, 1988); Celtic 9 Aberdeen 0 (Nov 6, 2010). **Record away win:** Hamilton 0 Celtic 8, Nov 5, 1988. **Record aggregate:** Motherwell 6 Hibernian 6, Prem, May 5, 2010; Motherwell 6 Hibernian 6, , Prem, May 5 2010.

Scottish League Div 1: Celtic 11 Dundee 0, Oct 26, 1895. **Record away win:** Hibs 11 *Airdrie 1, Oct 24, 1959.

Scottish League Div 2: Airdrieonians 15 Dundee Wanderers 1, Dec 1, 1894 (biggest win in history of League football in Britain).

Record modern Scottish League aggregate: 12 – Brechin 5 Cowdenbeath 7, Div 2, Jan 18, 2003.

Record British score since 1900: Stirling 20 Selkirk 0 (Scottish Cup 1, Dec 8, 1984). Winger Davie Thompson (7 goals) was one of 9 Stirling players to score.

LEAGUE GOALS – BEST IN SEASON (Before restructure in 1992)

Div		Goals	Games
1	WR (Dixie) Dean, Everton, 1927–28	60	39
2	George Camsell, Middlesbrough, 1926–27	59	37
3(S)	Joe Payne, Luton, 1936–37	55	39
3(N)	Ted Harston, Mansfield, 1936–37	55	41
3	Derek Reeves, Southampton, 1959–60	39	46
4	Terry Bly, Peterborough, 1960–61	52	46

(Since restructure in 1992)

Div		Goals	Games
1	Guy Whittingham, Portsmouth, 1992–93	42	46
2	Jordan Rhodes Huddersfield 2011-12	36	40
3	Andy Morrell, Wrexham, 2002–03	34	45

Premier League – BEST IN SEASON

Andy Cole **34 goals** (Newcastle – 40 games, 1993–94); Alan Shearer **34 goals**
(Blackburn – 42 games, 1994–95).

FOOTBALL LEAGUE – BEST MATCH HAULS

(Before restructure in 1992)

Div	Goals	
1	Ted Drake (Arsenal), away to Aston Villa, Dec 14, 1935	7
	James Ross (Preston) v Stoke, Oct 6, 1888	7
2	*Neville (Tim) Coleman (Stoke) v Lincoln, Feb 23, 1957	7
	Tommy Briggs (Blackburn) v Bristol Rov, Feb 5, 1955	7
3(S)	Joe Payne (Luton) v Bristol Rov, Apr 13, 1936	10
3(N)	Robert ('Bunny') Bell (Tranmere) v Oldham, Dec 26, 1935	
	he also missed a penalty	9
3	Barrie Thomas (Scunthorpe) v Luton, Apr 24, 1965	5
	Keith East (Swindon) v Mansfield, Nov 20, 1965	5
	Steve Earle (Fulham) v Halifax, Sep 16, 1969	5
	Alf Wood (Shrewsbury) v Blackburn, Oct 2, 1971	5
	Tony Caldwell (Bolton) v Walsall, Sep 10, 1983	5
	Andy Jones (Port Vale) v Newport Co., May 4, 1987	5
4	Bert Lister (Oldham) v Southport, Dec 26, 1962	6

*Scored from the wing

(Since restructure in 1992)

Div Goals

1 5 in match – Paul Barnes (Burnley v Stockport, 1996–97); Robert Taylor (all 5, Gillingham at Burnley, 1998–99); Lee Jones (all 5, Wrexham v Cambridge Utd, 2001–02).

3 5 in match – Tony Naylor (Crewe v Colchester, 1992–93); Steve Butler (Cambridge Utd v Exeter, 1993–4); Guiliano Grazioli (Peterborough at Barnet, 1998–99).

Lge 1 5 in match – Juan Ugarte (Wrexham at Hartlepool, 2004–05); Jordan Rhodes (Huddersfield at Wycombe, 2011–12).

Last player to score 6 in English League match: Geoff Hurst (West Ham 8 Sunderland 0, Div 1 Oct 19,1968.

PREMIER LEAGUE – BEST MATCH HAULS

5 goals in match: Andy Cole (Manchester Utd v Ipswich, Mar 4, 1995); Alan Shearer (Newcastle v Sheffield Wed, Sep 19, 1999); Jermain Defoe (Tottenham v Wigan, Nov 22, 2009); Dimitar Berbatov (Manchester Utd v Blackburn, Nov 27, 2010), Sergio Aguero (Manchester City v Newcastle, Oct 3, 2015).

SCOTTISH LEAGUE

Div		Goals
Prem	Gary Hooper (Celtic) v Hearts, May 13, 2012	5
	Kris Boyd (Rangers) v Dundee Utd, Dec 30, 2009	5
	Kris Boyd (Kilmarnock) v Dundee Utd, Sep 25, 2004	5
	Kenny Miller (Rangers) v St Mirren, Nov 4, 2000	5
	Marco Negri (Rangers) v Dundee Utd, Aug. 23, 1997	5
	Paul Sturrock (Dundee Utd) v Morton, Nov 17, 1984	5
1	Jimmy McGrory (Celtic) v Dunfermline, Jan 14, 1928	8
1	Owen McNally (Arthurlie) v Armadale, Oct 1, 1927	8
2	Jim Dyet (King's Park) v Forfar, Jan 2, 1930 on his debut for the club	8
2	John Calder (Morton) v Raith, Apr 18, 1936	8
2	Norman Haywood (Raith) v Brechin, Aug. 20, 1937	8

SCOTTISH LEAGUE – BEST IN SEASON

Div		Goals
Prem	Brian McClair (Celtic, 1986–87)	35
	Henrik Larsson (Celtic, 2000–01)	35
1	William McFadyen (Motherwell, 1931–32)	52
2	*Jimmy Smith (Ayr, 1927–28 – 38 appearances)	66
	(*British record)	

CUP FOOTBALL

Scottish Cup: John Petrie (Arbroath) v Bon Accord, at Arbroath, 1st round, Sep 12, 1885 — 13

FA Cup: Ted MacDougall (Bournemouth) v Margate, 1st round, Nov 20, 1971 — 9

FA Cup Final: Billy Townley (Blackburn) v Sheffield Wed, at Kennington Oval, 1890; Jimmy Logan (Notts Co) v Bolton, at Everton, 1894; Stan Mortensen (Blackpool) v Bolton, at Wembley, 1953 — 3

League Cup: Frank Bunn (Oldham) v Scarborough (3rd round), Oct 25, 1989 — 6

Scottish League Cup: Willie Penman (Raith) v Stirling, Sep 18, 1948 — 6

Scottish Cup: Most goals in match since war: 10 by **Gerry Baker** (St Mirren) in 15-0 win (1st round) v Glasgow Univ, Jan 30, 1960; 9 by his brother **Joe Baker** (Hibernian) in 15-1 win (2nd round) v Peebles, Feb 11, 1961.

AGGREGATE LEAGUE SCORING RECORDS

	Goals
*Arthur Rowley (1947–65, WBA, Fulham, Leicester, Shrewsbury)	434
†Jimmy McGrory (1922–38, Celtic, Clydebank)	410
Hughie Gallacher (1921–39, Airdrieonians, Newcastle, Chelsea, Derby, Notts Co, Grimsby, Gateshead)	387
William ('Dixie') Dean (1923–37, Tranmere, Everton, Notts Co)	379
Hugh Ferguson (1916–30, Motherwell, Cardiff, Dundee)	363
● Jimmy Greaves (1957–71, Chelsea, Tottenham, West Ham)	357
Steve Bloomer (1892–1914, Derby, Middlesbrough, Derby)	352
George Camsell (1923–39, Durham City, Middlesbrough)	345
Dave Halliday (1920–35, St Mirren, Dundee, Sunderland, Arsenal, Manchester City, Clapton Orient)	338
John Aldridge (1979–98, Newport, Oxford Utd, Liverpool, Tranmere)	329
Harry Bedford (1919–34), Nottm Forest, Blackpool, Derby, Newcastle, Sunderland, Bradford PA, Chesterfield	326
John Atyeo (1951–66, Bristol City)	315
Joe Smith (1908–29, Bolton, Stockport)	315
Victor Watson (1920–36, West Ham, Southampton)	312

Harry Johnson (1919–36, Sheffield Utd, Mansfield) **305**
Bob McPhail (1923–1939, Airdrie, Rangers) **306**
(*Rowley scored 4 for WBA, 27 for Fulham, 251 for Leicester, 152 for Shrewsbury.
● **Greaves'** 357 is record top-division total (he also scored 9 League goals for AC Milan). **Aldridge** also scored 33 League goals for Real Sociedad. †McGrory scored 397 for Celtic, 13 for Clydebank).
Most League goals for one club: 349 – Dixie Dean (Everton 1925–37); **326 – George Camsell** (Middlesbrough 1925–39); **315 – John Atyeo** (Bristol City 1951–66); **306 – Vic Watson** (West Ham 1920–35); **291 – Steve Bloomer** (Derby 1892–1906, 1910–14); **259 – Arthur Chandler** (Leicester 1923–35); **255 – Nat Lofthouse** (Bolton 1946–61); **251 – Arthur Rowley** (Leicester 1950–58).
More than 500 goals: Jimmy McGrory (Celtic, Clydebank and Scotland) scored a total of **550** goals in his first-class career (1922–38).
More than 1,000 goals: Brazil's **Pele** is reputedly the game's all-time highest scorer with **1,283** goals in 1,365 matches (1956–77), but many of them were scored in friendlies for his club, Santos. He scored his 1,000th goal, a penalty, against Vasco da Gama in the Maracana Stadium, Rio, on Nov 19, 1969. ● Pele (born Oct 23, 1940) played regularly for Santos from the age of 16. During his career, he was sent off only once. He played 95 'A' internationals for Brazil and in their World Cup-winning teams in 1958 and 1970. † Pele (Edson Arantes do Nascimento) was subsequently Brazil's Minister for Sport. He never played at Wembley, apart from being filmed there scoring a goal for a commercial. Aged 57, Pele received an 'honorary knighthood' (Knight Commander of the British Empire) from the Queen at Buckingham Palace on Dec 3, 1997.
Romario (retired Apr, 2008, aged 42) scored more than 1,000 goals for Vasco da Gama, Barcelona, PSV Eindhoven, Valencia and Brazil (56 in 73 internationals).

MOST LEAGUE GOALS IN SEASON: DEAN'S 60

WR ('Dixie') Dean, Everton centre-forward, created a League scoring record in 1927–28 with 60 in 39 First Division matches. He also scored three in FA Cup ties, and 19 in representative games, totalling 82 for the season.
George Camsell, of Middlesbrough, previously held the record with 59 goals in 37 Second Division matches in 1926–27, his total for the season being 75.

SHEARER'S RECORD 'FIRST'

Alan Shearer (Blackburn) is the only player to score more than 30 top-division goals in 3 successive seasons since the War: 31 in 1993–94, 34 in 1994–95, 31 in 1995–96.
Thierry Henry (Arsenal) is the first player to score more than 20 Premier League goals in five consecutive seasons (2002–06). **David Halliday** (Sunderland) topped 30 First Division goals in 4 consecutive seasons with totals of 38, 36, 36 and 49 from 1925–26 to 1928–29.

MOST GOALS IN A MATCH

Sep 12, 1885: John Petrie set the all-time British individual record for a first-class match when, in Arbroath's 36-0 win against Bon Accord (Scottish Cup 1), he scored **13.**
Apr 13, 1936: Joe Payne set the still-existing individual record on his debut as a centre-forward, for Luton v Bristol Rov (Div 3 South). In a 12-0 win he scored **10.**

ROWLEY'S ALL-TIME RECORD

Arthur Rowley is English football's top club scorer with a total of 464 goals for WBA, Fulham, Leicester and Shrewsbury (1947–65). There were 434 in the League, 26 FA Cup, 4 League Cup.
Jimmy Greaves is second with a total of 420 goals for Chelsea, AC Milan, Tottenham and West Ham, made up of 366 League, 35 FA Cup, 10 League Cup and 9 in Europe. He also scored nine goals for AC Milan.
John Aldridge retired as a player at the end of season 1997–98 with a career total of 329 League

goals for Newport, Oxford Utd, Liverpool and Tranmere (1979–98). In all competitions for those clubs he scored 410 in 737 appearances. He also scored 45 in 63 games for Real Sociedad.

MOST GOALS IN INTERNATIONAL MATCHES

13 by **Archie Thompson** for Australia v American Samoa in World Cup (Oceania Group qualifier) at Coff's Harbour, New South Wales, Apr 11, 2001. Result: 31-0.

7 by **Stanley Harris** for England v France in Amateur International in Paris, Nov 1, 1906. Result: 15-0.

6 by **Nat Lofthouse** for Football League v Irish League, at Wolverhampton, Sep 24, 1952. Result: 7-1.

Joe Bambrick for Northern Ireland against Wales (7-0) in Belfast, Feb 1, 1930 – a record for a Home Nations International. **WC Jordan** in Amateur International for England v France, at Park Royal, Mar 23, 1908. Result: 12-0. **Vivian Woodward** for England v Holland in Amateur International, at Chelsea, Dec 11,1909. Result: 9-1.

5 by **Howard Vaughton** for England v Ireland (Belfast) Feb 18, 1882. Result: 13-0.

Steve Bloomer for England v Wales (Cardiff) Mar 16, 1896. Result: 9-1.

Hughie Gallacher for Scotland against Ireland (Belfast), Feb 23, 1929. Result: 7-3.

Willie Hall for England v Northern Ireland, at Old Trafford, Nov 16, 1938. Five in succession (first three in 3'5 mins – fastest international hat-trick). Result: 7-0.

Malcolm Macdonald for England v Cyprus (Wembley) Apr 16, 1975. Result: 5-0.

Hughie Gallacher for Scottish League against Irish League (Belfast) Nov 11, 1925. Result: 7-3.

Barney Battles for Scottish League against Irish League (Firhill Park, Glasgow) Oct 31, 1928. Result: 8-2.

Bobby Flavell for Scottish League against Irish League (Belfast) Apr 30, 1947. Result: 7-4.

Joe Bradford for Football League v Irish League (Everton) Sep 25, 1929. Result: 7-2.

Albert Stubbins for Football League v Irish League (Blackpool) Oct 18, 1950. Result: 6-3.

Brian Clough for Football League v Irish League (Belfast) Sep 23, 1959. Result: 5-0.

LAST ENGLAND PLAYER TO SCORE ...

3 goals: Harry Kane v Bulgaria (4-0) Euro Champ qual, Wembley, Sept 7, 2019; Kane v Montenegro (7-0) Euro Champ qual, Wembley, Nov 14. 2019 (England's 1,000th international); Kane v Albania (5-0), World Cup qual, Wembley, Nov 12, 2021.

4 goals: Kane v San Marino (10-0), World Cup qual, Serravalle, Nov 15, 2021.

5 goals: Malcolm Macdonald v Cyprus (5-0), Euro Champ qual, Wembley, Apr 16, 1975.

INTERNATIONAL TOP SHOTS

		Goals	Games
England	Wayne Rooney (2003–2019)	53	120
N Ireland	David Healy (2000–13)	36	95
Scotland	Denis Law (1958–74)	30	55
	Kenny Dalglish (1971–86)	30	102
Wales	Gareth Bale (2006–22)	39	106
Rep of Ire	Robbie Keane (1998–2016)	68	146

ENGLAND'S TOP MARKSMEN

(As at start of season 2022–23)

	Goals	Games
Wayne Rooney (2003–17)	53	120
Harry Kane (2015–2022)	50	73
Bobby Charlton (1958–70)	49	106
Gary Lineker (1984–92)	48	80

Jimmy Greaves (1959–67)	44	57
Michael Owen (1998–2008)	40	89
Tom Finney (1946–58)	30	76
Nat Lofthouse (1950–58)	30	33
Alan Shearer (1992–2000)	30	63
Vivian Woodward (1903–11)	29	23
Frank Lampard (2003–14)	29	106
Steve Bloomer (1895–1907)	28	23
David Platt (1989–96)	27	62
Bryan Robson (1979–91)	26	90
Geoff Hurst (1966–72)	24	49
Stan Mortensen (1947–53)	23	25
Tommy Lawton (1938–48)	22	23
Peter Crouch (2005–11)	22	42
Mike Channon (1972–77)	21	46
Steven Gerrard (2000–14)	21	114
Kevin Keegan (1972–82)	21	63

ROONEY'S ENGLAND RECORD

Wayne Rooney reached 50 international goals with a penalty against Switzerland at Wembley on September 8, 2015 to become England's record scorer, surpassing Bobby Charlton's mark. Charlton's record was set in 106 games, Rooney's tally in 107.

CONSECUTIVE GOALS FOR ENGLAND

Steve Bloomer scored in **10** consecutive appearances (19 goals) between Mar 1895 and Mar 1899. **Jimmy Greaves** scored **11** goals in five consecutive matches from the start of season 1960–61.

ENGLAND'S TOP FINAL SERIES MARKSMEN

Gary Lineker with 6 goals at 1986 World Cup in Mexico.
Harry Kane with 6 goals at 2018 World Cup in Russia.

MOST ENGLAND GOALS IN SEASON

13 – Jimmy Greaves (1960–61 in 9 matches); **12** – Dixie Dean (1926–27 in 6 matches); **12** Harry Kane (2021–22 in 12 matches); **11** – Harry Kane (2017–18 in 11 matches); **10** – Gary Lineker (1990–91 in 10 matches); **10** – Wayne Rooney – (2008–09 in 9 matches).

MOST ENGLAND HAT-TRICKS

Jimmy Greaves 6; **Gary Lineker** 5, **Harry Kane** 5, **Bobby Charlton** 4, **Vivian Woodward** 4, **Stan Mortensen** 3.

MOST GOALS FOR ENGLAND U-21s

14 – Eddie Nketiah (12 apps), **13** – Alan Shearer (11 apps), Francis Jeffers (13 apps).

GOLDEN GOAL DECIDERS

The Football League, in an experiment to avoid penalty shoot-outs, introduced a new golden goal system in the 1994–95 **Auto Windscreens Shield** to decide matches in the knock-out stages of the competition in which scores were level after 90 minutes. The first goal scored in overtime ended play.

Iain Dunn (Huddersfield) became the first player in British football to settle a match by this sudden-death method. His 107th-minute goal beat Lincoln 3-2 on Nov 30, 1994, and to mark his 'moment in history' he was presented with a golden football trophy.

The AWS Final of 1995 was decided when Paul Tait headed the only goal for Birmingham against Carlisle 13 minutes into overtime – the first time a match at Wembley had been decided by the 'golden goal' formula.

First major international tournament match to be decided by sudden death was the Final of the **1996 European Championship** at Wembley in which Germany beat Czech Rep 2-1 by **Oliver Bierhoff's** goal in the 95th minute.

In the **1998 World Cup Finals** (2nd round), host country France beat Paraguay 1-0 with **Laurent Blanc's** goal (114).

France won the **2000 European Championship** with golden goals in the semi-final, 2-1 v Portugal (Zinedine Zidane pen, 117), and in the Final, 2-1 v Italy (David Trezeguet, 103).

Galatasaray (Turkey) won the **European Super Cup** 2-1 against Real Madrid (Monaco, Aug 25, 2000) with a 103rd minute golden goal, a penalty.

Liverpool won the **UEFA Cup** 5-4 against Alaves with a 117th-min golden goal, an own goal, in the Final in Dortmund (May 19, 2001).

In the **2002 World Cup Finals**, 3 matches were decided by Golden Goals: in the 2nd round Senegal beat Sweden 2-1 (Henri Camara, 104) and South Korea beat Italy 2-1 (Ahn Jung-hwan, 117); in the quarter-final, Turkey beat Senegal 1-0 (Ilhan Mansiz, 94).

France won the 2003 **FIFA Confederations Cup Final** against Cameroon (Paris, Jun 29) with a 97th-minute golden goal by Thierry Henry.

Doncaster won promotion to Football League with a 110th-minute golden goal winner (3-2) in the Conference Play-off Final against Dagenham at Stoke (May 10, 2003).

Germany won the **Women's World Cup Final** 2-1 v Sweden (Los Angeles, Oct 12, 2003) with a 98th-minute golden goal.

GOLD TURNS TO SILVER

Starting with the 2003 Finals of the UEFA Cup and Champions League/European Cup, UEFA introduced a new rule by which a silver goal could decide the winners if the scores were level after 90 minutes.

Team leading after 15 minutes' extra time win match. If sides level, a second period of 15 minutes to be played. If still no winner, result to be decided by penalty shoot-out.

UEFA said the change was made because the golden goal put too much pressure on referees and prompted teams to play negative football.

Although both 2003 European Finals went to extra-time, neither was decided by a silver goal. The new rule applied in the 2004 European Championship Finals, and Greece won their semi-final against the Czech Republic in the 105th minute.

The **International Board** decided (Feb 28 2004) that the golden/silver goal rule was 'unfair' and that from July 1 competitive international matches level after extra-time would, when necessary, be settled on penalties.

PREMIER LEAGUE TOP SHOTS (1992–2022)

Alan Shearer	260	Jimmy Floyd Hasselbaink	127
Wayne Rooney	208	Robbie Keane	126
Andy Cole	187	Nicolas Anelka	125
Sergio Aguero	184	Dwight Yorke	123
Harry Kane	183	Romelu Lukaku	121
Frank Lampard	177	Steven Gerrard	120
Thierry Henry	175	Mohamed Salah	120
Robbie Fowler	163	Ian Wright	113
Jermain Defoe	162	Dion Dublin	111
Michael Owen	150	Sadio Mane	111
Les Ferdinand	149	Emile Heskey	110
Teddy Sheringham	146	Ryan Giggs	109
Robin van Persie	144	Raheem Sterling	109
Jamie Vardy	133	Peter Crouch	108

Paul Scholes	107	Cristiano Ronaldo	102
Darren Bent	106	Matt Le Tissier	100
Didier Drogba	104		

LEAGUE GOAL RECORDS

The highest goal-scoring aggregates in the Football League, Premier and Scottish League are:

For

	Goals	Games	Club	Season
Prem	106	38	Manchester City	2017–18
Div 1	128	42	Aston Villa	1930–31
New Div 1	108	46	Manchester City	2001–02
New Champ	106	46	Fulham	2021–22
Div 2	122	42	Middlesbrough	1926–27
New Div 2	89	46	Millwall	2000–01
New Lge 1	106	46	Peterborough	2010–11
Div 3(S)	127	42	Millwall	1927–28
Div 3(N)	128	42	Bradford City	1928–29
Div 3	111	46	QPR	1961–62
New Div 3	96	46	Luton	2001–02
New Lge 2	96	46	Notts Co	2009–10
Div 4	134	46	Peterborough	1960–61
Scot Prem	106	38	Celtic	2015–17
Scot L 1	132	34	Hearts	1957–58
Scot L 2	142	34	Raith Rov	1937–38
Scot L 3 (Modern)	130	36	Gretna	2004–05

Against

Prem	100	42	Swindon	1993–94
Div 1	125	42	Blackpool	1930–31
New Div 1	102	46	Stockport	2001–02
New Champ	98	46	Rotherham	2016–17
Div 2	141	34	Darwen	1898–99
New Div 2	102	46	Chester	1992–93
New Lge 1	98	46	Stockport	2004–05
Div 3(S)	135	42	Merthyr T	1929–30
Div 3(N)	136	42	Nelson	1927–28
Div 3	123	46	Accrington Stanley	1959–60
New Div 3	113	46	Doncaster	1997–98
New Lge 2	96	46	Stockport	2010–11
Div 4	109	46	Hartlepool Utd	1959–60
Scot Prem	106	38	Celtic	2016–17
Scot L 1	137	38	Leith A	1931–32
Scot L 2	146	38	Edinburgh City	1931–32
Scot L 3 (Modern)	118	36	East Stirling	2003–04

BEST DEFENSIVE RECORDS *Denotes under old offside law

Div	Goals Agst	Games	Club	Season
Prem	15	38	Chelsea	2004–05
1	16	42	Liverpool	1978–79
1	*15	22	Preston	1888–89
New Div 1	28	46	Sunderland	1998–99
New Champ	30	46	Preston	2005–06
	30	46	Watford	2020–21
2	18	28	Liverpool	1893–94

Div	Goals Agst	Games	Club	Season
2	*22	34	Sheffield Wed	1899–1900
2	24	42	Birmingham	1947–48
2	24	42	Crystal Palace	1978–79
New Div 2	25	46	Wigan	2002–03
New Lge 1	29	46	Wigan	2017–18
3(S)	*21	42	Southampton	1921–22
3(S)	30	42	Cardiff	1946–47
3(N)	*21	38	Stockport	1921–22
3(N)	21	46	Port Vale	1953–54
3	30	46	Middlesbrough	1986–87
New Div 3	20	46	Gillingham	1995–96
New Lge 2	27	46	Cheltenham	2019–20
4	25	46	Lincoln	1980–81

SCOTTISH LEAGUE

Div	Goals Agst	Games	Club	Season
Prem	13	38	Rangers	2020–21
1	*12	22	Dundee	1902–03
1	*14	38	Celtic	1913–14
2	20	38	Morton	1966–67
2	*29	38	Clydebank	1922–23
2	29	36	East Fife	1995–96
New Div 3	21	36	Brechin	1995–96

TOP SCORERS (LEAGUE ONLY)

		Goals	Div
2021–22	Aleksandar Mitrovic (Fulham)	43	Champ
2020–21	Paul Mullin (Cambridge)	32	Lg 2
2019–20	Aleksandar Mitrovic (Fulham)	26	Champ
2018–19	Teemu Pukki (Norwich)	29	Champ
	James Norwood (Tranmere)	29	Lge 2
2017–18	Mohamed Salah (Liverpool)	32	Prem
2016–17	Billy Sharp (Sheffield Utd)	30	Lge 1
2015–16	Matt Taylor (Bristol Rov)	27	Lge 2
2014–15	Daryl Murphy (Ipswich)	27	Champ
2013–14	Luis Suarez (Liverpool)	31	Prem
2012–13	Tom Pope (Port Vale)	31	Lge 2
2011–12	Jordan Rhodes (Huddersfield)	36	Lge 1
2010–11	Clayton Donaldson (Crewe)	28	Lge 2
2009–10	Rickie Lambert (Southampton)	31	Lge 1
2008– 09	Simon Cox (Swindon)		
	Rickie Lambert (Bristol Rov)	29	Lge 1
2007–08	Cristiano Ronaldo (Manchester Utd)	31	Prem
2006–07	Billy Sharp (Scunthorpe)	30	Lge 1
2005–06	Thierry Henry (Arsenal)	27	Prem
2004–05	Stuart Elliott (Hull)	27	1
	Phil Jevons (Yeovil)	27	2
	Dean Windass (Bradford City)	27	1
2003–04	Thierry Henry (Arsenal)	30	Prem
2002–03	Andy Morrell (Wrexham)	34	3
2001–02	Shaun Goater (Manchester City)	28	1
	Bobby Zamora (Brighton)	28	2
2000–01	Bobby Zamora (Brighton)	28	3
1999–00	Kevin Phillips (Sunderland)	30	Prem

1998–99	Lee Hughes (WBA)	31	1
1997–98	Pierre van Hooijdonk (Nottm Forest)	29	1
	Kevin Phillips (Sunderland)	29	1
1996–97	Graeme Jones (Wigan)	31	3
1995–96	Alan Shearer (Blackburn)	31	Prem
1994–95	Alan Shearer (Blackburn)	34	Prem
1993–94	Jimmy Quinn (Reading)	35	2
1992–93	Guy Whittingham (Portsmouth)	42	1
1991–92	Ian Wright (Crystal Palace 5, Arsenal 24)	29	1
1990–91	Teddy Sheringham (Millwall)	33	2
1989–90	Mick Quinn (Newcastle)	32	2
1988–89	Steve Bull (Wolves)	37	3
1987–88	Steve Bull (Wolves)	34	4
1986–87	Clive Allen (Tottenham)	33	1
1985–86	Gary Lineker (Everton)	30	1
1984–85	Tommy Tynan (Plymouth Argyle)	31	3
	John Clayton (Tranmere)	31	4
1983–84	Trevor Senior (Reading)	36	4
1982–83	Luther Blissett (Watford)	27	1
1981–82	Keith Edwards (Hull 1, Sheffield Utd 35)	36	4
1980–81	Tony Kellow (Exeter)	25	3
1979–80	Clive Allen (Queens Park Rangers)	28	2
1978–79	Ross Jenkins (Watford)	29	3
1977–78	Steve Phillips (Brentford)	32	4
	Alan Curtis (Swansea City)	32	4
1976–77	Peter Ward (Brighton)	32	3
1975–76	Dixie McNeil (Hereford)	35	3
1974–75	Dixie McNeil (Hereford)	31	3
1973–74	Brian Yeo (Gillingham)	31	4
1972–73	Bryan (Pop) Robson (West Ham)	28	1
1971–72	Ted MacDougall (Bournemouth)	35	3
1970–71	Ted MacDougall (Bournemouth)	42	4
1969–70	Albert Kinsey (Wrexham)	27	4
1968–69	Jimmy Greaves (Tottenham)	27	1
1967–68	George Best (Manchester Utd)	28	1
	Ron Davies (Southampton)	28	1
1966–67	Ron Davies (Southampton)	37	1
1965–66	Kevin Hector (Bradford PA)	44	4
1964–65	Alick Jeffrey (Doncaster)	36	4
1963–64	Hugh McIlmoyle (Carlisle)	39	4
1962–63	Jimmy Greaves (Tottenham)	37	1
1961–62	Roger Hunt (Liverpool)	41	2
1960–61	Terry Bly (Peterborough)	52	4

100 LEAGUE GOALS IN SEASON

Manchester City, First Div Champions in 2001–02, scored 108 goals.

Bolton, First Div Champions in 1996–97, reached 100 goals, the first side to complete a century in League football since 103 by **Northampton** (Div 4 Champions) in 1986–87.

Last League Champions to reach 100 League goals: **Manchester City** (106 in 2017–18). Last century of goals in the top division: 111 by runners-up **Tottenham** in 1962–63.

Clubs to score a century of Premier League goals in season: **Manchester City** 106 in 2017-18, **Chelsea** 103 in 2009–10, Manchester City (102) and Liverpool (101) in 2013–14.

Wolves topped 100 goals in four successive First Division seasons (1957–58, 1958–59, 1959–60, 1960–61).

In **1930–31**, the top three all scored a century of League goals: 1 Arsenal (127), 2 Aston Villa (128), 3 Sheffield Wed (102).

100 GOALS AGAINST

Swindon, relegated with 100 goals against in 1993–94, were the first top-division club to concede a century of League goals since **Ipswich** (121) went down in 1964. Most goals conceded in the top division: 125 by **Blackpool** in 1930–31, but they avoided relegation.

MOST LEAGUE GOALS ON ONE DAY

A record of 209 goals in the four divisions of the Football League (43 matches) was set on **Jan 2, 1932**: 56 in Div 1, 53 in Div 2, 57 in Div 3 South and 43 in Div 3 North.

There were two 10-goal aggregates: Bradford City 9, Barnsley 1 in Div 2 and Coventry City 5, Fulham 5 in Div 3 South.

That total of 209 League goals on one day was equalled on **Feb 1, 1936** (44 matches): 46 in Div 1, 46 in Div 2, 49 in Div 3 South and 69 in Div 3 North. Two matches in the Northern Section produced 23 of the goals: Chester 12, York 0 and Crewe 5, Chesterfield 6.

MOST GOALS IN TOP DIV ON ONE DAY

This record has stood since **Dec 26, 1963**, when 66 goals were scored in the ten First Division matches played.

MOST PREMIER LEAGUE GOALS ON ONE DAY

47, in nine matches on **May 8, 1993** (last day of season). For the first time, all 20 clubs scored in the Premier League programme over the weekend of Nov 27-28, 2010.

FEWEST PREMIER LEAGUE GOALS IN ONE WEEK-END

10, in **10** matches on **Nov 24/25, 2001**.

FEWEST FIRST DIV GOALS ON ONE DAY

For full/near full programme: **Ten goals**, all by home clubs, in ten matches on Apr 28, 1923 (day of Wembley's first FA Cup Final).

SCORER OF LEAGUE'S FIRST GOAL

Kenny Davenport (2 mins) for Bolton v Derby, Sep 8, 1888.

VARDY'S RECORD

Jamie Vardy set a Premier League record by scoring in 11 consecutive matches for Leicester (Aug-Nov 2015). The all-time top division record of scoring in 12 successive games was set by **Jimmy Dunne** for Sheffield Utd in the old First Division in season 1931-32. **Stan Mortensen** scored in 15 successive matches for Blackpool (First Division) in season 1950-51, but that sequence included two injury breaks.

LUTON GOAL FEAST

Luton set a Football League record in season 2017–18 by scoring seven or more goals in three games before Christmas – beating Yeovil 8-2 on the opening day of the season, Stevenage 7-1 and Cambridge 7-0.

SCORERS FOR 7 PREMIER LEAGUE CLUBS

Craig Bellamy (Coventry, Newcastle, Blackburn, Liverpool, West Ham, Manchester City, Cardiff).

SCORERS FOR 6 PREMIER LEAGUE CLUBS

Les Ferdinand (QPR, Newcastle, Tottenham, West Ham, Leicester, Bolton); **Andy Cole** (Newcastle, Manchester Utd, Blackburn, Fulham, Manchester City, Portsmouth); **Marcus Bent** (Crystal Palace, Ipswich, Leicester, Everton, Charlton, Wigan); **Nick Barmby** (Tottenham, Middlesbrough, Everton, Liverpool, Leeds, Hull); **Peter Crouch** (Tottenham, Aston Villa, Southampton, Liverpool, Portsmouth, Stoke); **Robbie Keane** (Coventry, Leeds, Tottenham, Liverpool, West Ham, Aston Villa); **Nicolas Anelka** (Arsenal, Liverpool, Manchester City, Bolton, Chelsea, WBA); **Darren Bent** (Ipswich, Charlton, Tottenham, Sunderland, Aston Villa, Fulham).

SCORERS FOR 5 PREMIER LEAGUE CLUBS

Stan Collymore (Nottm Forest, Liverpool, Aston Villa, Leicester, Bradford); **Mark Hughes** (Manchester Utd, Chelsea, Southampton, Everton, Blackburn); **Benito Carbone** (Sheffield Wed, Aston Villa, Bradford, Derby, Middlesbrough); **Ashley Ward** (Norwich, Derby, Barnsley, Blackburn Bradford); **Teddy Sheringham** (Nottm Forest, Tottenham, Manchester Utd, Portsmouth, West Ham); **Chris Sutton** (Norwich, Blackburn, Chelsea, Birmingham, Aston Villa).

SCORERS IN MOST CONSECUTIVE LEAGUE MATCHES

Arsenal broke the record by scoring in 55 successive Premier League fixtures: the last match in season 2000–01, then all 38 games in winning the title in 2001–02, and the first 16 in season 2002–03. The sequence ended with a 2-0 defeat away to Manchester Utd on December 7, 2002. **Chesterfield** previously held the record, having scored in 46 consecutive matches in Div 3 (North), starting on Christmas Day, 1929 and ending on December 27, 1930.

HEADING FOR VICTORY

When **Oxford Utd** beat Shrewsbury 6-0 (Div 2) on Apr 23, 1996, all six goals were headers. Charlie Wyke scored four headed goals, all from Aiden McGeady crosses, when Sunderland beat Doncaster 4-1 (Lge 1) on Feb 13, 2021.

ALL–ROUND MARKSMEN

Alan Cork scored in four divisions of the Football League and in the Premier League in his 18-season career with Wimbledon, Sheffield Utd and Fulham (1977–95). **Brett Ormerod** scored in all four divisions (2, 1, Champ and Prem Lge) for Blackpool in two spells (1997–2002, 2008–11). **Grant Holt** (Sheffield Wed, Rochdale, Nottm Forest, Shrewsbury, Norwich) has scored in four Football League divisions and in the Premier League.

CROUCH AHEAD OF THE GAME

Peter Crouch holds the record for most headed goals in the Premier League with a total of 53, ahead of Alan Shearer (46) and Dion Dublin (45).

MOST CUP GOALS

FA Cup – most goals in one season: 20 by Jimmy Ross (Preston, runners-up 1887–88); 15 by **Alex (Sandy) Brown** (Tottenham, winners 1900–01). **Most FA Cup goals in individual careers:** 49 by Harry Cursham (Notts Co 1877–89); 20th century: 44 by **Ian Rush** (39 for Liverpool, 4 for Chester, 1 for Newcastle 1979–98). **Denis Law** was the previous highest FA Cup scorer in the 20th century with 41 goals for Huddersfield Town, Manchester City and Manchester Utd (1957–74). **Most FA Cup Final goals by individual:** 5 by Ian Rush for Liverpool (2 in 1986, 2 in 1989, 1 in 1992).

HOTTEST CUP HOT-SHOT

Geoff Hurst scored 21 cup goals in season 1965–66: 11 League Cup, 4 FA Cup and 2 Cup-Winners' Cup for West Ham, and 4 in the World Cup for England.

SCORERS IN EVERY ROUND

Twelve players have scored in every round of the FA Cup in one season, from opening to Final inclusive: **Archie Hunter** (Aston Villa, winners 1887); **Sandy Brown** (Tottenham, winners 1901); **Harry Hampton** (Aston Villa, winners 1905); **Harold Blackmore** (Bolton, winners 1929); **Ellis Rimmer** (Sheffield Wed, winners 1935); **Frank O'Donnell** (Preston, beaten 1937); **Stan Mortensen** (Blackpool, beaten 1948); **Jackie Milburn** (Newcastle, winners 1951); **Nat Lofthouse** (Bolton, beaten 1953); **Charlie Wayman** (Preston, beaten 1954); **Jeff Astle** (WBA, winners 1968); **Peter Osgood** (Chelsea, winners 1970).

Blackmore and the next seven completed their 'set' in the Final at Wembley; Osgood did so in the Final replay at Old Trafford.

Tony Brown became the first player to score in every round of the **League Cup**, including one in the final which WBA won 5-3 on aggregate against West Ham in 1966. The following season, the first to be contested in a single match at Wembley, Albion's Clive Clark also scored in every round, netting both goals in the 3-2 defeat by QPR in the final.

TEN IN A ROW

Dixie McNeill scored for Wrexham in ten successive FA Cup rounds (18 goals): 11 in Rounds 1-6, 1977–78; 3 in Rounds 3-4, 1978–79; 4 in Rounds 3-4, 1979–80.

Stan Mortensen (Blackpool) scored 25 goals in 16 FA Cup rounds out of 17 (1946–51).

TOP MATCH HAULS IN FA CUP

Ted MacDougall scored nine goals, a record for the competition proper, in the FA Cup first round on Nov 20, 1971, when Bournemouth beat Margate 11-0. On Nov 23, 1970 he had scored six in an 8-1 first round replay against Oxford City.

Other six-goal FA Cup scorers include **George Hilsdon** (Chelsea v Worksop, 9-1, 1907–08), **Ronnie Rooke** (Fulham v Bury, 6-0, 1938–39), **Harold Atkinson** (Tranmere v Ashington, 8-1, 1952–53), **George Best** (Manchester Utd v Northampton 1969–70, 8-2 away), **Duane Darby** (Hull v Whitby, 8-4, 1996–97).

Denis Law scored all six for Manchester City at Luton (6-2) in an FA Cup 4th round tie on Jan 28, 1961, but none of them counted – the match was abandoned (69 mins) because of a waterlogged pitch. He also scored City's goal when the match was played again, but they lost 3-1.

Tony Philliskirk scored **five** when Peterborough beat Kingstonian 9-1 in an FA Cup 1st round replay on Nov 25, 1992, but had them wiped from the records.

With the score at 3-0, the Kingstonian goalkeeper was concussed by a coin thrown from the crowd and unable to play on. The FA ordered the match to be replayed at Peterborough behind closed doors, and Kingstonian lost 1-0.

● Two players have scored **ten goals** in FA Cup preliminary round matches: **Chris Marron** for South Shields against Radcliffe in Sep 1947; **Paul Jackson** when Sheffield-based club Stocksbridge Park Steels beat Oldham Town 17-1 on Aug 31, 2002. He scored 5 in each half and all ten with his feet – goal times 6, 10, 22, 30, 34, 68, 73, 75, 79, 84 mins.

QUICKEST GOALS AND RAPID SCORING

A goal in **4 sec** was claimed by **Jim Fryatt**, for Bradford PA v Tranmere (Div 4, Apr 25, 1965), and by **Gerry Allen** for Whitstable v Danson (Kent League, Mar 3,1989). **Damian Mori** scored in **4 sec** for Adelaide v Sydney (Australian National League, December 6, 1995).

Goals after **6 sec** – **Albert Mundy** for Aldershot v Hartlepool, Oct 25, 1958; **Barrie Jones** for Notts Co v Torquay, Mar 31, 1962; **Keith Smith** for Crystal Palace v Derby, Dec 12, 1964.

9.6 sec by **John Hewitt** for Aberdeen at Motherwell, 3rd round, Jan 23, 1982 (fastest goal in Scottish Cup history).

Colin Cowperthwaite reputedly scored in **3.5 sec** for Barrow v Kettering (Alliance Premier League) on Dec 8, 1979, but the timing was unofficial.

Phil Starbuck for Huddersfield **3 sec** after entering the field as 54th min substitute at home to

Wigan (Div 2) on Easter Monday, Apr 12, 1993. Corner was delayed, awaiting his arrival and he scored with a header.

Malcolm Macdonald after **5 sec** (officially timed) in Newcastle's 7-3 win in a pre-season friendly at St Johnstone on Jul 29, 1972.

World's fastest goal: 2.8 sec, direct from kick-off, Argentinian **Ricardo Olivera** for Rio Negro v Soriano (Uruguayan League), December 26, 1998.

Fastest international goal: 7 sec, Christian Benteke for Belgium v Gibraltar (World Cup qual, Faro), Oct 10, 2016.

Fastest England goals: 17 sec, Tommy Lawton v Portugal in Lisbon, May 25, 1947. **27 sec, Bryan Robson** v France in World Cup at Bilbao, Spain on Jun 16, 1982; **37 sec, Gareth Southgate** v South Africa in Durban, May 22, 2003; **30 sec, Jack Cock** v Ireland, Belfast, Oct 25, 1919; **30 sec, Bill Nicholson** v Portugal at Goodison Park, May 19, 1951. **38 sec, Bryan Robson** v Yugoslavia at Wembley, Dec 13, 1989; **42 sec, Gary Lineker** v Malaysia in Kuala Lumpur, Jun 12, 1991.

Fastest international goal by substitute: 5 sec, John Jensen for Denmark v Belgium (Euro Champ), Oct 12, 1994.

Fastest goal by England substitute: 10 sec, Teddy Sheringham v Greece (World Cup qualifier) at Old Trafford, Oct 6, 2001.

Fastest FA Cup goal: 4 sec, Gareth Morris (Ashton Utd) v Skelmersdale, 1st qual round, Sep 15, 2001.

Fastest FA Cup goal (comp proper): 9.7 sec, Jimmy Kebe for Reading v WBA, 5th Round, Feb 13, 2010.

Fastest FA Cup Final goal: 25 sec, Louis Saha for Everton v Chelsea at Wembley, May 30, 2009.

Fastest goal by substitute in FA Cup Final: 96 sec, Teddy Sheringham for Manchester Utd v Newcastle at Wembley, May 22, 1999.

Fastest League Cup Final goal: 45 sec, John Arne Riise for Liverpool v Chelsea, 2005.

Fastest goal on full League debut: 7.7 sec, Freddy Eastwood for Southend v Swansea (Lge 2), Oct 16, 2004. He went on to score hat-trick in 4-2 win.

Fastest goal in cup final: 4.07 sec, 14-year-old **Owen Price** for Ernest Bevin College, Tooting, beaten 3-1 by Barking Abbey in Heinz Ketchup Cup Final at Arsenal on May 18, 2000. Owen, on Tottenham's books, scored from inside his own half when the ball was played back to him from kick-off.

Fastest Premier League goals: 7.69 sec, Shane Long for Southampton v Watford, Apr 23, 2019 **9.82 sec, Ledley King** for Tottenham away to Bradford, Dec 9, 2000; **10.52 sec, Alan Shearer for** Newcastle v Manchester City, Jan 18, 2003: **10.54 sec Christian Eriksen** for Tottenham v Manchester Utd, Jan 31, 2018; **11.9 sec, Mark Viduka** for Leeds v Charlton, Mar 17, 2001, **11.90 sec. James Beattie** for Southampton at Chelsea, Aug 28, 2004.

Fastest top-division goal: 7 sec, Bobby Langton for Preston v Manchester City (Div 1), Aug 25, 1948.

Fastest goal in Champions League: 10 sec, Roy Makaay for Bayern Munich v Real Madrid (1st ko rd), Mar 7, 2007.

Fastest Premier League goal by substitute: 9 sec, Shaun Goater, Manchester City's equaliser away to Manchester Utd (1-1), Feb 9, 2003. In Dec, 2011, Wigan's **Ben Watson** was brought off the bench to take a penalty against Stoke and scored.

Fastest goal on Premier League debut: 36 sec, Thievy Bifouma on as sub for WBA away to Crystal Palace, Feb 8, 2014.

Fastest Scottish Premiership goal: 10 sec, Kris Boyd for Kilmarnock v Ross Co, Jan 28, 2017.

Fastest-ever hat-trick: 90 sec, credited to 18-year-old **Tommy Ross** playing in a Highland match for Ross County against Nairn County on Nov 28, 1964.

Fastest goal by goalkeeper in professional football: 13 sec, Asmir Begovic for Stoke v Southampton (Prem Lge), Nov 2, 2013.

Fastest goal in Olympic Games: 14 sec, Neymar for Brazil in semi-finals v Honduras, Aug 17, 2016, Rio de Janeiro.

Fastest goal in women's football: 7 sec, Angie Harriott for Launton v Thame (Southern League, Prem Div), season 1998-99.

Fastest hat-trick in League history: 2 min 20 sec, Bournemouth's 84th-minute substitute **James Hayter** in 6-0 home win v Wrexham (Div 2) on Feb 24, 2004 (goal times 86, 87, 88 mins).

Fastest First Division hat-tricks since war: Graham Leggat, 3 goals in 3 minutes (first half) when Fulham beat Ipswich 10-1 on Boxing Day, 1963; **Nigel Clough,** 3 goals in **4 minutes** (81, 82, 85 pen) when Nottm Forest beat QPR 4-0 on Dec 13, 1987.

Fastest Premier League hat-trick: 2 min 56 sec (13, 14, 16) by Sadio Mane in Southampton 6, Aston Villa 1 on May 16, 2015.

Fastest international hat-trick: 2 min 35 sec, Abdul Hamid Bassiouny for Egypt in 8-2 win over Namibia in Abdallah, Libya, (African World Cup qual), Jul 13, 2001.

Fastest international hat-trick in British matches: 3.5 min, Willie Hall for England v N Ireland at Old Trafford, Manchester, Nov 16, 1938. (Hall scored 5 in 7-0 win); **3min 30 sec, Arif Erdem** for Turkey v N Ireland, European Championship qualifier, at Windsor Park, Belfast, on Sep 4, 1999.

Fastest FA Cup hat-tricks: In 3 min, Billy Best for Southend v Brentford (2nd round, Dec 7, 1968); **2 min 20 sec, Andy Locke** for Nantwich v Droylsden (1st Qual round, Sep 9, 1995).

Fastest Scottish hat-trick: 2 min 30 sec, Ian St John for Motherwell away to Hibernian (Scottish League Cup), Aug 15, 1959.

Fastest hat-trick of headers: Dixie Dean's 5 goals in Everton's 7-2 win at home to Chelsea (Div 1) on Nov 14, 1931 included 3 headers between **5th** and **15th-min.**

Scored first kick: Billy Foulkes (Newcastle) for Wales v England at Cardiff, Oct 20, 1951, in his first international match.

Preston scored six goals in **7 min** in record 26-0 FA Cup 1st round win v Hyde, Oct 15, 1887.

Notts Co scored six second-half goals in **12 min** (Tommy Lawton 3, Jackie Sewell 3) when beating Exeter 9-0 (Div 3 South) at Meadow Lane on Oct 16, 1948.

Arsenal scored six in **18 min** (71-89 mins) in 7-1 home win (Div 1) v Sheffield Wed, Feb 15, 1992.

Tranmere scored six in first **19 min** when beating Oldham 13-4 (Div 3 North), December 26, 1935.

Sunderland scored eight in **28 min** at Newcastle (9-1 Div 1), December 5, 1908. Newcastle went on to win the title.

Southend scored all seven goals in **29 min** in 7-0 win at home to Torquay (Leyland Daf Cup, Southern quarter-final), Feb 26, 1991. Score was 0-0 until 55th minute.

Plymouth scored five in first **18 min** in 7-0 home win v Chesterfield (Div 2), Jan 3, 2004.

Five in 20 min: Frank Keetley in Lincoln's 9-1 win over Halifax in Div 3 (North), Jan 16, 1932; **Brian Dear** for West Ham v WBA (6-1, Div 1) Apr 16, 1965. Kevin Hector for Bradford PA v Barnsley (7-2, Div 4), Nov 20, 1965.

Four in 5 min: John McIntyre for Blackburn v Everton (Div 1), Sep 16, 1922; WG (Billy) Richardson for WBA v West Ham (Div 1), Nov 7, 1931.

Three in 2˙5 min: Jimmy Scarth for Gillingham v Leyton Orient (Div 3S), Nov 1, 1952.

Three in three minutes: Billy Lane for Watford v Clapton Orient (Div 3S), December 20, 1933; **Johnny Hartburn** for Leyton Orient v Shrewsbury (Div 3S), Jan 22, 1955; **Gary Roberts** for Brentford v Newport, (Freight Rover Trophy, South Final), May 17, 1985; **Gary Shaw** for Shrewsbury v Bradford City (Div 3), December 22, 1990.

Two in 9 sec: Jamie Bates with last kick of first half, Jermaine McSporran 9 sec into second half when Wycombe beat Peterborough 2-0 at home (Div 2) on Sep 23, 2000.

Premier League – fastest scoring: Four goals in 4 min 44 sec, Tottenham home to Southampton on Sunday, Feb 7, 1993.

Premier League – fast scoring away: When **Aston Villa** won 5-0 at Leicester (Jan 31, 2004), all goals scored in **18 second-half min** (50-68).

Four in 13 min by Premier League sub: Ole Gunnar Solskjaer for Manchester Utd away to Nottm Forest, Feb 6, 1999.

Five in 9 mins by substitute: Robert Lewandowski for Bayern Munich v Wolfsburg (5-1, Bundesliga), Sep 22, 2015.

FASTEST GOALS IN WORLD CUP FINAL SERIES

10.8 sec, Hakan Sukur for Turkey against South Korea in 3rd/4th-place match at Taegu, Jun 29, 2002; **15 sec, Vaclav Masek** for Czechoslovakia v Mexico (in Vina, Chile, 1962); **27 sec, Bryan Robson** for England v France (in Bilbao, Spain, 1982).

TOP MATCH SCORES SINCE WAR

By English clubs: 13-0 by Newcastle v Newport (Div 2, Oct 1946); 13-2 by Tottenham v Crewe (FA Cup 4th. Rd replay, Feb 1960); 13-0 by Chelsea v Jeunesse Hautcharage, Lux. (Cup-Winners' Cup 1st round, 2nd leg, Sep 1971).

By Scottish club: 20-0 by Stirling v Selkirk (E. of Scotland League) in Scottish Cup 1st round. (Dec 1984). That is the highest score in British first-class football since Preston beat Hyde 26-0 in FA Cup, Oct 1887.

MOST GOALS IN CALENDAR YEAR

91 by Lionel Messi in 2012 (79 Barcelona, 12 Argentina).

ROONEY'S DOUBLE TOP

Wayne Rooney ended season 2016–17 as top scorer for England (53) and Manchester Utd (253).

PREMIER LEAGUE LONGEST-RANGE GOALS BY OUTFIELD PLAYERS

66 yards: Charlie Adam (Stoke at Chelsea, Apr 4, 2015)
64 yards: Xabi Alonso (Liverpool v Newcastle, Sep 20, 2006)
62 yards: Maynor Figueroa (Wigan at Stoke, Dec 12, 2009)
60 yards: Wayne Rooney (Everton v West Ham, Nov 29, 2017)
59 yards: David Beckham (Manchester Utd at Wimbledon, Aug 17, 1996)
55 yards: Wayne Rooney (Manchester Utd at West Ham, Mar 22, 2014)

GOALS BY GOALKEEPERS

(Long clearances unless stated)

Pat Jennings for Tottenham v Manchester Utd (goalkeeper Alex Stepney), Aug 12, 1967 (FA Charity Shield).
Peter Shilton for Leicester v Southampton (Campbell Forsyth), Oct 14, 1967 (Div 1).
Ray Cashley for Bristol City v Hull (Jeff Wealands), Sep 18, 1973 (Div 2).
Steve Sherwood for Watford v Coventry (Raddy Avramovic), Jan 14, 1984 (Div 1).
Steve Ogrizovic for Coventry v Sheffield Wed (Martin Hodge), Oct 25, 1986 (Div 1).
Andy Goram for Hibernian v Morton (David Wylie), May 7, 1988 (Scot Prem Div).
Andy McLean, on Irish League debut, for Cliftonville v Linfield (George Dunlop), Aug 20, 1988.
Alan Paterson for Glentoran v Linfield (George Dunlop), Nov 30, 1988 (Irish League Cup Final – only instance of goalkeeper scoring winner in a senior cup final in UK).
Ray Charles for East Fife v Stranraer (Bernard Duffy), Feb 28, 1990 (Scot Div 2).
Iain Hesford for Maidstone v Hereford (Tony Elliott), Nov 2, 1991 (Div 4).
Chris Mackenzie for Hereford v Barnet (Mark Taylor), Aug 12, 1995 (Div 3).
Peter Schmeichel for Manchester Utd v Rotor Volgograd, Sep 26, 1995 (header, UEFA Cup 1).
Mark Bosnich (Aston Villa) for Australia v Solomon Islands, Jun 11, 1997 (penalty in World Cup qual – 13-0).
Peter Keen for Carlisle away to Blackpool (goalkeeper John Kennedy), Oct 24, 2000 (Div 3).
Steve Mildenhall for Notts Co v Mansfield (Kevin Pilkington), Aug 21, 2001 (free-kick inside own half, League Cup 1).
Peter Schmeichel for Aston Villa v Everton (Paul Gerrard), Oct 20, 2001 (volley, first goalkeeper to score in Premier League).
Mart Poom for Sunderland v Derby (Andy Oakes), Sep 20, 2003 (header, Div 1).
Brad Friedel for Blackburn v Charlton (Dean Kiely), Feb 21, 2004 (shot, Prem).
Paul Robinson for Leeds v Swindon (Rhys Evans), Sep 24, 2003 (header, League Cup 2).
Andy Lonergan for Preston v Leicester (Kevin Pressman), Oct 12, 2004 (Champ).
Matt Glennon for St Johnstone away to Ross Co (Joe Malin), Mar 11, 2006 (shot, Scot Div 1).
Gavin Ward for Tranmere v Leyton Orient (Glenn Morris), Sep 2, 2006 (free-kick Lge 1).
Mark Crossley for Sheffield Wed v Southampton (Kelvin Davis), Dec 23, 2006 (header, Champ).
Paul Robinson for Tottenham v Watford (Ben Foster), Mar 17, 2007 (Prem).

Adam Federici for Reading v Cardiff (Peter Enckelman), Dec 28, 2008 (shot, Champ).
Chris Weale for Yeovil v Hereford (Peter Gulacsi), Apr 21, 2009 (header, Lge 1).
Scott Flinders for Hartlepool v Bournemouth (Shwan Jalal), Apr 30, 2011 (header, Lge 1).
Iain Turner for Preston v Notts Co (Stuart Nelson), Aug 27 2011 (shot, Lge 1).
Andy Leishman for Auchinleck v Threave (Vinnie Parker), Oct 22, 2011 (Scot Cup 2).
Tim Howard for Everton v Bolton (Adam Bogdan), Jan 4, 2012 (Prem).
Asmir Begovic for Stoke v Southampton (Artur Boruc), Nov 2, 2013 (Prem).
Mark Oxley for Hibernian v Livingston (Darren Jamieson), Aug 9, 2014 (Scot Champ).
Jesse Joronen for Stevenage v Wycombe (Matt Ingram), Oct 17, 2015 (Lge 2).
Barry Roche for Morecambe v Portsmouth (Ryan Fulton), Feb 2, 2016 (header, Lge 2).
Lewis McMinn for Brechin v Stirling (Blair Currie), Dec 7, 2019 (Scot Lge 2).
Tom King for Newport v Cheltenham (Josh Griffiths), Jan 19, 2021 (Lge 2)
Alisson for Liverpool v WBA (Sam Johnstone), May 16, 2021 (header, Prem)

MORE GOALKEEPING HEADLINES

Arthur Wilkie, sustained a hand injury in Reading's Div 3 match against Halifax on Aug 31, 1962, then played as a forward and scored twice in a 4-2 win.
Alex Stepney was Manchester Utd's joint top scorer for two months in season 1973–74 with two penalties.
Dundee Utd goalkeeper Hamish McAlpine scored three penalties in a ten-month period between 1976–77, two against Hibernian, home and away, and one against Rangers at Ibrox.
Alan Fettis scored twice for Hull in 1994–95 Div 2 season, as a substitute in 3-1 home win over Oxford Utd (Dec 17) and, when selected outfield, with last-minute winner (2-1) against Blackpool on May 6.
Roger Freestone scored for Swansea with a penalty at Oxford Utd (Div 2, Apr 30, 1995) and twice from the spot the following season against Shrewsbury (Aug 12) and Chesterfield (Aug 26).
Jimmy Glass, on loan from Swindon, kept Carlisle in the Football League on May 8, 1999. With ten seconds of stoppage-time left, he went upfield for a corner and scored the winner against Plymouth that sent Scarborough down to the Conference instead.
Paul Smith, Nottm Forest goalkeeper, was allowed to run through Leicester's defence unchallenged and score direct from the kick-off of a Carling Cup second round second match on Sep 18, 2007. It replicated the 1-0 score by which Forest had led at half-time when the original match was abandoned after Leicester defender Clive Clarke suffered a heart attack. Leicester won the tie 3-2.
Tony Roberts (Dagenham), is the only known goalkeeper to score from open play in the FA Cup, his last-minute goal at Basingstoke in the fourth qualifying round on Oct 27, 2001 earning a 2-2 draw. Dagenham won the replay 3-0 and went on to reach the third round proper.
The only known instance in first-class football in Britain of a goalkeeper scoring direct from a goal-kick was in a First Division match at Roker Park on Apr 14, 1900. The kick by Manchester City's **Charlie Williams** was caught in a strong wind and Sunderland keeper J. E Doig fumbled the ball over his line.
Jose Luis Chilavert, Paraguay's international goalkeeper, scored a hat-trick of penalties when his club Velez Sarsfield beat Ferro Carril Oeste 6-1 in the Argentine League on Nov 28, 1999. In all, he scored 8 goals in 72 internationals. He also scored with a free-kick from just inside his own half for Velez Sarsfield against River Plate on Sep 20, 2000.
Most goals by a goalkeeper in a League season: 5 (all penalties) by **Arthur Birch** for Chesterfield (Div 3 North), 1923–24.
When Brazilian goalkeeper **Rogerio Ceni** (37) converted a free-kick for Sao Paulo's winner (2-1) v Corinthians in a championship match on Mar 27, 2011, it was his 100th goal (56 free-kicks, 44 pens) in a 20-season career.

OWN GOALS

Most by player in one season: 5 by **Robert Stuart** (Middlesbrough) in 1934–35.

Three in match by one team: Sheffield Wed's **Vince Kenny**, **Norman Curtis** and **Eddie Gannon** in 5-4 defeat at home to WBA (Div 1) on Dec 26, 1952; Rochdale's **George Underwood**, **Kenny Boyle** and **Danny Murphy** in 7-2 defeat at Carlisle (Div 3 North), Dec 25, 1954; Sunderland's **Stephen Wright** and **Michael Proctor** (2) at home to Charlton (1-3, Prem), Feb 1, 2003; Brighton's **Liam Bridcutt** (2) and **Lewis Dunk** in 6-1 FA Cup 5th rd defeat at Liverpool, Feb 19, 2012.; Sunderland's **Santiago Vergini**, **Liam Bridcutt** and **Patrick van Aanholt** in 8-0 defeat at Southampton (Prem), Oct 18, 2014.

One-man show: Chris Nicholl (Aston Villa) scored all four goals in 2-2 draw away to Leicester (Div 1), Mar 20, 1976 – two for his own side and two own goals.

Fastest own goals: 8 sec by **Pat Kruse** of Torquay, for Cambridge Utd (Div 4), Jan 3, 1977; in First Division, **16 sec** by **Steve Bould** (Arsenal) away to Sheffield Wed, Feb 17, 1990.

Late own-goal man: Frank Sinclair (Leicester) put through his own goal in the 90th minute of Premier League matches away to Arsenal (L1-2) and at home to Chelsea (2-2) in Aug 1999.

Half an own goal each: Chelsea's second goal in a 3-1 home win against Leicester on December 18, 1954 was uniquely recorded as 'shared own goal'. Leicester defenders **Stan Milburn** and **Jack Froggatt**, both lunging at the ball in an attempt to clear, connected simultaneously and sent it rocketing into the net.

Match of 149 own goals: When Adama, Champions of Malagasy (formerly Madagascar) won a League match 149-0 on Oct 31, 2002, all 149 were own goals scored by opponents Stade Olympique De L'Emryne. They repeatedly put the ball in their own net in protest at a refereeing decision.

MOST SCORERS IN MATCH

Liverpool set a Football League record with **eight** scorers when beating Crystal Palace 9-0 (Div 1) on Sep 12, 1989. Marksmen were: Steve Nicol (7 and 88 mins), Steve McMahon (16), Ian Rush (45), Gary Gillespie (56), Peter Beardsley (61), John Aldridge (67 pen), John Barnes (79), Glenn Hysen (82).

Fifteen years earlier, **Liverpool** had gone one better with **nine** different scorers when they achieved their record win, 11-0 at home to Stromsgodset (Norway) in the Cup-Winners' Cup 1st round, 1st leg on Sep 17, 1974.

Eight players scored for **Swansea** when they beat Sliema, Malta, 12-0 in the Cup-Winners' Cup 1st round, 1st leg on Sep 15, 1982.

Nine Stirling players scored in the 20-0 win against Selkirk in the Scottish Cup 1st Round on December 8, 1984.

Premier League record: **Seven Chelsea** scorers in 8-0 home win over Aston Villa, Dec 23, 2012. An eighth player missed a penalty.

LONG SCORING RUNS

Tom Phillipson scored in 13 consecutive matches for Wolves (Div 2) in season 1926–27, which is still an English League record. In the same season, **George Camsell** scored in 12 consecutive matches for Middlesbrough (Div 2). **Bill Prendergast** scored in 13 successive League and Cup appearances for Chester (Div 3 North) in season 1938–39.

Dixie Dean scored in 12 consecutive games (23 goals) for Everton in Div 2 in 1930–31.

Danish striker **Finn Dossing** scored in 15 consecutive matches (Scottish record) for Dundee Utd (Div 1) in 1964–65.

50-GOAL PLAYERS

With **52** goals for **Wolves** in 1987–78 (34 League, 12 Sherpa Van Trophy, 3 Littlewoods Cup, 3 FA Cup), **Steve Bull** became the first player to score 50 in a season for a League club since **Terry Bly** for Div 4 newcomers Peterborough in 1960–61. Bly's 54 comprised 52 League goals and 2 in the FA Cup, and included 7 hat-tricks, still a post-war League record. Bull was again the country's top scorer with 50 goals in season 1988–89: 37 League, 2 Littlewoods Cup and 11 Sherpa Van Trophy. Between Bly and Bull, the highest individual scoring total for a season was 49 by two players: **Ted MacDougall** (Bournemouth 1970–71, 42 League, 7 FA Cup) and **Clive Allen** (Tottenham 1986–87, 33 League, 12 Littlewoods Cup, 4 FA Cup).

HOT SHOTS

Jimmy Greaves was top Div 1 scorer (League goals) six times in 11 seasons: 32 for Chelsea (1958–59), 41 for Chelsea (1960–61) and, for Tottenham, 37 in 1962–63, 35 in 1963–64, 29 in 1964–65 (joint top) and 27 in 1968–69.

Brian Clough (Middlesbrough) was leading scorer in Div 2 in three successive seasons: 40 goals in 1957–58, 42 in 1958–59 and 39 in 1959–60.

John Hickton (Middlesbrough) was top Div 2 scorer three times in four seasons: 24 goals in 1967–68, 24 in 1969–70 and 25 in 1970–71.

MOST HAT-TRICKS

Nine by George Camsell (Middlesbrough) in Div 2, 1926–27, is the record for one season. Most League hat-tricks in career: 37 by **Dixie Dean** for Tranmere and Everton (1924–38).

Most top division hat-tricks in a season since last War: six by **Jimmy Greaves** for Chelsea (1960–61). **Alan Shearer** scored five hat-tricks for Blackburn in the Premier League, season 1995–96.

Frank Osborne (Tottenham) scored three consecutive hat-tricks in Div 1 in Oct–Nov 1925, against Liverpool, Leicester (away) and West Ham.

Tom Jennings (Leeds) scored hat-tricks in three successive Div 1 matches (Sep–Oct, 1926): 3 goals v Arsenal, 4 at Liverpool, 4 v Blackburn. Leeds were relegated that season.

Jack Balmer (Liverpool) scored his three hat-tricks in a 17-year career in successive Div 1 matches (Nov 1946): 3 v Portsmouth, 4 at Derby, 3 v Arsenal. No other Liverpool player scored during that 10-goal sequence by Balmer.

Gilbert Alsop scored hat-tricks in three successive matches for Walsall in Div 3 South in Apr 1939: 3 at Swindon, 3 v Bristol City and 4 v Swindon.

Alf Lythgoe scored hat-tricks in three successive games for Stockport (Div 3 North) in Mar 1934: 3 v Darlington, 3 at Southport and 4 v Wrexham.

TRIPLE HAT-TRICKS

There have been at least three **instances of 3 hat-tricks being scored for one team in a Football League match:**

Apr 21, 1909: Enoch West, Billy Hooper and **Alfred Spouncer** for Nottm Forest (12-0 v Leicester Fosse, Div 1).

Mar 3, 1962: Ron Barnes, Wyn Davies and **Roy Ambler** in Wrexham's 10-1 win against Hartlepool (Div 4).

Nov 7, 1987: Tony Adcock, Paul Stewart and **David White** for Manchester City in 10-1 win at home to Huddersfield (Div 2).

For the first time in the Premier League, **three** hat-tricks were completed on one day (Sep 23, 1995): **Tony Yeboah** for Leeds at Wimbledon; **Alan Shearer** for Blackburn v Coventry; **Robbie Fowler** with 4 goals for Liverpool v Bolton.

In the FA Cup, **Jack Carr, George Elliott** and **Walter Tinsley** each scored 3 in Middlesbrough's 9-3 first round win against Goole in Jan, 1915. **Les Allen** scored 5, **Bobby Smith** 4 and **Cliff Jones** 3 when Tottenham beat Crewe 13-2 in a fourth-round replay in Feb 1960.

HAT-TRICKS v THREE 'KEEPERS

When West Ham beat Newcastle 8-1 (Div 1) on Apr 21, 1986 **Alvin Martin** scored 3 goals against different goalkeepers: Martin Thomas injured a shoulder and was replaced, in turn, by outfield players Chris Hedworth and Peter Beardsley.

Jock Dodds of Lincoln had done the same against West Ham on Dec 18, 1948, scoring past Ernie Gregory, Tommy Moroney and George Dick in 4-3 win.

David Herd (Manchester Utd) scored against Sunderland's Jim Montgomery, Charlie Hurley and Johnny Parke in 5-0 First Division home win on Nov 26, 1966.

Brian Clark, of Bournemouth, scored against Rotherham's Jim McDonagh, Conal Gilbert and Michael Leng twice in 7-2 win (Div 3) on Oct 10, 1972.

On Oct 16, 1993 (Div 3) **Chris Pike** (Hereford) scored a hat-trick in 5-0 win over Colchester, who became the first team in league history to have two keepers sent off in the same game.

On Dec 18, 2004 (Lge 1), in 6-1 defeat at Hull, Tranmere used **John Achterberg** and **Russell Howarth,** both retired injured, and defender **Theo Whitmore.**

On Mar 9, 2008, Manchester Utd had three keepers in their 0-1 FA Cup quarter-final defeat by Portsmouth. **Tomasz Kuszczak** came on at half-time for **Edwin van der Sar** but was sent off when conceding a penalty. **Rio Ferdinand** went in goal and was beaten by Sulley Muntari's spot-kick.

Derby used three keepers in a 4-1 defeat at Reading (Mar 10, 2010, Champ). **Saul Deeney,** who took over when **Stephen Bywater** was injured, was sent off for a foul and **Robbie Savage** replaced him.

EIGHT-DAY HAT-TRICK TREBLE

Joe Bradford, of Birmingham, scored three hat-tricks in eight days in Sep 1929–30 v Newcastle (won 5-1) on the 21st, 5 for the Football League v Irish League (7-2) on the 25th, and 3 in his club's 5-7 defeat away to Blackburn on the 28th.

PREMIER LEAGUE DOUBLE HAT-TRICK

Robert Pires and **Jermaine Pennant** each scored 3 goals in Arsenal's 6-1 win at home to Southampton (May 7, 2003).

TON UP – BOTH ENDS

Manchester City are the only club to score and concede a century of League goals in the same season. When finishing fifth in the 1957–58 season, they scored 104 and gave away 100.

TOURNAMENT TOP SHOTS

Most individual goals in a World Cup Final series: 13 by **Just Fontaine** for France, in Sweden 1958. Most in European Championship Finals: 9 by **Michel Platini** for France, in France 1984.

MOST GOALS ON CLUB DEBUT

Jim Dyet scored eight in King's Park's 12-2 win against Forfar (Scottish Div 2, Jan 2, 1930). **Len Shackleton** scored six times in Newcastle's 13-0 win v Newport (Div 2, Oct 5, 1946) in the week he joined them from Bradford Park Avenue.

MOST GOALS ON LEAGUE DEBUT

Five by **George Hilsdon,** for Chelsea (9-2) v Glossop, Div 2, Sep 1, 1906. **Alan Shearer,** with three goals for Southampton (4-2) v Arsenal, Apr 9, 1988, became, at 17, the youngest player to score a First Division hat-trick on his full debut.

FOUR-GOAL SUBSTITUTE

James Collins (Swindon), sub from 60th minute, scored 4 in 5-0 home win v Portsmouth (Lge 1) on Jan 1, 2013.

CLEAN-SHEET RECORDS

On the way to promotion from Div 3 in season 1995–96, Gillingham's ever-present goalkeeper **Jim Stannard** set a clean-sheet record. In 46 matches. He achieved 29 shut-outs (17 at home, 12 away), beating the 28 by **Ray Clemence** for Liverpool (42 matches in Div 1, 1978–79) and the previous best in a 46-match programme of 28 by Port Vale (Div 3 North, 1953–54). In conceding only 20 League goals in 1995–96, Gillingham created a defensive record for the lower divisions.

Chris Woods, Rangers' England goalkeeper, set a British record in season 1986–87 by going 1,196 minutes without conceding a goal. The sequence began in the UEFA Cup match against Borussia Moenchengladbach on Nov 26, 1986 and ended when Rangers were sensationally beaten 1-0 at home by Hamilton in the Scottish Cup 3rd round on Jan 31, 1987 with a 70th-minute goal by **Adrian Sprott.** The previous British record of 1,156 minutes without a goal conceded was held by Aberdeen goalkeeper **Bobby Clark** (season 1970–01).

Manchester Utd set a new Premier League clean-sheet record of 1,333 minutes (including 14 successive match shut-outs) in season 2008–09 (Nov 15–Feb 21). **Edwin van der Sar's** personal British league record of 1,311 minutes without conceding ended when United won 2-1 at Newcastle on Mar 4, 2009.

Most clean sheets in season in top English division: **28** by **Liverpool** (42 matches) in 1978–79; **25** by **Chelsea** (38 matches) in 2004–05.

There have been three instances of clubs keeping 11 consecutive clean sheets in the Football League: **Millwall** (Div 3 South, 1925–26), **York** (Div 3, 1973–74) and **Reading** (Div 4, 1978–79). In this sequence, Reading goalkeeper **Steve Death** set the existing League shut-out record of 1,103 minutes.

Sasa Ilic remained unbeaten for over 14 hours with 9 successive shut-outs (7 in Div 1, 2 in play-offs) to equal a Charlton club record in Apr/May 1998. He had 12 clean sheets in 17 first team games after winning promotion from the reserves with 6 successive clean sheets.

Sebastiano Rossi kept a clean sheet in 8 successive away matches for AC Milan (Nov 1993–Apr 1994).

A world record of 1,275 minutes without conceding a goal was set in 1990–01 by **Abel Resino,** the Atletico Madrid goalkeeper. He was finally beaten by Sporting Gijon's Enrique in Atletico's 3-1 win on Mar 19, 1991.

In international football, the record is held by **Dino Zoff** with a shut-out for Italy (Sep 1972 to Jun 1974) lasting 1,142 minutes.

LOW SCORING

Fewest goals by any club in season in Football League: 18 by **Loughborough** (Div 2, 34 matches, 1899–1900); in 38 matches 20 by **Derby** (Prem Lge, 2007–08), 20 by **Sheffield Utd** (Prem Lge, 2020–21); in 42 matches, 24 by **Watford** (Div 2, 1971–72) and by **Stoke** (Div 1, 1984–85)); in 46-match programme, 27 by **Stockport** (Div 3, 1969–70).

Arsenal were the lowest Premier League scorers in its opening season (1992–93) with 40 goals in 42 matches, but won both domestic cup competitions. In subsequent seasons the lowest Premier League scorers were **Ipswich** (35) in 1993–94, **Crystal Palace** (34) in 1994–95, **Manchester City** (33) in 1995–96 and **Leeds** (28) in 1996–97 until **Sunderland** set the Premier League's new fewest-goals record with only 21 in 2002–03. Then, in 2007–08, **Derby** scored just 20.

LONG TIME NO SCORE

The world international non-scoring record was set by **Northern Ireland** when they played 13 matches and 1,298 minutes without a goal. The sequence began against Poland on Feb 13, 2002 and ended 2 years and 5 days later when David Healy scored against Norway (1-4) in Belfast on Feb 18, 2004.

Longest non-scoring sequences in Football League: 11 matches by **Coventry** in 1919–20 (Div 2); 11 matches in 1992–93 (Div 2) by **Hartlepool,** who after beating Crystal Palace 1-0 in the FA Cup 3rd round on Jan 2, went 13 games and 2 months without scoring (11 League, 1 FA Cup, 1 Autoglass Trophy). The sequence ended after 1,227 blank minutes with a 1-1 draw at Blackpool (League) on Mar 6.

In the Premier League (Oct–Jan season 1994–95) **Crystal Palace** failed to score in nine consecutive matches.

The British non-scoring club record is held by **Stirling:** 14 consecutive matches (13 League, 1 Scottish Cup) and 1,292 minutes play, from Jan 31 1981 until Aug 8, 1981 (when they lost 4-1 to Falkirk in the League Cup).

In season 1971–72, **Mansfield** did not score in any of their first nine home games in Div 3. They were relegated on goal difference of minus two.

FA CUP CLEAN SHEETS

Most consecutive FA Cup matches without conceding a goal: 11 by **Bradford City.** The sequence spanned 8 rounds, from 3rd in 1910–11 to 4th. Round replay in 1911–12, and included winning the Cup in 1911.

GOALS THAT WERE WRONGLY GIVEN

Tottenham's last-minute winner at home to Huddersfield (Div 1) on Apr 2, 1952: Eddie Baily's corner-kick struck referee WR Barnes in the back, and the ball rebounded to Baily, who crossed for Len Duquemin to head into the net. Baily had infringed the Laws by playing the ball twice, but the result (1-0) stood. Those two points helped Spurs to finish Championship runners-up; Huddersfield were relegated.

The second goal (66 mins) in **Chelsea's** 2-1 home win v Ipswich (Div 1) on Sep 26, 1970: Alan Hudson's shot hit the stanchion on the outside of goal and the ball rebounded on to the pitch. But instead of the goal-kick, referee Roy Capey gave a goal, on a linesman's confirmation. TV pictures proved otherwise. The Football League quoted from the Laws of the Game: 'The referee's decision on all matters is final.'

When **Watford's** John Eustace and **Reading's** Noel Hunt challenged for a 13th minute corner at Vicarage Road on Sep 20, 2008, the ball was clearly diverted wide. But referee Stuart Attwell signalled for a goal on the instruction his assistant and it went down officially as a Eustace own goal. The Championship match ended 2-2.

Sunderland's 1-0 Premier League win over **Liverpool** on Oct 17, 2009 was decided by one of the most bizarre goals in football history when Darren Bent's shot struck a red beach ball thrown from the crowd and wrong-footed goalkeeper Jose Reina. Referee Mike Jones wrongly allowed it to stand. The Laws of the Game state: 'An outside agent interfering with play should result in play being stopped and restarted with a drop ball.'

Blackburn's 59th minute equaliser (2-2) in 3-3 draw away to Wigan (Prem) on Nov 19, 2011 was illegal. Morten Gamst Pedersen played the ball to himself from a corner and crossed for Junior Hoilett to net.

The Republic of Ireland were deprived of the chance of a World Cup place in the second leg of their play-off with France on Nov 18, 2009. They were leading 1-0 in Paris when Thierry Henry blatantly handled before setting up William Gallas to equalise in extra-time and give his side a 2-1 aggregate victory. The FA of Ireland's call for a replay was rejected by FIFA.

• The most notorious goal in World Cup history was fisted in by Diego Maradona in **Argentina's** 2-1 quarter-final win over England in Mexico City on Jun 22, 1986.

ATTENDANCES

GREATEST WORLD CROWDS

World Cup, Maracana Stadium, Rio de Janeiro, Jul 16, 1950. Final match (Brazil v Uruguay) attendance 199,850; receipts £125,000.

Total attendance in three matches (including play-off) between Santos (Brazil) and AC Milan for the Inter-Continental Cup (World Club Championship) 1963, exceeded 375,000.

BRITISH RECORD CROWDS

Most to pay: 149,547, Scotland v England, at Hampden Park, Glasgow, Apr 17, 1937. This was the first all-ticket match in Scotland (receipts £24,000).

At Scottish FA Cup Final: 146,433, Celtic v Aberdeen, at Hampden Park, Apr 24, 1937. Estimated another 20,000 shut out.

For British club match (apart from a Cup Final): 143,470, Rangers v Hibernian, at Hampden

Park, Mar 27, 1948 (Scottish Cup semi-final).

FA Cup Final: 126,047, Bolton v West Ham, Apr 28, 1923. Estimated 150,000 in ground at opening of Wembley Stadium.

New Wembley: 89,874, FA Cup Final, Cardiff v Portsmouth, May 17, 2008.

World Cup Qualifying ties: 120,000, Cameroon v Morocco, Yaounde, Nov 29, 1981; 107,580, Scotland v Poland, Hampden Park, Oct 13, 1965.

European Cup: 135,826, Celtic v Leeds (semi-final, 2nd leg) at Hampden Park, Apr 15, 1970.

European Cup Final: 127,621, Real Madrid v Eintracht Frankfurt, at Hampden Park, May 18, 1960.

European Cup-Winners' Cup Final: 100,000, West Ham v TSV Munich, at Wembley, May 19, 1965.

Scottish League: 118,567, Rangers v Celtic, Jan 2, 1939.

Scottish League Cup Final: 107,609, Celtic v Rangers, at Hampden Park, Oct 23, 1965.

Football League old format: First Div: 83,260, Manchester Utd v Arsenal, Jan 17, 1948 (at Maine Road); **Div 2** 70,302 Tottenham v Southampton, Feb 25, 1950; **Div 3S:** 51,621, Cardiff v Bristol City, Apr 7, 1947; **Div 3N:** 49,655, Hull v Rotherham, Dec 25, 1948; **Div 3:** 49,309, Sheffield Wed v Sheffield Utd, Dec 26, 1979; **Div 4:** 37,774, Crystal Palace v Millwall, Mar 31, 1961.

Premier League: 83,222, Tottenham v Arsenal (Wembley), Feb 10, 2018

Football League – New Div 1: 41,214, Sunderland v Stoke, Apr 25, 1998; **New Div 2:** 32,471, Manchester City v York, May 8, 1999; **New Div 3:** 22,319, Hull v Hartlepool Utd, Dec 26, 2002. **New Champs:** 52,181, Newcastle v Ipswich, Apr 24, 2010; **New Lge 1:** 46,039, Sunderland v Bradford, Dec 26, 2018; **New Lge 2:** 28,343, Coventry v Accrington, Feb 10, 2018.

In English Provinces: 84,569, Manchester City v Stoke (FA Cup 6), Mar 3, 1934.

Record for Under-21 International: 55,700, England v Italy, first match at New Wembley, Mar 24, 2007.

Record for friendly match: 104,679, Rangers v Eintracht Frankfurt, at Hampden Park, Glasgow, Oct 17, 1961.

FA Youth Cup: 38,187, Arsenal v Manchester Utd, Mar 14, 2007.

Record Football League aggregate (season): 41,271,414 (1948–49) – 88 clubs.

Record Football League aggregate (single day): 1,269,934, December 27, 1949, previous day, 1,226,098.

Record average home League attendance for season: 75,691 by Manchester Utd in 2007–08.

Long-ago League attendance aggregates: 10,929,000 in 1906–07 (40 clubs); 28,132,933 in 1937–38 (88 clubs).

Last 1m crowd aggregate, League (single day): 1,007,200, December 27, 1971.

Record Amateur match attendance: 100,000 for FA Amateur Cup Final, Pegasus v Harwich & Parkeston at Wembley, Apr 11, 1953.

Record Cup-tie aggregate: 265,199, at two matches between Rangers and Morton, in Scottish Cup Final, 1947–48.

Abandoned match attendance records: In England – 63,480 at Newcastle v Swansea City FA Cup 3rd round, Jan 10, 1953, abandoned 8 mins (0-0), fog.

In Scotland: 94,596 at Scotland v Austria (4-1), Hampden Park, May 8, 1963. Referee Jim Finney ended play (79 minutes) after Austria had two players sent off and one carried off.

Colchester's record crowd (19,072) was for the FA Cup 1st round tie v Reading on Nov 27, 1948, abandoned 35 minutes (0-0), fog.

SMALLEST CROWDS

Smallest League attendances: 450 Rochdale v Cambridge Utd (Div 3, Feb 5, 1974); 469, Thames v Luton (Div 3 South, December 6, 1930).

Only 13 people paid to watch Stockport v Leicester (Div 2, May 7, 1921) at Old Trafford, but up to 2,000 stayed behind after Manchester Utd v Derby earlier in the day. Stockport's ground was closed.

Lowest Premier League crowd: 3,039 for Wimbledon v Everton, Jan 26, 1993 (smallest top-division attendance since War).

Lowest Saturday post-war top-division crowd: 3,231 for Wimbledon v Luton, Sep 7, 1991 (Div 1).

Lowest Football League crowds, new format – Div 1: 849 for Wimbledon v Rotherham, (Div 1)

Oct 29, 2002 (smallest attendance in top two divisions since War); 1,054 Wimbledon v Wigan (Div 1), Sep 13, 2003 in club's last home match when sharing Selhurst Park; **Div 2:** 1,077, Hartlepool Utd v Cardiff, Mar 22, 1994; **Div 3:** 739, Doncaster v Barnet, Mar 3, 1998.

Lowest top-division crowd at a major ground since the war: 4,554 for Arsenal v Leeds (May 5, 1966) – fixture clashed with live TV coverage of Cup-Winners' Cup Final (Liverpool v Borussia Dortmund).

Smallest League Cup attendances: 612, Halifax v Tranmere (1st round, 2nd leg) Sep 6, 2000; 664, Wimbledon v Rotherham (3rd round), Nov 5, 2002.

Smallest League Cup attendance at top-division ground: 1,987 for Wimbledon v Bolton (2nd Round, 2nd Leg) Oct 6, 1992.

Smallest Wembley crowds for England matches: 15,628 v Chile (Rous Cup, May 23, 1989 – affected by Tube strike); 20,038 v Colombia (Friendly, Sep 6, 1995); 21,432 v Czech. (Friendly, Apr 25, 1990); 21,142 v Japan (Umbro Cup, Jun 3, 1995); 23,600 v Wales (British Championship, Feb 23, 1983); 23,659 v Greece (Friendly, May 17, 1994); 23,951 v East Germany (Friendly, Sep 12, 1984); 24,000 v N Ireland (British Championship, Apr 4, 1984); 25,756 v Colombia (Rous Cup, May 24, 1988); 25,837 v Denmark (Friendly, Sep 14, 1988).

Smallest international modern crowds: 221 for Poland v N Ireland (4-1, friendly) at Limassol, Cyprus, on Feb 13, 2002. Played at neutral venue at Poland's World Cup training base. 265 (all from N Ireland) at their Euro Champ qual against Serbia in Belgrade on Mar 25, 2011. Serbia ordered by UEFA to play behind closed doors because of previous crowd trouble.

Smallest international modern crowds at home: N Ireland: 2,500 v Chile (Belfast, May 26, 1989 – clashed with ITV live screening of Liverpool v Arsenal Championship decider); Scotland: 7,843 v N Ireland (Hampden Park, May 6, 1969); Wales: 2,315 v N Ireland (Wrexham, May 27, 1982).

Smallest attendance for post-war England match: 2,378 v San Marino (World Cup) at Bologna (Nov 17, 1993). Tie clashed with Italy v Portugal (World Cup) shown live on Italian TV.

Lowest England attendance at New Wembley: 40,181 v Norway (friendly), Sep 3, 2014

Smallest paid attendance for British first-class match: 29 for Clydebank v East Stirling, CIS Scottish League Cup 1st round, Jul 31, 1999. Played at Morton's Cappielow Park ground, shared by Clydebank. Match clashed with the Tall Ships Race which attracted 200,000 to the area.

FA CUP CROWD RECORD (OUTSIDE FINAL)

The first FA Cup-tie shown on closed-circuit TV (5th round, Saturday, Mar 11, 1967, kick-off 7pm) drew a total of 105,000 spectators to Goodison Park and Anfield. At Goodison, 64,851 watched the match 'for real', while 40,149 saw the TV version on eight giant screens at Anfield. Everton beat Liverpool 1-0.

LOWEST SEMI-FINAL CROWD

The smallest FA Cup semi-final attendance since the War was 17,987 for the Manchester Utd–Crystal Palace replay at Villa Park on Apr 12, 1995. Palace supporters largely boycotted tie after a fan died in car-park clash outside pub in Walsall before first match.

Previous lowest: 25,963 for Wimbledon v Luton, at Tottenham on Apr 9, 1988.

Lowest quarter-final crowd since the war: 8,735 for Chesterfield v Wrexham on Mar 9, 1997.

Smallest FA Cup 3rd round attendances for matches between League clubs: 1,833 for Chester v Bournemouth (at Macclesfield) Jan 5, 1991; 1,966 for Aldershot v Oxford Utd, Jan 10, 1987.

PRE-WEMBLEY CUP FINAL CROWDS

AT CRYSTAL PALACE

1895	42,560	1902	48,036	1908	74,967
1896	48,036	Replay	33,050	1909	67,651
1897	65,891	1903	64,000	1910	76,980

1898	62,017	1904	61,734	1911	69,098
1899	73,833	1905	101,117	1912	54,434
1900	68,945	1906	75,609	1913	120,028
1901	110,802	1907	84,584	1914	72,778

AT OLD TRAFFORD
1915 50,000

AT STAMFORD BRIDGE

| 1920 .... 50,018 | 1921 .... 72,805 | 1922 .... 53,000 |

England women's record crowd: 77,768 v Germany, 1-2 (Wembley, Nov 9, 2019).

INTERNATIONAL RECORDS

MOST APPEARANCES

Steven Davis became the most capped British player when captaining Northern Ireland in a World Cup qualifier against Bulgaria at Windsor Park on Mar 31, 2021. The 36-year-old Rangers midfielder overtook former England goalkeeper **Peter Shilton**'s record of 125 appearances which had stood since 1990. Davis won his first cap against Canada in 2005, when playing for Aston Villa, and was made captain by manager Nigel Worthington in his 50th international in 2011.

Nine players have completed a century of appearances in full international matches for England. **Billy Wright** of Wolves, was the first, retiring in 1959 with a total of 105 caps. **Bobby Charlton,** of Manchester Utd, beat Wright's record in the World Cup match against West Germany in Leon, Mexico, in Jun 1970 and **Bobby Moore**, of West Ham, overtook Charlton's 106 caps against Italy in Turin, in Jun 1973. Moore played 108 times for England, a record that stood until **Shilton** reached 109 against Denmark in Copenhagen (Jun 7, 1989). In season 2008–09, **David Beckham** (LA Galaxy/AC Milan) overtook Moore as England's most-capped outfield player. In the vastly different selection processes of their eras, Moore played 108 full games for his country, whereas Beckham's total of 115 to the end of season 2009–10, included 58 part matches, 14 as substitute and 44 times substituted. **Steven Gerrard** won his 100th cap against Sweden in Stockholm on Nov 14, 2012 and **Ashley Cole** reached 100 appearances against Brazil at Wembley on Feb 6, 2013. **Frank Lampard** played his 100th game against Ukraine in Kiev (World Cup qual) on Sep 10, 2013. **Wayne Rooney**'s 100th appearance was against Slovenia at Wembley (Euro Champ qual) on Nov 15, 2014.

Robbie Keane won his 126th Republic of Ireland cap, overtaking Shay Given's record, In a World Cup qualifier against the Faroe Islands on Jun 7, 2013. Keane scored all his team's goals in a 3-0 win.

Kenny Dalglish became Scotland's first 100-cap international v Romania (Hampden Park, Mar 26, 1986).

World's most-capped player: Soh Chin Ann, 195 (official) for Malaysia (1969–84).

Most-capped European player: Cristiano Ronaldo 189 for Portugal (2003–22)

Most-capped European goalkeeper: Thomas Ravelli, 143 Internationals for Sweden (1981–97).

BRITAIN'S MOST-CAPPED PLAYERS

(As at start of season 2022–23)

England		Ashley Cole	107
Peter Shilton	125	Bobby Charlton	106
Wayne Rooney	120	Frank Lampard	106
David Beckham	115	Billy Wright	105
Steven Gerrard	114	**Scotland**	
Bobby Moore	108	Kenny Dalglish	102

Jim Leighton	91	Pat Jennings	119
Darren Fletcher	80	Aaron Hughes	112
Alex McLeish	77	Jonny Evans	98
Paul McStay	76	David Healy	95
Tommy Boyd	72	Mal Donaghy	91
Wales		Sammy McIlroy	88
Chris Gunter	109	Maik Taylor	88
Gareth Bale	106		
Wayne Hennessey	104	**Republic of Ireland**	
Neville Southall	92	Robbie Keane	146
Ashley Williams	86	Shay Given	134
Gary Speed	85	John O'Shea	118
Craig Bellamy	78	Kevin Kilbane	110
Joe Ledley	77	Steve Staunton	102
Northern Ireland		Damien Duff	100
Steven Davis	138		

ENGLAND'S MOST-CAPPED PLAYER (either gender)

Fara Williams made 172 appearances for the England women's team. The midfielder played in three World Cups and four European Championships in a 20-year career. She retired, aged 37, at the end of the 2020–21 season.

MOST ENGLAND CAPS IN ROW

Most consecutive international appearances: 70 by **Billy Wright,** for England from Oct 1951 to May 1959. He played 105 of England's first 108 post-war matches.
England captains most times: Billy Wright and **Bobby Moore,** 90 each.
England captains – 4 in match (v Serbia & Montenegro at Leicester Jun 3, 2003): **Michael Owen** was captain for the first half and after the interval the armband passed to **Emile Heskey** (for 15 minutes), **Phil Neville** (26 minutes) and substitute **Jamie Carragher** (9 minutes, including time added).

MOST SUCCESSIVE ENGLAND WINS

10 (Jun 1908–Jun 1909. Modern: 8 (Oct 2005–Jun 2006).

ENGLAND'S LONGEST UNBEATEN RUN

19 matches (16 wins, 3 draws), Nov 1965–Nov 1966.

ENGLAND'S TALLEST

At **6ft 7in,** **Peter Crouch** became England's tallest-ever international when he made his debut against Colombia in New Jersey, USA on May 31, 2005.

MOST PLAYERS FROM ONE CLUB IN ENGLAND SIDES

Arsenal supplied seven men (a record) to the England team v Italy at Highbury on Nov 14, 1934. They were: Frank Moss, George Male, Eddie Hapgood, Wilf Copping, Ray Bowden, Ted Drake and Cliff Bastin. In addition, Arsenal's Tom Whittaker was England's trainer.
Since then until 2001, the most players from one club in an England team was six from **Liverpool** against Switzerland at Wembley in Sep 1977. The side also included a Liverpool old boy, Kevin Keegan (Hamburg).
Seven **Arsenal** men took part in the England – France (0-2) match at Wembley on Feb 10, 1999. Goalkeeper David Seaman and defenders Lee Dixon, Tony Adams and Martin Keown lined up for England. Nicolas Anelka (2 goals) and Emmanuel Petit started the match for France and Patrick Vieira replaced Anelka.

Manchester Utd equalled Arsenal's 1934 record by providing England with seven players in the World Cup qualifier away to Albania on Mar 28, 2001. Five started the match – David Beckham (captain), Gary Neville, Paul Scholes, Nicky Butt and Andy Cole – and two went on as substitutes: Wes Brown and Teddy Sheringham.

INTERNATIONAL SUBS RECORDS

Malta substituted all 11 players in their 1-2 home defeat against England on Jun 3, 2000. Six substitutes by England took the total replacements in the match to 17, then an international record.

Most substitutions in match by **England:** 11 in second half by Sven-Goran Eriksson against Holland at Tottenham on Aug 15, 2001; 11 against Italy at Leeds on Mar 27, 2002; Italy sent on 8 players from the bench – the total of 19 substitutions was then a record for an England match; 11 against Australia at Upton Park on Feb 12, 2003 (entire England team changed at half-time); 11 against Iceland at City of Manchester Stadium on Jun 5, 2004.

Forty three players, a record for an England match, were used in the international against Serbia & Montenegro at Leicester on Jun 3, 2003. England sent on 10 substitutes in the second half and their opponents changed all 11 players.

The **Republic of Ireland** sent on 12 second-half substitutes, using 23 players in all, when they beat Russia 2-0 in a friendly international in Dublin on Feb 13, 2002.

First England substitute: Wolves winger **Jimmy Mullen** replaced injured Jackie Milburn (15 mins) away to Belgium on May 18, 1950. He scored in a 4-1 win.

ENGLAND'S WORLD CUP-WINNERS

At Wembley, Jul 30, 1966, 4-2 v West Germany (2-2 after 90 mins), scorers Hurst 3, Peters. Team: Banks; Cohen, Wilson, Stiles, Jack Charlton, Moore (capt), Ball, Hurst, Bobby Charlton, Hunt, Peters. Manager **Alf Ramsey** fielded that same eleven in six successive matches (an England record): the World Cup quarter-final, semi-final and Final, and the first three games of the following season. England wore red shirts in the Final and The Queen presented the Cup to Bobby Moore. The players each received a £1,000 bonus, plus £60 World Cup Final appearance money, all less tax, and Ramsey a £6,000 bonus from the FA The match was shown live on TV (in black and white).

England's non-playing 'reserves' – there were no substitutes – also received the £1,000 bonus, but no medals. That remained the case until FIFA finally decided that non-playing members and staff of World Cup-winning squads should be given replica medals. England's 'forgotten heroes' received theirs at a reception in Downing Street on June 10, 2009 and were later guests of honour at the World Cup qualifier against Andorra at Wembley. The 11 'reserves' were: Springett, Bonetti, Armfield, Byrne, Flowers, Hunter, Paine, Connelly, Callaghan, Greaves, Eastham. Jimmy Greaves played in all three group games, against Uruguay, Mexico and France. John Connelly was in the team against Uruguay, Terry Paine against Mexico and Ian Callaghan against France.

BRAZIL'S RECORD RUN

Brazil hold the record for the longest unbeaten sequence in international football: 45 matches from 1993–97. The previous record of 31 was held by Hungary between Jun 1950 and Jul 1954.

ENGLAND MATCHES ABANDONED

May 17, 1953 v **Argentina** (Friendly, Buenos Aires) after 23 mins (0-0) – rain.

Oct 29, 1975 v **Czechoslovakia** (Euro Champ qual, Bratislava) after 17 mins (0-0) – fog. Played next day.

Feb 15, 1995 v **Rep of Ireland** (Friendly, Dublin) after 27 mins (1-0) – crowd disturbance.

ENGLAND POSTPONEMENTS

Nov 21, 1979 v **Bulgaria** (Euro Champ qual, Wembley, postponed for 24 hours – fog; Aug 10, 2011 v **Holland** (friendly), Wembley, postponed after rioting in London.
Oct 16, 2012 v **Poland** (World Cup qual, Warsaw) postponed to next day – pitch waterlogged. The friendly against **Honduras** (Miami, Jun 7, 2014) was suspended midway through the first half for 44 minutes – thunderstorm.

ENGLAND UNDER COVER

England played indoors for the first time when they beat Argentina 1-0 in the World Cup at the Sapporo Dome, Japan, on Jun 7, 2002.

ALL-SEATED INTERNATIONALS

The first **all-seated crowd** (30,000) for a full international in Britain saw **Wales** and **West Germany** draw 0-0 at Cardiff Arms Park on May 31, 1975. The terraces were closed.
England's first all-seated international at Wembley was against Yugoslavia (2-1) on December 13, 1989 (attendance 34,796). The terracing behind the goals was closed for conversion to seating.
The first **full-house all-seated** international at Wembley was for England v Brazil (1-0) on Mar 28, 1990, when a capacity 80,000 crowd paid record British receipts of £1,200,000.

MOST NEW CAPS IN ENGLAND TEAM

6, by Sir Alf Ramsey (v Portugal, Apr 3, 1974) and by Sven-Goran Eriksson (v Australia, Feb 12, 2003; 5 at half-time when 11 changes made).

PLAYED FOR MORE THAN ONE COUNTRY

Multi-nationals in senior international football include: **Johnny Carey** (1938–53) – caps Rep of Ireland 29, N Ireland 7; **Ferenc Puskas** (1945–62) – caps Hungary 84, Spain 4; **Alfredo di Stefano** (1950–56) – caps Argentina 7, Spain 31; **Ladislav Kubala** (1948–58) – caps, Hungary 3, Czechoslovakia 11, Spain 19, only player to win full international honours with 3 countries. Kubala also played in a fourth international team, scoring twice for FIFA v England at Wembley in 1953. Eleven players, including **Carey**, appeared for both N Ireland and the Republic of Ireland in seasons directly after the last war.
Cecil Moore, capped by N Ireland in 1949 when with Glentoran, played for USA v England in 1953.
Hawley Edwards played for England v Scotland in 1874 and for Wales v Scotland in 1876.
Jack Reynolds (Distillery and WBA) played for both Ireland (5 times) and England (8) in the 1890s.
Bobby Evans (Sheffield Utd) had played 10 times for Wales when capped for England, in 1910–11. He was born in Chester of Welsh parents.
In recent years, several players have represented USSR and one or other of the breakaway republics. The same applies to Yugoslavia and its component states. **Josip Weber** played for Croatia in 1992 and made a 5-goal debut for Belgium in 1994.

THREE-GENERATION INTERNATIONAL FAMILY

When Bournemouth striker **Warren Feeney** was capped away to Liechtenstein on Mar 27, 2002, he became the third generation of his family to play for Northern Ireland. He followed in the footsteps of his grandfather James (capped twice in 1950) and father Warren snr. (1 in 1976).

FATHERS & SONS CAPPED BY ENGLAND

George Eastham senior (pre-war) and **George Eastham junior**; **Brian Clough** and **Nigel Clough**; **Frank Lampard snr** and **Frank Lampard jnr**; **Mark Chamberlain** and **Alex Oxlade-Chamberlain**; **Ian Wright** and **Shaun Wright-Phillips**.

FATHER & SON SAME-DAY CAPS

Iceland made father-and-son international history when they beat Estonia 3-0 in Tallin on Apr 24, 1996. **Arnor Gudjohnsen** (35) started the match and was replaced (62 mins) by his 17-year-old son **Eidur**.

LONGEST UNBEATEN START TO ENGLAND CAREER

Steven Gerrard, 21 matches (W16, D5) 2000–03.

SUCCESSIVE ENGLAND HAT-TRICKS

The last player to score a hat-trick in consecutive England matches was **Harry Kane** who scored three goals against Albania (5-0) and four in another World Cup qualifier against San Marino (10-0) in November 2021.

MOST GOALS BY PLAYER v ENGLAND

4 by **Zlatan Ibrahimovic** (Sweden 4 England 2, Stockholm, Nov 14, 2012).

POST-WAR HAT-TRICKS v ENGLAND

Nov 25, 1953, **Nandor Hidegkuti** (England 3, Hungary 6, Wembley); May 11, 1958, **Aleksandar Petakovic** (Yugoslavia 5, England 0, Belgrade); May 17, 1959, **Juan Seminario** (Peru 4, England 1, Lima); Jun 15, 1988, **Marco van Basten** (Holland 3, England 1, European Championship, Dusseldorf). Six other players scored hat-tricks against England (1878–1930).

NO-SAVE GOALKEEPERS

Chris Woods did not have one save to make when England beat San Marino 6-0 (World Cup) at Wembley on Feb 17, 1993. He touched the ball only six times.

Gordon Banks had a similar no-save experience when England beat Malta 5-0 (European Championship) at Wembley on May 12, 1971. Malta did not force a goal-kick or corner, and the four times Banks touched the ball were all from back passes.

Robert Green was also idle in the 6-0 World Cup qualifying win over Andorra at Wembley on Jun 10, 2009.

Joe Hart was untroubled in England's 5-0 win over San Marino in a World Cup qualifier at Wembley on Oct 12, 2012.

WORLD/EURO MEMBERS

FIFA has 211 member countries, **UEFA** 55

NEW FIFA PRESIDENT

The 18-year reign of FIFA president **Sepp Blatter** ended in December 2015 amid widespread allegations of corruption. He was replaced in February 2016 by Gianni Infantino, a 45-year-old Swiss-Italian lawyer, who was previously general secretary of UEFA. Under new rules, he will serve four years.

FIFA WORLD YOUTH CUP (UNDER-20)

Finals: **1977** (Tunis) Soviet Union 2 Mexico 2 (Soviet won 9-8 on pens.); **1979** (Tokyo) Argentina 3 Soviet Union 1; **1981** (Sydney) W Germany 4 Qatar 0; **1983** (Mexico City) Brazil 1 Argentina 0; **1985** (Moscow) Brazil 1 Spain 0; **1987** (Santiago) Yugoslavia 1 W Germany 1 (Yugoslavia won 5-4 on pens.); **1989** (Riyadh) Portugal 2 Nigeria 0; **1991** (Lisbon) Portugal 0 Brazil 0 (Portugal won 4-2 on pens.); **1993** (Sydney) Brazil 2 Ghana 1; **1995** (Qatar) Argentina 2 Brazil 0; **1997** (Kuala Lumpur) Argentina 2 Uruguay 1; **1999** (Lagos) Spain 4 Japan 0; **2001** (Buenos Aires) Argentina 3 Ghana 0; **2003** (Dubai) Brazil 1 Spain 0; **2005**

(Utrecht) Argentina 2 Nigeria 1; **2007** (Toronto) Argentina 2 Czech Republic 1; **2009** (Cairo) Ghana 0 Brazil 0 (aet, Ghana won 4-3 on pens); **2011** (Bogota) Brazil 3 Portugal 2 (aet); **2013** (Istanbul) France 0 Uruguay 0 (aet, France won 4-1 on pens); **2015** (Auckland) Serbia 2 Brazil 1 (aet); **2017** (Suwon) England 1 Venezuela 0; **2019** (Lodz) Ukraine 3 South Korea 1. **2021** Tournament cancelled.

FAMOUS CLUB FEATS

Manchester City won the 2017–18 Premier League title under Pep Guardiola in record style. They became England's first champions to total 100 points and had the longest winning streak, 18 matches, in top-flight history. There were other new Premier League marks for goals scored (106), goal difference (79), overall wins (32), away victories (16), and for a 19-point gap to second-place. In season 2018–19, City made history with a domestic treble, winning the Premier League, FA Cup and League Cup. On their way to the 2020–21 title, City set a top-flight record of 21 straight wins in all competitions and a record for the top four tiers of English football with a 12 successive Premier League away victories.

Arsenal created an all-time English League record sequence of 49 unbeaten Premier League matches (W36, D13), spanning 3 seasons, from May 7, 2003 until losing 2-0 away to Manchester Utd on Oct 24, 2004. It included all 38 games in season 2003–04.

The Double: There have been 12 instances of a club winning the Football League/Premier League title and the FA Cup in the same season. **Preston** 1888–89; **Aston Villa** 1896–97; **Tottenham** 1960–61; **Arsenal** 1970–71, 1997–98, 2001–02; **Liverpool** 1985–86; **Manchester Utd** 1993–94, 1995–96, 1998–99; **Chelsea** 2009–10; **Manchester City** 2018-19.

The Treble: Liverpool were the first English club to win three major competitions in one season when in 1983–84, Joe Fagan's first season as manager, they were League Champions, League Cup winners and European Cup winners.

Sir Alex Ferguson's **Manchester Utd** achieved an even more prestigious treble in 1998–99, completing the domestic double of Premier League and FA Cup and then winning the European Cup. In season 2008–09, they completed another major triple success – Premier League, Carling Cup and World Club Cup.

Liverpool completed a unique treble by an English club with three cup successes under Gerard Houllier in season 2000–01: the League Cup, FA Cup and UEFA Cup.

Liverpool the first English club to win five major trophies in one calendar year (Feb– Aug 2001): League Cup, FA Cup, UEFA Cup, Charity Shield, UEFA Super Cup.

As Champions in season 2001–02, **Arsenal** set a Premier League record by winning the last 13 matches. They were the first top-division club since Preston in the League's inaugural season (1888–89) to maintain an unbeaten away record.

(See Scottish section for treble feats by Rangers and Celtic).

Record Home Runs: Liverpool went 85 competitive first-team games unbeaten at home between losing 2-3 to Birmingham on Jan 21, 1978 and 1-2 to Leicester on Jan 31, 1981. They comprised 63 in the League, 9 League Cup, 7 in European competition and 6 FA Cup.

Chelsea hold the record unbeaten home League sequence of 86 matches (W62, D24) between losing 1-2 to Arsenal, Feb 21, 2004, and 0-1 to Liverpool, Oct 26, 2008.

Third to First: Charlton, in 1936, became the first club to advance from the Third to First Division in successive seasons. **Queens Park Rangers** were the second club to achieve the feat in 1968, and **Oxford Utd** did it in 1984 and 1985 as Champions of each division. Subsequently, **Derby** (1987), **Middlesbrough** (1988), **Sheffield Utd** (1990) and **Notts Co** (1991) climbed from Third Division to First in consecutive seasons.

Watford won successive promotions from the modern Second Division to the Premier League in 1997–98, 1998–99. **Manchester City** equalled the feat in 1998–99, 1999–2000. **Norwich** climbed from League 1 to the Premier League in seasons 2009–10, 2010–11. **Southampton** did the same in 2010–11 and 2011–12.

Fourth to First: Northampton, in 1965 became the first club to rise from the Fourth to the

First Division. **Swansea** climbed from the Fourth Division to the First (three promotions in four seasons), 1977–78 to 1980–81. **Wimbledon** repeated the feat, 1982–83 to 1985–86. **Watford** did it in five seasons, 1977–8 to 1981–82. **Carlisle** climbed from Fourth Division to First, 1964–74.

Non-League to First: When **Wimbledon** finished third in the Second Division in 1986, they completed the phenomenal rise from non-League football (Southern League) to the First Division in nine years. Two years later they won the FA Cup.

Tottenham, in 1960–61, not only carried off the First Division Championship and the FA Cup for the first time that century but set up other records by opening with 11 successive wins, registering most First Division wins (31), most away wins in the League's history (16), and equalling Arsenal's First Division records of 66 points and 33 away points. They already held the Second Division record of 70 points (1919–20).

Arsenal, in 1993, became the first club to win both English domestic cup competitions (FA Cup and League Cup) in the same season. **Liverpool** repeated the feat in 2001 and 2022. **Chelsea** did it in 2007 and **Manchester City** in 2019.

Chelsea achieved the FA Cup/Champions League double in May 2012.

Preston, in season 1888–89, won the first League Championship without losing a match and the FA Cup without having a goal scored against them. Only other English clubs to remain unbeaten through a League season were **Liverpool** (Div 2 Champions in 1893–94) and **Arsenal** (Premier League Champions 2003–04).

Bury, in 1903, also won the FA Cup without conceding a goal.

Everton won Div 2, Div 1 and the FA Cup in successive seasons, 1930–31, 1931–32, 1932–33.

Wolves won the League Championship in 1958 and 1959 and the FA Cup in 1960.

Liverpool won the title in 1964, the FA Cup in 1965 and the title again in 1966. In 1978 they became the first British club to win the European Cup in successive seasons. Nottm Forest repeated the feat in 1979 and 1980.

Liverpool won the League Championship six times in eight seasons (1976–83) under **Bob Paisley's** management.

Sir Alex Ferguson's **Manchester Utd** won the Premier League in 13 of its 21 seasons (1992–2013). They were runners-up five times and third three times.

FA CUP/PROMOTION DOUBLE

WBA are the only club to achieve this feat in the same season (1930–31).

COVENTRY UNIQUE

Coventry are the only club to have played at every top level – the Premier League, Championship, League's One and Two, the old Divisions One, Two, Three and Four and the old Division Three North and South.

FAMOUS UPS & DOWNS

Sunderland: Relegated in 1958 after maintaining First Division status since their election to the Football League in 1890. They dropped into Division 3 for the first time in 1987.

Aston Villa: Relegated with Preston to the Third Division in 1970.

Arsenal up: When the League was extended in 1919, Woolwich Arsenal (sixth in Division Two in 1914–15, last season before the war) were elected to Division One. Arsenal have been in the top division ever since.

Tottenham down: At that same meeting in 1919 Chelsea (due for relegation) retained their place in Division One but the bottom club (Tottenham) had to go down to Division Two.

Preston and Burnley down: Preston, the first League Champions in season 1888–89, dropped into the Fourth Division in 1985. So did Burnley, also among the League's original members in 1888. In 1986, Preston had to apply for re-election.

Wolves' fall: Wolves, another of the Football League's original members, completed the fall from

First Division to Fourth in successive seasons (1984–85–86).

Lincoln out: Lincoln became the first club to suffer automatic demotion from the Football League when they finished bottom of Div 4, on goal difference, in season 1986–87. They were replaced by Scarborough, champions of the GM Vauxhall Conference. Lincoln regained their place a year later.

Swindon up and down: In the 1990 play-offs, Swindon won promotion to the First Division for the first time, but remained in the Second Division because of financial irregularities.

MOST CHAMPIONSHIP WINS

Manchester Utd have been champions of England a record 20 times (7 Football League, 13 Premier League).

LONGEST CURRENT MEMBERS OF TOP DIVISION

Arsenal (since 1919), **Everton** (1954), **Liverpool** (1962), **Manchester Utd** (1975).

CHAMPIONS: FEWEST PLAYERS

Liverpool used only **14** players (five ever-present) when they won the League Championship in season 1965–66. **Aston Villa** also called on no more than 14 players to win the title in 1980–81, with seven ever-present.

UNBEATEN CHAMPIONS

Only two clubs have become Champions of England with an unbeaten record: **Preston** as the Football League's first winners in 1888–89 (22 matches) and **Arsenal**, Premier League winners in 2003–04 (38 matches).

LEAGUE HAT-TRICKS

Huddersfield created a record in 1924–25–26 by winning the League Championship three years in succession.

Arsenal equalled this hat-trick in 1933–34–35, **Liverpool** in 1982–83–84 and **Manchester Utd** in 1999–2000–01. Sir Alex Ferguson's side became the first to complete two hat-tricks (2007–08–09).

'SUPER DOUBLE' WINNERS

Since the War, there have been three instances of players appearing in and then managing FA Cup and Championship-winning teams:

Joe Mercer: Player in Arsenal Championship teams 1948, 1953 and in their 1950 FA Cup side; manager of Manchester City when they won Championship 1968, FA Cup 1969.

Kenny Dalglish: Player in Liverpool Championship-winning teams 1979, 1980, 1982, 1983, 1984, player-manager 1986, 1988, 1990; player-manager when Liverpool won FA Cup (to complete Double) 1986; manager of Blackburn, Champions 1995.

George Graham: Played in Arsenal's Double-winning team in 1971, and as manager took them to Championship success in 1989 and 1991 and the FA Cup – League Cup double in 1993.

ORIGINAL TWELVE

The original 12 members of the Football League (formed in 1888) were: **Accrington, Aston Villa, Blackburn, Bolton, Burnley, Derby, Everton, Notts Co, Preston, Stoke, WBA** and **Wolves**. Results on the opening day (Sep 8, 1888): Bolton 3, Derby 6; Everton 2, Accrington 1; Preston 5, Burnley 2; Stoke 0, WBA 2; Wolves 1, Aston Villa 1. Preston had the biggest first-day crowd: 6,000. Blackburn and Notts Co did not play that day. They kicked off a week later (Sep 15) – Blackburn 5, Accrington 5; Everton 2, Notts Co 1.

Accrington FC resigned from the league in 1893 and later folded. A new club, Accrington Stanley, were members of the league from 1921 until 1962 when financial problems forced their demise. The current Accrington Stanley were formed in 1968 and gained league status in 2007.

FASTEST CLIMBS

Three promotions in four seasons by two clubs – **Swansea City**: 1978 third in Div 4; 1979 third in Div 3; 1981 third in Div 2; **Wimbledon:** 1983 Champions of Div 4; 1984 second in Div 3; 1986 third in Div 2.

MERSEYSIDE RECORD

Liverpool is the only city to have staged top-division football – through Everton and/or Liverpool – **in every season** since League football began in 1888.

EARLIEST PROMOTIONS TO TOP DIVISION POST-WAR

Mar 23, 1974, **Middlesbrough;** Mar 25, 2006, **Reading.**

EARLIEST RELEGATIONS POST-WAR

From top division: **QPR** went down from the old First Division on Mar 29, 1969; **Derby** went down from the Premier League on Mar 29, 2008, with 6 matches still to play. From modern First Division: **Stockport** on Mar 16, 2002, with 7 matches still to play; **Wimbledon** on Apr 6, 2004, with 7 matches to play.

LEAGUE RECORDS

CHAMPIONS OF ENGLAND 1888–2022

Football League and Premier league

Manchester Utd 20, Liverpool 19, Arsenal 13, Everton 9, Manchester City 8, Aston Villa 7, Chelsea 6, Sunderland 6, Newcastle 4, Sheffield Wed 4, Blackburn 3, Huddersfield 3, Leeds 3, Wolves 3, Burnley 2, Derby 2, Portsmouth 2, Preston 2, Tottenham 2, Ipswich 1, Leicester 1, Nottm Forest 1, Sheffield Utd 1, WBA 1

DOUBLE CHAMPIONS

Nine men have played in and managed League Championship-winning teams:

Ted Drake Player – Arsenal 1934, 1935, 1938. Manager – Chelsea 1955.
Bill Nicholson Player – Tottenham 1951. Manager – Tottenham 1961.
Alf Ramsey Player – Tottenham 1951. Manager – Ipswich 1962.
Joe Mercer Player – Everton 1939, Arsenal 1948, 1953. Manager – Manchester City 1968.
Dave Mackay Player – Tottenham 1961. Manager – Derby 1975.
Bob Paisley Player – Liverpool 1947. Manager – Liverpool 1976, 1977, 1979, 1980, 1982, 1983.
Howard Kendall Player – Everton 1970. Manager – Everton 1985, 1987.
Kenny Dalglish Player – Liverpool 1979, 1980, 1982, 1983, 1984. Player-manager – Liverpool 1986, 1988, 1990. Manager – Blackburn 1995.
George Graham Player – Arsenal 1971. Manager – Arsenal 1989, 1991.

CANTONA'S FOUR-TIMER

Eric Cantona played in four successive Championship-winning teams: Marseille 1990–01, Leeds 1991–92, Manchester Utd 1992–93 and 1993–94.

ARRIVALS AND DEPARTURES

The following are the Football League arrivals and departures since 1923:

Year	In	Out
1923	Doncaster	Stalybridge Celtic
	New Brighton	
1927	Torquay	Aberdare Athletic
1928	Carlisle	Durham
1929	York	Ashington
1930	Thames	Merthyr Tydfil
1931	Mansfield	Newport Co
	Chester	Nelson
1932	Aldershot	Thames
	Newport Co	Wigan Borough
1938	Ipswich	Gillingham
1950	Colchester, Gillingham	
	Scunthorpe, Shrewsbury	
1951	Workington	New Brighton
1960	Peterborough	Gateshead
1962	Oxford Utd	Accrington (resigned)
1970	Cambridge Utd	Bradford PA
1972	Hereford	Barrow
1977	Wimbledon	Workington
1978	Wigan	Southport
1987	Scarborough	Lincoln
1988	Lincoln	Newport Co
1989	Maidstone	Darlington
1990	Darlington	Colchester
1991	Barnet	
1992	Colchester	Aldershot, Maidstone (resigned)
1993	Wycombe	Halifax
1997	Macclesfield	Hereford
1998	Halifax	Doncaster
1999	Cheltenham	Scarborough
2000	Kidderminster	Chester
2001	Rushden	Barnet
2002	Boston	Halifax
2003	Yeovil, Doncaster	Exeter, Shrewsbury
2004	Chester, Shrewsbury	Carlisle, York
2005	Barnet, Carlisle	Kidderminster, Cambridge Utd
2006	Accrington, Hereford	Oxford Utd, Rushden & Diamonds
2007	Dagenham, Morecambe	Torquay, Boston
2008	Aldershot, Exeter	Wrexham, Mansfield
2009	Burton, Torquay	Chester, Luton
2010	Stevenage, Oxford Utd	Grimsby, Darlington
2011	Crawley, AFC Wimbledon	Lincoln, Stockport
2012	Fleetwood, York	Hereford, Macclesfield
2013	Mansfield, Newport	Barnet, Aldershot
2014	Luton, Cambridge Utd	Bristol Rov, Torquay
2015	Barnet, Bristol Rov	Cheltenham, Tranmere
2016	Cheltenham, Grimsby	Dagenham & Redbridge, York
2017	Lincoln, Forest Green	Hartlepool, Leyton Orient
2018	Macclesfield, Tranmere	Barnet, Chesterfield
2019	Leyton Orient, Salford	Notts Co Yeovil
2020	Barrow, Harrogate	Macclesfield
2021	Sutton, Hartlepool	Southend, Grimsby
2022	Stockport, Grimsby	Oldham, Scunthorpe

Leeds City were expelled from Div 2 in Oct, 1919; Port Vale took over their fixtures.

EXTENSIONS TO FOOTBALL LEAGUE

Clubs	Season	Clubs	Season
12 to 14	1891–92	44 to 66†	1920–21
14 to 28*	1892–93	66 to 86†	1921–22
28 to 31	1893–94	86 to 88	1923–24
31 to 32	1894–95	88 to 92	1950–51
32 to 36	1898–99	92 to 93	1991–92
36 to 40	1905–06	(Reverted to 92 when Aldershot closed, Mar 1992)	

*Second Division formed. † Third Division (South) formed from Southern League clubs.
†Third Division (North) formed.
Football League reduced to 70 clubs and three divisions on the formation of the FA Premier League in 1992; increased to 72 season 1994–95, when Premier League reduced to 20 clubs.

RECORD RUNS

Arsenal hold the record unbeaten sequence in the English League – 49 Premier League matches (36 wins, 13 draws) from May 7, 2003 until Oct 24, 2004 when beaten 2-0 away to Manchester Utd. The record previously belonged to **Nottm Forest** – 42 First Division matches (21 wins, 21 draws) from Nov 19, 1977 until beaten 2-0 at Liverpool on December 9, 1978.
Huddersfield set a new Football League record of 43 League 1 matches unbeaten from Jan 1, 2011 until Nov 28, 2011 when losing 2-0 at Charlton.
Best debuts: Ipswich won the First Division at their first attempt in 1961–62.
Peterborough in their first season in the Football League (1960–01) not only won the Fourth Division but set the all-time scoring record for the League of 134 goals. **Hereford** were promoted from the Fourth Division in their first League season, 1972–73.
Wycombe were promoted from the Third Division (via the play-offs) in their first League season, 1993–94. **Stevenage** were promoted from League 2 (via the play-offs) in their first League season, 2010–11. **Crawley** gained automatic promotion in their first season in 2011–12.
Record winning sequence in a season: 18 consecutive League victories by Manchester City, 2017-18, and Liverpool, 2019-20, longest in English top-flight.
Best winning start to League season: 13 successive victories in Div 3 by **Reading**, season 1985–86.
Best starts in 'old' First Division: 11 consecutive victories by **Tottenham** in 1960–61; 10 by **Manchester Utd in** 1985–86. In 'new' First Division, 11 consecutive wins by **Newcastle** in 1992–93 and by **Fulham** in 2000–01.
Longest unbeaten sequence (all competitions): 40 by **Nottm Forest,** Mar–December 1978. It comprised 21 wins, 19 draws (in 29 League matches, 6 League Cup, 4 European Cup, 1 Charity Shield).
Longest unbeaten starts to League season: 38 matches (26 wins, 12 draws) in **Arsenal's** undefeated Premier League season, 2003–04; 29 matches – **Leeds,** Div 1 1973–74 (19 wins, 10 draws); **Liverpool,** Div 1 1987–88 (22 wins, 7 draws).
Most consecutive League matches unbeaten in a season: 38 **Arsenal** Premier League season 2003–04 (see above); 33 **Reading** (25 wins, 8 draws) 2005–06.
Longest winning sequence in Div 1: 13 matches by **Tottenham** – last two of season 1959–60, first 11 of 1960–61.
Longest unbeaten home League sequence in top division: 86 matches (62 wins, 24 draws) by **Chelsea** (Mar 2004–Oct 2008).
League's longest winning sequence with clean sheets: 9 matches by **Stockport** (Lge 2, 2006–07 season).
Premier League – best starts to season: Arsenal, 38 games, 2003–04; **Liverpool** 27 games 2019–20
Best winning start to Premier League season: 9 consecutive victories by **Chelsea** in 2005–06.
Premier League – most consecutive home wins: 24 by **Liverpool** (last 7 season 2018-19, first 17 season 2019-20).
Most consecutive away League wins in top flight: 24 by **Liverpool** (last 7 2018–19, first 17 2019–20).
Premier League – longest unbeaten away run: 29 matches (W19, D10) by **Manchester Utd** (Feb 2020–Oct 2021).

Record home-win sequences: Bradford Park Avenue won 25 successive home games in Div 3 North – the last 18 in 1926–27 and the first 7 the following season. Longest run of home wins in the top division is 21 by **Liverpool** – the last 9 of 1971–72 and the first 12 of 1972–73.
British record for successive League wins: 25 by **Celtic** (Scottish Premier League), 2003–04.

WORST SEQUENCES

Cambridge Utd had the previous worst of 31 in 1983–84 (21 lost, 10 drawn). They were bottom of Div 2.
Longest sequence without home win: Sunderland, in the Championship, went an English record 21 games in all competitions without a victory in front of their own supporters (Dec 2016-Nov 2017).
Worst losing start to a League season : 12 consecutive defeats by **Manchester Utd** (Div 1), 1930–31.
Worst Premier League start: QPR 16 matches without win (7 draws, 9 defeats), 2012–13.
Premier League – most consecutive defeats: 20 **Sunderland** last 15 matches, 2002–03, first five matches 2005–06.
Premier League – most consecutive home defeats: 11 Watford (2021–22)
Longest non-winning start to League season: 25 matches (4 draws, 21 defeats) by **Newport**, Div 4. Worst no-win League starts since then: 16 matches by **Burnley** (9 draws, 7 defeats in Div 2, 1979–80); 16 by **Hull** (10 draws, 6 defeats in Div 2, 1989–90); 16 by **Sheffield Utd** (4 draws, 12 defeats in Div 1, 1990–91).
Most home League defeats in a season: 18 by Cambridge Utd (Div 3, 1984–85) and by Leyton Orient (Lg 2, 2016–17).
Fewest League wins in season: 1 by **Loughborough** (Div 2, season 1899–1900). They lost 27, drew 6, goals 18-100 and dropped out of the League. (See also Scottish section). 1 by **Derby** (Prem Lge, 2007–08). They lost 29, drew 8, goals 20-89.
Most consecutive League defeats in season: 18 by **Darwen** (Div 1, 1898–99); 17 by **Rochdale** (Div 3 North, 1931–32).
Fewest home League wins in season: 1 by **Loughborough** (Div 2, 1899–1900), **Notts Co** (Div 1, 1904–05), **Woolwich Arsenal** (Div 1, 1912–13), **Blackpool** (Div 1, 1966–67), **Rochdale** (Div 3, 1973–74), **Sunderland** (Prem Lge, 2005–06); **Derby** (Prem Lge, 2007–08).
Away League defeats record: 24 in a row by **Crewe** (Div 2) – all 15 in 1894–95 followed by 9 in 1895–96; by **Nelson** (Div 3 North) – 3 in Apr 1930 followed by all 21 in season 1930–31. They then dropped out of the League.
Biggest defeat in Champions' season: During **Newcastle's** title-winning season in 1908–09, they were beaten 9-1 at home by Sunderland on December 5.

WORST START BY EVENTUAL CHAMPIONS

Sunderland took only 2 points from their first 7 matches in season 1912–13 (2 draws, 5 defeats). They won 25 of the remaining 31 games to clinch their fifth League title.

DISMAL DERBY

Derby were relegated in season 2007–08 as the worst-ever team in the Premier League, having recorded the fewest wins (1), fewest points (11) and fewest goals (20). They experienced the longest run without a victory in League history – 32 games from Sept 22 to the end of the campaign. The sequence extended to 36 at the start of the following season. Macclesfield also went 36 matches without winning, 23 up to the end of their relegation season 2011–12 and 13 after returning to League Two in 2018–19.

UNBEATEN LEAGUE SEASON

Only three clubs have completed an English League season unbeaten: **Preston** (22 matches in 1888–89, the League's first season), **Liverpool** (28 matches in Div 2, 1893–94) and **Arsenal** (38 matches in Premier League, 2003–04).

100 PER CENT HOME RECORDS

Six clubs have won every home League match in a season: **Sunderland** (13 matches)' in 1891–92 and four teams in the old Second Division: **Liverpool** (14) in 1893–94, **Bury** (15) in 1894–95, **Sheffield Wed** (17) in 1899–1900 and **Small Heath,** subsequently **Birmingham** (17) in 1902–03. The last club to do it, **Brentford,** won all 21 home games in Div 3 South in 1929–30. **Rotherham** just failed to equal that record in 1946–47. They won their first 20 home matches in Div 3 North, then drew the last 3-3 v Rochdale.

BEST HOME LEAGUE RECORDS IN TOP FLIGHT

Sunderland, 1891–92 (P13, W13); **Newcastle,** 1906–07 (P19, W18, D1); **Chelsea,** 2005–06 (P19, W18, D1); **Manchester Utd,** 2010–11 (P19, W18, D1); **Manchester City,** 2011–12 (P19, W18, D1); **Liverpool,** 2019-20 (P19, W18, D1)

MOST CONSECUTIVE CLEAN SHEETS

Premier League – 14: **Manchester Utd** (2008–09); **Football League** – 11: **Millwall** (Div 3 South 1925–26); **York** (Div 3 1973–74); **Reading** (Div 4, 1978–79).

WORST HOME RUNS

Most consecutive home League defeats: 14 **Rochdale** (Div 3 North) seasons 1931–32 and 1932–33; 10 **Birmingham** (Div 1) 1985–86; 9 **Darwen** (Div 2) 1897–98; 9 **Watford** (Div 2) 1971–72.
Between Nov 1958 and Oct 1959 **Portsmouth** drew 2 and lost 14 out of 16 consecutive home games.
West Ham did not win in the Premier League at Upton Park in season 2002–03 until the 13th home match on Jan 29.

MOST AWAY WINS IN SEASON

Doncaster won 18 of their 21 away League fixtures when winning Div 3 North in 1946–47.

100 PER CENT HOME WINS ON ONE DAY

Div 1 – All 11 home teams won on Feb 13, 1926 and on Dec 10, 1955. **Div 2** – All 12 home teams won on Nov 26, 1988. **Div 3,** all 12 home teams won in the week-end programme of Oct 18–19, 1968.

NO HOME WINS IN DIV ON ONE DAY

Div 1 – 8 away wins, 3 draws in 11 matches on Sep 6, 1986. **Div 2** – 7 away wins, 4 draws in 11 matches on Dec 26, 1987. **Premier League** – 6 away wins, 5 draws in 11 matches on Dec 26, 1994.
The weekend **Premier League** programme on Dec 7–8–9, 1996 produced no home win in the ten games (4 aways, 6 draws). There was again no home victory (3 away wins, 7 draws) in the week-end **Premier League** fixtures on Sep 23–24, 2000.

MOST DRAWS IN A SEASON (FOOTBALL LEAGUE)

23 by **Norwich** (Div 1, 1978–79), **Exeter** (Div 4, 1986–87). **Cardiff** and **Hartlepool** (both Div 3, 1997–98). **Norwich** played 42 matches, the others 46.

MOST DRAWS IN PREMIER LEAGUE SEASON

18 (in 42 matches) by **Manchester City** (1993–94), **Sheffield Utd** (1993–94), **Southampton** (1994–95).

MOST DRAWS IN ONE DIVISION ON ONE DAY

On Sep 18, 1948 **nine** out of 11 First Division matches were drawn.

MOST DRAWS IN PREMIER DIV PROGRAMME

Over the week-ends of December 2–3–4, 1995, and Sep 23–24, 2000, **seven** out of the ten matches finished level.

FEWEST DRAWS IN SEASON

In 46 matches: 3 by **Reading** (Div 3 South, 1951–52); **Bradford Park Avenue** (Div 3 North, 1956–57); **Tranmere** (Div 4, 1984–85); **Southend** (Div 3, 2002–03); in 42 matches: 2 by **Reading** (Div 3 South, 1935–36); **Stockport** (Div 3 North, 1946–47); in 38 matches: 2 by **Sunderland** (Div 1, 1908–09).

HIGHEST-SCORING DRAWS IN LEAGUE

Leicester 6, **Arsenal** 6 (Div 1 Apr 21, 1930); **Charlton** 6, **Middlesbrough** 6 (Div 2. Oct 22, 1960)
Latest **6-6** draw in first-class football was between **Tranmere** and **Newcastle** in the Zenith Data Systems Cup 1st round on Oct 1, 1991. The score went from 3-3 at 90 minutes to 6-6 after extra time, and Tranmere won 3-2 on penalties. In Scotland: **Queen of the South** 6, **Falkirk** 6 (Div 1, Sep 20, 1947).
Most recent **5-5** draws in top division: **Southampton** v **Coventry** (Div 1, May 4, 1982); **QPR** v **Newcastle** (Div 1, Sep 22, 1984); **WBA** v **Manchester Utd** (Prem Lge, May 19, 2013).

DRAWS RECORDS

Most consecutive drawn matches in Football League: 8 by **Torquay** (Div 3, 1969–70), **Middlesbrough** (Div 2, 1970–71), **Peterborough** (Div 4, 1971–72), **Birmingham** (Div 3 (1990–91), **Southampton** (Champ, 2005–06), **Chesterfield** (Lge 1, 2005–06), **Swansea** (Champ, 2008–09).
Longest sequence of draws by the same score: six 1-1 results by **QPR** in season 1957–58. **Tranmere** became the first club to play **five consecutive 0-0 League draws**, in season 1997–98. Relegated **Chesterfield** drew nine successive National League games in season 2018–19.

IDENTICAL RECORDS

There is only **one instance** of two clubs in one division finishing a season with identical records. In 1907–08, **Blackburn** and **Woolwich Arsenal** were bracketed equal 14th in the First Division with these figures: P38, W12, D12, L14, Goals 51-63, Pts. 36.
The total of **1195 goals** scored in the Premier League in season 1993–94 was repeated in 1994–95.

DEAD LEVEL

Millwall's record in Division Two in season 1973–74 was P42, W14, D14, L14, F51, A51, Pts 42.

CHAMPIONS OF ALL DIVISIONS

Wolves, Burnley and **Preston** are the only clubs to have won titles in the old Divisions 1, 2, 3 and 4.

POINTS DEDUCTIONS

2000–01: Chesterfield 9 for breach of transfer regulations and falsifying gate receipts.
2002–03: Boston 4 for contractual irregularities.
2004–05: Wrexham, Cambridge Utd 10 for administration.
2005–06: Rotherham 10 for administration.
2006–07: Leeds, Boston 10 for administration; **Bury** 1 for unregistered player.
2007–08: Leeds 15 over insolvency rules; **Bournemouth, Luton, Rotherham** 10 for administration.
2008–09: Luton 20 for failing Insolvency rules, 10 over payments to agents; **Bournemouth,**

Rotherham 17 for breaking administration rules; **Southampton, Stockport** 10 for administration – **Southampton** with effect from season 2009–10 **Crystal Palace** 1 for ineligible player.

2009–10: Portsmouth 9, **Crystal Palace** 10 for administration; **Hartlepool** 3 for ineligible player.

2010–11: Plymouth 10 for administration; **Hereford** 3, **Torquay** 1, each for ineligible player

2011–12: Portsmouth and **Port Vale** both 10 for administration – Portsmouth from following season.

2013–14: Coventry 10 for administration; **AFC Wimbledon** 3 for ineligible player.

2014–15: Rotherham 3 for ineligible player.

2015–16: Bury 3 for ineligible player.

2018–19: Birmingham 9 for financial irregularities; **Bolton** 12 for administration, triggered in season 2019–20.

2021–22 Derby 12 for administration, 9 for breaking financial rules; **Reading** 6 for breaking financial rules

Among previous points penalties imposed:

Nov 1990: Arsenal 2, **Manchester Utd** 1 following mass players' brawl at Old Trafford.

Dec 1996: Brighton 2 for pitch invasions by fans.

Jan 1997: Middlesbrough 3 for refusing to play Premier League match at Blackburn because of injuries and illness.

Jun 1994: Tottenham 12 (reduced to 6) and banned from following season's FA Cup for making illegal payments to players. On appeal, points deduction annulled and club re-instated in Cup.

2019–20: Bury 12 for insolvency (club later expelled); **Wigan** 12 into administration; **Macclesfield** 17 for breaches of regulations; 12 **Sheffield Wed** for breaking spending rules, triggered in season 2020–21 and later reduced by half.

NIGHTMARE STARTS

Most goals conceded by a goalkeeper on League debut: 13 by Steve Milton when Halifax lost 13-0 at Stockport (Div 3 North) on Jan 6, 1934.

Post-war: 11 by Crewe's new goalkeeper **Dennis Murray** (Div 3 North) on Sep 29, 1951, when Lincoln won 11-1.

RELEGATION ODD SPOTS

None of the Barclays Premier League relegation places in season 2004–05 were decided until the last day (Sunday, May 15). **WBA** (bottom at kick-off) survived with a 2-0 home win against Portsmouth, and the three relegated clubs were **Southampton** (1-2 v Manchester Utd), **Norwich** (0-6 at Fulham) and **Crystal Palace** (2-2 at Charlton).

In season 1937–38, **Manchester City** were the highest-scoring team in the First Division with 80 goals (3 more than Champions Arsenal), but they finished in 21st place and were relegated – a year after winning the title. They scored more goals than they conceded (77).

That season produced the **closest relegation battle** in top-division history, with only 4 points spanning the bottom 11 clubs in Div 1. **WBA** went down with **Manchester City**.

Twelve years earlier, in 1925–26, City went down to Division 2 despite totalling 89 goals – still the most scored in any division by a team. Manchester City also scored 31 FA Cup goals that season, but lost the Final 1-0 to Bolton Wanderers.

Cardiff were relegated from Div 1 in season 1928–29, despite conceding fewest goals in the division (59). They also scored fewest (43).

On their way to relegation from the First Division in season 1984–85, **Stoke** twice lost ten matches in a row.

RELEGATION TREBLES

Two Football League clubs have been relegated three seasons in succession. **Bristol City** fell from First Division to Fourth in 1980–81–82 and **Wolves** did the same in 1984–85–86.

OLDEST CLUBS

Oldest Association Football Club is **Sheffield FC** (formed in 1857). The oldest Football League clubs are **Nottm Forest**, 1865; and **Sheffield Wed**, 1866.

NOTTS COUNTY RELEGATED

Notts County, formed in 1862 and the world's oldest professional club, were relegated from the Football League for the first time in season 2018–19.

FOUR DIVISIONS

In **May, 1957**, the Football League decided to re-group the two sections of the Third Division into Third and Fourth Divisions in **season 1958–59**.

The Football League was reduced to three divisions on the formation of the Premier League in **1992**. In season 2004–05, under new sponsors Coca-Cola, the titles of First, Second and Third Divisions were changed to League Championship, League One and League Two.

THREE UP – THREE DOWN

The Football League annual general meeting of Jun 1973 agreed to adopt the promotion and relegation system of three up and three down.

The **new system** came into effect in **season 1973–74** and applied only to the first three divisions; four clubs were still relegated from the Third and four promoted from the Fourth.

It was the first change in the promotion and relegation system for the top two divisions in 81 years.

MOST LEAGUE APPEARANCES (as at end of season 2021–22)

Players with more than 700 English League apps (as at end of season 2019–20)

1005   Peter Shilton 1966–97 (286 Leicester, 110 Stoke, 202 Nottm Forest, 188 Southampton, 175 Derby, 34 Plymouth Argyle, 1 Bolton, 9 Leyton Orient).

931   Tony Ford 1975–2002 (423 Grimsby, 9 Sunderland, 112 Stoke, 114 WBA, 5 Bradford City, 76 Scunthorpe, 103 Mansfield, 89 Rochdale).

840   Graham Alexander 1991–2012 (159 Scunthorpe, 152 Luton; 372 Preston, 157 Burnley)

824   Terry Paine 1956–77 (713 Southampton, 111 Hereford).

795   Tommy Hutchison 1968–91 (165 Blackpool, 314 Coventry City, 46 Manchester City, 92 Burnley, 178 Swansea). In addition, 68 Scottish League apps for Alloa 1965–68, giving career League app total of 863.

791   David James 1988-2013 (89 Watford, 217 Liverpool, 67 Aston Villa, 91 West Ham, 93 Manchester City, 134 Portsmouth, 81 Bristol City, 19 Bournemouth).

790   Neil Redfearn 1982–2004 (35 Bolton, 100 Lincoln, 46 Doncaster, 57 Crystal Palace, 24 Watford, 62 Oldham, 292 Barnsley, 30 Charlton, 17 Bradford City, 22 Wigan, 42 Halifax, 54 Boston, 9 Rochdale).

782   Robbie James 1973–94 (484 Swansea, 48 Stoke, 87 QPR, 23 Leicester, 89 Bradford City, 51 Cardiff).

777   Alan Oakes 1959–84 (565 Manchester City, 211 Chester, 1 Port Vale).

773   Dave Beasant 1980–2003 (340 Wimbledon, 20 Newcastle, 6 Grimsby, 4 Wolves, 133 Chelsea, 88 Southampton, 139 Nottm F, 27 Portsmouth, 16 Brighton).

770   John Trollope 1960–80 (all for Swindon, record total for one club).

768   Dean Lewington 2002–22 (29 Wimbledon, 739 MK Dons).

764   Jimmy Dickinson 1946–65 (all for Portsmouth).

763   Peter Clarke 2000–22 (9 Everton, 13 Blackpool, 13 Port Vale, 5 Coventry, 125 Southend, 192 Huddersfield, 63 Bury, 107 Oldham, 12 Fleetwood, 98 Tranmere).

761   Roy Sproson 1950–72 (all for Port Vale).

760   Mick Tait 1974–97 (64 Oxford Utd, 106 Carlisle, 33 Hull, 240 Portsmouth, 99 Reading, 79 Darlington, 139 Hartlepool Utd).

758	Billy Bonds 1964–88 (95 Charlton, 663 West Ham).
758	Ray Clemence 1966–88 (48 Scunthorpe, 470 Liverpool, 240 Tottenham).
757	Pat Jennings 1963–86 (48 Watford, 472 Tottenham, 237 Arsenal).
757	Frank Worthington 1966–88 (171 Huddersfield Town, 210 Leicester, 84 Bolton, 75 Birmingham, 32 Leeds, 19 Sunderland, 34 Southampton, 31 Brighton, 59 Tranmere, 23 Preston, 19 Stockport).
755	Wayne Allison 1986–2008 (84 Halifax, 7 Watford, 195 Bristol City, 103 Swindon, 76 Huddersfield, 102 Tranmere, 73 Sheffield Utd, 115 Chesterfield).
749	Ernie Moss 1968–88 (469 Chesterfield, 35 Peterborough, 57 Mansfield, 74 Port Vale, 11 Lincoln, 44 Doncaster, 26 Stockport, 23 Scarborough, 10 Rochdale).
748	Luke Chambers 2002–22 (124 Northampton, 205 Nottm Foret, 376 Ipswich, 43 Colchester).
746	Les Chapman 1966–88 (263 Oldham, 133 Huddersfield Town, 70 Stockport, 139 Bradford City, 88 Rochdale, 53 Preston).
744	Asa Hartford 1967–90 (214 WBA, 260 Manchester City, 3 Nottm Forest, 81 Everton, 28 Norwich, 81 Bolton, 45 Stockport, 7 Oldham, 25 Shrewsbury).
743	Alan Ball 1963–84 (146 Blackpool, 208 Everton, 177 Arsenal, 195 Southampton, 17 Bristol Rov.).
743	John Hollins 1963–84 (465 Chelsea, 151 QPR, 127 Arsenal).
743	Phil Parkes 1968–91 (52 Walsall, 344 QPR, 344 West Ham, 3 Ipswich).
737	Steve Bruce 1979–99 (205 Gillingham, 141 Norwich, 309 Manchester Utd 72 Birmingham, 10 Sheffield Utd).
734	Teddy Sheringham 1983–2007 (220 Millwall, 5 Aldershot, 42 Nottm Forest, 104 Manchester Utd, 236 Tottenham, 32 Portsmouth, 76 West Ham, 19 Colchester)
732	Mick Mills 1966–88 (591 Ipswich, 103 Southampton, 38 Stoke).
731	Ian Callaghan 1959–81 (640 Liverpool, 76 Swansea, 15 Crewe).
731	David Seaman 1982–2003 (91 Peterborough, 75 Birmingham, 141 QPR, 405 Arsenal, 19 Manchester City).
725	Steve Perryman 1969–90 (655 Tottenham, 17 Oxford Utd, 53 Brentford).
722	Martin Peters 1961–81 (302 West Ham, 189 Tottenham, 207 Norwich, 24 Sheffield Utd).
718	Mike Channon 1966–86 (511 Southampton, 72 Manchester City, 4 Newcastle, 9 Bristol Rov, 88 Norwich, 34 Portsmouth).
716	Ron Harris 1961–83 (655 Chelsea, 61 Brentford).
716	Mike Summerbee 1959–79 (218 Swindon, 357 Manchester City, 51 Burnley, 3 Blackpool, 87 Stockport).
714	Glenn Cockerill 1976–98 (186 Lincoln, 26 Swindon, 62 Sheffield Utd, 387 Southampton, 90 Leyton Orient, 40 Fulham, 23 Brentford).
710	Jamie Cureton 1992–2016 (98 Norwich, 5 Bournemouth, 174 Bristol Rov, 108 Reading, 43 QPR, 30 Swindon, 52 Colchester, 8 Barnsley, 12 Shrewsbury, 88 Exeter, 19 Leyton Orient, 35 Cheltenham, 38 Dagenham)
705	Keith Curle 1981–2003 (32 Bristol Rov, 16 Torquay, 121 Bristol City, 40 Reading, 93 Wimbledon, 171 Manchester City, 150 Wolves, 57 Sheffield Utd, 11 Barnsley, 14 Mansfield.
705	Phil Neal 1968–89 (186 Northampton, 455 Liverpool, 64 Bolton).
705	John Wile 1968–86 (205 Peterborough, 500 WBA).
705	Steve Fletcher 1990-2013 (32 Hartlepool, 629 Bournemouth, 38 Chesterfield, 6 Plymouth)
703	Rob Lee 1983-2006 (298 Charlton, 303 Newcastle, 48 Derby, 16 West Ham, 38 Wycombe).
703	Andy Melville 1986-2005 (175 Swansea, 135 Oxford, 204 Sunderland, 6 Bradford City, 153 Fulham, 17 West Ham, 13 Nottm F.).
701	Neville Southall 1980–2000 (39 Bury, 578 Everton, 9 Port Vale, 9 Southend, 12 Stoke, 53 Torquay, 1 Bradford City).

- **Stanley Matthews** made 701 League apps 1932–65 (322 Stoke, 379 Blackpool), incl. 3 for Stoke at start of 1939–40 before season abandoned (war).
- Goalkeeper **John Burridge** made a total of 771 League appearances in a 28-season career in English and Scottish football (1968–96). He played 691 games for 15 English clubs (Workington, Blackpool, Aston Villa, Southend, Crystal Palace, QPR, Wolves, Derby, Sheffield Utd, Southampton, Newcastle, Scarborough, Lincoln, Manchester City and Darlington) and 80 for 5 Scottish clubs (Hibernian, Aberdeen, Dumbarton, Falkirk and Queen of the South).

LONGEST LEAGUE APPEARANCE SEQUENCE

Harold Bell, centre-half of Tranmere, was ever-present for the first nine post-war seasons (1946–55), achieving a League record of 401 consecutive matches. Counting FA Cup and other games, his run of successive appearances totalled 459.

The longest League sequence since Bell's was 394 appearances by goalkeeper **Dave Beasant** for Wimbledon, Newcastle and Chelsea. His nine-year run began on Aug 29, 1981 and was ended by a broken finger sustained in Chelsea's League Cup-tie against Portsmouth on Oct 31, 1990. Beasant's 394 consecutive League games comprised 304 for Wimbledon (1981–88), 20 for Newcastle (1988–89) and 70 for Chelsea (1989–90).

Phil Neal made 366 consecutive First Division appearances for Liverpool between December 1974 and Sep 1983, a remarkable sequence for an outfield player in top-division football.

MOST CONSECUTIVE PREMIER LEAGUE APPEARANCES

310 by goalkeeper **Brad Friedel** (152 Blackburn, 114 Aston Villa, 44 Tottenham, May 2004–Oct 2012). He played in 8 **ever-present seasons** (2004–12, Blackburn 4, Villa 3, Tottenham 1).

EVER-PRESENT DEFENCE

The **entire defence** of **Huddersfield** played in all 42 Second Division matches in season 1952–53, namely, Bill Wheeler (goal), Ron Staniforth and Laurie Kelly (full-backs), Bill McGarry, Don McEvoy and Len Quested (half-backs). In addition, Vic Metcalfe played in all 42 League matches at outside-left.

FIRST SUBSTITUTE USED IN LEAGUE

Keith Peacock (Charlton), away to Bolton (Div 2) on Aug 21, 1965.

FROM PROMOTION TO CHAMPIONS

Clubs who have become Champions of England a year after winning promotion: **Liverpool** 1905, 1906; **Everton** 1931, 1932; **Tottenham** 1950, 1951; **Ipswich** 1961, 1962; **Nottm Forest** 1977, 1978. The first four were placed top in both seasons: Forest finished third and first.

PREMIER LEAGUE'S FIRST MULTI-NATIONAL LINE-UP

Chelsea made history on December 26, 1999 when starting their Premier League match at Southampton without a single British player in the side.

Fulham's Unique XI: In the Worthington Cup 3rd round at home to Bury on Nov 6, 2002, Fulham fielded 11 players of 11 different nationalities. Ten were full Internationals, with Lee Clark an England U–21 cap.

On Feb 14, 2005 **Arsenal** became the first English club to select an all-foreign match squad when Arsene Wenger named 16 non-British players at home to Crystal Palace (Premier League).

Fifteen nations were represented at Fratton Park on Dec 30, 2009 (Portsmouth 1 Arsenal 4) when, for the first time in Premier League history, not one Englishman started the match. The line-up comprised seven Frenchmen, two Algerians and one from each of 13 other countries.

Players from 22 nationalities (subs included) were involved in the Blackburn–WBA match at Ewood Park on Jan 23, 2011.

PREMIER LEAGUE'S FIRST ALL-ENGLAND LINE-UP

On Feb 27, 1999 **Aston Villa** (at home to Coventry) fielded the first all-English line up seen in the Premier League (starting 11 plus 3 subs).

ENTIRE HOME-GROWN TEAM

Crewe Alexandra's starting 11 in the 2-0 home win against Walsall (Lge 1) on Apr 27, 2013 all graduated from the club's academy.

THREE-NATION CHAMPIONS

David Beckham won a title in four countries: with Manchester Utd six times (1996–97–99–2000–01–03), Real Madrid (2007), LA Galaxy (2011 and Paris St Germain (2013).
Trevor Steven earned eight Championship medals in three countries: two with Everton (1985, 1987); five with Rangers (1990, 1991, 1993, 1994, 1995) and one with Marseille in 1992.

LEEDS NO WIN AWAY

Leeds, in 1992–93, provided the first instance of a club failing to win an away League match as reigning Champions.

PIONEERS IN 1888 AND 1992

Three clubs among the twelve who formed the Football League in 1888 were also founder members of the Premier League: **Aston Villa, Blackburn** and **Everton.**

CHAMPIONS (MODERN) WITH TWO CLUBS – PLAYERS

Francis Lee (Manchester City 1968, Derby 1975); **Ray Kennedy** (Arsenal 1971, Liverpool 1979, 1980, 1982); **Archie Gemmill** (Derby 1972, 1975, Nottm Forest 1978); **John McGovern** (Derby 1972, Nottm Forest 1978) **Larry Lloyd** (Liverpool 1973, Nottm Forest 1978); **Peter Withe** (Nottm Forest 1978, Aston Villa 1981); **John Lukic** (Arsenal 1989, Leeds 1992); **Kevin Richardson** (Everton 1985, Arsenal 1989); **Eric Cantona** (Leeds 1992, Manchester Utd 1993, 1994, 1996, 1997); **David Batty** (Leeds 1992, Blackburn 1995), **Bobby Mimms** (Everton 1987, Blackburn 1995), **Henning Berg** (Blackburn 1995, Manchester Utd 1999, 2000); **Nicolas Anelka** (Arsenal 1998, Chelsea 2010); **Ashley Cole** (Arsenal 2002, 2004, Chelsea 2010); **Gael Clichy** (Arsenal 2004, Manchester City 2012); **Robert Huth** (Chelsea 2005, 2006, Leicester 2016); **Kolo Toure** (Arsenal 2004, Manchester City 2012); **Carlos Tevez** (Manchester Utd 2008, 2009, Manchester City 2012; **James Milner** (Manchester City 2012, 2014, Liverpool 2020); **N'Golo Kante** (Leicester 2016, Chelsea 2017), **Riyad Mahrez** (Leicester 2016, Manchester City 2019, 2021, 2022).

TITLE TURNABOUTS

In Jan 1996, **Newcastle** led the Premier League by 13 points. They finished runners-up to Manchester Utd.
At Christmas 1997, **Arsenal** were 13 points behind leaders Manchester Utd and still 11 points behind at the beginning of Mar 1998. But a run of 10 wins took the title to Highbury.
On Mar 2, 2003, **Arsenal**, with 9 games left, went 8 points clear of Manchester Utd, who had a match in hand. United won the Championship by 5 points.
In Mar 2002, **Wolves** were in second (automatic promotion) place in Nationwide Div 1, 11 points ahead of WBA, who had 2 games in hand. They were overtaken by Albion on the run-in, finished third, then failed in the play-offs. A year later they won promotion to the Premier League via the play-offs.

CLUB CLOSURES

Five clubs have left the Football League in mid-season: **Leeds City** (expelled Oct 1919); **Wigan**

Borough (Oct 1931, debts of £20,000); **Accrington Stanley** (Mar 1962, debts £62,000); **Aldershot** (Mar 1992, debts £1.2m). **Maidstone**, with debts of £650,000, closed Aug 1992, on the eve of the season; **Bury** (expelled Aug 2019, financial mismanagement).

FOUR-DIVISION MEN

In season 1986–87, goalkeeper **Eric Nixon,** became the first player to appear in **all four divisions** of the Football League **in one season**. He served two clubs in Div 1: Manchester City (5 League games) and Southampton (4); in Div 2 Bradford City (3); in Div 3 Carlisle (16); and in Div 4 Wolves (16). Total appearances: 44.

Harvey McCreadie, a teenage forward, played in four divisions over two seasons inside a calendar year – from Accrington (Div 3) to Luton (Div 1) in Jan 1960, to Div 2 with Luton later that season and to Wrexham (Div 4) in Nov.

Tony Cottee played in all four divisions in season 2000–01, for Leicester (Premier League), Norwich (Div 1), Barnet (Div 3, player-manager) and Millwall (Div 2).

FATHERS AND SONS

When player-manager **Ian** (39) and **Gary** (18) **Bowyer** appeared together in the **Hereford** side at Scunthorpe (Div 4, Apr 21, 1990), they provided the first instance of father and son playing in the same team in a Football League match for 39 years. Ian played as substitute, and Gary scored Hereford's injury-time equaliser in a 3-3 draw.

Alec (39) and **David** (17) **Herd** were among previous father-and-son duos in league football – for Stockport, 2-0 winners at Hartlepool (Div 3 North) on May 5, 1951.

When Preston won 2-1 at Bury in Div 3 on Jan 13, 1990, the opposing goalkeepers were brothers: **Alan Kelly** (21) for Preston and **Gary** (23) for Bury. Their father, **Alan** (who kept goal for Preston in the 1964 FA Cup Final and won 47 Rep of Ireland caps) flew from America to watch the sons he taught to keep goal line up on opposite sides.

Other examples: **Bill Dodgin Snr** (manager, Bristol Rov) faced son **Bill Jnr** (manager of Fulham) four times between 1969 and 1971. On Apr 16, 2013 (Lge 1), Oldham, under **Lee Johnson,** won 1-0 at home to Yeovil, managed by his father **Gary.**

George Eastham Snr (manager) and son **George Eastham Jnr** were inside-forward partners for Ards in the Irish League in season 1954–55.

FATHER AND SON REFEREE PLAY-OFF FINALS

Father and son refereed two of the 2009 Play-off Finals. **Clive Oliver**, 46, took charge of Shrewsbury v Gillingham (Lge 2) and **Michael Oliver**, 26, refereed Millwall v Scunthorpe (Lge 1) the following day.

FATHER AND SON BOTH CHAMPIONS

John Aston snr won a Championship medal with Manchester Utd in 1952 and **John Aston jnr** did so with the club in 1967. **Ian Wright** won the Premier League title with Arsenal in 1998 and **Shaun Wright-Phillips** won with Chelsea in 2006.

FATHER AND SON RIVAL MANAGERS

When **Bill Dodgin snr** took Bristol Rov to Fulham for an FA Cup 1st Round tie in Nov 1971, the opposing manager was his son, **Bill jnr**. Rovers won 2-1. Oldham's new manager, **Lee Johnson**, faced his father **Gary's** Yeovil in a Lge 1 match in April, 2013. Oldham won 1-0.

FATHER AND SON ON OPPOSITE SIDES

It happened for the first time in FA Cup history (1st Qual Round on Sep 14, 1996) when 21-year-old **Nick Scaife** (Bishop Auckland) faced his father **Bobby** (41), who played for Pickering. Both were in midfield. Home side Bishops won 3-1.

THREE BROTHERS IN SAME SIDE

Southampton provided the first instance for 65 years of three brothers appearing together in a Div 1 side when **Danny Wallace** (24) and his 19-year-old twin brothers **Rodney** and **Ray** played against Sheffield Wed on Oct 22, 1988. In all, they made 25 appearances together for Southampton until Sep 1989.

A previous instance in Div 1 was provided by the Middlesbrough trio, **William, John** and **George Carr** with 24 League appearances together from Jan 1920 to Oct 1923.

The **Tonner** brothers, **Sam, James** and **Jack**, played together in 13 Second Division matches for Clapton Orient in season 1919–20.

Brothers **David, Donald** and **Robert Jack** played together in Plymouth's League side in 1920.

TWIN TEAM-MATES (see also Wallace twins above)

Twin brothers **David** and **Peter Jackson** played together for three League clubs (Wrexham, Bradford City and Tranmere) from 1954–62. The **Morgan** twins, **Ian** and **Roger**, played regularly in the QPR forward line from 1964–68. WBA's **Adam** and **James Chambers**, 18, were the first twins to represent England (v Cameroon in World Youth Championship, Apr 1999). They first played together in Albion's senior team, aged 19, in the League Cup 2nd. Round against Derby in Sep 2000. Brazilian identical twins **Rafael** and **Fabio Da Silva** (18) made first team debuts at full-back for Manchester Utd in season 2008–09. Swedish twins **Martin** and **Marcus Olsson** played together for Blackburn in season 2011–12. **Josh** and **Jacob Murphy**, 19, played for Norwich in season 2013–2014.

SIR TOM DOES THE HONOURS

Sir Tom Finney, England and Preston legend, opened the Football League's new headquarters on their return to Preston on Feb 23, 1999. Preston had been the League's original base for 70 years before the move to Lytham St Annes in 1959.

SHORTENED MATCHES

The 0-0 score in the **Bradford City v Lincoln** Third Division fixture on May 11, 1985, abandoned through fire after 40 minutes, was subsequently confirmed as a result. It is the shortest officially-completed League match on record, and was the fourth of only five instances in Football League history of the score of an unfinished match being allowed to stand.

The other occasions: **Middlesbrough 4, Oldham 1** (Div 1, Apr 3, 1915), abandoned after 55 minutes when Oldham defender Billy Cook refused to leave the field after being sent off; **Barrow 7, Gillingham 0** (Div 4, Oct 9, 1961), abandoned after 75 minutes because of bad light, the match having started late because of Gillingham's delayed arrival.

A crucial **Manchester** derby (Div 1) was abandoned after 85 minutes, and the result stood, on Apr 27, 1974, when a pitch invasion at Old Trafford followed the only goal, scored for City by Denis Law, which relegated United, Law's former club.

The only instance of a first-class match in England being abandoned **'through shortage of players'** occurred in the First Division at Bramall Lane on Mar 16, 2002. Referee Eddie Wolstenholme halted play after 82 minutes because **Sheffield Utd** were reduced to 6 players against **WBA.** They had had 3 men sent off (goalkeeper and 2 substitutes), and with all 3 substitutes used and 2 players injured, were left with fewer than the required minimum of 7 on the field. Promotion contenders WBA were leading 3-0, and the League ordered the result to stand.

The last 60 seconds of **Birmingham v Stoke** (Div 3, 1-1, on Feb 29, 1992) were played behind locked doors. The ground had been cleared after a pitch invasion.

A First Division fixture, **Sheffield Wed v Aston Villa** (Nov 26, 1898), was abandoned through bad light with Wednesday leading 3-1. The Football League ruled that the match should be completed, and the remaining 10.5 minutes were played four months later (Mar 13, 1899), when Wednesday added another goal to make the result 4-1.

SIX TRANSFER RECORDS

Sheffield Utd broke their transfer record six times during 2019-20, signing Luke Freeman (£5m), Callum Robinson (£8m), Lys Mousset £10m), Oliver McBurnie (£20m), Sander Berge (£22m) and Rhian Brewster (£23.5m)

FA CUP RECORDS
(See also Goalscoring section)

CHIEF WINNERS

14 Arsenal; **12** Manchester Utd; **8** Chelsea, Tottenham, Liverpool; **7** Aston Villa; **6** Blackburn, Manchester City, Newcastle.

Three times in succession: The Wanderers (1876–77–78) and Blackburn (1884–85–86).

Trophy handed back: The FA Cup became the Wanderers' absolute property in 1878, but they handed it back to the Association on condition that it was not to be won outright by any club.

In successive years by professional clubs: Blackburn (1890 and 1891); Newcastle (1951 and 1952); Tottenham (1961 and 1962); Tottenham (1981 and 1982); Arsenal (2002 and 2003); Chelsea (2009 and 2010); Arsenal (2014 and 2015).

Record Final-tie score: Bury 6, Derby 0 (1903); Manchester City 6 Watford 0 (2019)

Most FA Cup Final wins at Wembley: Arsenal 11, Manchester Utd 10, Chelsea 8, Liverpool 6, Tottenham 6, Manchester City 5, Newcastle 5.

SECOND DIVISION WINNERS

Notts Co (1894), **Wolves** (1908), **Barnsley** (1912), **WBA** (1931), **Sunderland** (1973), **Southampton** (1976), **West Ham** (1980). When **Tottenham** won the Cup in 1901 they were a Southern League club.

'OUTSIDE' SEMI-FINALISTS

Twelve clubs have reached the semi-finals of the competition while playing outside the top two divisions – **Millwall** (1900,1903,1937), **Southampton** (1900, 1902,1908), **Tottenham** (1901), **Swindon** (1910, 1912), **Port Vale** (1954), **York** (1955), **Norwich** (1959), **Crystal Palace** (1976), **Plymouth** (1984), **Chesterfield** (1997), **Wycombe** (2001) and **Sheffield United** (2014). **Southampton** twice, and **Tottenham** reached the final.

FOURTH DIVISION QUARTER-FINALISTS

Oxford Utd (1964), **Colchester** (1971), **Bradford City** (1976), **Cambridge Utd** (1990).

FOURTH ROUND – NO REPLAYS

No replays were necessary in the 16 fourth round ties in January 2008 (7 home wins, 9 away). This had not happened for 51 years, since 8 home and 8 away wins in season 1956–57.

FIVE TROPHIES

The trophy which Arsenal won in 2014 was the fifth in FA Cup history. These were its predecessors:

1872–95: First Cup stolen from shop in Birmingham while held by Aston Villa. Never seen again.

1910: Second trophy presented to Lord Kinnaird on completing 21 years as FA president.

1911–91: Third trophy used until replaced ('battered and fragile') after 80 years' service.

1992–2013 Fourth FA Cup lasted 21 years – now retained at FA headquarters at Wembley Stadium.

Traditionally, the Cup stays with the holders until returned to the FA in March.

FINALISTS RELEGATED

Six clubs have reached the FA Cup Final and been relegated. The first five all lost at Wembley

– **Manchester City** 1926, **Leicester** 1969, **Brighton** 1983, **Middlesbrough** 1997 and **Portsmouth** 2010. **Wigan,** Cup winners for the first time in 2013, were relegated from the Premier League three days later.

FA CUP – TOP SHOCKS

1922 (1)	Everton	0	Crystal Palace	6
1933 (3)	Walsall	2	Arsenal	0
1939 (F)	Portsmouth	4	Wolves	1
1948 (3)	Arsenal	0	Bradford PA	1
1948 (3)	Colchester	1	Huddersfield	0
1949 (4)	Yeovil	2	Sunderland	1
1954 (4)	Arsenal	1	Norwich	2
1955 (5)	York	2	Tottenham	1
1957 (4)	Wolves	0	Bournemouth	1
1957 (5)	Bournemouth	3	Tottenham	1
1958 (4)	Newcastle	1	Scunthorpe	3
1959 (3)	Norwich	3	Manchester Utd	0
1959 (3)	Worcester	2	Liverpool	1
1961 (3)	Chelsea	1	Crewe	2
1964 (3)	Newcastle	1	Bedford	2
1965 (4)	Peterborough	2	Arsenal	1
1971 (5)	Colchester	3	Leeds	2
1972 (3)	Hereford	2	Newcastle	1R
1973 (F)	Sunderland	1	Leeds	0
1975 (3)	Burnley	0	Wimbledon	1
1976 (F)	Southampton	1	Manchester Utd	0
1978 (F)	Ipswich	1	Arsenal	0
1980 (3)	Chelsea	0	Wigan	1
1980 (3)	Halifax	1	Manchester City	0
1980 (F)	West Ham	1	Arsenal	0
1981 (4)	Exeter	4	Newcastle	0R
1984 (3)	Bournemouth	2	Manchester Utd	0
1985 (4)	York	1	Arsenal	0
1986 (3)	Birmingham	1	Altrincham	2
1988 (F)	Wimbledon	1	Liverpool	0
1989 (3)	Sutton	2	Coventry	1
1991 (3)	WBA	2	Woking	4
1992 (3)	Wrexham	2	Arsenal	1
1994 (3)	Liverpool	0	Bristol City	1R
1994 (3)	Birmingham	1	Kidderminster	2
1997 (5)	Chesterfield	1	Nottm Forest	0
2001 (4)	Everton	0	Tranmere	3
2003 (3)	Shrewsbury	2	Everton	1
2005 (3)	Oldham	1	Manchester City	0
2008 (6)	Barnsley	1	Chelsea	0
2009 (2)	Histon	1	Leeds	0
2010 (4)	Liverpool	1	Reading	2R
2011 (3)	Stevenage	3	Newcastle	1
2012 (3)	Macclesfield	2	Cardiff	1
2013 (4)	Norwich	0	Luton	1
2013 (4)	Oldham	3	Liverpool	2
2013 (F)	Wigan	1	Manchester City	0
2014 (3)	Rochdale	2	Leeds	0
2015 (4)	Chelsea	2	Bradford City	4

2015 (5)	Bradford City	2	Sunderland	0
2016 (3)	Oxford	3	Swansea	2
2017 (5)	Burnley	0	Lincoln	1
2018 (5)	Wigan	1	Manchester City	0
2019 (3)	Fulham	1	Oldham	2
2019 (3)	Gillingham	1	Cardiff	0
2019 (3)	Newport	2	Leicester	1
2019 (3)	Sheffield Utd	0	Barnet	1
2019 (4)	AFC Wimbledon	4	West Ham	2
2020 (3)	Tranmere	2	Watford	1R
2021 (3)	Crawley	3	Leeds	0

YEOVIL TOP GIANT-KILLERS

Yeovil's victories over Colchester and Blackpool in season 2000–01 gave them a total of 20 FA Cup wins against League opponents. They set another non-League record by reaching the third round 13 times.

This was Yeovil's triumphant (non-League) Cup record against League clubs: 1924–25 Bournemouth 3-2; 1934–35 Crystal Palace 3-0, Exeter 4-1; 1938–39 Brighton 2-1; 1948–49 Bury 3-1, Sunderland 2-1; 1958–59 Southend 1-0; 1960–61 Walsall 1-0; 1963–64 Southend 1-0, Crystal Palace 3-1; 1970–71 Bournemouth 1-0; 1972–73 Brentford 2-1; 1987–88 Cambridge Utd 1-0; 1991–92 Walsall 1-0; 1992–93 Torquay 5-2, Hereford 2-1; 1993–94 Fulham 1-0; 1998–99 Northampton 2-0; 2000–01 Colchester 5-1, Blackpool 1-0.

NON-LEAGUE BEST

Since League football began in 1888, three non-League clubs have reached the FA Cup Final. **Sheffield Wed** (Football Alliance) were runners-up in 1890, as were **Southampton** (Southern League) in 1900 and 1902. **Tottenham** won the Cup as a Southern League team in 1901.

Lincoln won 1-0 at Burnley on Feb 18, 2017, to become the first non-league club to reach the last eight in 103 years. Two non-league sides – **Lincoln** and **Sutton** – had reached the last 16 for the first time.

Otherwise, the furthest progress by non-League clubs has been to the 5th round on 7 occasions: **Colchester** 1948, **Yeovil** 1949, **Blyth** 1978, **Telford** 1985, **Kidderminster** 1994, **Crawley** 2011, **Luton** 2013, **Boreham Wood** (2022).

Greatest number of non-League sides to reach the **3rd round** is **8** in 2009: **Barrow**, **Blyth**, **Eastwood**, **Forest Green**, **Histon**, **Kettering**, **Kidderminster** and **Torquay**.

Most to reach **Round 4: 3** in 1957 (**Rhyl**, **New Brighton**, **Peterborough**) and 1975 (**Leatherhead**, **Stafford** and **Wimbledon**).

Five non-League clubs reaching **round 3** in 2001 was a Conference record. They were **Chester**, **Yeovil**, **Dagenham**, **Morecambe** and **Kingstonian**.

In season 2002–03, **Team Bath** became the first University-based side to reach the FA Cup 1st Round since **Oxford University** (Finalists in 1880).

NON-LEAGUE 'LAST TIMES'

Last time no non-League club reached round 3: 2018. Last time only one did so: 1969 (**Kettering**).

TOP-DIVISION SCALPS

Victories in FA Cup by non-League clubs over top-division teams since 1900 include: 1900–01 (Final, replay): **Tottenham** 3 Sheffield Utd 1 (Tottenham then in Southern League); 1919–20 **Cardiff** 2, Oldham 0; Sheffield Wed 0, **Darlington** 2; 1923–24 **Corinthians** 1, Blackburn 0; 1947–48 **Colchester** 1, Huddersfield 0; 1948–9 **Yeovil** 2, Sunderland 1; 1971–72 **Hereford**

2, Newcastle 1; 1974–75 Burnley 0, **Wimbledon** 1; 1985–86 Birmingham 1, **Altrincham** 2; 1988–89 **Sutton** 2, Coventry 1; 2012–13 Norwich 0, **Luton** 1, 2016–17 Burnley 0 **Lincoln** 1.

MOST WINNING MEDALS

Ashley Cole has won the trophy seven times, with (Arsenal 2002–03–05) and Chelsea (2007–09–10–12). **The Hon Arthur Kinnaird** (The Wanderers and Old Etonians), **Charles Wollaston** (The Wanderers) and **Jimmy Forrest** (Blackburn) each earned five winners' medals. Kinnaird, later president of the FA, played in nine of the first 12 FA Cup Finals, and was on the winning side three times for The Wanderers, in 1873 (captain), 1877, 1878 (captain), and twice as captain of Old Etonians (1879, 1882).

MANAGERS' MEDALS BACKDATED

In 2010, the FA agreed to award Cup Final medals to all living managers who took their teams to the Final before 1996 (when medals were first given to Wembley team bosses). Lawrie McMenemy had campaigned for the award since Southampton's victory in 1976.

MOST WINNERS' MEDALS AT WEMBLEY

4 – Mark Hughes (3 for Manchester Utd, 1 for Chelsea), **Petr Cech, Frank Lampard, John Terry** (4 times winning captin), **Didier Drogba, Ashley Cole** (all Chelsea), **Olivier Giroud** (3 for Arsenal, 1 for Chelsea).

3 – Dick Pym (3 clean sheets in Finals), **Bob Haworth, Jimmy Seddon, Harry Nuttall, Billy Butler** (all Bolton); **David Jack** (2 Bolton, 1 Arsenal); **Bob Cowell, Jack Milburn, Bobby Mitchell** (all Newcastle); **Dave Mackay** (Tottenham); **Frank Stapleton** (1 Arsenal); **Bryan Robson** ((3 times winning captain), **Arthur Albiston, Gary Pallister, Roy Keane, Peter Schmeichel, Ryan Giggs** (all Manchester United); **Bruce Grobbelaar, Steve Nicol, Ian Rush** (all Liverpool); (all Manchester United); **Dennis Wise** (1 Wimbledon, 2 Chelsea); **Nicolas Anelka** (1 Arsenal, 2 Chelsea); **Per Mertesacker** (3 times winning captain), **Mesut Ozil, Aaron Ramsey** (all Arsenal)

Arsenal's **David Seaman** and **Ray Parlour** have each earned 4 winners' medals (2 at Wembley, 2 at Cardiff) as have Manchester Utd's **Roy Keane** and **Ryan Giggs** (3 at Wembley, 1 at Cardiff).

MOST WEMBLEY FINALS

Olivier Giroud appeared in his sixth FA Cup Final when he came off the bench in Chelsea's 1-0 defeat by Leicester in May 2021 – three for Arsenal and three for Chelsea.

MOST WEMBLEY/CARDIFF FINAL APPEARANCES

8 Ashley Cole (Arsenal, Chelsea); **7** Roy Keane (Nottm Forest, Manchester Utd), Ryan Giggs (Manchester Utd); **6** Paul Scholes (Manchester Utd), Olivier Giroud (Arsenal, Chelsea).

BIGGEST FA CUP SCORE AT WEMBLEY

6-0 by Manchester City v Watford (final, May 18, 2019).

WINNING GOALKEEPER-CAPTAINS

1988 **Dave Beasant** (Wimbledon); 2003 **David Seaman** (Arsenal); 2021 **Kasper Schmeichel** (Leicester).

MOST WINNING MANAGERS

7 Arsene Wenger (Arsenal) 1998, 2002, 2003, 2005, 2014, 2015, 2017; **6 George Ramsay** (Aston Villa) 1887, 1895, 1897, 1905, 1913, 1920; **5 Sir Alex Ferguson** (Manchester Utd) 1990, 1994, 1996, 1999, 2004.

PLAYER-MANAGERS IN FINAL

Kenny Dalglish (Liverpool, 1986); **Glenn Hoddle** (Chelsea, 1994); **Dennis Wise** (Millwall, 2004).

DEBUTS IN FINAL

Alan Davies (Manchester Utd v Brighton, 1983); **Chris Baird** (Southampton v Arsenal, 2003); **Curtis Weston** (Millwall sub v Manchester Utd, 2004).

SEMI-FINALS AT WEMBLEY

1991 Tottenham 3 Arsenal 1; **1993** Sheffield Wed 2 Sheffield Utd 1, Arsenal 1 Tottenham 0; **1994** Chelsea 2 Luton 0, Manchester Utd 1 Oldham 1; **2000** Aston Villa beat Bolton 4-1 on pens (after 0-0), Chelsea 2 Newcastle 1; **2008** Portsmouth 1 WBA 0, Cardiff 1 Barnsley 0; **2009** Chelsea 2 Arsenal 1, Everton beat Manchester Utd 4-2 on pens (after 0-0); **2010** Chelsea 3 Aston Villa 0, Portsmouth 2 Tottenham 0; **2011** Manchester City 1 Manchester Utd 0, Stoke 5 Bolton 0; **2012** Liverpool 2 Everton 1, Chelsea 5 Tottenham 1; **2013** Wigan 2 Millwall 0, Manchester City 2 Chelsea 1; **2014** Arsenal beat Wigan 4-2 on pens (after 1-1), Hull 5 Sheffield Utd 3; **2015** Arsenal 2 Reading 1, Aston Villa 2 Liverpool 1; **2016** Manchester Utd 2 Everton 1, Crystal Palace 2 Watford 1; **2017** Arsenal 2 Manchester City 1, Chelsea 4 Tottenham 2; **2018** Chelsea 2 Southampton 0, Manchester Utd 2 Tottenham 1; **2019** Manchester City 1 Brighton 0, Watford 3 Wolves 2; **2020** Arsenal 2 Manchester City 0, Chelsea 3 Manchester Utd 1; **2021** Chelsea 1 Manchester City 0, Leicester 1 Southampton 0; **2022** Liverpool 3 Manchester City 2, Chelsea 2 Crystal Palace 0

CHELSEA'S FA CUP MILESTONES

Their victory over Liverpool in the 2012 Final set the following records:

Captain **John Terry** first player to lift the trophy four times for one club; **Didier Drogba** first to score in four Finals; **Ashley Cole** first to earn seven winner's medals (Arsenal 3, Chelsea 4); **Roberto Di Matteo** first to score for and manage the same winning club (player for Chelsea 1997, 2000, interim manager 2012).

Chelsea's four triumphs in six seasons (2007–12) the best winning sequence since Wanderers won five of the first seven competitions (1872–78) and Blackburn won five out of eight (1884–91).

FIRST ENTRANTS (1871–72)

Barnes, Civil Service, Crystal Palace, Clapham Rov, Donnington School (Spalding), Hampstead Heathens, Harrow Chequers, Hitchin, Maidenhead, Marlow, Queen's Park (Glasgow), Reigate Priory, Royal Engineers, Upton Park and Wanderers. Total 15.

LAST ALL-ENGLISH WINNERS

Manchester City, in 1969, were the last club to win the final with a team of all English players.

FA CUP FIRSTS

Out of country: Cardiff, by defeating Arsenal 1-0 in the 1927 Final at Wembley, became the first and only club to take the FA Cup out of England.

All-English Winning XI: First club to win the FA Cup with all-English XI: Blackburn Olympic in 1883. Others since: WBA in 1888 and 1931, Bolton (1958), Manchester City (1969), West Ham (1964 and 1975).

Non-English Winning XI: Liverpool in 1986 (Mark Lawrenson, born Preston, was a Rep of Ireland player).

Won both Cups: Old Carthusians won the FA Cup in 1881 and the FA Amateur Cup in 1894 and 1897. **Wimbledon** won Amateur Cup in 1963, FA Cup in 1988.

MOST GAMES NEEDED TO WIN

Barnsley played a record 12 matches (20 hours' football) to win the FA Cup in season 1911–12. All six replays (one in round 1, three in round 4 and one in each of semi-final and Final) were brought about by goalless draws.

Arsenal played 11 FA Cup games when winning the trophy in 1979. Five of them were in the 3rd round against Sheffield Wed.

LONGEST TIES

6 matches: (11 hours): Alvechurch v Oxford City (4th qual round, 1971–72). Alvechurch won 1-0.

5 matches: (9 hours, 22 mins – record for competition proper): Stoke v Bury (3rd round, 1954–55). Stoke won 3-2.

5 matches: Chelsea v Burnley (4th round, 1955–56). Chelsea won 2-0.

5 matches: Hull v Darlington (2nd round, 1960–61). Hull won 3-0.

5 matches: Arsenal v Sheffield Wed (3rd round, 1978–79). Arsenal won 2-0.

Other marathons (qualifying comp, all 5 matches, 9 hours): Barrow v Gillingham (last qual round, 1924–25) – winners Barrow; Leyton v Ilford (3rd qual round, 1924–25) – winners Leyton; Falmouth v Bideford (3rd qual round, 1973–74) – winners Bideford.

End of Cup Final replays: The FA decided that, with effect from 1999, there would be no Cup Final replays. In the event of a draw after extra-time, the match would be decided on penalties. This happened for the first time in 2005, when Arsenal beat Manchester Utd 5-4 on penalties after a 0-0 draw. A year later, Liverpool beat West Ham 3-1 on penalties after a 3-3 draw.

FA Cup marathons ended in season 1991–92, when the penalty shoot-out was introduced to decide ties still level after one replay and extra-time.

In 1932–33 **Brighton** (Div 3 South) played 11 FA Cup games, including replays, and scored 43 goals, without getting past round 5. They forgot to claim exemption and had to play from 1st qual round.

LONGEST ROUND

The longest round in FA Cup history was the **3rd round** in **1962–63**. It took 66 days to complete, lasting from Jan 5 to Mar 11, and included 261 postponements because of bad weather.

LONGEST UNBEATEN RUN

23 matches by Blackburn In winning the Cup in three consecutive years (1884–05–06), they won 21 ties (one in a replay), and their first Cup defeat in four seasons was in a first round replay of the next competition.

RE-STAGED TIES

Sixth round, Mar 9, 1974: Newcastle 4, Nottm Forest 3. Match declared void by FA and ordered to be replayed following a pitch invasion after Newcastle had a player sent off. Forest claimed the hold-up caused the game to change its pattern. The tie went to two further matches at Goodison Park (0-0, then 1-0 to Newcastle).

Third round, Jan 5, 1985: Burton 1, Leicester 6 (at Derby). Burton goalkeeper Paul Evans was hit on the head by a missile thrown from the crowd and continued in a daze. The FA ordered the tie to be played again, behind closed doors at Coventry (Leicester won 1-0).

First round replay, Nov 25, 1992: Peterborough 9 (Tony Philliskirk 5), Kingstonian 1. Match expunged from records because, at 3-0 after 57 mins, Kingstonian were reduced to ten men when goalkeeper Adrian Blake was concussed by a 50 pence coin thrown from the crowd. The tie was re-staged on the same ground behind closed doors (Peterborough won 1-0).

Fifth round: Within an hour of holders Arsenal beating Sheffield Utd 2-1 at Highbury on Feb 13, 1999, the FA took the unprecedented step of declaring the match void because an unwritten rule of sportsmanship had been broken. With United's Lee Morris lying injured, their goalkeeper Alan Kelly kicked the ball into touch. Play resumed with Arsenal's Ray Parlour throwing it in the direction of Kelly, but Nwankwo Kanu took possession and centred for Marc Overmars to score the 'winning' goal. After four minutes of protests by manager Steve Bruce and his players, referee Peter Jones confirmed the goal. Both managers absolved Kanu of cheating but Arsenal's Arsene Wenger offered to replay the match. With the FA immediately approving, it was re-staged at Highbury ten days later (ticket prices halved) and Arsenal again won 2-1.

PRIZE FUND

The makeover of the FA Cup competition took off in 2001–02 with the introduction of round-by-round prize-money.

FA CUP FOLLIES

1999–2000 The FA broke with tradition by deciding the 3rd round be moved from its regular Jan date and staged before Christmas. Criticism was strong, gates poor and the 3rd round in 2000–01 reverted to the New Year. By allowing the holders Manchester Utd to withdraw from the 1999–2000 competition in order to play in FIFA's inaugural World Club Championship in Brazil in Jan, the FA were left with an odd number of clubs in the 3rd round. Their solution was a 'lucky losers' draw among clubs knocked out in round 2. Darlington, beaten at Gillingham, won it to re-enter the competition, then lost 2-1 away to Aston Villa.

HAT-TRICKS IN FINAL

There have been three in the history of the competition: **Billy Townley** (Blackburn, 1890), **Jimmy Logan** (Notts Co, 1894) and **Stan Mortensen** (Blackpool, 1953).

MOST APPEARANCES

88 by **Ian Callaghan** (79 for Liverpool, 7 for Swansea City, 2 for Crewe); 87 by **John Barnes** (31 for Watford, 51 for Liverpool, 5 for Newcastle); 86 by **Stanley Matthews** (37 for Stoke, 49 for Blackpool); 84 by **Bobby Charlton** (80 for Manchester Utd, 4 for Preston); 84 by **Pat Jennings** (3 for Watford, 43 for Tottenham, 38 for Arsenal); 84 by **Peter Shilton** for seven clubs (30 for Leicester, 7 for Stoke, 18 for Nottm Forest, 17 for Southampton, 10 for Derby, 1 for Plymouth Argyle, 1 for Leyton Orient); 82 by **David Seaman** (5 for Peterborough, 5 for Birmingham, 17 for QPR, 54 for Arsenal, 1 for Manchester City).

THREE-CLUB FINALISTS

Five players have appeared in the FA Cup Final for three clubs: **Harold Halse** for Manchester Utd (1909), Aston Villa (1913) and Chelsea (1915); **Ernie Taylor** for Newcastle (1951), Blackpool (1953) and Manchester Utd (1958); **John Barnes** for Watford (1984), Liverpool (1988, 1989, 1996) and Newcastle (1998); **Dennis Wise** for Wimbledon (1988), Chelsea (1994, 1997, 2000), Millwall (2004); **David James** for Liverpool (1996), Aston Villa (2000) and Portsmouth (2008, 2010).

CUP MAN WITH TWO CLUBS IN SAME SEASON

Stan Crowther, who played for Aston Villa against Manchester Utd in the 1957 FA Cup Final, appeared for both Villa and United in the 1957–58 competition. United signed him directly after the Munich air crash and, in the circumstances, he was given dispensation to play for them in the Cup, including the Final.

CAPTAIN'S CUP DOUBLE

Martin Buchan is the only player to have captained Scottish and English FA Cup-winning teams – Aberdeen in 1970 and Manchester Utd in 1977.

MEDALS BEFORE AND AFTER

Two players appeared in FA Cup Final teams before and after the Second World War: **Raich Carter** was twice a winner (Sunderland 1937, Derby 1946) and **Willie Fagan** twice on the losing side (Preston 1937, Liverpool 1950).

DELANEY'S COLLECTION

Scotland winger **Jimmy Delaney** uniquely earned Scottish, English, Northern Ireland and Republic of Ireland Cup medals. He was a winner with Celtic (1937), Manchester Utd (1948) and Derry City (1954) and a runner-up with Cork City (1956).

STARS WHO MISSED OUT

Internationals who never won an FA Cup winner's medal include: Tommy Lawton, Tom Finney, Johnny Haynes, Gordon Banks, George Best, Terry Butcher, Peter Shilton, Martin Peters, Nobby Stiles, Alan Ball, Malcolm Macdonald, Alan Shearer, Matthew Le Tissier, Stuart Pearce, Des Walker, Phil Neal, Ledley King.

CUP WINNERS AT NO COST

Not one member of **Bolton**'s 1958 FA Cup-winning team cost the club a transfer fee. Each joined the club for a £10 signing-on fee.

11-NATIONS LINE-UP

Liverpool fielded a team of 11 different nationalities in the FA Cup 3rd round at Yeovil on Jan 4, 2004.

HIGH-SCORING SEMI-FINALS

The **record team score** in FA Cup semi-finals is **6**: 1891–92 WBA 6, Nottm Forest 2; 1907–08 Newcastle 6, Fulham 0; 1933–34 Manchester City 6, Aston Villa 1.

Most goals in semi-finals (aggregate): 17 in 1892 (4 matches) and 1899 (5 matches). In modern times: 15 in 1958 (3 matches, including Manchester Utd 5, Fulham 3 – highest-scoring semi-final since last war); 16 in 1989–90 (Crystal Palace 4, Liverpool 3; Manchester Utd v Oldham 3-3, 2-1. All **16 goals** in those three matches were scored by **different players**.

Stoke's win against Bolton at Wembley in 2011 was the first 5-0 semi-final result since Wolves beat Grimsby at Old Trafford in 1939. In 2014, Hull defeated Sheffield Utd 5-3.

Last hat-trick in an FA Cup semi-final was scored by **Alex Dawson** for Manchester Utd in 5-3 replay win against Fulham at Highbury in 1958.

SEMI-FINAL VENUES

Villa Park has staged more such matches (55 including replays) than any other ground. Next is Wembley (35), the Hillsborough (33)

ONE IN A HUNDRED

The 2008 semi-finals included only one top-division club, Portsmouth, for the first time in 100 years – since Newcastle in 1908.

FOUR SPECIAL AWAYS

The only times that **all four quarter-finals** were won by the away team were in seasons 1986–87 and 2019–20

DRAWS RECORD

In season 1985–86, **seven** of the eight 5th round ties went to replays – a record for that stage of the competition.

SHOCK FOR TOP CLUBS

The fourth round on Jan 24, 2015 produced an astonishing set of home defeats for leading clubs. The top three in the Premier League, Chelsea, Manchester City and Southampton were all knocked out and sixth-place Tottenham also lost at home. Odds against this happening were put at 3825-1.

LUCK OF THE DRAW

In the FA Cup on Jan 11, 1947, eight of **London**'s ten Football League clubs involved in the 3rd round were drawn at home (including Chelsea v Arsenal). Only Crystal Palace played outside the capital (at Newcastle).

In the 3rd round in Jan 1992, Charlton were the only London club drawn at home (against Barnet), but the venue of the Farnborough v West Ham tie was reversed on police instruction. So Upton Park staged Cup ties on successive days, with West Ham at home on the Saturday and Charlton (who shared the ground) on Sunday.

Arsenal were drawn away in every round on the way to reaching the Finals of 1971 and 1972. **Manchester Utd** won the Cup in 1990 without playing once at home.

The 1999 finalists, **Manchester Utd** and **Newcastle**, were both drawn at home every time in Rounds 3–6.

On their way to the semi-finals of both domestic Cup competitions in season 2002–03, **Sheffield Utd** were drawn at home ten times out of ten and won all ten matches – six in the League's Worthington Cup and four in the FA Cup.

On their way to winning the Cup in 2014, **Arsenal** did not play once outside London. Home draws in rounds 3, 4, 5 and 6 were followed by the semi-final at Wembley.

ALL TOP-DIVISION VICTIMS

The only instance of an FA Cup-winning club meeting top-division opponents in every round was provided by Manchester Utd in 1947–48. They beat Aston Villa, Liverpool, Charlton, Preston, then Derby in the semi-final and Blackpool in the Final.

In contrast, these clubs have reached the Final without playing top-division opponents on the way: West Ham (1923), Bolton (1926), Blackpool (1948), Bolton (1953), Millwall (2004).

WON CUP WITHOUT CONCEDING GOAL

1873 **The Wanderers** (1 match; as holders, exempt until Final); 1889 **Preston** (5 matches); 1903 **Bury** (5 matches). In 1966 **Everton** reached Final without conceding a goal (7 matches), then beat Sheffield Wed 3-2 at Wembley.

HOME ADVANTAGE

For the first time in FA Cup history, all eight ties in the 1992–93 5th round were won (no replays) by the **clubs drawn at home**. Only other instance of eight home wins at the last 16 stage was in 1889–90, in what was then the 2nd round.

NORTH-EAST WIPE-OUT

For the first time in 54 years, since the 4th round in Jan, 1957, the North-East's 'big three' were knocked out on the same date, Jan 8, 2011 (3rd round). All lost to lower-division opponents – Newcastle 3-1 at Stevenage, **Sunderland** 2-1 at home to Notts County and **Middlesbrough** 2-1 at Burton.

SEMI-FINAL – DOUBLE DERBIES

There have been three instances of both FA Cup semi-finals in the same year being local derbies: **1950** Liverpool beat Everton 2-0 (Maine Road), Arsenal beat Chelsea 1-0 after 2-2 draw (both at Tottenham); **1993** Arsenal beat Tottenham 1-0 (Wembley), Sheffield Wed beat

Sheffield Utd 2-1 (Wembley); **2012** Liverpool beat Everton 2-1 (Wembley), Chelsea beat Tottenham 5-1 (Wembley).

TOP CLUB DISTINCTION

Since the Football League began in 1888, there has never been an FA Cup Final in which **neither club** represented the top division.

CLUBS THROWN OUT

Bury expelled (Dec 2006) for fielding an ineligible player in 3-1 2nd rd replay win at Chester. **Droylsden** expelled for fielding a suspended player in 2-1 2nd rd replay win at home to Chesterfield (Dec 2008).

SPURS OUT – AND IN

Tottenham were banned, pre-season, from the 1994–95 competition because of financial irregularities, but were re-admitted on appeal and reached the semi-finals.

FATHER & SON FA CUP WINNERS

Peter Boyle (Sheffield Utd 1899, 1902) and **Tommy Boyle** (Sheffield Utd 1925); **Harry Johnson Snr** (Sheffield Utd 1899, 1902) and **Harry Johnson Jnr** (Sheffield Utd 1925); **Jimmy Dunn Snr** (Everton 1933) and **Jimmy Dunn Jnr** (Wolves 1949); **Alec Herd** (Manchester City 1934) and **David Herd** (Manchester Utd 1963); **Frank Lampard Snr** (West Ham 1975, 1980) and **Frank Lampard Jnr** (Chelsea 2007, 2009, 2010, 2012).

BROTHERS IN FA CUP FINAL TEAMS (modern times)

1950 **Denis and Leslie Compton** (Arsenal); 1952 **George and Ted Robledo** (Newcastle); 1967 **Ron and Allan Harris** (Chelsea); 1977 **Jimmy and Brian Greenhoff** (Manchester Utd); 1996 and 1999 **Gary and Phil Neville** (Manchester Utd).

FA CUP SPONSORS

Littlewoods Pools became the first sponsors of the FA Cup in season 1994–95 in a £14m, 4-year deal. French insurance giants **AXA** took over (season 1998–99) in a sponsorship worth £25m over 4 years. German energy company **E.ON** agreed a 4-year deal worth £32m from season 2006–07 and extended it for a year to 2011. American beer company **Budweiser** began a three-year sponsorship worth £24m in season 2011–12. The **Emirates** airline became the first title sponsor (2015-18) in a reported £30m deal with the FA. This sponsorship has been extended to 2024.

FIRST GOALKEEPER-SUBSTITUTE IN FINAL

Paul Jones (Southampton), who replaced injured Antti Niemi against Arsenal in 2003.

LEAGUE CUP RECORDS
(See also Goalscoring section)

Most winning teams: 9 Liverpool; 8 Manchester City; 5 Aston Villa, Chelsea, Manchester United.

Most winning managers: 4 Brian Clough (Nottm Forest), Sir Alex Ferguson (Manchester United), Jose Mourinho (3 Chelsea, 1 Manchester United), Pep Guardiola (Manchester City, record four successive years, 2018–21)

Highest scores: West Ham 10-0 v Bury (2nd round, 2nd leg 1983–84; agg 12-1); Liverpool 10-0 v Fulham (2nd round, 1st leg 1986–87; agg 13-2).

Most League Cup goals (career): 49 Geoff Hurst (43 West Ham, 6 Stoke, 1960–75); 49 Ian Rush (48 Liverpool, 1 Newcastle, 1981–98).
Highest scorer (season): 12 Clive Allen (Tottenham 1986–87 in 9 apps).
Most goals in match: 6 Frank Bunn (Oldham v Scarborough, 3rd round, 1989–90).
Most winners' medals: 6 Fernandinho, Sergio Aguero (both Manchester City)
Most appearances in Final: 6 Kenny Dalglish (Liverpool 1978–87), Ian Rush (Liverpool 1981–95). Emile Heskey (Leicester 1997, 1999, 2000), Liverpool (2001, 2003), Aston Villa (2010), Fernandinho (Manchester City 2014–21).
Biggest Final win: Swansea City 5 Bradford City 0 (2013).
League Cup sponsors: Milk Cup 1981–86, Littlewoods Cup 1987–90, Rumbelows Cup 1991–92, Coca-Cola Cup 1993–98. Worthington Cup 1999–2003, Carling Cup 2003–12; Capital One Cup from season 2012–16; Carabao 2017–22.
Up for the cup, then down: In 2011, Birmingham became only the second club to win a major trophy (the Carling Cup) and be relegated from the top division. It previously happened to Norwich in 1985 when they went down from the old First Division after winning the Milk Cup.
Rush record: Ian Rush was the first to play in 8 winning teams in Cup Finals at Wembley, all with Liverpool (FA Cup 1986–89–92); League Cup 1981–82–83–84–95)
Britain's first under-cover Cup Final: Worthington Cup Final between Blackburn and Tottenham at Cardiff's Millennium Stadium on Sunday, Feb 24, 2002. With rain forecast, the retractable roof was closed on the morning of the match.
Record penalty shoot-out: Liverpool beat Middlesbrough 14-13 (3rd round, Sep 23, 2014) after 2-2. Derby beat Carlisle 14-13 (2nd round, Aug 23, 2016) after 1-1.

DISCIPLINE

SENDINGS-OFF

Season 2003–04 set an **all-time record** of 504 players sent off in English domestic football competitions. There were 58 in the Premier League, 390 Nationwide League, 28 FA Cup (excluding non-League dismissals), 22 League Cup, 2 in Nationwide play-offs, 4 in LDV Vans Trophy.
Most sendings-off in Premier League programme (10 matches): 9 (8 Sat, 1 Sun, Oct 31–Nov 1, 2009).
The 58 Premier League red cards was 13 fewer than the record English **top-division** total of 71 in 2002–03. **Bolton** were the only club in the English divisions without a player sent off in any first-team competition that season.
Worst day for dismissals in English football was Boxing Day, 2007, with **20 red cards** (5 Premier League and 15 Coca-Cola League). Three players, Chelsea's Ashley Cole and Ricardo Carvalho and Aston Villa's Zat Knight were sent off in a 4-4 draw at Stamford Bridge. Luton had three men dismissed in their game at Bristol Rov, but still managed a 1-1 draw.
Previous worst day was Dec 13, 2003, with **19 red cards** (2 Premier League and the 17 Nationwide League).
In the entire first season of post-war League football (1946–47) only 12 players were sent off, followed by 14 in 1949–50, and the total League dismissals for the first nine seasons after the War was 104.
The worst pre-War total was 28 in each of seasons 1921–22 and 1922–23.

ENGLAND SENDINGS-OFF

England had two players sent off in the same match for the first time on Oct 14, 2020 when losing 1-0 to Denmark in the Nations League at Wembley. Harry Maguire was dismissed for two yellow cards and Reece James shown a straight red for confronting Spanish referee Jesus Gil Manzano after the final whistle.

Jun 5, 1968	**Alan Mullery**	v Yugoslavia (Florence, Euro Champ)
Jun 6, 1973	**Alan Ball**	v Poland (Chorzow, World Cup qual)

Jun 12, 1977	**Trevor Cherry**	v Argentina (Buenos Aires, friendly)
Jun 6, 1986	**Ray Wilkins**	v Morocco (Monterrey, World Cup Finals)
Jun 30, 1998	**David Beckham**	v Argentina (St Etienne, World Cup Finals)
Sep 5, 1998	**Paul Ince**	v Sweden (Stockholm, Euro Champ qual)
Jun 5, 1999	**Paul Scholes**	v Sweden (Wembley, Euro Champ qual)
Sep 8, 1999	**David Batty**	v Poland (Warsaw, Euro Champ qual)
Oct 16, 2002	**Alan Smith**	v Macedonia (Southampton, Euro Champ qual)
Oct 8, 2005	**David Beckham**	v Austria (Old Trafford, World Cup qual)
Jul 1, 2006	**Wayne Rooney**	v Portugal (Gelsenkirchen, World Cup Finals)
Oct 10, 2009	**Robert Green**	v Ukraine (Dnipropetrovsk, World Cup qual)
Oct 7, 2011	**Wayne Rooney**	v Montenegro (Podgorica, Euro Champ qual)
Sep 11, 2012	**Steven Gerrard**	v Ukraine (Wembley, World Cup qual)
Jun 4, 2014	**Raheem Sterling**	v Ecuador (Miami, friendly)
Sep 5, 2020	**Kyle Walker** v Iceland (Reykjavik, Nations Lge)
Oct 14, 2020	**Harry Maguire** and **Reece James** v Denmark (Wembley, Nations Lge)
Jun 14,2022	**John Stones**v Hungary (Molineux, Nations League).

Other countries: Most recent sendings-off of players representing other Home Countries:
N Ireland – Jamal Lewis (World Cup qual v Switzerland, Geneva, Oct 9, 2021).
Scotland – John Souttar (Nations Lge v Israel, Haifa, Oct 11, 2018).
Wales – Ethan Ampadu (European Champ v Italy, Rome, Jun 20,2021; Harry Wilson (European Champ v Denmark, Amsterdam, Jun 26,2021)
Rep of Ireland – Jeff Hendrick (Nations Lge v Wales, Cardiff, Nov 15, 2020)
England dismissals at other levels:
U-23: Stan Anderson (v Bulgaria, Sofia, May 19, 1957); **Alan Ball** (v Austria, Vienna, Jun 2, 1965); **Kevin Keegan** (v E Germany, Magdeburg, Jun 1, 1972); **Steve Perryman** (v Portugal, Lisbon, Nov 19, 1974).
U-21: Sammy Lee (v Hungary, Keszthely, Jun 5, 1981); **Mark Hateley** (v Scotland, Hampden Park, Apr 19, 1982); **Paul Elliott** (v Denmark, Maine Road, Manchester, Mar 26, 1986); **Tony Cottee** (v W Germany, Ludenscheid, Sep 8, 1987); **Julian Dicks** (v Mexico, Toulon, France, Jun 12, 1988); **Jason Dodd** (v Mexico, Toulon, May 29, 1991; 3 Mexico players also sent off in that match); **Matthew Jackson** (v France, Toulon, May 28, 1992); **Robbie Fowler** (v Austria, Kafkenberg, Oct 11, 1994); **Alan Thompson** (v Portugal, Oporto, Sep 2, 1995); **Terry Cooke** (v Portugal, Toulon, May 30, 1996); **Ben Thatcher** (v Italy, Rieti, Oct 10, 1997); **John Curtis** (v Greece, Heraklion, Nov 13, 1997); **Jody Morris** (v Luxembourg, Grevenmacher, Oct 13, 1998); **Stephen Wright** (v Germany, Derby, Oct 6, 2000); **Alan Smith** (v Finland, Valkeakoski, Oct 10, 2000); **Luke Young** and **John Terry** (v Greece, Athens, Jun 5, 2001); **Shola Ameobi** (v Portugal, Rio Maior, Mar 28, 2003); **Jermaine Pennant** (v Croatia, Upton Park, Aug 19, 2003); **Glen Johnson** (v Turkey, Istanbul, Oct 10, 2003); **Nigel Reo-Coker** (v Azerbaijan, Baku, Oct 12, 2004); **Glen Johnson** (v Spain, Henares, Nov 16, 2004); **Steven Taylor** (v Germany, Leverkusen, Oct 10, 2006); **Tom Huddlestone** (v Serbia & Montenegro, Nijmegen, Jun 17, 2007); **Tom Huddlestone** (v Wales, Villa Park, Oct 14, 2008); **Michael Mancienne** (v Finland, Halmstad, Jun 15, 2009); **Fraizer Campbell** (v Sweden, Gothenburg, Jun 26, 2009); **Ben Mee** (v Italy, Empoli, Feb 8, 2011); **Danny Rose** (v Serbia, Krusevac, Oct 16, 2012); **Andre Wisdom** (v Finland, Tampere, Sep 9, 2013); **Jack Stephens** (v Bosnia-Herz, Sarajevo, Nov 12, 2015; **Jordon Ibe** (vSwitzerland, Thun, Mar 26, 2016; **Curtis Jones** (v Croatia, Koper, Mar 31, 2021); **U-21 Rhian Brewster** (v Andorra, La Velle, Oct 11, 2021).
England 'B' (1): **Neil Webb** (v Algeria, Algiers, Dec 11, 1990).

MOST DISMISSALS IN INTERNATIONAL MATCHES

19 (10 Chile, 9 Uruguay), Jun 25, 1975; **6** (2 Mexico, 4 Argentina), 1956; **6** (5 Ecuador, 1 Uruguay), Jan 4, 1977 (4 Ecuadorians sent off in 78th min, match abandoned, 1-1); **5** (Holland 3, Brazil 2), Jun 6, 1999 in Goianio, Brazil.

INTERNATIONAL STOPPED THROUGH DEPLETED SIDE

Portugal v Angola (5-1), friendly international in Lisbon on Nov 14, 2001, abandoned (68 mins) because Angola were down to 6 players (4 sent off, 1 carried off, no substitutes left).

MOST 'CARDS' IN WORLD CUP FINALS MATCH

20 in Portugal v Holland quarter-final, Nuremberg, Jun 25, 2006 (9 yellow, 2 red, Portugal; 7 yellow, 2 red, Holland).

FIVE OFF IN ONE MATCH

For the first time since League football began in 1888, five players were sent off in one match (two Chesterfield, three Plymouth) in Div 2 at Saltergate on **Feb 22, 1997**. Four were dismissed (two from each side) in a goalmouth brawl in the last minute. Five were sent off on Dec 2, 1997 (4 Bristol Rov, 1 Wigan) in Div 2 match at Wigan, four in the 45th minute. The third instance occurred at Exeter on **Nov 23, 2002** in Div 3 (three Exeter, two Cambridge United) all in the last minute. On **Mar 27, 2012** (Lge 2) three Bradford players and two from Crawley were shown red cards in the dressing rooms after a brawl at the final whistle at Valley Parade.

Matches with **four** Football League club players being sent off in one match:

Jan 8, 1955: Crewe v Bradford City (Div 3 North), two players from each side.

Dec 13, 1986: Sheffield Utd (1 player) v Portsmouth (3) in Div 2.

Aug 18, 1987: Port Vale v Northampton (Littlewoods Cup 1st Round, 1st Leg), two players from each side.

Dec 12, 1987: Brentford v Mansfield (Div 3), two players from each side.

Sep 6, 1992: First instance in British first-class football of four players from one side being sent off in one match. Hereford's seven survivors, away to Northampton (Div 3), held out for a 1-1 draw.

Mar 1, 1977: Norwich v Huddersfield (Div 1), two from each side.

Oct 4, 1977: Shrewsbury (1 player), Rotherham (3) in Div 3.

Aug 22, 1998: Gillingham v Bristol Rov (Div 2), two from each side, all after injury-time brawl.

Mar 16, 2001: Bristol City v Millwall (Div 2), two from each side.

Aug 17, 2002: Lincoln (1 player), Carlisle (3) in Div 3.

Aug 26, 2002: Wycombe v QPR (Div 2), two from each side.

Nov 1, 2005: Burnley (1 player) v Millwall (3) in Championship.

Nov 24, 2007: Swindon v Bristol Rov (Lge 1), two from each side.

Mar 4, 2008: Hull v Burnley (Champ) two from each side.

Four Stranraer players were sent off away to Airdrie (Scottish Div 1) on Dec 3, 1994, and that Scottish record was equalled when four Hearts men were ordered off away to Rangers (Prem Div) on Sep 14, 1996. Albion had four players sent off (3 in last 8 mins) away to Queen's Park (Scottish Div 3) on Aug 23, 1997.

In the **Island Games** in Guernsey (Jul 2003), five players (all from Rhodes) were sent off against Guernsey for violent conduct and the match was abandoned by referee Wendy Toms.

Most dismissals one team, one match: Five players of America Tres Rios in first ten minutes after disputed goal by opponents Itaperuna in Brazilian cup match in Rio de Janeiro on Nov 23, 1991. Tie then abandoned and awarded to Itaperuna.

Eight dismissals in one match: Four on each side in South American Super Cup quarter-final (Gremio, Brazil v Penarol, Uruguay) in Oct 1993.

Five dismissals in one season – Dave Caldwell (2 with Chesterfield, 3 with Torquay) in 1987–88.

First instance of four dismissals in Scottish match: three Rangers players (all English – Terry Hurlock, Mark Walters, Mark Hateley) and Celtic's Peter Grant in Scottish Cup quarter-final at Parkhead on Mar 17, 1991 (Celtic won 2-0).

Four players (3 Hamilton, 1 Airdrie) were sent off in Scottish Div 1 match on Oct 30, 1993.

Four players (3 Ayr, 1 Stranraer) were sent off in Scottish Div 1 match on Aug 27, 1994.

In Scottish Cup first round replays on Dec 16, 1996, there were two instances of three players of one side sent off: Albion Rov (away to Forfar) and Huntly (away to Clyde).

FASTEST SENDINGS-OFF

World record – 10 sec: Giuseppe Lorenzo (Bologna) for striking opponent in Italian League match v Parma, Dec 9, 1990. Goalkeeper **Preston Edwards** (Ebbsfleet) for bringing down opponent and conceding penalty in Blue Square Premier League South match v Farnborough, Feb 5, 2011.

World record (non-professional) – 3 sec: David Pratt (Chippenham) at Bashley (British Gas Southern Premier League, Dec 27, 2008).

Domestic – 13 sec: Kevin Pressman (Sheffield Wed goalkeeper at Wolves, Div 1, Sunday, Aug 14, 2000); **15 sec: Simon Rea** (Peterborough at Cardiff, Div 2, Nov 2, 2002). **19 sec: Mark Smith** (Crewe goalkeeper at Darlington, Div 3, Mar 12, 1994). **Premier League – 72 sec: Tim Flowers** (Blackburn goalkeeper v Leeds Utd, Feb 1, 1995).

In World Cup – 55 sec: Jose Batista (Uruguay v Scotland at Neza, Mexico, Jun 13, 1986).

In European competition – 90 sec: Sergei Dirkach (Dynamo Moscow v Ghent UEFA Cup 3rd round, 2nd leg, Dec 11, 1991).

Fastest FA Cup dismissal – 52 sec: Ian Culverhouse (Swindon defender, deliberate hand-ball on goal-line, away to Everton, 3rd Round, Sunday Jan 5, 1997).

Fastest League Cup dismissal – 33 sec: Jason Crowe (Arsenal substitute v Birmingham, 3rd Round, Oct 14, 1997). Also fastest sending off on debut.

Fastest Sending-off of substitute – 0 sec: Walter Boyd (Swansea City) for striking opponent before ball in play after he went on (83 mins) at home to Darlington, Div 3, Nov 23, 1999. **15 secs: Keith Gillespie** (Sheffield Utd) for striking an opponent at Reading (Premier League), Jan 20, 2007. **90 sec.**

MOST SENDINGS-OFF IN CAREER

21   **Willie Johnston** , 1964–82 (Rangers 7, WBA 6, Vancouver Whitecaps 4, Hearts 3, Scotland 1)
21   **Roy McDonough**, 1980–95 (13 in Football League – Birmingham, Walsall, Chelsea, Colchester, Southend, Exeter, Cambridge Utd plus 8 non-league)
13   **Steve Walsh** (Wigan, Leicester, Norwich, Coventry)
13   **Martin Keown** (Arsenal, Aston Villa, Everton)
13   **Alan Smith** (Leeds, Manchester Utd, Newcastle, England U–21, England)
12   **Dennis Wise** (Wimbledon, Chelsea, Leicester, Millwall)
12   **Vinnie Jones** (Wimbledon, Leeds, Sheffield Utd, Chelsea, QPR)
12   **Mark Dennis** (Birmingham, Southampton, QPR)
12   **Roy Keane** (Manchester Utd, Rep of Ireland)
10   **Patrick Vieira** (Arsenal)
10   **Paul Scholes** (Manchester Utd, England)

Most Premier League sendings-off: Patrick Vieira 8, Duncan Ferguson 8, Richard Dunne 8, Vinnie Jones 7, Roy Keane 7, Alan Smith 7. Lee Cattermole 7.

● **Carlton Palmer** holds the unique record of having been sent off with each of his five Premier League clubs: Sheffield Wed, Leeds, Southampton, Nottm Forest and Coventry.

FA CUP FINAL SENDINGS-OFF

Kevin Moran (Manchester Utd) v Everton, Wembley, 1985; **Jose Antonio Reyes** (Arsenal) v Manchester Utd, Cardiff, 2005; **Pablo Zabaleta** (Manchester City) v Wigan, Wembley 2013; **Chris Smalling** (Manchester Utd) v Crystal Palace , Wembley, 2016; **Victor Moses** (Chelsea) v Arsenal, Wembley, 2017. **Mateo Kovacic** (Chelsea) v Arsenal, Wembley 2020.

WEMBLEY SENDINGS-OFF

Aug 1948	**Branko Stankovic** (Yugoslavia) v Sweden, Olympic Games
Jul 1966	**Antonio Rattin** (Argentina captain) v England, World cup quarter-final
Aug 1974	**Billy Bremner** (Leeds) and **Kevin Keegan** (Liverpool), Charity Shield
Mar 1977	**Gilbert Dresch** (Luxembourg) v England, World Cup
May 1985	**Kevin Moran** (Manchester Utd) v Everton, FA Cup Final
Apr 1993	**Lee Dixon** (Arsenal) v Tottenham, FA Cup semi-final

May 1993	Peter Swan (Port Vale) v WBA, Div 2 Play-off Final
Mar 1994	Andrei Kanchelskis (Manchester Utd) v Aston Villa, League Cup Final
May 1994	Mike Wallace, Chris Beaumont (Stockport) v Burnley, Div 2 Play-off Final
Jun 1995	Tetsuji Hashiratani (Japan) v England, Umbro Cup
May 1997	Brian Statham (Brentford) v Crewe, Div 2 Play-off Final
Apr 1998	Capucho (Portugal) v England, friendly
Nov 1998	Ray Parlour (Arsenal) and Tony Vareilles (Lens), Champions League
Mar 1999	Justin Edinburgh (Tottenham) v Leicester, League Cup Final
Jun 1999	Paul Scholes (England) v Sweden, European Championship qual
Feb 2000	Clint Hill (Tranmere) v Leicester, League Cup Final
Apr 2000	Mark Delaney (Aston Villa) v Bolton, FA Cup semi-final
May 2000	Kevin Sharp (Wigan) v Gillingham, Div 2 Play-off Final
Aug 2000	Roy Keane (Manchester Utd captain) v Chelsea, Charity Shield
May 2007	Marc Tierney (Shrewsbury) v Bristol Rov, Lge 2 Play-off Final
May 2007	Matt Gill (Exeter) v Morecambe, Conf Play-off Final
May 2009	Jamie Ward (Sheffield Utd) and Lee Hendrie (Sheffield Utd) v Burnley, Champ Play-off Final (Hendrie after final whistle)
May 2009	Phil Bolland (Cambridge Utd) v Torquay, Blue Square Prem Lge Play-off Final
May 2010	Robin Hulbert (Barrow) and David Bridges (Stevenage), FA Trophy Final
Apr 2011	Paul Scholes (Manchester Utd) v Manchester City, FA Cup semi-final
Apr 2011	Toumani Diagouraga (Brentford) v Carlisle, Johnstone's Paint Trophy Final
Sep 2012	Steven Gerrard (England) v Ukraine, World Cup qual
Feb 2013	Matt Duke (Bradford) v Swansea, League Cup Final
May 2013	Pablo Zabaleta (Manchester City) v Wigan, FA Cup Final
Mar 2014	Joe Newell (Peterborough) v Chesterfield, Johnstone's Paint Trophy Final
May 2014	Gary O'Neil (QPR) v Derby, Champ Play-off Final
May 2016	Chris Smalling (Manchester Utd) v Crystal Palace, FA Cup Final
May 2017	Victor Moses (Chelsea) v Arsenal, FA Cup Final
Aug 2017	Pedro (Chelsea) v Arsenal, Community Shield
Sep 2017	Jan Vertonghen (Tottenham) v Borussia Dortmund, Champions League
May 2018	Liam Ridehalgh (Tranmere) v Boreham Wood, National League Play-off Final – after 48 secs
May 2018	Denis Odoi (Fulham) v Aston Villa, Championship Play-off Final
May 2019	Mark O'Brien (Newport) v Tranmere, Lge 2 Play-off Final
Jun 2020	Dean Moxey (Exeter) v Northampton, Lge 2 Play-off Final
Aug 2020	Mateo Kovacic (Chelsea) v Arsenal, FA Cup Final
Oct 2020	Harry Maguire, Reece James (England) v Denmark, Nations Lge
May 2021	Jay Fulton (Swansea) v Brentford, Champ Play-off Final
May 2022	Oli Hawkins (Mansfield) v Port Vale, Lge 2 Play-off Final

WEMBLEY'S SUSPENDED CAPTAINS

Suspension prevented four **club captains** playing at Wembley in modern finals, in successive years. Three were in FA Cup Finals – **Glenn Roeder** (QPR, 1982), **Steve Foster** (Brighton, 1983), **Wilf Rostron** (Watford, 1984). Sunderland's **Shaun Elliott** was banned from the 1985 Milk Cup Final. Roeder was banned from QPR's 1982 Cup Final replay against Tottenham, and Foster was ruled out of the first match in Brighton's 1983 Final against Manchester Utd.

RED CARD FOR KICKING BALL-BOY

Chelsea's **Eden Hazard** was sent off (80 mins) in the League Cup semi-final, second leg at Swansea on Jan 23, 2013 for kicking a 17-year-old ball-boy who refused to hand over the ball that had gone out of play. The FA suspended Hazard for three matches.

BOOKINGS RECORDS

Most players of one Football League club booked in one match is **TEN** – members of the Mansfield team away to Crystal Palace in FA Cup second round, Nov 1962. Most yellow cards for one team in Premier League match – **9** for Tottenham away to Chelsea, May 2, 2016.

Fastest bookings – 3 seconds after kick-off, **Vinnie Jones** (Chelsea, home to Sheffield Utd, FA Cup fifth round, Feb 15, 1992); 5 seconds after kick-off: **Vinnie Jones** (Sheffield Utd, away to Manchester City, Div 1, Jan 19, 1991). He was sent-off (54 mins) for second bookable offence.

FIGHTING TEAM-MATES

Charlton's **Mike Flanagan** and **Derek Hales** were sent off for fighting each other five minutes from end of FA Cup 3rd round tie at home to Southern League Maidstone on Jan 9, 1979.

Bradford City's **Andy Myers** and **Stuart McCall** had a fight during the 1-6 Premier League defeat at Leeds on Sunday, May 13, 2001.

On Sep 28, 1994 the Scottish FA suspended Hearts players **Graeme Hogg** and **Craig Levein** for ten matches for fighting each other in a pre-season 'friendly' v Raith.

Blackburn's England players **Graeme Le Saux** and **David Batty** clashed away to Spartak Moscow (Champions League) on Nov 22, 1995. Neither was sent off.

Newcastle United's England Internationals **Lee Bowyer** and **Kieron Dyer** were sent off for fighting each other at home to Aston Villa (Premier League on Apr 2, 2005).

Arsenal's **Emmanuel Adebayor** and **Nicklas Bendtner** clashed during the 5-1 Carling Cup semi-final 2nd leg defeat at Tottenham on Jan 22, 2008. Neither was sent off; each fined by their club.

Stoke's **Ricardo Fuller** was sent off for slapping his captain, Andy Griffin, at West Ham in the Premier League on Dec 28, 2008.

Preston's **Jermaine Beckford** and **Eoin Doyle** clashed in the Championship game against Sheffield Wednesday on Dec 3, 2016, and were sent off.

St Johnstone's **Richard Foster** and **Danny Swanson** were dismissed for brawling in the Scottish Premier League match with Hamilton on Apr 1, 2017.

FOOTBALL'S FIRST BETTING SCANDAL

A Football League investigation into the First Division match which ended Manchester Utd 2, Liverpool 0 at Old Trafford on Good Friday, Apr 2, 1915 proved that the result had been 'squared' by certain players betting on the outcome. Four members of each team were suspended for life, but some of the bans were lifted when League football resumed in 1919 in recognition of the players' war service.

PLAYERS JAILED

Ten professional footballers found guilty of conspiracy to fraud by 'fixing' matches for betting purposes were given prison sentences at Nottingham Assizes on Jan 26, 1965.

Jimmy Gauld (Mansfield), described as the central figure, was given four years. Among the others sentenced, **Tony Kay** (Sheffield Wed, Everton & England), **Peter Swan** (Sheffield Wed & England) and **David 'Bronco' Layne** (Sheffield Wed) were suspended from football for life by the FA.

DRUGS BANS

Abel Xavier (Middlesbrough) was the first Premier League player found to have taken a performance-enchancing drug. He was banned by UEFA for 18 months in Nov 2005 after testing positive for an anabolic steroid. The ban was reduced to a year in Jul 2006 by the Court of Arbitration for Sport. **Paddy Kenny** (Sheffield Utd goalkeeper) was suspended by an FA commission for 9 months from July, 2009 for failing a drugs test the previous May. Kolo Toure (Manchester City) received a 6-month ban in May 2011 for a doping offence. It was backdated to Mar 2.

LONG SUSPENSIONS

The longest suspension (8 months) in modern times for a player in British football was imposed on two Manchester Utd players. First was **Eric Cantona** following his attack on a spectator as he left the pitch after being sent off at Crystal Palace (Prem League) on Jan 25, 1995. The club immediately suspended him to the end of the season and fined him 2 weeks' wages (est £20,000). Then, on a disrepute charge, the FA fined him £10,000 (Feb 1995) and extended the ban to Sep 30 (which FIFA confirmed as world-wide). A subsequent 2-weeks' jail sentence on Cantona for assault was altered, on appeal, to 120 hours' community service, which took the form of coaching schoolboys in the Manchester area.

On **Dec 19, 2003** an FA Commission, held at Bolton, suspended **Rio Ferdinand** from football for 8 months (plus £50,000 fine) for failing to take a random drug test at the club's training ground on Sep 23. The ban operated from Jan 12, 2004.

Aug 1974: **Kevin Keegan** (Liverpool) and **Billy Bremner** (Leeds) both suspended for 10 matches and fined £500 after being sent off in FA Charity Shield at Wembley.

Jan 1988: **Mark Dennis** (QPR) given 8-match ban after 11th sending-off of his career.

Oct 1988: **Paul Davis** (Arsenal) banned for 9 matches for breaking the jaw of Southampton's Glenn Cockerill.

Oct 1998: **Paolo Di Canio** (Sheff Wed) banned for 11 matches and fined £10,000 for pushing referee Paul Alcock after being sent off at home to Arsenal (Prem), Sep 26.

Mar 2005: **David Prutton** (Southampton) banned for 10 matches (plus 1 for red card) and fined £6,000 by FA for shoving referee Alan Wiley when sent off at home to Arsenal (Prem), Feb 26.

Aug 2006: **Ben Thatcher** (Manchester City) banned for 8 matches for elbowing Pedro Mendes (Portsmouth).

Sep 2008: **Joey Barton** (Newcastle) banned for 12 matches (6 suspended) and fined £25,000 by FA for training ground assault on former Manchester City team-mate Ousmane Dabo.

May 2012: **Joey Barton** (QPR) suspended for 12 matches and fined £75,000 for violent conduct when sent off against Manchester City on final day of Premier League season.

Mar 2014: **Joss Labadie** (Torquay) banned for 10 matches and fined £2,000 for biting Chesterfield's Ollie Banks (Lge 2) on Feb 15, 2014.

Seven-month ban: **Frank Barson**, 37-year-old Watford centre-half, sent off at home to Fulham (Div 3 South) on Sep 29, 1928, was suspended by the FA for the remainder of the season.

Twelve-month ban: Oldham full-back **Billy Cook** was given a 12-month suspension for refusing to leave the field when sent off at Middlesbrough (Div 1), on Apr 3, 1915. The referee abandoned the match with 35 minutes still to play, and the score (4-1 to Middlesbrough) was ordered to stand.

Long Scottish bans: Sep 1954: **Willie Woodburn**, Rangers and Scotland centre-half, suspended for rest of career after fifth sending-off in 6 years.

Billy McLafferty, Stenhousemuir striker, was banned (Apr 14) for 8 and a half months, to Jan 1, 1993, and fined £250 for failing to appear at a disciplinary hearing after being sent off against Arbroath on Feb 1.

Twelve-match ban: On May 12, 1994 Scottish FA suspended Rangers forward **Duncan Ferguson** for 12 matches for violent conduct v Raith on Apr 16. On Oct 11, 1995, Ferguson (then with Everton) sent to jail for 3 months for the assault (served 44 days); Feb 1, 1996 Scottish judge quashed 7 matches that remained of SFA ban on Ferguson.

On Sep 29, 2001 the SFA imposed a **17-match suspension** on Forfar's former Scottish international **Dave Bowman** for persistent foul and abusive language when sent off against Stranraer on Sep 22. As his misconduct continued, he was shown **5 red cards** by the referee.

On Apr 3, 2009, captain **Barry Ferguson** and goalkeeper **Allan McGregor** were banned for life from playing for Scotland for gestures towards photographers while on the bench for a World Cup qualifier against Iceland.

On Dec 20, 2011 Liverpool and Uruguay striker **Luis Suarez** was given an 8-match ban and fined £40,000 by the FA for making 'racially offensive comments' to Patrice Evra of Manchester Utd (Prem Lge, Oct 15).

On Apr 25, 2013 **Luis Suarez** was given a 10-match suspension by the FA for 'violent conduct' – biting Chelsea defender Branislav Ivanovic, Prem Lge, Apr 21. The Liverpool player was also fined £200,000 by Liverpool. His ban covered the last 4 games of that season and the first 6 of 2013–14. On Jun 26, 2014, Suarez, while still a Liverpool player, received the most severe punishment in World Cup history – a four-month ban from 'all football activities' and £66,000 fine from FIFA for biting Giorgio Chiellini during Uruguay's group game against Italy.

On Nov 4, 2016 Rochdale's **Calvin Andrew** was banned by the FA for 12 matches – reduced to 9 on appeal – for elbowing Peter Clarke (Oldham) in the face.

On Apr 16, 2017 **Joey Barton** was banned by the FA for 18 months and fined £30,000 for breaching betting rules. The Burnley player admitted placing 1,260 bets on matches.

TWO-YEAR EUROPEAN BAN OVERTURNED

Manchester City received a two-season European ban and £25m fine in February 2020 after being charged with breaking UEFA's Financial Fair Play rules. The club lodged an appeal with the Court of Arbitration for Sport and the ban was quashed in July 2020. The fine, for not co-operating with UEFA, was reduced to £9m.

TOP FINES

Clubs: £49,000,000 (World record) Manchester City: May 2014 for breaking UEFA Financial Fair Play rules (**£32,600,000** suspended subject to City meeting certain conditions over two seasons). **£42m** settlement Queens Park Rangers: Jul 2018, breaching Financial Fair Play rules; **£7.6m** Bournemouth: May 2016, for breaking Financial Fair Play rules; **£5,500,000** West Ham: Apr 2007, for breaches of regulations involving 'dishonesty and deceit' over Argentine signings Carlos Tevez and Javier Mascherano; **£3.95m**: Watford: Aug 2017, forged banking letter; **£1,500,000** (increased from original £600,000) Tottenham: Dec 1994, financial irregularities; **£875,000** QPR: May 2011 for breaching rules when signing Argentine Alejandro Faurlin; **£500,000** (plus 2-year academy signings ban) Everton: Nov 2018, breaking recruitment rules; **£460,000** plus signings ban in two transfer windows (reduced on appeal to £230,000 and one transfer window) Chelsea: breaching rules relating to under-18 foreign players; **£390,000** FA: Feb 2019, failing to police recruitment of young players; **£375,000** (reduced to £290,000 on appeal) Chelsea: May 2016, players brawl v Tottenham; **£315.000** Manchester City: Aug 2019, breaching rules on signing youth players; **£300,000** (reduced to £75,000 on appeal) Chelsea: Jun 2005, illegal approach to Arsenal's Ashley Cole; **£300,000** (plus 2-year ban on signing academy players, part suspended) Manchester City: May 2017, approaching young players; **£225,000** (reduced to £175,000 on appeal) Tottenham: May 2016, players brawl v Chelsea; **£200,000** Aston Villa: May 2015 for fans' pitch invasion after FA Cup quarter-final v WBA; **£200,000** Leeds: Feb 2019, spying on other clubs' training sessions; **£200,000** (half suspended) Liverpool: Oct 2019, ineligible player, League Cup v MK Dons; **£175,000** Arsenal: Oct 2003, players' brawl v Manchester Utd; **£150,000** Leeds: Mar 2000, players' brawl v Tottenham; **£150,000** Tottenham: Mar 2000, players brawl v Leeds; **£145,000** Hull: Feb 2015, breaching Financial Fair Play rules; **£115,000** West Ham: Aug 2009, crowd misconduct at Carling Cup; v Millwall; **£105,000** Chelsea: Jan 1991, irregular payments; **£100,000** Boston Utd: Jul 2002, contract irregularities; **£100,000** Arsenal and Chelsea: Mar 2007 for mass brawl after Carling Cup Final; **£100,000** (including suspended fine) Blackburn: Aug 2007, poor disciplinary record; **£100,000** Sunderland: May 2014, breaching agents' regulations; **£100,000** Reading: Aug 2015, pitch invasion, FA Cup tie v Bradford (reduced to £40,000 on appeal); **£100,000** Chelsea: Dec 2016, players brawl v Manchester City; **£100,000** (plus 2-year ban on signing academy players, part suspended) Liverpool: Apr 2017, approaching young player; **£100,000** West Ham: Jan 2019, pitch invasions v Burnley; **£100,000** Derby: Jun 2021, prohibitive accounting policies;

£90,000 Brighton: Feb 2015, breaching rules on agents; **£71,000** West Ham: Feb 2015 for playing Diafra Sakho in FA Cup 4th round tie against Bristol City after declaring him unfit for Senegal's Africa Cup of Nations squad; **£65,000** Chelsea: Jan 2016, players brawl v WBA; **£62,000** Macclesfield: Dec 2005, funding of a stand at club's ground; Arsenal, Chelsea, Liverpool, Manchester City, Manchester Utd, Tottenham fined combined **£22m** for signing up to European Super League.

Players: £220,000 (plus 4-match ban) John Terry (Chelsea): Sep 2012, racially abusing Anton Ferdinand (QPR); **£150,000** Roy Keane (Manchester Utd): Oct 2002, disrepute offence over autobiography; **£150,000** plus 4-month ban (increased from £75,000 and two-week ban after appeal by FA) Daniel Sturridge (ex-Liverpool): Mar 2020, breaching betting rules; **£100,000** (reduced to £75,000 on appeal) Ashley Cole (Arsenal): Jun 2005, illegal approach by Chelsea; **£100,000 (plus 5-match ban)** Jonjo Shelvey (Newcastle): Dec 2016, racially abusing Romain Saiss (Wolves); **£100,000 (plus 3-match ban)** Edinson Cavani (Manchester Utd): Dec 2020, offensive social media post; **£70,000** plus world-wide 10-week ban Kieran Trippier (Atletico Madrid and England): Dec 2020, breaching FA betting rules; **£90,000** Ashley Cole (Chelsea): Oct 2012, offensive Tweet against FA; **£80,000 (plus 5-match ban)** Nicolas Anelka (WBA): Feb 2014, celebrating goal at West Ham with racially-offensive 'quenelle' gesture; **£75,000 (plus 12-match ban)** Joey Barton (QPR): May 2012, violent conduct v Manchester City; **£60,000 (plus 3-match ban)** John Obi Mikel (Chelsea): Dec 2012, abusing referee Mark Clattenburg after Prem Lge v Manchester Utd; **£60,000** Dexter Blackstock (Nottm Forest): May 2014, breaching betting rules; **£60,000** (plus 8-match ban) Kiko Casilla (Leeds): Feb 2020, racially abusing Jonathan Leko (Charlton);**£50,000** Cameron Jerome (Stoke): Aug 2013, breaching FA betting rules; **£50,000** Benoit Assou-Ekotto (Tottenham): Sep 2014, publicly backing Nicolas Anelka's controversial 'quenelle' gesture; **£50,000** (plus 1-match ban) Bernardo Silva (Manchester City): Nov 2019, offensive social message to team-mate Benjamin Mendy; **£50,000** (plus 1-match ban) Dele Alli (Tottenham): Jun 2020, offensive social media post; **£45,000** Patrick Vieira (Arsenal): Oct 1999, tunnel incidents v West Ham; **£45,000** Rio Ferdinand (Manchester Utd): Aug 2012, improper comments about Ashley Cole on Twitter; **£40,000** Lauren (Arsenal): Oct 2003, players' fracas v Manchester Utd; **£40,000 (plus 8-match ban)** Luis Suarez (Liverpool): Dec 2011, racially abusing Patrice Evra (Manchester Utd); **£40,000 (plus 3-match ban)** Dani Osvaldo (Southampton): Jan 2014, violent conduct, touchline Newcastle; **£40,000** Bacary Sagna (Manchester City): Jan 2017, questioning integrity of referee Lee Mason; **£40,000 (plus 4-match ban)** Eric Dier (Tottenham): Jul 2020, confronting spectator in the stand.

*In eight seasons with Arsenal (1996–2004) **Patrick Vieira** was fined a total of £122,000 by the FA for disciplinary offences.

Managers: £200,000 (reduced to £75,000 on appeal) Jose Mourinho (Chelsea): Jun 2005, illegal approach to Arsenal's Ashley Cole; **£60,000 (plus 7-match ban)** Alan Pardew (Newcastle): head-butting Hull player David Meyler (also fined £100,000 by club); **£60,000** Rafael Benitez (Newcastle): Oct 2018, talking about match referee ahead of fixture; **£60,000** Rafael Benitez (Newcastle): Oct 2018, talking about match referee ahead of fixture; **£58,000** Jose Mourinho (Manchester Utd): Nov 2016, misconduct involving referees Mark Clattenburg and Anthony Taylor; **£50,000** Jose Mourinho (Chelsea): Oct 2015, accusing referees of bias; **£45,000** Jurgen Klopp (Liverpool): Feb 2019, questioning integrity of referee Kevin Friend; **£40,000 (plus 1 match stadium ban)** Jose Mourinho (Chelsea): Nov 2015, abusive behaviour towards referee Jon Moss v West Ham; **£40,000 (plus 3-match Euro ban)** Arsene Wenger (Arsenal): Jan 2018, abuse towards referee Mike Dean v WBA; **£33,000 (plus 3-match Euro ban)** Arsene Wenger: Mar 2012, criticising referee after Champions League defeat by AC Milan; **£30,000** Sir Alex Ferguson (Manchester Utd): Mar 2011 criticising referee Martin Atkinson v Chelsea; **£30,000 (plus 6-match ban ((plus 6-match ban reduced to 4 on appeal);** Rui Faria (Chelsea assistant): May 2014, confronting match officials v Sunderland.

• Jonathan Barnett, Ashley Cole's agent was fined **£100,000** in Sep 2006 for his role in the 'tapping up' affair involving the player and Chelsea.

- Gillingham and club chairman Paul Scally each fined £75,000 in Jul 2015 for 'racial victimisation' towards player Mark McCammon. Club fine reduced to £50,000 on appeal.
- Leyton Orient owner Francesco Becchetti fined £40,000 and given six-match stadium ban in Jan 2016 for violent conduct towards assistant manager Andy Hessenthaler.

*£68,000 FA: May 2003, pitch invasions and racist chanting by fans during England v Turkey, Sunderland.

£50,000 FA: Dec 2014, for Wigan owner-chairman Dave Whelan, plus six-week ban from all football activity, for remarks about Jewish and Chinese people in newspaper interview.

*£250,000 FA: Dec 2016, for Leeds owner Massimo Cellino, plus 18-month ban, for breaking agent regulations (reduced to £100,000 and one year on appeal). Club fined £250,000 (reduced to £200,000 on appeal). Agent Derek Day fined £75,000 and banned for 18 months (11 months suspended).

MANAGERS

INTERNATIONAL RECORDS
(As at start of season 2021–2022

	P	W	D	L	F	A
Gareth Southgate (England – Sep 2016)	74	46	16	12	158	49
Steve Clarke (Scotland – May 2019)	37	17	9	11	51	45
Ryan Giggs (Wales –Jan 2018-Jun 2022)	24	12	4	8	28	20
Robert Page (Wales – caretaker)	26	10	9	7	31	29
Ian Baraclough (Northern Ireland – Jun 2020)	26	5	8	13	24	32
Stephen Kenny (Republic of Ireland – Apr 2020)	26	6	11	9	28	22

ENGLAND MANAGERS

		P	W	D	L
1946–62	**Walter Winterbottom**	139	78	33	28
1963–74	**Sir Alf Ramsey**	113	69	27	17
1974	**Joe Mercer**, caretaker	7	3	3	1
1974–77	**Don Revie**	29	14	8	7
1977–82	**Ron Greenwood**	55	33	12	10
1982–90	**Bobby Robson**	95	47	30	18
1990–93	**Graham Taylor**	38	18	13	7
1994–96	**Terry Venables**	23	11	11	1
1996–99	**Glenn Hoddle**	28	17	6	5
1999	**Howard Wilkinson**, caretaker	1	0	0	1
1999–2000	**Kevin Keegan**	18	7	7	4
2000	**Howard Wilkinson**, caretaker	1	0	1	0
2000	**Peter Taylor**, caretaker	1	0	0	1
2001–06	**Sven–Goran Eriksson**	67	40	17	10
2006–07	**Steve McClaren**	18	9	4	5
2007–12	**Fabio Capello**	42	28	8	6
2012	**Stuart Pearce**, caretaker	1	0	0	1
2012–16	**Roy Hodgson**	56	33	15	8
2016	**Sam Allardyce**	1	1	0	0

INTERNATIONAL MANAGER CHANGES

England: Walter Winterbottom 1946–62 (initially coach); **Alf Ramsey** (Feb 1963–May 1974); **Joe Mercer** (caretaker May 1974); **Don Revie** (Jul 1974–Jul 1977); **Ron Greenwood** (Aug 1977–Jul 1982); **Bobby Robson** (Jul 1982–Jul 1990); **Graham Taylor** (Jul 1990–Nov 1993); **Terry Venables**, coach (Jan 1994–Jun 1996); **Glenn Hoddle**, coach (Jun 1996–Feb 1999); **Howard Wilkinson** (caretaker Feb 1999); **Kevin Keegan** coach (Feb 1999–

Oct 2000); **Howard Wilkinson** (caretaker Oct 2000); **Peter Taylor** (caretaker Nov 2000); **Sven–Goran Eriksson** (Jan 2001–Aug 2006); **Steve McClaren** (Aug 2006–Nov 2007); **Fabio Capello** (Dec 2007–Feb 2012); **Roy Hodgson** (May 2012– Jun 2016); **Sam Allardyce** (Jul–Sep 2016); **Gareth Southgate** (Sep–Nov 2016 interim, then permanent appointment).

Scotland (modern): Bobby Brown (Feb 1967–Jul 1971); **Tommy Docherty** (Sep 1971–Dec 1972); **Willie Ormond** (Jan 1973–May 1977); **Ally MacLeod** (May 1977–Sep 1978); **Jock Stein** (Oct 1978–Sep 1985); **Alex Ferguson** (caretaker Oct 1985–Jun 1986); **Andy Roxburgh**, coach (Jul 1986–Sep 1993); **Craig Brown** (Sep 1993–Oct 2001); **Berti Vogts** (Feb 2002–Oct 2004); **Walter Smith** (Dec 2004–Jan 2007); **Alex McLeish** (Jan 2007–Nov 2007); **George Burley** (Jan 2008–Nov 2009); **Craig Levein** (Dec 2009–Nov 2012); **Billy Stark** (caretaker Nov–Dec 2012); **Gordon Strachan** (Jan 2013–Oct 2017); **Malky Mackay**, (caretaker Nov 2017); **Alex McLeish** (Feb 2018–Apr 2019); **Steve Clarke** (since May 2019).

Northern Ireland (modern): Peter Doherty (1951–62); **Bertie Peacock** (1962–67); **Billy Bingham** (1967–Aug 1971); **Terry Neill** (Aug 1971–Mar 1975); **Dave Clements** (player-manager Mar 1975–1976); **Danny Blanchflower** (Jun 1976–Nov 1979); **Billy Bingham** (Feb 1980–Nov 1993); **Bryan Hamilton** Feb 1994–Feb 1998); **Lawrie McMenemy** (Feb 1998–Nov 1999); **Sammy McIlroy** (Jan 2000–Oct 2003); **Lawrie Sanchez** (Jan 2004–May 2007); **Nigel Worthington** (May 2007–Oct 2011); **Michael O'Neill** (Oct 2011–Apr 2020); **Ian Baraclough** (since Jun 2020).

Wales (modern): Mike Smith (Jul 1974–Dec 1979); **Mike England** (Mar 1980–Feb 1988); **David Williams** (caretaker Mar 1988); **Terry Yorath** (Apr 1988–Nov 1993); **John Toshack** (Mar 1994, one match); **Mike Smith** (Mar 1994–Jun 1995); **Bobby Gould** (Aug 1995–Jun 1999); **Mark Hughes** (Aug 1999 – Oct 2004); **John Toshack** (Nov 2004–Sep 2010); Brian Flynn (caretaker Sep–Dec 2010); **Gary Speed** (Dec 2010–Nov 2011); **Chris Coleman** (Jan 2012-Nov 2017); **Ryan Giggs** (Jan 2018–Jun 2022).

Republic of Ireland (modern): Liam Tuohy (Sep 1971–Nov 1972); **Johnny Giles** (Oct 1973–Apr 1980, initially player–manager); **Eoin Hand** (Jun 1980–Nov 1985); **Jack Charlton** (Feb 1986–Dec 1995); **Mick McCarthy** (Feb 1996–Oct 2002); **Brian Kerr** (Jan 2003–Oct 2005); **Steve Staunton** (Jan 2006–Oct 2007); **Giovanni Trapattoni** (May 2008–Sep 2013); **Martin O'Neill** (Nov 2013–Nov 2018); **Mick McCarthy** (Nov 2018–Apr 2020); **Stephen Kenny** (since Apr 2020).

WORLD CUP-WINNING MANAGERS

1930 Uruguay (Alberto Suppici); 1934 and 1938 Italy (Vittorio Pozzo); 1950 Uruguay (Juan Lopez Fontana); 1954 West Germany (Sepp Herberger); 1958 Brazil (Vicente Feola); 1962 Brazil (Aymore Moreira); 1966 England (Sir Alf Ramsey); 1970 Brazil (Mario Zagallo); 1974 West Germany (Helmut Schon); 1978 Argentina (Cesar Luis Menotti); 1982 Italy (Enzo Bearzot); 1986 Argentina (Carlos Bilardo); 1990 West Germany (Franz Beckenbauer); 1994 Brazil (Carlos Alberto Parreira); 1998 France (Aimee Etienne Jacquet); 2002 Brazil (Luiz Felipe Scolari); 2006 Italy (Marcello Lippi); 2010 Spain (Vicente Del Bosque); 2014 Germany (Joachim Low); 2018 France (Didier Deschamps).

Each of the 21 winning teams had a manager/coach of that country's nationality.

YOUNGEST LEAGUE MANAGERS

Ivor Broadis, 23, appointed player-manager of Carlisle, Aug 1946; **Chris Brass**, 27, appointed player-manager of York, Jun 2003; **Terry Neill**, 28, appointed player manager of Hull, Jun 1970; **Graham Taylor**, 28, appointed manager of Lincoln, Dec 1972.

LONGEST-SERVING LEAGUE MANAGERS – ONE CLUB

Fred Everiss, secretary–manager of WBA for 46 years (1902–48); **George Ramsay**, secretary–manager of Aston Villa for 42 years (1884–1926); **John Addenbrooke**, Wolves, for 37 years (1885–1922). Since last war: **Sir Alex Ferguson** at Manchester Utd for 27 seasons (1986–2013); **Dario Gradi** at Crewe for 26 years (1983–2007, 2009–11); **Sir Matt Busby**, in charge of Manchester Utd for 25 seasons (1945–69, 1970–71; **Jimmy Seed** at Charlton for 23 years (1933–56); **Arsene Wenger** at Arsenal for 22 years (1996-2018); **Brian Clough** at Nottm Forest for 18 years (1975–93).

LAST ENGLISH MANAGER TO WIN CHAMPIONSHIP

Howard Wilkinson (Leeds), season 1991–92.

MANAGERS WITH MORE THAN 1000 MATCHES

Sir Alex Ferguson, Sir Bobby Robson, Sir Matt Busby, Arsene Wenger, Roy Hodgson, Harry Redknapp, Alec Stock, Brian Clough, Jim Smith, Graham Taylor, Dario Gradi, Tony Pulis, Dave Bassett, Lennie Lawrence, Alan Buckley, Denis Smith, Joe Royle, Ron Atkinson, Brian Horton, Neil Warnock, Len Ashurst, Lawrie McMenemy, Graham Turner, Steve Coppell, John Toshack, Rafael Benitez, Sven-Goran Eriksson, Claudio Ranieri and Carlo Ancelotti, Sam Allardyce, Danny Wilson, Mick McCarthy, Steve Bruce, Jose Mourinho, David Moyes.

SHORT-TERM MANAGERS

Departed

3 days	Bill Lambton (Scunthorpe)	Apr 1959
6 days	Tommy McLean (Raith Rov)	Sep 1996
7 days	Tim Ward (Exeter)	Mar 1953
7 days	Jack Crompton (Luton)	Jul 1962
7 days	Kevin Cullis (Swansea City)	Feb 1996
8 days	Billy McKinlay (Watford)	Oct 2014
10 days	Dave Cowling (Doncaster)	Oct 1997
10 days	Peter Cormack (Cowdenbeath)	Dec 2000
13 days	Johnny Cochrane (Reading)	Apr 1939
13 days	Micky Adams (Swansea City)	Oct 1997
16 days	Jimmy McIlroy (Bolton)	Nov 1970
19 days	Martin Allen (Barnet)	Apr 2011
20 days	Paul Went (Leyton Orient)	Oct 1981
27 days	Malcolm Crosby (Oxford Utd)	Jan 1998
27 days	Oscar Garcia (Watford)	Sep 2014
28 days	Tommy Docherty (QPR)	Dec 1968
28 days	Paul Hart (QPR)	Jan 2010
29 days	Carl Fletcher (Leyton Orient)	Nov 2019
29 days	John McGreal (Swindon)	Jun 2021
31 days	Paul Scholes (Oldham)	Mar 2019
32 days	Steve Coppell (Manchester City)	Nov 1996
32 days	Darko Milanic (Leeds)	Oct 2014
34 days	Niall Quinn (Sunderland)	Aug 2006
36 days	Steve Claridge (Millwall)	Jul 2005
39 days	Paul Gascoigne (Kettering)	Dec 2005
39 days	Kenny Jackett (Rotherham)	Nov 2016
40 days	Alex McLeish (Nottm Forest)	Feb 2013
41 days	Steve Wicks (Lincoln)	Oct 1995
41 days	Les Reed (Charlton)	Dec 2006
43 days	Mauro Milanese (Leyton Orient)	Dec 2014
44 days	Brian Clough (Leeds)	Sep 1974
44 days	Jock Stein (Leeds)	Oct 1978
45 days	Tony Pulis (Sheffield Wed)	Dec 2020
45 days	Paul Murray (Hartlepool)	Dec 2014
48 days	John Toshack (Wales)	Mar 1994
48 days	David Platt (Sampdoria coach)	Feb 1999

49 days	Brian Little (Wolves)	Oct 1986
49 days	Terry Fenwick (Northampton)	Feb 2003
52 days	Alberto Cavasin (Leyton Orient)	Nov 2016
54 days	Craig Levein (Raith Rov)	Oct 1996
54 days	Chris Lucketti (Bury)	Jan 2018
56 days	Martin Ling (Swindon)	Dec 2015
57 days	Henning Berg (Blackburn)	Dec 2012
59 days	Kevin Nugent (Barnet)	Apr 2017
60 days	Michael Jolley (Barrow)	Feb 2021
61 days	Bill McGarry (Wolves)	Nov 1985
63 days	Graham Westley (Stevenage)	Feb 2020

- In May 1984, Crystal Palace named **Dave Bassett** as manager, but he changed his mind four days later, without signing the contract, and returned to Wimbledon.
- In May 2007, **Leroy Rosenior** was reportedly appointed manager of Torquay after relegation and sacked ten minutes later when the club came under new ownership.
- **Brian Laws** lost his job at Scunthorpe on Mar 25, 2004 and was reinstated three weeks later.
- In an angry outburst after a play-off defeat in May 1992, Barnet chairman Stan Flashman sacked manager **Barry Fry** and re-instated him a day later.

EARLY-SEASON MANAGER SACKINGS

2012: Andy Thorn (Coventry) 8 days; John Sheridan (Chesterfield) 10 days; **2011:** Jim Jefferies (Hearts) 9 days; **2010** Kevin Blackwell (Sheffield Utd) 8 days; **2009** Bryan Gunn (Norwich) 6 days; **2007:** Neil McDonald (Carlisle) 2 days; Martin Allen (Leicester) 18 days; **2004:** Paul Sturrock (Southampton) 9 days; **2004:** Sir Bobby Robson (Newcastle) 16 days; **2003:** Glenn Roeder (West Ham) 15 days; **2000:** Alan Buckley (Grimsby) 10 days; **1997:** Kerry Dixon (Doncaster) 12 days; **1996:** Sammy Chung (Doncaster) on morning of season's opening League match; **1996:** Alan Ball (Manchester City) 12 days; **1994:** Kenny Hibbitt (Walsall) and Kenny Swain (Wigan) 20 days; **1993:** Peter Reid (Manchester City) 12 days; **1991:** Don Mackay (Blackburn) 14 days; **1989:** Mick Jones (Peterborough) 12 days; **1980:** Bill McGarry (Newcastle) 13 days; **1979:** Dennis Butler (Port Vale) 12 days; **1977:** George Petchey (Leyton O) 13 days; **1977:** Willie Bell (Birmingham) 16 days; **1971:** Len Richley (Darlington) 12 days.

DOUBLE DISMISSAL

Mark Hughes became the first manager to be sacked by two Premier League clubs in the same calendar year (2018) – Stoke in January and Southampton in December.

FOUR GAMES AND OUT

Frank de Boer was sacked as Crystal Palace manager after his first four Premier League matches at the start of the 2017–18 season – the competition's shortest reign in terms of games.

BRUCE'S FOUR-TIMER

Steve Bruce is the only manager to win four promotions to the Premier League – with Birmingham in 2002 and 2007 and with Hull in 2013 and 2016.

RECORD START FOR MANAGER

Russ Wilcox, appointed by Scunthorpe in Nov 2013, remained unbeaten in his first 28 league matches (14 won, 14 drawn) and took the club to promotion from League Two. It was the most successful start to a managerial career in English football, beating the record of 23 unbeaten games by Preston's William Sudell in 1889.

RECORD TOP DIVISION START

Arsenal were unbeaten in 17 league matches from the start of season 1947-48 under new manager **Tom Whittaker**.

SACKED, REINSTATED, FINISHED

Brian McDermott was sacked as Leeds manager on Jan 31, 2014. The following day, he was reinstated. At the end of the season, with the club under new ownership, he left by 'mutual consent.'

CARETAKER SUPREME

As Chelsea's season collapsed, Andre Villas-Boas was sacked in March 2012 after eight months as manager, 2012. Roberto Di Matteo was appointed caretaker and by the season's end his team had won the FA Cup and the Champions League.

MANAGER DOUBLES

Four managers have won the League Championship with different clubs: **Tom Watson**, secretary–manager with Sunderland (1892–93–95) and **Liverpool** (1901); **Herbert Chapman** with Huddersfield (1923–24, 1924–25) and Arsenal (1930–31, 1932–33); **Brian Clough** with Derby (1971–72) and Nottm Forest (1977–78); **Kenny Dalglish** with Liverpool (1985–86, 1987–88, 1989–90) and Blackburn (1994–95).

Managers to win the FA Cup with different clubs: **Billy Walker** (Sheffield Wed 1935, Nottm Forest 1959); **Herbert Chapman** (Huddersfield 1922, Arsenal 1930).

Kenny Dalglish (Liverpool) and **George Graham** (Arsenal) completed the Championship/FA Cup double as both player and manager with a single club. **Joe Mercer** won the title as a player with Everton, the title twice and FA Cup as a player with Arsenal and both competitions as manager of Manchester City.

CHAIRMAN–MANAGER

On Dec 20, 1988, after two years on the board, Dundee Utd manager **Jim McLean** was elected chairman, too. McLean, Scotland's longest-serving manager (appointed on Nov 24, 1971), resigned at end of season 1992–93 (remained chairman).

Ron Noades was chairman-manager of Brentford from Jul 1998–Mar 2001. **John Reames** did both jobs at Lincoln from Nov 1998–Apr 2000)

Niall Quinn did both jobs for five weeks in 2006 before appointing Roy Keane as manager of Sunderland.

TOP DIVISION PLAYER–MANAGERS

Les Allen (QPR 1968–69); **Johnny Giles** (WBA 1976–77); **Howard Kendall** (Everton 1981–82); **Kenny Dalglish** (Liverpool, 1985–90); **Trevor Francis** (QPR, 1988–89); **Terry Butcher** (Coventry, 1990–91); **Peter Reid** (Manchester City, 1990–93); **Trevor Francis** (Sheffield Wed, 1991–94); **Glenn Hoddle**, (Chelsea, 1993–95); **Bryan Robson** (Middlesbrough, 1994–97); **Ray Wilkins** (QPR, 1994–96); **Ruud Gullit** (Chelsea, 1996–98); **Gianluca Vialli** (Chelsea, 1998–2000).

FIRST FOREIGN MANAGER IN ENGLISH LEAGUE

Uruguayan **Danny Bergara** (Rochdale 1988–89).

COACHING KINGS OF EUROPE

Five coaches have won the European Cup/Champions League with two different clubs: · **Ernst Happel** with Feyenoord (1970) and Hamburg (1983); **Ottmar Hitzfeld** with Borussia Dortmund (1997) and Bayern Munich (2001); **Jose Mourinho** with Porto (2004) and Inter Milan (2010); **Jupp Heynckes** with Real Madrid (1998) and Bayern Munich (2013); **Carlo Ancelotti** with AC Milan (2003, 2007) and Real Madrid (2014).

FOREIGN TRIUMPH

Former Dutch star **Ruud Gullit** became the first foreign manager to win a major English competition when Chelsea took the FA Cup in 1997.

Arsene Wenger and **Gerard Houllier** became the first foreign managers to receive recognition when they were awarded honorary OBEs in the Queen's Birthday Honours in Jun 2003 'for their contribution to English football and Franco–British relations'.

MANAGERS OF POST-WAR CHAMPIONS (*Double winners)

1947 George Kay (Liverpool); **1948** Tom Whittaker (Arsenal); **1949** Bob Jackson (Portsmouth).

1950 Bob Jackson (Portsmouth); **1951** Arthur Rowe (Tottenham); **1952** Matt Busby (Manchester Utd); **1953** Tom Whittaker (Arsenal); **1954** Stan Cullis (Wolves); **1955** Ted Drake (Chelsea); **1956** Matt Busby (Manchester Utd); **1957** Matt Busby (Manchester Utd); **1958** Stan Cullis (Wolves); **1959** Stan Cullis (Wolves).

1960 Harry Potts (Burnley); **1961** *Bill Nicholson (Tottenham); **1962** Alf Ramsey (Ipswich); **1963** Harry Catterick (Everton); **1964** Bill Shankly (Liverpool); **1965** Matt Busby (Manchester Utd); **1966** Bill Shankly (Liverpool); **1967** Matt Busby (Manchester Utd); **1968** Joe Mercer (Manchester City); **1969** Don Revie (Leeds).

1970 Harry Catterick (Everton); **1971** *Bertie Mee (Arsenal); **1972** Brian Clough (Derby); **1973** Bill Shankly (Liverpool); **1974** Don Revie (Leeds); **1975** Dave Mackay (Derby); **1976** Bob Paisley (Liverpool); **1977** Bob Paisley (Liverpool); **1978** Brian Clough (Nottm Forest); **1979** Bob Paisley (Liverpool).

1980 Bob Paisley (Liverpool); **1981** Ron Saunders (Aston Villa); **1982** Bob Paisley (Liverpool); **1983** Bob Paisley (Liverpool); **1984** Joe Fagan (Liverpool); **1985** Howard Kendall (Everton); **1986** *Kenny Dalglish (Liverpool – player/manager); **1987** Howard Kendall (Everton); **1988** Kenny Dalglish (Liverpool – player/manager); **1989** George Graham (Arsenal).

1990 Kenny Dalglish (Liverpool); **1991** George Graham (Arsenal); **1992** Howard Wilkinson (Leeds); **1993** Alex Ferguson (Manchester Utd); **1994** *Alex Ferguson (Manchester Utd); **1995** Kenny Dalglish (Blackburn); **1996** *Alex Ferguson (Manchester Utd); **1997** Alex Ferguson (Manchester Utd); **1998** *Arsene Wenger (Arsenal); **1999** *Alex Ferguson (Manchester Utd).

2000 Sir Alex Ferguson (Manchester Utd); **2001** Sir Alex Ferguson (Manchester Utd); **2002** *Arsene Wenger (Arsenal); **2003** Sir Alex Ferguson (Manchester Utd); **2004** Arsene Wenger (Arsenal); **2005** Jose Mourinho (Chelsea); **2006** Jose Mourinho (Chelsea); **2007** Sir Alex Ferguson (Manchester Utd); **2008** Sir Alex Ferguson (Manchester Utd); **2009** Sir Alex Ferguson (Manchester Utd); **2010** *Carlo Ancelotti (Chelsea); **2011** Sir Alex Ferguson (Manchester Utd); **2012** Roberto Mancini (Manchester City); **2013** Sir Alex Ferguson (Manchester Utd); **2014** Manuel Pellegrini (Manchester City); **2015** Jose Mourinho (Chelsea) **2016** Claudio Ranieri (Leicester); **2017** Antonio Conte (Chelsea); **2018** Pep Guardiola (Manchester City); **2019** Pep Guardiola (Manchester City); **2020** Jurgen Klopp (Liverpool); **2021** Pep Guardiola (Manchester City; **2022** Pep Guardiola (Manchester City)

WORLD NO 1 MANAGER

When **Sir Alex Ferguson**, 71, retired in May 2013, he ended the most successful managerial career in the game's history. He took Manchester United to a total of 38 prizes – 13 Premier League titles, 5 FA Cup triumphs, 4 League Cups, 10 Charity/Community Shields (1 shared), 2 Champions League wins, 1 Cup-Winners' Cup, 1 FIFA Club World Cup, 1 Inter-Continental Cup and 1 UEFA Super Cup. Having played centre-forward for Rangers, the Glaswegian managed 3 Scottish clubs, East Stirling, St Mirren and then Aberdeen, where he broke the Celtic/Rangers duopoly with 9 successes: 3 League Championships, 4 Scottish Cups, 1 League Cup and 1 UEFA Cup. Appointed at Old Trafford in November 1986, when replacing Ron Atkinson, he did not win a prize there until his fourth season (FA Cup 1990), but thereafter the club's trophy cabinet glittered with silverware. His total of 1,500 matches in charge ended with a 5-5 draw away to West Bromwich Albion. The longest-serving manager in the club's history, he constructed 4 triumphant teams. Sir Alex was knighted in 1999 and in 2012 he received the FIFA award for services to football. On retirement from management, he became a director and club ambassador. United maintained the dynasty of long-serving Scottish managers (Sir Matt Busby for 24 seasons) by appointing David Moyes, who had been in charge at Everton for 11 years.

WENGER'S LEGACY

Arsene Wenger was a virtually unknown French manager when taking over Arsenal in 1996. He left 22 years later as the most successful in the club's history. Wenger led them to three Premier League titles, including the unbeaten season in 2003-04 achieved by the team known as the 'Invincibles.' There were seven FA Cup successes, one in 2002 when Arsenal completed the Double. He was also closely involved in planning the move from Highbury to the Emirates Stadium in 2006.

THE PROMOTION MAN

Neil Warnock set a record of eight promotions when he took Cardiff back to the Premier League in 2018. In 38 years as a manager, he was also successful with Scarborough, Notts County twice, Plymouth, Huddersfield, Sheffield United and Queens Park Rangers. Warnock's achievements were marked by a special award from the League Managers' Association.

MANAGERS' EURO TREBLES

Two managers have won the European Cup/Champions League three times. **Bob Paisley** did it with Liverpool (1977,78, 81).
Carlo Ancelotti's successes were with AC Milan in 2003 and 2007 and with Real Madrid in 2014.

WINNER MOURINHO

In winning the Premier League and League Cup in 2015, Jose Mourinho embellished his reputation as Chelsea's most successful manager. Those achievements took his total of honours in two spells at the club to 8: 3 Premier League, 3 League Cup, 1 FA Cup, 1 Community Shield. Joining from Portuguese champions Porto, Mourinho was initially with Chelsea from June 2004 to September 2007. He then successfully coached Inter Milan and Real Madrid before returning to Stamford Bridge in June 2013. His Premier League triumph in 2015 was his eighth title In 11 years in four countries (England 3, Portugal 2, Italy 2, Spain 1). In his first season with Manchester Utd (2016–17), he won three trophies – League Cup, Europa League and Community Shield.

WENGER'S CUP AGAIN

Arsenal's win against Aston Villa in the 2015 Final was a record 12th success for them in the FA Cup and a sixth triumph in the competition for manager Arsene Wenger, equalling the record of George Ramsay for Villa (1887-1920). With his sixth victory in seven Finals, Wenger made history as the first manager to win the Cup in successive seasons twice (previously in 2002 and 2003). He won it for a record seventh time – in eight finals – in 2017.

FATHER AND SON MANAGERS WITH SAME CLUB

Fulham: Bill Dodgin Snr 1949–53; Bill Dodgin Jnr 1968–72. **Brentford:** Bill Dodgin Snr 1953–57; Bill Dodgin Jnr 1976–80. **Bournemouth:** John Bond 1970–73; Kevin Bond 2006–08. **Derby:** Brian Clough 1967–73; Nigel Clough 2009–2013. **Bristol City:** Gary Johnson 2005–10; Lee Johnson 2016-present.

SIR BOBBY'S HAT-TRICK

Sir Bobby Robson, born and brought up in County Durham, achieved a unique hat-trick when he received the Freedom of Durham in Dec 2008. He had already been awarded the Freedom of

Ipswich and Newcastle. He died in July 2009 and had an express loco named after him on the East Coast to London line.

MANAGERS WITH MOST FA CUP SUCCESSES
7 Arsene Wenger (Arsenal); **6 George Ramsay** (Aston Villa); **5 Sir Alex Ferguson** (Manchester Utd); **3 Charles Foweraker** (Bolton), **John Nicholson** (Sheffield Utd), **Bill Nicholson** (Tottenham).

RELEGATION 'DOUBLES'
Managers associated with two clubs relegated in same season: **John Bond** in 1985–86 (Swansea City and Birmingham); **Ron Saunders** in 1985–86 (WBA – and their reserve team – and Birmingham); **Bob Stokoe** in 1986–87 (Carlisle and Sunderland); **Billy McNeill** in 1986–87 (Manchester City and Aston Villa); **Dave Bassett** in 1987–88 (Watford and Sheffield Utd); **Mick Mills** in 1989–90 (Stoke and Colchester); **Gary Johnson** in 2014-15 (Yeovil and Cheltenham)

THREE FA CUP DEFEATS IN ONE SEASON
Manager **Michael Appleton** suffered three FA Cup defeats in season 2012-13, with Portsmouth (v Notts Co, 1st rd); Blackpool (v Fulham, 3rd rd); Blackburn (v Millwall, 6th rd).

WEMBLEY STADIUM

NEW WEMBLEY
A new era for English football began in March 2007 with the completion of the new national stadium. The 90,000-seater arena was hailed as one of the world's finest – but came at a price. Costs soared, the project fell well behind schedule and disputes involving the FA, builders Multiplex and the Government were rife. The old stadium, opened in 1923, cost £750,000. The new one, originally priced at £326m in 2000, ended up at around £800m. The first international after completion was an Under-21 match between England and Italy. The FA Cup Final returned to its spiritual home after being staged at the Millennium Stadium in Cardiff for six seasons. Then, England's senior team were back for a friendly against Brazil.

DROGBA'S WEMBLEY RECORD
Didier Drogba's FA Cup goal for Chelsea against Liverpool in May 2012 meant that he had scored in all his 8 competitive appearances for the club at Wembley. (7 wins, 1 defeat). They came in: 2007 FA Cup Final (1-0 v Manchester Utd); 2008 League Cup Final (1-2 v Tottenham); 2009 FA Cup semi-final (2-1 v Arsenal); 2009 FA Cup Final (2-1 v Everton); 2010 FA Cup semi-final (3-0 v Aston Villa); 2010 FA Cup Final (1-0 v Portsmouth); 2012 FA Cup semi-final (5-1 v Tottenham); 2012 FA Cup Final (2-1 v Liverpool).

INVASION DAY
Memorable scenes were witnessed at the first **FA Cup Final at Wembley**, Apr 28, 1923, between **Bolton** and **West Ham**. An accurate return of the attendance could not be made owing to thousands breaking in, but there were probably more than 200,000 spectators present. The match was delayed for 40 minutes by the crowd invading the pitch. Official attendance was 126,047. Gate receipts totalled £27,776. The two clubs and the FA each received £6,365 and the FA refunded £2,797 to ticket-holders who were unable to get to their seats. Cup Final admission has since been by ticket only.

REDUCED CAPACITY
Capacity of the all-seated Wembley Stadium was 78,000. The last 100,000 attendance was

for the 1985 FA Cup Final between Manchester Utd and Everton. Crowd record for New Wembley: 89,874 for 2008 FA Cup Final (Portsmouth v Cardiff).

WEMBLEY'S FIRST UNDER LIGHTS

Nov 30, 1955 (England 4, Spain 1), when the floodlights were switched on after 73 minutes (afternoon match played in damp, foggy conditions).
First Wembley international played throughout under lights: England 8, N Ireland 3 on evening of Nov 20, 1963 (att: 55,000).

MOST WEMBLEY APPEARANCES

59 by **Tony Adams** (35 England, 24 Arsenal); 57 by **Peter Shilton** (52 England, 3 Nottm Forest, 1 Leicester, 1 Football League X1).

WEMBLEY HAT-TRICKS

Three players have scored hat-tricks in major finals at Wembley: **Stan Mortensen** for Blackpool v Bolton (FA Cup Final, 1953), **Geoff Hurst** for England v West Germany (World Cup Final, 1966) and **David Speedie** for Chelsea v Manchester City (Full Members Cup, 1985).

ENGLAND'S WEMBLEY DEFEATS

England have lost 27 matches to foreign opponents at Wembley:

Nov 1953	3-6 v Hungary	**Jun 1995**	1-3 v Brazil
Oct 1959	2-3 v Sweden	**Feb 1997**	0-1 v Italy
Oct 1965	2-3 v Austria	**Feb 1998**	0-2 v Chile
Apr 1972	1-3 v W Germany	**Feb 1999**	0-2 v France
Nov 1973	0-1 v Italy	**Oct 2000**	0-1 v Germany
Feb 1977	0-2 v Holland	**Aug 2007**	1-2 v Germany
Mar 1981	1-2 v Spain	**Nov 2007**	2-3 v Croatia
May 1981	0-1 v Brazil	**Nov 2010**	1-2 v France
Oct 1982	1-2 v W Germany	**Feb 2012**	2-3 v Holland
Sep 1983	0-1 v Denmark	**Nov 2013**	0-2 v Chile
Jun 1984	0-2 v Russia	**Nov 2013**	0-1 v Germany
May 1990	1-2 v Uruguay	**Mar 2016**	1-2 v Holland
Sep 1991	0-1 v Germany	**Sep 2018**	1-2 v Spain
		Oct 2020	0-1 v Denmark

England have lost two European Championship ties on penalties at Wembley – the Euro 1996 semi-final against Germany and the Euro 2020 Final against Italy.

FASTEST GOALS AT WEMBLEY

In first-class matches: **25 sec** by **Louis Saha** for Everton in 2009 FA Cup Final against Chelsea; **38 sec** by **Bryan Robson** for England's against Yugoslavia in 1989; **42 sec** by **Roberto Di Matteo** for Chelsea in 1997 FA Cup Final v Middlesbrough; **44 sec** by **Bryan Robson** for England v Northern Ireland in 1982.
Fastest goal in **any** match at Wembley: **20 sec** by **Maurice Cox** for Cambridge University against Oxford in 1979.

FOUR WEMBLEY HEADERS

When **Wimbledon** beat Sutton 4-2 in the FA Amateur Cup Final at Wembley on May 4, 1963, Irish centre-forward **Eddie Reynolds** headed all four goals.

WEMBLEY ONE-SEASON DOUBLES

In 1989, **Nottm Forest** became the first club to win two Wembley Finals in the same season (Littlewoods Cup and Simod Cup).

In 1993, **Arsenal** made history there as the first club to win the League (Coca-Cola) Cup and the FA Cup in the same season. They beat Sheffield Wed 2-1 in both finals.

In 2012, **York** won twice at Wembley in nine days at the end of the season, beating Newport 2-0 in the FA Trophy Final and Luton 2-1 in the Conference Play-off Final to return to the Football League.

SUDDEN-DEATH DECIDERS

First Wembley Final decided on sudden death (first goal scored in overtime): Apr 23, 1995 – **Birmingham** beat Carlisle (1-0, Paul Tait 103 mins) to win Auto Windscreens Shield.

First instance of a golden goal deciding a major international tournament was at Wembley on Jun 30, 1996, when **Germany** beat the Czech Republic 2-1 in the European Championship Final with Oliver Bierhoff's goal in the 95th minute.

WEMBLEY'S MOST ONE-SIDED FINAL (in major domestic cups)

Manchester City 6 **Watford** 0 (FA Cup, May 18,2019).

FOOTBALL TRAGEDIES

DAYS OF TRAGEDY – CLUBS

Season 1988–89 brought the worst disaster in the history of British sport, with the death of 96 Liverpool supporters (200 injured) at the **FA Cup semi-final** against Nottm Forest at **Hillsborough, Sheffield**, on Saturday, Apr 15. The tragedy built up in the minutes preceding kick-off, when thousands surged into the ground at the Leppings Lane end. Many were crushed in the tunnel between entrance and terracing, but most of the victims were trapped inside the perimeter fencing behind the goal. The match was abandoned without score after six minutes' play. The dead included seven women and girls, two teenage sisters and two teenage brothers. The youngest victim was a boy of ten, the oldest 67-year-old Gerard Baron, whose brother Kevin played for Liverpool in the 1950 Cup Final. (*Total became 96 in Mar 1993, when Tony Bland died after being in a coma for nearly four years). A two-year inquest at Warrington ended on April 26, 2016 with the verdict that the 96 were 'unlawfully killed.' It cleared Liverpool fans of any blame and ruled that South Yorkshire Police and South Yorkshire Ambulance Service 'caused or contributed' to the loss of life.

The two worst disasters in one season in British soccer history occurred at the end of 1984–85. On May 11, the last Saturday of the League season, 56 people (two of them visiting supporters) were burned to death – and more than 200 taken to hospital – when fire destroyed the main stand at the **Bradford City–Lincoln** match at Valley Parade.

The seventh, 77-year-old stand was full for City's last fixture before which, amid scenes of celebration, the club had been presented with the Third Division Championship trophy. The fire broke out just before half-time and, within five minutes, the entire stand was engulfed.

Heysel Tragedy

Eighteen days later, on May 29, at the European Cup Final between **Liverpool** and **Juventus** at the Heysel Stadium, Brussels, 39 spectators (31 of them Italian) were crushed or trampled to death and 437 injured. The disaster occurred an hour before the scheduled kick-off when Liverpool supporters charged a Juventus section of the crowd at one end of the stadium, and a retaining wall collapsed. The sequel was a 5-year ban by UEFA on English clubs generally in European competition, with a 6-year ban on Liverpool.

On May 26 1985 ten people were trampled to death and 29 seriously injured in a crowd panic on the way into the **Olympic Stadium, Mexico City** for the Mexican Cup Final between local clubs National University and America.

More than 100 people died and 300 were injured in a football disaster at **Nepal's national stadium** in Katmandu in Mar 1988. There was a stampede when a violent hailstorm broke over the capital. Spectators rushed for cover, but the stadium exits were locked, and hundreds were trampled in the crush.

In South Africa, on Jan 13 1991 40 black fans were trampled to death (50 injured) as they tried to escape from fighting that broke out at a match in the gold-mining town of Orkney, 80 miles from Johannesburg. The friendly, between top teams **Kaiser Chiefs** and **Orlando Pirates**, attracted a packed crowd of 20,000. Violence erupted after the referee allowed Kaiser Chiefs a disputed second-half goal to lead 1-0.

Disaster struck at the French Cup semi-final (May 5, 1992), with the death of 15 spectators and 1,300 injured when a temporary metal stand collapsed in the Corsican town of Bastia. The tie between Second Division **Bastia** and French Champions **Marseille** was cancelled. Monaco, who won the other semi-final, were allowed to compete in the next season's Cup-Winners' Cup.

A total of 318 died and 500 were seriously injured when the crowd rioted over a disallowed goal at the National Stadium in Lima, Peru, on May 24, 1964. **Peru** and **Argentina** were competing to play in the Olympic Games in Tokyo.

That remained **sport's heaviest death** toll until Oct 20, 1982, when (it was revealed only in Jul 1989) 340 Soviet fans were killed in Moscow's Lenin Stadium at the UEFA Cup second round first leg match between **Moscow Spartak** and **Haarlem** (Holland). They were crushed on an open stairway when a last-minute Spartak goal sent departing spectators surging back into the ground.

Among other crowd disasters abroad: Jun, 1968 – 74 died in Argentina. Panic broke out at the end of a goalless match between River Plate and Boca Juniors at Nunez, Buenos Aires, when Boca supporters threw lighted newspaper torches on to fans in the tiers below.

Feb 1974 – 49 killed in **Egypt** in crush of fans clamouring to see Zamalek play Dukla Prague.

Sep 1971 – 44 died in **Turkey**, when fighting among spectators over a disallowed goal (Kayseri v Siwas) led to a platform collapsing.

The then worst disaster in the history of British football, in terms of loss of life, occurred at Glasgow Rangers' ground at **Ibrox Park**, Jan 2 1971. Sixty-six people were trampled to death (100 injured) as they tumbled down Stairway 13 just before the end of the **Rangers v Celtic** New Year's match. That disaster led to the 1975 Safety of Sports Grounds legislation.

The Ibrox tragedy eclipsed even the Bolton disaster in which 33 were killed and about 500 injured when a wall and crowd barriers collapsed near a corner-flag at the **Bolton v Stoke** FA Cup sixth round tie on Mar 9 1946. The match was completed after half an hour's stoppage.

In a previous crowd disaster at **Ibrox** on Apr 5, 1902, part of the terracing collapsed during the Scotland v England international and 25 people were killed. The match, held up for 20 minutes, ended 1-1, but was never counted as an official international.

Eight leading players and three officials of **Manchester Utd** and eight newspaper representatives were among the 23 who perished in the air crash at **Munich** on Feb 6, 1958, during take-off following a European Cup-tie in Belgrade. The players were Roger Byrne, Geoffrey Bent, Eddie Colman, Duncan Edwards, Mark Jones, David Pegg, Tommy Taylor and Liam Whelan, and the officials were Walter Crickmer (secretary), Tom Curry (trainer) and Herbert Whalley (coach). The newspaper representatives were Alf Clarke, Don Davies, George Follows, Tom Jackson, Archie Ledbrooke, Henry Rose, Eric Thompson and Frank Swift (former England goalkeeper of Manchester City).

On May 14, 1949, the entire team of Italian Champions **Torino**, 8 of them Internationals, were killed when the aircraft taking them home from a match against Benfica in Lisbon crashed at Superga, near Turin. The total death toll of 28 included all the club's reserve players, the manager, trainer and coach.

On Feb 8, 1981, 24 spectators died and more than 100 were injured at a match in **Greece**. They were trampled as thousands of the 40,000 crowd tried to rush out of the stadium at Piraeus after Olympiacos beat AEK Athens 6-0.

On Nov 17, 1982, 24 people (12 of them children) were killed and 250 injured when fans stampeded at the end of a match at the Pascual Guerrero stadium in **Cali, Colombia**. Drunken spectators hurled fire crackers and broken bottles from the higher stands on to people below and started a rush to the exits.

On Dec 9, 1987, the 18-strong team squad of **Alianza Lima**, one of Peru's top clubs, were wiped out, together with 8 officials and several youth players, when a military aircraft taking them home from Puccalpa crashed into the sea off Ventillana, ten miles from Lima. The only survivor among 43 on board was a member of the crew.

On Apr 28, 1993, 18 members of **Zambia's international squad** and 5 ZFA officials died when the aircraft carrying them to a World Cup qualifying tie against Senegal crashed into the Atlantic soon after take-off from Libreville, Gabon.

On Oct 16 1996, 81 fans were crushed to death and 147 seriously injured in the '**Guatemala Disaster**' at the World Cup qualifier against Costa Rica in Mateo Flores stadium. The tragedy happened an hour before kick-off, allegedly caused by ticket forgery and overcrowding – 60,000 were reported in the 45,000-capacity ground – and safety problems related to perimeter fencing.

On Jul 9, 1996, 8 people died, 39 injured in riot after derby match between **Libya's two top clubs** in Tripoli. Al-Ahli had beaten Al-Ittihad 1-0 by a controversial goal.

On Apr 6, 1997, 5 spectators were crushed to death at **Nigeria's national stadium** in Lagos after the 2-1 World Cup qualifying victory over Guinea. Only two of five gates were reported open as the 40,000 crowd tried to leave the ground.

It was reported from the **Congo** (Oct 29, 1998) that a bolt of lightning struck a village match, killing all 11 members of the home team Benatshadi, but leaving the opposing players from Basangana unscathed. It was believed the surviving team wore better-insulated boots.

On Jan 10, 1999, eight fans died and 13 were injured in a stampede at **Egypt's Alexandria Stadium**. Some 25,000 spectators had pushed into the ground. Despite the tragedy, the cup-tie between Al-Ittihad and Al-Koroum was completed.

Three people suffocated and several were seriously injured when thousands of fans forced their way into **Liberia's national stadium** in Monrovia at a goalless World Cup qualifying match against Chad on Apr 23, 2000. The stadium (capacity 33,000) was reported 'heavily overcrowded'.

On Jul 9, 2000, 12 spectators died from crush injuries when police fired tear gas into the 50,000 crowd after South Africa scored their second goal in a World Cup group qualifier against Zimbabwe in **Harare**. A stampede broke out as fans scrambled to leave the national stadium. Players of both teams lay face down on the pitch as fumes swept over them. FIFA launched an investigation and decided that the result would stand, with South Africa leading 2-0 at the time of the 84th-minute abandonment.

On Apr 11, 2001, at one of the biggest matches of the South African season, 43 died and 155 were injured in a crush at **Ellis Park, Johannesburg**. After tearing down a fence, thousands of fans surged into a stadium already packed to its 60,000 capacity for the Premiership derby between top Soweto teams Kaizer Chiefs and Orlando Pirates. The match was abandoned at 1-1 after 33 minutes. In Jan 1991, 40 died in a crowd crush at a friendly between the same clubs at Orkney, 80 miles from Johannesburg.

On Apr 29, 2001, seven people were trampled to death and 51 injured when a riot broke out at a match between two of Congo's biggest clubs, Lupopo and Mazembe at **Lubumbashi**, southern Congo.

On May 6, 2001, two spectators were killed in Iran and hundreds were injured when a glass fibre roof collapsed at the over-crowded Mottaqi Stadium at Sari for the match between Pirouzi and Shemshak Noshahr.

On May 9, 2001, in Africa's worst football disaster, 123 died and 93 were injured in a stampede at the national stadium in **Accra, Ghana**. Home team Hearts of Oak were leading 2-1 against Asante Kotoko five minutes from time, when Asanti fans started hurling bottles on to the pitch. Police fired tear gas into the stands, and the crowd panicked in a rush for the exits, which were locked. It took the death toll at three big matches in Africa in Apr/May to 173.

On Aug 12, 2001, two players were killed by lightning and ten severely burned at a **Guatemala** Third Division match between Deportivo Culquimulilla and Pueblo Nuevo Vinas.

On Nov 1, 2002, two players died from injuries after lightning struck Deportivo Cali's training ground in **Colombia**.

On Mar 12 2004, five people were killed and more than 100 injured when spectators stampeded shortly before the Syrian Championship fixture between Al-Jihad and Al-Fatwa in **Qameshli**, Northern Syria. The match was cancelled.

On Oct 10, 2004, three spectators died in a crush at the African Zone World Cup qualifier between **Guinea** and **Morocco** (1-1) at Conakry, Guinea.

On Mar 25, 2005, five were killed as 100,000 left the Azadi Stadium, **Tehran**, after Iran's World Cup qualifying win (2-1) against Japan.

On Jun 2, 2007, 12 spectators were killed and 46 injured in a crush at the Chillabombwe Stadium, **Zambia**, after an African Nations Cup qualifier against Congo.

On Mar 29, 2009, 19 people died and 139 were injured after a wall collapsed at the Ivory Coast stadium in **Abidjan** before a World Cup qualifier against Malawi. The match went ahead, Ivory Coast winning 5-0 with two goals from Chelsea's Didier Drogba. The tragedy meant that, in 13 years, crowd disasters at club and internationals at ten different grounds across Africa had claimed the lives of 283 people.

On Jan 8, 2010, terrorists at **Cabinda**, Angola machine-gunned the Togo team buses travelling to the Africa Cup of Nations. They killed a driver, an assistant coach and a media officer and injured several players. The team were ordered by their Government to withdraw from the tournament.

On Oct 23, 2010, seven fans were trampled to death when thousands tried to force their way into the Nyayo National Stadium in **Nairobi** at a Kenya Premier League match between the Gor Mahia and AFC Leopards clubs.

On Feb 1, 2012, 74 died and nearly 250 were injured in a crowd riot at the end of the Al-Masry v Al-Ahly match in **Port Said** – the worst disaster in Egyptian sport.

On Nov 28, 2016, 71 died in the worst air crash in world football history when a charter flight carrying players, officials and staff of leading Brazilian club Chapecoense from **Bolivia** to **Colombia** hit a mountain ridge at 8,500 feet. The victims included 65 people from the club.

On Feb 8, 2019, ten young players died when fire engulfed a dormitory at the youth team training centre of one of Brazil's biggest clubs, Flamengo in Rio de Janeiro.

DAYS OF TRAGEDY – PERSONAL

Sam Wynne, Bury right-back, collapsed five minutes before half-time in the First Division match away to Sheffield Utd on Apr 30, 1927, and died in the dressing-room.

John Thomson, Celtic and Scotland goalkeeper, sustained a fractured skull when diving at an opponent's feet in the Rangers v Celtic League match on Sep 5, 1931, and died the same evening.

Sim Raleigh (Gillingham), injured in a clash of heads at home to Brighton (Div 3 South) on Dec 1, 1934, continued to play but collapsed in second half and died in hospital the same night.

James Thorpe, Sunderland goalkeeper, was injured during the First Division match at home to Chelsea on Feb 1, 1936 and died in a diabetic coma three days later.

Derek Dooley, Sheffield Wed centre-forward and top scorer in 1951–52 in the Football League with 46 goals in 30 matches, broke a leg in the League match at Preston on Feb 14, 1953, and, after complications set in, had to lose the limb by amputation.

John White, Tottenham's Scottish international forward, was killed by lightning on a golf course at Enfield, North London in Jul, 1964.

Tony Allden, Highgate centre-half, was struck by lightning during an Amateur Cup quarter-final with Enfield on Feb 25, 1967. He died the following day. Four other players were also struck but recovered.

Roy Harper died while refereeing the York v Halifax (Div 4) match on May 5, 1969.

Jim Finn collapsed and died from a heart attack while refereeing Exeter v Stockport (Div 4) on Sep 16, 1972.

Scotland manager **Jock Stein**, 62, collapsed and died at the end of the Wales-Scotland World Cup qualifying match (1-1) at Ninian Park, Cardiff on Sep 10, 1985.

David Longhurst, York forward, died after being carried off two minutes before half-time in the Fourth Division fixture at home to Lincoln on Sep 8, 1990. The match was abandoned (0-0). The inquest revealed that Longhurst suffered from a rare heart condition.

Mike North collapsed while refereeing Southend v Mansfield (Div 3) on Apr 16, 2001 and died shortly afterwards. The match was abandoned and re-staged on May 8, with the receipts donated to his family.

Marc-Vivien Foe, on his 63rd appearance in Cameroon's midfield, collapsed unchallenged in the centre circle after 72 minutes of the FIFA Confederations Cup semi-final against Colombia in Lyon, France, on Jun 26, 2003, and despite the efforts of the stadium medical staff he could not be revived. He had been on loan to Manchester City from Olympique Lyonnais in season 2002–03, and poignantly scored the club's last goal at Maine Road.

Paul Sykes, Folkestone Invicta (Ryman League) striker, died on the pitch during the Kent Senior Cup semi-final against Margate on Apr 12, 2005. He collapsed after an innocuous off-the-ball incident.

Craig Gowans, Falkirk apprentice, was killed at the club's training ground on Jul 8, 2005 when he came into contact with power lines.

Peter Wilson, Mansfield goalkeeping coach, died of a heart attack after collapsing during the warm-up of the League Two game away to Shrewsbury on Nov 19, 2005.

Matt Gadsby, Hinckley defender, collapsed and died while playing in a Conference North match at Harrogate on Sep 9, 2006.

Phil O'Donnell, 35-year-old Motherwell captain and Scotland midfield player, collapsed when about to be substituted near the end of the SPL home game against Dundee Utd on Dec 29, 2007 and died shortly afterwards in hospital.

Vichai Srivaddhanaprabha, Leicester owner, died in a helicopter crash following the club's Premier League match against West Ham. The pilot and three others on board also died in the crash outside the King Power Stadium, seconds after the helicopter's take-off from the pitch on Oct 27, 2018

Emiliano Sala, Argentine striker, died in a plane crash in the English Channel on Jan 21, 2019 two days after signing for Cardiff from Nantes. The pilot of the light aircraft also died.

Justin Edinburgh, Leyton Orient manager, suffered a cardiac arrest and died five days later on Apr 8, 2019

GREAT SERVICE

'For services to Association Football', **Stanley Matthews** (Stoke, Blackpool and England), already a CBE, became the first professional footballer to receive a knighthood. This was bestowed in 1965, his last season. Before he retired and five days after his 50th birthday, he played for Stoke to set a record as the oldest First Division footballer (v Fulham, Feb 6, 1965).

Over a brilliant span of 33 years, he played in 886 first-class matches, including 54 full Internationals (plus 31 in war time), 701 League games (including 3 at start of season 1939–40, which was abandoned on the outbreak of war) and 86 FA Cup-ties, and scored 95 goals. He was never booked in his career.

Sir Stanley died on Feb 23, 2000, three weeks after his 85th birthday. His ashes were buried under the centre circle of Stoke's Britannia Stadium. After spending a number of years in Toronto, he made his home back in the Potteries in 1989, having previously returned to his home town, Hanley in Oct, 1987 to unveil a life-size bronze statue of himself. The inscription reads: 'Sir Stanley Matthews, CBE. Born Hanley, 1 Feb 1915.

His name is symbolic of the beauty of the game, his fame timeless and international, his sportsmanship and modesty universally acclaimed. A magical player, of the people, for the people.' On his home-coming in 1989, Sir Stanley was made President of Stoke, the club he joined as a boy of 15 and served as a player for 20 years between 1931 and 1965, on either side of his spell with Blackpool.

In Jul 1992 FIFA honoured him with their 'Gold merit award' for outstanding services to the game.

Former England goalkeeper **Peter Shilton** has made more first-class appearances (1,387) than any other footballer in British history. He played his 1,000th. League game in Leyton Orient's 2-0 home win against Brighton on Dec 22, 1996 and made 9 appearances for Orient in his final season. He retired from international football after the 1990 World Cup in Italy with 125 caps, then a world record. Shilton kept a record 60 clean sheets for England.

Shilton's career spanned 32 seasons, 20 of them on the international stage. He made his League debut for Leicester in May 1966, two months before England won the World Cup.

His 1,387 first-class appearances comprise a record 1,005 in the Football League, 125 Internationals, 102 League Cup, 86 FA Cup, 13 for England U-23s, 4 for the Football League and 52 other matches (European Cup, UEFA Cup, World Club Championship, Charity Shield, European Super Cup, Full Members' Cup, Play-offs, Screen Sports Super Cup, Anglo-Italian Cup, Texaco Cup, Simod Cup, Zenith Data Systems Cup and Autoglass Trophy).

Shilton appeared 57 times at Wembley, 52 for England, 2 League Cup Finals, 1 FA Cup Final, 1 Charity Shield match, and 1 for the Football League. He passed a century of League appearances with each of his first five clubs: Leicester (286), Stoke (110), Nottm Forest (202), Southampton (188) and Derby (175) and subsequently played for Plymouth, Bolton and Leyton Orient.

He was awarded the MBE and OBE for services to football. At the Football League Awards ceremony in March 2013, he received the League's Contribution award.

Six other British footballers have made more than 1,000 first-class appearances:

Ray Clemence, formerly with Tottenham, Liverpool and England, retired through injury in season 1987–88 after a goalkeeping career of 1,119 matches starting in 1965–66.

Clemence played 50 times for his first club, Scunthorpe; 665 for Liverpool; 337 for Tottenham; his 67 representative games included 61 England caps.

A third great goalkeeper, **Pat Jennings**, ended his career (1963–86) with a total of 1,098 first-class matches for Watford, Tottenham, Arsenal and N Ireland. They were made up of 757 in the Football League, 119 full Internationals, 84 FA Cup appearances, 72 League/Milk Cup, 55 European club matches, 2 Charity Shield, 3 Other Internationals, 1 Under-23 cap, 2 Texaco Cup, 2 Anglo-Italian Cup and 1 Super Cup. Jennings played his 119th and final international on his 41st birthday, Jun 12, 1986, against Brazil in Guadalajara in the Mexico World Cup.

Yet another outstanding 'keeper, **David Seaman**, passed the 1,000 appearances milestone for clubs and country in season 2002–03, reaching 1,004 when aged 39, he captained Arsenal to FA Cup triumph against Southampton.

With Arsenal, Seaman won 3 Championship medals, the FA Cup 4 times, the Double twice, the League Cup and Cup-Winners' Cup once each. After 13 seasons at Highbury, he joined Manchester City (Jun 2003) on a free transfer. He played 26 matches for City before a shoulder injury forced his retirement in Jan 2004, aged 40.

Seaman's 22-season career composed 1,046 first-class matches: 955 club apps (Peterborough 106, Birmingham 84, QPR 175, Arsenal 564, Manchester City 26); 75 senior caps for England, 6 'B' caps and 10 at U-21 level.

Defender **Graeme Armstrong**, 42-year-old commercial manager for an Edinburgh whisky company and part-time assistant-manager and captain of Scottish Third Division club Stenhousemuir, made the 1000th first team appearance of his career in the Scottish Cup 3rd Round against Rangers at Ibrox on Jan 23, 1999. He was presented with the Man of the Match award before kick-off.

Against East Stirling on Boxing Day, he had played his 864th League game, breaking the British record for an outfield player set by another Scot, Tommy Hutchison, with Alloa, Blackpool, Coventry, Manchester City, Burnley and Swansea City.

Armstrong's 24-year career, spent in the lower divisions of the Scottish League, began as a 1-match trialist with Meadowbank Thistle in 1975 and continued via Stirling Albion, Berwick Rangers, Meadowbank and, from 1992, Stenhousemuir.

Tony Ford became the first English outfield player to reach 1000 senior appearances in Rochdale's 1-0 win at Carlisle (Auto Windscreens Shield) on Mar 7, 2000. Grimsby-born, he began his 26-season midfield career with Grimsby and played for 7 other League clubs: Sunderland (loan), Stoke, WBA, Bradford City (loan), Scunthorpe, Mansfield and Rochdale. He retired, aged 42, in 2001 with a career record of 1072 appearances (121 goals) and his total of 931 League games is exceeded only by Peter Shilton's 1005.

On Apr 16, 2011, **Graham Alexander** reached 1,000 appearances when he came on as a sub for Burnley at home to Swansea. Alexander, 40, ended a 22-year career with the equaliser for Preston against Charlton (2-2, Lge 1) on Apr 28, 2012 – his 1,023rd appearance. He also played for Luton and Scunthorpe and was capped 40 times by Scotland.

RECORD FOR BARRY

Gareth Barry surpassed Ryan Giggs's record of 632 Premier League appearances in West Bromwich Albion's 2-0 defeat by Arsenal in the 2017–18 season. His record now stands at 653 appearances (1997–2018).

GIGGS RECORD COLLECTION

Ryan Giggs (Manchester Utd) has collected the most individual honours in English football with a total of 34 prizes. They comprise: 13 Premier League titles, 4 FA Cups, 3 League Cups, 2 European Cups, 1 UEFA Super Cup, 1 Inter-Continental Cup, 1 World Club Cup, 9 Charity Shields/Community Shields. One-club man Giggs played 24 seasons for United, making a record 963 appearances. He won 64 Wales caps and on retiring as a player, aged 40, in May 2014, became the club's assistant manager. He ended a 29-year association with the club in June 2016.

KNIGHTS OF SOCCER

Players, managers and administrators who have been honoured for their services to football: **Charles Clegg** (1927), **Stanley Rous** (1949), **Stanley Matthews** (1965), **Alf Ramsey** (1967), **Matt Busby** (1968), **Walter Winterbottom** (1978) **John Smith** (1990), **Bert Millichip** (1991), **Bobby Charlton** (1994), **Tom Finney** (1998), **Geoff Hurst** (1998), **Alex Ferguson** (1999), **Bobby Robson** (2002), **Trevor Brooking** (2004), **Dave Richards** (2006), **Doug Ellis** (2011), **Kenny Dalglish** (2018).

● On Nov 6, 2014, **Karren Brady**, vice-chairman of West Ham, was elevated to the Lords as Karren, Baroness Brady, OBE, of Knightsbridge, life peer

PENALTIES

The **penalty-kick** was introduced to the game, following a proposal to the Irish FA in 1890 by William McCrum, son of the High Sheriff for Co Omagh, and approved by the International Football Board on Jun 2, 1891.

First penalty scored in a first-class match in England was by John Heath, for Wolves v Accrington Stanley (5-0 in Div 1, Sep 14, 1891).

The greatest influence of the penalty has come since the 1970s, with the introduction of the shoot-out to settle deadlocked ties in various competitions.

Manchester Utd were the first club to win a competitive match in British football via a shoot-out (4-3 away to Hull, Watney Cup semi-final, Aug 5, 1970); in that penalty contest, George Best was the first player to score, Denis Law the first to miss.

The shoot-out was adopted by FIFA and UEFA the same year (1970).

In season 1991–92, penalty shoot-outs were introduced to decide FA Cup ties still level after one replay and extra time.

Wembley saw its first penalty contest in the 1974 Charity Shield. Since then many major matches across the world have been settled in this way, including:

1976   **European Championship Final (Belgrade):** Czechoslovakia beat West Germany 5-3 (after 2-2)

1980	**Cup-Winners' Cup Final (Brussels):** Valencia beat Arsenal 5-4 (after 0-0)
1984	**European Cup Final (Rome):** Liverpool beat Roma 4-2 (after 1-1)
1984	**UEFA Cup Final:** Tottenham (home) beat Anderlecht 4-3 (2-2 agg)
1986	**European Cup Final (Seville):** Steaua Bucharest beat Barcelona 2-0 (after 0-0).
1987	**Freight Rover Trophy Final (Wembley):** Mansfield beat Bristol City 5-4 (after 1-1)
1987	**Scottish League Cup Final (Hampden Park):** Rangers beat Aberdeen 5-3 (after 3-3)
1988	**European Cup Final (Stuttgart):** PSV Eindhoven beat Benfica 6-5 (after 0-0)
1988	**UEFA Cup Final:** Bayer Leverkusen (home) beat Espanyol 3-2 after 3-3 (0-3a, 3-0h)
1990	**Scottish Cup Final (Hampden Park):** Aberdeen beat Celtic 9-8 (after 0-0)
1991	**European Cup Final (Bari):** Red Star Belgrade beat Marseille 5-3 (after 0-0)
1991	**Div 4 Play-off (Wembley):** Torquay beat Blackpool 5-4 (after 2-2)
1992	**Div 4 Play-off (Wembley):** Blackpool beat Scunthorpe 4-3 (after 1-1)
1993	**Div 3 Play-off(Wembley):** York beat Crewe 5-3 (after 1-1)
1994	**Autoglass Trophy Final (Wembley):** Swansea City beat Huddersfield 3-1 (after 1-1)
1994	**World Cup Final (Los Angeles):** Brazil beat Italy 3-2 (after 0-0)
1994	**Scottish League Cup Final (Ibrox Park):** Raith beat Celtic 6-5 (after 2-2)
1995	**Copa America Final (Montevideo):** Uruguay beat Brazil 5-3 (after 1-1)
1996	**European Cup Final (Rome):** Juventus beat Ajax 4-2 (after 1-1)
1996	**European U-21 Champ Final (Barcelona):** Italy beat Spain 4-2 (after 1-1)
1997	**Auto Windscreens Shield Final (Wembley):** Carlisle beat Colchester 4-3 (after 0-0)
1997	**UEFA Cup Final:** FC Schalke beat Inter Milan 4-1 (after 1-1 agg)
1998	**Div 1 Play-off (Wembley):** Charlton beat Sunderland 7-6 (after 4-4)
1999	**Div 2 Play-off (Wembley):** Manchester City beat Gillingham 3-1 (after 2-2)
1999	**Women's World Cup Final (Pasedena):** USA beat China 5-4 (after 0-0)
2000	**African Nations Cup Final (Lagos):** Cameroon beat Nigeria 4-3 (after 0-0)
2000	**UEFA Cup Final (Copenhagen):** Galatasaray beat Arsenal 4-1 (after 0-0)
2000	**Olympic Final (Sydney):** Cameroon beat Spain 5-3 (after 2-2)
2001	**League Cup Final (Millennium Stadium):** Liverpool beat Birmingham 5-4 (after 1-1)
2001	**Champions League Final (Milan):** Bayern Munich beat Valencia 5-4 (after 1-1)
2002	**Euro U-21 Champ Final (Basle):** Czech Republic beat France 3-1 (after 0-0)
2002	**Div 1 Play-off Final (Millennium Stadium):** Birmingham beat Norwich 4-2 (after 1-1)
2003	**Champions League Final (Old Trafford):** AC Milan beat Juventus 3-2 (after 0-0)
2004	**Div 3 Play-off Final (Millennium Stadium):** Huddersfield beat Mansfield 4-1 (after 0-0)
2004	**Copa America Final (Lima):** Brazil beat Argentina 4-2 (after 2-2)
2005	**FA Cup Final (Millennium Stadium):** Arsenal beat Manchester Utd 5-4 (after 0-0)
2005	**Champions League Final (Istanbul):** Liverpool beat AC Milan 3-2 (after 3-3)
2006	**African Cup of Nations Final (Cairo):** Egypt beat Ivory Coast 4-2 (after 0-0)
2006	**FA Cup Final (Millennium Stadium):** Liverpool beat West Ham 3-1 (after 3-3)
2006	**Scottish Cup Final (Hampden Park):** Hearts beat Gretna 4-2 (after 1-1)
2006	**Lge 1 Play-off Final (Millennium Stadium):** Barnsley beat Swansea City 4-3 (after 2-2)
2006	**World Cup Final (Berlin):** Italy beat France 5-3 (after 1-1)
2007	**UEFA Cup Final (Hampden Park):** Sevilla beat Espanyol 3-1 (after 2-2)
2008	**Champions League Final (Moscow):** Manchester Utd beat Chelsea 6-5 (after 1-1)
2008	**Scottish League Cup Final (Hampden Park):** Rangers beat Dundee Utd 3-2 (after 2-2)
2009	**League Cup Final (Wembley):** Manchester Utd beat Tottenham 4-1 (after 0-0)
2011	**Women's World Cup Final (Frankfurt):** Japan beat USA 3-1 (after 2-2)
2012	**League Cup Final (Wembley):** Liverpool beat Cardiff 3-2 (after 2-2)
2012	**Champions League Final (Munich):** Chelsea beat Bayern Munich 4-3 (after 1-1)
2012	**Lge 1 Play-off Final (Wembley):** Huddersfield beat Sheffield Utd 8-7 (after 0-0)
2012	**Africa Cup of Nations Final (Gabon):** Zambia beat Ivory Coast 8-7 (after 0-0)
2013	**FA Trophy Final (Wembley):** Wrexham beat Grimsby 4-1 (after 1-1)
2013	**European Super Cup (Prague):** Bayern Munich beat Chelsea 5-4 (after 2-2)

2014	**Scottish League Cup Final (Celtic Park):** Aberdeen beat Inverness 4-2 (after 0-0)
2014	**Lge 1 Play-off Final (Wembley):** Rotherheam beat Leyton Orient 4-3 (after 2-2)
2014	**Europa Lge Final (Turin):** Sevilla beat Benfica 4-2 (after 0-0)
2015	**Africa Cup of Nations Final (Equ Guinea):** Ivory Coast beat Ghana 9-8 (after 0-0)
2015	**Conference Play-off Final (Wembley):** Bristol Rov beat Grimsby 5-3 (after 1-1)
2015	**Lge 2 Play-off Final (Wembley):** Southend beat Wycombe 7-6 (after 1-1)
2015	**FA Trophy Final (Wembley)** North Ferriby beat Wrexham 5-4 (after3-3)
2015	**Euro U-21 Champ Final (Prague):** Sweden beat Portugal 4-3 (after 0-0)
2015	**Copa America Final (Santiago):** Chile beat Argentina 4-1 (after 0-0)
2016	**League Cup Final (Wembley):** Manchester City beat Liverpool 3-1 (after 1-1)
2016	**Champions League Final (Milan):** Real Madrid beat Atletico Madrid 5-3 (after 1-1)
2016	**Olympic Men's Final (Rio de Janeiro):** Brazil beat Germany 5-4 (after 1-1)
2017	**Champ Play-off Final (Wembley):** Huddersfield beat Reading 4-3 (after 0-0)
2017	**Community Shield (Wembley):** Arsenal beat Chelsea 4-1 (after 1-1)
2019	**League Cup Final (Wembley):** Manchester City beat Chelsea 4-3 (after 0-0)
2019	**Football League Trophy Final (Wembley):** Portsmouth beat Sunderland 5-4 (after 2-2)
2019	**Community Shield (Wembley):** Manchester City beat Liverpool 5-4 (after 1-1)
2020	**Community Shield (Wembley):** Arsenal beat Liverpool 5-4 (after 1-1)
2020	**Euro 2020 Qualifying Play-off Final (Belgrade):** Scotland beat Serbia 5-4 (after 1-1)
2020	**League Trophy Final (Wembley):** Salford beat Portsmouth 4-1 (after 0-0)
2021	**Europa League Final (Godansk):** Villarreal beat Manchester Utd 11-10 (after 1-1)
2021	**Europa League Final (Gdansk):** Villarreal beat Manchester Utd 11-10 (after 1-1)
2021 (20)	**European Championship Final (Wembley):** Italy beat England 3-2 (after 1-1)
2021	**European Super Cup (Windsor Park):** Chelsea beat Villarreal 6-5 (after 1-1)
2022	**League Cup Final (Wembley):** Liverpool beat Chelsea 11-10 (after 0-0)
2022	**FA Cup Final (Wembley):** Liverpool beat Chelsea 6-5 (after 0-0)
2022	**Europa League Final (Seville):** Eintracht Frankfurt beat Rangers 5-4 (after 1-1)

In South America in 1992, in a 26-shot competition, **Newell's Old Boys** beat America 11-10 in the Copa Libertadores.

Longest-recorded penalty contest in first-class matches was in Argentina in 1988 – from 44 shots, **Argentinos Juniors** beat Racing Club 20-19. Genclerbirligi beat Galatasaray 17-16 in a Turkish Cup-tie in 1996. Only one penalty was missed.

Highest-scoring shoot-outs in international football: **North Korea** beat Hong Kong 11-10 (after 3-3 draw) in an Asian Cup match in 1975; and **Ivory Coast** beat Ghana 11-10 (after 0-0 draw) in African Nations Cup Final, 1992.

Most penalties needed to settle an adult game in Britain: **44** in Norfolk Primary Cup 4th round replay, Dec 2000. Aston Village side **Freethorpe** beat Foulsham 20-19 (5 kicks missed). All 22 players took 2 penalties each, watched by a crowd of 20. The sides had drawn 2-2, 4-4 in a tie of 51 goals.

Penalty that took 24 days: That was how long elapsed between the award and the taking of a penalty in an Argentine Second Division match between **Atalanta** and Defensores in 2003. A riot ended the original match with 5 minutes left. The game resumed behind closed doors with the penalty that caused the abandonment. Lucas Ferreiro scored it to give Atalanta a 1-0 win.

INTERNATIONAL PENALTIES, MISSED

Four penalties out of five were missed when **Colombia** beat Argentina 3-0 in a Copa America group tie in Paraguay in Jul 1999. Martin Palmermo missed three for Argentina and Colombia's Hamilton Ricard had one spot-kick saved.

In the European Championship semi-final against Italy in Amsterdam on Jun 29, 2000, **Holland** missed five penalties – two in normal time, three in the penalty contest which Italy won 3-1 (after 0-0). Dutch captain Frank de Boer missed twice from the spot.

ENGLAND'S SHOOT-OUT RECORD

1990 (World Cup semi-final, Turin) 3-4 v West Germany after 1-1.
1996 (Euro Champ quarter-final, Wembley) 4-2 v Spain after 0-0.
1996 (Euro Champ semi-final, Wembley) 5-6 v Germany after 1-1.
1998 (World Cup 2nd round., St Etienne) 3-4 v Argentina after 2-2.
2004 (Euro Champ quarter-final, Lisbon) 5-6 v Portugal after 2-2.
2006 (World Cup quarter-final, Gelsenkirchen) 1-3 v Portugal after 0-0.
2012 (Euro Champ quarter-final, Kiev) 2-4 v Italy after 0-0.
2018 (World Cup round of 16, Moscow) 4-3 v Colombia after 1-1.
2019 (Euro Champ final, Wembley) 2-3 v Italy after 1-1
2021 (Euro Champ Final, Wembley) 2-3 v Italy after 1-1

FA CUP SHOOT-OUTS

First penalty contest in the FA Cup took place in 1972. In the days of the play-off for third place, the match was delayed until the eve of the following season when losing semi-finalists Birmingham and Stoke met at St Andrew's on Aug 5. The score was 0-0 and Birmingham won 4-3 on penalties.

Highest-scoring: Preliminary round replay (Aug 30, 2005): Tunbridge Wells beat Littlehampton 16-15 after 40 spot-kicks (9 missed).

Competition proper: Scunthorpe beat Worcester 14-13 in 2nd round replay (Dec 17, 2014) after 1-1 (32 kicks).

Shoot-out abandoned: The FA Cup 1st round replay between Oxford City and Wycombe at Wycombe on Nov 9, 1999 was abandoned (1-1) after extra-time. As the penalty shoot-out was about to begin, a fire broke out under a stand. Wycombe won the second replay 1-0 at Oxford Utd's ground.

First FA Cup Final to be decided by shoot-out was in 2005 (May 21), when Arsenal beat Manchester Utd 5-4 on penalties at Cardiff's Millennium Stadium (0-0 after extra time). A year later (May 13) Liverpool beat West Ham 3-1 (3-3 after extra-time).

ENGLISH RECORD SHOOT-OUT

Total of 34 spot-kicks: Football League Trophy group match, Nov 8, 2016, won 13-12 by Chelsea under-23 v Oxford United. Also: Southern League Challenge Cup 2nd rd, Nov 20, 2019, won 12-11 by Taunton v Truro.

SHOOT-OUT RECORD WINNERS AND LOSERS

When **Bradford** beat Arsenal 3-2 on penalties in a League Cup fifth round tie, it was the club's ninth successive shoot-out victory in FA Cup, League Cup and Johnstone's Paint Trophy ties between Oct 2009 and Dec 2012.

Tottenham's 4-1 spot-kick failure against Basel in the last 16 of the Europa League was their seventh successive defeat in shoot-outs from Mar 1996 to Apr 2013 (FA Cup, League Cup, UEFA Cup, Europa League)

MISSED CUP FINAL PENALTIES

John Aldridge (Liverpool) became the first player to miss a penalty in an FA Cup Final at Wembley when Dave Beasant saved his shot in 1988 to help Wimbledon to a shock 1-0 win. Seven penalties before had been scored in the Final at Wembley.

Previously, **Charlie Wallace**, of Aston Villa, had failed from the spot in the 1913 Final against Sunderland at Crystal Palace, which his team won 1-0

Gary Lineker (Tottenham) had his penalty saved by Nottm Forest's Mark Crossley in the 1991 FA Cup Final.

For the first time, two spot-kicks were missed in an FA Cup Final. In 2010, Petr Cech saved from Portsmouth's **Kevin-Prince Boateng** while Chelsea's **Frank Lampard** put his kick wide.

Another miss at Wembley was by Arsenal's **Nigel Winterburn**, Luton's Andy Dibble saving his spot-kick in the 1988 Littlewoods Cup Final, when a goal would have put Arsenal 3-1 ahead. Instead, they lost 3-2.

Winterburn was the third player to fail with a League Cup Final penalty at Wembley, following **Ray Graydon** (Aston Villa) against Norwich in 1975 and **Clive Walker** (Sunderland), who shot wide in the 1985 Milk Cup Final, also against Norwich who won 1-0. Graydon had his penalty saved by Kevin Keelan, but scored from the rebound and won the cup for Aston Villa (1-0).

Derby's Martin Taylor saved a penalty from **Eligio Nicolini** in the Anglo-Italian Cup Final at Wembley on Mar 27, 1993, but Cremonese won 3-1.

LEAGUE PENALTIES RECORD

Most penalties in Football League match: Five – 4 to Crystal Palace (3 missed), 1 to Brighton (scored) in Div 2 match at Selhurst Park on Mar 27 (Easter Monday), 1989. Crystal Palace won 2-1. Three of the penalties were awarded in a 5-minute spell. The match also produced 5 bookings and a sending-off. Other teams missing 3 penalties in a match: Burnley v Grimsby (Div 2), Feb 13, 1909; Manchester City v Newcastle (Div 1), Jan 17, 1912.

HOTTEST MODERN SPOT-SHOTS

Matthew Le Tissier ended his career in season 2001–02 with the distinction of having netted 48 out of 49 first-team penalties for Southampton. He scored the last 27 after his only miss when Nottm Forest keeper Mark Crossley saved in a Premier League match at The Dell on Mar 24, 1993.

Graham Alexander scored 78 out of 84 penalties in a 22-year career (Scunthorpe, Luton, Preston twice and Burnley) which ended in 2012.

SPOT-ON BRANNAGAN

Cameron Brannagan scored an English record four penalties for Oxford in their 7-2 win at Gillingham (Lge 1, Jan 29, 2022).

SPOT-KICK HAT-TRICKS

Right-back **Joe Willetts** scored three penalties when Hartlepool beat Darlington 6-1 (Div 3N) on Good Friday 1951.

Danish international **Jan Molby**'s only hat-trick in English football, for Liverpool in a 3-1 win at home to Coventry (Littlewoods Cup, 4th round replay, Nov 26, 1986) comprised three goals from the penalty spot.

It was the first such hat-trick in a major match for two years – since **Andy Blair** scored three penalties for Sheffield Wed against Luton (Milk Cup 4th round, Nov 20 1984).

Portsmouth's **Kevin Dillon** scored a penalty hat-trick in the Full Members Cup (2nd round) at home to Millwall (3-2) on Nov 4, 1986.

Alan Slough scored a hat-trick of penalties in an away game, but was on the losing side, when Peterborough were beaten 4-3 at Chester (Div 3, Apr 29, 1978).

Josh Wright's three penalties in the space of 11 minutes enabled Gillingham to come from 2-0 down to defeat his former club Scunthorpe 3-2 in League One on Mar 11, 2017

Penalty hat-tricks in **international football: Dimitris Saravakos** (in 9 mins) for Greece v Egypt in 1990. He scored 5 goals in match. **Henrik Larsson**, among his 4 goals in Sweden's 6-0 home win v Moldova in World Cup qualifying match, Jun 6, 2001.

MOST PENALTY GOALS (LEAGUE) IN SEASON

13 out of 13 by **Francis Lee** for Manchester City (Div 1) in 1971–72. His goal total for the season was 33. In season 1988–89, **Graham Roberts** scored 12 League penalties for Second Division Champions Chelsea. In season 2004–05, **Andrew Johnson** scored 11 Premier League penalties for Crystal Palace, who were relegated.

PENALTY-SAVE SEQUENCES

Ipswich goalkeeper **Paul Cooper** saved eight of the ten penalties he faced in 1979–80. **Roy Brown** (Notts Co) saved six in a row in season 1972–73.

Andy Lomas, goalkeeper for Chesham (Diadora League) claimed a record eighth **consecutive** penalty saves – three at the end of season 1991–92 and five in 1992–93.

Mark Bosnich (Aston Villa) saved five in two consecutive matches in 1993–94: three in Coca-Cola Cup semi-final penalty shoot–out v Tranmere (Feb 26), then two in Premier League at Tottenham (Mar 2).

MISSED PENALTIES SEQUENCE

Against Wolves in Div 2 on Sep 28, 1991, **Southend** missed their seventh successive penalty (five of them the previous season).

RANGERS SPOT-ON

Rangers were awarded four penalties in their 4-0 win Scottish Premiership win over St Mirren on Feb 2, 2019, converting three of them.

SCOTTISH RECORDS
(See also under 'Goals' & 'Discipline')

CELTIC SUPREME

In winning the Treble for the fourth time in 2016–17, **Celtic** rewrote the Scottish records. In the first season under **Brendan Rodgers**, previously Liverpool manager, they did not lose a domestic match, the first to stay unbeaten in the league since Rangers in 1899. They set new records for points (106), goals (106), victories (34) and for a 30-point winning margin. In 2017–18, Celtic became the first in Scotland to win back-to-back domestic trebles and stretched an unbeaten run to a British record 69 games in domestic competitions. Their 25 consecutive victories in season 2003–04 also represents a British best, while the 1966–67 record was the most successful by a British side in one season. They won the Treble and became the first to win the European Cup. Under Jock Stein, there were nine titles in a row (1966–74). In season 2018–19, Celtic completed a third successive domestic treble, this one under **Brendan Rodgers** and **Neil Lennon**, who took over when Rodgers left to become Leicester manager in late February. After a ninth straight title in the curtailed 2019–20 season Celtic set their sights on a record tenth in the new campaign. **Rangers** ended the run, but Celtic and Lennon still made history with victory over Hearts in the delayed 2020 Scottish Cup Final. It gave the club a fourth straight domestic treble and the manager a domestic treble as player and manager.

RANGERS BACK ON TOP

Rangers denied arch-rivals Celtic a record tenth straight title with a runaway triumph under Steven Gerrard in season 2020–21. They finished 25 points ahead, were unbeaten in their 38 matches and set a new British defensive record by conceding only 13 goals.

RANGERS' MANY RECORDS

Rangers' record-breaking feats include:

League Champions: 55 times (once joint holders) – world record.

Winning every match in Scottish League (18 games, 1898–99 season).

Major hat-tricks: Rangers have completed the domestic treble (League Championship, League Cup and Scottish FA Cup) a record seven times (1948–49, 1963–64, 1975–76, 1977–78, 1992–93, 1998–99, 2002–03).

League & Cup double: 17 times.

Nine successive Championships (1989–97). Four men played in all nine sides: Richard Gough, Ally McCoist, Ian Ferguson and Ian Durrant.

117 major trophies: Championships 55, Scottish Cup 34, League Cup 27, Cup-Winners' Cup 1.

UNBEATEN SCOTTISH CHAMPIONS

Celtic and **Rangers** have each won the Scottish Championship with an unbeaten record; Celtic in 1897–98 (P18, W15, D3) and in 2016–17 (P38, W34; D4); Rangers in 1898–99 (P18, W18) and in 2020-21 (P38 W32, D6).

FORSTER'S SHUT-OUT RECORD

Celtic goalkeeper **Fraser Forster** set a record in Scottish top-flight football by not conceding a goal for 1,256 consecutive minutes in season 2013–14.

TRIO OF TOP CLUBS MISSING

Three of Scotland's leading clubs were missing from the 2014–15 Premiership season. With **Hearts** finishing bottom and **Rangers** still working their way back through the divisions after being demoted, they were joined in the second tier by **Hibernian**, who lost the play-off final on penalties to Hamilton.

CELTIC CUP JOY

Celtic became the first team to win the Scottish Cup four times in a row by beating Hearts on penalties in the delayed 2020 Final.

SCOTTISH CUP FINAL DISMISSALS

Five players have been sent off in the Scottish FA Cup Final: **Jock Buchanan** (Rangers v Kilmarnock, 1929); **Roy Aitken** (Celtic v Aberdeen, 1984); **Walter Kidd** (Hearts captain v Aberdeen, 1986); **Paul Hartley** (Hearts v Gretna, 2006); **Pa Kujabi** (Hibernian v Hearts, 2012); **Carl Tremarco** (Inverness v Falkirk, 2015).

HIGHEST-SCORING SHOOT-OUT

In Scottish football's highest-scoring penalty shoot-out, **Albion Rovers** beat **Stranraer** 15-14 after 30 spot-kicks in their League Cup group match (2-2) on Oct 13, 2020.

MCGRORY RECORD

Jimmy McGrory set a British top-flight record when scoring eight goals in Celtic's 9-0 win over Dunfermline on Jan 14, 1928.

RECORD SEQUENCES

Celtic hold Britain's League record of 62 matches undefeated, from Nov 13, 1915 to Apr 21, 1917, when Kilmarnock won 2-0 at Parkhead. They won 49, drew 13 (111 points) and scored 126 goals to 26.
Greenock Morton in 1963–64 accumulated 67 points out of 72 and scored 135 goals.
Queen's Park did not have a goal scored against them during the first seven seasons of their existence (1867–74, before the Scottish League was formed).

EARLIEST PROMOTIONS IN SCOTLAND

Dundee promoted from Div 2, Feb 1, 1947; **Greenock Morton** promoted from Div 2, Mar 2, 1964; **Gretna** promoted from Div 3, Mar 5, 2005; **Hearts** promoted from Championship, Mar 21, 2015.

WORST HOME SEQUENCE

After gaining promotion to Div 1 in 1992, **Cowdenbeath** went a record 38 consecutive home League matches without a win. They ended the sequence (drew 8, lost 30) when beating Arbroath 1-0 on Apr 2, 1994, watched by a crowd of 225.

ALLY'S RECORDS

Ally McCoist became the first player to complete 200 goals in the Premier Division when he scored Rangers' winner (2-1) at Falkirk on Dec 12, 1992. His first was against Celtic in Sep 1983, and he reached 100 against Dundee on Boxing Day 1987.

When McCoist scored twice at home to Hibernian (4-3) on Dec 7, 1996, he became Scotland's record post-war League marksman, beating Gordon Wallace's 264.

Originally with St Johnstone (1978–81), he spent two seasons with Sunderland (1981–83), then joined Rangers for £200,000 in Jun 1983.

In 15 seasons at Ibrox, he scored 355 goals for Rangers (250 League), and helped them win 10 Championships (9 in succession), 3 Scottish Cups and earned a record 9 League Cup winner's medals. He won the European Golden Boot in consecutive seasons (1991–92, 1992–93).

His 9 Premier League goals in three seasons for Kilmarnock gave him a career total of 281 Scottish League goals when he retired at the end of 2000–01. McCoist succeeded Walter Smith as manager of Rangers in May 2011.

SCOTLAND'S MOST SUCCESSFUL MANAGER

Bill Struth, 30 trophies for Rangers, 1920–54 (18 Championships, 10 Scottish Cups, 2 League Cups.

SMITH'S IBROX HONOURS

Walter Smith, who retired in May, 2011, won a total of 21 trophies in two spells as Rangers manager (10 League titles, 5 Scottish Cups, 6 League Cups).

RANGERS PUNISHED

In April 2012, **Rangers** (in administration) were fined £160,000 by the Scottish FA and given a 12-month transfer ban on charges relating to their finances. The ban was later overturned in court. The club had debts estimated at around £135m and on June 12, 2012 were forced into liquidation. A new company emerged, but Rangers were voted out of the Scottish Premier League and demoted to Division Three for the start of the 2012-13 season. They returned to the top division in 2016 via three promotions in four seasons.

FIVE IN A MATCH

Paul Sturrock set an individual scoring record for the Scottish Premier Division with 5 goals in Dundee Utd's 7-0 win at home to Morton on Nov 17, 1984. **Marco Negri** equalled the feat with all 5 when Rangers beat Dundee Utd 5-1 at Ibrox (Premier Division) on Aug 23, 1997, and **Kenny Miller** scored 5 in Rangers' 7-1 win at home to St Mirren on Nov 4, 2000. **Kris Boyd** scored all Kilmarnock's goals in a 5-2 SPL win at home to Dundee Utd on Sep 25, 2004. Boyd scored another 5 when Rangers beat Dundee Utd 7-1 on Dec 30, 2009. That took his total of SPL goals to a record 160. **Gary Hooper** netted all Celtic's goals in 5-0 SPL win against Hearts on May 13, 2012.

NEGRI'S TEN-TIMER

Marco Negri scored in Rangers' first ten League matches (23 goals) in season 1997–98, a Premier Division record. The previous best was 8 by **Ally MacLeod** for Hibernian in 1978.

DOUBLE SCOTTISH FINAL

Rangers v Celtic drew **129,643** and **120,073** people to the Scottish Cup Final and replay at Hampden Park, Glasgow, in 1963. Receipts for the two matches totalled £50,500.

MOST SCOTTISH CHAMPIONSHIP MEDALS

13 by **Sandy Archibald** (Rangers, 1918–34). Post-war record: 10 by **Bobby Lennox** (Celtic, 1966–79).

Alan Morton won **nine** Scottish Championship medals with Rangers in 1921–23–24–25–27–28–29–30–31. **Ally McCoist** played in the Rangers side that won nine successive League titles (1989–97).

Between 1927 and 1939 **Bob McPhail** helped Rangers win nine Championships, finish second twice and third once. He scored 236 League goals but was never top scorer in a single season.

TOP SCOTTISH LEAGUE SCORERS IN SEASON

Raith Rovers (Div 2) 142 goals in 1937–38; **Morton** (Div 2) 135 goals in 1963–64; **Hearts** (Div 1) 132 goals in 1957–58; **Falkirk** (Div 2) 132 goals in 1935–36; **Gretna** (Div 3) 130 goals in 2004–05.

SCOTTISH CUP – NO DECISION

The **Scottish FA** withheld their Cup and medals in 1908–09 after Rangers and Celtic played two drawn games in the Final. Spectators rioted.

NO WIN ALL SEASON

Brechin did not win any of their 36 Championship matches in season 2017-18. They lost every away game and finished with four points, the joint lowest-ever in British football

HAMPDEN'S £63M REDEVELOPMENT

On completion of redevelopment costing £63m **Hampden Park**, home of Scottish football and the oldest first-class stadium in the world, was re-opened full scale for the Rangers-Celtic Cup Final on May 29, 1999.

Work on the 'new Hampden' (capacity 52,000) began in 1992. The North and East stands were restructured (£12m); a new South stand and improved West stand cost £51m. The Millennium Commission contributed £23m and the Lottery Sports Fund provided a grant of £3.75m.

FIRST FOR INVERNESS

Inverness Caledonian Thistle won the Scottish Cup for the Highlands for the first time when beating Falkirk 2-1 in the Final on May 30, 2015.

FASTEST GOALS IN SPL

10.4 sec by **Kris Boyd** for Kilmarnock in 3-2 win over Ross Co, Jan 28, 2017; 12.1 sec by **Kris Commons** for Celtic in 4-3 win over Aberdeen, Mar 16, 2013; 12.4 sec by **Anthony Stokes** for Hibernian in 4-1 home defeat by Rangers, Dec 27, 2009.

YOUNGEST SCORER IN SPL

Fraser Fyvie, aged 16 years and 306 days, for Aberdeen v Hearts (3-0) on Jan 27, 2010.

12 GOALS SHARED

There was a record aggregate score for the SPL on May 5, 2010, when **Motherwell** came from 6-2 down to draw 6-6 with **Hibernian.**

25POINT DEDUCTION

Dundee were deducted 25 points by the Scottish Football League in November 2010 for going into administration for the second time. It left the club on minus 11 points, but they still managed to finish in mid-table in Division One.

GREAT SCOTS

In Feb 1988, the Scottish FA launched a national **Hall of Fame**, initially comprising the first 11

Scots to make 50 international appearances, to be joined by all future players to reach that number of caps. Each member receives a gold medal, invitation for life at all Scotland's home matches, and has his portrait hung at Scottish FA headquarters in Glasgow.

MORE CLUBS IN 2000

The **Scottish Premier League** increased from 10 to 12 clubs in season 2000–01. The **Scottish Football League** admitted two new clubs – Peterhead and Elgin City from the Highland League – to provide three divisions of 10 in 2000–01.

FIRST FOR EDINBURGH CITY

In May 2016, **Edinburgh City** became the first club to be promoted to Scottish League Two through the pyramid system with a 2-1 aggregate play-off aggregate win over East Stirling, whose 61 years in senior football came to an end.

NOTABLE SCOTTISH 'FIRSTS'

- The father of League football was a Scot, **William McGregor**, a draper in Birmingham. The 12-club Football League kicked off in Sep 1888, and McGregor was its first president.
- **Hibernian** were the first British club to play in the European Cup, by invitation. They reached the semi-final when it began in 1955–56.
- **Celtic** were Britain's first winners of the European Cup, in 1967.
- Scotland's First Division became the **Premier Division** in season 1975–76.
- Football's **first international** was staged at the West of Scotland cricket ground, Partick, on Nov 30, 1872: Scotland 0, England 0.
- Scotland introduced its **League Cup** in 1945–46, the first season after the war. It was another 15 years before the Football League Cup was launched.
- Scotland pioneered the use in British football of **two subs** per team in League and Cup matches.
- The world's **record football score** belongs to Scotland: Arbroath 36, Bon Accord 0 (Scottish Cup 1st rd) on Sep 12, 1885.
- The Scottish FA introduced the penalty **shoot-out** to their Cup Final in 1990.
- On Jan 22, 1994 all six matches in the **Scottish Premier Division** ended as draws.
- Scotland's new Premier League introduced a **3-week shut-down** in Jan 1999 – first instance of British football adopting the winter break system that operates in a number of European countries. The SPL ended its New Year closure after 2003. The break returned from season 2016–17.
- **Rangers** made history at home to St Johnstone (Premier League, 0-0, Mar 4, 2000) when fielding a team entirely without Scottish players.
- **John Fleck**, aged 16 years, 274 days, became the youngest player in a Scottish FA Cup Final when he came on as a substitute for Rangers in their 3-2 win over Queen of the South at Hampden Park on May 24, 2008

SCOTTISH CUP SHOCK RESULTS

1885–86	(1)	Arbroath 36 Bon Accord 0
1921–22	(F)	Morton 1 Rangers 0
1937–38	(F)	East Fife 4 Kilmarnock 2 (replay, after 1-1)
1960–61	(F)	Dunfermline 2 Celtic 0 (replay, after 0-0)
1966–67	(1)	Berwick 1 Rangers 0
1979–80	(3)	Hamilton 2 Keith 3
1984–85	(1)	Stirling 20 Selkirk 0
1984–85	(3)	Inverness 3 Kilmarnock 0
1986–87	(3)	Rangers 0 Hamilton 1
1994–95	(4)	Stenhousemuir 2 Aberdeen 0
1998–99	(3)	Aberdeen 0 Livingston 1

1999–2000	(3)	Celtic 1 Inverness 3
2003–04	(5)	Inverness 1 Celtic 0
2005–06	(3)	Clyde 2 Celtic 1
2008–09	(6)	St Mirren 1 Celtic 0
2009–10	(SF)	Ross Co 2 Celtic 0
2013–14	(4)	Albion 1 Motherwell 0
2020–21	(2)	Brora 2 Hearts 1

Scottish League (Coca-Cola) Cup Final
1994–95   Raith 2, Celtic 2 (Raith won 6-5 on pens)

Europa League first qualifying round
2017–18   Progres Niederkorn (Luxembourg) 2 Rangers 1 (on agg)
2019–20   Connah's Quay (Wales) 3 Kilmarnock 2 (on agg)

MISCELLANEOUS

NATIONAL ASSOCIATIONS FORMED

FA	1863
FA of Wales	1876
Scottish FA	1873
Irish FA	1904
Federation of International Football Associations (FIFA)	1904

NATIONAL & INTERNATIONAL COMPETITIONS LAUNCHED

FA Cup	1871
Welsh Cup	1877
Scottish Cup	1873
Irish Cup	1880
Football League	1888
Premier League	1992
Scottish League	1890
Scottish Premier League	1998
Scottish League Cup	1945
Football League Cup	1960
Home International Championship	1883–84
World Cup	1930
European Championship	1958
European Cup	1955
Fairs/UEFA Cup	1955
Cup-Winners' Cup	1960
European Champions League	1992
Olympic Games Tournament, at Shepherd's Bush	1908

INNOVATIONS

Size of Ball: Fixed in **1872**.

Shinguards: Introduced and registered by Sam Weller Widdowson (Nottm Forest & England) in **1874**.

Referee's whistle: First used on Nottm Forest's ground in **1878**.

Professionalism: Legalised in England in the summer of **1885** as a result of agitation by Lancashire clubs.

Goal-nets: Invented and patented in **1890** by Mr JA Brodie of Liverpool. They were first used in the North v South match in Jan, **1891**.

Referees and linesmen: Replaced umpires and referees in Jan, **1891**.

Penalty-kick: Introduced at Irish FA's request in the season **1891–92**. The penalty law ordering the goalkeeper to remain on the goal-line came into force in Sep, **1905**, and the order to stand on his goal-line until the ball is kicked arrived in **1929–30**.

White ball: First came into official use in **1951**.

Floodlighting: First FA Cup-tie (replay), Kidderminster Harriers v Brierley Hill Alliance, **1955**. First Football League match: Portsmouth v Newcastle (Div 1), **1956**.

Heated pitch to beat frost tried by Everton at Goodison Park in **1958**.

First soccer closed-circuit TV: At Coventry ground in Oct **1965** (10,000 fans saw their team win at Cardiff, 120 miles away).

Substitutes (one per team) were first allowed in Football League matches at the start of season **1965–66**. Three substitutes (one a goalkeeper) allowed, two of which could be used, in Premier League matches, **1992–93**. The Football League introduced three substitutes for **1993–94**.

Three points for a win: Introduced by the Football League in **1981–82**, by FIFA in World Cup games in **1994**, and by the Scottish League in the same year.

Offside law amended, player 'level' no longer offside, and 'professional foul' made sending-off offence, **1990**.

Penalty shoot-outs introduced to decide FA Cup ties level after one replay and extra time, **1991–92**.

New back-pass rule: goalkeeper must not handle ball kicked to him by team-mate, **1992**.

Linesmen became 'referees' assistants', **1998**.

Goalkeepers not to hold ball longer than 6 seconds, **2000**.

Free-kicks advanced by ten yards against opponents failing to retreat, **2000**. This experimental rule in England was scrapped in 2005).

YOUNGEST AND OLDEST

Youngest Caps

Harry Wilson (Wales v Belgium, Oct 15, 2013)	16 years 207 days
Norman Whiteside (N Ireland v Yugoslavia, Jun 17, 1982)	17 years 41 days
Theo Walcott (England v Hungary, May 30, 2006)	17 years 75 days
Johnny Lambie (Scotland v Ireland, Mar 20, 1886)	17 years 92 days
Jimmy Holmes (Rep of Ireland v Austria, May 30, 1971)	17 years 200 days

Youngest England scorer: Wayne Rooney (17 years, 317 days) v Macedonia, Skopje, Sep 6, 2003.

Youngest scorer on England debut: Marcus Rashford (18 years, 208 days) v Australia, Sunderland, May 27, 2016.

Youngest England hat-trick scorer: Theo Walcott (19 years, 178 days) v Croatia, Zagreb, Sep 10, 2008.

Youngest England captains: Bobby Moore (v Czech., Bratislava, May 29, 1963), 22 years, 47 days; Michael Owen (v Paraguay, Anfield, Apr 17, 2002), 22 years, 117 days.

Youngest England goalkeeper: Jack Butland (19 years, 158 days) v Italy, Bern, Aug 15, 2012

Youngest England players to reach 50 caps: Michael Owen (23 years, 6 months) v Slovakia at Middlesbrough, Jun 11, 2003; Bobby Moore (25 years, 7 months) v Wales at Wembley, Nov 16, 1966.

Youngest player in World Cup Final: Pele (Brazil) aged 17 years, 237 days v Sweden in Stockholm, Jun 12, 1958.

Youngest player to appear in World Cup Finals: Norman Whiteside (N Ireland v Yugoslavia in Spain – Jun 17, 1982, age 17 years and 42 days).

Youngest First Division player: Derek Forster (Sunderland goalkeeper v Leicester, Aug 22, 1964) aged 15 years, 185 days.

Youngest First Division scorer: At 16 years and 57 days, schoolboy Jason Dozzell (substitute after 30 minutes for Ipswich at home to Coventry on Feb 4, 1984). Ipswich won 3-1 and Dozzell scored their third goal.

Youngest Premier League player: Harvey Elliott (Fulham on loan from Liverpool, sub away to

Wolves, May 4, 2019), 16 years and 30 days.

Youngest Premier League scorer: James Vaughan (Everton, home to Crystal Palace, Apr 10, 2005), 16 years, 271 days.

Youngest Premier League scorer on first start: Daniel Jebbison (Sheffield Utd away to Everton, May 16, 2021) aged 17 years, 309 days.

Youngest Premier League captain: Lee Cattermole (Middlesbrough away to Fulham, May 7, 2006) aged 18 years, 47 days.

Youngest player sent off in Premier League: Wayne Rooney (Everton, away to Birmingham, Dec 26, 2002) aged 17 years, 59 days.

Youngest First Division hat-trick scorer: Alan Shearer, aged 17 years, 240 days, in Southampton's 4-2 home win v Arsenal (Apr 9, 1988) on his full debut. Previously, Jimmy Greaves (17 years, 309 days) with 4 goals for Chelsea at home to Portsmouth (7-4), Christmas Day, 1957.

Youngest to complete 100 Football League goals: Jimmy Greaves (20 years, 261 days) when he did so for Chelsea v Manchester City, Nov 19, 1960.

Youngest players in Football League: Reuben Noble-Lazarus (Barnsley 84th minute sub at Ipswich, Sep 30, 2008, Champ) aged 15 years, 45 days; Mason Bennett (Derby at Middlesbrough, Champ, Oct 22, 2011) aged 15 years, 99 days; Albert Geldard (Bradford PA v Millwall, Div 2, Sep 16, 1929) aged 15 years, 158 days; Ken Roberts (Wrexham v Bradford Park Avenue, Div 3 North, Sep 1, 1951) also 15 years, 158 days.

Youngest Football League scorer: Ronnie Dix (for Bristol Rov v Norwich, Div 3 South, Mar 3, 1928) aged 15 years, 180 days.

Youngest player in Scottish League: Goalkeeper Ronnie Simpson (Queens Park) aged 15 in 1946.

Youngest player in FA Cup: Andy Awford, Worcester City's England Schoolboy defender, aged 15 years, 88 days when he substituted in second half away to Boreham Wood (3rd qual round) on Oct 10, 1987.

Youngest player in FA Cup proper: Luke Freeman, Gillingham substitute striker (15 years, 233 days) away to Barnet in 1st round, Nov 10, 2007.

Youngest FA Cup scorer: Sean Cato (16 years, 25 days), second half sub in Barrow Town's 7-2 win away to Rothwell Town (prelim rd), Sep 3, 2011.

Youngest Wembley Cup Final captain: Barry Venison (Sunderland v Norwich, Milk Cup Final, Mar 24, 1985 – replacing suspended captain Shaun Elliott) – aged 20 years, 220 days.

Youngest FA Cup-winning captain: Bobby Moore (West Ham, 1964, v Preston), aged 23 years, 20 days.

Youngest FA Cup Final captain: David Nish aged 21 years and 212 days old when he captained Leicester against Manchester City at Wembley on Apr 26, 1969.

Youngest FA Cup Final player: Curtis Weston (Millwall sub last 3 mins v Manchester Utd, 2004) aged 17 years, 119 days.

Youngest FA Cup Final scorer: Norman Whiteside (Manchester Utd v Brighton, 1983 replay, Wembley) aged 18 years, 19 days.

Youngest FA Cup Final managers: Stan Cullis, Wolves (32) v Leicester, 1949; Steve Coppell, Crystal Palace (34) v Manchester Utd, 1990; Ruud Gullit, Chelsea (34) v Middlesbrough, 1997.

Youngest player in Football League Cup: Harvey Elliott (Fulham) sub v Millwall, 3rd round, Sep 25, 2018, aged 15 years and 174 days.

Youngest Wembley scorer: Norman Whiteside (Manchester Utd v Liverpool, Milk Cup Final, Mar 26, 1983) aged 17 years, 324 days.

Youngest Wembley Cup Final goalkeeper: Chris Woods (18 years, 125 days) for Nottm Forest v Liverpool, League Cup Final on Mar 18, 1978.

Youngest Wembley FA Cup Final goalkeeper: Peter Shilton (19 years, 219 days) for Leicester v Manchester City, Apr 26, 1969.

Youngest senior international at Wembley: Salomon Olembe (sub for Cameroon v England, Nov 15, 1997), aged 16 years, 342 days.

Youngest winning manager at Wembley: Stan Cullis, aged 32 years, 187 days, as manager of Wolves, FA Cup winners on April 30 1949.

Youngest scorer in full international: Mohamed Kallon (Sierra Leone v Congo, African Nations Cup, Apr 22, 1995), reported as aged 15 years, 192 days.

Youngest English player to start a Champions League game: Phil Foden (Manchester City v Shakhtar Donetsk, Dec 6, 2017) aged 17 years, 192 days.

Youngest English scorer in Champions League: Alex Oxlade-Chamberlain (Arsenal v Olympíacos, September 28 2011) aged 18 years, 1 month 13 days.

Youngest player sent off in World Cup Final series: Rigobert Song (Cameroon v Brazil, in USA, Jun 1994) aged 17 years, 358 days.

Youngest FA Cup Final referee: Kevin Howley, of Middlesbrough, aged 35 when in charge of Wolves v Blackburn, 1960.

Youngest player in England U-23 team: Duncan Edwards (v Italy, Bologna, Jan 20, 1954), aged 17 years, 112 days.

Youngest player in England U-21 team: Theo Walcott (v Moldova, Ipswich, Aug 15, 2006), aged 17 years, 152 days.

Youngest player in Scotland U-21 team: Christian Dailly (v Romania, Hampden Park, Sep 11, 1990), aged 16 years, 330 days.

Youngest player in senior football: Cameron Campbell Buchanan, Scottish-born outside right, aged 14 years, 57 days when he played for Wolves v WBA in War-time League match, Sep 26, 1942.

Youngest player in peace-time senior match: Eamon Collins (Blackpool v Kilmarnock, Anglo-Scottish Cup quarter-final 1st leg, Sep 9, 1980) aged 14 years, 323 days.

World's youngest player in top division match: Centre-forward Fernando Rafael Garcia, aged 13, played for 23 minutes for Peruvian club Juan Aurich in 3-1 win against Estudiantes on May 19, 2001.

Oldest player to appear in Football League: New Brighton manager Neil McBain (51 years, 120 days) as emergency goalkeeper away to Hartlepool (Div 3 North, Mar 15, 1947).

Other oldest post-war League players: Sir Stanley Matthews (Stoke, 1965, 50 years, 5 days); Peter Shilton (Leyton Orient 1997, 47 years, 126 days); Kevin Poole (Burton, 2010, 46 years, 291 days); Dave Beasant (Brighton 2003, 44 years, 46 days); Alf Wood (Coventry, 1958, 43 years, 199 days); Tommy Hutchison (Swansea City, 1991, 43 years, 172 days).

Oldest Football League debutant: Andy Cunningham, for Newcastle at Leicester (Div 1) on Feb 2, 1929, aged 38 years, 2 days.

Oldest post-war debut in English League: Defender David Donaldson (35 years, 7 months, 23 days) for Wimbledon on entry to Football League (Div 4) away to Halifax, Aug 20, 1977.

Oldest player to appear in First Division: Sir Stanley Matthews (Stoke v Fulham, Feb 6, 1965), aged 50 years, 5 days – on that his last League appearance, the only 50-year-old ever to play in the top division.

Oldest players in Premier League: Goalkeepers John Burridge (Manchester City v QPR, May 14, 1995), 43 years, 5 months, 11 days; Alec Chamberlain (Watford v Newcastle, May 13, 2007) 42 years, 11 months, 23 days; Steve Ogrizovic (Coventry v Sheffield Wed, May 6, 2000, 42 years, 7 months, 24 days.)

Oldest player for British professional club: John Ryan (owner-chairman of Conference club Doncaster, played as substitute for last minute in 4-2 win at Hereford on Apr 26, 2003), aged 52 years, 11 months, 3 weeks.

Oldest FA Cup Final player: Walter (Billy) Hampson (Newcastle v Aston Villa on Apr 26, 1924), aged 41 years, 257 days.

Oldest captain and goalkeeper in FA Cup Final: David James (Portsmouth v Chelsea, May 15, 2010) aged 39 years, 287 days.

Oldest FA Cup Final scorers: Bert Turner (Charlton v Derby, Apr 27, 1946) aged 36 years, 312 days. Scored for both sides. Teddy Sheringham (West Ham v Liverpool, May 13, 2006) aged 40 years, 41 days. Scored in penalty shoot-out.

Oldest FA Cup-winning team: Arsenal 1950 (average age 31 years, 2 months). Eight of the players were over 30, with the three oldest centre-half Leslie Compton 37, and skipper Joe Mercer and goalkeeper George Swindin, both 35.

Oldest World Cup-winning captain: Dino Zoff, Italy's goalkeeper v W Germany in 1982 Final, aged 40 years, 92 days.

Oldest player capped by England: Stanley Matthews (v Denmark, Copenhagen, May 15, 1957), aged 42 years, 103 days.

Oldest England scorer: Stanley Matthews (v N Ireland, Belfast, Oct 6, 1956), aged 41 years, 248 days.

Oldest British international player: Billy Meredith (Wales v England at Highbury, Mar 15, 1920), aged 45 years, 229 days.

Oldest 'new caps': Goalkeeper Alexander Morten, aged 41 years, 113 days when earning his only England Cap against Scotland on Mar 8, 1873; Arsenal centre-half Leslie Compton, at 38 years, 64 days when he made his England debut in 4-2 win against Wales at Sunderland on Nov 15, 1950. **For Scotland:** Goalkeeper Ronnie Simpson (Celtic) at 36 years, 186 days v England at Wembley, Apr 15, 1967.

Oldest scorer in Wembley Final: Chris Swailes, 45, for Morpeth in 4-1 win over Hereford (FA Vase), May 22, 2016.

Longest Football League career: This spanned 32 years and 10 months, by Stanley Matthews (Stoke, Blackpool, Stoke) from Mar 19, 1932 until Feb 6, 1965.

Shortest FA Cup-winning captain: 5ft 4in – Bobby Kerr (Sunderland v Leeds, 1973).

KANTE'S PEAK

N'Golo Kante became the first player in English football to win back-to-back titles with different clubs while playing a full season with each – Leicester (2015-16), Chelsea (2016–17).

EURO FIRST FOR REFEREE

Liverpool's defeat of Chelsea on penalties in the Super Cup on Aug 14, 2019, was refereed by Stephanie Frappart, of France, who became the first woman to take charge of a major European men's match.

SHIRT NUMBERING

Numbering players in Football League matches was made compulsory in 1939. Players wore numbered shirts (1-22) in the FA Cup Final as an experiment in 1933 (Everton 1-11 v Manchester City 12-22).

Squad numbers for players were introduced by the Premier League at the start of season 1993–94. They were optional in the Football League until made compulsory in 1999–2000.

Names on shirts: For first time, players wore names as well as numbers on shirts in League Cup and FA Cup Finals, 1993.

FIRST SUBSTITUTE

The first substitute used in the Football League was **Keith Peacock** (Charlton) away to Bolton in Div 2, Aug 21, 1965.

END OF WAGE LIMIT

Freedom from the maximum wage system – in force since the formation of the Football League in 1888 – was secured by the Professional Footballers' Association in 1961. About this time Italian clubs renewed overtures for the transfer of British stars and Fulham's **Johnny Haynes** became the first British player to earn £100 a week.

THE BOSMAN RULING

On Dec 15, 1995 the **European Court of Justice** ruled that clubs had no right to transfer fees for out-of-contract players, and the outcome of the 'Bosman case' irrevocably changed football's player-club relationship. It began in 1990, when the contract of 26-year-old **Jean-Marc Bosman**, a midfield player with FC Liege, Belgium, expired. French club Dunkirk wanted him but were unwilling to pay the £500,000 transfer fee, so Bosman was compelled to remain with Liege. He responded with a lawsuit against his club and UEFA on the grounds of 'restriction of trade', and after five years at various court levels the European Court of Justice ruled not only in favour of Bosman but of all professional footballers.

The end of restrictive labour practices revolutionised the system. It led to a proliferation of transfers, rocketed the salaries of elite players who, backed by an increasing army of agents, found themselves in a vastly improved bargaining position as they moved from team to team, league to league, nation to nation. Removing the limit on the number of foreigners clubs could field brought an increasing ratio of such signings, not least in England and Scotland.

Bosman's one-man stand opened the way for footballers to become millionaires, but ended his own career. All he received for his legal conflict was 16 million Belgian francs (£312,000) in compensation, a testimonial of poor reward and martyrdom as the man who did most to change the face of football.

By 2011, he was living on Belgian state benefits, saying: 'I have made the world of football rich and shifted the power from clubs to players. Now I find myself with nothing.'

INTERNATIONAL SHOCK RESULTS

1950	USA 1 England 0 (World Cup).
1953	England 3 Hungary 6 (friendly).
1954	Hungary 7 England 1 (friendly)
1966	North Korea 1 Italy 0 (World Cup).
1982	Spain 0, Northern Ireland 1; Algeria 2, West Germany 1 (World Cup).
1990	Cameroon 1 Argentina 0; Scotland 0 Costa Rica 1; Sweden 1 Costa Rica 2 (World Cup).
1990	Faroe Islands 1 Austria 0 (European Champ qual).
1992	Denmark 2 Germany 0 (European Champ Final).
1993	USA 2 England 0 (US Cup tournament).
1993	Argentina 0 Colombia 5 (World Cup qual).
1993	France 2 Israel 3 (World Cup qual).
1994	Bulgaria 2 Germany 1 (World Cup).
1994	Moldova 3 Wales 2; Georgia 5 Wales 0 (European Champ qual).
1995	Belarus 1 Holland 0 (European Champ qual).
1996	Nigeria 4 Brazil 3 (Olympics).
1998	USA 1 Brazil 0 (Concacaf Gold Cup).
1998	Croatia 3 Germany 0 (World Cup).
2000	Scotland 0 Australia 2 (friendly).
2001	Australia 1 France 0; Australia 1, Brazil 0 (Confederations Cup).
2001	Honduras 2 Brazil 0 (Copa America).
2001	Germany 1 England 5 (World Cup qual).
2002	France 0 Senegal 1; South Korea 2 Italy 1 (World Cup).
2003:	England 1 Australia 3 (friendly)
2004:	Portugal 0 Greece 1 (European Champ Final).
2005:	Northern Ireland 1 England 0 (World Cup qual).
2014:	Holland 5 Spain 1 (World Cup).
2014:	Brazil 1 Germany 7 (World Cup).
2016	England 1 Iceland 2 (European Champ)
2018	South Korea 2 Germany 0 (World Cup)

GREAT RECOVERIES – DOMESTIC FOOTBALL

On Dec 21, 1957, **Charlton** were losing 5-1 against Huddersfield (Div 2) at The Valley with only 28 minutes left, and from the 15th minute, had been reduced to ten men by injury, but they won 7-6, with left-winger Johnny Summers scoring five goals. **Huddersfield** (managed by Bill Shankly) remain the only team to score six times in a League match and lose. On Boxing

Day, 1927 in Div 3 South, **Northampton** won 6-5 at home to Luton after being 1-5 down at half-time.

Season 2010–11 produced a Premier League record for **Newcastle**, who came from 4-0 down at home to Arsenal to draw 4-4. Previous instance of a team retrieving a four-goal deficit in the top division to draw was in 1984 when Newcastle trailed at QPR in a game which ended 5-5. In the 2012-13 League Cup, **Arsenal** were 0-4 down in a fourth round tie at Reading, levelled at 4-4 and went on to win 7-5 in extra-time.

MATCHES OFF

Worst day for postponements: Feb 9, 1963, when 57 League fixtures in England and Scotland were frozen off. Only 7 Football League matches took place, and the entire Scottish programme was wiped out.

Other weather-hit days:

Jan 12, 1963 and Feb 2, 1963 – on both those Saturdays, only 4 out of 44 Football League matches were played.

Jan 1, 1979 – 43 out of 46 Football League fixtures postponed.

Jan 17, 1987 – 37 of 45 scheduled Football League fixtures postponed; only 2 Scottish matches survived.

Feb 8–9, 1991 – only 4 of the week-end's 44 Barclays League matches survived the freeze-up (4 of the postponements were on Friday night). In addition, 11 Scottish League matches were off.

Jan 27, 1996 – 44 Cup and League matches in England and Scotland were frozen off.

On the weekend of Jan 9, 10, 11, 2010, 46 League and Cup matches in England and Scotland were victims of the weather. On the weekend of Dec 18-21, 2010, 49 matches were frozen off in England and Scotland.

Fewest matches left on one day by postponements was during the Second World War – Feb 3, 1940 when, because of snow, ice and fog only one out of 56 regional league fixtures took place. It resulted Plymouth Argyle 10, Bristol City 3.

The Scottish Cup second round tie between Inverness Thistle and Falkirk in season 1978–79 was **postponed 29 times** because of snow and ice. First put off on Jan 6, it was eventually played on Feb 22. Falkirk won 4-0.

Pools Panel's busiest days: Jan 17, 1987 and Feb 9, 1991 – on both dates they gave their verdict on 48 postponed coupon matches.

FEWEST 'GAMES OFF'

Season 1947–48 was the best since the war for English League fixtures being played to schedule. Only six were postponed.

LONGEST SEASON

The latest that league football has been played in a season was July 26, 2020, following a three-month shutdown from the middle of March caused by the coronavirus pandemic. The Premier League and Championship were completed, with Leagues One and Two curtailed and final positions decided on a points-per-game basis. This system was used in Scotland, where all four divisions were cut short. The FA Cup was completed on August 1, Arsenal defeating Chelsea 2-1. The Scottish Cup, paused after the quarter-finals, was completed in the 2020–21 season.

Worst winter hold-up was in season 1962–63. The Big Freeze began on Boxing Day and lasted until Mar, with nearly 500 first-class matches postponed. The FA Cup 3rd round was the longest on record – it began with only three out of 32 ties playable on Jan 5 and ended 66 days and 261 postponements later on Mar 11. The Lincoln–Coventry tie was put off 15 times. The Pools Panel was launched that winter, on Jan 26, 1963.

HOTTEST DAYS

The Nationwide League kicked off season 2003–04 on Aug 9 with pitch temperatures of 102 degrees recorded at Luton v Rushden and Bradford v Norwich. On the following day, there was a pitch temperature of 100 degrees for the Community Shield match between Manchester Utd and Arsenal at Cardiff's Millennium Stadium. Wembley's pitch-side thermometer registered 107 degrees for the 2009 Chelsea–Everton FA Cup Final.

FOOTBALL LEAGUE NAME CHANGE

From the start of the 2016-17 season, the Football League was renamed the English Football League, as part of a corporate and competition rebranding.

FOOTBALL ASSOCIATION SECRETARIES/CHIEF EXECUTIVES

1863–66 Ebenezer Morley; 1866–68 **Robert Willis**; 1868–70 **RG Graham**; 1870–95 **Charles Alcock** (paid from 1887); 1895–1934 **Sir Frederick Wall**; 1934–62 **Sir Stanley Rous**; 1962–73 **Denis Follows**; 1973–89 **Ted Croker** (latterly chief executive); 1989–99 **Graham Kelly** (chief executive); 2000–02 **Adam Crozier** (chief executive); 2003–04 **Mark Palios** (chief executive); 2005–08: **Brian Barwick** (chief executive); 2009–10 **Ian Watmore** (chief executive); 2010-15 **Alex Horne** (chief executive); 2015–19 **Martin Glenn** (chief executive); 2019 **Mark Bullingham** (chief executive).

FOOTBALL'S SPONSORS

Football League: Canon 1983–86; Today Newspaper 1986–87; Barclays 1987–93; Endsleigh Insurance 1993–96; Nationwide Building Society 1996–2004; Coca-Cola 2004–10; npower 2010–14; Sky Bet from 2014.

League Cup: Milk Cup 1982–86; Littlewoods 1987–90; Rumbelows 1991–92; Coca-Cola 1993–98; Worthington 1998–2003; Carling 2003–12; Capital One 2012–16; Carabao from 2017.

Premier League: Carling 1993–2001; Barclaycard 2001–04; Barclays 2004–16.

FA Cup: Littlewoods 1994–98; AXA 1998–2002; E.ON 2006–11; Budweiser 2011–15; Emirates (title sponsor) from 2015.

NEW HOMES FOR CLUBS

Newly-constructed League grounds in England since the war: 1946 Hull (Boothferry Park); 1950 Port Vale (Vale Park); 1955 Southend (Roots Hall); 1988 Scunthorpe (Glanford Park); 1990 Walsall (Bescot Stadium); 1990 Wycombe (Adams Park); 1992 Chester (Deva Stadium); 1993 Millwall (New Den); 1994 Huddersfield (McAlpine Stadium); 1994 Northampton (Sixfields Stadium); 1995 Middlesbrough (Riverside Stadium); 1997 Bolton (Reebok Stadium); 1997 Derby (Pride Park); 1997 Stoke (Britannia Stadium); 1997 Sunderland (Stadium of Light); 1998 Reading (Madejski Stadium); 1999 Wigan (JJB Stadium); 2001 Southampton (St Mary's Stadium); 2001 Oxford Utd (Kassam Stadium); 2002 Leicester (Walkers Stadium); 2002 Hull (Kingston Communications Stadium); 2003 Manchester City (City of Manchester Stadium); 2003 Darlington (New Stadium); 2005 Coventry (Ricoh Arena); Swansea (Stadium of Swansea, Morfa); 2006 Arsenal (Emirates Stadium); 2007 Milton Keynes Dons (Stadium: MK); Shrewsbury (New Meadow); Doncaster (Keepmoat Stadium); 2008 Colchester (Community Stadium); 2009 Cardiff City Stadium; 2010 Chesterfield (b2net Stadium), Morecambe (Globe Arena); 2011 Brighton (American Express Stadium); 2012 Rotherham (New York Stadium). 2016 West Ham (Olympic Stadium); 2019 Tottenham (Tottenham Hotspur Stadium); 2020 Brentford (Community Stadium); AFC Wimbledon (Plough Lane Stadium).

NATIONAL FOOTBALL CENTRE

The FA's new £120m centre at St George's Park, Burton upon Trent, was opened on Oct 9, 20012 by the Duke of Cambridge, president of the FA. The site covers 330 acres, has 12 full-size pitches (5 with undersoil heating and floodlighting). There are 5 gyms, a 90-seat lecture theatre, a hydrotherapy unit with swimming pool for the treatment of injuries and two hotels. It is the base for England teams, men and women, at all levels.

GROUND-SHARING

Manchester Utd played their home matches at **Manchester City's** Maine Road ground for 8 years after Old Trafford was bomb-damaged in Aug 1941. **Crystal Palace** and **Charlton** shared Selhurst Park (1985–91); **Bristol Rov** and **Bath City** (Twerton Park, Bath, 1986–96); **Partick Thistle** and **Clyde** (Firhill Park, Glasgow, 1986–91; in seasons 1990–01, 1991–92 **Chester** shared **Macclesfield's** ground (Moss Rose).

Crystal Palace and **Wimbledon** shared Selhurst Park, from season 1991–92, when **Charlton** (tenants) moved to rent Upton Park from **West Ham**, until 2003 when Wimbledon relocated to Milton Keynes. **Clyde** moved to Douglas Park, **Hamilton Academical's** home, in 1991–92. **Stirling Albion** shared **Stenhousemuir's** ground, Ochilview Park, in 1992–93. In 1993–94, **Clyde** shared **Partick's** home until moving to Cumbernauld. In 1994–95, **Celtic** shared Hampden Park with **Queen's Park** (while Celtic Park was redeveloped); **Hamilton** shared **Partick's** ground. **Airdrie** shared **Clyde's** Broadwood Stadium. **Bristol Rov** left **Bath City's** ground at the start of season 1996–97, sharing Bristol Rugby Club's Memorial Ground. **Clydebank** shared **Dumbarton's** Boghead Park from 1996–97 until renting **Greenock Morton's** Cappielow Park in season 1999–2000. **Brighton** shared **Gillingham's** ground in seasons 1997–98, 1998–99. **Fulham** shared **QPR's** home at Loftus Road in seasons 2002–03, 2003–04, returning to Craven Cottage in Aug 2004. **Coventry** played home fixtures at Northampton in season 2013–14, returning to their own ground, the Ricoh Arena, in Sept 2014 **Coventry** were unable to agree terms to play at the Ricoh Arena in season 2019–20 and moved home games to Birmingham's St Andrew's Stadium. Coventry returned home for season 2021–22, with the Ricoh Arena having been renamed the Coventry Building Society Stadium.

Inverness Caledonian Thistle moved to share **Aberdeen's** Pittodrie Stadium in 2004–05 after being promoted to the SPL; **Gretna's** home matches on arrival in the SPL in 2007–08 were held at Motherwell and Livingston. Stenhousemuir (owners) share Ochilview with East Stirling (tenants).

ARTIFICIAL TURF

QPR were the first British club to install an artificial pitch, in 1981. They were followed by **Luton** in 1985, and **Oldham** and **Preston** in **1986**. QPR reverted to grass in 1988, as did Luton and promoted Oldham in season 1991–92 (when artificial pitches were banned in Div 1). **Preston** were the last Football League club playing 'on plastic' in 1993–94, and their Deepdale ground was restored to grass for the start of 1994–95.

Stirling were the **first Scottish club** to play on plastic, in season 1987–88.

CORNER-KICK RECORDS

Not a single corner-kick was recorded when **Newcastle** drew 0-0 at home to **Portsmouth** (Div 1) on Dec 5, 1931.

The record for **most corners** in a match for one side is believed to be **Sheffield Utd's 28** to West Ham's 1 in Div 2 at Bramall Lane on Oct 14, 1989. For all their pressure, Sheffield Utd lost 2-0.

Nottm Forest led **Southampton** 22-2 on corners (Premier League, Nov 28, 1992) but lost the match 1-2.

Tommy Higginson (Brentford, 1960s) once passed back to his own goalkeeper from a corner kick.

When **Wigan** won 4-0 at home to Cardiff (Div 2) on Feb 16, 2002, all four goals were headed in from corners taken by N Ireland international **Peter Kennedy**.

Steve Staunton (Rep of Ireland) is believed to be the only player to score direct from a corner in **two** Internationals.

In the 2012 Champions League Final, **Bayern Munich** forced 20 corners without scoring, while **Chelsea** scored from their only one.

SACKED AT HALF-TIME

Tottenham sacked **Martin Jol** after a poor start to the 2007-08 season, with the manager learning of his fate at half-time of a UEFA Cup group match against the Spanish side Getafe at White Hart Lane on the night of October 25.

Leyton Orient sacked **Terry Howard** on his 397th appearance for the club – at half-time in a Second Division home defeat against Blackpool (Feb 7, 1995) for 'an unacceptable performance'. He was fined two weeks' wages, given a free transfer and moved to Wycombe.

Bobby Gould resigned as **Peterborough's** head coach at half-time in their 1-0 defeat in the LDV Vans Trophy 1st round at Bristol City on Sep 29, 2004.

Harald Schumacher, former Germany goalkeeper, was sacked as Fortuna Koln coach when they were two down at half-time against Waldhof Mannheim (Dec 15, 1999). They lost 5-1.

MOST GAMES BY 'KEEPER FOR ONE CLUB

Alan Knight made 683 League appearances for Portsmouth, over 23 seasons (1978–2000), a record for a goalkeeper at one club. The previous holder was Peter Bonetti with 600 League games for Chelsea (20 seasons, 1960–79).

PLAYED TWO GAMES ON SAME DAY

Jack Kelsey played full-length matches for both club and country on Wednesday Nov 26, 1958. In the afternoon he kept goal for Wales in a 2-2 draw against England at Villa Park, and he then drove to Highbury to help Arsenal win 3-1 in a prestigious floodlit friendly against Juventus.

On the same day, winger **Danny Clapton** played for England (against Wales and Kelsey) and then in part of Arsenal's match against Juventus.

On Nov 11, 1987, **Mark Hughes** played for Wales against Czechoslovakia (European Championship) in Prague, then flew to Munich and went on as substitute that night in a winning Bayern Munich team, to whom he was on loan from Barcelona.

On Feb 16, 1993 goalkeeper **Scott Howie** played in Scotland's 3-0 U-21 win v Malta at Tannadice Park, Dundee (ko 1.30pm) and the same evening played in Clyde's 2-1 home win v Queen of South (Div 2).

Ryman League **Hornchurch**, faced by end-of-season fixture congestion, played **two matches** on the same night (May 1, 2001). They lost 2-1 at home to Ware and drew 2-2 at Clapton.

FIRST 'MATCH OF THE DAY'

BBC TV (recorded highlights): Liverpool 3, Arsenal 2 on Aug 22, 1964. **First complete match to be televised:** Arsenal 3, Everton 2 on Aug 29, 1936. **First League match televised in colour:** Liverpool 2, West Ham 0 on Nov 15, 1969.

'MATCH OF THE DAY' – BIGGEST SCORES

Football League: Tottenham 9, Bristol Rov 0 (Div 2, 1977–78). **Premier League:** Nottm Forest 1, Manchester Utd 8 (1998–99); Portsmouth 7 Reading 4 (2007–08).

FIRST COMMENTARY ON RADIO

Arsenal 1 Sheffield Utd 1 (Div 1) broadcast on BBC, Jan 22, 1927.

OLYMPIC FOOTBALL WINNERS

1908 Great Britain (in London); **1912** Great Britain (Stockholm); **1920** Belgium (Antwerp); **1924** Uruguay (Paris); **1928** Uruguay (Amsterdam); **1932** No soccer in Los Angeles Olympics; **1936** Italy (Berlin); **1948** Sweden (London); **1952** Hungary (Helsinki); **1956** USSR (Melbourne); **1960** Yugoslavia (Rome); **1964** Hungary (Tokyo); **1968** Hungary (Mexico City); **1972** Poland (Munich); **1976** E Germany (Montreal); **1980** Czechoslovakia (Moscow); **1984** France (Los Angeles); **1988** USSR (Seoul); **1992** Spain (Barcelona); **1996** Nigeria (Atlanta); **2000** Cameroon (Sydney); **2004** Argentina (Athens); **2008** Argentina (Beijing);

2012 Mexico (Wembley); **2016** Brazil (Rio de Janeiro); **2020** Brazil (Yokohama).
Highest scorer in Final tournament: Ferenc Bene (Hungary) 12 goals, 1964.
Record crowd for Olympic Soccer Final: 108,800 (France v Brazil, Los Angeles 1984).

MOST AMATEUR CUP WINS

Bishop Auckland set the FA Amateur Cup record with 10 wins, and in 1957 became the only club to carry off the trophy in three successive seasons. The competition was discontinued after the Final on Apr 20, 1974. (Bishop's Stortford 4, Ilford 1, at Wembley).

FOOTBALL FOUNDATION

This was formed (May 2000) to replace the **Football Trust**, which had been in existence since 1975 as an initiative of the Pools companies to provide financial support at all levels, from schools football to safety and ground improvement work throughout the game.

SEVEN-FIGURE TESTIMONIALS

The first was **Sir Alex Ferguson**'s at Old Trafford on Oct 11, 1999, when a full-house of 54,842 saw a Rest of the World team beat Manchester Utd 4-2. United's manager pledged that a large percentage of the estimated £1m receipts would go to charity.

Estimated receipts of £1m and over came from testimonials for **Denis Irwin** (Manchester Utd) against Manchester City at Old Trafford on Aug 16, 2000 (45,158); **Tom Boyd** (Celtic) against Manchester Utd at Celtic Park on May 15, 2001 (57,000) and **Ryan Giggs** (Manchester Utd) against Celtic on Aug 1, 2001 (66,967).

Tony Adams' second testimonial (1-1 v Celtic on May 13, 2002) two nights after Arsenal completed the Double, was watched by 38,021 spectators at Highbury. Of £1m receipts, he donated £500,000 to Sporting Chance, the charity that helps sportsmen/women with drink, drug, gambling problems.

Sunderland and a Republic of Ireland XI drew 0-0 in front of 35,702 at the Stadium of Light on May 14, 2002. The beneficiary, **Niall Quinn**, donated his testimonial proceeds, estimated at £1m, to children's hospitals in Sunderland and Dublin, and to homeless children in Africa and Asia.

A record testimonial crowd of 69,591 for **Roy Keane** at Old Trafford on May 9, 2006 netted more than £2m for charities in Dublin, Cork and Manchester. Manchester Utd beat Celtic 1-0, with Keane playing for both teams.

Alan Shearer's testimonial on May 11, 2006, watched by a crowd of 52,275 at St James' Park, raised more than £1m. The club's record scorer, in his farewell match, came off the bench in stoppage time to score the penalty that gave Newcastle a 3-2 win over Celtic. Total proceeds from his testimonial events, £1.64m, were donated to 14 charities in the north-east.

Ole Gunnar Solskjaer, who retired after 12 years as a Manchester Utd player, had a crowd of 68,868, for his testimonial on Aug 2, 2008 (United 1 Espanyol 0). He donated the estimated receipts of £2m to charity, including the opening of a dozen schools In Africa.

Liverpool's **Jamie Carragher** had his testimonial against Everton (4-1) on Sep 4, 2010. It was watched by a crowd of 35,631 and raised an estimated £1m for his foundation, which supports community projects on Merseyside.

Gary Neville donated receipts of around £1m from his testimonial against Juventus (2-1) in front of 42,000 on May 24, 2011, to charities and building a Supporters' Centre near Old Trafford.

Paul Scholes had a crowd of 75,000 for his testimonial, Manchester United against New York Cosmos, on Aug 5, 2011. Receipts were £1.5m.

Steven Gerrard, Liverpool captain, donated £500,000 from his testimonial to the local Alder Hey Children's Hospital after a match against Olympiacos was watched by a crowd of 44,362 on Aug 3, 2013. Gerrard chose the Greek champions because he scored a special goal against them in the season Liverpool won the 2005 Champions League.

Wayne Rooney's match against Everton on Aug 3, 2016, raised £1.2m, which the Manchester United captain donated to local children's charities.

WHAT IT USED TO COST

Minimum admission to League football was one shilling in 1939 After the war, it was increased to 1s 3d in 1946; 1s 6d in 1951; 1s 9d in 1952; 2s in 1955; 2s 6d; in 1960; 4s in 1965; 5s in 1968; 6s in 1970; and 8s (40p) in 1972 After that, the fixed minimum charge was dropped.

Wembley's first Cup Final programme in 1923 cost three pence ($1\frac{1}{4}$p in today's money). The programme for the 'farewell' FA Cup Final in May, 2000 was priced £10.

FA Cup Final ticket prices in 2011 reached record levels – £115, £85, £65 and £45.

WHAT THEY USED TO EARN

In the 1930s, First Division players were on £8 a week (£6 in close season) plus bonuses of £2 win, £1 draw. The maximum wage went up to £12 when football resumed post-war in 1946 and had reached £20 by the time the limit was abolished in 1961.

EUROPEAN TROPHY WINNERS

European Cup/Champions League: 14 Real Madrid; 7 AC Milan; 6 Liverpool, Bayern Munich; 5 Barcelona; 4 Ajax; 3 Inter Milan, Manchester Utd; 2 Benfica, Chelsea, Juventus, Nottm Forest, Porto; 1 Aston Villa, Borussia Dortmund, Celtic, Feyenoord, Hamburg, Marseille, PSV Eindhoven, Red Star Belgrade, Steaua Bucharest

Cup-Winners' Cup: 4 Barcelona; 2 Anderlecht, Chelsea, Dynamo Kiev, AC Milan; 1 Aberdeen, Ajax, Arsenal, Atletico Madrid, Bayern Munich, Borussia Dortmund, Dynamo Tbilisi, Everton, Fiorentina, Hamburg, Juventus, Lazio, Magdeburg, Manchester City, Manchester Utd, Mechelen, Paris St Germain, Parma, Rangers, Real Zaragoza, Sampdoria, Slovan Bratislava, Sporting Lisbon, Tottenham, Valencia, Werder Bremen, West Ham.

UEFA Cup: 3 Barcelona, Inter Milan, Juventus, Liverpool, Valencia; 2 Borussia Moenchengladbach, Feyenoord, Gothenburg, Leeds, Parma, Real Madrid, Sevilla, Tottenham; 1 Anderlecht, Ajax, Arsenal, Bayer Leverkusen, Bayern Munich, CSKA Moscow, Dynamo Zagreb, Eintracht Frankfurt, Ferencvaros, Galatasaray, Ipswich, Napoli, Newcastle, Porto, PSV Eindhoven, Real Zaragoza, Roma, Schalke, Shakhtar Donetsk, Zenit St Petersburg.

Europa League: 4 Sevilla; 3 Atletico Madrid; 2 Chelsea; 1 Manchester Utd, Porto, Villarreal, Eintracht Frankfurt.

- The Champions League was introduced into the European Cup in 1992–93 to counter the threat of a European Super League. The UEFA Cup became the Europa League, with a new format, in season 2009–10.

BRITAIN'S 38 TROPHIES IN EUROPE

Euro Cup/Champs Lge (15)	Cup-Winners' Cup (10)	Fairs/UEFA Cup/Europa Lge (13)
1967 Celtic	1963 Tottenham	1968 Leeds
1968 Manchester Utd	1965 West Ham	1969 Newcastle
1977 Liverpool	1970 Manchester City	1970 Arsenal
1978 Liverpool	1971 Chelsea	1971 Leeds
1979 Nottm Forest	1972 Rangers	1972 Tottenham
1980 Nottm Forest	1983 Aberdeen	1973 Liverpool
1981 Liverpool	1985 Everton	1976 Liverpool
1982 Aston Villa	1991 Manchester Utd	1981 Ipswich
1984 Liverpool	1994 Arsenal	1984 Tottenham
1999 Manchester Utd	1998 Chelsea	2001 Liverpool
2005 Liverpool		2013 Chelsea
2008 Manchester Utd		2017 Manchester Utd
2012 Chelsea		2019 Chelsea
2019 Liverpool		
2021 Chelsea		

ENGLAND'S EUROPEAN RECORD

England had an unprecedented clean sweep of finalists in the two European club competitions in season 2018–19, with Liverpool defeating Tottenham in the Champions League and Chelsea beating Arsenal in the Europa League.

END OF CUP-WINNERS' CUP

The **European Cup-Winners' Cup**, inaugurated in 1960–61, terminated with the 1999 Final. The competition merged into a revamped **UEFA Cup**.

From its inception in 1955, the **European Cup** comprised only championship-winning clubs until 1998–99, when selected runners-up were introduced. Further expansion came in 1999–2000 with the inclusion of clubs finishing third in certain leagues and fourth in 2002.

EUROPEAN CLUB COMPETITIONS – SCORING RECORDS

European Cup – record aggregate: 18-0 by Benfica v Dudelange (Lux) (8-0a, 10-0h), prelim rd, 1965–66.

Record single-match score: 12-2 by Feyenoord v KR Reykjavic, 1st rd, 1st leg, 1969–70.

Biggest win: 11-0 by Dinamo Bucharest v Crusaders, 1st rd, 2nd leg, 1973–74.

Champions League – record single-match score: Liverpool 8-0 v Besiktas, Group A qual (Nov 6, 2007).

Cup-Winners' Cup – *record aggregate: 21-0 by Chelsea v Jeunesse Hautcharage (Lux) (8-0a, 13-0h), 1st rd, 1971–72.

Record single-match score: 16-1 by Sporting Lisbon v Apoel Nicosia, 2nd round, 1st leg, 1963–64 (aggregate was 18-1).

UEFA Cup (prev Fairs Cup) – *Record aggregate: 21-0 by Feyenoord v US Rumelange (Lux) (9-0h, 12-0a), 1st round, 1972–73.

Record single-match score: 14-0 by Ajax Amsterdam v Red Boys (Lux) 1st rd, 2nd leg, 1984–85 (aggregate also 14-0).

Record British score in Europe: 13-0 by **Chelsea** at home to Jeunesse Hautcharage (Lux) in Cup-Winners' Cup 1st round, 2nd leg, 1971–72. Chelsea's overall 21-0 win in that tie is highest aggregate by British club in Europe.

Individual scoring record for European tie (over two legs): 10 goals (6 home, 4 away) by **Kiril Milanov** for Levski Spartak in 19-3 agg win Cup-Winners' Cup 1st round v Lahden Reipas, 1976–77. Next highest: **8 goals** by Jose Altafini for AC Milan v US Luxembourg (European Cup, prelim round, 1962–63, agg 14-0) and by **Peter Osgood** for Chelsea v Jeunesse Hautcharage (Cup-Winners' Cup, 1st round 1971–72, agg 21-0). Altafini and Osgood each scored 5 goals at home, 3 away.

Individual single-match scoring record in European competition: **6** by **Mascarenhas** for Sporting Lisbon in 16-1 Cup-Winner's Cup 2nd round, 1st leg win v Apoel, 1963–64; and by **Lothar Emmerich** for Borussia Dortmund in 8-0 CWC 1st round, 2nd leg win v Floriana 1965–66; and by **Kiril Milanov** for Levski Spartak in 12-2 CWC 1st round, 1st leg win v Lahden Reipas, 1976–77.

Most goals in single European campaign: 15 by **Jurgen Klinsmann** for Bayern Munich (UEFA Cup 1995–96).

Most goals by British player in European competition: 30 by **Peter Lorimer** (Leeds, in 9 campaigns).

Most individual goals in Champions League match: 5 by **Lionel Messi** (Barcelona) in 7-1 win at home to Bayer Leverkusen in round of 16 second leg, 2011–12.

Most Champions League goals by individual player 140 by **Cristiano Ronaldo** in 183 apps for Manchester Utd, Real Madrid, Juventus (2003–22)

Most European Cup goals by individual player: 49 by **Alfredo di Stefano** in 58 apps for Real Madrid (1955–64).

(*Joint record European aggregate)

First European treble: Clarence Seedorf became the first player to win the European Cup with three clubs: Ajax in 1995, Real Madrid in 1998 and AC Milan in 2003.

EUROPEAN FOOTBALL – BIG RECOVERIES

In the most astonishing Final in the history of the European Cup/Champions League, **Liverpool** became the first club to win it from a 3-0 deficit when they beat AC Milan 3-2 on penalties after a 3-3 draw in Istanbul on May 25, 2005. Liverpool's fifth triumph in the competition meant that they would keep the trophy.

The following season, **Middlesbrough** twice recovered from three-goal aggregate deficits in the **UEFA Cup**, beating Basel 4-3 in the quarter finals and Steaua Bucharest by the same scoreline in the semi-finals. In 2010, **Fulham** beat Juventus 5-4 after trailing 1-4 on aggregate in the second leg of their Europa League, Round of 16 match at Craven Cottage.

Two Scottish clubs have won a European tie from a 3-goal, first leg deficit: **Kilmarnock** 0-3, 5-1 v Eintracht Frankfurt (Fairs Cup 1st round, 1964–65); **Hibernian** 1-4, 5-0 v Napoli (Fairs Cup 2nd Round, 1967–68).

English clubs have three times gone out of the **UEFA Cup** after leading 3-0 from the first leg: 1975–76 (2nd Rd) **Ipswich** lost 3-4 on agg to Bruges; 1976–77 (quarter-final) **QPR** lost on penalties to AEK Athens after 3-3 agg; 1977–78 (3rd round) **Ipswich** lost on penalties to Barcelona after 3-3 agg.

● In the **1966 World Cup quarter-final** (Jul 23) at Goodison Park, North Korea led Portugal 3-0, but Eusebio scored 4 times to give **Portugal** a 5-3 win.

RONALDO'S EURO CENTURY

Cristiano Ronaldo became the first player to reach a century of goals in European club competitions when scoring twice for Real Madrid away to Bayern Munich on Apr 12, 2017. He reached the hundred in 143 matches (84 for Real, 16 for Manchester Utd) in the Champions League (97), UEFA Super Cup (2) and Champions League qualifying round (1).

RECORD COMEBACK

The greatest turnaround in Champions League history took place in a round of 16 match on Mar 8, 2017. **Barcelona**, 0-4 down to Paris St Germain, won the return leg 6-1, scoring three goals in the last seven minutes.

HEAVIEST ENGLISH-CLUB DEFEATS IN EUROPE

(Single-leg scores)

Champions League: Porto 5 Leicester 0 (group, Dec 6, 2016); Tottenham 2 Bayern Munich 7 (group, Oct 1, 2019).

European Cup: Artmedia Bratislava 5, **Celtic** 0 (2nd qual round), Jul 2005 (agg 5-4); Ajax 5, **Liverpool** 1 (2nd round), Dec 1966 (agg 7-3); Real Madrid 5, **Derby** 1 (2nd round), Nov 1975 (agg 6-5).

Cup-Winners' Cup: Sporting Lisbon 5, **Manchester Utd** 0 (quarter-final), Mar 1964 (agg 6-4).

Fairs/UEFA Cup: Bayern Munich 6, **Coventry** 1 (2nd round), Oct 1970 (agg 7-3). **Combined London** team lost 6-0 (agg 8-2) in first Fairs Cup Final in 1958. Barcelona 5, **Chelsea** 0 in Fairs Cup semi-final play-off, 1966, in Barcelona (after 2-2 agg).

SHOCK ENGLISH CLUB DEFEATS

1968–69 (Eur Cup, 1st round): **Manchester City** beaten by Fenerbahce, 1-2 agg.

1971–72 (CWC, 2nd round): **Chelsea** beaten by Atvidaberg on away goals.

1993–94 (Eur Cup, 2nd round): **Manchester Utd** beaten by Galatasaray on away goals.

1994–95 (UEFA Cup, 1st round): **Blackburn** beaten by Trelleborgs, 2-3 agg.

2000–01 (UEFA Cup, 1st round): **Chelsea** beaten by St Gallen, Switz 1-2 agg.

RECORD MEDAL SALES

At Sotherby's in London on Nov 11, 2014, the FA Cup winner's medal which **Sir Stanley Matthews** earned with Blackpool in 1953 was sold for £220,000 – the most expensive medal in British sporting history. At the same auction, **Ray Wilson's** 1966 World Cup winner's medal fetched £136,000, while **Jimmy Greaves**, who was left out of the winning England team, received £44,000 for the medal the FA belatedly awarded him in 2009

West Ham bought (Jun 2000) the late **Bobby Moore**'s collection of medals and trophies for £1.8m at Christie's auction. It was put up for sale by his first wife Tina and included his World Cup-winner's medal.

A No. 6 duplicate red shirt made for England captain **Bobby Moore** for the 1966 World Cup Final fetched £44,000 at an auction at Wolves' ground in Sep, 1999. Moore kept the shirt he wore in that Final and gave the replica to England physio Harold Shepherdson.

Sir Geoff Hurst's 1966 World Cup-winning shirt fetched a record £91,750 at Christie's in Sep, 2000. His World Cup Final cap fetched £37,600 and his Man of the Match trophy £18,800. Proceeds totalling £274,410 from the 129 lots went to Hurst's three daughters and charities of his choice, including the Bobby Moore Imperial Cancer Research Fund.

In Aug, 2001, Sir Geoff sold his World Cup-winner's medal to his former club West Ham Utd (for their museum) at a reported £150,000.

'The **Billy Wright** Collection' – caps, medals and other memorabilia from his illustrious career – fetched over £100,000 at Christie's in Nov, 1996.

At the sale in Oct 1993, trophies, caps and medals earned by **Ray Kennedy**, former England, Arsenal and Liverpool player, fetched a then record total of £88,407. Kennedy, suffering from Parkinson's Disease, received £73,000 after commission. The PFA paid £31,080 for a total of 60 lots – including a record £16,000 for his 1977 European Cup winner's medal – to be exhibited at their Manchester museum. An anonymous English collector paid £17,000 for the medal and plaque commemorating Kennedy's part in the Arsenal Double in 1971.

Previous record for one player's medals, shirts etc collection: £30,000 (**Bill Foulkes**, Manchester Utd in 1992). The sale of **Dixie Dean**'s medals etc in 1991 realised £28,000.

In Mar, 2001, **Gordon Banks**' 1966 World Cup-winner's medal fetched a new record £124,750. TV's Nick Hancock, a Stoke fan, paid £23,500 for **Sir Stanley Matthews's** 1953 FA Cup-winner's medal. He also bought one of Matthews's England caps for £3,525 and paid £2,350 for a Stoke Div 2 Championship medal (1963).

Dave Mackay's 1961 League Championship and FA Cup winner's medals sold for £18,000 at Sotherby's. Tottenham bought them for their museum.

A selection of England World Cup-winning manager **Sir Alf Ramsey**'s memorabilia – England caps, championship medals with Ipswich etc. – fetched more than £80,000 at Christie's. They were offered for sale by his family, and his former clubs Tottenham and Ipswich were among the buyers.

Ray Wilson's 1966 England World Cup-winning shirt fetched £80,750. Also in Mar, 2002, the No. 10 shirt worn by **Pele** in Brazil's World Cup triumph in 1970 was sold for a record £157,750 at Christies. It went to an anonymous telephone bidder.

In Oct, 2003, **George Best**'s European Footballer of the Year (1968) trophy was sold to an anonymous British bidder for £167,250 at Bonham's. It was the then most expensive item of sporting memorabilia ever auctioned in Britain.

England captain **Bobby Moore**'s 1970 World Cup shirt, which he swapped with Pele after Brazil's 1-0 win in Mexico, was sold for £60,000 at Christie's in Mar, 2004.

Sep, 2004: England shirt worn by tearful **Paul Gascoigne** in 1990 World Cup semi-final v Germany sold at Christie's for £28,680. At same auction, shirt worn by Brazil's **Pele** in 1958 World Cup Final in Sweden sold for £70,505.

May, 2005: The **second FA Cup** (which was presented to winning teams from 1896 to 1909) was bought for £420,000 at Christie's by Birmingham chairman David Gold, a world record for an item of football memorabilia. It was presented to the National Football Museum, Preston. At the same auction, the World Cup-winner's medal earned by England's **Alan Ball** in 1966 was sold for £164,800.

Oct, 2005: At auction at Bonham's, the medals and other memorabilia of Hungary and Real Madrid legend **Ferenc Puskas** were sold for £85,000 to help pay for hospital treatment.

Nov, 2006: A ball used in the 2006 World Cup Final and signed by the winning **Italy** team was sold for £1.2m (a world record for football memorabilia) at a charity auction in Qatar. It was bought by the Qatar Sports Academy.

Feb, 2010: A pair of boots worn by **Sir Stanley Matthews** in the 1953 FA Cup Final was sold at Bonham's for £38,400.

Oct, 2010: Trophies and memorabilia belonging to **George Best** were sold at Bonham's for £193,440. His 1968 European Cup winner's medal fetched £156,000.

Oct–Nov 2010: **Nobby Stiles** sold his 1966 World Cup winner's medal at an Edinburgh auction for a record £188,200. His old club, Manchester Utd, also paid £48,300 for his 1968 European Cup medal to go to the club's museum at Old Trafford. In London, the shirt worn by Stiles in the 1966 World Cup Final went for £75,000. A total of 45 items netted £424,438. **George Cohen** and **Martin Peters** had previously sold their medals from 1966.

Oct 2011: **Terry Paine** (who did not play in the Final) sold his 1966 World Cup medal for £27,500 at auction.

Mar 2013: **Norman Hunter** (Leeds and England) sold his honours' collection on line for nearly £100,000

Nov 2013: A collection of **Nat Lofthouse's** career memorabilia was sold at auction for £100,000. Bolton Council paid £75,000 for items including his 1958 FA Cup winner's medal to go on show at the local museum.

LONGEST UNBEATEN CUP RUN

Liverpool established the longest unbeaten Cup sequence by a Football League club: 25 successive rounds in the League/Milk Cup between semi-final defeat by Nottm Forest (1-2 agg) in 1980 and defeat at Tottenham (0-1) in the third round on Oct 31, 1984. During this period Liverpool won the tournament in four successive seasons. The only other club to achieve this feat was **Manchester City** also in the League Cup, in seasons 2017–18 to 2021–22

BIG HALF-TIME SCORES

Tottenham 10, Crewe 1 (FA Cup 4th round replay, Feb 3, 1960; result 13-2); Tranmere 8, Oldham 1 (Div 3N., Dec 26, 1935; result 13-4); **Chester City 8, York 0** (Div 3N., Feb 1, 1936; result 12-0; believed to be record half-time scores in League football).

Nine goals were scored in the first half – **Burnley 4, Watford 5** in Div 1 on Apr 5, 2003. Result: 4-7.

Stirling Albion led Selkirk 15-0 at half-time (result 20-0) in the Scottish Cup 1st round, Dec 8, 1984.

World record half-time score: **16-0** when **Australia** beat **American Samoa** 31-0 (another world record) in the World Cup Oceania qualifying group at Coff's Harbour, New South Wales, on Apr 11 2001.

• On Mar 4 1933 **Coventry** beat QPR (Div 3 South) 7-0, having led by that score at half-time. This repeated the half-time situation in Bristol City's 7-0 win over Grimsby on Dec 26, 1914.

TOP SECOND-HALF TEAM

Most goals scored by a team in one half of a League match is **11. Stockport** led Halifax 2-0 at half-time in Div 3 North on Jan 6 1934 and won 13-0.

FIVE NOT ENOUGH

Last team to score **5** in League match and lose: **Burton**, beaten 6-5 by Cheltenham (Lge 2, Mar 13, 2010).

LONG SERVICE WITH ONE CLUB

Bill Nicholson, OBE, was associated with Tottenham for 67 years – as a wing-half (1938–55), then the club's most successful manager (1958–74) with 8 major prizes, subsequently chief advisor and scout. He became club president, and an honorary freeman of the borough, had an executive suite named after him at the club, and the stretch of roadway from Tottenham High Road to the main gates has the nameplate Bill Nicholson Way. He died, aged 85, in Oct 2004.

Ted Bates, the Grand Old Man of Southampton with 66 years of unbroken service to the club, was awarded the Freedom of the City in Apr, 2001. He joined Saints as an inside-forward from Norwich in 1937, made 260 peace-time appearances for the club, became reserve-team trainer in 1953 and manager at The Dell for 18 years (1955–73), taking Southampton into the top division in 1966. He was subsequently chief executive, director and club president. He died in Oct 2003, aged 85.

Bob Paisley was associated with Liverpool for 57 years from 1939, when he joined them from Bishop Auckland, until he died in Feb 1996. He served as player, trainer, coach, assistant-manager, manager, director and vice-president. He was Liverpool's most successful manager, winning 13 major trophies for the club (1974–83).

Dario Gradi, MBE, stepped down after completing 24 seasons and more than 1,000 matches as manager of Crewe (appointed Jun 1983). Never a League player, he previously managed Wimbledon and Crystal Palace. At Crewe, his policy of finding and grooming young talent has earned the club more than £20m in transfer fees. He stayed with Crewe as technical director, and twice took charge of team affairs again following the departure of the managers who succeeded him, Steve Holland and Gudjon Thordarson.

Ronnie Moran, who joined Liverpool in as a player 1952, retired from the Anfield coaching staff in season 1998–99.

Ernie Gregory served West Ham for 52 years as goalkeeper and coach. He joined them as boy of 14 from school in 1935, retired in May 1987.

Ryan Giggs played 24 seasons for Manchester Utd (1990-2014), then became assistant manager under Louis van Gaal.

Ted Sagar, Everton goalkeeper, 23 years at Goodison Park (1929–52, but only 16 League seasons because of war).

Alan Knight, goalkeeper, played 23 seasons (1977–2000) for his only club, Portsmouth.

Sam Bartram was recognised as one of the finest goalkeepers never to play for England, apart from unofficial wartime games. He was with Charlton from 1934–56

Jack Charlton, England World Cup winner, served Leeds from 1952–73.

Roy Sproson, defender, played 21 League seasons for his only club, Port Vale (1950–71).

John Terry had a 22-year association with Chelsea from 1994–2017.

TIGHT AT HOME

Fewest home goals conceded in League season (modern times): 4 by **Liverpool** (Div 1, 1978–9); 4 by **Manchester Utd** (Premier League, 1994–95) – both in 21 matches.

TRANSFER WINDOW

This was introduced to Britain in Sep 2002 via FIFA regulations to bring uniformity across Europe (the rule previously applied in a number of other countries).

The transfer of contracted players is restricted to two periods: Jun 1–Aug 31 and Jan 1–31).

On appeal, Football League clubs continued to sign/sell players (excluding deals with Premier League clubs).

PROGRAMME PIONEERS

Chelsea pioneered football's magazine-style programme by introducing a 16-page issue for the First Division match against Portsmouth on Christnmas Day 1948. It cost sixpence (2.5p). A penny programme from the 1909 FA Cup Final fetched £23,500 at a London auction in May, 2012.

WORLD'S OLDEST FOOTBALL ANNUAL

Now in its 136th edition, this publication began as the 16-page Athletic News Football Supplement & Club Directory in 1887. From the long-established Athletic News, it became the Sunday Chronicle Annual in 1946, the Empire News in 1956, the News of the World & Empire News in 1961 and the News of the World Annual from 1965 until becoming the Nationwide Annual in 2008.

PREMIER LEAGUE CLUB DETAILS AND SQUADS 2022–23

(at time of going to press)

ARSENAL

Ground: Emirates Stadium, Highbury, London, N5 IBU
Telephone: 0207 619 5003. **Club nickname:** Gunners
Capacity: 60,704. **Colours:** Red and white. **Shirt sponsor:** Emirates
Record attendance: Highbury: 73,295 v Sunderland (Div 1) Mar 9, 1935. Emirates Stadium: 60,161 v Manchester Utd (Prem Lge) Nov 3, 2007. Wembley: 73,707 v Lens (Champ Lge) Nov 25, 1998
Record transfer fee: £72m to Lille for Nicolas Pepe, Aug 2019
Record fee received: £40m from Liverpool for Alex Oxlade-Chamberlain, Aug 2017
League Championship: Winners 1930–31, 1932–33, 1933–34, 1934–35, 1937–38, 1947–48, 1952–53, 1970–71, 1988–89, 1990–91, 1997–98, 2001–02, 2003–04
FA Cup: Winners 1930, 1936, 1950, 1971, 1979, 1993, 1998, 2002, 2003, 2005, 2014, 2015, 2017, 2020
League Cup: Winners 1987, 1993
European competitions: Winners Fairs Cup 1969–70; Cup-Winners' Cup 1993–94
Finishing positions in Premier League: 1992–93 10th, 1993–94 4th, 1994–95 12th, 1995–96 5th, 1996–97 3rd, 1997–98 1st, 1998–99 2nd, 1999–2000 2nd, 2000–01 2nd, 2001–02 1st, 2002–03 2nd, 2003–04 1st, 2004–05 2nd, 2005–06 4th, 2006–07 4th, 2007–08 3rd, 2008–09 4th, 2009–10 3rd, 2010–11 4th, 2011–12 3rd, 2012–13 4th, 2013–14 4th, 2014–15 3rd, 2015–16 2nd, 2016–17 5th, 2017–18 6th, 2018–19 5th, 2019–20 8th, 2020–21 8th, 2021–22 5th
Biggest win: 12-0 v Loughborough (Div 2) Mar 12, 1900
Biggest defeat: 0-8 v Loughborough (Div 2) Dec 12, 1896
Highest League scorer in a season: Ted Drake 42 (1934–35)
Most League goals in aggregate: Thierry Henry 175 (1999–2007) (2012)
Longest unbeaten League sequence: 49 matches (2003–04). **Longest sequence without a League win:** 23 matches (1912–13). **Most capped player:** Thierry Henry (France) 81

Height Name	ft in	Previous club	Birthplace	Birthdate
Goalkeepers				
Leno, Bernd	6.3	Bayer Leverkusen	Bietighem-Bissingen, Ger	04.03.92
Ramsdale, Aaron	6.2	Sheffield Utd	Stoke	14.05.98
Turner, Matt	6.3	New England	Park Ridge, US	24.06.94
Defenders				
Cedric Soares	5.8	Southampton	Singen, Ger	31.08.91
Gabriel	6.3	Lille	Sao Paulo, Br	19.12.97
Holding, Rob	6.0	Bolton	Tameside	12.09.95
Mari, Pablo	6.4	Flamengo	Valencia, Sp	31.08.93
Saliba, William	6.4	Saint-Etienne	Bondy, Fr	24.03.01
Marquinhos	6.0	Sao Paulo	Sao Paulo, Br	14.05.94
Nuno Tavares	6.0	Benfica	Lisbon Por	26.01.00
Tierney, Kieran	5.10	Celtic	Douglas, IOM	05.06.97
Tomiyasu, Takehiro	6.2	Bologna	Fukuoka, Jap	05.11.98
Midfielders				
Elneny, Mohamed	5.11	Basle	El-Mahalla, Egy	11.07.92
Fabio Vieira	5.8	Porto	Santa Maria, Por	30.05.00

Maitland-Niles, Ainsley	5.10	–	Goodmayes	29.08.97
Odegaard, Martin	5.8	Real Madrid	Drammen, Nor	17.12.98
Partey, Thomas	6.1	Atletico Madrid	Krobo Odumase, Gha	13.06.93
Pepe, Nicolas	5.10	Lille	Mantes-la-Jolie, Fr	29.05.95
Sambi Lokonga, Albert	6.0	Anderlecht	Brussels, Bel	22.10.99
Smith Rowe, Emile	6.0	–	Croydon	28.07.00
Torreira, Lucas	5.6	Sampdoria	Fray Bentos, Uru	11.02.96
Xhaka, Granit	6.1	Borussia M'gladbach	Basle, Swi	27.09.92
Forwards				
Balogun, Folarin	5.10	–	New York, US	03.07.01
Gabriel Jesus	5.9	Manchester City	Sao Paulo, Br	03.04.97
Martinelli, Gabriel	5.11	Ituano	Guarulhos, Br	18.06.01
Nelson, Reiss	5.9	–	Elephant and Castle	10.12.99
Nketiah, Eddie	5.9	–	Lewisham	30.05.99
Saka, Bukayo	5.10	–	Ealing	05.09.01

ASTON VILLA

Ground: Villa Park, Trinity Road, Birmingham, B6 6HE
Telephone: 0333 323 1874. **Club nickname:** Villans
Capacity: 42,682. **Colours:** Claret and blue. **Shirt sponsor:** Cazoo
Record attendance: 76,588 v Derby (FA Cup 6) Mar 2, 1946
Record transfer fee: £33m to Norwich for Emiliano Buendia, Jun 2021.
Record fee received: £100m from Manchester City for Jack Grealish, Aug 2021
League Championship: Winners 1893–94, 1895–96, 1896–97, 1898–99, 1899–1900, 1909–10, 1980–81.
FA Cup: Winners 1887, 1895, 1897, 1905, 1913, 1920, 1957
League Cup: Winners 1961, 1975, 1977, 1994, 1996
European competitions: Winners European Cup 1981–82; European Super Cup 1982
Finishing positions in Premier League: 1992–93 2nd, 1993–94 10th, 1994–95 18th, 1995–96 4th, 1996–97 5th, 1997–98 7th, 1998–99 6th, 1999–2000 6th, 2000–01 8th, 2001–02 8th, 2002–03 16th, 2003–04 6th,2004–05 10th, 2005–06 16th, 2006–07 11th, 2007–08 6th, 2008–09 6th, 2009–10 6th, 2010–11 9th, 2011–12 16th, 2012–13th 15th, 2013–14 15th,2014–15 17th, 2015–16 20th 2019–20 17th, 2020–21 11th, 2021–22 14th
Biggest win: 12-2 v Accrington (Div 1) Mar 12, 1892; 11-1 v Charlton (Div 2) Nov 24, 1959; 10-0 v Sheffield Wed (Div 1) Oct 5, 1912, v Burnley (Div 1) Aug 29, 1925. Also: 13-0 v Wednesbury (FA Cup 1) Oct 30, 1886
Biggest defeat: 0-8 v Chelsea (Prem Lge) Dec 23, 2012
Highest League scorer in a season: 'Pongo' Waring 49 (1930–31)
Most League goals in aggregate: Harry Hampton 215 (1904–15)
Longest unbeaten League sequence: 15 matches (1897, 1909–10 and 1949. **Longest sequence without a League win:** 19 matches (2015–16). **Most capped player:** Steve Staunton (Republic of Ireland) 64

Goalkeepers				
Martinez, Emiliano	6.4	Arsenal	Mar del Plata, Arg	02.09.92
Olsen, Robin	6.5	Roma	Malmo, Swe	08.01.90
Steer, Jed	6.3	Norwich	Norwich	23.09.92
Defenders				
Cash, Matty	6.1	Nottm Forest	Slough	07.08.97
Chambers, Calum	6.0	Arsenal	Petersfield	20.01.9
Diego Carlos	6.1	Sevilla	Sao Paulo, Br	15.03.93
Digne, Lucas	5.10	Everton	Meaux, Fr	20.07.93
Guilbert, Frederic	5.10	Caen	Valognes, Fr	24.12.94

Hause, Kortney	6.3	Wolves	Goodmayes	16.07.95
Konsa, Ezri	6.0	Brentford	Newham	23.10.97
Mings, Tyrone	6.3	Bournemouth	Bath	13.03.93
Young, Ashley	5.9	Inter Milan	Stevenage	09.07.85
Midfielders				
Bailey, Leon	5.10	Bayer Leverkusen	Kingston, Jam	09.08.97
Buendia, Emiliano	5.8	Norwich	Mar del Plata, Arg	25.12.96
Chukwuemeka, Carney	6.0	Northampton	Eisenstadt, Aut	20.10.03
Coutinho, Philippe	5.8	Barcelona	Rio de Janeiro, Br	12.06.92
Douglas Luiz	5.9	Manchester City	Rio de Janeiro, Br	09.05.98
El Ghazi, Anwar	6.2	Lille	Barendrecht, Hol	03.05.95
Kamara, Boubacar	6.1	Marseille	Marseille	23.11.99
Marvelous Nakamba	5.10	Club Bruges	Hwange, Zim	19.01.94
McGinn, John	5.10	Hibernian	Glasgow	18.10.94
Ramsey, Jacob	5.11	–	Birmingham	28.05.01
Sanson, Morgan	6.0	Marseille	Saint-Doulchard, Fr	18.08.94
Traore, Bertrand	5.11	Lyon	Burkina Faso	06.09.95
Forwards				
Davis, Keinan	6.3	–	Stevenage	13.02.98
Ings, Danny	5.10	Southampton	Winchester	16.03.92
Watkins, Ollie	5.10	Brentford	Torbay	30.12.95
Wesley	6.2	Club Bruges	Juiz de Fora, Br	26.11.96

BOURNEMOUTH

Ground: Vitality Stadium, Dean Court, Bournemouth BH7 7AF.
Telephone: 0344 576 1910. **Club nickname:** Cherries
Capacity: 11,364. **Colours:** Red and black. **Shirt sponsor:** Dafabet
Record attendance: 28,799 v Manchester Utd (FA Cup 6) Mar 2, 1957
Record transfer fee: £25 to Levante for Jefferson Lerma, Aug 2018
Record fee received: £40m from Manchester City for Nathan Ake, Aug 2018
League Championship: 9th 2016–17
FA Cup: 6th rd, 1957
League Cup: 5th rd 2014
Finishing position in Premier League: 2015–16 16th, 2016–17 9th, 2 20017–18 12th, 2018–19 14th, 2019–20 18th
Biggest win: 8-0 v Birmingham (Champ) Oct 15, 2014. Also: 11-0 v Margate (FA Cup 1) Nov20, 1971
Biggest defeat: 0-9 v Lincoln (Div 3) Dec 18, 1982
Highest League scorer in a season: Ted MacDougall 42 (1970–71)
Most League goals in aggregate: Ron Eyre 202 (1924–33)
Longest unbeaten League sequence: 18 matches (1982). **Longest sequence without a League win:** 14 matches (1974). **Most capped player:** Gerry Peyton (Republic of Ireland) 7

Goalkeepers				
Dennis, Will	6.2	Watford	–	10.07.00
Travers, Mark	6.3	Shamrock Rov	Maynooth, Ire	18.05.99
Defenders				
Fredericks, Ryan	5.8	West Ham	Potters Bar	10.10.92
Hill, James	6.1	Fleetwood	Bristol	10.01.02
Kelly, Lloyd	5.10	Bristol City	Bristol	01.10.98
Mepham, Chris	6.3	Brentford	Hammersmith	05.11.97
Smith, Adam	5.11	Tottenham	Leystonstone	29.04.91
Stacey, Jack	5.11	Luton	Bracknell	06.04.96
Zemura, Jordan	5.9	Charlton	Lambeth	14.11.99

Midfielders

Billing, Philip	6.4	Huddersfield	Esbjerg, Den	11.06.96
Brooks, David	5.8	Sheffield Utd	Warrington	08.07.97
Christie, Ryan	5.10	Celtic	Inverness	22.02.95
Cook, Lewis	5.9	Leeds	Leeds	03.02.97
Dembele, Siriki	5.8	Peterborough	Ivory Coast	07.09.96
Lerma, Jefferson	5.10	Levante	Cerrito, Col	25.10.94
Marcondes, Emiliano	6.0	Brentford	Hvidovre, Den	09.03.95
Pearson, Ben	5.5	Preston	Oldham	04.01.95
Rothwell, Joe	6.1	Blackburn	Manchester	11.01.95
Stanislas, Junior	6.0	Burnley	Eltham	26.11.89

Forwards

Anthony, Jaidon	6.0	Arsenal	Hackney	01.12.99
Lowe, Jamal	6.0	Swansea	Harrow	21.07.94
Moore, Kieffer	6.4	Cardiff	Torquay	08.08.92
Solanke, Dominic	6.1	Liverpool	Reading	14.09.97

BRENTFORD

Ground: Community Stadium, Lionel Road, Brentford TW8 7BW
Telephone: 0208 847 2511. **Club nickname:** Bees
Capacity: 17,250. **Colours:** Red, white and black. **Shirt sponsor:** Hollywoodbets
Record attendance: Griffin Park: 38,678 v Leicester (FA Cup 6) Feb 26, 1949. Community Stadium: 17,094 v Manchester Utd (Prem Lge) Jan 19, 2022
Record transfer fee: £13.5m to Celtic for Kristoffer Ajer, July 2021
Record fee received: £28m from Aston Villa for Ollie Watkins, Sep 2020
League Championship: 5th 1935–36
FA Cup: 6th rd 1938, 1946, 1949, 1989
League Cup: Semi-finals 2021
European competitions: Semi-finals Anglo-Italian Cup 1992–93
Finishing position in Premier League: 2021–22 13th
Biggest win: 9-0 v Wrexham (Div 3) Oct 15, 1963
Biggest defeat: 0-7 v Swansea (Div 3 south) Nov 8, 1924; 0-7 v Walsall (Div 3 South) Jan 19, 1957; 0-7 v Peterborough (Lg 2) Nov 24, 2007
Highest League scorer in a season: Jack Holliday 38 (1932–33)
Most League goals in aggregate: Jim Towers 153 (1954–61)
Longest unbeaten League sequence: 26 matches (1999). **Longest sequence without a League win:** 16 (1994). **Most capped player:** Henrik Dalsgaard (Denmark) 22

Goalkeepers

Raya, David	6.0	Blackburn	Barcelona, Sp	15.09.95

Defenders

Ajer, Kristoffer	6.6	Celtic	Raelingen, Nor	17.04.98
Goode, Charlie	6.5	Northampton	Watford	03.08.95
Henry, Rico	5.8	Walsall	Birmingham	08.07.97
Jansson, Pontus	6.5	Leeds	Arlov, Swe	13.02.91
Jorgensen, Mathias	6.3	Fenerbahce	Copenhagen, Den	23.04.90
Pinnock, Ethan	6.2	Barnsley	Lambeth	29.05.93
Roersley, Mads	6.0	FC Copenhagen	Copenhagen, Den	24.06.99
Sorensen, Mads Bech	6.2	AC Horsens	Horsens, Den	07.01.99

Midfielders

Baptiste, Shandon	5.10	Oxford	Grenada	08.04.98
Bidstrup, Mads	5.9	Copenhagen	Koge, Den	25.02.01
Dasilva, Josh	6.0	Arsenal	Ilford	23.10.98
Eriksen, Christian	5.10	Inter Milan	Middelfart, Den	14.02.92

Fosu-Henry, Tarique	5.11	Oxford	Wandsworth	05.11.95
Ghoddos, Saman	5.10	Amiens	Malmo, Swer	06.09.93
Janelt, Vitaly	6.1	Bochum	Hamburg, Ger	10.05.98
Jensen, Mathias	5.10	Celta Vigo	Jerslev, Den	01.01.96
Mbeumo, Bryan	5.7	Troyes	Avallon, Fr	07.08.99
Norgaard, Christian	6.1	Fiorentina	Copenhagen, Den	10.03.94
Onyeka, Frank	6.0	Midtjylland	Maiduguri, Nig	01.01.98
Zamburek, Jan	6.0	Slavia Prague	Czech	13.02.01
Forwards				
Canos, Sergi	5.9	Norwich	Nules, Sp	02.02.97
Forss, Marcus	6.0	WBA	Turku, Fin	18.06.99
Toney, Ivan	5.10	Peterborough	Northampton	16.03.96
Wissa, Yoanne	5.10	Lorient	Epinay, Fr	03.09.96

BRIGHTON AND HOVE ALBION

Ground: Amex Stadium, Village Way, Brighton BN1 9BL
Telephone: 0344 324 6282. **Club nickname:** Seagulls
Capacity: 31,800. **Colours:** Blue and white. **Shirt sponsor:** American Express
Record attendance: Goldstone Ground: 36,747 v Fulham (Div 2) Dec 27, 1958; Withdean Stadium: 8,729 v Manchester City (League Cup 2) Sep 24, 2008; Amex Stadium: 31,637 v Manchester Utd (Prem Lge) May 7 2022
Record transfer fee: £20.7m to RB Salzburg for Enock Mwapo, Jul 2021
Record fee received: £50m from Arsenal forBen White , Jul 2021
League Championship: 9th 2021–22
FA Cup: Runners-up 1983
League Cup: Fifth round 1979
Finishing position in Premier League: 2017–18 15th, 2018–19 17th, 2019–20 15th, 2020–21 16th, 2021–22 9th
Biggest win: 10-1 v Wisbech (FA Cup 1) Nov 13, 1965
Biggest defeat: 0-9 v Middlesbrough (Div 2) Aug 23, 1958
Highest League scorer in a season: Peter Ward 32 (1976–77)
Most League goals in aggregate: Tommy Cook 114 (1922–29)
Longest unbeaten League sequence: 22 matches (2015). **Longest sequence without a League win:** 15 matches (1972–73). **Most capped player:** Shane Duffy (Republic of Ireland) 50

Goalkeepers				
Sanchez, Robert	6.6	Levante	Cartagena, Sp	18.11.97
Steele, Jason	6.2	Sunderland	Newton Aycliffe	18.08.90
Defenders				
Duffy, Shane	6.4	Blackburn	Derry	01.01.92
Dunk, Lewis	6.4	–	Brighton	01.11.91
Lamptey, Tariq	5.6	Chelsea	Hillingdon	30.09.00
Veltman, Joel	6.0	Ajax	Ijmuiden, Hol	15.01.92
Webster, Adam	6.3	Bristol City	Chichester	04.01.95
Midfielders				
Adingra, Simon	5.9	Nordsjaelland	Iv C	01.01.02
Alzate, Steven	5.11	Leyton Orient	Camden	08.09.98
Caicedo, Moises	5.10	Ind del Valle	Santo Domingo, Ec	02.11.01
Cucurella, Marc	5.8	Getafe	Alella, Sp	22.07.98
Gross, Pascal	6.0	Ingolstadt	Mannheim, Ger	15.06.91
Lallana, Adam	5.10	Liverpool	Bournemouth	10.05.8
Mac Allister, Alexis	5.9	Argentinos	La Pampa, Arg	24.12.98
March, Solly	5.11	Lewes	Eastbourne	20.07.94
Mitoma, Kaoru	5.10	Frontale	Oita, Jap	20.05.97

| Moder, Jakub | 6.3 | Lech Poznan | Szczecinek, Pol | 07.04.99 |
| Mwepu, Enock | 6.0 | Salzburg | Lusaka, Zam | 01.01.98 |

Forwards

Connolly, Aaron	5.10	Mervue	Galway, Ire	28.01.00
Enciso, Julio	5.7	Libertad Asuncion	Caaguazu, Par	23.01.04
Maupay, Neal	5.7	Brentford	Versailles, Fr	14.08.96
Sarmiento, Jeremy	6.0	Benfica	Madrid, Sp	16.06.02
Trossard, Leandro	5.8	Genk	Waterschei, Bel	04.12.94
Welbeck, Danny	5.10	Watford	Manchester	26.11.90
Zeqiri, Andi	6.1	Lausanne	Lausanne, Switz	22.06.99

CHELSEA

Ground: Stamford Bridge Stadium, London SW6 1HS
Telephone: 0371 811 1955. **Club nickname:** Blues
Capacity: 40,834. **Colours:** Blue. **Shirt sponsor:** Three
Record attendance: 82,905 v Arsenal (Div 1) Oct 12, 1935
Record transfer fee: £97.5m to Inter Milan for Romelu Lukaku, Aug 2021
Record fee received: £89m from Real Madrid for Eden Hazard, Jun 2019
League Championship: Winners 1954–55, 2004–05, 2005–06, 2009–10, 2014–15, 2016–17
FA Cup: Winners 1970, 1997, 2000, 2007, 2009, 2010, 2012, 2018
League Cup: Winners 1965, 1998, 2005, 2007, 2015
European competitions: Winners Champions League 2011–12, 2020–21; Cup-Winners' Cup 1970–71, 1997–98; Europa League 2012–13, 2018–19; European Super Cup 1998
Finishing positions in Premier League: 1992–93 11th, 1993–94 14th, 1994–95 11th, 1995–96 11th, 1996–97 6th, 1997–98 4th, 1998–99 3rd, 1999–2000 5th, 2000–01 6th, 2001–02 6th, 2002–03 4th, 2003–04 2nd, 2004–05 1st, 2005–06 1st, 2006–07 2nd, 2007–08 2nd, 2008–09 3rd, 2009–10 1st, 2010–11 2nd, 2011–12 6th, 2012–13 3rd, 2013–14 3rd, 2014–15 1st, 2015–16 10th, 2016–17 1st, 2017–18 5th, 2018–19 3rd, 2019–20 4th, 2020–21 4th, 2021–22 3rd
Biggest win: 8-0 v Aston Villa (Prem Lge) Dec 23, 2012. Also: 13-0 v Jeunesse Hautcharage, (Cup-Winners' Cup 1) Sep 29, 1971
Biggest defeat: 1-8 v Wolves (Div 1) Sep 26, 1953; 0-7 v Leeds (Div 1) Oct 7, 1967, v Nottm Forest (Div 1) Apr 20, 1991
Highest League scorer in a season: Jimmy Greaves 41 (1960–61)
Most League goals in aggregate: Bobby Tambling 164 (1958–70)
Longest unbeaten League sequence: 40 matches (2004–05). **Longest sequence without a League win:** 21 matches (1987–88). **Most capped player:** Frank Lampard (England) 104

Goalkeepers

Arrizabalaga, Kepa	6.2	Athletic Bilbao	Ondarroa. Sp	03.10.94
Bettinelli, Marcus	6.4	Fulham	Camberwell	24.05.92
Mendy, Edouard	6.6	Rennes	Montivilliers, Fr	01.03.92

Defenders

Azpilicueta, Cesar	5.10	Marseille	Pamplona, Sp	28.08.89
Chalobah, Trevor	6.3	–	Freetown, SLeone	05.07.99
Chilwell, Ben	5.10	Leicester	Milton Keynes	21.12.96
Emerson	5.9	Roma	Santos, Br	03.08.94
James, Reece	6.0	–	Redbridge	08.12.99
Malang Sarr	6.0	Nice	Nice, Fr	23.01.99
Thiago Silva	6.0	Paris SG	Rio de Janeiro, Br	22.09.84

Midfielders

Barkley, Ross	6.2	Everton	Liverpool	05.12.93
Hudson-Odoi, Callum	6.0	–	Wandsworth	07.11.00
Jorginho	5.11	Napoli	Imbituba, Bra	20.12.91

Kante, N'Golo	5.7	Leicester	Paris, Fr	29.03.91
Kenedy	6.0	Fluminense	Santa Rita, BNr	08.02.96
Kovacic, Mateo	5.10	Real Madrid	Linz, Aut	06.05.94
Havertz, Kai	6.2	Bayer Leverkusen	Aachen, Ger	11.06.99
Loftus-Cheek, Ruben	6.3	–	Lewisham	23.01.96
Marcos Alonso	6.2	Fiorentina	Madrid, Sp	28.12.90
Mount, Mason	5.10	–	Portsmouth	10.01.99
Ziyech, Hakim	5.11	Ajax	Dronten, Hol	19.03.93
Forwards				
Batshuayi, Michy	6.0	Marseille	Brussels, Bel	02.10.93
Broja, Armando	6.3	Tottenham	Slough	10.09.01
Pulisic, Christian	5.8	Borussia Dortmund	Hershey, US	18.09.98
Werner, Timo	5.11	Leipzig	Stuttgart, Ger	06.03.96

CRYSTAL PALACE

Ground: Selhurst Park, Whitehorse Lane, London SE25, 6PU
Telephone: 0208 768 6000. **Club nickname:** Eagles
Capacity: 25,486. **Colours:** Red and blue. **Shirt sponsor:** cinch
Record attendance: 51,482 v Burnley (Div 2), May 11, 1979
Record transfer fee: £27m to Liverpool for Christian Benteke, Aug 2016. **ecord fee received:** £50m
from Manchester Utd for Aaron Wan-Bissaka, Jun 2019. **eague Championship:** 3rd 1990–91
FA Cup: Runners-up 1990, 2016
League Cup: Semi-finals 1993, 1995, 2001, 2012
Finishing positions in Premier League: 1992–93 20th, 1994–95 19th, 1997–98 20th,.
2004–05 18th, 2013–14 11th, 2014–15 10th, 2015–16 15th, 2016–17 14th, 2017–18
11th, 2018–19 12th, 2019–20 14th, 2020–21 14th, 2021–22 12th
Biggest win: 9-0 v Barrow (Div 4) Oct 10, 1959.
Biggest defeat: 0-9 v Liverpool (Div 1) Sep 12, 1989. Also: 0-9 v Burnley (FA Cup 2 rep) Feb 10, 1909
Highest League scorer in a season: Peter Simpson 46 (1930–31)
Most League goals in aggregate: Peter Simpson 153 (1930–36)
Longest unbeaten League sequence: 18 matches (1969). **Longest sequence without a League
win:** 20 matches (1962). **Most capped player:** Wayne Hennessey (Wales) 50

Goalkeepers				
Butland, Jack	6.4	Stoke	Bristol	10.03.93
Guaita, Vicente	6.3	Getafe	Torrente, Sp	10.01.87
Defenders				
Andersen, Joachim	6.4	Lyon	Solrod Strand, Den	31.05.96
Ferguson, Nathan	5.11	WBA	Birmingham	06.10.00
Guehi, Marc	6.0	Chelsea	Abidjan Iv C	13.07.00
Kouyate, Cheikhou	6.4	West Ham	Dakar, Sen	21.12.89
Mitchell, Tyrick	5.9	–	Brent	01.09.99
Riedewald, Jairo	6.0	Ajax	Haarlem, Hol	09.09.96
Tomkins, James	6.3	West Ham	Basildon	29.03.89
Ward, Joel	6.2	Portsmouth	Emsworth	29.10.89
Midfielders				
Eze, Eberechi	5.8	QPR	Greenwich	29.06.98
Hughes, Will	6.1	Watford	Weybridge	07.04.95
McArthur, James	5.7	Wigan	Glasgow	07.10.87
Milivojevic, Luka	6.0	Olympiacos	Kragujevac, Serb	07.04.91
Olise, Michael	6.2	Reading	Hammersmith	12.12.01
Schlupp, Jeffrey	5.8	Leicester	Hamburg, Ger	23.12.92
Forwards				
Ayew, Jordan	6.0	Swansea	Marseille, Fr	11.09.91

Benteke, Christian	6.3	Liverpool	Kinshasa, DR Cong	03.12.90
Edouard, Odsonne	6.2	Celtic	Kouro, Fr Guin	16.01.98
Mateta, Jean-Philippe	6.4	Mainz	Sevran, Fr	28.06.97
Plange, Luke	5.11	Derby	Kingston upon Thames	04.11.02
Zaha, Wilfried	5.10	Man Utd	Abidjan, Iv C	10.11.92

EVERTON

Ground: Goodison Park, Liverpool L4 4EL
Telephone: 0151 556 1878. **Club nickname:** Stake
Capacity: 39,414. **Colours:** Blue and white. **Shirt sponsor:** Stake
Record attendance: 78,299 v Liverpool (Div 1) Sep 18, 1948
Record transfer fee: £45m to Swansea for Gylfi Sigurdsson, Aug 2017
Record fee received: £75m from Manchester Utd for Romelu Lukaku, Jul 2017
League Championship: Winners 1890–91, 1914–15, 1927–28, 1931–31, 1938–39, 1962–63, 1969–70, 1984–85, 1986–87
FA Cup: Winners 1906, 1933, 1966, 1984, 1995
League Cup: Runners-up 1977, 1984
European competitions: Winners Cup-Winners' Cup 1984–85
Finishing positions in Premier League: 1992–93 13th, 1993–94 17th, 1994–95 15th, 1995–96 6th 1996–97 15th 1997–98 17th 1998–99 14th, 1999–2000 13th, 2000–01 16th, 2001–02 15th, 2002–03 7th, 2003–04 17th, 2004–05 4th, 2005–06 11th, 2006–07 6th, 2007–08 5th, 2008–09 5th, 2009–10 8th, 20010–11 7th, 2011–12 7th, 2012–13 6th, 2013–14 5th, 2014–15 11th, 2015–16 11th, 2016–17 7th, 2017–18 8th, 2018–19 8th, 2019–20 12th, 2020–21 10th, 2021–22 16th
Biggest win: 9-1 v Manchester City (Div 1) Sep 3, 1906, v Plymouth (Div 2) Dec 27, 1930. Also: 11-2 v Derby (FA Cup 1) Jan 18, 1890
Biggest defeat: 0-7 v Portsmouth (Div 1) Sep 10, 1949, v Arsenal (Prem Lge) May 11, 2005
Highest League scorer in a season: Ralph 'Dixie' Dean 60 (1927–28)
Most League goals in aggregate: Ralph 'Dixie' Dean 349 (1925–37)
Longest unbeaten League sequence: 20 matches (1978). **Longest sequence without a League win:** 14 matches (1937). **Most capped player:** Neville Southall (Wales) 92

Goalkeepers

Begovic, Asmir	6.5	Bournemouth	Trebinje, Bos	20.06.87
Joao Virginia	6.3	–	Faro Por	10.09.99
Pickford, Jordan	6.1	Sunderland	Washington, Co Dur	07.03.94

Defenders

Branthwaite, Jarrad	6.5	Carlisle	Carlisle	27.06.02
Coleman, Seamus	5.10	Sligo	Donegal, Ire	11.10.88
Godfrey, Ben	6.0	Norwich	York	1501.98
Holgate, Mason	5.11	Barnsley	Doncaster	22.10.96
Keane, Michael	6.3	Burnley	Stockport	11.01.93
Mina, Yerry	6.4	Barcelona	Guachene, Col	23.09.94
Mykolenko, Vitaly	5.11	Dynamo Kiev	Cherksay, Ukr	29.05.99
Patterson, Nathan	6.0	Rangers	Glasgow	16.10.01
Tarkowski, James	6.1	Burnley	Manchester	19.11.92

Midfielders

Allan	5.9	Napoli	Rio de Janeiro, Br	08.01.91
Alli, Dele	6.1	Tottenham	Milton Keynes	11.04.96
Andre Gomes	6.2	Barcelona	Grijo, Por	30.07.93
Davies, Tom	5.11	–	Liverpool	30.06.98
Doucoure, Abdoulaye	6.0	Watford	Meulan, Fr	01.01.93
Gbamin, Jean-Philippe	6.1	Mainz	San Pedro Iv C	25.09.95
Gordon, Anthony	6.0	–	Kirkdale	24.02.01

Townsend, Andros	6.0	Crystal Palace	Leytonstone	16.07.91

Forwards

Calvert-Lewin, Dominic	6.2	Sheffield Utd	Sheffield	16.03.97
Gordon, Anthony	5.10	–	Liverpool	24.02.01
Gray, Demarai	5.10	Bayer Leverkusen	Birmingham	28.06.96
Iwobi, Alex	5.11	Arsenal	Lagos, Nig	03.05.96
Kean, Moise	6.0	Juventus	Vercelli, It	28.02.00
Rondon, Salomon	6.1	Dalia Pro	Caracas, Ven	16.09.89

FULHAM

Ground: Craven Cottage, Stevenage Road, London SW6 6HH
Telephone: 0870 442 1222. **Club nickname:** Cottagers
Capacity: 20,000. **Colours:** White and black. **Shirt sponsor:** World Mobile
Record attendance: 49,335 v Millwall (Div 2) Oct 8, 1938
Record transfer fee: £25m to Nice for Jean Michael Seri, Jul 2018
Record fee received: £25m from Tottenham for Ryan Sessegnon, Aug 2019
League Championship: 7th 2008–09
FA Cup: Runners-up 1975
League Cup: 5th rd 1968, 1971, 2000
European competitions: Runners-up Europa League 2009–10
Finishing positions in Premier League: 2001–02 13th, 2002–03 14th, 2003–04 9th, 2004–05 13th, 2005–06 12th, 2006–07 16th, 2007–08 17th, 2008–09 7th, 2009–10 12th, 2010–11 8th, 2011–12 9th, 2012–13 12th, 2013–14 19th, 2018–19th, 2020–21 18th
Biggest win: 10-1 v Ipswich (Div 1) Dec 26, 1963
Biggest defeat: 0-10 v Liverpool (League Cup 2), Sep 23, 1986
Highest League scorer in a season: Frank Newton 43 (1931–32), Aleksandar Mitrovic 43 (2021–22)
Most League goals in aggregate: Gordon Davies 159 (1978–84 and 1986–91)
Longest unbeaten League sequence: 23 matches (2017–18). **Longest sequence without a League win:** 15 matches (1950). **Most capped player:** Johnny Haynes (England) 56

Goalkeepers

Gazzaniga, Paulo	6.5	Tottenham	Murphy, Arg	02.01.92
Rodak, Marek	6.5	–	Kosice, Slovak	13.02.96

Defenders

Bryan, Joe	5.7	Bristol City	Bristol	17.09.93
Kongolo, Terence	6.2	Huddersfield	Fribourg, Switz	14.02.94
Ream, Tim	6.1	Bolton	St Louis, US	05.10.87
Robinson, Antonee	6.0	Wigan	Milton Keynes	08.08.97
Tete, Kenny	5.11	Lyon	Amsterdam, Hol	09.10.95
Tosin Adarabioyo	6.5	Manchester City	Manchester	24.09.97

Midfielders

Cairney, Tom	6.0	Blackburn	Nottingham	20.01.91
Chalobah, Nathaniel	6.1	Watford	Freetown, SLeone	12.12.94
Joao Palhinha	6.3	Sporting	Lisbon, Por	09.07.95
Kebano, Neeskens	5.11	Genk	Montereau, Fr	10.03.92
Onomah, Josh	5.11	Tottenham	Enfield	27.04.97
Reed, Harrison	5.11	Southampton	Worthing	27.01.95
Wilson, Harry	5.8	Liverpool	Wrexham	22.03.97

Forwards

Decordova-Reid, Bobby	5.8	Carfdiff	Bristol	02.02.93
Mitrovic, Aleksandar	6.3	Newcastle	Smederevo, Serb	16.09.94
Muniz Rodrigo	6.1	Flamengo	Sao Domingos, Br	04.05.01

LEEDS UNITED

Ground: Elland Road, Leeds LS11 OES
Telephone: 0871 334 1919. **Club nickname:** Whites
Capacity: 37,792. **Colours:** White. **Shirt sponsor:** Sbotop.
Record attendance: 57,892 v Sunderland (FA Cup 5 rep) Mar 15, 1967
Record transfer fee: £26m to Valencia for Rodrigo, Aug 2020
Record fee received: £29.1m from Manchester Utd for Rio Ferdinand, Jul 2002
League Championship: Winners 1968–69, 1973–74, 1991–92
FA Cup: Winner 1972
League Cup: Winners 1968
European competitions: Winners Fairs Cup 1967–68, 1970–71
Finishing positions in Premier League: 1992–93 17th, 1993–94 5th, 1994–95 5th, 1995–96
13th, 1996–97 11th, 1997–98 5th, 1998–99 4th, 1999–2000 3rd, 2000–01 4th, 2001–02
5th, 2002–03 15th, 2003–04 19th, 2020–21 9th, 2021–22 17th
Biggest win: 8-0 v Leicester (Div 1) Apr 7, 1934
Biggest defeat: 1-8 v Stoke (Div 1) Aug 27, 1934
Highest League scorer in a season: John Charles 43 (1953–54)
Most League goals in aggregate: Peter Lorimer 168 (1965–79, 1983–86)
Longest unbeaten League sequence: 34 matches (1968–69). **Longest sequence without a
League win:** 17 matches (1947). **Most capped player:** Billy Bremner (Scotland) 54

Goalkeepers

Klaesson, Kristoffer	6.2	Valerenga	Oslo, Nor	27.11.00
Meslier, Illan	6.5	Lorient	Lorient, Fr	02.03.00

Defenders

Ayling, Luke	6.1–	Bristol City	Lambeth	25.08.91
Cooper, Liam	6.0	Chesterfield	Hull	30.08.91
Drameh, Cody	5.8	Fulham	London	08.12.01
Junior Firpo	6.0	Barcelona	Santo Domingo, Dom	22.08.96
Koch, Robin	6.3	Freiburg	Kaiserslautern, Ger	17.07.96
Kristensen, Rasmus	6.2	RB Salzburg	Brande, Den	11.07.97
Llorente, Diego	6.1	Real Sociedad	Madrid, Sp	16.08.93
Struijk, Pascal	6.3	Ajax	Deurne, Bel	11.08.99

Midfielders

Aaronson, Brenden	5.10	RB Salzburg	Medford, US	22.10.00
Adams, Tyler	5.9	RB Leipzig	Wappinger, US	14.02.99
Dallas, Stuart	6.0	Brentford	Cookstown	19.04.91
Forshaw, Adam	6.1	Middlesbrough	Liverpool	08.10.91
Harrison, Jack	5.9	Manchester City	Stoke	20.11.96
James, Daniel	5.8	Manchester Utd	Beverley	10.11.97
Klich, Mateusz	6.0	FC Twente	Tarnow, Pol	13.06.90
Roca, Marc	6.0	Bayern Munich	Vilafranca, Sp	26.11.96
Shackleton, Jamie	5.7	–	Leeds	08.10.99
Sinisterra, Luis	5.8	Feyenoord, Santander, Col		17.06.99

Forwards

Bamford, Patrick	6.1	Middlesbrough	Grantham	05.09.93
Gelhardt, Joe	5.10	Wigan	Liverpool	04.05.92
Helder Costa	5.10	Wolves	Luanda, Ang	12.01.94
Raphina	5.9	Rennes	Porto Alegre, Br	14.12.96
Rodrigo	6.0	Valencia	Rio de Janeiro, Br	06.03.91

LEICESTER CITY

Ground: King Power Stadium, Filbert Way, Leicester, LE2 7FL

Telephone: 0344 815 5000. **Club nickname:** Foxes
Capacity: 32,312. **Colours:** Blue and white. **Shirt sponsor:** FBS
Record attendance: Filbert Street: 47,298 v. Tottenham (FA Cup 5) Feb 18, 1928; King Power Stadium: 32,148 v Newcastle (Prem Lge) Dec 26, 2003. Also: 32,188 v Real Madrid (friendly) Jul 30, 2011
Record transfer fee: £40m to Monaco for Youri Tielemans, Jul 2019
Record fee received: £80m from Manchester United for Harry Maguire, Aug 2019
League Championship: Winners 2015–16
FA Cup: Winners 2020–21
League Cup: Winners 1964, 1997, 2000
European competitions: Champions League quarter-finals 2016–17
Finishing positions in Premier League: 1994–95 21st, 1996–97 9th, 1997–98 10th, 1998–99 10th, 1999–2000 8th, 2000–01 13th, 2001–02 20th, 2003–04 18th, 2014–15 14th, 2015–16 1st, 2016–17 12th, 2017–18 9th, 2018–19 9th, 2019–2020 5th, 2020–21 5th 2021–22 8th
Biggest win: 10-0 v Portsmouth (Div 1) Oct 20, 1928. Also: 13-0 v Notts Olympic (FA Cup) Oct 13, 1894. **Biggest defeat (while Leicester Fosse):** 0-12 v Nottm Forest (Div 1) Apr 21, 1909
Highest League scorer in a season: Arthur Rowley 44 (1956–57)
Most League goals in aggregate: Arthur Chandler 259 (1923–35)
Longest unbeaten League sequence: 23 matches (2008–09). **Longest sequence without a League win:** 19 matches (1975). **Most capped player:** Kasper Schmeichel (Denmark) 84

Goalkeepers

Schmeichel, Kasper	6.0	Leeds	Copenhagen, Den	05.11.86
Ward, Danny	6.4	Liverpool	Wrexham	22.06.93

Defenders

Bertrand, Ryan	5.10	Southampton	Southwark	05.08.89
Caglar Soyuncu	6.1	Freiburg	Izmir, Tur	23.05.96
Castagne, Timothy	6.1	Atalanta	Arlon, Bel	05.12.95
Evans, Jonny	6.2	WBA	Belfast	02.01.88
Fofana, Wesley	6.3	St Etienne	Marseille, Fr	17.12.00
Justin, James	6.3	Luton	Luton	11.07.97
Ricardo Pereira	5.9	Porto	Lisbon, Por	06.10.93
Thomas, Luke	5.11	–	Syston	10.06.01
Vestergaard, Jannik	6.6	Southampton	Copenhagen, Den	03.08.92

Midfielders

Albrighton, Mark	6.1	Aston Villa	Tamworth	18.11.89
Amartey, Daniel	6.0	Copenhagen	Accra, Gh	01.12.94
Barnes, Harvey	5.9	–	Burnley	09.12.97
Choudhury, Hamza	5.10	–	Loughborough	01.10.97
Dewsbury-Hall, Kieran	5.10	–	Nottingham	06.09.98
Maddison, James	5.10	Norwich	Coventry	23.11.96
Mendy, Nampalys	5.6	Nice	La Seyne, Fr	23.06.92
Ndidi, Wilfred	6.0	Genk	Lagos, Nig	16.12.96
Praet, Dennis	5.11	Sampdoria	Leuven, Bel	14.05.94
Soumare, Boubakary	6.2	Lille	Noisy-le-Sec, Fr	27.02.99
Tielemans, Youri	5.10	Monaco	Sint-Pieters, Bel	07.05.97

Forward

Ayoze Perez	5.11	Newcastle	Santa Cruz, Ten	23.07.93
Daka, Patson	6.1	RB Salzburg	Kafue, Zam	09.10.98
Hirst, George	6.3	Leuven	Sheffield	15.02.99
Vardy, Jamie	5.10	Fleetwood	Sheffield	11.01.87

LIVERPOOL

Ground: Anfield, Liverpool L4 OTH
Telephone: 0151 263 2361. **Club nickname:** Reds or Pool
Capacity: 53,394. **Colours:** Red. **Shirt sponsor:** Standard Chartered
Record attendance: 61,905 v Wolves, (FA Cup 4), Feb 2, 1952
Record transfer fee: £75m to Southampton for Virgil van Dijk, Jan 2018
Record fee received: £142m from Barcelona for Philippe Coutinho, Jan 2018
League Championship: Winners 1900–01, 1905–06, 1921–22, 1922–23, 1946–47, 1963–64, 1965–66, 1972–73, 1975–76, 1976–77, 1978–79, 1979–80, 1981–82, 1982–83,1983–84, 1985–86, 1987–88, 1989–90, 2019–20 1st, 2020–21
FA Cup: Winners 1965, 1974, 1986, 1989, 1992, 2001, 2006, 2022
League Cup: Winners 1981, 1982, 1983, 1984, 1995, 2001, 2003, 2012, 2022
European competitions: Winners European Cup/Champions League 1976–77, 1977–78,1980–81, 1983–84, 2004–05, 2018–19; UEFA Cup 1972–73, 1975–76, 2000–01; European Super Cup 1977, 2001, 2005
Finishing positions in Premier League: 1992–93 6th, 1993–94 8th, 1994–95 4th, 1995–96 3rd, 1996–97 4th, 1997–98 3rd, 1998–99 7th, 1999–2000 4th, 2000–01 3rd, 2001–02 2nd, 2002–03 5th, 2003–04 4th, 2004–05 5th, 2005–06 3rd, 2006–07 3rd, 2007–08 4th, 2008–09 2nd, 2009–10 7th, 2010–11 6th, 2011–12 8th, 2012–13 7th, 2013–14 2nd, 2014–15 6th, 2015–16 8th, 2016–17 4th, 2017–18 4th, 2018–19 2nd, 2019–20 1st, 2020–21 3rd, 2021–22 2nd
Biggest win: 10-1 v Rotherham (Div 2) Feb 18, 1896. Also: 11-0 v Stromsgodset (Cup-Winners' Cup 1) Sep 17, 1974
Biggest defeat: 1-9 v Birmingham (Div 2) Dec 11, 1954
Highest League scorer in a season: Roger Hunt 41 (1961–62)
Most League goals in aggregate: Roger Hunt 245 (1959–69). 31 matches (1987–88))
Longest unbeaten League sequence: 44 matches (2019–20). **Longest sequence without a League win:** 14 matches (1953–54). **Most capped player:** Steven Gerrard (England) 114

Goalkeepers				
Adrian	6.3	West Ham	Seville, Sp	03.01.87
Alisson	6.4	Roma	Novo Hamburgo, Bra	02.10.92
Kelleher, Caoimhin	6.2	–	Cork, Ire	23.11.98
Defenders				
Alexander-Arnold, Trent	5.10	–	Liverpool	07.10.98
Davies, Ben	5.11	Preston	Barrow	11.08.95
Gomez, Joe	6.1	Charlton	Catford	23.05.97
Konate, Ibrahima	6.4	RB Leipzig	Paris, Fr	25.05.99
Matip, Joel	6.5	Schalke	Bochum, Ger	08.08.91
Phillips, Nat	6.3	–	Bolton	21.03.97
Ramsay, Calvin	5.10	Aberdeen	Aberdeen	31.07.03
Robertson, Andrew	5.10	Hull	Glasgow	11.03.94
Tsimikas, Kostas	5.10	Olympiacos	Thessaloniki, Gre	12.05.96
Van Dijk, Virgil	6.4	Southampton	Breda, Hol	08.07.91
Williams, Neco	6.0	–	Wrexham	13.04.01
Williams, Rhys	6.5	–	Preston	03.02.01
Midfielders				
Elliott, Harvey	5.8	Fulham	Chertsey	04.04.03
Fabio Carvalho	5.8	Fulham	Torres Vedras, Por	30.08.02
Fabinho	6.2	Monaco	Campinas, Bra	23.10.93
Henderson, Jordan	5.10	Sunderland	Sunderland	17.06.90
Jones, Curtis	6.0	–	Liverpool	30.01.01
Keita, Naby	5.8	Leipzig	Conakry, Guin	10.02.95
Diaz, Luis	5.10	Porto	Barrancas, Col	13.01.97

Milner, James	5.11	Man City	Leeds	04.01.86
Oxlade-Chamberlain, Alex	5.11	Arsenal	Portsmouth	15.08.93
Thiago Alcantara	5.9	Bayern Munich	San Pietro, It	11.04.91
Forwards				
Darwin Nunez	6.2	Benfica	Artigas, Uru	24.06.99
Diogo Jota	5.10	Wolves	Porto, Por	04.12.96
Firmino, Roberto	6.0	Hoffenheim	Maceio, Br	02.10.91
Salah, Mohamed	5.9	Roma	Basyoun, Egy	15.06.92

MANCHESTER CITY

Ground: Etihad Stadium, Etihad Campus, Manchester M11 3FF
Telephone: 0161 444 1894. **Club nickname:** City
Capacity: 55,017. **Colours:** Sky blue and white. **Shirt sponsor:** Etihad.
Record attendance: Maine Road: 84,569 v Stoke (FA Cup 6) Mar 3, 1934 (British record for any game outside London or Glasgow). Etihad Stadium: 54,693 v Leicester (Prem Lge) February 6, 2016
Record transfer fee: £100m to Aston Villa for Jack Grealish, Aug 2021
Record fee received: £46.3m from Barcelona for Ferran Torres, Dec 2021
League Championship: Winners 1936–37, 1967–68, 2011–12, 2013–14, 2017–18, 2018–19, 2020–21, 2021–22
FA Cup: Winners 1904, 1934, 1956, 1969, 2011, 2019
League Cup: Winners 1970, 1976, 2014, 2016, 2018, 2019, 2020, 2021
European competitions: Winners Cup-Winners' Cup 1969–70
Finishing positions in Premier League: 1992–93 9th, 1993–94 16th, 1994–95 17th, 1995–96 18th, 2000–01: 18th, 2002–03 9th, 2003–04 16th, 2004–05 8th, 2005–06 15th, 2006–07 14th, 2007–08 9th, 2008–09 10th, 2009–16 5th, 2010–11 3rd, 2011–12 1st, 2012–13 2nd, 2013–14 1st, 2014–15 2nd, 2015–16 4th, 2016–17 3rd, 2017–18 1st, 2018–19 1st, 2019–20 2nd, 2020–21 1st, 2021–22 1st
Biggest win: 10-1 v Huddersfield (Div 2) Nov 7, 1987. Also: 10-1 v Swindon (FA Cup 4) Jan 29, 1930
Biggest defeat: 1-9 v Everton (Div 1) Sep 3, 1906
Highest League scorer in a season: Tommy Johnson 38 (1928–29)
Most League goals in aggregate: Tommy Johnson, 158 (1919–30)
Longest unbeaten League sequence: 22 matches (1946–47) and (2017–18). **Longest sequence without a League win:** 17 matches (1979–80). **Most capped player:** Joe Hart (England) 75

Goalkeepers				
Ederson	6.2	Benfica	Osasco, Br	17.08.93
Ortega, Stefan	6.1	Arminia Bielefeld	Hofgeismar, Ger	06.11.92
Steffen, Zack	6.3	Columbus Crew	Coatesville, US	02.04.95
Defenders				
Ake, Nathan	5.11	Bournemouth	The Hague, Hol	18.02.95
Joao Cancelo	6.0	Juventus	Barrreiro, Por	27.05.94
Laporte, Aymeric	6.3	Athletic Bilbao	Agen, Fr	27.05.94
Ruben Dias	6.2	Benfica	Amadora, Por	14.05.97
Stones, John	6.2	Everton	Barnsley	28.05.94
Walker, Kyle	6.0	Tottenham	Sheffield	28.05.90
Zinchenko, Oleksandr	5.9	FC Ufa	Radomyshl, Ukr	15.12.96
Midfielders				
Bernardo Silva	5.8	Monaco	Lisbon, Por	10.08.94
De Bruyne, Kevin	5.11	Wolfsburg	Drongen, Bel	28.06.91
Foden, Phil	5.7	–	Stockport	28.05.00
Grealish, Jack	5.9	Aston Villa	Solihull	10.09.95
Gundogan, Ilkay	5.11	Borussia Dortmund	Gelsenkirchen, Ger	24.10.90

Mahrez, Riyad	5.10	Leicester	Sarcelles, Fr	21.02.91
Phillips, Kalvin	5.10	Leeds	Leeds	02.12.95
Rodri	6.3	Atletico Madrid	Madrid, Sp	23.06.96
Forwards				
Alvarez, Julian	5.7	River Plate	Cordoba, Arg	31.01.00
Delap, Liam	6.1	Derby	Winchester	08.02.03
Haaland, Erling	6.4	Borussia Dortmund	Leeds	21.07.00
Sterling, Raheem	5.7	Liverpool	Kingston, Jam	08.12.94

MANCHESTER UNITED

Ground: Old Trafford Stadium, Sir Matt Busby Way, Manchester, M16 ORA
Telephone: 0161 868 8000. **Club nickname:** Red Devils
Capacity: 74,140. **Colours:** Red and white. **Shirt sponsor:** TeamViewer
Record attendance: 75,811 v Blackburn (Prem Lge), Mar 31, 2007. Also: 76,962 Wolves v Grimsby (FA Cup semi-final) Mar 25, 1939. Crowd of 83,260 saw Manchester Utd v Arsenal (Div 1) Jan 17, 1948 at Maine Road – Old Trafford out of action through bomb damage
Record transfer fee: £89.3m to Juventus for Paul Pogba, Aug 2016
Record fee received: £80m from Real Madrid for Cristiano Ronaldo, Jun 2009
League Championship: Winners 1907–08, 1910–11, 1951–52, 1955–56, 1956–7, 1964–65, 1966–67, 1992–93, 1993–94, 1995–96, 1996–97, 1998–99, 1999–2000, 2000–01, 2002–03, 2006–07, 2007–08, 2008–09, 2010–11, 2012–13
FA Cup: Winners 1909, 1948, 1963, 1977, 1983, 1985, 1990, 1994, 1996, 1999, 2004, 2016
League Cup: Winners 1992, 2006, 2009, 2010, 2017
European competitions: Winners European Cup/Champions League 1967–68, 1998–99, 2007–08; Cup-Winners' Cup 1990–91; European Super Cup 1991; Europa League 2016–17
World Club Cup: Winners 2008
Finishing positions in Premier League: 1992–93 1st, 1993–94 1st, 1994–95 2nd, 1995–96 1st, 1996–97 1st, 1997–98 2nd, 1998–99 1st, 1999–2000 1st, 2000–01 1st, 2001–02 3rd, 2002–03 1st, 2003–04 3rd, 2004–05 3rd, 2005–06 2nd, 2006–07 1st, 2007–08 1st, 2000–09 1st, 2009–10 2nd, 2010–11 1st, 2011–12 2nd, 2012–13 1st, 2013–14 7th, 2014–15 4th, 2015–16 5th, 2016–17 6th, 2017–18 2nd, 2018–19 6th, 2019–20 3rd, 2020–21 2nd, 2021–22 6th
Biggest win: As Newton Heath: 10-1 v Wolves (Div 1) Oct 15, 1892. As Manchester Utd: 9-0 v Ipswich (Prem Lge), Mar 4, 1995;. 9-0 v Southampton (Prem Lge), Feb 2, 2021. Also: 10-0 v Anderlecht (European Cup prelim rd) Sep 26, 1956
Biggest defeat: 0-7 v Blackburn (Div 1) Apr 10, 1926, v Aston Villa (Div 1) Dec 27, 1930, v Wolves (Div 2) 26 Dec, 1931 **Highest League scorer in a season:** Dennis Viollet 32 (1959–60)
Most League goals in aggregate: Sir Bobby Charlton 199 (1956–73)
Longest unbeaten League sequence: 29 matches (1998–99). **Longest sequence without a League win:** 16 matches (1930). **Most capped player:** Sir Bobby Charlton (England) 106

Goalkeepers				
De Gea, David	6.4	Atletico Madrid	Madrid, Sp	07.11.90
Henderson, Dean	6.3	–	Whitehaven	12.03.97
Heaton, Tom	6.1	Aston Villa	Chester	15.04.86
Defenders				
Bailly, Eric	6.1	Villarreal	Bingerville, Iv C	12.04.94
Diogo Dalot	6.0	Porto	Braga, Por	18.03.99
Jones, Phil	5.11	Blackburn	Blackburn	21.02.92
Lindelof, Victor	6.2	Benfica	Vasteras, Swe	17.07.94
Maguire, Harry	6.2	Leicesterl	Sheffield	05.03.93
Malacia, Tyrell	5.8	Feyenoord	Rotterdam	17.08.99
Shaw, Luke	6.1	Southamptonn	Kingston upon Thames	12.07.95
Telles, Alex	5.11	Porto	Caxias do Sul, Br	15.12.92

| Varane, Raphael | 6.3 | Real Madrid | Lille, Fr | 25.04.93 |
| Wan-Bissaka, Aaron | 6.0 | Crystal Palace | Croydon | 26.11.97 |

Midfielders

Bruno Fernandes	5.8	Sporting Lisbon	Maia, Por	08.09.84
Diallo, Amad	5.8	Atalanta	Abidjan, Iv C	11.07.02
Elanga, Anthony	5.10	Malmo	Malmo, Swe	27.04.02
Fred	5.7	Shakhtar Donetsk	Belo Horizonte, Bra	05.03.93
McTominay, Scott	6.4	–	Lancaster	08.12.96
Sancho, Jadon	5.11	Borussia Dortmund	Camberwell	25.03.00
Van de Beek, Donny	6.1	Ajax	Nijkerkerveen, Hol	18.04.97

Forwards

Greenwood, Mason	5.11	–	Bradford	01.10.01
Martial, Anthony	5.11	Monaco	Massy, Fr	05.12.95
Rashford, Marcus	6.0	–	Wythensawe	31.10.97
Ronaldo, Cristiano	6.2	Juventus	Funchal, Mad	05.02.85

NEWCASTLE UNITED

Ground: St James' Park, Newcastle-upon-Tyne, NE1 4ST
Telephone: 0844 372 1892. **Club nickname:** Magpies
Capacity: 52,305. **Colours:** Black and white. **Shirt sponsor:** TBC
Record attendance: 68,386 v Chelsea (Div 1) Sep 3, 1930
Record transfer fee: £40m to Hoffenheim for Joelinton, Jul 2019
Record fee received: £35m from Liverpool or Andy Carroll, Jan 2011
League Championship: Winners 1904–05, 1906–07, 1908–09, 1926–27
FA Cup: Winners: 1910, 1924, 1932, 1951, 1952,1955
League Cup: Runners-up 1976
European competitions: Winners Fairs Cup 1968–69; Anglo-Italian Cup 1972–73
Finishing positions in Premier League: 1993–94 3rd, 1994–95 6th, 1995–96 2nd, 1996–97 2nd, 1997–98 13th, 1998–99 13th, 1999–2000 11th, 2000–01 11th, 2001–02 4th, 2002–03 3rd, 2003–04 5th, 2004–05 14th, 2005–06 7th, 2006–07 13th, 2007–08 12th, 2008–09 18th, 2010–11 12th, 2011–12 5th, 2012–13 16th, 2013–14 10th, 2014–15 15th, 2015–16 18th, 2017–18 10th, 2018–19 13th, 2019–20 13th, 2020–21 12th, 2021–22 11th
Biggest win: 13-0 v Newport (Div 2) Oct 5, 1946
Biggest defeat: 0-9 v Burton (Div 2) Apr 15, 1895
Highest League scorer in a season: Hughie Gallacher 36 (1926–27)
Most League goals in aggregate: Jackie Milburn 177 (1946–57)
Longest unbeaten League sequence: 14 matches (1950). **Longest sequence without a League win:** 21 matches (1978). **Most capped player:** Shay Given (Republic of Ireland) 83

Goalkeepers

Darlow, Karl	6.1	Nottm Forest	Northampton	08.10.90
Dubravka, Martin	6.3	Sparta Prague	Zilina, Slovak	15.01.89
Gillespie, Mark	6.3	Motherwell	Newcastle	27.03.92
Pope, Nick	6.3	Burnley	Cambridge	19.04.92

Defenders

Burn, Dan	6.7	Brighton	Blyth	09.05.92
Clark, Ciaran	6.2	Aston Villa	Harrow	26.09.89
Dummett, Paul	6.0	–	Newcastle	26.09.91
Fernandez, Federico	6.3	Swansea	Tres Algarrobos, Arg	21.02.89
Krafth, Emil	6.1	Amiens	Stockholm, Swe	02.08.94
Lascelles, Jamaal	6.2	Nottm Forest	Derby	11.11.93
Lewis, Jamal	5.10	Norwch	Luton	25.01.98
Manquillo, Javier	6.0	Atletico Madrid	Madrid, Sp	05.05.94
Schar, Fabian	6.2	Dep La Coruna	Wil, Switz	20.12.91

Trippier, Kieran	5.8	Atletico Madrid	Bury	19.09.90
Midfielders				
Almiron, Miguel	5.9	Atlanta	Asuncion, Par	10.02.94
Bruno Guimaraes	6.0	Lyon	Rio de Janeiro, Br	16.11.97
Fraser, Ryan	5.4	Bournemouth	Aberdeen	24.02.94
Longstaff, Sean	5.1	–	North Shields	30.10.97
Murphy, Jacob	5.10	Norwich	Wembley	24.02.95
Ritchie, Matt	5.8	Bournemouth	Gosport	10.09.89
Saint-Maximin, Allan	5.9	Nice	Chatenay-Malabry, Fr	12.03.97
Shelvey, Jonjo	6.0	Swansea	Romford	27.02.92
Targett, Matt	6.0	Aston Villa	Eastleigh	18.09.95
Willock, Joe	5.10	Arsenal	Waltham Forest	20.08.99
Forwards				
Gayle, Dwight	5.10	Crystal Palace	Walthamstow	20.10.90
Joelinton	6.1	Hoffenheim	Alianca, Br	14.08.96
Wilson, Callum	5.11	Bournemouth	Coventry	27.02.92
Wood, Chris	6.3	Burnley	Auckland, NZ	07.12.91

NOTTINGHAM FOREST

Ground: City Ground, Pavilion Road, Nottingham NG2 5FJ
Telephone: 0115 982 4444. **Club nickname:** Forest
Capacity: 30,445. **Colours:** Red and white. **Shirt sponsor:** TBC
Record attendance: 49,946 v Manchester Utd (Div 1) Oct 28, 1967
Record transfer fee: £17 to Union Berlin for Taiwo Awoniyi, Jun 2022
Record fee received: £15m from Middlesbrough for Britt Assombalonga, Jul 2017
League Championship: Winners 1977–78
FA Cup: Winners 1898, 1959
League Cup: Winners 1978, 1979, 1989, 1990
European competitions: Winners European Cup 1979, 1980
Finishing positions in Premier League: 1992–93 22nd, 1994–95 3rd, 1995–96 9th,1996–97 20th,1998–99 20th
Biggest win: 12-0 v Leicester Fosse (Div 1) Apr 12, 1909
Biggest defeat: 1-9 Blackburn (Div 2) Apr 10, 1937
Highest League scorer in a season: Wally Ardron 36 (1950–51)
Most League goals in aggregate: Grenville Morris 199 (1898–1913)
Longest unbeaten League sequence:42 matches (1977–78). **Longest sequence without a League win:** 19 matches (1998–99). **Most capped player:** Stuart Pearce (England) 76

Goalkeepers				
Henderson, Dean	6.3	Manchester Utd (loan)	Whitehaven	12.03.97
Defenders				
Biancone, Giulian	6.2	Troyes	Frejus, Fr	31.03.00
Cook, Steve	6.1	Bournemouth	Hastings	19.04.91
Laryea, Richie	5.9	Toronto	Toronto, Can	07.01.95
Mbe Soh, Loic	6.2	Paris SG	Nanga, Cam	13.06.01
McKenna, Scott	6.2	Aberdeen	Kirriemuir	12.11.96
Niakhate, Moussa	6.3	Mainz	Roubaix, Fr	08.03.96
Worrall, Joe	6.4	–	Hucknall	10.01.97
Midfielders				
Cafu	6.1	Olympiacos	Guimaraes, Por	26.02.93
Colback, Jack	5.10	Newcastle	Killingworth	24.10.89
Lolley, Joe	5.10	Huddersfield	Redditch	25.08.92
Ojeda, Braian	5.9	Olimpia	Itaugua, Par	27.06.00
Xande Silva	5.10	West Ham	Porto, Por	16.03.97

| Yates, Ryan | 6.3 | – | Lincoln | 21.11.97 |

Forwards

Awoniyi, Taiwo	6.0	Union Berlin	Ilorin, Nig	12.08.97
Grabban, Lewis	6.0	Bournemouth	Croydon	12.01.88
Johnson, Brennan	5.10	–	Nottingham	23.05.01
Mighten, Alex	5.9	–	Nottingham	11.04.02
Surridge, Sam	6.3	Stoke	Slough	28.07.98
Taylor, Lyle	6.2	Charlton	Greenwich	29.03.90

SOUTHAMPTON

Ground: St Mary's Stadium, Britannia Road, Southampton, SO14 5FP
Telephone: 0845 688 9448. **Club nickname:** Saints
Capacity: 32,384. **Colours:** Red and white. **Shirt sponsor:** Sportsbet
Record attendance: The Dell: 31,044 v Manchester Utd (Div 1) Oct 8, 1969. St Mary's:.32,363 v Coventry (Champ) Apr 28, 2012
Record transfer fee: £20m to Liverpool for Danny Ings, Jul 2019
Record fee received: £75m from Liverpool for Virgil van Dijk, Jan 2018
League Championship: Runners-up 1983–84
FA Cup: Winners 1976
League Cup: Runners-up 1979, 2017
European competitions: Fairs Cup rd 3 1969–70; Cup-Winners' Cup rd 3 1976–77
Finishing positions in Premier League: 1992–93 18th, 1993–94 18th, 1994–5 10th, 1995–96 17th, 1996–97 16th, 1997–98 12th, 1998–99 17th, 1999–200 15th, 2000–01 10th, 2001–02 11th, 2002–03 8th, 2003–04 12th, 2004–05 20th, 2012–13 14th, 2013–14 8th, 2014–15 7th, 2015–16 6th, 2016–17 8th, 2017–18 17th, 2018–19 16th, 2019–20 11th, 2020–21 15th, 2021–22 15th
Biggest win: 8-0 v Northampton (Div 3S) Dec 24, 1921, v Sunderland (Prem Lge) Oct 18, 2014
Biggest defeat: 0-9 v Leicester (Prem Lge) Oct 25, 2019; 0-9 v Manchester Utd (Prem Lge) Feb 2, 2021
Highest League scorer in a season: Derek Reeves 39 (1959–60)
Most League goals in aggregate: Mick Channon 185 (1966–82)
Longest unbeaten League sequence: 19 matches (1921). **Longest sequence without a League win:** 20 matches (1969). **Most capped player:** Steven Davis (Northern Ireland)) 59

Goalkeepers

Bazunu, Gavin	6.2	Manchester City	Dublin, Ire	20.02.02
Caballero, Willy	6.1	Chelsea	Santa Elena, Arg	28.09.81
McCarthy, Alex	6.4	Crystal Palace	Guildford	03.12.89

Defenders

Bednarek, Jan	6.2	Lech Poznan	Slupca, Pol	12.04.96
Bella-Kotchap, Armel	6.3	Bochum	Paris, Fr	11.12.01
Lyanco	6.2	Torino	Vitoria, Br	01.02.97
Perraud, Romain	5.8	Brest	Toulouse, Fr	22.09.97
Stephens, Jack	6.1	Plymouth	Torpoint	27.01.94
Valery, Yan	5.11	Rennes	Champigny, Fr	22.02.99
Walker-Peters, Kyle	5.8	Tottenham	Edmonton	13.04.97

Midfielders

Armstrong, Stuart	6.0	Celtic	Inverness	30.03.92
Diallo, Ibrahima	5.10	Brest	Tours, Fr	08.03.99
Djenepo, Moussa	5.10	Standard Liege	Bamako, Mali	15.06.98
Lavia, Romeo	5.11	Manchester City	Brussels, Bel	06.01.04
Redmond, Nathan	5.8	Norwich	Birmingham	06.03.94
Romeu, Oriol	6.0	Chelsea	Ulldecona, Sp	24.09.91
Salisu, Mohammed	6.3	Valladolid	Accra, Gh	17.04.99

Smallbone, Will	5.8	–	Basingstoke	21.02.00
Ward-Prowse, James	5.8	–	Portsmouth	01.11.94
Forwards				
Adams, Che	5.10	Birmingham	Leicester	13.07.96
Armstrong, Adam	5.8	Blackburn	Newcastle	10.02.97
Obafemi, Michael	5.7	–	Dublin, Ire	06.07.00
Tella, Nathan	5.9	Arsenal	Stevenage	05.07.99
Walcott, Theo	5.8	Everton	Newbury	16.03.89

TOTTENHAM HOTSPUR

Ground: Tottenham Hotspur Stadium, High Road, Tottenham N17 0BX
Telephone: 0344 499 5000. **Club nickname:** Spurs
Capacity: 62,850. **Colours:** White. **Shirt sponsor:** AIA
Record attendance: White Hart Lane: 75,038 v Sunderland (FA Cup 6) Mar 5, 1938. Wembley: 85,512 v Bayer Leverkusen (Champs Lge group) Nov 2, 2016. Tottenham Hotspur Stadium: 62,027 v Arsenal (Prem Lge) May 12, 2022
Record transfer fee: £53.8m to Lyon for Tanguy Ndombele, Jul 2019
Record fee received: £85.3m from Real Madrid for Gareth Bale, Aug 2013
League Championship: Winners 1950–51, 1960–61
FA Cup: Winners 1901, 1921, 1961, 1962, 1967, 1981, 1982, 1991
League Cup: Winners 1971, 1973, 1999, 2008
European competitions: Winners Cup-Winners' Cup 1962–63; UEFA Cup 1971–72, 1983–84
Finishing positions in Premier League: 1992–93 8th, 1993–94 15th, 1994–95 7th, 1995–96 8th, 1996–97 10th, 1997–98 14th, 1998–99 11th, 1999–2000 10th, 2000–01 12th, 2001–02 9th, 2002–03 10th, 2003–04 14th, 2004–05 9th, 2005–06 5th, 2006–07 5th, 2007–08 11th, 2008–09 8th, 2009–10 4th, 2010–11 5th, 2011–12 4th, 2012–13 5th, 2013–14 6th, 2014–15 5th, 2015–16 3rd, 2016–17 2nd, 2017–18 3rd, 2018–19 4th, 2019–20 6th, 2020–21 7th, 2021–22 4th
Biggest win: 9-0 v Bristol Rov (Div 2) Oct 22, 1977. Also: 13-2 v Crewe (FA Cup 4 replay) Feb 3, 1960
Biggest defeat: 0-7 v Liverpool (Div 1) Sep 2, 1979. Also: 0-8 v Cologne (Inter Toto Cup) Jul 22, 1995
Highest League scorer in a season: Jimmy Greaves 37 (1962–63)
Most League goals in aggregate: Jimmy Greaves 220 (1961–70)
Longest unbeaten League sequence: 22 matches (1949). **Longest sequence without a League win:** 16 matches (1934–35). **Most capped player:** Pat Jennings (Northern Ireland) 74

Goalkeepers				
Forster, Fraser	6.7	Southampton	Hexham	17.03.88
Lloris, Hugo	6.2	Lyon	Nice, Fr	26.12.86
Defenders				
Davies, Ben	5.6	Swansea	Neath	24.04.93
Dier, Eric	6.2	Sporting Lisbon	Cheltenham	15.01.94
Doherty, Matt	5.11	Wolves	Dublin, Ire	16.01.92
Emerson Royal	6.0	Barcelona	Sao Paulo, Br	14.01.99
Reguilon, Sergio	5.10	Real Madrid	Madrid, Sp	16.12.96
Rodon, Joe	6.4	Swansea	Llangyfelach	22.10.97
Romero, Cristian	6.1	Atalanta	Cordoba, Arg	27.04.98
Sanchez, Davinson	6.2	Ajax	Caloto, Col	12.06.96
Tanganga, Japhet	6.1	–	Hackney	31.03.99
Midfielders				
Bentancur, Rodrigo	6.2	Juventus	Nueva Helvecia, Uru	25.06.97
Bissouma, Yves	6.0	Brighton	Issia, Iv C	30.08.96
Gil, Bryan	5.9	Sevilla	L'Hospitalet, Sp	11.02.01
Hojbjerg, Pierre-Emile	6.1	Soutyhampton	Copenhagen, Den	05.08.95
Lo Celso, Giovani	5.10	Real Betis	Rosario, Arg	09.04.96

Ndombele, Tanguy	5.11	Lyon	Longjumeau, Fr	28.12.96
Sessegnon, Ryan	5.10	Fulham	Roehampton	18.05.00
Skipp, Oliver	5.9	–	Welwyn Garden City	16.09.00
Winks, Harry	5.10	–	Hemel Hempstead	02.02.96
Forwards				
Kane, Harry	6.2	–	Walthamstow	28.07.93
Lucas Moura	5.8	Paris SG	Sao Paulo, Br	13.08.92
Richarlison	6.0	Everton	Venecia, Br	10.05.97
Son Heung-Min	6.1	Bayer Leverkusen	Chuncheon, S Kor	08.07.92

WEST HAM UNITED

Ground: London Stadium, Olympic Park, London E20 2ST
Telephone: 0208 548 2748. **Club nickname:** Hammers
Capacity: 62,500. **Colours:** Claret and blue. **Shirt sponsor:** Betway
Record attendance: Upton Park: 43,322 v Tottenham (Div 1) Oct 17, 1970. London Stadium: 59.988 v Everton (Prem Lge) Mar 30, 2019
Record transfer fee: £45m to Eintracht Frankfurt for Sebastien Haller, Jul 2019
Record fee received: £25m from Marseille for Dimitri Payet, Jan 2017
League Championship: 3rd 1985–86
FA Cup: Winners 1964, 1975, 1980
League Cup: Runners-up 1966, 1981
European competitions: Winners Cup-Winners' Cup 1964–65
Finishing positions in Premier League: 1993–94 13th, 1994–95 14th, 1995–96 10th, 1996–97 14th, 1997–98 8th, 1998–99 5th, 1999–2000 9th, 2000–01 15th, 2001–02 7th, 2002–03 18th, 2005–06 9th, 2006–07 15th, 2007–08 10th, 2008–09: 9th, 2009–10 17th, 2010–11 20th, 2012–13 10th, 2013–14 13th, 2014–15 12th, 2015–16 7th, 2016–17 11th, 2017–18 13th, 2018–19 10th, 2019–20 16th, 2020–21 6th, 2021–22 7th
Biggest win: 8-0 v Rotherham (Div 2) Mar 8, 1958, v Sunderland (Div 1) Oct 19, 1968. Also: 10-0 v Bury (League Cup 2) Oct 25, 1983
Biggest defeat: 0-7 v Barnsley (Div 2) Sep 1, 1919, v Everton (Div 1) Oct 22, 1927, v Sheffield Wed (Div 1) Nov 28, 1959 **Highest League scorer in a season:** Vic Watson 42 (1929–30)
Most League goals in aggregate: Vic Watson 298 (1920–35)
Longest unbeaten League sequence: 27 matches (1980–81). **Longest sequence without a League win:** 17 matches (1976). **Most capped player:** Bobby Moore (England) 108.

Goalkeepers				
Areola, Alphonse	6.5	Paris SG	Paris, Fr	27.02.93
Fabianski, Lukasz	6.3	Swansea	Kostrzyn, Pol	18.04.85
Randolph, Darren	6.1	Middlesbrough	Bray, Ire	12.05.87
Defenders				
Aguerd, Nayef	6.2	Rennes	Kenitra, Mor	30.03.96
Coufal, Vladimir	5.10	Slavia Prague	Ostrava, Cz	22.08.92
Cresswell, Aaron	5.7	Ipswich	Liverpool	15.12.89
Dawson, Craig	6.2	Watford	Rochdale	06.05.90
Diop, Issa	6.4	Toulouse	Toulouse	09.01.97
Downes, Flynn	5.9	Swansea	Brentwood	20.01.99
Johnson, Ben	5.9	–	Waltham Forest	24.01.00
Masuaku, Arthur	5.11	Olympiacos	Lille, Fr	07.11.93
Ogbonna, Angelo	6.3	Juventus	Cassino, It	23.05.88
Zouma, Kurt	6.3	Chelsea	Lyon, Fr	27.10.94
Midfielders				
Fornals, Pablo	5.10	Villarreal	Castellon, Sp	22.02.96
Lanzini, Manuel	5.6	Al Jazira	Ituzaingo, Arg	15.02.93
Rice, Declan	6.1	–	London	14.01.99

Soucek, Tomas	6.3	Slavia Prague	Havlicku Brod, Cz	27.02.95
Vlasic, Nikola	5.10	CSKA Moscow	Split, Cro	04.10.97
Forwards				
Antonio, Michail	5.11	Nottm Forest	Wandsworth	28.03.90
Benrahma, Said	5.8	Brentford	Temouchent, Alg	10.08.95
Bowen, Jarrod	5.10	Hull	Leominster	20.12.96

WOLVERHAMPTON WANDERERS

Ground: Molineux Stadium, Waterloo Road, Wolverhampton WV1 4QR
Telephone: 0871 222 1877. **Club nickname:** Wolves
Capacity: 32,050. **Colours:** Yellow and black. **Shirt sponsor:** AstroPay
Record attendance: 61,315 v Liverpool (FA Cup 5) Feb 11, 1939
Record transfer fee: £35.6m to Porto for Fabio Silva, Sep 2020
Record fee received: £41m from Liverpool for Diogo Jota, Sep 2020
League Championship: Winners 1953–54, 1957–58, 1958–59
FA Cup: Winners 1893, 1908, 1949, 1960
League Cup: Winners 1974, 1980
European competitions: UEFA Cup runners-up 1971–72
Finishing positions in Premier League: 2003–04 20th, 2009–10 15th, 2003–04 20th, 2011–12 20th, 2018–19 7th, 2019–20 7th, 2020–21 13th, 2021–22 10th
Biggest win: 10-1 v Leicester (Div 2) Apr 15, 1938. Also: 14-0 v Crosswell's Brewery (FA Cup 2) Nov 13, 1886
Biggest defeat: 1-10 v Newton Heath (Div 1) Oct 15, 1892
Highest League scorer in a season: Dennis Westcott 38 (1946–47)
Most League goals in aggregate: Steve Bull 250 (1986–90)
Longest unbeaten League sequence: 20 matches (1923–24). **Longest sequence without a League win:** 19 matches (1984–85). **Most capped player:** Billy Wright (England) 105.

Goalkeepers				
Jose Sa	6.4	Olympiacos	Braga, Por	17.01.93
Defenders				
Ait-Nouri, Rayan	5.10	Angers	Montreuil, Fr	06.06.01
Boly, Willy	6.2	Porto	Melun, Fr	03.02.91
Coady, Conor	6.1	Huddersfield	St Helens	25.02.93
Hoever, Ki-Jana	5.11	Liverpool	Amsterdam, Hol	18.01.02
Jonny	5.9	Atletico Madrid	Vigo, Sp	03.03.94
Kilman, Max	5.10	Maidenhead	Kensington	23.05.97
Nelson Semedo	5.10	Barcelona	Lisbon, Por	16.11.93
Ruben Vinagre	5.9	Monaco	Charneca, Por	09.04.99
Midfielders				
Chiquinho	5.10	Estoril	Cascais, Por	05.02.00
Dendoncker, Leander	6.2	Anderlecht	Passendale, Bel	15.04.95
Gibbs-White, Morgan	5.11	–	Stafford	27.01.00
Joao Moutinho	5.7	Monaco	Portimao, Por	08.09.86
Podence, Daniel	5.6	Olympiacos	Oeiras, Por	21.10.95
Ruben Neves	6.0	Porto	Mozelos, Por	13.03.97
Forwards				
Cutrone, Patrick	6.0	AC Milan	Como, It	03.01.98
Fabio Silva	6.1	Porto	Porto, Por	19.07.02
Hwang Hee-chan	5.10	RB Leipzig	Chuncheon, S Kor	26.01.96
Pedro Neto	5.8	Braga	Viana do Castelo, Por	09.03.00
Raul Jimenez	6.2	Benfica	Tepeji del Rio, Mex	05.05.91
Traore, Adama	5.10	Middlesbrough	L'Hospitalet, Sp	25.01.96
Trincao, Francisco	6.0	Barcelona (loan)	Viana do Castelo, Por	29.12.99

CHAMPIONSHIP

BIRMINGHAM CITY

Ground: St Andrew's, Birmingham B9 4NH. **Telephone:** 0844 557 1875. **Club nickname:** Blues. **Colours:** Blue and white. **Capacity:** 29,409. **Record attendance:** 66,844 v Everton (FA Cup 5) Feb 11, 1939

Goalkeepers
Jeacock, Zach	6.3	–	Birmingham	08.05.01
Etheridge, Neil	6.3	Cardiff	Enfield	07.02.90

Defenders
Colin, Maxime	5.11	Brentford	Arras, Fr	15.11.91
Dean, Harlee	5.10	Brentford	Basingstoke	26.07.91
Friend, George	6.0	Middlesbrough	Barnstaple	19.10.87
Gordon, Nico	6.0	–	Birmingham	28.04.02
Roberts, Marc	6.0	Barnsley	Wakefield	26.07.90
Sanderson, Dion	6.2	Wolves (loan)	Wednesfield	15.12.99

Midfielders
Gardner, Gary	6.2	Aston Villa	Solihull	29.06.92
Graham, Jordan	6.0	Gillingham	Coventry	05.03.95
James, Jordan	6.2	–	Hereford	02.07.04
Juninho Bacuna	5.10	Rangers	Groningen, Hol	07.08.97
Placheta, Przemyslaw	5.10	Norwich (loan)	Lowicz, Pol	23.03.98
Woods, Ryan	5.8	Stoke	Norton Canes	13.12.93

Forwards
Cosgrove, Sam	6.2	Aberdeen	Beverley	02.12.96
Deeney, Troy	6.0	Watford	Birmingham	29.06.88
Hogan, Scott	5.1	Aston Villa	Salford	13.04.92
Jutkiewicz, Lukas	6.1	Burnley	Southampton	20.03.89
Leko, Jonathan	6.0	WBA	Kinshasa, DR Cong	24.04.99

BLACKBURN ROVERS

Ground: Ewood Park, Blackburn BB2 4JF. **Telephone:** 0871 702 1875. **Club nickname:** Rovers. **Colours:** Blue and white. **Capacity:** 31,367. **Record attendance:** 62,522 v Bolton (FA Cup 6) Mar 2, 1929

Goalkeepers
Kaminski, Thomas	6.3	Gent	Dendermonde, Bel	23.10.92
Pears, Aynsley	6.1	Middlesbrough	Durham	23.04.98

Defenders
Ayala, Daniel	6.3	Middlesbrough	El Saucejo, Sp	07.11.90
Pickering, Harry	6.1	Crewe	Chester	29.12.98
Wharton, Scott	6.0	–	Blackburn	03.10.97

Midfielders
Buckley, John	5.8	–	Manchester	13.10.99
Dack, Bradley	5.8	Gillingham	Greenwich	31.12.93
Dolan, Tyrhys	5.8	Preston	Manchester	28.12.01
Hedges, Ryan	6.1	Aberdeen	Northampton	08.07.95
Rankin-Costello, Joe	6.0	Manchester Utd	–	26.07.99
Tayo Edun	5.10	Lincoln	Islington	14.05.98

Travis, Lewis	6.0	Liverpool	Whiston	16.10.97
Forwards				
Brereton Diaz, Ben	6.0	Nottm Forest	Blythe Bridge	18.04.99
Gallagher, Sam	6.4	Southampton	Crediton	15.09.95
Markanday, Dilan	5.10	Tottenham	Barnet	20.08.01
Twine, Scott	5.10	MK Dons	Swindon	14.07.99

BLACKPOOL

Ground: Bloomfield Road, Blackpool FY1 6JJ. **Telephone:** 0871 622 1953. **Club nickname:** Seasiders. **Colours:** Tangerine and white. **Capacity:** 17,338. **Record attendance:** 38,098 v Wolves (Div 1) Sep 17, 1955

Goalkeepers				
Maxwell, Chris	6.1	Preston	St Asaph	30.07.90
Grimshaw, Daniel	6.1	Manchester City	Salford	16.01.98
Defenders				
Connolly, Callum	6.1	Everton	Liverpool	23.09.97
Ekpiteta, Marvin	6.4	Leyton Orient	Enfield	26.08.95
Gabriel, Jordan	5.10	Nottm Forest	London	25.09.98
Garbutt, Luke	5.11	Everton	Harrogate	21.05.93
Husband, James	5.11	Norwich	Leeds	03.01.94
James, Reece	5.7	Dopncaster	Bacup	07.11.93
Keogh, Richard	6.2	Huddersfield	Harlow	11.08.86
Thorniley, Jordan	5.11	Sheffield Wed	Warrington	24.11.96
Midfielders				
Bowler, Josh	5.9	Everton	Chertsey	05.03.99
Carey, Sonny	6.1	King's Lynn	Norwich	20.01.01
Dale, Owen	5.9	Crewe	Warrington	01.11.98
Dougall, Kenny	6.0	Barnsley	Brisbane, Aus	07.05.93
Hamilton CJ	5.7	Mansfield	Harrow	23.03.95
Stewart, Kevin	5.7	Hull	Enfield	07.09.93
Virtue, Matty	5.10	Liverpool	Epsom	02.05.97
Forwards				
Anderson, Keshi	5.10	Swindon	Luton	06.04.95
Beesley, Jake	6.1	Rochdale	Sheffield	02.12.96
Madine, Gary	6.3	Cardiff	Gateshead	24.08.90
Lavery, Shayne	5.11	Linfield	Aghagallon	08.12.98
Lubula, Bez	5.10	Crawley	DR Cong	08.01.98
Yates, Jerry	5.10	Rotherham	Doncaster	10.11.96

BRISTOL CITY

Ground: Ashton Gate, Bristol BS3 2EJ. **Telephone:** 0871 222 6666. **Club nickname:** Robins. **Colours:** Red and white. **Capacity:** 27,000. **Record attendance:** 43,335 v Preston (FA Cup 5) Feb 16, 1935

Goalkeepers				
Bajic, Stefan	6.3	Pau	Saint-Etienne, Fr	23.12.01
Bentley, Daniel	6.2	Brentford	Basildon	13.07.93
O'Leary, Max	6.1	–	Bath	10.10.96
Defenders				
Atkinson, Rob	6.4	Oxford	Chesterfield	13.07.98
Dasilva, Jay	5.7	Chelsea	Luton	22.04.98
Kalas, Tomas	6.0	Chelsea	Olomouc, Cz	15.05.93

Klose, Timm	6.4	Norwich	Frankfurt, Ger	09.05.88
Pring, Cameron	6.1	–	Cheltenham	22.01.98
Tanner, George	5.11	Carlisle	Blackpool	16.11.99
Wilson, Kane	5.10	Forest Green	Birmingham	11.03.00
Vyner, Zak	6.2	–	London	14.05.97
Midfielders				
James, Matty	5.11	Leicester	Bacup	22.07.91
King, Andy	6.0	Leuven	Barnstaple	29.10.88
Massengo, Han-Noah	5.9	Monaco	Villepinte, Fr	07.07.01
Naismith, Kai	6.1	Luton	Glasgow	18.12.92
Semenyo, Antoine	5.10	–	Chelsea	07.01.00
Sykes, Mark	6.0	Oxford	Belfast	04.08.97
Williams, Joe	5.10	Wigan	Liverpool	08.12.96
Forwards				
Martin, Chris	5.10	Derby	Beccles	04.11.88
Weimann, Andreas	6.2	Derby	Vienna, Aut	05.08.91
Wells, Nahki	5.8	Burnley	Hamilton, Berm	01.06.90

BURNLEY

Ground: Turf Moor, Harry Potts Way, Burnley BB10 4BX. **Telephone:** 0871 221 1882. **Club nickname:** Clarets. **Colours:** Claret and clue. **Capacity:** 22,546. **Record attendance:** 54,775 v Huddersfield (FA Cup 3) Feb 23, 1924

Goalkeepers				
Norris, Will	6.4	Wolves	Watford	12.08.93
Peacock-Farrell, Bailey	6.2	Leeds	Darlington	29.10.96
Defenders				
Collins, Nathan	6.4	Stoke	Leixlip, Ire	30.04.01
Egan-Riley CJ	6.0	Manchester City	Manchester	02.01.03
Harwood-Bellis, Taylor	6.2	Manchester City (loan)	Stockport	30.01.02
Long, Kevin	6.2	Cork	Cork, Ire	18.08.90
Lowton, Matthew	5.11	Aston Villa	Chesterfield	09.06.89
McNally, Luke	6.4	Oxford	Co Meath, Ire	20.09.99
Roberts, Connor	5.10	Swansea	Neath	23.09.95
Taylor, Charlie	5.9	Leeds	York	18.09.93
Midfielders				
Bastien, Samuel	5.8	Standard Liege	Meux, Bel	26.09.96
Brownhill, Josh	5.10	Bristol City	Warrington	19.12.95
Cork, Jack	6.1	Swansea	Carshalton	25.06.89
Gudmundsson, Johann Berg	6.1	Charlton	Reykjavik, Ice	27.10.90
McNeil, Dwight	6.1	–	Rochdale	22.11.99
Westwood, Ashley	5.7	Aston Villa	Nantwich	01.04.90
Forwards				
Barnes, Ashley	6.0	Brighton	Bath	31.10.89
Cornet, Maxwel	5.10	Lyon	Bregbo Iv C	27.9.96
Rodriguez, Jay	6.1	WBA	Burnley	29.07.89
Twine, Scott	5.10	MK Dons	Swindon	14.07.99
Vydra, Matej	5.11	Derby	Chotebor, Cz	01.05.92

CARDIFF CITY

Ground: Cardiff City Stadium, Leckwith Road, Cardiff CF11 8AZ. **Telephone:**0845 365 1115. **Club nickname:** Bluebirds. **Colours:** Blue and white. **Capacity:** 33,280. **Record attendance:** Ninian Park: 62,634 Wales v England, Oct 17, 1959; Club: 57,893 v Arsenal (Div 1) Apr

22, 1953, Cardiff City Stadium: 33,280 (Wales v Belgium) Jun 12, 2015. Club: 33,082 v Liverpool (Prem Lge) Apr 21, 2019

Goalkeepers

Alnwick, Jak	6.2	St Mirren	Hexham	17.06.93
Allsop, Ryan	6.2	Derby	Birmingham	17.06.92
Phillips, Dillon	6.2	Charlton	Hornchurch	11.06.95

Defenders

Bagan, Joel	6.3	Southampton	Basingstoke	03.09.01
Daley-Campbell, Vontae	6.0	Leicester	Lambeth	02.04.01
Collins, Jamilu	5.10	Paderborn	Kaduna, Nig	05.08.94
McGuinness, Mark	6.4	Arsenal	Slough	05.01.01
Morrison, Sean	6.1	Reading	Plymouth	08.01.91
Nelson, Curtis	6.0	Oxford	Newcastle-under-Lyme	21.05.93
Ng, Perry	5.11	Crewe	Liverpool	27.04.96

Midfielders

Adams, Ebou	5.11	Forest Green	Greenwich	15.01.96
Colwill, Rubin	5.8	–	Neath	27.04.02
Giles, Ryan	6.0	Wolves (loan)	Telford	26.01.00
Harris, Mark	6.0	–	Swansea	29.12.98
Murphy, Josh	5.8	Norwich	Wembley	24.02.95
O'Dowda, Callum	5.11	Bristol City	Oxford	23.04.95
Ralls, Joe	6.0	–	Aldershot	13.10.93
Romeo, Mahlon	5.10	Millwall	Westminster	19.09.95
Sawyers, Romaine	5.9	WBA	Birmingham	02.11.91
Tanner, Ollie	5.10	Lewes	Farnborough	13.05.02
Whyte, Gavin	5.8	Oxford	Belfast	31.01.96
Wintle, Ryan	5.6	Crewe	Newcastle-under-Lyme	13.06.97

Forwards

Collins, James	6.2	Luton	Coventry	01.12.90
Watters, Max	5.11	Crawley	Camden	23.03.99
Tanner, Ollie	5.10	Lewes	Farnborough	13.05.02

COVENTRY CITY

Ground: Coventry Building Society Arena, Phoenix Way, Coventry CV6 6GE. **Telephone:** 02476 991987. **Club nickname:** Sky Blues. **Colours:** Sky blue. **Capacity:** 32,753. **Record attendance:** Highfield Road: 51,455 v Wolves (Div 2) Apr 29, 1967. Coventry Building Society Arena: 31,407 v Chelsea (FA Cup 6) Mar 7, 2009

Goalkeepers

Moore, Simon	6.3	Sheffield Utd	Sandown, IOW	19.05.90
Wilson, Ben	6.1	Bradford	Stanley	09.08.92

Defenders

Bidwell, Jake	6.1	Swansea	Southport	21.03.93
Dabo, Fankaty	5.11	Chelsea	Southwark	11.10.95
Hyam, Dominic	6.2	Reading	Dundee	20.12.95
Kane, Todd	5.11	QPR	Huntingdon	17.09.93
McFadzean, Kyle	6.1	Burton	Sheffield	28.02.87
Rose, Michael	5.11	Ayr	Aberdeen	11.10.95

Midfielders

Allen, Jamie	5.11	Burton	Rochdale	29.01.95
Eccles, Josh	6.0	–	Coventry	02.04.00
Hamer, Gustavo	5.7	Zwolle	Itajai, Br	24.06.97
Kelly, Liam	6.2	Leyton Orient	Milton Keynes	10.02.90

O'Hare, Callum	5.9	–	Solihull	01.05.98
Palmer, Kasey	5.8	Bristol City	Lewisham	09.11.96
Sheaf, Ben	6.1	Arsenal	Dartford	05.02.98
Forwards				
Godden, Matt	6.1	Peterborough	Canterbury	29.07.91
Gyokeres, Viktor	6.2	Brighton	Stockholm, Swe	04.06.98
Tavares, Fabio	5.11	Rochdale	Porto, Por	22.01.01
Waghorn, Martyn	5.10	Derby	South Shields	23.01.93
Walker, Tyler	5.11	Nottm Forest	Nottingham	17.10.96

HUDDERSFIELD TOWN

Ground: John Smith's Stadium, Huddersfield HD1 6PX. **Telephone**:0870 444 4677. **Club nickname**: Terriers. **Colours**: Blue and white. **Capacity**: 24,121. **Record attendance**: Leeds Road: 67,037 v Arsenal (FA Cup 6) Feb 27, 1932; John Smith's Stadium: 24,426 v Manchester Utd (Prem Lge), Oct 21, 2017

Goalkeepers				
Nicholls, Lee	6.3	MK Dons	Huyton	05.10.92
Schofield, Ryan	6.3	–	Huddersfield	11.12.99
Defenders				
Boyle, Will	6.2	Cheltenham	Garforth	01.09.95
Colwill, Levi	6.2	Chelsea (loan)	Southampton	26.02.03
Edmonds-Green, Rarmani	6.0	–	Peckham	14.04.00
Lees, Tom	6.1	Sheffield Wed	Birmingham	28.11.90
Pearson, Matty	6.3	Luton	Keighley	03.08.93
Toffolo, Harry	6.0	Lincoln	Welwyn Garden City	19.08.95
Turton, Ollie	5.11	Blackpool	Manchester	06.12.92
Midfielders				
Aarons, Rolando	5.10	Newcastle	Kingston, Jam	16.11.95
High, Scott	5.10	–	Dewsbury	15.02.01
Hogg, Jonathan	5.7	Watford	Middlesbrough	06.12.88
Holmes, Duane	5.6	Derby	Columbus, US	06.11.94
Kasumu, David	5.11	MK Dons	Lambeth	05.10.99
Mahoney, Connor	5.9	Millwall	Blackburn	12.02.97
O'Brien, Lewis	5.8	–	Colchester	14.10.98
Russell, Jon	6.4	Chelsea	Hounslow	09.10.00
Thomas, Sorba	6.1	Boreham Wood	Newham	25.01.99
Forwards				
Koroma, Josh	5.10	Leyton Orient	Southwark	09.11.98
Rhodes, Jordan	6.1	Sheff Wed	Oldham	05.02.90
Ward, Danny	5.11	Cardiff	Bradford	09.12.90

HULL CITY

Ground: MKM Stadium, Anlaby Road, Hull, HU3 6HU. **Telephone**: 01482 504 600. **Club nickname**: Tigers. **Capacity**: 25,586. **Colours**: Amber and black. **Record attendance**: Boothferry Park: 55,019 v Manchester Utd (FA Cup 6) Feb 26, 1949. KC Stadium: 25,030 v Liverpool (Prem Lge) May 9, 2010. Also: 25,280 (England U21 v Holland) Feb 17, 2004

Goalkeepers				
Baxter, Nathan	6.3	Chelsea (loan)	Westminster	08.11.98
Ingram, Matt	6.3	QPR	High Wycombe	18.12.93
Defenders				
Coyle, Lewie	5.8	Fleetwood	Hull	15.10.95

Elder, Callum	5.11	Leicester	Sydney, Aus	23.01.95
Emmanuel, Josh	6.0	Bolton	London	18.08.97
Festus Arthur	6.3	Stockport	Hamburg, Ger	27.02.01
Figueiredo, Tobias	6.2	Nottm Forest	Satao, Por	0202.94
Fleming, Brandon	5.10	–	Dewsbury	03.12.99
Greaves, Jacob	6.1	–	Cottingham	12.09.00
Jones, Alfie	6.3	Southampton	Bristol	07.10.97
McLoughlin, Sean	6.3	Cork City	Cork, Ire	13.11.96
Midfielders				
Docherty, Greg	5.10	Rangers	Milngavie	10.09.96
Honeyman, George	5.8	Sunderland	Prudhoe	02.09.94
Longman, Ryan	5.11	Brighton	Redhill	06.11.00
Seri, Jean Michael	5.6	Fulham	Grand-Bereby, Iv C	19.07.91
Slater, Regan	5.8	Sheffied Utd	Gleadless	11.09.99
Tufan, Ozan	5.10	Fenerbahce	Orhaneli, Tur	23.03.95
Williams, Randell	5.9	Exeter	Lambeth	30.12.96
Forwards				
Lewis-Potter, Keane	5.11	–	Hull	22.02.01
Scott, James	6.2	Motherwell	Glasgow	30.08.00
Smith, Tyler	5.10	Sheffield Utd	Sheffield	04.12.98
Wilks, Mallik	5.11	Barnsley	Leeds	15.12.98

LUTON TOWN

Ground: Kenilworth Road, Maple Road, Luton LU4 8AW. **Telephone:** 01582 411622. **Club nickname:** Hatters. **Colours:** Orange and black. **Capacity:** 10,073. **Record attendance:** 30,069 v Blackpool (FA Cup 6) Mar 4, 1959

Goalkeepers				
Horvath, Ethan	6.3	Nottm Forest (loan)	Highlands Ranch, US	09.06.95
Isted, Harry	6.1	Stoke	Chichester	05.03.97
Macey, Matt	6.7	Hibernian	Bath	09.09.94
Shea, James	5.11	AFC Wimbledon	Islington	16.06.91
Defenders				
Bell, Amari'i	5.11	Blackburn	Burton	05.05.94
Bradley, Sonny	6.4	Plymouth	Hull	13.09.91
Bree, James	5.10	Aston Villa	Wakefield	11.10.97
Burke, Reece	6.2	Hull	Newham	02.09.96
Lockyer, Tom	6.1	Charlton	Cardiff	03.12.94
Osho, Gabriel	6.1	Reading	Reading	14.08.98
Potts, Dan	5.8	West Ham	Romford	13.04.94
Midfielders				
Berry, Luke	5.9	Cambridge	Cambridge	12.07.92
Campbell, Allan	5.9	Motherwell	Glasgow	04.07.98
Clark, Jordan	6.0	Accrington	Hoyland	22.09.93
Doughty, Alfie	6.0	Stoke	Hatfield	21.12.99
Freeman, Luke	5.9	Sheffield Utd	Dartford	22.03.92
Lansbury, Henri	6.0	Bristol City	Enfield	12.10.90
Ruddock, Pelly	5.9	West Ham	Hendon	17.07.93
Rea, Glen	6.1	Brighton	Brighton	03.09.94
Watson, Louie	5.10	Derby	Croydon	07.06.01
Forwards				
Adebayo, Elijah	6.4	Walsall	Brent	07.01.98
Admiral Muskwe	6.0	Leicester	Harare, Zim	21.08.98
Cornick, Harry	5.11	Bournemouth	Poole	06.03.95

Jerome, Cameron	6.1	MK Dons	Huddersfield	14.08.86
Mendes Gomes, Carlos	5.10	Morecambe	Yeumbeul, Sen	14.11.98
Oyedinma, Fred	6.1	Wycombe	Plumstead	24.11.96
Woodrow, Cauley	6.1	Barnsley	Hemel Hempstead	21.12.94

MIDDLESBROUGH

Ground: Riverside Stadium, Middlesbrough, TS3 6RS. **Telephone:** 0844 499 6789. **Club nickname:** Boro. **Capacity:** 34,742. **Colours:** Red. **Record attendance:** Ayresome Park: 53,596 v Newcastle (Div 1) Dec 27, 1949; Riverside Stadium: 35,000 (England v Slovakia) Jun 11, 2003. Club: 34,836 v Norwich (Prem Lge) Dec 28, 2004

Goalkeepers
| Daniels, Luke | 6.4 | Brentford | Bolton | 05.01.88 |
| Roberts, Liam | 6.0 | Northampton | Walsall | 24.11.94 |

Defenders
Bola, Marc	6.1	Blackpool	Greenwich	09.12.97
Coulson, Hayden	5.11	–	Gateshead	17.06.98
Dijksteel, Anfernee	6.0	Charlton	Amsterdam, Hol	27.10.96
Fisher, Darnell	5.9	Preston	Reading	04.04.94
Fry, Dael	6.0	–	Middlesbrough	30.08.97
Hall, Grant	6.4	QPR	Brighton	29.10.91
Lenihan, Darragh	5.10	Blackburn	Dunboyne, Ire	16.03.94
Spence, Djed	6.1	Fulham	London	09.08.00

Midfielders
Ameobi, Sammy	6.4	Nottm Forest	Newcastle	01.05.92
Boyd-Munce Caolan	5.10	Birmingham	Belfast	26.01.00
Crooks, Matt	6.1	Rotherham	Leeds	20.01.94
Giles, Ryan	6.0	Wolves (loan)	Telford	26.01.00
Payero, Martin	6.0	Banfield	Pascanas, Arg	11.09.98
Howson, Jonny	5.11	Norwich	Leeds	21.05.88
Jones, Isaiah	5.10	Tooting & Mitcham	Lambeth	26.06.99
McGree, Riley	5.10	Charlotte	Gawler, Aus	02.11.98
McNair, Paddy	6.0	Sunderland	Ballyclare	27.04.95
Tavernier, Marcus	5.10	Newcastle	Leeds	22.03.99

Forwards
Akpom, Chuba	6.0	PAOK Salonica	Canning Town	09.10.95
Ikpeazu, Uche	6.2	Wycombe	Harrow	28.02.95
Watmore, Duncan	5.10	Sunderland	Manchester	08.03.94

MILLWALL

Ground: The Den, Zampa Road, London SE16 3LN. **Telephone:** 0207 232 1222. **Club nickname:** Lions. **Colours:** Blue. **Capacity:** 20,146. **Record attendance:** The Den: 48,672 v Derby (FA Cup 5) Feb 20, 1937. New Den: 20,093 v Arsenal (FA Cup 3) Jan 10, 1994

Goalkeepers
| Bialkowski, Bartosz | 6.0 | Ipswich | Braniewo, Poil | 06.07.87 |
| Long, George | 6.4 | Hull | Sheffield | 05.11.93 |

Defenders
Ballard, Daniel	6.2	Arsenal (loan)	Stevenage	22.09.99
Cooper, Jake	6.4	Reading	Bracknell	03.02.95
Cresswell, Charlie	6.3	Leeds (loan)	Preston	17.08.02
Hutchinson, Shaun	6.2	Fulham	Newcastle	23.11.90
Malone, Scott	6.2	Derby	Rowley Regis	25.03.91
McNamara, Danny	5.11	–	Sidcup	27.12.98
Mitchell, Alex	6.3	–	–	07.10.01

Wallace, Murray	6.2	Scunthorpe	Glasgow	10.01.93
Midfielders				
Evans, George	6.1	Derby	Cheadle	13.12.94
Flemming, Zian	6.0	Fortuna Sittard	Amsterdam, Hol	01.08.98
Kieftenbeld, Maikel	5.11	Birmingham	Lemelerveld, Hol	26.06.90
Leonard, Ryan	6.1	Sheffield Utd	Plymouth	24.05.92
Mitchell, Billy	5.9	–	Orpington	07.04.01
Muller, Hayden	6.3	–	Croydon	07.02.02
Saville, George	5.9	Wolves	Camberley	01.06.93
Forwards				
Afobe, Benik	6.0	Stoke	Leyton	12.02.93
Bennett, Mason	5.10	Derby	Shirebrook	15.07.96
Bradshaw, Tom	5.10	Barnsley	Shrewsbury	27.07.92

NORWICH CITY

Ground: Carrow Road, Norwich NR1 1JE. **Telephone:** 01603 760760. **Club nickname:** Canaries. **Capacity:** 27,244. **Colours:** Yellow and green. **Record attendance:** 43,984 v Leicester (FA Cup 6), Mar 30, 1963

Goalkeepers				
Gunn, Angus	6.5	Southampton	Norwich	22.01.96
Krul, Tim	6.3	Brighton	Den Haag, Hol	03.04.88
McGovern, Michael	6.3	Hamilton	Enniskillen	12.07.84
Defenders				
Aarons, Max	5.10	Luton	Hammersmith	04.01.00
Byram, Sam	5.11	West Ham	Thurrock	16.09.93
Hanley, Grant	6.2	Newcastle	Dumfries	20.11.91
Giannoulis, Dimitris	5.10	PAOK	Katerini, Gre	17.10.95
Omobamidele, Andrew	6.2	Leeds	Leixlip, Ire	23.06.02
Zimmermann, Christoph	6.4	Borussia Dortmund	Dusseldorf, Ger	12.01.93
Midfielders				
Cantwell, Todd	6.0	–	Dereham	27.02.98
Hernandez, Onel	5.8	Braunschweig	Moron, Cub	01.12.93
Dowell, Kieran	6.0	Everton	Ormskirk	10.10.97
Lees-Melou, Pierre	6.1	Nice	Langon, Fr	25.05.93
McLean, Kenny	6.0	Aberdeen	Rutherglen	08.01.92
Rashica, Milot	5.10	Werder Bremen	Vucitrn, Kos	28.06.96
Sinani, Daniel	6.1	Dudelange	Belgrade, Serb	05.04.97
Sorensen, Jacob	6.0	Esbjerg	Esbjerg, Den	03.03.98
Tzolis, Christos	5.9	PAOK	Thessaloniki, Gre	30.01.02
Forwards				
Hugill, Jordan	6.0	West Ham	Middlesbrough	04.06.92
Idah, Adam	6.3	College Corinthians	Cork, Ire	11.02.01
Pukki, Teemu	5.11	Brondby	Kotka, Fin	29.03.90
Rowe, Jon	5.9	Wembley	Westminster	30.04.03
Sargent, Josh	6.1	Werder Bremen	O'Fallon, US	20.02.00

PRESTON NORTH END

Ground: Deepdale, Sir Tom Finney Way, Preston PR1 6RU. **Telephone:** 0844 856 1964. **Club nickname:** Lilywhites. **Colours:** White and navy. **Capacity:** 23,404. **Record attendance:** 42,684 v Arsenal (Div 1) Apr 23, 1938

Goalkeepers				
Cornell, David	6.2	Peterborough	Waunarlwydd	28.03.91

| Woodman, Freddie | 6.2 | Newcastle | Croydon | 04.03.97 |

Defenders

Bauer, Patrick	6.4	Charlton	Backnang, Ger	28.10.92
Cunningham, Greg	6.0	Cardiff	Galway, Ire	31.01.91
Diaby, Bambo	6.2	Barnsley	Mataro, Sp	17.12.97
Hughes, Andrew	5.11	Peterborough	Cardiff	05.06.92
Lindsay, Liam	6.3	Stoke	Paisley	12.10.95
Olosunde, Matthew	6.1	Rotherham	Philadelphia, US	07.03.98
Storey, Jordan	6.2	Exeter	Yeovil	02.09.97

Midfielders

Brady, Robbie	5.9	Bournemouth	Dublin, Ire	14.01.92
Browne, Alan	5.8	Cork	Cork, Ire	15.04.95
Harrop, Josh	5.9	Manchester Utd	Stockport	15.12.95
Johnson, Daniel	5.8	Aston Villa	Kingston, Jam	08.10.92
Ledson, Ryan	5.9	Oxford	Liverpool	19.08.97
McCann, Ali	5.9	St Johnstone	Edinburgh	04.12.99
Potts, Brad	6.2	Barnsley	Hexham	07.03.94
Whiteman, Ben	6.0	Doncaster	Rochdale	17.06.96
Woodburn, Ben	5.10	Liverpool	Nottingham	15.10.99

Forwards

Evans, Ched	6.0	Fleetwood	St Asaph	28.12.88
Maguire, Sean	5.9	Cork	Luton	01.05.94
Riis, Emil	6.3	Randers	Hobro, Denmark	24.06.98

QUEENS PARK RANGERS

Ground: Loftus Road, South Africa Road, London W12 7PA. **Telephone:** 0208 743 0262.
Club nickname: R's. **Colours:** Blue and white. **Capacity:** 18,439. **Record attendance:** 35,353 v Leeds (Div 1) 27 Apr, 1974

Goalkeepers

| Archer, Jordan | 6.2 | Middlesbrough | Walthamstow | 12.04.93 |
| Dieng, Seny | 6.4 | Duisburg | Zurich, Switz | 23.11.94 |

Defenders

Clarke-Salter, Jake	6.2	Chelsea	Carshalton	22.09.97
Dickie, Rob	6.4	Oxford	Wokingham	03.03.96
Dunne, Jimmy	6.0	Burnley	Dundalk, Ire	19.10.97
Hamalainen, Niko	5.9	Dallas	West Palm Beach, US	05.03.97
Kakay, Osman	5.11	–	Westminster	25.08.97
Masterson, Conor	6.1	Liverpool	Cellbridge, Ire	08.09.98
Odubajo, Moses	5.10	Sheffield Wed	Greenwich	28.07.93
Paal, Kenneth	5.9	Zwolle	Arnhem, Hol	24.06.97

Midfielders

Adomah, Albert	6.1	Notttm Forest	Lambeth	13.12.87
Amos, Luke	5.11	Tottenham (loan)	Welwyn Garden City	23.02.97
Chair, Ilias	5.4	Lierse	Antwerp, Bel	14.06.96
Dozzell, Andre	5.10	Ipswich	Ipswich	02.05.99
Field, Sam	5.11	WBA	Stourbridge	08.05.98
Johansen, Stefan	6.0	Fulham	Vardo, Nor	08.01.91
Shodipo, Olamide	5.10	–	Leixlip, Ire	05.07.97
Thomas, George	5.8	Leicester	Leicester	24.03.97

Forwards

Bonne, Macauley	5.11	Charlton	Ipswich	26.10.95
Dykes, Lyndon	6.2	Livingston	Gold Coast, Aus	07.10.95
Kelman, Charlie	5.11	Southend	Basildon	02.11.01

| Roberts, Tyler | 5.11 | Leeds (loan) | Gloucester | 12.11.99 |
| Willock, Chris | 5.11 | Benfica | Waltham Forest | 31.01.98 |

READING

Ground: Select Car Leasing Stadium, Junction 11 M4, Reading RG2 0FL. **Telephone:** 0118 968 1100. **Club nickname:** Royals. **Colours:** Blue and white. **Capacity:** 24,161. **Record attendance:** Elm Park: 33,042 v Brentford (FA Cup 5) Feb 19, 1927; Madejski Stadium: 24,184 v Everton (Prem Lge) Nov 17, 2012

Goalkeepers

Andresson, Jopkull	6.4	–	Mossfellsbaer, Ice	25.08.01
Lumley, Joe	6.4	Middlesbrough (loan)	Harlow	15.02.95
Southwood, Luke			Oxford	06.12.97

Defenders

Dann, Scott	6.2	Crystal Palace	Liverpool	14.02.87
Holmes, Tom	6.1	–	London	12.03.00
McIntyre, Tom	6.1	–	Reading	06.11.98
Moore, Liam	6.1	Leicester	Leicester	31.01.93
Yiadom, Andy	5.11	Barnsley	Holloway	02.12.91

Midfielders

Camara, Mamadi	5.9	Feirense	Catio, Guin-Bass	31.12.03
Ejaria, Ovie	6.0	Liverpool	Southwark	18.11.97
Fornah, Tyrese	6.3	Nottm Forest (loan)	Canning Town	11.09.99
Hoilett, Junior	5.8	Cardiff	Brampton, Can	05.06.90
Rinomhota, Andy	5.9	Portchester	Leeds	21.04.97
Tetek, Dejan	5.11	–	Oxford	24.09.02

Forwards

Azeez, Femi	5.11	Wealdstone	–	05.06.01
Lucas Joao	6.4	Sheffield Wed	Lisbon, Por	04/09.93
Meite, Yakou	6.1	Paris SG	Paris, Fr	11.02.96
Puscas, George	6.2	Inter Milan	Marghita, Rom	08.04.96

ROTHERHAM UNITED

Ground: New York Stadium, New York Way, Rotherham S60 1AH. **Telephone:** 08444 140733. **Club nickname:** Millers. **Colours:** Red and white. **Capacity:** 12,021. **Record attendance:** Millmoor: 25,170 v Sheffield Wed (Div 2) Jan 26, 1952 and v Sheffield Wed (Div 2) Dec 13, 1952; Don Valley Stadium: 7,082 v Aldershot (Lge 2 play-off semi-final, 2nd leg) May 19, 2010; New York Stadium: 11,758 v Sheffield Utd (Lge 1) Sep 7, 2013

Goalkeepers

| Johansson, Viktor | 6.1 | Leicester | Sweden | 14.09.98 |
| Vickers, Josh | 6.4 | Lincoln | Brentwood | 01.12.95 |

Defenders

Bola, Tolaji	6.2	Arsenal	Camden	04.01.99
Bramall, Cohen	5.10	Lincoln	Crewe	02.04.96
Harding, Wes	5.11	Birmingham	Leicester	20.10.96
Hull, Jake	6.6	–	Sheffield	20.10.01
Humphreys, Cameron	6.2	Zulte Waregem	Manchester	22.08.98
Kioso, Peter	6.0	Luton	Dublin, Ire	15.08.99
Wood, Richard	6.3	Charlton	Ossett	05.07.85

Midfielders

| Barlaser, Dan | 5.10 | Newcastle | Gateshead | 18.01.97 |
| Ferguson, Shane | 5.10 | Millwall | Derry | 12.07.91 |

Lindsay, Jamie	6.0	Ross Co	Rutherglen	11.10.95
Odoffin, Hakeem	6.3	Hailton	Barnet	13.04.98
Ogbene, Chiedozie	5.11	Brentford	Lagos, Nig	01.05.97
Rathbone, Ollie	5.11	Rochdale	Blackburn	10.10.96
Wiles, Ben	5.8	–	Rotherham	17.04.99
Forwards				
Eaves, Tom	6.4	Hull	Liverpool	14.01.92
Kayode, Joshua	6.3	–	Lagos, Nig	04.05.00
Kelly, Georgie	6.2	Bohemians	Donegal, Ire	12.11.96
Washington, Conor	5.11	Charlton	Chatham	18.05.92

SHEFFIELD UNITED

Ground: Bramall Lane, Sheffield S2 4SU. **Telephone:** 0114 253 7200. **Club nickname:** Blades. **Colours:** Red and white. **Capacity:** 32,125. **Record attendance:** 68,287 v Leeds (FA Cup 5) Feb 15, 1936

Goalkeepers				
Davies, Adam	6.1	Stoke	Rintein, Ger	17.07.92
Foderingham, Wes	6.1	Rangers	Hammersmith	14.01.91
Defenders				
Baldock, George	5.9	MK Dons	Buckingham	09.03.93
Basham, Chris	5.11	Blackpool	Hebburn	18.02.88
Bogle, Jayden	5.10	Derby	Reading	27.07.00
Egan, John	6.2	Brentford	Cork, Ire	20.10.92
Lowe, Max	5.9	Derby	Birmingham	11.05.97
Norrington-Davies, Rhys	6.0	–	Riyadh, Saudi	22.04.99
O'Connell, Jack	6.3	Brentford	Liverpool	29.03.94
Robinson, Jack	5.7	Nottm Forest	Warrington	01.09.93
Stevens, Enda	6.0	Portsmouth	Dublin, Ire	09.07.90
Midfielders				
Berge, Sander	6.4	Genk	Baerum, Nor	14.02.98
Doyle, Tommy	5.9	Manchester City (loan)	Manchester	17.10.01
Fleck, John	5.7	Coventry	Glasgow	24.08.91
Jebbison, Daniel	6.3	–	Oakville, Can	11.07.03
Norwood, Oliver	5.11	Brighton	Burnley	12.04.91
Ndiaye, Iliman	5.11	Boreham Wood	Rouen, Fr	06.03.00
Osborn, Ben	5.10	Nottm Forest	Derby	05.08.94
Forwards				
Brewster, Rhian	5.11	Liverpool	Chadwell Heath	01.04.00
McBurnie, Oliver	6.2	Swansea	Leeds	04.06.96
Sharp, Billy	5.9	Leeds	Sheffield	05.02.86

STOKE CITY

Ground: bet365 Stadium, Stanley Matthews Way, Stoke-on-Trent ST4 7EG. **Telephone:** 01782 367598. **Club nickname:** Potters. **Colours:** Red and white. **Capacity:** 30,089. **Record attendance:** Victoria Ground: 51,380 v Arsenal (Div 1) Mar 29, 1937. bet365 Stadium: 30,022 v Everton (Prem Lge) Mar 17, 2018

Goalkeepers				
Bonham, Jack	6.4	Gillingham	Stevenage	14.09.93
Bursik, Josef	6.2	AFC Wimbledon	Lambeth	12.07.00
Defenders				
Clarke, Harry	5.11	Arsenal (loan)	Ipswich	02.03.01

Duhaney, Demeaco	5.11	Huddersfield	Manchester	13.10.98
Flint, Aden	6.2	Cardiff	Pinxton	11.07.89
Forrester, Will	5.11	–	Alsager	29.06.01
Jagielka, Phil	5.11	Derby	Manchester	17.08.82
Souttar, Harry	6.6	Dundee Utd	Aberdeen	22.10.98
Taylor, Connor	6.0	Stafford	Stoke	25.10.01
Tymon, Josh	5.10	Hull	Hull	22.05.99
Wilmot, Ben	6.2	Watford	Stevenage	04.11.99
Midfielders				
Baker, Lewis	6.0	Chelsea	Luton	25.04.95
Brown, Jacob	5.11	Barnsley	Halifax	10.04.98
Clucas, Sam	5.10	Swansea	Lincoln	25.09.90
Etebo, Peter	5.9	Feirense	Warri, Nig	09.11.95
Fox, Morgan	6.1	Sheffield Wed	Chelmsford	21.09.93
Kilkenny, Gavin	5.8	Bournemouth (loan)	Dublin, Ire	01.02.00
Laurent, Josh	6.2	Reading	Leytonstone	06.05.95
McCarron, Liam	5.9	Leeds	Preston	07.03.01
Powell, Nick	6.0	Wigan	Crewe	23.03.94
Thompson, Jordan	5.9	Blackpool	Belfast	03.01.97
Forwards				
Campbell, Tyrese	6.0	Manchester City	Cheadle Hulme	28.12.99
Wright-Phillips, D'Margio	5.9	Manchester City-	Manchester	24.09.01

SUNDERLAND

Ground: Stadium of Light, Sunderland SR5 1SU. **Telephone:** 0871 911 1200. **Club nickname:** Black Cats. **Capacity:** 49,400. **Colours:** Red and white. **Record attendance:** Roker Park: 75,118 v Derby (FA Cup 6 rep) Mar 8, 1933. Stadium of Light: 48,353 v Liverpool (Prem Lge) Apr 13, 2002

Goalkeepers				
Patterson, Anthony	6.2	–	North Shields	10.05.00
Defenders				
Ballard, Dan	6.2	Arsenal	Stevenage	22.09.99
Batth, Danny	6.3	Stoke	Brierley Hill	21.09.90
Cirkin, Dennis	6.0	Tottenham	Dublin, Ire	06.04.02
Huggins, Niall	5.8	Leeds	York	18.12.00
Hume, Trai	5.11	Linfield	Ballymena	18.03.02
Wright, Bailey	5.10	Bristol City	Mebourne, Aus	28.07.92
Midfielders				
Diamond, Jack	5.9	–	Gateshead	12.01.00
Embleton, Elliot	5.8	–	Durham	02.04.99
Evans, Corry	5.11	Blackburn	Belfast	30.07.90
Gooch, Lyndon	5.8	–	Santa Cruz, US	24.12.95
Matete, Jay	5.7	Fleetwood	Lambeth	11.02.01
Neil, Dan	5.10	–	South Shields	13.12.01
O'Nien, Luke	5.9	Wycombe	Hemel Hempstead	21.11.94
Pritchard, Alex	5.9	Huddersfield	Orsett	03.05.93
Roberts, Patrick	5.6	Manchester City	Kingston upon Thames	05.02.97
Winchester, Carl	6.0	Forest Green	Belfast	12.04.93
Forwards				
Dajaku, Leon	5.11	Union Berlin	Waiblingen, Ger	12.04.01
Stewart, Ross	6.2	Ross Co	Irvine	11.07.96

SWANSEA CITY

Ground: Swansea.com Stadium, Morfa, Swansea SA1 2FA. **Telephone:** 01792 616600. **Club nickname:** Swans. **Colours:** White. **Capacity:** 21,088. **Record attendance:** Vetch Field: 32,796 v Arsenal (FA Cup 4) Feb 17, 1968. Liberty Stadium: 20,972 v Liverpool (Prem Lge) May 1, 2016

Goalkeepers

Benda, Steven	6.3	1860 Munich	Stuttgart, Ger	01.10.98
Fisher, Andy	6.0	MK Dons	Wigan	12.02.98

Defenders

Bennett, Ryan	6.2	Wolves	Orsett	06.03.90
Cabango, Ben	6.1	Newport	Cardiff	30.05.00
Cooper, Brandon	6.1	–	Porthcawl	14.01.00
Latibeaudiere, Joel	5.11	Manchester City	Doncaster	06.01.00
Naughton, Kyle	5.10	Tottenham	Sheffield	11.11.88
Ogbeta, Nathaniel	6.0	Shrewsbury	Salford	28.04.01
Sorinola, Matthew	5.8	Union SG (loan)	Lambeth	19.12.01
Wood, Nathan	6.2	Middlesbrough	Ingleby-Barwick	31.05.02

Midfielders

Allen, Joe	5.7	Stoke	Carmarthen	14.03.90
Congreve, Cameron	5.11	–	Blaenu Gwent	24.01.04
Fulton, Jay	5.10	Falkirk	Bolton	04.04.94
Grimes, Matt	5.10	Exeter	Exeter	15.07.95
Manning, Ryan	5.11	QPR	Galway, Ire	14.06.96
Ntcham, Olivier	5.11	Celtic	Longjumeau, Fr	09.02.96
Walsh, Liam	5.8	Bristol City	Huyton	15.09.97

Forwards

Cullen, Liam	5.10	–	Kilgetty	23.04.99
Garrick, Jordan	5.11	–	Jamaica	15.07.98
Joseph, Kyle	6.1	Wigan	Chipping Barnet	10.09.01
Obafemi, Michael	5.7	Southampton	Dublin	06.07.00
Paterson, Jamie	5.11	Bristol City	Coventry	20.12.91
Piroe, Joel	5.11	PSV Eindhoven	Wijchen, Hol	02.08.99
Whittaker, Morgan	6.0	Derby	Derby	07.01.01

WATFORD

Ground: Vicarage Road Stadium, Vicarage Road, Watford WD18 0ER. **Telephone:** 01923 496000. **Club nickname:** Hornets. **Colours:** Yellow and black. **Capacity:** 21,577. **Record attendance:** 34,099 v Manchester Utd (FA Cup 4 rep) Feb 3, 1969

Goalkeepers

Bachmann, Daniel	6.3	Stoke	Vienna, Aut	09.07.94

Defenders

Cathcart, Craig	6.2	Blackpool	Belfast	06.02.89
Kabasele, Christian	6.1	Genk	Lubumbashi, DR Cong	24.01.91
Kamara, Hassane	5.8	Nice	Saint Denis, Fr	05.03.94
Kiko	5.9	Alaves	Sanet Negrals, Sp	02.02.91
Masina, Adam	6.2	Bologna	Khouribga, Mor	02.01.94
Ngakia, Jeremy	6.1	West Ham	Lewisham	07.09.00
Rose, Danny	5.8	Tottenham	Doncaster	02.07.90
Samir	6.3	Udinese	Rio de Janeiro, Br	05.12.94
Sierralta, Francisco	6.4	Udinese	Las Condes,ß Chil	06.05.97
Troost-Ekong, William	6.3	Udinese	Haarlem, Hol	01.09.93

Midfielders

Cleverley, Tom	5.10	Everton	Basingstoke	12.08.89

Gosling, Dan	5.10	Bournemouth	Brixham	02.02.90
Kayembe, Edo	6.0	Eupen	Kananga, DR Cong	03.08.98
Forwards				
Baah, Kwadwo	6.0	Rochdale	Stuttgart	27.01.03
Bayo, Vakoun	6.0	Charleroi	Daloa, 1v C	10.01.97
Dennis, Emmanuel	5.10	Club Bruges	Yola, Nig	15.11.97
Fletcher, Ashley	6.1	Middlesbrough	Keighley	02.10.95
Joao Pedro	6.0	Fluminense	Ribeirao Preto, Br	26.09.01
Mebude, Dapo	5.9	Rangers	London	29.07.01
Sarr, Ismaila	6.1	Rennes	Saint-Louis, Sen	25.02.98
Sema, Ken	5.10	Ostersunds	Norrkoping, Swe	30.09.93

WEST BROMWICH ALBION

Ground: The Hawthorns, Halfords Lane, West Bromwich B71 4LF. **Telephone:** 0871 271 1100. **Club nickname:** Baggies. **Colours:** Blue and white. **Capacity:** 26,850. **Record attendance:** 64,815 v Arsenal (FA Cup 6) Mar 6, 1937

Goalkeepers				
Button, David	6.3	Brighton	Stevenage	27.02.89
Palmer, Alex	6.3	–	Kidderminster	10.08.96
Defenders				
Ajayi, Semi	6.4	Rotherham	Crayford	09.11.93
Bartley, Kyle	6.1	Swansea	Stockport	22.05.91
Bryan, Kean	6.1	Sheffield Utd	Manchester	01.11.96
Furlong, Darnell	5.11	QPR	Luton	31.10.95
Kipre, Cedric	6.4	Wigan	Paris, Fr	09.12.96
O'Shea Dara	6.2	–	Dublin, Ire	04.03.99
Townsend, Conor	5.6	Scunthorpe	Hessle	04.03.93
Midfielders				
Diangana, Grady	5.11	West Ham	DR Cong	19.04.98
Gardner-Hickman, Taylor	6.2	–	Telford	30.12.01
Livermore, Jake	6.0	Hull	Enfield	14.11.89
Molumby, Jayson	5.10	Brighton	Cappoquin, Ire	06.08.99
Mowatt, Alex	5.10	Barnsley	Doncaster	13.02.95
Phillips, Matt	6.0	QPR	Aylesbury	13.03.91
Reach, Adam	6.1	Sheffield Wed	Chester-le-Street	03.02.93
Swift, John	6.0	Reading	Portsmouth	23.06.95
Wallace, Jed	5.10	Millwall	Reading	26.03.94
Forwards				
Dike, Daryl	6.2	Orlando	Edmond, US	03.06.00
Grant, Karlan	6.0	Huddersfield	Greenwich	19.12.97
Robinson, Callum	5.10	Sheffield Utd	Northampton	02.02.95
Zohore, Kenneth	6.2	Cardiff	Copenhagen, Den	31.01.94

WIGAN ATHLETIC

Ground: DW Stadium, Robin Park, Wigan WN5 0UZ. **Telephone:** 01942 774000. **Club nickname:** Latics. **Colours:** Blue. **Capacity:** 25,138. **Record attendance:** Springfield Park: 27,526 v Hereford (FA Cup 2) Dec 12, 1953; DW Stadium: 25,133 v Manchester Utd (Prem Lge) May 11, 2008

Goalkeepers				
Amos, Ben	6.3	Charlton	Macclesfield	10.04.90
Jones, Jamie	6.2	Stevenage	Kirkby	18.02.89

Defenders

Bennett, Joe	5.10	Cardiff	Rochdale	28.03.90
Darikwa, Tendayi	6.2	Nottm Forest	Nottingham	13.12.91
Kerr, Jason	6.0	St Johnstone	Edinburgh	06.02.97
Long, Adam	6.1	–	Douglas, IOM	14.11.00
Naylor, Tom	6.2	Portsmouth	Kirkby-in-Ashfield	28.06.91
Pearce, Tom	6.1	Leeds	Ormskirk	12.04.98
Robinson, Luke	5.9	Wrexham	Birkenhead	19.11.01
Tilt, Curtis	6.4	Rotherham	Walsall	04.08.91
Whatmough, Jack	6.0	Portsmouth	Gosport	19.08.96

Midfielders

Aasgaard, Thelo	6.1	–	Liverpool	02.05.02
Edwards, Gwion	5.9	Ipswich	Lampeter	01.03.93
Jones, Jordan	5.9	Rangers	Redcar	24.10.94
McClean, James	5.11	Stoke	Derry	22.04.89
McGrath, Jamie	5.9	St Mirren	Athboy, Ire	30.09.96
Power, Max	5.11	Sunderland	Birkenhead	27.07.93
Shinnie, Graeme	5.9	Derby	Aberdeen	04.08.91

Forwards

Humphrys, Stephen	6.1	Rochdale	Oldham	15.09.97
Keane, Will	6.2	Ipswich	Stockport	11.01.93
Lang, Callum	6.0	Liverpool	Liverpool	08.09.98
Magennis, Josh	6.2	Hull	Bangor, NI	15.08.90
Wyke, Charlie	5.11	Sunderland	Middlesbrough	06.12.92

LEAGUE ONE

ACCRINGTON STANLEY

Ground: Wham Stadium, Livingstone Road, Accrington BB5 5BX. **Telephone**: 0871 434 1968. **Club nickname**: Stanley. **Colours**: Red. **Capacity**: 5,450. **Record attendance**: 5,397 v Derby (FA Cup 4) Jan 26, 2019

Goalkeepers

Jensen, Lukas	6.6	Burnley (loan)	Helsingor, Den	13.03.99
Savin, Toby	6.4	Crewe	Southport	26.05.00

Defenders

Clark, Mitch	5.8	Leicester	Nuneaton	13.03.99
Conneely, Seamus	6.1	Sligo	Lambeth	09.07.88
Nottingham, Michael	6.4	Blackpool	Birmingham	14.04.89
Rich-Baghuelou, Jay	6.5	Crystal Palace	Sydney, Aus	22.10.99
Rodgers, Harvey	5.11	Fleetwood	York	20.10.96

Midfielders

Coyle, Liam	–	Liverpool	Liverpool	06.12.99
Hamilton, Ethan	6.2	Peterborough	Edinburgh	18.10.98
Lowe, Matt	5.10	Brackley	Warwick	11.03.96
McConville, Sean	5.11	Chester	Burscough	06.03.89
Morgan, David	5.8	Southport	Belfast	04.07.94
O'Sullivan, John	5.11	Morecambe	Dublin, Ire	18.09.93
Pell, Harry	6.4	Colchester	Tilbury	21.10.91
Pritchard, Joe	5.8	Bolton	Watford	10.09.96
Sangare, Mo	6.1	Newcastle	Monrovia, Lib	28.12.98

Forwards

Bishop, Colby	5.11	Leamington	Nottingham	04.11.96

| Hardy, Joe | 5.8 | Liverpool | Wirral | 26.09.98 |
| Whalley, Shaun | 5.10 | Shrewsbury | Whiston | 07.08.87 |

BARNSLEY

Ground: Oakwell Stadium, Barnsley S71 1ET. **Telephone:** 01226 211211. **Club nickname:**
Tykes. **Colours:** Red and white. **Capacity:** 23,287. **Record attendance:** 40,255 v Stoke (FA Cup
5) Feb 15, 1936

Goalkeepers

Collins, Brad	6.0	Chelsea	Southampton	18.02.97
Searle, Jamie	6.6	Swansea	Whakatane, NZ	25.11.00
Walton, Jack	6.1	–	Bury	23.04.98

Defenders

Andersen, Mads	6.4	Horsens	Albertsund, Den	27.12.97
Brittain, Callum	5.10	MK Dons	Bedford	12.03.98
Cundy, Robbie	6.2	Bristol City	Oxford	30.05.97
Helik, Michal	6.3	Cracovia	Chorzow, Pol	09.09.95
Kitching, Liam	6.1	Forest Green	Harrogate	01.10.99
McCarthy, Conor	6.4	St Mirren	Blarney, Ire	11.04.98
Moon, Jasper	6.1	Leicester	Coventry	24.11.00
Oduor, Clarke	5.10	Leeds	Siaya, Ken	25.06.99
Williams, Jordan	5.10	Huddersfield	Huddersfield	22.10.99

Midfielders

Benson, Josh	5.10	Burnley	Brentwood	05.12.99
Connell, Luca	5.11	Celtic	Liverpool	20.04.01
Hondermarck, William	6.1	Norwich	Orleans, Fr	21.11.00
Kane, Herbie	5.8	Liverpool	Bristol	23.11.98
Styles, Callum	5.6	Burnley	Bury	28.03.00

Forwards

Adeboyejo, Victor	5.11	Leyton Orient	Ibadan, Nig	12.01.98
Cole, Devante	6.1	Motherwell	Alderley Edge	10.05.95
Leya Iseka, Aaron	6.0	Toulouse	Brussels, Bel	15.11.97
Morris, Carlton	6.2	Norwich	Cambridge	16.12.95
Oulare, Obbi	6.4	Standard Liege	Waregem, Bel	08.01.96

BOLTON WANDERERS

Ground: University of Bolton Stadium, Burnden Way, Lostock, Bolton BL6 6JW. **Telephone:**
0844 871 2932. **Club nickname:** Trotters. **Colours:** White and navy. **Capacity:** 28,723. **Record
attendance:** Burnden Park: 69,912 v Manchester City (FA Cup 5) Feb 18, 1933. University of
Bolton Stadium: 28,353 v Leicester (Prem Lge) Dec 28, 2003

Goalkeepers

| Dixon, Joel | 6.4 | Barrow | Middlesbrough | 09.12.93 |
| Trafford, James | 6.5 | Manchester City (loan) | Cockermouth | 10.10.02 |

Defenders

Aimson, Will	5.10	Plymouth	Christchurch	01.01.94
Bradley, Conor	5.11	Liverpool	Castlederg	09.07.03
Iredale, Jack	6.1	Cambridge	Greenock	02.05.96
John, Declan	5.10	Swansea	Merthyr Tydfil	30.06.95
Johnston, George	6.0	Feyenoord	Manchester	01.09.98
Jones, Gethin	5.10	Carlisle	Perth, Aus	13.20.95
Santos, Ricardo	6.6	Barnet	Almada, Por	18.06.95

Midfielders

| Dempsey, Kyle | 5.10 | Gillingham | Whitehaven | 19.09.95 |

Lee, Kieran	6.1	Sheffield Wed	Stalybridge	22.06.88
Morley, Aaron	5.10	Rochdale	Bury	27.02.00
Sadlier, Kieran	6.0	Rotherham	Haywards Heath	14.09.94
Sheehan, Josh	6.0	Newport	Pembrey	30.03.95
Thomason, George	5.10	Longridge	Barrow	12.01.01
Williams MJ	6.0	Blackpool	Bangor, Wal	06.11.95
Forwards				
Afolayan, Oladapo	5.11	West Ham	Harrow	11.09.97
Bakayoko, Amadou	6.3	Coventry	Kenema, SL	01.01.96
Bodvarsson, Jon Dadi	6.3	Millwall	Selfoss, Ice	25.05.92
Charles, Dion	6.0	Accrington	Preston	07.10.95
Isgrove, Lloyd	5.10	Swindon	Yeovil	12.01.93
Kachunga, Elias	5.10	Sheffield Wed	Haan, Ger	22.04.92

BRISTOL ROVERS

Ground: Memorial Stadium, Filton Avenue, Horfield, Bristol BS7 0BF. **Telephone:** 0117 909 6648. **Club nickname:** Pirates. **Colours:** Blue and white. **Capacity:** 12,300. **Record attendance:** Eastville: 38,472 v Preston (FA Cup 4) Jan 30, 1960. Memorial Stadium: 12,011 v WBA (FA Cup 6) Mar 9, 2008

Goalkeepers				
Belshaw, James	6.3	Harrogate	Nottingham	12.10.90
Jaakkola, Anssi	6.5	Reading	Kemi, Fin	13.03.87
Defenders				
Anderton, Nick	6.2	Carlisle	Preston	22.04.96
Clarke, Trevor	5.9	Rotherham	Dublin, Ire	26.03.98
Gibbons, James	5.9	Port Vale	Stoke	16.03.98
Grant, Josh	6.1	Chelsea	Brixton	11.10.98
Hoole, Luca	5.10	–	Newport	02.06.02
Kilgour, Alfie	5.10	–	Bath	18.05.98
Midfielders				
Anderson, Harry	5.9	Lincoln	Slough	09.01.97
Coutts, Paul	6.1	Fleetwood	Aberdeen	22.07.88
Evans, Antony	6.1	Crewe	Liverpool	23.09.98
Finley, Sam	5.7	Fleetwood	Liverpool	04.08.92
Rossiter, Jordan	5.10	Fleetwood	Liverpool	24.03.97
Westbrooke, Zain	5.11	Coventry	Chertseyy	28.10.96
Forwards				
Collins, Aaron	6.1	Forest Green	Newport	27.05.97
Loft, Ryan	6.3	Scunthorpe	Gravesend	14.09.87
Marquis, John	6.1	Lincoln	Leisham	16.05.92
Rodman, Alex	6.2	Shrewsbury	Sutton Coldfield	15.12.87
Saunders, Harvey	5.10	Fleetwood	Wolverhampton	20.07.97

BURTON ALBION

Ground: Pirelli Stadium, Princess Way, Burton upon Trent DE13 AR. **Telephone:** 01283 565938. **Club nickname:** Brewers. **Colours:** Yellow and black. **Capacity:** 6,912. **Record attendance:** 6,746 v Derby (Champ), Aug 26, 2016

Goalkeepers				
Garratt, Ben	6.1	Crewe	Market Drayton	25.04.94
Hawkins, Callum	6.2	–	Rotherham	12.12.99
Defenders				
Blake-Tracy, Frazer	6.0	Peterborough	Dereham	10.09.95

Borthwick-Jackson, Cameron	6.0	Oldham	Manchester	02.02.97
Brayford, John	5.8	Sheffield Utd	Stoke	29.12.87
Hamer, Tom	6.2	Oldham	Bolton	16.11.99
Hughes, Sam	6.2	Leicester	West Kirby	15.04.97
Kokolo, Will	5.11	Middlesbrough	France	09.06.00
Leak, Ryan	6.3	Burgos	Burton	28.02.98
Mancienne, Michael	6.0	New England	Feltham	08.01.88
O'Connor, Thomas	5.11	Southampton	Kilkenny, Ire	21.04.99
Oshilaja, Deji	6.0	Charlton	Bermondsey	16.07.93
Shaughnessy, Conor	6.3	Rochdale	Galway, Ire	30.06.96
Midfielders				
Lakin, Charlie	5.11	Birmingham	Solihull	08.05.95
Morris, Bryn	6.0	Portsmotuh	Hartlepool	25.04.96
Powell, Joe	5.11	West Ham	Newham	30.10.98
Smith, Jonny	5.10	Bristol City	Liverpool	28.07.97
Taylor, Terry	6.1	Wolves	Irvine	29.06.01
Forwards				
Ahadme, Gassan	6.2	Norwich	Vic, Sp	17.11.00
Moult, Lewis	6.0	Preston	Stoke	14.05.92

CAMBRIDGE UNITED

Ground: Abbey Stadium, Newmarket Road, Cambridge CB5 8LN. **Telephone:** 01223 566500. **Club nickname:** U's. **Colours:** Yellow and black. **Capacity:** 8,127. **Record attendance:** 14,000 v Chelsea (friendly) May 1, 1970

Goalkeepers				
Mannion, Will	6.2	Pafos	Hillingdon	05.05.98
Mitov, Dimitar	6.2	Charlton	Montana, Bul	22.01.97
Defenders				
Brophy, James	5.10	Leyton Orient	Brent	25.07.94
Dunk, Harrison	6,0	Bromley	London	25.10.90
Jones, Lloyd	6.3	Northampton	Plymouth	07.10.95
Taylor, Greg	6.1	Luton	Bedford	15.01.90
Williams, George	5.9	Bristol Rov	Hillingdon	14.04.93
Midfielders				
Digby, Paul	6.3	Stevenage	Sheffield	02.02.95
Lankester, Jack	5.10	Ipswich	Bury St Edmunds	19.01.00
May, Adam	6.0	Portsmouth	Southampton	06.12.97
O'Neil, Liam	5.11	Chesterfield	Cambridge	31.07.93
Tracey, Shilow	5.10	Tottenham	Newham	29.04.98
Worman, Ben	5.8	–	Cambridge	30.08.01
Forwards				
Ironside, Joe	5.11	Macclesfield	Middlesbrough	16.10.93
Janneh, Saikou	5.11	Bristol City	Gunjur, Gam	11.01.00
Knibbs, Harvey	6.1	Aston Villa	Bristol	26.04.99
Smith, Sam	6.0	Reading	Manchester	08.03.98

CHARLTON ATHLETIC

Ground: The Valley, Floyd Road, London SE7 8BL. **Telephone:** 0208 333 4000. **Club nickname:** Addicks. **Colours:** Red and white. **Capacity:** 27,111. **Record attendance:** 75,031 v Aston Villa (FA Cup 5) Feb 12, 1938

Goalkeepers				
MacGillivray, Craig	6.2	Portsmouth	Harrogate	12.01.93

Maynard-Brewer, Ashley	6.2	–	Joondalup, Aus	25.06.99
Wollacott, Joe	6.3	Swindon	Bristol	08.09.96
Defenders				
Egbo, Mandela	5.11	Swindon	Brent	17.08.97
Inniss, Ryan	6.5	Crystal Palace	Penge	05.06.95
Lavelle, Sam	6.0	Morecambe	Blackpool	03.10.96
Morgan, Albie	5.11	–	Rochester	02.02.00
O'Connell, Eoghan	6.2	Rochdale	Cork, Ire	13.08.95
Sessegnon, Steve	5.9	Fulham (loan)	Roehampton	18.05.00
Midfielders				
Blackett-Taylor, Corey	5.8	Tranmere	Erdington	23.09.97
Clare, Sean	6.3	Oxford	Hackney	18.09.96
Dobson, George	6.1	Sunderland	Harold Wood	15.11.97
Forster-Caskey, Jake	5.10	Brighton	Southend	05.04.94
Fraser, Scott	6.0	Ipswich	Dundee	30.03.95
Gilbey, Alex	6.0	MK Dons	Dagenham	09.12.94
Jaiyesimi, Diallang	6.0	Swindon	Southwark	07.05.98
Kirk, Charlie	5.7	Crewe	Winsford	24.12.97
McGrandles, Conor	6.0	Lincoln	Falkirk	24.09.95
Forwards				
Aneke, Chuks	6.3	Birmingham	Newham	03.07.93
Davison, Josh	5,11	Peterborough	Enfield	16.09.99
Stockley, Jayden	6.3	Preston	Poole	15.09.93

CHELTENHAM TOWN

Ground: Jonny-Rocks Stadium, Whaddon Road, Cheltenham GL52 5NA. **Telephone:** 01242 573558. **Club nickname:** Robins. **Colours:** Red and white. **Capacity:** 7,066. **Record attendance:** 8,326 v Reading (FA Cup 1) Nov 17, 1956

Goalkeepers				
Harris, Max	6.2	Oxford	Gloucester	14.09.99
Defenders				
Freestone, Lewis	5.9	Brighton	King's Lynn	26.10.99
Horton. Grant	6.3	–	Colchester	13.09.01
Hutchnson, Reece	5.8	Burton	Birmingham	14.04.00
Long, Sean	5.10	Lincoln	Dublin	02.05.95
Raglan, Charlie	6.0	Oxford	Wythenshawe	28.04.93
Williams, Ben	5.10	Barnsley	Preston	31.03.99
Midfielders				
Adshead, Dan	5.10	Norwich	Manchester	02.09.01
Blair, Matty	5.10	Doncaster	Warwick	30.11.87
Bonds, Elliot	5.10	Hull	Brent	23.03.00
Chapman, Ellis	6.3	Leicester	Lincoln	08.01.01
Sercombe, Liam	5.10	Bristol Rov	Exeter	25.04.90
Forwards				
Brown, Charlie	6.1	MK Dons	Ipswich	23.09.99
Lloyd, George	5.8	–	Gloucester	11.02.00
May, Alfie	5.10	Doncaster	Gravesend	02.07.93
Nlundulu, Dan	6.0	Southampton (loan)	–	05.02.99

DERBY COUNTY

Ground: Pride Park, Derby DE24 8XL. **Telephone:** 0871 472 1884. **Club nickname:** Rams. **Colours:** White and black. **Capacity:** 33,597. **Record attendance:** Baseball Ground: 41,826 v

Tottenham (Div 1) Sep 20, 1969; Pride Park: 33,597 (England v Mexico) May 25, 2011; Club: 33,475 v Rangers (Ted McMinn testimonial) May 1, 2006

Goalkeepers

Wildsmith, Joe	6.2	Sheffield Wed	Sheffield	28.12.95

Defenders

Bielik, Krystian	6.2	Arsenal	Konin, Pol	04.01.98
Buchanan, Lee	5.9	–	Mansfield	07.03.01
Byrne, Nathan	5.11	Wigan	St Albans	05.06.92
Cashin, Eiran	6.0	–	Mansfield	09.11.01
Chester, James	5.11	Stoke	Warrington	23.01.89
Davies, Curtis	6.2	Hull	Waltham Forest	15.03.85
Forsyth, Craig	6.0	Watford	Carnoustie	24.02.89
Stearman, Richard	6.3	Huddersfield	Wolverhampton	19.08.87

Midfielders

Bird, Max	6.0	–	Burton	08.09.00
Hourihane, Conor	6.0	Aston Villa	Bandon, Ire	02.02.91
Knight, Jason	5.9	Cabinteely	Dublin, Ire	13.02.01
Merndez-Laing, Nathaniel	5.10	Sheffield Wed	Birmingham	15.04.92
Robinson, Darren	5,11	Dungannon	–	29.12.04
Sibley, Louie	5.11	–	Birmingham	13.09.01

Forwards

Barkhuizen, Tom	5.11	Preston	Blackpool	04.07.93
Ebiowei, Malcolm	6.1	Rangers	–	04.09.03
Kazim-Richards, Colin	6.1	Panucha	Leytonstone	26.08.86
McGoldrick, David	6.1	Sheffield Utd	Nottingham	29.11.87

EXETER CITY

Ground: St James Park, Stadium Way, Exeter EX4 6PX. **Telephone:** 01392 411243. **Club nickname:** Grecians. **Colours:** Red and white. **Capacity:** 8,696. **Record attendance:** 20,984 v Sunderland (FA Cup 6 replay) Mar 4, 1931

Goalkeepers

Brown, Scott	6.0	Port Vale	Wolverhampton	26.04.85

Defenders

Caprice, Jake	5.11	Tranmere	Lambeth	11.11.92
Diabate, Cheick	6.2	Stevenage	London	21.01.02
Grounds, Jonathan	6.1	Swindon	Thornaby	02.02.88
Hartridge, Alex	6.1	–	Torquay	09.03.99
Pond, Alfie	6.3	Tiverton	Exeter	01.03.04
Stubbs, Sam	6.0	Fleetwood	Liverpool	20.11.98
Sweeney, Pierce	6.0	Swindon	Dublin, Ire	11.09.94

Midfielders

Brown, Jevani	5.9	Colchester	Letchworth	16.10.94
Coley, Josh	5.10	Maidenhead	Stevenage	24.07.98
Collins, Archie	5.9	–	Taunton	31.08.99
Dieng, Timothee	6.2	Southend	Grenoble, Fr	09.04.92
Key, Josh	5.1	Torquay	Exeter	19.11.99
Kite, Harry	5.9	–	Crediton	29.06.00
Sparkes, Jack	5.9	–	Exeter	29.09.00
Taylor, Kyle	5.7	Bournemouth	Poole	26.05.99

Forwards

Jay, Matt	5.10	–	Torbay	27.02.96
Nombe, Sam	5.11	MK Dons	Croydon	22.10.98

FLEETWOOD TOWN

Ground: Highbury Stadium, Park Avenue, Fleetwod FY7 6TX. **Telephone:** 01253 775080. **Club nickname:** Fishermen. **Colours:** Red and white. **Capacity:** 5,327. **Record attendance:** 5,194 v York (Lge 2 play-off semi-final, 2nd leg) May 16, 2014

Goalkeepers				
Cairns, Alex	6.0	Rotherham	Doncaster	04.01.93
Lynch, Jay	6.2	Rochdale	Salford	31.03.93
Wright, Harry	6.0	Ipswich	Ipswich	03.11.98
Defenders				
Andrew, Danny	5.11	Doncaster	Holbeach	23.12.90
Clarke, Tom	5.11	Salford	Halifax	21.12.87
Earl, Josh	6.4	Preston	Southport	24.10.98
Holgate, Harrison	6.1	–	Leeds	01.07.00
Johnson, Darnell	6.1	Leicester	Leicester	03.09.98
Nsiala, Toto	6.4	Ipswich	Kinshasa, DR Cong	25.03.92
Rooney, Shaun	6.3	St Johnstone	Bellshill	26.07.96
Midfielders				
Baggley, Barry	5.9	Glentoran	Belfast	11.01.02
Batty, Dan	5.11	Hull	Pontefract	10.12.97
Boyle, Dylan	5.9	–	Belfast	15.01.02
Johnston, Carl	5.10	Linfield	Belfast	30.03.02
Vela, Josh	5.11	Shrewsbury	Salford	14.12.93
Wiredu, Brendan	6.3	Colchester	London	07.11.99
Forwards				
Garner, Gerard	6.2	–	Liverpool	02.11.98
Garner, Joe	5.11	Apoel	Clitheroe	12.04.88
Harrison, Ellis	5.11	Portsmouth	Newport	29.01.94
Morris, Shayden	6.0	Southend	Newham	03.11.02
Morton, Callum	5.10	WBA	Torquay	19.01.00

FOREST GREEN ROVERS

Ground: New Lawn, Another Way, Nailsworth GL6 OFG. **Telephone:** 01453 835291. **Club nickname:** Green Devils. **Colours:** Green. **Capacity:** 5,140. **Record attendance:** 4,836 v Derby (FA Cup 3, Jan 3, 2009)

Goalkeepers				
McGee, Luke	6.2	Portsmouth	Edgware	02.09.95
Thomas, Lewis	6.1	Swansea	Swansea	20.09.97
Defenders				
Bernard, Dom	6.0	Birmingham	Gloucester	29.03.97
Cargill, Baily	6.2	MK Dons	Winchester	05.07.95
Casey, Oliver	6.2	Blackpool (loan)	Leeds	14.10.00
Moore-Taylor, Jordan	5.10	MK Dons	Exeter	21.01.94
Udoka Godwin-Malife	5.11	Oxford City	–	09.05.00
Midfielders				
Brown, Reece	5.9	Huddersfield	Derby	03.03.96
Bunker, Harvey	5.11	Southampton	Portsmouth	15.04.03
Cadden, Nicky	5.10	Morton	Bellshill	19.09.96
Davis, David	5.0	Shrewsbury	Smethwick	20.02.91
Diallo, Sadou	6.2	Wolves	Guinea	10.06.99
Hendry, Regan	5.10	Raith Rov	Edinburgh	21.01.98
Little, Armani	5.9	Torquay	Portsmouth	05.04.97

McAllister, Kyle	5.10	St Mirren	Paisley	21.01.99
O'Keefe, Corey	6.0	Rochdale	Birmingham	05.06.98
Stevenson, Ben	6.0	Colchester	Leicester	23.03.97
Forwards				
March, Josh	5.10	Leamington	Stourbridge	18.03.97
Matt, Jamille	6.1	Newport	Kingston, Jam	20.10.89
Stevens, Matty	5.11	Peterborough	Guildford	12.02.98

IPSWICH TOWN

Ground: Portman Road, Ipswich IP1 2DA. **Telephone:** 01473 400500. **Club nickname:** Blues/Town. **Colours:** Blue and white. **Capacity:** 30,311. **Record attendance:** 38,010 v Leeds (FA Cup 6) Mar 8, 1975

Goalkeepers				
Hladky, Vaclav	6.2	Salford	Bron, Cz	14.11.90
Walton, Christian	6.5	Brighton	Truro	09.11.95
Defenders				
Ball, Dominic	6.1	QPR	Welwyn Garden City	02.08.95
Burgess, Cameron	6.4	Accrington	Aberdeen	21.10.95
Donacien, Janoi	6.0	Accrington	Castries, St Luc	03.11.93
Edmundson, George	6.3	Rangers	Manchester	15.08.97
Leigh, Greg	5.11	Morecambe	Sale	30.09.94
Ndaba, Corrie	6.2	–	Dublin, Ire	25.12.99
Penney, Matt	5.8	Sheffield Wed	Chesterfield	11.02.98
Vincent-Young, Kane	5.11	Colchester	Camden	15.03.96
Woolfenden, Luke	6.1	–	Ipswich	21.10.98
Midfielders				
El Mizouni, Idris	5.10	–	Paris, Fr	26.09.00
Evans, Lee	6.1	Wigan	Newport	24.07.94
Harper, Rekeem	6.0	WBA	Birmingham	08.03.00
Morsy, Sam	5.9	Middlesbrough	Wolverhampton	10.09.91
Tunnicliffe, Ryan	6.0	Luton	Heywood	30.12.92
Forwards				
Aluko, Sone	5.9	Reading	Hounslow	19.02.89
Burns, Wes	5.8	Fleetwood	Cardiff	23.11.94
Chaplin, Conor	5.10	Barnsley	Worthing	16.02.97
Edwards, Kyle	5.10	WBA	Dudley	17.02.98
Hawkins, Oli	6.4	Portsmouth	Ealing	08.04.92
Jackson, Kayden	5.11	Accrington	Bradford	22.02.94
John-Jules, Tyreece	6.0	Arsenal (loan)	Westminster	14.02.01
Ladapo, Freddie	6.0	Rotherham	Romford	01.02.93
Pigott, Joe	6.2	AFC Wimbledon	Maidstone	24.11.93

LINCOLN CITY

Ground: LNER Stadium, Lincoln LN5 8LD. **Telephone:** 01522 880011. **Club nickname:** Imps. **Colours:** Red and white. **Capacity:** 10,300. **Record attendance:** 23,196 v Derby (League Cup 4) Nov 15, 1967

Goalkeepers				
Long, Sam	6.0	Crystal Palace	Redbridge	12.11.02
Wright, Jordan	6.3	Nottm Forest	Stoke	28.02.99
Defenders				
Benn, Jay	6.0	Halifax	Brighouse	22.08.01

Eyoma TJ	6.0	Tottenham	Hackney	29.01.00
Jackson, Adam	6.2	Hibernian	Darlington	18.05.94
Montsma, Lewis	6.3	Dordrecht	Amsterdam, Hol	25.04.98
O'Connor, Paudie	6.3	Bradford	Limerick, Ire	14.07.97
Poole, Regan	6.0	MK Dons	Cardiff	18.06.98
Robson, Jamie	5.8	Dundee Utd	Perth, Sco	19.12.97
Walsh, Joe	5.11	MK Dons	Cardiff	13.05.92
Midfielders				
Bishop, Teddy	5.11	Ipswich	Cambridge	15.07.96
Bridcutt, Liam	5.9	Nottm Forest	Reading	08.05.89
Maguire, Chris	5.8	Sunderland	Bellshill	16.01.89
Mandroiu, Danny	5.10	Shamrock Rov	Dublin, Ire	20.10.98
Sanders, Max	5.9	Brighton	Horsham	04.01.99
Sorensen, Lasse	6.1	Stoke	Vejen, Den	21.10.99
Forwards				
Adelakun, Hakeeb	6.3	Bristol City	Hackney	11.06.96
Hopper, Tom	6.1	Southend	Boston	14.12.93
Kendall, Charley	6.0	Eastbourne	Eastbourne	15.12.00
Scully, Anthony	5.10	West Ham	London	19.04.99
Vernam, Charles	5.9	Bradford	Lincoln	08.10.96

MILTON KEYNES DONS

Ground: stadiummk, Stadium Way West, Milton Keynes MK1 1ST. **Telephone:** 01908 622922. **Club nickname:** Dons. **Colours:** White. **Capacity:** 30,500. **Record attendance:** 28,127 v Chelsea (FA Cup 4) Jan 31, 2016

Goalkeepers				
Ravizzoli, Franco	6.1	Eastbourne	Mar del Plata, Arg	09.07.97
Defenders				
Darling, Harry	5.11	Cambridge	Cambridge	08.08.99
Harvie, Daniel	6.0	Ayr	Glasgow	14.07.98
Jules, Zak	6.3	Walsall	Islington	02.07.97
Kemp, Dan	5.7	Leyton Orient	Sidcup	11.01.99
Lewington, Dean	5.11	Wimbledon	Kingston upon Thames	18.05.84
O'Hora, Warren	6.2	Brighton	Dublin, Ire	19.04.99
Tucker, Jack	6.2	Gillingham	Whitstable	12.11.99
Watson, Tennai	6.0	Reading	Hillingdon	04.03.97
Midfielders				
Burns, Darragh	5.10	St Patrick's	Stamullen, Ire	06.08.02
Grant, Conor	5.10	Rochdale	Dublin, Ire	18.12.97
Holland, Nathan	5.10	West Ham	Wythenshawe	19.06.98
McEachran, Josh	5.10	Birmingham	Oxford	01.03.93
Robson, Ethan	6.0	Blackpool	Houghton-le-Spring	25.10.96
Smith, Matt	5.9	Manchester City	Redditch	22.11.99
Forwards				
Eisa, Mo	6.0	Peterborough	Khartoum, Sud	12.07.94

MORECAMBE

Ground: Mazuma Stadium, Christie Way, Westgate, Morecambe LA4 4TB. **Telephone:** 01524 411797. **Club nickname:** Shrimps. **Colours:** Red. **Capacity:** 6,476. **Record attendance:** Christie Park: 9,234 v Weymouth (FA Cup 3) Jan 6, 1962. Mazuma Stadium: 5,831 v Sunderland (Lge 1) Apr 30, 2022

Goalkeepers

Ripley, Connor	6.3	Preston	Middlesbrough	13.02.93
Smith, Adam	6.4	Stevenage	Sunderland	23.11.92

Defenders

Cooney, Ryan	5.10	Burnley	Manchester	26.02.00
Gibson, Liam	6.1	Newcastle	Stanley	25.04.97
Love, Donald	5.10	Salford	Rochdale	02.12.94
Melbourne, Max	5.10	Lincoln	Solihull	24.10.98
McLaughlin, Ryan	6.0	Rochdale	Belfast	30.09.94
O'Connor, Anthony	6.2	Bradford	Cork, Ire	25.10.92
Rawson, Farrend	6.4	Mansfield	Nottingham	11.07.96

Midfielders

Connolly, Dylan	5.9	Northampton	Dublin, Ire	02.05.95
Fane, Ousmane	6.4	UITM	Paris, Fr	13.12.96
McDonald, Wes	5.9	Walsall	Lambeth	04.05.97
McLoughlin, Shane	5.9	AFC Wimbledon	New York, US	01.03.97
Taylor, Jake	5.10	Port Vale	Manchester	08.09.98

Forwards

Duffus, Courtney	6.2	Bromley	Cheltenham	24.10.95
Gnahoua, Arthur	5.11	Bolton	London	18.09.92
Obika, Jon	6.0	St Mirren	Enfield	12.09.90
Stockton, Cole	6.1	Tranmere	Huyton	13.03.94

OXFORD UNITED

Ground: Kassam Stadium, Grenoble Road, Oxford OX4 4XP. **Telephone:** 01865 337500.
Club nickname: U's. **Colours:** Yellow and black. **Capacity:** 12,500. **Record attendance:** Manor Ground: 22,750 v Preston (FA Cup 6) Feb 29, 1964. Kassam Stadium: 12,243 v Leyton Orient (Lge 2) May 6, 2006

Goalkeepers

Eastwood, Simon	6.2	Blackburn	Luton	26.06.89
Stevens, Jack	6.2	–	–	02.08.97

Defenders

Long, Sam	5.10	–	Oxford	16.01.95
Moore, Elliott	6.5	Leicester	Coalville	16.03.97
Mousinho, John	6.1	Burton	Isleworth	30.04.86
Seddon, Steve	5.10	Birmingham	Reading	25.12.97

Midfielders

Brannagan, Cameron	5.11	Liverpool	Manchester	09.05.96
Browne, Marcus	5.10	Middlesbrough	Tower Hamlets	18.12.97
Davis, Ben	5.9	Fulham	Phuket, Thai	24.11.00
Forde, Anthony	6.1	Rotherham	Ballingarry, Ire	16.11.93
Gorrin, Alex	6.0	Motherwell	Tenerife, Sp	01.08.93
Henry, James	6.1	Wolves	Reading	10.06.89
McGuane, Marcus	5.10	Nottm Forest	Greenwich	02.12.99

Forwards

Baldock, Sam	5.8	Derby	Buckingham	15.03.89
Bodin, Billy	5.11	Preston	Swindon	24.03.92
Osei, Derick	6.2	Brest	Toulouse, Fr	10.09.98
Taylor, Matty	5.9	Bristol City	Oxford	30.03.90

PETERBOROUGH UNITED

Ground: Western Homes Stadium, London Road, Peterborough PE2 8AL. **Telephone:** 01733

563947. **Club nickname:** Posh. **Colours:** Blue and white. **Capacity:** 15,314. **Record attendance:** 30,096 v Swansea (FA Cup 5) Feb 20, 1965

Goalkeepers

Bergstrom, Lucas	6.7	Chelsea (loan)	Pargas, Fin	05.09.02
Cartwright, Harvey	6.4	Hull (loan)	Grimsby	09.05.02
Pym, Christy	5.11	Exeter	Exeter	24.04.95

Defenders

Butler, Dan	5.9	Newport	Cowes	26.08.94
Edwards, Ronnie	5.11	Barnet	Harlow	28.03.03
Kent, Frankie	6.2	Colchester	Romford	21.11.95
Knight, Josh	6.1	Leicester	Fleckney	07.09.97
Thompson, Nathan	5.10	Portsmouth	Chester	22.04.91

Midfielders

Burrows, Harrison	5.10	–	Murrow	12.01.02
Fuchs, Jeandro	5.9	Dundee Utd	Yaounde, Cam	11.10.97
Jade-Jones, Ricky	6.0	–	Peterborough	08.11.02
Kyprianou, Hector	6.1	Leyton Orient	Enfield	27.05.01
Norburn, Ollie	6.1	Shrewsbury	Bolton	26.10.92
Poku, Kwame	5.9	Colchester	Croydon	11.08.01
Randall, Joel	5.10	Exeter	Salisbury	01.11.99
Szmodics, Sammie	5.7	Bristol City	Colchester	24.09.95
Taylor, Jack	6.1	Barnet	Hammersmith	23.06.98
Thompson, Ben	5.11	Gillingham	Sidcup	03.10.95
Ward, Joe	5.6	Woking	Chelmsford	22.08.95

Forwards

Ajiboye, David	5.8	Sutton	Bromley	28.09.98
Clarke-Harris, Jonson	6.0	Bristol Rov	Leicester	20.07.94
Kanu, Idris	6.0	Aldershot	London	05.12.99
Marriott, Jack	5.9	Derby	Beverley	09.09.84

PLYMOUTH ARGYLE

Ground: Home Park, Plymouth PL2 3DQ. **Telephone:** 01752 562561. **Club nickname:** Pilgrims **Colours:** Green and white. **Capacity:** 18,600. **Record attendance:** 43,596 v Aston Villa (Div 2) Oct 10, 1936

Goalkeepers

Burton, Callum	6.2	Cambridge	Newport, Salop	15.08.96
Cooper, Michael	6.1	–	Exeter	08.10.99

Defenders

Bolton, James	6.0	Portsmouth	Stone	13.08.94
Butcher, Matt	6.2	Accrington	Portsmouth	14.05.97
Galloway, Brendan	6.1	Luton	Harare, Zim	17.03.96
Gillesphey, Macaulay	5.11	Brisbane	Ashington	24.11.95
Law, Ryan	5.10	–	Kingsteignton	08.09.99
Scarr, Dan	6.2	Walsall	Bromsgrove	24.12.94
Wilson, James	6.2	Lincoln	Newport	26.02.89

Midfielders

Camara, Panutche	6.1	Crawley	Guin-Bass	28.02.97
Edwards, Joe	5.9	Walsall	Gloucester	31.10.90
Grant, Conor	5.9	Everton	Fazakerley	18.04.95
Houghton, Jordan	6.0	MK Dons	Chertsey	09.11.95
Mayor, Danny	6.0	Bury	Leyland	18.10.90
Pack, Marlon	6.2	Cardiff	Portsmouth	25.03.91

Randell, Adam	5.9	–	Plymouth	01.10.00
Forwards				
Ennis, Niall	5.10	Wolves	Wolverhampton	20.05.99
Hardie, Ryan	6.2	Blackpool	Stranraer	17.03.97
Jephcott, Luke	5.10	–	Truro	26.01.00
Miller, Mickel	5.9	Rotherham	Croydon	02.12.95

PORTSMOUTH

Ground: Fratton Park, Frogmore Road, Portsmouth, PO4 8RA. **Telephone:** 0239 273 1204. **Club nickname:** Pompey. **Colours:** Blue and white. **Capacity:** 21,000. **Record attendance:** 51,385 v Derby (FA Cup 6) Feb 26, 1949

Goalkeepers				
Bass, Alex	6.2	–	Southampton	01.04.98
Bazunu, Gavin	6.2	Manchester City (loan)	Dublin, Ire	20.02.02
Defenders				
Freeman, Kieron	5.10	Swansea	Arnold	21.03.92
Hume, Denver	5.10	Sunderland	Newbiggin	11.08.98
Mnoga, Haji	6.1	–	Portsmouth	16.04.02
Ogilvie, Connor	6.1	Gillingham	Waltham Abbey	14.02.96
Raggett, Sean	6.6	Norwich	Gillingham	25.01.94
Robertson, Clark	6.2	Rotherham	Aberdeen	05.09.93
Swanson, Zak	6.2	Arsenal	Cambridge	28.09.00
Vincent, Liam	5.8	Bromley	Bromley	11.02.03
Midfielders				
Curtis, Ronan	6.0	Derry	Donegal, Ire	29.03.96
Harness, Marcus	6.0	Burton	Coventry	01.08.94
Jacobs, Michael	5.9	Wigan	Rothwell	04.11.91
Morrell, Joe	5.8	Luton	Ipswich	03.01.97
Thompson, Louis	5.11	Norwich	Bristol	19.12.94
Tunnicliffe, Ryan	6.0	Luton	Heywood	30.12.92
Forwards				
Hackett-Fairchild, Reeco	6.3	Bromley	Redbridge	09.01.98
Reid, Jayden	6.1	Birmingham	Luton	22.04.01

PORT VALE

Ground: Vale Park, Hamil Road, Burslem, Stoke-on-Trent ST6 1AW. **Telephone:** 01782 655800. **Club nickname:** Valiants. **Colours:** White and black. **Capacity:** 19,052. **Record attendance:** 49,768 v Aston Villa (FA Cup 5) Feb 20, 1960

Goalkeepers				
Covolan, Lucas	6.4	Torquay	Curitiba, Br	06.06.91
Stone, Aidan	6.1	Mansfield	Stafford	20.07.99
Defenders				
Benning, Mal	5.10	Mansfield	Sandwell	02.11.93
Cass, Lewis	6.1	Newcastle	North Shields	27.02.00
Hall, Connor	6.4	Harrogate	Slough	23.05.93
Hussey, Chris	6.0	Cheltenham	Hammersmith	02.01.89
Jones, Dan	6.0	Salford	Bishop Auckland	14.12.94
Martin, Aaron	6.3	Hamilton	Newport, IOW	29.09.89
Smith, Nathan	6.0	–	Madeley	03.04.96
Midfielders				
Charsley, Harry	5.10	Mansfield	Birkenhead	01.11.96

Conlon, Tom	5.9	Stevenage	Stoke	03.02.96
Garrity, Ben	6.0	Blackpool	Liverpool	21.02.97
Ojo, Funso	5.10	Aberdeen	Antwerp, Bel	28.08.91
Pett, Tom	5.8	Stevenage	Potters Bar	03.12.91
Walker, Brad	6.1	Shrewsbury	Billingham	25.04.96
Worrall, David	6.0	Millwall	Manchester	12.06.90
Forwards				
Proctor, Jamie	6.2	Wigan	Preston	25.03.92
Wilson, James	6.1	Salford	Biddulph	01.12.95

SHEFFIELD WEDNESDAY

Ground: Hillsborough, Sheffield, S6 1SW. **Telephone:** 0871 995 1867. **Club nickname:** Owls.
Colours: Blue and white. **Capacity:** 39,732. **Record attendance:** 72,841 v Manchester City (FA
Cup 5) Feb 17, 1934

Goalkeepers				
Dawson, Cameron	6.0	Sheffield Utd	Sheffield	07.07.95
Stockdale, David	6.3	Wycombe	Leeds	20.09.85
Defenders				
Brown, Jaden	5.9	Huddersfield	Lewisham	24.01.99
Famewo, Akin	5.9	Norwich	Lewisham	09.11.98
Heneghan, Ben	6.3	AFC Wimbledon	Manchester	19.09.93
Hunt, Jack	5.9	Bristol City Leeds	06.12.90	
Ihiekwe, Michael	6.1	Rotherham	Liverpool	29.11.92
Iorfa, Dominic	6.4	Wolves	Southend	24.06.95
Palmer, Liam	6.2	–	Worksop	19.09.91
Midfielders				
Adeniran, Dennis	5.11	Everton	Southwark	02.01.99
Bannan, Barry	5.11	Crystal Palace	Airdrie	01.12.89
Byers, George	5.11	Swansea	Ilford	29.05.96
Dele-Bashiru, Fisayo	5.10	Manchester City	Hamburg, Ger	06.02.01
Hunt, Alex	5.9	–	Sheffield	29.05.00
Johnson, Marvin	5.10	Middlesbrough	Birmingham	01.12.90
Mendez-Laing, Nathaniel	5.10	Middlesbrough	Birmingham	15.04.92
Sow, Sylla	6.0	Waalwijk	Nijmegen, Hol	08.08.96
Vaulks, Will	5.11	Cardiff	Wirral	13.09.93
Forwards				
Gregory, Lee	6.2	Stoke	Sheffield	26.08.88
Paterson, Callum	6.0	Cardiff	–	13.10.94
Smith, Michael	6.4	Rotherham	Wallsend	17.10.91
Windass, Josh	5.9	Wigan	Hull	09.01.94

SHREWSBURY TOWN

Ground: Montgomery Waters Meadow, Oteley Road, Shrewsbury SY2 6ST. **Telephone:** 01743
289177. **Club nickname:** Shrews. **Colours:** Blue and yellow. **Capacity:** 9,875. **Record attendance:** Gay Meadow: 18,917 v Walsall (Div 3) Apr 26, 1961. Montgmery Waters Meadow:
10,210 v Chelsea (Lge Cup 4) Oct 28, 2014

Goalkeepers				
Burgoyne, Harry	6.4	Wolves	Ludlow	28.12.96
Marosi, Marko	6.3	Coventry	Slovakia	23.10.93
Defenders				
Dacosta, Julien	6.0	Coventry (loan)	Marseille, Fr	29.05.96

Dunkley, Chey	6.2	Sheffield Wed	Wolverhampton	13.02.92
Flanagan, Tom	6.2	Sunderland	Hammersmith	21.10.91
Leahy, Luke	5.10	Bristol Rov	Coventry	19.11.92
Moore, Taylor	6.1	Bristol City (loan)	Walthamstow	12.05.97
Nurse, George	5.11	Bristol City	Bristol	30.04.99
Pennington, Matthew	6.1	Everton	Warrington	06.10.94
Midfielders				
Bayliss, Tom	6.0	Preston	Leicester	06.04.99
Bennett, Elliott	5.10	Blackburn	Telford	18.12.88
Shipley, Jordan	6.0	Coventry	Leamington Spa	26.09.97
Forwards				
Bloxham, Tom	6.5	–	Leicester	02.11.03
Bowman, Ryan	6.2	Exeter	Carlisle	30.11.91
Caton, Charlie	6.1	–	Bodelwyddan	25.11.02
O'Brien, Aiden	6.3	Portsmouth	Islington	04.10.93
Udoh, Daniel	6.1	AFC Telord	Lagos, Nig	30.08.96

WYCOMBE WANDERERS

Ground: Adams Park, Hillbottom Road, High Wycombe HP12 4HJ. **Telephone:** 01494 472100.
Club nickname: Chairboys. **Colours:** Light and dark blue. **Capacity:** 10,137. **Record attendance:**
10,000 v Chelsea (friendly) July 13, 2005

Goalkeepers				
Dickinson, Tyla	6.1	QPR	–	03.04.01
Defenders				
Grimmer, Jack	6.1	Coventry	Aberdeen	25.01.94
Jacobson, Joe	5.11	Shrewsbury	Cardiff	17.11.86
McCarthy, Jason	6.1	Millwall	Southampton	07.11.95
Obita, Jordan	5.11	Oxford	Oxford	08.12.93
Tafazolli, Ryan	6.5	Hull	Sutton	28.09.91
Wakely, Jack	6.4	Chelsea	High Wycombe	25.10.00
Midfielders				
Freeman, Nick	5.11	Biggleswade	Stevenage	07.11.95
Gape, Dominic	5.11	Southampton	Burton Bradstock	09.09.94
Horgan, Daryl	5.8	Hibernian	Galway, Ire	10.08.92
McCleary, Garath	6.0	Reading	Oxford	15.05.87
Mehmeti, Anis	5.11	Woodford	Islington	09.01.01
Scowen, Josh	5.10	Sunderland	Enfield	28.03.93
Thompson, Curtis	5.7	Notts Co	Nottingham	02.09.93
Wheeler, David	5.11	QPR	Brighton	04.10.90
Wing, Lewis	6.1	Middlesbrough	Newton Aycliffe	23.05.95
Forwards				
De Barr, Tjay	5.10	Lincoln Red Imps	Gibraltar	13.03.00
Hanlan, Brandon	6.0	Bristol Rov	Chelsea	31.05.97
Kaikai, Sullay	6.0	Blackpool	Southwark	26.08.95
Mellor, D'Mani	6.1	Manchester Utd	Manchester	20.10.00
Vokes, Sam	5.11	Stoke	Lymington	21.10.89

LEAGUE TWO

AFC WIMBLEDON

Ground: Plough Lane, London SW17 0NR. **Telephone:** 0208 547 3528. **Club nickname:** Dons.

Goalkeepers

Broome, Nathan	6.1	Stoke	Manchester	03.01.02
Tzanev, Nik	6.5	Brentford	Wellington, NZ	23.12.96

Defenders

Brown, Lee	6.0	Portsmouth	Farnborough	10.08.90
Gunter, Chris	5.11	Charlton	Newport	21.07.89
Kalambay, Paul	6.0	–	Dulwich	09.07.99
Nightingale, Will	6.1	–	Wandsworth	02.08.95
Osew, Paul	5.7	Brentford	London	25.11.00
Pearce, Alex	6.2	Millwall	Wallingford	09.11.88

Midfielders

Assai, Ayoub	5:9	–	Maidstone	21.01.02
Chislett, Ethan	5.10	Aldershot	Guildford	22.02.00
Marsh, George	5.11	Tottenham	Pembury	05.11.98
McCormick, Luke	5.9	Chelsea	Bury St Edmunds	21.01.99
Woodyard, Alex	5.9	Peterborough	Gravesend	03.05.93

Forwards

Cosgrave, Aaron	6.0	Lewes	Shenfield	17.07.99
Robinson, Zach	6.2	–	Lambeth	11.06.02
Rudoni, Jack	6.1	–	Carshalton	14.06.01

BARROW

Ground: Holker Street Stadium, Wilkie Road, Barrow LA14 5UW. **Telephone:** 01229 666010. **Club nickname:** Bluebirds. **Colours:** Blue and white. **Capacity:** 5,045. **Record attendance:** 16,874 v Swansea (FA Cup 3) Jan 9, 1954

Goalkeepers

Farman, Paul	6.5	Carlisle	North Shields	02.11.89
Lillis, Josh	6.2	Rochdale	Derby	24.06.87

Defenders

Brough, Patrick	6.3	Falkirk	Carlisle	20.02.96
Brown, Connor	5.9	York	Sheffield	02.10.91
Canavan, Niall	6.3	Bradford	Leeds	11.04.91
Ellis, Mark	6.2	Tranmere	Plymouth	30.09.88
Grayson, Joe	5.10	Blackburn	Leicester	26.03.99
Grayson, Joe	5.10	Blackburn	Leicester	26.03.99
Hutton, Remeao	5.10	Birmingham	Walsall	28.09.98
Jones, James	6.0	Altrincham	Wrexham	13.03.97
McClelland, Sam	6.3	Chelsea (loan)	Coleraine	04.01.02
Ray, George	6.0	Exeter	Warrington	03.10.93
Warren, Tyrell	5.11	FC Halifax	Manchester	05.10.98

Midfielders

Banks, Ollie	6.3	Tranmere	Rotherham	21.09.92
Foley, Sam	6.0	Tranmere	Upton-on-Severn	17.10.86
Gotts, Robbie	5.10	Leeds	Harrogate	09.11.99
Kay, Josh	6.0	Chesterfield	Blackpool	30.01.97
Rooney, John	5.10	Stockport	Liverpool	17.12.90
Stevens, Jordan	5.10	Leeds	Gloucester	25.03.00
Taylor, Jason	6.1	Eastleigh	Droylsden	28.01.87
White, Tom	5.10	Blackburn	–	09.05.97

Forwards

Bennett, Richie	6.3	Sutton	Oldham	03.03.91

| Gordon, Josh | 5.10 | Walsall | Stoke | 19.01.95 |
| Waters, Billy | 5.10 | Halifax | Epsom | 15.10.94 |

BRADFORD CITY

Ground: Utilita Energy Stadium, Valley Parade, Bradford BD8 7DY. **Telephone:** 01274 773355. **Club nickname:** Bantams. **Colours:** Claret and amber. **Capacity:** 25,136. **Record attendance:** 39,146 v Burnley (FA Cup 4) Mar 11, 1911

Goalkeepers
| Lewis, Harry | 6.3 | Southampton | Shrewsbury | 20.12.97 |

Defenders
Cousin-Dawson, Finn	6.0	–	Stockton	04.07.02
Foulds, Matty	5.10	Como	Bradford	17.02.98
Kelleher, Fiacre	6.3	Wrexham	Cork, Ire	10.03.96
Ridehalgh, Liam	5.10	Tranmere	Halifax	20.04.91
Staunton, Reece	6.0	–	Bradford	10.12.01
Threlkeld, Oscar	6.0	Salford	Radcliffe	15.12.94

Midfielders
Chapman, Harry	5.8	Blackburn	Hartlepool	05.11.97
Gilliead, Alex	6.0	Scunthorpe	Shotley Bridge	11.02.96
Osadebe, Emmanuel	6.2	Walsall	Dundalk, Ire	01.10.96
Scales, Kian	5.11	–	Leeds	10.05.02
Smallwood, Richie	5.11	Hull	Redcar	29.12.90
Songo'o, Yann	6.1	Morecambe	Toulon, Fr	19.11.91
Sutton, Levi	5.11	Scunthorpe	Scunthorpe	24.03.96
Walker, Jamie	5.9	Hearts	Edinburgh	25.06.93

Forwards
Angol, Lee	6.2	Leyton Orieny	Sutton	04.08.94
Cook, Andy	6.1	Mansfield	Bishop Auckland	18.10.90
Eisa, Abou	5.11	Scunthorpe	Khartoum, Sud	05.01.96
Harratt, Kian	6.0	Huddersfield (loan)	Pontefract	21.06.02
Hendrie, Luke	6.2	Hartlepool	Leeds	27.08.94
Young, Jake	5.11	Forest Green	Huddersfield	22.07.02

CARLISLE UNITED

Ground: Brunton Park, Warwick Road, Carlisle CA1 1LL. **Telephone:** 01228 526237. **Club nickname:** Cumbrians. **Colours:** Blue. **Capacity:** 17,949. **Record attendance:** 27,500 v Birmingham City (FA Cup 3) Jan 5, 1957, v Middlesbrough (FA Cup 5) Jan 7, 1970

Goalkeepers
| Holy, Tomas | 6.9 | Ipswich | Rychnov, Cz | 10.12.91 |

Defenders
Armer, Jack	6.1	Preston	Preston	16.04.01
Barclay, Ben	6.2	Stockport (loan)	Manchester	07.10.96
Feeney, Morgan	6.3	Sunderland	Bootle	05.02.99
Senior, Joel	5.11	Altrincham	Manchester	24.06.99
Whelan, Corey	6.0	Wigan	Chester	12.12.97

Midfielders
Charters, Taylor	6.1	–	Whitehaven	02.10.01
Dickenson, Brennan	6.0	Exeter	Ferndown	26.02.93
Dixon, Josh	5.11	–	Carlisle	07.02.01
Gibson, Jordan	5.10	Sligo	Birmingham	28.02.98
Guy, Callum	5.10	Blackpool	Nottingham	25.11.96
Hilton, Sonny	5.6	Fulham (loan)	Liverpool	30.01.01

Mellish, Jon	6.2	Gateshead	South Shields	19.09.97
Moxon, Owen	6.1	Annan	Carlisle	17.01.98
Forwards				
Abrahams, Tristan	6.1	Newport	Lewisham	29.12.98
Dennis, Kristian	5.11	St Mirren	Manchester	12.03.90
Edmondson, Ryan	6.2	Leeds	Harrogate	20.05.01
Patrick, Omari	6.1	Burton	Slough	24.05.96
Sho-Silva, Tobi	6.0	Sutton	Thamesmead	27.03.95

COLCHESTER UNITED

Ground: JobServe Community Stadium, United Way, Colchester CO4 5HE. **Telephone:** 01206 755100. **Club nickname:** U's. **Colours:** Blue and. **Capacity:** 10,105. **Record attendance:** Layer Road:19,072 v Reading (FA Cup 1) Nov 27, 1948. Community Stadium: 10,064 v Norwich (Lge 1) Jan 16, 2010

Goalkeepers				
Hornby, Sam	6.3	Bradford	Birmingham	02.02.95
George, Shamal	6.3	Liverpool	Wirral	06.01.98
Defenders				
Chambers, Luke	5.11	Ipswich	Kettering	29.08.85
Clampin, Ryan	5.11	–	Colchester	29.01.99
Coxe, Cameron	6.1	Solihull	Merthyr Tydfil	18.12.98
Daniels, Charlie	5.10	Portsmouth	Harlow	07.09.86
Dallison, Tom	6.1	Crawley	Romford	02.02.96
Eastman, Tom	6.3	Ipswich	Colchester	21.10.91
Smith, Tommy	6.2	Sunderland	Macclesfield	31.03.90
Midfielders				
Chilvers, Noah	5.8	–	Chelmsford	22.02.01
Hannant, Luke	5.11	Cambridge	Great Yarmouth	04.11.93
Huws, Emyr	6.1	Ipswich	Llanelli	30.09.93
Judge, Alan	6.0	Ipswich	Dublin, Ire	11.11.88
Newby, Alex	5.8	Rochdale	Barrow	21.11.95
Skuse, Cole	5.9	Ipswich	Bristol	29.03.86
Forwards				
Akinde, John	6.2	Gillingham	Gravesend	08.07.89
Junior Tchamadeu	6.1	Charlton	Redbridge	22.12.03
Nouble, Frank	6.3	Plymouth	Lewisham	24.09.91
Sears, Freddie	5.10	Ipswich	Hornchurch	27.11.89

CRAWLEY TOWN

Ground: People's Pension Stadium, Winfield Way, Crawley RH11 9RX. **Telephone:** 01293 410000. **Club nickname:** Reds. **Colours:** Red. **Capacity:** 6,134. **Record attendance:** 5,880 v Reading (FA Cup 3) Jan 5, 2013

Goalkeepers				
Addai, Corey	6.5	Esbjerg	Hackney	10.10.97
Morris, Glenn	6.0	Gillingham	Woolwich	20.12.83
Defenders				
Adebowale, Emmanuel	6.5	Eastbourne	Stratford	19.09.97
Craig, Tony	6.0	Bristol Rov	Greenwich	20.04.85
Francillette, Ludwig	6.4	Newcastle	Basse-Terre, Guad	01.05.99
Gallacher, Owen	5.9	Burton	Newcastle	06.04.99
Johnson, Travis	6.1	Crewe	Stoke	28.08.00
Lynch, Joel	6.1	Sunderland	Eastbourne	03.10.87
Tsaroulla, Nick	5.10	Brentford	Bristol	29.03.99

Tunnicliffe, Jordan	6.1	AFC Fylde	Nuneaton	13.20.93
Midfielders				
Francomb, George	6.0	AFC Wimbledon	Hackney	08.09.91
Hessenthaler, Jake	5.10	Grimsby	Gravesend	20.04.90
Payne, Jack	5.9	Eastleigh	Gravesend	05.12.91
Powell, Jack	5.10	Maidstone	Canning Town	29.01.94
Forwards				
Appiah, Kwesi	5.11	North East Utd	Camberwell	12.08.90
Nadesan, Ashley	6.2	Fleetwood	Redhill	09.09.94
Nichols, Tom	5.10	Bristol Rov	Taunton	28.08.93
Oteh, Aramide	5.9	Salford	Lewisham	10.09.98
Rodari, Davide	5.11	Hastings	Switzerland	23.06.99
Telford, Dom	5.9	Newport	Burnley	05.12.96
Tilley, James	5.10	Grimsby	Billingshurst	13.06.98

CREWE ALEXANDRA

Ground: Alexandra Stadium, Gresty Road, Crewe CW2 6EB. **Telephone:** 01270 213014.
Club nickname: Railwaymen. **Colours:** Red and white. **Capacity:** 10,153. **Record attendance:** 20,000 v Tottenham (FA Cup 4) Jan 30, 1960

Goalkeepers				
Richards, Dave	6.0	Bristol City	Abergavenny	31.12.93
Defenders				
Adebisi, Rio	5.10	–	Croydon	27.09.00
McDonald, Rod	6.3	Carlisle	Crewe	11.04.92
Offord, Luke	5.7	–	Chichester	19.11.99
O'Riordan, Connor	6.4	–	Crewe	19.10.03
Sass-Davies, Billy	6.1	–	Abergele	17.02.00
Williams, Zac	6.0	–	Denbigh	27.03.04
Midfielders				
Ainley, Callum	5.8	–	Middlewich	02.11.97
Colkett, Charlie	5.9	Cheltenham	Newham	04.09.96
Finney, Oliver	5.7	–	Stoke	15.12.97
Gomes, Madger	5.11	Doncaster	Alicante, Sp	01.02.97
Griffiths, Regan	5.11	–	Liverpool	01.05.00
Lowery, Tom	5.6	–	Holmes Chapel	31.12.97
Mellor, Kelvin	6.2	Carlisle	Crewe	25.01.91
Tabiner, Joel	6.0	–	Liverpool	30.11.03
Thomas, Conor	6.1	Cheltenham	Coventry	29.10.93
Uwakwe, Tariq	6.0	Chelsea	Islington	19.11.99
Forwards				
Agyei, Dan	6.0	Oxford	Kingston upon Thames	01.06.97
Baker-Richardson, Courtney	6.2	Newport	Coventry	05.12.95
Long, Chris	5.11	Motherwell	Huyton	25.02.95
Sambou, Bassala	6.0	Fortuna Sittard	Hannover, Ger	15.10.97

DONCASTER ROVERS

Ground: Eco-Power Stadium, Stadium Way, Doncaster DN4 5JW. **Telephone:** 01302 764664.
Club nickname: Rovers. **Colours:** Red and white. **Capacity:** 15,231. **Record attendance:** Belle Vue: 37,149 v Hull (Div 3 N) Oct 2, 1948. Keepmoat Stadium: 15,001 v Leeds (Lge 1) Apr 1, 2008

Goalkeepers				
Jones, Louis	6.1	–	Doncaster	12.10.98

Mitchell, Jonathan	5.11	Hartlepool	Hartlepool	24.11.94
Defenders				
Anderson, Tom	6.3	Burnley	Burnley	02.09.93
Knoyle, Kyle	5.10	Cambridge	Newham	24.09.96
Seaman, Charlie	5.8	Bournemouth	–	30.09.99
Williams, Ro-Shaun	6.0	Shrewsbury	Manchester	03.09.98
Younger, Ollie	6.0	Sunderland	Skipton	14.11.99
Midfielders				
Barlow, Aidan	5.9	Manchester Utd	Salford	10.01.00
Biggins, Harrison	5.10	Fleetwood	Sheffield	15.03.96
Clayton, Adam	5.9	Birmingham	Manchester	14.01.89
Close, Ben	5.9	Portsmouth	Portsmouth	08.08.96
Molyneux, Luke	5.11	Hartlepool	Bishop Auckland	29.03.98
Rowe, Tommy	5.11	Bristol City	Wythenshawe	24.09.88
Taylor, Jon	5.11	Rotherham	Liverpool	20.07.92
Forwards				
Agard, Kieran	5.10	Plymouth	Newham	10.10.89
Dodoo, Joe	6.0	Wigan	Kumasi, Gha	29.06.95
Griffiths, Reo	5.11	Lyon	London	27.06.00
Miller, George	5.10	Barnsley	Bolton	11.08.98

GILLINGHAM

Ground: Mems Priestfield Stadium, Redfern Avenue, Gillingham ME7 4DD. **Telephone:** 01634 300000. **Club nickname:** Gills. **Colours:** Blue and white. **Capacity:** 11,582. **Record attendance:** 23,002 v QPR. (FA Cup 3) Jan 10, 1948

Goalkeepers				
Turner, Jake	6.4	Newcastle	Wilmslow	25.02.99
Defenders				
Ehmer, Max	6.2	Bristol Rov	Frankfurt, Ger	03.02.92
McKenzie, Robbie	6.1	Hull	Hull	25.09.98
Tutonda, David	5.11	Bristol Rov	Kinshasa, Zai	11.10.95
Wright, Will	6.3	Dagenham	Luton	12.06.97
Midfielders				
Jefferies, Dominic	5.11	Brentford	–	22.05.02
Lee, Olly	5.11	Hearts	Hornchurch	11.07.91
MacDonald, Alex	5.7	Mansfield	Nottingham	14.04.90
O'Keefe, Stuart	5.8	Cardiff	Norwich	04.03.91
Reeves, Ben	5.10	Plymouth	Verwood	19.11.91
Forwards				
Kashket, Scott	5.10	Crewe	Chigwell	25.02.96

GRIMSBY TOWN

Ground: Blundell Park, Cleethorpes DN35 7PY. **Telephone:** 01472 605050. **Club nickname:** Mariners. **Colours:** Black and white. **Capacity:** 9,052. **Record attendance:** 31,651 v Wolves (FA Cup 5) Feb 20,1937

Goalkeepers				
Battersby, Ollie	6.3	Sheffield Utd	Grimsby	23.07.01
Crocombe, Max	6.4	Melbourne	Auckland, NZ	12.08.93
Defenders				
Danny Amos	5.11	Port Vale	Sheffield	22.12.99
Cropper, Jordan				
Efete, Michee	5.11	Wealdstone	Ealing	11.03.97

Glennon, Anthony	5.11	Burnley	Bootle	26.11.99
Goundry, Jaz	6.3	–	Mansfield	01.11.03
Maher, Niall	5.10	Halifax	Manchester	31.07.95
Longe-King, David	6.4	Newport	Brent	26.01.95
Pearson, Shaun	6.0	Wrexham	York	28.04.89
Waterfall, Luke	6.2	Shrewsbury	Sheffield	30.07.90
Midfielders				
Clifton, Harry	5,11	–	Grimsby	12.06.98
Holohan, Gavan	5.11	Hartlepool	Kilkenny	15.12.91
Khan, Otis	5.9	Leyton Orient	Ashton-under-Lyne	05.09.95
Scannell, Sean	5.9	Blackpool	Croydon	17.09.90
Wearne, Stephen	5.11	Sunderland	Stockton	16.12.00
Forwards				
Maguire-Drew, Jordan	5.9	Woking	Crawley	19.09.97
McAtee, John	5,11	Scunthorpe	Salford	23.07.99
Orsi, Danilo	6.2	Harrogate	Camden	19.04.96
Taylor, Ryan	6.2	Newport	Rotherham	04.05.88

HARROGATE TOWN

Ground: EnviroVent Stadium, Wetherby Road, Harrogate, HG2 7SA. **Telephone**: 01423 210600. **Club nickname**: Town. **Colours**: Yellow and black. **Capacity**: 4,108. **Record attendance**: 4,280 v Harrogate Railway (Whitworth Cup Final, 1949-50)

Goalkeepers				
Jameson, Pete	6.3	York	Sunderland	21/04/93
Oxley, Mark	6.2	Southend	Sheffield	28.09.90
Defenders				
Burrell, Warren	6.1	Buxton	Sheffield	03.06.90
Ferguson, Kyle	6.4	Altrincham	Bellshill	24.09.99
Legge, Leon	6.1	Port Vale	Hastings	28.04.85
Mattock, Joe	5.11	Rotherham	Leicester	15.05.90
McArdle, Rory	6.1	Exeter	Sheffield	01.05.87
Sheron Nathan	6.1	Fleetwood	Whiston	04.10.97
Smith, Will	6.1	Barnsley	Leeds	04.11.98
Welch-Hayes, Miles	5.11	Colchester	Oxford	25.10.96
Midfielders				
Austerfield, Josh	5.10	Huddersfield (loan)	Morley	02.11.01
Daly, Matty	5.11	Huddersfield (loan)	Stockport	10.03.01
Dooley, Stephen	5.11	Rochdale	Ballymoney	19.10.91
Falkingham, Josh	5.7	Darlington	Leeds	25.08.90
Pattison, Alex	6.0	Wycombe	Darlington	06.09.97
Thomson, George	5.9	FC United	Melton Mowbray	19.05.92
Forwards				
Armstrong, Luke	6.1	Salford	Durham	02.07.96
Martin, Aaron	6.0	Guisely	Sheffield	06.07.91
Muldoon, Jack	5.10	AFC Fylde	Scunthorpe	19.05.89

HARTLEPOOL UNITED

Ground: Suit Direct Stadium, Clarence Road, Hartlepool TS24 8BZ. **Telephone**: 01429 272584. **Club nickname**: Pool. **Colours**: Blue and white. **Capacity**: 7,865. **Record attendance**: 17,426 v Manchester Utd (FA Cup 3) Jan 5,1957

| **Goalkeepers** | | | | |
| Killip, Ben | 6.2 | Braintree | Isleworth | 24.11.95 |

| Letheren, Kyle | 6.2 | Morecambe | Llanelli | 26.12.87 |

Defenders

Ferguson, David	5.10	York	Sunderland	07.06.94
Lacey, Alex	6.2	Notts Co	Milton Keynes	31.05.93
Murray, Euan	6.1	Kilmarnock	Rutherglen	20.01.94
Odusina, Timi	6.1	Norwich	Croydon	28.10.99
Ogle, Reagan	5.9	Accrington	Wollongong, Aus	29.03.99
Paterson, Brody	5.10	Celtic	Kirkcaldy	24.04.01
Sterry, Jamie	5.11	South Shields	Newcastle	21.11.95
Tumilty, Reghan	5.11	Raith Rov	Glasgow	26.02.97

Midfielders

Crawford, Tom	6.1	Notts Co	Chester	30.05.99
Featherstone, Nicky	5.8	Harrogate	Goole	22.09.88
Hastie, Jake	5.11	Rangers	Law	18.03.99
Niang, Mouhamed	6.2	Partick	Dakar, Sen	08.10.99
Shelton, Mark	6.0	Salford	Nottingham	12.09.96

Forwards

Carver, Marcus	6.1	Southport	Blackburn	22.10.93
Cook, Jordan	5.10	Hateshead	Hetton	20.03.90
Grey, Joe	5.9	–	Newcastle	04.05.03

LEYTON ORIENT

Ground: Breyer Group Stadium, Brisbane Road, London E10 5NF. **Telephone:** 0208 926 1111. **Club nickname:** O's. **Colours:** Red. **Capacity:** 9,271. **Record attendance:** 34,345 v West Ham (FA Cup 4) Jan 25, 1964

Goalkeepers

| Sargeant, Sam | 6.0 | – | Greenwich | 23.09.97 |
| Vigouroux, Lawrence | 6.4 | Everton de Vina | Camden | 19.11.93 |

Defenders

Beckles, Omar	6.3	Crewe	Kettering	19.10.91
Happe, Dan	6.5	–	Tower Hamlets	28.09.98
James, Tom	5.11	Hibernian	Cardiff	15.04.96
Ogie, Shadrach	6.1	–	Limerick, Ire	26.08.01
Sweeney, Jayden	5.10	–	Camden	04.12.01
Thompson, Adam	6.1	Rotherham	Harlow	28.09.92
Wood, Connor	5.11	Bradford	Harlow	17.07.96

Midfielders

Archibald, Theo	6.1	Lincoln	Glasgow	05.03.98
Brown, Jordan	5.11	Derby	Stoke	21.06.01
Clay, Craig	5.11	Motherwell	Nottingham	05.05.92
Coleman, Ethan	5.11	King's Lynn	Reading	28.01.00
Georgiou, Anthony	5.10	Limassol	Lewisham	24.02.97
Moncur, George	5.9	Hull	Swindon	18.08.93
Pratley, Darren	6.0	Charlton	Barking	22.04.85

Forwards

Drinan, Aaron	6.0	Ipswich	Cork, Ire	06.05.98
Smith, Harry	6.5	Northampton	Chatham	18.05.95
Smyth, Paul	5.8	QPR	Belfast	10.09.97
Sotiriou, Ruel	5.11	–	Edmonton	24.08.00

MANSFIELD TOWN

Ground: One Call Stadium, Quarry Lane, Mansfield NG18 5DA. **Telephone:** 01623 482482.

Club nickname: Stags. **Colours:** Amber and blue. **Capacity:** 9,186. **Record attendance:** 24,467 v Nottm Forest (FA Cup 3) Jan 10, 1953

Goalkeepers

Flinders, Scott	6.4	Cheltenham	Rotherham	12.06.86

Defenders

Gordon, Kellan	5.11	Derby	Burton	25.12.97
Hewitt, Elliott	5.11	Grimsby	Bodelwyddan	30.05.94
McLaughlin, Stephen	5.10	Southend	Donegal, Ire	14.06.90
Perch, James	6.0	Scunthorpe	Mansfield	28.09.85
Wallace, Kieran	6.1	Burton	Nottingham	26.01.95

Midfielders

Boateng, Hiram	6.0	MK Dons	London	08.01.96
Clarke, Ollie	5.11	Bristol Rov	Bristol	29.06.92
Lapslie, George	5.9	Charlton	Waltham Forest	05.09.97
Law, Jason	5.10	Carlton	Nottingham	26.04.99
Maris, George	5.11	Cambridge	Sheffield	06.03.96
O'Toole, John-Joe	6.2	Burton	Harrow	30.09.88
Quinn, Stephen	5.6	Burton	Dublin, Ire	01.04.86

Forwards

Akins, Lucas	6.0	Burton	Huddersfield	25.02.89
Bowery, Jordan	6.1	MK Dons	Nottingham	02.07.91
Hawkins, Oli	6.4	Ipswich	Ealing	08.04.92
Johnson, Danny	5.10	Leyton Orient	Middlesbrough	28.02.93
Knowles, Jimmy	6.0	Nottm Forest	Sutton-in-Ashfield	25.01.02
Oates, Rhys	6.0	Hartlepool	Pontefract	04.12.94

NEWPORT COUNTY

Ground: Rodney Parade, Newport NP19 0UU. **Telephone:** 01633 670690. **Club nickname:** Exiles. **Colours:** Amber and black. **Capacity:** 11,676. **Record attendance:** Somerton Park: 24,268 v Cardiff (Div 3S) Oct 16, 1937. Rodney Parade: 9,836 v Tottenham (FA Cup 4) Jan 27, 2018

Goalkeepers

Day, Joe	6.1	Cardiff	Brighton	13.08.90
Townsend, Nick	5.11	Barnsley	Solihull	01.11.94

Defenders

Bennett, Scot	5.10	Notts Co	Newquay	30.11.90
Clarke, James	6.0	Walsall	Aylesbury	17.11.89
Demetriou, Mickey	6.2	Shrewsbury	Dorrington	12.03.90
Drysdale, Declan	6.5	Coventry	Birkenhead	14.11.99
Farquharson, Priestley	6.3	Connah's Quay	London	15.03.97
Lewis, Aaron	6.0	Lincoln	Swansea	26.06.98
Lewis, Adam	5.9	Liverpool (loan)	Liverpool	08.11.99
Norman, Cameron	6.2	Walsall	Norwih	12.10.95

Midfielders

Bowen, Sam	5.11	Cardiff	–	14.01.01
Collins, Lewis	5.10	–	Newport	09.05.01
Dolan, Matt	5.9	Yeovil	Hartlepool	11.02.93
Waite, James	5.9	Penybont	Cwmbran	11.05.99
Wildig, Aaron	5.9	Morecambe	Hereford	15.04.92
Willmott, Robbie	5.9	Chelmsford	Harlow	16.05.90

Forwards

Bogle, Omar	6.3	Hartlepool	Sandwell	26.07.93
Collins, Lewis	5.11	–	Newport	09.05.01

| Twamley, Lewys | 5.7 | Cardiff | Cardiff | 26.05.03 |
| Zanzala, Offrande | 6.1 | Barrow | Brazzaville, Rep Con | 08.11.96 |

NORTHAMPTON TOWN

Ground: Sixfields Stadium, Upton Way, Northampton NN5 5QA. **Telephone:** 01604 683700.
Club nickname: Cobblers. **Colours:** Claret and white. **Capacity:** 7,789. **Record attendance:**
County Ground: 24,523 v Fulham (Div 1) Apr 23, 1966. Sixfields Stadium: 7,798 v Manchester Utd (Lge Cup 3) Sep 21, 2016

Goalkeepers

Maxted, Jonny	6.0	Exeter	Tadcaster	26.10.93
Defenders				
Guthrie, Jon	6.3	Livingston	Devizes	29.07.92
Haynes, Ryan	6.1	Newport	Northampton	27.09.95
Koiki, Ali	6.2	Bristol Rov	Kensington	22.08.99
McGowan, Aaron	6.0	Kilmarnock	Liverpool	24.07.96
Odimayo, Akin	6.0	Swindon	Camden	28.11.99
Sherring, Sam	5.11	Bournemouth	Dorchester	08.05.00
Midfielders				
Fox, Ben	5.11	Grimsby	Burton	01.02.98
Hoskins, Sam	5.8	Yeovil	Dorchester	04.02.93
McWilliams, Shaun	5.11	–	Northampton	14.08.98
Pinnock, Mitch	6.1	Kilmarnock	Gravesend	12.12.94
Sowerby, Jack	5.9	Fleetwood	Preston	23.03.95
Forwards				
Appere, Louis	6.1	Dundee Utd	Perth, Sco	26.03.99
Hylton, Danny	6.0	Luton	Camden	25.02.89

ROCHDALE

Ground: Crown Oil Arena, Wilbutts Lane, Rochdale OL11 5DS. **Telephone:** 01706 644648.
Club nickname: Dale. **Colours:** Blue and black. **Capacity:** 10,249. **Record attendance:** 24,231
v Notts Co (FA Cup 2) Dec 10, 1949

Goalkeepers

O'Donnell, Richard	6.2	Bradford	Sheffield	12.09.88
Defenders				
Ebanks-Landell, Ethan	6.2	Shrewsbury	West Bromwich	16.12.92
Graham, Sam	6.2	Sheffield Utd	Sheffield	13.08.00
John, Cameron	5.11	Doncaster	Havering	24.08.99
McNulty, Jim	6.0	Bury	Liverpool	13.02.85
O'Connell, Eoghan	6.2	Bury	Cork, Ire	13.08.95
Taylor, Max	6.2	Manchester Utd	Manchester	10.01.00
White, Aidy	5.9	Hearts	Otley	10.10.91
Midfielders				
Ball, James	6.2	Solihull	Bolton	01.12.95
Brierley, Ethan	5.6	–	Rochdale	23.11.03
Kelly, Liam	5.4	Feyenoord	Basingstoke	22.11.95
Keohane, Jimmy	5.11	Cork	Aylesbury	22.01.91
Diagourage, Toumani	6.2	Morecambe	Paris, Fr	10.06.87
Forwards				
Campbell, Tahvon	6.1	Woking	Birmingham	10.01.97
Charman, Luke	6.1	Darlington	Durham	09.12.97
Odoh, Abraham	5.7	Charlton	Lambeth	25.06.00
Rodney, Devante	6.2	Walsall	Manchester	19.05.98

SALFORD CITY

Ground: Peninsula Stadium, Moor Lane, Salford M7 3PZ. **Telephone**: 0161 792 6287. **Club nickname**: Ammies. **Colours**: Red and white. **Capacity**: 5,106. **Record attendance**: 4,518 v Leeds (League Cup 1) Aug 13, 2019

Goalkeepers

King, Tom	6.1	Newport	Plymouth	09.03.95

Defenders

Eastham, Ashley	6.3	Fleetwood	Preston	22.03.91
Shephard, Liam	5.10	Newport	Pentre	22.11.94
Touray, Ibou	5.11	Newport	Gambia	30.07.99
Turnbull, Jordan	6.1	Northampton	Trowbridge	30.10.94
Vassell, Theo	6.0	Wrexham	Stoke	02.01.97

Midfielders

Bolton, Luke	5.9	Manchester City	Stockport	07.10.99
Lowe, Jason	5.10	Bolton	Wigan	02.09.91
Lund, Matty	6.0	Rochdale	Manchester	21.11.90
Mallan, Stevie	5.11	Malatyaspor	Glasgow	25.03.96
Morris, Josh	5.10	Fleetwood	Preston	30.09.91
Watson, Ryan	6.1	Tranmere	Crewe	07.07.93
Watt, Elliot	5.11	Bradford	Preston	11.03.00

Forwards

Hendry, Callum	5.10	St Johnstone	Lytham	08.12.97
McAleny, Conor	5.10	Oldham	Liverpool	12.08.92
Smith, Matt	6.6	Millwall	Birmingham	07.06.89
Thomas-Asante, Brandon	5.11	Ebbsfleet	Milton Keynes	29.12.98

STEVENAGE

Ground: Lamex Stadium, Broadhall Way, Stevenage SG2 8RH. **Telephone**: 01438 223223. **Club nickname**: Boro. **Colours**: White and red. **Capacity**: 7,318. **Record attendance**: 8,040 v Newcastle (FA Cup 4) January 25, 1998

Goalkeepers

Chapman, Aaron	6.8	Gillingham	Rotherham	29.05.90
Walker, Laurie	6.5	MK Dons	Bedford	14.10.89

Defenders

Bostwick, Michael	6.3	Burton	Eltham	17.05.88
Clark, Max	5.11	Rochdale	Hull	19.01.96
Piergianni, Carl	6.1	Oldham	Peterborough	03.05.92
Sweeney, Dan	6.3	Forest Green	Kingston upon Thames	25.04.94
Vancooten, Terence	6.1	Reading	Kingston upon Thames	29.12.97
Wildin, Luther	5.10	Nuneaton	Leicester	03.12.97

Midfielders

List, Elliott	5.10	Gillingham	Camberwell	12.05.97
Read, Arthur	5.10	Brentford	Camden	03.11.99
Reeves, Jake	5.8	Notts Co	Lewisham	30.05.93
Taylor, Jake	5.10	Exeter	Ascot	01.12.91

Forwards

Norris, Luke	6.1	Colchester	Stevenage	03.06.93
Reid, Jamie	5.11	Mansfield	Torquay	15.07.94
Roberts, Jordan	6.1	Motherwell	Watford	05.01.94
Rose, Danny	5.10	Northampton	Barnsley	10.12.93

STOCKPORT COUNTY

Ground: Edgeley Park, Hardcastle Road, Stockport SK3 9DD. **Telephone:** 0161 286 8888.
Colours: Blue and white. **Capacity:** 10,852. **Record attendance:** 27,833 v Liverpool (FA Cup 5)
February 11, 1950

Goalkeepers

Hincliffe, Ben	6.1	Fylde	Preston	10.09.87
Jaros, Vitezslav	6.3	Liverpool (loan)	Pribram, Cz	23.07.01

Defenders

Horsfall, Fraser	6.3	Northampton	Huddersfield	12.11.96
Johnson, Ryan	6.2	Port Vale	Birmingham	01.10.96
Kitching, Mark	6/2	Hartlepool	Guisborough	04.09.95
Lewis, Joe	6.2	Torquay	Neath	20.09.99
Minihan, Sam	6.1	Worcester	Rochdale	16.02.94
Palmer, Ash	6.1	Guiseley	Pontefract	09.11.92
Rydel, Ryan	5.11	Fleetwood	Oldham	09.01.01
Southam-Hales, Macauley	5.9	Fleetwood	Cardiff	02.02.96

Midfielders

Camps, Callum	5.11	Fleetwood	Stockport	14.03.96
Croasdale, Ryan	5.9	Fylde	Lancaster	26.09.94
Collar, Will	5.10	Hamilton	Horsham	03.02.97
Hippolyte, Myles	6.0	Scunthorpe	Harrow	09.11.94
Keane, Jordan	6.3	Boston	Nottingham	19.09.93
Lemonheigh-Evans, Connor	5.10	Torquay	Swansea	24.01.97
Newby, Eliot	5.10	Chorley	Barrow	21.11.95
Sarcevic, Antoni	6.0	Bolton	Manchester	13.03.92
Whitfield, Ben	5.6	Torquay	Bingley	28.02.96
Wright, Akil	6.0	York	Derby	13.05.90

Forwards

Crankshaw, Ollie	6.0	Bradford	Preston	12.08.98
Jennings, Connor	6.0	Tranmere	Manchester	29.10.91
Madden Paddy	6.0	Fleetwood	Dublin	04.03.90
Quigley, Scott	6.4	Barrow	Shrewsbury	02.09.92
Reid, Alex	6.3	Stevenage	Birmingham	06.09.95
Wootton, Kyle	6.2	Notts Co	Kidderminster	11.10.96

SUTTON UNITED

Ground: Borough Sports Ground, Sutton SM1 2EY. **Telephone:** 0208 644 444:. **Colours:** Amber
and brown. **Capacity:** 5,013. **Record attendance:** 14,000 v Leeds (FA Cup 4) Jan 24, 1970

Goalkeepers

House, Brad	6.2	Horsham	Worthing	19.10.98
Rose, Jack	6.3	Walsall	Solihull	31.0195

Defenders

Goodliffe, Ben	6.2	Wolves	Watford	19.06.99
John, Louis	6.3	Cambridge Utd	Croydon	19.04.94
Kizzi, Joe	6.4	Bromley	Enfield	24.06.93
Milsom, Rob	5.10	Notts Co	Redhill	02.01.87
Rowe, Coby	6.3	Haringey	Waltham Forest	02.10.95
Wyatt, Ben	5.8	St Albans	Norwich	04.02.96

Midfielders

Barden, Jon	6.0	St Louis	Harrow	09.11.92
Beautyman, Harry	5.10-	Stevenage	Newham	01.04.92

Boldewijn, Enzio	6.1	Notts Co	Almere, Hol	17.11.92
Dundas, Craig	6.2	Hampton & Richmond	Lambeth	16.02.81
Eastmond, Craig	6.0	Yeovil	Wandsworth	09.12.90
Lovatt, Adam	–	Hastingss	–	11.05.99
Randall, Will	5.11	Newport	Swindon	02.05.97
Smith, Alistair	6.2	Altrincham	Beverley	19.05.99
Forwards				
Bugiel, Omar	6.1	Bromley	Berlin, Ger	03.01.94
Thomas, Kwame	6.3	Wrexham	Nottingham	28.09.95
Wilson, Donovan	5.11	Bath	Yate	14.03.97

SWINDON TOWN

Ground: County Ground, County Road, Swindon SN1 2ED. **Telephone:** 0871 423 6433. **Club nickname:** Robins. **Colours:** Red and white. **Capacity:** 15,728. **Record attendance:** 32,000 v Arsenal (FA Cup 3) Jan 15, 1972

Goalkeepers				
Brynn, Sol	6.1	Middlesbrough (loan)	Middlesbrough	30.10.00
Ward, Lewis	6.5	Exeter	–	05.03.97
Defenders				
Baudry, Mathieu	6.2	MK Dons	Le Havre, Fr	24.02.88
Brennan, Ciaran	6.2	Sheffield Wed (loan)	Kilkenny, Ire	05.05.00
Curran, Taylor	6.0	Southend	Redbridge	07.07.00
Devine, Reece	6.1	Manchester Utd	Stourbridge	18.12.01
Grounds, Jonathan	6.1	Birmingham	Thornaby	02.02.88
Harries, Cian	6.1	Bristol Rov	Birmingham	01.04.97
Hunt, Rob	5.8	Oldham	Dagenham	07.07.95
Midfielders				
Gladwin, Ben	6.3	MK Dons	Reading	08.06.92
Iandolo, Ellis	6.0	Maidstone	Chatham	22.08.97
Lyden, Jordan	6.0	Aston Villa	Perth, Aus	30.01.96
Payne, Jack	5.7	Lincoln	Tower Hamlets	25.10.94
Reed, Louis	5.8	Peterborough	Barnsley	25.07.97
Shade, Tyrese	6.0	Leicester	Birmingham	09.06.00
Williams, Jonny	5.6	Cardiff	Pemburey	09.10.93
Forwards				
McKirdy, Harry	5.10	Port Vale	London	29.03.97

TRANMERE ROVERS

Ground: Prenton Park, Prenton Road, West Birkenhead CH42 9PY. **Telephone:** 0871 221 2001. **Club nickname:** Rovers. **Colours:** White and blue. **Capacity:** 16,587. **Record attendance:** 24,424 v Stoke (FA Cup 4) Feb 5, 1972

Goalkeepers				
Doohan, Ross	6.1	Celtic (loan)	Clydebank	29.03.98
Murphy, Joe	6.2	Shrewsbury	Dublin, Ire	21.08.81
Defenders				
Bristow, Ethan	6.2	Reading	Maidenhead	27.11.01
Byrne, Neil	6.3	Hartlepool	Portmarnock, Ire	02.02.93
Gogley, Josh	5.10	Birmingham	Coventry	12.03.96
Davies, Tom	5.11	Bristol Rov	Warrington	18.04.92
MacDonald, Calum	5.11	Blackpool	Norwich	18.12.97
O'Connor, Lee	5.9	Celtic	Waterford, Ire	28.07.00

Midfielders

Hawkes, Josh	6.0	Sunderland	Stockton	28.01.99
Merrie, Chris	5.11	Wigan	Liverpool	02.11.98
Morris, Kieron	5.10	Walsall	Hereford	03.06.94
Nolan, Jon	5.11	Bristol Rov	Huyton	22.04.92

Forwards

Hemmings, Kane	6.1	Burton	Burton	08.04.91
Jolley, Charlie	5.10	Wigan	Liverpool	13.01.01
Nevitt, Elliott	6.1	–	Liverpool	30.10.96

WALSALL

Ground: Banks's Stadium, Bescot Crescent, Walsall WS1 4SA. **Telephone:** 01922 622791. **Club nickname:** Saddlers. **Colours:** Red and white. **Capacity:** 11,300. **Record attendance:** Fellows Park: 25,453 v Newcastle (Div 2) Aug 29, 1961. Banks's Stadium: 11,049 v Rotherham (Div 1) May 10, 2004

Goalkeepers

Evans, Owen	6.2	Cheltenham	Newport	28.11.96
Przybek, Adam	6.2	Wycombe	Nuneaton	02.04.00

Defenders

Clarke, Peter	6.0	Tranmere	Southport	03.01.82
Daniels, Donervon	6.1	Crewe	Montserratt	24.11.93
Gordon, Liam	6.1	Bolton	Croydon	15.05.99
McEntree, Oisin	6.3	Newcastle	New York, US	05.01.01
Menayesse, Rollin	6.3	Mansfield	Kinshasa, DR Cong	04.12.97
Monthe, Manny	6.1	Tranmere	Cameroon	26.01.95
Ward, Stephen	5.11	Ipswich	Dublin, Ire	20.08.85
White, Hayden	6.1	Mansfield	Greenwich	15.04.95

Midfielders

Allen, Taylor	5.10	Forest Green	Walsall	16.06.00
Comley, Brandon	5.11	Dagenham	Islington	18.11.95
Earing, Jack	6.0	Halifax	Bury	21.09.99
Holden, Rory	5.7	Bristol City	Derry	23.08.97
Hutchinson, Isaac	5.10	Derby	Eastbourne	10.04.00
Kiernan, Brendan	5.9	Harrogate	Lambeth	10.11.92
Kinsella, Liam	5.9	–	Colchester	23.02.96
Labadie, Joss	6.3	Newport	Croydon	30.08.90
Perry, Sam	6.0	Aston Villa	Walsall	29.12.01
Riley, Joe	5.10	Carlisle	Blackpool	06.12.96

Forwards

James-Taylor, Douglas	6.1	Stoke (loan)	Camden	18.12.01
Wilkinson, Conor	6.3	Leyton Orient	Croydon	23.01.95
Williams, Andy	5.10	Cheltenham	Hereford	14.08.86

SCOTTISH PREMIERSHIP SQUADS 2022–23

(at time of going to press)

ABERDEEN

Ground: Pittodrie Stadium, Pittodrie Street, Aberdeen AB24 5QH.
Capacity: 22,199. **Telephone:** 01224 650400
Manager: Jim Goodwin. **Colours:** Red and white. **Nickname:** Dons
Goalkeepers: Joe Lewis, Kelle Roos, Gary Woods

Defenders: David Bates, Jonny Hayes, Jack MacKenzie, Ross McCrorie, Jayden Richardson, Liam Scales (loan), Anthony Stewart
Midfielders: Connor Barron, Lewis Ferguson, Matty Kennedy, Dante Polvara, Yiber Ramadani
Forwards: Vicente Besuijen, Connor McLennan, Bojan Miovski, Christian Ramirez, Marley Watkins

CELTIC

Ground: Celtic Park, Glasgow G40 3RE.
Capacity: 60,832. **Telephone:** 0871 226 1888
Manager: Angelos Postecoglou. **Colours:** Green and white. **Nickname:** Bhoys
Goalkeepers: Scott Bain, Joe Hart, Benjamin Siegrist
Defenders: Alexandro Bernabei, Boli Bolingoli, Cameron Carter-Vickers, Christopher Jullien, Josip Juranovic, Anthony Ralston, Carl Starfelt, Greg Taylor, Osaze Urhoghide, Stephen Welch
Midfielders: James Forrest, Reo Hatate, Yosuke Ideguchi, Mikey Johnston, Jota, James McCarthy, Callum McGregor, Matt O'Riley, Scott Robertson, Liam Shaw, Ismaila Soro, David Turnbull
Forwards: Liel Abada, Albian Ajeti, Kyogo Furuhashi, Giorgos Giakoumakis, Leigh Griffiths, Johnny Kenny, Daizen Maeda

DUNDEE UNITED

Ground: Tannadice Park, Tannadice Street, Dundee DD3 7JW.
Capacity: 14,209. **Telephone:** 01382 833166
Manager: Jack Ross. **Colours:** Tangerine and black. **Nickname:** Terrors
Goalkeepers: Carljohan Eriksson, Jack Newman
Defenders: Mark Connolly, Nathan Cooney, Ryan Edwards, Kieran Freeman, Ross Graham, Scott McMann, Charlie Mulgrew, Ilmari Niskanen, Liam Smith, Kerr Smith
Midfielders: Calum Butcher, Declan Glass, Ian Harkes, Dylan Levitt, Archie Meekison, Chris Mochrie, Craig Moore, Peter Pawlett
Forwards: Logan Chalmers, Nicky Clark, Steven Fletcher, Kai Fotheringham, Rory MacLeod, Darren Watson, Tony Watt

HEART OF MIDLOTHIAN

Ground: Tynecastle Stadium, McLeod Street Edinburgh EH11 2NL.
Capacity: 20,099. **Telephone:** 0871 663 1874.
Manager: Robbie Neilson. **Colours:** Maroon and white. **Nickname:** Jam Tarts
Goalkeepers: Craig Gordon, Ross Stewart
Defenders: Nathaniel Atkinson, Jamie Brandon, Alex Cochrane, Craig Halkett, Stephen Kingsley, Cammy Logan, Lewis Neilson, Michael Smith, Kye Rowles, Toby Sibbick
Midfielders: Beni Baningime, Loic Damour, Cameron Devlin. Alan Forrest, Josh Ginnelly,Jorge Grant, Andy Halliday, Peter Haring, Barrie McKay, Gary Mackay-Steven, Aaron McEneff, Scott McGill, Connor Smith
Forwards: Liam Boyce, Euan Henderson

HIBERNIAN

Ground: Easter Road, Albion Place, Edinburgh EH7 5QG
Capacity: 20,451. **Telephone:** 0131 661 2159.
Manager: Lee Johnson. **Colours:** Green and white. **Nickname:** Hibees
Goalkeepers: Kevin Dabrowski, Murray Johnson, David Marshall
Defenders: Rocky Bushiri, Chris Cadden, Allan Delferriere, Josh Doig, Paul Hanlon, Darren McGregor, Lewis Miller, Demetri Mitchell, Ryan Porteous, Lewis Stevenson
Midfielders: Steven Bradley, Josh Campbell, Jake Doyle-Hayes, Ewan Henderson, Nohan Kenneh, Daniel Mackay, Kyle Magennis, Aiden McGeady, Joe Newell, Dylan Tait, Jair Tavares
Forwards: Momodou Bojang, Christian Doidge, Runar Hauge, Elias Melkersen, Kevin Nisbet, Elie Youan

KILMARNOCK

Ground: Rugby Park, Kilmarnock KA 1 2DP.
Capacity: 18,128. **Telephone:** 01563 545300
Manager: Derek McInnes. **Colours:** Blue and white. **Nickname:** Killie
Goalkeepers: Zach Hemming (loan), Curtis Lyle, Sam Walker
Defenders: Liam Donnelly, Lee Hodson, Dylan McGowan, Lewis May (loan), Jack Sanders, Chris Stokes, Ash Taylor, Calum Waters
Midfielders: Blair Alston, Daniel Armstrong, Brad Lyons, Kerr McInroy, Rory McKenzie, Liam Polworth, Alan Power, Steven Warnock
Forwards: Kyle Connell, Innes Cameron, Kyle Lafferty, Scott Robinson, Oli Shaw

LIVINGSTON

Ground: Tony Macaroni Arena, Alderstone Road, Livingston EH54 7DN
Capacity: 10,016. **Telephone:** 01506 417000
Manager: David Martindale. **Colours:** Gold and black. **Nickname:** Livvy's Lions
Goalkeepers: Zach Hemming (loan), Ivan Konovalov, Max Stryjek
Defenders: Morgan Boyes, Jamie Brandon, Phillip Cancar, Nicky Devlin, Jack Fitzwater, Sean Kelly, Jackson Longridge, Lewis Mayo (loan), Ayo Obileye, Tom Parkes, James Penrice,
Midfielders: Scott Bitsindou, Jason Holt, Cristian Montano, Josh Mullin, Stephane Omeonga, Scott Pittman, Andrew Shinnie
Forwards: Bruce Anderson, Esmael Goncalves, Jack Hamilton, Jaze Kabi, Joel Nouble

MOTHERWELL

Ground: Fir Park, Firpark Street, Motherwell ML1 2QN.
Capacity: 13,742. **Telephone:** 01698 333333
Manager: Graham Alexander. **Colours:** Claret and amber. **Nickname:** Well
Goalkeepers: Scott Fox, Liam Kelly
Defenders: Jake Carroll, David Devine, Sondre Solholm Johansen, Max Johnston, Ricki Lamie, Nathan McGinley, Paul McGinn, Bevis Mugabi, Stephen O'Donnell, Juhani Ojala
Midfielders: Dean Cornelius, Sean Goss, Barry Maguire, Callum Slattery, Blair Spittal, Ross Tierney
Forwards: Joe Efford, Robbie Mahon, Connor Shields, Kevin van Veen, Kayne Woolery

RANGERS

Ground: Ibrox Stadium, Edmison Drive, Glasgow G51 2XD
Capacity: 50,411. **Telephone:** 0871 702 1972
Manager: Giovanni van Bronckhorst. **Colours:** Blue. **Nickname:** Gers
Goalkeepers: Allan McGregor, Robby McCrorie, Jon McLaughlin
Defenders: Borna Barisic, Calvin Bassey, Connor Goldson, Filip Helander, Nikola Katic, Jack Simpson, John Souttar, James Tavernier, Ben Williamson, Mateusz, Zukowski
Midfielders: Scott Arfield, Joe Aribo, Steven Davis, Ianis Hagi, Ryan Jack, Glen Kamara, Stephen Kelly, Ryan Kent, John Lundstram, Glen Middleton, Nnamdi Ofoborh, Tom Lawrence
Forwards: Antonio Colak, Jake Hastie, Alfredo Morelos, Kemar Roofe, Fashion Sakala, Scott Wright

ROSS COUNTY

Ground: Global Energy Stadium, Victoria Park, Jubilee Road, Dingwall IV15 9QZ. **Capacity:** 6,541. **Telephone:** 01738 459090
Manager: Malky Mackay. **Colours:** Blue and white. **Nickname:** Staggies
Goalkeepers: Ross Laidlaw, Ross Munro, Logan Ross
Defenders: Jack Baldwin, Coll Donaldson, George Harmon, Ben Purrington, Connor Randall, Keith Watson, Ben Williamson

Midfielders: Ross Callachan, David Cancola, Yan Dandha, Owura Edwards (loan), Victor Loturi, Adam Mackinnon, Ben Paton, Harry Paton, Josh Sims, Jordan Tillson
Forwards: Jordy Hiwula, Kazeem Olaigbe, Alex Samuel, Dominic Samuel, Jordan White, Matthew Wright

ST JOHNSTONE

Ground: McDiarmid Park, Crieff Road, Perth PH1 2SJ
Capacity: 10,673. **Telephone:** 01738 459090
Manager: Callum Davidson. **Colours:** Blue and white. **Nickname:** Saints
Goalkeepers: Zander Clark, Elliot Parish, Ross Sinclair
Defenders: Callum Booth, James Brown, Dan Cleary, Andrew Considine, Tony Gallacher, Liam Gordon, Melker Hallberg, John Mahon, Jamie McCart, Adam Montgomery (loan)
Midfielders: Cammy Ballantyne, Graham Carey, Ali Crawford, Murray Davidson, Charlie Gilmour, Cammy MacPherson, David Wotherspoon, Drey Wright
Forwards: Theo Bair, Chris Kane, Stevie May, Michael O'Halloran, Jamie Murphy, Eetu Vertainen

ST MIRREN

Ground: Simple Digital Arena Greenhill Road, Paisley PA3 IRU
Capacity: 8,006. **Telephone:** 0141 889 2558
Manager: Stephen Robinson. **Colours:** Black and white. **Nickname:** Buddies
Goalkeepers: Trevor Carson, Dean Lyness, Peter Urminsky
Defenders: Charles Dunne, Marcus Fraser, Declan Gallagher, Joe Shaughnessy, Ryan Strain, Richard Tait, Scott Tanser
Midfielders: Ethan Erhahon, Ryan Flynn, Jay Henderson, Greg Kiltie, Mark O'Hara, Dylan Reid
Forwards: Jonah Ayunga, Eamonn Brophy, Alex Greive, Lewis Jamieson, Curtis Main, Keiran Offord, Toyosi Olusanya

THE THINGS THEY SAY ...

'There are no excuses for my actions which I sincerely regret' – **Kurt Zouma**, West Ham defender, apologises after being filmed kicking and slapping his pet cat and being taken to court.

'I probably don't have the vocabulary to describe that properly – **Michael Duff**, Cheltenham manager, after a 5-5 draw at Wycombe.

'You are watching an all-time great at the peak of his powers' – **Jurgen Klopp**, Liverpool manager, after Mohamed Salah's 150th goal for the club.

'It is maybe a bit of a surprise, but do not be put off by that. I am here to make Bradford City a team people want to watch and be proud of' – **Mark Hughes**, former Wales and Manchester City manager, after taking over at the League Two club.

'To see where we are in the league, that's utopia' – **Nathan Jones**, Luton manager, after his side climbed to third after beating Hull.

'My heart was going mad when I came through those doors. The responsibility of things going wrong was on me and the world was watching'- **Jermaine Jenas**, former Tottenham and England midfielder, on stage conducting the World Cup draw in Qatar – a job he handled perfectly.

ENGLISH FIXTURES 2022–2023
Premier League and Football League

Friday 29 July
Championship
Huddersfield v Burnley

Saturday 30 July
Championship
Blackburn v QPR
Blackpool v Reading
Cardiff v Norwich
Hull v Bristol City
Luton v Birmingham
Middlesbrough v WBA
Millwall v Stoke
Rotherham v Swansea
Wigan v Preston

League One
Accrington v Charlton
Bristol Rov v Forest Green
Cambridge v MK Dons
Cheltenham v Peterborough
Derby v Oxford
Ipswich v Bolton
Lincoln v Exeter
Morecambe v Shrewsbury
Plymouth v Barnsley
Port Vale v Fleetwood
Sheff Wed v Portsmouth
Wycombe v Burton

League Two
AFC Wimbledon v Gillingham
Bradford v Doncaster
Carlisle v Crawley
Harrogate v Swindon
Leyton Orient v Grimsby
Northampton v Colchester
Rochdale v Crewe
Salford v Mansfield
Stockport v Barrow
Sutton v Newport
Tranmere v Stevenage
Walsall v Hartlepool

Sunday 31 July
Championship
Sunderland v Coventry

Monday 1 August
Championship
Watford v Sheff Utd

Friday 5 August
Premier League
Crystal Palace v Arsenal

Saturday 6 August
Premier League
Everton v Chelsea
Fulham v Liverpool
Bournemouth v Aston Villa
Leeds v Wolves
Newcastle v Nottm Forest
Tottenham v Southampton

Championship
Birmingham v Huddersfield
Bristol City v Sunderland
Burnley v Luton
Norwich v Wigan
Preston v Hull
QPR v Middlesbrough
Reading v Cardiff
Sheff Utd v Millwall
Stoke v Blackpool
Swansea v Blackburn

League One
Barnsley v Cheltenham
Bolton v Wycombe
Burton v Bristol Rov
Charlton v Derby
Exeter v Port Vale
Fleetwood v Plymouth
Forest Green v Ipswich
MK Dons v Sheff Wed
Oxford v Cambridge
Peterborough v Morecambe
Portsmouth v Lincoln
Shrewsbury v Accrington

League Two
Barrow v Bradford
Colchester v Carlisle
Crawley v Leyton Orient
Crewe v Harrogate
Doncaster v Sutton
Gillingham v Rochdale
Grimsby v Northampton
Hartlepool v AFC Wimbledon
Mansfield v Tranmere
Newport v Walsall
Stevenage v Stockport
Swindon v Salford

Sunday 7 August
Premier League
Leicester v Brentford
Man Utd v Brighton
West Ham v Man City

Championship
Coventry v Rotherham

Monday 8 August
Championship
WBA v Watford

Saturday 13 August
Premier League
Arsenal v Leicester
Aston Villa v Everton
Brentford v Man Utd
Brighton v Newcastle
Man City v Bournemouth
Southampton v Leeds
Wolves v Fulham

Championship
Blackpool v Swansea
Cardiff v Birmingham
Huddersfield v Stoke
Hull v Norwich
Luton v Preston
Millwall v Coventry
Rotherham v Reading
Sunderland v QPR
Watford v Burnley
Wigan v Bristol City

League One
Accrington v Burton
Bristol Rov v Oxford
Cambridge v Exeter
Cheltenham v Portsmouth
Derby v Barnsley
Ipswich v MK Dons
Lincoln v Forest Green
Morecambe v Fleetwood
Plymouth v Peterborough
Port Vale v Bolton
Sheff Wed v Charlton
Wycombe v Shrewsbury

League Two
AFC Wimbledon v Doncaster
Bradford v Newport
Carlisle v Swindon
Harrogate v Crawley
Leyton Orient v Mansfield
Northampton v Hartlepool
Rochdale v Grimsby
Salford v Crewe
Stockport v Colchester
Sutton v Barrow
Tranmere v Gillingham
Walsall v Stevenage

Sunday 14 August
Premier League
Chelsea v Tottenham
Nottm Forest v West Ham

Championship

Blackburn v WBA
Middlesbrough v Sheff Utd

Monday 15 August
Premier League

Liverpool v Crystal Palace

Tuesday 16 August
Championship

Birmingham v Watford
Bristol City v Luton
Burnley v Hull
Coventry City v Wigan
Norwich v Huddersfield
Preston v Rotherham
QPR v Blackpool
Swansea v Millwall

League One

Barnsley v Bristol Rov
Bolton v Morecambe
Burton v Ipswich
Charlton v Plymouth
Exeter v Wycombe
Fleetwood v Cheltenham
Forest Green v Accrington
MK Dons v Port Vale
Oxford v Lincoln
Peterborough v Sheff Wed
Portsmouth v Cambridge
Shrewsbury v Derby

League Two

Barrow v Walsall
Colchester v Bradford
Crawley v Northampton
Crewe v Sutton
Doncaster v Stockport
Gillingham v Harrogate
Grimsby v Carlisle
Hartlepool v Tranmere
Mansfield v AFC Wimbledon
Newport v Salford
Stevenage v Rochdale
Swindon v Leyton Orient

Wednesday 17 August
Championship

Reading v Blackburn
Sheff Utd v Sunderland
Stoke v Middlesbrough
WBA v Cardiff

Saturday 20 August
Premier League

Bournemouth v Arsenal
Crystal Palace v Aston Villa
Everton v Nottm Forest
Fulham v Brentford
Leicester v Southampton
Tottenham v Wolves

Championship

Birmingham v Wigan
Bristol City v Cardiff
Burnley v Blackpool
Coventry City v Huddersfield
Norwich v Millwall
Preston v Watford
QPR v Rotherham
Reading v Middlesbrough
Sheff Utd v Blackburn
Stoke v Sunderland
Swansea v Luton
WBA v Hull

League One

Barnsley v Wycombe
Bolton v Sheff Wed
Burton v Port Vale
Charlton v Cambridge
Exeter v Cheltenham
Fleetwood v Derby
Forest Green v Plymouth
MK Dons v Accrington
Oxford v Morecambe
Peterborough v Lincoln
Portsmouth v Bristol Rov
Shrewsbury v Ipswich

League Two

Barrow v Harrogate
Colchester v Leyton Orient
Crawley v AFC Wimbledon
Crewe v Northampton
Doncaster v Salford
Gillingham v Walsall
Grimsby v Sutton
Hartlepool v Bradford
Mansfield v Stockport
Newport v Tranmere
Stevenage v Carlisle
Swindon v Rochdale

Sunday 21 August
Premier League

Leeds v Chelsea
Newcastle v Man City
West Ham v Brighton

Monday 22 August
Premier League

Man Utd v Liverpool

Saturday 27 August
Premier League

Arsenal v Fulham
Brentford v Everton
Brighton v Leeds
Chelsea v Leicester
Liverpool v Bournemouth
Man City v Crystal Palace
Southampton v Man Utd

Championship

Blackburn v Stoke
Blackpool v Bristol City
Cardiff v Preston
Huddersfield v WBA
Hull v Coventry
Luton v Sheff Utd
Middlesbrough v Swansea
Millwall v Reading
Rotherham v Birmingham
Sunderland v Norwich
Watford v QPR
Wigan v Burnley

League One

Accrington v Exeter
Bristol Rov v Shrewsbury
Cambridge v Burton
Cheltenham v Oxford
Derby v Peterborough
Ipswich v Barnsley
Lincoln v Fleetwood
Morecambe v MK Dons
Plymouth v Bolton
Port Vale v Portsmouth
Sheff Wed v Forest Green
Wycombe v Charlton

League Two

AFC Wimbledon v Barrow
Bradford v Crewe
Carlisle v Gillingham
Harrogate v Newport
Leyton Orient v Hartlepool
Northampton v Doncaster
Rochdale v Crawley
Salford v Stevenage
Stockport v Swindon
Sutton v Mansfield
Tranmere v Colchester
Walsall v Grimsby

Sunday 28 August
Premier League

Aston Villa v West Ham
Nottm Forest v Tottenham
Wolves v Newcastle

Tuesday 30 August
Premier League

Crystal Palace v Brentford
Fulham v Brighton
Leeds v Everton
Southampton v Chelsea

Championship

Birmingham v Norwich
Burnley v Millwall
Cardiff v Luton
QPR v Hull
Watford v Middlesbrough
Wigan v WBA

Wednesday 31 August
Premier League
Arsenal v Aston Villa
Bournemouth v Wolves
Liverpool v Newcastle
Man City v Nottm Forest
West Ham v Tottenham

Championship
Blackpool v Blackburn
Bristol City v Huddersfield
Coventry City v Preston
Sheff Utd v Reading
Sunderland v Rotherham
Stoke v Swansea

Thursday 1 September
Premier League
Leicester v Man Utd

Saturday 3 September
Premier League
Aston Villa v Man City
Brentford v Leeds
Everton v Liverpool
Newcastle v Crystal Palace
Nottm Forest v Bournemouth
Tottenham v Fulham
Wolves v Southampton

Championship
Blackburn v Bristol City
Huddersfield v Blackpool
Hull v Sheff Utd
Luton v Wigan
Middlesbrough v Sunderland
Millwall v Cardiff
Norwich v Coventry
Preston v Birmingham
Reading v Stoke
Rotherham v Watford
Swansea v QPR
WBA v Burnley

League One
Accrington v Ipswich
Bolton v Charlton
Bristol Rov v Morecambe
Cambridge v Lincoln
Derby v Plymouth
Exeter v MK Dons
Fleetwood v Wycombe
Forest Green v Shrewsbury
Oxford v Burton
Port Vale v Cheltenham
Portsmouth v Peterborough
Sheff Wed v Barnsley

League Two
Bradford v Walsall
Carlisle v Rochdale
Colchester v Hartlepool
Crewe v Stevenage

Doncaster v Mansfield
Gillingham v Swindon
Leyton Orient v Tranmere
Newport v Grimsby
Northampton v Barrow
Salford v Crawley
Stockport v AFC Wimbledon
Sutton v Harrogate

Sunday 4 September
Premier League
Brighton v Leicester.
Chelsea v West Ham
Man Utd v Arsenal

Saturday 10 September
Premier League
Bournemouth v Brighton
Fulham v Chelsea
Leicester v Aston Villa
Liverpool v Wolves
Man City v Tottenham
Southampton v Brentford

Championship
Birmingham v Swansea
Blackpool v Middlesbrough
Bristol City v Preston
Burnley v Norwich
Cardiff v Hull
Coventry v WBA
QPR v Huddersfield
Sheff Utd v Rotherham
Stoke v Luton
Sunderland v Millwall
Watford v Reading
Wigan v Blackburn

League One
Barnsley v Portsmouth
Burton v Fleetwood
Charlton v Exeter
Cheltenham v Bolton
Ipswich v Cambridge
Lincoln v Accrington
MK Dons v Bristol Rov
Morecambe v Derby
Peterborough v Forest Green
Plymouth v Sheff Wed
Shrewsbury v Oxford
Wycombe v Port Vale

League Two
AFC Wimbledon v Leyton Orient
Barrow v Colchester
Crawley v Gillingham
Grimsby v Crewe
Harrogate v Carlisle
Hartlepool v Doncaster
Mansfield v Bradford
Rochdale v Salford
Stevenage v Sutton

Swindon v Newport
Tranmere v Stockport
Walsall v Northampton

Sunday 11 September
Premier League
Arsenal v Everton
Crystal Palace v Man Utd
West Ham v Newcastle

Monday 12 September
Premier League
Leeds v Nottm Forest

Tuesday 13 September
Championship
Blackburn v Watford
Huddersfield v Wigan
Hull v Stoke
Middlesbrough v Cardiff
Preston v Burnley
Swansea v Sheff Utd

League Two
AFC Wimbledon v Northampton
Barrow v Doncaster
Crawley v Stockport
Grimsby v Gillingham
Harrogate v Salford
Hartlepool v Crewe
Mansfield v Carlisle
Rochdale v Leyton Orient
Stevenage v Newport
Swindon v Sutton
Tranmere v Bradford
Walsall v Colchester

Wednesday 14 September
Luton v Coventry
Millwall v QPR
Norwich v Bristol City
Rotherham v Blackpool
Reading v Sunderland
WBA v Birmingham

League One
Barnsley v Port Vale
Burton v Portsmouth
Charlton v Forest Green
Cheltenham v Cambridge
Ipswich v Bristol Rov
Lincoln v Derby
MK Dons v Bolton
Morecambe v Sheff Wed
Peterborough v Fleetwood
Plymouth v Oxford
Shrewsbury v Exeter
Wycombe v Accrington

Friday, 16 September
Premier League
Nottm Forest v Fulham

Saturday 17 September
Premier League
Aston Villa v Southampton
Brighton v Crystal Palace
Everton v West Ham
Newcastle v Bournemouth
Tottenham v Leicester
Wolves v Man City

Championship
Birmingham v Coventry
Burnley v Bristol City
Huddersfield v Cardiff
Luton v Blackburn
Middlesbrough v Rotherham
Millwall v Blackpool
Norwich v WBA
Preston v Sheff Utd
QPR v Stoke
Swansea v Hull
Watford v Sunderland
Wigan v Reading

League One
Accrington v Cheltenham
Bolton v Peterborough
Bristol Rov v Lincoln
Cambridge v Barnsley
Derby v Wycombe
Exeter v Burton
Fleetwood v Charlton
Forest Green v Morecambe
Oxford v MK Dons
Port Vale v Shrewsbury
Portsmouth v Plymouth
Sheff Wed v Ipswich

League Two
Bradford v Stevenage
Carlisle v AFC Wimbledon
Colchester v Grimsby
Crewe v Crawley
Doncaster v Swindon
Gillingham v Mansfield
Leyton Orient v Walsall
Newport v Barrow
Northampton v Rochdale
Salford v Tranmere
Stockport v Harrogate
Sutton v Hartlepool

Sunday 18 September
Premier League
Brentford v Arsenal
Chelsea v Liverpool
Man Utd v Leeds

Saturday 24 September
League One
Barnsley v Charlton
Bristol Rov v Accrington
Derby v Cheltenham
Forest Green v Exeter
Lincoln v MK Dons
Morecambe v Cambridge
Oxford v Fleetwood
Peterborough v Port Vale
Plymouth v Ipswich
Portsmouth v Bolton
Sheff Wed v Wycombe
Shrewsbury v Burton

League Two
Barrow v Leyton Orient
Bradford v AFC Wimbledon
Colchester v Rochdale
Crewe v Mansfield
Doncaster v Crawley
Grimsby v Swindon
Hartlepool v Gillingham
Newport v Carlisle
Northampton v Stockport
Stevenage v Harrogate
Sutton v Salford
Walsall v Tranmere

Saturday 1 October
Premier League
Arsenal v Tottenham
Bournemouth v Brentford
Crystal Palace v Chelsea
Fulham v Newcastle
Leeds v Aston Villa
Leicester v Nottm Forest
Liverpool v Brighton
Man City v Man Utd
Southampton v Everton
West Ham v Wolves

Championship
Blackburn v Millwall
Blackpool v Norwich
Bristol City v QPR
Cardiff v Burnley
Coventry City v Middlesbrough
Hull v Luton
Reading v Huddersfield
Rotherham v Wigan
Sheff Utd v Birmingham
Stoke v Watford
Sunderland v Preston
WBA v Swansea

League One
Accrington v Morecambe
Bolton v Lincoln
Burton v Forest Green
Cambridge v Derby
Charlton v Oxford

Cheltenham v Shrewsbury
Exeter v Bristol Rov
Fleetwood v Barnsley
Ipswich v Portsmouth
MK Dons v Peterborough
Port Vale v Sheff Wed
Wycombe v Plymouth

League Two
AFC Wimbledon v Colchester
Carlisle v Crewe
Crawley v Stevenage
Gillingham v Sutton
Harrogate v Bradford
Leyton Orient v Newport
Mansfield v Hartlepool
Rochdale v Doncaster
Salford v Grimsby
Stockport v Walsall
Swindon v Northampton
Tranmere v Barrow

Tuesday 4 October
Championship
Bristol City v Coventry
Cardiff v Blackburn
Luton v Huddersfield
Reading v Norwich
Sheff Utd v QPR
Sunderland v Blackpool

Wednesday 5 October
Championship
Burnley v Stoke
Hull v Wigan
Middlesbrough v Birmingham
Preston v WBA
Rotherham v Millwall
Watford v Swansea

Saturday 8 October
Premier League
Arsenal v Liverpool
Bournemouth v Leicester
Brighton v Tottenham
Chelsea v Wolves
Crystal Palace v Leeds
Everton v Man Utd
Man City v Southampton
Newcastle v Brentford
Nottm Forest v Aston Villa
West Ham v Fulham

Championship
Birmingham v Bristol City
Blackburn v Rotherham
Blackpool v Watford
Coventry City v Burnley
Huddersfield v Hull
Millwall v Middlesbrough
Norwich v Preston
QPR v Reading
Stoke v Sheff Utd

Swansea v Sunderland
WBA v Luton
Wigan v Cardiff

League One
Barnsley v Exeter
Bristol Rov v Cambridge
Derby v Port Vale
Forest Green v Bolton
Lincoln v Charlton
Morecambe v Ipswich
Oxford v Wycombe
Peterborough v Burton
Plymouth v Accrington
Portsmouth v Fleetwood
Sheff Wed v Cheltenham
Shrewsbury v MK Dons

League Two
Barrow v Mansfield
Bradford v Stockport
Colchester v Harrogate
Crewe v Gillingham
Doncaster v Leyton Orient
Grimsby v Crawley
Hartlepool v Carlisle
Newport v Rochdale
Northampton v Salford
Stevenage v Swindon
Sutton v Tranmere
Walsall v AFC Wimbledon

Saturday 15 October
Premier League
Aston Villa v Chelsea
Brentford v Brighton
Fulham v Bournemouth
Leeds v Arsenal
Leicester v Crystal Palace
Liverpool v Man City
Man Utd v Newcastle
Southampton v West Ham
Tottenham v Everton
Wolves v Nottm Forest

Championship
Bristol City v Millwall
Burnley v Swansea
Cardiff v Coventry
Hull v Birmingham
Luton v QPR
Middlesbrough v Blackburn
Preston v Stoke
Reading v WBA
Rotherham v Huddersfield
Sheff Utd v Blackpool
Sunderland v Wigan
Watford v Norwich

League One
Accrington v Derby
Bolton v Barnsley

Burton v Morecambe
Cambridge v Sheff Wed
Charlton v Portsmouth
Cheltenham v Bristol Rov
Exeter v Oxford
Fleetwood v Shrewsbury
Ipswich v Lincoln
MK Dons v Plymouth
Port Vale v Forest Green
Wycombe v Peterborough

League Two
AFC Wimbledon v Sutton
Carlisle v Doncaster
Crawley v Newport
Gillingham v Stevenage
Harrogate v Hartlepool
Leyton Orient v Northampton
Mansfield v Walsall
Rochdale v Barrow
Salford v Bradford
Stockport v Grimsby
Swindon v Colchester
Tranmere v Crewe

Tuesday 18 October
Premier League
Arsenal v Man City
Bournemouth v Southampton
Brentford v Chelsea
Brighton v Nottm Forest
Crystal Palace v Wolves
Fulham v Aston Villa
Leicester v Leeds

Championship
Blackburn v Sunderland
Huddersfield v Preston
Norwich v Luton
Stoke v Rotherham
Swansea v Reading
WBA v Bristol City

Wednesday 19 October
Premier League
Liverpool v West Ham
Man Utd v Tottenham
Newcastle v Everton

Championship
Birmingham v Burnley
Blackpool v Hull
Coventry City v Sheff Utd
Millwall v Watford
QPR v Cardiff
Wigan v Middlesbrough

Saturday 22 October
Premier League
Aston Villa v Brentford
Chelsea v Man Utd

Everton v Crystal Palace
Leeds v Fulham
Man City v Brighton
Nottm Forest v Liverpool
Southampton v Arsenal
Tottenham v Newcastle
West Ham v Bournemouth
Wolves v Leicester

Championship
Blackburn v Birmingham
Blackpool v Preston
Middlesbrough v Huddersfield
Millwall v WBA
QPR v Wigan
Reading v Bristol City
Rotherham v Hull
Sheff Utd v Norwich
Stoke v Coventry
Sunderland v Burnley
Swansea v Cardiff
Watford v Luton

League One
Accrington v Bolton
Bristol Rov v Plymouth
Burton v Cheltenham
Cambridge v Port Vale
Exeter v Fleetwood
Forest Green v Portsmouth
Ipswich v Derby
Lincoln v Sheff Wed
MK Dons v Wycombe
Morecambe v Barnsley
Oxford v Peterborough
Shrewsbury v Charlton

League Two
Carlisle v Leyton Orient
Crawley v Mansfield
Crewe v Doncaster
Gillingham v Barrow
Grimsby v Bradford
Harrogate v Tranmere
Newport v Colchester
Rochdale v AFC Wimbledon
Salford v Stockport
Stevenage v Northampton
Sutton v Walsall
Swindon v Hartlepool

Tuesday 25 October
League One
Barnsley v Lincoln
Bolton v Burton
Charlton v MK Dons
Cheltenham v Morecambe
Derby v Exeter
Fleetwood v Forest Green
Peterborough v Accrington
Plymouth v Shrewsbury
Port Vale v Ipswich

Portsmouth v Oxford
Sheff Wed v Bristol Rov
Wycombe v Cambridge

League Two
AFC Wimbledon v Crewe
Barrow v Grimsby
Bradford v Swindon
Colchester v Crawley
Hartlepool v Salford
Leyton Orient v Gillingham
Mansfield v Newport
Northampton v Sutton
Stockport v Carlisle
Tranmere v Rochdale
Walsall v Harrogate
Doncaster v Stevenage

Saturday 29 October
Premier League
Arsenal v Nottm Forest
Bournemouth v Tottenham
Brentford v Wolves
Brighton v Chelsea
Crystal Palace v Southampton
Fulham v Everton
Leicester v Man City
Liverpool v Leeds
Man Utd v West Ham
Newcastle v Aston Villa

Championship
Birmingham v QPR
Bristol City v Swansea
Burnley v Reading
Cardiff v Rotherham
Coventry City v Blackpool
Huddersfield v Millwall
Hull v Blackburn
Luton v Sunderland
Norwich v Stoke
Preston v Middlesbrough
WBA v Sheff Utd
Wigan v Watford

League One
Barnsley v Forest Green
Bolton v Oxford
Charlton v Ipswich
Cheltenham v MK Dons
Derby v Bristol Rov
Fleetwood v Accrington
Peterborough v Cambridge
Plymouth v Exeter
Port Vale v Lincoln
Portsmouth v Shrewsbury
Sheff Wed v Burton
Wycombe v Morecambe

League Two
AFC Wimbledon v Harrogate
Barrow v Crewe

Bradford v Crawley
Colchester v Stevenage
Doncaster v Gillingham
Hartlepool v Grimsby
Leyton Orient v Salford
Mansfield v Swindon
Northampton v Newport
Stockport v Sutton
Tranmere v Carlisle
Walsall v Rochdale

Tuesday 1 November
Championship
Bristol City v Sheff Utd
Coventry City v Blackburn
Hull v Middlesbrough
Luton v Reading
Preston v Swansea
WBA v Blackpool

Wednesday 2nd November
Championship
Birmingham v Millwall
Burnley v Rotherham
Cardiff v Watford
Huddersfield v Sunderland
Norwich v QPR
Wigan v Stoke

Saturday 5 November
Premier League
Aston Villa v Man Utd
Chelsea v Arsenal
Everton v Leicester
Leeds v Bournemouth
Man City v Fulham
Nottm Forest v Brentford
Southampton v Newcastle
Tottenham v Liverpool
West Ham v Crystal Palace
Wolves v Brighton

Championship
Blackburn v Huddersfield
Blackpool v Luton
Middlesbrough v Bristol City
Millwall v Hull
QPR v WBA
Reading v Preston
Rotherham v Norwich
Sheff Utd v Burnley
Stoke v Birmingham
Sunderland v Cardiff
Swansea v Wigan
Watford v Coventry

Saturday 12 November
Premier League
Bournemouth v Everton
Brighton v Aston Villa
Fulham v Man Utd

Liverpool v Southampton
Man City v Brentford
Newcastle v Chelsea
Nottm Forest v Crystal Palace
Tottenham v Leeds
West Ham v Leicester
Wolves v Arsenal

Championship
Birmingham v Sunderland
Bristol City v Watford
Burnley v Blackburn
Cardiff v Sheff Utd
Coventry City v QPR
Huddersfield v Swansea
Hull v Reading
Luton v Rotherham
Norwich v Middlesbrough
Preston v Millwall
WBA v Stoke
Wigan v Blackpool

League One
Accrington v Sheff Wed
Bristol Rov v Fleetwood
Burton v Charlton
Cambridge v Bolton
Exeter v Peterborough
Forest Green v Wycombe
Ipswich v Cheltenham
Lincoln v Plymouth
MK Dons v Derby
Morecambe v Portsmouth
Oxford v Port Vale
Shrewsbury v Barnsley

League Two
Carlisle v Walsall
Crawley v Barrow
Crewe v Colchester
Gillingham v Northampton
Grimsby v Doncaster
Harrogate v Leyton Orient
Newport v Stockport
Rochdale v Mansfield
Salford v AFC Wimbledon
Stevenage v Hartlepool
Sutton v Bradford
Swindon v Tranmere

Saturday 19 November
League One
Barnsley v MK Dons
Bristol Rov v Peterborough
Burton v Plymouth
Cambridge v Accrington
Cheltenham v Wycombe
Exeter v Ipswich
Fleetwood v Bolton
Lincoln v Morecambe
Oxford v Forest Green
Port Vale v Charlton

Portsmouth v Derby
Sheff Wed v Shrewsbury

League Two
Barrow v Hartlepool
Bradford v Northampton
Colchester v Doncaster
Grimsby v Stevenage
Harrogate v Mansfield
Newport v Gillingham
Salford v Carlisle
Stockport v Leyton Orient
Sutton v Rochdale
Swindon v Crewe
Tranmere v AFC Wimbledon
Walsall v Crawley

Saturday 3 December
League One
Accrington v Oxford
Bolton v Bristol Rov
Charlton v Cheltenham
Derby v Sheff Wed
Forest Green v Cambridge
Ipswich v Fleetwood
MK Dons v Burton
Morecambe v Exeter
Peterborough v Barnsley
Plymouth v Port Vale
Shrewsbury v Lincoln
Wycombe v Portsmouth

League Two
AFC Wimbledon v Grimsby
Carlisle v Sutton
Crawley v Swindon
Crewe v Newport
Doncaster v Walsall
Gillingham v Salford
Hartlepool v Stockport
Leyton Orient v Bradford
Mansfield v Colchester
Northampton v Tranmere
Rochdale v Harrogate
Stevenage v Barrow

Saturday 10 December
Championship
Blackburn v Preston
Blackpool v Birmingham
Middlesbrough v Luton
Millwall v Wigan
QPR v Burnley
Reading v Coventry
Rotherham v Bristol City
Sheff Utd v Huddersfield
Stoke v Cardiff
Sunderland v WBA
Swansea v Norwich
Watford v Hull

League One
Accrington v Portsmouth
Bristol Rov v Port Vale
Burton v Derby
Cambridge v Plymouth
Exeter v Sheff Wed
Forest Green v Cheltenham
Ipswich v Peterborough
Lincoln v Wycombe
MK Dons v Fleetwood
Morecambe v Charlton
Oxford v Barnsley
Shrewsbury v Bolton

League Two
Carlisle v Barrow
Crawley v Hartlepool
Crewe v Leyton Orient
Gillingham v Bradford
Grimsby v Tranmere
Harrogate v Northampton
Newport v Doncaster
Rochdale v Stockport
Salford v Walsall
Stevenage v Mansfield
Sutton v Colchester
Swindon v AFC Wimbledon

Saturday 17 December
Championship
Birmingham v Reading
Bristol City v Stoke
Burnley v Middlesbrough
Cardiff v Blackpool
Coventry City v Swansea
Huddersfield v Watford
Hull v Sunderland
Luton v Millwall
Norwich v Blackburn
Preston v QPR
WBA v Rotherham
Wigan v Sheff Utd

League One
Barnsley v Burton
Bolton v Exeter
Charlton v Bristol Rov
Cheltenham v Lincoln
Derby v Forest Green
Fleetwood v Cambridge
Peterborough v Shrewsbury
Plymouth v Morecambe
Port Vale v Accrington
Portsmouth v MK Dons
Sheff Wed v Oxford
Wycombe v Ipswich

League Two
AFC Wimbledon v Stevenage
Barrow v Swindon
Bradford v Rochdale
Colchester v Salford
Doncaster v Harrogate

Hartlepool v Newport
Leyton Orient v Sutton
Mansfield v Grimsby
Northampton v Carlisle
Stockport v Gillingham
Tranmere v Crawley
Walsall v Crewe

Monday 26 December
Premier League
Arsenal v West Ham
Aston Villa v Liverpool
Brentford v Tottenham
Chelsea v Bournemouth
Crystal Palace v Fulham
Everton v Wolves
Leeds v Man City
Leicester v Newcastle
Man Utd v Nottm Forest
Southampton v Brighton

Championship
Bristol City v WBA
Burnley v Birmingham
Cardiff v QPR
Hull v Blackpool
Luton v Norwich
Middlesbrough v Wigan
Preston v Huddersfield
Reading v Swansea
Rotherham v Stoke
Sheff Utd v Coventry
Sunderland v Blackburn
Watford v Millwall

League One
Accrington v Barnsley
Bolton v Derby
Burton v Lincoln
Cambridge v Shrewsbury
Charlton v Peterborough
Cheltenham v Plymouth
Exeter v Portsmouth
Fleetwood v Sheff Wed
Ipswich v Oxford
MK Dons v Forest Green
Port Vale v Morecambe
Wycombe v Bristol Rov

League Two
AFC Wimbledon v Newport
Carlisle v Bradford
Crawley v Sutton
Gillingham v Colchester
Harrogate v Grimsby
Leyton Orient v Stevenage
Mansfield v Northampton
Rochdale v Hartlepool
Salford v Barrow
Stockport v Crewe
Swindon v Walsall
Tranmere v Doncaster

Thursday 29 December
Championship
Birmingham v Hull
Blackburn v Middlesbrough
Blackpool v Sheff Utd
Coventry City v Cardiff
Huddersfield v Rotherham
Millwall v Bristol City
Norwich v Reading
QPR v Luton
Swansea v Watford
Wigan v Sunderland
Stoke v Burnley
WBA v Preston

League One
Barnsley v Fleetwood
Bristol Rov v Exeter
Derby v Cambridge
Forest Green v Burton
Lincoln v Bolton
Morecambe v Accrington
Oxford v Charlton
Peterborough v MK Dons
Plymouth v Wycombe
Portsmouth v Ipswich
Sheff Wed v Port Vale
Shrewsbury v Cheltenham

League Two
Barrow v Tranmere
Bradford v Harrogate
Colchester v AFC Wimbledon
Crewe v Carlisle
Doncaster v Rochdale
Grimsby v Salford
Hartlepool v Mansfield
Newport v Leyton Orient
Northampton v Swindon
Stevenage v Crawley
Sutton v Gillingham
Walsall v Stockport

Saturday 31 December
Premier League
Bournemouth v Crystal Palace
Brighton v Arsenal
Fulham v Southampton
Liverpool v Leicester
Man City v Everton
Newcastle v Leeds
Nottm Forest v Chelsea
Tottenham v Aston Villa
West Ham v Brentford
Wolves v Man Utd

Sunday 1 January
Championship
Birmingham v Middlesbrough
Blackburn v Cardiff
Blackpool v Sunderland

Coventry City v Bristol City
Huddersfield v Luton
Millwall v Rotherham
Norwich v Watford
QPR v Sheff Utd
Stoke v Preston
Swansea v Burnley
WBA v Reading
Wigan v Hull

League One
Barnsley v Bolton
Bristol Rov v Cheltenham
Derby v Accrington
Forest Green v Port Vale
Lincoln v Ipswich
Morecambe v Burton
Oxford v Exeter
Peterborough v Wycombe
Plymouth v MK Dons
Portsmouth v Charlton
Sheff Wed v Cambridge
Shrewsbury v Fleetwood

League Two
Barrow v Rochdale
Bradford v Salford
Colchester v Swindon
Crewe v Tranmere
Doncaster v Carlisle
Grimsby v Stockport
Hartlepool v Harrogate
Newport v Crawley
Northampton v Leyton Orient
Stevenage v Gillingham
Sutton v AFC Wimbledon
Walsall v Mansfield

Monday 2 January
Premier League
Arsenal v Newcastle
Aston Villa v Wolves
Brentford v Liverpool
Chelsea v Man City
Crystal Palace v Tottenham
Everton v Brighton
Leeds v West Ham
Leicester v Fulham
Man Utd v Bournemouth
Southampton v Nottm Forest

Saturday 7 January
League One
Accrington v Plymouth
Bolton v Forest Green
Burton v Peterborough
Cambridge v Bristol Rov
Charlton v Lincoln
Cheltenham v Sheff Wed
Exeter v Barnsley
Fleetwood v Portsmouth
Ipswich v Morecambe

MK Dons v Shrewsbury
Port Vale v Derby
Wycombe v Oxford

League Two
AFC Wimbledon v Walsall
Carlisle v Hartlepool
Crawley v Grimsby
Gillingham v Crewe
Harrogate v Colchester
Leyton Orient v Doncaster
Mansfield v Barrow
Rochdale v Newport
Salford v Northampton
Stockport v Bradford
Swindon v Stevenage
Tranmere v Sutton

Saturday 14 January
Premier League
Aston Villa v Leeds
Brentford v Bournemouth
Brighton v Liverpool
Chelsea v Crystal Palace
Everton v Southampton
Man Utd v Man City
Newcastle v Fulham
Nottm Forest v Leicester
Tottenham v Arsenal
Wolves v West Ham

Championship
Bristol City v Birmingham
Burnley v Coventry
Cardiff v Wigan
Hull v Huddersfield
Luton v WBA
Middlesbrough v Millwall
Preston v Norwich
Reading v QPR
Rotherham v Blackburn
Sheff Utd v Stoke
Sunderland v Swansea
Watford v Blackpool

League One
Accrington v Bristol Rov
Bolton v Portsmouth
Burton v Shrewsbury
Cambridge v Morecambe
Charlton v Barnsley
Cheltenham v Derby
Exeter v Forest Green
Fleetwood v Oxford
Ipswich v Plymouth
MK Dons v Lincoln
Port Vale v Peterborough
Wycombe v Sheff Wed

League Two
AFC Wimbledon v Bradford
Carlisle v Newport

Crawley v Doncaster
Gillingham v Hartlepool
Harrogate v Stevenage
Leyton Orient v Barrow
Mansfield v Crewe
Rochdale v Colchester
Salford v Sutton
Stockport v Northampton
Swindon v Grimsby
Tranmere v Walsall

Saturday 21 January
Premier League
Arsenal v Man Utd
Bournemouth v Nottm Forest
Crystal Palace v Newcastle
Fulham v Tottenham
Leeds v Brentford
Leicester v Brighton
Liverpool v Chelsea
Man City v Wolves
Southampton v Aston Villa
West Ham v Everton

Championship
Birmingham v Preston
Blackpool v Huddersfield
Bristol City v Blackburn
Burnley v WBA
Cardiff v Millwall
Coventry City v Norwich
QPR v Swansea
Sheff Utd v Hull
Stoke v Reading
Sunderland v Middlesbrough
Watford v Rotherham
Wigan v Luton

League One
Barnsley v Accrington
Bristol Rov v Wycombe
Derby v Bolton
Forest Green v MK Dons
Lincoln v Burton
Morecambe v Port Vale
Oxford v Ipswich
Peterborough v Charlton
Plymouth v Cheltenham
Portsmouth v Exeter
Sheff Wed v Fleetwood
Shrewsbury v Cambridge

League Two
Barrow v Salford
Bradford v Carlisle
Colchester v Gillingham
Crewe v Stockport
Doncaster v Tranmere
Grimsby v Harrogate
Hartlepool v Rochdale
Newport v AFC Wimbledon
Northampton v Mansfield

Stevenage v Leyton Orient
Sutton v Crawley
Walsall v Swindon

Saturday 28 January
Championship
Blackburn v Blackpool
Huddersfield v Bristol City
Hull v QPR
Luton v Cardiff
Middlesbrough v Watford
Millwall v Burnley
Norwich v Birmingham
Preston v Coventry
Reading v Sheff Utd
Rotherham v Sunderland
Swansea v Stoke
WBA v Wigan

League One
Barnsley v Sheff Wed
Burton v Oxford
Charlton v Bolton
Cheltenham v Port Vale
Ipswich v Accrington
Lincoln v Cambridge
MK Dons v Exeter
Morecambe v Bristol Rov
Peterborough v Portsmouth
Plymouth v Derby
Shrewsbury v Forest Green
Wycombe v Fleetwood

League Two
AFC Wimbledon v Stockport
Barrow v Northampton
Crawley v Salford
Grimsby v Newport
Harrogate v Sutton
Hartlepool v Colchester
Mansfield v Doncaster
Rochdale v Carlisle
Stevenage v Crewe
Swindon v Gillingham
Tranmere v Leyton Orient
Walsall v Bradford

Saturday 4 February
Premier League
Aston Villa v Leicester
Brentford v Southampton
Brighton v Bournemouth
Chelsea v Fulham
Everton v Arsenal
Man Utd v Crystal Palace
Newcastle v West Ham
Nottm Forest v Leeds
Tottenham v Man City
Wolves v Liverpool

Championship
Blackburn v Wigan

Huddersfield v QPR
Hull v Cardiff
Luton v Stoke
Middlesbrough v Blackpool
Millwall v Sunderland
Norwich v Burnley
Preston v Bristol City
Reading v Watford
Rotherham v Sheff Utd
Swansea v Birmingham
WBA v Coventry

League One
Accrington v Lincoln
Bolton v Cheltenham
Bristol Rov v MK Dons
Cambridge v Ipswich
Derby v Morecambe
Exeter v Charlton
Fleetwood v Burton
Forest Green v Peterborough
Oxford v Shrewsbury
Port Vale v Wycombe
Portsmouth v Barnsley
Sheff Wed v Plymouth

League Two
Bradford v Mansfield
Carlisle v Harrogate
Colchester v Barrow
Crewe v Grimsby
Doncaster v Hartlepool
Gillingham v Crawley
Leyton Orient v AFC Wimbledon
Newport v Swindon
Northampton v Walsall
Salford v Rochdale
Stockport v Tranmere
Sutton v Stevenage

Saturday 11 February
Premier League
Arsenal v Brentford
Bournemouth v Newcastle
Crystal Palace v Brighton
Fulham v Nottm Forest
Leeds v Man Utd
Leicester v Tottenham
Liverpool v Everton
Man City v Aston Villa
Southampton v Wolves
West Ham v Chelsea

Championship
Birmingham v WBA
Blackpool v Rotherham
Bristol City v Norwich
Burnley v Preston
Cardiff v Middlesbrough
Coventry City v Luton
QPR v Millwall
Sheff Utd v Swansea

Stoke v Hull
Sunderland v Reading
Watford v Blackburn
Wigan v Huddersfield

League One
Barnsley v Cambridge
Burton v Exeter
Charlton v Fleetwood
Cheltenham v Accrington
Ipswich v Sheff Wed
Lincoln v Bristol Rov
MK Dons v Oxford
Morecambe v Forest Green
Peterborough v Bolton
Plymouth v Portsmouth
Shrewsbury v Port Vale
Wycombe v Derby

League Two
AFC Wimbledon v Carlisle
Barrow v Newport
Crawley v Crewe
Grimsby v Colchester
Harrogate v Stockport
Hartlepool v Sutton
Mansfield v Gillingham
Rochdale v Northampton
Stevenage v Bradford
Swindon v Doncaster
Tranmere v Salford
Walsall v Leyton Orient

Tuesday 14 February
Championship
Birmingham v Cardiff
Burnley v Watford
Coventry City v Millwall
Norwich v Hull
QPR v Sunderland
Reading v Rotherham

League One
Accrington v Wycombe
Bolton v MK Dons
Bristol Rov v Ipswich
Cambridge v Cheltenham
Derby v Lincoln
Exeter v Shrewsbury
Fleetwood v Peterborough
Forest Green v Charlton
Oxford v Plymouth
Port Vale v Barnsley
Portsmouth v Burton
Sheff Wed v Morecambe

League Two
Bradford v Tranmere
Carlisle v Mansfield
Colchester v Walsall
Crewe v Hartlepool
Doncaster v Barrow

Gillingham v Grimsby
Leyton Orient v Rochdale
Newport v Stevenage
Northampton v AFC Wimbledon
Salford v Harrogate
Stockport v Crawley
Sutton v Swindon

Wednesday 15 February
Championship
Bristol City v Wigan
Preston v Luton
Sheff Utd v Middlesbrough
Stoke v Huddersfield
Swansea v Blackpool
WBA v Blackburn

Saturday 18 February
Premier League
Aston Villa v Arsenal
Brentford v Crystal Palace
Brighton v Fulham
Chelsea v Southampton
Everton v Leeds
Man Utd v Leicester
Newcastle v Liverpool
Nottm Forest v Man City
Tottenham v West Ham
Wolves v Bournemouth

Championship
Blackburn v Swansea
Blackpool v Stoke
Cardiff v Reading
Huddersfield v Birmingham
Hull v Preston
Luton v Burnley
Middlesbrough v QPR
Millwall v Sheff Utd
Rotherham v Coventry
Sunderland v Bristol City
Watford v WBA
Wigan v Norwich

League One
Accrington v Shrewsbury
Bristol Rov v Burton
Cambridge v Oxford
Cheltenham v Barnsley
Derby v Charlton
Ipswich v Forest Green
Lincoln v Portsmouth
Morecambe v Peterborough
Plymouth v Fleetwood
Port Vale v Exeter
Sheff Wed v MK Dons
Wycombe v Bolton

League Two
AFC Wimbledon v Hartlepool
Bradford v Barrow
Carlisle v Colchester
Harrogate v Crewe
Leyton Orient v Crawley

Northampton v Grimsby
Rochdale v Gillingham
Salford v Swindon
Stockport v Stevenage
Sutton v Doncaster
Tranmere v Mansfield
Walsall v Newport

Saturday 25 February
Premier League
Bournemouth v Man City
Crystal Palace v Liverpool
Everton v Aston Villa
Fulham v Wolves
Leeds v Southampton
Leicester v Arsenal
Man Utd v Brentford
Newcastle v Brighton
Tottenham v Chelsea
West Ham v Nottm Forest

Championship
Birmingham v Luton
Bristol City v Hull
Burnley v Huddersfield
Coventry City v Sunderland
Norwich v Cardiff
Preston v Wigan
QPR v Blackburn
Reading v Blackpool
Sheff Utd v Watford
Stoke v Millwall
Swansea v Rotherham
WBA v Middlesbrough

League One
Barnsley v Derby
Bolton v Port Vale
Burton v Accrington
Charlton v Sheff Wed
Exeter v Cambridge
Fleetwood v Morecambe
Forest Green v Lincoln
MK Dons v Ipswich
Oxford v Bristol Rov
Peterborough v Plymouth
Portsmouth v Cheltenham
Shrewsbury v Wycombe

League Two
Barrow v Stockport
Colchester v Northampton
Crawley v Carlisle
Crewe v Rochdale
Doncaster v Bradford
Gillingham v AFC Wimbledon
Grimsby v Leyton Orient
Hartlepool v Walsall
Mansfield v Salford
Newport v Sutton
Stevenage v Tranmere
Swindon v Harrogate

Saturday 4 March

Premier League
Arsenal v Bournemouth
Aston Villa v Crystal Palace
Brentford v Fulham
Brighton v West Ham
Chelsea v Leeds
Liverpool v Man Utd
Man City v Newcastle
Nottm Forest v Everton
Southampton v Leicester
Wolves v Tottenham

Championship
Blackburn v Sheff Utd
Blackpool v Burnley
Cardiff v Bristol City
Huddersfield v Coventry
Hull v WBA
Luton v Swansea
Middlesbrough v Reading
Millwall v Norwich
Rotherham v QPR
Sunderland v Stoke
Watford v Preston
Wigan v Birmingham

League One
Accrington v Forest Green
Bristol Rov v Barnsley
Cambridge v Portsmouth
Cheltenham v Fleetwood
Derby v Shrewsbury
Ipswich v Burton
Lincoln v Oxford
Morecambe v Bolton
Plymouth v Charlton
Port Vale v MK Dons
Sheff Wed v Peterborough
Wycombe v Exeter

League Two
AFC Wimbledon v Mansfield
Bradford v Colchester
Carlisle v Grimsby
Harrogate v Gillingham
Leyton Orient v Swindon
Northampton v Crawley
Rochdale v Stevenage
Salford v Newport
Stockport v Doncaster
Sutton v Crewe
Tranmere v Hartlepool
Walsall v Barrow

Saturday 11 March

Premier League
Bournemouth v Liverpool
Crystal Palace v Man City
Everton v Brentford
Fulham v Arsenal
Leeds v Brighton

Leicester v Chelsea
Man Utd v Southampton
Newcastle v Wolves
Tottenham v Nottm Forest
West Ham v Aston Villa

Championship
Birmingham v Rotherham
Bristol City v Blackpool
Burnley v Wigan
Coventry City v Hull
Norwich v Sunderland
Preston v Cardiff
QPR v Watford
Reading v Millwall
Sheff Utd v Luton
Stoke v Blackburn
Swansea v Middlesbrough
WBA v Huddersfield

League One
Barnsley v Plymouth
Bolton v Ipswich
Burton v Wycombe
Charlton v Accrington
Exeter v Lincoln
Fleetwood v Port Vale
Forest Green v Bristol Rov
MK Dons v Cambridge
Oxford v Derby
Peterborough v Cheltenham
Portsmouth v Sheff Wed
Shrewsbury v Morecambe

League Two
Barrow v Sutton
Colchester v Stockport
Crawley v Harrogate
Crewe v Salford
Doncaster v AFC Wimbledon
Gillingham v Tranmere
Grimsby v Rochdale
Hartlepool v Northampton
Mansfield v Leyton Orient
Newport v Bradford
Stevenage v Walsall
Swindon v Carlisle

Tuesday 14 March

Championship
Blackpool v QPR
Middlesbrough v Stoke
Millwall v Swansea
Rotherham v Preston
Watford v Birmingham
Wigan v Coventry

Wednesday 15 March

Championship
Blackburn v Reading
Cardiff v WBA
Huddersfield v Norwich
Hull v Burnley

Luton v Bristol City
Sunderland v Sheff Utd

Saturday 18 March

Premier League
Arsenal v Crystal Palace
Aston Villa v Bournemouth
Brentford v Leicester
Brighton v Man Utd
Chelsea v Everton
Liverpool v Fulham
Man City v West Ham
Nottm Forest v Newcastle
Southampton v Tottenham
Wolves v Leeds

Championship
Blackburn v Burnley
Blackpool v Coventry
Middlesbrough v Preston
Millwall v Huddersfield
QPR v Birmingham
Reading v Hull
Rotherham v Cardiff
Sheff Utd v WBA
Stoke v Norwich
Sunderland v Luton
Swansea v Bristol City
Watford v Wigan

League One
Accrington v MK Dons
Bristol Rov v Portsmouth
Cambridge v Charlton
Cheltenham v Exeter
Derby v Fleetwood
Ipswich v Shrewsbury
Lincoln v Peterborough
Morecambe v Oxford
Plymouth v Forest Green
Port Vale v Burton
Sheff Wed v Bolton
Wycombe v Barnsley

League Two
AFC Wimbledon v Crawley
Bradford v Hartlepool
Carlisle v Stevenage
Harrogate v Barrow
Leyton Orient v Colchester
Northampton v Crewe
Rochdale v Swindon
Salford v Doncaster
Stockport v Mansfield
Sutton v Grimsby
Tranmere v Newport
Walsall v Gillingham

Saturday 25 March

League One
Barnsley v Ipswich
Bolton v Plymouth
Burton v Cambridge

Charlton v Wycombe
Exeter v Accrington
Fleetwood v Lincoln
Forest Green v Sheff Wed
MK Dons v Morecambe
Oxford v Cheltenham
Peterborough v Derby
Portsmouth v Port Vale
Shrewsbury v Bristol Rov

League Two
Barrow v AFC Wimbledon
Colchester v Tranmere
Crawley v Rochdale
Crewe v Bradford
Doncaster v Northampton
Gillingham v Carlisle
Grimsby v Walsall
Hartlepool v Leyton Orient
Mansfield v Sutton
Newport v Harrogate
Stevenage v Salford
Swindon v Stockport

Saturday 1 April
Premier League
Arsenal v Leeds
Bournemouth v Fulham
Brighton v Brentford
Chelsea v Aston Villa
Crystal Palace v Leicester
Everton v Tottenham
Man City v Liverpool
Newcastle v Man Utd
Nottm Forest v Wolves
West Ham v Southampton

Championship
Birmingham v Blackburn
Bristol City v Reading
Burnley v Sunderland
Cardiff v Swansea
Coventry City v Stoke
Huddersfield v Middlesbrough
Hull v Rotherham
Luton v Watford
Norwich v Sheff Utd
Preston v Blackpool
WBA v Millwall
Wigan v QPR

League One
Barnsley v Morecambe
Bolton v Accrington
Charlton v Shrewsbury
Cheltenham v Burton
Derby v Ipswich
Fleetwood v Exeter
Peterborough v Oxford
Plymouth v Bristol Rov
Port Vale v Cambridge
Portsmouth v Forest Green

Sheff Wed v Lincoln
Wycombe v MK Dons

League Two
AFC Wimbledon v Rochdale
Barrow v Gillingham
Bradford v Grimsby
Colchester v Newport
Doncaster v Crewe
Hartlepool v Swindon
Leyton Orient v Carlisle
Mansfield v Crawley
Northampton v Stevenage
Stockport v Salford
Tranmere v Harrogate
Walsall v Sutton

Friday 7 April
Championship
Blackburn v Norwich
Blackpool v Cardiff
Middlesbrough v Burnley
Millwall v Luton
QPR v Preston
Reading v Birmingham
Rotherham v WBA
Sheff Utd v Wigan
Stoke v Bristol City
Sunderland v Hull
Swansea v Coventry
Watford v Huddersfield

League One
Accrington v Port Vale
Bristol Rov v Charlton
Burton v Barnsley
Cambridge v Fleetwood
Exeter v Bolton
Forest Green v Derby
Ipswich v Wycombe
Lincoln v Cheltenham
MK Dons v Portsmouth
Morecambe v Plymouth
Oxford v Sheff Wed
Shrewsbury v Peterborough

League Two
Carlisle v Tranmere
Crawley v Bradford
Crewe v Barrow
Gillingham v Doncaster
Grimsby v Hartlepool
Harrogate v AFC Wimbledon
Newport v Northampton
Rochdale v Walsall
Salford v Leyton Orient
Stevenage v Colchester
Sutton v Stockport
Swindon v Mansfield

Saturday 8 April
Premier League
Aston Villa v Nottm Forest

Brentford v Newcastle
Fulham v West Ham
Leeds v Crystal Palace
Leicester v Bournemouth
Liverpool v Arsenal
Man Utd v Everton
Southampton v Man City
Tottenham v Brighton
Wolves v Chelsea

Monday 10 April
Championship
Birmingham v Stoke
Bristol City v Middlesbrough
Burnley v Sheff Utd
Cardiff v Sunderland
Coventry City v Watford
Huddersfield v Blackburn
Hull v Millwall
Luton v Blackpool
Norwich v Rotherham
Preston v Reading
WBA v QPR
Wigan v Swansea

League One
Barnsley v Shrewsbury
Bolton v Cambridge
Charlton v Burton
Cheltenham v Ipswich
Derby v MK Dons
Fleetwood v Bristol Rov
Peterborough v Exeter
Plymouth v Lincoln
Port Vale v Oxford
Portsmouth v Morecambe
Sheff Wed v Accrington
Wycombe v Forest Green

League Two
AFC Wimbledon v Salford
Barrow v Crawley
Bradford v Sutton
Colchester v Crewe
Doncaster v Grimsby
Hartlepool v Stevenage
Leyton Orient v Harrogate
Mansfield v Rochdale
Northampton v Gillingham
Stockport v Newport
Tranmere v Swindon
Walsall v Carlisle

Saturday 15 April
Premier League
Aston Villa v Newcastle
Chelsea v Brighton
Everton v Fulham
Leeds v Liverpool
Man City v Leicester
Nottm Forest v Man Utd
Southampton v Crystal Palace

Tottenham v Bournemouth
West Ham v Arsenal
Wolves v Brentford

Championship
Blackburn v Hull
Blackpool v Wigan
Middlesbrough v Norwich
Millwall v Preston
QPR v Coventry
Reading v Burnley
Rotherham v Luton
Sheff Utd v Cardiff
Stoke v WBA
Sunderland v Birmingham
Swansea v Huddersfield
Watford v Bristol City

League One
Accrington v Fleetwood
Bristol Rov v Derby
Burton v Sheff Wed
Cambridge v Peterborough
Exeter v Plymouth
Forest Green v Barnsley
Ipswich v Charlton
Lincoln v Port Vale
MK Dons v Cheltenham
Morecambe v Wycombe
Oxford v Bolton
Shrewsbury v Portsmouth

League Two
Carlisle v Northampton
Crawley v Tranmere
Crewe v Walsall
Gillingham v Stockport
Grimsby v Mansfield
Harrogate v Doncaster
Newport v Hartlepool
Rochdale v Bradford
Salford v Colchester
Stevenage v AFC Wimbledon
Sutton v Leyton Orient
Swindon v Barrow

Tuesday 18 April
Championship
Blackpool v WBA
Millwall v Birmingham
Rotherham v Burnley
Sheff Utd v Bristol City
Stoke v Wigan
Sunderland v Huddersfield

League One
Accrington v Peterborough
Bristol Rov v Sheff Wed
Burton v Bolton
Cambridge v Wycombe
Exeter v Derby
Forest Green v Fleetwood

Ipswich v Port Vale
Lincoln v Barnsley
MK Dons v Charlton
Morecambe v Cheltenham
Oxford v Portsmouth
Shrewsbury v Plymouth

League Two
Carlisle v Stockport
Crawley v Colchester
Crewe v AFC Wimbledon
Gillingham v Leyton Orient
Grimsby v Barrow
Harrogate v Walsall
Newport v Mansfield
Rochdale v Tranmere
Salford v Hartlepool
Stevenage v Doncaster
Sutton v Northampton
Swindon v Bradford

Wednesday 19 April
Championship
Blackburn v Coventry
Middlesbrough v Hull
QPR v Norwich
Reading v Luton
Swansea v Preston
Watford v Cardiff

Saturday 22 April
Premier League
Arsenal v Southampton
Bournemouth v West Ham
Brentford v Aston Villa
Brighton v Man City
Crystal Palace v Everton
Fulham v Leeds
Leicester v Wolves
Liverpool v Nottm Forest
Man Utd v Chelsea
Newcastle v Tottenham

Championship
Birmingham v Blackpool
Bristol City v Rotherham
Burnley v QPR
Cardiff v Stoke
Coventry City v Reading
Huddersfield v Sheff Utd
Hull v Watford
Luton v Middlesbrough
Norwich v Swansea
Preston v Blackburn
WBA v Sunderland
Wigan v Millwall

League One
Barnsley v Oxford
Bolton v Shrewsbury
Charlton v Morecambe

Cheltenham v Forest Green
Derby v Burton
Fleetwood v MK Dons
Peterborough v Ipswich
Plymouth v Cambridge
Port Vale v Bristol Rov
Portsmouth v Accrington
Sheff Wed v Exeter
Wycombe v Lincoln

League Two
AFC Wimbledon v Swindon
Barrow v Carlisle
Bradford v Gillingham
Colchester v Sutton
Doncaster v Newport
Hartlepool v Crawley
Leyton Orient v Crewe
Mansfield v Stevenage
Northampton v Harrogate
Stockport v Rochdale
Tranmere v Grimsby
Walsall v Salford

Tuesday 25 April
Premier League
Aston Villa v Fulham
Everton v Newcastle
Leeds v Leicester
Nottm Forest v Brighton
Tottenham v Man Utd
West Ham v Liverpool
Wolves v Crystal Palace

Wednesday 26 April
Premier League
Chelsea v Brentford
Man City v Arsenal
Southampton v Bournemouth

Saturday 29 April
Premier League
Arsenal v Chelsea
Bournemouth v Leeds
Brentford v Nottm Forest
Brighton v Wolves
Crystal Palace v West Ham
Fulham v Man City
Leicester v Everton
Liverpool v Tottenham
Man Utd v Aston Villa
Newcastle v Southampton

Championship
Blackburn v Luton
Blackpool v Millwall
Bristol City v Burnley
Cardiff v Huddersfield
Coventry City v Birmingham
Hull v Swansea
Reading v Wigan

Rotherham v Middlesbrough
Sheff Utd v Preston
Stoke v QPR
Sunderland v Watford
WBA v Norwich

League One

Accrington v Cambridge
Bolton v Fleetwood
Charlton v Port Vale
Derby v Portsmouth
Forest Green v Oxford
Ipswich v Exeter
MK Dons v Barnsley
Morecambe v Lincoln
Peterborough v Bristol Rov
Plymouth v Burton
Shrewsbury v Sheff Wed
Wycombe v Cheltenham

League Two

AFC Wimbledon v Tranmere
Carlisle v Salford
Crawley v Walsall
Crewe v Swindon
Doncaster v Colchester
Gillingham v Newport
Hartlepool v Barrow
Leyton Orient v Stockport
Mansfield v Harrogate
Northampton v Bradford
Rochdale v Sutton
Stevenage v Grimsby

Saturday 6 May
Premier League

Bournemouth v Chelsea
Brighton v Everton
Fulham v Leicester
Liverpool v Brentford
Man City v Leeds
Newcastle v Arsenal
Nottm Forest v Southampton
Tottenham v Crystal Palace

West Ham v Man Utd
Wolves v Aston Villa

Championship

Birmingham v Sheff Utd
Burnley v Cardiff
Huddersfield v Reading
Luton v Hull
Middlesbrough v Coventry
Millwall v Blackburn
Norwich v Blackpool
Preston v Sunderland
QPR v Bristol City
Swansea v WBA
Watford v Stoke
Wigan v Rotherham

League One

Barnsley v Peterborough
Bristol Rov v Bolton
Burton v MK Dons
Cambridge v Forest Green
Cheltenham v Charlton
Exeter v Morecambe
Fleetwood v Ipswich
Lincoln v Shrewsbury
Oxford v Accrington
Port Vale v Plymouth
Portsmouth v Wycombe
Sheff Wed v Derby

League Two

Barrow v Stevenage
Bradford v Leyton Orient
Colchester v Mansfield
Grimsby v AFC Wimbledon
Harrogate v Rochdale
Newport v Crewe
Salford v Gillingham
Stockport v Hartlepool
Sutton v Carlisle
Swindon v Crawley
Tranmere v Northampton
Walsall v Doncaster

Saturday 13 May
Premier League

Arsenal v Brighton
Aston Villa v Tottenham
Brentford v West Ham
Chelsea v Nottm Forest
Crystal Palace v Bournemouth
Everton v Man City
Leeds v Newcastle
Leicester v Liverpool
Man Utd v Wolves
Southampton v Fulham

Saturday 20 May
Premier League

Bournemouth v Man Utd
Brighton v Southampton
Fulham v Crystal Palace
Liverpool v Aston Villa
Man City v Chelsea
Newcastle v Leicester
Nottm Forest v Arsenal
Tottenham v Brentford
West Ham v Leeds
Wolves v Everton

Sunday 28 May
Premier League

Arsenal v Wolves
Aston Villa v Brighton
Brentford v Man City
Chelsea v Newcastle
Crystal Palace v Nottm Forest
Everton v Bournemouth
Leeds v Tottenham
Leicester v West Ham
Man Utd v Fulham
Southampton v Liverpool

THE THINGS THEY SAY ...

'For me, I would like to keep Wembley for finals. We should play semi-finals at another neutral venue, like it used to be - **Jordan Henderson**, Liverpool captain.

'I've seen snow stops play, hail stops play, floodlight failure stops play, fog stops play and mist stops play. Drone stops play, that's a new one on me' – **Jonathan Pearce**, *Match of the Day* commentator, when Brentford against Wolves was halted on safety grounds by a drone flying above the Community Stadium.

'The road to success isn't easy and sadly, nowadays, there is a search for immediate results. There is less and less patience' – **Rafael Benitez**, sacked after six months as Everton manager.

SCOTTISH FIXTURES 2022–2023
Premiership Championship League One and League Two

Saturday 30 July
Premiership
Livingston v Rangers
Hearts v Ross Co
Kilmarnock v Dundee Utd
St Johnstone v Hibernian
St Mirren v Motherwell

Championship
Ayr v Arbroath
Cove v Raith
Dundee v Partick
Hamilton v Greenock
Inverness v Queen's Park

League One
Dunfermline v Alloa
Falkirk v Montrose
Kelty v Edinburgh City
Peterhead v Airdrieonians
Queen of South v Clyde

League Two
Bonnyrigg v Forfar
Dumbarton v Stirling
Elgin v East Fife
Stenhousemuir v Albion Rov
Stranraer v Annan

Sunday 31 July
Premiership
Celtic v Aberdeen

Saturday 6 August
Premiership
Aberdeen v St Mirren
Dundee Utd v Livingston
Hibernian v Hearts
Motherwell v St Johnstone
Rangers v Kilmarnock
Ross Co v Celtic

Championship
Arbroath v Inverness
Greenock v Cove
Partick v Hamilton
Queen's Park v Ayr
Raith v Dundee

League One
Airdrieonians v Falkirk
Alloa v Kelty
Clyde v Peterhead
Edinburgh City v Dunfermline
Montrose v Queen of South

League Two
Albion Rov v Dumbarton
Annan v Stenhousemuir
East Fife v Bonnyrigg
Forfar v Stranraer
Stirling v Elgin

Saturday 13 August
Premiership
Aberdeen v Motherwell
Hearts v Dundee Utd
Kilmarnock v Celtic
Livingston v Hibernian
Rangers v St Johnstone
St Mirren v Ross Co

Championship
Ayr v Hamilton
Dundee v Arbroath
Inverness v Cove
Queen's Park v Partick
Raith v Greenock

League One
Alloa v Edinburgh City
Clyde v Kelty
Dunfermline v Montrose
Falkirk v Peterhead
Queen of South v Airdrieonians

League Two
Albion Rov v East Fife
Dumbarton v Annan
Forfar v Elgin
Stirling v Stenhousemuir
Stranraer v Bonnyrigg

Saturday 20 August
Premiership
Celtic v Hearts
Dundee Utd v St Mirren
Hibernian v Rangers
Motherwell v Livingston
Ross Co v Kilmarnock
St Johnstone v Aberdeen

Championship
Arbroath v Queen's Park
Cove v Ayr
Hamilton v Raith
Greenock v Dundee
Partick v Inverness

League One
Airdrieonians v Alloa
Edinburgh City v Falkirk
Kelty v Dunfermline

Montrose v Clyde
Peterhead v Queen of South

League Two
Annan v Stirling
Bonnyrigg v Albion Rov
East Fife v Forfar
Elgin v Stranraer
Stenhousemuir v Dumbarton

Saturday 27 August
Premiership
Aberdeen v Livingston
Dundee Utd v Celtic
Hearts v St Johnstone
Kilmarnock v Motherwell
Rangers v Ross Co
St Mirren v Hibernian

Championship
Ayr v Dundee
Hamilton v Arbroath
Inverness v Greenock
Partick v Raith
Queen's Park v Cove

League One
Alloa v Peterhead
Dunfermline v Airdrieonians
Edinburgh City v Clyde
Falkirk v Queen of South
Montrose v Kelty

League Two
Albion Rov v Annan
Bonnyrigg v Stirling
Dumbarton v Elgin
Forfar v Stenhousemuir
Stranraer v East Fife

Saturday 3 September
Premiership
Celtic v Rangers
Hibernian v Kilmarnock
Livingston v Hearts
Motherwell v Dundee Utd
Ross Co v Aberdeen
St Johnstone v St Mirren

Championship
Arbroath v Partick
Cove v Hamilton
Dundee v Queen's Park
Greenock v Ayr
Raith v Inverness

League One
Airdrieonians v Edinburgh City
Clyde v Alloa
Kelty v Falkirk
Peterhead v Montrose
Queen of South v Dunfermline

League Two
Annan v Forfar
East Fife v Dumbarton
Elgin v Bonnyrigg
Stenhousemuir v Stranraer
Stirling v Albion Rov

Saturday 10 September
Premiership
Aberdeen v Rangers
Celtic v Livingston
Dundee Utd v Hibernian
Hearts v St Mirren
Kilmarnock v St Johnstone
Ross Co v Motherwell

Championship
Arbroath v Raith
Ayr v Partick
Cove v Dundee
Inverness v Hamilton
Queen's Park v Greenock

League One
Clyde v Dunfermline
Edinburgh City v Peterhead
Falkirk v Alloa
Kelty v Queen of South
Montrose v Airdrieonians

League Two
Bonnyrigg v Annan
East Fife v Stenhousemuir
Elgin v Albion Rov
Forfar v Stirling
Stranraer v Dumbarton

Saturday 17 September
Premiership
Hibernian v Aberdeen
Livingston v Kilmarnock
Motherwell v Hearts
Rangers v Dundee Utd
St Johnstone v Ross Co
St Mirren v Celtic

Championship
Dundee v Inverness
Hamilton v Queen's Park
Greenock v Arbroath
Partick v Cove
Raith v Ayr

League One
Airdrieonians v Clyde
Alloa v Montrose
Dunfermline v Falkirk
Peterhead v Kelty
Queen of South v Edinburgh City

League Two
Albion Rov v Forfar
Annan v East Fife
Dumbarton v Bonnyrigg
Stenhousemuir v Elgin
Stirling v Stranraer

Saturday 1 October
Premiership
Aberdeen v Kilmarnock
Celtic v Motherwell
Dundee Utd v St Johnstone
Hearts v Rangers
Ross Co v Hibernian
St Mirren v Livingston

Championship
Ayr v Inverness
Cove v Arbroath
Hamilton v Dundee
Partick v Greenock
Queen's Park v Raith

League One
Dunfermline v Peterhead
Falkirk v Clyde
Kelty v Airdrieonians
Montrose v Edinburgh City
Queen of South v Alloa

League Two
Bonnyrigg v Stenhousemuir
East Fife v Stirling
Elgin v Annan
Forfar v Dumbarton
Stranraer v Albion Rov

Saturday 8 October
Premiership
Dundee Utd v Aberdeen
Hibernian v Motherwell
Kilmarnock v Hearts
Livingston v Ross Co
Rangers v St Mirren
St Johnstone v Celtic

Championship
Arbroath v Dundee
Ayr v Queen's Park
Inverness v Partick
Greenock v Hamilton
Raith v Cove

League One
Airdrieonians v Queen of South
Alloa v Dunfermline
Clyde v Montrose
Edinburgh City v Kelty
Peterhead v Falkirk

League Two
Albion Rov v Bonnyrigg
Forfar v East Fife
Stenhousemuir v Annan
Stirling v Dumbarton
Stranraer v Elgin

Saturday 15 October
Premiership
Aberdeen v Hearts
Celtic v Hibernian
Livingston v St Johnstone
Motherwell v Rangers
Ross Co v Dundee Utd
St Mirren v Kilmarnock

Championship
Cove v Inverness
Dundee v Ayr
Hamilton v Partick
Greenock v Raith
Queen's Park v Arbroath

League One
Alloa v Airdrieonians
Dunfermline v Edinburgh City
Kelty v Clyde
Montrose v Falkirk
Queen of South v Peterhead

League Two
Annan v Stranraer
Bonnyrigg v East Fife
Dumbarton v Albion Rov
Elgin v Forfar
Stenhousemuir v Stirling

Saturday 22 October
Premiership
Hearts v Celtic
Hibernian v St Johnstone
Kilmarnock v Ross Co
Motherwell v Aberdeen
Rangers v Livingston
St Mirren v Dundee Utd

Championship
Arbroath v Hamilton
Ayr v Cove
Dundee v Greenock
Inverness v Raith
Partick v Queen's Park

League One
Clyde v Queen of South
Edinburgh City v Airdrieonians
Falkirk v Kelty
Montrose v Dunfermline
Peterhead v Alloa

Saturday 29 October
Premiership
Dundee Utd v Motherwell
Hibernian v St Mirren
Livingston v Celtic
Rangers v Aberdeen
Ross Co v Hearts
St Johnstone v Kilmarnock

Championship
Arbroath v Ayr
Hamilton v Cove
Greenock v Inverness
Queen's Park v Dundee
Raith v Partick

League One
Airdrieonians v Montrose
Alloa v Clyde
Dunfermline v Kelty
Peterhead v Edinburgh City
Queen of South v Falkirk

League Two
Albion Rov v Stenhousemuir
Annan v Dumbarton
East Fife v Elgin
Stirling v Bonnyrigg
Stranraer v Forfar

Saturday 5 November
Premiership
Aberdeen v Hibernian
Celtic v Dundee Utd
Hearts v Motherwell
Kilmarnock v Livingston
Ross Co v St Mirren
St Johnstone v Rangers

Championship
Ayr v Greenock
Cove v Queen's Park
Inverness v Arbroath
Partick v Dundee
Raith v Hamilton

League One
Clyde v Airdrieonians
Edinburgh City v Queen of South
Falkirk v Dunfermline
Kelty v Alloa
Montrose v Peterhead

League Two
Albion Rov v Stirling
Bonnyrigg v Elgin
Dumbarton v Stranraer
Forfar v Annan
Stenhousemuir v East Fife

Wednesday 9 November
Premiership
Dundee Utd v Kilmarnock
Hibernian v Ross Co
Livingston v Aberdeen
Motherwell v Celtic
Rangers v Hearts
St Mirren v St Johnstone

Saturday 12 November
Premiership
Aberdeen v Dundee Utd
Celtic v Ross Co
Hearts v Livingston
Kilmarnock v Hibernian
St Johnstone v Motherwell
St Mirren v Rangers

Championship
Arbroath v Cove
Dundee v Raith
Hamilton v Ayr
Greenock v Partick
Queen's Park v Inverness

League One
Airdrieonians v Peterhead
Alloa v Queen of South
Dunfermline v Clyde
Falkirk v Edinburgh City
Kelty v Montrose

League Two
East Fife v Albion Rov
Elgin v Dumbarton
Forfar v Bonnyrigg
Stirling v Annan
Stranraer v Stenhousemuir

Saturday 19 November
Championship
Cove v Greenock
Dundee v Hamilton
Inverness v Ayr
Partick v Arbroath
Raith v Queen's Park

League One
Airdrieonians v Kelty
Clyde v Falkirk
Edinburgh City v Alloa
Peterhead v Dunfermline
Queen of South v Montrose

League Two
Albion Rov v Stranraer
Annan v Elgin
Dumbarton v Forfar
Stenhousemuir v Bonnyrigg
Stirling v East Fife

Saturday 3 December
Championship
Arbroath v Greenock
Ayr v Raith
Cove v Partick
Inverness v Dundee
Queen's Park v Hamilton

League One
Clyde v Edinburgh City
Dunfermline v Queen of South
Falkirk v Airdrieonians
Kelty v Peterhead
Montrose v Alloa

League Two
Bonnyrigg v Dumbarton
East Fife v Annan
Elgin v Stenhousemuir
Forfar v Albion Rov
Stranraer v Stirling

Saturday 17 December
Premiership
Aberdeen v Celtic
Hearts v Kilmarnock
Livingston v Dundee Utd
Motherwell v St Mirren
Rangers v Hibernian
Ross Co v St Johnstone

Championship
Dundee v Cove
Hamilton v Inverness
Greenock v Queen's Park
Partick v Ayr
Raith v Arbroath

League One
Airdrieonians v Dunfermline
Alloa v Falkirk
Edinburgh City v Montrose
Peterhead v Clyde
Queen of South v Kelty

League Two
Albion Rov v Elgin
Annan v Bonnyrigg
Dumbarton v Stenhousemuir
East Fife v Stranraer
Stirling v Forfar

Saturday 24 December
Premiership
Celtic v St Johnstone
Dundee Utd v Hearts
Hibernian v Livingston
Motherwell v Kilmarnock
Ross Co v Rangers
St Mirren v Aberdeen

Championship
Arbroath v Queen's Park
Ayr v Dundee
Cove v Hamilton
Partick v Inverness
Raith v Greenock

League One
Clyde v Alloa
Edinburgh City v Peterhead
Falkirk v Queen of South
Kelty v Dunfermline
Montrose v Airdrieonians

League Two
Annan v Albion Rov
Bonnyrigg v Stranraer
Dumbarton v East Fife
Elgin v Stirling
Stenhousemuir v Forfar

Wednesday 28 December
Premiership
Dundee Utd v Ross Co
Hibernian v Celtic
Kilmarnock v Aberdeen
Livingston v St Mirren
Rangers v Motherwell
St Johnstone v Hearts

Monday 2 January
Premiership
Aberdeen v Ross Co
Hearts v Hibernian
Kilmarnock v St Mirren
Livingston v Motherwell
Rangers v Celtic
St Johnstone v Dundee Utd

Championship
Dundee v Arbroath
Hamilton v Raith
Inverness v Cove
Greenock v Ayr
Queen's Park v Partick

League One
Airdrieonians v Edinburgh City
Alloa v Kelty
Dunfermline v Falkirk
Peterhead v Montrose
Queen of South v Clyde

League Two
Albion Rov v Dumbarton
East Fife v Bonnyrigg
Forfar v Elgin
Stirling v Stenhousemuir
Stranraer v Annan

Saturday 7 January
Premiership
Aberdeen v St Johnstone
Celtic v Kilmarnock
Dundee Utd v Rangers
Motherwell v Hibernian
Ross Co v Livingston
St Mirren v Hearts

Championship
Arbroath v Inverness
Ayr v Hamilton
Partick v Greenock
Queen's Park v Cove
Raith v Dundee

League One
Clyde v Kelty
Edinburgh City v Dunfermline
Falkirk v Montrose
Peterhead v Airdrieonians
Queen of South v Alloa

League Two
Annan v Forfar
Bonnyrigg v Albion Rov
Dumbarton v Stirling
Elgin v East Fife
Stenhousemuir v Stranraer

Saturday 14 January
Premiership
Celtic v St Mirren
Hearts v Aberdeen
Hibernian v Dundee Utd
Kilmarnock v Rangers
Motherwell v Ross Co
St Johnstone v Livingston

Championship
Ayr v Arbroath
Cove v Raith
Dundee v Partick
Hamilton v Greenock
Inverness v Queen's Park

League One
Alloa v Edinburgh City
Dunfermline v Peterhead
Falkirk v Clyde
Kelty v Airdrieonians
Montrose v Queen of South

League Two
Albion Rov v Dumbarton
East Fife v Bonnyrigg
Forfar v Elgin
Stirling v Stenhousemuir
Stranraer v Annan

League Two
Bonnyrigg v Stirling
East Fife v Stenhousemuir
Elgin v Annan
Forfar v Dumbarton
Stranraer v Albion Rov

Saturday 28 January
Premiership
Dundee Utd v Celtic
Hibernian v Aberdeen
Livingston v Hearts
Rangers v St Johnstone
Ross Co v Kilmarnock
St Mirren v Motherwell

Championship
Cove v Ayr
Dundee v Queen's Park
Greenock v Arbroath
Partick v Hamilton
Raith v Inverness

League One
Airdrieonians v Alloa
Clyde v Dunfermline
Edinburgh City v Falkirk
Montrose v Kelty
Peterhead v Queen of South

League Two
Albion Rov v Forfar
Annan v East Fife
Dumbarton v Bonnyrigg
Stenhousemuir v Elgin
Stirling v Stranraer

Wednesday 1 February
Premiership
Aberdeen v St Mirren
Celtic v Livingston
Hearts v Rangers
Kilmarnock v Dundee Utd
Motherwell v St Johnstone
Ross Co v Hibernian

Saturday 4 February
Premiership
Aberdeen v Motherwell
Hearts v Dundee Utd
Livingston v Kilmarnock
Rangers v Ross Co
St Johnstone v Celtic
St Mirren v Hibernian

Championship
Arbroath v Raith
Hamilton v Dundee
Inverness v Greenock
Partick v Cove
Queen's Park v Ayr

League One
Airdrieonians v Clyde
Alloa v Peterhead
Dunfermline v Montrose
Kelty v Falkirk
Queen of South v Edinburgh City

League Two
Bonnyrigg v Annan
East Fife v Stirling
Elgin v Albion Rov
Forfar v Stranraer
Stenhousemuir v Dumbarton

Saturday 11 February
League Two
Albion Rov v East Fife
Dumbarton v Annan
Forfar v Stenhousemuir
Stirling v Elgin
Stranraer v Bonnyrigg

Saturday 18 February
Premiership
Celtic v Aberdeen
Dundee Utd v St Johnstone
Hibernian v Kilmarnock
Livingston v Rangers
Motherwell v Hearts
St Mirren v Ross Co

Championship
Ayr v Partick
Cove v Arbroath
Inverness v Hamilton
Greenock v Dundee
Queen's Park v Raith

League One
Clyde v Peterhead
Dunfermline v Airdrieonians
Falkirk v Alloa
Kelty v Queen of South
Montrose v Edinburgh City

League Two
Annan v Stirling
Bonnyrigg v Forfar
East Fife v Dumbarton
Elgin v Stranraer
Stenhousemuir v Albion Rov

Saturday 25 February
Premiership
Aberdeen v Livingston
Celtic v Hearts
Hibernian v Rangers
Kilmarnock v Motherwell
Ross Co v Dundee Utd
St Johnstone v St Mirren

Championship
Arbroath v Partick
Dundee v Inverness
Hamilton v Queen's Park
Greenock v Cove
Raith v Ayr

League One
Airdrieonians v Falkirk
Alloa v Montrose
Edinburgh City v Clyde
Peterhead v Kelty
Queen of South v Dunfermline

League Two
Albion Rov v Annan
Bonnyrigg v Stenhousemuir
Dumbarton v Elgin
Forfar v Stirling
Stranraer v East Fife

Saturday 4 March
Premiership
Dundee Utd v Aberdeen
Hearts v St Johnstone
Livingston v Hibernian
Rangers v Kilmarnock
Ross Co v Motherwell
St Mirren v Celtic

Championship
Ayr v Inverness
Cove v Dundee
Hamilton v Arbroath
Partick v Raith
Queen's Park v Greenock

League One
Dunfermline v Alloa
Falkirk v Peterhead
Kelty v Edinburgh City
Montrose v Clyde
Queen of South v Airdrieonians

League Two
Annan v Stenhousemuir
East Fife v Forfar
Elgin v Bonnyrigg
Stirling v Albion Rov
Stranraer v Dumbarton

Saturday 11 March
Championship
Cove v Queen's Park
Dundee v Ayr
Inverness v Arbroath
Greenock v Partick
Raith v Hamilton
League One
Airdrieonians v Kelty
Clyde v Queen of South
Edinburgh City v Alloa

Montrose v Falkirk
Peterhead v Dunfermline

League Two
Albion Rov v Stranraer
Annan v Elgin
Dumbarton v Forfar
Stenhousemuir v East Fife
Stirling v Bonnyrigg

Saturday 18 March
Premiership
Aberdeen v Hearts
Celtic v Hibernian
Dundee Utd v St Mirren
Kilmarnock v St Johnstone
Livingston v Ross Co
Motherwell v Rangers

Championship
Arbroath v Greenock
Hamilton v Ayr
Partick v Dundee
Queen's Park v Inverness
Raith v Cove

League One
Airdrieonians v Peterhead
Alloa v Clyde
Dunfermline v Edinburgh City
Kelty v Montrose
Queen of South v Falkirk

League Two
Bonnyrigg v East Fife
Dumbarton v Albion Rov
Elgin v Stenhousemuir
Forfar v Annan
Stranraer v Stirling

Saturday 25 March
Championship
Ayr v Cove
Dundee v Raith
Inverness v Partick
Greenock v Hamilton
Queen's Park v Arbroath

League One
Clyde v Airdrieonians
Edinburgh City v Queen of South
Falkirk v Kelty
Montrose v Dunfermline
Peterhead v Alloa

League Two
Albion Rov v Bonnyrigg
Annan v Stranraer
East Fife v Elgin
Stenhousemuir v Forfar
Stirling v Dumbarton

Saturday 1 April

Premiership
Hibernian v Motherwell
Kilmarnock v Hearts
Rangers v Dundee Utd
Ross Co v Celtic
St Johnstone v Aberdeen
St Mirren v Livingston

Championship
Arbroath v Ayr
Cove v Partick
Dundee v Hamilton
Greenock v Inverness
Raith v Queen's Park

League One
Alloa v Airdrieonians
Clyde v Falkirk
Dunfermline v Kelty
Edinburgh City v Montrose
Queen of South v Peterhead

League Two
Bonnyrigg v Stranraer
Dumbarton v Stenhousemuir
East Fife v Annan
Elgin v Stirling
Forfar v Albion Rov

Saturday 8 April

Premiership
Aberdeen v Kilmarnock
Celtic v Rangers
Dundee Utd v Hibernian
Hearts v St Mirren
Motherwell v Livingston
St Johnstone v Ross Co

Championship
Arbroath v Dundee
Ayr v Greenock
Hamilton v Cove
Inverness v Raith
Partick v Queen's Park

League One
Airdrieonians v Montrose
Alloa v Queen of South
Falkirk v Dunfermline
Kelty v Clyde
Peterhead v Edinburgh City

League Two
Albion Rov v Elgin
Annan v Dumbarton
Stenhousemuir v Bonnyrigg

Stirling v East Fife
Stranraer v Forfar

Saturday 15 April

Premiership
Hibernian v Hearts
Kilmarnock v Celtic
Livingston v St Johnstone
Motherwell v Dundee Utd
Rangers v St Mirren
Ross Co v Aberdeen

Championship
Cove v Inverness
Dundee v Greenock
Partick v Ayr
Queen's Park v Hamilton
Raith v Arbroath

League One
Clyde v Edinburgh City
Dunfermline v Queen of South
Falkirk v Airdrieonians
Kelty v Alloa
Montrose v Peterhead

League Two
Annan v Albion Rov
Bonnyrigg v Dumbarton
East Fife v Stranraer
Elgin v Forfar
Stenhousemuir v Stirling

Saturday 22 April

Premiership
Aberdeen v Rangers
Celtic v Motherwell
Dundee Utd v Livingston
Hearts v Ross Co
St Johnstone v Hibernian
St Mirren v Kilmarnock

Championship
Arbroath v Cove
Ayr v Queen's Park
Hamilton v Partick
Inverness v Dundee
Greenock v Raith

League One
Airdrieonians v Dunfermline
Alloa v Falkirk
Edinburgh City v Kelty
Peterhead v Clyde
Queen of South v Montrose

League Two
Albion Rov v Stenhousemuir
Dumbarton v East Fife
Forfar v Bonnyrigg
Stirling v Annan
Stranraer v Elgin

Saturday 29 April

Championship
Ayr v Raith
Dundee v Cove
Hamilton v Inverness
Greenock v Queen's Park
Partick v Arbroath

League One
Airdrieonians v Queen of South
Dunfermline v Clyde
Falkirk v Edinburgh City
Kelty v Peterhead
Montrose v Alloa

League Two
Annan v Bonnyrigg
East Fife v Albion Rov
Elgin v Dumbarton
Stirling v Forfar
Stranraer v Stenhousemuir

Friday 5 May

Championship
Arbroath v Hamilton
Cove v Greenock
Inverness v Ayr
Queen's Park v Dundee
Raith v Partick

Saturday 6 May

League One
Alloa v Dunfermline
Clyde v Montrose
Edinburgh City v Airdrieonians
Peterhead v Falkirk
Queen of South v Kelty

League Two
Albion Rov v Stirling
Bonnyrigg v Elgin
Dumbarton v Stranraer
Forfar v East Fife
Stenhousemuir v Annan

NATIONAL LEAGUE FIXTURES 2022–2023

Saturday 6 August
Aldershot v Solihull
Altrincham v Maidstone
Barnet v Halifax
Dag & Red v Gateshead
Dorking v Chesterfield
Notts Co v Maidenhead
Scunthorpe v Yeovil
Southend v Boreham Wood
Torquay v Oldham
Wealdstone v Bromley
Wrexham v Eastleigh
York v Woking

Saturday 13 August
Boreham Wood v Notts Co
Bromley v Altrincham
Chesterfield v Aldershot
Eastleigh v Wealdstone
Halifax v Torquay
Gateshead v Barnet
Maidenhead v Scunthorpe
Maidstone v York
Oldham v Dorking
Solihull v Southend
Woking v Dag & Red
Yeovil v Wrexham

Tuesday 16 August
Boreham Wood v Aldershot
Bromley v Torquay
Chesterfield v Wrexham
Eastleigh v Dag & Red
Halifax v Southend
Gateshead v Notts Co
Maidenhead v Altrincham
Maidstone v Dorking
Oldham v Wealdstone
Solihull v York
Woking v Scunthorpe
Yeovil v Barnet

Saturday 20 August
Aldershot v Bromley
Altrincham v Yeovil
Barnet v Woking
Dag & Red v Maidenhead
Dorking v Gateshead
Notts Co v Chesterfield
Scunthorpe v Solihull
Southend v Oldham
Torquay v Boreham Wood
Wealdstone v Halifax
Wrexham v Maidstone
York v Eastleigh

Saturday 27 August
Boreham Wood v Altrincham
Bromley v Scunthorpe

Chesterfield v Barnet
Eastleigh v Southend
Halifax v Notts Co
Gateshead v Wealdstone
Maidenhead v York
Maidstone v Torquay
Oldham v Aldershot
Solihull v Dorking
Woking v Wrexham
Yeovil v Dag & Red

Monday 29 August
Aldershot v Maidstone
Altrincham v Chesterfield
Barnet v Eastleigh
Dag & Red v Bromley
Dorking v Boreham Wood
Notts Co v Solihull
Scunthorpe v Halifax
Southend v Maidenhead
Torquay v Woking
Wealdstone v Yeovil
Wrexham v Gateshead
York v Oldham

Saturday 3 September
Aldershot v Barnet
Bromley v Eastleigh
Dag & Red v Notts Co
Dorking v Wrexham
Gateshead v Maidstone
Maidenhead v Halifax
Oldham v Chesterfield
Scunthorpe v Boreham Wood
Solihull v Altrincham
Southend v Torquay
Wealdstone v Woking
Yeovil v York

Saturday 10 September
Altrincham v Wealdstone
Barnet v Southend
Boreham Wood v Oldham
Chesterfield v Gateshead
Eastleigh v Scunthorpe
Halifax v Dorking
Maidstone v Solihull
Notts Co v Bromley
Torquay v Aldershot
Woking v Yeovil
Wrexham v Maidenhead
York v Dag & Red

Tuesday 13 September
Altrincham v Scunthorpe
Barnet v Dorking
Boreham Wood v Maidenhead
Chesterfield v Southend
Eastleigh v Yeovil
Halifax v Gateshead

Maidstone v Wealdstone
Notts Co v Aldershot
Torquay v Solihull
Woking v Oldham
Wrexham v Dag & Red
York v Bromley

Saturday 17 September
Aldershot v Halifax
Bromley v Maidstone
Dag & Red v Altrincham
Dorking v Notts Co
Gateshead v Boreham Wood
Maidenhead v Woking
Oldham v Eastleigh
Scunthorpe v York
Solihull v Barnet
Southend v Wrexham
Wealdstone v Torquay
Yeovil v Chesterfield

Saturday 24 September
Altrincham v Aldershot
Bromley v Oldham
Dag & Red v Barnet
Eastleigh v Halifax
Maidenhead v Gateshead
Maidstone v Chesterfield
Scunthorpe v Dorking
Wealdstone v Southend
Woking v Solihull
Wrexham v Torquay
Yeovil v Boreham Wood
York v Notts Co

Saturday 1 October
Aldershot v Wealdstone
Barnet v York
Boreham Wood v Maidstone
Chesterfield v Maidenhead
Dorking v Dag & Red
Halifax v Woking
Gateshead v Eastleigh
Notts Co v Altrincham
Oldham v Wrexham
Solihull v Bromley
Southend v Yeovil
Torquay v Scunthorpe

Tuesday 4 October
Aldershot v Eastleigh
Barnet v Maidstone
Boreham Wood v Bromley
Chesterfield v Dag & Red
Dorking v Yeovil
Halifax v York
Gateshead v Altrincham
Notts Co v Wrexham
Oldham v Scunthorpe
Solihull v Wealdstone

Southend v Woking
Torquay v Maidenhead

Saturday 8 October
Altrincham v Dorking
Bromley v Gateshead
Dag & Red v Southend
Eastleigh v Chesterfield
Maidenhead v Oldham
Maidstone v Halifax
Scunthorpe v Aldershot
Wealdstone v Boreham Wood
Woking v Notts Co
Wrexham v Barnet
Yeovil v Solihull
York v Torquay

Saturday 22 October
Aldershot v York
Barnet v Maidenhead
Boreham Wood v Wrexham
Chesterfield v Bromley
Dorking v Wealdstone
Halifax v Dag & Red
Gateshead v Woking
Notts Co v Maidstone
Oldham v Yeovil
Solihull v Eastleigh
Southend v Scunthorpe
Torquay v Altrincham

Tuesday 25 October
Altrincham v Oldham
Bromley v Barnet
Dag & Red v Boreham Wood
Eastleigh v Torquay
Maidenhead v Solihull
Maidstone v Southend
Scunthorpe v Gateshead
Wealdstone v Notts Co
Woking v Dorking
Wrexham v Halifax
Yeovil v Aldershot
York v Chesterfield

Saturday 29 October
Barnet v Scunthorpe
Chesterfield v Boreham Wood
Dag & Red v Wealdstone
Dorking v Aldershot
Halifax v Oldham
Gateshead v Solihull
Maidenhead v Bromley
Maidstone v Yeovil
Notts Co v Torquay
Woking v Eastleigh
Wrexham v Altrincham
York v Southend

Tuesday 8 November
Aldershot v Dag & Red
Altrincham v Barnet

Boreham Wood v York
Bromley v Woking
Eastleigh v Maidstone
Oldham v Gateshead
Scunthorpe v Wrexham
Solihull v Halifax
Southend v Notts Co
Torquay v Dorking
Wealdstone v Chesterfield
Yeovil v Maidenhead

Saturday 12 November
Aldershot v Maidenhead
Altrincham v York
Boreham Wood v Woking
Bromley v Halifax
Eastleigh v Notts Co
Oldham v Barnet
Scunthorpe v Maidstone
Solihull v Dag & Red
Southend v Dorking
Torquay v Chesterfield
Wealdstone v Wrexham
Yeovil v Gateshead

Saturday 19 November
Barnet v Torquay
Chesterfield v Solihull
Dag & Red v Scunthorpe
Dorking v Bromley
Halifax v Boreham Wood
Gateshead v Southend
Maidenhead v Eastleigh
Maidstone v Oldham
Notts Co v Yeovil
Woking v Altrincham
Wrexham v Aldershot
York v Wealdstone

Saturday 26 November
Aldershot v Southend
Altrincham v Eastleigh
Boreham Wood v Solihull
Chesterfield v Woking
Dorking v York
Maidstone v Maidenhead
Notts Co v Barnet
Oldham v Dag & Red
Torquay v Gateshead
Wealdstone v Scunthorpe
Wrexham v Bromley
Yeovil v Halifax

Saturday 3 December
Barnet v Wealdstone
Bromley v Yeovil
Dag & Red v Torquay
Eastleigh v Boreham Wood
Halifax v Chesterfield
Gateshead v Aldershot
Maidenhead v Dorking
Scunthorpe v Notts Co

Solihull v Oldham
Southend v Altrincham
Woking v Maidstone
York v Wrexham

Saturday 10 December
Boreham Wood v Southend
Bromley v Wealdstone
Chesterfield v Dorking
Eastleigh v Wrexham
Halifax v Barnet
Gateshead v Dag & Red
Maidenhead v Notts Co
Maidstone v Altrincham
Oldham v Torquay
Solihull v Aldershot
Woking v York
Yeovil v Scunthorpe

Tuesday 13 December
Aldershot v Boreham Wood
Altrincham v Maidenhead
Barnet v Yeovil
Dag & Red v Eastleigh
Dorking v Maidstone
Notts Co v Gateshead
Scunthorpe v Woking
Southend v Halifax
Torquay v Bromley
Wealdstone v Oldham
Wrexham v Chesterfield
York v Solihull

Monday 26 December
Aldershot v Woking
Altrincham v Halifax
Barnet v Boreham Wood
Dag & Red v Maidstone
Dorking v Eastleigh
Notts Co v Oldham
Scunthorpe v Chesterfield
Southend v Bromley
Torquay v Yeovil
Wealdstone v Maidenhead
Wrexham v Solihull
York v Gateshead

Sunday 1 January
Boreham Wood v Barnet
Bromley v Southend
Chesterfield v Scunthorpe
Eastleigh v Dorking
Halifax v Altrincham
Gateshead v York
Maidenhead v Wealdstone
Maidstone v Dag & Red
Oldham v Notts Co
Solihull v Wrexham
Woking v Aldershot
Yeovil v Torquay

Saturday 7 January

Aldershot v Chesterfield
Altrincham v Bromley
Barnet v Gateshead
Dag & Red v Woking
Dorking v Oldham
Notts Co v Boreham Wood
Scunthorpe v Maidenhead
Southend v Solihull
Torquay v Halifax
Wealdstone v Eastleigh
Wrexham v Yeovil
York v Maidstone

Saturday 21 January

Boreham Wood v Torquay
Bromley v Aldershot
Chesterfield v Notts Co
Eastleigh v York
Halifax v Wealdstone
Gateshead v Dorking
Maidenhead v Dag & Red
Maidstone v Wrexham
Oldham v Southend
Solihull v Scunthorpe
Woking v Barnet
Yeovil v Altrincham

Tuesday 24 January

Boreham Wood v Dorking
Bromley v Dag & Red
Chesterfield v Altrincham
Eastleigh v Barnet
Halifax v Scunthorpe
Gateshead v Wrexham
Maidenhead v Southend
Maidstone v Aldershot
Oldham v York
Solihull v Notts Co
Woking v Torquay
Yeovil v Wealdstone

Saturday 28 January

Aldershot v Oldham
Altrincham v Boreham Wood
Barnet v Chesterfield
Dag & Red v Yeovil
Dorking v Solihull
Notts Co v Halifax
Scunthorpe v Bromley
Southend v Eastleigh
Torquay v Maidstone
Wealdstone v Gateshead
Wrexham v Woking
York v Maidenhead

Saturday 4 February

Aldershot v Dorking
Altrincham v Wrexham
Boreham Wood v Chesterfield
Bromley v Maidenhead

Eastleigh v Woking
Oldham v Halifax
Scunthorpe v Barnet
Solihull v Gateshead
Southend v York
Torquay v Notts Co
Wealdstone v Dag & Red
Yeovil v Maidstone

Saturday 11 February

Barnet v Oldham
Chesterfield v Torquay
Dag & Red v Solihull
Dorking v Southend
Halifax v Bromley
Gateshead v Yeovil
Maidenhead v Aldershot
Maidstone v Scunthorpe
Notts Co v Eastleigh
Woking v Boreham Wood
Wrexham v Wealdstone
York v Altrincham

Saturday 18 February

Aldershot v Wrexham
Altrincham v Woking
Boreham Wood v Halifax
Bromley v Dorking
Eastleigh v Maidenhead
Oldham v Maidstone
Scunthorpe v Dag & Red
Solihull v Chesterfield
Southend v Gateshead
Torquay v Barnet
Wealdstone v York
Yeovil v Notts Co

Tuesday 21 February

Barnet v Altrincham
Chesterfield v Wealdstone
Dag & Red v Aldershot
Dorking v Torquay
Halifax v Solihull
Gateshead v Oldham
Maidenhead v Yeovil
Maidstone v Eastleigh
Notts Co v Southend
Woking v Bromley
Wrexham v Scunthorpe
York v Boreham Wood

Saturday 25 February

Altrincham v Solihull
Barnet v Aldershot
Boreham Wood v Scunthorpe
Chesterfield v Oldham
Eastleigh v Bromley
Halifax v Maidenhead
Maidstone v Gateshead
Notts Co v Dag & Red
Torquay v Southend

Woking v Wealdstone
Wrexham v Dorking
York v Yeovil

Saturday 4 March

Aldershot v Torquay
Bromley v Notts Co
Dag & Red v York
Dorking v Maidstone
Gateshead v Chesterfield
Maidenhead v Wrexham
Oldham v Boreham Wood
Scunthorpe v Eastleigh
Solihull v Maidstone
Southend v Barnet
Wealdstone v Altrincham
Yeovil v Woking

Tuesday 7 March

Aldershot v Notts Co
Bromley v Yeovil
Dag & Red v Wrexham
Dorking v Barnet
Gateshead v Halifax
Maidenhead v Boreham Wood
Oldham v Woking
Scunthorpe v Altrincham
Solihull v Torquay
Southend v Chesterfield
Wealdstone v Maidstone
Yeovil v Eastleigh

Saturday 11 March

Altrincham v Dag & Red
Barnet v Solihull
Boreham Wood v Gateshead
Chesterfield v Yeovil
Eastleigh v Oldham
Halifax v Aldershot
Maidstone v Bromley
Notts Co v Dorking
Torquay v Wealdstone
Woking v Maidenhead
Wrexham v Southend
York v Scunthorpe

Saturday 18 March

Barnet v Notts Co
Bromley v Wrexham
Dag & Red v Oldham
Eastleigh v Altrincham
Halifax v Yeovil
Gateshead v Torquay
Maidenhead v Maidstone
Scunthorpe v Wealdstone
Solihull v Boreham Wood
Southend v Aldershot
Woking v Chesterfield
York v Dorking

Saturday 25 March

Aldershot v Gateshead
Altrincham v Southend
Boreham Wood v Eastleigh
Chesterfield v Halifax
Dorking v Maidenhead
Maidstone v Woking
Notts Co v Scunthorpe
Oldham v Solihull
Torquay v Dag & Red
Wealdstone v Barnet
Wrexham v York
Yeovil v Bromley

Saturday 1 April

Altrincham v Notts Co
Bromley v Solihull
Dag & Red v Dorking
Eastleigh v Gateshead
Maidenhead v Chesterfield
Maidstone v Boreham Wood
Scunthorpe v Torquay
Wealdstone v Aldershot
Woking v Halifax
Wrexham v Oldham
Yeovil v Southend
York v Barnet

Friday 7 April

Aldershot v Yeovil
Barnet v Bromley
Boreham Wood v Dag & Red
Chesterfield v York
Dorking v Woking
Halifax v Wrexham

Gateshead v Scunthorpe
Notts Co v Wealdstone
Oldham v Altrincham
Solihull v Maidenhead
Southend v Maidstone
Torquay v Eastleigh

Monday 10 April

Altrincham v Gateshead
Bromley v Boreham Wood
Dag & Red v Chesterfield
Eastleigh v Aldershot
Maidenhead v Torquay
Maidstone v Barnet
Scunthorpe v Oldham
Wealdstone v Solihull
Woking v Southend
Wrexham v Notts Co
Yeovil v Dorking
York v Halifax

Saturday 15 April

Aldershot v Scunthorpe
Barnet v Wrexham
Boreham Wood v Wealdstone
Chesterfield v Eastleigh
Dorking v Altrincham
Halifax v Maidstone
Gateshead v Bromley
Notts Co v Woking
Oldham v Maidenhead
Solihull v Yeovil
Southend v Dag & Red
Torquay v York

Saturday 22nd April

Altrincham v Torquay
Bromley v Chesterfield
Dag & Red v Halifax
Eastleigh v Solihull
Maidenhead v Barnet
Maidstone v Notts Co
Scunthorpe v Southend
Wealdstone v Dorking
Woking v Gateshead
Wrexham v Boreham Wood
Yeovil v Oldham
York v Aldershot

Saturday 29 April

Aldershot v Altrincham
Barnet v Dag & Red
Boreham Wood v Yeovil
Chesterfield v Maidstone
Dorking v Scunthorpe
Halifax v Eastleigh
Gateshead v Maidenhead
Notts Co v York
Oldham v Bromley
Solihull v Woking
Southend v Wealdstone
Torquay v Wrexham

THE THINGS THEY SAY ...

'I've had a good run. Now it's time for a rest – **Neil Warnock**,73, announcing his retirement after 42 years of management spanning 1,603 games with 16 clubs.

'I thought the reception was a joke, an absolute joke. He has between phenomenal for us. We are either all in this together or we're not, - **Gareth Southgate**, England manager, criticising supporters booing Harry Maguire during the match against the Ivory Coast.

'A goal for West Ham, a goal for Ukraine' – **London stadium announcer** after Andriy Yarmolenko scored against Aston Villa on his first appearance since his homeland was invaded by Russia.

'It was so emotional for me. It is difficult to think about football because every day the Russian army is killing Ukraine people. I thank my team-mates, West Ham supporters and all British people because you support us' – **Andriy Yarmolenko**.